CLARKE HALL AND MORRISON

ON

CHILDREN

ENGLAND: BUTTERWORTH & CO. (PUBLISHERS) LTD.
              LONDON: 88 Kingsway, WC2B 6AB

AUSTRALIA: BUTTERWORTH PTY. LTD.
              SYDNEY: 586 Pacific Highway, Chatswood, NSW 2067
              MELBOURNE: 343 Little Collins Street, 3000
              BRISBANE: 240 Queen Street, 4000

CANADA: BUTTERWORTH & CO. (CANADA) LTD.
              TORONTO: 14 Curity Avenue, 374

NEW ZEALAND: BUTTERWORTHS OF NEW ZEALAND LTD.
              WELLINGTON: 26–28 Waring Taylor Street, 1

SOUTH AFRICA: BUTTERWORTH & CO. (SOUTH AFRICA) (PTY.) LTD.
              DURBAN: 152–154 Gale Street

ISBN – Standard Edition: 0 406 15804 5
Special Edition: 0 406 15805 3

MADE AND PRINTED IN GREAT BRITAIN BY
WILLIAM CLOWES & SONS, LIMITED,
LONDON, BECCLES AND COLCHESTER

CLARKE HALL AND MORRISON'S
LAW RELATING TO

CHILDREN

AND

YOUNG PERSONS

EIGHTH EDITION

BY

L. GOODMAN, LL.B.
BARRISTER, SENIOR CHIEF CLERK,
INNER LONDON JUVENILE COURTS

LONDON
BUTTERWORTHS
1972

First Edition 1934
Second Edition 1942
Third Edition 1947
Fourth Edition 1951
Fifth Edition 1956
Sixth Edition 1961
First reprint of Sixth Edition 1962
Second reprint of Sixth Edition 1965
Seventh Edition 1967
Reprinted 1967
Eighth Edition 1972

PREFACE TO EIGHTH EDITION

IT is somewhat daunting to undertake the editorship of this work, which task has for some years now been performed by joint editors who were my predecessors at the Inner London Juvenile Courts. The changes in the law consequent on the Social Work (Scotland) Act, 1968, and the Children and Young Persons Act, 1969, have created particular difficulty. Many of the provisions have not yet been brought into force, and many provisions are subject to "transitional modifications". An outline of these changes and the effects of the Criminal Justice Act, 1967, the Administration of Justice Act, 1970, and the Courts Act, 1971, would be out of place in a preface, and it is hoped that an adequate account is given in the material printed. In the preface to the last edition the editors invited suggestions for improvement, and it may be that future editions will have to take greater account of the need for social workers to understand the implications of legislation and case law which affect the rights and welfare of the young. The Houghton Committee has already produced a report on the law and procedure on Adoption and any major revision may well start with this section of the work. Further revisions will be indicated by the acceptance of the Redcliffe-Maud report on Local Government and any consolidation of the Children and Young Persons Acts.

It has been thought convenient to add a section on legal aid and the opportunity is taken of printing the various regulations and sections of the Criminal Justice Act 1967 as amended.

Various sections of the book have been expanded so that reference may be made, for example, to the Crown Court Rules, and the provisions for the enforcement of fines and sums adjudged to be paid on conviction.

The Law Commission are currently examining the anomalies in jurisdiction between the Magistrates' Courts and the High Court created by the Divorce Reform Act, 1969 and the Matrimonial Proceedings and Property Act, 1970. There may well be an opportunity for a more logical and less piecemeal approach to welfare reports in guardianship and matrimonial proceedings, and indeed the constitution and jurisdiction of "family courts" is also to be considered. A prime question which arises is which of the matters currently assigned to juvenile courts are appropriate for a family court. Any such major reforms should not lead us to neglect the need for a review of the operation of the Children and Young Persons Act, 1969.

Some dissatisfaction has been expressed at the lack of resources available to local authorities to whose care a child or young person is committed; coupled with this is the difficulty caused by social service departments becoming "generic" under the Local Authority Social Services Act, 1970. The problems arising from an increase in the staffing of social work departments and the introduction of inexperienced workers into court work need to be tackled by an effective training programme. Magistrates themselves need an understanding of how these departments work and much benefit could be derived from a close co-operation between the agencies involved in juvenile courts and regular meetings along the lines recommended by the Home Office in the guide to Part I of the Children and Young Persons Act, 1969.

Acknowledgement is made to the Controller of H.M. Stationery Office for permission to print certain official circulars in respect of which Crown copyright is reserved. Acknowledgement is also made to the Home Office, Department of Health and Social Security, the Inner London Education Authority and the Church of England Committee for liaison with the Social Services for permission to reproduce circulars and by-laws included in the work, and for their valuable assistance. Finally I must acknowledge the forbearance of the Committee of Magistrates for the Inner London Area, and my colleagues. I have been given much help and encouragement, but must take sole responsibility for any views expressed. The law is stated as at 1 January 1972.

March 1972   L. GOODMAN

PREFACE TO FIRST EDITION

WHEN Sir William Clarke Hall did me the honour of inviting me to collaborate with him in the preparation of this book it was his intention that it should cover the whole of the law relating to children and young persons. Subsequently, however, we came to the conclusion that the better course would be to annotate the Children Act, 1908, and the Children and Young Persons Act, 1932 (this was before the Consolidation Act of 1933), and such other statutes or portions of statutes as affected the work of magistrates, with the exception of the Adoption of Children Act and the Guardianship of Infants Acts, which he and his son, Mr. Justin Clarke Hall, had treated fully in their recent book, " The Law of Adoption." *

Sir William was able to furnish me with a considerable share of his work on this book, but unfortunately his death deprived me of any opportunity of going through it with him. I have attempted to revise it and bring it up to date, much of it having been written some time ago. Thus it happens that whereas I have considered all that he wrote, he had no opportunity of reading my contribution, and for any mistakes or defects in the book I alone must be held responsible.

Acknowledgement is due to Mr. Justin Clarke Hall, barrister-at-law, for much valuable help given to his father in connection with the portion of the work which he had undertaken.

I have also to thank Mr. Albert Lieck, chief clerk of the Bow Street Police Court, for much assistance, and Mr. C. J. Collinge, of the same court, who has prepared the tables of cases and statutes and the index.

It was Sir William's wish, and not less mine, that he should write a preface, setting forth fully his conception of the juvenile court, its work and its mission. Inasmuch as I do not feel able to take his place for that purpose, the book must be so much the poorer. This I know : Sir William, whose devotion to work for children and whose respect for the child have not been surpassed, rejoiced at the increasing recognition, both by the public and by the legislature, of the importance of the juvenile court. As a text for his preface he would, I think, have taken words from sect. 44 (1) of the Children and Young Persons Act, 1933, which enshrine in a statute a principle upon which he himself had always acted :

" Every court in dealing with a child or young person who is brought before it, either as being in need of care or protection or as an offender or otherwise, shall have regard to the welfare of the child or young person."

A. C. L. M.

LONDON,
October 31, 1933.

* Butterworth & Co. (Publishers) Ltd., London.

TABLE OF CONTENTS

DIVISION 2

CHILD PROTECTION

DIVISION 3

ADOPTION

INDEX

TABLE OF STATUTES

References in this Table to *"Statutes"* are to Halsbury's Statutes of England (Third Edition) showing the volume and page at which the annotated text of the Act will be found. Page references printed in bold type indicate where the Act is set out in part or in full.

TABLE OF CASES

In the following Table references are given to the English and Empire Digest
where a Digest of each Case will be found.

A.

B.

G.

H.

PAGE

DIVISION 1

GENERAL

CONTENTS

SECTION 1.—INTRODUCTORY NOTE

Modern legislation has laid it down clearly that in dealing with juveniles welfare is to be a principal consideration. Thus the Guardianship of Minors Act, 1971, states in s. 1, p. 1198, *post*: "Where in any proceeding before any court (whether or not a court as defined in s. 15 of the Guardianship of Minors Act, 1971, p. 1207, *post*) the custody or upbringing of a minor, or the administration of any property belonging to or held on trust for a minor, or the application of the income thereof, is in question, the court, in deciding that question, shall regard the welfare of the minor as the first and paramount consideration." Again, in s. 44 (1) of the Children and Young Persons Act, 1933, p. 50, *post*, the court is required when dealing with any child or young person brought before it, whether as an offender or otherwise, to have regard to its welfare. This does not mean that the courts may travel outside the law in order to achieve what they believe to be welfare.

Where a child or a young person is accused of an offence, he is entitled to be tried on precisely the same principles as those regulating the trial of an adult, although the procedure is or should be simpler in form. Only if he is proved guilty can the court proceed to exercise its powers, and it is in that event that it must have regard to welfare. The fact that the court has due regard to the welfare of the juvenile does not necessarily exclude punishment, but it does mean that in deciding whether or not to punish or whether to adopt some alternative treatment instead of punishment, it should have regard to what is likely to prove best for the juvenile, and should not attempt the difficult task of measuring the degree of guilt, and the degree of punishment which it considers corresponds to that measure of guilt. Similarly, where a juvenile is brought before a juvenile court not charged with an offence, but as in need of care, protection or control, the first business of the court is to try the issue whether or not the case is brought within the terms of the statute, and only if this be proved by proper evidence can the court proceed to decide upon treatment. If the case be not proved, then whatever be the ground upon which the juvenile has been brought before the court he must be released from custody. The liberty of the subject, however small that subject may be, must be safeguarded by the courts, and as the case of *R. v. Toynbee Hall Juvenile Court Justices, Ex parte Joseph*, [1939] 3 All E. R. 16; 103 J. P. 279 showed, the High Court will intervene where that liberty has been invaded without proper legal justification.

The juvenile is to be guarded from association with older persons accused or convicted of crime. At the police station he must be kept apart from them. Generally, if he is to appear before a court, it must be a juvenile court and not the ordinary magistrates' court. No court can impose imprisonment on an offender under seventeen. For certain juvenile offenders punishment may take the form of detention in a detention centre or attendance at an attendance centre, these two types

5

of institution having been created by the Criminal Justice Act, 1948, although the power to make these orders may be withdrawn when schemes of intermediate treatment are proposed under the Children and Young Persons Act, 1969 (*ibid.*, s. 7).

When a juvenile gives evidence in certain classes of case, he may be protected from publicity, and in certain circumstances his evidence can even be taken out of court. If he has to be punished, or if through no fault of his own he has to be removed from evil surroundings, special forms of treatment are available, such as committal to a borstal institution, or to the care of a local authority. It is the duty of parents to secure the regular attendance of their children at school, and the parents may be prosecuted if they fail to do this. The court before which the parent appears may direct that the child be brought before a juvenile court. If a child fails to attend regularly the local education authority may bring the child before a juvenile court, and in either case the court may make in respect of the child any order it could make in the case of a child found to be in need of care or control under s. 1 of the Children and Young Persons Act, 1969.

There are many statutes restricting the employment of young people or imposing special conditions in relation to such employment. It has not been possible to deal fully with this branch of the law within the compass of this work, and reference must be had to special treatises on the Factory Acts and similar statutes for precise information on this branch of the law. There are certain sections of the Children and Young Persons Acts, 1933 and 1963 which deal with the employment of children and young persons, and these are dealt with in their appropriate place. The Young Persons (Employment) Act, 1938 ; 17 Halsbury's Statutes, 3rd Edn., 529, which was amended by the Shops Act, 1950; 13 Halsbury's Statutes, 3rd Edn., 317, makes it unlikely that s. 19 of the Children and Young Persons Act, 1933, p. 30, *post*, will be brought into force.

SECTION 2.—CHILDREN AND YOUNG PERSONS LEGISLATION

CHILDREN AND YOUNG PERSONS ACT, 1933

[23 & 24 Geo. 5, c. 12]

ARRANGEMENT OF SECTIONS

PART I

PREVENTION OF CRUELTY AND EXPOSURE TO MORAL AND PHYSICAL DANGER

Offences

PART II

EMPLOYMENT

General Provisions as to Employment

PART III

PROTECTION OF CHILDREN AND YOUNG PERSONS IN RELATION TO CRIMINAL
AND SUMMARY PROCEEDINGS

*An Act to consolidate certain enactments relating to persons under the age
of eighteen years.*   [13th April, 1933.]

PART I.—PREVENTION OF CRUELTY AND EXPOSURE TO MORAL AND PHYSICAL DANGER

Offences

1. Cruelty to persons under sixteen.—(1) If any person who has
attained the age of sixteen years and has the custody, charge, or care of
any child or young person under that age, wilfully assaults, ill-treats,
neglects, abandons, or exposes him, or causes or procures him to be
assaulted, ill-treated, neglected, abandoned, or exposed, in a manner
likely to cause him unnecessary suffering or injury to health (including
injury to or loss of sight, or hearing, or limb, or organ of the body, and
any mental derangement), that person shall be guilty of a misdemeanour,
and shall be liable—

(a) on conviction on indictment, to a fine not exceeding one hundred
    pounds, or alternatively, or in addition thereto, to imprison-
    ment for any term not exceeding two years ;

(b) on summary conviction, to a fine not exceeding one hundred
    pounds, or alternatively, or in addition thereto, to imprison-
    ment for any term not exceeding six months.

(2) For the purposes of this section—

(a) a parent or other person legally liable to maintain a child or young person shall be deemed to have neglected him in a manner likely to cause injury to his health if he has failed to provide adequate food, clothing, medical aid or lodging for him, or if, having been unable otherwise to provide such food, clothing, medical aid or lodging, he has failed to take steps to procure it to be provided under the enactments applicable in that behalf ;

(b) where it is proved that the death of an infant under three years of age was caused by suffocation (not being suffocation caused by disease or the presence of any foreign body in the throat or air passages of the infant) while the infant was in bed with some other person who has attained the age of sixteen years, that other person shall, if he was, when he went to bed, under the influence of drink, be deemed to have neglected the infant in a manner likely to cause injury to its health.

(3) A person may be convicted of an offence under this section—

(a) notwithstanding that actual suffering or injury to health, or the likelihood of actual suffering or injury to health, was obviated by the action of another person ;

(b) notwithstanding the death of the child or young person in question.

(4) [*Repealed by the Criminal Law Act, 1967.*]

(5) If it is proved that a person convicted under this section was directly or indirectly interested in any sum of money accruing or payable in the event of the death of the child or young person, and had knowledge that that sum of money was accruing or becoming payable, then—

(a) in the case of a conviction on indictment, the maximum amount of the fine which may be imposed under this section shall be two hundred pounds, and the court shall have power, in lieu of awarding any other penalty under this section, to sentence the person convicted to penal servitude for any term not exceeding five years ; and

(b) in the case of a summary conviction, the court in determining the sentence to be awarded shall take into consideration the fact that the person was so interested and had such knowledge.

(6) For the purposes of the last foregoing subsection :—

(a) a person shall be deemed to be directly or indirectly interested in a sum of money if he has any share in or any benefit from the payment of that money, notwithstanding that he may not be a person to whom it is legally payable ; and

(b) a copy of a policy of insurance, certified to be a true copy by an officer or agent of the insurance company granting the policy, shall be evidence that the child or young person therein stated to be insured has in fact been so insured, and that the person in whose favour the policy has been granted is the person to whom the money thereby insured is legally payable.

(7) Nothing in this section shall be construed as affecting the right of any parent, teacher, or other person having the lawful control or charge of a child or young person to administer punishment to him.

NOTES

This section is printed as amended by the National Assistance (Adaptation of Enactments) Regulations, 1950 (S.I. 1951 No. 174), the Children and Young Persons Act, 1963, ss. 31, 64, 65 and Sched. III, and the Criminal Law Act, 1967, s. 10 and Sched. III.

" **Age of sixteen.** "—Strict proof of age is not necessary when the court can judge from appearance, or from the circumstances of the case (*R*. v. *Cox*, [1898] 1 Q. B. 179; 67 L. J. Q. B. 293; and see s. 99, p. 77, *post*).

Where the appearance of the accused is such as to leave a possibility of doubt, the age should, it is submitted, be proved by the prosecution.

In *R*. v. *Viasani* (1866), 31 J. P. 260; 15 L. T. 240; a case under the Vagrancy Act, 1824; 8 Halsbury's Statutes, 3rd Edn., 71, it was held that the justices were justified in coming to the conclusion, from the appearance of the child, that he was fourteen, although he gave his age as sixteen. See also *R*. v. *Turner*, [1910] 1 K. B. 346; 74 J. P. 81.

See also note " **Attained the age** " at p. 53, *post*.

" **Custody, charge or care.** "—See s. 17, p. 28, *post*, for definitions of these terms.

In *R*. v. *Connor*, [1908] 2 K. B. 26; 72 J. P. 212, it was held that a father cannot by living apart from his wife divest himself of the custody of the child. The leading case on the father living apart is *Brooks* v. *Blount*, [1923] 1 K.B. 257; 87 J. P. 64, where it was decided that where parents enter into a written agreement, by which a father undertakes to pay the mother a weekly sum, and the mother is to maintain the children and herself, and to have the custody of the children, if the father fails to perform his obligations as to payments, the separation agreement does not get rid of the presumption that he has the custody of the children.

" The words ' as between father and mother ' in s. 38 (2) of the Children Act, 1908 [now s. 17 of this Act, p. 26, *post*]," said Lord Hewart, " appear to be used by the legislature in order to draw a distinction between that which may be done by either of them to regulate their relation as individuals, and that which may be done by either of them in purported subtraction from the obligations which they owe to the community in regard to their children . . ." " In my opinion it is not possible for a parent by his own act to get rid of this legal presumption (*i.e.*, that he has the custody of the child). . . ." Salter, J.: " The person who has the custody of the child cannot be heard to say that he has not the custody of the child unless he is deprived of the custody by the order of a competent court."

And even if the father, being separated from his wife, remits sufficient money for the support of the children, and she neglects them to his knowledge, he is liable (*Poole* v. *Stokes* (1914), 78 J. P. 231; 110 L. T. 1020; and see s. 17, p. 28, *post*).

See, on illegitimate children, the case of *Humphrys* v. *Polak*, [1901] 2 K. B. 385; 70 L. J. K. B. 752.

This rule does not, however, relieve the person who undertakes the duty of supplying the child with food and clothing and is provided by the father with means of doing so, for he or she has the charge. If he fails in this duty and the child dies he will be guilty of murder, and the father if he is conscious of the neglect will be guilty of manslaughter (*R*. v. *Bubb*, *R*. v. *Hook* (1850), 14 J. P. 562; 4 Cox, C. C. 455). The test of charge seems to be immediate control.

Whether or not a person has the custody, charge, or care, may be a question of fact for the jury (*R*. v. *Cox*, [1898] 1 Q. B. 179; 18 Cox, C. C. 672). Another case on this point is *The Liverpool Society for the Prevention of Cruelty to Children* v. *Jones*, [1914] 3 K. B. 813; 79 J. P. 20. The respondent was the father of four illegitimate children, and lived with them and their mother. No affiliation order had been made against him. It was held that, although in law the mother was the custodian of the children, yet it was a question of fact whether the respondent had the custody, charge, or care of the children within the meaning of the Act.

" **Child.** "—By s. 107, p. 81, *post*, this expression means a person under fourteen years old.

"**Young person.**"—By s. 107 this means a person between the ages of four-teen and seventeen, but here the section deals with persons under sixteen. As to proof of age, see note "Age of sixteen", p. 12, *ante*.

"**Wilfully.**"—This word governs all the following words : "assaults," "ill-treats," "neglects," etc., in the same way that the phrase "in a manner likely to cause unnecessary suffering or injury to health" also qualifies them. (See below.)

Wilfulness may be inferred from the whole conduct of the defendant, and from the circumstances of the case, and it is no longer necessary to prove malice, as was essential under the Offences against the Person Act, 1861, s. 20; 8 Halsbury's Statutes, 3rd Edn., 154.

The leading case on the meaning of the word is *R.* v. *Senior*, [1899] 1 Q. B 283 ; 63 J. P. 8. The defendant was a member of the "Peculiar People," and omitted to supply his child (which died of diarrhoea and pneumonia) with any medical aid or medicine, although aware of the danger of the case. The medical evidence called was to the effect that the child's life might have been saved, and most certainly would have been prolonged, had medical assistance been obtained.

"Wilfully," said Lord Russell, C.J. (at p. 290), "means that the act is done deliberately, and intentionally, not by accident or inadvertence, but so that the mind of the person doing the act goes with it."

"**Assaults.**"—Common assault is the *attempt* to apply any force to a person : if the force be actually applied it becomes battery.

The case of *R.* v. *Hatton*, [1925] 2 K. B. 322 ; 19 Cr. App. Rep. 29 ; 89 J. P. 164, has made it clear, however, that there must be something more than a common assault in order to bring a prosecution under this section, and that therefore the ordinary definitions of assault do not apply, nor again do a large number of cases on common assault. It was decided in the above case that the words "in a manner likely to cause . . . unnecessary suffering" qualify the words "assaults," "ill-treats," "neglects," "abandons," "exposes," etc., and that therefore a mere common assault, unless it produced, or was likely to produce, or cause, unnecessary suffering, was not within the section.

It seems, therefore, that in practice it may be advisable to add a second count of common assault under s. 42 of the Offences against the Person Act, 1861; 8 Halsbury's Statutes, 3rd Edn., 162, when proceeding under this section, and it must be remembered that many of the cases on assault might not have succeeded under this section, as they were decided under a different Act, or before the above case, and must all be read in the light of *R.* v. *Hatton* for the purpose of this Act.

Proceedings under s. 42 of the Offences against the Person Act, 1861, must be upon the information of the person aggrieved or on his behalf. If, however, the person assaulted is so feeble, old and infirm as to be incapable of instituting proceedings, and is not a free agent but under the control of the person committing the assault, the information may be laid by a third person; *Pickering* v. *Willoughby*, [1907] 2 K. B. 296; 71 J. P. 311, distinguishing *Nicholson* v. *Booth and Naylor* (1888), 52 J. P. 662. It would seem therefore that in certain circumstances it may be proper for a police officer or other person to prosecute under s. 42, *supra*, where a child has been assaulted.

The facts in *R.* v. *Hatton, supra,* were these: A child aged twelve years was alone in the house with a male lodger, the defendant. She was in a room when the defendant entered, shut the door, and then did an act, not to her, but in her presence. When she screamed he put his hand over her mouth, and for some time prevented her leaving the room. He subsequently denied that he had done anything.

"The words 'in a manner likely to cause such child or young person unnecessary suffering or injury to his health,'" said Lord Hewart, C.J., "govern the words 'wilfully assaults,' and the sentence which is provided by that section, a sentence of two years' imprisonment, with or without hard labour, makes it plain that what is contemplated by the section is something more than ordinary assault, namely, a wilful assault, such as is likely to cause the child unnecessary suffering. . . . It is quite obvious, when one looks at the case as a whole, that what might very easily be in the minds of the jury was the reflection that that which was done in the presence of the child, if it was done, was likely to cause, if not suffering, at any rate considerable anguish of mind, and astonishment, and disgust.

"That, however, is not assault. That the appellant might be convicted under this section of the statute, it was necessary to show that there was a wilful assault in a manner likely to cause the child unnecessary suffering."

The Lord Chief Justice then went on to say that though the above was sufficient to quash the conviction, it was also a case in which emphatic warning ought to have been given to the jury of the danger of convicting on the uncorroborated evidence of a child.

" **Consent.**"—An assault coming within the rule that fraud vitiates consent (*R. v. Bennett* (1866), 4 F. & F. 1105), for a medical man to take off the clothes of a female patient, under the pretence that he cannot otherwise judge her illness, is an assault (*R. v. Rosinski* (1824), 1 Lew, C. C. 11 ; 1 Mood, C. C. 19). Subject to this rule, the act must be done without the consent of the passive party in order to constitute an assault. " Mere submission, however, is not consent, for there may be submission without consent, and while the feelings are repugnant to the act that is being done." Per Kelly, C. B., *R. v. Wollaston* (1872), 26 L. T. 403 ; 12 Cox, C. C. 180. (In that case, however, the conviction was quashed, as there was consent.) See also *R. v. Dimes* (1911), 7 Cr. App. Rep. 43 ; 76 J. P. 47.

So where there is complete ignorance, on the part of the person submitting to the act, of its real nature there is no consent (*R. v. Lock* (1872), L. R. 2 C. C. R. 10 ; 42 L. J. M. C. 5). Neither does submission to an assault by a person in authority necessarily imply consent (*R. v. Nichol* (1807), Russ. & Ry. 130 ; and see also p. 13, *post*, "Assaults by Schoolmasters"). Nor the submission of a child to the act of a strong man (*R. v. Day* (1841), 9 C. & P. 722).

Putting a child in a bag and leaving it hanging on palings was held to be an assault (*R. v. March* (1844), 1 Car. & Kir. 496). So too might be the exposing of a child of tender years to the inclemency of the weather (see *R. v. Ridley* (1811), 2 Camp. 650), but such exposure where, in the result, no inconvenience or injury actually happens to the child, cannot amount to an assault (*R. v. Renshaw* (1847), 9 L. T. (o.s.) 395 ; 2 Cox, C. C. 285).

The effect of the use of the word " assault " in this section would seem from the above decisions to be to make such acts as the following, when committed by persons having the " custody, charge, or care " of children, punishable under this section in all cases in which unnecessary suffering is likely directly to supervene— *e.g.*, shutting a child in a room where suffering would be likely to be caused by terror of the dark, or cold, or hunger ; threatening it with some instrument, as with a stick or poker ; terrifying it with a dog, etc. It has always been held that mere words cannot be an assault, but mere words, it has been suggested, might amount to ill-treatment.

So if a child has simply been left in a dark room and not shut into it, this would not be an assault (*R. v. Smith* (1826), 2 C. & P. 449), though it might be neglect or ill-treatment.

The " injury " need not be effected directly by the hand of the party ; thus there may be a battery by encouraging a dog to bite. Russell on Crimes, 12th Edn., I, 656

" **Punishment.**"—A parent, or person standing *in loco parentis*, has of course the right to punish a child under his charge, and this right is expressly guarded by s. 1 (7) of the Act (p. 12, *ante*). Such punishment will not therefore be an assault if it is inflicted in moderation and with a proper instrument. When excessive punishment has resulted in the death of a child, the law has always held the person who inflicted the punishment guilty of manslaughter, but under this Act any excessive punishment causing " unnecessary suffering or injury to its (the child's) health " will be punishable as an assault. It will therefore be well to see what has in the past been held to be " excessive punishment."

The ancient common law on this subject is thus laid down by Hale (Pleas of the Crown, vol. i, p. 473) : " If a schoolmaster corrects his scholar, or a master his servant, or a parent his child, and by struggling or otherwise the child, or scholar, or servant dies, this is only *per infortuniam*." " If done," says East (Pleas of the Crown, vol. i, p. 261), " with a cudgel, or other thing not likely to kill, it will be manslaughter ; if with a dangerous weapon likely to kill, or maim . . . murder. . . . Yet though the correction exceeds the bounds of moderation, the court will pay a tender regard to the nature of the provocation." On this principle, as he goes on to add, the court having consulted " the principal counsel on the circuit," came to the conclusion that a father who beat his son to death for theft was guilty of manslaughter.

In *R.* v. *Hopley* (1860), 2 F. & F. 202, a schoolmaster took a boy of thirteen from his bed at night and beat him with a thick stick, and also a skipping rope, for two hours and a half, at the end of which time the boy died ; held by Cockburn, C. J., that the prisoner was liable to a charge of manslaughter, and the jury accordingly convicted him.

" If it (the punishment) be administered for the gratification of passion or of rage, or if it be immoderate or excessive in its nature or degree, or if it be protracted beyond the child's power of endurance, or with an instrument unfitted for the purpose and calculated to produce danger to life or limb ; in all such cases the punishment is excessive, and the violence is unlawful, and if evil consequences to life or limb ensue, then the person inflicting it is answerable to the law, and if death ensues, it will be manslaughter." Per Cockburn, C.J., *R.* v. *Hopley, supra* ; see also "Assaults by Schoolmasters", *infra.*

In *R.* v. *Cheeseman* (1836), 7 C. & P. 455, the prisoner kept a girl of fifteen working for fourteen and sometimes fifteen hours a day, and when the required quantity of work was not done, beat the child, who subsequently died of consumption accelerated by ill-treatment. The prisoner pleaded guilty to manslaughter.

In *R.* v. *Griffin* (1869), 11 Cox, C. C. 402, a father had beaten his child, a little girl of two and a half years of age, with a leather strap, in consequence of which she died. It was contended for the defence that no crime had been committed, the father having a perfect right to correct the child.

Martin, B., however, held that the child must be capable of appreciating the correction, and that in the case before him this capacity was wanting.

As will be seen from the above cases it was the *causing* of the death of the child which was punishable as a crime. The effect of the statutes has been to make such excessive punishments as these criminal offences in all cases. It is only necessary to prove the infliction of unnecessary suffering, or the likelihood of its ensuing to constitute an offence under this section.

Assaults by Schoolmasters.—A schoolmaster, being a person *in loco parentis*, has the same right of inflicting punishment as a parent, and has also the same liabilities should the punishment prove excessive. His rights in this respect are, however, only co-extensive with the authority deputed to him and cease as soon as that ceases.

In the case of *Cleary* v. *Booth*, [1893] 1 Q. B. 465 ; 57 J. P. 375, the Divisional Court held that the master of a board-school was entitled to inflict corporal punishment on a pupil for an offence committed outside the school ; but for a board-school master to punish a child for not learning a lesson not authorised by the education code has been held to be an assault (*Hunter* v. *Johnson* (1884), 13 Q. B. D. 225 ; 48 J. P. 663 ; *Fitzgerald* v. *Northcote* (1865), 4 F. & F. 656). As to punishment for breaking a rule of the school, outside the school, see *R.* v. *Newport (Salop) Justices, Ex parte Wright*, [1929] 2 K. B. 416 ; 93 J. P. 179.

A schoolmaster who has taken improper liberties with a female pupil may be convicted of an indecent assault even though she was over thirteen (the same might now apply if she was over sixteen, the present statutory age), and had merely submitted to the assault (*R.* v. *M'Gavaran* (1852), 3 Car. & Kir. 320 ; 6 Cox, C. C. 64), the ground for this decision being that the fact that the master held a position of authority vitiated the consent (*R.* v. *Nichol* (1807), Russ. & Ry. 130). " Mere submission to an assault does not necessarily imply consent." Per Coleridge, J., *R.* v. *Day* (1841), 9 C. & P. 722.

Assaults under other Acts.—Where the accused has not the " custody charge, or care " (see p. 12, *ante*), or the assault is not " likely to cause unnecessary suffering " (see p. 18, *post*), a summons may be taken out for common assault under s. 42 of the Offences against the Person Act, 1861 ; 8 Halsbury's Statutes, 3rd Edn., 162. If the assault prove to be aggravated, it may be dealt with under s. 43, *op. cit.* 163.

If serious injury has been done to the child the accused should be charged with an assault occasioning actual bodily harm (s. 47 ; 8 Halsbury's Statutes, 3rd Edn., 165) or unlawful wounding (s. 20 ; *op. cit.* 154).

" Ill-treats.''—This is a word which is intended to cover a continuous course of active misconduct towards a child, calculated to cause " unnecessary suffering or injury to health." It is also submitted that it meets cases where, though there is no assault, threatening or terrifying language is used to or in the presence of a child so as to cause it suffering or injury to health. Thus, where one beating might not be sufficiently excessive to constitute an assault within the meaning of the Act, continuous beatings of the same nature might constitute ill-treatment. Ill-treatment need not be inflicted by actual physical violence. It may be ill-treatment wantonly to terrify a child, as by making a dog bark at it.

This important point as to how far a criminal injury may be inflicted by one person upon another without any actual physical "impact" is one on which unfortunately there is a great dearth of legal precedent. At common law it was undoubtedly held that actual violence was necessary. "If any man," says Hale (Pleas of the Crown, vol. i, p. 429), "either by working on the fancy of another, or possibly by harsh and unkind usage, puts another into such passion of grief or fear that the party dies," this, though it may be murder in the sight of God, "cannot come under the judgment of felony." "The great improvements," says Stephen (History of the Criminal Law, vol. iii, p. 6), commenting on this passage, "which have taken place in medical knowledge since Hale's time, of course make it possible in the present day to speak much more decisively on the question whether death has been caused by a given act, or set of acts, than was formerly possible." . . . "To shout in the ear of a sleeping man who has certain diseases of the heart may be as effectual a way of killing him as a stab with a knife, but at first sight such a death would not be described as being caused by any definite bodily injury. Should such a case occur in the present day I think it would be regarded as killing" (History of the Criminal Law, vol. iii, p. 5). Where B, having in her arms an infant, was assaulted by A, and the infant was so terrified that it died within six weeks of the assault from shock of fear, A was held guilty of manslaughter (*R. v. Towers* (1874), 12 Cox, C. C. 530).

"Mere intimidation," said Denman, J., in *R. v. Towers, supra,* "causing a person to die by working on his fancy was not murder. But there were cases in which intimidations have been held to be murder. If, for instance, four or five persons were to stand round a man, and so threaten and frighten him as to make him believe that his life was in danger, and he were to back away from them and tumble over a precipice to avoid them, then murder would have been committed. . . ."

It seems, therefore, that an offence under this section may be committed by one person against another without direct physical violence. Manifestly in the case of a child the effect of terror is likely to be more dangerous than in that of an adult, and the instances in which "injury to health" or "unnecessary suffering" can be proved to be likely to supervene as a direct consequence must be numerous.

Briefly, then, any course of conduct likely to cause injury to a child, whether such injury be mental or physical, is, it is submitted, ill-treatment. See, however, *R. v. Hatton*, p. 13, *ante*. The words "Assaults, ill-treats, neglects" etc., do not create separate and watertight offences and if the evidence can fairly be said to indicate "ill-treatment" even though the same conduct might equally well be called neglect, it is no misdirection to a jury to say that neglect is to be regarded as sufficient to support a charge of ill-treatment. (Per Widgery, L.J.) *R. v. Hayles*, [1969] 1 Q. B. 364; [1969] 1 All E. R. 34, C. A. where a conviction for wilfully ill-treating a child was upheld, the appellant having put his child to bed after a fall without any medical attention or treatment.

"**Neglects.**"—"Neglect," said Lord Russell, C.J., "is the want of reasonable care—that is, the omission of such steps as a reasonable parent would take, such as are usually taken in the ordinary experience of mankind—that is, in such a case as the present, provided that the parent had such means as would enable him to take the necessary steps" (*R. v. Senior*, [1899] 1 Q. B. 283; 63 J. P. 8). The question of means has become of little importance since the coming into operation of various statutes by which medical and other assistance is provided.

Even at common law it was a misdemeanor to neglect to supply necessaries to a child servant or apprentice, being of tender years and unable to provide for itself, and whom the defendant was bound either by duty or contract to support (*R. v. Friend* (1802), Russ, & Ry. 20); but it was not sufficient to support an indictment for neglect, abandonment, or exposure, to prove "that the child had suffered injury, but not to any serious extent" (*R. v. Phillpot* (1853), Dears, C. C. 179; 17 J. P. 280).

Where a man and woman are jointly summoned for neglect of children, the man is equally guilty with the woman if he has seen what was going on (see *R. v. Bubb*, *R. v. Hook* (1850), 14 J. P. 562 ; 4 Cox, C. C. 455).

In the case of *Oakey v. Jackson*, [1914] 1 K. B. 216 ; 78 J. P. 87, it was held that a refusal to allow an operation on a child may be an offence under the above section if the circumstances are such as to make the refusal unreasonable.

" The justices in deciding whether there was wilful neglect must consider in each case the nature of the operation and the reasonableness of the refusal to have it performed " (per Darling, J., at p. 88).   See also *R. v. De Crespigny, Ex parte Carter* (1912), *Times*, May 21.

" Means."—It has been held that the word " neglect " sufficiently alleges the ability of the parent to provide for the child, and that it is not necessary to aver in the indictment that the parent had means (*R. v. Ryland* (1867), L. R. 1 C. C. R. 99 ; 31 J. P. 790).

Where a man deliberately abstains from doing work which he might obtain if he wished, and leaves his children to be provided for by others, this is " wilful neglect " within the meaning of the Act.   It is for the magistrates or the jury to infer from all the circumstances in the case how far the neglect was " wilful " or merely unavoidable, and the degrees of guilt to a certain extent depend on the amount of means.

The view has generally been adopted that frequent drunkenness is some evidence of means.   A presumption that the defendant had means may also be raised when it is proved that he or she certainly had means at some time shortly before the alleged neglect, and this is a question of fact to be left to the jury (*R. v. Jones* (1901), 19 Cox, C. C. 678).

" Abandons or exposes."—There is also s. 27 of the Offences against the Person Act, 1861; 8 Halsbury's Statutes, 3rd Edn., 156, relating to the abandonment of infants under two years.   In *R. v. White* (1871), L. R. 1 C. C. R. 311 ; 36 J. P. 134 ; 12 Cox, C. C. 83, the defendant was convicted under s. 27 of the Offences against the Person Act, 1861, of abandoning a child within the meaning of that Act.

The facts were that the mother of the child, who lived apart from her husband, and who had the actual custody of the child, brought it and left it at the father's door, telling him she had done so.   The father knowingly allowed it to remain there for six hours, till it was found by a constable stiff with cold.   It was held that though the father had not had actual custody and possession, his allowing it to remain where it was constituted abandonment and exposure by him.

In *R. v. Falkingham* (1870), L. R. 1 C. C. R. 222 ; 34 J. P. 149, a child five weeks old was put in a hamper, wrapped in a shawl and padded with shavings and cotton wool, and sent by train to its putative father's lodgings.   After a journey of half an hour the hamper was delivered twenty-five minutes later to his father's address, and the child was found to be alive and unharmed.   The mother and another woman who assisted her were found guilty of abandoning the child within the meaning of the Offences against the Persons Act, 1861 ; 8 Halsbury's Statutes, 3rd Edn., 147.

In *R. v. Williams* (1910), 4 Cr. App. Rep. 89 ; 74 J. P. N. 99 ; 26 T. L. R. 290 ; it was held that to constitute the offence under s. 12 of the Children Act, 1908 (now s. 1 of this Act, p. 10, *ante*), the exposure need not necessarily consist of the physical placing of the child somewhere with intent to injure it.

In *R. v. Whibley*, [1938] 3 All E. R. 777 ; 102 J. P. 326, on appeal to the Court of Criminal Appeal against a sentence for wilfully abandoning five children, who had been left at a juvenile court, it was held that to leave the children at a juvenile court was not likely to cause them unnecessary suffering or injury to health, and the appeal was allowed.

" Abandonment."—It would be the duty of the local authority to receive an abandoned child into care under s. 1 of the Children Act, 1948, p. 880, *post*.

" Causes or procures."—" Procure " is one of the words used in the Accessories and Abettors Act, 1861, s. 8; 8 Halsbury's Statutes, 3rd Edn., 114, "whosoever shall aid, abet, counsel or procure," etc.   It is also used in s. 35 of the Magistrates' Courts Act, 1952; 21 Halsbury's Statutes, 3rd Edn., 218.

The procurement may take place through a third party (*Foster's Crown Cases*, 125 ; and see *R. v. Cooper* (1833), 5 C. & P. 535 ; 1 Nev. & M. M. C. 371), but there must be some active proceedings on the part of the defendant.

" Likely to cause unnecessary suffering or injury to health."—Deliberate omission to supply medical or surgical aid is within these words (*R.* v. *Senior,* [1899] 1 Q. B. 283; 63 J. P. 8; and *Oakey* v. *Jackson,* [1914] 1. K. B. 216; 78 J. P. 87).

Direct proof that the neglect, etc., did in fact, or was likely to, cause unnecessary suffering or injury to health is not required, since it may be inferred from the evidence of neglect (*R.* v. *Brenton* (1904), 111 C. C. C. Sessions Pap. 309; and see also *Cole* v. *Pendleton* (1896), 60 J. P. 359; 40 Sol. Jo. 480).

It is no defence that the actual injury was caused by the act of a third person (*R.* v. *Connor,* [1908] 2 K. B. 26, at p. 31; 72 J. P. 212).

The words " likely to cause," etc., qualify all the preceding words : " assaults," " ill-treats," " neglects," etc. (*R.* v. *Hatton,* [1925] 2 K. B. 322; 19 Cr. App. Rep. 29; 89 J. P. 164).

" Evidence."—(i) Proof of likelihood of suffering being caused.

Medical evidence is usually most satisfactory in these cases, but it is not essential. See *R.* v. *Brenton, supra.*

In many, or indeed most, cases where a prosecution has been instituted under this Act, it will be found that either an officer of a society or a police constable has seen the accused and has informed him of the complaint made against him. In such a case it is of the utmost importance to bear in mind that no threat or induce-ment of any sort must be used, and it rests upon the prosecution, before seeking to give evidence of the statement of an accused person, to show affirmatively that no such threat or inducement was used (*R.* v. *Thompson,* [1893] 2 Q. B. 12; 57 J. P. 312). If, however, the accused when informed of the complaint voluntarily makes a statement, such statement may properly be given in evidence; there is nothing wrong or unfair in the conduct of the officer of a society in communicating to a person not yet charged with an offence the nature of the complaint against him and in taking down his answer even when no caution has been given (*Rogers* v. *Hawken* (1898), 62 J. P. 279; 67 L. Q. B. 526; *Lewis* v. *Harris* (1913), 78 J. P. 68; 110 L. T. 337). The Judges' Rules, 1964 (see Home Office Circular No. 31/1964), r. VI applies the rules to persons other than police officers charged with the duty of investigating offences or charging offenders: as to the meaning of professional investigators see *R.* v. *Nichols* (1967), 51 Cr. App. Rep. 233; [1967] Crim. L. R. 296.

(ii) Evidence of child.

If it should happen that the evidence of a child of tender years is relied upon by the prosecution, the need of corroboration must be borne in mind (*R.* v. *Hatton, supra*). In the case of unsworn evidence this is a statutory requirement (see s. 38, p. 44, *post*); but apparently, in *R.* v. *Hatton,* p. 13, *ante.,* the child's evidence was sworn.

See s. 27 of the Children and Young Persons Act, 1963, p. 98, *post,* as to the evidence of children in committal proceedings for sexual offences.

" Prosecutions."—Local education authorities have power to institute proceed-ings for offences under Part I and Part II of the Act; see s. 98, p. 76, *post.*

" Procedure."—Even where it is proposed to proceed summarily the defendant is entitled to go for trial if he desires to do so and he must be informed of his right to do so before the charge is gone into (Magistrates' Courts Act, 1952, s. 25, p. 276, *post*).

Under section one, however, there is the alternative procedure by indictment, and the justices may therefore commit for trial without giving the defendant the option of a summary trial if, in all the circumstances, they think this the proper course. The procedure in this type of prosecution is laid down in s. 18 of the Magis-trates' Courts Act, 1952.

" Six months."—The effect of this is to give the court power to sentence to six months imprisonment or to impose a fine not exceeding £100 or both. In default of payment of a fine, imprisonment regulated by the scale laid down in Sched. 3 to the Magistrates' Courts Act, 1952, may be imposed, and may be made consecutive to a term of imprisonment imposed in addition to the fine. (See s. 108 of the Magi-strates' Courts Act, 1952; 21 Halsbury's Statutes, 3rd Edn., 278.)

The Ingleby Committee recommended that full use be made of facilities for rehabilitation, although the power to impose imprisonment should be retained.

"**Other person.**"—If it can be proved that the defendant is legally liable to maintain the child, proof of means is no longer necessary. See note "Means" p. 17, *ante*.

"**Deemed.**"—This is so even if religious grounds are given as the reason for not supplying medical aid (*R.* v. *Senior*, [1899] 1 Q. B. 283 ; 63 J. P. 8).

"**Fails.**"—In *R.* v. *De Crespigny, Ex parte Carter* (1912), *Times*, May 21, when the justices convicted a man under this section for refusing to allow an operation for a cleft palate, a Divisional Court refused to make absolute a rule *nisi* for *certiorari* on the ground that the question for the justices was simply one of fact.

Justices must consider the nature of the operation and the reasonableness of the refusal in dealing with cases of neglect under this section (*Oakey* v. *Jackson*, [1914] 1 K. B. 216 ; 78 J. P. 87).

"**Action of another person.**"—See, for illustrations of this subsection, the intervention of the relieving officer in *R.* v. *Falkingham* (1870), L. R. 1 C. C. R. 222 ; 34 J. P. 149 ; and the constable in *R.* v. *White* (1871), L. R. 1 C. C. R. 311 ; 36 J. P. 134.

"**Manslaughter.**"—The fact that a person has been already convicted of neglect under sub-s. (1), p. 10, *ante*, is no bar to further proceedings for manslaughter should the child subsequently die.

"Death is a new fact, and not a mere matter of aggravation or a mere consequence." Per Williams, J., *R.* v. *Friel* (1890), 17 Cox, C. C. 325 ; and see *R.* v. *Tonks*, [1916] 1 K. B. 443 ; 80 J. P. 165.

A verdict of neglect under sub-s. (1) cannot be given if the jury are satisfied on the facts that the accused was guilty of manslaughter (*R.* v. *Tonks, supra*).

"**Directly or indirectly interested.**"—These words were introduced in order to catch those who insured the children in their care in the name of a third person, since strictly at law no one could be said to be interested except the person named in the policy as the holder of the policy. See sub-s. (6), p. 11, *ante*.

"**Such knowledge.**"—Under the Prevention of Cruelty to Children Act, 1904, which referred to a person "indicted," actual proof of the insurance of the child could be given as part of the case for the prosecution when the defendant was tried on indictment.

Now, since the statute refers to a person "convicted," such proof can only be given after the conviction. Though it can be given in every case, the court has no power to increase the punishment in case of a summary conviction.

"**Penal servitude.**"—Penal servitude was abolished by s. 1 of the Criminal Justice Act, 1948; 8 Halsbury's Statutes, 3rd Edn., 337.

Neglecting to provide food for and assaulting apprentices or servants.

S. 26 of the Offences against the Person Act, 1861, is as follows:

> "Whosoever, being legally liable, either as a master or mistress, to provide for any apprentice or servant necessary food, clothing, or lodging, shall wilfully and without lawful excuse refuse or neglect to provide the same, or shall unlawfully and maliciously do or cause to be done any bodily harm to any such apprentice or servant, so that the life of such apprentice or servant shall be endangered, or the health of such apprentice or servant shall have been or shall be likely to be permanently injured, shall be guilty of a misdemeanor.

In practice proceedings would now probably be taken under s. 1 of the Children and Young Persons Act, 1933, p. 10, *ante*, where the servant or apprentice is under sixteen. For a similar section to s. 26 of the 1861 Act see the Conspiracy and Protection of Property Act, 1875, s. 6; *op. cit.* 888. Under that section an offence is triable summarily, unless the offender claims trial by jury.

"**Endangered.**"—There seems to be no decided case on the question whether the words "so that the life of such persons shall be endangered" qualify all the preceding words, or only those as to the actual doing of bodily harm to the servant. On the analogy of the words "likely to cause unnecessary suffering" in s. 1 of the Children and Young Persons Act, 1933, and the decision given in the case of *R* v. *Hatton*, [1925] 2 K. B. 322 ; 19 Cr. App. Rep. 29 ; 89 J. P. 164 (see p. 13, *ante*), it is suggested that they qualify all the words.

Visiting Forces Act, 1952.—An offence punishable under this section is an " offence against the person " within the meaning of s. 3 of the Visiting Forces Act, 1952; 29 Halsbury's Statutes, 3rd Edn., 925. See that section as to the limitation of the liability of a member of a visiting force or a member of a civilian component of such a force to be tried by a United Kingdom court for such an offence.

2. Causing or encouraging seduction or prostitution of girl under sixteen. [*Repealed by the Sexual Offences Act, 1956, s. 51 and Sched. IV, and replaced by s. 28 of that Act, p. 396, post.*]

3. Allowing persons under sixteen to be in brothels.—(1) If any person having the custody, charge or care of a child or young person who has attained the age of four years and is under the age of sixteen years, allows that child or young person to reside in or to frequent a brothel, he shall be guilty of a misdemeanour and shall be liable on conviction on indictment, or on summary conviction, to a fine not exceeding twenty-five pounds, or alternatively, or in addition thereto, to imprisonment for any term not exceeding six months.

NOTES

This section is printed as amended by the Sexual Offences Act, 1956, Sched. IV and the Children and Young Persons Act, 1963.

" **Custody, charge or care.**"—See note at p. 12, *ante.*

" **Six months.**"—See note on p. 18, *ante.*

" **Brothel.**"—A brothel means a place resorted to by persons of both sexes for the purpose of illicit intercourse, whether the women are common prostitutes or not (*Winter* v. *Woolfe*, [1931] 1 K. B. 549; 95 J. P. 20). A prostitute who receives men in her own room but does not allow other women to use her premises for the purpose is not keeping a brothel (*Singleton* v. *Ellison*, [1895] 1 Q. B. 607; 59 J. P. 119. In *Caldwell* v. *Leech* (1913), 77 J. P. 254; 109 L. T. 188, a woman allowed one prostitute to use premises for receiving different men, and this was held not to be keeping a brothel. A block of flats inhabited by different prostitutes may constitute a brothel (*Durose* v. *Wilson* (1907), 71 J. P. 263; 96 L. T. 645).

The defendant has a right to claim trial by jury under s. 25 of the Magistrates' Courts Act, 1952, p. 276, *post.* The court may, however, independently of this, decide to commit for trial, since the procedure may be by indictment or summary proceedings.

Procedure.—This being an offence punishable either on indictment or on summary conviction, s. 18 of the Magistrates' Courts Act, 1952, applies, but it is to be noted that the punishment upon conviction on indictment is no greater than that on summary conviction.

Visiting Forces Act, 1952.—See note to s. 1, *supra.*

4. Causing or allowing persons under sixteen to be used for begging.—(1) If any person causes or procures any child or young person under the age of sixteen years or, having the custody, charge, or care of such a child or young person, allows him to be in any street, premises, or place for the purpose of begging or receiving alms, or of inducing the giving of alms (whether or not there is any pretence of singing, playing, performing, offering anything for sale, or otherwise) he shall, on summary conviction, be liable to a fine not exceeding twenty-five pounds, or alternatively, or in addition thereto, to imprisonment for any term not exceeding three months.

(2) If a person having the custody, charge, or care of a child or young person is charged with an offence under this section, and it is proved that the child or young person was in any street, premises, or place for any such purpose as aforesaid, and that the person charged allowed the child or young person to be in the street, premises, or place, he shall be presumed to have allowed him to be in the street, premises, or place for that purpose unless the contrary is proved.

(3) If any person while singing, playing, performing or offering anything for sale in a street or public place has with him a child who has been lent or hired out to him, the child shall, for the purposes of this section, be deemed to be in that street or place for the purpose of inducing the giving of alms.

NOTES

This section is printed as amended by the Children and Young Persons Act, 1963.

" Causes or procures."—See p. 17, ante.

" Allows."—This is evidently something less than causing or procuring ; it is the failure by a person having custody, etc., to prevent what he could and should have prevented.

" Child, young person."—See s. 107, p. 81, post.

" Custody, charge or care."—See p. 12, ante.

" Street."—Defined by s. 107, p. 81, post, and includes any highway and any public bridge, road, lane, footway, square, court, alley, or passage, whether a thoroughfare or not.

" Begging or receiving alms."—As to begging on behalf of other persons, see Pointon v. Hill (1884), 12 Q. B. D. 306 ; 48 J. P. 341, where miners went round the town with a cart inscribed " Children's Bread Waggon," soliciting alms on behalf of the wives and children of miners on strike. It was held that they were not begging within the meaning of the Vagrancy Act, 1824 ; 8 Halsbury's Statutes, 3rd Edn., 71.

Visiting Forces Act, 1952.—See note to s. 1, p. 20, ante.

5. Giving intoxicating liquor to children under five.—If any person gives, or causes to be given, to any child under the age of five years any intoxicating liquor, except upon the order of a duly qualified medical practitioner, or in case of sickness, apprehended sickness, or other urgent cause, he shall, on summary conviction, be liable to a fine not exceeding ten pounds.

NOTE

This section is printed as amended by the Criminal Justice Act, 1967, s. 92 and Sched. III.

Intoxicating liquor is defined in s. 107, p. 81, post.

6. Causing or allowing children to be in bars of licensed premises.—[Repealed by Licensing Act, 1953, s. 168 and Tenth Schedule. See now s. 168 of the Licensing Act, 1964, p. 428, post.]

7. Sale of tobacco, etc., to persons under sixteen.—(1) Any person who sells to a person apparently under the age of sixteen years any tobacco or cigarette papers, whether for his own use or not, shall be

liable, on summary conviction, in the case of a first offence to a fine not exceeding twenty-five pounds, in the case of a second offence to a fine not exceeding fifty pounds, and in the case of a third or subsequent offence to a fine not exceeding one hundred pounds :

Provided that a person shall not be guilty of an offence under this section in respect of any sale of tobacco otherwise than in the form of cigarettes, if he did not know and had no reason to believe that the tobacco was for the use of the person to whom it was sold.

(2) If on complaint to a court of summary jurisdiction it is proved to the satisfaction of the court that any automatic machine for the sale of tobacco kept on any premises is being extensively used by persons apparently under the age of sixteen years, the court may order the owner of the machine, or the person on whose premises the machine is kept, to take such precautions to prevent the machine being so used as may be specified in the order or, if necessary, to remove the machine, within such time as may be specified in the order, and if any person against whom such an order has been made fails to comply therewith, he shall be liable, on summary conviction, to a fine not exceeding fifty pounds, and to a further fine not exceeding ten pounds for each day during which the offence continues.

(3) It shall be the duty of a constable and of a park-keeper being in uniform to seize any tobacco or cigarette papers in the possession of any person apparently under the age of sixteen years whom he finds smoking in any street or public place, and any tobacco or cigarette papers so seized shall be disposed of, if seized by a constable, in such manner as the police authority may direct, and if seized by a park-keeper, in such manner as the authority or person by whom he was appointed may direct.

(4) Nothing in this section shall make it an offence to sell tobacco or cigarette papers to, or shall authorise the seizure of tobacco or cigarette papers in the possession of, any person who is at the time employed by a manufacturer of or dealer in tobacco, either wholesale or retail, for the purposes of his business, or is a boy messenger in uniform in the employment of a messenger company and employed as such at the time.

(5) For the purposes of this section the expression " tobacco " includes cigarettes and smoking mixtures intended as a substitute for tobacco, and the expression " cigarettes " includes cut tobacco rolled up in paper, tobacco leaf, or other material in such form as to be capable of immediate use for smoking.

NOTES

This section is printed as amended by the Children and Young Persons Act, 1963.

" **Owner.**"—Under sub-s. (2) there will, of course, be a summons against the owner or other person, so that he may he heard to show cause why an order should not be made.

"**Appeal.**"—There is a right of appeal to the Crown Court against an order (see s. 102, p. 78, *post*).

" **Second offence.**"—See *R.* v. *South Shields Licensing Justices*, p. 26, *post*.

Street and **public place** are defined in s. 107, p. 81, *post*.

8. Taking pawns from persons under fourteen.—If a pawnbroker takes an article in pawn from any person apparently under the age of fourteen years, whether offered by that person on his own behalf or on behalf of any other person, he shall be guilty of an offence against the Pawnbrokers Act, 1872.

NOTES

" **Pawnbroker.**"—By s. 5 of the Pawnbrokers Act, 1872 ; 24 Halsbury's Statutes, 3rd Edn., 705, a pawnbroker includes any person who carries on business of taking goods and chattels in pawn, and by s. 45; *op. cit.* 780, an offence against the Act for which no special penalty is provided, is punishable by a penalty not exceeding £10.

By s. 50 of the Metropolitan Police Act, 1839 ; *op. cit.* 702, a pawnbroker (including his agent or servant) is liable to a fine of £5 if he purchases or takes in pawn any goods from any child apparently under the age of *sixteen.*

9. Prohibition of purchase of old metals from persons under sixteen.—[*Repealed by the Scrap Metal Dealers Act, 1964, s. 10 and Schedule, Part I (37 Halsbury's Statutes, 3rd Edn., 627, 628). It is now replaced by s. 5 (1) of that Act as follows*]:

" **5. Other offences relating to scrap metal.**—(1) If a scrap metal dealer acquires any scrap metal from a person apparently under the age of sixteen years, whether the scrap metal is offered by the person on his own behalf or on behalf of another person, he shall be guilty of an offence and liable on summary conviction to a fine not exceeding £10:

Provided that, where a person is charged with an offence under this subsection, it shall be a defence to prove that the person from whom he acquired the scrap metal was in fact of or over the age of sixteen years."

NOTES

" **Scrap metal** ".—By s. 9, *ibid.*, " scrap metal " includes any old metal, and any broken, worn out, defaced or partly manufactured articles made wholly or partly of metal, and any metallic wastes, and also includes old, broken, worn out or defaced tooltips or dies made of any of the materials commonly known as hard metal or of cemented or sintered metallic carbides.

" **Article.**"—This includes any part of an article.

10. Vagrants preventing children from receiving education.— (1) If a person habitually wanders from place to place and takes with him any child who has attained the age of five years or any young person who has not attained the age at which under the enactments relating to education children cease to be of compulsory school age he shall, unless he proves that the child or young person is not, by being so taken with him, prevented from receiving efficient full-time education suitable to his age, ability and aptitude, be liable on summary conviction to a fine not exceeding ten pounds :

(1A) Proceedings for an offence under this section shall not be instituted except by a local education authority; and before instituting such proceedings the authority shall consider whether it would be appropriate, instead of or as well as instituting the proceedings, to bring the child or young person in question before a juvenile court under section 1 of the Children and Young Persons Act, 1969.

(2) Any constable who finds a person wandering from place to place and taking a child or young person with him may, if he has reasonable ground for believing that the person is guilty of an offence under this section, apprehend him without a warrant.

(3) Where in any proceedings for an offence against this section it is proved that the parent or guardian of the child or young person is engaged in any trade or business of such a nature as to require him to travel from place to place, the person against whom the proceedings were brought shall be acquitted if it is proved that the child or young person has attended a school at which he was a registered pupil as regularly as the nature of the trade or business of the parent or guardian permits :

Provided that in the case of a child or young person who has attained the age of six years the person against whom the proceedings were brought shall not be entitled to be acquitted under this subsection unless it is proved that the child or young person has made at least two hundred attendances during the period of twelve months ending with the date on which the proceedings were instituted.

(4) The Board of Education shall have power to make regulations as to the issue of certificates of attendance for the purposes of the last foregoing subsection, and any such regulations shall be laid before Parliament as soon as may be after they are made.

NOTES

This section is printed as amended by the Education Act, 1944, s. 120, Sched. VIII, Part I, the Criminal Justice Act, 1967, and the Children and Young Persons Act, 1969, s. 72 (3) and Sched. V.

Regulations.—None have been made under this subsection, and those dated April 20, 1909, which were kept in force under Sched. V, para. 1, were repealed by the Employment of Children in Entertainments Provisional Amending Rules, 1945. Those Rules were in turn replaced by the 1946 Amending Rules, which make no special reference to the issue of certificates of attendance.

"Detaining child or young person.—See Children and Young Persons Act, 1969, s. 28 (2)."

11. Exposing children under twelve to risk of burning.—If any person who has attained the age of sixteen years, having the custody, charge or care of any child under the age of twelve years, allows the child to be in any room containing an open fire grate or any heating appliance liable to cause injury to a person by contact therewith, not sufficiently protected to guard against the risk of his being burnt or scalded without taking reasonable precautions against that risk, and by reason thereof the child is killed or suffers serious injury, he shall on summary conviction be liable to a fine not exceeding ten pounds:

Provided that neither this section, nor any proceedings taken thereunder, shall affect any liability of any such person to be proceeded against by indictment for any indictable offence.

NOTES

This section is printed as amended by the Children and Young Persons (Amendment) Act, 1952.

" Custody, charge or care."—See p. 12, *ante.*

" Any indictable offence."—A person might, for example, be guilty, in certain circumstances, of manslaughter.

Visiting Forces Act, 1952.—See note to s. 1, p. 20, *ante.*

12. Failing to provide for safety of children at entertainments.—

(1) Where there is provided in any building an entertainment for children, or an entertainment at which the majority of the persons attending are children, then, if the number of children attending the entertainment exceeds one hundred, it shall be the duty of the person providing the entertainment to station and keep stationed wherever necessary a sufficient number of adult attendants, properly instructed as to their duties, to prevent more children or other persons being admitted to the building, or to any part thereof, than the building or part can properly accommodate, and to control the movement of the children and other persons admitted while entering and leaving the building or any part thereof, and to take all other reasonable precautions for the safety of the children.

(2) Where the occupier of a building permits, for hire or reward, the building to be used for the purpose of an entertainment, he shall take all reasonable steps to secure the observance of the provisions of this section.

(3) If any person on whom any obligation is imposed by this section fails to fulfil that obligation, he shall be liable, on summary conviction, to a fine not exceeding, in the case of a first offence fifty pounds, and in the case of a second or subsequent offence one hundred pounds, and also, if the building in which the entertainment is given is licensed under the Cinematograph Act, 1909, or under any of the enactments relating to the licensing of theatres and of houses and other places for music or dancing, the licence shall be liable to be revoked by the authority by whom the licence was granted.

(4) A constable may enter any building in which he has reason to believe that such an entertainment as aforesaid is being, or is about to be, provided, with a view to seeing whether the provisions of this section are carried into effect, and an officer authorised for the purpose by an authority by whom licences are granted under any of the enactments referred to in the last foregoing subsection shall have the like power of entering any building so licensed by that authority.

(5) The institution of proceedings under this section shall—

    (a) in the case of a building licensed by the Lord Chamberlain, or licensed by the council of a county or county borough under the Cinematograph Act, 1909, or under the enactments relating to the licensing of theatres or of houses and other places for music or dancing, be the duty of the council of the county or county borough in which the building is situated ; and

    (b) in any other case, be the duty of the police authority.

(6) This section shall not apply to any entertainment given in a private dwelling-house.

NOTES

" Providing the entertainment."—It will, we submit, be a question of fact, to be decided by the justices, who is the person " who provides the entertainment."

Generally, no doubt, it would be the person who arranges to hire the building and is responsible for the programme. The occupier who permits the use of the building, for hire or reward, is always liable (sub-s. (2)) ; but this does not exclude the possibility that others may also be liable.

" **Second offence.**"—This means an offence committed after a conviction for a previous offence (*R. v. South Shields Licensing Justices*, [1911] 2 K. B. 1 ; 75 J. P. 299).

Subsection (4).—It is desirable that the authority of an officer other than a constable should be in writing. Wilfully to obstruct a constable in the execution of his duty under this section would no doubt be an offence under the Police Act, 1964 ; 25 Halsbury's Statutes, 3rd Edn., 330 ; but in the case of obstruction of some other authorised person wishing to enter a building there appears to be no statutory offence. The obligation to admit is implied, and not expressed, so that it is very doubtful whether sub-s. (3) could be applied. Refusal to admit might possibly be a common law misdemeanour. In practice, however, no difficulty need arise. An authorised person who is refused admittance can call a constable, and a refusal to admit a constable is, as we submit, clearly an offence.

Cinematograph entertainments.—See the Cinematograph (Children) (No. 2) Regulations, 1955, S.I. 1955 No. 1909.

Special Provisions as to Prosecutions for Offences specified in First Schedule

13. Power to take offenders into custody.—(1) Any constable may take into custody, without warrant—

(a) any person who within his view commits any of the offences mentioned in the First Schedule to this Act, if the constable does not know and cannot ascertain his name and residence ;

(b) any person who has committed, or whom he has reason to believe to have committed, any of the offences mentioned in the First Schedule to this Act, if the constable has reasonable ground for believing that that person will abscond or does not know and cannot ascertain his name and address.

(2) Where, under the powers conferred by this section, a constable arrests any person without warrant, the superintendent or inspector of police or an officer of police of equal or superior rank, or the officer in charge of the police station to which the person is brought, shall, unless in his belief the release of the person on bail would tend to defeat the ends of justice, or to cause injury or danger to the child or young person against whom the offence is alleged to have been committed, release the person arrested on his entering into such a recognisance, with or without sureties, as may in the judgment of the officer of police be required to secure his attendance upon the hearing of the charge.

NOTES

"**Without warrant.**"—For common law powers of arrest without warrant see s. 2 Criminal Law Act, 1967.

" **Cannot ascertain.**"—It seems clear that this must mean " cannot ascertain at the time."

It is not necessary that a person seen committing an offence should be arrested at the time. Application for a summons or a warrant can be made later. An officer of a society saw a man driving a horse in an unfit state and delayed taking any proceedings until he had communicated with his society, and on their instructions waited to see the effect of a warning. When a fortnight later he applied to the justices for a summons they refused it on the ground that he had delayed too long in applying for it. The Divisional Court held that the fact that the accused was not given in charge at once constituted no bar to future proceedings (*R.* v. *Paget* (1889), 53 J. P. 469). The ordinary law is that a police constable has no general power to arrest a person without warrant merely on suspicion of having committed a misdemeanour, but see s. 2 (4) Criminal Law Act, 1967.

" **Bail.**"—See Magistrates' Courts Act, 1952, s. 38, p. 381, *post.*

First Schedule.—See p. 83, *post,* and list of offences at p. 245, *post.*

Suicide Act, 1961.—As to the prohibition on instituting proceedings for an offence under s. 2, *ibid.* (subject to s. 13, *supra,* and s. 40, *post*) except by or with the consent of the Director of Public Prosecutions, see s. 2 (4), *ibid.*

14. Mode of charging offences and limitation of time.—(1) Where a person is charged with committing any of the offences mentioned in the First Schedule to this Act in respect of two or more children or young persons, the same information or summons may charge the offence in respect of all or any of them, but the person charged shall not, if he is summarily convicted, be liable to a separate penalty in respect of each child or young person except upon separate informations.

(2) The same information or summons may also charge any person as having the custody, charge, or care, alternatively or together, and may charge him with the offences of assault, ill-treatment, neglect, abandonment, or exposure, together or separately, and may charge him with committing all or any of those offences in a manner likely to cause unnecessary suffering or injury to health, alternatively or together, but when those offences are charged together the person charged shall not, if he is summarily convicted, be liable to a separate penalty for each.

(3) [*Repealed by the Children and Young Persons Act,* 1963].

(4) When any offence mentioned in the First Schedule to this Act charged against any person is a continuous offence, it shall not be necessary to specify in the information, summons, or indictment, the date of the acts constituting the offence.

NOTES

This section is printed as amended by the Children and Young Persons Act, 1963.

" **Date of the acts.**"—In *R.* v. *Miller* (1901), 65 J. P. 313, an indictment for neglect of children alleged the neglect as on April 9, 1901, and on divers dates between November 9, 1900, and April 9, 1901. Phillimore, J., did not admit evidence tendered on behalf of the prosecution of neglect before those dates.

The subsection is not affected by the Indictment Rules, 1971 (S.I. 1971 No. 1253).

15. Evidence of husband or wife of accused person.—As respects proceedings against any person for any of the offences mentioned in the First Schedule to this Act otherwise than in the entry relating to the Sexual Offences Act, 1956, the Criminal Evidence Act, 1898, shall apply as if the Schedule to that Act included references to those offences.

NOTES

This section is printed as amended by the Sexual Offences Act, 1956; 8 Halsbury's Statutes 3rd Edn., 415.

This section enables husband or wife to give evidence for the prosecution against the other. Such witness is competent, but not compellable. See *Leach* v. *R.,*

[1912] A. C. 305; 76 J. P. 203. The witness should be informed that he (or she) is not bound to give evidence; see *R.* v. *Acaster* (1912), 106 L. T. 384. See also the Sexual Offences Act, 1956, s. 39; 8 Halsbury's Statutes 3rd Edn., 438, and the Indecency with Children Act, 1960, s. 1 (2), p. 398, *post*.

Indecency with Children Act, 1960.—References in this section to the offences mentioned in the First Schedule, do not include offences under s. 1 of the Indecency with Children Act, 1960, *ibid.*, p. 398, *post*.

Supplemental

16. [*Repealed by Administration of Justice (Miscellaneous Provisions) Act, 1933, s.* 10 (3) *and Sched. III.*]

17. Interpretation of Part I.—For the purposes of this Part of this Act—

Any person who is the parent or legal guardian of a child or young person or who is legally liable to maintain him shall be presumed to have the custody of him, and as between father and mother the father shall not be deemed to have ceased to have the custody of him by reason only that he has deserted, or otherwise does not reside with, the mother and the child or young person ;

Any person to whose charge a child or young person is committed by any person who has the custody of him shall be presumed to have charge of the child or young person ;

Any other person having actual possession or control of a child or young person shall be presumed to have the care of him.

NOTES

" **Parent.**"—" Parent " does not include a putative father against whom no affiliation order has been made (*Butler* v. *Gregory* (1902), 18 T. L. R. 370; but see *Liverpool Society for Prevention of Cruelty to Children* v. *Jones*, [1914] 3 K. B. 813; 79 J. P. 20. The Court of Appeal held in *Re M. (an infant)*, [1955] 2 All E. R. 911; 119 J. P. 535; 99 Sol. J. 539; that the natural father of an illegitimate child is not a " parent " of the child within the meaning of the Adoption Act, 1950. See also note "Custody, charge, or care," p. 12, *ante*).

As to adopted children, see the Adoption Act, 1958, s. 13, p. 1047, *post*.

" **Legal guardian.**"—Defined by s. 107, p. 81, *post*, as meaning " a person appointed according to law to be his guardian, by deed or will or by order of a court of competent jurisdiction."

" **Person legally liable to maintain the child.**"—By s. 42 of the National Assistance Act, 1948; 23 Halsbury's Statutes, 3rd Edn., 662, the only persons liable are the father and the mother, and this only until the child becomes sixteen years of age. For this purpose a man's children include an illegitimate child of which he has been adjudged to be the putative father, and a woman's children include her illegitimate children. It is submitted that in certain circumstances a person might be legally liable under an agreement to maintain a child.

The section creates a presumption but this may be rebutted by evidence. It is not stated to be conclusive.

PART II.—EMPLOYMENT

General Provisions as to Employment

PRELIMINARY NOTE

Children and Young Persons Act, 1963.—Part II of that Act, in its application to England and Wales, and, as regards section 42, in its application elsewhere, shall be construed, and Part II of the Children and Young Persons Act, 1933, shall have effect, as if this Part were included in that Part (1963 Act, ss. 44, 65, pp. 109, 117, *post*).

Child.—By s. 58 of the Education Act, 1944, p. 266, *post*, any person, who is not for the purposes of that Act over compulsory school age shall be deemed to be a child within the meaning of any enactment relating to the prohibition or regulation of the employment of children or young persons.

18. Restrictions on employment of children.—(1) Subject to the provisions of this section and of any byelaws made thereunder no child shall be employed—

(a) until he has attained the age two years below that which is for the time being the upper limit of the compulsory school age by virtue of section thirty-five of the Education Act, 1944, together with any Order in Council made under that section (without regard to the provisions of subsection (1) of section thirty-eight of that Act as to the age of pupils at special schools, or to the provisions of section eight of the Education Act, 1946, as to deeming a person not to have attained a given age until the end of a school term).

(b) before the close of school hours on any day on which he is required to attend school ; or

(c) before seven o'clock in the morning or after seven o'clock in the evening on any day ; or

(d) for more than two hours on any day on which he is required to attend school ; or

(e) for more than two hours on any Sunday ; or

(f) to lift, carry or move anything so heavy as to be likely to cause injury to him.

(2) A local authority may make byelaws with respect to the employment of children, and any such byelaws may distinguish between children of different ages and sexes and between different localities, trades, occupations and circumstances, and may contain provisions—

(a) authorising—

(i) the employment of children before they attain the age at which employment ceases to be prohibited under paragraph (a) of the last foregoing subsection by their parents or guardians in light agricultural or horticultural work;

(ii) the employment of children (notwithstanding anything in paragraph (b) of the last foregoing subsection) for not more than one hour before the commencement of school hours on any day on which they are required to attend school ;

(b) prohibiting absolutely the employment of children in any specified occupation ;

(c) prescribing—

(i) the age below which children are not to be employed ;

(ii) the number of hours in each day, or in each week, for which, and the times of day at which, they may be employed ;

   (iii) the intervals to be allowed to them for meals and rest ;
   (iv) the holidays or half holidays to be allowed to them ;
   (v) any other conditions to be observed in relation to their
   employment ;

so, however, that no such byelaws shall modify the restrictions contained
in the last foregoing subsection save in so far as is expressly permitted
by paragraph (a) of this subsection, and any restriction contained in any
such byelaws shall have effect in addition to the said restrictions.

   (3) Nothing in this section, or in any byelaw made under this section,
shall prevent a child from taking part in a performance—

   (a) under the authority of a licence granted under this Part of this
       Act; or
   (b) in a case where by virtue of section 37 (3) of the Children and
       Young Persons Act, 1963, no licence under that section is
       required for him to take part in the performance.

NOTES

   This section is printed as amended by the Education Act, 1944, s. 120, Sched.
VIII, Part I, the Education (Miscellaneous Provisions) Act, 1948, s. 11, Sched. I,
Part II, and the Children and Young Persons Act, 1963, ss. 34, 64 and 65, and Sched.
III.
   " Age."—See note "Age of sixteen" to s. 1, p. 12, *ante.*
   " Employed."—See s. 30, p. 41, *post.*
   " Local authority."—See s. 96, p. 75, *post.*
   " Licence."—Sub-s. (3). See s. 24, p. 34, *post.*
   See also ss. 58 and 59 of the Education Act, 1944, pp. 266–267, *post.*
   Byelaws as to hours.—For a case in which a byelaw as to hours was upheld,
see *Roberts* v. *Williams* (1922), 86 J. P. 153 ; 127 L. T. 363.
   Byelaws must be confirmed by the Secretary of State; see s. 27, p. 39, *post.*
   Greater London Council Byelaws.—These are printed at pp. 668 *et seq., post.*

   19. Power of local authority to make byelaws with respect to
employment of persons under eighteen other than children.—
(1) Subject to the provisions of this section, a local authority may make
byelaws with respect to the employment of persons under the age of
eighteen years other than children, and any such byelaws may distinguish
between persons of different ages and sexes, and between different
localities, trades, occupations and circumstances, and may contain
provisions prescribing—

   (a) the number of hours in each day or in each week for which, and
       the times of day at which, they may be employed ;
   (b) the intervals to be allowed to them for meals and rest ;
   (c) the holidays or half-holidays to be allowed to them ;
   (d) any other conditions to be observed in relation to their employ-
       ment.

   (2) Nothing in this section shall empower a local authority to make
byelaws with respect to—

   (a) employment in or about the delivery, collection, or transport of
       goods, except in the capacity of van boy, errand boy, or
       messenger ;

(b) employment in or in connection with factories, workshops, mines, quarries, shops, or offices, except in the capacity of van boy, errand boy, or messenger ;

(c) employment in the building or engineering trades, except in the capacity of van boy, errand boy, or messenger ;

(d) employment in agriculture ;

(e) employment in domestic service, except as non-resident daily servant ;

(f) employment in any ship or boat registered in the United Kingdom as a British ship or in any British fishing boat entered in the fishing boat register.

(3) This section shall not come into operation until such date as may be appointed by an order of the Secretary of State, and the Secretary of State shall not make such an order until a draft thereof has been laid before both Houses of Parliament and has been approved by resolutions passed in the same session of Parliament by both Houses.

NOTE

This section has not yet been brought into force.

See the Young Persons (Employment) Acts, 1938 and 1964, the Shops Act, 1950, Part VI of the Factories Act, 1961, and Rules made under s. 118 of the last mentioned Act.

20. Street trading.—(1) No person under the age of seventeen years shall engage or be employed in street trading :

Provided that byelaws made under this section may permit young persons who have not attained the age of seventeen years to be employed by their parents in street trading.

(2) A local authority may make byelaws regulating or prohibiting street trading by persons under the age of eighteen years, and byelaws so made may distinguish between persons of different ages and sexes and between different localities, and may contain provisions—

(a) forbidding any such person to engage or be employed in street trading unless he holds a licence granted by the authority, and regulating the conditions on which such licences may be granted, suspended, and revoked ;

(b) determining the days and hours during which, and the places at which, such persons may engage or be employed in street trading ;

(c) requiring such persons so engaged or employed to wear badges ;

(d) regulating in any other respect the conduct of such persons while so engaged or employed.

(3) No person under the age of eighteen shall on a Sunday engage or be employed in street trading of a description to which, notwithstanding section 58 of the Shops Act, 1950 (which extends certain provisions to any place where a retail trade or business is carried on), those provisions do not extend.

NOTES

This section is printed as amended by the Children and Young Persons Act, 1963, s. 35, p. 102, *post.*

"Nothing in this section or section 30 of the principal Scottish Act or in any bye-law made under either of those sections shall restrict the engagement or employment of any person in the carrying on in any place of a retail trade or business (within the meaning of the Shops Act, 1950) on any occasion on which it is customary for retail trades or businesses to be carried on in that place." (Children and Young Persons Act, 1963, s. 35, p. 102, *post.*)

The principal Scottish Act means the Children and Young Persons (Scotland) Act, 1937. It is not reproduced in this work.

Section 35 (2) of the Children and Young Persons Act, 1963 frees from the restrictions on street trading, employment in established markets and other places where it is customary to carry on a retail trade or business (within the meaning of the Shops Act, 1950). Authorities may wish to add a note to their byelaws explaining the effect of this subsection. Suggested notes included in the Appendix to Home Office Circular No. 253/1968 are as follows.—

Suggested notes for inclusion in local authority byelaws regulating or prohibiting street trading by persons under 18.

1. By virtue of s. 35 (2) of the Children and Young Persons Act, 1963, the restrictions on street trading imposed by s. 20 (1) of the Children and Young Persons Act, 1933 and byelaws made under s. 20 (2) of that Act, do not apply to persons employed at established open air markets, or in any other place where it is customary for a retail trade or business (within the meaning of the Shops Act, 1950) to be carried on.

2. By virtue of s. 35 (3) of the Children and Young Persons Act, 1963 no person under 18 may engage or be employed in street trading on Sunday, except (a) where the employment is at a place where the occupier is allowed to trade up to 2 p.m. on Sunday subject to a requirement to close on Saturday; or (b), in any specified area in London, on any other day fixed by the local authority for that area. (Appendix to Home Office Circular No. 253/1968 dated November 8, 1968, circulated to Clerks to County Councils, etc.)

Shops Act, 1950.—13 Halsbury's Statutes, 3rd Edn., 317.

" **Age.**"—See note "Age of sixteen" to s. 1, p. 12, *ante.*

As to meaning of " street trading," see s. 30, p. 41, *post.*

The prohibition is against street trading by a child or young person on his own account or in the service of some other person, even if he receives no reward for his labour; see s. 30. Young persons may, however, if the byelaws permit it, be employed by their parents, but not otherwise. Children may not be employed.

"**Local authority.**"—See s. 96, p. 75, *post.* It will be observed that the byelaws will be in respect of young persons only, and not children.

21. Penalties and legal proceedings in respect of general provisions as to employment.—(1) If a person is employed in contravention of any of the foregoing provisions of this Part of this Act, or of the provisions of any byelaw made thereunder, the employer and any person (other than the person employed) to whose act or default the contravention is attributable shall be liable on summary conviction to a fine not exceeding twenty pounds or, in the case of a second or subsequent offence, not exceeding fifty pounds:

Provided that, if proceedings are brought against the employer, the employer, upon information duly laid by him and on giving to the prosecution not less than three days' notice of his intention, shall be entitled to have any person (other than the person employed) to whose act or default he alleges that the contravention was due, brought before the court as a party to the proceedings, and if, after the contravention has been proved, the employer proves to the satisfaction of the court that the contravention was due to the act or default of the said other person, that person may be convicted of the offence ; and if the employer further proves to the satisfaction of the court that he has used all due diligence to secure that the provisions in question should be complied with, he shall be acquitted of the offence.

(2) Where an employer seeks to avail himself of the proviso to the last foregoing subsection,

> (a) the prosecution shall have the right to cross-examine him, if he gives evidence, and any witness called by him in support of his charge against the other person, and to call rebutting evidence ; and
>
> (b) the court may make such order as it thinks fit for the payment of costs by any party to the proceedings to any other party thereto.

(3) A person under the age of eighteen years, who engages in street trading in contravention of the provisions of the last foregoing section, or of any byelaw made thereunder, shall be liable on summary conviction to a fine not exceeding ten pounds, or in the case of a second or subsequent offence, not exceeding twenty pounds.

NOTES

This section is printed as amended by the Children and Young Persons Act, 1963, s. 36, p. 103, *post.*

Powers of entry.—See s. 28, p. 40, *post.*

" **Second offence.**"—This means an offence committed after a conviction for a previous offence (*R.* v. *South Shields Licensing Justices*, [1911] 2 K. B. 1 ; 75 J. P. 299).

"**Employer.**" The special form of defence open to an alleged employer is not the only defence. See *Robinson* v. *Hill*, [1910] 1 K. B. 94 ; 73 J. P. 514, a case in which there was in fact no contract of employment between the defendant and the child.

Note that, in order to secure his own acquittal under the proviso, the employer must prove his own diligence in addition to proving the act or default of some other person.

"**Brought before the court.**"—This will be by summons. If the "other person" appears by counsel or solicitor that is no doubt equivalent to his having been brought before the court (s. 99 Magistrates' Courts Act, 1952 ; 21 Halsbury's Statutes, 3rd Edn., 271). If a summons is served and he fails to appear the court can proceed to hear the case in his absence.

In a case under a similar provision in the Food and Drugs Act, 1938, s. 83 ; 10 Halsbury's Statutes, 2nd Edn., 458, it was held that the defence was available even though the police had not been able to serve the summons upon the person alleged to be in default, who could not, therefore, be convicted; *Malcolm* v. *Cheek*, [1948] 1 K. B. 400; [1947] 2 All E. R. 881.

Entertainments and Performances.

22. [*Repealed by Children and Young Persons Act*, 1963, *ss.* 64, 65 *and Sched. V.*]

23. Prohibition against persons under sixteen taking part in performances endangering life or limb.—No person under the age of sixteen years shall take part in any performance to which section 37 of the Children and Young Persons Act, 1963, applies and in which his life or limbs are endangered and every person who causes or procures such a person, or being his parent or guardian allows him, to take part in such a performance, shall be liable on summary conviction to a fine not exceeding fifty pounds or, in the case of a second or subsequent offence, not exceeding one hundred pounds:

Provided that no proceedings shall be taken under this subsection except by or with the authority of a chief officer of police.

NOTES

This section is printed as amended by the Children and Young Persons Act, 1963, ss. 64, 65 and Sched. III, and the Criminal Justice Act, 1967.

"**Age.**"—See note "Age of sixteen" to s. 1, p. 12, *ante*.

"**Allows.**"—The word "knowingly" is not inserted here, and the effect is doubtless to cast the burden of proof of absence of knowledge upon the parent or guardian. It is arguable that actual knowledge need not be shown, or even inferred ; in the case of a parent or guardian negligence or indifference to parental duty amounts to allowing. But, as was said by Darling, J., in *Crabtree* v. *Fern Spinning Co. Ltd.* (1901), 66 J. P. 181 ; 85 L. T. 549 ; 20 Cox, C. C. 82. " A man cannot be said to allow that of which he is unaware, or that which he cannot prevent." That was a Factory Act case. In the case of parents and guardians, with their special responsibilities, we submit that instead of " is unaware " it would be appropriate to say " cannot be aware."

"**Fine not exceeding.**"—The maximum fine which may be imposed on summary conviction is fifty pounds for a first offence and one hundred pounds for a second or subsequent offence (Criminal Justice Act, 1967, s. 92 and Sched. III).

" **Second offence.**"—See note at p. 33, *ante*.

" **Chief officer of police.**"—See s. 107, p. 81, *post*.

24. Restrictions on training for performances of a dangerous nature.—(1) No person under the age of twelve years shall be trained to take part in performances of a dangerous nature, and no person under the age of sixteen years shall be trained to take part in such performances except under and in accordance with the terms of a licence granted and in force under this section ; and every person who causes or procures a person, or being his parent or guardian allows him, to be trained to take part in performances of a dangerous nature in contravention of this section, shall be liable on summary conviction to a fine not exceeding five pounds or, in the case of a second or subsequent offence, not exceeding twenty pounds.

(2) A local authority may grant a licence for a person who has attained the age of twelve years but is under the age of sixteen years to be trained to take part in performances of a dangerous nature.

(3) [*Repealed by Children and Young Persons Act, 1963, ss. 64, 65 and Sched. V.*]

(4) A licence under this section shall specify the place or places at which the person is to be trained and shall embody such conditions as are, in the opinion of the authority, necessary for his protection, but a licence shall not be refused if the authority is satisfied that the person is fit and willing to be trained and that proper provision has been made to secure his health and kind treatment.

(5) [*Repealed by Children and Young Persons Act, 1963, ss. 64, 65 and Sched. V.*]

NOTES

This section is printed as amended by the Children and Young Persons Act, 1963, ss. 64, 65 and Sched. III, p. 117, *post*.

"Fine not exceeding."—The maximum fine which may be imposed under sub-s. (1) on summary conviction is twenty pounds for a first offence and fifty pounds for a second or subsequent offence (Criminal Justice Act, 1967, s. 92 and Sched. III).

Licences: Children and Young Persons Act, 1963.—:

(1) The power to grant licences under this section shall be exercisable by the local authority for the area or one of the areas in which the training is to take place instead of by a magistrates' court.

(2) A licence under this section or under section 34 of the principal Scottish Act may be revoked or varied by the authority who granted it if any of the conditions embodied therein are not complied with or if it appears to them that the person to whom the licence relates is no longer fit and willing to be trained or that proper provision is no longer being made to secure his health and kind treatment.

(3) Where an authority refuse an application for such a licence or revoke or vary such a licence they shall state their grounds for doing so in writing to the applicant, or, as the case may be, to the holder of the licence, and the applicant or holder may appeal to a magistrates' court or, in Scotland, to the sheriff, against the refusal, revocation or variation (ss. 41, 65, *ibid.*, pp. 108, 117, *post*).

" Age."—See note " Age of sixteen " to s. 1, p. 12, *ante*.

" Performance of a dangerous nature."—See s. 30, p. 41, *post*. The definition, however, does not appear to be exhaustive.

" Allows."—See note to s. 23, p. 34, *ante*.

" Second offence."—See note at p. 33, *ante*.

Employment Abroad

25. Restrictions on persons under eighteen going abroad for the purpose of performing for profit.—(1) No person having the custody, charge or care of any person under the age of eighteen years shall allow him, nor shall any person cause or procure any person under that age, to go abroad for the purpose of singing, playing, performing, or being exhibited, for profit, unless a licence has been granted in respect of him under this section:

Provided that this subsection shall not apply in any case where it is proved that the person under the age of eighteen years was only temporarily resident within the United Kingdom.

(2) A police magistrate may grant a licence in such form as the Secretary of State may prescribe, and subject to such restrictions and conditions as the police magistrate thinks fit, for any person who has attained the age of fourteen years but is under the age of eighteen years to go abroad for the purpose of singing, playing, performing, or being exhibited, for profit, but no such licence shall be granted in respect of any person unless the police magistrate is satisfied—

  (a) that the application for the licence is made by or with the consent of his parent or guardian ;
  (b) that he is going abroad to fulfil a particular engagement ;
  (c) that he is fit for the purpose, and that proper provision has been made to secure his health, kind treatment, and adequate

supervision while abroad, and his return from abroad at the expiration or revocation of the licence ;

(d) that there has been furnished to him a copy of the contract of employment or other document showing the terms and conditions of employment drawn up in a language understood by him.

(3) A person applying for a licence under this section, shall, at least seven days before making the application, give to the chief officer of police for the district in which the person resides to whom the application relates, notice of the intended application together with a copy of the contract of employment or other document showing the terms and conditions of employment, and the chief officer of police shall send that copy to the police magistrate and may make a report in writing on the case to him or may appear, or instruct some person to appear, before him and show cause why the licence should not be granted, and the police magistrate shall not grant the licence unless he is satisfied that notice has been properly so given :

Provided that if it appears that the notice was given less than seven days before the making of the application, the police magistrate may nevertheless grant a licence if he is satisfied that the officer to whom the notice was given has made sufficient enquiry into the facts of the case and does not desire to oppose the application.

(4) A licence under this section shall not be granted for more than three months but may be renewed by a police magistrate from time to time for a like period, so, however, that no such renewal shall be granted, unless the police magistrate—

(a) is satisfied by a report of a British consular officer or other trustworthy person that the conditions of the licence are being complied with ;

(b) is satisfied that the application for renewal is made by or with the consent of the parent or guardian of the person to whom the licence relates.

(5) A police magistrate—

(a) may vary a licence granted under this section and may at any time revoke such a licence for any cause which he, in his discretion, considers sufficient ;

(b) need not, when renewing or varying a licence granted under this section, require the attendance before him of the person to whom the licence relates.

(6) The police magistrate to whom application is made for the grant, renewal or variation of a licence shall, unless he is satisfied that in the circumstances it is unnecessary, require the applicant to give such security as he may think fit (either by entering into a recognisance with or without sureties or otherwise) for the observance of the restrictions and conditions in the licence or in the licence as varied, and the recognisance may be enforced in like manner as a recognisance for the doing of some matter or thing required to be done in a proceeding before a court of summary jurisdiction is enforceable.

(7) If in any case where a licence has been granted under this section, it is proved to the satisfaction of a police magistrate that by reason of exceptional circumstances it is not in the interests of the person to whom the licence relates to require him to return from abroad at the expiration of the licence, then, notwithstanding anything in this section or any restriction or condition attached to the licence, the magistrate may by order release all persons concerned from any obligation to cause that person to return from abroad.

(8) Where a licence is granted, renewed or varied under this section, the police magistrate shall send the prescribed particulars to the Secretary of State for transmission to the proper consular officer, and every consular officer shall register the particulars so transmitted to him and perform such other duties in relation thereto as the Secretary of State may direct.

(9) In this section the expression " police magistrate " means one of the following magistrates, that is to say—

(a) the chief magistrate of the metropolitan police courts ;

(b) any magistrate of the metropolitan police court in Bow Street ;

(c) any stipendiary magistrate appointed by Order in Council to exercise jurisdiction under this section,

and the powers conferred by this section on a police magistrate shall in every case be exercisable by any of the magistrates aforesaid.

(10) This and the next following section extend to Scotland and to Northern Ireland.

NOTES

This section is printed as amended by the Children and Young Persons Act, 1963, ss. 64, 65 and Scheds. III and V.

Form of licence and regulation.—See S. R. & O. 1933, No. 992, p. 471, *post*.

" Custody, charge or care."—See notes at p. 12, *ante*.

" Allow."—See note at p. 34, *ante*.

" To go abroad."—It is to be noted that the licence is to go abroad for a particular purpose, and the restrictions are in respect of going abroad for such purpose. A person who goes abroad *bonâ fide* for some other purpose and subsequently while abroad sings, plays, performs, or is exhibited for profit, does not come within the section, save so far as s. 26 (2), p. 38, *post*, may apply. For meaning of " abroad," see s. 30, p. 41, *post*.

" Chief officer of police."—See s. 107, p. 81, *post*.

" Resides."—See note " Residence " at p. 162, *post*.

"Instruct some person to appear."—Evidently this means some person other than counsel or solicitor; usually a responsible police officer would be sent.

" Revocation of licence."—It will be observed that the magistrate may revoke a licence, even though its conditions are being fulfilled, if at any time in his discretion he considers there is sufficient cause. This power might be used, if, for example, the place at which the young person was performing proved to be undesirable.

" Recognisance."—As to enforcement, see Magistrates' Courts Act, 1952, s. 96 (21 Halsbury's Statutes, 3rd Edn. 266).

" Stipendiary magistrate."—No Order in Council under sub-s. (9) (c) has yet been made.

"Singing, playing, performing or being exhibited".—These words are to have effect as if they included taking part in any broadcast performance or any performance recorded (by whatever means) with a view to its use in a broadcast or in a film intended for public exhibition (Children and Young Persons Act, 1963, ss. 42 (1), 37 (2), 65, pp. 103, 108, 117, *post*).

Licences, under the age of fourteen.—A licence under this section may be granted in respect of a person notwithstanding that he is under the age of fourteen if—

    (a) the engagement which he is to fulfil is for acting and the application for the licence is accompanied by a declaration that the part he is to act cannot be taken except by a person of about his age; or

    (b) the engagement is for dancing in a ballet which does not form part of an entertainment of which anything other than ballet or opera also forms part and the application for the licence is accompanied by a declaration that the part he is to dance cannot be taken except by a child of about his age; or

    (c) the engagement is for taking part in a performance the nature of which is wholly or mainly musical or which consists of only opera and ballet and the nature of his part in the performance is wholly or mainly musical (Children and Young Persons Act, 1963, ss. 42, 65, *ibid.*, pp. 108, *post*).

Lay justices for the inner London area.—Lay justices for the inner London area are precluded from exercising the jurisdiction conferred on metropolitan stipendiary magistrates by this section. (Administration of Justice Act, 1964, s. 9. (3) (e); 20 Halsbury's Statutes, 3rd Edn., 661).

Procedure for dealing with applications for licences.—See the Appendix to Home Office Circular No. 255/1968, pp. 702 *et seq.*, *post*.

About to leave United Kingdom.—See Children and Young Persons Act, 1969, s. 28 (1) (c), p. 173, *post*.

26. Punishment of contraventions of last foregoing section and proceedings with respect thereto.—(1) If any person acts in contravention of the provisions of subsection (1) of the last foregoing section he shall be guilty of an offence under this section and be liable, on summary conviction, to a fine not exceeding one hundred pounds, or, alternatively, or in addition thereto, to imprisonment for any term not exceeding three months:

Provided that if he procured the person to go abroad by means of any false pretence or false representation, he shall be liable on conviction on indictment to imprisonment for any term not exceeding two years.

(2) Where, in proceedings under this section against a person, it is proved that he caused, procured, or allowed a person under the age of eighteen years to go abroad and that that person has while abroad been singing, playing, performing, or being exhibited, for profit, the defendant shall be presumed to have caused, procured, or allowed him to go abroad for that purpose, unless the contrary is proved:

Provided that where the contrary is proved, the court may order the defendant to take such steps as the court directs to secure the return of the person in question to the United Kingdom, or to enter into a recognisance to make such provision as the court may direct to secure his health, kind treatment, and adequate supervision while abroad, and his return to the United Kingdom at the expiration of such period as the court may think fit.

(3) Proceedings in respect of an offence under this section or for enforcing a recognisance under this or the last foregoing section may be instituted at any time within a period of three months from the first

discovery by the person taking the proceedings of the commission of the offence or, as the case may be, the non-observance of the restrictions and conditions contained in the licence, or, if at the expiration of that period the person against whom it is proposed to institute the proceedings is outside the United Kingdom, at any time within six months after his return to the United Kingdom.

(4) In any such proceedings as aforesaid, a report of any British consular officer and any deposition made on oath before a British consular officer and authenticated by the signature of that officer, respecting the observance or non-observance of any of the conditions or restrictions contained in a licence granted under the last foregoing section shall, upon proof that the consular officer, or deponent, cannot be found in the United Kingdom, be admissible in evidence, and it shall not be necessary to prove the signature or official character of the person appearing to have signed any such report or deposition.

(5) The wife or husband of a person charged with an offence under this section may be called as a witness either for the prosecution or defence, and without the consent of the person charged.

(6) [*Repealed by Children and Young Persons Act*, 1969, s. 72 (4) *and Sched. VI.*]

NOTES

This section is printed as amended by the Children and Young Persons Act, 1963, ss. 64, 65 and Scheds. III and V.

Order to secure return.—Presumably failure to comply with such an order can be dealt with under s. 54 of the Magistrates' Courts Act, 1952 (21 Halsbury's Statutes, 3rd Edn. 230).

Evidence of wife or husband.—The wife or husband is a competent witness, but not compellable (see *Leach* v. *R.*, [1912] A. C. 305; 76 J. P. 203, and *R.* v. *Acaster* (1912), 106 L. T. 384).

" Authority."—It would seem desirable that the authority should be in writing. Though the restrictions on going abroad apply to young persons under eighteen, it is to be noted that sub-s. (6) applies only to those under seventeen. In some cases it may be desirable to bring the young person before a juvenile court, if s. 1 of the Children and Young Persons Act, 1969, p. 130, *post*, be applicable to the facts of the case.

Scotland and Northern Ireland.—This section applies; see s. 25 (10), p. 37, *ante*.

Time limit.—Sub-s. (3) is an enabling provision by which the general time limit of six months under s. 104 of the Magistrates' Courts Act, 1952; 21 Halsbury's Statutes, 3rd Edn., 273, may be extended, and it appears that an information laid within six months of the offence is always in time; see *Ross* v. *English Steel Corporation, Ltd.*, [1945] 2 All E. R. 606; 109 J. P. 226.

" Singing, playing, performing or being exhibited."—See note to s. 25, p. 37, *ante*.

Supplemental

27. Byelaws.—(1) A byelaw made under this Part of this Act shall not have effect until confirmed by the Secretary of State and shall not be so confirmed until at least thirty days after the local authority have published it in such manner as the Secretary of State directs.

(2) Before confirming such a byelaw the Secretary of State shall consider any objections thereto which may be addressed to him by persons

affected or likely to be affected thereby, and may order a local enquiry to be held, and where such an enquiry is held, the person holding it shall receive such remuneration as the Secretary of State determines, and that remuneration and the expenses of the enquiry shall be paid by the local authority.

(3) [*Repealed.*]

NOTE

Proof of byelaws.—See s. 252 of the Local Government Act, 1933, which is as follows:

" The production of a printed copy of a byelaw purporting to be made by a local authority, upon which is endorsed a certificate purporting to be signed by the clerk of the authority stating—

(a) that the byelaw was made by the authority;

(b) that the copy is a true copy of the byelaw;

(c) that on a specified date the byelaw was confirmed by the authority named in the certificate or, as the case may require, was sent to the Secretary of State and has not been disallowed;

(d) the date, if any, fixed by the confirming authority for the coming into operation of the byelaw;

shall be *prima facie* evidence of the facts stated in the certificate, and without proof of the handwriting or official position of any person purporting to sign a certificate in pursuance of this section."

28. Powers of entry.—(1) If it is made to appear to a justice of the peace by the local authority, or by any constable, that there is reasonable cause to believe that the provisions of this Part of this Act, other than those relating to employment abroad, or of a byelaw made under the said provisions, are being contravened with respect to any person, the justice may by order under his hand addressed to an officer of the local authority, or to a constable, empower him to enter, at any reasonable time within forty-eight hours of the making of the order, any place in or in connection with which the person in question is, or is believed to be, employed, or as the case may be, in which he is, or is believed to be, taking part in a performance, or being trained, and to make enquiries therein with respect to that person.

(2) Any authorised officer of the said authority or any constable may—

(a) at any time enter any place used as a broadcasting studio or film studio or used for the recording of a performance with a view to its use in a broadcast or in a film intended for public exhibition and make inquiries therein as to any children taking part in performances to which section 37 of the Children and Young Persons Act, 1963 applies;

(b) at any time during the currency of a licence granted under the said section 37 or under the provisions of this Part of this Act, relating to training for dangerous performances enter any place (whether or not it is such a place as is mentioned in paragraph (a) of this subsection) where the person to whom the licence relates is authorised by the licence to take part in a performance or to be trained, and may make inquiries therein with respect to that person.

(3) Any person who obstructs any officer or constable in the due exercise of any powers conferred on him by or under this section, or who refuses

to answer or answers falsely any enquiry authorised by or under this section to be made, shall be liable on summary conviction in respect of each offence to a fine not exceeding twenty pounds.

NOTES

This section is printed as amended by the Children and Young Persons Act, 1963, ss. 44 and 64.

"**Local authority.**"—See s. 96, p. 75, *post*.

Order.—The order is not a search warrant, and the section does not require an information on oath, but the order is very much like a warrant, and it may be thought advisable to insist upon the sworn information. The order must be carried out within forty-eight hours, and should therefore bear not only the date but the hour at which it is made.

The constable or other person may enter at any reasonable time. What is reasonable must depend on the facts of each case, but in suitable cases entry may be made by night no less than by day.

The use of force is not specifically authorised, and we think it could not be justified.

"**At any time.**"—The word " reasonable " is not used in sub-s. (2).

"**Obstructs.**"—The word " wilfully " is not employed here, but it would perhaps, be a defence to show that the obstruction was not intentional.

Application of section.—See also Education Act, 1944, s. 59 (4), p. 267, *post*.

29. Savings.—(1) [*Repealed by the Children and Young Persons Act, 1963, ss. 64, 65 and Sched. V.*]

(2) [*Repealed by the Children and Young Persons Act, 1963, ss. 64, 65 and Sched. V.*]

(3) *Repealed by the Children and Young Persons Act, 1969, s. 72 (4) and Sched. V.*]

(4) The said provisions shall be in addition to and not in substitution for any enactments relating to employment in factories, workshops, mines and quarries, or for giving effect to any international convention regulating employment.

NOTES

This section is printed as amended by the Children and Young Persons Act, 1963, ss. 64, 65 and Scheds. III and V.

"**The said provisions.**"—The words refer to the repealed sub-s. (1) which referred to the provisions of this Part of this Act.

30. Interpretation of Part II.—For the purposes of this Part of this Act and of any byelaws made thereunder—

The expression " performance of a dangerous nature " includes all acrobatic performances and all performances as a contortionist ;

The expression " street trading " includes the hawking of newspapers, matches, flowers and other articles, playing, singing or performing for profit, shoe-blacking and other like occupations carried on in streets or public places ;

A person who assists in a trade or occupation carried on for profit shall be deemed to be employed notwithstanding that he receives no reward for his labour ;

A chorister taking part in a religious service or in a choir practice for a religious service shall not, whether he receives any reward or not, be deemed to be employed ; and

The expression " abroad " means outside Great Britain and Ireland.

NOTES

This section is printed as amended by the Education Act, 1944, s. 121, and Sched. IX, Part I.

" **Child.**"—For the purposes of enactments relating to employment child means a person who is not for the purposes of the Education Act, 1944, over compulsory school age.   See Education Act, 1944, s. 58, p. 266, *post*.

" **Performance of a dangerous nature.**"—The definition is inclusive, but not apparently exclusive.   It is easy to think of dangerous performances which are neither acrobatic nor contortionist.

" **Street trading.**"—This means seeking custom in the streets.   It does not apply to business between a shop and customers in their own homes (*Stratford Co-operative Society, Ltd.* v. *East Ham Corporation*, [1915] 2 K. B. 70 ; 79 J. P. 227). There is employment where the the relation is principal and agent as well as where it is master and servant (*Morgan* v. *Parr*, [1921] 2. K. B. 379 ; 85 J. P. 165 ; *Sweet* v. *Williams* (1922), 87 J. P. 51 ; 128 L. T. 379).

PART III.—PROTECTION OF CHILDREN AND YOUNG PERSONS IN RELATION TO CRIMINAL AND SUMMARY PROCEEDINGS

General Provisions as to Preliminary Proceedings

The local authorities for the purposes of this Part of this Act are the councils of counties and county boroughs (Children Act, 1948, s. 38, p. 914, *post*).   The council of each London borough shall as respects the borough, and the Common Council shall as respects the City, have the functions of the council of a county borough under Part III of this Act and be the local authority for such purposes of that Part as refer to a local authority (London Government Act, 1963, s. 47 ; 43 Halsbury's Statutes, 2nd Edn., 732).

As to Social Services Committees, see s. 2 and Sched. I of the Local Authority Social Services Act, 1970.

31. Separation of children and young persons from adults in police stations, courts, etc.—Arrangements shall be made for preventing a child or young person while detained in a police station, or while being conveyed to or from any criminal court, or while waiting before or after attendance in any criminal court, from associating with an adult (not being a relative) who is charged with any offence other than an offence with which the child or young person is jointly charged, and for ensuring that a girl (being a child or young person) shall while so detained, being conveyed, or waiting, be under the care of a woman.

NOTES

Juvenile court.—A juvenile court is included in the term " criminal court." Much of its jurisdiction is in criminal matters.

Waiting arrangements.—See Home Office letter 208/1964, p. 676, *post*, and see also Home Office Circular on juvenile court accommodation at p. 848, *post*.

32. [*Repealed by the Children and Young Persons Act*, 1969, *s.* 72 (4) *and Sched. VI. See now s.* 29, ibid.]

33. [*Repealed by the Criminal Justice Act*, 1948, *s.* 83 (3) *and Sched. X, Part I. Replaced by s.* 27 *of that Act, now repealed by the children and Young Persons Act*, 1969, *s.* 72(4) *and Sched. VI. See now s.* 23, ibid., *p.* 166, post.]

34. Attendance at court of parents of child or young person brought before court.—(1) Where a child or young person is charged with any offence or is for any other reason brought before a court, any person who is a parent or guardian of his may be required to attend at the court before which the case is heard or determined during all the stages of the proceedings, and any such person shall be so required at any stage where the court thinks it desirable, unless the court is satisfied that it would be unreasonable to require his attendance.

(2) Where a child or young person is arrested, such steps shall be taken by the person who arrested him as may be practicable to inform at least one person whose attendance may be required under this section.

NOTES

This section is printed as substituted by the Children and Young Persons Act, 1963, s. 25 (1), p. 97, *post*, and as amended by the Children and Young Persons Act, 1969, ss. 72 (3), (4) and Scheds. V and VI.

Attendance of parent.—The court will generally desire the parent to be present if the offence is serious, if the ground for bringing the child or young person before the court involves the conduct or character of the parent, or if the case is likely to result in committal to the care of a local authority On the other hand, it may be disposed to dispense with the parent's attendance when the charge is trivial and involves no moral turpitude and is likely to result in a small fine or a dismissal with a caution.   If, however, it is intended to order the fine to be paid by the parent, the provisions of s. 55, p. 59, *post*, must be complied with.   Rule 26 Magistrates' Courts (Children and Young Persons) Rules, 1970 (p. 580, *post*) allows for the issue of process to enforce attendance under this section.

" **Parent** " includes adopter; see s. 13 (1) of the Adoption Act, 1958, p. 1047, *post*.

35. [*Repealed by the Children and Young Persons Act*, 1969, *s.* 72 (4) *and Sched. VI. See now s.* 9, ibid.]

General Provisions as to Proceedings in Court

36. Prohibition against children being present in court during the trial of other persons.—No child (other than an infant in arms) shall be permitted to be present in court during the trial of any other person charged with an offence, or during any proceedings preliminary thereto, except during such time as his presence is required as a witness or otherwise for the purposes of justice ; and any child present in court when under this section he is not to be permitted to be so shall be ordered to be removed :

Provided that this section shall not apply to messengers, clerks, and other persons required to attend at any court for purposes connected with their employment.

NOTE

The term " in court " here is wide enough to include all courts dealing with criminal cases.

37. Power to clear court while child or young person is giving evidence in certain cases.—(1) Where, in any proceedings in relation to an offence against, or any conduct contrary to, decency or morality, a person who, in the opinion of the court, is a child or young person is called as a witness, the court may direct that all or any persons, not being members or officers of the court or parties to the case, their counsel or solicitors, or persons otherwise directly concerned in the case, be excluded from the court during the taking of the evidence of that witness :

Provided that nothing in this section shall authorise the exclusion of *bonâ fide* representatives of a newspaper or news agency.

(2) The powers conferred on a court by this section shall be in addition and without prejudice to any other powers of the court to hear proceedings in camerâ.

NOTES

There is, it is generally considered, an inherent power in every court to hear cases *in camerâ* if it is necessary on the ground that justice cannot otherwise be administered at all. Such a power is, however, very rarely used, and could be used only in the most exceptional circumstances. See an article at 92 J. P. N. 79, and *cf. Scott* v. *Scott*, [1913] A. C. 417, see also s. 6 (1) Criminal Justice Act, 1967.

The power conferred by this section, which is a re-enactment, has often been found useful in relieving a child witness of the embarrassment of full publicity.

" Decency or morality."—We suggest that these words should not be too widely interpreted. In a broad sense, stealing is an offence against morality. What seems to be in contemplation here, however, is an offence against sexual morality or decency. See the similar words in s. 39, p. 46, *post*.

Protection from publicity.—See Home Office Circular No. 208/1964, p. 676, *post*.

Statement of exclusion of public.—See Home Office Circular, No. 17/1964, p. 677, *post*.

38. Evidence of child of tender years.—(1) Where, in any proceedings against any person for any offence, any child of tender years called as a witness does not in the opinion of the court understand the nature of an oath, his evidence may be received, though not given upon oath, if, in the opinion of the court, he is possessed of sufficient intelligence to justify the reception of the evidence, and understands the duty of speaking the truth ; and his evidence, though not given on oath, but otherwise taken and reduced into writing in accordance with the provisions of section seventeen of the Indictable Offences Act, 1848, or of this Part of this Act, shall be deemed to be a deposition within the meaning of that section and that Part respectively :

Provided that where evidence admitted by virtue of this section is given on behalf of the prosecution the accused shall not be liable to be convicted of the offence unless that evidence is corroborated by some other material evidence in support thereof implicating him.

(2) If any child whose evidence is received as aforesaid wilfully gives false evidence in such circumstances that he would, if the evidence had been given on oath, have been guilty of perjury, he shall be liable on summary conviction to be dealt with as if he had been summarily convicted of an indictable offence punishable in the case of an adult with imprisonment.

NOTES

This section applies to all proceedings for a criminal offence, but not to proceedings in other matters—*e.g.* cases under the Matrimonial Proceedings (Magistrates' Courts) Act, 1960.

It is important to remember that this section does not make admissible the evidence of children who do not understand the duty of speaking the truth. There is still a limitation upon the reception of the evidence of young children ; they must be sufficiently intelligent, and they must understand the duty of telling the truth. See *R.* v. *Southern* (1929), 22 Cr. App. Rep. 6, at p. 12 ; 142 L. T. 383.

It would be quite improper to take the unsworn evidence of a tiny child without a test on these points (see *R.* v. *Lyons, infra*), and it is particularly necessary to see that nothing approaching a leading question is permitted. A child must not be prevented from giving evidence because of the objectionable nature of the case (*R.* v. *Moscovitch* (1924), 18 Cr. App. Rep. 37).

In *Peters* v. *Shaw* (1965), *Times,* May 4, a boy aged nine gave unsworn evidence in an action for damages. In reviewing the evidence Mr. Justice Widgery told the jury that a mistake had been made in allowing the boy to give unsworn evidence, for that was permissible only in criminal cases and that they must put what the boy said out of their minds.

The general requirement that evidence must be given on oath is contained in s. 78 of the Magistrates' Courts Act, 1952; 21 Halsbury's Statutes, 3rd Edn., 251. A witness who objects to taking an oath on the ground that he has no religious belief or that taking an oath is contrary to his religious belief may affirm instead (Oaths Act, 1888, s. 1 ; 12 Halsbury's Statutes, 3rd Edn., 857). See also the Oaths Act, 1961, which provides that the Oaths Act, 1888, shall apply also in relation to a person to whom it is not reasonably practicable (without inconvenience or delay) to administer an oath in the manner appropriate to his religious belief.

The proper and usual course, when a witness asks whether he can affirm, is for the judge to ask him whether he desires to affirm because he has no religious belief or because the taking of an oath is contrary to his religious belief. If the answer is " Yes " to one of those questions the judge will without more ado be satisfied, and should be satisfied, that the proposed witness comes within the terms of the section, and he should, accordingly, be allowed to affirm. *R.* v. *Clark*, [1962] 1 All E. R. 428, per Parker, C. J., at p. 430.

" **Opinion of the court.** "—A few preliminary questions should be put in order to form this opinion (*R.* v. *Lyons* (1921), 15 Cr. App. Rep. 144). In *R.* v. *Reynolds,* [1950] 1 K. B. 606; [1950] 1 All E. R. 335, evidence as to the child's degree of understanding was given in the absence of the jury, and the conviction was quashed. In that case Lord Goddard, C.J., said no member of the Court had known of a case in which witnesses were called on this issue, but there might be cases, and perhaps this was one, where such a course was proper.

In *R.* v. *Wallwork* (1958), 122 J. P. 299; 42 Cr. App. Rep. 153, the Court of Criminal Appeal expressed the opinion that it was undesirable for a child as young as five to give evidence.

" **Indictable Offences Act, 1848.** "—Section 17 was repealed by the Criminal Justice Act, 1925 and the Magistrates' Courts Act, 1952. By s. 13 of the Criminal Justice Act, 1925, the depositions of witnesses who have died or who are absent for reasons there specified, may be read in evidence at the trial provided it is proved by oath or by certificate that the deposition was taken in the presence of the defendant and that he or his counsel or solicitor had full opportunity of cross-examining such witness; and the deposition must purport to be signed by the justice before whom it purports to have been taken. Such evidence may be read without further proof unless it shall be proved that the deposition or certificate was not signed by the justice purporting to have signed the same, or that a witness who was excused as unnecessary has since been notified that his attendance is required. See now Magistrates' Courts Act, 1952, ss. 4 and 78; 21 Halsbury's Statutes, 3rd Edn., 191, 251, and Rule 4 of the Magistrates' Courts Rules, 1968.

" **Corroboration.**"—The attention of the jury should be called to the necessity for corroboration (*R*. v. *Southern, supra*).

The court will not quash a conviction merely because there has not been a specific direction to the jury that the evidence of a child, not sworn, under this section, must be corroborated, if in fact there has been corroboration (*R*. v. *Murray* (1913), 9 Cr. App. Rep. 248; 30 T. L. R. 196; *R*. v. *Davies* (1915), 79 J. P. N. 556; 85 L. J. K. B. 208; *R*. v. *Schiff* (1920), 15 Cr. App. Rep. 63). The unsworn testimony of other children and the answers of a child to its mother do not constitute the corroboration under this section (*R*. v. *Coyle*, [1926] N. I. 208; *R*. v. *Manser* (1934), 25 Cr. App. Rep. 18; 78 Sol. J. 769). Nor does a complaint made by a child immediately after the occurrence (*R*. v. *Evans* (1924), 18 Cr. App. Rep. 123; 88 J. P. 196); nor a refusal by the defendant to be medically examined (*R*. v. *Gray* (1904), 68 J. P. 327).

The mere fact that a defendant tells a lie to a police officer does not of itself amount to corroboration, but a lie may be corroboration on the facts of a particular case (*Credland* v. *Knowler* (1951), 115 J. P. N. 279).

In *R*. v. *Campbell*, [1956] 2 Q. B. 432; [1956] 2 All E. R. 272; 120 J. P. 359, in the Court of Criminal Appeal it was stated that a child's unsworn evidence could be corroboration of sworn evidence on a charge against another person. This view was not followed in *R*. v. *E.*, [1964] 1 All E. R. 205, where the court ruled as a preliminary ruling before the jury was sworn that the unsworn testimony of a child aged seven could not be corroboration of the sworn testimony of another child aged eight.

Note the provisions of ss. 2 (3A) and 9 (3A) of the Criminal Justice Act, 1967, pp. 432, 434, *post* (as amended by Children and Young Persons Act, 1969). These provisions are not yet in force and will not come into force until the minimum age for prosecution under s. 4, *ibid.*, is raised.

Protection from publicity.—See Home Office letter 208/1964 p. 676, *post*.

39. Power to prohibit publication of certain matter in newspapers.—(1) In relation to any proceedings in any court, the court may direct that—

   (a) no newspaper report of the proceedings shall reveal the name, address, or school, or include any particulars calculated to lead to the identification, of any child or young person concerned in the proceedings, either as being the person by or against or in respect of whom the proceedings are taken, or as being a witness therein ;

   (b) no picture shall be published in any newspaper as being or including a picture of any child or young person so concerned in the proceedings as aforesaid ;

except in so far (if at all) as may be permitted by the direction of the court.

(2) Any person who publishes any matter in contravention of any such direction shall on summary conviction be liable in respect of each offence to a fine not exceeding fifty pounds.

NOTES

This section is printed as amended by the Children and Young Persons Act, 1963.

See Home Office letter No. 18/56, p. 674, *post*, as to drawing the attention of the court to cases to which this section applies.

This section is widely drawn, and can include proceedings in a civil as well as a criminal court. The court may give directions restricting publicity in any proceedings; but, in the absence of such directions, the ordinary rules as to newspaper reports of judicial proceedings will apply. See also s. 49, p. 56, *post*.

"Court"—In the section "court" does not include any court in Scotland. See the Children and Young Persons Act, 1963, s. 57 (3) as amended by the Act of 1969 (p. 115, *post*).

"Calculated."—Here evidently means "likely," and not necessarily "intended."

Sound and Television broadcasts.—For extension of this section to sound and television broadcasts see the Children and Young Persons Act, 1963, s. 57 (4), p. 115, *post*.

Protection from publicity.—See Home Office Circular No. 208/1964, p. 676, *post*.

Statement of use of court's powers.—See Home Office Circular No. 17/1964, p. 677, *post*.

Scotland.—For application to Scotland see s. 57 (3) Children and Young Persons Act, 1963, p. 115, *post*.

Special Procedure with regard to Offences specified in First Schedule

40. Warrant to search for or remove a child or young person.—
(1) If it appears to a justice of the peace on information on oath laid by any person who, in the opinion of the justice, is acting in the interests of a child or young person, that there is reasonable cause to suspect—

(a) that the child or young person has been or is being assaulted, ill-treated, or neglected in any place within the jurisdiction of the justice, in a manner likely to cause him unnecessary suffering, or injury to health ; or

(b) that any offence mentioned in the First Schedule to this Act has been or is being committed in respect of the child or young person,

the justice may issue a warrant authorising any constable named therein to search for the child or young person, and, if it is found that he has been or is being assaulted, ill-treated, or neglected in manner aforesaid, or that any such offence as aforesaid has been or is being committed in respect of him, to take him to a place of safety, or authorising any constable to remove him with or without search to a place of safety, and a child or young person taken to a place of safety in pursuance of such a warrant may be detained there until he can be brought before a juvenile court.

(2) A justice issuing a warrant under this section may by the same warrant cause any person accused of any offence in respect of the child or young person to be apprehended and brought before a court of summary jurisdiction, and proceedings to be taken against him according to law.

(3) Any constable authorised by warrant under this section to search for any child or young person, or to remove any child or young person

with or without search, may enter (if need be by force) any house, building, or other place specified in the warrant, and may remove him therefrom.

(4) Every warrant issued under this section shall be addressed to and executed by a constable, who shall be accompanied by the person laying the information, if that person so desires, unless the justice by whom the warrant is issued otherwise directs, and may also, if the justice by whom the warrant is issued so directs, be accompanied by a duly qualified medical practitioner.

(5) It shall not be necessary in any information or warrant under this section to name the child or young person.

NOTES

This section is printed as amended by the Children and Young Persons Act, 1963. For list of offences mentioned in the First Schedule, see p. 245, *post*.

"**Reasonable cause to suspect.**"—It is of course the duty of any person applying for a warrant fairly and fully to state the ground of his suspicion. Compare the similar protection given by the repealed s. 10 of the Criminal Law Amendment Act, 1885; 5 Halsbury's Statutes, 2nd Edn., 911, and see the dictum of Lord Coleridge, C.J., in *Hope* v. *Evered* (1886), 17 Q. B. D. 338; 55 L. J. M. C. 146.

S. 8 of the Children Act, 1958, p. 965, *post*, provides that any refusal to allow the visiting of a foster child or the inspection of any premises by a person authorised to do so under Part I of that Act shall be treated as giving reasonable cause for such a suspicion.

S. 45 of the Adoption Act, 1958, p. 1075, *post*, makes similar provisions in respect of a protected child as defined in that Act.

Refusal to allow an authorised person to enter premises is deemed to be a reasonable cause to suspect that a child or young person is neglected, etc. (Children and Young Persons Act, 1969, s. 59 (3), p. 206, *post*.)

"**Young person.**"—This means over fourteen and under seventeen (s. 107, p. 81, *post*), but see the limit of sixteen years in s. 1, p. 10, *ante*.

"**Warrant.**"—It appears that the justice has a discretion to issue a warrant in one of two alternative forms : (i) the constable may be authorised to search for the child, and if he shall find the offence has been or is being committed, he may proceed to take the child ; (ii) the constable may be authorised unconditionally to remove the child.

Thus, under (i) there is a discretion in the constable, who may use his own judgment whether he should or should not remove the child, while under (ii) he must do so.

It may be thought well to employ (i) where the evidence upon which the warrant is granted is not strong ; otherwise to act under (ii). In any event, the constable will of course report to the justice the state of affairs he found.

Though the child or young person need not be named, it is obviously necessary that he should be identified in some way.

See s. 43 of the Sexual Offences Act, 1956, p. 397, *post*, as to further powers to search for and remove a woman (or girl) detained for immoral purposes.

Detention in place of safety.—The warrant authorising a constable to take a child or young person to a place of safety under this section must specify a period not exceeding twenty-eight days beyond which a child or young person must not be detained without being brought before a juvenile court (see the Children and Young Persons Act, 1963, s. 23, p. 95, *post*).

41. Power to proceed with case in absence of child or young person.—Where in any proceedings with relation to any of the offences mentioned in the First Schedule to this Act, the court is satisfied that the attendance before the court of any child or young person in respect of whom the offence is alleged to have been committed is not essential to the just hearing of the case, the case may be proceeded with and determined in the absence of the child or young person.

NOTES

Care proceedings under s. 1 (2) (a) Children and Young Persons Act, 1969, unlike the provisions of s. 2 (2) (c) of the 1963 Act (now repealed) are not "specifically related" to any of the offences mentioned in the First Schedule. The section is generally considered to relate to criminal proceedings. For the power to continue care proceedings in the absence of a child see Children and Young Persons Act, 1969, s. 2 (9).

For list of offences mentioned in the First Schedule, see p. 245, *post*.

" **Attendance.**"—According to Lord Alverstone, C.J., in *R.* v. *Hale*, [1905] 1 K. B. 126; 69 J. P. 83, this is equivalent to attendance for the purpose of giving evidence. In the interests of the accused, however, where the child's evidence is essential to the just hearing of the case, his presence should not be dispensed with. See the remarks of Lord Alverstone in *R.* v. *Hale*, *supra*, a case decided under a similar [repealed] section.

42. Extension of power to take deposition of child or young person.—(1) Where a justice of the peace is satisfied by the evidence of a duly qualified medical practitioner that the attendance before a court of any child or young person in respect of whom any of the offences mentioned in the First Schedule to this Act is alleged to have been committed would involve serious danger to his life or health, the justice may take in writing the deposition of the child or young person on oath, and shall thereupon subscribe the deposition and add thereto a statement of his reason for taking it and of the day when and place where it was taken, and of the names of the persons (if any) present at the taking thereof.

(2) The justice taking any such deposition shall transmit it with his statement—

    (a) if the deposition relates to an offence for which any accused person is already committed for trial, to the proper officer of the court for trial at which the accused person has been committed ; and

    (b) in any other case, to the clerk of the court before which proceedings are pending in respect of the offence.

NOTES

This section must be read in conjunction with s. 43. It applies to summary as well as to indictable offences.

" **Proper officer.**"—Presumably the appropriate officer of the Crown Court.

Sexual offences.—As to the evidence of children in committal proceedings for sexual offences see s. 27 of the Children and Young Persons Act, 1963, p. 98, *post*.

43. Admission of deposition of child or young person in evidence. —Where, in any proceedings in respect of any of the offences mentioned in the First Schedule to this Act, the court is satisfied by the evidence of a duly qualified medical practitioner that the attendance before the court of any child or young person in respect of whom the offence is alleged to have been committed would involve serious danger to his life or health, any deposition of the child or young person taken under the Indictable Offences Act, 1848, or this Part of this Act, shall be admissible in evidence either for or against the accused person without further proof thereof if it purports to be signed by the justice by or before whom it purports to be taken :

Provided that the deposition shall not be admissible in evidence against the accused person unless it is proved that reasonable notice of the intention to take the deposition has been served upon him and that he or his counsel or solicitor had, or might have had if he had chosen to be present, an opportunity of cross-examining the child or young person making the deposition.

NOTES

See s. 42, *supra*.

Indictable Offences Act.—See now the Magistrates' Courts Act, 1952.

" **Reasonable notice.**"—The notice should apparently be in writing. In *R.* v. *Shurmer* (1886), 17 Q. B. D. 323 ; 50 J. P. 743, the Court for Crown Cases Reserved quashed the conviction on the ground that written notice (under another statute in similar terms) had not been given, although in fact the accused was present.

Sexual offences.—As to the evidence of children in committal proceedings for sexual offences see s. 27 of the Children and Young Persons Act, 1963, p. 98, *post*.

Principles to be observed by all Courts in dealing with Children and Young Persons

44. General considerations.—(1) Every court in dealing with a child or young person who is brought before it, either as an offender or otherwise, shall have regard to the welfare of the child or young person and shall in a proper case take steps for removing him from undesirable surroundings, and for securing that proper provision is made for his education and training.

(2) [*Repealed by Children and Young Persons Act, 1969, s. 72* (4) *and Sched. VI.*]

NOTES

This section is printed as amended by the Children and Young Persons Act, 1969, s. 72 (4) and Sched. VI.

" **Shall have regard to the welfare of the child or young person.**"—This section removed doubts which, quite reasonably, existed before. It was felt by some that it was not permissible to send a child away for years, upon a trivial charge, if he was of good character and the only justification would be that such a course would be for his welfare.

It is now laid down that questions of welfare, including environment, education and training, are to be taken into account in all cases. Even so, however, it must be remembered that nothing can override the principle that the court must first of all try the case and determine whether what is alleged is proved. Whether it be an offence or a proceeding under s. 1 of the Act of 1969, p. 130, *post*, the case must be made out before questions of welfare can be entertained. If a case fails for want of proof, the court cannot act, however much the welfare of the child may demand action.

In the case of *In re McGrath (Infants)*, [1893] 1 Ch. 143; 62 L. J. Ch. 208, Lindley L. J., said " The dominant matter for the consideration of the court is the welfare of the child. But the welfare of a child is not to be measured by money only, or by physical comfort only. The word "welfare" must be taken in its widest sense. The moral and religious welfare of the child must be considered as well as its physical well being. Nor can the ties of affection be disregarded."

See also note to s. 1 of the Guardianship of Minors Act, 1971, p. 1198, *post.*

Juvenile Courts

45. Constitution of juvenile courts.—Courts of summary jurisdiction constituted in accordance with the provisions of the Second Schedule to this Act and sitting for the purpose of hearing any charge against a child or young person or for the purpose of exercising any other jurisdiction conferred on juvenile courts by or under this or any other Act, shall be known as juvenile courts and in whatever place sitting shall be deemed to be petty sessional courts.

NOTES

"**Court of summary jurisdiction.**"—This means "any justice or justices of the peace, or other magistrate, by whatever name called, to whom jurisdiction is given by, or who is authorised to act under, the Summary Jurisdiction Acts, whether in England, Wales, or Ireland, and whether acting under the Summary Jurisdiction Acts or any of them, or under any other Act, or by virtue of his commission, or under the common law" (Interpretation Act, 1889, s. 13 (11)). The relevant sections of the Summary Jurisdiction Acts were repealed by the Magistrates' Courts Act, 1952. See the corresponding provisions of that Act, and the definition of "Magistrates' Court" in s. 124, *ibid.*, 8 Halsbury's Statutes, 3rd Edn., 286.

"**Petty sessional court.**"—This, as respects England and Wales, means "a court of summary jurisdiction consisting of two or more justices when sitting in a petty sessional court-house, and shall include the Lord Mayor of the City of London, and any alderman of that city, and any metropolitan or borough police magistrate or other stipendiary magistrate when sitting in a court-house or place at which he is authorised by law to do alone any act authorised to be done by more than one justice of the peace." (Interpretation Act, 1889, s. 13 (12)).

Thus, every petty sessional court is a court of summary jurisdiction, but not every court of summary jurisdiction is a petty sessional court. A juvenile court, however, is, under this section, always a petty sessional court.

Saving for juvenile courts. As to the saving for juvenile courts from the provisions of the Magistrates' Courts Act, 1952, relating to the constitution, place of sitting and procedure of Magistrates' Courts, see s. 130 of that Act which is as follows:—

> "**130. Saving for juvenile courts.**—The provisions of this Act relating to the constitution, place of sitting and procedure of magistrates' courts shall, in their application to juvenile courts, have effect subject to any provision contained in the rules or any enactment regulating the constitution, place of sitting or procedure of juvenile courts."

It should be noted that the procedure in juvenile courts remains as laid down in the Children and Young Persons Acts, 1933–1969, and the Magistrates' Courts (Children and Young Persons) Rules, 1970, pp. 571 *et seq., post.*

Appearance by advocate.—We are of opinion that s. 99 of the Magistrates' Courts Act, 1952, which provides that an absent party represented by counsel or solicitor shall be deemed not to be absent, read in conjunction with s. 130, *supra.* does not apply to proceedings in juvenile courts.

46. Assignment of certain matters to juvenile courts.—(1) Subject as hereinafter provided, no charge against a child or young person, and no application whereof the hearing is by rules made under this section assigned to juvenile courts, shall be heard by a court of summary jurisdiction which is not a juvenile court :

Provided that—

(a) a charge made jointly against a child or young person and a person who has attained the age of seventeen years shall be heard by a court of summary jurisdiction other than a juvenile court ; and

(b) where a child or young person is charged with an offence, the charge may be heard by a court of summary jurisdiction which is not a juvenile court if a person who has attained the age of seventeen years is charged at the same time with aiding, abetting, causing, procuring, allowing or permitting that offence ; and

(c) where, in the course of any proceedings before any court of summary jurisdiction other than a juvenile court, it appears that the person to whom the proceedings relate is a child or young person, nothing in this subsection shall be construed as preventing the court, if it thinks fit so to do, from proceeding with the hearing and determination of those proceedings.

(1A) If a notification that the accused desires to plead guilty without appearing before the court is received by the clerk of a court in pursuance of section 1 of the Magistrates' Courts Act, 1957 and the court has no reason to believe that the accused is a child or young person, then, if he is a child or young person he shall be deemed to have attained the age of seventeen for the purposes of subsection (1) of this section in its application to the proceedings in question.

(2) No direction, whether contained in this or any other Act, that a charge shall be brought before a juvenile court shall be construed as restricting the powers of any justice or justices to entertain an application for bail or for a remand, and to hear such evidence as may be necessary for that purpose.

(3) [*Repealed by the Justices of the Peace Act*, 1949.]

NOTES

This section is printed as amended by the Education Act, 1944, s. 121, and Sched. IX, Part I, and the Justices of the Peace Act, 1949 and the Children and Young Persons Act, 1969, s. 72 (3) and Sched. V.

Rules.—Sub-s. (3) was repealed by the Justices of the Peace Act, 1949, ss. 15, 46 and Sched. VII, Part II, but rules having effect under this section have effect as if contained in rules made under that Act; *ibid.*, s. 15 (8).

" **Juvenile courts.** "—From para. (a) of the proviso to s. 46 (1) it seems clear that charges made jointly against a child or a young person and an adult must not be heard in a juvenile court.

This section prohibits, with two exceptions, the hearing of charges against children and young persons (save joint charges already referred to) in the ordinary magistrates' court. The case of an adult charged with an offence and a child or young person aiding, abetting, causing, procuring, allowing or permitting is now provided for in s. 18 of the Children and Young Persons Act, 1963 (p. 94, *post*), which allows a court which is not a juvenile court to deal with the juvenile. The same section also empowers a court which is not a juvenile court to deal with a juvenile charged with an offence arising out of circumstances which are the same as or connected with those giving rise to an offence with which an adult is charged at the same time.

" **Attained the age.**"—Subject to statutory exceptions, a person attains the age of seventeen years at the commencement of the relevant anniversary of the date of his birth, Family Law Reform Act, 1969, s. 9 (1); and see note "Age of sixteen" to s. 1, p. 12, *ante*.

" **Bail** "—Sub-s. (2) is applicable to cases where the child or young person cannot be brought before a juvenile court for some days after his arrest. He can be brought before a justice or justices and remanded, with or without bail.

Affiliation proceedings.—It sometimes happens that the defendant to an application for an affiliation order is a young person. Apparently, such a case must be heard in the adult court, but it is a domestic proceeding within the meaning of s. 56 of the Magistrates' Courts Act, 1952. See Legitimacy Act, 1959, s. 5, p. 1298, *post*.

Jurisdiction.—Statutes such as the Dogs Act, 1871, provide that courts of summary jurisdiction may make orders on complaint, and provide penalties for disobedience of such orders. It is submitted that, in the case of children and young persons, the first stage being neither a charge nor an application whereof the hearing is by rules assigned to juvenile courts, application should be made for such orders to a court of summary jurisdiction which is not a juvenile court. See *R*. v. *Nottingham JJ*., *Ex parte Brown*, [1960] 3 All E. R. 625 ; 125 J. P. 49, in which it was held that the first stage is in the nature of a civil proceeding, and that no offence is involved until there is failure to comply with the order.

47. Procedure in juvenile courts.—(1) Juvenile courts shall sit as often as may be necessary for the purpose of exercising any jurisdiction conferred on them by or under this or any other Act.

(2) A juvenile court shall not sit in a room in which sittings of a court other than a juvenile court are held if a sitting of that other court has been or will be held there within an hour before or after the sitting of the juvenile court ; and no person shall be present at any sitting of a juvenile court except—

    (a) members and officers of the court ;

    (b) parties to the case before the court, their solicitors and counsel, and witnesses and other persons directly concerned in that case ;

    (c) bonâ fide representatives of newspapers or news agencies ;

    (d) such other persons as the court may specially authorise to be present :

(3) [*Repealed by the Justices of the Peace Act*, 1949.]

NOTES

The section is printed as amended by the Justices of the Peace Act, 1949, and the Children and Young Persons Act, 1963.

Premises.—A juvenile court is no longer required to sit in a different building or room or on different days.

" **Jurisdiction.**"—" Under any other Act." There may be jurisdiction under some Acts to deal with certain matters concerning adults. For example, it is usually considered that under s. 96 of the Magistrates' Courts Act, 1952, p. 317, *post*, a recognizance entered into before a juvenile court by an adult may be enforced by the juvenile court.

" **Specially.**"—" Specially " authorise to be present. This word seems to indicate the intention that general permission should not be given to classes of persons, but that applications for permission should be individually considered.

Rules.—Sub-s. (3) made it possible for the Rules to modify the statutes, but only in respect of procedure.

Sub-s. (3) was repealed by the Justices of the Peace Act, 1949, but rules having effect under this section have effect as if contained in rules made under that Act; *ibid.*, s. 15 (8).

Rules made under the Justices of the Peace Act are printed at pp. 571 *et seq.*, *post*.

Clearing court.—As to power to clear the court, see s. 37 and notes thereto, p. 44, *ante*.

Magistrates' Courts Act, 1952; saving for juvenile courts.—See note to s. 45, p. 51, *ante*.

Adoption Act, 1958, Part IV.—Sub.-s. 47 (2) does not apply to any sitting of a juvenile court in any proceedings under Part IV of the Adoption Act, 1958. See s. 47, *ibid.*, p. 1075, *post*.

Children Act, 1958.—Sub-s. (2) does not apply to any sitting of a juvenile court in any proceedings under Part I of the Children Act, 1958. See s. 10, *ibid.*, p. 965, *post*.

48. Miscellaneous provisions as to powers of juvenile courts.—(1) A juvenile court sitting for the purpose of hearing a charge against a person who is believed to be a child or young person may, if it thinks fit to do so, proceed with the hearing and determination of the charge, notwithstanding that it is discovered that the person in question is not a child or young person.

(2) The attainment of the age of seventeen years by *a probationer, or* a person in whose case an order for conditional discharge has been made, shall not deprive a juvenile court of jurisdiction to enforce his attendance and deal with him in respect of *any failure to comply with the requirements of the probation order* or the commission of a further offence *or to amend or discharge the probation order*.

(3) When a juvenile court has remanded a child or young person for information to be obtained with respect to him, any juvenile court acting for the same petty sessional division or place—

(a) may in his absence extend the period for which he is remanded, so, however, that he appears before a court or a justice of the peace at least once in every twenty-one days ;

(b) when the required information has been obtained, may deal with him finally;

(4) A juvenile court may sit on any day for the purpose of hearing and determining a charge against a child or young person in respect of an indictable offence.

(5) A juvenile court sitting in the metropolitan police court area shall have all the powers of a metropolitan police magistrate ; and for the purposes of any enactment by virtue of which any powers are exercisable—

(a) by a court of summary jurisdiction acting for the same petty sessional division or place as a juvenile court by which some previous act has been done ; or

(b) by a juvenile court acting for the same petty sessional division or place as a court of summary jurisdiction by which some previous act has been done, the metropolitan police court area shall be deemed to be the place for which all metropolitan police magistrates sitting in that area and all juvenile courts sitting in that area act.

(6) [*Repealed by the Justices of the Peace Act*, 1949, *ss.* 15, 46 *and Sched. VII, Part III.*]

NOTES

This section is printed as amended by the Criminal Justice Act, 1948, the Justices of the Peace Act, 1949, the Magistrates' Courts Act, 1952, the Children and Young Persons Act, 1963, and the Children and Young Persons Act, 1969, s. 72 (4) and Sched. VI. The words printed in italics are repealed (Sched. VI, *ibid.*) but by para. 2, Sched. 3 Children and Young Persons Act, 1969 (Commencement No. 3) Order, 1970 (S.I. 1970 No. 1498), nothing in any provision of Sched. V or VI of the 1969 Act brought into force by that order shall affect the operation of this section or s. 9, Criminal Justice Act, 1961, in relation to a probation order which continues in force by virtue of para. 5 (2) of the said Sched. V. A juvenile court may therefore still deal with a probationer who has attained the age of seventeen where the order was made before 1st January, 1971.

"**A charge against.**"—A juvenile court has no power to start hearing an application under s. 1 of the 1969 Act in respect of a person who is discovered to be over seventeen. It has power, however, to hear such an application where before the conclusion of the proceedings a young person attains the age of seventeen. See s. 29 (1) of the Children and Young Persons Act, 1963 (p. 99, *post*).

"**Discovers.**"—The use of this word and the previous reference to belief as to age appear to indicate a reference to cases where there has been some mistake or misrepresentation, and not to cases where the age of a young person is known to the court throughout. However where proceedings are begun and he becomes an adult during the course of the proceedings s. 29 (1) of the Act of 1963 as amended by the Act of 1969 allows the court to deal with such a case and make any order which it could have made if he had not attained that age. For further provisions as to the attainment of the age of seventeen during the course of proceedings see Children and Young Persons Act, 1969, s. 16 (11). In *R.* v. *Chelsea Justices, Ex parte Director of Public Prosecutions*, [1963] 3 All E. R. 657; 128 J. P. 18, it was held that this section did not apply where the court knew when the charge was first preferred, that the defendant was seventeen.

"**In his absence.**"—These remands are apparently limited to cases in which the court has remanded for inquiries, and is considering the manner in which the child or young person is to be dealt with. The section would not apply to cases where the court had not yet determined that the case was proved.

In case of illness or accident, a person accused of an offence may be further remanded, in his absence, under s. 106 of the Magistrates' Courts Act, 1952, p. 384, *post*.

Notice should be sent to the defendant (and his sureties if any).

See Form 19 to the Magistrates' Courts (Children and Young Persons) Rules, 1970, pp. 592, *post*.

"**Remands.**"—As to powers of remand where the defendant is before the court, see Magistrates' Courts Act, 1952, ss. 6, 14 (p. 378 *post*), 26 (p. 379, *post*), 98 (7) (21 Halsbury's Statutes, 3rd Edn., 268), 105 and 106 (pp. 383, 384, *post*).

"**Finding of guilt.**"—The convenient practice of acting upon a finding of guilt, by a differently constituted court from that which convicted or found guilty is authorised by s. 98 (7) of the Magistrates' Courts Act, 1952; 21 Halsbury's Statutes, 3rd Edn., 268.

The similar provision in relation to care or protection cases under s. 5 of the Children and Young Persons Act, 1938, has now been repealed; see note to s. 2 (10), Act of 1969, p. 136, *post*.

Indictable offences.—Sub-s. (4) abolishes the necessity for giving public notice, so far as the trial of children and young persons is concerned, of sittings for the purpose of trying indictable offences summarily.

" **Metropolitan police court area.**"—This is now to be read as " Inner London area " (Administration of Justice Act, 1964, Sched. 3). Schedule 2 to the Children and Young Persons Act, 1963 (which related to the constitution of juvenile courts) is amended in this respect by s. 12 of the Administration of Justice Act, 1964.

"**All the powers of a metropolitan police magistrate.**"—These magistrates have certain special powers conferred upon them by the Metropolitan Police Courts Acts. See, for example, s. 36 of the 1839 Act; 21 Halsbury's Statutes, 3rd Edn., 21. Part of s. 36 was repealed by the Magistrates' Courts Act, 1952. See also ss. 6, 105 and 106 of that Act, pp. 378, 383 and 384, *post*.

" **Shall be deemed to be the place.**"—This removes difficulties that might be raised as to jurisdiction. Every metropolitan magistrate may sit in any metropolitan police court and in any metropolitan juvenile court and exercise jurisdiction in any one of them over cases arising anywhere in the whole metropolitan police court area.

Lay justices for the inner London area who are on the juvenile court panel are eligible to sit in any metropolitan juvenile court.

49. Restrictions on newspaper reports of proceedings in juvenile courts.—(1) Subject as hereinafter provided, no newspaper report of any proceedings in a juvenile court shall reveal the name, address or school, or include any particulars calculated to lead to the identification, of any child or young person concerned in those proceedings, either as being the person against or in respect of whom the proceedings are taken or as being a witness therein, nor shall any picture be published in any newspaper as being or including a picture of any child or young person so concerned in any such proceedings as aforesaid :

Provided that the court or the Secretary of State may in any case, if satisfied that it is appropriate to do so for the purpose of avoiding injustice to a child or young person, by order dispense with the requirements of this section in relation to him to such extent as may be specified in the order.

(2) Any person who publishes any matter in contravention of this section shall on summary conviction be liable in respect of each offence to a fine not exceeding fifty pounds.

NOTES

This section and s. 39, *ante*, extend to Scotland but references to a court in these sections shall not include a court in Scotland (s. 57 (3), Children and Young Persons Act, 1963, p. 115, *post* as amended by the Act of 1969).

General note.—The section is printed as amended by s. 10 of the Act of 1969. For construction of references to "juvenile court," "young person" see s. 10. In proceedings in pursuance of ss. 15 and 16, Children and Young Persons Act, 1969, in a magistrates' court other than a juvenile court and on appeal therefrom from it shall be the duty of the court to announce that this section applies; and if the court fails to do so the section shall not apply to the proceedings in question (s. 10 (2), *ibid.*).

Scotland.—For application to Scotland see s. 57 (3) of the Children and Young Persons Act, 1963, p. 115, *post*.

Appeals.—This section, with the necessary modifications, applies in relation to proceedings on appeal from a juvenile court as it applies in relation to proceedings in a juvenile court. (s. 57 (2) of the Children and Young Persons Act, 1963, p. 115, *post*).

Broadcasts.—This section, with the necessary modifications, applies in relation to sound and television broadcasts as it applies in relation to newspapers (s. 57 (4) of the Children and Young Persons Act, 1963, p. 115, *post*).

" **Calculated.**"—Here evidently means " likely " and not necessarily " intended."

Proviso.—The order referred to in the proviso should be specific in details, and it may be advisable that it should be drawn up in writing. Publicity may occasionally be desirable, even in a juvenile court, in order to assist the course of justice but is not permissible unless to avoid *injustice* to the person to whom the order relates.

Juvenile Offenders

50. Age of criminal responsibility.—It shall be conclusively presumed that no child under the age of ten years can be guilty of any offence.

NOTES

This section is printed as amended by the Children and Young Persons Act, 1963, which raised the age from eight to ten.

The old presumption that a child between seven (now ten) and fourteen has not reached the age of discretion and is *doli incapax* must still be borne in mind. This presumption is, however, rebuttable by strong evidence of a mischievous discretion.

Malitia supplet aetatem. In practice, it will be found that the child of average intelligence shows a capacity for knowing good from evil; but the presumption should be borne in mind when a charge against a child involves guilty knowledge and it is not obvious that such guilty knowledge must have existed.

Although not amounting to criminal acts, the child's actions may show a need of care, protection or control. Cf. Children and Young Persons Act, 1969, s. 1, p. 130, *post.*

Receiving from child.—In the case of *Walters* v. *Lunt*, [1951] 2 All E. R. 645, it was held that as a child under the age of eight cannot be found guilty of larceny, property taken by the child was not property stolen, and that a receiver of the property could not be convicted under s. 33 (1) of the Larceny Act, 1916, of receiving the property knowing it to have been stolen. *Semble* he could have been convicted of larceny as bailee or of larceny by finding. It would now seem that a person would not be guilty of handling stolen property s. 22, Theft Act, 1968, in such circumstances but could be convicted of theft provided there was a dishonest appropriation.

Evidence of understanding and capacity.—In the case of *X.* v. *X.* (1958), 122 J. P. Jo. 752, the Divisional Court dismissed the appeal by case stated of a boy nearly nine years old found guilty of breaking and entering a house and stealing. The Lord Chief Justice, giving judgment, said that there was evidence before the justices rebutting the presumption, and that in his view there was some evidence, for example, that the defendant was a respectable child, who had been properly brought up.

In *R.* v. *Padwick* (1959), *Times*, April 24th, an appeal by case stated relating to a boy aged 8 years, Lord Parker, C.J., said that before the justices rule on a case of this sort they should hear evidence of the boy's home background and all his circumstances; in a bad home it would be likely that a child would be brought up without knowledge of right or wrong. See also *Ex parte N.*, [1959] Crim. L. R. 523.

The cases seem to be authority for the admission of evidence, however prejudicial, to show that the defendant knew the difference between right and wrong, even if it entailed leading evidence of a previous finding of guilt.

51. [*Repealed by Criminal Law Act, 1967, s. 10 and Sched. III.*]

52. [*Repealed by the Criminal Justice Act, 1948. See now s. 17 of that Act and s. 107 of the Magistrates' Courts Act, 1952, pp. 372, 385, post.*]

53. Punishment of certain grave crimes.—(1) A person convicted of an offence who appears to the court to have been under the age of eighteen years at the time the offence was committed, shall not if he is convicted of murder, be sentenced to imprisonment for life nor shall sentence of death be pronounced on or recorded against any such person; but in lieu thereof the court shall (notwithstanding anything in this or any other Act) sentence him to be detained during Her Majesty's pleasure; and if so sentenced he shall be liable to be detained in such place and under such conditions as the Secretary of State may direct.

(2) Where a child or young person is convicted on indictment of any offence punishable in the case of an adult with imprisonment for fourteen years or more, not being an offence the sentence for which is fixed by law, and the court is of opinion that none of the other methods in which the case may legally be dealt with is suitable, the court may sentence the offender to be detained for such period not exceeding the maximum term of imprisonment with which the offence is punishable in the case of an adult as may be specified in the sentence ; and where such a sentence has been passed the child or young person shall, during that period, be liable to be detained in such place and on such conditions as the Secretary of State may direct.

(3) A person detained pursuant to the directions of the Secretary of State under this section shall, while so detained, be deemed to be in legal custody.

(4) [*Repealed as to England and Wales by the Criminal Justice Act*, 1967, s. 103 *and Sched. VII.*]

NOTES

Sub-s. (1) is printed as substituted by the Murder (Abolition of Death Penalty) Act, 1965, s. 1 (5).   Sub-s. (2) is printed as amended by the Criminal Justice Act, 1961, and the Children and Young Persons Act, 1963.

Determination of age.—See note to s. 17 of the Criminal Justice Act, 1948, p. 372, *post*.

Family Allowances.—See leaflet at p. 1006, *post*.

Supervision.—As to the supervision of persons released on licence from sentences of detention during Her Majesty's Pleasure, or for life, imposed under this section, and for the arrangements for informing the police of the release on licence of such persons see Home Office Circulars Nos. 171/1968 and 172/1968 dated July 23, 1968.

Detention in community homes.—(1) The power to give directions under this section shall include power to direct detention by a local authority specified in the directions in a home so specified which is a community home provided by the authority or a controlled community home for the management, equipment and maintenance of which the authority are responsible; but a person shall not be liable to be detained in the manner provided by this section after he attains the age of nineteen.

(2) It shall be the duty of a local authority specified in directions given in pursuance of this section to detain the person to whom the directions relate in the home specified in the directions subject to and in accordance with such instructions relating to him as the Secretary of State may give to the authority from time to time; and the authority shall be entitled to recover from the Secretary of State any expenses reasonably incurred by them in discharging that duty (Children and Young Persons Act, 1969, s. 30, p. 177, *post*).

" **Appeal.**"—There is no appeal against sentence under sub-s. (1), the sentence being fixed by law. (*R. v. Collins*, [1943] 1 All E. R. 203).

In *R. v. G.* (1971), *Times*, September 27th, G. pleaded guilty of 8 burglaries with eighteen similar offences taken into consideration.   An order was made for his detention for 18 months as he was just too young for Borstal training.   He had been sent to an approved school.   On appeal against the detention order held: a care order under s. 20, Children and Young Persons Act, 1969, should be substituted as there was no possibility of after care and supervision under the original order and that the best thing for all would be for him to remain at a community home for an indefinite period, which could only be achieved by a care order.

After care of persons released from custody.—As to the duty of probation officers to undertake the supervision of any person while on licence under this section on behalf of the Central After-Care Association see r. 30 (1) of the Probation Rules, 1965, p. 527, *post.*

Firearms.—A person holding a licence issued under this section is prohibited from having a firearm or ammunition in his possession. Firearms Act, 1968, s. 21 (3).

Life imprisonment.—Life is a period that may validly be specified for an offender's detention in a sentence passed under sub-s. (2), *R.* v. *Abbott*, [1964] 1 Q. B. 489; [1963] 1 All E. R. 738; 127 J. P. 273.

Release on licence.—The Secretary of State may, if recommended by the Parole Board, release on licence a person detained under this section, but shall not do so in the case of a person sentenced to detention during Her Majesty's pleasure except after consultation with the Lord Chief Justice of England together with the trial judge if available.

A licence granted under s. 61 of the Criminal Justice Act, 1967 to any person sentenced under s. 53 (2), *supra*, to be detained otherwise than for life shall unless previously revoked under s. 62 of the first mentioned Act remain in force until a date specified in the licence, being the date of the expiration of the sentence (Criminal Justice Act, 1967, s. 61).

Offenders sentenced to detention during Her Majesty's pleasure under sub-s. (1) or to be detained for life under sub-s. (2) are to be treated for review and licensing purposes as offenders sentenced to life imprisonment. Offenders subject to fixed terms of detention under sub-s. (2) will in accordance with the Local Review Committee Rules, 1967, be considered for release on licence, initially after serving one third of their sentences or twelve months, whichever is the greater, as are adult offenders serving fixed terms of imprisonment. See Home Office Circular No. 46/1968, dated February 26, 1968, paras. 52 and 53.

Transitional arrangements.—A person subject immediately before the commencement of s. 61 of the Criminal Justice Act, 1967, to a licence under s. 53 (4) of the Children and Young Persons Act, 1933, shall be treated as if he had been released on licence under the said s. 61 and as if the conditions contained in a licence under the said s. 53 (4) had been specified in a licence under the said s. 61 and, in the case of a person released after being sentenced under s. 53 (2) of the said Act of 1933 to be detained otherwise than for life, as if a licence granted to him under the said s. 61 had specified the date of the expiration of his sentence as the date until which the licence is to remain in force.

Where any person sentenced under s. 53 of the Children and Young Persons Act, 1933, to be detained was notified before the commencement of s. 61 of this Act that the Secretary of State proposed to release him under the said s. 53 the Secretary of State may release him on licence under the said s. 61, whether or not recommended to do so by the Parole Board or the Parole Board for Scotland.

(Criminal Justice Act, 1967, s. 102 and Sched. V, paras. 10 and 11.)

Parole Board.—See Part III of the Criminal Justice Act, 1967.

Social inquiry report.—A sentence to be detained under this section is a sentence to which s. 57 of the Criminal Justice Act, 1967, p. 303, *post* applies, and the Secretary of State may by rules provide that before passing such a sentence a court must consider a social inquiry report.

Section 57 of the Criminal Justice Act, 1967, was not in force at the time of going to press, but see Home Office Circular No. 188/1968, *Social Enquiry Reports before sentence,* where courts are requested to obtain such reports before passing certain sentences although the rule-making power has not been implemented.

54. [*Repealed by Children and Young Persons Act,* 1969, *s.* 72 (4) *and Sched. VI.*]

55. Power to order parent to pay fine, etc., instead of child or young person.—(1) Where a *child or* young person is found guilty of any offence for the commission of which a fine, damages, or costs may be imposed, if the court is of opinion that the case would be best met by the imposition of a fine, damages, or costs, whether with or without any other punishment, the court may *in any case, and shall if the offender is a child*, order that the fine, damages, or costs awarded be paid by the parent or guardian of the *child or* young person instead of by the *child or* young person, unless the court is satisfied that the parent or guardian cannot be found or that he has not conduced to the commission of the offence by neglecting to exercise due care or control of the *child or* young person.

(2) [*Repealed by Children and Young Persons Act*, 1969, *s. 72 (4) and Sched. VI.*]

(3) An order under this section may be made against a parent or guardian who, having been required to attend, has failed to do so, but, save as aforesaid, no such order shall be made without giving the parent or guardian an opportunity of being heard.

(4) [*Repealed by the Administration of Justice Act*, 1970, *s. 54 and Sched. XI. See now s. 41 and Sched. IX*, ibid.]

(5) A parent or guardian may appeal against an order under this section—

> (a) if made by a court of summary jurisdiction to the Crown Court; and
>
> (b) if made by the Crown Court to the Criminal Division of the Court of Appeal in accordance with Part I of the Criminal Appeal Act, 1968, as if the parent or guardian against whom the order was made had been convicted on indictment, and the order were a sentence passed on his conviction.

NOTES

This section is printed as amended by the Criminal Justice Act, 1967, s. 103, Sched. VI, the Criminal Appeal Act, 1968, ss. 52, 55 (2), and Sched. 5, the Children and Young Persons Act, 1969, ss. 72 (3), (4) and Scheds. V and VI and the Courts Act, 1971. From a date to be appointed, the words in italics are repealed, Children and Young Persons Act, 1969, s. 72 (4) and Sched. VI.

Under sub-s. (1), it will be noticed, it is not necessary for the court to be satisfied affirmatively that the parent has conduced to the commission of the offence ; the penalty may be enforced against the parent unless the court is satisfied that he has not conduced to the offence. The question of enforcement will naturally be decided at the time the fine is imposed.

Compensation, etc.—Sub-s. (1) applies in relation to compensation for loss under sub-s. (2) of s. 11 of the Criminal Justice Act, 1948, and to any sums which the court has power to award under s. 4 of the Forfeiture Act, 1870, as amended by the Criminal Law Act, 1967, or s. 34 of the Magistrates' Courts Act, 1952, as it applies in relation to damages or costs (Criminal Justice Act, 1961, s. 8 (4), p. 318, *post*).

"A parent or guardian."—Sub-s. (3) must be noted. The parent must not be ordered to pay the fine unless he has had notice or had an opportunity of being heard. As to enquiry into his means, see s. 70 of the Magistrates' Courts Act, 1952, p. 315, *post*, and Rule 45 of the Magistrates' Courts Rules, 1968.

Fine and costs.—A child tried summarily may not be fined more than ten pounds. Ss. 6 (3) and 34 (5) Children and Young Persons Act, 1969, p. 144, *post*. A young person tried summarily may not be fined more than fifty pounds, s. 6 (3), *ibid*.

If a child or young person is ordered to pay his own fine, etc., the amount of costs must not exceed the amount of the fine. See s. 6 of the Costs in Criminal Cases Act, 1952, 21 Halsbury's Statutes, 3rd Edn., 176.

" With or without any other punishment."—In certain cases a statute authorises both imprisonment and fine.

56. Power of other courts to remit juvenile offenders to juvenile courts.—(1) Any court by or before which a *child or* young person is found guilty of an offence other than homicide, may, and if it is not a juvenile court, shall unless satisfied that it would be undesirable to do so, remit the case to a juvenile court acting for the place where the offender was committed for trial, or, if he was not committed for trial, to a juvenile court acting either for the same place as the remitting court or for the place where the offender habitually resides; and, where any such case is so remitted, the offender shall be brought before a juvenile court accordingly, and that court may deal with him in any way in which it might have dealt with him if he had been tried and found guilty by that court.

(2) Where any case is so remitted—

(a) the offender shall have the same right of appeal against any order of the court to which the case is remitted as if he had been found guilty by that court, but shall have no right of appeal against the order of remission ; and

(b) [*Repealed by the Courts Act,* 1971.]

(3) A court by which an order remitting a case to a juvenile court is made under this section may give such directions as appear to be necessary with respect to the custody of the offender or for his release on bail until he can be brought before the juvenile court, and shall cause to be transmitted to the clerk of the juvenile court a certificate setting out the nature of the offence and stating that the offender has been found guilty thereof, and that the case has been remitted for the purpose of being dealt with under this section.

NOTES

This section is printed as amended by the Children and Young Persons Act, 1963, the Courts Act, 1971, and s. 72 (3) and Sched. V, Children and Young Persons Act, 1969. From a date to be appointed the words in italics are repealed. S. 72 (4) and Sched. VI, *ibid.*

Procedure.—It will not be necessary to call witnesses before the juvenile court to prove the offence, though that court may sometimes find it desirable to have some of the witnesses before them in order that they may know more about the case than the bare certificate discloses, upon the question of the best means of disposing of the case. So far as the finding of guilt is concerned, it would seem that the juvenile court to which a case is remitted can go behind the finding at any time before making an order upon the finding of guilt *S. (an infant)* v. *Manchester City Recorder,* [1969] 3 All E. R. 1230.

The amendment to sub-s. (1) makes it clear that one juvenile court may remit an offender to another juvenile court.

"Directions as to custody."—If this be a remand, s. 23 of the Children and Young Persons Act, 1969, p. 166, *post,* will apply and the defendant may be remanded to the care of a local authority or, in the case of a young person, sent to a remand centre when available, if he is unruly or depraved. If a remand centre is not available such a young person may be committed to prison.

Rule 27 of the Magistrates' Courts (Children and Young Persons) Rules, 1970, makes no reference to this section, but this may be by an oversight. Although the procedure is analogous to committal for sentence the remand procedure seems more appropriate.

" Certificate."—No form of certificate is prescribed by the Rules, but by s. 106, p. 80, *post,* a copy of the order shall be evidence of the order if it purports to be certified as a true copy by the clerk of the court.

Requirement to remit.—See Children and Young Persons Act, 1969, s. 7 (8), p. 146, *post.*

57. [*Repealed by the Children and Young Persons Act*, 1969, *s.* 72 (4) *and Sched. VI.*]

58. Power of Secretary of State to send certain juvenile offenders to approved schools.—*The Secretary of State may by order direct that—*

(*a*) *a person who is under the age of eighteen years and is undergoing detention in a Borstal institution; or*

(*b*) *a child or young person with respect to whom he is authorised to give directions under subsection* (2) *of section fifty-three of this Act; or*

(*c*) *a young person who has been ordered to be imprisoned and has been pardoned by His Majesty on condition of his agreeing to undergo training in a school,*

shall be transferred or sent to and detained in an approved school specified in the order; and any such order shall be an authority for his detention in that approved school or in such other approved school as the Secretary of State may from time to time determine until such date as may be specified in the order:

Provided that the date to be so specified shall be not later than that on which he will in the opinion of the Secretary of State attain the age of nineteen years nor later—

(*a*) *in the case of a person who was sentenced to detention under the said sub-section* (2), *than the date on which his detention would have expired;*

(*b*) *in the case of a young person who has been sentenced to imprisonment and pardoned as aforesaid, than three years from the date as from which his sentence began to run.*

(*c*) *in the case of a person who was undergoing detention in a Borstal institution, than the end of the period for which he would have been liable to be detained therein.*

NOTES

From a date to be appointed this section is repealed by the Children and Young Persons Act, 1969, s. 72 (4) and Sched. VI, this will be presumably when approved schools are absorbed into the system of community homes, under s. 36 of the Act of 1969.

This section is printed as amended by the Criminal Justice Act, 1948, and the Children and Young Persons Act, 1963.

Borstal transfers.—See s. 44 of the Prison Act, 1952, p. 308, *post*, as to transfers from prison to borstal and vice versa.

" Attainment of age."—See note to s. 46, p. 53, *ante*.

59. Miscellaneous provisions as to summary proceedings against juvenile offenders.—(1) The words " conviction " and "sentence" shall cease to be used in relation to *children and* young persons dealt with summarily and any reference to any enactment whether passed before or after the commencement of this Act to a person convicted, a conviction or a sentence shall, in the case of a *child or* young person, be construed as including a reference to a person found guilty of an offence, a finding of guilt or an order made upon such a finding, as the case may be.

(2) [*Repealed by the Costs in Criminal Cases Act*, 1952.]

NOTES

This section is printed as amended by the Criminal Justice Act, 1948, and the Costs in Criminal Cases Act, 1952.

From a date to be appointed the words in italics are repealed by the Children and Young Persons Act, 1969, s. 72 (4) and Sched. VI.

"**Sentence.**"—By s. 80 of the Criminal Justice Act, 1948, as amended, the word "sentence" has the following meaning for the purposes of that Act—

> "'Sentence' includes an order for detention in a detention centre, but does not include a committal in default of payment of any sum of money or failing to do or abstain from doing anything required to be done or left undone;"

60. Amendments of certain enactments relating to criminal proceedings and courts of summary jurisdiction.—[*Repealed by the Magistrates' Courts Act*, 1952.]

Children and Young Persons in need of Care or Protection

61. Definition of " in need of care or protection." [*Repealed by the Children and Young Persons Act*, 1963].

NOTE

The Children and Young Persons Act, 1963, repealed and extended the definition formerly contained in this section. That Act has itself been repealed (see now Children and Young Persons Act, 1969, s. 1.)

Sections 62–76 of this Act are repealed by the Children and Young Persons Act, 1969, s. 72 (4) and Sched. VI. For provisions relating to powers of juvenile courts in care proceedings see the Children and Young Persons Act, 1969, ss. 1–3, pp. 130, 138, *post*. The repealed provisions relating to supervision, approved schools and fit person orders are superseded by the provisions of the 1969 Act which, *inter alia*, provide for a system of community homes for the accommodation of juveniles who are the subject of care orders. Care orders are defined in s. 20 of that Act, and supervision orders in s. 11. Although s. 66 is repealed, in relation to supervision orders made under the 1933 to 1963 Acts before 1st January, 1971, the court will have power to amend the order and may instead of committal to the care of a fit person, or to an approved school, discharge the supervision order and make a care order, provided the court is satisfied that the subject of the order is unlikely to receive the care and control he needs unless a care order is made (s. 72 (1) and Sched. IV, para. 12, p. 229, *post*).

PART IV.—REMAND HOMES, APPROVED SCHOOLS, AND PERSONS TO WHOSE CARE CHILDREN AND YOUNG PERSONS MAY BE COMMITTED

Part IV applies to an order made on an application under s. 26 (1) of the Children Act, 1948, or to an affiliation order revived under s. 26 (4) of that Act, as if it were an affiliation order in respect of which an order had been made under sub-s. (1) of s. 88 of the Children and Young Persons Act, 1933. See s. 26 (5) of the Children Act, 1948, p. 904, *post*.

Local authorities.—Local authorities for the purpose of this Part of the Act are the councils of counties and county boroughs (Children Act, 1948, s. 38, p. 914, *post*).

As to social services committees, see the Local Authority Social Services Act, 1970, s. 2, p. 927 *post*.

The Council of each London borough shall as respects the borough, and the Common Council shall as respects the City, have the functions of the council of a county borough under Part IV of this Act and be the local authority for such purposes of that Part as refer to a local authority. (London Government Act, 1963, s. 47; 20 Halsbury's Statutes, 3rd Edn., 504).

The Administration of Children's Homes Regulations 1951 (S.I. 1951 No. 1217), pp. 979 *et seq., post,* do not apply to remand homes within the meaning of this Part of this Act (*ibid.,* r. 17).

Remand Homes

77. Provision of remand homes by councils of counties and county boroughs.—(1) *It shall be lawful for the council of every county and county borough to provide for their area remand homes, which may be situate either within or without the area, and for that purpose they may arrange with the occupiers of any premises for the use thereof, or may themselves establish, or join with the council of another county or county borough in establishing, such homes.*

(2) The authority or persons responsible for the management of any institution other than a prison may, subject in the case of an institution supported wholly or partly out of public funds to the consent of the Government department concerned, arrange with the council of a county or county borough for the use of the institution, or any part thereof, as a remand home upon such terms as may be agreed.

(2A) The council of a county or county borough may contribute towards the expenditure incurred by any society or person in establishing, enlarging or improving an institution for the purpose of its being used, in accordance with an arrangement with the council, as a remand home for that county or county borough, such sums, and subject to such conditions, as the council think fit; and subsection (5) of section seventy-seven of the Criminal Justice Act, 1948, shall apply to any sums so paid as it applies to the payments referred to in that subsection.

(3) [*Subsections* (3) *and* (4) *are repealed by the Children and Young Persons Act,* 1969. *See S.I.* 1970 *No.* 1498.]

NOTES

The words in italics are repealed by the Children and Young Persons Act, 1969, s. 72 (4) and Sched. VI, and the Children and Young Persons Act (Commencement No. 2) Order, 1969 (S.I. 1969 No. 1565). However s. 77 (1) continues to apply to a local authority by virtue of para. 13 (1) (c), Sched. IV Children and Young Persons Act, 1969 (p. 230, *post*), and s. 78 (3) of the Act of 1933, shall notwithstanding the repeal of that section continue to apply in relation to remand homes provided by that authority as if for the words "detained in custody" there were substituted the word "accommodated" (S.I. 1970 No. 1498, p. 614, *post*). The repeal of sub-s. (2), (2A) by s. 72 (4) and Sched. VI is not yet operative.

This section is printed as amended by the Criminal Justice Act, 1948 and the Children and Young Persons Act, 1969, s. 72 (1) and Sched. IV.

Remand Home Rules.—See p. 468, *post.*

Stamford House Remand Home.—Secure accommodation. See Home Office letter 118/61/D.1, p. 679, *post.*

78. Provisions as to custody of children and young persons in remand homes.—[*Subsections* (1) *and* (2) *are repealed by the Children and Young Persons Act,* 1969, *s.* 72 (4) *and Sched. VI.*]

(3) *The Secretary of State shall cause remand homes to be inspected and may make rules for their inspection, regulation and management, and for*

the classification, treatment, employment, discipline and control of persons accommodated therein, and for the visitation of such persons from time to time by persons appointed in accordance with the rules.

(4) [*Subsections* (4) *and* (5) *are repealed by the Children and Young Persons Act,* 1969.]

NOTES

Section 78 (3) although repealed by the Act of 1969 continues to apply in relation to remand homes as modified by S.I. 1970 No. 1498, Sched. III, para. 5.   See notes to s. 77, *ante*.

Approved Schools

79. Approval of schools.—(1) *The managers of any school intended for the education and training of persons to be sent there in pursuance of this Act may apply to the Secretary of State to approve the school for that purpose, and the Secretary of State may, after making such inquiries as he thinks fit, approve the school for that purpose and issue a certificate of approval to the managers.*

(2) *If at any time the Secretary of State is dissatisfied with the condition or management of an approved school, or considers its continuance as an approved school unnecessary, he may by notice served on the managers withdraw the certificate of approval of the school as from a date specified in the notice, not being less than six months after the date of the notice, and upon the date so specified (unless the notice is previously withdrawn) the withdrawal of the certificate shall take effect and the school shall cease to be an approved school:*

Provided that the Secretary of State, instead of withdrawing the certificate of approval, may by a notice served on the managers of the school prohibit the admission of persons to the school for such time as may be specified in the notice, or until the notice is revoked.

(3) *The managers of an approved school may, on giving six months' notice in writing to the Secretary of State of their intention so to do, surrender the certificate of approval of the school, and at the expiration of six months from the date of the notice (unless the notice is previously withdrawn), the surrender of the certificate shall take effect, and the school shall cease to be an approved school.*

(4) [*Repealed by Children and Young Persons Act,* 1969, *s.* 72 (4) *and Sched. VI and S.I.* 1970 *No.* 1498.]

(5) *The Secretary of State shall cause any grant of a certificate of approval of an approved school, and any notice of the withdrawal of, or intention to surrender, such a certificate, to be advertised within one month from the date thereof in the London Gazette.*

NOTES

From a date to be appointed the words in italics are repealed by the Children and Young Persons Act, 1969, s. 72 (4) and Sched. VI.

For definition of " managers," see s. 107, p. 81, *post*.

Directions as to management.—As to the power of the Secretary of State to give directions as to the management of approved schools, and as to the application of this section in the event of failure to give effect to such directions, see s. 18 of the

Criminal Justice Act, 1961, p. 407, *post*, and para. 3 (2) (b), Sched. III Children and Young Persons Act, 1969. (The repeal of this section by the Children and Young Persons Act, 1969, s. 72 (4) and Sched. VI is not yet operative.)

Remand Homes.—The provisions of this section may be applied to remand homes by rules made by the Secretary of State; see the Criminal Justice Act, 1948, s. 49 (2), p. 377, *post*, and the Remand Home Rules, 1939 p. 468, *post*. The repeal of s. 49 (2) is not yet operative.

80. Provision of approved schools by local authorities.—(1) *A local authority may, with the approval of the Secretary of State, undertake, or combine with any other local authority in undertaking, or contribute such sums of money upon such conditions as they may think fit towards the purchase, establishment, building, alteration, enlargement, rebuilding or management of an approved school:*

Provided that, before giving his approval, the Secretary of State shall satisfy himself that the proposed expenditure is reasonable and, where it is proposed to purchase, build or establish a new school, that there is a deficiency of approved school accommodation which cannot properly be remedied in any other way.

(2) *In the event of a deficiency of approved school accommodation, it shall be the duty of every local authority concerned to take, either alone or in combination with other local authorities, appropriate steps under this section to remedy the deficiency.*

NOTES

From a date to be appointed the words in italics are repealed by the Children and Young Persons Act, 1969, s. 72 (4) and Sched. VI.

"**Local authority.**"—See s. 96, p. 75, *post*.

It is not clear who are the local authorities " concerned." At present, courts often send children to schools outside their own areas, and a shortage of schools does not appear to concern one authority more than another. Possibly the fact that a large number of places in schools were required by courts in a particular county would place a responsibility upon that county to provide more accommodation.

See s. 104, p. 79, *post*, as to Exchequer grants. (The repeal of this section by s. 72 (4) and Sched. VI of the Act of 1969 is not yet operative.)

81. Classification, administration, and management.—(1) *The Secretary of State may classify approved schools according to the age of the persons for whom they are intended, the religious persuasion of such persons, the character of the education and training given therein, their geographical position, and otherwise as he thinks best calculated to secure that a person sent to an approved school is sent to a school appropriate to his case, or as may be necessary for the purposes of this Act.*

(2) *[Repealed by the Children and Young Persons Act, 1969, s. 72 (4) and Sched. VI and S.I. 1970, No. 1498.]*

(3) *The provisions set out in the Fourth Schedule to this Act shall have effect in relation to the administration of approved schools and the treatment of persons sent thereto.*

NOTES

From a date to be appointed the words in italics are repealed by the Children and Young Persons Act, 1969, s. 72 (4) and Sched. VI.

Home leave and visits.—Geographical position is important as affecting home leave and visits by parents ; schools try in all suitable cases to maintain and improve a child's relationship with his home. The Approved School Rules (p. 459, *post*) provide for children to be visited by their parents.

82. [*Repealed by the Children and Young Persons Act, 1969, s. 72 (4) and Sched. VI. See now s. 32, ibid. See also s. 75, Social Work (Scotland) Act, 1968, which by s. 97, ibid. (p. 76, post) applies to England and Wales. See also Home Office Circular No. 19/1969, p. 704, post, which presumably is still relevant.*]

83. [*Repealed by the Children and Young Persons Act, 1969, s. 72 (4) and Sched. VI. See now s. 26, ibid., and Part V, Social Work (Scotland) Act, 1968, pp. 171, 234, post.*]

84. [*Repealed by the Children and Young Persons Act, 1969, s. 72 (4) and Sched. VI. See now ss. 20, 27 and 43, ibid., and s. 75 Social Work (Scotland) Act, 1968.*]

85. [*Repealed by the Children and Young Persons Act, 1969, s. 72 (4) and Sched. VI. See now s. 32, ibid.*]

Provisions as to Contributions towards Expenses

86. Contributions to be made by parents, etc., of children and young persons committed to the care of fit persons, or to approved schools.—(1) Where a care order which is not an interim order has been made in respect of a child or young person, it shall be the duty of the persons specified in section twenty-four of the Children Act, 1948, to make contributions in respect of him.

(2) [*Repealed by the Children and Young Persons Act, 1969, s. 72 (4) and Sched. VI.*]

(3) Where the child or young person has been committed to the care of a local authority, the contributions shall be payable to the council of the county or county borough within which the person liable to make the contributions is for the time being residing.

(4) [*Repealed by the Children and Young Persons Act, 1969, s. 72 (4) and Sched. VI.*]

NOTES

This section is printed as amended by the Children Act, 1948, the Children and Young Persons Act, 1969, s. 72 (3), (4) and Scheds. V and VI, and the Local Government Act, 1958. Sched. VIII of the latter Act also modifies the section as follows:—

2.—(1) Where contributions under section eighty-six of the Children and Young Persons Act, 1933, in respect of a child or young person committed to, or received into, the care of a local authority are payable, by the person liable to make the contributions, to an authority other than the authority responsible for maintenance, the authority receiving the contributions from the said person shall pay them over to the authority responsible for maintenance, subject however to such deductions in respect of services rendered by the authority paying the contributions over as may be agreed between the two authorities or as in default of agreement may be determined by the Secretary of State.

(2) In the foregoing sub-paragraph references to the authority responsible for maintenance—

    (a) in relation to a child or young person committed to the care of a local authority, are references to that authority;

    (b) in relation to a child received into the care of a local authority, are references to the local authority into whose care the child has been received, except that where the authority to whom the contributions are payable by the person liable to make them has been notified that under subsection (4) of section one of the Children Act, 1948, expenses are being recovered from another authority, the said references shall be construed as references to that other authority.

Children Act, 1948.—For s. 24 see p. 903, *post*. For the application of this section to children in the care of a local authority, see s. 23, *ibid.*, p. 903, *post*.

Agreements.—The local authority and the person liable to contribute may enter into an agreement, the consideration being an undertaking by the local authority not to institute proceedings for an order. See s. 62 of the Act of 1969.

Contribution Orders.—See note to s. 24 of the Children Act, 1948, p. 903, *post*, and s. 62 Children and Young Persons Act, 1969, p. 208, *post*.

Scotland and Northern Ireland.—Sub-s. (3) is modified by the Maintenance Orders Act, 1950, s. 14 and Sched. I, as follows:—

" Where the person liable to make contributions in respect of a child or young person is for the time being residing in Scotland or Northern Ireland, subsection (3) shall have effect as if for references to the council of the county or county borough in which the person liable as aforesaid is for the time being residing there were substituted references to the local authority having the care of the child or young person."

By s. 74 (6) Social Work Scotland Act, 1968, where an order under s. 72 (3) *ibid.*, has been made committing a child to the care of a local authority in England or Wales, it shall have effect as if it were a care order under the Children and Young Persons Act, 1969 (subject to certain modifications). Parental contributions therefore would be payable under s. 62, *ibid.*

Revocation, variation, etc., of order for periodical payment.—See s. 53 of the Magistrates' Courts Act, 1952, which is as follows:—

" Where a magistrates' court has made an order for the periodical payment of money, the court may, by order on complaint, revoke, revive or vary the order."

S. 53 of the Magistrates' Courts Act, 1952, *supra*, applies to such orders as affiliation orders, orders under the Guardianship of Minors Act and orders for parental contributions under the Children and Young Persons Act, 1933, and the Children Act, 1948. So far as costs are concerned, as the procedure is by way of complaint for an order, s. 55 of that Act applies.

See also the Magistrates' Courts Rules 1968.

" Where the person liable is residing."—Apparently where there are different persons, living in different districts, there may be different county councils to whom contributions should be paid. But see Local Government Act, 1958, Sched. VIII, para. 2 (1), *supra*.

Arrears.—For the recovery of arrears where no order is in force, see s. 30 of the Children and Young Persons Act, 1963, p. 99, *post*.

Children Act, 1948.—Subject to the provisions of Part III of the Children Act, 1948, this section and ss. 87 and 88 apply to children received into the care of a local authority under s. 1 of that Act as they apply to children in the care of a local authority by virtue of such an order as mentioned in sub.-s. (1) (*ibid.*, s. 23 (1)).

Forms.—For forms of order, etc., see p. 612, *post*.

Adoption.—For the effect on a contribution order of notice of intention to apply for an adoption order in respect of an infant in the care of a local authority, see s. 36 of the Adoption Act, 1958, p. 1068, *post*.

"Transitional Provisions".—See para. 9, Sched. IV of the Act of 1969 as to fit person orders other than to local authorities, and also paras. 7 (6), 8 (2), *ibid.* See also para. 6 of Sched. III, S.I. 1970 No. 1498, p. 614, *post*.

Where no contribution order is in force in relation to a child who is deemed to be the subject of a care order (see paras. 7 (2) and 8 (1), Sched. IV, Act of 1969) and the contribution paid is in excess of the amount that could be proposed under s. 62 (3) of the Act of 1969 a local authority should propose a fresh reduced contribution. Where the amount is less than above a higher amount may be requested under s. 62 (5), *ibid.*

87. Enforcement of duty of parent, etc., to make contributions.

—(1) Where a care order which is not an interim order has been made in respect of a child or young person then, subject to section 62 of the Children and Young Persons Act, 1969, any court of summary jurisdiction having jurisdiction in the place where the person to be charged is for the time being residing may subsequently at any time, make an order (hereafter in this Act referred to as a "contribution order") on any person who is under the last foregoing section liable to make contributions in respect of the child or young person, requiring him to contribute such weekly sum as the court having regard to his means thinks fit:

(2) A contribution order in respect of a child or young person may be made on the application of the local authority entitled to receive contributions in respect of him.

(3) A contribution order shall remain in force, as long as the child or young person to whom it relates is in the care of the local authority concerned.

(4) Subject to the provisions of this subsection—

(a) a contribution order shall be enforceable as an affiliation order and the enactments relating to the enforcement of affiliation orders shall apply accordingly, subject to any necessary modifications ; and

(b) sections fifty-two and fifty-three of the Magistrates' Courts Act, 1952 (which contains provisions as to orders for the periodical payment of money made by courts of summary jurisdiction) shall apply to every contribution order whether the court which made it was, or was not, a court of summary jurisdiction;

but any powers conferred by any of the enactments aforesaid on any justices or courts of summary jurisdiction shall be exercisable, and exercisable only, by justices and courts of summary jurisdiction having jurisdiction in the place where the person liable is for the time being residing.

(5) [*Repealed by the Children and Young Persons Act, 1963.*]

NOTES

This section is printed as amended by the Children Act, 1948, the Criminal Justice Act, 1961, and the Children and Young Persons Acts, 1963 and 1969. The section is further modified by the Local Government Act, 1958, Sched. VIII, which provides that references in sub-s. (2) to a council entitled to receive contributions shall be construed as references to the council to whom the contributions are payable by the person under a duty to make them.

Contribution orders.—There is no longer power for a juvenile court to make a contribution order.

Parental contributions cease when the juvenile attains the age of sixteen, but the juvenile himself may be liable to contribute (Children Act, 1948, s. 24, p. 903, *post*).

Where a child or young person is in the care of a local authority and has been allowed by the local authority to be under the charge and control of a parent, guardian, relative or friend, although remaining in the care of a local authority, no contribution shall be payable, whether or not a contribution order has been made, in respect of that period (s. 62 (2) Children and Young Persons Act, 1969).

" **Enforceable as an affiliation order.**"—That is by an order on complaint in accordance with s. 74 of the Magistrates' Courts Act, 1952; 21 Halsbury's Statutes, 3rd Edn., 247. There is no time limit except that complaint may not be made until after fifteen days from the making of the order (s. 74 (2)). There is power to remit arrears under *ibid.*, s. 76; 21 Halsbury's Statutes, 3rd Edn., 249. Enforcement may be by distress, attachment of earnings or imprisonment.

Attachment of earnings.—See the Magistrates' Courts (Attachment of Earnings) Rules, 1971, S.I. 1971 No. 809, and the Attachment of Earnings Act, 1971. By Sched. I, para. 7 an order under this section or s. 30, Children and Young Persons Act, 1963, is a maintenance order to which the Act applies.

Arrears.—See s. 30 of the Children and Young Persons Act, 1963, p. 99, *post.*

" **Venue.**"—This is an exception to the general rule that proceedings may be taken where the person entitled to the payments is residing. Here, it must be where the defendant is residing.

Variation, etc.—It is suggested that the local authority named in the order, and also the authority responsible for receiving the contributions should be made defendants to a summons to show cause why the order should not be varied. Probably they will arrange for only one authority to appear.

Change of address.—Parents are under a duty to notify the local authority of any change of address (Children and Young Persons Act, 1969, s. 24 (8), p. 168, *post*).

Children Act, 1948.—As to the application of this section to children received into the care of a local authority under that Act, see note to s. 86, p. 68, *ante.*

Scotland and Northern Ireland.—A court in England has jurisdiction under this section to make, revoke, revive or vary an order against a person residing in Scotland or Northern Ireland (Maintenance Orders Act, 1950, s. 4).

Sub-s. (1) is modified by the Maintenance Orders Act, 1950, s. 14 and Sched. I, as follows:—

> " Where the person to be charged under a contribution order resides in Scotland or Northern Ireland, subsection (1) shall have effect as if for the reference to a court of summary jurisdiction having jurisdiction in the place where the said person is for the time being residing there were substituted a reference to a court of summary jurisdiction having jurisdiction in the place in which the person entitled under section eighty-six to receive the contributions resides or, if that person is a local authority, having jurisdiction within the area of that authority.
> Where the person on whom a contribution order has been made is for the time being residing in Scotland or Northern Ireland, subsection (4) shall have effect as if the words from ' but any powers ' to the end of the subsection were omitted."

As to the jurisdiction of a court of summary jurisdiction in England, see ss. 4 and 27 of that Act.

As to rules of procedure, see the Maintenance Orders Act, 1950 (Summary Jurisdiction) Rules, 1950 (S.I. 1950 No. 2035 (L. 30)).

88. Provision as to affiliation orders.—(1) Where a child or young person who is the subject of a care order (other than an interim order), is illegitimate, and an affiliation order for his maintenance is in force, the court which makes the order may at the same time, and any court of summary jurisdiction having jurisdiction in the place where the putative father is for the time being residing, may subsequently at any time order the payments under the affiliation order to be paid to the local authority who are from time to time entitled under section eighty-six of this Act to receive contributions in respect of the child or young person.

Applications for orders under this subsection may be made by the local authority by whom applications for contribution orders may be made.

(2) Where an order made under this section with respect to an affiliation order is in force—

(a) any powers conferred on any justices or courts of summary jurisdiction by the enactments relating to the enforcement of affiliation orders or by section thirty of the Criminal Justice Administration Act, 1914, shall as respects the affiliation order in question be exercisable, and exercisable only, by justices and courts of summary jurisdiction having jurisdiction in the place where the person liable is for the time being residing ;

(b) any sums received under the affiliation order shall be applied in like manner as if they were contributions received under a contribution order ;

(c) if the putative father changes his address, he shall forthwith give notice thereof to the local authority who were immediately before the change entitled to receive payments under the order and, if he fails so to do, he shall be liable on summary conviction to a fine not exceeding ten pounds;

(d) [*Repealed by the Magistrates' Courts Act, 1952.*]

(3) [*Repealed by the Children Act, 1948.*]

(4) The making of an order under this section with respect to an affiliation order shall not extend the duration of that order, and that order shall not in any case remain in force (except for the purpose of the recovery of arrears) after the child or young person to whom that order relates has ceased to be the subject of a care order by virtue of which the order under this section was made or, where this section applies by virtue of section 23 of the Children Act, 1948, after he has ceased to be in the care of the local authority under section 1 of that Act, or in either case, if he is allowed by local authority to be under the charge and control of a parent, guardian, relative or friend, although remaining in the care of the local authority.

Provided that, where an affiliation order would, but for the provisions of this subsection have continued in force, the mother, or any person entitled to make an application for an order under section three of the Affiliation Orders Act, 1914, may apply to a court of summary jurisdiction having jurisdiction in the place where she or he is for the time residing, for an order that the affiliation order may be revived, and that payments thereunder may until the expiration thereof be made to the applicant at such rate (not exceeding the maximum rate allowed by the law in the case of affiliation orders) as may be proper, and the court may make such an order accordingly, and where such an order is so made, any power to vary, revoke or again revive the affiliation order or any part thereof, being a power which would but for the provisions of this subsection be vested in the court which originally made the affiliation order, shall be exercisable, and exercisable only, by the court which made the order under this subsection.

NOTES

This section is printed as amended by the Children Act, 1948, the Magistrates' Courts Act, 1952, the Family Allowances and National Insurance Act, 1956, the Criminal Justice Acts, 1961 and 1967, and the Children and Young Persons Act,

1969. It is further modified by the Local Government Act, 1958, Sched. VIII, which provides that references in sub-s. (1) to a council entitled to receive contributions shall be construed as references to the council to whom the contributions are payable by the person under a duty to make them.

Subsection (1).—The appropriate procedure is by summons addressed to the putative father and to the person hitherto receiving the payments, calling on them to show cause why the proposed variation should not be made, unless the variation is made at the time of committal. It seems just that the order should not be made at the time of committal unless the persons interested are present and are given an opportunity of being heard.

Payment through court. Payments may be ordered to be made through a justices clerk as collecting officer by virtue of s. 52 of the Magistrates' Courts Act, 1952.

By Rule 25 of the Magistrates' Courts (Children and Young Persons) Rules, 1970, p. 580, *post*, the clerk of the court must notify the collecting officer. The Rule does not require the court which made the order to be notified, but this will no doubt be thought a convenient practice.

Subsection (4).—" That order " evidently refers to the original affiliation order, which is extinguished but can be revived. As to power to vary, revoke or revive orders for the periodical payment of money, see Magistrates' Courts Act, 1952, s. 53, which replaced s. 30 (3) of the Criminal Justice Administration Act, 1914. Note the change of jurisdiction at the end of this subsection.

The person entitled to make application under s. 3 of the Affiliation Orders Act, 1914; 489, was the person for the time being having the custody of the child either legally or by any arrangement approved by the court. That Act was repealed by the Affiliation Proceedings Act, 1957. See now s. 5 of that Act, which contains similar provisions.

"The maximum rate."—By virtue of the Maintenance Orders Act, 1968, there is no statutory maximum.

Children Act, 1948.—For further provisions as to affiliation orders, see s. 26 of the Children Act, 1948, p. 903, *post*.

Scotland and Northern Ireland.—Sub-s. (1) is modified by the Maintenance Orders Act, 1950, s. 14 and Sched. I, as follows:—

> " Where the putative father of an illegitimate child or young person resides in Scotland or Northern Ireland, subsection (1) shall have effect as if for the reference to the place where the putative father is for the time being residing there were substituted a reference to the place where the mother of the child is for the time being residing.
> Where the person liable under an affiliation order in respect of which an order under section eighty-eight is in force is for the time being residing in Scotland or Northern Ireland, paragraph (a) of subsection (2) shall not apply."

As to the jurisdiction of a court in England, see ss. 3 and 27 of that Act.

Amount and duration.—Under the Affiliation Proceedings Act, 1957, s. 4 as amended there is now no statutory maximum sum; 1 Halsbury's Statutes, 3rd Edn., 78. See s. 7 of that Act and s. 5, Family Law Reform Act, 1969, as to payments after the child has attained the age of sixteen and restrictions upon such payments when the child is in care of a local authority under s. 1 Children Act, 1948, or by virtue of a care order (other than interim order) within the meaning of the Children and Young Persons Act, 1969.

89. Miscellaneous provisions as to contribution orders.—
[Repealed by the Children and Young Persons Act, 1969, s. 72 (4) and Sched. VI.]

(2) Where, by virtue of an order made under either of the two last foregoing sections, any sum is payable to the council of a county or county borough, the council of the county or county borough in which the person liable under the order is for the time being residing shall be entitled to receive and give a discharge for, and, if necessary, enforce

payment of, any arrears accrued due under the order, notwithstanding that those arrears may have accrued at a time when he was not resident in that county or county borough.

(3) In any proceedings under either of the two last foregoing sections a certificate purporting to be signed by the clerk to a council for the time being entitled to receive contributions, or by some other officer of the council duly authorised in that behalf, and stating that any sum due to the council under an order is overdue and unpaid shall be evidence of the facts stated therein.

(4) [*Repealed by the National Assistance Act,* 1948, *s.* 62 (3) *and Sched. VII.*]

NOTES

This section is printed as amended by the Children Act, 1948, and the Children and Young Persons Act, 1969.

" **Purporting to be signed.**"—Proof of the signature is therefore unnecessary unless it be disputed.

" **Shall be evidence.**"—Not conclusive evidence, of course ; so it may be rebutted by other evidence. In case of dispute it may be necessary to call witnesses to prove the arrears.

" **Arrears.**"—As to recovery of arrears of contributions where no order is in force, see s. 30 of the Children and Young Persons Act, 1963, p. 99, *post.*

Scotland and Northern Ireland.—Sub-s. (2) is modified by the Maintenance Orders Act, 1950, s. 14 and Sched. I, as follows:—

" Where the person liable under a contribution order made under section eighty-seven, or under an affiliation order in respect of which an order under section eighty-eight is in force, is for the time being residing in Scotland or Northern Ireland, sub-section (2) shall have effect as if for the reference to the council of the county or county borough in which the person liable under the order is for the time being residing there were substituted a reference to the local authority to whom sums are payable under the order and as if for the words ' when he was not resident in the county or county borough ' there were substituted the words ' when that authority were not entitled to sums payable under the order."

90. [*Repealed by the Children and Young Persons Act,* 1969, *s.* 72 (4) *and Sched. VI. See now Sched. III, para.* 8, ibid.]

91. [*Repealed by the Children and Young Persons Act,* 1969, *s.* 72 (4) *and Sched. VI.*]

PART V.—HOMES SUPPORTED BY VOLUNTARY CONTRIBUTIONS

Children Act, 1948.—See s. 54 (3) of the Children Act, 1948, p. 919, *post,* as to the duty of local authorities to cause children in a voluntary home other than a community home, not subject to the special exemption in favour of a home inspected as a whole by a Government department (cf. s. 54 (5)), to be visited, and as to the penalties for obstructing the entry of any person authorised by a local authority.

Since the end of the year 1948 no voluntary home can be carried on unless it is for the time being registered in a register to be kept for the purposes of this section by the Secretary of State (*ibid.*, s. 29 (1)). See the remainder of that section for further provisions as to registration, and s. 30 for appeals against a refusal to register or a proposal to remove from the register.

The Secretary of State may give directions as to the number of persons who may at any one time be accommodated in a voluntary home. See the Administration of Children's Homes Regulations, 1951, p. 979, *post.*

92. Definition of voluntary homes.—In this Part of this Act the expression " voluntary home " means any home or other institution for the boarding, care, and maintenance of poor children or young persons, being a home or other institution supported wholly or partly by voluntary contributions, but does not include any mental nursing home or residential home for mentally disordered persons within the meaning of Part III of the Mental Health Act, 1959.

NOTES

This section is printed as amended by the National Health Service Act, 1946 and the Mental Health Act, 1959.

Definition of Voluntary Home.—By s. 27 of the Children Act, 1948, it is provided that this section is to have effect as if to the reference therein to a home or other institution, supported wholly or partly by voluntary contributions there were added a reference to a home or other institution supported wholly or partly by endowments, not being a school within the meaning of the Education Act, 1944, or the Education (Scotland) Act, 1946.

The words of this section are intentionally wide. As it applies to institutions, wholly or partly supported by voluntary contributions or by endowments the requirements of s. 93 will apply to almost all homes and hostels taking poor children or young persons other than State or local government institutions maintained out of public funds. It would seem to apply to such approved schools as receive voluntary donations towards their upkeep.

93. Notification of particulars with respect to voluntary homes.—(1) It shall be the duty of the person in charge of any voluntary home to send the prescribed particulars with respect to the home to the Secretary of State within three months after the commencement of this Act, or in the case of a home established after the commencement of this Act within three months from the establishment of the home and to send such particulars in every subsequent year before such date as may be prescribed.

(2) If default is made in sending the prescribed particulars with respect to any voluntary home in accordance with the requirements of this section, the person in charge of the home shall, on summary conviction, be liable to a fine not exceeding five pounds and to a further fine not exceeding twenty shillings in respect of each day during which the default continues after conviction.

NOTES

This section does not apply to a voluntary home which is a controlled or assisted community home (Children and Young Persons Act, 1969, s. 44).

" Person in charge."—Who is the person in charge will be a question of fact for magistrates to determine.

Regulations.—See pp. 972 et seq., post.

Children Act, 1948.—See s. 32 of that Act, p. 911, post, as to provisions where particulars to be sent of voluntary homes are varied.

94. [Repealed by the Children and Young Persons Act, 1969, s. 72 (4) and Sched. VI. See now s. 58, ibid.]

95. [Repealed by the Children Act, 1948. See now s. 29 of that Act, p. 908, post.]

PART VI.—SUPPLEMENTAL

Local authorities.—The council of each London borough shall as respects the borough, and the Common Council shall as respects the City, have the functions of the council of a county borough under Part IV of this Act so far as it relates to Parts III, IV and V and be the local authority for such purposes of as refer to a local authority (London Government Act, 1963, s. 47 ; 20 Halsbury's Statutes, 3rd Edn., 504.)

Local Authorities

96. Provisions as to local authorities.—(1) Subject to the modifications hereinafter contained as to the City of London, where any powers or duties are by [Part II of this Act] conferred or imposed on local authorities (by that description), those powers and duties shall, . . . be powers and duties of local education authorities . . .

(2) [*Repealed by the Education Act, 1944, s. 121, and Sched. IX, Part I.*]

(3) Expenses incurred by a local authority in connection with powers and duties which are, under this Act, exercised and performed by them as local education authorities [shall be defrayed as expenses under the enactments relating to education].

(4) Expenses incurred under this Act by the council of a county or county borough, exclusive of any expenses to be defrayed [in accordance with] the last foregoing subsection . . . shall be defrayed—

(a) . . .

(b) . . . as expenses for general county purposes or, as the case may be, out of the general rate.

(5) A local authority may, for the purposes of their functions under this Act, acquire, dispose of, or otherwise deal with land—

(a) . . .

(b) in the case of the council of a county borough . . . in like manner as for the purposes of the Public Health Act, 1875, and sections one hundred and seventy-five to one hundred and seventy-eight of that Act shall apply accordingly.

(6) [*Repealed by the London Government Act, 1963, s. 93 and Sched. XVIII.*]

(7) Subject to the provisions of sections 2 and 3 of the Local Authority Social Services Act, 1970 (which require certain matters to be referred to the Social Services Committee and restrict the reference of other matters to that committee) a local authority may refer to a committee appointed for the purposes of this Act, or to any committee appointed for the purposes of any other Act, any matter relating to the exercise by the authority of any of their powers under this Act and may delegate any of the said powers (other than any power to borrow money) to any such committee.

(8) A local authority, or a committee to whom any powers of a local authority under this Act have been delegated, may by resolution empower the clerk or the chief education officer of the authority to exercise in the name of the authority in any case which appears to him to be one of urgency any powers of the authority or, as the case may be, of the committee with respect to the institution of proceedings under this Act.

NOTES

This section is printed as amended by the Local Government Act, 1933, the London Government Act, 1939, the Education Act, 1944, the Children Act, 1948, the National Assistance Act, 1948, and the Local Authority Social Services Act, 1970.

"**Local Education Authorities.**"—See Education Act, 1944, s. 114, p. 270, *post*.

Subsection (4).—This subsection does not apply to expenses incurred by the Common Council, (London Government Act, 1963, s. 47) and s. 49 of the Children Act, 1948, does not apply to London Borough Councils nor to the Council of a County borough who keep accounts under s. 8 Local Authority Social Services Act, 1970, or if the Common Council of the City of London keep accounts thereunder, to that Council, s. 8, *ibid*.

Subsection (5).—This subsection is to have effect, in relation to the compulsory purchase of land, as if it provided that the council of a county borough or urban district may be authorised by the Ministry of Health to purchase land compulsorily for the provisions of their functions under that Act (Acquisition of Land (Authorisation Procedure) Act, 1946, s. 6 and Sched. IV; 6 Halsbury's Statutes, 3rd Edn., 160).

Subsection (8).—The clerk or the chief education officer cannot, it appears, delegate his authority, but must exercise it personally. It seems clear that it is the clerk or the education officer who is to judge of the urgency of a case. This being so it would seem that the council or committee can give him a general authority to act in cases of urgency. But see s. 277 of the Local Government Act, 1933; 19 Halsbury's Statutes, 3rd Edn., 556, as to the wide powers now possessed by local authorities to delegate.

97. Modifications of last foregoing section as to City of London.
—The last foregoing section shall, in its application to the City of London, have effect subject to the modifications that the powers and duties of a local authority under this Act as respects street trading and employment, shall be powers and duties of the Common Council and any expenses of the Common Council shall be defrayed out of the general rate:

Provided that—
    (a) the powers and duties of a local authority with respect to the granting of licences for children to take part in entertainments shall be powers and duties of the education authority; and
    (b) nothing in this section shall exempt the City of London from the liability to contribute towards the expenses incurred by the Local Education authority under this Act.

NOTE

This section is printed as amended by the Education Act, 1944, the Children Act, 1948, and the London Government Act, 1963, ss. 30 (8), 93, and Sched. XVIII. As to responsibility under the Education Act, 1944, see s. 117, *ibid.*, p. 271, *post*.

98. Institution of proceedings by local authorities.
—Without prejudice to the provisions of the last foregoing section, a local education authority may institute proceedings for any offence under Part I or Part II of this Act.

NOTES

This section was substituted by the Children Act, 1948.

Children Act, 1948.—Ss. 38 and 55 (1) of the Children Act, 1948, p. 914, *post*, provide that in England and Wales a local authority may institute proceedings for any offence under the provisions of the Children and Young Persons Act, 1933, other than the provisions of Parts I and II thereof.

As to disqualification of a justice who is a member of local authority, see the Justices of the Peace Act, 1949, s. 3; 21 Halsbury's Statutes, 3rd Edn., 112.

" **Local education authority.**"—Without prejudice, proceedings may be instituted by the council of a county or county borough, whether or not the council are the local education authority, and may, where the council are the local education authority, be instituted by them otherwise than in that capacity. See s. 56 of the Children and Young Persons Act, 1963, p. 114, *post.*

Supplementary Provisions as to Legal Proceedings

99. Presumption and determination of age.—(1) Where a person, whether charged with an offence or not, is brought before any court otherwise than for the purpose of giving evidence, and it appears to the court that he is a child or young person, the court shall make due inquiry as to the age of that person, and for that purpose shall take such evidence as may be forthcoming at the hearing of the case, but an order or judgment of the court shall not be invalidated by any subsequent proof that the age of that person has not been correctly stated to the court, and the age presumed or declared by the court to be the age of the person so brought before it shall, for the purposes of this Act, be deemed to be the true age of that person, and, where it appears to the court that the person so brought before it has attained the age of seventeen years, that person shall for the purposes of this Act be deemed not to be a child or young person.

(2) Where in any charge or indictment for any offence under this Act or any of the offences mentioned in the First Schedule to this Act, except as provided in that schedule, it is alleged that the person by or in respect of whom the offence was committed was a child or young person or was under or had attained any specified age, and he appears to the court to have been at the date of the commission of the alleged offence a child or young person, or to have been under or to have attained the specified age, as the case may be, he shall for the purposes of this Act be presumed at that date to have been a child or young person or to have been under or to have attained that age, as the case may be, unless the contrary is proved.

(3) Where, in any charge or indictment for any offence under this Act or any of the offences mentioned in the First Schedule to this Act, it is alleged that the person in respect of whom the offence was committed was a child or was a young person, it shall not be a defence to prove that the person alleged to have been a child was a young person or the person alleged to have been a young person was a child in any case where the acts constituting the alleged offence would equally have been an offence if committed in respect of a young person or child respectively.

(4) Where a person is charged with an offence under this Act in respect of a person apparently under a specified age it shall be a defence to prove that the person was actually of or over that age.

NOTES

This section is printed as amended by the Sexual Offences Act, 1956, s. 48 and Sched. III.

" **Due inquiry.**"—As to proof of age, see note to s. 1, p. 12, *ante.* It will be observed that there is a duty upon the court to obtain such evidence as is available.

"For the purposes of this Act."—See s. 70 (3), *ibid.*, and the Childrens and Young Persons Act, 1969.

" Attained the age."—See note at p. 53, *ante*.

Subsection (2).—See the entry in the Third Schedule to the Sexual Offences Act, 1956 (relating to the First Schedule to the Children and Young Persons Act, 1933), which provides that for the purposes of sub-s. (2), *supra*, that entry applies so far as it relates to offences under ss. 10, 11, 12, 14, 15, 16, 20 and 28 of that Act, and attempts to commit offences under ss. 10, 11 and 12 of that Act.

The presumption as to age does not apply to offences in the entry other than those in the proviso, and in the case of offences not included in the proviso the age will have to be proved if it is material to the charge.

100. Evidence of wages of defendant.—In any proceedings under this Act a copy of an entry in the wages book of any employer of labour, or if no wages book be kept a written statement signed by the employer or by any responsible person in his employ, shall be evidence that the wages therein entered or stated as having been paid to any person, have in fact been so paid.

NOTE

The copy or written statement will have to be proved by a witness. It then becomes *primâ facie* evidence ; it can be contradicted by other evidence.

In certain matters, however, a written statement of wages paid may be received in evidence without such proof by virtue of s. 80 of the Magistrates' Courts Act, 1952; 21 Halsbury's Statutes, 3rd Edn., 252.

101. Application of Summary Jurisdiction Acts.—Subject to the provisions of this Act, all orders of a court of summary jurisdiction, whether a petty sessional court or not, under this Act shall be made, and all proceedings in relation to any such orders shall be taken, in manner provided by the Summary Jurisdiction Acts.

NOTES

This section is printed as amended by the Justices of the Peace Act, 1949. Rules which were made under it have effect as if contained in rules made under s. 15 of that Act (*ibid.*, s. 15(8)).

Most of the provisions of the Summary Jurisdiction Acts, were repealed by the Magistrates' Courts Act, 1952; 21 Halsbury's Statutes, 3rd Edn., 181. See the relevant provisions of that Act.

102. Appeals to the Crown Court.—(1) Appeals to the Crown Court from orders of a court of summary jurisdiction under this Act may be brought in the following cases and by the following persons, that is to say—

(a)–(b) [*Repealed by the Children and Young Persons Act, 1969, s. 72 (4) and Sched. VI.*]

(c) in the case of an order requiring a person to contribute in respect of himself or any other person, by the person required to contribute;

(d) in the case of an order requiring all or any part of the payments accruing due under an affiliation order to be paid to some other person, by the person who would but for the order be entitled to the payments ;

(e) in the case of an order requiring the owner of an automatic machine for the sale of tobacco or the person on whose premises such a machine is kept, to take precautions to prevent the machine being extensively used by persons apparently under the age of sixteen years or to remove the machine, by any person aggrieved ;

(2) Nothing in this section shall be construed as affecting any other right of appeal conferred by this or any other Act.

NOTES

This section is printed as amended by the Children Act, 1948, and the Children and Young Persons Acts, 1963 and 1969, and the Courts Act, 1971.

Right of appeal.—There is a general right of appeal against convictions and sentences conferred by s. 83 of the Magistrates' Courts Act, 1952; 21 Halsbury's Statutes, 3rd Edn., 254.

The words " conviction " and " sentence " cease to be used in relation to children and young persons dealt with summarily, by virtue of s. 59 of this Act, p. 62, *ante*, but the same rights of appeal as in the case of adults were continued.

"Quarter Sessions."—See the Courts Act, 1971, s. 8 and Sched. I, which vests all appellate jurisdiction in the Crown Court.

Appeal against order.—There is no general right of appeal against orders. Such appeals must be authorised expressly by statute, see *R. v. London County Quarter Sessions Appeals Committee, Ex parte Metropolitan Police Commissioner*, [1948] 1 K. B. 760; [1948] 1 All E. R. 72.

Supplementary Provisions as to Secretary of State

103. Power of Secretary of State to appoint inspectors.—*The Secretary of State may appoint for the purposes of the enactments relating to children and young persons a chief inspector, and such number of inspectors to act under the direction of the chief inspector as the Treasury may approve, and may pay to the persons so appointed such remuneration and allowances as with the consent of the Treasury he may determine, and they shall perform such duties as the Secretary of State may from time to time direct.*

NOTE

From a date to be appointed the words in italics are repealed by the Children and Young Persons Act, 1969, s. 72 (4) and Sched. VI.

Children Act, 1948.—References in this section to enactments relating to children and young persons included references to the Children Act, 1948 (*ibid.*, s. 54 (1)).

104. Exchequer grants and expenses of Secretary of State.— (1) *There shall be paid out of money provided by Parliament—*

(a) *such sums on such conditions as the Secretary of State with the approval of the Treasury may recommend towards—*

(i) *the expenses of the managers of an approved school;*
(ii) *[Repealed by the Children Act, 1948.]*
(iii) *the expenses of a council of a county or county borough in respect of remand homes;*

(b) *[Repealed by the Local Government Act, 1958.]*
(c) *any expenses incurred by the Secretary of State in the administration of this Act.*

(2) *The conditions on which any sums are paid under this section towards the expense incurred in connection with the provision of a site for, or with the erection, enlargement, improvement or repair of, an approved school, may*

*include conditions for securing the repayment in whole or in part of the sums
paid in the event of the school ceasing to be an approved school, and, notwithstanding anything in the constitution of the school or of the managers thereof,
or in the trusts, if any, to which the property of the school or of the managers is
subject, the managers and any persons who are trustees of any of the said
property may accept those sums on those conditions, and execute any instrument required for carrying into effect those conditions, and shall be bound by
those conditions and by any instrument so executed and have power to fulfil
the conditions and the obligations created by the instrument.*

NOTES

From a date to be appointed the words in italics are repealed by the Children and
Young Persons Act, 1969, s. 72 (4) and Sched. VI.

This section is printed as amended by the Education Act, 1944, the Children Act,
1948, and the Local Government Act, 1958.

Any expenses incurred by the council of a county or county borough in giving
effect to arrangements made under s. 49 (4) of the Criminal Justice Act, 1948,
shall be treated for the purposes of any grant under s. 104 of this Act as expenses of
the council in respect of remand homes (Criminal Justice Act, 1948, s. 49 (6)).

For s. 49 (4), see p. 377, *post.*

General

105. Variation of Orders in Council.—An Order in Council under
this Act may be revoked or varied by any subsequent Order in Council.

106. Provisions as to documents, etc.—(1) An order or other act
of the Secretary of State under this Act may be signified under the hand
of the Secretary of State or an Under-Secretary of State or an Assistant
Under-Secretary.

(2) A document purporting to be a copy—

(a) of an order made by a court under or by virtue of any of the
provisions contained in sections fifty-six, fifty-seven and sixty-
two to ninety of this Act or in the Fourth Schedule to this
Act ; or

(b) [*Repealed by the Education Act, 1944.*]

(c) of an affiliation order referred to in an order under section eighty-
eight of this Act,

shall, if it purports to be certified as a true copy by the clerk of the court,
be evidence of the order.

(3) *The production of a copy of the London Gazette containing a notice of
the grant, or of the withdrawal or surrender, of a certificate of approval of an
approved school shall be sufficient evidence of the fact of a certificate having
been duly granted to the school named in the notice, or of the withdrawal or
surrender of such a certificate, and the grant of a certificate of approval of an
approved school may also be proved by the production of the certificate itself,
or of a document purporting to be a copy of the certificate and to be authenticated as such by an Under-Secretary of State or Assistant Under-Secretary.*

(4) *Any notice or other document required or authorised by this Act to be
served on the managers of an approved school, may if those managers are a
local authority or a joint committee representing two or more local authorities,*

be served either personally or by post upon their clerk, and in any other case, may be served either personally or by post upon any one of the managers, or their secretary, or the headmaster of the school.

(5) *An order, licence, or other document may be authenticated on behalf of the managers of an approved school, if they are a local authority or a joint committee representing two or more local authorities, by the signature of their clerk, or some other officer of the local authority duly authorised in that behalf, and in any other case, by the signature of one of the managers of their secretary, or of the headmaster.*

NOTES

From a date to be appointed the words in italics are repealed by the Children and Young Persons Act, 1969, s. 72 (4) and Sched. VI.

This section is printed as amended by the Education Act, 1944.

As to proof of orders, regulations, etc., of the Secretary of State, see Documentary Evidence Act, 1868, s. 2; 12 Halsbury's Statutes, 3rd Edn., 843. Under sub-s. (2) it will not be necessary to prove the signature of the clerk unless it be disputed. The document is " evidence," but is not made conclusive evidence, so that it can be contradicted by other evidence.

The provisions of sub-s. (3) of this section may be applied to remand homes by rules made by the Secretary of State; see the Criminal Justice Act, 1948, s. 49 (2), p. 377, *post.*

"**A copy of an order.**"—From a date to be appointed in sub-s. (2) (a) for the words from "fifty-seven" to "Schedule to" there shall be substituted the words "eighty-seven and eighty-eight of" (Children and Young Persons Act, 1969, s. 72 (3) and Sched. V).

107. Interpretation.—(1) In this Act, unless the context otherwise requires, the following expressions have the meanings hereby respectively assigned to them, that is to say,—

"Care order and interim order" have the same meaning as in the Children and Young Persons Act, 1969;

" Approved school " means a school approved by the Secretary of State under section seventy-nine of this Act ;

" Approved school order " means an order made by a court sending a person to an approved school ;

" Chief officer of police " as regards England has the same meaning as in the Police Act, 1964, as regards Scotland has the same meaning as in the Police (Scotland) Act, 1890, and as regards Northern Ireland means a district inspector of the Royal Ulster Constabulary;

" Child " means a person under the age of fourteen years ;

" Guardian," in relation to a child or young person, includes any person who, in the opinion of the court having cognisance of any case in relation to the child or young person or in which the child or young person is concerned, has for the time being the charge of or control over the child or young person ;

" Intoxicating liquor " means any fermented, distilled or spirituous liquor which cannot according to any law for the time being in force be legally sold without a licence from the Commissioners of Customs and Excise ;

" Legal guardian," in relation to a child or young person, means a person appointed, according to law, to be his guardian by deed or will, or by order of a court of competent jurisdiction ;

" Managers," in relation to an approved school established or taken over by a local authority or by a joint committee representing two or more local authorities, means the local authority or the joint committee as the case may be, and in relation to any other approved school, means the persons for the time being having the management or control thereof :

" Metropolitan police court area " means the area consisting of the police court divisions for the time being constituted under the Metropolitan Police Courts Acts, 1839 and 1840 and the City of London ;

"Place of safety" means a community home provided by a local authority or a controlled community home, any police station, or any hospital, surgery, or any other suitable place, the occupier of which is willing temporarily to receive a child or young person;

" Prescribed " means prescribed by regulations made by the Secretary of State ;

" Public place " includes any public park, garden, sea beach or railway station, and any ground to which the public for the time being have or are permitted to have access, whether on payment or otherwise ;

" Special reception centre " means accommodation for the temporary reception of children provided under subsection (2) of section fifteen of the Children Act, 1948, which a local authority has given notice is for the time being available for the custody of children sent there for that purpose from the area specified in the notice, and any reference to the area of a special reception centre shall be construed as a reference to the area so specified;

"Street" includes any highway and any public bridge, road, lane, footway, square, court, alley or passage, whether a thoroughfare or not;

" Young person " means a person who has attained the age of fourteen years and is under the age of seventeen years.

(2) [*Repealed by the Children and Young Persons Act, 1969, s. 72 (3), (4) and Scheds. V and VI.*]

(3) References in this Act to any enactment or to any provision in any enactment shall, unless the context otherwise requires, be construed as references to that enactment or provision as amended by any subsequent enactment including this Act.

NOTES

This section is printed as amended by the National Assistance Act, 1948, the Children Act, 1948 the Children and Young Persons (Amendment) Act, 1952, the Children and Young Persons Act, 1963, the Police Act, 1964, and the Children and Young Persons Act, 1969.

Chief Officer of Police.—By s. 62 and Sch. 8 of the Police Act, 1964, the Chief Officer of Police for Police Areas is as follows :—

The City of London	The Commissioner of City of London Police
The Metropolitan Police District	The Commissioner of Police of the Metropolis.
Other Police Areas	The Chief Constable.

The City of London in Sched. 8 means the City as defined for the purposes of the Acts relating to the City of London Police. The metropolitan police district means that district as defined in s. 76 of the London Government Act, 1963.

For other definitions relating to police authorities see ss. 2, 3, 62, *ibid.*

" Child."—See s. 58 of the Education Act, 1944, p. 266, *post*, for definition in relation to the employment of children.

" Child ; Young person."—" Child " in s. 1 of the Children and Young Persons Act, 1963, means a person under the age of eighteen. See s. 1, *ibid.*, p. 91.

Attained the age.—See note at p. 53, *ante.*

" Place of safety."—This does not include a prison. See article at 101 J. P. N. 797. Local authorities are required to make provision, in community homes provided by them or in controlled community homes, for the reception and maintenance of children removed to a place of safety under the Children and Young Persons Act, 1933 and ss. 2 (5), 16 (3) or 28 of the Act of 1969, (Children Act, 1948, s. 51 (1)).

108. Transitory provisions.—*[Not reproduced.]*

109. Short title, commencement, extent and repeals.—(1) This Act may be cited as the Children and Young Persons Act, 1933.

(2) *[Repealed by the Statute Law Revision Act, 1950.]*

(3) Save as therein otherwise expressly provided, this Act shall not extend to Scotland or Northern Ireland.

(4) *[Repealed by the Statute Law Revision Act, 1950.]*

SCHEDULES

FIRST SCHEDULE

[SECTIONS 13, 14, 15, 40, 41, 42, 43, 63, 67, 99 AND 108]

OFFENCES AGAINST CHILDREN AND YOUNG PERSONS, WITH RESPECT TO WHICH SPECIAL PROVISIONS OF THIS ACT APPLY

The murder or manslaughter of a child or young person.

Infanticide.

Any offence under sections twenty-seven or fifty-six of the Offences against the Person Act, 1861, and any offence against a child or young person under sections five, forty-two or forty-three of that Act.

Any offence under sections one, three, four, eleven or twenty-three of this Act.

Any offence against a child or young person under any of the following sections of the Sexual Offences Act, 1956, that is to say sections two to seven, ten to sixteen, nineteen, twenty, twenty-two to twenty-six and twenty-eight, and any attempt to commit against a child or young person an offence under sections two, five, six, seven, ten, eleven, twelve, twenty-two or twenty-three of that Act:

Provided that for the purposes of subsection (2) of section ninety-nine of this Act this entry shall apply so far only as it relates to offences under sections ten, eleven, twelve, fourteen, fifteen, sixteen, twenty and twenty-eight of the Sexual Offences Act, 1956, and attempts to commit offences under sections ten, eleven and twelve of that Act.

Any other offence involving bodily injury to a child or young person.

NOTES

This schedule is printed as amended by the Sexual Offences Act, 1956.

As to England and Wales only this Schedule is amended so that the reference to the murder or manslaughter of a child or young person applies also to ai ding, abetting, counselling or procuring the suicide of a child or young person. See the Suicide Act, 1961, s. 2 and Sched. I (8 Halsbury's Statutes, 3rd Edn., 519, 520).

For detailed list, see Section 3 of this book, p. 245, *post.*

" **Any offence involving bodily injury.**"—The following decisions have been made on this expression :—*R.* v. *Beer* (1898), 62 J. P. 120, where Darling, J., held that indecent assault is not such an offence; *H.M. Advocate* v. *Lee*, [1923] S. C. (J.) 1, in which Lord Blackburn held that an indecent assault on a young girl which did not involve actual injury was an offence involving bodily injury; and *H.M. Advocate* v. *Macphie*, [1926] S. C. (J.) 91; 91 J. P. N. 143; where the Court of Justiciary decided that an attempted murder in which no actual injury was inflicted was " an offence involving bodily injury."

Indecency with Children Act, 1960.—By s. 1 (3) of the Indecency with Children Act, 1960, references in the Children and Young Persons Act, 1933, except those in s. 15, to the offences mentioned in this Schedule shall include offences under s. 1 of the Indecency with Children Act, 1960. See s. 1, *ibid.*, p. 398, *post.*

SECOND SCHEDULE

[SECTION 45]

CONSTITUTION OF JUVENILE COURTS

[Repealed by the Children and Young Persons Act, 1963. See now Sched. 2 to that Act, pp. 120, et seq., post.]

THIRD SCHEDULE

[Repealed by the Magistrates' Courts Act, 1952.]

FOURTH SCHEDULE

[SECTIONS 81 AND 106]

NOTE

From a date to be appointed this schedule is repealed by the Children and Young Persons Act, 1969, s. 72 (4) and Sched. VI.

PROVISIONS AS TO ADMINISTRATION OF APPROVED SCHOOLS AND TREATMENT OF PERSONS SENT THERETO

Formerly, to the extent that a remand home was designated under s. 11 of the Children and Young Persons Act, 1963, and used as a classifying centre, the provisions of this Schedule (except paras. 1–3, 7 and 14) applied to it and s. 78 (4) of the Children and Young Persons Act, 1933, did not. Both these sections have now been repealed.

General Provisions

1.—(1) The Secretary of State may make rules for the management and discipline of approved schools, and different rules may be made as respects different schools or classes of school.

(2) The managers of an approved school may make supplementary rules for the management and discipline of the school, but rules so made shall not have effect unless approved by the Secretary of State.

NOTES

Formerly rules were made by managers, subject to approval by the Secretary of State. Managers can now make supplementary rules only.
  For definition of managers, see s. 107, p. 81, *ante*.
  For Rules, see p. 459, *post*.

2. No substantial addition to, or diminution or alteration of, the buildings or grounds of an approved school shall be made without the approval in writing of the Secretary of State.

Treatment of Pupils

3. A minister of the religious persuasion to which a person in an approved school belongs may visit him at the school on such days, at such times, and on such conditions, as may be fixed by rules made by the Secretary of State, for the purpose of affording him religious assistance and instruction.

4. [*Repealed by the Children and Young Persons Act, 1969, s. 72 (4) and Sched. VI.*]

Power to Place out Pupils

5. [*Repealed by the Children and Young Persons Act, 1969, s. 72 (4) and Sched. VI.*]

6. [*Repealed by the Criminal Justice Act, 1961.*]

7. [*Paras. 7, 8, 9, 11, 12 and 13 are repealed by the Children and Young Persons Act, 1969, s. 72 (4) and Sched. VI.*]

Superannuation of Officers

14. The managers of any approved school may, as part of the expenses of the management of the school, pay, or contribute towards the payment of—

(a) a superannuation allowance or gratuity—

(i) to any officer who retires by reason of old age or permanent infirmity of mind or body ;

(ii) to any officer, who, in accordance with the terms of his appointment, is required to vacate his office by reason of the death, or the retirement on account of old age or permanent infirmity, of another officer ;

NOTE

This will include such a case as that of husband and wife holding joint appointments, or where they are respectively headmaster and matron, and one dies or retires.

(b) a gratuity to any dependant of an officer who has died in the service of the school :

Provided that no payment or contribution in respect of any such superannuation allowance or gratuity shall be made unless it is made in accordance with rules approved by the Secretary of State with the concurrence of the Treasury for regulating the grant of such allowances and gratuities, or unless it is specially sanctioned by the Secretary of State.

FIFTH SCHEDULE

[SECTION 108]

TRANSITORY PROVISIONS

[NOTE.—*The provisions of this schedule are now considered obsolete, and the text is therefore not reprinted.*]

SIXTH SCHEDULE

[*Repealed by the Statute Law Revision Act, 1950.*]

CHILDREN AND YOUNG PERSONS (AMENDMENT) ACT, 1952

[15 & 16 Geo. 6 & 1 Eliz. 2, c. 50]

ARRANGEMENT OF SECTIONS

An Act to amend the Children and Young Persons Act, 1933, and section twenty-seven of the Criminal Justice Act, 1948; and for purposes connected therewith.   [1st August, 1952]

1. Definition of " in need of care or protection ".—[*Repealed by the Children and Young Persons Act, 1963.*]

[*Sections 2–5 are repealed by the Children and Young Persons Act, 1969, s. 72 (4) and Sched. VI.*]

6. Approved school orders.—[*Repealed by the Children and Young Persons Act, 1963.*]

7. Arrangements between managers of approved school and local authority.—[*Repealed by the Children and Young Persons Act, 1963.*]

8. Exposing children under twelve to risk of burning.—Section eleven of the principal Act shall be amended as follows:—

(a) by the substitution of the word " twelve " for the word " seven ";
and

(b) by inserting after the words " fire grate " the words " or any heating appliance liable to cause injury to a person by contact therewith ".

NOTE

For s. 11 of the principal Act, see p. 24, *ante.* Note also the provisions of the Heating Appliances (Fireguards) Act, 1952.

9. Consequential amendments of enactments.—[*Not printed.*]

10. Interpretation.—(1) In this Act the expression " the principal Act " means the Children and Young Persons Act, 1933.

(2) Save in so far as the context otherwise requires, any reference in this Act to any other enactment shall be construed as a reference to that enactment as amended by or under any other enactment, including this Act.

(3) Subject to the foregoing provisions of this section, this Act shall be construed as one with the Children and Young Persons Acts, 1933 and 1938.

11. Short title, citation, extent and commencement.—(1) This Act may be cited as the Children and Young Persons (Amendment) Act, 1952, and this Act and the Children and Young Persons Acts, 1933 and 1938, may be cited together as the Children and Young Persons Acts, 1933 to 1952.

(2) This Act shall not extend to Scotland or Northern Ireland.

(3) This Act shall come into operation on the first day of October, nineteen hundred and fifty-two.

SCHEDULE   Section 9

CONSEQUENTIAL AMENDMENTS OF ENACTMENTS

This Schedule makes a number of amendments to the Children and Young Persons Act, 1933, the Children and Young Persons Act, 1938, and the Criminal Justice Act, 1948. The affected sections have been printed as amended. The amendments contained in paras. 1, 3, 5, 8, 9 and 11 to 16 are repealed by the Children and Young Persons Act, 1969.

CHILDREN AND YOUNG PERSONS ACT, 1963

[1963 c. 37]

INTRODUCTORY NOTE

Much of this Act is based upon recommendations made by the Committee on Children and Young Persons (the Ingleby Committee) Cmnd, 1191. It received the Royal Assent on July 31, 1963, and s. 65 (6) provides that it shall come into operation on such day as the Secretary of State may by order by statutory instrument appoint, and different days may be appointed for different purposes. The Children and Young Persons Act, 1963 (Commencement No. 1) Order 1963 brought into operation certain provisions of the Act from October 1, 1963, and the Children and Young Persons Act 1963 (Commencement No. 2) Order, 1963 brings into operation the remainder of Parts I and III from February 1, 1964. The regulations required for the purposes of Part II came into force on March 3, 1969.

Section 1 provides express authority for local authorities to perform and co-ordinate preventive work and to remove conditions that might result in children coming into, or remaining in, care, or being brought before juvenile courts. It is now their duty to ensure that the necessary advice, guidance or assistance is provided, either directly through their own service, or through voluntary organisations. Assistance in cash is to be given only in exceptional circumstances. The section does not give power to impose guidance on parents who are not willing to receive it.

Section 2 superseded s. 61 of the Children and Young Persons Act, 1933, both of which are now repealed, together with the definition of "in need of care or protection" in s. 107 of that Act. References in any enactment to a child or young person in need of care or protection were to be construed as references to a child or young person in need of care, protection or control as defined by s. 2. A parent or guardian is no longer able to bring a child or young person before a court as beyond control under s. 1 of the 1969 Act; such a child or young person will come within the definition in s. 1, and will be brought before a court by the local authority, the police, or an authorised person. If the local authority does not bring the child or young person before the court after a request in writing by the parent or guardian, the latter may apply to a juvenile court for an order directing them to do so (s. 3).

The age of criminal responsibility, as defined by s. 50 of the 1933 Act is raised from eight to ten (s. 16) and offences of which a person of or over twenty-one was found guilty while under fourteen are to be disregarded for the purposes of any evidence relating to his previous convictions.

Section 18 adds to the categories of offences with which a child or young person is charged which may be dealt with by a magistrates' court which is not a juvenile court.

Section 27 makes it possible for a child in committal proceedings for sexual offences to make a statement in writing which shall be admissible in evidence in certain circumstances, and the child is not then to be called as a witness for the prosecution before the magistrates' court.

A modified form of oath for use in juvenile courts and by a child or young person before any court is provided by s. 28.

Section 29 makes provisions as to persons who become over the age of seventeen in proceedings before juvenile courts.

Under s. 30, a magistrates' court may make an arrears order requiring a person liable to make contributions in respect of a child where no order was in force requiring him to make the contributions to pay such weekly sum, for such a period as the court thinks fit. Such an arrears order is to be treated as a contribution order for the purposes of the enactments referred to in sub-s. (3).

Sections 31 and 32 increase the maximum penalties for some offences under the 1933 Act.

Sections 34 to 36 modify the provisions of the 1933 Act as to the employment of children, and ss. 37 to 39 replace ss. 22 and 29 (1) and (2) of the 1933 Act as regards restrictions on persons under sixteen taking part in public performances, etc. and on licences for performances by children under 13. Sections 41 to 43 modify the provisions in the 1933 Act as to licences for performances of a dangerous nature, for children and young persons performing abroad, and as to powers of entry by authorised officers of local authorities or by constables in that connection.

By s. 48, where a child has been received into the care of a local authority under s. 1 of the Children Act, 1948, and the whereabouts of his parent or guardian have remained unknown for not less than twelve months, the parent or guardian is to be deemed to have abandoned the child, for the purposes of s. 2, *ibid.* The power of the local authority under the last mentioned section is further extended by s. 48 (2).

Section 57 modifies the provisions in the 1933 Act as to newspaper reports of proceedings involving children and young persons.

Schedule 2 of the 1963 Act which relates to the constitution of juvenile courts is substituted for Sched. 2 of the 1933 Act.

Substantial alterations are made to the Children and Young Persons Act, 1933, the Children Act, 1948 and other statutes. The statutes are printed as amended.

ARRANGEMENT OF SECTIONS

PART I

CARE AND CONTROL OF CHILDREN AND YOUNG PERSONS

An Act to amend the law relating to children and young persons; and for purposes connected therewith   [*31st July 1963*]

PART I

CARE AND CONTROL OF CHILDREN AND YOUNG PERSONS

Welfare powers of local authorities

1. Extension of power to promote welfare of children.—(1) It shall be the duty of every local authority to make available such advice, guidance and assistance as may promote the welfare of children by diminishing the need to receive children into or keep them in care under the Children Act, 1948, the principal Act or the principal Scottish Act or to bring children before a juvenile court; and any provisions made by a local authority under this subsection may, if the local authority think fit, include provision for giving assistance in kind, or in exceptional circumstances, in cash.

(2) In carrying out their duty under subsection (1) of this section a local authority may make arrangements with voluntary organisations or other persons for the provision by those organisations or other persons of such advice, guidance or assistance as is mentioned in that subsection.

(3) Where any provision which may be made by a local authority under subsection (1) of this section is made (whether by that or any other authority) under any other enactment the local authority shall not be required to make the provision under this section but shall have power to do so.

(4) [*Repealed by the Children and Young Persons Act*, 1969, *s. 72* (4) *and Sched. VI. See now s. 63* (1) (a), *ibid.*]

(5) In this section " child " means a person under the age of eighteen.

NOTES

General note.—As to the treatment of children in care of local authorities see Part II of the Children Act, 1948, pp. 892, *et seq., ante.* This section requires the local authority to use its welfare powers in order to avoid receiving children into care.

This section is repealed as to Scotland by the Social Work (Scotland) Act, 1968, ss. 95 (2), 98 and Sched. IX, Part II, and S.I. 1969 No. 1274.

Principal Act.—*I.e.*, the Children and Young Persons Act, 1933. The name of the Act is used in the notes to the sections of this Act.

The principal Scottish Act.—*I.e.*, the Children and Young Persons (Scotland) Act, 1937 (1 Edw. 8 & 1 Geo. 6 c. 37) not reproduced in this work.

" Local authority ".—Local authorities for the purposes of Part I are the councils of counties and county boroughs. See s. 38 (1) of the Children Act, 1948, p. 914, *ante.* As to social services committees required to be established by those authorities see Local Authority Social Services Act, 1970, s. 2 and Sched. I, p. 927, *ante.*

" **Juvenile court.**"—See s. 45 of the Children and Young Persons Act, 1933, p. 51, *ante.*

" **Receiving into care.**"—See s. 1 of the Children Act, 1948, p. 880, *ante.*

" **Age of eighteen.**"—See notes " Age of sixteen " and " Attained the age " at pp. 12, 53, *ante.*   See also s. 99 of the Children and Young Persons Act, 1933, p. 77, *ante.*

Children and young persons in need of care, protection or control

2. Children and young persons in need of care, protection or control.—[*Repealed by the Children and Young Persons Act,* 1969, *s.* 72 (4) *and Sched. VI. See now s.* 1, *ibid., p.* 130, *post.*]

3. Children and young persons beyond control.—(1) No child or young person shall be brought before a juvenile court by his parent or guardian on the ground that he is unable to control him ; but where the parent or guardian of a child or young person has, by notice in writing, requested the local authority within whose area the child or young person resides to bring him before a juvenile court under section 1 of the Children and Young Persons Act, 1969 and the local authority refuse to do so or fail to do so within twenty-eight days from the date on which the notice is given the parent or guardian may apply by complaint to a juvenile court for an order directing them to do so.

(2) Where a complaint has been made under this section for an order against a local authority, the local authority shall make available to the court such information as to the home surroundings, school record, health and character of the child or young person as appears to them likely to assist the court and shall for that purpose make such investigations as may be necessary.

(3) On the hearing of a complaint under this section the child or young person shall not be present.

NOTES

This section is printed as amended by the Children and Young Persons Act, 1969, s. 72 (3) and Sched. V.

General note.—The procedure under this section replaces that under s. 64 of the Children and Young Persons Act, 1933, under which a parent or guardian could bring a child or young person before a juvenile court as being beyond his control. That section is repealed by this Act, and a child or young person beyond the control of his parent or guardian can be dealt with under s. 1 of the Children and Young Persons Act, 1969 (p. 130, *post*) by virtue of the definition in s. 1, *post.* See also Magistrates' Courts (Children and Young Persons) Rules, 1970 r. 22, p. 579, *post.*

" **Juvenile court.**"—See note to s. 1, p. 91, *ante.*

" **Parent.**"—This expression is not defined in this Act nor the Children and Young Persons Acts, 1933 and 1969. It does not include the natural father of an illegitimate child (see *Re M. (an infant),* [1955] 2 Q. B. 479; [1955] 2 All E. R. 911; 119 J. P. 535), but appears to include its natural mother (see *Re G. (an infant),* [1956] 2 All E. R. 876). Under Part I of the Children Act, 1958 it includes the person or one of the persons by whom the child is adopted (s. 17, *ibid., p.* 969, *post*).

As to attendance of parent at court see s. 34 of the Children and Young Persons Act, 1933, p. 43, *ante.*

Cf. also the definition of parent in s. 59 of the Children Act, 1948, p. 923, *post.*

" **Local authority.**"—See note to s. 1, p. 91, *ante.*

" Within twenty-eight days."—The day on which the notice is given is not to be reckoned ; Cf. *Stewart* v. *Chapman*, [1951] 2 K. B. 792 ; [1951] 2 All E. R. 613.

Definitions.—By virtue of s. 65 (3), p. 117, *post*, the definitions of child, guardian, young person etc. in s. 107 of the Children and Young Persons Act, 1933, as amended, p. 81, *ante*, apply.

" Shall make available."—There is a duty on the local authority to furnish to the court all the information in its possession about the child or young person. If an order directing the local authority to bring the juvenile before the court is made, it would obviously be undesirable that the same court should adjudicate in the beyond control proceedings, and therefore r. 22 (2) of the Magistrates' Courts (Children and Young Persons) Rules, 1970, p. 579, *post* precludes any member of the court who sat in proceedings under s. 3 from sitting in subsequent proceedings under s. 1.

" Shall not be present."—This presumably means present in court during the proceedings. It is conceivable that in certain cases the local authority may wish to call the juvenile as a witness, and it is doubtful that sub-s. (3) is enough to preclude its doing so.

Legal aid.—Legal aid may be given in connection with proceedings under this section. See the Legal Aid (Extension of Proceedings) Regulations, 1969, S.I. 1969 No. 921.

4. [*Sections 4–15 are repealed by the Children and Young Persons Act, 1969, s. 72 (4) and Sched. VI. For provisions as to remitting care proceedings see s. 2 (11), ibid., as to supervision, ss. 11–19, and as to care orders, ss. 20–22.*]

NOTE

It should be noted that as regards supervision orders made before January 1, 1971 this Act and the Act of 1933 continue in force as if the Children and Young Persons Act, 1969 had not been passed. As to the orders that may be made see now Sched. IV, para. 12, *ibid.*, p. 229, *post*.

Juvenile courts and proceedings in connection with children and young persons

16. Offences committed by children.—(1) Section 50 of the principal Act shall be amended by substituting therein the word " ten " for the word " eight ".

(2) In any proceedings for an offence committed or alleged to have been committed by a person of or over the age of twenty-one, any offence of which he was found guilty while under the age of fourteen shall be disregarded for the purposes of any evidence relating to his previous convictions ; and he shall not be asked, and if asked shall not be required to answer, any question relating to such an offence, notwithstanding that the question would otherwise be admissible under section 1 of the Criminal Evidence Act, 1898.

NOTES

General note.—Subsection (1) increases the age of criminal responsibility to ten. Subsection (2) is a new provision with reference to previous convictions.

"Disregarded".—Findings of guilt excluded by sub-s. (2) should be included in police officers' proof of evidence but not in the attached factual statement. See Practice Direction, p. 532, *post*.

" Age."—See note " Attained the age ", at p. 53, *ante*. See also s. 99 of the Children and Young Persons Act, 1933, p. 384, *ante*.

Children and Young Persons Act, 1933, s. 50.—See p. 57, *ante*.

Criminal Evidence Act, 1898.—See 12 Halsbury's Statutes, 3rd Edn., 865.

" **Principal Act.**"—*I.e.*, the Children and Young Persons Act, 1933, see s. 63 (1), p. 117, *post*.

17. Constitution and place of sitting of juvenile courts.—(1) For Schedule 2 to the principal Act (which relates to the constitution of juvenile courts) there shall be substituted Schedule 2 to this Act.

(2) In section 47 (2) of the principal Act (which relates to sittings of juvenile courts) for the words from " subject as hereinafter provided " to " other courts are held " there shall be substituted the words " not sit in a room in which sittings of a court other than a juvenile court are held if a sitting of that other court has been or will be held there within an hour before or after the sitting of the juvenile court ".

NOTES

" **Juvenile court.**"—See note to s. 1, p. 91, *ante*.

Children and Young Persons Act, 1933, Sch. 2.—The substituted schedule is reproduced at pp. 120 *et seq., post*.

" **Principal Act.**"—*I.e.*, the Children and Young Persons Act, 1933, see s. 63 (1), p. 117, *post*.

See also s. 12 of the Administration of Justice Act, 1964, which is as follows :—

> **12.—Composition of juvenile courts.**—(1) Without prejudice to the general adaptations of enactments for which provision is made hereafter in this Act, Sched. 2 to the Children and Young Persons Act, 1963 (constitution of juvenile courts), shall have effect as if for any reference to the metropolitan stipendiary court area there were substituted a reference to the inner London area, and Part II of that Schedule shall apply accordingly to the inner London area and the City subject to the following provisions of this section.
>
> (2) In para. 15 of the said Sched. 2 for any reference to a justice or justices of the peace for the county of London there shall be substituted a reference to a lay justice or justices for the inner London area.
>
> (3) The functions of the Secretary of State under the said Part II with respect to the nomination or selection of the chairmen and other members of the juvenile courts shall be transferred to the Lord Chancellor, and accordingly for any reference to the Secretary of State in paras. 15,16 and 18 of the said Sched. 2 there shall be substituted a reference to the Lord Chancellor.

18. Jurisdiction of magistrates' courts in certain cases involving children and young persons.—Notwithstanding section 46 (1) of the principal Act (which restricts the jurisdiction of magistrates' courts which are not juvenile courts in cases where a child or young person is charged with an offence) a magistrates' court which is not a juvenile court may hear an information against a child or young person if he is charged—

(a) with aiding, abetting, causing, procuring, allowing or permitting an offence with which a person who has attained the age of seventeen is charged at the same time ; or

(b) with an offence arising out of circumstances which are the same as or connected with those giving rise to an offence with which a person who has attained the age of seventeen is charged at the same time.

NOTES

" **Age.**"—See note " attained the age ", at p. 53, *ante*.

Definitions ; " Child, young person ".—See s. 107, p. 81, *ante*.

Children and Young Persons Act, 1933, s. 46.—See p. 51, *ante*.

" **Principal Act.**"—*I.e.*, the Children and Young Persons Act, 1933, see s. 63 (1), p. 117, *post*.

" **May hear an information.**"—The adult court is not compelled to deal with the case. *Cf.* the mandatory " shall be heard " and the permissive " may be heard " in provisos (a) and (b) of s. 46 (1) of the principal Act, p. 52, *ante*. Para. (a) of this section deals with the converse of proviso (b) of s. 46 (1) of the principal Act. The effect is to enable one court to deal with a principal and an aider and abettor at the same time, whatever their respective ages. The provisions of para. (b) of this section will avoid the necessity for two trials in such cases as larceny and receiving, cross-summonses for assault, and summonses arising out of collisions between two vehicles, where both drivers are prosecuted, irrespective of the ages of the parties.

19. Assessors for recorder in appeals and committals from juvenile courts.—[*Repealed by the Courts Act, 1971, s. 56 (4) and Sched. XI. See now s. 5 (2) ibid., and the Crown Court Rules, p. 654, post.*]

20. Constitution of London Sessions for purposes of committals from juvenile courts.—[*Repealed.*]

21. Abolition of special time limit for indictable offences in Sch. 1 to principal Act.—Section 14 (3) of the principal Act (which, as respects the summary trial of the offences mentioned in Schedule 1 to that Act, makes provision, similar to that made as respects summary trial generally by section 104 of the Magistrates' Courts Act, 1952, for limiting the time within which proceedings may be begun, but unlike that section, extends to summary trial under section 19, 20 or 21 of the said Act of 1952) is hereby repealed.

22. Children and young persons arrested and not released.—[*Repealed by the Children and Young Persons Act, 1969, s. 72 (4) and Sched. VI. See now s. 29, ibid., p. 175, post.*]

23. Children and young persons detained in places of safety.—(1) A court or justice of the peace—

   (a) [*Repealed by the Children and Young Persons Act, 1969.*]
   (b) issuing a warrant under section 40 of the principal Act authorising a constable to take a child or young person to a place of safety; or
   (c) ordering the removal of a child or young person to a place of safety under section 7 of the Children Act, 1958 or section 43 of the Adoption Act, 1958 ;

shall specify in the warrant, or order a period, which shall not exceed twenty-eight days, beyond which the child or young person must not be detained in a place of safety without being brought before a juvenile court; and accordingly the child or young person shall be brought before a juvenile court not later than the end of that period unless he has been released or received into the care of a local authority.

   (2) [*Repealed by the Children and Young Persons Act, 1969.*]

   (3) A child or young person required to be brought before a juvenile court or a justice of the peace under subsection (1) of this section shall (if

not otherwise brought before the court or justice) be brought before the court or justice by the local authority in whose area the place of safety is situated; and the person occupying or in charge of a place of safety not provided by that local authority shall as soon as practicable notify that local authority whenever a child or young person is taken there as mentioned in subsection (1) of this section.

(4) Notwithstanding anything in the preceding provisions of this section, where the person to be brought before a court or justice is under the age of five or cannot be brought before the court or justice by reason of illness or accident, the duty to bring him before the court or justice may be discharged by the making of an application for an order under subsection (5) of this section.

(5) Where a person is brought before a juvenile court or justice of the peace in pursuance of subsection (3) of this section or an application is made in respect of any person to a juvenile court or justice of the peace in pursuance of subsection (4) thereof, the court or justice may either order him to be released or make an interim order within the meaning of the Children and Young Persons Act, 1969.

[*Subsections 6–8 are repealed by the Children and Young Persons Act*, 1969.]

NOTES

This section is printed as amended by the Children and Young Persons Act, 1969, s. 72 (3), (4) and Scheds. V and VI.

General note.—The provisions of sub-s. (1) (a) and s. 67 (1) of the 1933 Act are substantially re-enacted in s. 28 of the 1969 Act (p. 173, *post*). Under sub-s. (1) it is not made clear in what circumstances the juvenile may be "released or received into care," while, under s. 28 of the 1969 Act there is no obligation for a juvenile "detained" to be brought to court. It is clear that after consultations it may appear that proceedings are not necessary.

" **Received into care.**"—See s. 1 of the Children Act, 1948, p. 880, *post*.

Definitions: " child; place of safety; young person."—See s. 107 of the 1933 Act, p. 81, *ante*. The definition of young person was extended by sub-s. (8) of this section, to include a person of or over the age of seventeen who is to be brought before a juvenile court under s. 66 of the principal Act. The provisions of this Act and the principal Act in relation to supervision orders made before January 1, 1971, have effect as if the Children and Young Persons Act, 1969, had not been passed. For the powers of a juvenile court in relation to such orders see para. 12 (2), Sched. IV, *ibid*.

" **Juvenile court.**"—See note to s. 1, p. 91, *ante*.

" **Or a justice of the peace.**"—The repeal of sub-s. (2) creates some difficulty. That subsection, dealing with juveniles who had taken refuge in a place of safety or been taken there otherwise than under the authority of a court or a justice (under s. 23 (1) (a) now repealed) *e.g.* by a *constable* under s. 67 (1) of the 1933 Act, required that the juvenile be brought before a juvenile court *or a justice of the peace within eight days*. Subsection (3) now refers to a juvenile brought before a court or a justice under sub-s. (1) which in fact only allows of appearance before a juvenile court. The remaining provisions of this section all relate back to sub-s. (3) and it is therefore doubtful whether the section in fact allows a justice of the peace to make an interim order. An interim order made by a court commences with the date of the making of the order: if made by a justice, *e.g.* s. 28 (6) Children and Young Persons Act, 1969, from the date when the person to whom it relates was first in legal custody (s. 20 (1) (b), *ibid.*).

" **Local authority.**"—See note to s. 1, p. 91, *ante*.

Children Act, 1958, s. 7.—See p. 964, *post*.

Adoption Act, 1958, s. 43.—See p. 1073, *post.*

" **Principal Act.**"—*I.e.,* the Children and Young Persons Act, 1933, see s. 63 (1), p. 117, *post.*

24. Age limits for children sent to special reception centres.— [*Repealed by the Children and Young Persons Act, 1969, s. 72 (4) and Sched. VI.*]

25. Attendance at court of parents of child or young person brought before court.—(1) For section 34 of the principal Act there shall be substituted the following section :—

" 34.—(1) Where a child or young person is charged with any offence or is for any other reason brought before a court, any person who is a parent or guardian of his may be required to attend at the court before which the case is heard or determined during all the stages of the proceedings, and any such person shall be so required at any stage where the court thinks it desirable, unless the court is satisfied that it would be unreasonable to require his attendance.

(2) Where a child or young person is arrested, such steps shall be taken by the person who arrested him as may be practicable to inform at least one person whose attendance may be required under this section ".

(2) [*Repealed by the Children and Young Persons Act, 1969, s. 72 (4) and Sched. VI.*]

NOTES

This section is printed as amended by the Children and Young Persons Act, 1969.

General note.—The provision in sub-s. (5) of the original s. 34 regarding the attendance of a parent from whose custody or charge a child or young person had been removed by an order of a court is not reproduced in the substituted section, but the existence of such an order might satisfy the court that the attendance of that parent would be unreasonable. If he is the only person whose attendance might be required he must be informed. See also the notes to the original section at p. 43, *ante,* as modified by the substituted section, a further amendment makes it clear that the person who arrests must inform. The previous Acts did not lay the duty on any specified person to see that a parent was informed.

" **Parent.**"—See note to s. 1 of the 1969 Act, p. 132, *post.*

Definitions.— For " child, young person, guardian, place of safety "; see note to s. 107, p. 81, *ante.*

26. Medical evidence by certificate.—In any proceedings, other than proceedings for an offence, before a juvenile court, and on any appeal from a decision of a juvenile court in any such proceedings, any document purporting to be a certificate of a fully registered medical practitioner as to any person's physical or mental condition shall be admissible as evidence of that condition.

NOTES

" **Juvenile court.**"—See note to s. 1, p. 91, *ante.*

" **Fully registered medical practitioner.**"—See the Medical Act, 1956, ss. 52, 54, 57; 21 Halsbury's Statutes 3rd Edn., pp. 665, 667.

" **Admissible as evidence.**"—Although there is no express provision (as in the Mental Health Act, 1959, s. 63 (2)) the parties might require the practitioner to be called to give oral evidence.

27. Evidence of children in committal proceedings for sexual offences.—(1) In any proceedings before a magistrates' court inquiring into a sexual offence as examining justices—

    (a) a child shall not be called as a witness for the prosecution ; but

    (b) any statement made in writing by or taken in writing from the child shall be admissible in evidence of any matter of which his oral testimony would be admissible ;

except in a case where the application of this subsection is excluded under subsection (2) of this section.

    (2) Subsection (1) of this section shall not apply—

    (a) where at or before the time when such a statement is tendered in evidence the defence objects to the application of that subsection ; or

    (b) where the prosecution requires the attendance of the child for the purpose of establishing the identity of any person ; or

    (c) where the court is satisfied that it has not been possible to obtain from the child a statement that may be given in evidence under this section ; or

    (d) where the inquiry into the offence takes place after the court has discontinued to try it summarily and the child has given evidence in the summary trial.

    (3) Section 23 of the Magistrates' Courts Act, 1952 (which, in a case where an inquiry into an offence is followed by summary trial, treats evidence given for the purposes of the inquiry as having been given for the purposes of the trial) shall not apply to any statement admitted in pursuance of subsection (1) of this section.

    (4) In this section " sexual offence " means any offence under the Sexual Offences Act, 1956, or the Indecency with Children Act, 1960, or any attempt to commit such an offence.

NOTES

" **Examining justices.**"—The object of the section is to save a child having to give oral evidence twice, and therefore applies to committal proceedings only.

Treatment of child witnesses.—See Home Office circular 208/1964, p. 676, *post*.

Magistrates' Courts Act, 1952, s. 23.—See 21 Halsbury's Statutes, 3rd Edn., 208.

Sexual Offences Act, 1956.—See 8 Halsbury's Statutes 3rd Edn., 415. Sections 28 and 43 are reproduced at p. 396, *post*.

Indecency with Children Act, 1960.—See pp. 398 to 400, *post*.

" **Explanation to child.**"—See Rule 4 (4) of the Magistrates' Courts Rules, 1968, p. 550, *post*.

Treatment of child witness in proceedings in respect of sexual offences.—See Home Office Circular No. 208/1964, p. 676, *post*.

Oral evidence.—As to note to be made on the papers sent to court of trial; see Home Office circulars Nos. 17 and 19/1964, pp. 675 *et seq.*, *post*.

Advice to police as to child witnesses.—See Home Office circular No. 17/1964, p. 677, *post*.

28. Form of oath for use in juvenile courts and by children and young persons in other courts.—(1) Subject to subsection (2) of this section, in relation to any oath administered to and taken by any person before a juvenile court or administered to and taken by any child or young person before any other court, section 2 of the Oaths Act, 1909 shall have effect as if the words " I promise before Almighty God " were set out in it instead of the words " I swear by Almighty God that ".

(2) Where in any oath otherwise duly administered and taken either of the forms mentioned in this section is used instead of the other, the oath shall nevertheless be deemed to have been duly administered and taken.

NOTES

As to the evidence of a child of tender years see the Children and Young Persons Act, 1933, s. 38, p. 44, *ante*. See the notes to that section at pp. 44 *et seq.*, *ante.*, as to evidence on oath.

Definitions.—For " child, young person ", see note to s. 107, p. 81, *ante*.

29. Provisions as to persons between the ages of 17 and 18.—(1) Where proceedings in respect of a young person are begun under section 1 of the Children and Young Persons Act, 1969, or for an offence and he attains the age of seventeen before the conclusion of the proceedings, the court may deal with the case and make any order which it could have made if he had not attained that age.

(2) [*Repealed by the Children and Young Persons Act, 1969, s. 72 (4) and Sched. VI.*]

NOTES

This section is printed as amended by the Children and Young Persons Act, 1969, s. 72 (3), (4) and Scheds. V and VI.

General note.—The power of courts to make these orders was previously restricted to persons who had not attained the age of seventeen at the time of the making of the order.

"Make any order."—This will include an interim order under s. 2 (11) of the Act of 1969, p. 136, *post*.

Age.—See note to s. 16, p. 93, *ante*.

Recovery of arrears of contributions

30. Recovery of arrears of contributions.—(1) Where during any period (in this section referred to as " the period of default ")—

   (a) a person was liable to make contributions in respect of a child; but

   (b) no order was in force requiring him to make the contributions;

a magistrates' court acting for the petty sessions area where he is for the time being residing may, on the application of the local authority who would have been entitled to receive payment under such an order, make an order (in this section referred to as an "arrears order") requiring him to pay such weekly sum, for such period, as the court, having regard to his means, thinks fit; but the aggregate of the payments required to be made by any person under an arrears order shall not exceed the aggregate that, in the opinion of the court, would have been payable by him under a contribution order in respect of the period of default or, if it exceeded three months, the last part thereof, less the aggregate of the payments (if any) made by him in respect of his liability during that period or, as the case may be, the last part thereof.

For the purposes of this subsection the last part of the period of default shall be taken to be the last three months thereof and such time, if any, preceding the last three months as is equal to the time during which it continued after the making of the application for the arrears order.

(2) No application for an arrears order shall be made later than three months after the end of the period of default.

(3) An arrears order shall be treated as a contribution order, and payments under it as contributions, for the purposes of the following enactments, that is to say—

> in the principal Act, subsection (3) of section 86, sections 87 (4), 89 and 102 (1) (c).
> the Maintenance Orders Act, 1950,
> the Maintenance Orders Act, 1958,
> paragraph 2 of Schedule 8 to the Local Government Act, 1958,
> section 62 of the Children and Young Persons Act, 1969.

(4) Where the person who was liable to make contributions resides in Scotland or Northern Ireland, subsection (1) of this section shall have effect as if for the magistrates' court therein mentioned there were substituted a magistrates' court acting for the area or part of the area of the local authority which is the applicant.

(5) A person liable to make payments under an arrears order shall, except at a time when he is under a duty to give information of his address under section 24 (8) of the Children and Young Persons Act, 1969, keep the local authority to whom the payments are to be made informed of his address; and if he fails to do so he shall be liable on summary conviction to a fine not exceeding ten pounds.

(6) In this section—

> " child " has the same meaning as in the Children Act, 1948.
> " contributions " means contributions under section 86 of the principal Act, and
> " contribution order " means an order under section 87 of the principal Act.

NOTES

This section is printed as amended by the Children and Young Persons Act, 1969, s. 72 (3) and Sched. V and the Criminal Justice Act, 1967, s. 92 and Sched. III.

" Later than three months " (sub-s. (2)).—*Cf.* note " within twenty eight days " to s. 3, p. 93, *ante.*

Definition ; " child."—In this section it means a person under the age of eighteen years and any person who has attained that age and is the subject of a care order within the meaning of the Children and Young Persons Act, 1969 (Children Act, 1948, s. 59, p. 923, *post*).

Children and Young Persons Act, 1933, ss. 86, 87, 89, 102.—See pp. 67, 69, 72, 78, *ante.*

Maintenance Orders Act, 1950.—See 17 Halsbury's Statutes, 3rd Edn., 594.

Maintenance Orders Act, 1958.—See 17 Halsbury's Statutes, 3rd Edn., 293.

Local Government Act, 1958, Sch. VIII.—See 19 Halsbury's Statutes, 3rd Edn., 816.

" Principal Act."—*I.e.*, the Children and Young Persons Act, 1933, see s. 63 (1), p. 117, *post.*

Attachment of Earnings.—See the Attachment of Earnings Act, 1971, s. 2 and Sched. I (41 Halsbury's Statutes, 3rd Edn., 451).

Increase of certain penalties

31. Increase of penalty for cruelty.—In section 1 of the principal Act (cruelty to persons under sixteen) paragraph (b) of subsection (1) (which provides for a fine not exceeding twenty-five pounds on summary conviction) shall be amended, as respects offences committed after the commencement of this Act, by the substitution for the words " twenty-five pounds " of the words " one hundred pounds ".

NOTES

Children and Young Persons Act, 1933, s. 1.—See p. 10, *ante.*

" Commencement of this Act."—*I.e.*, February 1, 1964, see s. 65 (6), p. 117, *post.*

" Principal Act."—*I.e.*, the Children and Young Persons Act, 1933, see s. 63 (1), p. 117, *post.*

32. Increase of penalty for sales of tobacco, etc., to persons under 16.—Section 7 of the principal Act and section 18 of the principal Scottish Act (which, in subsection (1), prohibit the sale of tobacco and cigarette papers to persons apparently under the age of sixteen and, in subsection (2), enable a court to order measures to be taken to prevent the use by such persons of automatic machines for the sale of tobacco) shall each be amended, as respects offences committed after the commencement of this Act, by substituting—

(a) in subsection (1) (which provides for fines not exceeding two, five and ten pounds on a first, second or subsequent conviction) for the words " two ", " five " and " ten " the words " twenty-five ", " fifty " and " one hundred ", respectively ; and

(b) in subsection (2) (which provides for fines not exceeding five pounds for failure to comply with the order of the court and further fines not exceeding one pound for each day during which the offence continues) for the words " five " and " one " the words " fifty " and " ten ", respectively.

NOTES

Children and Young Persons Act, 1933, s. 7.—See p. 21, *ante.*

" Second or subsequent offence."—See note at p. 26, *ante.*

" Commencement of this Act."—*I.e.*, February 1, 1964, see s. 65 (6), p. 117, *post.*

" Principal Act."—*I.e.*, the Children and Young Persons Act, 1933; see s. 63 (1), p. 21, *post.*

New appeals

33. New appeals.—[*Repealed by the Children and Young Persons Act,* 1969, *s.* 72 (4) *and Sched. VI. See now s.* 21 (4), (5), ibid.]

PART II

EMPLOYMENT OF CHILDREN AND YOUNG PERSONS

General provisions as to employment

NOTE

By virtue of s. 44 (1), p. 109, *post*, in its application to England and Wales and as regards s. 42, p. 108, *post*, in its application elsewhere this Part of this Act shall be construed, and Part II of the Children and Young Persons Act, 1933, shall have effect, as if this Part were included in that Part.

34. Hours of employment.—For paragraph (c) of section 18 (1) of the principal Act (which prohibits the employment of children before six o'clock in the morning or after eight o'clock in the evening) and for paragraph (c) of section 28 (1) of the principal Scottish Act (which prohibits such employment before six o'clock in the morning or after seven o'clock in the evening, or at certain times of the year eight o'clock in the evening) there shall be substituted the following paragraph :—

" (c) before seven o'clock in the morning or after seven o'clock in the evening on any day ; or ".

NOTES
Children and Young Persons Act, 1933, s. 18.—See p. 29, *ante.*

35. Street trading.—(1) In section 20 (1) of the principal Act (which subject to certain exceptions, prohibits persons under the age of sixteen from engaging or being employed in street trading) for the word " sixteen ", in both places where it occurs, there shall be substituted the word " seventeen ".

(2) Nothing in the said section 20 or section 30 of the principal Scottish Act or in any byelaw made under either of those sections shall restrict the engagement or employment of any person in the carrying on in any place of a retail trade or business (within the meaning of the Shops Act, 1950) on any occasion on which it is customary for retail trades or businesses to be carried on in that place.

(3) At the end of the said section 20 there shall be added the following subsection :—

" (3) No person under the age of eighteen shall on a Sunday engage or be employed in street trading of a description to which, notwithstanding section 58 of the Shops Act, 1950 (which extends certain provisions to any place where a retail trade or business is carried on), those provisions do not extend."

NOTES
" **Age.**"—See note to s. 16, p. 93, *ante.*

Definitions; " Street trading ".—See Children and Young Persons Act, 1933, s. 30, p. 41, *ante.*

Children and Young Persons Act, 1933, s. 20.—See p. 31, *ante.*

Shops Act, 1950.—See 13 Halsbury's Statutes, 3rd Edn., 317.

36. Increase of certain penalties.—Section 21 of the principal Act and section 31 of the principal Scottish Act (which impose penalties for contraventions of the general provisions of those Acts as to employment) shall each be amended, as respects offences committed after the commencement of this Act, as follows :—

(a) in subsection (1) (which provides for fines not exceeding five pounds and twenty pounds for first and subsequent offences respectively) for the words " five pounds " there shall be substituted the words " twenty pounds " and for the words " twenty pounds " the words " fifty pounds " ; and

(b) in subsection (3) (which provides for fines of twenty shillings and forty shillings for first and subsequent offences respectively) for the words " twenty shillings " there shall be substituted the words " ten pounds " and for the words " forty shillings " the words " twenty pounds ".

NOTES

" **Subsequent offences.**"—*Cf.* note at p. 33, *ante.*

Children and Young Persons Act, 1933, s. 21.—See p. 32, *ante.*

" **Commencement of this Act.**"—*I.e.*, the time at which this provision comes into operation, s. 65, (6), p. 117, *post.* This provision came into force on March 3, 1969 (S.I. 1968 No. 1727).

" **Principal Act.**"—*I.e.*, the Children and Young Persons Act, 1933, see s. 63 (1), p. 117, *post.*

Entertainment

37. Restriction on persons under 16 taking part in public performances, etc.—(1) Subject to the provisions of this section, a child shall not take part in a performance to which this section applies except under the authority of a licence granted by the local authority in whose area he resides or, if he does not reside in Great Britain, by the local authority in whose area the applicant or one of the applicants for the licence resides or has his place of business.

(2) This section applies to—

(a) any performance in connection with which a charge is made (whether for admission or otherwise) ;

(b) any performance in licensed premises within the meaning of the Licensing Act, 1953, or the Licensing (Scotland) Act, 1959, or in premises in respect of which a club is registered under the said Act of 1959 or the Licensing Act, 1961 ;

(c) any broadcast performance ;

(d) any performance recorded (by whatever means) with a view to its use in a broadcast or in a film intended for public exhibition ;

and a child shall be treated for the purposes of this section as taking part in a performance if he takes the place of a performer in any rehearsal or in any preparation for the recording of the performance.

(3) A licence under this section shall not be required for any child to take part in a performance to which this section applies if—

(a) in the six months preceding the performance he has not taken part in other performances to which this section applies on more than three days; or

(b) the performance is given under arrangements made by a school (within the meaning of the Education Act, 1944 or the Education (Scotland) Act, 1962) or made by a body of persons approved for the purposes of this section by the Secretary of State or by the local authority in whose area the performance takes place, and no payment in respect of the child's taking part in the performance is made, whether to him or to any other person, except for defraying expenses;

but the Secretary of State may by regulations made by statutory instrument prescribe conditions to be observed with respect to the hours of work, rest or meals of children taking part in performances as mentioned in paragraph (a) of this subsection.

(4) The power to grant licences under this section shall be exercisable subject to such restrictions and conditions as the Secretary of State may by regulations made by statutory instrument prescribe and a local authority shall not grant a licence for a child to take part in a performance or series of performances unless they are satisfied that he is fit to do so, that proper provision has been made to secure his health and kind treatment and that, having regard to such provision (if any) as has been or will be made therefor, his education will not suffer; but if they are so satisfied, in the case of an application duly made for a licence under this section which they have power to grant, they shall not refuse to grant the licence.

(5) Regulations under this section may make different provision for different circumstances and may prescribe, among the conditions subject to which a licence is to be granted, conditions requiring the approval of a local authority and may provide for that approval to be given subject to conditions imposed by the authority.

(6) Without prejudice to the generality of the preceding subsection, regulations under this section may prescribe, among the conditions subject to which a licence may be granted, a condition requiring sums earned by the child in respect of whom the licence is granted in taking part in a performance to which the licence relates to be paid into the county court (or, in Scotland, consigned in the sheriff court) or dealt with in a manner approved by the local authority.

(7) A licence under this section shall specify the times, if any, during which the child in respect of whom it is granted may be absent from school for the purposes authorised by the licence; and for the purposes of the enactments relating to education a child who is so absent during any times so specified shall be deemed to be absent with leave granted by a

person authorised in that behalf by the managers, governors or proprietor of the school or, in Scotland, with reasonable excuse.

(8) Any statutory instrument made under this section shall be subject to annulment in pursuance of a resolution of either House of Parliament.

NOTES

General note.—This section with ss. 38 to 40, *post*, replaces s. 22 of the Children and Young Persons Act, 1933, which is repealed and s. 29 which is repealed in part.

Although by s. 44 this Part of the Act is to be construed and Part II of the principal Act is to take effect as if this Part were included in that part, the definition of "child" is governed by the provisions of the Education Act, 1944, s. 58 (p. 266).

" **Resides ".**—See note " Residence " at p. 162, *ante*.

" **Great Britain."**—See note at p. 1047, *post*.

" **Licence under this section shall not be required." (sub-s. (3)).**—In such case nothing in the Children and Young Persons Act, 1933, s. 18 (p. 29, *ante*) or in any byelaw made under that section shall prevent a child taking part in a performance. Subsection (3) is not expressly restricted to amateur productions but it would appear to apply primarily to them.

"**Taking part in a performance."**—This is not defined in the Act, and it will be for a court to decide in a particular case whether the activity involved constitutes a performance.

"**Local authority."**—Where approval is sought for performance in the area of one local authority application should presumably be made to that authority.

Where the application is in respect of performances in the areas of two or more authorities it should generally be made to the Children's Department, Home Office, Norman Shaw Building South, Victoria Embankment, London, S.W.1, but see para. 15 of the Guide to the Law on Performances by Children, published by Her Majesty's Stationery Office. See also note to s. 1, p. 91, *ante*.

Other employment.—While a child is taking part in performances he may not do any other work: see S.I. 1968 No. 1728, reg. 18, p. 508, *post*.

"**Absent from school."**—Neither the Act nor the Regulations make any provision under which absence from school may be authorised for a performance unless licensed.

"**Regulations."**—See the Children (Performances) Regulations, 1968, pp. 502, *et seq., post*.

" **Powers of entry."**—See the Children and Young Persons Act, 1933, s. 28, p. 40, *ante*.

" **Offences."**—See s. 40, p. 107, *post*.

" **Performances of dangerous nature."**—See the Children and Young Persons Act, 1933, ss. 23, 24, p. 33, *ante*, and s. 41 of this Act, p. 108, *post*.

" **Going abroad to perform for profit."**—See the Children and Young Persons Act, 1933, s. 25, p. 35, *ante.*, and s. 42 of this Act, p. 108, *post*.

Education Act, 1944.—For meaning of "school" see s. 114 (1), p. 270, *post*.

Licensing Act, 1953 ; Licensing Act, 1961.—These Acts are repealed by the Licensing Act, 1964.

For the meaning of "licensed premises" see s. 200, *ibid.*, p. 431, *post*.

38. Restriction on licences for performances by children under 13.—(1) A licence under the preceding section in respect of a child under the age of thirteen shall not be granted unless—

> (a) the licence is for acting and the application therefor is accompanied by a declaration that the part he is to act cannot be taken except by a child of about his age ; or

(b) the licence is for dancing in a ballet which does not form part of an entertainment of which anything other than ballet or opera also forms part and the application for the licence is accompanied by a declaration that the part he is to dance cannot be taken except by a child of about his age ; or

(c) the nature of his part in the performance is wholly or mainly musical and either the nature of the performance is also wholly or mainly musical or the performance consists only of opera and ballet.

(2) On the extension of the compulsory school age (or, in Scotland, school age) to sixteen years, that is to say—

(a) in England and Wales, on the coming into force of an Order in Council under section 35 of the Education Act, 1944 ; and

(b) in Scotland, on the coming into force of regulations under section 32 of the Education (Scotland) Act, 1962 ;

subsection (1) of this section shall have effect as if for the word " thirteen " there were substituted the word " fourteen ".

NOTES

"**Acting.**"—This is not defined in the Act, and it will be for the licensing authority to decide whether what a child under 13 is doing in a particular case is "acting".

Rehearsals.—Licences are not required for rehearsals as such but see S.I. 1968 No. 1728, reg. 6, p. 503, *post.*

Order in Council.—No Order in council has been made under the Education Act, 1944, s. 35, (p. 252, *post*) at the time of going to press.

39. Supplementary provisions as to licences under section 37.— (1) A licence under section 37 of this Act may be varied on the application of the person holding it by the local authority by whom it was granted or by any local authority in whose area the performance or one of the performances to which it relates takes place.

(2) The local authority by whom such a licence was granted, and any local authority in whose area the performance or one of the performances to which it relates takes place, may vary or revoke the licence if any condition subject to which it was granted is not observed or they are not satisfied as to the matters mentioned in subsection (4) of the said section 37, but shall, before doing so, give to the holder of the licence such notice (if any) of their intention as may be practicable in the circumstances.

(3) Where a local authority grant such a licence authorising a child to take part in a performance in the area of another local authority they shall send to that other authority such particulars as the Secretary of State may by regulations made by statutory instrument prescribe ; and where a local authority vary or revoke such a licence which was granted by, or relates to a performance in the area of, another local authority, they shall inform that other authority.

(4) A local authority proposing to vary or revoke such a licence granted by another local authority shall, if practicable, consult that other authority.

(5) The holder of such a licence shall keep such records as the Secretary of State may by regulations made by statutory instrument prescribe and

shall on request produce them to an officer of the authority who granted the licence, at any time not later than six months after the performance or last performance to which it relates.

(6) Where a local authority refuse an application for a licence under section 37 of this Act or revoke or, otherwise than on the application of the holder, vary such a licence they shall state their grounds for doing so in writing to the applicant or, as the case may be, the holder of the licence ; and the applicant or holder may appeal to a magistrates' court or, in Scotland, the sheriff, against the refusal, revocation or variation, and against any condition subject to which the licence is granted or any approval is given, not being a condition which the local authority are required to impose.

(7) Any statutory instrument made under this section shall be subject to annulment in pursuance of a resolution of either House of Parliament.

NOTES

Regulations.—See the Children (Performances) Regulations, 1968, pp. 501, *et seq., post.*

40. Offences.—(1) If any person—

(a) causes or procures any child or, being his parent or guardian, allows him, to take part in any performance in contravention of section 37 of this Act ; or

(b) fails to observe any condition subject to which a licence under that section is granted, or any condition prescribed under subsection (3) of that section ; or

(c) knowingly or recklessly makes any false statement in or in connection with an application for a licence under that section ;

he shall be liable on summary conviction to a fine not exceeding one hundred pounds or imprisonment for a term not exceeding three months or both.

(2) If any person fails to keep or produce any record which he is required to keep or produce under section 39 of this Act, he shall be liable on summary conviction to a fine not exceeding fifty pounds or imprisonment for a term not exceeding three months or both.

(3) The court by which the holder or one of the holders of a licence under section 37 of this Act is convicted of an offence under this section may revoke the licence.

(4) In any proceedings for an offence under this section alleged to have been committed by causing, procuring or allowing a child to take part in a performance without a licence under section 37 of this Act it shall be a defence to prove that the accused believed that the condition specified in paragraph (a) of subsection (3) of that section was satisfied and that he had reasonable grounds for that belief.

NOTES

" Parent."—See note to s. 3, p. 92, *ante.*

" Reasonable grounds for that belief."—See *R.* v. *Harrison,* [1938] 3 All E. R. 134.

41. Licences for training persons between 12 and 16 for perform-ances of a dangerous nature.—(1) The power to grant licences under section 24 of the principal Act (which relates to the training of persons under the age of sixteen to take part in performances of a dangerous nature) shall be exercisable by the local authority for the area or one of the areas in which the training is to take place instead of by a magistrates' court.

(2) A licence under the said section 24 or under section 34 of the principal Scottish Act (which makes provision in Scotland similar to that made in England and Wales by the said section 24 as amended by sub-section (1) of this section) may be revoked or varied by the authority who granted it if any of the conditions embodied therein are not complied with or if it appears to them that the person to whom the licence relates is no longer fit and willing to be trained or that proper provision is no longer being made to secure his health and kind treatment.

(3) Where an authority refuse an application for such a licence or revoke or vary such a licence they shall state their grounds for doing so in writing to the applicant, or, as the case may be, to the holder of the licence, and the applicant or holder may appeal to a magistrates' court or, in Scotland, to the sheriff, against the refusal, revocation or variation.

NOTES

General note.—Subsection (2) replaces s. 24 (5) of the Children and Young Persons Act, 1933, which is repealed by this Act. The right to appeal under sub-s. (3) is new.

" **Age.**"—See note to s. 16, p. 93, *ante*.

" **Local authority.**"—See note to s. 1, p. 91, *ante*.

" **Appeal to magistrates' court.**"—The appeal is by way of complaint for an order. See the Magistrates' Courts Rules, 1968, r. 30, and the Magistrates' Courts Act, 1952, ss. 43 *et seq.*; 21 Halsbury's Statutes, 3rd Edn. 224.

42. Licences for children and young persons performing abroad.—(1) Section 25 of the principal Act (which prohibits persons under eighteen from going abroad for the purpose of performing for profit except under the authority of a licence granted under that section) and section 26 of that Act (which imposes penalties for contraventions) shall have effect as if the words " singing, playing, performing or being exhibited " included taking part in any such performance as is mentioned in paragraph (c) or (d) of section 37 (2) of this Act.

(2) A licence under the said section 25 may be granted in respect of a person notwithstanding that he is under the age of fourteen if—

(a) the engagement which he is to fulfil is for acting and the application for the licence is accompanied by a declaration that the part he is to act cannot be taken except by a person of about his age ; or

(b) the engagement is for dancing in a ballet which does not form part of an entertainment of which anything other than ballet or opera also forms part and the application for the licence is accompanied by a declaration that the part he is to dance cannot be taken except by a child of about his age ; or

(c) the engagement is for taking part in a performance the nature of which is wholly or mainly musical or which consists only of opera and ballet and the nature of his part in the performance is wholly or mainly musical.

NOTES

" Age."—See note to s. 16, p. 93, *ante*.

Children and Young Persons Act, 1933, ss. 25, 26.—See pp. 35, 38, *ante*.

" **Principal Act.**"—*I.e.*, the Children and Young Persons Act, 1933, see s. 63 (1), p. 117, *post*.

43. Extended powers of entry.—For subsection (2) of section 28 of the principal Act and for subsection (2) of section 36 of the principal Scottish Act there shall be substituted the following subsection :—

" (2) Any authorised officer of the said authority or any constable may—

(a) at any time enter any place used as a broadcasting studio or film studio or used for the recording of a performance with a view to its use in a broadcast or in a film intended for public exhibition and make inquiries therein as to any children taking part in performances to which section 37 of the Children and Young Persons Act, 1963 applies ;

(b) at any time during the currency of a licence granted under the said section 37 or under the provisions of this Part of this Act relating to training for dangerous performances enter any place (whether or not it is such a place as is mentioned in paragraph (a) of this subsection) where the person to whom the licence relates is authorised by the licence to take part in a performance or to be trained, and may make inquiries therein with respect to that person."

NOTES

" **Children.**"—By virtue of s. 65 (3) the definitions of child, guardian, etc., in s. 107 of the Children and Young Persons Act, 1933, p. 81, *ante*, apply.

" **Authorised officer.**"—*Cf.* the note " Conduct of proceedings " at p. 920, *post*.

" **Local authority.**"—See note to s. 1, p. 91, *ante*.

Children and Young Persons Act, 1933, s. 28.—See p. 40, *ante*.

" **Dangerous performances.**"—See note " Performances of dangerous nature," to s. 37, p. 105, *ante*.

" **Principal Act.**"—*I.e.*, the Children and Young Persons Act, 1933, see s. 63 (1), p. 117, *post*.

Construction of Part II

44. Construction of Part II.—(1) This Part of this Act, in its application to England and Wales, and, as regards section 42, in its application elsewhere, shall be construed, and Part II of the principal Act shall have effect, as if this Part were included in that Part.

(2) This Part of this Act, except section 42, shall, in its application to Scotland, be construed as if it were included in Part III of the principal Scottish Act and as if references to a local authority were references to an

education authority ; and the said Part III shall have effect as if this Part of this Act (except section 42) were included in it.

NOTE

"**Principal Act.**"—*I.e.*, the Children and Young Persons Act, 1933, see s. 63 (1), p. 117, *post.*

PART III

MISCELLANEOUS AND GENERAL

Research and financial assistance

45. Research.—(1) The Secretary of State may conduct or assist other persons in conducting research into any matter connected with his functions or the functions of local authorities under the Children and Young Persons Acts, 1933 to 1956, the Children Act, 1948, the Children Act, 1958, the Children and Young Persons Act, 1969 or this Act, or any matter connected with the adoption of children.

(2) Any local authority may conduct or assist other persons in conducting research into any matter connected with their functions under the enactments mentioned in subsection (1) of this section or their functions connected with the adoption of children.

NOTE

This section is printed as amended by the Social Work (Scotland) Act, 1968, ss. 95 (2), 98 and Sched. IX, and the Children and Young Persons Act, 1969, s. 72 (3) and Sched. V.

"**Local authorities.**"—See note to s. 1, p. 91, *ante.*

Scotland.—From November 19, 1969, this section is repealed as to Scotland only (Social Work (Scotland) Act, 1968, ss. 95 (2), 98 and Sched. IX, Part I and S.I. 1969 No. 1274).

46. Financial assistance under s. 20 of Children Act, 1948.—(1) In subsection (1) of section 20 of the Children Act, 1948 (which authorises a local authority to contribute towards the cost of accommodation and maintenance of certain persons over the age of eighteen who have been in the care of a local authority) after the word " being " there shall be inserted the words " either a person who has attained the age of seventeen but has ceased to be in the care of a local authority, or ".

(2) In subsection (2) of the said section 20 (which authorises a local authority to make grants towards the education or training of certain persons over the age of eighteen who immediately before they attained that age were in the care of a local authority) for the word " eighteen ", in the first place where it occurs, there shall be substituted the word " seventeen" and for the words " immediately before they attained the age of eighteen " there shall be substituted the words " at or after the time when they attained the age of seventeen ".

NOTES

Scotland.—From November 19, 1969, this section is repealed as to Scotland only (Social Work (Scotland) Act, 1968, ss. 95 (2), 98 and Sched. IX, Part I and S.I. 1969 No. 1274).

" **Age.**"—See note to s. 16, p. 93, *ante.*

" **Local authority.**"—See note to s. 1, p. 91, *ante.*

Children Act, 1948, s. 20.—See p. 900, *post.*

" **In care of a local authority.**"—See Part II of the Children Act, 1948, pp. 892, *et seq., post.*

47. Power of local authority to guarantee apprenticeship deeds etc. of persons in their care.

—While a person is in the care of a local authority under the principal Act, the principal Scottish Act or the Children Act, 1948 or by virtue of an order under the Matrimonial Proceedings (Children) Act, 1958 or the Matrimonial Proceedings (Magistrates' Courts) Act, 1960, the local authority may undertake any obligation by way of guarantee under any deed of apprenticeship or articles of clerkship entered into by that person ; and where the local authority have undertaken any such obligation under any deed or articles they may at any time (whether or not the person concerned is still in their care) undertake the like obligation under any deed or articles supplemental thereto.

NOTES

Scotland.—From November 19, 1969, this section is repealed as to Scotland only (Social Work (Scotland) Act, 1968, ss. 95 (2), 98 and Sched. IX, Part I and S.I. 1969 No. 1274).

In the care of a local authority under the principal Act.—This would have been under a fit person order. Such orders are now care orders by virtue of para. 8, Sched. IV Children and Young Persons Act, 1969, and although references in Part II Children Act, 1948 to a child in care include references to a child who is the subject of a care order (s. 11, *ibid.*) the reference here would not include such children.

" **Local authority.**"—See note to s. 1, p. 91, *ante.*

Matrimonial Proceedings (Children) Act, 1958.—See now Matrimonial Causes Act, 1965, s. 36, p. 1240, *post.*

Matrimonial Proceedings (Magistrates' Courts) Act, 1960.—See 17 Halsbury's Statutes 3rd Edn., 241.

" **Principal Act.**"—*I.e.*, the Children and Young Persons Act, 1933, see s. 63 (1), p. 117, *post.*

Children in respect of whom parental rights may be or have been assumed by local authority

48. Extension of power of local authority to assume parental rights.

—(1) Where, after a child has been received into the care of a local authority under section 1 of the Children Act, 1948, the whereabouts of any parent or guardian of his have remained unknown for not less than twelve months, then, for the purposes of section 2 of that Act (which enables a local authority in certain circumstances to assume parental rights) the parent or guardian shall be deemed to have abandoned the child.

(2) The power of a local authority under paragraph (b) of section 2 (1) of the Children Act, 1948 to resolve that all rights and powers of a parent or guardian shall vest in them may be exercised, as well as in the cases mentioned in that paragraph, in any case, where it appears to them—

    (a) that the parent or guardian suffers from a mental disorder (within the meaning of the Mental Health Act, 1959 or the Mental Health (Scotland) Act 1960) which renders him unfit to have the care of the child ; or

(b) that the parent or guardian has so persistently failed without reasonable cause to discharge the obligations or a parent or guardian as to be unfit to have the care of the child ;

and the power of the court or sheriff, under subsection (3) of that section, to order that the resolution shall not lapse may also be exercised if the court or sheriff is satisfied that the person who objected to the resolution is unfit to have the care of the child by reason of his persistent failure to discharge the obligation of a parent or guardian.

(3) In this section " child " has the same meaning as in the Children Act, 1948.

NOTES

Scotland.—From November 19, 1969, this section is repealed as to Scotland only (Social Work (Scotland) Act, 1968, ss. 95 (2), 98 and Sched. IX, Part I and S.I. 1969 No. 1274).

" **Local Authority.**"—See note to s. 1, p. 91, *ante.*

" **Parent.**"—See note to s. 3, p. 92, *ante.*

Definitions.—See note to s. 43, p. 109, *ante.*   " Child " means a person under the age of eighteen years ; Children Act, 1948, s. 59, p. 923, *post.*

Children Act, 1948.—See pp. 880 *et seq., post.*

" **Persistently failed without reasonable cause.**"—*Cf.* the similar wording in s. 5 (2) of the Adoption Act, 1958, p. 1034, *post.*

49. Harbouring or concealing child required to return to local authority.—(1) Where a local authority have, in accordance with section 13 (2) of the Children Act, 1948, allowed any person to take charge of a child with respect to whom a resolution under section 2 of that Act is in force and have by notice in writing required that person to return the child at a time specified in the notice (which, if that person has been allowed to take charge of the child for a fixed period, shall not be earlier than the end of that period) any person who harbours or conceals the child after that time or prevents him from returning as required by the notice shall be liable on summary conviction to a fine not exceeding twenty pounds or to imprisonment for a term not exceeding two months or to both.

(2) In this section " child " has the same meaning as in the Children Act, 1948.

NOTES

Scotland.—From November 19, 1969, this section is repealed as to Scotland only (Social Work (Scotland) Act, 1968, ss. 95 (2), 98 and Sched. IX, Part I and S.I. 1969 No. 1274).

" **Local authority.**"—See note to s. 1, p. 91, *ante.*

" **Child.**"—See note "Definitions," to s. 48, *supra.*

Children Act 1948, s. 13.—See p. 893, *post.*

50. Extension of power to appoint guardian.—[*Repealed by the Guardianship of Minors Act, 1971, s. 18 and Sched. II. See now s. 5 (2), ibid.*]

Persons under supervision changing country of residence

51. Supervision of persons moving to Scotland.—[*Repealed as to England and Wales by the Social Work (Scotland) Act, 1968, ss. 95 (2), 98, and Sched. IX, Part II.*]

See now Part V, ibid., pp. 234, et seq., post. The interim provisions in Sched. IV, Part II Children and Young Persons Act are now spent (S.I. 1971 No. 589, p. 654, post.]

52. Supervision orders by Scottish courts in respect of persons residing in England.—*[Repealed by Social Work (Scotland) Act, 1968, ss. 95 (2), 98, and Sched. IX, Part II. See now Part V, ibid., pp. 234 et seq., post.]*

Children and young persons escaping to other parts of British Islands

53. Arrest in one part of British Islands of children or young persons escaping in other part.—*[Subsections (1) and (2) were repealed by the Children and Young Persons Act, 1969, s. 72 (4) and Sched. VI. See now s. 32 (1), ibid., and Part V, Social Work (Scotland) Act, 1968.]*

(3) Every person who is authorised by the managers of a training school within the meaning of the Children and Young Persons Act (Northern Ireland) 1950 to arrest a person under their care and bring him back to his school shall, for the purpose of acting on that authority, have all the powers, protection and privileges—

(a) in Great Britain or the Isle of Man, of a constable ;

(b) in Jersey, of a member of the police ;

(c) in any other part of the Channel Islands, of an officer of police within the meaning of section 43 of the Larceny (Guernsey) Law 1958, or any corresponding law for the time being in force.

Amendment of Adoption Act, 1958

54. Extension of scope of Adoption Rules.—(1) Section 9 of the Adoption Act, 1958 (which enables Adoption Rules within the meaning of that Act to be made with respect to matters arising out of Part I thereof) shall have effect as if—

(a) in subsection (3) thereof the reference to Part I of that Act included references to sections 34 and 35 thereof (under which the right of a parent, adoption society or local authority to remove an infant from the care and possession of a person who has applied for an adoption order cannot be exercised without the leave of the court) ; and

(b) subsection (5) thereof included applications for the leave of the court under the said sections 34 or the said section 35 among the applications for the hearing and determination of which otherwise than in open court provision may be made by Adoption Rules.

(2) In the application of this section to Scotland, the references to section 9 of the Adoption Act, 1958 and to subsections (3) and (5) thereof shall be construed as references to section 11 of that Act and subsections (2) and (3) thereof, and references to Adoption Rules shall be construed as references to an act of sederunt made in pursuance of the said subsection (2).

NOTES

Adoption Act, 1958, s. 9.—See p. 1043, *post.*

Sections 34, 35.—See pp. 1066, 1067, *post.* These sections are in Part III of that Act.

Rules.—The Adoption (Juvenile Courts) Rules, 1965, S.I. 1965, No. 2072, The Adoption (County Courts) (Amendment) Rules, 1965, S.I. 1965, No. 2070 amend the existing rules in accordance with this extension of their scope. The rules, as amended, are printed at pp. 1109, *et seq.*, *post.* As regards the High Court see the Adoption (High Court) Rules, 1971, p. 1156, *post.*

55. Emigration with consent of Secretary of State.—Section 52 of the Adoption Act, 1958 (which, subject to exceptions, requires the authority of a provisional adoption order for the taking or sending abroad for adoption of infants who are British subjects) shall not apply in the case of any infant emigrating under the authority of the Secretary of State given under section 17 of the Children Act, 1948 or section 23 of the Social Work (Scotland) Act, 1968.

NOTES

This section is printed as amended by the Social Work (Scotland) Act, 1968, ss. 95, 97, 98, and Sched. VIII and the Children and Young Persons Act, 1969, s. 72 (4) and Sched. VI.

Adoption Act, 1958, s. 52.—See p. 1077, *post.*

Children Act, 1948, s. 17.—See p. 898, *post.*

Miscellaneous

56. Prosecution of offences under Part I or Part II of principal Act.—(1) Without prejudice to section 98 of the principal Act (which authorises a local education authority to institute proceedings for an offence under Part I or Part II of that Act) any such proceedings may be instituted by the council of a county or county borough, whether or not the council are the local education authority, and may, where the council are the local education authority, be instituted by them otherwise than in that capacity.

(2) So much of subsection (5) of section 85 of the Local Government Act, 1933 and subsection (1) of section 3 of the Local Authority Social Services Act, 1970 as restricts the matters that may be referred to or dealt with by committees established under the said section 85 and section 2 of the said Act of 1970 respectively shall not apply in relation to functions exercisable by a council in pursuance of this section.

NOTES

This section is printed as amended by the Local Authority Social Services Act, 1970.

Definition.—For " local education authority ", see note to s. 43, p. 109, *ante.*

Children and Young Persons Act, 1933, s. 98.—See p. 76, *ante.*

Local Government Act, 1933, s. 85 (5).—See 19 Halsbury's Statutes 3rd Edn., 445.

Local Authority Social Services Act, 1970.—See p. 927, *post.*

" **Principal Act.**"—*I.e.*, the Children and Young Persons Act, 1933, see s. 63 (1), p. 117, *post.*

57. Newspaper and broadcast reports of proceedings involving children and young persons.—(1) In section 39 of the principal Act and in section 46 of the principal Scottish Act (which empower a court to prohibit the publication in newspapers of pictures or matter leading to the identification of children and young persons concerned in certain proceedings) the words " which arise out of any offence against, or any conduct contrary to, decency or morality " shall be omitted and for the word " against " in paragraph (a) there shall be substituted the words " by or against ".

(2) Section 49 of the principal Act and section 54 of the principal Scottish Act (which restrict newspaper reports of proceedings in juvenile courts) shall, with the necessary modifications, apply in relation to any proceedings on appeal from a juvenile court (including an appeal by case stated or, in Scotland, stated case) as they apply in relation to proceedings in a juvenile court.

(3) The said sections 39 and 49 shall extend to Scotland and the said sections 46 and 54 shall extend to England and Wales, but—

(a) references to a court in the said sections 39 and 49 shall not include a court in Scotland; and

(b) references to a court in the said sections 46 and 54 shall not include a court in England or Wales.

(4) The said sections 39 and 49 and the said sections 46 and 54 shall, with the necessary modifications, apply in relation to sound and television broadcasts as they apply in relation to newspapers.

NOTES

Amendments: Social Work (Scotland) Act, 1968.—From April 15, 1971, in sub-s. (2) any reference to a juvenile court shall, in relation to Scotland, be construed as a reference to the sheriff sitting summarily in respect of an offence by a child (Social Work (Scotland) Act, 1968, ss. 95, 97, 98 and Sched. VIII and S.I. 1971 No. 184).

Children and Young Persons Act, 1933, ss. 39, 49.—See pp. 46, 47, *ante.*

" Principal Act."—*I.e.*, the Children and Young Persons Act, 1933, see s. 63 (1), p. 117, *post.*

" Proceedings on appeal from a juvenile court." This provision cures an anomaly which existed under s. 49 of the principal Act, p. 56, *ante.*

Scotland.—As to prohibition of publication of proceedings in Scotland see s. 58 of the Social Work (Scotland) Act, 1968, p. 233, *post*, which by s. 97, *ibid.*, applies to England and Wales.

58. Powers of local authority to visit and assist persons formerly in their care.—Where a person was at or after the time when he attained the age of seventeen in the care of a local authority under the Children Act, 1948, the principal Act or the principal Scottish Act, or by virtue of an order under the Matrimonial Proceedings (Children) Act, 1958 or the Matrimonial Proceedings (Magistrates' Courts) Act, 1960, but has ceased to be in their care, then, while he is under the age of twenty-one, the local authority, if so requested by him, may cause him to be visited, advised and befriended and, in exceptional circumstances, to be given financial assistance.

NOTES

This section is repealed as to Scotland only by the Social Work (Scotland) Act, 1968, ss. 95 (2), 98, and Sched. IX.

General note.—This is a new power conferred on local authorities. It is a power to be exercised only on the request of the person concerned.

In the care of a local authority under the Children Act, 1948.—See s. 1, *ibid.*, p. 880, *post*, and as to financial assistance towards expenses of person over compulsory school age s. 20, *ibid.*, p. 900, *post*, as amended by this Act, and the Act of 1969.

Matrimonial Proceedings (Children) Act, 1958.—This Act was repealed and consolidated in the Matrimonial Causes Act, 1965. See s. 36, *ibid.*, p. 1240, *post*.

Matrimonial Proceedings (Magistrates Courts) Act, 1960.—See 17 Halsbury's Statutes, 3rd Edn., 323.

" Principal Act."—*I.e.*, the Children and Young Persons Act, 1933, see s. 63 (1), p. 117, *post*.

London Government Act, 1963, Transfers.—See note to s. 1 of the Children Act, 1948, p. 880, *ante*.

59. Adjustment between local authorities of expenses of maintaining persons in remand homes.—[*Repealed by the Children and Young Persons Act*, 1969, s. 72 (4) *and Sched. VI.*]

Supplementary provisions

60. Expenses.—There shall be paid out of moneys provided by Parliament any expenses incurred by the Secretary of State under this Act and any increase attributable to this Act in the moneys so payable under any other enactment.

61. Effect of Act on general grants in England and Wales.—(1) [*Repealed by the Children and Young Persons Act*, 1969, s. 72 (4) *and Sched. VI.*]

62. Effect of Act on general grants in Scotland.—(1) Any expenditure incurred by virtue of this Act by the council of a county or of a large burgh shall be relevant expenditure for the purposes of sections 2 and 3 of the Local Government and Miscellaneous Financial Provisions (Scotland) Act, 1958 (which relate to general grants) whether or not it is expenditure specified in Schedule 1 to that Act.

(2) The Secretary of State shall have power, by an order made in the like manner and subject to the like provisions as a general grant order, to vary the provisions of any general grant order made before the commencement of this Act for a grant period ending after the commencement of this Act.

(3) Any order made by virtue of this section may be made for all or any of the years comprised in the said grant period, as may be specified in the order, and in respect of the year or years so specified shall increase the annual aggregate amount of the general grants to such extent as may appear to the Secretary of State to be appropriate having regard to any additional expenditure incurred or likely to be incurred by councils of counties or of large burghs in consequence of the passing of this Act.

(4) The provisions of this section shall have effect without prejudice to the exercise of any power conferred by section 2 (2) of the Local Government and Miscellaneous Financial Provisions (Scotland) Act, 1958 (which confers power to vary general grant orders in consequence of unforeseen increases in the level of prices, costs or remuneration).

(5) In this section the expressions " general grant order " and " grant period " have the meanings respectively assigned to them by subsection (5) and subsection (6) of section 1 of the Local Government and Miscellaneous Financial Provisions (Scotland) Act, 1958.

(6) This section extends to Scotland only.

63. Interpretation.—(1) In this Act " the principal Act " means the Children and Young Persons Act, 1933 and " the principal Scottish Act " means the Children and Young Persons (Scotland) Act, 1937.

(2) References in this Act to any enactment are references thereto as amended and include references thereto as applied, by any other enactment including, except where the context otherwise requires, any enactment contained in this Act.

64. Amendments, transitional provisions, and repeals.—[*Not printed.*]

65. Citation, construction, commencement and extent.—(1) This Act may be cited as the Children and Young Persons Act, 1963.

(2) This Act and the Children and Young Persons Acts, 1933 to 1956 may be cited as the Children and Young Persons Acts, 1933 to 1963, and this Act and the Children and Young Persons (Scotland) Acts, 1937 and 1956 may be cited as the Children and Young Persons (Scotland) Acts, 1937 to 1963.

(3) This Act, except in so far as it amends any Act not construed as one with the principal Act or the principal Scottish Act, shall be construed, in its application to England and Wales, as one with the principal Act and, in its application to Scotland, as one with the principal Scottish Act.

(4) The following provisions of this Act do not extend to Scotland, that is to say, Part I except sections 1, 10 and 32, sections 56 and 61, and Schedules 1 and 2 and Schedule 4 except paragraph 3.

(5) Section 42 of this Act, paragraphs 7, 8 and 50 of Schedule 3, and so much of Schedule 5 as relates to section 25 and section 26 of the principal Act, extend to Northern Ireland.

(6) This Act shall come into operation on such day as the Secretary of State may by order made by statutory instrument appoint, and different days may be so appointed for different purposes; and any reference in any provision of this Act to the commencement of this Act shall be construed as a reference to the time at which that provision comes into operation.

NOTES

This section is printed as amended by the Children and Young Persons Act, 1969, s. 72 (4), Sched. VI.

"Come into operation": Part II.—See the Children and Young Persons Act, 1963 (Commencement No. 3) Order, 1968, p. 500, *post.*

SCHEDULES

SCHEDULE 1

SUPERVISION ORDERS

NOTE

[This Schedule was repealed by the Children and Young Persons Act, 1969, s. 72 (4) and Sched. VI.   By virtue of Sched. IV, para. 12, *ibid.*, in relation to supervision orders made before January 1, 1971 this Schedule has effect as if the Act of 1969 had not been passed.]

Contents and duration of supervision orders

1. *Subject to the provisions of this Schedule, a supervision order may contain such provisions as the court, having regard to the particular circumstances of the case, considers necessary for effecting the purposes of the order.*

2. *A supervision order shall cease to have effect when the person placed under supervision attains the age of eighteen.*

Discharge and amendment

3.—(1) *A juvenile court may, upon the application of the person under supervision, or of the person under whose supervision he is, discharge the supervision order.*

(2) *Without prejudice to its power under the preceding sub-paragraph, where an order is in force committing the person under supervision to the care of a fit person, the juvenile court may discharge the supervision order on the application of that person or, where the other order is revoked, without any application.*

NOTE

" **Discharge the supervision order.**"—Paragraph 3 (1) read in conjunction with s. 5 (1) (a), now repealed makes it clear that only the court named in the order has jurisdiction to discharge it.

4.—(1) *Subject to sub-paragraph (2) of this paragraph, if a juvenile court is satisfied that a person under supervision proposes to change, or has changed, his residence to another petty sessions area, the court may, and if an application in that behalf is made by the person under whose supervision he is shall, by order amend the supervision order by substituting for the petty sessions area named therein (or, as the case may be, by inserting therein) the petty sessions area where the person under supervision proposes to reside or is residing.*

(2) *If the supervision order contains requirements which, in the opinion of the court, cannot be complied with unless the person under supervision continues to reside in the same petty sessions area, the court shall not amend the order as aforesaid, unless, in accordance with the following provisions of this Schedule, it cancels those requirements or substitutes therefor other requirements which can be so complied with.*

NOTE

" **Proposes to change, or has changed, his residence.**"—See r. 39 of the Probation Rules, 1965, p. 526, *post*.   For provisions as to change of residence to Scotland, see s. 73 of the Social Work (Scotland) Act, 1968.   Supervision order in that section has the meaning (*inter alia*) assigned to it by s. 5 of the 1963 Act, (s. 94, *ibid.*).

5.—(1) *Subject to sub-paragraph (2) of this paragraph, a juvenile court may, on the application of any person, by order amend a supervision order—*

(a) *by substituting for the supervision of a probation officer supervision by a person appointed for the purpose by the court; or*

(b) *by substituting for the supervision of a person appointed for the purpose by the court supervision by some other person so appointed or supervision by a probation officer; or*

(c) *by cancelling any of the requirements of the order or by inserting therein (either in addition to or in substitution for any such requirement) any requirement which could be included in the order if it were then being made by the court.*

(2) *A court shall not amend a supervision order under this paragraph—*

(a) *by reducing the period of supervision specified in the order, or by extending that period beyond the end of three years from the date of the original order; or*

(b) *by inserting therein a requirement that the person under supervision shall submit to treatment for his mental condition unless the amending order is made within three months after the date of the original order.*

6.—(1) *Where an application for the discharge or amendment of a supervision order made in respect of any person is made by the person under whose supervision he is, the applicant may, for the purposes of the application, bring the person under supervision before the court.*

(2) *Where a court proposes to amend a supervision order by imposing a requirement that the person under supervision shall reside in an institution or submit to treatment for his mental condition the court shall summon the person under supervision to appear before the court.*

Requirements as to residence and treatment

7. *A supervision order may not contain any requirement as to the place of residence of the person placed under supervision or as to treatment for his mental condition unless he either is under the age of fourteen or consents to the requirement.*

8. *The period for which a person may be required by a supervision order to reside in an approved probation hostel, an approved probation home or any other institution or to submit to treatment for his mental condition shall not exceed twelve months.*

9. *A supervision order requiring the person under supervision to submit to treatment for his mental condition shall specify one of the following as the treatment required, that is to say—*

(a) *treatment as a resident patient in a hospital or mental nursing home within the meaning of the Mental Health Act, 1959, but not in a special hospital within the meaning of that Act;*

(b) *treatment as a non-resident patient at an institution or place specified in the order; or*

(c) *treatment by or under the direction of a fully registered medical practitioner specified in the order.*

10. *Where a medical practitioner by whom or under whose direction a person (in this paragraph referred to as "the patient") is being treated for his mental condition in pursuance to any requirement of a supervision order is of opinion—*

(a) *that the treatment should be continued beyond the period specified in that behalf in the order; or*

(b) *that the patient needs different treatment; or*

(c) *that the patient is not susceptible to treatment; or*

(d) *that the patient does not require further treatment;*

or where the practitioner is for any reason unwilling to continue to treat or direct the treatment of the patient, he shall make a report in writing to that effect to the person under whose supervision the patient is and that person shall apply to a juvenile court for the variation or cancellation of the requirement.

Selection of probation officers

11. *The probation officer under whose supervision a person is to be placed shall be selected under arrangements made by the probation committee.*

12. *If the probation officer so selected dies or is unable for any reason to carry out his duties, or if the case committee dealing with the case think it desirable that another person should take his place, another probation officer shall be selected in like manner.*

13. [*Repealed as to England and Wales by the Criminal Justice Act, 1967, ss. 55, 103 and Sched. VII.*]

Notification of orders

14. *The court by which a supervision order is made or amended shall forthwith give or send a copy of its order—*

    (a) *to the person under supervision; and*
    (b) *to the person under whose supervision he is placed; and*
    (c) *where the person under supervision is required to reside in an institution, to the person in charge of the institution; and*
    (d) *where the person under supervision is required to reside in an institution which is neither an approved probation hostel or home or a mental nursing home or hospital within the meaning of the Mental Health Act, 1959 in which he is required to reside for the purpose of treatment as a resident patient, to the Secretary of State; and*
    (e) *where the petty sessions area named in the order is not the petty sessions area for which the court acts, to the clerk to the justices for the petty sessions area named in the order;*

and, in the case mentioned in sub-paragraph (e) of this paragraph, shall also send to the clerk to the said justices such documents and information relating to the case as the court considers likely to be of assistance to them.

NOTES

Supervision order.—See note to s. 4, p. 93, *ante.*

" Place of residence."—See note " Residence " at p. 162, *post.*

" Age."—See note to s. 16, p. 93, *ante.*

" Approved probation home, hostel."—See Criminal Justice Act, 1948, s. 46, p. 292, *post.*

" Shall not exceed twelve months."—A supervision order containing a requirement to reside in an approved probation hostel or home need no longer be reviewed after six months. Both the Ingleby Committee and the Morison Committee on the Probation Service (Cmd. 1800) recommended that the requirement for six-monthly review should be abolished, but the opportunity has been taken to abolish it for supervision orders only.

" Fully registered medical practitioner."—See note to s. 26, p. 97, *ante.*

" Juvenile court."—See note to s. 1, p. 91, *ante.*

Mental Health Act, 1959.—For meaning of "hospital, mental nursing home, special hospital" see s. 147, *ibid.*, 25 Halsbury's Statutes (3rd Edn.) p. 162.

SCHEDULE 2

CONSTITUTION OF JUVENILE COURTS

PART I

OUTSIDE METROPOLITAN AREA

Juvenile court panels

1. The following provisions of this Part of this Schedule shall have effect as respect any area outside the [inner London area] and the City of London.

NOTES

The words in square brackets were substituted by the Administration of Justice Act, 1964, ss. 12, 39 and Sched. 3 (20 Halsbury's Statutes (3rd Edn.) 664, 678, 683).

Age of justices.—The age limit for appointment has been fixed at 65, see the Juvenile Courts (Constitution) Rules, 1954, pp. 472 *et seq., post.*

The Children and Young Persons Act, 1969, s. 61, provides that the Lord Chancellor (and not the justices in a petty session area) may by rules provide for the appointment of juvenile court panels. No such rules have yet been made.

2. A justice shall not be qualified to sit as a member of a juvenile court unless he is a member of a juvenile court panel, that is to say, a panel of justices specially qualified to deal with juvenile cases.

3. Subject to the following provisions of this Part of this Schedule, a juvenile court panel shall be formed for every petty sessions area.

Combined juvenile court panels

4. A magistrates' courts committee may make recommendations to the Secretary of State—

(a) for the formation of a combined juvenile court panel for two or more petty sessions areas, or

(b) for the dissolution of any such combined juvenile court panel.

if the committee's area comprises at least one of the petty sessions areas concerned.

5. It shall be the duty of the magistrates' courts committee for any area, if directed to do so by the Secretary of State, to review the functioning of juvenile courts in their area and on completion of the review to submit to the Secretary of State either a report making such recommendations as are mentioned in paragraph 4 of this Schedule or a report giving reasons for making no such recommendations.

6. Subject to the provisions of this Schedule—

(a) where a magistrates' courts committee make such recommendations to the Secretary of State, he may make an order giving effect to them subject to any modifications he thinks fit ; and

(b) where a magistrates' courts committee fail to comply within six months with a direction of the Secretary of State under the preceding paragraph, or the Secretary of State is dissatisfied with the report submitted in pursuance of such a direction, he may make such order as he thinks fit for the purposes mentioned in paragraph 4 of this Schedule.

NOTE

Rules.—For the Juvenile Courts (Constitution) Rules 1954 made under ss. 14, 15 of the Justices of the Peace Act, 1949 (18 Halsbury's Statutes, 3rd Edn., 20, 21 see p. 472, *post*.

Effect of order establishing combined panel

7. Where a combined juvenile court panel is formed for any petty sessions areas any justice who is a member of the panel may exercise in relation to each of the areas any jurisdiction exercisable by him as a member of a juvenile court.

Restrictions on formation of combined panels

8. No order under this Schedule shall provide for the formation of a combined juvenile court panel for an area which includes—

(a) a county or part of a county and the whole or part of another county ; or

(b) two county boroughs.

9. An order under this Schedule providing for the formation of a combined juvenile court panel for an area which comprises a borough having a separate magistrates' courts committee shall not be made except with the consent of every magistrates' courts committee the whole or part of whose area is included in the area for which the combined panel is formed.

Consultations and notices

10. A magistrates' courts committee, before submitting recommendations for an order under this Schedule, shall consult and, when submitting any such recommendations, shall give notice to—

   (a) the justices acting for any petty sessions area concerned which is within the committee's area (except where the committee's area is a borough) ; and
   (b) any other magistrates' courts committee the whole or part of whose area is concerned ;

and shall also consult the said justices before commenting on any recommendations on which they are consulted under this paragraph by another magistrates' courts committee.

11. Where the Secretary of State proposes to make an order under this Schedule in a case where either no recommendations have been made to him or the proposed order departs from the recommendations made to him, he shall send a copy of the proposed order to the magistrates' courts committee for any area the whole or part of which is concerned and to the justices acting for any petty sessions area concerned.

12. Where notice of recommendations or a copy of a proposed order is required to be sent under the preceding paragraphs to any justices or committee, the Secretary of State shall, before making an order, consider any representations made to him by the justices or committee, or by any juvenile court panel concerned, within one month from the time the notice was given or the copy of the proposed order was sent.

PART II

METROPOLITAN AREA

13. The following provisions of this Part of this Schedule shall have effect as respects the [inner London Area] and the City of London (in this Part of this Schedule referred to as the metropolitan area).

14. Juvenile courts shall be constituted for the whole of the metropolitan area but shall sit for such divisions and in such places as the Secretary of State may by order specify, without prejudice, however, to their jurisdiction with respect to the whole area.

15. Subject to the following provisions of this Schedule—

   (a) each juvenile court shall consist of a chairman and two other members and shall have both a man and a woman among its members ;
   (b) the chairman shall be a person nominated by the [Lord Chancellor] to act as chairman of juvenile courts for the metropolitan area and shall be either a metropolitan stipendiary magistrate or a [lay justice for the inner London area] selected, in such manner as may be provided by an order of the [Lord Chancellor] from a panel of such [lay justices] from time to time nominated by him ; and
   (c) the other members shall be [lay justices] so selected from that panel.

NOTE

As to special powers of metropolitan juvenile courts, see s. 48 (5) of the Children and Young Persons Act, 1933, p. 54, ante.

16. If at any time, by reason of illness or other emergency, no person nominated under paragraph 15 (b) of this Schedule is available to act as chairman of a juvenile court, any metropolitan stipendiary magistrate or, with the consent of the [Lord Chancellor], any lay justice selected as aforesaid from the said panel, may act temporarily as chairman.

17. Where it appears to the chairman that a juvenile court cannot, without adjournment, be fully constituted, and that an adjournment would not be in the interests of justice, the chairman may sit with one other member (whether a man or a woman) or, if a metropolitan stipendiary magistrate, may sit alone.

18. The [Lord Chancellor], in nominating any persons under this Part of this Schedule, shall have regard to the previous experience of the persons available and their special qualifications for dealing with juvenile cases; and every such nomination shall be for a specified period and shall be revocable by the [Lord Chancellor].

19. [*This paragraph was repealed by the Administration of Justice Act, 1964, s. 41 and Schedule 5.*]

NOTES

The words in square brackets were substituted by the Administration of Justice Act, 1964, ss. 12, 39 and Sched. 3.

May by order specify.—The Juvenile Courts (London) Order, 1965, S.I. 1965 No. 584 has been made under this Schedule.

Regulations.—For power to make rules affecting the provisions of paras. 15–18 see s. 61 (4) Children and Young Persons Act, 1969.

PART III

GENERAL

20. An order of the Secretary of State under this Schedule shall be made by statutory instrument and may be revoked or varied by a subsequent order thereunder.

21. Any such order may contain supplementary, incidental and consequential provisions.

NOTE

Magistrates Courts Act, 1952; saving for juvenile courts.—See note to s. 45, p. 51, *ante*.

SCHEDULE 3

MINOR AND CONSEQUENTIAL AMENDMENTS

NOTE

Paragraphs 10, 16 to 23, 25 to 27, 33 to 36, 44, 46, 48 and 49 and in para. 50 the words "Special Reception Centre or other" and "'Special Reception Centre' has the same meaning as in the Children and Young Persons Act, 1933, and", are repealed by the Children and Young Persons Act, 1969, s. 72 (4) and Sched. VI. As regards the remaining paragraphs the statutes are printed as amended.

The principal Act

1–3. [*Not printed.*]

4. For subsection (3) of section 18 there shall be substituted the following subsection:—

" (3) Nothing in this section or in any byelaw made under this section, shall prevent a child from taking part in a performance—

    (a) under the authority of a licence granted under this Part of this Act;
      or

(b) in a case where by virtue of section 37 (3) of the Children and Young Persons Act, 1963 no licence under that section is required for him to take part in the performance."

5. In section 23, for the words " public performance " there shall be substituted the words " performance to which section 37 of the Children and Young Persons Act, 1963 applies and ".

6.—(1) In subsection (2) of section 24 for the words " petty sessional court " there shall be substituted the words " local authority."

(2) In subsection (4) of that section for the word " court ", in both places where it occurs, there shall be substituted the word " authority ".

7. In the proviso to section 25 (1), for the words " Great Britain and Ireland " there shall be substituted the words " the United Kingdom ".

8. In section 26 (1), the words " or in default of payment of such a fine " shall be omitted.

9. In section 28 (1) for the words " an entertainment or performance " there shall be substituted the words " a performance ".

10. In section 29 (3), for the words " The said provisions " there shall be substituted the words " The provisions of this Part of this Act relating to employment ".

11–51. [Not printed.]

SCHEDULE 4

TRANSITIONAL PROVISIONS

NOTE

The provisions of this Schedule are now considered obsolete and the text is therefore not reprinted.

Section 64   ## SCHEDULE 5

ENACTMENTS REPEALED

[Effect is given to the repeals in the sections as printed.]

CHILDREN AND YOUNG PERSONS ACT, 1969

[1969 c. 54]

ARRANGEMENT OF SECTIONS

PART I

CARE AND OTHER TREATMENT OF JUVENILES THROUGH COURT PROCEEDINGS

Care of children and young persons through juvenile courts

*An Act to amend the law relating to children and young persons; and for
purposes connected therewith.*   [*22nd October* 1969]

INTRODUCTORY NOTE

The Act is based largely upon proposals set out in the White Papers "The Child,
the Family, and the Young Offender " (Command 2742) and "Children in Trouble"
(Command 3601).   The first of the White Papers published in August 1965 invited discussion "of possible measures to support the family, forestall and reduce
delinquency and revise the law and practice relating to young offenders in England
and Wales".   One major result of the discussion was that the proposals to change
the system of courts for dealing with offenders both over and under 17 were not
implemented.   In July 1968 and after the publication of "Children in Trouble" the
"Report of the Committee on Local Authority and Allied Personal Social Services"
(Command 3703–The Seebohm Report) was published.   The terms of reference of
that Committee were clearly such as to make the report complementary to the provisions enacted, and its recommendations are now enacted in the Local Authority
Social Services Act, 1970.

Section 73 (2) of the Act provides that it shall come into force "on such day as the
Secretary of State may by order appoint and different days may be appointed for
different provision, or for different provisions so far as they apply to such cases only
as may be specified in the order".   A number of provisions enable the Secretary of
State to make orders or give directions and by s. 69 (3) such orders or directions may
be varied or revoked.   Additionally any order or regulation under the Act may make
different provisions for different circumstances, provide for exemptions and certain
incidental and supplemental provisions.   Further s. 73 (3) empowers the Secretary
of State to make such transitional provisions as he considers appropriate including
adaptations of provisions of the Act brought into force by the order or of any other
provisions then in force.   It will be seen that there is a high degree of flexibility
which enables the Act to be phased into operation both in relation to the various
sections and by reference to the age of children and young persons. The new system of
community homes (ss. 35 to 50) is in the planning stage and existing facilities will
have to be used until each regional plan is finally approved and the necessary staff
recruited and the building programme completed.

The Social Work (Scotland) Act, 1968, has now been brought into force.   The

Children and Young Persons Act, 1969 (Commencement No. 1 Order), 1969, S.I. 1969 No. 1552, and the other commencement orders printed at p. 561, *post*, bring into operation the main provisions and enable a start to be made on the system of community homes.   Part I of the Act deals with the new style "Care Proceedings" and related provisions while Part II deals with community homes and amendments to the Children Acts, 1948 and 1958.

Section 1.—Supersedes s. 2 of the Children and Young Persons Act, 1963, and substitutes a new form of care proceedings in juvenile courts. This now includes "Truancy" cases and children and young persons who are found guilty of offences. "Beyond control" proceedings come within the section but there is a reversion to the Act of 1933 in that there is a double test; it must be shown that the juvenile is beyond control and that he is in need of care or control which he is unlikely to receive unless the court makes an order. Under this section truancy cases must be brought by a local education authority. Legal aid will be granted by the court under the Criminal Justice Act, 1967 and not under the Legal Aid and Advice Act, 1949.

Section 2.—Substantially re-enacts existing law and provides for the issue of a summons or warrant. It clarifies the law by providing for a witness summons or warrant in care proceedings, and provision is made for the court acting for the area where the relevant infant resides to deal with care proceedings.

Section 3.—Imports the safeguards of the criminal law in "offence condition" care proceedings and allows compensation to be awarded.

Section 4.—The consequences of a criminal act by a child are altered by this section but the age of criminal responsibility is not affected.

Section 5.—Restricts the prosecution of young offenders and lends statutory emphasis to informal action outside the courts, *e.g.* police caution. Private prosecutions are not permitted.

Section 6.—Abolishes a young person's right to claim trial by jury.

Section 7.—Abolishes the approved school and fit person order, provides for supervision orders in place of probation orders and raises the minimum age for borstal. Presumably the section will be phased in (see s. 34).

Section 8.—The restrictions imposed by s. 5 render this section necessary in order to have full information before considering a prosecution.

Section 9.—Substantially re-enacts existing law. There is a change of emphasis in that a local authority has a *duty* to provide, *e.g.* psychiatric reports if a court so requests.

Section 10.—Restricts the cases in which a court can authorise the names, etc., of juveniles to be reported.

Sections 11 to 19.—Deal with the making and varying of supervision orders and related provisions; the maximum period of a "condition of residence" is 90 days; and the Act contemplates that a longer period required in say a hostel will be under a care order. Regional planning committees are charged with the duty of making arrangements for facilities for supervisors. Normally a child will be supervised by a local authority. Supervisors will determine if any requirements of the order will be carried out or not.

Sections 20 to 22.—Deal with care orders and allow for appeal against the refusal to discharge an interim order, and also an application to the high court for discharge of an interim order. An application to discharge a care order may not be made less than three months after a previous application.

Section 23.—Replaces s. 27 of the Criminal Justice Act, 1948, in so far as it deals with the remand of children and young persons and provides for remands to be to the care of a local authority.

Section 24.—Provides for the appointment of a visitor to advise and befriend children in care who have had little or no communication with their parents.

Section 25 and 26.—Deal with transfers between England or Wales and Ireland or the Channel Islands or the Isle of Man.

Section 27.—Takes account of changes made by the Act and provides a new definition of a child in care for the purposes of Part II of the Children Act, 1948.

Section 28.—Replaces s. 67 of the Children and Young Persons Act, 1933, taking account of the changes made by the Act.

Section 29.—Replaces s. 22 of the Children and Young Persons Act, 1963, taking account of the changes made by the Act.

Section 30.—Provides for the Secretary of State to direct detention by a local authority in a community home of young offenders convicted of grave crime.

Section 31.—Replaces the existing provision for removal from approved school to borstal.

Section 32.—Substantially re-enacts existing law relating to the detention of absentees.

Section 33.—Provides for legal aid in care proceedings and others to be under the Criminal Justice Act, 1967, and Sched. I makes the necessary modifications and provides for a parent's income to be considered as part of the defendant's for the purposes of a contribution order.

Section 34.—Empowers the Secretary of State to specify different ages for the purposes of Part I of the Act.

Sections 35 to 50.—Are concerned with the establishment of a comprehensive system of community homes for the accommodation and treatment of children in the care of local authorities in England and Wales. The Act provides for the making of plans by local authorities on a regional basis to meet the needs of their regions as a whole for the provision of community homes of various types, affording residential accommodation suitable to children in care whose ages may differ widely and the possibility of the joint management by a local authority and a voluntary organisation of a voluntary home which caters for children in local authority care. The sections provide for the powers and duties of local authorities and require a local authority to give effect to so much of the regional plan as contemplates provisions of homes by them, details the manners in which local authorities may accommodate children in their care, and regulates the conduct of community homes, and finally makes a transitional provision in relation to the discontinuance of existing establishments.

Sections 51 to 59.—Amend the Children Act, 1958, and the Adoption Act, 1958, and provide a new definition of "foster child".

Section 60.—Amends the Extradition Act, 1870, and the Fugitive Offenders Act, 1967.

Section 61.—Makes provision for the Lord Chancellor to make rules affecting juvenile court panels and their composition.

Section 62.—Provides a uniform basis for the making of contribution orders in respect of children and young persons committed to the care of a local authority by a care order.

Section 63.—Following the recommendations of the Adams Committee on civil judicial statistics, provides for the clerk to be responsible for providing such particulars with respect to the proceedings of a juvenile court as the Secretary of State may require, and requires local authorities and voluntary organisations to make returns of certain information.

Schedule 1.—Modifies Part IV of the Criminal Justice Act, 1967.

Schedule 2.—Deals with the composition of children's regional planning committees.

Schedule 3.—Relates to approved schools and other institutions.

Schedule 4.—Contains transitional provisions and savings.

Schedules 5 and 6.—Make substantial alterations in the various Acts there referred to.

Schedule 7.—Reprints the Children Act, 1958, ss. 1 to 6 and s. 14 as amended by this Act.

PART I

CARE AND OTHER TREATMENT OF JUVENILES THROUGH COURT PROCEEDINGS

NOTE

The majority of the provisions of Part I are in force, although ss. 4 and 5 have not yet been brought into force. The Government have announced that they do not intend to bring s. 5 into force, and that the minimum age for prosecution will not be raised above the age of 12 in the life of the present Government. The withdrawal of the powers to make attendance centre and detention centre orders, and the raising of the minimum age for borstal are all matters which will largely depend on the success of regional plans in providing alternative methods of treatment. The transitional modifications (see S.I. 1970 No. 1882, p. 624, *post*) as to age affect the operation of Part I of the Act and will need to be borne in mind in relation to children who are of prosecutable age.

Care of children and young persons through juvenile courts

1. Care proceedings in juvenile courts.—(1) Any local authority, constable or authorised person who reasonably believes that there are grounds for making an order under this section in respect of a child or young person may, subject to section 2 (3) and (8) of this Act, bring him before a juvenile court.

(2) If the court before which a child or young person is brought under this section is of opinion that any of the following conditions is satisfied with respect to him, that is to say—

    (a) his proper development is being avoidably prevented or neglected or his health is being avoidably impaired or neglected or he is being ill-treated; or

    (b) it is probable that the condition set out in the preceding paragraph will be satisfied in his case, having regard to the fact that the court or another court has found that that condition is or was satisfied in the case of another child or young person who is or was a member of the household to which he belongs; or

    (c) he is exposed to moral danger; or

    (d) he is beyond the control of his parent or guardian; or

    (e) he is of compulsory school age within the meaning of the Education Act 1944, and is not receiving efficient full-time education suitable to his age, ability and aptitude; or

    (f) he is guilty of an offence, excluding homicide,

and also that he is in need of care or control which he is unlikely to receive unless the court makes an order under this section in respect of him, then, subject to the following provisions of this section and sections 2 and 3 of this Act, the court may if it thinks fit make such an order.

(3) The order which a court may make under this section in respect of a child or young person is—

    (a) an order requiring his parent or guardian to enter into a recognisance to take proper care of him and exercise proper control over him; or

    (b) a supervision order; or

    (c) a care order (other than an interim order); or

    (d) a hospital order within the meaning of Part V of the Mental Health Act, 1959; or

    (e) a guardianship order within the meaning of that Act.

(4) In any proceedings under this section the court may make orders in pursuance of paragraphs (c) and (d) of the preceding subsection but subject to that shall not make more than one of the orders mentioned in the preceding subsection, without prejudice to any power to make a further order

in subsequent proceedings of any description; and if in proceedings under this section the court makes one of those orders and an order so mentioned is already in force in respect of the child or young person in question, the court may discharge the earlier order unless it is a hospital or guardianship order.

(5) An order under this section shall not be made in respect of a child or young person—

(a) in pursuance of paragraph (a) of subsection (3) of this section unless the parent or guardian in question consents;

(b) in pursuance of paragraph (d) or (e) of that subsection unless the conditions which, under section 60 of the said Act of 1959, are required to be satisfied for the making of a hospital or guardianship order in respect of a person convicted as mentioned in that section are satisfied in his case so far as they are applicable;

(c) if he has attained the age of sixteen and is or has been married.

(6) In this section "authorised person" means a person authorised by order of the Secretary of State to bring proceedings in pursuance of this section and any officer of a society which is so authorised, and in sections 2 and 3 of this Act "care proceedings" means proceedings in pursuance of this section and "relevant infant" means the child or young person in respect of whom such proceedings are brought or proposed to be brought.

NOTES

General note.—This section with certain modifications re-enacts previous law. Since the Children and Young Persons Act, 1963, when the age of criminal responsibility was raised to ten it has been possible to deal with an under ten offender as being in need of care, protection or control. Read together with s. 4 (restrictions on prosecution of under fourteens) the section gives effect to the White Paper "Children in Trouble" and brings the offender who is under the minimum age for prosecution but above the age of criminal responsibility within the ambit of civil proceedings. It should be remembered that both children *and* young persons may be dealt with in care proceedings for an offence despite the fact that s. 5 has not been brought into force. With the inclusion of para. (e) of sub-s. 2 it is now possible to make a Hospital or Guardianship Order in truancy cases. The conditions in s. 2 (2) (c), (d) and (e) of the Children and Young Persons Act, 1963, are not re-enacted and situations in which a child or young person is the victim of a first schedule offence may well be covered by paras. (a) and (c) of sub-s. 2 of s. 1.

Definitions.—"Child", "young person".—See s. 70 (3) p. 214, *post.* See also s. 34, transitional modifications specifying ages. "Care order" see ss. 20 and 22, *post.*

Summons or warrant.—Subsection (4) of s. 2 provides for the issue of a summons or warrant; s. 28 provides for the detention of a child or young person in a place of safety pending appearances before a juvenile court.

"Proper development" (sub-s. (2) (a)).—It is submitted that these words are wide enough to cover mental as well as physical development. This condition and para. (c) replace the previous provisions regarding the commission of an offence mentioned in the First Sched. to the Children and Young Persons Act, 1933.

Difficulty may arise where in fact an offence is alleged to have been committed and is either the subject of a prosecution, or a prosecution is under consideration. Previously when the commission of an offence was alleged it had been the practice to decline to hear care proceedings until the criminal case was dealt with, and the child could be protected by a series of interim orders. Although this presents difficulty in preparing any plans for the child and his parents the interests of a parent charged with an offence must also be protected. A parent must be warned of the danger of self-incrimination and it would be invidious if a criminal court subject to a higher burden of proof were to come to a verdict which was inconsistent with the findings of a juvenile court in civil proceedings. We submit that magistrates should decline to entertain applications which would lead to concurrent jurisdiction in different courts. The operation of the Crown Court Rules, p. 654, *post*, should reduce delays in the hearing of charges against a parent.

If courts hear such applications after a conviction the provisions of s. 11 of the Civil Evidence Act, 1968 may facilitate proof.

"Court ... has found" (sub-s. (2) (b)).—It would seem that sub-s. (2) (b) replaces paras. (c), (d) and (e) of s. 2 (2) of the Children and Young Persons Act, 1963. Section 2 (7) provides that the probability must be assessed on the basis of what is likely to happen if no order is made. The reference to a court must be construed as a reference to a juvenile court, as no other has jurisdiction to make a finding in relation to the conditions in s. 1 (2) (a). The inclusion of the words "is or was" enables the court to make a finding under the paragraph in relation to a child or young person who has died before the proceedings.

An extract from the court register is admissible in any legal proceedings as evidence of the proceedings of the court entered in the register. (Rule 56 of the Magistrates' Court Rules, 1968, S.I. 1969 No. 1920). The Civil Evidence Act, 1968, ss. 11–19, are in force, but Part I, in particular, ss. 2, 3, 6 and 7 is not in force in relation to Magistrates' Courts (Civil Evidence Act, 1968 (Commencement No. 2 Order), 1969, S.I. 1969 No. 1104).

"Member of the household".—The word household has never been defined in the Children and Young Persons Acts.

"Not receiving efficient fulltime education" (Sub-s. (2) (e)).—Section 2 (8) provides that proceedings under s. 1 (2) (e) must be brought by a local education authority and s. 2 (8) (b) provides that if the child is not attending regularly the condition is deemed to be satisfied unless it is proved that he is receiving the education mentioned in the condition.

"Offence excluding homicide".—This includes not only murder, but any offence involving unlawful killing, *e.g.* death by dangerous driving (Road Traffic Acts, 1960, s. 1). Homicide remains a prosecutable offence in relation to a child (s. 4).

Police cautions.—Evidence of a caution being administered is not in itself evidence of the need for care or control. It would be necessary to show the commission of an offence, and this would not be excluded in cases brought under sub-s. (2) (e) (s. 3 (2), *post*).

"Care or control".—The conditions 2 (a) to (f) inclusive are all subject to the second test that he is also in need of care or control. Care includes protection and guidance; and control includes discipline, s. 70 (1), *post*. The wording of the conditions is designed to overcome the criticisms voiced of the "good parent" test in s. 2 of the Children and Young Persons Act, 1963. We submit that the test expresses the same principle, as if a child is receiving proper care and guidance it is unlikely that a court order is needed. The phrase perhaps makes it clear that the test is to be objective and not what would be reasonable in the circumstances of the parents in question.

"Moral danger". See *Bowers* v. *Smith*, [1953] 1 All E. R. 320. In *Re An Infant* (1965), 109 Sol. Jo. 455, the Divisional Court allowed an appeal by Dudley Corporation against the dismissal of an application that a girl was in need of care, protection or control on the grounds that the evidence produced was insufficient to establish a *prima facie* case, and stated that the justices should have heard the parent or parents, after evidence had been given that a man had unlawful sexual intercourse with her when she was eleven years old.

"Beyond control".—This is subject to the double test and is a reversion to the Children and Young Persons Act, 1933, although only a local authority, constable, or authorised person may bring proceedings. The further evidence to satisfy the conditions that he is in need of care or control which he is unlikely to receive unless an order is made would be to show that action outside the Court (*e.g.* reception into care) would be inappropriate or ineffective.

"Parent".—This expression is not defined. It does not include the natural father of an illegitimate child, *Re M. (an infant)*, [1955] 2 Q. B. 479; [1955] 2 All E. R. 911; 119 J. P. 535, but appears to include its natural mother (see *Re G. (an infant)*, [1956] 2 All E. R. 876), under Part I of the Children Act 1958, it includes the person or one of the persons by whom the child is adopted (s. 17, *ibid.*, p. 969, *post*).   As to attendance of parent at court see s. 34 of the Act of 1933, p. 43, *ante.* *Cf.* also the definition of parent in s. 59 Children Act, 1948, p. 923, *post.*

Orders in pursuance of paras. (c) and (d) (sub-s. (4)).—This imposes a new limitation on the court's powers; previously the court could combine a supervision order with a binding over or fit person order.

"The court may discharge" (sub.-s. (4)).—There is no power to discharge a hospital or guardianship order as under the provisions of the Mental Health Act there are no provisions for discharge by a court.   The Act provides for their discharge administratively in accordance with medical advice, and the power to discharge previous orders is new.   See also Sched. 4, para. 1 for power to discharge orders made under the Children and Young Persons Act, 1933.

"Care order."—This replaces an approved school order or fit person order (ss. 7 (5) and (6)).   For definition see s. 20.

Refusal of parental consent to a life-saving blood transfusion or operation for a child.—See Home Office Circular No. 63/1968, March 5, 1968, and Ministry of Health Circular F/P9/IB dated April 14, 1967, pp. 693, 694, *post.*

Married woman, living with husband.—In *Alhaji Mohamed* v. *Knott,* [1969] 1 Q. B. 1; [1968] 2 All E. R. 563; 132 J. P. 349 the appellant, a Nigerian Moslem married in Nigeria to a girl then aged 13 who was also a Nigerian Moslem.   The marriage was valid according to Moslem law of domicil.   It was potentially a poly-gamous marriage.   Justices in a juvenile court held that the marriage was not one recognised in England and that accordingly or alternatively because the girl had no parent or guardian in England she was exposed to moral danger.

On appeal to the Queen's Bench Division against a fit person order it was held that the marriage would be recognised by the English Court as a valid marriage giving the wife the status of wife and in considering whether the wife was in moral danger in living with the appellant the justices had misdirected themselves by ignoring the way of life in which the parties had been brought up, and the fit person order should be revoked.

Per curiam (a) a fit person order may be made in appropriate circumstances in respect of a wife validly married to her husband ([1968] 2 All E. R., p. 567).

(b) in such circumstances as those in the present case, where a wife validly married to a husband by foreign law was under sixteen years of age, a prosecution should not be brought under s. 6 (1) of the Sexual Offences Act, 1956, for sexual intercourse between the parties, nor did the existence in English law of the criminal offence of unlawful sexual intercourse with a person under the age of sixteen render the wife a person who was exposed to moral danger for the purposes of s. 2 (2) (a) of the Children and Young Persons Act, 1963.

With reference to note (a) above it should be noted that sub-s. (5) provides that a person of or over the age of sixteen who is or has been married shall not be brought before or dealt with by a juvenile court under that section.

Unless the parent . . . consents (sub-s. (5)).—Under previous legislation a court could order parents to enter into a recognizance, but would presumably have allowed parents to make representations.   The effectiveness of such an order will depend to a large extent on parental co-operation and to require their consent is consistent with this view.   In any event it is now clear that where a parent refuses to enter into such a recognizance the court must make another order.   For amount and period of recognizance see s. 2 (13).   For recognizance of young person see s. 3 (7).

Family Allowance.—See s. 11 Family Allowances Act, 1965, as to exclusion from family of children subject to a care order.

S. 60—Mental Health Act, 1959.—See p. 445, *post.*

"Authorised person" (sub-s. (6)).—The officers of the N.S.P.C.C. (S.I. 1970 No. 1500, p. 571, *post.*)

"Child or young person" (sub-s. (6)).—These words govern the whole section and a young person may be dealt with under the offence condition, which is not limited to child offenders.

Legal Aid.—See notes to s. 33 and Sched. 1.   Legal aid takes the form of a legal aid order granted by the court as in criminal proceedings.

Evidence.—The proceedings are civil, and therefore the juvenile and his parent are both competent and compellable witnesses. This does not apply to the proof of the "offence condition" (see s. 3 (3), *post*). See s. 26 of the 1963 Act, p. 97, *ante*, as to medical evidence by certificate.

Transitional Provisions.—See Sched. 4, para. 2 (1).

2. Provisions supplementary to s. 1.—(1) If a local authority receive information suggesting that there are grounds for bringing care proceedings in respect of a child or young person who resides or is found in their area, it shall be the duty of the authority to cause enquiries to be made into the case unless they are satisfied that such enquiries are unnecessary.

(2) If it appears to a local authority that there are grounds for bringing care proceedings in respect of a child or young person who resides or is found in their area, it shall be the duty of the authority to exercise their power under the proceding section to bring care proceedings in respect of him unless they are satisfied that it is neither in his interest nor the public interest to do so or that some other person is about to do so or to charge him with an offence.

(3) No care proceedings shall be begun by any person unless that person has given notice of the proceedings to the local authority for the area in which it appears to him that the relevant infant resides or, if it appears to him that the relevant infant does not reside in the area of a local authority, to the local authority for any area in which it appears to him that any circumstances giving rise to the proceedings arose; but the preceding provisions of this subsection shall not apply where the person by whom the notice would fall to be given is the local authority in question.

(4) Without prejudice to any power to issue a summons or warrant apart from this subsection, a justice may issue a summons or warrant for the purpose of securing the attendance of the relevant infant before the court in which care proceedings are brought or proposed to be brought in respect of him; but subsections (3) and (4) of section 47 of the Magistrates' Courts Act, 1952 (which among other things restrict the circumstances in which a warrant may be issued) shall apply with the necessary modifications to a warrant under this subsection as they apply to a warrant under that section and as if in subsection (3) after the word "summons" there were inserted the words "cannot be served or".

(5) Where the relevant infant is arrested in pursuance of a warrant issued by virtue of the preceding subsection and cannot be brought immediately before the court aforesaid, the person in whose custody he is—

(a) may make arrangements for his detention in a place of safety for a period of not more than seventy-two hours from the time of the arrest (and it shall be lawful for him to be detained in pursuance of the arrangements); and

(b) shall within that period, unless within it the relevant infant is brought before the court aforesaid, bring him before a justice;

and the justice shall either make an interim order in respect of him or direct that he be released forthwith.

(6) Section 77 of the Magistrates' Courts Act, 1952 (under which a summons or warrant may be issued to secure the attendance of a witness) shall apply to care proceedings as it applies to the hearing of a complaint.

(7) In determining whether the condition set out in subsection (2) (b) of the preceding section is satisfied in respect of the relevant infant, it shall be assumed that no order under that section is to be made in respect of him.

(8) In relation to the condition set out in subsection (2) (e) of the preceding section the references to a local authority in that section and subsections (1), (2) and (11) (b) of this section shall be construed as references to a local education authority; and in any care proceedings—

   (a) the court shall not entertain an allegation that that condition is satisfied unless the proceedings are brought by a local education authority; and
   (b) the said condition shall be deemed to be satisfied if the relevant infant is of the age mentioned in that condition and it is proved that he—
      (i) is the subject of a school attendance order which is in force under section 37 of the Education Act, 1944 and has not been complied with, or
      (ii) is a registered pupil at a school which he is not attending regularly within the meaning of section 39 of that Act, or
      (iii) is a person whom another person habitually wandering from place to place takes with him,
      unless it is also proved that he is receiving the education mentioned in that condition;

but nothing in paragraph (a) of this subsection shall prevent any evidence from being considered in care proceedings for any purpose other than that of determining whether that condition is satisfied in respect of the relevant infant.

(9) If on application under this subsection to the court in which it is proposed to bring care proceedings in respect of a relevant infant who is not present before the court it appears to the court that he is under the age of five and either—

   (a) it is proved to the satisfaction of the court, on oath or in such other manner as may be prescribed by rules under section 15 of the Justices of the Peace Act, 1949, that notice of the proposal to bring the proceedings at the time and place at which the application is made was served on the parent or guardian of the relevant infant at what appears to the court to be a reasonable time before the making of the application; or
   (b) it appears to the court that his parent or guardian is present before the court

the court may if it thinks fit, after giving the parent or guardian if he is present an opportunity to be heard, give a direction under this subsection in respect of the relevant infant; and a relevant infant in respect of whom such a direction is given by a court shall be deemed to have been brought before the court under section 1 of this Act at the time of the direction, and care proceedings in respect of him may be continued accordingly.

(10) If the court before which the relevant infant is brought in care proceedings is not in a position to decide what order, if any, ought to be made under the preceding section in respect of him, the court may make an interim order in respect of him.

(11) If it appears to the court before which the relevant infant is brought in care proceedings that he resides in a petty sessions area other than that for which the court acts, the court shall, unless it dismisses the case and subject to subsection (5) of the following section, direct that he be brought under the preceding section before a juvenile court acting for the petty sessions area in which he resides; and where the court so directs—

(a) it may make an interim order in respect of him and, if it does so, shall cause the clerk of the court to which the direction relates to be informed of the case;

(b) if the court does not make such an order it shall cause the local authority in whose area it appears to the court that the relevant infant resides to be informed of the case, and it shall be the duty of that authority to give effect to the direction within twenty-one days.

(12) The relevant infant may appeal to the Crown Court against any order made in respect of him under the preceding section except such an order as is mentioned in subsection (3) (a) of that section.

(13) Such an order as is mentioned in subsection (3) (a) of the preceding section shall not require the parent or guardian in question to enter into a recognisance for an amount exceeding fifty pounds or for a period exceeding three years or, where the relevant infant will attain the age of eighteen in a period shorter than three years, for a period exceeding that shorter period; and section 96 of the Magistrates' Courts Act, 1952 (which relates to the forfeiture of recognisances) shall apply to a recognisance entered into in pursuance of such an order as it applies to a recognisance to keep the peace.

(14) For the purposes of this Act, care proceedings in respect of a relevant infant are begun when he is first brought before a juvenile court in pursuance of the preceding section in connection with the matter to which the proceedings relate.

NOTES

General note.—Subsections (1), (2) and (3) substantially re-enact existing law embodied in s. 35 of the Children and Young Persons Act, 1933, now repealed.

Section 34 (2) (transitional modifications) preserves the requirement to notify a probation officer as well as the local authority in relation to juveniles above a specified age.

"A justice may issue a summons or warrant" (sub-s. (4)).—A similar provision appeared in Rule 16 of the Summary Jursidiction (Children and Young Persons) Rules, 1933. Doubt has been expressed whether a warrant may be issued without a summons having first been served or at least an attempt made to serve a summons. The form prescribed (p. 585, *post*) provides that *the* summons has been or cannot be served. In civil cases generally the power to issue warrants is heavily circumscribed, and it may be better practice to issue a summons in the first instance. If a child is at risk and in circumstances where he may be in need of care or control he may be detained without warrant (s. 28, *post*).

"Interim Order" (sub-s. (5)).—It is preferable that this be made in a court house. For definition see s. 20. See also s. 22 for special provisions relating to interim orders.

"Section 77 of the Magistrates' Court Act, 1952" (sub-s. (6)).—This provision enables a summons or warrant to be issued for the attendance of a witness to an offence. Having regard to the proviso to s. 77 (2), it is submitted that the issue of a warrant in the first instance is not authorised.

"The court may make an interim order."—Formerly under s. 5 Children and Young Persons Act, 1938 a finding that a child or young person is in need of care or protection could be recorded, and the record was admissible as evidence of that fact for the purpose of any further hearing. This section was applied to certain proceedings under the Act of 1933 which had commenced before s. 1 was brought into force and where immediately before that date the court had neither made any order nor dismissed the case. (Administration of Justice Act, 1970, s. 51 (2)).

As regards trial of an information see s. 98 (7) Magistrates' Courts' Act.

The repeal of s. 5 presents difficulties as there is now no corresponding provision, although s. 3 (5) allows for the determination of a *finding of guilt* to be binding on the court to which the case is remitted. The questions raised are whether different justices may deal with the juvenile after a finding that he is in need of care or control, and if so, whether the finding is conclusive. The position is now similar to that in domestic proceedings before magistrates, and the same justices should adjudicate in any adjourned hearing.

The said condition shall be deemed to be satisfied (sub-s. (8)). The onus is on the parent to show that the child is receiving efficient fulltime education. Where the child is a registered pupil and has failed to attend regularly the court may not now make an order where it is proved that he is receiving efficient fulltime education. Previously it was only a defence to failure to register the child.

"But nothing in paragraph (a) of this subsection" (sub-s. (8)).—There may well be evidence from a local authority or the police that the child is in need of care or control, indeed such evidence must be provided if an order is to be made.

"Shall be deemed to have been brought" (sub-s. (9)).—Accordingly the court may direct that he be brought before a juvenile court acting for the petty sessions area in which he resides (under sub-s. 11), and indeed such a child may never actually appear as by sub-s. 14 proceedings are begun when he is first brought before a juvenile court in pursuance of s. 1.

"Notice of the proposal."—See rules 55, 82 Magistrates' Courts Rules, 1968.

He resides in a petty sessions area other than that for which the court Acts (sub-s. (11)).—Under s. 4 of the Children and Young Persons Act, 1963 (now repealed) the court had a discretion to remit, but subject to s. 3 (5) the court *must* now remit.

The inclusion of the words "unless it dismisses the case" presents difficulty, s. 3 (5) deals with the situation where a court makes a finding on the offence condition; if that condition is not proved that is the end of the case. The subsection would seem to allow a court (a) to hear sufficient evidence to be satisfied that there is a case. There may be circumstances in which it becomes apparent at an early stage that the case should be dismissed and if some evidence is led there is less likelihood of remission of cases where for example the basis of jurisdiction does not exist or (b) without hearing the case to make such a direction.

"Under the age of five" (sub-s. (9)).—A child under five need never now appear before the court. See also sub-s. (14).

Appeal to the Crown Court (sub-s. (12)).—(See also s. 3 (8)). Legal aid on an appeal will be under the provisions of the Criminal Justices Act, 1967, as amended—see p. 326, *post*. The hearing of an appeal will be at the location of the Crown Court designated by a Presiding judge as the appropriate location for such proceedings originating in the areas concerned (Directions by the Lord Chief Justice, October 14, 1971 under ss. 4 (5), 5 (4) and Sched. X, Courts Act, 1971.) Before the Courts Act the venue for an appeal where an offence condition was alleged was the court of quarter sessions for the area of the court which made the finding whether or not an order was made. This was clearly more convenient as the appellant might wish to challenge both the order and finding, and witnesses travelling might be saved.

The directions allow for different locations according to circumstances and presumably the former considerations will apply. The venue for appeals where a case is remitted under s. 56 of the 1933 Act is subject to the same direction, and where the finding of guilt is contested the location may now be at a court more convenient to witnesses, whereas formerly the venue was the court for the area to which the case was remitted.

The right of appeal against a hospital order is now under s. 2 (12). S. 70 (2) of the Mental Health Act, 1959, is repealed.

3. Further supplementary provisions relating to s. 1 (2) (f).—(1) In any care proceedings, no account shall be taken for the purposes of the condition set out in paragraph (f) of subsection (2) of section 1 of this Act (hereafter in this section referred to as "the offence condition") of an offence alleged to have been committed by the relevant infant if—

    (a) in any previous care proceedings in respect of him it was alleged that the offence condition was satisfied in consequence of the offence; or

    (b) the offence is a summary offence within the meaning of the Magistrates' Courts Act, 1952 and, disregarding section 4 of this Act, the period for beginning summary proceedings in respect of it expired before the care proceedings were begun; or

    (c) disregarding section 4 of this Act, he would if charged with the offence be entitled to be discharged under any rule of law relating to previous acquittal or conviction.

(2) In any care proceedings the court shall not entertain an allegation that the offence condition is satisfied in respect of the relevant infant unless the proceedings are brought by a local authority or a constable; but nothing in this or the preceding subsection shall prevent any evidence from being considered in care proceedings for any purpose other than that of determining whether the offence condition is satisfied in respect of the relevant infant.

(3) If in any care proceedings the relevant infant is alleged to have committed an offence in consequence of which the offence condition is satisfied with respect to him, the court shall not find the offence condition satisfied in consequence of the offence unless, disregarding section 4 of this Act, it would have found him guilty of the offence if the proceedings had been in pursuance of an information duly charging him with the offence and the court had had jurisdiction to try the information; and without prejudice to the preceding provisions of this subsection the same proof shall be required to substantiate or refute an allegation that the offence condition is satisfied in consequence of an offence as is required to warrant a finding of guilty, or as the case may be, of not guilty of the offence.

(4) A person shall not be charged with an offence if in care proceedings previously brought in respect of him it was alleged that the offence condition was satisfied in consequence of that offence.

(5) If in any care proceedings in which it is alleged that the offence condition is satisfied in respect of the relevant infant it appears to the court that the case falls to be remitted to another court in pursuance of subsection (11) of the preceding section but that it is appropriate to determine whether the condition is satisfied before remitting the case, the court may determine accordingly; and any determination under this subsection shall be binding on the court to which the case is remitted.

(6) Where in any care proceedings the court finds the offence condition satisfied with respect to the relevant infant in consequence of an indictable offence within the meaning of the Magistrates' Courts Act, 1952, then, whether or not the court makes an order under section 1 of this Act—

(a) section 34 of that Act (which relates to compensation for loss of property or damage to it) shall apply as if the finding were a finding of guilty of the offence and as if the maximum amount of an award under that section were one hundred pounds; and

(b) the court shall if the relevant infant is a child, and may if he is not, order any sum awarded by virtue of this subsection to be paid by his parent or guardian instead of by him unless it is satisfied that the parent or guardian cannot be found or has not conduced to the commission of the offence by neglecting to exercise due care or control of him, so however that an order shall not be made in pursuance of this paragraph unless the parent or guardian has been given an opportunity of being heard or has been required to attend the proceedings and failed to do so;

but where the finding in question is made in pursuance of the preceding subsection, the powers conferred by this subsection shall be exercisable by the court to which the case is remitted instead of by the court which made the finding.

(7) Where in any care proceedings the court finds the offence condition satisfied with respect to the relevant infant and he is a young person, the court may if it thinks fit and he consents, instead of making such an order as is mentioned in section 1 (3) of this Act, order him to enter into a recognisance for an amount not exceeding twenty-five pounds and for a period not exceeding one year to keep the peace or to be of good behaviour; and such an order shall be deemed to be an order under section 1 of this Act but no appeal to the Crown Court may be brought against an order.

(8) Where in any care proceedings the court finds the offence condition satisfied with respect to the relevant infant in consequence of an offence which was not admitted by him before the court, then—

(a) if the finding is made in pursuance of subsection (5) of this section and the court to which the case is remitted decides not to make any order under section 1 of this Act in respect of the relevant infant; or

(b) if the finding is not made in pursuance of that subsection and the court decides as aforesaid,

the relevant infant may appeal to the Crown Court against the finding, and in a case falling within paragraph (a) of this subsection any notice of appeal shall be given within twenty-one days after the date of the decision mentioned in that paragraph; and a person ordered to pay compensation by virtue of subsection (6) of this section may appeal to the Crown Court against the order.

NOTES

This section is printed as amended by the Criminal Damage Act, 1971, s. 11 and Sched. I., the Administration of Justice Act, 1970, s. 54 and Sched. XI, and the Courts Act, 1971, s. 56 and Sched. XI and the Crown Court Rules, Rule 6 and Sched. I, part II, p. 656, *post*.

General note.—Subsections (1)–(4) import the safeguards of the criminal law in care proceedings where an offence is alleged, *i.e.*, "autrefois acquit" or "autrefois convict". Also the time limit in s. 104 of the Magistrates' Courts Act, 1952 applies.

"Care proceedings were begun."—See s. 2 (4).

"But nothing . . . shall prevent any evidence from being considered" (sub-s. (2)).—Where an offence is alleged it will still be necessary to prove that the juvenile is in need of care or control which he is unlikely to receive unless the court makes an order and the subsection will allow evidence of an offence on that point. Similarly in care proceedings brought under s. 1 (2) (a)–(e) evidence of an offence would not be excluded by the operation of sub-s. 1 if otherwise admissible.

"Shall not find the offence condition satisfied" (sub-s. (3)).—This subsection imports the criminal burden of proof, *i.e.*, beyond reasonable doubt, and also, it is submitted, the laws of evidence. Although care proceedings are "civil" presumably the respondent and his parents would not be compellable at this stage of the proceedings. As the court will have to be satisfied that the juvenile is in need of care or control, great care must be taken to avoid hearing any evidence on this point which would not be admissible in relation to the offence, until that condition is found to be satisfied. To do otherwise would defeat the whole object of the sub-section, which is to make proof of the offence condition no easier than in criminal proceedings.

"It is appropriate to determine . . . before remitting the case" (sub-s. (5)).—This will enable a court to make a finding without the necessity of requiring witnesses etc. to travel to the court acting for the area where the juvenile resides.

Appeal to the Crown Court (sub-s. (8)).—If an order is made, an appeal will be under s. 2 (12). If the court finds the offence condition satisfied, but makes no order, sub-s. (8) gives a right of appeal against the finding.

Venue.—Where after a finding of guilt by one court, the case is remitted under sub-s. (5) to another court and an order is made, the appeal was formerly to the quarter sessions for the area of the first mentioned court. See note to s. 2, as to location of the Crown Court for appeals. With the repeal of sub-s. (9), the appeal is simply to the Crown Court. For location of the Crown Court see directions by the Lord Chief Justice under ss. 4 (5), 5 (4) Courts Act, 1971, p. 663, *post*.

Bail pending appeal.—An appellant "in custody pursuant to a sentence imposed by a magistrates' court" may be admitted to bail by the Crown Court. By s. 59 of the Act of 1933, reference to a sentence is to be construed as an order on a finding of guilt. It would appear that the Crown Court may not therefore bail the subject of a care order made in care proceedings. By s. 89 of the Magistrates' Courts Act, 1952, the magistrates' court may release an appellant against the *decision of the court* if he is in custody. Under previous law bail was granted where an approved school order was made whether in criminal or civil proceedings and in an unreported case Mr. Justice Jones decided that magistrates had power to admit to bail the subject of a care order made on a finding of guilt. Presumably application in that case was made to the High Court under s. 22 Criminal Justice Act, 1967. There seems, however, no reason why a person should not be "in custody" even if the care order is made in care proceedings and there are no limitations on the magistrates' court which require that the appeal arise from criminal proceedings as there are in respect of the higher courts.

Legal aid.—Legal aid may be granted by the court (Criminal Justice Act, 1967, as amended by s. 33 and Sched. I of the Children and Young Persons Act, 1969) (pp. 180, 326, *post*).

Compensation.—In view of *R. v. Forest, JJ., Ex parte Coppin*, [1969] 2 All E.R. 668; *R. v. Taylor*, [1969] 2 All E.R. 662, there may be difficulty in awarding compensation where a case is remitted, as application should be made by the "aggrieved person" immediately after conviction. This is so even where the offence is under s. 1 Criminal Damage Act, 1971. The finding of the juvenile court is only a finding of guilt for the purposes of s. 34 of the Magistrates' Courts Act 1952 and the provisions of the former Act for compensation on "application or *otherwise*" apply to a finding of guilt as such.

Consequential changes in criminal proceedings etc.

4. Prohibition of criminal proceedings for offences by children.—
A person shall not be charged with an offence, except homicide, by reason of anything done or omitted while he was a child.

NOTES

General note.—This section is not yet in force. The government have announced that the minimum age for prosecution may be raised to 12. See s. 34 (1) (a), *post*, for power to modify reference to a child and s. 34 (7) as to the raising of the age above that of 12. The age of criminal responsibility remains unchanged. Powers of arrest without warrant are not affected. The consequences of criminal responsibility, *i.e.*, liability to prosecution, are however changed.

Where property comes into the possession of the police in connection with any criminal charge, the Police Property Act, 1897 makes provision for a court of summary jurisdiction to make an order for the delivery of the property to the person who appears to be the owner. The prohibition of criminal charges against a child does not, however, affect the position as the Police Property Act is amended by Sched. V, para. 1, (*post*), to include property which has come into the possession of the police in connection with an allegation, in proceedings under s. 1 of this act, that the condition set out in sub-s. (2) (f) of that section is satisfied.

Homicide.—*I.e.* any offence of unlawful killing, which it is submitted will include causing death by dangerous driving (Road Traffic Act, 1960, s. 1).

5. Restrictions on criminal proceedings for offences by young persons.—(1) A person other than a qualified informant shall not lay an information in respect of an offence if the alleged offender is a young person.

(2) A qualified informant shall not lay an information in respect of an offence if the alleged offender is a young person unless the informant is of opinion that the case is of a description prescribed in pursuance of sub-section (4) of this section and that it would not be adequate for the case to be dealt with by a parent, teacher or other person or by means of a caution from a constable or through an exercise of the powers of a local authority or other body not involving court proceedings or by means of proceedings under section 1 of this Act.

(3) A qualified informant shall not come to a decision in pursuance of the preceding subsection to lay an information unless—

(a) he has told the appropriate local authority that the laying of the information is being considered and has asked for any observations which the authority may wish to make on the case to the informant; and

(b) the authority either have notified the informant that they do not wish to make such observations or have not made any during the period or extended period indicated by the informant as that which in the circumstances he considers reasonable for the purpose or the informant has considered the observations made by the authority during that period;

but the informant shall be entitled to disregard the foregoing provisions of this subsection in any case in which it appears to him that the requirements of the preceding subsection are satisfied and will continue to be satisfied notwithstanding any observarions which might be made in pursuance of this subsection.

(4) The Secretary of State may make regulations specifying, by reference to such considerations as he thinks fit, the descriptions of cases in which a qualified informant may lay an information in respect of an offence if the alleged offender is a young person; but no regulations shall be made under this subsection unless a draft of the regulations has been approved by a resolution of each House of Parliament.

(5) An information laid by a qualified informant in a case where the offender is a young person shall be in writing and shall—

(a) state the alleged offender's age to the best of the informant's knowledge; and
(b) contain a certificate signed by the informant stating that the requirements of subsections (2) and (3) of this section are satisfied with respect to the case or that the case is one in which the requirements of the said subsection (2) are satisfied and the informant is entitled to disregard the requirements of the said subsection (3).

(6) If at the time when justices begin to inquire into a case, either as examining justices or on the trial of an information, they have reason to believe that the alleged offender is a young person and either—

(a) it appears to them that the person who laid the information in question was not a qualified informant when he laid it; or
(b) the information is not in writing or does not contain such a certificate as is mentioned in subsection (5) (b) of this section,

it shall be their duty to quash the information, without prejudice to the laying of a further information in respect of the matter in question; but no proceedings shall be invalidated by reason of a contravention of any provision of this section and no action shall lie, by reason only of such a contravention, in respect of proceedings in respect of which such a contravention has occurred.

(7) Nothing in the preceding provisions of this section applies to an information laid with the consent of the Attorney General or laid by or on behalf or with the consent of the Director of Public Prosecutions.

(8) It shall be the duty of a person who decides to lay an information in respect of an offence in a case where he has reason to believe that the alleged offender is a young person to give notice of the decision to the appropriate local authority unless he is himself that authority—

(9) In this section—

"the appropriate local authority", in relation to a young person, means the local authority for the area in which it appears to the informant in question that the young person resides or, if the young person appears to the informant not to reside in the area of a local authority, the local authority in whose area it is alleged that the relevant offence or one of the relevant offences was committed; and

"qualified informant" means a servant of the Crown, a police officer and a member of a designated police force acting in his capacity as such a servant, officer or member, a local authority, the Greater London Council, the council of a county district and any body designated as a public body for the purposes of this section;

and in this subsection "designated" means designated by an order made by the Secretary of State; but nothing in this section shall be construed as preventing any council or other body from acting by an agent for the purposes of this section.

NOTES

General note.—This section with the exception of sub-ss. (8) and (9) has not been brought into force. The section was substituted at a fairly late stage when the Bill was before Parliament. The Magistrates Association and other bodies had felt unhappy at the discretion regarding prosecution being given to a magistrate rather than the police. The section as enacted to some extent still follows the proposals set out in the White Paper "Children in Trouble" but the decision regarding prosecution has been left with the police. Section 34 (1 (b)) (transitional modifications of Part I for persons of specified ages) provides that references in this section (except sub-s. (8)) shall be construed as including a child or excluding a young person, who has attained such age as may be specified. Read together with s. 34 (1) (a) this enables regulations to provide that while s. 4 does not apply to children over a certain age s. 5 will apply. Subsection (2) envisages, *inter alia*, young persons being dealt with by care proceedings rather than prosecution. This is consistent with the aims of the White Paper in avoiding the "stigma" of criminality. With the abolition of the right to claim trial by jury (s. 6) and the protection afforded by s. 3 it is submitted that the rights of young persons are in no way adversely affected by a decision to institute proceedings under s. 1. The section uses the phrase "lay an information". It has been the practice of many police forces to deal with juveniles by way of summons where possible rather than to charge them. In serious cases the police will undoubtedly wish to proceed by way of charge and the appearance of a defendant in answer to a charge which complies with the provisions of sub-s. (5) may be regarded as the laying of an information provided that the charge complies with Rule 83 of the Magistrates Courts Rules, 1968 (S.I. 1968 No. 1920).

"Is a young person."—See the regulation making power in s. 34. References in sub-s. (8) include a child who has attained the age of 10. (S.I. 1970 No. 1882, p. 624, *post.*)

"Of a description prescribed in pursuance of sub-s. (4)" (sub-s. (2)).—No regulations have been made but it may be that the criteria proposed in the White Paper "Children in Trouble" (Command No. 3601, Appendix A.) will give some indication of the descriptions and considerations to which qualified informants must have regard. The regulations will ensure uniformity of approach to the discretion which the police are given by this section.

"By means of a caution" (sub-s. (2)).—A variety of cautioning schemes exist throughout the country. For a description of police cautioning and juvenile liaison schemes see the "Report of the Committee on Children and Young Persons", 1960 (Command No. 1199), paras. 138–149. (The Metropolitan Police have since the report evolved a juvenile bureau and cautioning system.) With express statutory emphasis lent to the system it may well be necessary in order to achieve uniformity for rules to be made or administrative directions given to the police. Problems arise when a defendant is found guilty and has had a previous caution or cautions. Some courts incline to ignore the caution while others regard it as properly part of the defendant's antecedents. It is important to recognise that the fact of a caution does not of itself imply the commission of an offence and magistrates may wish to adopt the procedure set out in "The Magistrate", July, 1970.

The subsection requires both the test of the offence being of a description prescribed and also the inadequacy of informal action to be satisfied.

The powers of a local authority.—sub-s. (2)).—*E.g.* under the Children Act, 1948, s. 1.

"Told the appropriate local authority" (sub-s. (3)).—The section does not prescribe any form which the consultation should take. Presumably this will be worked out locally.

"**Shall be entitled to disregard**" (**sub-s. (3)**).—The informant is not entitled to disregard the provisions of any regulations made under sub-s. (4).

"**Quash the information**" (**sub-s. (6)**).—It is arguable that this does not involve a dismissal under s. 13 of the Magistrates' Courts Act, 1952, and would not therefore allow a court to award costs under ss. 5 or 6 of the Costs in Criminal Cases Act, 1952.

"**Qualified informant**" (**sub-s. (9)**).—The private prosecution is effectively abolished.

Previous care proceedings.—See the provisions of s. 3 (4).

6. Summary trial of young persons.—(1) Where a person under the age of seventeen appears or is brought before a magistrates court on an information charging him with an offence, other than homicide, which is an indictable offence within the meaning of the Magistrates' Courts Act, 1952, he shall be tried summarily unless—

    (a) he is a young person and the offence is such as is mentioned in subsection (2) of section 53 of the Act of 1933 (under which young persons convicted on indictment of certain grave crimes may be sentenced to be detained for long periods) and the court considers that if he is found guilty of the offence it ought to be possible to sentence him in pursuance of that subsection; or

    (b) he is charged jointly with a person who has attained the age of seventeen and the court considers it necessary in the interests of justice to commit them both for trial;

and accordingly in a case falling within paragraph (a) or paragraph (b) of this subsection the court shall, if it is of opinion that there is sufficient evidence to put the accused on trial, commit him for trial.

(2) In sections 18 (1) and 25 (1) of the said Act of 1952 (which provide for the trial on indictment of persons aged fourteen or over who are charged with certain summary offences within the meaning of that Act) for the word "fourteen" there shall be substituted the word "seventeen".

(3) If on trying a person summarily in pursuance of subsection (1) of this section the court finds him guilty, it may impose a fine of an amount not exceeding fifty pounds or may exercise the same powers as it could have exercised if he had been found guilty of an offence for which, but for section 107 (2) of the said Act of 1952, it could have sentenced him to imprisonment for a term not exceeding three months.

NOTES

General note.—This section restricts the committal for trial of children and young persons (other than for an offence of homicide) to cases falling within sub-s. (1) (a) and (b). The right to claim trial by jury is abolished by sub-s. (2).

"**Under the age of 17**" (**sub-s. (1)**).—This section covers children *and* young persons, as under s. 34 (1) (a) there may be children under 14 who will still for a time be "prosecutable".

Committal for trial.—This may not be under the provisions of s. 1 Criminal Justice Act, 1971 (*R. v. Coleshill JJ., Ex parte Whitehouse*, [1971] 3 All E. R. 929 *R. v. L. and W.*, [1971] Crim. L. R. 481) nor seemingly is it appropriate for a voluntary bill of indictment to be preferred (*ibid.*) per Thompson, J. to grant such a bill "would defeat the spirit of s. 6 . . . and the intention of Parliament that young persons should not be committed for trial on indictment unless and until the evidence . . . has been considered".

"The court considers."—In order for a court to consider that a young person needs to be detained under s. 53 of the Act of 1933 it may be necessary to enquire into the circumstances of the case or the defendants antecedent history.

Appeal to the Crown Court.—An appeal will lie under s. 83 of the Magistrates' Courts Act, 1952. Note that a supervision order is not excluded from the definition of sentence.

Legal aid.—See s. 73 of the Criminal Justice Act, 1967, p. 326, *post*. If legal aid is granted this will cover the making of an application to the Crown Court for bail where a juvenile is committed for sentence or gives notice of appeal. An unrepresented defendant who applies to the High Court for bail may be represented by the Official Solicitor, but legal aid does not extend to an application to a judge in chambers. An application to the Crown Court however, may be taken into account when assessing fees under the Legal Aid in Criminal Proceedings (Fees and Expenses) Regulations, 1968, S.I. 1968 No. 1230.

Release of appellant.—See ss. 89 and 124 of the Magistrates' Courts Act, 1952. See also s. 37 (1) of the Criminal Justice Act, 1948, s. 22 Criminal Justice Act, 1967. As to the Crown Court, see s. 13, Courts Act, 1971.

"Fine ... not exceeding fifty pound (sub-s. (3)).—By s. 34 (5) in the case of a "prosecutable" child the maximum fine is ten pounds.

"Term not exceeding three months".—Any detention centre order therefore must be for a maximum of three months, even though the defendant has attained the age of 17 before sentence.

Magistrates' Courts Act, 1952.—In ss. 2 (4) and 104 there are references to ss. 20 and 21 which are repealed by this Act. In effect this would create a limitation period of six months for indictable cases in respect of a juvenile. By s. 51 (1) of the Administration of Justice Act, 1970, the references to the said sections 20 and 21, shall be construed as references to this section. See also note **Proof of Age,** p. 215, *post*.

7. Alterations in treatment of young offenders etc.—(1) *The minimum age at conviction which qualifies for a sentence of borstal training under section 20 of the Criminal Justice Act, 1948 shall be seventeen instead of fifteen years; and accordingly in subsection (1) of that section and section 28 (1) of the Magistrates' Courts Act, 1952 for the word "fifteen" there shall be substituted the word "seventeen".*

(2) In section 3 (1) of the said Act of 1948 (which authorises the court by or before which a person is convicted of an offence to make a probation order in respect of him) after the word "person" there shall be inserted the words "who has attained the age of seventeen".

(3) *If a court having power to order children or young persons of any class or description to be detained in a detention centre in pursuance of section 4 of the Criminal Justice Act, 1961 or to attend at an attendance centre in pursuance of section 19 of the said Act of 1948 is notified in pursuance of this subsection by the Secretary of State that a detention centre or, as the case may be, an attendance centre will not be available for the reception from that court of children or young persons of that class or description after a date specified in the notification, the power in question shall not be exercisable by that court after that date; and the Secretary of State shall cause a copy of any notification under this subsection to be published in the London Gazette before the date specified in the notification.*

(4) Section 5 of the said Act of 1961 (which provides for detention for defaults) shall cease to apply to young persons.

(5) An order sending a person to an approved school shall not be made after such day as the Secretary of State may by order specify for the purposes of this subsection.

(6) Sections 54 and 57 of the Act of 1933 (which among other things enable a child or young person found guilty of an offence to be sent to a remand home or committed to the care of a fit person) shall cease to have effect.

(7) Subject to the enactments requiring cases to be remitted to juvenile courts and to section 53 (1) of the Act of 1933 (which provides for detention for certain grave crimes), where a child is found guilty of homicide or a young person is found guilty of any offence by or before any court, that court or the court to which his case is remitted shall have power—

(a) if the offence is punishable in the case of an adult with imprisonment, to make a care order (other than an interim order) in respect of him; or

(b) to make a supervision order in respect of him; or

(c) with the consent of his parent or guardian, to order the parent or guardian to enter into a recognisance to take proper care of him and exercise proper control over him,

and, if it makes such an order as is mentioned in this subsection while another such order made by any court is in force in respect of the child or young person, shall also have power to discharge the earlier order; and subsection (13) of section 2 of this Act shall apply to an order under paragraph (c) of this subsection as it applies to such an order as is mentioned in that subsection.

(8) Without prejudice to the power to remit any case to a juvenile court which is conferred on a magistrates' court other than a juvenile court by section 56 (1) of the Act of 1933, in a case where such a magistrates' court finds a person guilty of an offence and either he is a young person or was a young person when the proceedings in question were begun it shall be the duty of the court to exercise that power unless the court decides to deal with the case by exercising a power to make one or more of the following orders, that is to say, an order discharging him absolutely or conditionally, an order for the payment of a fine, damages or costs, an order requiring his parent or guardian to enter into a recognisance to take proper care of him and exercise proper control over him or an order under section 5 or 7 of the Road Traffic Act, 1962 (which relate respectively to the disqualification of drivers and the endorsement of licences).

NOTES

General note.—Subsections (1) and (3) have not yet been brought into force. The provisions of s. 34 and any order thereunder must be borne in mind, as references to a particular age may be modified. The section provides for the abolition of approved school order, fit person order, probation order, attendance centre order, detention centre order and borstal training for those under seventeen. For transitional provisions see Scheds. III and IV.

Probation order (sub-s. (2)).—Supervision orders will take the place of probation orders for persons under the age of 17. For definition see s. 11, *post*, see also ss. 15 (3) and (4) for provisions which operate when a supervised person has attained the age of eighteen.

"To make a supervision order in respect of him" (sub-s. (7)).—Where the subject of the order resides or will reside in Scotland, see the Social Work (Scotland) Act, 1968, s. 73 (1A), *post*. "Supervision order" is not included in the list of orders made on conviction by a magistrates' court excluded from the expression "sentence" in s. 83 (3) of the Magistrates' Courts Act, 1952.

There will therefore be a right of appeal against the making of a supervision order in criminal proceedings as well as the right of appeal against the making of such order in care proceedings under s. 2 (12), *ante*.

By s. 34 (1) (c), p. 181, *post*, the Secretary of State may by order provide that any reference to a young person in this subsection shall be construed as including a child who has attained such age as may be specified. The age of 10 is specified by S.I. 1970 No. 1882, p. 624, *post*.

"Where such a magistrates' court finds a young person guilty" (sub-s. (8)).—Remittals by higher courts remain covered by the provisions of s. 56 (1) of the Children and Young Persons Act, 1933, as amended and the law in respect of such remittals is unchanged.

"Or was a young person when the proceedings . . . were begun" (sub-s. (8)).—This is an extension of the previous law, and it would appear that the court to which such a case is remitted may make a care order.

The effect of sub-s. (8) is to "spell out" the cases where it would be "undesirable to remit", and accordingly unless the magistrates' court makes one of those orders, the court must remit the case. S.I. 1970 No. 1882 provides that references in this subsection to a young person shall include a child who has attained the age of 10 years.

8. Finger-printing of suspected young persons.—(1) If a police officer not below the rank of inspector makes an application on oath to a justice stating—

(a) that there is evidence sufficient to justify the laying of an information that a young person has or is suspected of having committed an offence punishable with imprisonment in the case of an adult; and

(b) that with a view to deciding, in accordance with section 5 of this Act, whether the information should be laid it is appropriate in the opinion of the officer for an order under subsection (2) of this section to be made in respect of the young person,

the justice may if he thinks fit issue a summons or warrant for the purpose of securing the attendance of the young person before a magistrates' court with a view to the making of such an order in respect of him.

(2) The court before which a young person appears in pursuance of a summons or warrant under the preceding subsection may if it thinks fit order his finger and palm prints to be taken by a constable.

(3) Subsections (2) and (4) of section 40 of the Magistrates' Courts Act, 1952 (which respectively relate to the taking and destruction of finger and palm prints) shall have effect as if references to an order under that section included references to an order under the preceding subsection and, in relation to an order under the preceding subsection as if for the words from "remanded" to "committed" in subsection (2) there were substituted the words "lawfully detained at any place, at that place" and as if the reference to acquittal in subsection (4) included a reference to a finding of a court that the condition set out in section 1 (2) (f) of this Act is not satisfied in consequence of the offence specified in the application mentioned in subsection (1) of this section.

NOTES

General note.—This section is not yet in force and its implementation is dependant upon s. 5.

"Evidence sufficient to justify the laying of an information" (sub-s. (1)).— In the exercise of police powers under s. 5 it may be necessary to determine whether an offender is involved in other offences, and the section enables finger prints to be taken before a decision to prosecute has been reached.

Makes an application on oath . . . stating.—It is not necessary for the court to enquire into the evidence.

9. Investigations by local authorities.—(1) Where a local authority or a local education authority bring proceedings under section 1 of this Act or proceedings for an offence alleged to have been committed by a young person or are notified that any such proceedings are being brought, it shall be the duty of the authority, unless they are of opinion that it is unnecessary to do so, to make such investigations and provide the court before which the proceedings are heard with such information relating to the home surroundings, school record, health and character of the person in respect of whom the proceedings are brought as appear to the authority likely to assist the court.

(2) If the court mentioned in subsection (1) of this section requests the authority aforesaid to make investigations and provide information or to make further investigations and provide further information relating to the matters aforesaid, it shall be the duty of the authority to comply with the request.

NOTES

General note.—Under ss. 2 (3) and 5 (3) local authorities will be notified of impending proceedings and the Act repeals the provisions of the Children and Young Persons Act, 1933, s. 35 which required a local authority to provide information to the court. As to social enquiry reports before sentence see Home Office circular No. 188/1968.

"If the court . . . requests."—The local authority are under a duty to make investigatons if the court requests as well as any report made of their own motion under sub-s. (1). For investigation by probation officers see s. 34 (2) and (3).

Young person.—This includes a reference to a child who has attained the age of 10 (S.I. 1970 No. 1882). For attainment of age see Family Law Reform Act, 1969, s. 9.

10. Further limitations on publication of particulars of children and young persons etc.—(1) In subsection (1) of section 49 of the Act of 1933 (which among other things imposes restrictions on reports of certain court proceedings concerning children or young persons but authorises the court or the Secretary of State, if satisfied that it is in the interests of justice to do so, to dispense with the requirements of that section)—

(a) the references to a young person concerned in the proceedings as the person in respect of whom they are taken shall be construed as including references to any person who has attained the age of seventeen but not eighteen and against or in respect of whom the proceedings are taken and, in the case of proceedings under Part I of this Act, any other person in respect of whom those proceedings are taken; and

(b) the references to a juvenile court shall, in relation to proceedings in pursuance of the provisions of sections 15 and 16 of this Act or on appeal from such proceedings, be construed as including a reference to any other magistrates' court or, as the case may be, the court in which the appeal is brought; and

(c) for the words "in the interests of justice so to do" there shall be substituted the words "appropriate to do so for the purpose of avoiding injustice to a child or young person" and after the word "section" there shall be inserted the words "in relation to him".

(2) Where by virtue of paragraph (b) of the preceding subsection the said section 49 applies to any proceedings, it shall be the duty of the court in which the proceedings are taken to announce in the course of the proceedings that that section applies to them; and if the court fails to do so that section shall not apply to the proceedings in question.

(3) A notice displayed in pursuance of section 4 of the Criminal Justice Act, 1967 (which requires the publication of a notice stating the result of proceedings before examining justices and containing particulars of the person to whom the proceedings related) shall not contain the name or address of any child or young person unless the justices in question have stated that in their opinion he would be mentioned in the notice apart from the foregoing provisions of this subsection and should be mentioned in it for the purpose of avoiding injustice to him.

NOTE

General note.—The modifications to s. 49 of the Children and Young Persons Act, 1933, extend protection to those over the age of 17 but under 18 and make clear that the type of case where a court may consider an order is where another child or young person may have his name cleared by the publication of the offender's name.

Supervision

11. Supervision orders.—Any provision of this Act authorising a court to make a supervision order in respect of any person shall be construed as authorising the court to make an order placing him under the supervision of a local authority designated by the order or of a probation officer; and in this Act "supervision order" shall be construed accordingly and "supervised person" and "supervisor", in relation to a supervision order, mean respectively the person placed or to be placed under supervision by the order and the person under whose supervision he is placed or to be placed by the order.

NOTE

Any provision of this Act.—Supervision orders under the Matrimonial Proceedings (Magistrates' Courts) Act, 1960 are not affected.

For transitional provisions affecting supervision orders made under the Children and Young Persons Act, 1963, see Sched. 4, p. 226, *post.*

12. Power to include requirements in supervision orders.—(1) A supervision order may require the supervised person to reside with an individual named in the order who agrees to the requirement, but a requirement imposed by a supervision order in pursuance of this subsection shall be subject to any such requirement of the order as is authorised by the following provisions of this section.

(2) Subject to section 19 (6) of this Act, a supervision order may require the supervised person to comply with such directions of the supervisor

as are mentioned in paragraph (a) or (b) or paragraphs (a) and (b) of this subsection, that is to say—

> (a) directions requiring the supervised person to live for a single period specified in the directions at a place so specified;
>
> (b) directions given from time to time requiring him to do all or any of the following things—
>
>> (i) to live at a place or places specified in the directions for a period or periods so specified,
>>
>> (ii) to present himself to a person or persons specified in the directions at a place or places and on a day or days so specified,
>>
>> (iii) to participate in activities specified in the directions on a day or days so specified;

but it shall be for the supervisor to decide whether and to what extent he exercises any power to give directions conferred on him by virtue of the preceding provisions of this subsection and to decide the form of any directions; and a requirement imposed by a supervision order in pursuance of this subsection shall be subject to any such requirement of the order as is authorised by subsection (4) of this section.

(3) The periods specified in directions given by virtue of subsection (2) of this section in pursuance of a supervision order shall be in accordance with the following provisions, that is to say—

> (a) the aggregate of the periods specified in directions given by virtue of paragraph (a) and paragraph (b) of that subsection shall not exceed ninety days;
>
> (b) the period specified in directions given by virtue of the said paragraph (a) shall not exceed ninety days and subject to paragraph (e) below shall not begin after the expiration of one year beginning with the date of the order or, if the directions are authorised solely by a variation of the order, with the date of the variation;
>
> (c) the aggregate of the periods specified in directions given by virtue of the said paragraph (b) shall not exceed thirty days in the year beginning with the date aforesaid and thirty days in any year beginning with an anniversary of that date;
>
> (d) if the order provides that any of the preceding paragraphs of this subsection is to have effect in relation to the order as if for a reference to ninety days or thirty days there were substituted a reference to a shorter period specified in the order, the paragraph in question shall have effect accordingly;
>
> (e) for the purpose of calculating the period or periods in respect of which directions may be given in pursuance of the order—
>
>> (i) the supervisor shall be entitled to disregard any day in respect of which directions were previously given in pursuance of the order and on which the directions were not complied with;
>>
>> (ii) a direction given in respect of one or more parts of a day shall be treated as given in respect of the whole of the day,

and if during the year mentioned in paragraph (b) of this sub-section the supervised person is given such directions as are there mentioned specifying a period beginning in that year but does not begin to comply with the directions during that year, the supervisor shall be entitled to disregard so much of that paragraph as prevents that period from beginning after the expiration of that year.

(4) Where a court which proposes to make a supervision order is satis-fied, on the evidence of a medical practitioner approved for the purposes of section 28 of the Mental Health Act, 1959, that the mental condition of a supervised person is such as requires and may be susceptible to treatment but is not such as to warrant his detention in pursuance of a hospital order under Part V of that Act, the court may include in the super-vision order a requirement that the supervised person shall, for a period specified in the order, submit to treatment of one of the following de-scriptions so specified, that is to say—

(a) treatment by or under the direction of a fully registered medical practitioner specified in the order;
(b) treatment as a non-resident patient at a place specified in the order; or
(c) treatment as a resident patient in a hospital or mental nursing home within the meaning of the said Act of 1959, but not a special hospital within the meaning of that Act.

(5) A requirement shall not be included in a supervision order in pur-suance of the preceding subsection—

(a) in any case, unless the court is satisfied that arrangements have been or can be made for the treatment in question and, in the case of treatment as a resident patient, for the reception of the patient;
(b) in the case of an order made or to be made in respect of a person who has attained the age of fourteen, unless he consents to its inclusion;

and a requirement so included shall not in any case continue in force after the supervised person becomes eighteen.

NOTES

"**Subject to any such requirement . . . as is authorised**" (**sub-s. 1**).—A requirement as to residence will be subject to any directions under sub-s. (2).

"**Subject to section 19 (6).**"—A scheme under s. 19 must be in force for a plan-ning area in which the supervised person resides before any requirement under sub-s. (2) may be included in a supervision order. See p. 161, *post*.

"**Comply with such directions**" (**sub-s. (2)).**—See also s. 18 (2) (b) for pre-scribed minor requirements. Directions under paras. (a) and (b) may be made in the same order, but sub-s. (3) lays down the maximum permitted period of any such requirements. The content of the directions will depend upon the scheme drawn up under s. 19. The Act does not seem to contemplate the situation where a supervised person under 17 fails to comply with such directions. Presumably a refusal could lead to the supervisor making an application under s. 15 (1), however, unless the court then finds it appropriate to make a care order, there would not appear to be any sanction. Where the supervised person has attained the age of 17 the court has the power, subject to the restrictions of s. 15 (2), to fine or impose any punishment which it could have imposed if it then had power to try him for the offence in consequence of which the supervision order was made (s. 15 (4)).

If a requirement under s. (2) (a) for 90 days is inserted it will not be possible to include a requirement under 12 (2) (b). However whether any directions at all are given are entirely within the discretion of the supervisor.

There is no power to include a requirement in a supervision order other than a requirement under sub-s. (2) or s. 18 (2) (b), p. 159, *post*. The "prescribed requirements" appear in the scheduled forms of supervision order, see forms 43, 44 and 45 and Rule 28 (2), Magistrates' Courts (Children and Young Persons) Rules, 1970, pp. 604–606 and 581, *post*. Cf. the provisions of s. 3 (3) Criminal Justice Act, 1948, p. 279, *post*.

Intermediate treatment.—This is the term used to refer to requirements under sub-s. 2. Until a scheme is in force under s. 19 for the planning area in which the supervised person resides, no such requirement may be inserted in the order (s. 19 (6), *post*).

"The period specified . . . by virtue of the said paragraphs (a) and (b)" **(sub-s. (3) (b)).**—There is no provision corresponding to a supervision order with a condition of residence for one year in an approved hostel.

Such provision can only be given under a care order provided that the system of community homes includes such hostels.

"Shall submit to treatment of one of the following descriptions" (sub-s. (4)).—The history of such conditions in supervision orders is unusual. Until the Children and Young Persons Act, 1963 the provisions of the Criminal Justice Act, 1948, applied to supervision orders and accordingly the evidence of a medical practitioner approved etc. was required. This provision was repealed when supervision orders come under Sched. I of the Children and Young Persons Act, 1963 although the period of treatment could still not exceed 12 months. Now the evidence of an approved medical practitioner is necessary but there is no limit to the period. For variation or cancellation of such a requirement see s. 15 (5). By virtue of s. 16 (6) (a) and (c) the condition may only be made or inserted if the court is satisfied that the supervised person is unlikely to receive the care or control he needs unless the court makes the order or is likely to receive it notwithstanding the order. There is no provision corresponding to s. 4 (7) Criminal Justice Act, 1948, regarding written evidence.

"Require the supervised person to reside" (sub-s. (1)).—See s. 18 (1), *post*.

Scotland.—No requirement authorised by this section may be excluded in a supervision order made by virtue of s. 7A (4) of the Criminal Justice (Scotland) Act, 1949, or s. 72 (1A) of the Social Work (Scotland) Act, 1968, unless the supervised person is before the court (sub-ss. (5) and (1A), *ibid*.).

13. Selection of supervisor.—(1) A court shall not designate a local authority as the supervisor by a provision of a supervision order unless the authority agree or it appears to the court that the supervised person resides or will reside in the area of the authority.

(2) A court shall not insert in a supervision order a provision placing a child under the supervision of a probation officer unless the local authority of which the area is named or to be named in the order in pursuance of section 18 (2) (a) of this Act so request and a probation officer is already exercising or has exercised, in relation to another member of the household to which the child belongs, duties imposed by paragraph 3 (5) of Schedule 5 to the Criminal Justice Act, 1948 or by rules under paragraph 6 (b) of that Schedule.

(3) Where a provision of a supervision order places a person under the supervision of a probation officer, the supervisor shall be a probation officer appointed for or assigned to the petty sessions area named in the order in pursuance of section 18 (2) (a) of this Act and selected under arrangements made by the probation and after-care committee; but if the probation officer selected as aforesaid dies or is unable to carry out his

duties or if the case committee dealing with the case think it desirable that another officer should take his place, another probation officer shall be selected as aforesaid for the purposes of the order.

NOTES

"**Unless the authority agrees**" **(sub-s. (1)).**—The petty sessions area where the supervised person resides or will reside must be included in the order (s. 18 (2) (a)) and the appropriate court for variation will be the one acting for that area (s. 16 (11)).

Child.—The reference shall be construed as excluding a child who has attained the age of 10 (S.I. 1970 No. 1882, p. 624, *post*). So long as there are children of prosecutable age, the intention is that they may also be supervised by a probation officer.

"**Under the supervision of a probation officer**" **(sub-s. (2) and (3)).**— Section 34 (2) provides for notice of proceedings in relation to a person who has attained a specified age to be given to a probation officer. See also s. 34 (3).

14. Duty of supervisor.—While a supervision order is in force it shall be the duty of the supervisor to advise, assist and befriend the supervised person.

NOTE

This section substantially re-enacts the present law. It is to be noted that probation officers are subject to the Probation Rules, 1965 and 1967, S.I. 1965 No. 723 and S.I. 1967 No. 1884. No rules governing a local authority supervisor have yet been made, but in view of the wide discretion given to supervisors by s. 12 (2) it may be felt that some such rules would be helpful.

15. Variation and discharge of supervision orders.—(1) If while a supervision order is in force in respect of a supervised person who has not attained the age of eighteen it appears to a juvenile court, on the application of the supervisor or the supervised person, that it is appropriate to make an order under this subsection, the court may make an order discharging the supervision order or varying it by—

 (a) cancelling any requirement included in it in pursuance of section 12 or section 18 (2) (b) of this Act; or

 (b) inserting in it (either in addition to or in substitution for any of its provisions) any provision which could have been included in the order if the court had then had power to make it and were exercising the power,

and may on discharging the supervision order make a care order (other than an interim order) in respect of the supervised person; but the powers of variation conferred by this subsection do not include power to insert in the supervision order, after the expiration of twelve months beginning with the date when the order was originally made, a requirement in pursuance of section 12 (2) (a) of this Act, or, after the expiration of three months beginning with that date, a requirement in pursuance for section 12 (4) of this Act, unless in either case it is in substitution for such a requirement already included in the order.

(2) If on an application in pursuance of the preceding subsection, in a case where the supervised person has attained the age of seventeen and the supervision order was not made by virtue of section 1 of this Act or on the

occasion of the discharge of a care order, it appears to the court appropriate to do so it may proceed as if the application were in pursuance of subsection (3) or, if it is made by the supervisor, in pursuance of subsections (3) and (4) of this section and as if in that subsection or those subsections, as the case may be, the word "seventeen" were substituted for the word "eighteen" and the words "a magistrates' court other than" were omitted.

(3) If while a supervision order is in force in respect of a supervised person who has attained the age of eighteen it appears to a magistrates' court other than a juvenile court, on the application of the supervisor or the supervised person, that it is appropriate to make an order under this subsection, the court may make an order discharging the supervision order or varying it by—

(a) inserting in it a provision specifying the duration of the order or altering or cancelling such a provision already included in it; or

(b) substituting for the provisions of the order by which the supervisor is designated or by virtue of which he is selected such other provisions in that behalf as could have been included in the order if the court had then had power to make it and were exercising the power; or

(c) substituting for the name of an area included in the order in pursuance of section 18 (2) (a) of this Act the name of any other area of a local authority or petty sessions area, as the case may be, in which it appears to the court that the supervised person resides or will reside; or

(d) cancelling any provision included in the order by virtue of section 18 (2) (b) of this Act or inserting in it any provision prescribed for the purposes of that paragraph ; or

(e) cancelling any requirement included in the order in pursuance of section 12 (1) or (2) of this Act.

(4) If while a supervision order is in force in respect of a supervised person who has attained the age of eighteen it is proved to the satisfaction of a magistrates' court other than a juvenile court, on the application of the supervisor, that the supervised person has failed to comply with any requirement included in the supervision order in pursuance of section 12 or section 18 (2) (b) of this Act, the court may—

(a) whether or not it also makes an order under subsection (3) of this section, order him to pay a fine of an amount not exceeding twenty pounds or, subject to subsection (10) of the following section, make an attendance centre order in respect of him;

(b) if it also discharges the supervision order, make an order imposing on him any punishment which it could have imposed on him if it had then had power to try him for the offence in consequence of which the supervision order was made and had convicted him in the exercise of that power;

and in a case where the offence in question is of a kind which the court has no power to try or has no power to try without appropriate consents, the punishment imposed by virtue of paragraph (b) of this subsection shall not exceed that which any court having power to try such an offence could have imposed in respect of it and shall not in any event exceed imprisonment for a term of six months and a fine of four hundred pounds.

(5) If a medical practitioner by whom or under whose direction a supervised person is being treated for his mental condition in pursuance of a requirement included in a supervision order by virtue of section 12 (4) of this Act is unwilling to continue to treat or direct the treatment of the supervised person or is of opinion—

(a) that the treatment should be continued beyond the period specified in that behalf in the order; or
(b) that the supervised person needs different treatment; or
(c) that he is not susceptible to treatment; or
(d) that he does not require further treatment,

the practitioner shall make a report in writing to that effect to the supervisor; and on receiving a report under this subsection the supervisor shall refer it to a juvenile court, and on such a reference the court may make an order cancelling or varying the requirement.

(6) The preceding provisions of this section shall have effect subject to the provisions of the following section.

NOTES

General note.—The provisions of sub-s. (1) substantially re-enact the previous law. For power to bring a supervised person before the court see s. 16 (2). Sub-s. (2) does not apply to a supervision order made by virtue of s. 72 of the Social Work (Scotland) Act, 1968 (p. 235, *ante*).

"On the application of the ... supervised person" (sub-s. (1)).—Or by his parent or guardian (s. 70 (2)).

"On discharging the supervision order make a care order" (sub-s. (1)).—By s. 16 (6) the power to make a care order or indeed any other order under s. 15 (1) except minor variations is only to be exercised where the court is satisfied that the supervised person either is unlikely to receive the care or control he needs unless the court makes the order or is likely to receive it, notwithstanding the order.

Other than interim order (sub-s. (1)).—See sub-s. 16 (4) (b).

"Who has attained the age of 18." (sub-s. (3)).—A supervision order made under ss. 1 or 21 (2) must expire at the age of 18. Subsections (3) and (4) only apply to supervision orders for an offence. These subsections confer jurisdiction on adult courts and the court's powers are similar to those in respect of a person on probation.

Fails to comply (sub-s. (4)). See note to s. 12, **Comply with such directions** (p. 151, *ante*).

"To the satisfaction of a magistrates' court (sub-s. (4)).—Section 16 (11) confers jurisdiction on the court acting for the petty sessions area named in the order in pursuance of s. 18 (2) (a).

"Whether or not it makes an order under subsection (3)" (sub-s. (4)).—Unlike a probation order, a fine of £20 or an attendance centre order may be imposed even though the supervision order is discharged. The power to make a probation order must be in doubt as the Act does not use the wording of ss. 6 and 8 of the Criminal Justice Act, 1948 "deal with him in any manner in which the court could deal with him if he had just been convicted". Although the subsection is confined to orders made for an offence, it may be possible in the appropriate case to extend the supervision order to a maximum of three years from the date on which the order was originally made.

Treatment should be continued beyond the period specified (sub-s. 15 (5) (a)).—There is no limit of 12 months as in the case of probation orders. The condition of treatment could therefore be extended to the length of the supervision order.

Attaining the age of 17 or 18.—See s. 16 (1), *post*.

Legal aid.—Legal aid may be granted by the court (Criminal Justice Act, 1967, Part IV, as amended by s. 33 of and Sched. I to the Children and Young Persons Act, 1969), pp. 326, 181, *post*.

Scotland.—As to transfers to and from Scotland, see Social Work (Scotland) Act, 1968, p. 232, *post*. As to adjustments between authorities see ss. 86 and 87, *ibid*., p. 240, *post* (which applies to England and Wales by s. 97, *ibid*.).

Subsection (4) shall have effect as if paragraph (b) and the words following it were omitted in relation to orders made under s. 7A (4) of the Criminal Justice (Scotland) Act, 1949 (sub-s. (5), *ibid*.).

In relation to supervision orders made under s. 72 (1A) of the Social Work (Scotland) Act, 1968, this section has effect as if sub-s. (2) were omitted.

16. Provisions supplementary to s. 15.—(1) Where the supervisor makes an application or reference under the preceding section to a court he may bring the supervised person before the court, and subject to subsection (5) of this section a court shall not make an order under that section unless the supervised person is present before the court.

(2) Without prejudice to any power to issue a summons or warrant apart from this subsection, a justice may issue a summons or warrant for the purpose of securing the attendance of a supervised person before the court to which any application or reference in respect of him is made under the preceding section; but subsections (3) and (4) of section 47 of the Magistrates' Courts Act, 1952 (which among other things restrict the circumstances in which a warrant may be issued) shall apply with the necessary modifications to a warrant under this subsection as they apply to a warrant under that section and as if in subsection (3) after the word "summons" there were inserted the words "cannot be served or".

(3) Where the supervised person is arrested in pursuance of a warrant issued by virtue of the preceding subsection and cannot be brought immediately before the court referred to in that subsection, the person in whose custody he is—

(a) may make arrangements for his detention in a place of safety for a period of not more than seventy-two hours from the time of the arrest (and it shall be lawful for him to be detained in pursuance of the arrangements); and

(b) shall within that period, unless within it the relevant infant is brought before the court aforesaid, bring him before a justice;

and the justice shall either direct that he be released forthwith or—

(i) if he has not attained the age of eighteen, make an interim order in respect of him;

(ii) if he has attained that age, remand him.

(4) If on an application to a court under subsection (1) of the preceding section—

(a) the supervised person is brought before the court under a warrant issued or an interim order made by virtue of the preceding provisions of this section; or

(b) the court considers that it is likely to exercise its powers under that subsection to make an order in respect of the supervised person but, before deciding whether to do so, seeks information with respect to him which it considers is unlikely to be obtained unless the court makes an interim order in respect of him,

the court may make an interim order in respect of the supervised person.

(5) A court may make an order under the preceding section in the absence of the supervised person if the effect of the order is confined to one or more of the following, that is to say—

   (a) discharging the supervision order;

   (b) cancelling a provision included in the supervision order in pursuance of section 12 or section 18 (2) (b) of this Act;

   (c) reducing the duration of the supervision order or any provision included in it in pursuance of the said section 12;

   (d) altering in the supervision order the name of any area;

   (e) changing the supervisor.

(6) A juvenile court shall not—

   (a) exercise its powers under subsection (1) of the preceding section to make a care order or an order discharging a supervision order or inserting in it a requirement authorised by section 12 of this Act or varying or cancelling such a requirement except in a case where the court is satisfied that the supervised person either is unlikely to receive the care or control he needs unless the court makes the order or is likely to receive it notwithstanding the order;

   (b) exercise its powers to make an order under subsection (5) of the preceding section except in such a case as is mentioned in paragraph (a) of this subsection;

   (c) exercise its powers under the said subsection (1) to make an order inserting a requirement authorised by section 12 (4) of this Act in a supervision order which does not already contain such a requirement unless the court is satisfied as mentioned in the said section 12 (4) on such evidence as is there mentioned.

(7) Where the supervised person has attained the age of fourteen, then except with his consent a court shall not make an order under the preceding section containing provisions which insert in the supervision order a requirement authorised by section 12 (3) of this Act or which alter such a requirement already included in the supervision order otherwise than by removing it or reducing its duration.

(8) The supervised person may appeal to the Crown Court against—

   (a) any order made under the preceding section, except an order made or which could have been made in the absence of the supervised person and an order containing only provisions to which he consented in pursuance of the preceding subsection;

   (b) the dismissal of an application under that section to discharge a supervision order.

(9) Where an application under the preceding section for the discharge of a supervision order is dismissed, no further application for its discharge shall be made under that section by any person during the period of three

months beginning with the date of the dismissal except with the consent of a court having jurisdiction to entertain such an application.

(10) In paragraph (a) of subsection (4) of the preceding section "attendance centre order" means such an order to attend an attendance centre as is mentioned in subsection (1) of section 19 of the Criminal Justice Act, 1948; and the provisions of that section shall accordingly apply for the purposes of that paragraph as if for the words from "has power" to "probation order" in subsection (1) there were substituted the words "considers it appropriate to make an attendance centre order in respect of any person in pursuance of section 15 (4) of the Children and Young Persons Act, 1969" and for references to an offender there were substituted references to the supervised person and as if subsection (5) were omitted.

(11) In this and the preceding section references to a juvenile court or any other magistrates' court, in relation to a supervision order, are references to such a court acting for the petty sessions area for the time being named in the order in pursuance of section 18 (2) (a) of this Act; and if while an application to a juvenile court in pursuance of the preceding section is pending the supervised person to whom it relates attains the age of seventeen or eighteen, the court shall deal with the application as if he had not attained the age in question.

NOTES

Magistrates' Courts Act, 1952, s. 47 (sub-s. (2)).—See note to s. 2 (4), *ante*.

"Exercise its power under subsection 1 of section 15" (sub-s. (6) (c)).— This applies the test of care or control when a condition of mental treatment is varied.

A young person's consent is always required before such a requirement is inserted (s. 12 (5), *ante*).

Where an application is dismissed (sub-s. (9)).—See similar provision in respect of care orders in s. 21 (3), *post*.

Appeal to the Crown Court (sub-s. (8)).—Legal aid may be granted by the court (Criminal Justice Act, 1967, Part IV, as amended by s. 33 of and Sched. I to the Children and Young Persons Act, 1969, *post*).

17. Termination of supervision.—A supervision order shall, unless it has previously been discharged, cease to have effect—

    (a) in any case, on the expiration of the period of three years, or such shorter period as may be specified in the order, beginning with the date on which the order was originally made;

    (b) if the order was made by virtue of section 1 of this Act or on the occasion of the discharge of a care order and the supervised person attains the age of eighteen on a day earlier than that on which the order would expire under paragraph (a) above, on that earlier day.

NOTES

"Attains the age".—See s. 9 of the Family Law Reform Act, 1969, p. 1310, *post*.

"Supervision order".—This will include a supervision order made after a reference under the Criminal Justice (Scotland) Act, 1949, s. 7A (p. 299, *ante*) and also an order under s. 72 of the Social Work (Scotland) Act, 1968 but in relation to the latter order para. (a) shall have effect as if the reference to three years and the date on which the order was originally made were respectively references to one year and the date on which the said notification was sent, and as if in para. (b) the words from "the order was" to "and" were omitted (s. 72, *ibid.*). In relation to orders under s. 7A (4) para. (a) shall have effect as if the second reference to the supervision order were a reference to the probation order in consequence of which the order was made (sub-s. (5), *ibid.*).

18. Supplementary provisions relating to supervision orders.— (1) A court shall not make a supervision order unless it is satisfied that the supervised person resides or will reside in the area of a local authority; and a court shall be entitled to be satisfied that the supervised person will so reside if he is to be required so to reside by a provision to be included in the order in pursuance of section 12 (1) of this Act.

(2) A supervision order—

(a) shall name the area of the local authority and the petty sessions area in which it appears to the court making the order, or to the court varying any provision included in the order in pursuance of this paragraph, that the supervised person resides or will reside; and

(b) may contain such prescribed provisions as the court aforesaid considers appropriate for facilitating the performance by the supervisor of his functions under section 14 of this Act, including any prescribed provisions for requiring visits to be made by the supervised person to the supervisor,

and in paragraph (b) of this subsection " prescribed"means prescribed by rules under section 15 of the Justices of the Peace Act, 1949.

(3) A court which makes a supervision order or an order varying or discharging a supervision order shall forthwith send a copy of its order—

(a) to the supervised person and, if the supervised person is a child, to his parent or guardian; and

(b) to the supervisor and any person who has ceased to be the supervisor by virtue of the order; and

(c) to any local authority who is not entitled by virtue of the preceding paragraph to such a copy and whose area is named in the supervision order in pursuance of the preceding subsection or has ceased to be so named by virtue of the court's order; and

(d) where the supervised person is required by the order, or was required by the supervision order before it was varied or discharged, to reside with an individual or to undergo treatment by or under the direction of an individual or at any place, to the individual or the person in charge of that place; and

(e) where a petty sessions area named in the order or discharged order in pursuance of subsection (2) of this section is not that for which the court acts, to the clerk to the justices for the petty sessions area so named;

and, in a case falling within paragraph (e) of this subsection, shall also send to the clerk to the justices in question such documents and information relating to the case as the court considers likely to be of assistance to them.

(4) Where a supervision order requires compliance with such directions as are mentioned in section 12 (2) of this Act, any expenditure incurred by the supervisor for the purposes of the directions shall be defrayed by the local authority of which the area is named in the order in pursuance of subsection (2) of this section.

NOTES

"**Resides**" (sub-s. (1)).—This means habitually resides (s. 70, *post*) or residence under a requirement in a supervision order.

"**Shall name the area of the local authority**" (sub-s. (2)).—This is so even where a probation officer supervises under s. 13 (2). The local authority is responsible for the payment of the cost of requirements under s. 12 (2) (sub-s. (4)).

"**Prescribed provisions**" (sub-s. (2) (b)).—See Rule 28 (2) Magistrates' Courts (Children and Young Persons) Rules, 1970, p. 581, *post*, and forms 43, 44 and 45. For duty of court to explain effect of order see Rule 21 (2) and note thereto.

"**Such documents and information**" (sub-s. (3)).—For example social enquiry reports, psychiatric reports, notes of evidence.

"**Any expenditure incurred**" (sub-s. (4)).—At present, a probation and after care committee has no authority to pay for such expenditure and there is considerable local variation in the use of charitable funds etc. for these purposes.

Scotland.—Section 73 (1A) of the Social Work Scotland Act, 1968 (p. 237, *post*) makes provision for supervision orders to be made in respect of persons residing or proposing to reside in Scotland. For amendment of an existing supervision order where the subject resides or proposes to reside in Scotland see s. 73 (1), *ibid.*, p. 236, *post*. The situation where a probationer or subject of a supervision requirement lives or proposes to live in England or Wales is covered by s. 7A Criminal Justice (Scotland) Act, 1949, and s. 72 (1A), *ibid.*, *post*.

19. Facilities for the carrying out of supervisors' directions.—(1) It shall be the duty of the children's regional planning committee for each planning area (hereafter in this section referred to as "the committee") to make arrangements, with such persons as the committee thinks fit, for the provision by those persons of facilities for enabling directions given by virtue of section 12 (2) of this Act to persons resident in the area to be carried out effectively.

(2) The committee shall specify the arrangements made in pursuance of the preceding subsection in a scheme and shall submit the scheme to the Secretary of State for him to determine the date on which it is to come into force; and the Secretary of State shall, after consultation with the committee and the relevant authorities, determine that date and notify his determination to the committee.

(3) On receiving a notification in pursuance of subsection (2) of this section in respect of a scheme, the committee shall send copies of the scheme and notification to each of the relevant authorities and to the clerk to the justices for each petty sessions area of which any part is included in the planning area in question; and each of the relevant authorities shall, as soon as practicable after receiving those documents, keep a copy of them available at their principal offices for inspection by members of the public at all reasonable hours and on demand by any person furnish him with a copy of them free of charge.

(4) If, after the scheme prepared by the committee under this section has come into force, any arrangements specified in it are cancelled or the

committee makes arrangements for the purposes of this section other than arrangements so specified, the committee shall send notice of the cancellations or other arrangements, stating the date on which they are to come into force and the alterations in the scheme which they entail, to the Secretary of State and the authorities and clerks mentioned in subsection (3) of this section; and on and after that date the scheme shall have effect subject to those alterations and the relevant authorities shall have, in relation to the notice, the same duty as is imposed on them by that subsection in relation to the scheme.

(5) Arrangements in pursuance of this section shall not be made for any facilities unless the facilities are approved or are of a kind approved by the Secretary of State for the purposes of this section; but where arrangements in pursuance of this section are made by the committee with any of the relevant authorities for the provision of facilities by the authority it shall be the duty of the authority to provide those facilities while the scheme is in force and those arrangements are specified in it.

(6) A court shall not include in a supervision order any such requirements as are mentioned in section 12 (2) of this Act unless the court is satisfied that a scheme under this section is in force for the planning area in which the supervised person resides or will reside or that the date on which such a scheme is to come into force has been determined; and a supervisor authorised to give directions by virtue of any such requirements shall not, in pursuance of those requirements, give directions involving the use of facilities which are not for the time being specified in a scheme in force under this section for the planning area aforesaid.

NOTES

Children's regional planning committee (sub-s. (1)).—For definition of planning area see s. 35 (1), *post*. For composition etc. of planning committees see Sched. II. See also the Children and Young Persons (Planning Areas) Order, 1970, S.I. 1970 No. 335.

"Such persons as the committee think fit" (sub-s. (1)).—*e.g.* local authority or voluntary organisations.

"Facilities" (sub-s. (1)).—The determination of the Secretary of State is necessary before directions for the use of facilities can be included in a supervision order (sub-s. (6)).

When an approved scheme contains such provisions for "intermediate treatment" as will take the place of detention centres and attendance centres, the secretary of State may give notice to courts under s. 7 (3) of the Act.

"Relevant authorities".—For definition see s. 35 (3).

"It shall be the duty of the authority" (sub-s. (5)).—Where a *local authority* has agreed to provide facilities they must be provided for as long as the facilities are included in the scheme. No similar duty is placed upon other organisations.

Committal to care of local authorities

20. Orders for committal to care of local authorities.—(1) Any provision of this Act authorising the making of a care order in respect of any person shall be construed as authorising the making of an order committing him to the care of a local authority; and in this Act "care order" shall be construed accordingly and "interim order" means a care order containing provision for the order to expire with the expiration of twenty-eight days, or of a shorter period specified in the order, beginning—

    (a) if the order is made by a court, with the date of the making of the order; and

    (b) if it is made by a justice, with the date when the person to whom it relates was first in legal custody in connection with the matter in consequence of which the order is made.

(2) The local authority to whose care a person is committed by a care order shall be—

    (a) except in the case of an interim order, the local authority in whose area it appears to the court making the order that that person resides or, if it does not appear to the court that he resides in the area of a local authority, any local authority in whose area it appears to the court that any offence was committed or any circumstances arose in consequence of which the order is made; and

    (b) in the case of an interim order, such one of the local authorities mentioned in paragraph (a) of this subsection as the court or justice making the order thinks fit (whether or not the person in question appears to reside in their area).

(3) Subject to the provisions of the following section, a care order other than an interim order shall cease to have effect—

    (a) if the person to whom it relates had attained the age of sixteen when the order was originally made, when he attains the age of nineteen; and

    (b) in any other case, when that person attains the age of eighteen.

(4) A care order shall be sufficient authority for the detention by any local authority or constable of the person to whom the order relates until he is received into the care of the authority to whose care he is committed by the order.

NOTES

"**If it is made by a justice**" (**sub-s. (1))**.—*I.e.* under ss. 22 (5); 28 (6); see note "or a justice of the peace" to s. 23 of the Act of 1963, p. 95, *ante*.

Effectively a person cannot be detained for a period exceeding 28 days without being brought before a court as opposed to a single justice.

"**In the case of an interim order**" (**sub-s. (1))**.—The local authority would normally be the authority acting for the area where the relevant infant resides, as under s. 2 (11) the court shall direct that the infant be brought before his "home" court.

"**That person resides**" (**sub-s. (2))**.—Resides means "habitually resides" (s. 70, *post*). Presumably the relevant time is the making of the order, see s. 21 (5).

In an offence condition care proceeding where the court proposes to act under s. 3 (5) the appropriate authority before a finding would be the one acting for the court proposing to make the finding.

Residence.—An individual resides where he eats, drinks and sleeps, or where his family or his servants eat, drink and sleep (per Bailey, J., in *R.* v. *North Curry (Inhabitants)* (1825), 4 B. & C. 953). "A person resides where he lives, where he has his bed, and where he dwells" (per Lord Reading, C.J. in *Stoke-on-Trent Borough Council* v. *Cheshire County Council*, [1915] 3 K. B. 699). The importance of determining the question of residence lies in its application to the question of liability for maintenance.

Effect of Adoption order.—See s. 15 (4) Adoption Act, 1958, p. 1049, *post*.

"The local authority ... shall be".—In the case of a care order taking effect by virtue of s. 74 Social Work (Scotland) Act, 1968, this section has effect as if sub-s. (2) were omitted. The Scottish Act provides that the Secretary of State will name the local authority.

"Detention by any local authority or constable" (sub-s. (4)).—Police or local authority may therefore convey the subject of a care order.

"Shall cease to have effect".—In sub-s. (3) para (a) and in para (b) the words "in any other case" does not apply to care orders made by virtue of s. 74 of the Social Work (Scotland) Act, 1968 (sub-s. (6), *ibid.*).

Transitional provisions.—See para. 11, Sched. IV. Where a fit person order is converted into a care order it will expire at the age of 18; otherwise the effect might be to extend the period during which a person who is already subject to a fit person order is liable to remain in care.

Family Allowances.—See leaflet at p. 1006, *post.*

Northern Ireland.—See note to. 21. Sub-sections (2), (3) do not apply to a care order made by virtue of s. 25 (*post*).

Isle of Man, Channel Islands.—See s. 26, *post.*

21. Variation and discharge of care orders.—(1) If it appears to a juvenile court, on the application of a local authority to whose care a person is committed by a care order which would cease to have effect by virtue of subsection (3) (b) of the preceding section, that he is accommodated in a community home or a home provided by the Secretary of State and that by reason of his mental condition or behaviour it is in his interest or the public interest for him to continue to be so accommodated after he attains the age of eighteen, the court may order that the care order shall continue in force until he attains the age of nineteen; but the court shall not make an order under this subsection unless the person in question is present before the court.

(2) If it appears to a juvenile court, on the application of a local authority to whose care a person is committed by a care order or on the application of that person, that it is appropriate to discharge the order, the court may discharge it and on discharging it may, unless it was an interim order and unless the person to whom the discharged order related has attained the age of eighteen, make a supervision order in respect of him.

(3) Where an application under the preceding subsection for the discharge of a care order is dismissed, then—

(a) in the case of an interim order, no further application for its discharge shall be made under that subsection except with the consent of a juvenile court (without prejudice to the power to make an application under subsection (4) of the following section) and

(b) in any other case, no further application for its discharge shall be made under this subsection by any person during the period of three months beginning with the date of the dismissal except with the consent of a juvenile court.

(4) The person to whom the relevant care order relates or related may appeal to the Crown Court against an order under subsection (1) of this section or a supervision order made in pursuance of subsection (2) of this

section or the dismissal of an application under the said subsection (2) for the discharge of the care order.

(5) The local authority to whose care a person is committed by a care order (other than an interim order) may, within the period of three months beginning with the date of the order, appeal to the Crown Court against the provision of the order naming their area on the ground that at the time the order was made the person aforesaid resided in the area of another local authority named in the notice of appeal; but no appeal shall be brought by a local authority under this subsection unless they give notice in writing of the proposal to bring it to the other local authority in question before giving notice of appeal.

(6) References in this section to a juvenile court, in relation to a care order, are references to a juvenile court acting for any part of the area of the local authority to whose care a person is committed by the order or for the place where that persons resides.

NOTES

On the application of that person (sub-s. (2)). This also applies to his parent or guardian, See s. 70 (2), *post*.

"It is appropriate to discharge" (sub-s. (2)).—This provision includes the discharge of interim care orders. Section 22 (4) provides for an application to discharge an interim order to be made to the High Court. This is not an appeal. The right to appeal to the Crown Court against a refusal to discharge an interim order (s. 21 (4)) may give rise to difficulty. If notice of appeal is given a court may be inhibited from taking further steps in the case till the appeal is heard, which may be some time after the expiration of the interim order. If further interim orders are then made in respect of the infant an endless succession of appeals may ensue. The difficulty arises from the definition of care order in s. 20 (1) so as to include an interim care order. In sub-s. (4) the use of the word "relates or related" seems to imply the possibility of appeal against an order which has expired.

"Community home".—See para. 3, Sched. III, *post*, for application to approved schools.

"During the period of three months" (sub-s. (3) (b)).—This provision is new and effectively limits the number of applications that may be made.

Presumably before a court grants a summons to discharge it would be satisfied that there is "fresh evidence".

Appeal against the provision naming that area. (sub-s. (5)).—This subsection corresponds to s. 90 of the Children and Young Persons Act, 1933 and s. 33 of the Children and Young Persons Act, 1963 (now repealed). The appeal now lies direct to the Crown Court. The provisions allowing appeal on the ground that residence is not known have not been re-enacted and the ground set out in sub-s. (5) is the only ground.

The time limit for appeal is not affected by the Crown Court Rules, p. 654, *post* (Rule 6 (2) and Sched. I, part I. Subsection (5) does not apply to orders made under s. 74, Social Work (Scotland) Act, 1968, (sub-s. (6), *ibid*.).

Legal aid.—Legal aid may be granted by the court—(Criminal Justice Act, 1967, Part IV, as amended by s. 33 and Sched. I of the Children and Young Persons Act, 1969).

Northern Ireland.—For transfer from training school in Northern Ireland and from care of local authority to care of managers of a training school, see s. 25, *post*, sub-ss. (1), (5) do not apply to a care order under s. 25 (1).

Isle of Man, Channel Islands.—See s. 26, *post*.

22. Special provisions relating to interim orders.—(1) A juvenile court or a justice shall not make an interim order in respect of any person unless either—

(a) that person is present before the court or justice; or
(b) the court or justice is satisfied that he is under the age of five or cannot be present as aforesaid by reason of illness or accident.

(2) An interim order shall contain provision requiring the local authority to whose care a person is committed by the order to bring that person before a court specified in the order on the expiration of the order or at such earlier time as the specified court may require, so however that the said provision shall, if the court making the order considers it appropriate so to direct by reason of the fact that that person is under the age of five or by reason of illness or accident, require the local authority to bring him before the specified court on the expiration of the order only if the specified court so requires.

(3) A juvenile court acting for the same area as a juvenile court by which or a justice by whom an interim order has been made in respect of any person may, at any time before the expiration of the order, make a further interim order in respect of him; and the power to make an interim order conferred by this subsection is without prejudice to any other power to make such an order.

(4) The High Court may, on the application of a person to whom an interim order relates, discharge the order on such terms as the court thinks fit; but if on such an application the discharge of the order is refused, the local authority to whose care he is committed by the order shall not exercise in his case their powers under section 13 (2) of the Children Act, 1948 (which enables them to allow a parent or other person to be in charge of him) except with the consent and in accordance with any directions of the High Court.

(5) If a court which has made or, apart from this subsection, would make an interim order in respect of a person who has attained the age of fourteen certifies that he is of so unruly a character that he cannot safely be committed to the care of a local authority and has been notified by the Secretary of State that a remand centre is available for the reception from the court of persons of his class or description, then, subject to the following provisions of this section, the court shall commit him to a remand centre for twenty-eight days or such shorter period as may be specified in the warrant; but in a case where an interim order is in force in respect of the person in question, a warrant under this subsection shall not be issued in respect of him except on the application of the local authority to whose care he is committed by the order and shall not be issued for a period extending beyond the date fixed for the expiration of the order, and on the issue of a warrant under this subsection in such a case the interim order shall cease to have effect.

In this subsection "court" includes a justice.

(6) Subsections (1), (3) and (4) of this section, so much of section 2 (11) (a) as requires the clerk to be informed and section 21 (2) to (4) of this Act shall apply to a warrant under subsection (5) of this section as they apply to an interim order but as if the words "is under the age of five or" in subsection (1) of this section were omitted.

NOTES

"**Court specified in the order**" (**sub-s. (2)**).—*I.e.* not necessarily the committing court.

"**Expiration of the order" (sub-s. (2)).**—See s. 20 (1) (a) and (b).

"**So unruly a character" (sub-s. (5)).**—This re-enacts the provisions of s. 75 (2), Criminal Justice Act, 1948. As yet no remand centres are available. A number of establishments have been set up for use as remand centres but no remand centre rules have yet been made and the establishments are in law, prisons.

Note that s. 34 (1) (f) enables the minimum age of fourteen to be raised.

"**Court includes a justice" (sub-s. (5)).**—It will only rarely be necessary for a single justice to exercise these powers; there are difficulties if no clerk is present. The necessity for the presence of the young person (sub-s. (1) will probably rule out application being made at a justice's home).

"**The High Court may" (sub-s. (4)).**—There is a right of appeal against an interim order (s. 21 (4)), and a right to apply for discharge (s. 21 (2)).

23. Remand to care of local authorities etc.—(1) Where a court—

    (a) remands or commits for trial a child charged with homicide or remands a child convicted of homicide; or

    (b) remands a young person charged with or convicted of one or more offences or commits him for trial or sentence,

and he is not released on bail, then, subject to the following provisions of this section, the court shall commit him to the care of a local authority in whose area it appears to the court that he resides or that the offence or one of the offences was committed.

(2) If the court aforesaid certifies that a young person is of so unruly a character that he cannot safely be committed to the care of a local authority under the preceding subsection, then if the court has been notified by the Secretary of State that a remand centre is available for the reception from the court of persons of his class or description, it shall commit him to a remand centre and, if it has not been so notified, it shall commit him to a prison.

(3) If, on the application of the local authority to whose care a young person is committed by a warrant under subsection (1) of this section, the court by which he was so committed or any magistrates' court having jurisdiction in the place where he is for the time being certifies as mentioned in subsection (2) of this section, the provisions of the said subsection (2) relating to committal shall apply in relation to him and he shall cease to be committed in pursuance of the said subsection (1).

(4) The preceding provisions of this section shall have effect subject to the provisions of section 28 of the Magsitrates' Courts Act, 1952 (which relates to committal to quarter sessions with a view to a borstal sentence).

(5) In this section "court" and "magistrates' court" include a justice: and notwithstanding anything in the preceding provisions of this section, section 105 (5) of the said Act of 1952 (which provides for remands to the custody of a constable for periods not exceeding three clear days) shall have effect in relation to a child or young person as if for the reference to three clear days there were substituted a reference to twenty-four hours.

NOTES

General note.—Previous law governing remand and committals of young persons contained in s. 27 Criminal Justice Act, 1948, is repealed and a new s. 27, dealing with seventeen to twenty year-olds has been substituted. This section now contains provisions affecting "prosecutable" children and young persons.

"Remands a young person" (sub-s. (1) (b)).—Section 34 (1) (c) enables sub-s. (1) to be applied to children who are still of prosecutable age; the reference to "young person" includes a child who has attained the age of 10 (S.I. 1970 No. 1882, p. 624, *post*). **"Keep him in their care".**—See note to s. 24, *infra*.

"Subject to the provisions of section 28 of the Magistrates' Courts Act, 1952" (sub-s. (4)).—This provides that committals are to be to remand centres, or prison, and for further provisions regarding remands see ss. 46 (2) and 48 (3) Children and Young Persons Act, 1933 (pp. 51, 54, *ante*). For s. 28 of the Magistrates' Courts Act, 1952, see p. 307.

"Remands to the custody of a constable" (sub-s. (5)).—This may be necessary in some cases to avoid a long journey to a community home in an adjourned case. For s. 105 (5) of the Magistrates' Courts Act, 1952, see p. 383.

24. Powers and duties of local authorities etc. with respect to persons committed to their care.—(1) It shall be the duty of a local authority to whose care a person is committed by a care order or by a warrant under subsection (1) of the preceding section to receive him into their care and, notwithstanding any claim by his parent or guardian, to keep him in their care while the order or warrant is in force.

(2) A local authority shall, subject to the following provisions of this section, have the same powers and duties with respect to a person in their care by virtue of a care order or such a warrant as his parent or guardian would have apart from the order or warrant and may (without prejudice to the preceding provisions of this subsection but subject to regulations made in pursuance of section 43 of this Act) restrict his liberty to such extent as the authority consider appropriate.

(3) A local authority shall not cause a person in their care by virtue of a care order to be brought up in any religious creed other than that in which he would have been brought up apart from the order.

(4) It shall be the duty of a local authority to comply with any provision included in an interim order in pursuance of section 22 (2) of this Act and, in the case of a person in their care by virtue of the preceding section, to permit him to be removed from their care in due course of law.

(5) If a person who is subject to a care order and has attained the age of five is accommodated in a community home or other establishment which he has not been allowed to leave during the preceding three months for the purpose of ordinary attendance at an educational institution or at work and it appears to the local authority to whose care he is committed by the order that—

(a) communication between him and his parent or guardian has been so infrequent that it is appropriate to appoint a visitor for him; or

(b) he has not lived with or visited or been visited by either of his parents or his guardian during the preceding twelve months,

it shall be the duty of the authority to appoint an independent person to be his visitor for the purposes of this subsection; and a person so appointed shall—

(i) have the duty of visiting, advising and befriending the person to whom the care order relates; and

(ii) be entitled to exercise on behalf of that person his powers under section 21 (2) of this Act; and

(iii) be entitled to recover from the authority who appointed him any expenses reasonably incurred by him for the purposes of his functions under this subsection.

In this section "independent person" means a person satisfying such conditions as may be prescribed by regulations made by the Secretary of State with a view to securing that he is independent of the local authority in question and unconnected with any community home.

(6) A person's appointment as a visitor in pursuance of the preceding subsection shall be determined if the care order in question ceases to be in force or he gives notice in writing to the authority who appointed him that he resigns the appointment or the authority give him notice in writing that they terminate it; but the determination of such an appointment shall not prejudice any duty under the preceding subsection to make a further appointment.

(7) The functions conferred on a local authority by the preceding provisions of this section in respect of any person are in addition to the functions which, by virtue of section 27 of this Act, are conferred on the authority in respect of him by Part II of the Children Act, 1948.

(8) While a care order other than an interim order is in force in respect of a person who has not attained the age of eighteen, it shall be the duty of his parent to keep the local authority to whose care he is committed by the order informed of the parent's address; and if the parent knows of the order and fails to perform his duty under this subsection, the parent shall be liable on summary conviction to a fine not exceeding ten pounds unless he shows that at the material time he was residing at the address of the other parent and had reasonable cause to believe that the other parent had kept the authority informed of their address.

NOTES

"Keep him in their care".—A reference in s. 11 of the Children Act, 1948 (p. 892) to a child in care is a reference, *inter alia*, to a child in the care of a local authority under s. 23 (1) of this act. (*Ibid.*, s. 27, p. 172, *post*.)

By virtue of s. 13 of the Children Act, 1948, as substituted by s. 49 of this Act, p. 196, *post*, such a child may be allowed to be "under the charge and control of a parent, guardian, relative or friend".

The same powers and duties (sub-s. (2)).—But see s. 4 (3) of the Adoption Act, 1958, (p. 1031) as amended and note **"Consents required"** to s. 3 of the Marriage Act, 1949, p. 1216.

"Regulations" (sub-s. (2)).—No regulations have yet been made.

"Independent person".—See the Children and Young Persons (Definition of Independent Persons) Regulations, 1971, S.I. 1971 No. 486, p. 652, *post*.

Religious creed (sub-s. (3)).—This represents a change of emphasis. By s. 75 of the Children and Young Persons Act, 1933, a local authority or the fit person had to be of the same religious persuasion as the child or give an undertaking that the child would be brought up in accordance with that religious persuasion. Sub-s. (3) would seem to allow a local authority either positively to undertake a child's religious education in the creed in which he would have been brought up apart from the order or simply to refrain from educating him in the ways of any other religion.

In the case of young children, it is the right of the parents to choose the child's religion, and this naturally involves the right to change the child's religion, if the parents conscientiously change their own, in spite of baptism or other ceremonies.

See, as to change of religion, *R.* v. *Clarke, Re Race* (1857), 7 E. & B. 186; 21 J. P. N. 53; *Re Turner, Ex parte Turner* (1872), 36 J. P. 613; 41 L. J. Q. B. 142; *R.* v. *Williams* (1888), 58 L. J. Q. B. 176; 5 T. L. R. 104; *R.* v. *Barnardo (No.* 2) (1889), 58 L. J. Q. B. 522; *Stevenson* v. *Florant,* [1927] A. C. 211; 96 L. J. P. C. 1; *In Re Collins, an Infant,* [1950] Ch. 498; [1950] 1 All E. R. 1057.

If the parents disagree, the court will have to decide between them. Formerly the rights of the father were held to be superior to those of the mother, but since the passing of the Guardianship of Infants Act, 1925; 17 Halsbury's Statutes, 3rd Edn., 424, decisions to that effect are not necessarily binding. See *In Re Collins, supra.* The interests of the child are now the paramount consideration. The conduct of each parent, the religious education of the child in the past, and the probable effects of a change of religion, are all matters to be considered. If the child is of sufficient age, it may be consulted as to its own wishes (*Re W., W.* v. *M.,* [1907] 2 Ch. 557; 77 L. J. Ch. 147. In that case a boy of thirteen, an orphan, signified his wish to become a Christian, though he was the son of a Jewish father and was being brought up as a Jew. The Court of Appeal affirmed the order of the Chancery judge that the boy should be brought up as a Christian.

It has also been held by the House of Lords in *Ward* v. *Laverty,* [1925] A. C. 101; 94 L. J. P. C. 17, that where the eldest of a family had acquired strong convictions it would not be for her benefit to remove her to a household of a different faith and that it would not be for the benefit of the younger children to separate them from their elder sister; it was for the welfare of all the children that they should be brought up together with the relatives in whose custody they then were.

Where there is a parent, the responsibility for religious views is that of the parent, not of the court, and where the child is too young to have intelligent views of its own and the character of the parent is not attacked, the court must give effect to the wishes of the parent (*In Re Carroll,* [1931] 1 K. B. 317; 95 J. P. 25).

At what age the infant is allowed to exercise a choice contrary to the wishes of his parent is not clear. In *Re May, Eggar* v. *May,* [1917] 2 Ch. 126; 86 L. J. Ch. 698, Neville, J., seems to have taken the view that the father has the right to decide up to the time the child becomes twenty-one years of age. But in *R.* v. *Gyngall,* [1893] 2 Q. B. 232; 57 J. P. 773, Lord Esher, M.R., speaks of sixteen as the age at which a child is of an age to act upon his own wishes. In that case it was held that although at common law the parent had an absolute right to the custody and guardianship of the child unless that right was forfeited by misconduct, yet the court, exercising the paternal jurisdiction of the old Court of Chancery, may supersede that right, and will, in the circumstances of each case, decree what is best for the welfare of the child. The same learned judge, however, in *Re Agar-Ellis, Agar-Ellis* v. *Lascelles* (1883), 24 Ch. D. 317, at p. 326; 53 L. J. Ch. 10, said that the father has the control over the person, education and conduct of his children until they are twenty-one years of age. This, of course, is subject to the reservation that he may forfeit those rights.

Generally speaking, infants are considered to be capable of self-support at sixteen years of age (compare s. 15 (2) (a) of the Guardianship of Minors Act, 1971, p. 1208, *post*). In religious matters they may have opinions of their own at an even earlier age, as was recognised by s. 73 (1) of the Poor Law Act, 1930 [*Repealed*].

The cases of *Re Thain, Thain* v. *Taylor,* [1926] Ch. 676; 95 L. J. Ch. 292, and *McClement* v. *McClement* (1958), 122 J. P. Jo. 181, may also be consulted.

Transfer

25. Transfers between England or Wales and Northern Ireland. —(1) If it appears to the Secretary of State, on the application of the welfare authority or the managers of the training school to whose care a person is committed by a fit person order or by virtue of a training school order, that his parent or guardian resides or will reside in the area of a local authority in England or Wales, the Secretary of State may make an order committing him to the care of that local authority; and while an order under this subsection is in force it shall have effect as if it were a care order and as if sections 20 (2) and (3) and 21 (1) and (5) of this Act were omitted and in section 31 (3) (a) of this Act for the reference to section 20 (3) there were substituted a reference to subsection (3) of this section.

(2) If it appears to the Minister of Home Affairs for Northern Ireland on the application of the local authority to whose care a person is committed by a care order other than an interim order, that his parent or guardian resides or will reside in Northern Ireland, the said Minister may make an order committing him to the care of the managers of a training school or to the care of the welfare authority in whose area his parent or guardian resides or will reside; and the provisions of the Children and Young Persons Act (Northern Ireland), 1968 (except sections 83 (3) (a), 88 (3), 90 and 91 (3)) shall apply to an order under this subsection as if it were a training school order made on the date of the care order or, as the case may be, a fit person order.

If an order under this subsection commits a person to the care of the managers of a training school, the contributions to be made in respect of him under section 161 of the said Act of 1968 shall be made by such council as may be named in that order, being the council within whose district his parent proposes to reside or is residing at the time of the order.

(3) When a person is received into the care of a local authority or welfare authority or the managers of a training school in pursuance of an order under this section, the training school order, fit person order or care order in consequence of which the order under this section was made shall cease to have effect; and the order under this section shall, unless it is discharged earlier, cease to have effect—

    (a) in the case of an order under subsection (1), on the earlier of the following dates, that is to say, the date when the person to whom the order relates attains the age of nineteen or the date when, by the effluxion of time, the fit person order aforesaid would have ceased to have effect or, as the case may be, the period of his detention under the training school order aforesaid would have expired;

    (b) in the case of an order under subsection (2), on the date when the care order aforesaid would have ceased to have effect by the effluxion of time or—

        (i) if the person to whom the order relates is committed by it to the care of a welfare authority and will attain the age of eighteen before that date, when he attains that age;

        (ii) if the order has effect by virtue of subsection (2) as a training school order and the period of supervision following the detention of the person in question in pursuance of the order expires before that date, when that period expires.

(4) An order under this section shall be sufficient authority for the detention in Northern Ireland, by any constable or by a person duly authorised by a local authority or welfare authority or the managers of a training school, of the person to whom the order relates until he is received into the care of the authority or managers to whose care he is committed by the order.

(5) In this section "training school", "training school order" and "welfare authority" have the same meaning as in the said Act of 1968, and "fit

person order" means an order under that Act committing a person to the care of a fit person.

NOTES

General note.—As a transfer under sub-s. (1) depends upon the residence of the parent, the right of the English court to discharge is not excluded. Transfer may now operate to and from Northern Ireland (cf. the former provisions of s. 83 of the Children and Young Persons Act, 1933).

"**Northern Ireland**"—Detention in transit in England or Wales is covered by *ibid.*, s. 20 (4).

26. Transfers between England or Wales and the Channel Islands or Isle of Man.—(1) The Secretary of State may by order designate for the purposes of this section an order of any description which—

(a) a court in the Isle of Man or any of the Channel Islands is authorised to make by the law for the time being in force in that country; and

(b) provides for the committal to the care of a public authority of a person who has not attained the age of eighteen; and

(c) appears to the Secretary of State to be of the same nature as a care order other than an interim order;

and in this section "relevant order" means an order of a description for the time being so designated and "the relevant authority", in relation to a relevant order, means the authority in the Isle of Man or any of the Channel Islands to whose care the person to whom the order relates is, under the law of that country, committed by the order.

(2) The Secretary of State may authorise a local authority to receive into their care any person named in the authorisation who is the subject of a relevant order; and while such an authorisation is in force in respect of any person he shall, subject to the following subsection, be deemed to be the subject of a care order committing him to the care of the local authority.

(3) This Act shall have effect, in relation to a person in respect of whom an authorisation under this section is in force, as if sections 20 (2) and (3), 21 and 31 and in section 27 (4) the words from "and if" onwards were omitted; and it shall be the duty of a local authority who propose, in exercise of their powers under section 13 (2) of the Children Act, 1948, to allow such a person residing outside England and Wales to consult the relevant authority before exercising those powers.

(4) An authorisation given to a local authority under this section shall cease to have effect when—

(a) the local authority is informed by the Secretary of State that he has revoked it; or

(b) the relevant order to which the authorisation relates ceases to have effect by the effluxion of time under the law of the place where the order was made or the local authority is informed by the relevant authority that the order has been discharged under that law; or

(c) the person to whom the relevant order relates is again received into the care of the relevant authority;

and if a local authority having by virtue of this section the care of a person to whom a relevant order relates is requested by the relevant authority to make arrangements for him to be received again into the care of the relevant authority, it shall be the duty of the local authority to comply with the request.

NOTES

General note.—Corresponding provisions were made in s. 83 of the Children and Young Persons Act, 1933.

"May by order designate" (sub-s. (1)).—The order to be designated by the Secretary of State is one of those authorised by the relevant authority and which "appears to be of the same nature as a care order". At present there is the equivalent of a fit person order in the Isle of Man for example and such an order has been designated. (S.I. 1971 No. 1288, p. 667, *post*). A special care order within the meaning of the Children and Young Persons (Guernsey) Law, 1967 as amended has also been designated, S.I. 1971 No. 348, p. 652, *post*.

The exclusion of the review provisions in s. 27 (4) does not over-ride the power of the Secretary of State to revoke the authorisation. The right to discharge under s. 21, which is excluded, is given to the relevant authority making the order (sub-s. (4) (b)).

Consequential modifications of ss. 11 and 12 of Children Act, 1948

27. Consequential modifications of 1948 c. 43 ss. 11 and 12.—(1) For section 11 of the Children Act, 1948 (which specifies the children in respect of whom functions are conferred on local authorities by Part II of that Act) there shall be substituted the following section:—

> **11. Children to whom Part II applies.**—Except where the contrary intention appears, any reference in this Part of this Act to a child who is or was in the care of a local authority is a reference to a child who is or was in the care of the authority under section 1 of this Act or by virtue of a care order within the meaning of the Children and Young Persons Act, 1969 or a warrant under section 23 (1) of that Act (which relates to remands in the care of local authorities);

but nothing in the said section 11 as replaced by this subsection prejudices the application of any provision of the said Part II to any person by virtue of an enactment passed after that Act and before this Act.

(2) If it appears to a local authority that it is necessary, for the purpose of protecting members of the public, to exercise their powers in relation to a particular child in their care in a manner which may not be consistent with their general duty under section 12 (1) of the said Act of 1948 to further his best interests and afford him opportunity for proper development, the authority may, notwithstanding that duty, act in that manner.

(3) If the Secretary of State considers it necessary, for the purpose of protecting members of the public, to give directions to a local authority with respect to the exercise of their powers in relation to a particular child in their care, he may give such directions to the authority; and it shall be the duty of the authority, notwithstanding their general duty aforesaid, to comply with any such directions.

(4) Without prejudice to their general duty aforesaid, it shall be the duty of a local authority who have at any time had a child in their care

throughout the preceding six months and have not during that period held a review of his case in pursuance of this subsection to review his case as soon as is practicable after the expiration of that period and, if a care order is in force with respect to him, to consider in the course of the review whether to make an application for the discharge of the order.

NOTES

General note.—The new s. 11 of the Children Act, 1948, is necessary to take account of the changes made by this Act.

"Passed after that Act and or before this Act" (sub-s. (1)).—*E.g.* s. 2 (e) of the Matrimonial Proceedings (Magistrates' Courts) Act, 1960 and s. 36 of the Matrimonial Causes Act, 1965.

Isle of Man, Channel Islands.—See s. 26, *ante.*

"Protecting members of the public" (sub-s. (2)).—Presumably with the passing of approved schools, community homes with a closed provision will be made available to serve this purpose. By s. 43 (1) (d) the Secretary of State may give directions to a local authority.

"Hold a review of his case" (sub-s. (4)).—The Act is silent as to how the review should be made but see "The Report of the Committee on Local Authority and Allied Personal Social Services" (Command No. 3703) where the suggestion is made that parents be given the right to challenge decisions and to be legally represented. The review is that of the local authority who may nevertheless wish to have an independent person on the review body. It is particularly important that the decisions of a local authority, which may ultimately involve detention in borstal type accommodation should be carefully reviewed. It may well be that regulations under s. 43 will specify the period of such detention and other matters.

Detention

28. Detention of child or young person in place of safety.—(1) If, upon an application to a justice by any person for authority to detain a child or young person and take him to a place of safety, the justice is satisfied that the applicant has reasonable cause to believe that—

(a) any of the conditions set out in section 1 (2) (a) to (e) of this Act is satisfied in respect of the child or young person; or

(b) an appropriate court would find the condition set out in section 1 (2) (b) of this Act satisfied in respect of him; or

(c) the child or young person is about to leave the United Kingdom in contravention of section 25 of the Act of 1933 (which regulates the sending abroad of juvenile entertainers),

the justice may grant the application; and the child or young person in respect of whom an authorisation is issued under this subsection may be detained in a place of safety by virtue of the authorisation for twenty-eight days beginning with the date of authorisation, or for such shorter period beginning with that date as may be specified in the authorisation.

(2) Any constable may detain a child or young person as respects whom the constable has reasonable cause to believe that any of the conditions set out in section 1 (2) (a) to (d) of this Act is satisfied or that an appropriate court would find the condition set out in section 1 (2) (b) of this Act satisfied or that an offence is being committed under section 10 (1) of the Act of 1933 (which penalises a vagrant who takes a juvenile from place to place).

(3) A person who detains any person in pursuance of the preceding provisions of this section shall, as soon as practicable after doing so, inform him of the reason for his detention and take such steps as are practicable for informing his parent or guardian of his detention and of the reason for it.

(4) A constable who detains any person in pursuance of subsection (2) of this section or who arrests a child without a warrant otherwise than for homicide shall as soon as practicable after doing so secure that the case is enquired into by a police officer not below the rank of inspector or by the police officer in charge of a police station, and that officer shall on completing the enquiry either—

    (a) release the person in question; or

    (b) if the officer considers that he ought to be further detained in his own interests or, in the case of an arrested child, because of the nature of the alleged offence, make arrangements for his detention in a place of safety and inform him, and take such steps as are practicable for informing his parent or guardian, of his right to apply to a justice under subsection (5) of this section for his release;

and subject to the said subsection (5) it shall be lawful to detain the person in question in accordance with any such arrangements.

(5) It shall not be lawful for a child arrested without a warrant otherwise than for homicide to be detained in consequence of the arrest or such arrangements as aforesaid, or for any person to be detained by virtue of subsection (2) of this section or any such arrangements, after the expiration of the period of eight days beginning with the day on which he was arrested or, as the case may be, on which his detention in pursuance of the said subsection (2) began; and if during that period the person in question applies to a justice for his release, the justice shall direct that he be released forthwith unless the justice considers that he ought to be further detained in his own interests or, in the case of an arrested child, because of the nature of the alleged offence.

(6) If while a person is detained in pursuance of this section an application for an interim order in respect of him is made to a magistrates' court or a justice, the court or justice shall either make or refuse to make the order and, in the case of a refusal, may direct that he be released forthwith.

NOTES

General note.—During any period before s. 4 is in full operation up to the age of fourteen, regulations under s. 34 (1) (a) may apply s. 28 (4) to a child of prosecutable age, and accordingly references to a child in sub-ss. (4) and (5) may be and have been modified so as to restrict the meaning to a child below a specified age. The reference to a child excludes a child who has attained the age of 10 (S.I. 1970 No. 1882, p. 624, *post*). The power to arrest a child for an offence with or without a warrant is not affected by this section.

"Application" (sub-s. (1)).—The mode of application is not specified. In many cases it will be convenient for a court, rather than a single justice, to entertain the application, and either hear evidence on oath or require a written information.

"Conditions set out in s. 1 (2) (a) to (e)" (sub-s. (1)).—Paragraph (f) is not included but a child over ten is still capable of crime and liable to arrest without a warrant.

"Place of safety." (sub-s. (1)).—For definition see s. 107 of the Children and Young Persons Act, 1933, as amended by para. 12 (2) of Sched. V to this Act.

"Any constable may detain" (sub-s. (2)).—A child or young person who is truanting cannot be detained as s. 1 (2) (e) is omitted although application may be made under sub-s. (1) or s. 2 (4).

"Has reasonable cause to believe" (sub-s. (2)).—Compare the powers under s. 67 (1) of the Children and Young Persons Act, 1933, now repealed, where the phrase used is "about to be brought before a juvenile court". Now a constable or authorised person may detain or remove the child or young person before any decision as to court appearance has been made.

"Inform him of the reason" (sub-s. (3)).—This substantially re-enacts existing law. The subsection now makes it clear that the duty of informing lies upon the person detaining.

"Police officer."—For definition see s. 70, *ibid.*, s. 62 of and Sched. VIII to the Police Act, 1964.

"After the expiration of the period of eight days" (sub-s. (5)).—A child arrested without a warrant, and a child or young person detained under sub-s. (2) will both be liable to be detained for up to eight days in a place of safety. However at present as children over 10 are excluded and children under 10 are incapable of crime, a child arrested with or without warrant will be dealt with under s. 29, *post.*

"Applies to a justice" (sub-s. (5)).—It is submitted that application may also be made to a court and this is clearly more convenient administratively.

This represents a change from previous law under s. 22 of the Children and Young Persons Act, 1963. Instead of appearing in seventy-two hours a child on arrest for an offence may be detained for up to eight days, as also may be a young person detained under sub-s. (2). However he will have been informed of his right to apply (sub-s. (4)). A young person arrested for an offence must still be brought before court within seventy-two hours (s. 29 (5)). See the Ingleby Committee Report (Cmnd. 1191) which recommended that where a child is brought before a single justice under s. 23 (2) of the Act of 1963 it should be a justice who is a member of a juvenile court panel.

"The person in question" (sub-s. (5)).—Or his parent or guardian (s. 70 (2)).

"Application for an interim order" (sub-s. (6)).—The person must be present before the court (s. 22 (1)) except where s. 22 (1) (b) applies.

An application for an interim order may also be made if it is not possible by reason of illness or accident to bring the person before the court before the expiration of the period (s. 23 (5) of the Children and Young Persons Act, 1963).

29. Release or further detention of arrested child or young person.—(1) Where a person is arrested with or without a warrant and cannot be brought immediately before a magistrates' court, then if either—

(a) he appears to be a child and his arrest is for homicide; or

(b) he appears to be a young person and his arrest is for any offence,

the police officer in charge of the police station to which he is brought or another police officer not below the rank of inspector shall forthwith enquire into the case and, subject to subsection (2) of this section, shall release him unless—

(i) the officer considers that he ought in his own interests to be further detained; or

(ii) the officer has reason to believe that he has committed homicide or another grave crime or that his release would defeat the ends of justice or that if he were released (in a case where he was arrested without a warrant) he would fail to appear to answer to any charge which might be made.

(2) A person arrested in pursuance of a warrant shall not be released in pursuance of subsection (1) of this section unless he or his parent or guardian (with or without sureties) enters into a recognisance for such amount as the officer aforesaid considers will secure his attendance at the hearing of the charge; and a recognisance entered into in pursuance of this subsection may, if the said officer thinks fit, be conditioned for the attendance of the parent or guardian at the hearing in addition to the person arrested.

(3) An officer who enquires into a case in pursuance of subsection (1) of this section and does not release the person to whom the enquiry relates shall, unless the officer certifies that it is impracticable to do so or that he is of so unruly a character as to make it inappropriate to do so, make arrangements for him to be taken into the care of a local authority and detained by the authority, and it shall be lawful to detain him in pursuance of the arrangements; and a certificate made under this subsection in respect of any person shall be produced to the court before which that person is first brought thereafter.

(4) *Where an officer decides in pursuance of subsection (1) of this section not to release a person arrested without a warrant and it appears to the officer that a decision falls to be taken in pursuance of section 5 of this Act whether to lay an information in respect of an offence alleged to have been committed by that person, it shall be the duty of the officer to inform him that such a decision falls to be taken and to specify the offence.*

(5) A person detained by virtue of subsection (3) of this section shall be brought before a magistrates' court within seventy-two hours from the time of his arrest unless within that period a police officer not below the rank of inspector certifies to a magistrates' court that by reason of illness or accident he cannot be brought before a magistrates' court within that period.

(6) Where in pursuance of the preceding subsection a person is brought before a court or a certificate in respect of any person is produced to a court and the court does not proceed forthwith to inquire into the case, then—

(a) except in a case falling within paragraph (b) of this subsection, the court shall order his release; and

(b) in a case where he was arrested in pursuance of a warrant or the court considers that he ought in his own interests to be further detained or the court has reason to believe as mentioned in subsection (1) (ii) of this section, the court shall remand him;

and where a court remands a person in pursuance of this subsection otherwise than on bail it shall, if he is not represented by counsel or a solicitor, inform him that he may apply to a judge of the High Court to be admitted to bail and shall, if he is not so represented or his counsel or solicitor so requests, give him a written notice stating the reason for so remanding him.

NOTES

General note.—Subsection (4) and s. 5, *ante*, are not yet in force.

"Appears to be a young person" (sub-s. (1) (b)).—Regulations under s. 34 (1) (c) may include additionally a child who has attained a specified age. By S.I. 1970 No. 1882, the age of 10 is so specified.

"In his own interests" (sub-s. (1)).—Although this section substantially re-enacts existing law this provision is more compendious.

"In pursuance of a warrant" (sub-s. (2)).—If arrest is without a warrant it may not be known whether there is to be a prosecution. Section 38 of the Magistrates' Courts Act, 1952, p. 381, allows a recognisance to attend a police station to be taken. The repeal of the proviso to s. 38 (1) and the repeal of s. 32 of the Act of 1933 has the effect that if arrest is without warrant the child must either be detained or released. There is no power to require a recognisance from the parent or juvenile to attend court.

"Shall remand him".—The words that follow make it clear that the remand may be on bail. The fact that arrest was by warrant is not of itself justification for a remand in care.

30. Detention of young offenders in community homes.—(1) The power to give directions under section 53 of the Act of 1933 (under which young offenders convicted on indictment of certain grave crimes may be detained in accordance with directions given by the Secretary of State) shall include power to direct detention by a local authority specified in the directions in a home so specified which is a community home provided by the authority or a controlled community home for the management, equipment and maintenance of which the authority are responsible; but a person shall not be liable to be detained in the manner provided by this section after he attains the age of nineteen.

(2) It shall be the duty of a local authority specified in directions given in pursuance of this section to detain the person to whom the directions relate in the home specified in the directions subject to and in accordance with such instructions relating to him as the Secretary of State may give to the authority from time to time; and the authority shall be entitled to recover from the Secretary of State any expenses reasonably incurred by them in discharging that duty.

NOTES

General note.—Corresponding provisions were made in s. 58 of the Children and Young Persons Act, 1933, p. 62.

Section 53 of the Children and Young Persons Act, 1933.—See p. 57.

"Community home"; "controlled community home" (sub-s. (1)).—See s. 39, *post*.

The Secretary of State may agree with managers of an assisted community home to place a juvenile in an assisted home, but the managers are not under a duty to receive such a juvenile under the section. See also the regulation making power in s. 43 (2) (c), *post*.

31. Removal to borstal institutions of persons committed to care of local authorities.—(1) Where a person who has attained the age of fifteen is for the time being committed to the care of a local authority by a care order (other than an interim order) and accommodated in a community home and the authority consider that he ought to be removed to a borstal institution under this section, they may with the consent of the Secretary of State bring him before a juvenile court.

(2) If the court before which a person is brought in pursuance of this section is satisfied that his behaviour is such that it will be detrimental to

the persons accommodated in any community home for him to be accommodated there, the court may order him to be removed to a borstal institution.

(3) Where an order is made under subsection (2) of this section with respect to any person, the care order aforesaid shall cease to have effect and he shall be treated as if he had been sentenced to borstal training on the date of the other order, except that—

(a) where the day on which the care order would have ceased to have effect by virtue of section 20 (3) of this Act (disregarding section 21 (1)) is earlier than the end of the period of two years beginning with the date aforesaid he shall, subject to paragraph (b) of this subsection, not be liable to be detained by virtue of this subsection after that day; and

(b) section 45 (4) of the Prison Act, 1952 shall apply to him as if for the reference to two years from the date of his sentence there were substituted a reference to that day.

(4) If the court before which a person is brought in pursuance of this section is not in a position to decide whether to make an order under subsection (2) of this section in respect of him, it may make an order for his detention in a remand centre for a period not exceeding twenty-one days.

(5) An order under the preceding subsection may from time to time be varied or extended by the court which made the order or by any other magistrates' court acting for the same area as that court, but a court shall not exercise its powers under this subsection—

(a) if the person to whom the order relates is not before the court, unless the court is satisfied that by reason of illness or accident he cannot be present;

(b) so as to authorise the detention of that person after the expiration of the period of eight weeks beginning with the date when the order was originally made.

(6) The provisions of the Magistrates' Courts Act, 1952 and of any other enactment relating to summary proceedings (other than provisions relating to remand or legal aid) shall apply to proceedings for the removal of a person under this section as they apply to proceedings against a person charged with a summary offence.

(7) Where immediately before an order under paragraph (f) of section 34 (1) of this Act comes into force an order under this section is in force with respect to any person, the order under that paragraph shall not affect the other order or the application of this section to that person while the other order remains in force.

NOTES

General note.—Removal from approved schools to borstal was covered by para. 8 of Sched. IV to the Children and Young Persons Act, 1933, s. 82 of that Act, and s. 16 of the Criminal Justice Act, 1961. All are now repealed. The test in s. 16 of the Criminal Justice Act, 1961, seems to have been adopted, and absconding by itself is no longer a criterion.

"Committed to the care of a local authority" (sub-s. (1)).—*I.e.* whether for an offence or not.

Detention in a remand centre.—If no such centre is available, the local authority must retain the person in their care, as the section unlike s. 23 (2), does not include power to detain in a prison.

Community home.—See paras. 3 (2) and 4 (3) (c) of Sched. III, for application to approved schools.

"Magistrates' Courts Act, 1952" (sub-s. (6)).—As the person is to be treated as though charged with a summary offence the provisions of the Magistrates' Courts Act, 1952, in respect of appeal to the Crown Court will apply.
Legal aid under s. 73 of the Criminal Justice Act, 1967, as amended by Sched. I to this Act is available for applications under this section, and on appeal.

"On the date of the other order" (sub-s. (3)).—Removal under the Children and Young Persons Act, 1933, was treated differently from the removal under the Criminal Justice Act, 1961.
Removal under the Children and Young Persons Act, 1933, was for two years from the date of removal even if the approved school order would have expired by then. This subsection follows the Criminal Justice Act, 1961, and a young person is not liable to be detained beyond the day on which the care order would have expired.

"Section 20 (3) of this Act".—In relation to a care order on transfer from a training school in Northern Ireland or a fit person order (s. 25, *ante*), a reference to s. 25 (3) is to be substituted (s. 25 (1), *ante*).

Isle of Man, Channel Islands.—For modification of this section in respect of designated orders, see s. 26, *ante*.

32. Detention of absentees.—(1) If any of the following persons, that is to say—

(a) a person committed to the care of a local authority by a care order or by a warrant under section 23 of this Act; or

(b) a person who, in pursuance of section 2 (5), 16 (3) or 28 of this Act, has been taken to a place of safety which is a community home provided by a local authority or a controlled community home; or

(c) a person in the care of a local authority in pursuance of arrangements under section 29 (3) of this Act; or

(d) a person sent to a remand home, special reception centre or training school or committed to the care of a fit person under the Children and Young Persons Act (Northern Ireland), 1968;

is absent from premises at which he is required by the local authority or the relevant Northern Ireland authority to live, or as the case may be is absent from the home, remand home, special reception centre or training school, at a time when he is not permitted by the local authority or the managers of the home or the relevant Northern Ireland authority to be absent from it, he may be arrested by a constable anywhere in the United Kingdom or the Channel Islands without a warrant and shall if so arrested be conducted, at the expense of the authority or managers, to the premises or other place aforesaid or such other premises as the authority or managers may direct.

(2) If a magistrates' court is satisfied by information on oath that there are reasonable grounds for believing that a person specified in the information can produce a person who is absent in subsection (1) of this section, the court may issue a summons directed to the person so specified and requiring him to attend and produce the absent person before the court; and a person who without reasonable excuse fails to comply with any such requirement shall, without prejudice to any liability apart from this

subsection, be guilty of an offence and liable on summary conviction to a fine of an amount not exceeding twenty pounds.

In the application of this subsection to Northern Ireland, "magistrates' court" means a magistrates' court within the meaning of the Magistrates' Courts Act (Northern Ireland), 1964.

(3) A person who knowingly compels, persuades, incites or assists another person to become or continue to be absent as mentioned in subsection (1) of this section shall be guilty of an offence and liable on summary conviction to imprisonment for a term not exceeding six months or a fine of an amount not exceeding one hundred pounds or both.

(4) The reference to a constable in subsection (1) of this section includes a reference to a person who is a constable under the law of any part of the United Kingdom, to a member of the police in Jersey and to an officer of police within the meaning of section 43 of the Larceny (Guernsey) Law, 1958 or any corresponding law for the time being in force, and in that subsection "the relevant Northern Ireland authority" means in the case of a person committed to the care of a fit person, the fit person, and in the case of a person sent to a remand home, special reception centre or training school, the person in charge of that home or centre or the managers of that school.

(5) Nothing in this section authorises the arrest in Northern Ireland of, or the taking there of any proceedings in respect of, such a person as is mentioned in paragraph (d) of subsection (1) of this section.

NOTES

Compare the previous provisions of ss. 78, 82 and 85 of the Children and Young Persons Act, 1933.

"A place of safety which is a community home" (sub-s. (1) (b)).—There is no provision for arrest under this section of an absconder from a place of safety unless it is one of the class defined in para. (a) and (d). This corresponds to previous law. For transitional provision see para. 7 (4) of Sched. IV.

Legal aid

33. Legal aid.—(1) Part IV of the Criminal Justice Act, 1967 (which relates to legal aid in criminal proceedings) shall have effect subject to the provisions of Schedule 1 to this Act (being provisions for applying the said Part IV to certain proceedings under this Part of this Act and for modifying the said Part IV in certain minor respects in relation to juveniles).

(2) Legal aid in pursuance of the Legal Aid and Advice Act, 1949, shall not be given in respect of any proceedings in respect of which legal aid may be given by virtue of the preceding subsection.

NOTES

General note.—The amendment and modifications are noted under Sched. I, and under the title **Legal Aid**, p. 325, *post.*

Legal Aid and Advice Act, 1949 (sub-s. (2)).—See the Legal Aid (General) (Amendment) Regulations, 1964, S.I. 1964 No. 1893 and the Legal Aid (Extension of Proceedings) Regulations, 1969, S.I. 1969 No. 921.

By virtue of s. 24 (2) a local authority to whose care a child or young person is committed has the same powers and duties as his parent or guardian, and, it is submitted, should consider legal representation in appropriate cases.

Transitional modifications of Part I for
persons of specified ages

34. Transitional modifications of Part I for persons of specified ages.—(1) The Secretary of State may by order provide—

(a) that any reference to a child in section 4, 13 (2) or 28 (4) or (5) of this Act shall be construed as excluding a child who has attained such age as may be specified in the order;

(b) that any reference to a young person in section 5 of this Act (except subsection (8)) shall be construed as including a child, or excluding a young person, who has attained such age as may be so specified;

(c) that any reference to a young person in section 5 (8), 7, (7), 7 (8), 9 (1), 23 (1) or 29 (1) of this Act shall be construed as including a child who has attained such age as may be so specified;

(d) that section 7 (1) of this Act shall have effect as if for references to seventeen years there were substituted references to sixteen years;

(e) that section 23 (2) or (3) of this Act shall have effect as if the references to a young person excluded a young person who has not attained such age as may be so specified;

(f) that section 22 (5) of this Act shall have effect as if for the reference to the age of fourteen, or section 31 (1) of this Act shall have effect as if for the reference to the age of fifteen, there were substituted a reference to such greater age as may be so specified.

(2) In the case of a person who has not attained the age of seventeen but has attained such lower age as the Secretary of State may by order specify, no proceedings under section 1 of this Act or for an offence shall be begun in any court unless the person proposing to begin the proceedings has, in addition to any notice falling to be given by him to a local authority in pursuance of section 2 (3) or 5 (8) of this Act, given notice of the proceedings to a probation officer for the area for which the court acts; and accordingly in the case of such a person the reference in section 1 (1) of this Act to the said section 2 (3) shall be construed as including a reference to this subsection.

(3) In the case of a person who has attained such age as the Secretary of State may by order specify, an authority shall, without prejudice to subsection (2) of section 9 of this Act, not be required by virtue of subsection (1) of that section to make investigations or provide information which it does not already possess with respect to his home surroundings if, by direction of the justices or probation and after-care committee acting for any relevant area, arrangements are in force for information with respect to his home surroundings to be furnished to the court in question by a probation officer.

(4) Except in relation to section 13 (2) of this Act, references to a child in subsection (1) of this section do not include references to a person under the age of ten.

(5) In relation to a child tried summarily in pursuance of section 6 of this Act, for the words "fifty pounds" in subsection (3) of that section there shall be substituted the words "ten pounds".

(6) Without prejudice to the generality of section 69 (4) of this Act, an order under this section may specify different ages for the purposes of different provisions of this Act specified in the order.

(7) A draft of any order proposed to be made under this section shall be laid before Parliament and, in the case of an order of which the effect is that the reference to a child in section 4 of this Act includes a child who has attained an age of more than twelve, shall not be made unless the draft has been approved by a resolution of each House of Parliament.

NOTE

General note.—The full implementation of the Act will require additional resources in the community home system and the social work service. The abolition of attendance centres and detention centres will also have to be phased. This section provides the necessary machinery; under sub-s. (1) regulations may provide, *e.g.* that where a child is prosecutable the courts will have power to order them to be supervised by probation officers. Paragraph (c) is complementary to para. (a) and applies provisions relating to criminal proceedings to prosecutable children. Paragraph (e) will enable the Home Secretary to raise the age above which a young person may be committed to a prison or remand centre. Paragraph (f) will enable the gradual phasing out of the power to remove to borstal any person subject to a care order in a community home.

Subsections (2) and (3) are complementary to para. (a) and make ancillary provision for the supervision by probation officers of children who are of prosecutable age. Any order made under this section is subject to variation or revocation by a subsequent order (s. 69 (3)). Transitional modifications are made by S.I. 1970 No. 1882, p. 624, *post*, and the modifications are noted under the appropriate sections. For the purposes of sub-ss. (2) and (3), the age of 10 is specified by the order.

PART II

ACCOMMODATION ETC. FOR CHILDREN IN CARE, AND FOSTER CHILDREN

NOTE

Sections 35–48 inclusive came into force on December 1, 1969 (S.I. 1969 No. 1565). and see the Community Homes Regulations 1972, S. I. 1972 No. 319.

Community homes

35. Regional planning of accommodation for children in care.— (1) With a view to the preparation, in pursuance of the provisions of this Part of this Act, of regional plans for the provision of accommodation for children in the care of local authorities and for the equipment and maintenance of the accommodation, the Secretary of State may by order provide that any area specified in the order shall by a separate area (in this Act referred to as a "planning area") for the purposes of those provisions.

(2) Before making an order under subsection (1) of this section, the Secretary of State shall consult each local authority whose area or any part of whose area is included in the planning area which he proposes should be specified in the order and such other local authorities, if any, as he thinks fit.

(3) It shall be the duty of the local authorities whose areas are wholly or partly included in a planning area (in this Act referred to, in relation to such an area, as "the relevant authorities") to establish for the area, within such period as may be provided by the order specifying the planning

area or such longer period as the Secretary of State may allow, a body to be called the children's regional planning committee.

(4) The provisions of Schedule 2 to this Act shall have effect in relation to children's regional planning committees.

(5) In the case of an order under subsection (1) of this section which (by virtue of section 69 (3) of this Act) varies or revokes a previous order under that subsection—

(a) the reference in subsection (2) of this section to the planning area which the Secretary of State proposes should be specified in the order shall be construed as a reference to the planning area as it would be if the variation were made or, as the case may be, to the planning area as it is before the revocation; and

(b) the order may contain such transitional provisions (including provisions as to the expenses and membership of any existing or former children's regional planning committee for a planning area) as the Secretary of State thinks fit.

NOTES

Order specifying the planning area (sub-s. (3)).—See the Children and Young Persons (Planning Area) Order, 1970 (S.I. 1970 No. 335).

Variation or revocation of order.—Before varying or revoking a planning area order the Secretary of State must therefore consult each local authority in the area as it was or as it would become if the variation or revocation were made.

The power to vary will enable changes in local government regions to be reflected in the planning areas.

"Community Homes."—See Home Office Circular No. 239/1969, pp. 707 *et seq. post*, and S. I. 1972 No. 319.

36. Regional plans for community homes.—(1) The children's regional planning committee for a planning area (in this and the following section referred to as "the committee") shall prepare and submit to the Secretary of State, in accordance with the following provisions of this section, a plan (in this Act referred to as a "regional plan") for the provision and maintance of homes, to be known as community homes, for the accommodation and maintenance of children in the care of the relevant authorities.

(2) The community homes for which provision may be made by a regional plan shall be—

(a) community homes provided by the relevant authorities; and

(b) voluntary homes provided by voluntary organisations but in the management of each of which the plan proposes that a relevant authority should participate in accordance with an instrument of management.

(3) Where a regional plan makes provision for any such voluntary home as is referred to in paragraph (b) of subsection (2) of this section, the plan shall designate the home as either a controlled community home or an assisted community home, according as it is proposed in the plan that the management, equipment and maintenance of the home should be the responsibility of one of the relevant authorities or of the voluntary organisation by which the home is provided.

(4) Every regional plan shall contain proposals—

   (a) with regard to the nature and purpose of each of the community homes for which the plan makes provision; and

   (b) for the provision of facilities for the observation of the physical and mental condition of children in the care of the relevant authorities and for the assessment of the most suitable accommodation and treatment for those children.

(5) Before including provision in a regional plan that a community home should be provided by any of the relevant authorities or that a voluntary home provided by a voluntary organisation should be designated as a controlled or assisted community home, the committee shall obtain the consent of the authority or voluntary organisation by which the home is or is to be provided and, in the case of a home which is to be designated as a controlled or assisted community home, the consent of the local authority which it is proposed should be specified in the instrument of management for the home.

(6) A regional plan shall be prepared in such form and shall contain such information as the Secretary of State may direct, either generally or in relation to a particular planning area or particular kinds of plans; and the Secretary of State may direct that the regional plan for a particular planning area shall be submitted to him within such period as may be specified in the direction or such longer period as he may allow.

NOTES

General note.—Community homes are for the accommodation and maintenance of children in the care of the relevant local authorities; thus the range of homes to be provided will include reception centres and children's homes, residential nurseries (as provided under ss. 15 and 19 of the Children Act, 1948), children's homes provided by voluntary organisations, and the equivalent of approved schools, approved hostels and ultimately borstals in so far as they accommodate persons under 17.

They may be provided by local authorities or by voluntary organisations. If the latter, then one local authority will participate in the management. See para. 8 of Home Office Circular, No. 239/1969, dated November 18, 1969 and the Community Homes Regulations 1972, S. I. 1972 No. 319.

"Facilities for observation" (sub-s. (4)).—The wording of the subsection is mandatory and accordingly facilities for observation must be provided in each regional plan.

At present some individual authorities are unable to provide such homes. See also Sched. III, para. 3.

37. Approval and variation of regional plans.—(1) After considering any regional plan submitted to him under section 36 of this Act and after making in the plan such modifications (if any) as he may agree with the committee by which the plan was submitted and as he may consider appropriate for securing that the plan makes proper provision for the accommodation and maintenance of children in the care of the relevant authorities, the Secretary of State may approve the plan.

(2) Where the Secretary of State considers that, either with or without such modifications as are referred to in subsection (1) of this section, part but not the whole of a plan submitted to him under section 36 of this Act makes proper provision for the accommodation and maintenance of the children to whom that part of the plan relates, the Secretary of State may approve that part of the plan.

(3) Where the Secretary of State has approved part only of a regional plan, the committee for the planning area concerned shall prepare and submit to him under section 36 of this Act a further regional plan containing proposals to supplement that part of the previous plan which was approved by the Secretary of State.

(4) If, at any time after the approval of the whole or part of a regional plan by the Secretary of State, the committee for the planning area concerned consider that the plan, or such part of it as was approved, should be varied or replaced, they shall prepare and submit to the Secretary of State under section 36 of this Act a further regional plan for that purpose; and any such further regional plan may—

(a) take the form of a replacement for the regional plan or part thereof which was previously approved by the Secretary of State; or

(b) contain proposals for the amendment of that regional plan or part thereof.

(5) In relation to a further regional plan which contains proposals for supplementing or amending a regional plan or part of a regional plan which has been previously approved by the Secretary of State (in this subsection referred to as "the approved plan")—

(a) section 36 (4) of this Act shall have effect as if references to a regional plan were references to the approved plan as it would have effect if supplemented or amended in accordance with the proposals contained in the further regional plan; and

(b) subsection (1) of this section shall have effect as if the reference therein to children in the care of the relevant authorities were a reference to the children to whom the proposals in the plan relate; and

(c) in so far as the further regional plan contains proposals under which a home would cease to be a community home, or would become a community home of a different description, or would be used for a purpose different from that provided for in the approved plan, the committee preparing the further plan shall, before submitting it to the Secretary of State, obtain the consent of the local authority or voluntary organisation by which the home is provided and, if the proposal is for a home to become or to cease to be a controlled or assisted community home, the consent of the local authority which it is proposed should be, or which is, specified in the instrument of management for the home.

(6) Where the Secretary of State approves a regional plan, in whole or in part, he shall give notice in writing of his approval to the committee for the planning area concerned specifying the date on which the plan is to come into operation, and the committee shall send a copy of the notice to each of the relevant authorities and to any voluntary organisation whose consent was required to any provision of the plan.

NOTE

"**Modifications**" (**sub-s. (1)**).—The Secretary of State has no power to amend a regional plan against the wishes of the Committee.

There is no provision corresponding to s. 19 (3) whereby the regional plan is to be published.

38. Provision of community homes by local authorities.—Where a regional plan for a planning area includes provision for a community home to be provided by one of the relevant authorities, it shall be the duty of the local authority concerned to provide, manage, equip and maintain that home.

NOTE

General note.—Section 15 of the Children Act, 1948 (duty of local authority to provide homes) is repealed and this section replaces it.

The responsibilities of a local authority in relation to controlled or assisted community homes are set out in ss. 41 and 42.

39. Instruments of management for assisted and controlled community homes.—(1) The Secretary of State may by order make an instrument of management providing for the constitution of a body of managers for any voluntary home which, in accordance with a regional plan approved by him, is designated as a controlled or assisted community home.

(2) Where in accordance with a regional plan approved by the Secretary of State, two or more voluntary homes are designated as controlled community homes or as assisted community homes, then if—

(a) those homes are, or are to be, provided by the same voluntary organisation; and

(b) the same local authority is to be represented on the body of managers for those homes,

a single instrument of management may be made by the Secretary of State under this section constituting one body of managers for those homes or for any two or more of them.

(3) The number of persons who, in accordance with an instrument of management under this section, constitute the body of managers for a voluntary home shall be such number, being a multiple of three, as may be specified in the instrument of management, but the instrument shall provide that a proportion of the managers shall be appointed by such local authority as may be so specified and—

(a) in the case of a voluntary home which is designated in a regional plan as a controlled community home, the proportion shall be two-thirds; and

(b) in the case of a voluntary home which is so designated as an assisted community home, the proportion shall be one-third.

(4) An instrument of management shall provide that the "foundation managers", that is to say, those of the managers of the voluntary home to which the instrument relates who are not appointed by a local authority in accordance with subsection (3) of this section, shall be appointed, in such manner and by such persons as may be specified in the instrument,—

(a) so as to represent the interests of the voluntary organisation by which the home is, or is to be, provided; and

(b) for the purpose of securing that, as far as practicable, the character of the home as a voluntary home will be preserved and that, subject to section 40 (3) of this Act, the terms of any trust deed relating to the home are observed.

(5) An instrument of management under this section shall come into force on such date as may be specified in the instrument, and if such an instrument is in force in relation to a voluntary home the home shall be and be known as a controlled community home or an assisted community home, according to its designation in the regional plan.

NOTE

"Regional plan".—See s. 36 and Sched. II.

Instruments of management.—See Home Office Circular 196/1970, p. 813, *post.*

40. Supplementary provisions as to instruments of management and trust deeds.—(1) An instrument of management for a controlled or assisted community home shall contain such provisions as the Secretary of State considers appropriate for giving effect to the provisions of the regional plan by which the home is designated as a controlled or assisted community home, but nothing in the instrument of management for such a home shall affect the purposes for which the premises comprising the home are held.

(2) Without prejudice to the generality of subsection (1) of this section, an instrument of management may contain—

   (a) provisions specifying the nature and purpose of the home or each of the homes to which it relates;
   (b) provisions requiring a specified number or proportion of the places in that home or those homes to be made available to local authorities and to any other body specified in the instrument; and
   (c) provisions relating to the management of that home or those homes and the charging of fees in respect of children placed therein or places made available to any local authority or other body.

(3) Subject to subsection (1) of this section, in the event of any inconsistency between the provisions of any trust deed and the instrument of management relating to a controlled or assisted community home, the instrument shall prevail over the provisions of the trust deed in so far as they relate to that home.

(4) After consultation with the voluntary organisation by which a controlled or assisted community home is provided and with the local authority specified in the instrument of management for the time being in force for that home, the Secretary of State may vary or revoke any provisions of that instrument of management by a further instrument of management.

(5) In this Act the expression "trust deed", in relation to a voluntary home, means any instrument (other than an instrument of management) regulating the maintenance, management or conduct of the home or the constitution of a body of managers or trustees of the home.

NOTES

General note.—The instrument of management (see s. 39) made by the Secretary of State cannot alter the basic purposes for which premises comprising a voluntary home are held.

Subject to certain provisions relating to approved schools and probation hostels (see para. 5 of Sched. III), where an organisation holds premises on trust for purposes inconsistent with use as a community home it is for that organisation to secure appropriate modification of the trust deed. This cannot by virtue of sub-s. 1 be done by the instrument of management, and sub-s. (3) which deals with inconsistencies between the instrument of management and a trust deed is expressly made subject to sub-s. 1.

"**Trust Deed**".—The definition in sub-s. (5) is wide and is not confined to trust deeds properly so described.

41. Management of controlled community homes.—(1) The management, equipment and maintenance of a controlled community home shall be the responsibility of the local authority specified in the instrument of management for that home, and in the following provisions of this section "the responsible authority", in relation to such a home, means the local authority responsible for its management, equipment and maintenance.

(2) Subject to the following provisions of this section, the responsible authority shall exercise their functions in relation to a controlled community home through the body of managers constituted by the instrument of management for the home, and any thing done, liability incurred or property acquired by the managers shall be done, incurred or acquired by the managers as agents of the responsible authority.

(3) In so far as any matter is reserved for the decision of the responsible authority, either by subsection (4) of this section or by the instrument of management for the controlled community home in question or by the service by the responsible authority on the managers or any of them of a notice reserving any matter, that matter shall be dealt with by the responsible authority themselves and not by the managers, but in dealing with any matter so reserved, the responsible authority shall have regard to any representations made to them by the managers.

(4) The employment of persons at a controlled community home shall be a matter reserved for the decision of the responsible authority, but where the instrument of management so provides the responsible authority may enter into arrangements with the voluntary organisation by which the home is provided whereby, in accordance with such terms as may be agreed between the responsible authority and the voluntary organisation, persons who are not in the employment of the responsible authority shall undertake duties at the home.

(5) The accounting year of the managers of a controlled community home shall be such as may be specified by the responsible authority and, before such date in each accounting year as may be so specified, the managers of a controlled community home shall submit to the responsible authority estimates, in such form as the authority may require, of expenditure and receipts in respect of the next accounting year; and any expenses incurred by the managers of a controlled community home with the approval of the responsible authority shall be defrayed by that authority.

(6) The managers of a controlled community home shall keep proper accounts in respect of that home and proper records in relation to the accounts, but where an instrument of management relates to more than

one controlled community home, one set of accounts and records may be kept in respect of all the homes to which the instrument relates.

NOTE

Arrangements for employment (sub-s. (4)).—These arrangements would enable (if the instrument of management so provides) the employees of the voluntary organisation or, for example, members of religious orders, to undertake the care of children in a controlled community home.

42. Management of assisted community homes.—(1) The management, equipment and maintenance of an assisted community home shall be the responsibility of the voluntary organisation by which the home is provided, and in the following provisions of this section "the responsible organisation", in relation to such a home, means the voluntary organisation responsible for its management, equipment and maintenance.

(2) Subject to the following provisions of this section, the responsible organisation shall exercise its functions in relation to the home through the body of managers constituted by the instrument of management for the home, and any thing done, liability incurred or property acquired by the managers shall be done, incurred or acquired by the managers as agents of the responsible organisation.

(3) In so far as any matter is reserved for the decision of the responsible organisation, either by subsection (4) of this section or by the instrument of management for the assisted community home in question or by the service by the responsible organisation on the managers or any of them of a notice reserving any matter, that matter shall be dealt with by the responsible organisation itself and not by the managers, but in dealing with any matter so reserved the responsible organisation shall have regard to any representations made to the organisation by the managers.

(4) The employment of persons at an assisted community home shall be a matter reserved for the decision of the responsible organisation but, subject to subsection (5) of this section,—

   (a) where the responsible organisation proposes to engage any person to work at the home or to terminate without notice the employment of any person at the home, the responsible organisation shall consult the local authority specified in the instrument of management and, if the local authority so directs, the responsible organisation shall not carry out its proposal without the consent of the local authority; and
   (b) the local authority may, after consultation with the responsible organisation, require the organisation to terminate the employment of any person at the home.

(5) Paragraphs (a) and (b) of subsection (4) of this section shall not apply—

   (a) in such cases or circumstances as may be specified by notice in writing given by the local authority to the responsible organisation; and
   (b) in relation to the employment of any persons or class of persons specified in the instrument of management.

(6) The accounting year of the managers of an assisted community home shall be such as may be specified by the responsible organisation and, before such date in each accounting year as may be so specified, the managers of an assisted community home shall submit to the responsible organisation estimates, in such form as the organisation may require, of expenditure and receipts in respect of the next financial year; and all expenses incurred by the managers of an assisted community home with the approval of the responsible organisation shall be defrayed by the organisation.

(7) The managers of an assisted community home shall keep proper accounts in respect of that home and proper records in relation to those accounts, but where an instrument of management relates to more than one assisted community home, one set of accounts and records may be kept in respect of all the homes to which the instrument relates.

NOTE

General note.—The powers of the local authority in respect of assisted community homes are intended to give a measure of control over the employment of persons in regular contact with children in the homes most of whom are likely to be in the care of a local authority.

Where there is little contact between staff and children, *e.g.* cleaners, a local authority may well be prepared to waive their rights under sub-s. (4) (a) and (b). The other excepted case is such staff as are specified in the instrument of management. This could allow, for example, for members of religious orders employed in a community home to be exempt from local authority consultation over engagement or summary dismissal.

See sub-s. (5).

43. Control of premises used for, and conduct of, community homes.—(1) The Secretary of State may make regulations with respect to the conduct of community homes and for securing the welfare of the children in community homes.

(2) Without prejudice to the generality of subsection (1) of this section, regulations under this section may—

(a) impose requirements as to the accommodation and equipment to be provided in community homes and as to the medical arrangements to be made for protecting the health of the children in the homes;

(b) impose requirements as to the facilities which are to be provided for giving religious instruction to children in community homes;

(c) require the approval of the Secretary of State for the provision and use of accommodation for the purpose of restricting the liberty of children in community homes and impose other requirements as to the placing of a child in accommodation provided for that purpose, including a requirement to obtain the permission of the local authority or voluntary organisation in whose care the child is;

(d) authorise the Secretary of State to give and revoke directions requiring the local authority by whom a community home is provided or who are specified in the instrument of management for a controlled community home or the voluntary organisation by which an assisted community home is provided to accommodate in the home a child in the care of a local authority for whom no places are made available in that home or to take such action in relation to a child accommodated in the home as may be specified in the directions;

(e) require reviews of any permission given in pursuance of paragraph (c) above and provide for such a review to be conducted in a manner approved by the Secretary of State by a committee of persons representing the local authority or voluntary organisation in question but including at least one person satisfying such conditions as may be prescribed by the regulations with a view to securing that he is independent of the authority or organisation and unconnected with any community home containing such accommodation as is mentioned in the said paragraph (c);

(f) prescribe standards to which premises used for community homes are to conform;

(g) require the approval of the Secretary of State to the use of buildings for the purpose of community homes and to the doing of anything (whether by way of addition, diminution or alteration) which materially affects the buildings or grounds or other facilities or amenities available for children in community homes;

(h) provide that, to such extent as may be provided for in the regulations, the Secretary of State may direct that any provision of regulations under this section which is specified in the direction and makes any such provision as is referred to in paragraph (a), (f) or (g) above shall not apply in relation to a particular community home or the premises used for it, and may provide for the variation or revocation of any such direction by the Secretary of State.

(3) Without prejudice to the power to make regulations under this section conferring functions on the local authority or voluntary organisation by which a community home is provided or on the managers of a controlled or assisted community home, regulations under this section may confer functions in relation to a controlled or assisted community home on the local authority named in the instrument of management for the home.

(4) Where it appears to the Secretary of State that any premises used for the purposes of a community home are unsuitable for those purposes, or that the conduct of a community home is not in accordance with regulations made by him under this section or is otherwise unsatisfactory, he may by notice in writing served on the responsible body, direct that as from such date as may be specified in the notice the premises shall not be used for the purposes of a community home.

(5) Where the Secretary of State has given a direction in relation to a controlled or assisted community home under subsection (4) of this section and the direction has not been revoked, the Secretary of State may at any time by order revoke the instrument of management for that home.

(6) For the purposes of subsection (4) of this section the responsible body—

(a) in relation to a community home provided by a local authority, is that local authority;

(b) in relation to a controlled community home, is the local authority specified in the instrument of management for that home; and

(c) in relation to an assisted community home, is the voluntary organisation by which the home is provided.

NOTES

General note.—This replaces s. 15 of the Children Act, 1948 (and s. 31 of that Act, as regards voluntary community homes, is replaced by s. 44).

For regulations made under this section, see the Community Homes Regulations, 1972, S. I. 1972 No. 319.

Approval of Secretary of State (sub-s. (2) (c)).—Compare the provisions of s. 13 (b) of the Children Act, 1948, which required a local authority to obtain authorisation before placing a child in care in, for example, a remand home. The right of a local authority to restrict a child's liberty under s. 24 (2) is subject to regulations under this section.

"Give and revoke directions" (sub-s. (2) (d)).—See also s. 27 (3), *ante.*

The Secretary of State may require a child to be accommodated in a community home in order to protect the public and the home need not be in the area of the "caring" authority.

Note that references in Part II of the Act and Sched. III to a child means a person under eighteen and a person over eighteen still subject to a care order (s. 70).

"Revoke the instrument of management" (sub-s. (5)).—For financial arrangements in consequence of revocation, see s. 48.

44. Controlled and assisted community homes exempted from certain provisions as to voluntary homes.—While a voluntary home is a controlled or assisted community home, the following enactments shall not apply in relation to it, that is to say,—

(a) sections 29 and 30 of the Children Act, 1948 (compulsory registration of voluntary homes);

(b) section 31 of that Act (regulations as to conduct of voluntary homes); and

(c) section 93 of the Act of 1933 and section 32 of the Children Act, 1948 (notification to Secretary of State of certain particulars relating to voluntary homes).

45. Determination of disputes relating to controlled and assisted community homes.—(1) Subject to subsection (5) of this section, where any dispute relating to a controlled community home arises between the local authority specified in the instrument of management and either the voluntary organisation by which the home is provided or any other local authority who have placed, or desire or are required to place, a child in their care in the home, the dispute may be referred by either party to the Secretary of State for his determination.

(2) Subject to subsection (5) of this section, where any dispute relating to an assisted community home arises between the voluntary organisation by which the home is provided and any local authority who have placed, or desire to place, a child in their care in the home, the dispute may be referred by either party to the Secretary of State for his determination.

(3) Where a dispute is referred to the Secretary of State under this section he may, in order to give effect to his determination of the dispute, give such directions as he thinks fit to the local authority or voluntary organisation concerned.

(4) The provisions of this section shall apply notwithstanding that the matter in dispute may be one which, under or by virtue of the preceding provisions of this Part of this Act, is reserved for the decision, or is the responsibility, of the local authority specified in the instrument of management or, as the case may be, the voluntary organisation by which the home is provided.

(5) Where any trust deed relating to a controlled or assisted community home contains provision whereby a bishop or any other ecclesiastical or denominational authority has power to decide questions relating to religious instruction given in the home, no dispute which is capable of being dealt with in accordance with that provision shall be referred to the Secretary of State under this section.

NOTE

" Trust Deed ".—See s. 40 (5).

46. Discontinuance of approved schools etc. on establishment of community homes.—(1) If in the case of any approved school, remand home, approved probation hostel or approved probation home within the meaning of the Criminal Justice Act, 1948 (hereafter in this section referred to as an "approved institution") it appears to the Secretary of State that in consequence of the establishment of community homes for a planning area the institution as such is no longer required, he may by order provide that it shall cease to be an approved institution on a date specified in the order.

(2) The provisions of Schedule 3 to this Act shall have effect in relation to institutions which are, or by virtue of this section have ceased to be, approved institutions.

NOTES

General note.—When any of these institutions are no longer required as such in consequence of the establishment of community homes then either,

(a) Under the regional plan the institution may become an assisted or controlled community home or be sold for use as a local authority home, or
(b) There is no room for the institution as a community home.

Although it is anticipated that remand homes (all but two are provided by local authorities) and most approved schools will become community homes, there is no compulsion. They may transfer to local authorities (Sched. III, para. 6) or become special or boarding schools under the Education Acts or change to some charitable purpose, see ss. 13 (2) and 33 of the Education Act, 1944.

"Approved school".—See the Children and Young Persons Act, 1933, s. 79 at p. 65 *ante*.

"Remand home".—See the Children and Young Persons Act, 1933, s. 77 at pp. 64 *et seq.*, *ante*.

"Approved probation home or hostel".—See Criminal Justice Act, 1948, s. 46 at p. 292, *ante*.

Transitional provisions.—See Sched. III.

"Cease to be an approved institution" (sub-s. (1)).—This power is not in substitution for the power to withdraw a certificate of approval under s. 79 (2) of the Children and Young Persons Act, 1933, p. 65 which remains in force until that part of Sched. V (Repeals) is brought into force in relation to that section.

47. Discontinuance by voluntary organisation of controlled or assisted community home.—(1) The voluntary organisation by which a controlled or assisted community home is provided shall not cease to provide the home except after giving to the Secretary of State and the local authority specified in the instrument of management not less than two years' notice in writing of their intention to do so.

(2) A notice under subsection (1) of this section shall specify the date from which the voluntary organisation intends to cease to provide the home as a community home; and where such a notice is given and is not withdrawn before the date specified in it, then, subject to subsection (4) of this section the instrument of management for the home shall cease to have effect on that date and accordingly the home shall then cease to be a controlled or assisted community home.

(3) Where a notice is given under subsection (1) of this section, the local authority to whom the notice is given shall inform the children's regional planning committee responsible for the regional plan under which the voluntary home in question was designated as a controlled or assisted community home of the receipt and content of the notice.

(4) Where a notice is given under subsection (1) of this section and the body of managers for the home to which the notice relates give notice in writing to the Secretary of State that they are unable or unwilling to continue as managers of the home until the date specified in the first-mentioned notice, the Secretary of State may by order—

  (a) revoke the instrument of management; and
  (b) require the local authority who were specified in that instrument to conduct the home, until the date specified in the notice under subsection (1) of this section or such earlier date (if any) as may be specified for the purposes of this paragraph in the order, as if it were a community home provided by the local authority.

(5) Where the Secretary of State makes such a requirement as is specified in subsection (4) (b) of this section,—

  (a) nothing in the trust deed for the home in question shall affect the conduct of the home by the local authority; and
  (b) the Secretary of State may by order direct that for the purposes of any provision specified in the direction and made by or under any enactment relating to community homes (other than this section) the home shall, until the date or earlier date specified as mentioned in subsection (4) (b) of this section, be treated as an assisted community home or as a controlled community home, but except in so far as the Secretary of State so directs, the home shall until that date be treated for the purposes of any such enactment as a community home provided by the local authority; and
  (c) on the date or earlier date specified as mentioned in subsection (4) (b) of this section the home shall cease to be a community home.

NOTES

See Home Office Circular No. 246/1969, pp. 716 *et seq., post.* This Circular contains a speculative timetable for action under the various provisions of Part II of this Act.

"**Shall not cease to provide the home**" **(sub-s. (1)).**—A change of status for the home, for example from controlled to assisted, would be effected under s. 40 (4) and is not affected by the operation of the section which relates to the provision of the facility and not the management of the home.

"**Trust deed**".—See s. 40 (3).

48. Financial provisions applicable on cessation of controlled or assisted community home.—(1) Where the instrument of management for a controlled or assisted community home ceases to have effect by virtue either of an order under section 43 (5) of this Act or of subsection (2) or subsection (4) (a) of section 47 of this Act, the voluntary organisation by which the home was provided or, if the premises used for the purposes of the home are not vested in that organisation, the persons in whom those premises are vested (in this section referred to as "the trustees of the home"), shall become liable, in accordance with the following provisions of this section, to make repayment in respect of any increase in the value of the premises and other property belonging to the voluntary organisation or the trustees of the home which is attributable to the expenditure of public money thereon.

(2) Where an instrument of management has ceased to have effect as mentioned in subsection (1) of this section and the instrument related—

    (a) to a controlled home; or

    (b) to an assisted community home which, at any time before that instrument of management came into force, was a controlled community home,

then, on the home ceasing to be a community home, the voluntary organisation by which the home was provided or, as the case may be, the trustees of the home, shall pay to the local authority specified in that instrument of management a sum equal to that part of the value of any relevant premises which is attributable to expenditure by the local authority who at the time the expenditure was incurred had responsibility for the management, equipment and maintenance of the home by virtue of section 41 (1) of this Act.

(3) For the purposes of subsection (2) of this section, "relevant premises", in relation to a controlled 'or assisted community home, means premises used for the purposes of the home and belonging to the voluntary organisation or the trustees of the home but erected, extended or improved at any time while the home was a controlled community home, by the local authority having, at that time, such responsibility in relation to the home as is mentioned in subsection (2) of this section.

(4) Where an instrument of management has ceased to have effect as mentioned in subsection (1) of this section and the instrument related—

    (a) to an assisted community home; or

    (b) to a controlled community home which, at any time before that instrument of management came into force, was an assisted community home,

then, on the home ceasing to be a community home, the voluntary organisation by which the home was provided or, as the case may be, the trustees of the home, shall pay to the Secretary of State a sum equal to that part of the value of the premises and any other property used for the purposes of the home which is attributable to the expenditure of money provided by way of grant under section 65 of this Act.

(5) Where an instrument of management has ceased to have effect as mentioned in subsection (1) of this section and the controlled or assisted community home to which it related was conducted in premises which formerly were used as an approved school or were an approved probation hostel or home but which were designated as a community home in a regional plan approved by the Secretary of State, then, on the home ceasing to be a community home, the voluntary organisation by which the home was provided or, as the case may be, the trustees of the home, shall pay to the Secretary of State a sum equal to that part of the value of the premises concerned and of any other property used for the purposes of the home and belonging to the voluntary organisation or the trustees of the home which is attributable to the expenditure—

> (a) of sums paid towards the expenses of the managers of an approved school under section 104 of the Act of 1933; or
> (b) of sums paid under section 77 (3) (b) of the Criminal Justice Act, 1948 in relation to expenditure on approved probation hostels or homes.

(6) The amount of any sum payable under this section by the voluntary organisation by which a controlled or assisted community home was provided or by the trustees of the home shall be determined in accordance with such arrangements—

> (a) as may be agreed between the voluntary organisation by which the home was provided and the local authority concerned or, as the case may be, the Secretary of State; or
> (b) in default of agreement, as may be determined by the Secretary of State;

and with the agreement of the local authority concerned or the Secretary of State, as the case may be, the liability to pay any sum under this section may be discharged, in whole or in part, by the transfer of any premises or other property used for the purposes of the home in question.

(7) The provisions of this section shall have effect notwithstanding anything in any trust deed for a controlled or assisted community home and notwithstanding the provisions of any enactment or instrument governing the disposition of the property of a voluntary organisation.

(8) Any sums received by the Secretary of State under this section shall be paid into the Consolidated Fund.

NOTE
"Controlled or assisted community home".—See s. 39 (3).

Consequential modifications of ss. 13 and 19 of
Children Act, 1948

49. Provision of accommodation and maintenance for children in care.—For section 13 of the Children Act, 1948 there shall be substituted the following section:—

13. Provision of accommodation and maintenance for children in care.—(1) A local authority shall discharge their duty to provide accommodation and maintenance for a child in their care in such one of the following ways as they think fit, namely,—

(a) by boarding him out on such terms as to payment by the authority and otherwise as the authority may, subject to the provisions of this Act and regulations thereunder, determine; or

(b) by maintaining him in a community home or in any such home as is referred to in section 64 of the Children and Young Persons Act, 1969; or

(c) by maintaining him in a voluntary home (other than a community home) the managers of which are willing to receive him;

or by making such other arrangements as seem appropriate to the local authority.

(2) Without prejudice to the generality of subsection (1) of this section, a local authority may allow a child in their care, either for a fixed period or until the local authority otherwise determine, to be under the charge and control of a parent, guardian, relative or friend.

(3) The terms, as to payment and other matters, on which a child may be accommodated and maintained in any such home as is referred to in section 64 of that Act shall be such as the Secretary of State may from time to time determine.

NOTES

This section came into force on December 1, 1969, S.I. 1969 No. 1565.

"Boarding out".—The Boarding Out of Children Regulations, 1955, S.I. 1955 No. 1377, made under the Children Act, 1948, s. 14, have not yet been revoked.

Voluntary home (other than a community home).—*I.e.* a home registered under ss. 29 and 30 of the Children Act, 1948.

"Such other arrangements".—By virtue of para. 3 (1) of Sched. III, in any interim period as defined in that paragraph, children in care may be accommodated in the premises of an approved school but this power is in addition to the schedule and operates from the coming into force of this section.

"A local authority may" (s. 13 (2)).—But see s. 22 (4) of this Act for restriction on the exercise of this power. Subsection (2) applies to all children in care and unlike the previous position under s. 5 of the Family Allowance and National Insurance Act, 1956, a child received into care under s. 1 of the Children Act, 1948, may be allowed home on trial. Sub-ss. (3) and (4) of s. 3 of the Children Act, 1948, are redundant in view of the subsection and are repealed. (See Home Office Circular Nos. 239/1969, pp. 707 *et seq.*, *post*, and 240/1969, pp. 714 *et seq.*, *post*.)

"Terms as to payment".—By s. 62 (2) no contribution is payable in respect of a period during which a child is "allowed home".

50. Accommodation of persons over school age in convenient community home.—For section 19 of the Children Act, 1948 there shall be substituted the following section:—

19. Accommodation of persons over school age in convenient community home.—(1) A local authority may provide accommodation in a community home for any person who is over compulsory school age but has not attained the age of twenty-one if the community home is provided for children who are over compulsory school age and is near the place where that person is employed or seeking employment or receiving education or training.

NOTE

General note.—The former section allowed a local authority to provide hostels for certain purposes. Community homes now supersede the various classes of establishment which formerly had a separate statutory existence.

This section came into force on December 1, 1969, (S.I. 1969 No. 1565).

Foster children

NOTE

General note.—As regards the effect of amendments to the Children Act, 1958, see the notes to those sections, pp. 956, 957, *post.*

51. Modification of general duty of local authorities with respect to foster children.—For section 1 of the Children Act, 1958 (which imposes a duty on every local authority to secure that foster children are visited by officers of the authority) there shall be substituted the following section:—

1. Duty of local authorities to ensure well-being of foster children.—It shall be the duty of every local authority to satisfy themselves as to the well-being of children within their area who are foster children within the meaning of this Part of this Act, and, for that purpose, to secure that, so far as appears to the authority to be appropriate, the children are visited from time to time by officers of the authority and that such advice is given as to the care and maintenance of the children as appears to be needed.

NOTE

General note.—For ss. 1 to 6 and 14 of the Children Act, 1958, as amended by this Act, see pp. 956, 957, *post.*

The requirement to "visit" is only so far as it appears appropriate. This contrasts with the former provisions to visiting irrespective of whether supervision was really necessary or not.

52. Amendments of definitions of "foster child" and "protected child".—(1) In subsection (1) of section 2 of the Children Act, 1958 (which, subject to the following provisions of that section, defines a foster child for the purposes of Part I of that Act as a child below the upper limit of the compulsory school age whose care and maintenance are undertaken for reward for a period exceeding one month by a person who is not a relative or guardian of his) the words from "for reward" to "one month" shall be omitted.

(2) At the end of paragraph (c) of subsection (3) of the said section 2 (which provides that a child is not a foster child while he is in the care of any person in a school) there shall be added the words "in which he is receiving full time education".

(3) After subsection (3) of the said section 2 there shall be inserted the following subsection:—

(3A) A child is not a foster child within the meaning of this Part of this Act at any time while his care and maintenance are undertaken by a person, other than a relative or guardian of his, if at that time—

(a) that person does not intend to, and does not in fact, undertake his care and maintenance for a continuous period of more than six days; or

(b) that person is not a regular foster parent and does not intend to, and does not in fact, undertake his care and maintenance for a continuous period of more than twenty-seven days;

and for the purposes of this subsection a person is a regular foster parent if, during the period of twelve months immediately preceding the date on which he begins to undertake the care and maintenance of the child in question, he had, otherwise than as a relative or guardian, the care and maintenance of one or more children either for a period of, or periods amounting in the aggregate to, not less than three months or for at least three continuous periods each of which was of more than six days.

(4) Section 37 of the Adoption Act, 1958 (which defines "protected child" for the purposes of Part IV of that Act) shall have effect subject to the following modifications:—

(a) in paragraph (a) of subsection (1) (which refers to arrangements for placing a child in the care of a person who is not a parent, guardian or relative of his) after the words "relative of his" there shall be inserted the words "but who proposes to adopt him";

(b) in subsection (1) (which among other matters excludes a foster child from the definition of a "protected child") the words "but is not a foster child within the meaning of Part I of the Children Act, 1958" shall be omitted; and

(c) in subsection (2) (which excludes certain children from the definition of protected child, including children only temporarily in the care and possession of a person under such arrangements as are referred to in subsection (1) (a) of that section) the words from "by reason" to "that subsection, not" shall be omitted.

(5) In consequence of the modifications of the definition of "protected child" specified in subsection (4) of this section, after subsection (4) of section 2 of the Children Act, 1958 there shall be inserted the following subsection:—

"(4A) A child is not a foster child for the purposes of this Part of this Act while he is placed in the care and possession of a person who proposes to adopt him under arrangements made by such a local authority or registered adoption society as is referred to in Part II of the Adoption Act, 1958 or while he is a protected child within the meaning of Part IV of that Act."

NOTES

For s. 2 of the Children Act, 1958, as amended, see p. 956 *post*.

"For reward and for a period exceeding one month, shall be omitted" (sub-s. (1)).—The effect of this amendment is to bring within the ambit of the Act those placements where no payment is made and which because there is no application to adopt do not fall within the Adoption Act, 1958. A local authority may supervise whether or not foster parents receive payment. Further any private person other than a relative or guardian or proposed adopter who undertakes the care and maintenance of a child becomes a foster parent unless either the period of care is six days or less (such children being protected by the Nurseries and Child-minders Regulation Act, 1948, as amended), or he is not a regular foster parent as defined by the subsection.

In which he is receiving full time education (sub-s. (2)).—Children under school age and children living on school premises and receiving education elsewhere are not excluded from the definition of a foster child.

Transitional provisions.—A person who is subject to an order committing him to the care of a fit person other than a local authority is not a foster child within the meaning of s. 2 of the Children Act, 1958 (Sched. IV, para. 10).

53. Modification of duty of persons maintaining foster children to notify local authority.—(1) Section 3 of the Children Act, 1958 (which requires any person maintaining foster children to notify the local authority on each occasion on which he receives a foster child) shall have effect subject to the following provisions of this section.

(2) In subsection (1) of the section (which requires at least two weeks advance notice of, or, in an emergency, notice within one week after, the reception of a foster child) at the beginning there shall be inserted the words "Subject to the following provisions of this section", after the words "two weeks" there shall be inserted the words "and not more than four weeks" and for the words "one week" there shall be substituted the words "forty-eight hours".

(3) In subsection (2) of the section (which relates to the content of the notice) after the word "specify" there shall be inserted the words "the date on which it is intended that the child should be received or, as the case may be, on which the child was in fact received or became a foster child and".

(4) After subsection (2) of the section there shall be inserted the following subsection:—

(2A) A person shall not be required to give notice under subsection (1) of this section in relation to a child if—

(a) he has on a previous occasion given notice under that subsection in respect of that or any other child, specifying the premises at which he proposes to keep the child in question; and

(b) he has not, at any time since that notice was given, ceased to maintain at least one foster child at those premises and been required by virtue of the following provisions of this section to give notice under subsection (5A) of this section in respect of those premises.

(5) In subsection (3) of the section (which relates to notification of changes of address of foster parents and requires similar periods of notice as under subsection (1))—

(a) for the words "a foster child" there shall be substituted the words "one or more foster children";

(b) for the words "the child is kept" there shall be substituted the words "the child is, or the children are, kept";

(c) after the words "two weeks" there shall be inserted the words "and not more than four weeks"; and

(d) for the words "one week" there shall be substituted the words "forty-eight hours".

(6) So much of subsection (4) of the section as requires notification that a foster child has been removed or has removed himself from the care of the person maintaining him shall cease to have effect and, accordingly, in that subsection for the words "that person" there shall be substituted the words "the person who was maintaining him" and in subsection (5) of the section (which dispenses with the need for such a notice where a child ceases to be a foster child on his removal from a foster parent but empowers the local authority concerned to require certain particulars in such a case)—

(a) for the words "ceases to be a foster child on his removal" there shall be substituted the words "is removed or removes himself";

(b) the words "need not give notice under subsection (4) of this section but" shall be omitted; and

(c) for the words from "the same" onwards there shall be substituted the words "the name and address, if known, of the person (if any) into whose care the child has been removed".

(7) After subsection (5) of the section there shall be inserted the following subsections:—

(5A) Subject to the provisions of the following subsection, where a person who has been maintaining one or more foster children at any premises ceases to maintain foster children at those premises and the circumstances are such that no notice is required to be given under subsection (3) or subsection (4) of this section, that person shall, within forty-eight hours after he ceases to maintain any foster child at those premises, give notice in writing thereof to the local authority.

(5B) A person need not give the notice required by the preceding subsection in consequence of his ceasing to maintain foster children at any premises if, at the time he so ceases, he intends within twenty-seven days again to maintain any of them as a foster child at those premises; but if he subsequently abandons that intention or the said period expires without his having given effect to it he shall give the said notice within forty-eight hours of that event.

NOTES

For s. 3 of the Children Act, 1958, as amended by this Act, see p. 958, *post*.

General note.—Notice is now required not of the reception of each foster child but of the intention to receive a foster child for the first time.

"In respect of that or any other child" (new sub-s. (2 A)).—*I.e.*, separate notices are not required in respect of individual foster children but see s. 4 (2) of the Children Act, 1958, as amended, which allows a local authority to require particulars in cases where this is considered necessary.

54. Inspection of premises in which foster children are kept.—(1) In section 4 (1) of the Children Act, 1958 (which empowers an officer of a local authority to inspect premises in the local authority's area in which foster children are being kept) after the word "in" in the second place where it occurs there shall be inserted the words "the whole or any part of".

(2) After the said section 4 (1) there shall be inserted the following subsection:—

> (1A) If it is shown to the satisfaction of a justice of the peace on sworn information in writing—
>> (a) that there is reasonable cause to believe that a foster child is being kept in any premises, or in any part thereof, and
>> (b) that admission to those premises or that part thereof has been refused to a duly authorised officer of the local authority or that such a refusal is apprehended or that the occupier is temporarily absent,
>
> the justice may by warrant under his hand authorise an officer of the local authority to enter the premises, if need be by force, at any reasonable time within forty-eight hours of the issue of the warrant, for the purpose of inspecting the premises.

(3) At the end of paragraph (b) of section 14 (1) of the Children Act, 1958 (which makes it an offence under that section to refuse to allow an inspection of any premises under section 4 (1) of that Act) there shall be added the words "or wilfully obstructs a person entitled to enter any premises by virtue of a warrant under subsection (1A) of that section".

NOTE

General note.—For s. 4 of the Children Act, 1958, see p. 960, *post*.

The new s. 4 (1A) introduces a new power to issue a warrant. Formerly cases arose where there were good grounds for suspecting that foster children were kept in particular premises but, where admission was refused, nothing could be done. There is similar power in respect of daily minded children under s. 7 (2) of the Nurseries and Child-Minders Regulation Act, 1948. As to extension of power to issue warrants to search for and remove a child see s. 8 of the Children Act, 1958, at p. 965, *post*.

55. Imposition of requirements and prohibitions relating to the keeping of foster children.—(1) In section 4 (2) of the Children Act, 1958 (which empowers a local authority to impose certain requirements on a person who keeps or proposes to keep foster children in premises used wholly or mainly for that purpose) for the word "mainly" there shall be substituted the word "partly".

(2) After paragraph (f) of the said section 4 (2) there shall be inserted the following paragraphs:—

> (g) the fire precautions to be taken in the premises;
> (h) the giving of particulars of any foster child received in the premises and of any change in the number or identity of the foster children kept therein.

(3) In the words following the several paragraphs of the said section 4 (2), after the word "but" there shall be inserted the words "any such

requirement may be limited to a particular class of foster children kept in the premises and" and for the words "(b) to (f)" there shall be substituted the words "(b) to (h)".

(4) For subsection (3) of section 4 of the Children Act, 1958 (which empowers a local authority to prohibit a person from keeping a particular foster child or any foster children at particular premises) there shall be substituted the following subsections:—

(3) Where a person proposes to keep a foster child in any premises and the local authority are of the opinion that—

    (a) the premises are not suitable premises in which to keep foster children; or

    (b) that person is not a suitable person to have the care and maintenance of foster children; or

    (c) it would be detrimental to that child to be kept by that person in those premises;

the local authority may impose a prohibition on that person under subsection (3A) of this section.

(3A) A prohibition imposed on any person under this subsection may—

    (a) prohibit him from keeping any foster child in premises specified in the prohibition; or

    (b) prohibit him from keeping any foster child in any premises in the area of the local authority; or

    (c) prohibit him from keeping a particular child specified in the prohibition in premises so specified.

(3B) Where a local authority have imposed a prohibition on any person under subsection (3A) of this section, the local authority may, if they think fit, cancel the prohibition, either of their own motion or on an application made by that person on the ground of a change in the circumstances in which a foster child would be kept by him.

(5) In section 5 (1) of the Children Act, 1958 (which confers a right of appeal to a juvenile court within fourteen days of the imposition of a requirement or prohibition under section 4 of that Act) after the word "prohibition", in the second place where it occurs, there shall be inserted the words "or, in the case of a prohibition imposed under subsection (3A) of that section, within fourteen days from the refusal by the local authority to accede to an application by him for the cancellation of the prohibition".

NOTE

For s. 4 of the Children Act, 1958, see p. 960, post.

"Partly" (sub-s. (1)).—This amendment clarifies the previous law. Private fostering in an ordinary home is now subject to inspection as to any part of the premises, whether children are kept in that part or not, and requirements may also be imposed as to, for example, the maximum number of foster children to be kept at the premises. See s. 57 for modifications of this provision.

56. Extension of disqualification for keeping foster children.—(1)

In section 6 of the Children Act, 1958 (which provides that a person shall not, without the consent of the local authority, maintain a foster child if one or more of a variety of orders has been made against him) there shall be made the following amendments, that is to say—

    (a) in paragraph (b), after the word "1933", there shall be inserted the words "the Children and Young Persons Act, 1969" and for the words from "in respect of" to "of which the" there shall be substituted the words "and by virtue of the order or requirement a";

    (b) at the end of paragraph (c) there shall be inserted the words "or has been placed on probation or discharged absolutely or conditionally for any such offence";

    (c) in paragraph (e), after the word "subsection" there shall be inserted the words "(3) or" and for the words from "refusing" onwards there shall be substituted the words "refusing, or an order under section five of that Act cancelling, the registration of any premises occupied by him or his registration"; and

    (d) after paragraph (e) there shall be inserted the following paragraph:—

        (f) an order has been made under section 43 of the Adoption Act, 1958 for the removal of a protected child who was being kept or was about to be received by him.

(2) At the end of the said section 6 there shall be added the following subsection:—

    (2) Where this section applies to any person, otherwise than by virtue of this subsection, it shall apply also to any other person who lives in the same premises as he does or who lives in premises at which he is employed;

and accordingly the said section 6 as amended by the preceding subsection shall be subsection (1) of that section.

NOTES

For s. 6 of the Children Act, 1958, as amended, see p. 963, post.

"Or has been placed on probation." (sub-s. (1) (b)).—A conviction followed by probation is not a conviction for the purposes of any enactment other than the Criminal Justice Act, 1948 (Criminal Justice Act, 1948, s. 12) and the inclusion of these words is necessary to give a local authority an opportunity to consider the case.

Section 43 of the Adoption Act, 1958 (sub-s. (1) (a)).—This fills a gap that was seen to exist in previous enactments. For s. 43 of the Adoption Act, 1958, see p. 1073, post.

"Any other person" (sub-s. (2)).—Up to now the disqualification attached solely to the foster parent. The disqualification will apparently cover any employee living in the premises, or a lodger.

57. Modifications of provisions as to offences.—(1) After subsection (1) of section 14 of the Children Act, 1958 (which, among other matters, makes it an offence to maintain a foster child in contravention of section 6 of that Act) there shall be inserted the following subsection:—

    (1A) Where section 6 of this Act applies to any person by virtue only of subsection (2) of that section, he shall not be guilty of an offence under paragraph (d) of subsection (1) of this section if he proves that he did not know, and had no reasonable ground for believing, that a person living or employed in the premises in which he lives was a person to whom that section applies.

(2) After subsection (2) of the said section 14 (which provides that offences under that section are punishable summarily) there shall be added the following subsection:—

(2A) If any person who is required, under any provision of this Part of this Act, to give a notice fails to give the notice within the time specified in that provision, then, notwithstanding anything in section 104 of the Magistrates' Courts Act, 1952 (time limit for proceedings) proceedings for the offence may be brought at any time within six months from the date when evidence of the offence came to the knowledge of the local authority.

NOTE

General note.—For s. 14 of the Children Act, 1958, as amended, see p. 967, *post*. The new sub-s. (1A) takes account of the amendments made by the preceding section whereby a person other than the foster parent may be disqualified.

Inspection

58. Inspection of children's homes etc. by persons authorised by Secretary of State.—(1) Subject to subsection (2) of this section, the Secretary of State may cause to be inspected from time to time—

(a) any community home provided by a local authority under section 38 of this Act;

(b) any voluntary home (whether a community home or not);

(c) any other premises at which one or more children in the care of a local authority are being accommodated and maintained;

(d) any other premises at which one or more children are being boarded out by a voluntary organisation; and

(e) any other premises where a foster child within the meaning of Part I of the Children Act, 1958 or a child to whom any of the provisions of that Part are extended by section 12 or section 13 of that Act, or a protected child within the meaning of Part IV of the Adoption Act, 1958 is being accommodated or maintained.

(2) Subsection (1) of this section does not apply to any home or other premises which is, as a whole, subject to inspection by or under the authority of a government department.

(3) An inspection under this section shall be conducted by a person authorised in that behalf by the Secretary of State, but an officer of a local authority shall not be so authorised except with the consent of that authority.

(4) Any person inspecting a home or other premises under this section may inspect the children therein and make such examination into the state and management of the home or other premises and the treatment of children therein as he thinks fit.

NOTES

This section came into force on December 1, 1969 (S.I. 1969 No. 1565).

Inspection.—This section and the following section restate the provisions of s. 94 of the Children and Young Persons Act, 1933 and s. 54 (1) and (2) of the Children Act, 1948, taking account of changes made in this Part of this Act.

59. Powers of entry supplemental to s. 58.—(1) A person authorised to inspect any home or other premises under section 58 of this Act
shall have a right to enter the home or other premises for that purpose and
for any other purpose specified in subsection (4) of that section, but shall
if so required produce some duly authenticated document showing his
authority to exercise the power of entry conferred by this subsection.

(2) A person who obstructs the exercise by a person authorised as
mentioned in subsection (1) of this section of a power of entry conferred
thereby shall be liable on summary conviction to a fine not exceeding
five pounds or, in the case of a second or subsequent conviction, to a fine
not exceeding twenty pounds.

(3) A refusal to allow any such person as is mentioned in subsection (1)
of this section to enter any such home or other premises as are mentioned
in section 58 (1) of this Act shall be deemed, for the purposes of section 40
of the Act of 1933 (which relates to search warrants), to be a reasonable
cause to suspect that a child or young person in the home or other premises
is being neglected in a manner likely to cause him unnecessary suffering or
injury to health.

NOTE

This section came into force on December 1, 1969 (S.I. 1969 No. 1565).
Obstruction (sub-s. (2)).—See s. 54 (7) of the Children Act, 1948, p. 919.

PART III

MISCELLANEOUS AND GENERAL

Miscellaneous

60. Extradition offences.—(1) There shall be included—

(a) in the list of extradition crimes contained in Schedule 1 to the
    Extradition Act, 1870; and
(b) among the descriptions of offences set out in Schedule 1 to the
    Fugitive Offenders Act, 1967,

any offence of the kind described in section 1 of the Act of 1933 (which
relates to cruelty to persons under sixteen) and any offence of the kind
described in section 1 of the Indecency with Children Act, 1960.

(2) Nothing in this Act shall be construed as derogating from the provisions of section 17 of the said Act of 1870 or section 16 (2) or 17 of the
said Act of 1967 in their application to any provisions of those Acts
respectively as amended by the preceding subsection.

NOTES

General note.—This section came into force on December 1, 1969 (S.I. 1969
No. 1565). This section remedies the situation whereby offences under s. 1 of the
Children and Young Persons Act, 1933, were not included in the provisions re-
ferred to.

Any offence of the kind described.—These offences need to be identified for
the purpose of other laws (*e.g.* in British dependencies) which have similar legislation.

61. Rules relating to juvenile court panels and composition of juvenile courts.—(1) Without prejudice to the generality of the power to make rules under section 15 of the Justices of the Peace Act, 1949 relating to the procedure and practice to be followed by magistrates' courts, provision may be made by such rules with respect to any of the following matters, namely,—

(a) the formation and revision of juvenile court panels, that is to say, panels of justices specially qualified to deal with juvenile cases and the eligibility of justices to be members of such panels;

(b) the appointment of persons as chairmen of juvenile courts; and

(c) the composition of juvenile courts.

(2) Rules making any such provisions as are referred to in subsection (1) of this section may confer powers on the Lord Chancellor with respect to any of the matters specified in the rules and may, in particular, provide for the appointment of juvenile court panels by him and for the removal from a juvenile court panel of any justice who, in his opinion, is unsuitable to serve on a juvenile court.

(3) Rules made by virtue of this section may make different provision in relation to different areas for which juvenile court panels are formed; and in the application of this section to the county palatine of Lancaster, for any reference in the preceding subsection to the Lord Chancellor there shall be substituted a reference to the Chancellor of the Duchy.

(4) Nothing in this section or in any rules made under section 15 of the said Act of 1949 shall affect—

(a) the areas for which juvenile court panels are formed and juvenile courts are constituted;

(b) the provisions of Part I of Schedule 2 to the Act of 1963 (and, as it has effect by virtue of section 17 (1) of that Act, Part I of Schedule 2 to the Act of 1933) with respect to the making of recommendations and orders relating to the formation of combined juvenile court panels; or

(c) the provision of paragraph 14 of that Schedule relating to the divisions of the metropolitan area for which juvenile courts sit;

but rules under the said section 15 may repeal, either generally or with respect to any part of the metropolitan area, any provision contained in paragraphs 15 to 18 of that Schedule (which contain provisions applicable in the metropolitan area with respect to certain of the matters referred to in subsection (1) of this section) and in subsections (2) and (3) of section 12 of the Administration of Justice Act, 1964 (which amend those paragraphs).

(5) In this section "the metropolitan area" means the inner London area and the City of London.

NOTE

General note.—Rules may provide for appointment of panels by the Lord Chancellor and not by the justices in a petty sessions area as under the Juvenile Courts (Constitution) Rules, 1954.

The effect of sub-ss. (2) and (3) is that the method of appointment of juvenile panels may differ from area to area.

62. Contributions in respect of children and young persons in care.—(1) The provisions of sections 86 to 88 of the Act of 1933 (which, as originally enacted, provided for contributions in respect of children and young persons committed to the care of a fit person or sent to an approved school) shall apply in relation to children and young persons committed to the care of a local authority by a care order which is not an interim order.

(2) Whether or not a contribution order has been made in respect of any child or young person in the care of a local authority, no contribution shall be payable in respect of him for any period during which he is allowed by the local authority to be under the charge and control of a parent, guardian relative or friend, although remaining in the care of the local authority.

(3) Where a person (in this section referred to as a "contributory") is liable under section 86 of the Act of 1933 to make a contribution in respect of a child or young person in the care of a local authority, then, subject to the following provisions of this section, the amount of his contribution shall be such as may be proposed by the local authority and agreed by the contributory or, in default of agreement, as may be determined by a court in proceedings for, or for the variation of, a contribution order.

(4) The maximum contribution which may be proposed by a local authority in respect of a child or young person in their care shall be a weekly amount equal to the weekly amount which, in the opinion of the local authority, they would normally be prepared to pay if a child or young person of the same age were boarded out by them (whether or not the child or young person in respect of whom the contribution is proposed is in fact so boarded out and, if he is, whether or not the local authority are in fact paying that amount).

(5) No contribution order shall be made on a contributory in respect of a child or young person unless—

(a) the local authority in whose care he is have, by notice in writing given to the contributory, proposed an amount as the amount of his contribution; and

(b) either the contributory and the local authority have not, within the period of one month beginning with the day on which the notice was given to the contributory, agreed on the amount of his contribution or the contributory has defaulted in making one or more contributions of an amount which has been agreed.

(6) In proceedings for a contribution order, the court shall not order a contributory to pay a contribution greater than that proposed in the notice given to him under subsection (5) (a) of this section.

(7) In proceedings for the variation of a contribution order, the local authority concerned shall specify the weekly amount which, having regard to subsection (4) of this section, they propose should be the amount of the contribution and the court shall not vary the contribution order so as to require the contributory to pay a contribution greater than that proposed by the local authority.

(8) In this section—

"contribution" means a contribution under section 86 of the Act of
1933; and

"contribution order" means an order under section 87 of that Act.

NOTE

General note.—The practice of local authorities and courts in the fixing of the
amount of a contribution varies considerably. This section is designed to achieve
greater uniformity, in that a basis for the charge is for the first time laid down, that
of a boarding out fee (whether or not the child is in fact boarded out).

Arrears of contribution.—See s. 30 of the Children and Young Persons Act,
1963.

"Parent, guardian etc.".—See note p. 164, *ante*, and s. 70, *post*, for definition of
guardian.

"Liable under s. 86".—This section of the Act of 1933 is applied to children
received into care by ss. 23, 24 of the Childrens Act, 1948.

"By notice in writing".—Notice may be sent by post (s. 287A of the Local
Government Act, 1933). Contributions are payable to the authority wherever
the person liable to contribute resides, but by paras. 2 (1), (2) Sched. VIII of the
Local Government Act, 1958, the authority receiving them must pay them over to
the authority responsible for maintenance less any deductions for services agreed
between them or determined by the Secretary of State. See Home Office Circular
285/1970, p. 860, *post*, which suggests that if notice is given on behalf of another
authority this should be clearly expressed, or that the caring authority should send
copies of the notice to the authority entitled to receive payment.

**63. Returns of information and presentation of reports etc. to
Parliament.**—(1) Every local authority shall, at such times and in such
form as the Secretary of State may direct, transmit to the Secretary of
State such particulars as he may require—

(a) with respect to the performance by the local authority of all or
any of their functions under the enactments mentioned in subsection (6) of this section; and

(b) with respect to the children in relation to whom the authority
have exercised those functions.

(2) Every voluntary organisation shall, at such times and in such form
as the Secretary of State may direct, transmit to him such particulars as
he may require with respect to the children who are accommodated and
maintained in voluntary homes provided by the organisation or who have
been boarded out by the organisation.

(3) The clerk of each juvenile court shall, at such times and in such form
as the Secretary of State may direct, transmit to him such particulars
as he may require with respect to the proceedings of the court.

(4) The Secretary of State shall in each year lay before Parliament a
consolidated and classified abstract of the information transmitted to him
under the preceding provisions of this section.

(5) The Secretary of State shall lay before Parliament in 1973 and in
every third subsequent year a report with respect to the exercise by local
authorities of their functions under the enactments mentioned in subsection (6) of this section, the provision by voluntary organisations of

facilities for children and such other matters relating to children as he thinks fit.

(6) The enactments referred to in subsections (1) and (5) of this section are—

(a) Parts III and IV of the Children and Young Persons Act, 1933;

(b) the Children Act, 1948;

(c) the Children Act, 1958;

(d) the Adoption Act, 1958;

(e) section 9 of the Mental Health Act, 1959 and section 10 of that Act so far as it relates to children and young persons in respect of whom the rights and powers of a parent are vested in a local authority as mentioned in subsection (1) (a) of that section;

(f) section 10 of the Mental Health (Scotland) Act, 1960 so far as it relates to children and young persons in respect of whom the rights and powers of a parent are vested in a local authority as mentioned in subsection (1) (a) of that section;

(g) section 2 (1) (f) of the Matrimonial Proceedings (Magistrates' Courts) Act 1960, section 37 of the Matrimonial Causes Act, 1965 and section 7 (4) of the Family Law Reform Act, 1969;

(h) the Children and Young Persons Act, 1963, except Part II and section 56;

(i) this Act.

NOTES

This section is printed as amended by the Local Authority Social Services Act, 1970.

General note.—This section came into force on December 1, 1969 (S.I. 1969 No. 1565).

The Adams Committee on Civil Judicial Statistics recommended that publication of statistics of non-criminal proceedings in magistrates' courts in the Criminal Statistics should be discontinued and that *courts* should be responsible rather than police for the supply of information.

"As the Secretary of State may direct".—Section 69 (orders and regulations etc.) does not refer to this section, and it would seem that any directions would be by a Home Office Circular, rather than Statutory Instrument. By s. 69 (3) any directions given may be varied or revoked. See Home Office Circular 270/1970, p. 827, *post*.

Section 1 (4) of the Children and Young Persons Act, 1963 (which required local authorities to make reports) was repealed from December 1, 1969 (S.I. 1969 No. 1565).

Child.—See s. 70, *post*, for definition.

Financial provisions

64.—Expenses of Secretary of State in providing homes offering specialised facilities.—There shall be defrayed out of moneys provided by Parliament any expenses incurred by the Secretary of State in providing, equipping and maintaining homes for the accommodation of children who are in the care of local authorities and are in need of particular facilities and services which are provided in those homes and are, in the opinion of the Secretary of State, unlikely to be readily available in community homes.

NOTE

This section came into force on December 1, 1969 (S.I. 1969 No. 1565).

Home.—For powers of local authority to maintain a child in such a home see s. 13 (1) (b) of the Children Act, 1948, p. 893, *post*, as amended by this Act, and see also s. 53 (2) of the Children and Young Persons Act, 1933, p. 57, *ante*, for power of the Secretary of State to direct the detention of children and young persons convicted on indictment of certain offences.

Such homes may be established to meet the need of the disturbed adolescent who cannot be contained in a school type residential care nor purely hospital setting.

The Department of Health and Social Security has issued a pamphlet (H.M.S.O. 1971) Youth Treatment Centres which describes the provision envisaged for severely disturbed children. One such centre, St. Charles, Brentwood, is in operation; for admission procedures, see D.H.S.S. Circular 26/1971, p. 855, *post*.

Child.—See s. 70, *post*.

65. Grants to voluntary organisations etc.—(1) The Secretary of State may make out of moneys provided by Parliament grants to voluntary organisations of such amounts and subject to such conditions as he may with the consent of the Treasury determine towards expenditure incurred by them in connection with the establishment, maintenance or improvement of voluntary homes which at the time the expenditure was incurred were assisted community homes or were designated as such in a regional plan which was then in operation, including expenses incurred by them in respect of the borrowing of money to defray any such expenditure.

(2) The power of the Secretary of State to make grants to voluntary organisations under section 46 of the Children Act, 1948 (which relates to grants in respect of certain expenses incurred in connection with voluntary homes) shall not apply to expenditure incurred in connection with a voluntary home which at the time the expenditure was incurred, was a controlled or assisted community home or was designated as such in a regional plan which was then in operation.

(3) Where an order has been made under section 46 of this Act in relation to an approved institution within the meaning of that section and no such provision as is referred to in paragraph 9 (1) of Schedule 3 to this Act is made by a regional plan in relation to any part of the premises of the institution, the Secretary of State may with the consent of the Treasury make out of moneys provided by Parliament grants towards the discharge by any person of any liability, other than an obligation to which paragraph 11 of that Schedule applies, which was incurred by that person in connection with the establishment, maintenance or improvement of the institution.

(4) No grant shall be made under subsection (3) of this section in respect of a liability relating to an institution unless it appears to the Secretary of State that, on or within a reasonable time after the date specified in the order referred to in that subsection, the premises of the institution are to be used for a purpose which is of benefit to children; and any grant made under that subsection shall be subject to such conditions as the Secretary of State may with the approval of the Treasury determine, including conditions with respect to the repayment in whole or in part of the grant, either by the person to whom the grant was made or by some other person who, before the grant was made, consented to accept the liability.

(5) Any sums received by the Secretary of State by virtue of any such condition as is referred to in subsection (4) of this section shall be paid into the Consolidated Fund.

NOTE

General note.—This section came into force on December 1, 1969 (S.I. 1969 No. 1565).

Controlled assisted community homes.—See s. 39, *ante*.

Child.—See s. 70, *post*, for definition.

66. Increase of rate support grants.—(1) The power to make an order under section 3 (1) of the Local Government Act, 1966, increasing the amounts fixed by a rate support grant order for a particular year shall be exercisable, in accordance with subsection (2) of this section, in relation to any rate support grant order made before the date of the coming into operation of any provision of this Act (in this section referred to as "the relevant provision") for a grant period ending after that date.

(2) Without prejudice to subsection (4) of the said section 3 (which empowers an order under subsection (1) of that section to vary the matters prescribed by a rate support grant order), an order under subsection (1) of that section made by virtue of this section may be made for such year or years comprised in the grant period concerned as may be specified in the order and in respect of the year or each of the years so specified shall increase the amounts fixed by the relevant rate support grant order as the aggregate amounts of the rate support grants and any elements of the grants for that year to such extent and in such a manner as may appear to the Minister of Housing and Local Government to be appropriate, having regard to any additional expenditure incurred or likely to be incurred by local authorities in consequence of the coming into operation of the relevant provision.

(3) In this section "grant period" means the period for which a rate support grant order is made.

(4) There shall be defrayed out of moneys provided by Parliament any increase in rate support grants attributable to this Act.

NOTE

This section came into force on December 1, 1969. (S.I. 1969 No. 1565).

67. Administrative expenses.—Any administrative expenses of the Secretary of State under this Act shall be defrayed out of moneys provided by Parliament.

NOTE

This section came into force on December 1, 1969 (S.I. 1969 No. 1565).

Supplemental

68. Compulsory acquisition of land.—(1) A local authority other than a county council may be authorised by the Secretary of State to purchase compulsorily any land, whether situated inside or outside their area, for the purposes of their functions under this Act or section 1 of the Act of 1963.

(2) The Acquisition of Land (Authorisation Procedure) Act, 1946 shall apply in relation to the compulsory purchase of land in pursuance of subsection (1) of this section as if that subsection were contained in an Act in force immediately before the commencement of that Act.

(3) In the application to the functions of a county council under this Act or section 1 of the Act of 1963 of section 159 (1) of the Local Government Act, 1933 (under which a county council may be authorised to purchase land compulsorily) the power to authorise a compulsory purchase shall be vested in the Secretary of State.

NOTE

This section came into force on December 1, 1969 (S.I. 1969 No. 1565).

69. Orders and regulations etc.—(1) Any power conferred on the Secretary of State by this Act to make an order or regulations, except an order under section 25, 39 or 43 (5) or paragraph 23 or 24 of Schedule 4, shall be exercisable by statutory instrument; and any statutory instrument made in pursuance of this subsection, except an instrument containing only regulations under paragraph 8 (2) of Schedule 3 or an order under section 1 (6), 26, 46, 47, 72 (2) or 73 (2), or paragraph 11 (2) of Schedule 3, shall be subject to annulment in pursuance of a resolution of either House of Parliament.

(2) A statutory instrument containing regulations under subsection (3) of section 5 or an order under section 34 of this Act shall not be subject to annulment as aforesaid, but no such regulations or order shall be included in a statutory instrument containing provisions which do not require approval in pursuance of the said subsection (4) or, as the case may be, to which subsection (7) of the said section 34 does not apply.

(3) An order made or directions given by the Secretary of State under any provision of this Act, except an order under section 7 (5), may be revoked or varied by a subsequent order or subsequent directions under that provision.

(4) Any order or regulations made by the Secretary of State under this Act may—

(a) make different provision for different circumstances;
(b) provide for exemptions from any provisions of the order or regulations; and
(c) contain such incidental and supplemental provisions as the Secretary of State considers expedient for the purposes of the order or regulations.

NOTE

This section came into force on December 1, 1969 (S.I. 1969 No. 1565).

70. Interpretation and ancillary provisions.—(1) In this Act, unless the contrary intention appears, the following expressions have the following meanings:—

"the Act of 1933" means the Children and Young Persons Act, 1933;

"the Act of 1963" means the Children and Young Persons Act, 1963;

"approved school order", "guardian" and "place of safety" have the same meanings as in the Act of 1933;

"care order" has the meaning assigned to it by section 20 of this Act;

"child", except in Part II (including Schedule 3) and sections 27, 63, 64 and 65 of this Act, means a person under the age of fourteen, and in that Part (including that Schedule) and those sections means a person under the age of eighteen and a person who has attained the age of eighteen and is the subject of a care order;

"instrument of management" means an instrument of management made under section 39 of this Act;

"interim order" has the meaning assigned to it by section 20 of this Act;

"local authority" means the council of a county, county borough or London borough or the Common Council of the City of London;

"petty sessions area" has the same meaning as in the Magistrates' Courts Act, 1952 except that, in relation to a juvenile court constituted for the metropolitan area within the meaning of Part II of Schedule 2 to the Act of 1963, it means such a division of that area as is mentioned in paragraph 14 of that Schedule;

"planning area" has the meaning assigned to it by section 35 (1) of this Act;

"police officer" means a member of a police force;

"regional plan" has the meaning assigned to it by section 36 (1) of this Act;

"the relevant authorities", in relation to a planning area, has the meaning assigned to it by section 35 (3) of this Act;

"reside" means habitually reside, and cognate expressions shall be construed accordingly except in section 12 (4) and (5) of this Act;

"supervision order", "supervised person" and "supervisor" have the meanings assigned to them by section 11 of this Act;

"trust deed", in relation to a voluntary home, has the meaning assigned to it by section 40 (5) of this Act;

"voluntary home" has the same meaning as in Part V of the Act of 1933;

"voluntary organisation" has the same meaning as in the Children Act, 1948; and

"young person" means a person who has attained the age of fourteen and is under the age of seventeen;

and it is hereby declared that, in the expression "care or control", "care" includes protection and guidance and "control" includes discipline.

(2) Without prejudice to any power apart from this subsection to bring proceedings on behalf of another person, any power to make an application which is exercisable by a child or young person by virtue of section 15 (1), 21 (2), 22 (4) or (6) or 28 (5) of this Act shall also be exercisable on his behalf by his parent or guardian; and in this subsection "guardian" includes any person who was a guardian of the child or young person in question at the time when any supervision order, care order or warrant to which the application relates was originally made.

(3) In section 99 (1) of the Act of 1933 (under which the age which a court presumes or declares to be the age of a person brought before it is deemed to be his true age for the purposes of that Act) the references to that Act shall be construed as including references to this Act.

(4) Subject to the following subsection, any reference in this Act to any enactment is a reference to it as amended, and includes a reference to it as applied, by or under any other enactment including this Act.

(5) Any reference in this Act to an enactment of the Parliament of Northern Ireland shall be construed as a reference to that enactment as amended by any Act of that Parliament, whether passed before or after this Act, and to any enactment of that Parliament for the time being in force which re-enacts the said enactment with or without modifications.

NOTE

Proof of age.—Section 6, p. 144, *ante*, is deemed to be a provision of the Magistrates' Courts Act, 1952 and not of this Act (Administration of Justice Act, 1970, s. 51 (1)).

71. Application to Isles of Scilly.—This Act shall have effect, in its application to the Isles of Scilly, with such modifications as the Secretary of State may by order specify.

NOTE

This section came into force on December 1, 1969 (S.I. 1969 No. 1565).

72. Transitional provisions, minor amendments and repeals etc.
—(1) The transitional provisions and savings set out in Part I of Schedule 4 to this Act shall have effect.

(2) The transitional provisions set out in Part II of Schedule 4 to this Act shall have effect until such day as the Secretary of State may by order specify for the purposes of this subsection (being the day on and after which those provisions will in his opinion be unnecessary in consequence of the coming into force of provisions of the Social Work (Scotland) Act, 1968) and shall be deemed to have been repealed on that day by an Act of Parliament passed after this Act.

(3) The enactments mentioned in Schedule 5 to this Act shall have effect subject to the amendments specified in that Schedule (which are minor amendments and amendments consequential on the provisions of this Act).

(4) Subject to subsection (1) of this section, the enactments mentioned in the first and second columns of Schedule 6 to this Act are hereby repealed to the extent specified in the third column of that Schedule.

(5) In accordance with Part II of this Act and the said Schedules 5 and 6, sections 1 to 6 and 14 of the Children Act, 1958 are to have effect, after

the coming into force of so much of that Part and those Schedules as relates to those sections, as set out in Schedule 7 to this Act, but without prejudice to any other enactment affecting the operation of those sections.

NOTE

Parts of this section are brought into operation from various dates by the Children and Young Persons Act, 1969 (Commencement Nos. 1 to 4) Orders, 1969, pp. 561 *et seq.*, *post*. The effect of these Orders is shown against the appropriate section in the text.

"**Transitional provisions**".—See note to Sched. IV, part II, p. 230, *post*, and S.I. 1971 No. 589, p. 654, *post*.

73. Citation commencement and extent.—(1) This Act may be cited as the Children and Young Persons Act, 1969, and this Act and the Children and Young Persons Act, 1933 to 1963 may be cited together as the Children and Young Persons Acts, 1933 to 1969.

(2) This Act shall come into force on such day as the Secretary of State may by order appoint, and different days may be appointed under this subsection for different provisions of this Act so far as they apply to such cases only as may be specified in the order.

(3) Without prejudice to the generality of section 69 (4) of this Act, an order under the preceding subsection may make such transitional provision as the Secretary of State considers appropriate in connection with the provisions brought into force by the order, including such adaptations of those provisions and of any other provisions of this Act then in force as appear to him appropriate for the purposes or in consequence of the operation of any provision of this Act before the coming into force of any other provision of this Act or of a provision of the Social Work (Scotland) Act, 1968.

(4) This section and the following provisions only of this Act extend to Scotland, that is to say—

   (a) sections 10 (1) and (2), 32 (1), (3) and (4), 56 and 57 (1);
   (b) section 72 (2) and Part II of Schedule 4;
   (c) paragraphs 25, 26, 33, 35, 38, 42, 53, 54 and 57 to 83 of Schedule 5 and section 72 (3) so far as it relates to those paragraphs;
   (d) section 72 (4) and Schedule 6 so far as they relate to the Merchant Shipping Act, 1894, the Superannuation (Miscellaneous Provisions) Act, 1948, sections 10, 53, 55 and 59 of the Act of 1963, the Family Allowances Act, 1965 and the Social Work (Scotland) Act, 1968.

(5) This section and the following provisions only of this Act extend to Northern Ireland, that is to say—

   (a) sections 25 and 32;
   (b) section 72 (3) and Schedule 5 so far as they relate to section 29 of the Criminal Justice Act, 1961 and provisions of the Social Work (Scotland) Act, 1968 which extend to Northern Ireland; and
   (c) section 72 (4) and Schedule 6 so far as they relate to section 83 of the Act of 1933, paragraph 13 of Schedule 2 to the Children and

Young Persons (Scotland) Act, 1937, section 29 of the Criminal Justice Act, 1961, sections 10 (1) and (2), 53 (1) and 65 (5) of, and paragraphs 27, 34 and 50 of Schedule 3 to, the Act of 1963 and sections 73 (2), 76 (1) and (2) and 77 (1) (b) of the Social Work (Scotland) Act, 1968;

and section 32 (2) and (3) of this Act shall be treated for the purposes of section 6 of the Government of Ireland Act, 1920 as if it had been passed before the day appointed for the said section 6 to come into operation.

(6) Section 26 of this Act and this section, and section 72 (4) of this Act and Schedule 6 to this Act so far as they relate to paragraph 13 of Schedule 2 to the Children and Young Persons (Scotland) Act, 1937 and section 53 (1) of, and paragraph 34 of Schedule 3 to, the Act of 1963, extend to the Channel Islands and the Isle of Man, and section 32 (1) and (4) of this Act and this section extend to the Channel Islands.

(7) It is hereby declared that the provisions of sections 69 and 70 of this Act extend to each of the countries aforesaid so far as is appropriate for the purposes of any other provisions of this Act extending to the country in question.

NOTES

General note.—This section came into force on November 16, 1969 (S.I. 1969 No. 1552).

"On such day" (sub-s. (2)).—The following orders have been made bringing into operation provisions of the Act on the dates stated therein:—
The Children and Young Persons Act, 1969
   (Commencement No. 1) Order, 1969, pp. 561 *et seq.*, *post.*
   (Commencement No. 2) Order, 1969, pp. 563 *et seq.*, *post.*
   (Commencement No. 3) Order, 1970, pp. 614 *et seq.*, *post.*
   (Commencement No. 4) Order, 1970, pp. 653 *et seq.*, *post.*

SCHEDULES

SCHEDULE 1
MODIFICATIONS OF PART IV OF CRIMINAL JUSTICE ACT, 1967

NOTE

General note.—These modifications enable, *inter alia*, a contribution order to be made against an "appropriate contributor" (defined in s. 84 of the Criminal Justice Act, 1967, as amended by this Act as follows:—"appropriate contributor", in relation to a person who has not attained the age of sixteen, means his father, any person who has been adjudged to be his putative father and (whether or not he is legitimate) his mother, as well as the applicant for legal aid himself who may well have no means).

The schedule provides a useful sanction in that parents who are required and fail to produce a statement of means are deemed to have sufficient means to support a contribution order. This is so even where the defendant becomes sixteen after the legal aid order has been made.

Where a defendant under sixteen desires legal aid, but his parents do not, the court has a discretion whether to require a statement of means from the parent. A parent who is "deemed" to have sufficient means may seek to vary any contribution order that has been made.

One further consequence is that all care proceedings and some proceedings consequent upon them are now the subject of "criminal" legal aid as against civil aid.

This may well save delay inherent in the latter system. Para. 5 is consequential upon the appropriate contributor provisions.

The Criminal Justice Act, 1967, as amended by this Schedule is printed at p. 326, *post.*

SCHEDULE 2
CHILDREN'S REGIONAL PLANNING COMMITTEES

1.—(1) Subject to the following provisions of this Schedule, the children's regional planning committee for a planning area (in this Schedule referred to as "the committee") shall consist of such number of persons selected and appointed in such manner and holding office on such terms as the relevant authorities may from time to time approve.

(2) No person who is disqualified by virtue of section 59 of the Local Government Act, 1933 from being a member of any local authority which is one of the relevant authorities for a planning area may be a member of the committee for that area.

2.—(1) Subject to sub-paragraph (2) of this paragraph, the relevant authorities for a planning area shall so exercise their powers under paragraph (1) 1 of this Schedule as to secure that each authority nominates as a member of the committee for the area at least one person who is not so nominated by any other of the relevant authorities.

(2) If the Secretary of State considers that owing to special circumstances the requirement imposed by sub-paragraph (1) of this paragraph should be dispensed with in the case of a particular authority he may direct accordingly.

(3) The members of the committee for a planning area who are nominated by the relevant authorities are in the following provisions of this Schedule referred to as "the nominated members".

3.—(1) Without prejudice to any power of co-option conferred on the committee for a planning area under paragraph 1 (1) of this Schedule, but subject to paragraph 4 of this Schedule, the nominated members of the committee may co-opt other persons to serve as members of the committee, either generally or in relation only to such matters as may be specified by the nominated members.

(2) Where any persons are co-opted to serve as members of the committee for a planning area in relation only to such matters as are specified by the nominated members then, subject to any directions given by the relevant authorities, the extent to which those persons shall be entitled to attend, speak and vote at meetings of the committee shall be such as may be determined by the nominated members.

4. The relevant authorities for a planning area shall so exercise their powers under paragraph 1 (1) of this Schedule, and the nominated members of the committee for a planning area shall so limit any exercise of their power under paragraph 3 of this Schedule, as to secure that at all times a majority of the members of the committee for the planning area are members of the relevant authorities.

5. Subject to any directions given by the relevant authorities, the procedure and quorum of the committee for a planning area shall be such as may be determined by the nominated members.

6. Section 93 (1) of the Local Government Act, 1933 (which relates to the expenses of joint committees of local authorities) shall apply to the committee

for a planning area as it applies to such a joint committee as is mentioned in that section, but as if—

(a) for references to the local authorities by whom the committee is appointed there were substituted references to the relevant authorities; and

(b) for paragraphs (a) and (b) of subsection (1) of that section there were substituted the words "by the Secretary of State";

and Part X of that Act (which relates to accounts and audit) shall apply to the accounts of the committee for a planning area as it applies to the accounts of such a joint committee as is mentioned in section 219 (c) of that Act.

NOTES

This Schedule came into force on December 1, 1969, Children and Young Persons Act, 1969 (Commencement No. 2) Order, 1969, S.I. 1969 No. 1565.

"Disqualified" (para. 1 (2)).—This includes those who hold paid office under the authority.

"Special circumstances" (para. 2 (2)).—The circumstances are not outlined further.

"May co-opt other persons" (para. 3 (1)).—The committee is left entirely free as to co-opted members, but it may be that representatives of education, health, police, courts, voluntary child care, etc. would be thought to have a large contribution to make.

Expenses (para. 6).—Subsistence allowances and other expenses for members of the committee could be covered by the prescribing of these committees under s. 111 (1) (h) of the Local Government Act, 1948, as bodies to which Part VI of that Act applies. The schedule itself makes no provisions for members allowances. Joint committees of local authorities for the exercise of such functions may fall within the provisions of the Public Bodies (Admission to Meetings) Act, 1960.

SCHEDULE 3

APPROVED SCHOOLS AND OTHER INSTITUTIONS

Provisions as to staff

1.—(1) This paragraph applies where it appears to the Secretary of State that on the date specified in an order under section 46 of this Act (in the following provisions of this Schedule referred to as a "section 46 order") all or any of the premises used for the purposes of the institution to which the order relates are to be used for the purposes—

(a) of a community home, or

(b) of a school of any of the following descriptions, namely, a county school, a voluntary school which is a controlled or aided school, or a special school;

and in this Schedule "the specified date", in relation to an institution to which a section 46 order relates, means the date specified in that order.

(2) Where this paragraph applies the Secretary of State may, by the section 46 order, make such provision as he considers appropriate with respect to—

(a) the transfer of existing staff to the employment of the authority, voluntary organisation or other body of persons responsible for the employment of persons at the community home or school, as the case may be; and

(b) the transfer to a local authority or voluntary organisation specified in the order of any liabilities (including contingent and future liabilities) with respect to the payment of superannuation and other benefits to or in respect of existing staff and retired staff.

(3) If any such superannuation or other benefits as are referred to in sub-paragraph (2) (b) of this paragraph are not benefits to which the Pensions (Increase) Acts, 1920 to 1969 or any of those Acts apply, the section 46 order may contain such provisions as the Secretary of State considers appropriate—

(a) for securing the continued payment of additional accounts (calculated by reference to increases under those Acts) which were paid before the specified date in respect of any such benefits; and

(b) for securing the payment of additional amounts (calculated by reference to increases under those Acts) in respect of any such benefits to which any person became entitled before the specified date but in respect of which no similar additional amounts were paid before that date.

(4) Where this paragraph applies the section 46 order—

(a) shall contain provisions for the protection of the interests of any existing staff whose employment is transferred as mentioned in sub-paragraph (2) (a) of this paragraph;

(b) may contain provisions for the protection of the interests of existing staff whose employment is not so transferred; and

(c) may contain provisions applying, amending or repealing any provision made by or under any enactment and relating to the conditions of service of existing staff or the payment of superannuation and other benefits to or in respect of existing or retired staff;

and in a case falling within sub-paragraph (1) (b) of this paragraph any provisions made under paragraph (a) of this sub-paragraph shall have effect notwithstanding any provision made by or under any enactment and relating to the remuneration of teachers.

(5) In this paragraph "existing staff" in relation to a section 46 order means persons who, immediately before the specified date, were employed for the purposes of the institution to which the order relates, and "retired staff" in relation to such an order means persons who, at some time before the specified date, were employed for those purposes but ceases to be so employed before the specified date.

2.—(1) Regulations under section 60 of the Local Government Act, 1958 may make provision in relation to persons who suffer loss of employment or loss or diminution of emoluments as a result of a section 46 order, and if in such a case the Minister by whom the regulations are made thinks fit, the regulations may provide for the payment of compensation by the Secretary of State instead of by an authority prescribed by or determined under the regulations.

(2) In accordance with sub-paragraph (1) of this paragraph, subsection (2) of the said section 60 shall be amended as follows:

(a) after the words "under the regulations" there shall be inserted the words "or, in a case to which paragraph 2 of Schedule 3 to the Children and Young Persons Act, 1969, applies, by the Secretary of State"; and

(b) after the words "order under Part I of the Police Act, 1964" there shall be inserted the words "or of an order under section 46 of the Children and Young Persons Act, 1969".

(3) Where a section 46 order is made in relation to an approved institution but paragraph 1 of this Schedule does not apply in relation to that institution, the section 46 order may make such provision as the Secetary of State considers appropriate with respect to the transfer to him of any such liabilities as are

referred to in sub-paragraph (2) (b) of that paragraph and the payment by him of any such additional amount as is referred to in sub-paragraph (3) of that paragraph.

Use of premises as homes for children in care

3.—(1) If on the day specified for the purposes of section 7 (5) of this Act premises are used for the purposes of an approved school, then during the period (in this Schedule referred to, in relation to an approved school, as "the interim period") beginning immediately after that day and ending on the day on which the school ceases to be an approved school (whether by virtue of a section 46 order or otherwise) those premises may be used for the accommodation and maintenance of children in the care of local authorities.

(2) If during the interim period the premises of an approved school are used for the accommodation and maintenance of children in the care of a local authority then, during that period,

    (a) any reference in section 21 (1) or section 31 of this Act to a community home includes a reference to those premises; and

    (b) for the reference in section 18 (1) (c) of the Criminal Justice Act, 1961 (directions of Secretary of State as to management of approved schools) to persons under the care of the managers there shall be substituted a reference to the children in the care of local authorities who are accommodated and maintained in those premises.

(3) At the request of the managers of an approved school the Secretary of State may, at any time during the interim period, give a direction–

    (a) that so much as may be specified in the direction of any rules made under paragraph (1) 1 of Schedule 4 to the Act of 1933 (approved school rules) and of any rules made by the managers and approved by him under paragraph 1 (2) of that Schedule shall no longer apply in relation to that school; and

    (b) that, in place of those rules, so much as may be specified in the **direction** of any regulations made under section 43 of this Act shall apply, subject to such adaptations and modifications as may be so specified, in relation to the approved school as if it were a community home.

(4) If the effect of the application, by a direction under sub-paragraph (3) above, of any provision of regulations made under section 43 of this Act in relation to an approved school would be to impose any duty or confer any power on a local authority in relation to that school, the Secretary of State shall not give a direction applying that provision except with the consent of the local authority concerned.

4.—(1) If on the day specified for the purposes of section 7 (5) of this Act a remand home was designated under section 11 of the Act of 1963 as a classifying centre then, during the period beginning immediately after that day and ending on the date specified in a section 46 order relating to that home, the home may be used for the accommodation and maintenance of children in the care of local authorities.

(2) In this Schedule "classifying centre" means a remand home designated as mentioned in sub-paragraph (1) of this paragraph and, in relation to a classifying centre, the period in that sub-paragraph is referred to as "the interim period".

(3) During the interim period—

    (a) the expenses of a local authority in providing and maintaining a classifying centre in relation to the whole or part of the expenses of which a direction has been given by the Secretary of State under section 11 (3) of the Act of 1963 shall be treated for the purposes of section 104 of the Act of 1933 as if they were expenses incurred by the authority as managers of an approved school;

(b) subsections (4) and (5) of section 106 of the Act of 1933 shall apply in relation to a classifying centre as they apply in relation to an approved school the managers of which are a local authority; and

(c) any reference in section 21 (1) or section 31 of this Act to a community home includes a reference to a classifying centre.

5.—(1) Where a section 46 order is made in relation to an approved school or approved probation hostel or home and, in a regional plan approved by the Secretary of State, the whole or any part of the premises of the institution is designated as a controlled or assisted community home, the premises so designated may, after the specified date, be used for the purpose specified in the regional plan.

(2) Without prejudice to any power to vary the provisions of a trust deed relating to a community home consisting of premises designated as mentioned in sub-paragraph (1) of this paragraph, the purpose referred to in that sub-paragraph shall be deemed to be included among the purposes for which the premises are held in accordance with a trust deed relating to that home.

6.—(1) Where a section 46 order is made in relation to an approved institution (other than an institution provided by a local authority) and, in a regional plan approved by the Secretary of State, the whole or any part of the premises of the institution is designated as a community home to be provided by a local authority, then if the Secretary of State is satisfied that the premises so designated were to a substantial extent provided with the assistance of grants under section 104 of the Act of 1933 or section 77 of the Criminal Justice Act, 1948, he may, by an authorisation in writing under this paragraph, authorise the transfer of the premises so designated to that local authority.

(2) The transfer of any premises in pursuance of an authorisation under this paragraph—

(a) shall be on such terms, as to payment and other matters, as may be agreed between the local authority concerned and the trustees or other persons in whom the premises are vested and, if the authorisation so provides, as may be approved by the Secretary of State;

(b) shall not take effect before the specified date; and

(c) shall operate to vest the premises transferred in the local authority free from any charitable trust and from any other obligation requiring the use of the premises for the purposes of an approved institution.

(3) Before giving an authorisation under this paragraph authorising the transfer of any premises belonging to a charity or otherwise held on charitable trusts, the Secretary of State shall consult the Charity Commissioners.

7. The provisions of paragraphs 3 to 6 of this Schedule shall have effect notwithstanding anything in the law relating to charities or in any deed or other instrument the purposes for which any premises may be used.

Financial provisions

8.—(1) During the period which is the interim period in relation to an approved school or to a classifying centre falling within paragraph 4 (3) (a) of this Schedule contributions shall be payable by local authorities to the managers of that school or, as the case may be, the local authority providing the classifying centre in respect of children in the care of the authorities who are accommodated and maintained in the school premises or the classifying centre in accordance with paragraph 3 (1) or paragraph 4 (1) of this Schedule.

(2) The contributions payable by a local authority under sub-paragraph (1) above in respect of a child in their care shall be payable throughout the time during which the child is accommodated and maintained in the approved school or classifying centre concerned and shall be such as may be prescribed by regulations made by the Secretary of State.

9.—(1) Where a section 46 order is made in relation to an approved institution other than an institution provided by a local authority, and in a regional plan approved by the Secretary of State the whole or any part of the premises of the approved institution is designated as a community home, then,—

(a) on the coming into force of an instrument of management for a voluntary home which consists of or includes the premises so designated; or
(b) on the transfer of the premises so designated to a local authority in pursuance of an authorisation under paragraph 6 of this Schedule,

any such obligation relating to that institution as is referred to in sub-paragraph (2) of this paragraph shall cease.

(2) Sub-paragraph (1) of this paragraph applies to any obligation arising by virtue of a condition imposed under either of the following enactments, namely,-

(a) section 104 of the Act of 1933 (expenses of managers of an approved school); or
(b) section 77 of the Criminal Justice Act, 1948 (expenditure in connection with approved probation hostels or homes).

(3) In a case falling within sub-paragraph (1) of this paragraph, the section 46 order may contain provisions requiring the responsible authority or organisation or, as the case may be, the local authority to whom the premises are transferred, to pay to the Secretary of State such sum as he may determine in accordance with sub-paragraph (4) of this paragraph by way of repayment of a proportion of any grants made in relation to the former approved institution under either of the enactments referred to in sub-paragraph (2) of this paragraph, but where the community home concerned is an assisted community home, the section 46 order may provide that, with the consent of the Treasury, the Secretary of State may reduce the sum to be paid to him in accordance with the preceding provisions of this sub-paragraph to such sum as he thinks fit.

(4) For the purpose of determining any such sum as is mentioned in sub-paragraph (3) of this paragraph, the Secretary of State shall assess—

(a) the amount which in his opinion represents the proportion of the total amount of the grants paid in respect of expenditure in connection with the former approved institution which was attributable to expenditure of a capital nature; and
(b) the amount which in his opinion represents the proportion of the contributions paid by local authorities under section 90 of the Act of 1933 or, as the case may be, the proportion of the sums paid by probation committees under rules made under Schedule 5 to the Criminal Justice Act, 1948 which (in either case) should be treated as having been paid on account of expenditure of a capital nature in connection with the former approved institution;

and the sum determined by the Secretary of State for the purpose of sub-paragraph (3) of this paragraph shall be equal to the amount by which the amount assessed under paragraph (a) above exceeds twice the amount assessed under paragraph (b) above.

(5) If the instrument of management for an assisted community home ceases to have effect as mentioned in subsection (1) of section 48 of this Act there shall

be deducted from any sum which is payable to the Secretary of State under subsection (5) of that section any sums paid to him by the responsible organisation in respect of the assisted community home in pursuance of any such provisions of a section 46 order relating to the former approved institution as are referred to in sub-paragraph (3) of this paragraph.

(6) In this paragraph "the former approved institution", in relation to a community home, means the approved institution the whole or part of the premises of which are comprised in that home.

10.—(1) The provisions of this paragraph apply where in a regional plan approved by the Secretary of State, the whole or any part of the premises of an approved institution to which a section 46 order relates is designated as a controlled or assisted community home and an instrument of management for a community home which consists of or includes the premises so designated has come into force; and in this paragraph "the former approved institution", in relation to such a community home, means the approved institution the whole or part of the premises of which are comprised in that home.

(2) Where this paragraph applies and the community home concerned is a controlled community home, then—

   (a) the Secretary of State may, by the section 46 order, make such provision as he considers appropriate for the transfer to the responsible authority of any rights, liabilities and obligations which, immediately before the specified date, were rights, liabilities and obligations of the managers of, or the society or person carrying on, the former approved institution and

   (b) except in so far as the section 46 order otherwise provides, any legal proceedings pending immediately before the specified date by or against those managers or that society or person shall be continued on and after that date, with the substitution of the responsible authority for those managers or that society or person as a party to the proceedings.

(3) Where this paragraph applies and the community home concerned is an assisted community home but the responsible organisation does not consist of the persons who were the managers of or, as the case may be, is not the society or person who carried on, the former approved institution, paragraphs (a) and (b) of sub-paragraph (2) of this paragraph shall apply with the substitution for any reference to the responsible authority of a reference to the responsible organisation.

(4) If any liabilities of a voluntary organisation which is the responsible organisation in relation to an assisted community home falling within sub-paragraph (1) of this paragraph were incurred by the organisation before the specified date or were transferred to the organisation by the section 46 order (by virtue of sub-paragraph (3) of this paragraph) and, in either case, had the former approved institution continued to be an approved institution, any expenditure incurred in meeting those liabilities would have been eligible for a grant out of moneys provided by Parliament—

   (a) under section 104 (1) (a) of the Act of 1933 as the expenses of the managers of an approved school, or

   (b) under section 77 (3) (b) of the Criminal Justice Act, 1948, as expenditure falling within that section and relating to an approved probation hostel or home,

then any expenditure incurred after the specified date by the responsible organisation in meeting those liabilities shall be deemed for the purposes of section 65 (1) of this Act to be expenditure incurred by the responsible organisation in connection with the assisted community home in question.

11.—(1) Where a section 46 order is made in relation to an approved institution and no such provision as is referred to in sub-paragraph (1) of paragraph 9 of this Schedule is made by a regional plan in relation to any part of the premises of the institution, the person or persons on whom falls any such obligation (in this paragraph referred to as a "repayment obligation") relating to the institution as is referred to in sub-paragraph (2) of that paragraph may apply to the Secretary of State for an order under this paragraph.

(2) If, on an application under sub-paragraph (1) of this paragraph, it appears to the Secretary of State that on or within a reasonable time after the specified date the premises of the institution concerned or the proceeds of sale of the whole or any part of those premises are to be used for a purpose which is of benefit to children, he may with the consent of the Treasury make an order—

    (a) substituting for the conditions under which the repayment obligation arose such different conditions as he considers appropriate with respect to the repayment of any sum to which the repayment obligation relates; and

    (b) if the person or persons on whom the repayment obligation falls so request, imposing any liability to repay a sum in pursuance of the substituted conditions referred to in paragraph (a) above on such other person or persons as consent to accept the liability and as, in the opinion of the Secretary of State, will be able to discharge that liability.

Interpretation

12. In this Schedule—

"approved institution" has the same meaning as in section 46 of this Act;

"the responsible authority", in relation to a controlled community home, has the same meaning as in section 41 of this Act;

"the responsible organisation", in relation to an assisted community home, has the same meaning as in section 42 of this Act; and

"section 46 order" and, in relation to an institution to which such an order relates, "specified date" have the meanings assigned to them by paragraph (1) 1 of this Schedule.

NOTE

Paragraphs 3 to 7 secure that after the abolition of the approved school under s. 7 (5) schools will be able to accommodate children in care, and this is so, even before they have acquired a new status as a community home, and makes further provision as to charity law so that any inconsistencies between a trust deed and the purposes of the home will be over ridden until the trust deed is varied. Until a direction under para. 3 is given Approved School Rules under Sched. IV to the Children and Young Persons Act, 1933, will apply (para. 3 (4)). Paragraph 4, in relation to classifying centres, takes account of the fact that since the approved school order is abolished there is no longer any distinction between expenditure relating to children who are the subject of approved school orders and other expenditure. As a result, during the transitional period the entire cost of a remand home in respect of which a direction has been made under s. 11 (3) of the Children and Young Persons Act, 1963, will count as approved school expenditure instead of that part only which is attributable to its use as a classifying centre. Hence the cost of classification of children on remand will no longer be accounted for as remand home expenditure nor will it qualify for rate support grant.

SCHEDULE 4

TRANSITIONAL PROVISIONS AND SAVINGS

PART I

GENERAL

NOTE

General note.—Paragraphs 2, 3 and 5 (1) are not yet in force and their implementation depends upon the coming into operation of ss. 4, 5 and 7 (1) of the Act. Paragraph 1A was added by s. 51 (2) of the Administration of Justice Act, 1970.

1. For the purposes of subsection (4) of section 1 and subsection (7) of section 7 of this Act, any order under the Act of 1933 committing a child or young person to the care of a fit person other than a local authority, any supervision order under that Act and any order to enter into recognisances in pursuance of section 62 (1) (c) of that Act shall be deemed to be such an earlier order as is mentioned in those subsections.

1A.—(1) Where—

    (a) before the date when section 1 of this Act comes into force any child or young person (hereafter in this paragraph referred to as "the relevant infant") has been brought before a juvenile court under section 62 of the Children and Young Persons Act, 1933 or has been brought before such a court by virtue of a provision of section 40 or 40A of the Education Act, 1944; and

    (b) immediately before that date that court has neither made any order which it has power to make in respect of the relevant infant under the said section 62 nor dismissed the case,

nothing in paragraph 13 of Schedule 5 to this Act nor in any provision of Schedule 6 thereto shall prevent the proceedings before that court in respect of the relevant infant being continued; but the court shall in those proceedings have power to make any order which it has power to make in proceedings under section 1 of this Act and shall not have the power to make any other order, and subsections (3), (4) and (5) of the said section 1 and subsections (10) and (13) of section 2 of this Act shall have effect accordingly with any necessary modifications.

(2) For the purposes of subsection (12) of the said section 2, any order made in respect of the relevant infant by virtue of sub-paragraph (1) of this paragraph shall be deemed to be made under section 1 of this Act.

(3) Any record of a finding of the fact that the relevant infant is in need of care or protection made in pursuance of section 5 of the Children and Young Persons Act, 1938 in any such proceedings as are referred to in sub-paragraph (1) of this paragraph shall, notwithstanding the repeal of the said section 5 by this Act, be admissible as evidence of that fact in those proceedings.

2.—(1) *Nothing in section 4 of this Act affects any proceedings against a person for an offence with which by virtue of that section he has ceased to be chargeable since the proceedings were begun; but where a person is found guilty of an offence and by reason of that section could not have been charged with it on the date of finding, then, subject to sections 1 (5) and 2 (13) of this Act, the court may make an order under section 1 of this Act in respect of the offender or an order discharging him absolutely but shall not have power to make any other order in consequence of the finding.*

(2) *Nothing in section 4 of this Act shall be construed as preventing any act or omission which occurred outside the United Kingdom from being a civil offence for the purposes of the Army Act, 1955, the Air Force Act, 1955, or the Naval Discipline Act, 1957, or from being dealt with under any of those Acts.*

3. *Nothing in section 5 of this Act affects any information laid in respect of a person before the date on which apart from this paragraph the information would have been required by virtue of that section to contain a statement of his age.*

4. Where a person is committed for trial by a jury before subsection (1) of section 6 of this Act comes into force, or claims to be tried by a jury before subsection (2) of that section comes into force, proceedings in respect of the offence in question shall not be affected by the coming into force of that subsection.

5.—(1) *The coming into force of section 7 (1) or of an order under section 34 (1) (d) of this Act shall not affect any sentence of borstal training passed before the date when the said section 7 (1) or the order came into force or any committal for sentence before that date under section 28 (1) of the Magistrates' Courts Act, 1952; but a sentence of borstal training shall not be passed on any person (including a person to whom such a committal relates) if on the date of the relevant conviction he had not attained the minimum age which is for the time being specified in section 20 (1) of the Criminal Justice Act, 1948.*

(2) Nothing in section 7 (2) of this Act affects a probation order made before the coming into force of the said section 7 (2).

6. No order shall be made under section 19 (1) of the Criminal Justice Act, 1948, at any time after the coming into force of this paragraph and before the coming into force of paragraph 23 of Schedule 5 to this Act, in respect of a person under the age of seventeen in consequence of a default within the meaning of the Criminal Justice Act, 1961.

7.—(1) Every approved school order in force on the specified day shall cease to have effect at the end of that day; and after that day—

(a) no person shall be detained by virtue of section 73 or section 82 of the Act of 1933 or an order under paragraph 2 of Schedule 2 to the said Act of 1961 or be subject to supervision in pursuance of that Schedule; and

(b) no person who has attained the age of nineteen shall be detained by virtue of a warrant under section 15 of the said Act of 1961.

(2) A person who has not attained the age of nineteen on the specified day and who, but for sub-paragraph (1) of this paragraph, would after that day have been the subject of an approved school order or liable to be detained or subject to supervision as mentioned in that sub-paragraph shall be deemed from the end of that day—

(a) to be the subject of a care order made by the court which made the approved school order in question on the same day as that order and committing him to the care of the local authority named in the approved school order in pursuance of section 70 (2) of the Act of 1933, or if no authority is so named, of a local authority nominated in relation to him by the Secretary of State; and

(b) in the case where he would have been subject to supervision as aforesaid, to have been allowed by the said local authority to be under the charge and control of the person last nominated in relation to him in pursuance of paragraph 1 (1) of Schedule 2 to the said Act of 1961;

but nothing in this paragraph shall be construed as affecting the validity of a warrant under the said section 15 in relation to a person who has not attained the age of nineteen.

In relation to a person in respect of whom two or more approved school orders would have been in force after the specified day but for sub-paragraph (1) of this paragraph, references to such an order in paragraph (a) of this sub-paragraph are to the later or latest of the orders.

(3) The Secretary of State may from time to time nominate another local authority in the place of a local authority nominated by him in pursuance of the preceding sub-paragraph or this sub-paragraph.

(4) A person who is the subject of a care order by virtue of sub-paragraph (2) of this paragraph and who was unlawfully absent on the specified day from an approved school in which he was then required to be shall, until the local authority to whose care he is committed by the order direct otherwise, be deemed for the purposes of section 32 of this Act to be duly required by the authority to live after that day in the premises which on that day constituted the school.

(5) A person who on the specified day is the subject of an approved school order or subject to supervision in pursuance of the said Schedule 2 or eligible for assistance under paragraph 7 of that Schedule and is not the subject of a care order from the end of that day by virtue of sub-paragraph (2) of this paragraph shall be deemed for the purposes of section 20 of the Children Act, 1948 and section 58 of the Act of 1963 (which authorise local authorities to provide assistance for persons formerly in care) to have been in the care of a local authority under the Children Act, 1948 on that day, notwithstanding that he may then have attained the age of eighteen; and in relation to such a person the reference in the said section 58 to the local authority shall be construed as a reference to any local authority.

(6) If an order under section 88 of the Act of 1933 is in force at the end of the specified day in respect of payments under an affiliation order made for the maintenance of a person who is deemed by virtue of this paragraph to be subject to a care order after that day, the order under that section shall after that day be deemed to have been made, by virtue of the care order, under that section as modified by this Act

(7) A direction restricting discharge which was given under section 74 of the Mental Health Act, 1959 in respect of a person detained by virtue of an approved school order and which is in force at the end of the specified day shall cease to have effect at the end of that day.

(8) References to an approved school order in this paragraph, except in sub-paragraph (2) (a), include references to an order of the competent authority under subsection (1) of section 83 of the Act of 1933 and such an order as is mentioned in subsection (3) of that section; and in relation to those orders this paragraph shall have effect as if for sub-paragraph (2) (a) there were substituted the following—

"(a) to be the subject of a care order made by a court in England on the date when the order for his detention in a school was made under the relevant law mentioned in section 83 of the Act of 1933 and committing him to the care of a local authority nominated in relation to him by the Secretary of State; and

(9) In this paragraph "the specified day" means the day specified for the purposes of section 7 (5) of this Act.

8.—(1) An order under the Act of 1933 committing a child or young person to the care of a local authority as a fit person and in force on the date when section 7 (6) of this Act comes into force shall be deemed on and after that date to be a care order committing him to the care of that authority.

(2) Sub-paragraph (6) of the preceding paragraph shall have effect for the purposes of this paragraph as if for references to that paragraph and the specified day there were substituted respectively references to this paragraph and the day preceding the date mentioned in the preceding sub-paragraph.

9. Except as provided by paragraph 1 of this Schedule and this paragraph, nothing in this Act affects—

    (a) an order under the Act of 1933 committing a child or young person to the care of a fit person other than a local authority and in force on the date when section 7 (6) of this Act comes into force; or

    (b) the operation of any enactment in relation to such an order;

but where an application for the variation or revocation of the order is considered on or after that date by a juvenile court in pursuance of section 84 (6) of the Act of 1933, the court shall have power (to the exclusion of its powers under the said section 84 (6)) to refuse the application or to revoke the order and, where it revokes the order, to make a care order in respect of the child or young person in question.

10. Without prejudice to the preceding paragraph, a person who is subject to such an order as is mentioned in sub-paragraph (a) of that paragraph is not a foster-child within the meaning of Part I of the Children Act, 1958.

11. Notwithstanding anything in section 20 (3) or 21 (1) of this Act, an order which is a care order by virtue of paragraph 8 of this Schedule and a care order made by virtue of paragraph 9 of this Schedule shall, unless previously revoked, cease to have effect when the child or young person in question attains the age of eighteen.

12.—(1) Where a supervision order under the Children and Young Persons Acts, 1933 to 1963 is in force on the date when this paragraph comes into force or where an order under section 52 of the Act of 1963 (whether made before, on or after that date) falls to be treated by virtue of subsection (3) of that section as a supervision order under the Act of 1933, the order and, in relation to the order, any enactment amended or repealed by this Act, shall, subject to the following provisions of this paragraph, have effect as if this Act had not been passed; and the order may be altered or revoked accordingly.

(2) A juvenile court before which the person to whom such a supervision order relates is brought after the date aforesaid in pursuance of subsection (1) of section 66 of the Act of 1933 shall not have power to make such an order as is mentioned in that subsection in respect of him but shall instead have power to revoke the supervision order and make a care order in respect of him on being satisfied that he is unlikely to receive the care or control he needs unless the court makes a care order; and section 6 (1) of the Act of 1963 shall not apply in a case where the court exercises its power under this sub-paragraph.

(3) Where such a supervision order contains a provision requiring residence in an institution which has become a community home, the provision shall be construed as requiring residence in the home; and in such a case any reference to an institution of the kind in question in rules under the Criminal Justice Act, 1948 providing for the making of payments to the body or person by whom the institution is managed shall be construed as a reference to the home.

(4) References to a supervision order in sub-paragraphs (2) and (3) of this paragraph include references to an order under the said section 52.

13.—(1) During the period beginning with the coming into force of section 35 of this Act and ending with the coming into operation of a regional plan for a particular planning area—

    (a) sections 15 and 16 of the Children Act, 1948, shall continue to apply in relation to each of the relevant authorities; and

    (b) each of the relevant authorities may continue to exercise the power conferred by subsection (2) of section 19 of that Act, as it had effect immediately before the passing of this Act, to accommodate persons in hostels provided under that section; and

(c) section 77 (1) of the Act of 1933 shall continue to apply in relation to each of the relevant authorities as if for the words "the duty of" there were substituted the words "lawful for".

(2) Where different parts of the area of a local authority are comprised in different planning areas then, in relation to that local authority, the period specified in sub-paragraph (1) of this paragraph shall not expire until a regional plan has come into operation for each of those planning areas.

(3) If on the submission of a regional plan for a planning area to the Secretary of State part only of the plan is approved by him, any reference in the preceding provisions of this paragraph to the coming into operation of a regional plan for that area shall be construed as a reference to the coming into operation of a further regional plan containing all necessary supplementary proposals for that area.

14. If immediately before the coming into force of section 49 of this Act any person has, under section 3 (3) of the Children Act, 1948, the care and control of a child (within the meaning of that Act) with respect to whom a resolution under section 2 of that Act is in force, then after the coming into force of that section the child shall again be in the care of the local authority by whom the resolution was passed but shall be deemed to have been allowed by that authority, under section 13 (2) of that Act (as substituted by the said section 49), to be under the charge and control of that person, on the same terms as were applicable under the said section 3 (3).

15. It shall be lawful for a person detained in any place in pursuance of section 27 of the Criminal Justice Act, 1948, at the time when paragraph 24 of Schedule 5 to this Act comes into force to be detained there thereafter, until he is next delivered thence in due course of law, as if that paragraph had not come into force.

16. Nothing in paragraph 29 of Schedule 5 to this Act affects the operation of section 2 (4) of the Children Act, 1958 in relation to a supervision order made under the Children and Young Persons (Scotland) Act, 1937.

17. Nothing in Schedule 6 to this Act affects the operation of section 15 (3) of the Adoption Act, 1958 in relation to a fit person order made under the Children and Young Persons (Scotland) Act, 1937.

18. Nothing in any provision of Schedule 6 to this Act affects any order which, immediately before the coming into force of that provision, is in force by virtue of any enactment repealed by that provision.

PART II

INTERIM PROVISIONS PENDING COMMENCEMENT OF PROVISIONS OF
SOCIAL WORK (SCOTLAND) ACT, 1968

[The provisions of this Part are now spent as the relevant provisions of the Scottish Act are in force. See the Children and Young Persons Act (Termination of Transitional Provisions) Order, 1971, S.I. 1971 No. 589.].

NOTES

The paras. in italics have not yet been brought into force.

Paragraph 1: "A fit person other than a local authority".—By paras. 7 and 8 an approved school order or fit person order to a local authority are deemed to be care orders. See para. 9 for provisions affecting such orders.

Paragraph 2 (2): "Act or omission ... outside the United Kingdom."—
A serviceman's child abroad may, therefore, continue to be dealt with for a "civil offence" though the act or omission could not have led to a prosecution here.

Paragraph 6.—Under s. 7 (3) the power to make attendance centre orders will be withdrawn in stages from individual courts as schemes under s. 19 are made. During the interim period, to avoid different provisions for enforcement in different areas, the power to make an attendance centre order in default is therefore withdrawn by this Schedule.

Paragraph 7.—The broad effect of this paragraph is to cancel all approved school orders and powers of detention and supervision connected therewith and to provide that those subject to such orders shall be deemed to have been committed to the care of a local authority for a period determined in accordance with s. 20 (3). Where the person concerned is over nineteen the effect of sub-para. (1) is that he will automatically be released.

Those under nineteen and liable to supervision will remain under the charge and control of the person last nominated.

Duration of care order.—All children and young persons subject to an approved school order will remain in care till eighteen, or if aged sixteen or over when the order was made nineteen (para. 7 (2) (a) and s. 20 (3)) subject to the right to apply for discharge (s. 21 (2)).

If no authority is named (sub-para. (2) (a)).—For example, where the person is resident outside England or Wales or an order is made under s. 40A of the Education Act, 1944, in respect of a vagrant child.

"Is not the subject of a care order" (sub-para. (5)).—*I.e.* because over nineteen on the specified day.

Section 88 of the Children and Young Persons Act, 1933 (sub-para. (6)).—See p. 70, *ante.*

Paragraph 9.—**"To refuse the application or revoke the order."**—The court also has power to discharge any fit person order when making a care or supervision order, under ss. 1 (4) and 7 (7) as affected by para. 1.

Paragraphs 12 to 18.—The effect of these paragraphs is noted where appropriate.

SCHEDULE 5

MINOR AND CONSEQUENTIAL AMENDMENTS OF ENACTMENTS

The Police (Property) Act, 1897

1. The Police (Property) Act, 1897 (which makes provision for the disposal of property in the possession of the police) shall apply to property which has come into the possession of the police in connection with an allegation, in proceedings under section 1 of this Act, that the condition set out in subsection (2) (f) of that section is satisfied as it applies to property which has come into the possession of the police in the circumstances mentioned in that Act.

The Act of 1933

[*Paragraphs 2–83: effect is given to these amendments in the sections as printed. See the Commencement Orders at pp. 561–563, et seq., post.*]

SCHEDULE 6

REPEALS

[*Effect is given to the repeals and prospective repeals in the sections as printed. See the Commencement Orders at pp. 561–563 et seq., post.*]

SCHEDULE 7

SECTIONS I TO 6 AND 14 OF THE CHILDREN ACT, 1958
AS AMENDED

[*The relevant sections of the Children Act,* 1958, *are printed at pp.* 956-967 *et seq., post.*]

SOCIAL WORK (SCOTLAND) ACT, 1968
[1968 c. 49]

PART III
CHILDREN IN NEED OF COMPULSORY MEASURES OF CARE

30. Definition of child and parent for Part III.—(1) Except where otherwise expressly provided, a child for the purposes of this Part of this Act means—

    (a) a child who has not attained the age of sixteen years;

    (b) a child over the age of sixteen years who has not attained the age of eighteen years and in respect of whom a supervision requirement of a children's hearing is in force under this Part of this Act;

    (c) a child whose case has been referred to a children's hearing in pursuance of Part V of this Act.

(2) For the said purposes the expression "parent" includes a guardian.

44. Disposal of case by children's hearing other than by discharge of referral.—(1) Subject to the provisions of this Part of this Act a children's hearing, where, after the consideration of his case, they decide that a child is in need of compulsory measures of care, may make a requirement, in this Act referred to as a supervision requirement, requiring him—

    (a) to submit to supervision in accordance with such conditions as they may impose; or

    (b) to reside in a residential establishment named in the requirement and be subject to such conditions as they may impose;

and a condition imposed by virtue of head (a) of this subsection may be a condition as to the place where the child is to reside, being a place other than a residential establishment, and the place may be a place in England or Wales where arrangements have been made in that behalf.

(1A) A supervision requirement imposing a condition as to the place where a child is to reside in England or Wales shall be a like authority as in Scotland for the person in charge of the place to restrict the child's liberty to such an extent as that person may consider appropriate having regard to the terms of the supervision requirement.

(2) In making a supervision requirement requiring a child to reside in a residential establishment a children's hearing shall have regard to the religious persuasion of the child.

(3) Without prejudice to the provisions of this Part of this Act relating to the review of supervision requirements, a children's hearing may, where they are satisfied that such a course is proper, postpone the operation of a supervision requirement, but otherwise a supervision requirement shall have effect as from the date it is made.

(4) Where it appears to a children's hearing that the functions of the education authority under section 63 of the Education (Scotland) Act 1962 (ascertainment of children suffering from disability) may require to be exercised, they shall, in addition to any other course which they may take under this section, send a report to that effect to the education authority concerned.

(5) It shall be the duty of the local authority to give effect to a supervision requirement made by a children's hearing for their area, and a child who is subject to such a supervision requirement shall, for the purposes of sections 16 to 18, 20, 24 to 26, 28 and 29 of this Act, be in their care:

Provided that where the performance of a function under any of the said sections in relation to the child requires, or would be facilitated by, the variation or discharge of the supervision requirement, the local authority shall recommend a review of the requirement under this Part of this Act.

(6) In any case of urgent necessity in the interests of the child, or of the other children in a place, a director of social work may direct that a child who is required to reside in that place under this section be transferred to another place.

(7) Any child transferred under the last foregoing subsection shall have his case reviewed by a children's hearing within seven days of his transfer, in accordance with the following provisions of this Act.

(8) A supervision requirement shall be in such form as the Secretary of State may prescribe.

NOTE

This section is printed as amended by the Children and Young Persons Act, 1969, s. 72 (3) and Sched. V.

58. Prohibition of publication of proceedings.—(1) Subject to the provisions of this section, no report of any proceedings in any children's hearing, or of any proceedings before the sheriff under section 42 of this Act, or of any appeal under this Part of this Act, which is made in a newspaper or a sound or television broadcast shall—

    (a) reveal the name, address or school; or
    (b) include any particulars calculated to lead to the identification,

of any child in any way concerned in a hearing and no picture shall be published in any newspaper or television broadcast as being or including a picture of a child concerned as aforesaid.

(2) Any person guilty of any offence against this section shall on summary conviction be liable to a fine not exceeding two hundred and fifty pounds in respect of each offence.

See ss. 39, 49 of the Children and Young Persons Act, 1933, p. 46, *ante*, and s. 57 of the Act of 1963, p. 115, *ante*, for provisions as to proceedings in England and Wales.

(3) The Secretary of State may in any case, if satisfied that it is in the interests of justice to do so, by order dispense with the requirements of subsection (1) of this section to such extent as may be specified in the order.

(4) This section shall extend to England and Wales.

PART V

RETURN AND REMOVAL OF CHILDREN WITHIN UNITED KINGDOM

NOTE

By s. 97 (1), *ibid.*, the provisions of this Part of the Act extend to England and Wales.

Absence without leave

69. Abscondment from a place of safety, or from the control of a person imposed by a supervision requirement.—(1) If a child—

(a) absconds from a place of safety in which he has been detained by virtue of this Act, or

(b) absconds from the control of a person under which he has been placed by a supervision requirement or by virtue of rules made by the Secretary of State under section 45 of this Act,

he may be arrested without a warrant in any part of the United Kingdom or the Channel Islands.

(2) A child arrested in pursuance of this section shall be brought back—

(a) in a case falling within paragraph (a) of subsection (1), to the place of safety.

(b) in a case falling within paragraph (b) of that subsection, to the person under whose control he has been placed.

(3) If, in the case of a child required to be brought back in pursuance of the last foregoing subsection—

(a) the occupier of the place of safety, or

(b) the person under whose control he has been placed,

is unwilling or unable to receive him, the child shall be detained in a place of safety until the reporter has considered, in pursuance of section 37 of this Act, whether the child may be in need of compulsory measures of care, or as the case may be, until he can be brought before a children's hearing for the consideration of his case or for a review of the supervision requirement to which he is subject.

(4) A children's hearing arranged for the purposes of the last foregoing subsection shall meet within a period of seven days from the date of the commencement of the detention of the child, and no child shall be detained under that subsection after the hearing have met or beyond that period.

(5) In this and the next following section any reference to a child absconding includes a reference to his being unlawfully taken away.

NOTE

Definitions.—For definition of "child" see s. 30, *ante*, and s. 77, *post*. For definition of "place of safety", "supervision requirement", "compulsory measures of care", "children's hearing", see s. 94, *post*.

70. Abscondment from residential establishments.—If a child who is required by a supervision requirement to reside in a residential establishment—

(a) absconds from the establishment in which he resides; or

(b) absconds from any hospital or other institution in which he is temporarily residing; or

(c) being absent on leave from the residential establishment, either runs away from the person in whose charge he is or fails to return to the establishment at the end of his leave;

he may be arrested without a warrant in any part of the United Kingdom or the Channel Islands and brought back—

(i) in a case falling within paragraph (b) to the place from which he absconded; or

(ii) where he has run away from the person mentioned in paragraph (c) to that person; or

(iii) in any case, to the residential establishment.

NOTE

Definition.—See note to s. 69, *supra*. For definition of "residential establishment" see s. 94, *post*.

71. Harbouring.—Any person who knowingly—

(a) assists or induces or persistently attempts to induce a child so to act as to be liable to be brought back in pursuance of either of the two last foregoing sections, or

(b) harbours or conceals a child so liable or prevents him from returning to a place or person mentioned in either of those sections,

shall be liable on summary conviction to a fine not exceeding one hundred pounds or to imprisonment for a term not exceeding six months or to both such fine and such imprisonment.

NOTE

Definitions.—See note to s. 69, *ante*.

Transfer

72. Supervision of children moving to England or Wales or Northern Ireland.—(1) Where a children's hearing are satisfied that a child in respect of whom a supervision requirement under section 44 (1) (a) of this Act is in force proposes to reside or is residing in England or Wales or in Northern Ireland they may either—

(a) discharge the supervision requirement; or

    (b) send notification of the requirement to a juvenile court acting for the petty sessions area in which the child proposes to reside or is residing.

(1A) The juvenile court in England or Wales to which notification of a supervision requirement is sent under this section may make a supervision order in respect of the person to whom the notification relates, but, notwithstanding anything in section 76 (1) of this Act, shall not include in the order a requirement authorised by section 12 of the Children and Young Persons Act, 1969 unless that person is before the court when the supervision order is made; and in relation to a supervision order made by virtue of this subsection—

    (a) section 15 of that Act shall have effect as if subsection (2) were omitted; and

    (b) section 17 of that Act shall have effect as if in paragraph (a) the references to three years and the date on which the order was originally made were respectively references to one year and the date on which the said notification was sent and as if in paragraph (b) the words from "the order was" to "and" were omitted.

(2) The juvenile court in Northern Ireland to which notification of a supervision requirement is sent under this section may make in respect of the child subject to that requirement a supervision order placing him under the supervision of a probation officer for a period not exceeding one year beginning with the day on which the notification was sent; and the provisions of the Children and Young Persons Act (Northern Ireland), 1950 shall apply to any such order as those provisions apply to a supervision order within the meaning of section 63 (1) (d) of the said Act of 1950.

(3) Where a case is disposed of by a juvenile court in pursuance of this section in respect of a child subject to a supervision requirement, the requirement shall cease to have effect.

(4) In this section "petty sessions area" in relation to England and Wales has the same meaning as in the said Act of 1969 and in relation to Northern Ireland means "petty sessions district" within the meaning of Part III of the Magistrates' Courts Act (Northern Ireland), 1964.

NOTES

    This section is printed as amended by the Children and Young Persons Act, 1969, s. 72 (3), (4) and Scheds. V and VI.

    Definitions.—See notes to ss. 69, 70, *ante*. For definition of "supervision order" see s. 94, *post*.

73. Supervision of children moving to Scotland.—(1) Where a juvenile court in England or Wales or in Northern Ireland is satisfied that a child in respect of whom a probation order or a supervision order is in force proposes to reside or is residing in Scotland, the court may either—

    (a) discharge the probation order or supervision order; or

    (b) send notification of that order to the reporter of the local authority for the area in which the child proposes to reside or is residing;

and on the receipt of such a notification it shall be the duty of the reporter

(i) in the case of a supervision order made by virtue of section 7A (4) of the Criminal Justice (Scotland) Act, 1949, to notify the appropriate court and to transmit to that court all documents and certified copies of documents relating to the case which the reporter has received by virtue of section 76 of that Act;

(ii) in any other case

to arrange a children's hearing for the consideration and determination of the case under Part III of this Act. In this subsection "the appropriate court" means the sheriff having jurisdiction in the area in which the child proposes to reside or is residing or, where the original probation order was imposed by the High Court of Justice, that Court.

(1A) Where a court in England or Wales is satisfied that a child in respect of whom the court proposes to make a supervision order is residing or proposes to reside in Scotland, the court may make the order notwithstanding anything in subsection (1) of section 18 of the Children and Young Persons Act, 1969 (which relates to residence of the supervised person in England or Wales); and where the court makes a supervision order by virtue of this subsection—

(a) the areas to be named in the order in pursuance of subsection (2) (a) of the said section 18 shall be those in which the court is sitting;

(b) the order may require the supervised person to comply with directions of the supervisor with respect to his departure to Scotland, and any such requirement shall, for the purposes of sections 15 and 16 of that Act (which relate to the variation and discharge of supervision orders), be deemed to be included in the order in pursuance of section 12 (2) of that Act; and

(c) the court shall send notification of the order as mentioned in paragraph (b) of the foregoing subsection and the provisions of that subsection relating to the duty of the reporter shall apply accordingly.

(2) For the purposes of a children's hearing arranged in pursuance of the foregoing provisions of this section the notification by a court of a probation order or supervision order shall be conclusive evidence of the existence of that order in relation to the child.

(3) When a children's hearing have disposed of a case referred to them under this section the probation order or the supervision order in respect of the child shall cease to have effect.

NOTES

This section is printed as amended by the Children and Young Persons Act, 1969, s. 72 (3), (4) and Scheds. V and VI.

74. Parent of a child in a residential establishment under a supervision requirement moving to England or Wales or Northern Ireland.—(1) Where a children's hearing are satisfied that the parent of a child who is required to reside in a residential establishment under a supervision requirement made under section 44 (1) (b) of this Act proposes to reside or is residing in England or Wales or in Northern Ireland they shall review the requirement, and on such review they may as they think proper—

    (a) discharge the supervision requirement;

    (b) continue the supervision requirement;

    (c) vary the supervision requirement by making a supervision requirement under subsection (1) (a) of the said section 44 and send notification of that requirement in accordance with section 72 (1) (b) of this Act; or

    (d) make a report on the case to the Secretary of State with a recommendation for the transfer of the child in accordance with the following provisions of this section.

(2) If the Secretary of State is for any reason unable to accept a recommendation for the transfer of a child made under paragraph (d) of subsection (1) of this section, he may refer the matter back to the children's hearing for their reconsideration of the case, or himself discharge the supervision requirement.

(3) Where such a recommendation is made and is not dealt with under subsection (2) of this section, the Secretary of State may make an order transferring the child to the care of the managers of a school in Northern Ireland, being a training school within the meaning of the Children and Young Persons Act (Northern Ireland), 1950, or committing him to the care of the local authority or, as the case may be, of the welfare authority in whose area the parent of the child proposes to reside or is residing.

(4) The provisions of the said Act of 1950 shall apply to any order under this section transferring a child to the care of the managers of a training school as if it were a training school order made by a court on the date on which the supervision requirement was originally made under section 44 of this Act in respect of the child:

Provided that—

    (a) notwithstanding anything in section 75 of the said Act of 1950, the order under this section shall not be authority for his detention in a training school after he has attained the age of eighteen years,

    (b) the contributions to be made in respect of him under section 126 of the said Act of 1950 shall be made by such council as may be named in the order under this section, being the council within whose district his parent proposes to reside or is residing at the time of the order.

(5) The provisions of the said Act of 1950 shall apply to any order under this section committing a child to the care of a welfare authority as if it were an order made by a court under that Act.

(6) An order under this section committing a child to the care of a local authority shall have effect as if it were a care order under the Children and Young Persons Act, 1969, but as if sections 20 (2) and 21 (5) of that Act and in section 20 (3) of that Act paragraph (a) and the words "in any other case" in paragraph (b) were omitted.

This section is printed as amended by the Children and Young Persons Act, 1969, s. 72 (3), (4) and Scheds. V and VI.

Definitions.—See notes to ss. 69, 70, *ante*. For the definitions of "approved school" and "training school" see s. 94, p. 242, *post*.

75. Parent of a child subject to an approved school order or a committal order moving to Scotland.—(1) Where the Minister of Home Affairs for Northern Ireland is satisfied that the parent of a child who is subject to a training school order or an order under section 74 (3) of this Act relating to a training school order proposes to reside or is residing in Scotland, he may refer the case to the reporter of the local authority of the area in which the parent of the child is proposing to reside or is residing and if the case is so referred the reporter shall arrange a children's hearing for the consideration and determination of the case under Part III of this Act.

(2) Where a child has been committed to the care of a local authority in England or Wales by a care order (other than an interim order) within the meaning of the Children and Young Persons Act, 1969, or an order under section 74 (3) of this Act, or committed to the care of a welfare authority in Northern Ireland under Part III of the Children and Young Persons Act (Northern Ireland), 1950 or Part I of the Education Act (Northern Ireland), 1947 or the said section 74 (3) and that authority are satisfied that the parent of the child proposes to reside or is residing in Scotland, the authority may make the like reference of the case as mentioned in the foregoing subsection and the reporter shall arrange a children's hearing accordingly.

(3) Any reference under subsection (1) or subsection (2) of this section shall include particulars of the training school or training school order or order under the said section 74 (3) relating to a training school or, as the case may be, of the order committing the child to the care of the local or welfare authority; and for the purposes of any children's hearing arranged pursuant to the reference those particulars shall be conclusive evidence of the existence of that order in relation to the child.

(4) When a children's hearing have disposed of a case referred to them under this section the order under the said section 74 (3) or of the court in England or Wales or in Northern Ireland in respect of the child shall cease to have effect.

This section is printed as amended by the Children and Young Persons Act, 1969, s. 72 (3), (4), and Scheds. V and VI.

Definitions.—See s. 94, p. 242, *post*.

76. Procedure.—(1) A children's hearing or court, in exercising any jurisdiction under this Part of this Act in respect of a child, may proceed in the absence of the child or his parents or both.

(2) It shall be the duty of the reporter at any children's hearing arranged for the purposes of section 72 of this Act and of the clerk to any court referring a case to a reporter for the purposes of section 73 of this

Act to ensure that all documents relating to the case or certified copies thereof are transmitted to the juvenile court, or as the case may be, to the reporter to which the case stands referred.

(3) Where a child is to be transferred from a residential establishment in Scotland to any place in England or Wales or in Northern Ireland under this Part of this Act, it shall be the duty of the local authority responsible for the child to ensure the transfer of the child to that place.

(4) Where a children's hearing is arranged under this Part of this Act in respect of a child subject to a training school order or order under section 74 (3) of this Act relating to a training school or committed to the care of a local authority in England or Wales or of a welfare authority in Northern Ireland, it shall be the duty of the managers of the training school or, as the case may be, of that local or welfare authority to ensure the transfer of the child to the place notified to them by the reporter.

NOTES

This section is printed as amended by the Children and Young Persons Act, 1969, s. 72 (3), (4) and Scheds. V and VI.

Definitions.—See s. 94, p. 242, *post.*

77. Meaning of child for the purposes of this Part of this Act.—
(1) "Child" in this Part of this Act means—

    (a) for the purpose of sections 69 to 71, a child within the meaning of Part III of this Act,

    (b) [*Repealed by the Children and Young Persons Act, 1969.*]

    (c) for any other purpose, a person under eighteen.

(2) "Parent" in this Part of this Act includes a guardian.

NOTES

This section is printed as amended by the Children and Young Persons Act, 1969, s. 72 (4) and Sched. VI.

Definition.—For the definition of "child" in Part III see s. 30, p. 232, *ante.*

86. Adjustments between authority providing accommodation etc., and authority of area of residence.—(1) Any expenditure which apart from this section would fall to be borne by a local authority—

    (a) in the provision under this Act of accommodation for a person ordinarily resident in the area of another local authority, or

    (b) in the provision under Part II of this Act of services and facilities for a person ordinarily so resident (including, in the case of a child, any expenses incurred after he has ceased to be a child, and, in the event of his care being taken over by virtue of section 15 (4) of this Act including also any travelling or other expenses incurred in connection with the taking over), or

    (c) for the conveyance of a person ordinarily resident as aforesaid, or

    (d) in administering a supervision requirement in respect of a person ordinarily resident as aforesaid,

shall be recoverable from the other local authority, and in this subsection any reference to another local authority includes a reference to a local authority in England or Wales.

(2) Any question arising under this section as to the ordinary residence of a person shall be determined by the Secretary of State, and the Secretary of State may determine that a person has no ordinary residence.

(3) In determining for the purposes of subsection (1) of this section the ordinary residence of any person or child, any period during which he was a patient in a hospital forming part of the hospital and specialist services provided under Part II of the National Health Service Act 1946 or Part II of the National Health Service (Scotland) Act 1947 or, in the case of a child, any period during which he resided in any place as an inmate of a school or other institution, or in accordance with the requirements of a supervision requirement, supervision order or probation order or the conditions of a recognizance, or while boarded out under this Act or under the Children Act, 1948, the Children and Young Persons Act, 1933 or the Children and Young Persons (Scotland) Act 1937, by a local authority or education authority shall be disregarded.

87. Charges that may be made for services and accommodation.—(1) Subject to the provisions of section 14 of this Act, and of this section, a local authority may recover from persons availing themselves of any service provided under this Act such charges (if any) as, having regard to the cost of the service, the authority may determine, whether generally or in the circumstances of any particular case.

(2) Persons, other than maintainable children, for whom accommodation is provided under this Act, shall be required to pay for that accommodation in accordance with the subsequent provisions of this section.

(3) Subject to the following provisions of this section, accommodation provided under this Act shall be regarded as accommodation provided under Part III of the National Assistance Act, 1948, and sections 22 (2) to (9) and 26 (2) to (4) (charges for accommodation and provision of accommodation in premises maintained by voluntary organisations) and sections 42 to 44 of the said Act of 1948 (which make provision for the mutual maintenance of wives and husbands and the maintenance of their children by recovery of assistance from persons liable for maintenance and for affiliation orders, etc.) shall apply accordingly.

(4) In the application of the said section 22, for any reference to the Minister there shall be substituted a reference to the Secretary of State, and in the application for the said section 26, any references to arrangements under a scheme for the provision of accommodation shall be construed as references to arrangements made by a local authority with a voluntary organisation for the provision of accommodation under this Act.

(5) The Secretary of State may, with the consent of the Treasury, make regulations for modifying or adjusting the rates at which payments under this section are made, where such a course appears to him to be justified, and any such regulations may provide for the waiving of any such payment in whole or in part in such circumstances as may be specified in the regulations.

(6) A local authority may refer to the Supplementary Benefits Commission for investigation any question arising as to the resources or other circumstances of a person applying for accommodation under this Act or for whom such accommodation is being provided.

94. Interpretation.—(1) In this Act, except where otherwise expressly provided or the context otherwise requires, the following expressions have the meanings hereby respectively assigned to them—

"approved school" means a school approved by the Secretary of State under section 79 of the Children and Young Persons Act, 1933,

'approved school order" has the meaning assigned to it by section 107 (1) of the Children and Young Persons Act 1933,

"children's panel" and "children's hearing" have the meanings respectively assigned to them by sections 33 (1) and 34 (1) of this Act,

"compulsory measures of care" means, in relation to a child, such measure of care as may be imposed upon him by a children's hearing,

*   *   *   *

"contributor" and "contribution order" have the meanings respectively assigned to them by sections 78 and 80 of this Act,

"establishment" means an establishment managed by a local authority, voluntary organisation or any other person, which provides non-residential accommodation for the purposes of this Act, whether for reward or not,

"functions" shall include powers and duties,

"guardian" means a person appointed by deed or will or by order of a court of competent jurisdiction to be the guardian of a child, or in relation to a child includes any person who, in the opinion of the court or children's hearing having cognizance of any case in relation to the child or in which the child is concerned, has for the time being the charge of or control over the child,

*   *   *   *

"local authority", in relation to Scotland, has the meaning assigned to it by section 1 (2) of this Act,

*   *   *   *

"parent" means either or both parents and,—

    (a) in relation to a child adopted in pursuance of any enactment, means the person or persons by whom he was adopted to the exclusion of his natural parents,

    (b) in relation to a child who is illegitimate, means his mother to the exclusion of his father,

*   *   *   *

"place of safety" means any residential or other establishment provided by a local authority, a police station, or any hospital, surgery or other suitable place, the occupier of which is willing temporarily to receive a child,

"prescribed" means—

    (a) in section 3, prescribed by regulations,

    (b) in section 44, prescribed by rules, and

    (c) in sections 62 (2), 66 (1) and (2), 94, paragraphs 2 (2) and (3), 4 (3) and (4) of Schedule 7, prescribed by order, "probation order", in relation to an order imposed by a court in England or Wales, has the meaning assigned to it by section 3 of the Criminal Justice Act, 1948, and in relation to such an order, imposed by a court in Northern Ireland, has the same meaning as in the Probation Act (Northern Ireland), 1950,

"residential establishment" means an establishment managed by a local authority, voluntary organization or any other person, which provides residential accommodation for the purposes of this Act, whether for reward or not,

"school age" has the meaning assigned to it by section 32 (1) of the Education (Scotland) Act, 1962,

"supervision order", in relation to an order imposed by a court in England or Wales, has the meaning assigned to it by section 5 of the Children and Young Persons Act, 1963 and includes a supervision order within the meaning of the Children and Young Persons Act, 1969 and in relation to an order imposed by a court in Northern Ireland has the meaning assigned to it by section 63 (1) (d) of the Children and Young Persons Act (Northern Ireland), 1950,

"supervision requirement" has the meaning assigned to it by section 44 (1) of this Act,

"training school" means a school approved by the Ministry of Home Affairs for Northern Ireland under section 106 of the Children and Young Persons Act (Northern Ireland), 1950,

"training school order" means an order made by a court in Northern Ireland sending a child or young person to a training school,

*   *   *   *

"welfare authority" means a welfare authority constituted under the Public Health and Local Government (Administrative Provisions) Act (Northern Ireland), 1946.

(2) Unless the context otherwise requires, any reference in this Act to any other enactment is a reference thereto as amended, and includes a reference thereto as extended or applied by or under any other enactment including this Act.

(3) Without prejudice to the last foregoing subsection, any reference in this Act to an enactment of the Parliament of Northern Ireland, or to an enactment which that Parliament has power to amend, shall be construed, in relation to Northern Ireland, as a reference to that enactment as amended by any Act of that Parliament, whether passed before or after this Act, and to any enactment of that Parliament passed after this Act and re-enacting the said enactment with or without modifications.

NOTE

This section is printed as amended by the Children and Young Persons Act, 1969, s. 72 (3) and Sched. V.

97. Extension of certain provisions of Act to England and Wales, Northern Ireland and the Channel Islands.—(1) The following provisions of this Act shall extend to England and Wales, that is to say—

section 44 (1) (except head (b) and (1A)
section 58
sections 86 and 87
Part V
section 98 (3) and Schedule 2, paragraphs 7 and 13
Schedule 8
Part II of Schedule 9.

(2) The following provisions of this Act shall extend to Northern Ireland, that is to say—

Part V
section 96
Schedule 8.

(3) The following provisions of this Act shall extend to the Channel Islands, that is to say sections 69 to 71.

(4) Save as aforesaid, and except in so far as it relates to the interpretation or commencement of the provisions, this Act shall extend only to Scotland.

98. Commencement.—(1) This Act (except this section) shall come into operation on such date as the Secretary of State may by order appoint.

(2) Different dates may be appointed by order under this section for different purposes of this Act; and any reference in any provision of this Act to the commencement of this Act shall, unless otherwise provided by any such order, be construed as a reference to the date on which that provision comes into operation.

(3) An order under this section may make such transitional provisions as appear to the Secretary of State to be necessary or expedient in connection with the provisions thereby brought into force, including such adaptations of those provisions or of any provision of this Act then in force as appear to the Secretary of State necessary or expedient for the purposes or in consequence of the operation of any provision of this Act before the coming into force of any other provision of this Act or of the Children and Young Persons Act, 1969.

NOTES

See the Social Work (Scotland) Act, 1968, Commencement Orders Nos. 1–6, Order 1969 (pp. 533, 626, *post*).

This section is printed as amended by the Children and Young Persons Act, 1969, s. 72 (3) and Sched. V.

SECTION 3.—LIST OF OFFENCES INCLUDED IN FIRST SCHEDULE OF CHILDREN AND YOUNG PERSONS ACT, 1933

(as amended by the Sexual Offences Act, 1956,
ss. 48 and 51 and Schedules III and IV)

OFFENCES AGAINST CHILDREN OR YOUNG PERSONS

The murder or manslaughter of a child or young person.
Infanticide.
Offences under the Offences against the Person Act, 1861:—

- s. 5—manslaughter of a child or young person.
- s. 27—the abandonment or exposure of a child under two so as to endanger its life or health.
- s. 42—common assault on a child or young person.
- s. 43—aggravated assault on a female child or young person or on a boy under fourteen.
- s. 56—taking away or detaining a child with intent to deprive a person having the lawful care or charge of such child of the possession of such child or receiving or harbouring a child with such intent knowing it to have been so taken away or detained.

Offences under the Children and Young Persons Act, 1933:—

- s. 1—cruelty to a person under sixteen.
- s. 3—allowing a person under sixteen to be in a brothel.
- s. 4—causing or allowing a person under sixteen to be used for begging.
- s. 11—exposing a child under twelve to risk of burning.
- s. 23—causing, procuring or allowing a person under sixteen to take part in a dangerous performance.

Offences under the Sexual Offences Act, 1956, against a child or young person:—

- s. 2—procurement of woman by threats.
- s. 3—procurement of woman by false pretences.
- s. 4—administering drugs to obtain or facilitate intercourse.
- s. 5—intercourse with girl under thirteen.
- s. 6—intercourse with girl between thirteen and sixteen.
- s. 7—intercourse with an idiot or imbecile.
- s. 10—incest by a man.
- s. 11—incest by a woman.
- s. 12—buggery.
- s. 13—indecency between men.
- s. 14—indecent assault on a woman.
- s. 15—indecent assault on a man.
- s. 16—assault with intent to commit buggery.
- s. 19—abduction of unmarried girl under eighteen from parent or guardian.
- s. 20—abduction of unmarried girl under sixteen from parent or guardian.
- s. 22—causing prostitution of women.
- s. 23—procuration of girl under twenty-one.
- s. 24—detention of woman in brothel or other premises.
- s. 25—permitting girl under thirteen to use premises for intercourse.

s. 26—permitting girl between thirteen and sixteen to use premises for intercourse.

s. 28—causing or encouraging prostitution of, intercourse with, or indecent assault on, girl under sixteen.

any attempt to commit against a child or young person an offence under sections 2, 5, 6, 7, 10, 11, 12, 22 or 23 of the Sexual Offences Act, 1956.

Any other offence involving bodily injury to a child or young person.

NOTES

Indecency with Children Act, 1960.—By s. 1 (3) of that Act references in the Children and Young Persons Act, 1933, except those in s. 15, to the offences mentioned in the First Schedule to the last mentioned Act shall include offences under s. 1 of the Indecency with Children Act, 1960.

Suicide Act, 1961.—As to England and Wales only the reference to the murder or manslaughter of a child or young person shall apply, also to aiding, abetting, counselling or procuring the suicide of a child or young person.

SECTION 4.—SCHOOL ATTENDANCE

INTRODUCTORY NOTE

For a full exposition of the Education Act, 1944, recourse should be had to *The New Law of Education* (Seventh Edition, 1971) by George Taylor, Esq., M.A., and John B. Saunders, Esq., published by Butterworths.

Here no more has been attempted than to include and annotate those sections to which users of this book are most likely to wish to refer.

The Act of 1944 created various new types of schools and colleges and entrusts the duties of local education authority to the councils of counties and county boroughs. The question of compulsory school age which is to be raised eventually so that the upper limit is sixteen years is dealt with in s. 35.

The method of enforcing school attendance was revised. School attendance orders are now made by the local education authorities and not by the courts, and such orders require the parent to cause the child to become a registered pupil at a school named in the order. If a registered pupil fails to attend regularly, or if there is failure to comply with an attendance order, the parent becomes liable to penalties which in the case of a third or subsequent conviction may include imprisonment without the option of a fine. Proceedings are in the adult court and not the juvenile court.

What is, in the eyes of most people, more important still, is to deal with the child. Widespread truancy and irregular attendance such as existed many years ago is a thing of the past. It is a tribute to the schools and the teachers of the present day that almost all children are happy at school. Where irregular attendance persists, it may be taken as an indication that there is something wrong with the parents and the home, or that the child is unhappy, handicapped or maladjusted in some way. There was a time when truants were sent away to approved schools or industrial schools as they were then called, without having been seen by the court which made the order. Gradually, it became the practice of many courts to take all possible steps to secure the attendance of the child and so to obtain more information about him and his troubles. Proceedings under the Education Act, 1921, were still before the adult court, but in 1938 the Lord Chancellor made Rules by which proceedings under ss. 44, 45 and 54 of that Act, were assigned to the juvenile courts. The juvenile courts were able to obtain reports from probation officers, local authorities, and sometimes from psychologists in much the same way as they were accustomed to do in respect of children brought before the court as in need of care or protection. Their hands were strengthened by the passing of the Children and Young Persons Act, 1938, s. 3 (3) (now repealed), of which gave them power to authorise some person to bring the child before the court.

It having been felt by many that most of the children who were the subject of proceedings for irregular attendance could best be dealt with

247

in precisely the same way as children in need of care or protection, and the powers of the court to make orders being almost exactly the same, it was not surprising to find that the Education Act, 1944, provided for such children being dealt with by the juvenile court as in need of care or protection. By s. 40 the adult court before which the parent is prosecuted may direct that the child shall be brought before the juvenile court. The local education authority has also the right to bring a child before the juvenile court under section 1, Children and Young Persons Act, 1969 if it considers that the child is not receiving efficient full time education and is in need of care or control, although no such direction has been given or applied for. The Children and Young Persons Act, 1969 (as did the Act of 1963), extends this power to include cases where the parent has failed to comply with the requirement of a school attendance order served on him and cases of vagrant children. Now the relevant sections of the Children and Young Persons Act, 1969, apply to the proceedings. The Magistrates' Courts (Children and Young Persons) Rules, 1970, must also be read accordingly.

Provision is made for ascertaining what children are in need of special educational treatment, and for the establishment of special schools for these handicapped pupils. Regulations have been made under ss. 33 and 100 (see notes to s. 9, p. 250, *post*), and these, *inter alia*, define the categories of handicapped pupils. The Mental Health Act, 1959, substituted a new section for s. 57 of the 1944 Act, dealing with children suffering from disability of mind. This has now been repealed by the Education (Handicapped Children) Act, 1970.

Certain other sections of the Act deal with questions of employment and matters connected therewith. Other sections relate to evidence and the conduct of proceedings. As to the power of local authorities to appear by an officer, see s. 277 of the Local Government Act, 1933; 19 Halsbury's Statutes, 3rd Edn., 556.

The right of a person summoned to appear by a member of his family or other person, which was conferred by s. 146 of the Education Act, 1921, is not re-enacted in the Act of 1944. By the Secretary of State for Education and Science Order, 1964 (S.I. 1964 No. 490) the Ministry of Education and the Office of the Minister for Science are dissolved and the nctions of those Ministers are transferred to the Secretary of State for Education and Science.

Section 9 of the Education Act, 1962, (p. 273, *post*), made new provisions for ascertaining school leaving dates in England and Wales.

EDUCATION ACT, 1944

[7 & 8 Geo. 6, c. 31]

6. Local education authorities.—(1) Subject to the provisions of Part I of the First Schedule to this Act, the local education authority for each county shall be the council of the county, and the local education authority for each county borough shall be the council of the county borough.

NOTES

" Local education authority."—For further definition, see s. 114 (1), p. 210, *post*.

Application.—As to application of the Act to London, and to the Isles of Scilly, see the London Government Act, 1963, Part IV, and s. 118; (20 Halsbury's Statutes, 3rd Edn., 448).

PRIMARY AND SECONDARY EDUCATION

Provision and Maintenance of Primary and Secondary Schools

8. Duty of local education authorities to secure provision of primary and secondary schools.—(1) It shall be the duty of every local education authority to secure that there shall be available for their area sufficient schools—

(a) for providing primary education, that is to say, full-time education suitable to the requirements of junior pupils who have not attained the age of ten years and six months, and full-time education suitable to the requirements of junior pupils who have attained that age and whom it is expedient to educate together with junior pupils who have not attained that age, and

(b) for providing secondary education, that is to say, full-time education suitable to the requirements of senior pupils, other than such full-time education as may be provided for senior pupils in pursuance of a scheme made under the provisions of this Act relating to further education and full-time education suitable to the requirements of junior pupils who have attained the age of ten years and six months and whom it is expedient to educate with senior pupils.

and the schools available for an area shall not be deemed to be sufficient unless they are sufficient in number, character, and equipment to afford for all pupils opportunities for education offering such variety of instruction and training as may be desirable in view of their different ages, abilities, and aptitudes, and of the different periods for which they may be expected to remain at school, including practical instruction and training appropriate to their respective needs.

(2) In fulfilling their duties under this section, a local education authority shall, in particular, have regard—

(a) to the need for securing that primary and secondary education are provided in separate schools;

(b) to the need for securing that provision is made for pupils who have not attained the age of five years by the provision of nursery schools or, where the authority consider the provision of such schools to be inexpedient, by the provision of nursery classes in other schools;

(c) to the need for securing that provision is made for pupils who suffer from any disability of mind or body by providing, either in special schools or otherwise, special educational treatment, that is to say, education by special methods appropriate for persons suffering from that disability; and

(d) to the expediency of securing the provision of boarding accommodation, either in boarding schools or otherwise, for pupils for whom education as boarders is considered by their parents and by the authority to be desirable:

Provided that paragraph (a) of this subsection shall not have effect with respect to special schools.

NOTES

This section is printed as amended by the Education (Miscellaneous Provisions) Act, 1948, s. 3 (2), and its provisions are restricted by *ibid.*, s. 4 (2).

" **Local education authority.**"—See note to s. 6, *ante.*

Compulsory attendance at special schools.—See s. 38, p. 255, *post.*

9. County schools, voluntary schools, nursery schools, and special schools.—

(5) Schools which are especially organised for the purpose of providing special educational treatment for pupils requiring such treatment and are approved by the Minister for that purpose shall be known as special schools.

NOTES

" **Special educational treatment.**"—For definition, see s. 114, p. 270, *post*, and s. 8 (2) (c), p. 249, *ante.*

Regulations.—See the Handicapped Pupils and Special Schools Regulations, 1959, S.I. 1959, No. 365, the Special Schools and Establishments (Grants) Regulations, 1959, S.I. 1959, No. 366, as amended by the Handicapped Pupils and Special Schools Amending Regulations, 1966, S.I. 1966, No. 1576; the Handicapped Pupils (Certificate) Regulations, 1961, S.I. 1961, No. 416, and the Special Schools and Establishments (Grant) (Amendment) Regulations, 1969, S.I. 1969 No. 410.

Primary and Secondary Education of pupils requiring Special Educational Treatment

33. Education of pupils requiring special educational treatment.

—(1) The Minister shall make regulations defining the several categories of pupils requiring special educational treatment and making provision as to the special methods appropriate for the education of pupils of each category.

(2) The arrangements made by a local education authority for the special educational treatment of pupils of any such category shall, so far as is practicable, provide for the education of pupils in whose case the disability is serious in special schools appropriate for that category, but where that is impracticable, or where the disability is not serious, the arrangements may provide for the giving of such education in any school maintained by a local authority or in any school not so maintained, other that one notified by the Secretary of State to the local education authority to be, in his opinion, unsuitable for the purpose.

(3) The Minister may by regulations make provision as to the requirements to be complied with by any school as a condition of approval of the school as a special school, and as to the withdrawal of approval from any school which fails to comply with requirements so prescribed, and, notwithstanding that the provisions of this Act requiring local education

authorities to have regard to the need for securing that primary and secondary education are provided in separate schools do not apply with respect to special schools, such regulations may impose requirements as to the organisation of any special school as a primary school or as a secondary school.

(4) The regulations made under this section with respect to special schools shall be such as to secure that, so far as practicable, every pupil in attendance at any such school will attend religious worship and religious instruction or will be withdrawn from attendance at such worship or instruction in accordance with the wishes of his parent.

NOTES

This section is printed as amended by the Education (Miscellaneous Provisions) Act, 1953, s. 17 and Sched. I.

"**The Minister**".—A reference to the Secretary of State is substituted by S.I. 1964 No. 490.

" **Special educational treatment.**"—See definition in s. 114, p. 270, *post*, and s. 8 (2) (c), p. 249, *ante*.

" **Parent.**"—See definition in s. 114, p. 270, *post*.

" **Local education authority.**"—See s. 6, p. 248, *ante* and s. 114, p. 270, *post*.

34. Duty of local education authorities to ascertain what children require special educational treatment.—(1) It shall be the duty of every local education authority to ascertain what children in their area require special educational treatment; and for the purpose of fulfilling that duty any officer of a local education authority authorised in that behalf by the authority may by notice in writing served upon the parent of any child who has attained the age of two years require him to submit the child for examination by a medical officer of the authority for advice as to whether the child is suffering from any disability of mind or body and as to the nature and extent of any such disability; and if a parent upon whom such a notice is served fails without reasonable excuse to comply with the requirements thereof, he shall be liable on summary conviction to a fine not exceeding ten pounds.

(2) If the parent of any child who has attained the age of two years requests the local education authority for the area to cause the child to be so medically examined as aforesaid, the authority shall comply with the request unless in their opinion the request is unreasonable.

(3) Before any child is so medically examined as aforesaid the authority shall cause notice to be given to the parent of the time and place at which the examination will be held, and the parent shall be entitled to be present at the examination if he so desires.

(4) If, after considering the advice given with respect to any child by a medical officer in consequence of any such medical examination as aforesaid and any reports or information which the local education authority are able to obtain from teachers or other persons with respect to the ability and aptitude of the child, the authority decide that the child requires special educational treatment, they shall give to the parent notice of their decision and shall provide such treatment for the child, unless the parent makes suitable arrangements for the provision of such treatment for the child otherwise than by the authority.

252

(5) The advice given with respect to any child by a medical officer in consequence of any such medical examination as aforesaid shall be communicated to the parent of the child and to the local education authority; and the medical officer by whom the examination was made shall, if required by the parent or by the authority so to do, issue to the authority and to the parent a certificate in the prescribed form showing whether the child is suffering from any such disability as aforesaid and, if so, the nature and extent thereof:

Provided that a local education authority shall not require the issue of such a certificate in respect of any child unless the certificate is, in their opinion, necessary for the purpose of securing the attendance of the child at a special school in accordance with the provisions of this Act relating to compulsory attendance at primary and secondary schools.

(6) Any certificate issued under the last foregoing subsection may be cancelled by the Minister or by a medical officer of the local education authority; and upon the cancellation of such a certificate the local education authority shall if they are providing special educational treatment for the child with respect to whom the certificate was issued cease to provide such treatment for the child and shall notify the parent accordingly.

NOTES

This section is printed as amended by the Education Act, 1946, s. 14 and Sched. II, Pt. II, and the Criminal Justice Act, 1967, s. 92 and Sched. III.

" Served."—As to service, see s. 113, p. 269, *post.*

" Parent "; " child "; " medical officer."—See definitions in s. 114, p. 270, *post.*

Minister.—As to complaint to the Minister about unreasonable exercise of powers, see s. 68, *ibid.* See also note to s. 33.

Regulations.—See note to s. 9, p. 250, *ante.*

Compulsory Attendance at Primary and Secondary Schools

35. Compulsory school age.—In this Act the expression " compulsory school age " means any age between five years and fifteen years, and accordingly a person shall be deemed to be of compulsory school age if he has attained the age of five years and has not attained the age of fifteen years and a person shall be deemed to be over compulsory school age as soon as he has attained the age of fifteen years :

Provided that, as soon as the Minister is satisfied that it has become practicable to raise to sixteen the upper limit of the compulsory school age, he shall lay before Parliament the draft of an Order in Council directing that the foregoing provisions of this section shall have effect as if for references therein to the age of fifteen years there were substituted references to the age of sixteen years ; and unless either House of Parliament, within the period of forty days beginning with the day on which any such draft as aforesaid is laid before it, resolves that the draft be not presented to His Majesty, His Majesty may by Order in Council direct accordingly.

In reckoning any such period of forty days, no account shall be taken of any time during which Parliament is dissolved or prorogued or during which both Houses are adjourned for more than four days.

NOTES

"**The Minister**".—See note to s. 33. See also s. 4 (2) of the Education (Miscellaneous Provisions) Act, 1948, and ss. 1, 2 of the Children and Young Persons Act, 1969, for provisions relating to compulsory attendance at school.

Attainment of age.—See note, p. 56, *ante*; but see s. 114 (6), p. 270, *post*, and see also s. 9 of the Education Act, 1962, p. 273, *post*, as to provisions for avoiding broken terms.

"**The age of sixteen years**".—It is anticipated that the age will be raised in 1973.

"**Special school.**"—The upper limit of the compulsory school age for a child registered at a special school is sixteen. See s. 38, p. 255, *post*.

"**Age.**"—As to evidence of age, see s. 95, p. 269, *post*.

"**Order in Council.**"—As to statutory instruments of which drafts are to be laid before Parliament, see s. 6 of the Statutory Instruments Act, 1946; 32 Halsbury's Statutes, 3rd Edn., 668.

36. Duty of parents to secure the education of their children.—

It shall be the duty of the parent of every child of compulsory school age to cause him to receive efficient full-time education suitable to his age, ability, and aptitude, either by regular attendance at school or otherwise.

NOTES

This section does not apply where it is not practicable for the parent to arrange for the child to become a registered pupil after the beginning of, but during the currency of, a school term (s. 4 (2) of the Education (Miscellaneous Provisions) Act, 1948).

Attendance.—As to enforcement, see ss. 39, 40, pp. 256, 257, *post*.

"**Parent**" includes guardian, etc.; see s. 114 (1), p. 270, *post*, and apparently for this purpose it includes the mother even when the child is living with both parents (*Plunkett* v. *Alker*, [1954] 1 All E. R. 396; 118 J. P. 156).

"**Regular attendance.**"—See s. 39 (2), p. 256, *post*.

37. School attendance orders.—(1) If it appears to a local education authority that the parent of any child of compulsory school age in their area is failing to perform the duty imposed on him by the last foregoing section, it shall be the duty of the authority to serve upon the parent a notice requiring him, within such time as may be specified in the notice not being less than fourteen days from the service thereof, to satisfy the authority that the child is receiving efficient full-time education suitable to his age, ability, and aptitude either by regular attendance at school or otherwise.

(2) If, after such a notice has been served upon a parent by a local education authority, the parent fails to satisfy the authority in accordance with the requirements of the notice that the child to whom the notice relates is receiving efficient full-time education suitable to his age, ability, and aptitude, then, if in the opinion of the authority it is expedient that he should attend school, the authority shall serve upon the parent an order in the prescribed form (hereinafter referred to as a " school attendance order ") requiring him to cause the child to become a registered pupil at a school named in the order :

Provided that—

(a) no such order shall be served by the authority upon the parent until the expiration of the period of fourteen days beginning with the day next following that on which they have served upon him a written notice of their intention to serve the order stating that if, before the expiration of that period, he selects a school at which he desires the child to become a registered pupil, that school will, unless the Minister otherwise directs, be named in the order; and

(b) if, before the expiration of that period, the parent selects such a school as aforesaid, that school shall, unless the Minister otherwise directs, be so named.

(3) If the local education authority are of opinion that the school selected by the parent as the school to be named in a school attendance order is unsuitable to the age, ability, or aptitude of the child with respect to whom the order is to be made, or that the attendance of the child at the school so selected would involve unreasonable expense to the authority, the authority may, after giving to the parent notice of their intention to do so, apply to the Minister for a direction determining what school is to be named in the order.

(4) If at any time while a school attendance order is in force with respect to any child the parent of the child makes application to the local education authority by whom the order was made requesting that another school be substituted for that named in the order, or requesting that the order be revoked on the ground that arrangements have been made for the child to receive efficient full-time education suitable to his age, ability, and aptitude otherwise than at school, the authority shall amend or revoke the order in compliance with the request unless they are of opinion that the proposed change of school is unreasonable or inexpedient in the interests of the child, or that no satisfactory arrangements have been made for the education of the child otherwise than at school, as the case may be ; and if a parent is aggrieved by a refusal of the authority to comply with any such request, he may refer the question to the Minister, who shall give such direction thereon as he thinks fit.

(5) If any person upon whom a school attendance order is served fails to comply with the requirements of the order, he shall be guilty of an offence against this section unless he proves that he is causing the child to receive efficient full-time education suitable to his age, ability, and aptitude otherwise than at school.

(6) If in proceedings against any person for a failure to comply with a school attendance order that person is acquitted, the court may direct that the school attendance order shall cease to be in force, but without prejudice to the duty of the local education authority to take further action under this section if at any time the authority are of opinion that having regard to any change of circumstances it is expedient so to do.

(7) Save as provided by the last foregoing subsection, a school attendance order made with respect to any child shall, subject to any amendment thereof which may be made by the local education authority, continue in force so long as he is of compulsory school age unless revoked by that authority.

NOTES

This section is printed as amended by the Education (Miscellaneous Provisions) Act, 1953, s. 10.

See notes to s. 36, p. 253, *ante*.

"**Notice**".—In *R*. v. *Appeals Committee of Surrey Quarter Sessions Ex parte Tweedie* (1963), 107 Sol. Jo. 555, the local authority were not satisfied, after service of notice, that the children were getting efficient full-time education, and served school attendance orders which were followed by convictions. The applicants' appeal to quarter sessions against convictions was dismissed. An application for an order of *certiorari* to quash the decision of quarter sessions was dismissed by the Queen's Bench Division and the Lord Chief Justice said that there could be cases where the local authority could say that reports of the work done by the children were not sufficient and that only inspection would satisfy them in all the circumstances of the case.

School attendance order.—The form is prescribed by the School Attendance Order Regulations, 1944. If the parent does not select a school in accordance with s. 37 (2) (a) the local education authority may name a school.

See an article at 129 J.P.N.48.

Service of notice.—See s. 113, p. 269, *post*.

"**Offence.**"—See s. 40, p. 257, *post*.

Defence.—Sub-s. (5) does not provide that it shall be a defence to prove that the child is attending some other school, not named in the order.

Presumption of age.—See s. 9 of the Education (Miscellaneous Provisions) Act, 1948, p. 272, *post*.

"**Parent.**"—See note to s. 36, p. 253, *ante*.

Care proceedings.—See s. 2 (8) Children and Young Persons Act, 1969.

38. Additional provisions as to compulsory attendance at special schools.

—(1) While the upper limit of the compulsory school age is, in relation to other children, less than sixteen, a person who is a registered pupil at a special school shall nevertheless be deemed to be of compulsory school age until he attains the age of sixteen years and shall not be deemed to be over compulsory school age until he has attained that age.

(2) A child who has under arrangements made by a local education authority become a registered pupil at a special school shall not be withdrawn from the school without the consent of that authority ; but if the parent of any such child is aggrieved by a refusal of the authority to comply with an application made by the parent requesting such consent, he may refer the question to the Minister, who shall give such direction thereon as he thinks fit.

(3) No direction given by the Minister under the last foregoing subsection or under subsection (3) or subsection (4) of the last foregoing section shall be such as to require a pupil to be a registered pupil at a special school unless either the parent consents to his attending such a school or there is in force a certificate issued by a medical officer of the local education authority showing that the child is suffering from some disability of mind or body of such a nature and extent that, in the opinion of the Minister, it is expedient that the child should attend a special school.

NOTES

Compulsory school age.—See s. 35, p. 252, *ante*.

"**Registered pupil.**"—See ss. 80, 114 (1), pp. 268, 270, *post*.

" **Special school.**"—This is defined in s. 9 (5), p. 250, *ante*, as a school specially organised for the purpose of providing special educational treatment for pupils requiring it, and approved by the Minister.

Attainment of age.—See note at p. 53, *ante*.

" **Parent.**"—This includes guardian, etc.; see s. 114 (1), p. 270, *post*, and apparently for this purpose it includes the mother, even when the child is living with both parents, see *Plunkett* v. *Alker*, [1954] 1 All E. R. 396; 118 J. P. 156.

39. Duty of parents to secure regular attendance of registered pupils.—(1) If any child of compulsory school age who is a registered pupil at a school fails to attend regularly thereat, the parent of the child shall be guilty of an offence against this section.

(2) In any proceedings for an offence against this section in respect of a child who is not a boarder at the school at which he is a registered pupil, the child shall not be deemed to have failed to attend regularly at the school by reason of his absence therefrom with leave or—

(a) at any time when he was prevented from attending by reason of sickness or any unavoidable cause ;

(b) on any day exclusively set apart for religious observance by the religious body to which his parent belongs ;

(c) if the parent proves that the school at which the child is a registered pupil is not within walking distance of the child's home, and that no suitable arrangements have been made by the local education authority either for his transport to and from the school or for boarding accommodation for him at or near the school or for enabling him to become a registered pupil at a school nearer to his home.

(3) Where in any proceedings for an offence against this section it is proved that the child has no fixed abode, paragraph (c) of the last foregoing subsection shall not apply, but if the parent proves that he is engaged in any trade or business of such a nature as to require him to travel from place to place and that the child has attended at a school at which he was a registered pupil as regularly as the nature of the trade or business of the parent permits, the parent shall be acquitted :

Provided that, in the case of a child who has attained the age of six years, the parent shall not be entitled to be acquitted under this subsection unless he proves that the child has made at least two hundred attendances during the period of twelve months ending with the date on which the proceedings were instituted.

(4) In any proceedings for an offence against this section in respect of a child who is a boarder at the school at which he is a registered pupil, the child shall be deemed to have failed to attend regularly at the school if he is absent therefrom without leave during any part of the school term at a time when he was not prevented from being present by reason of sickness or any unavoidable cause.

(5) In this section the expression " leave " in relation to any school means leave granted by any person authorised in that behalf by the managers, governors or proprietor of the school, and the expression " walking distance " means, in relation to a child who has not attained

the age of eight years, two miles, and in the case of any other child three miles, measured by the nearest available route.

NOTES

" Registered pupil."—It will be observed that the section applies only to pupils who have been registered.

" Regularly thereat."—What is regular attendance is not defined.

" Parent."—See note to s. 36, p. 253, *ante*.

" Offence."—See s. 40, *infra*.

Defence.—Exclusion of a child suspected of being verminous is a defence under s. 54 (7), p. 266, *post*.

The other defences open to the parent are defined in sub-s. (2) and where a head mistress refused to admit a girl in trousers unless a medical certificate was produced, and the parent continued to send the child in trousers, with the result that the child was excluded, the parent was guilty of an offence under this section (*Spiers* v. *Warrington Corporation*, [1953] 2 All E. R. 1052; 117 J. P. 564).

Attainment of age.—See note at p. 53, *ante*.

Presumption of age.—See s. 9 of the Education (Miscellaneous Provisions) Act, 1948, p. 272, *post*.

Prosecutions.—Section 40 (2), *infra*, defines the duties of local education authorities as to taking proceedings, and it would appear that the appropriate authority can take such proceedings before the court where the school is situate or where the child belongs, or in the case of failure to comply with a school attendance order, before the court in whose area the school attendance order was made.

"Unavoidable cause."—In the case of *Jenkins* v. *Howells*, [1949] 2 K. B. 218; [1949] 1 All E. R. 942, it was held that the " cause " must affect the child and not other members of the family. In that case the child's mother, whose health was bad, kept her at home. The justices held that the facts constituted an unavoidable cause and dismissed the information. On appeal by case stated the case was remitted to the justices with a direction to find the case proved.

Walking distance.—Distance, not safety, is the test for determining " the nearest available route " (*Shaxted* v. *Ward*, [1954] 1 All E. R. 336; 118 J. P. 168).

Late arrival at school.—In the case of *Hinchley* v. *Rankin*, [1961] 1 All E. R. 692 ; 125 J. P. 293, evidence was given that the attendance register was closed at 9.45 a.m., and that pupils arriving after that would be marked absent and shown as non-attendant for that session. On appeal to the Divisional Court against the decision of Birmingham Quarter Sessions allowing an appeal by the father from his conviction for that his child had failed to attend regularly at school, the Lord Chief Justice said that even if the child had arrived only a minute or two after the attendance register was closed, that would be a failure to attend within the meaning of the Act. The appeal was allowed.

40. Enforcement of school attendance.—(1) Subject to the provisions of this section, any person guilty of an offence against section thirty-seven or section thirty-nine of this Act shall be liable on summary conviction, in the case of a first offence against that section to a fine not exceeding one pound, in the case of a second offence against that section to a fine not exceeding five pounds, and in the case of a third or subsequent offence against that section to a fine not exceeding ten pounds or to imprisonment for a term not exceeding one month or to both such fine and such imprisonment.

(2) Proceedings for such offences as aforesaid shall not be instituted except by a local education authority; and before instituting such proceedings the authority shall consider whether it would be appropriate, instead of or as well as instituting the proceedings, to bring the child in

question before a juvenile court under section 1 of the Children and Young Persons Act, 1969.

(3) The court by which a person is convicted of an offence against section 37 of this Act or before which a person is charged with an offence against section 39 of this Act may if it thinks fit direct the authority who instituted the proceedings to bring the child to whom the proceedings relate before a juvenile court under the said section 1; and it shall be the duty of the authority to comply with the direction.

(4) Where a child in respect of whom a school attendance order is in force is brought before a juvenile court by a local education authority under the said section 1 and the court finds that the condition mentioned in subsection (2) (e) of that section is not satisfied with respect to him, the court may direct that the order shall cease to be in force.

NOTES

This section is printed as amended by the Education (Miscellaneous Provisions) Act, 1948, the Education (Miscellaneous Provisions) Act, 1953, and the Children and Young Persons Acts, 1963 and 1969.

" **Second offence; subsequent offence.**"—See note at p. 26, *ante*.

"**Fine not exceeding.**"—The maximum fine which may now be imposed under subsection (1) is ten pounds for a first offence and twenty pounds for a second or subsequent offence (Criminal Justice Act, 1967, s. 92 and Sched. III).

" **Parent.**"—See note to s. 36, p. 253, *ante*.

" **Direction.**"—Where a direction is given, it may be well that it should be in writing.

"**Brought before a juvenile court.**"—See now the Magistrates' Courts (Children and Young Persons) Rules, 1970.

Child brought by local education authority.—Sub-s. (2) enables the local education authority to bring a child before a juvenile court without first having to take proceedings against a parent for an offence against ss. 37 or 39 of this Act.

Wardship proceedings.—In the case of *Re Baker (Infants)*, [1962] Ch. 201; [1961] 3 All E.R. 276; 125 J.P. 591, it was held that the Education Act, 1944, restricted the inherent jurisdiction of the Sovereign as exercised by the Court in relation to infants by disabling it from giving any direction as to their education at variance with the provisions of the Act, and it was not proper to use that jurisdiction as a means of enforcing an attendance order. In that case school attendance orders had been made under s. 37 (p. 253, *ante*) and not obeyed. The remaining subsections of s. 40, dealing with the position after children became registered pupils were not directly in point.

The local education authority appealed to the Court of Appeal, where it was held that although the court had jurisdiction to continue the wardship of the children, the court would not do so in the present case for the following reasons:

(i) (*per* Ormerod, L. J.; Pearson, L. J., concurring) the prerogative of the Crown in relation to infants had been restricted in that it might no longer be exercised in relation to the particular matters placed by the Education Act, 1944, within the ambit of the local education authority's discretion and powers;

(ii) (*per* Upjohn and Pearson, L.JJ.) the Education Act, 1944, had established a comprehensive code which it was the duty of local education authorities to carry out, and it would not be proper for the court to exercise wardship jurisdiction solely to assist a local education authority in the enforcement of their statutory functions, or, in the absence of special circumstances, to exercise the court's discretionary control over a ward in a sphere of activity which had been entrusted by statute to a local education authority;

(iii) (*per* Ormerod and Pearson, L.JJ.) moreover the remedy provided by the statute had not been fully used.

In the judgments of the court attention was drawn to the fact that the remedy specifically provided under the Act had not been fully tried out. On a third summons for neglect to obey an order the magistrates might inflict a penalty of imprisonment. No third summons had been issued and it was therefore impossible to say how the mother of the infants would behave if threatened with a sentence of imprisonment. The appeal was dismissed.

40a. School attendance of vagrant children. [*Repealed by the Children and Young Persons Act*, 1969, *s.* 72 (4) *and Sched. VI. See now s.* 2 (8) (*b*) (iii).]

43. County colleges.—(1) It shall be the duty of every local education authority to establish and maintain county colleges, that is to say, centres approved by the Minister for providing for young persons who are not in full-time attendance at any school or other educational institution such further education including physical practical and vocational training, as will enable them to develop their various aptitudes and capacities and will prepare them for the responsibilities of citizenship.

(2) As soon after the date of the commencement of this Part of this Act as the Minister considers it practicable so to do, he shall direct every local education authority to estimate the immediate and prospective needs of their area with respect to county colleges having regard to the provisions of this Act, and to prepare and submit to him within such time and in such form as may be specified in the direction a plan showing the provision which the authority propose to make for such colleges for their area, and the plan shall contain such particulars as to the colleges proposed to be established as may be specified in the direction.

(3) The Minister shall, after considering the plan submitted by a local education authority and after consultation with them, make an order for the area of the authority specifying the county colleges which it is the duty of the authority to maintain, and the order shall require the authority to make such provision for boarding accommodation at county colleges as the Minister considers to be expedient: the order so made for any area shall continue to regulate the duties of the local education authority in respect of the matters therein mentioned and shall be amended by the Minister, after consultation with the authority, whenever in his opinion the amendment thereof is expedient by reason of any change or proposed change of circumstances.

(4) The Minister may make regulations as to the maintenance government and conduct of county colleges and as to the further education to be given therein.

NOTES

This section is printed as amended by the Statute Law Revision Act, 1950.

Date.—The County Colleges Order, 1947, S. R. & O. 1947 No. 527, laid down April 1, 1947, as the date on and after which local education authorities were to establish and maintain county colleges.

"The minister."—See note to s. 33, p. 251, *ante*.

44. Duty to attend county colleges in accordance with college attendance notices.—(1) This section shall come into operation on such date as soon as practicable after the date determined by Order in Council under the last foregoing section as the Minister may by order direct.

(2) It shall be the duty of the local education authority to serve upon every young person residing in their area who is not exempt from compulsory attendance for further education a notice (hereinafter referred to as a " college attendance notice ") directing him to attend at a county college, and it shall be the duty of every young person upon whom such a notice is served to attend at the county college named in the notice in accordance with the requirements specified therein.

(3) Subject to the provisions of the next following subsection, the requirements specified in a college attendance notice shall be such as to secure the attendance of the person upon whom it is served at a county college—

    (a) for one whole day, or two half-days, in each of forty-four weeks in every year while he remains a young person; or
    (b) where the authority are satisfied that continuous attendance would be more suitable in the case of that young person, for one continuous period of eight weeks, or two continuous periods of four weeks each, in every such year;

and in this section the expression " year " means, in relation to any young person, in the case of the first year the period of twelve months beginning with the first day on which he is required by a college attendance notice served on him to attend a county college, and in the case of every subsequent year the period of twelve months beginning immediately after the expiration of the last preceding year:

Provided that in respect of the year in which the young person attains the age of eighteen the requirements specified in the notice shall be reduced to such extent as the local education authority think expedient for securing that the attendances required of him until he attains that age shall be as nearly as may be proportionate to those which would have been required of him during a full period of twelve months.

(4) If, by reason of the nature of the employment of any young person or of other circumstances affecting him, the local education authority are satisfied that attendance in accordance with the provisions of the last foregoing subsection would not be suitable in his case, a college attendance notice may, with the consent of the young person, require his attendance in accordance with such other arrangements as may be specified in the notice, so, however, that the requirements specified in the notice in accordance with such arrangements as aforesaid shall be such as to secure the attendance of the young person for periods amounting in the aggregate to three hundred and thirty hours in each year, or, in the case of the year in which he attains the age of eighteen, to the proportionately reduced number of hours.

(5) Except where continuous attendance is required, no college attendance notice shall require a young person to attend a county college on a Sunday or on any day or part of a day exclusively set apart for religious observance by the religious body to which he belongs, or during any holiday or half-holiday to which by any enactment regulating his employment or by agreement he is entitled, or, so far as practicable, during any holiday or half-holiday which is allowed in accordance with any custom of his employment, or between the hours of six in the evening and half past eight in the morning:

Provided that the Minister may, on the application of any local education authority, direct that in relation to young persons in their area or in any part thereof employed at night or otherwise employed at abnormal times this subsection shall have effect as if for the reference to the hours of six in the evening and half past eight in the morning there were substituted a reference to such other times as may be specified in the direction.

(6) The place, days, times, and periods, of attendance required of a young person, and the period for which the notice is to be in force, shall be specified in any college attendance notice served on him; and the requirements of any such notice in force in the case of a young person may be amended as occasion may require either by the authority by whom it was served on him or by any other local education authority in whose area he may for the time being reside, so, however, that the provisions of every such notice shall be such as to secure that the requirements imposed on the young person during each year while he remains a young person shall comply with the provisions of the last three foregoing subsections.

(7) In determining what requirements shall be imposed upon a young person by a college attendance notice or by any amendments to such a notice, the local education authority shall have regard, so far as practicable, to any preference which he, and in the case of a young person under the age of sixteen years his parent, may express, to the circumstances of his employment or prospective employment, and to any representations that may be made to the authority by his employer or any other person proposing to employ him.

(8) The following persons shall be exempt from compulsory attendance for further education, that is to say—

(a) any person who is in full time attendance at any school or other educational institution (not being a county college);

(b) any person who is shown to the satisfaction of the local education authority to be receiving suitable and efficient instruction either full-time or for such times as in the opinion of the authority are equivalent to not less than three hundred and thirty hours instruction in a period of twelve months;

(c) any person who having been exempt under either of the last two foregoing paragraphs did not cease to be so exempt until after he had attained the age of seventeen years and eight months;

(d) any person who is undergoing a course of training for the mercantile marine or the sea fishing industry approved by the Minister or who, having completed such a course, is engaged in the mercantile marine or in the said industry;

(e) any person to whom, by reason of section one hundred and fifteen or section one hundred and sixteen of this Act, the duties of local education authorities do not relate;

(f) any person who attained the age of fifteen years before the date on which this section comes into operation, not being a person who immediately before that date was required to attend a continuation school under the provisions of the Education Act, 1921.

If any person is aggrieved by a decision of a local education authority given under paragraph (b) of this subsection, he may refer the question to the Minister, who shall give such direction thereon as he thinks fit.

(9) If any young person upon whom a college attendance notice has been served fails to comply with any requirement of the notice, he shall be guilty of an offence against this section unless he proves either—

(a) that he was at the material time exempt from compulsory attendance for further education; or

(b) that he was prevented from complying with the requirement by reason of sickness or any unavoidable cause; or

(c) that the requirement does not comply with the provisions of this section.

NOTES

" Serve."—See s. 113, p. 269, *post.*

" Young person," " parent."—See definition in s. 114, p. 270, *post.*

Age.—As to evidence see s. 95, p. 269, *post.* As to provisions for avoiding broken terms, see s. 9 of the Education Act, 1962, p. 273, *post.*

Exemption.—As to certificates of exemption, see s. 45 (5), p. 263, *post.*

Sub-s. (8) (e).—S. 115 relates to persons in the service of the Crown, and s. 116 to persons of unsound mind or detained by order of a court.

Attendance.—As to enforcement, see s. 46, p. 263, *post.*
As to evidence of attendance, see s. 95, p. 269, *post.*

" Unavoidable cause."—See note to s. 39, p. 257, *ante.*

45. Administrative provisions for securing attendance at county colleges.—(1) For the purpose of facilitating the execution by local education authorities of their functions under the last foregoing section, the following provisions shall, on and after the date on which that section comes into operation, have effect, that is to say:—

(a) every young person who is not exempt from compulsory attendance for further education shall at all times keep the local education authority in whose area he resides informed of his proper address;

(b) any person by whom such a young person as aforesaid is employed otherwise than by way of casual employment shall notify the local education authority for the area in which the young person resides when the young person enters his employment and again when he ceases to be employed by him, and shall also notify the authority of any change of address of the employer, and, if known to him, of the young person, which occurs during the continuance of the employment;

and any person who fails to perform any duty imposed on him by the foregoing provisions of this section shall be guilty of an offence against this section.

(2) The local education authority by whom a college attendance notice is served upon any young person shall serve a copy thereof upon any person who notifies the authority that the young person is employed by him.

(3) The Minister may by regulations make provision as to the form of college attendance notices, as to consultation and the exchange of information between different local education authorities, as to the issue of certificates of exemption in respect of young persons who are exempt from compulsory attendance for further education, and generally for the purpose of facilitating the administration by local authorities of the provisions of this Part of this Act as to attendance at county colleges.

(4) The Minister and the Minister of Labour shall issue instructions to local education authorities and to local offices of the Ministry of Labour respectively for ensuring due consultation and exchange of information between such authorities and offices.

(5) Any certificate of exemption in the prescribed form purporting to be authenticated in the prescribed manner shall be received in evidence in any legal proceeding, and shall unless the contrary is proved, be sufficient evidence of the fact therein stated.

NOTES

" **Local education authority.**"—See s. 6, p. 248, *ante* and s. 114, p. 270, *post.*

" **Serve.**"—See s. 113, p. 269, *post.*

"**The minister.**"—See note to s. 33, p. 251, *ante.*

46. Enforcement of attendance at county colleges.—(1) Any person guilty of an offence against either of the last two foregoing sections shall be liable on summary conviction, in the case of a first offence against that section to a fine not exceeding one pound, in the case of a second offence against that section to a fine not exceeding five pounds, and in the case of a third or subsequent offence against that section to a fine not exceeding ten pounds or to imprisonment for a term not exceeding one month or to both such fine and such imprisonment.

(2) It shall be the duty of the local education authority in whose area the young person in question resides to institute proceedings for such offences as aforesaid wherever, in their opinion, the institution of such proceedings is expedient, and no such proceedings shall be instituted except by or on behalf of a local education authority.

(3) If, in furnishing any information for the purposes of either of the last two foregoing sections, any person makes any statement which he knows to be false in any material particular, or recklessly makes any statement which is false in any material particular, he shall be liable on summary conviction to a fine not exceeding twenty pounds or to imprisonment for a term not exceeding three months or to both such fine and such imprisonment.

(4) Without prejudice to the provisions of any enactment or rule of law relating to the aiding and abetting of offences, if the parent of a young person or any person by whom a young person is employed or the servant or agent of any such person has conduced to or connived at any offence committed by the young person against either of the last two foregoing sections, the person who has conduced to or connived at the offence shall, whether or not any person is proceeded against or convicted in respect of the offence conduced to or connived at, be guilty of the like offence and punishable accordingly.

NOTES

" **Local education authority.**"—See s. 6, p. 248, *ante* and s. 114, p. 270, *post.*

" **Young person** "—" **parent.**"—See definition in s. 114, p. 270, *post.*

" **Second offence.**"—See *R.* v. *South Shields Licensing Justices,* [1911] 2 K. B. 1; 75 J. P. 299.

Imprisonment of person under 18.—See note at p. 373, *post.*

52. Recovery of cost of boarding accommodation and of clothing.

—(1) Where a local education authority have, under the powers conferred by the foregoing provisions of this Act, provided a pupil with board and lodging otherwise than at a boarding school or college the authority shall require the parent to pay to the authority in respect thereof such sums, if any, as in the opinion of the authority he is able without financial hardship to pay:

Provided that—

(a) where the board and lodging provided for the pupil were so provided under arrangements made by the local education authority on the ground that in their opinion education suitable to his age, ability, and aptitude could not otherwise be provided by the authority for him, no sum shall be recoverable in respect thereof under this section ; and

(b) where the board and lodging have been so provided for a pupil in attendance at a county college, the authority, if satisfied that the pupil is in a financial position to pay the whole or any part of a sum recoverable from the parent under this section, may recover that sum or that part thereof from the pupil instead of from the parent.

(2) The sums recoverable under this section shall not exceed the cost to the local education authority of providing the board and lodging.

(3) Any sums payable by virtue of this section may be recovered summarily as a civil debt.

NOTES

This section is printed as amended by the Education (Miscellaneous Provisions) Act, 1948.

" **Parent.**"—See note to s. 36, p. 253, *ante.*

" **Civil debt.**"—See Magistrates' Courts Act, 1952, ss. 47 (8), 50 (1), 64 (3), 73, Sched. III, para. 4; 21 Halsbury's Statutes, 3rd Edn., 226, 227, 238, 246, 295, and Rules 43 and 48 of the Magistrates' Courts Rules, 1968. Even where the pupil is summoned, and is under seventeen, proceedings will have to be in the adult court, unless assigned to the juvenile court by Rules.

Clothing.—Cost of clothing formerly dealt with in this section is now dealt with in s. 5 of the Education (Miscellaneous Provisions) Act, 1948; 11 Halsbury's Statutes, 3rd Edn., 295.

54. Power to ensure cleanliness.—(1) A local education authority

may, by directions in writing issued with respect to all schools maintained by them or with respect to any of such schools named in the directions, authorise a medical officer of the authority to cause examinations of the persons and clothing of pupils in attendance at such schools to be made whenever in his opinion such examinations are necessary in the interests of cleanliness; and if a medical officer of a local education authority has reasonable cause to suspect that the person or clothing of a pupil in attendance at any county college is infested with vermin or in a foul condition, he may cause an examination thereof to be made.

(2) Any such examination as aforesaid shall be made by a person authorised by the local education authority to make such examinations, and if the person or clothing of any pupil is found upon such an examination to be infested with vermin or in a foul condition, any officer of the authority may serve upon the parent of the pupil, or in the case of a pupil in attendance at a county college upon the pupil, a notice requiring him to cause the person and clothing of the pupil to be cleansed.

(3) A notice served under the last foregoing subsection shall inform the person upon whom it is served that unless within the period limited by the notice, not being less than twenty-four hours after the service thereof, the person and clothing of the pupil to whom the notice relates are cleansed to the satisfaction of such person as may be specified in the notice the cleansing thereof will be carried out under arrangements made by the local education authority; and if, upon a report being made to him by that person at the expiration of that period, a medical officer of the authority is not satisfied that the person and clothing of the pupil have been properly cleansed, the medical officer may issue an order directing that the person and clothing of the pupil be cleansed under such arrangements.

(4) It shall be the duty of the local education authority to make arrangements for securing that any person or clothing required under this section to be cleansed may be cleansed (whether at the request of a parent or pupil or in pursuance of an order issued under this section) at suitable premises by suitable persons and with suitable appliances; and where the council of any county district in the area of the authority are entitled to the use of any premises or appliances for cleansing the person or clothing of persons infested with vermin, the authority may require the council to permit the authority to use those premises or appliances for such purposes upon such terms as may be determined by agreement between the authority and the council or, in default of such agreement, by the Minister of Health.

(5) Where an order has been issued by a medical officer under this section directing that the person and clothing of a pupil be cleansed under arrangements made by a local education authority, the order shall be sufficient to authorise any officer of the authority to cause the person and clothing of the pupil named in the order to be cleansed in accordance with arrangements made under the last foregoing subsection, and for that purpose to convey him to, and detain him at, any premises provided in accordance with such arrangements.

(6) If, after the cleansing of the person or clothing of any pupil has been carried out under this section, his person or clothing is again found to be infested with vermin or in a foul condition at any time while he is in attendance at a school maintained by a local education authority or at a county college, and it is proved that the condition of his person or clothing is due to neglect on the part of his parent, or in the case of a

pupil in attendance at a county college to his own neglect, the parent or the pupil, as the case may be, shall be liable on summary conviction to a fine not exceeding twenty shillings.

(7) Where a medical officer of a local education authority suspects that the person or clothing of any pupil in attendance at a school maintained by the authority or at any county college is infested with vermin or in a foul condition, but action for the examination or cleansing thereof cannot immediately be taken, he may, if he considers it necessary so to do either in the interest of the pupil or of other pupils in attendance at the school or college, direct that the pupil be excluded from the school or college until such action has been taken ; and such a direction shall be a defence to any proceedings under this Act in respect of the failure of the pupil to attend school or to comply with the requirements of a college attendance notice, as the case may be, on any day on which he is excluded in pursuance of the direction, unless it is proved that the issue of the direction was necessitated by the wilful default of the pupil or his parent.

(8) No girl shall be examined or cleansed under the powers conferred by this section except by a duly qualified medical practitioner or by a woman authorised for that purpose by a local education authority.

NOTES

" **Directions.**"—S. 111; 11 Halsbury's Statutes, 3rd Edn., 254, gives power to vary such directions.

" **Clothing.**"—See s. 114, p. 270, *post*, for definition.

" **Notice.**"—As to service, see s. 113, p. 269, *post*.

" **Penalty.**"—See s. 120 (2) for restrictions upon the punishment of young persons, p. 272, *post*.

Parent.—See note to s. 36, p. 253, *ante*.

57. Medical examination and classification of children unsuitable for education. [*Sections 57, 57A, 57B were repealed by the Education (Handicapped Children) Act, 1970, and S.I. 1971 No. 187.*]

58. Adaptation of enactments relating to the employment of children or young persons.—For the purposes of any enactment relating to the prohibition or regulation of the employment of children or young persons, any person who is not for the purposes of this Act over compulsory school age shall be deemed to be a child within the meaning of that enactment.

NOTE

Enactments.—See the Employment of Women, Young Persons and Children Act, 1920; (12 Halsbury's Statutes, 3rd Edn., 57) the Children and Young Persons Act, 1933, ss. 18–30, pp. 29 *et seq.*, *ante*; the Young Persons (Employment) Acts, 1938 and 1964 (17 Halsbury's Statutes, 3rd Edn., 751, 261) Part VI of the Factories Act, 1961 (13 Halsbury's Statutes, 3rd Edn., 400) and Rules made under the last mentioned Act.

59. Power of local education authorities to prohibit or restrict employment of children.—(1) If it appears to a local education authority that any child who is a registered pupil at a county school, voluntary school, or special school, is being employed in such manner as to be prejudicial to his health or otherwise to render him unfit to obtain the full benefit of the education provided for him, the authority may, by notice in writing, served upon the employer, prohibit him from employing the child, or impose such restrictions upon his employment of the child as appear to them to be expedient in the interests of the child.

(2) A local education authority may, by notice in writing served upon the parent or employer of any child who is a registered pupil at a county school, voluntary school, or special school, require the parent or employer to provide the authority, within such period as may be specified in the notice, with such information as appears to the authority to be necessary for the purpose of enabling them to ascertain whether the child is being employed in such a manner as to render him unfit to obtain the full benefit of the education provided for him.

(3) Any person who employs a child in contravention of any prohibition or restriction imposed under subsection (1) of this section, or who fails to comply with the requirements of a notice served under subsection (2) of this section, shall be guilty of an offence against this section and liable on summary conviction, in the case of a first offence to a fine not exceeding one pound, in the case of a second offence to a fine not exceeding five pounds, and in the case of a third or subsequent offence to a fine not exceeding ten pounds or to imprisonment for a term not exceeding one month or to both such fine and such imprisonment.

(4) Subsection (1) and subsection (3) of section twenty-eight of the Children and Young Persons Act, 1933 (which relate to powers of entry for the enforcement of the provisions of Part II of that Act with respect to the employment of children) shall apply with respect to the provisions of any notice served under this section as they apply with respect to the provisions of the said Part II.

NOTES

" **Notice.**"—As to service of notice, see s. 113, p. 269, *post.*

" **Parent.**"—See note to s. 36, p. 253, *ante.*

" **Second Offence.**"—See note at p. 33, *ante.*

Children and Young Persons Act, 1933, s. 28.—See p. 40, *ante.*

" **Penalty.**"—See s. 120 (2), p. 272, *post,* for restrictions upon the punishment of young persons.

Cf. Children and Young Persons Act, 1933, ss. 18 to 20, pp. 29 *et seq., ante.*

76. Pupils to be educated in accordance with the wishes of their parents.

—In the exercise and performance of all powers and duties conferred and imposed on them by this Act the Minister and local education authorities shall have regard to the general principle that, so far as is compatible with the provision of efficient instruction and training and the avoidance of unreasonable public expenditure, pupils are to be educated in accordance with the wishes of their parents.

NOTE

In *Watt* v. *Kesteven C.C.,* [1955] 1 All E. R. 473; 119 J. P. 220, the Court of Appeal held that under this section a local authority, while having regard to the general principle stated were entitled to take administrative matters into account, and, while under a duty to make available education and to pay full tuition fees at an independent school with which they had made arrangements, they were not under a duty to do so at any independent school of the parent's choice.

In *Wood* v. *Ealing London Borough Council*, [1967] Ch. 364; [1966] 3 All E. R. 514, the objection was held not to relate to the size of the school or the conditions of entry. See also *Cumings* v. *Birkenhead Corporation*, [1971] 2 All E. R. 881.

80. Registration of pupils at schools.—(1) The proprietor of every school (that is to say in the case of a county school or voluntary school the managers or governors thereof) shall cause to be kept in accordance with regulations made by the Minister a register containing the prescribed particulars with respect to all persons who are pupils at the school, and such regulations may make provision for enabling such registers to be inspected, for enabling extracts therefrom to be taken for the purposes of this Act by persons duly authorised in that behalf under the regulations, and for requiring the persons by whom any such register is required to be kept to make to the Minister, and to local education authorities, such periodical or other returns as to the contents thereof as may be prescribed.

(2) If any person contravenes or fails to comply with any requirement imposed on him by regulations made under this section, he shall be liable on summary conviction to a fine not exceeding ten pounds.

(3) [*Repealed by the Education (Miscellaneous Provisions) Act*, 1948, ss. 4 (5), 11 (2) *and Sched. II. The provisions of this subsection are substantially re-enacted by* ibid., s. 4.]

NOTES

This section is printed as amended by the Education (Miscellaneous Provisions) Act, 1948.

"**The Minister.**"—See note to s. 33, p. 253, *ante*.

"**Registered pupil.**"—See s. 114 (1), p. 270, *post*.

"**School attendance order.**"—See s. 37, p. 253, *ante*.

"**Regulations.**"—See the Pupils Registration Regulations, 1956 (S.I. 1956 No. 357). The regulations made under this section shall prescribe the grounds on which names are to be deleted from a register kept thereunder, and the name of a person entered in such a register as a registered pupil shall be deleted therefrom when occasion arises on some one or other of the prescribed grounds and shall not be deleted therefrom on any other ground (Education (Miscellaneous Provisions) Act, 1948, s. 4 (6); 11 Halsbury's Statutes, 3rd Edn., 295).

94. Certificates of birth and registrars' returns.—(1) Where the age of any person is required to be proved for the purposes of this Act or of any enactment relating to the employment of children or young persons, the registrar having the custody of the register of births and deaths containing the entry relating to the birth of that person shall, upon being presented by any person with a written requisition in such form and containing such particulars as may be determined by regulations made by the Minister of Health, and upon payment of a fee of [two shillings], supply that person with a copy of the entry certified under his hand.

Every registrar shall, upon being requested so to do, supply free of charge a form of requisition for the purposes of this subsection.

NOTES

Sub-ss. (2), (3); 11 Halsbury's Statutes, 3rd Edn., 244, are not printed here.

'' **Child** '' **and** '' **young person.**''—See definitions in s. 114 (1), p. 270, *post.*

"**A fee of.**"—The fee was raised from sixpence by S.I. 1968 No. 1242; see the Decimal Currency Act 1969, s. 10.

95. Provisions as to evidence.—(1) Where in any proceedings, under this Act the person by whom the proceedings are brought alleges that any person whose age is material to the proceedings is under, of or over, any age, and satisfies the court that having used all reasonable diligence to obtain evidence as to the age of that person he has been unable to do so, then, unless the contrary is proved, the court may presume that person to be under, of, or over, the age alleged.

(2) In any legal proceedings any document purporting to be—

(a) a document issued by a local education authority, and to be signed by the clerk of that authority or by the chief education officer of that authority or by any other officer of the authority authorised to sign it ;

(b) an extract from the minutes of the proceedings of the managers or governors of any county school or voluntary school, and to be signed by the chairman of the managers or governors or by their clerk ;

(c) a certificate giving particulars of the attendance of a child or young person at a school or at a county college, and to be signed by the head teacher of the school or college ; or

(d) a certificate issued by a medical officer of a local education authority and to be signed by such an officer ;

shall be received in evidence and shall, unless the contrary is proved, be deemed to be the document which it purports to be, and to have been signed by the person by whom it purports to have been signed, without proof of his identity, signature, or official capacity, and any such extract or certificate as is mentioned in paragraphs (b) (c) or (d) of this subsection shall be evidence of the matters therein stated.

NOTES

Attainment of age.—See notes at p. 53, *ante.*

'' **Child** '' **and** '' **young person.**''—See definitions in s. 114 (1), *infra.*

Onus of proof.—Before the age alleged by the prosecutor or complainant can be presumed, he must prove reasonable diligence to the satisfaction of the court.

Presumption of age.—See s. 9 of the Education (Miscellaneous Provisions) Act, 1948, p. 272, *post,* as to the presumption of a child to have been of compulsory school age, which is in substitution for the power conferred on the court by sub-s. (1) of this section.

113. Notices.—Any order, notice or other document required or authorised by this Act to be served upon any person may be served by delivering it to that person, or by leaving it at his usual or last known place of residence, or by sending it in a pre-paid letter addressed to him at that place.

NOTES

This section is printed as amended by the Education Act, 1946.

" **Person.**"—This word generally includes bodies, corporate or unincorporate; see s. 19, of the Interpretation Act, 1889; 32 Halsbury's Statutes, 3rd Edn., 449; but by s. 2 (1) of that Act, in criminal matters it does not include bodies unincorporate. As to service on local authorities, see also s. 286, of the Local Government Act, 1933; 19 Halsbury's Statutes, 3rd Edn., 562.

" **Residence.**"—See note at p. 162, *ante*.

Service by post.—See s. 26 of the Interpretation Act, 1889; 32 Halsbury's Statutes, 3rd Edn., 452.

114. Interpretation.—(1) In this Act, unless the context otherwise requires, the following expressions have the meanings hereby respectively assigned to them, that is to say :—

*   *   *   *   *

" Child " means a person who is not over compulsory school age ;

" Clothing " includes boots and other footwear ;

" Compulsory school age " has, subject to the provisions of section thirty-eight of this Act, the meaning assigned to it by section thirty-five of this Act ;

" County " means an administrative county within the meaning of the Local Government Act, 1933 ;

*   *   *   *   *

" Further education " has the meaning assigned to it by section forty-one of this Act ;

*   *   *   *   *

" Local education authority " means, in relation to any area for which a joint education board is constituted as the local education authority under the provisions of Part I of the First Schedule to this Act, the board so constituted, and, save as aforesaid, means, in relation to a county, the council of the county, and, in relation to a county borough, the council of the county borough ;

*   *   *   *   *

" Medical inspection " means inspection by or under the directions of a medical officer of a local education authority or by a person registered in the dentists register under the Dentists Acts, 1878 to 1923, employed or engaged, whether regularly or for the purposes of any particular case, by a local education authority;

" Medical officer " means, in relation to any local education authority, a duly qualified medical practitioner employed or engaged, whether regularly or for the purposes of any particular case, by that authority ;

" Medical treatment" includes treatment by any duly qualified medical practitioner, but does not, in relation to any pupil other than a pupil receiving primary or secondary education otherwise than at school under arrangements made by a local education authority include treatment in that pupil's home;

*   *   *   *   *

" Parent," in relation to any child or young person, includes a guardian and every person who has the actual custody of the child or young person ;

* * * * *

" Prescribed " means prescribed by regulations made by the Minister;

* * * * *

" Pupil," where used without qualification, means a person of any age for whom education is required to be provided under this Act ;

" Registered pupil " means, in relation to any school, a pupil registered as such in the register kept in accordance with the requirements of this Act.

* * * * *

" School " means an institution for providing primary or secondary education or both primary and secondary education, being a school maintained by a local education authority, an independent school, or a school in respect of which grants are made by the Minister to the proprietor of the school ; and the expression " school " where used without qualification includes any such school or all such schools as the context may require ;

* * * * *

" Special educational treatment " has the meaning assigned to it by paragraph (c) of subsection (2) of section eight of this Act *i.e.* " education by special methods appropriate for persons suffering from that disability."

* * * * *

" Young person " means a person over compulsory school age who has not attained the age of eighteen years.

* * * * *

(5) [*Repealed by the Education Act*, 1946, s. 8 (4).]

(6) Any person who before the commencement of Part II of this Act had attained an age at which his parent had ceased to be under any obligation imposed under section forty-six of the Education Act, 1921, shall be deemed to be over compulsory school age, and any person who after the said date ceases to be of compulsory school age shall not, in the event of any subsequent change in the upper limit of the compulsory school age, again become a person of compulsory school age.

NOTES

This section is printed as amended by the Education (Miscellaneous Provisions) Acts, 1948 and 1953.

Attainment of age.—See notes at p. 53, *ante*.

S. 115; 11 Halsbury's Statutes, 3rd Edn., 261, contains savings in relation to persons in the service of the Crown and their children.

S. 116; 11 Halsbury's Statutes, 3rd Edn., 261, contains savings as to persons of unsound mind and persons detained by order of a court.

117. Application to London. [*Repealed by the London Government Act, 1963, s. 93 and Sched. XVIII. See that Act, Part I, and Sched. I and Part IV, s. 30.*]

118. Application to Isles of Scilly.—[*Not printed.*]

119. Commencement.—[*Not printed.*]

120. Amendment of enactments.—(2) In relation to any young person punishable under this Act or under section seventy-eight of the Unemployment Insurance Act, 1935, section fifty-four of the Children and Young Persons Act, 1933 (which relate to the substitution of other punishments for imprisonment), shall have effect as if references therein to a young person included references to any person who has not attained the age of eighteen years.

NOTES

This section is printed as amended by the Criminal Justice Act, 1948.

See note " Imprisonment under 18," to s. 17 of the Criminal Justice Act, 1948, p. 373, *post*, and see s. 107 of the Magistrates' Courts Act, 1952; 21 Halsbury's Statutes, 3rd Edn., 277.

"**Section 54 of the Children and Young Persons Act, 1933.**"—This section is now repealed, see p. 59, *ante*.

EDUCATION (MISCELLANEOUS PROVISIONS) ACT, 1948
[11 & 12 Geo. 6, c. 40]

8. Cancellation of report that a child is incapable of receiving education at school owing to disability of mind.—[*Repealed by the Mental Health Act*, 1959].

9. Presumption of age in proceedings to enforce attendance at school.—(1) For the purposes of a prosecution of the parent of a child for an offence against section thirty-seven or section thirty-nine of the principal Act (which relate respectively to failure to comply with a school attendance order and to failure of a child to attend regularly at school), in so far as the child's having been of compulsory school age at any time is material, the child shall be presumed to have been of compulsory school age at that time unless the parent proves the contrary.

(2) An obligation under the preceding subsection to presume a child to have been of compulsory school age at any time shall be in substitution, so far as regards the purposes for which that presumption is required to be made, for the power conferred on the court by subsection (1) of section ninety-five of the principal Act (which is a power to presume a person to be under, of, or over, an age alleged by the person by whom any proceedings under the principal Act are brought on his satisfying the court that, having used all reasonable diligence to obtain evidence as to the age of that person, he has been unable to do so).

NOTE

" **Principal Act.**"—*I.e.*, the Education Act, 1944.   For ss. 37, 39 and 95 (1), see pp. 253, 256, 269, *ante*.

EDUCATION ACT, 1962
[10 & 11 Eliz. 2, c. 12]

9. School leaving dates in England and Wales.—(1) The provisions of sub-ss. (2) to (4) of this section shall have effect in relation to any person who on a date when either—

(a) he is a registered pupil at a school, or

(b) not being such a pupil, he has been a registered pupil at a school within the preceding period of twelve months, attains an age (which apart from this section) would in his case be the upper limit of the compulsory school age.

(2) If he attains that age on any date from the beginning of September to the end of January, he shall be deemed not to have attained that age until the end of the appropriate spring term at his school.

(3) If he attains that age on any date on or after the beginning of February but before the end of the appropriate summer term at his school, he shall be deemed not to have attained that age until the end of that summer term.

(4) If he attains that age on any date between the end of the appropriate summer term at his school and the beginning of September next following the end of that summer term (whether another term has then begun or not) he shall be deemed to have attained that age at the end of that summer term.

(5) The provisions of this section shall have effect for the purposes of the Act of 1944, and for the purposes of any enactment whereby the definition of compulsory school age in that Act is applied or incorporated; and for references in any enactment to s. 8 of the Education Act, 1946, there shall, in relation to compulsory school age, be substituted references to this section:

Provided that for the purposes of any enactment relating to family allowances or national insurance (including industrial injuries insurance) the provisions of this section shall have effect as if sub-s. (4) thereof were omitted.

(6) This section shall not apply where the date referred to in sub-s. (1) thereof is a date before the beginning of September nineteen hundred and sixty-three.

(7) In this section " the appropriate spring term " in relation to a person, means the last term at his school which ends before the month of May next following the date on which he attains the age in question, and the " appropriate summer term ", in relation to a person means the last term at his school which ends before the month of September next following that date; and any reference to a person's school is a reference to the last school at which he is a registered pupil for a term ending before the said month of May or month of September (as the case may be) or for part of such a term.

NOTES

The Act of 1944 is the Education Act, 1944.

Education Act, 1946, s. 8.—This section is repealed by the Education Act, 1962.

"**Attains an age.**"—This section does not affect children who have stayed on beyond the limit of compulsory education. These cases apart, there are effectively two school leaving dates; at Easter and summer.

SECTION 5.—SUMMARY TRIAL OF INDICTABLE OFFENCES

INTRODUCTORY NOTE

Apart from homicide and the other exceptions contained in s. 6 of the Children and Young Persons Act, 1969, charges against a juvenile are to be tried summarily. For trial on indictment, see *Stone's Justices' Manual*, 104th Edn.

MAGISTRATES' COURTS ACT, 1952
[15 & 16 Geo. 6 & 1 Eliz. 2, c. 55]

20. Summary trial of information against young person for indictable offence.—[*Repealed by the Children and Young Persons Act, 1969, s. 72 (4) and Sched. VI. See now the provisions of section 6 (1) of the 1969 Act.*]

NOTE

Effect of repeal.—Reference to this section and s. 21 (*post*) in s. 104 of the Magistrates' Courts Act, 1952 are to be construed as a reference to s. 6 of the Children and Young Persons Act, 1969 (Administration of Justice Act, 1970, s. 51 (1)).

21. Summary trial of information against child.—[*Repealed by the Children and Young Persons Act, 1969, s. 72 (4) and Sched. VI. See now the provisions of section 6 (1) of the 1969 Act. See note to s. 20, Effect of Repeal,* supra.]

*　　　　*　　　　*　　　　*

24. Restriction on discontinuing trial and then taking depositions.—Except as provided in subsection (5) of section eighteen of this Act, or section 13 of the Criminal Justice Administration Act, 1962 a magistrates' court, having begun to try an information for any indictable offence summarily, shall not thereafter proceed to inquire into the information as examining justices.

NOTE

This section is printed as amended by the Criminal Justice Administration Act, 1962.

Section 18 of the 1952 Act as amended by s. 6 (2) of the 1969 Act applies only in the case of a person who has attained the age of seventeen who appears before a magistrates' court. Similarly by reason of the repeal of s. 20 of the 1952 Act by Sched. V of the 1969 Act, s. 13 of the Criminal Justice Administration Act 1962 does not apply to defendants who have not attained the age of seventeen.

The provisions as to the summary trial of juveniles are now contained in s. 6 of the 1969 Act, p. 144, *post.*

25. Right to claim trial by jury for certain summary offences.—
(1) Where a person who has attained the age of seventeen is charged
before a magistrates' court with a summary offence for which he is liable,
or would if he were adult be liable, to be sentenced by the court to
imprisonment for a term exceeding three months, he may, subject to the
provisions of this section, claim to be tried by a jury, unless the offence
is an assault or an offence under sections thirty or thirty-one of the
Sexual Offences Act, 1956, or an offence under section thirty-two of that
Act where the immoral purpose is other than the commission of a homosexual act.

(2) Where under the preceding subsection or any other enactment a
person charged with a summary offence is entitled to claim to be tried
by a jury, his claim shall be of no effect unless he appears in person and
makes it before he pleads to the charge; and, where under any enactment the prosecutor is entitled to claim that the accused shall be tried
by a jury, his claim shall be of no effect unless he makes it before the
accused pleads to the charge.

(3) A magistrates' court before which a person is charged with a
summary offence for which he may claim to be tried by a jury shall,
before asking him whether he pleads guilty, inform him of his right and,
if the court thinks it desirable for the information of the accused, explain
what is meant by being tried summarily; and shall then ask him whether
he wishes, instead of being tried summarily, to be tried by a jury.

(4) Where the accused is charged with an offence for which he is
entitled under subsection (1) of this section to be tried by a jury if he has
been previously convicted of a like offence but not otherwise, the court
shall explain to him that he may have a right to claim trial by a jury and,
after giving him the same information as is provided by the last preceding
subsection, shall ask him whether, if he has that right, he wishes, instead
of being tried summarily, to be tried by a jury.

(5) Where the accused is charged with an offence that is both—

    (a) a summary offence for which the accused may claim to be tried
        by a jury and

    (b) an indictable offence,

then, if the court, having begun under subsection (1) of section eighteen
of this Act to proceed as if the offence were not a summary one, proceeds
under subsection (3) of that section with a view to summary trial, it shall,
before asking the accused whether he wishes to be tried by a jury, explain
to him that if he is tried summarily and is convicted he may be committed for sentence to the Crown Court under section twenty-nine of this
Act if the court, on obtaining information of his character and antecedents, is of opinion that they are such that greater punishment should
be inflicted than the court has power to inflict.

(6) If—

    (a) under this section or under any other enactment a person charged
        with a summary offence is entitled to claim to be tried by a
        jury and claims to be so tried; or

(b) the prosecutor exercises a right conferred on him by any enactment to claim that the accused shall be tried by a jury,

the court shall thereupon deal with the information in all respects as if it were for an offence punishable on conviction on indictment only; and the offence, whether or not indictable otherwise than by virtue of any such claim, shall as respects the accused be deemed to be an indictable offence.

NOTES

This section is printed as amended by the Sexual Offences Act, 1967, s. 9, Criminal Law Act 1967, Sched. III, and the Children and Young Persons Act, 1969, s. 6 (2), and the Courts Act, 1971, s. 56 and Sched. XI.

As from 1st January 1971 this section applies only in cases where the defendant has attained the age of 17 (Children and Young Persons Act, 1969, s. 6 (2)).

For the provisions as to the summary trial of juveniles, see now s. 6 (1) of the 1969 Act, p. 144, *ante.*

*   *   *   *

32. Fines in respect of children.—*A magistrates' court shall not on finding guilty a person under fourteen years old impose a fine of more than ten pounds.*

NOTE

From a date to be appointed this section is repealed (Children and Young Persons Act, 1969, s. 72 (4) and Sched. VI).

*   *   *   *

125. " Summary " and " Indictable " offence.—*[This section is reproduced with notes at p.* 386, post.]

126. Interpretation of other terms.—*[This section is reproduced with notes at p.* 386, post.]

SECTION 6.—PROBATION AND ABSOLUTE OR CONDITIONAL DISCHARGE

INTRODUCTORY NOTE

One of the effects of the Children and Young Persons Act, 1969, was to abolish the probation order for those under the age of seventeen. The treatment of a juvenile offender is now in most respects on a par with the juvenile in need of care or control.

The supervision order, entailing supervision by a probation officer or local authority social worker, requires the supervisor to advise, assist and befriend, and in the case of a child below the minimum age for prosecution the local authority will normally supervise. Nevertheless, these provisions relating to probation orders are included as, for a while, juvenile courts will still be concerned with them. The repeal of s. 48 of the Children and Young Persons Act, 1933, does not affect its operation in relation to a person subject to a probation order made before January 1, 1971 (S.I. 1971 No. 1498, Sched. III, para. 2). The provisions as to breach of probation and commission of a further offence are still relevant therefore. Further a juvenile who attains the age of seventeen before sentence *may* be placed on probation by a juvenile court although s. 29 of the Children and Young Persons Act clearly envisages supervision.

Sched. 5, para 6, to the Criminal Justice Act, 1948, confers on the Secretary of State the power to make rules with relation to the functions of probation and case committees and other matters. The Probation Rules 1965 were made on March 31, 1965 under that Schedule, and the following extracts are printed at pp. 527, *et seq., post :—*

> Part IV.—Duties of probation officers.
> Part V.—Expenditure on persons for whom probation officer is responsible.
> S. 52.—Interpretation.
> Sched. I.—Payments in respect of persons under supervision.

The Approved Probation Hostel and Home Rules, 1949, were made under s. 46 (2) of the Criminal Justice Act, 1948.

The relevant provisions of the Criminal Justice Act, 1948, are printed below with notes. A court of summary jurisdiction, on finding a juvenile guilty of an offence, may discharge him absolutely, or conditionally upon his committing no further offence during a stated period of not more than three years, or may make a supervision order. A probation order may be discharged upon the application of the probation officer or the probationer. Probation and conditional discharge are without recognisance, and there is a separate procedure in respect of the breach of the requirements of a probation order and of the commission of a further offence. Requirements as to mental treatment during probation may be inserted in a probation order. The organisation of probation committees, case committees and supervising courts is dealt with in Sched. V.

CRIMINAL JUSTICE ACT, 1948
[11 & 12 Geo. 6, c. 58]

Probation and Discharge

3. Probation.—(1) Where a court by or before which a person who has attained the age of seventeen is convicted of an offence (not being an offence the sentence for which is fixed by law) is of opinion that having regard to the circumstances, including the nature of the offence and the character of the offender, it is expedient to do so, the court may, instead of sentencing him, make a probation order, that is to say, an order requiring him to be under the supervision of a probation officer for a period to be specified in the order of not less than one year nor more than three years.

(2) A probation order shall name the petty sessional division in which the offender resides or will reside; and the offender shall (subject to the provisions of the First Schedule to this Act relating to probationers who change their residence) be required to be under the supervision of a probation officer appointed for or assigned to that division.

(3) Subject to the provisions of the next following section, a probation order may in addition require the offender to comply during the whole or any part of the probation period with such requirements as the court, having regard to the circumstances of the case, considers necessary for securing the good conduct of the offender or for preventing a repetition by him of the same offence or the commission of other offences:

Provided that (without prejudice to the power of the court to make an order under subsection (2) of section eleven of this Act) the payment of sums by way of damages for injury or compensation for loss shall not be included among the requirements of a probation order.

(4) Without prejudice to the generality of the last foregoing subsection, a probation order may include requirements relating to the residence of the offender:

Provided that—

(a) before making an order containing any such requirements, the court shall consider the home surroundings of the offender; and

(b) where the order requires the offender to reside in an approved probation hostel, an approved probation home or any other institution, the name of the institution and the period for which he is so required to reside shall be specified in the order, and that period shall not extend beyond twelve months from the date of the order.

(5) Before making a probation order, the court shall explain to the offender in ordinary language the effect of the order (including any additional requirements proposed to be inserted therein under subsection (3) or subsection (4) of this section or under the next following section) and that if he fails to comply therewith or commits another offence he will be liable to be sentenced for the original offence; and the court shall not make the order unless he expresses his willingness to comply with the requirements thereof.

(6) The court by which a probation order is made shall forthwith give copies of the order to a probation officer assigned to the court, and he shall give a copy to the offender, to the probation officer responsible for the supervision of the offender and to the person in charge of any institution in which the probationer is required by the order to reside; and the court shall, except where it is itself the supervising court, send to the clerk to the justices for the petty sessional division named in the order a copy of the order, together with such documents and information relating to the case as it considers likely to be of assistance to the supervising court.

(7) Where a probation order requires the offender to reside in any institution, not being—

(a) an approved probation hostel or approved probation home; or
(b) an institution in which he is required to reside for the purposes of any such treatment as is mentioned in paragraph (a) or paragraph (b) of subsection (2) of the next following section,

the court shall forthwith give notice of the terms of the order to the Secretary of State.

NOTES

This section is printed as amended by the Children and Young Persons Act, 1969, s. 7 (2) and Sched. VI.

" **Offence the sentence for which is fixed by law.**"—See the definition in s. 80 (1), p. 293.

" **Having regard to . . .**"—The various factors to which the court may give consideration in deciding to deal with a case under the Act show how wide a discretion is conferred upon the justices, but it must be exercised judicially, and in a number of cases the High Court has overruled the decision of the justices when the earlier law had been unsuitably used, or where they have taken extraneous matters into consideration. The principles laid down in those cases will often apply. It is possible to apply these provisions in spite of previous convictions (*Vinters* v. *Freedman* (1901), 71 L. J. K. B. 48; 66 J. P. 135). They must not be used as a means of evading the law or of encouraging persistent offenders in their contumacy (*Eversfield* v. *Story*, [1942] 1 K. B. 437; [1942] 1 All E. R. 268; 106 J. P. 113).

Residence.—Where a person is required by a probation order to reside in an institution it will be the duty of the probation and after-care committee to make such payments as may be prescribed in respect of him, and the sums required will be defrayed by the local authority, but the Secretary of State may relieve the local authority of the liability in certain cases (Criminal Justice Act, 1948, s. 45 (1) and Sched. V, paras. 3 and 5). The Secretary of State may with the approval of the Treasury direct the payment of grants towards the expenditure of local authorities under Sched. V (*ibid.*, s. 77 (3)).

See s. 46, *post*, as to probation hostels and homes, and s. 47 as to inspection of institutions for residence of probationers. The period of residence, whether required by the original order or upon variation under Sched. I, must not exceed twelve months. See the Approved Probation Hostel and Home Rules, 1949.

As to fines outstanding against approved probation hostel and home residents see Home office Circular No. 178/1969.

Young person.—For power to make a supervision order where a young person is found guilty of an offence see the Children and Young Persons Act, 1969, ss. 7 (7) and 12.

Approved probation hostels and homes.—As to the obligation to receive a probationer or a person who is the subject of a supervision order, see r. 9 of the Approved Probation Hostel and Home Rules, 1949 (S.I. 1949 No. 1376).

Residents in approved probation hostels and homes—hospital cases.— When a resident goes to hospital the warden is required to notify the supervising probation officer immediately so that application may be made to the supervising court, if necessary, to cancel the requirement as to residence. If the resident is likely to return to the hostel or home a place is to be reserved for him. See Home Office Circular 56/57 dated March 22, 1957.

Irish offenders.—In the case of *R. v. McCartan*, [1958] 3 All E. R. 140; 122 J. P. 465, C. C. A., referred by the Secretary of State under s. 18 (b) of the Criminal Appeal Act, 1907 (now repealed and replaced by s. 17 of the Criminal Appeal Act, 1968) the Lord Chief Justice in giving the judgment of the Court of Criminal Appeal said that in the opinion of that Court an order could not be made under this section including a requirement that the probationer should return to Ireland and stay there, and that the way to obtain this result was to bind the offender over in the form of a common law recognizance, and make it a condition of the recognizance that he returns to Ireland and does not return to this country for such a period as the court may think fit.

This case had been dealt with in a Court of Assize, and no mention was made in the judgment of courts of inferior jurisdiction. Apart from this reference we are not aware of any authority for such courts to require an offender to enter into such a recognizance.

In Home Office letter 134/60/N dated August 31, 1960, it is stated that where a court of record makes use of this power and the offender is without means, the Prison Commissioners will meet the cost of his journey.

Explanation.—A probation officer is required to endeavour to ensure that a person under his supervision understands the effect of the order, and a court's power to amend or discharge it. Rule 33 of the Probation Rules 1965, p. 528.

Rules.—See the Probation Rules, 1965, S.I. 1965 No. 723, as amended by the Probation Rules, 1967, S.I. 1967 No. 1884.

As to expenses in hostels and homes see Rule 40 *ibid.*, p. 530, and Home Office circulars, pp. 692, *post.*

Supervision.—A probation officer under whose supervision a woman or girl may be placed in pursuance of an order under this section may be a man or a woman (Criminal Justice Act, 1967, s. 55).

Discharge.—See s. 5 and Sched. I, as modified by the Criminal Justice Act, 1967, s. 54.

Conditional discharge.—As to the power to substitute an order of conditional discharge see Criminal Justice Act, 1967, s. 53.

4. Probation orders requiring treatment for mental condition.—

(1) Where the court is satisfied, on the evidence of a duly qualified medical practitioner approved for the purposes of section twenty-eight of the Mental Health Act, 1959, that the mental condition of an offender is such as requires and may be susceptible to treatment but is not such as to warrant his detention in pursuance of a hospital order under Part V of that Act, the court may, if it makes a probation order, include therein a requirement that the offender shall submit, for such period not extending beyond twelve months from the date of the order as may be specified therein, to treatment by or under the direction of a duly qualified medical practitioner with a view to the improvement of the offender's mental condition.

(2) The treatment required by any such order shall be such one of the following kinds of treatment as may be specified in the order, that is to say—

    (a) treatment as a resident patient in a hospital or mental nursing home within the meaning of the Mental Health Act, 1959, not being a special hospital within the meaning of the Act.

    (b) . . .

(c) treatment as a non-resident patient at such institution or place as may be specified in the order; or

(d) treatment by or under the direction of such duly qualified medical practitioner as may be specified in the order;

but except as aforesaid the nature of the treatment shall not be specified in the order.

(3) A court shall not make a probation order containing such a requirement as aforesaid unless it is satisfied that arrangements have been made for the treatment intended to be specified in the order, and, if the offender is to be treated as a resident patient as aforesaid, for his reception.

(4) While the probationer is under treatment as a resident patient in pursuance of a requirement of the probation order, the probation officer responsible for his supervision shall carry out the supervision to such extent only as may be necessary for the purpose of the discharge or amendment of the order.

(5) Where the medical practitioner by whom or under whose direction a probationer is being treated for his mental condition in pursuance of a probation order is of opinion that part of the treatment can be better or more conveniently given in or at an institution or place not specified in the order, being an institution or place in or at which the treatment of the probationer will be given by or under the direction of a duly qualified medical practitioner, he may, with the consent of the probationer, make arrangements for him to be treated accordingly; and the arrangements may provide for the probationer to receive part of his treatment as a resident patient in an institution or place notwithstanding that the institution or place is not one which could have been specified in that behalf in the probation order.

(6) Where any such arrangements as are mentioned in the last foregoing section are made for the treatment of a probationer—

(a) the medical practitioner by whom the arrangements are made shall give notice in writing to the probation officer responsible for the supervision of the probationer, specifying the institution or place in or at which the treatment is to be carried out; and

(b) the treatment provided for by the arrangements shall be deemed to be treatment to which he is required to submit in pursuance of the probation order.

(7) Subsections (2) and (3) of section sixty-two of the Mental Health Act, 1959, shall apply for the purposes of this section as if for the reference in the said subsection (2) to paragraph (a) of subsection (1) of section sixty of that Act there were substituted a reference to subsection (1) of this section.

(8) . . .

(9) Except as provided by this section, a court shall not make a probation order requiring a probationer to submit to treatment for his mental condition.

NOTES

This section is printed as amended by the Mental Health Act, 1959.

Change of arrangements.—Sub-ss. (5) and (6) allow change of arrangements without prior reference to the court or the probation officer. The probation officer has to be informed, however, and he would no doubt inform the supervising court and the case committee.

Further provisions dealing with treatment are in para. 4 of the First Schedule.

There is an exception to sub-s. (9) for probationers residing or intending to reside in Scotland. See Criminal Justice Act, 1967, s. 54 (7), p. 302.

5. Discharge, amendment and review of probation orders.— (1) The provisions of the First Schedule to this Act shall have effect in relation to the discharge and amendment of probation orders.

(2) and (3) [*From October 1st, 1967 these subsections are repealed as to England and Wales. (Criminal Justice Act, 1967, ss. 54 and 103 and Sched. VII.)*

The parallel provisions relating to Scotland in ss. 4 (2) and 4 (3) of the Criminal Justice (Scotland) Act, 1949, are repealed from April 1st, 1969 (Social Work (Scotland) Act, 1968, s. 95 (2) and Sched. IX).]

(4) Where, under the following provisions of this Part of this Act, a probationer is sentenced for the offence for which he was placed on probation, the probation order shall cease to have effect.

NOTE

Cease to have effect.—This is without prejudice to the continuance of an order for costs, damages or compensation made in accordance with s. 11 (2) Criminal Justice Act, 1948. (*R. v. Evans*, [1963] 1 Q. B. 979; [1961] 1 All E. R. 313; 125 J. P. 134.)

Conditional discharge.—As to the power to substitute for a probation order an order of conditional discharge see Criminal Justice Act, 1967, s. 53.

6. Breach of requirement of probation order.—(1) If at any time during the probation period it appears on information to a justice of the peace on whom jurisdiction is hereinafter conferred that the probationer has failed to comply with any of the requirements of the order, the justice may issue a summons requiring the probationer to appear at the place and time specified therein, or may, if the information is in writing and on oath, issue a warrant for his arrest.

(2) The following justices shall have jurisdiction for the purposes of the foregoing subsection, that is to say—

    (a) if the probation order was made by a court of summary juris-diction, any justice acting for the petty sessional division or place for which that court or the supervising court acts;

    (b) in any other case, any justice acting for the petty sessional division or place for which the supervising court acts;

and any summons or warrant issued under this section shall direct the probationer to appear or be brought before a court of summary jurisdiction for the petty sessional division or place for which the justice issuing the summons or warrant acts.

(3) If it is proved to the satisfaction of the court before which a pro-bationer appears or is brought under this section that the probationer has failed to comply with any of the requirements of the probation order, that court may without prejudice to the continuance of the probation order, impose on him a fine not exceeding twenty pounds or, in a case to which

section nineteen of this Act applies, make an order under that section requiring him to attend at an attendance centre, or may—

(a) if the probation order was made by a court of summary jurisdiction, deal with the probationer, for the offence in respect of
which the probation order was made, in any manner in which
the court could deal with him if it had just convicted him of that
offence;

(b) if the probation order was made by the Crown Court, commit him
to custody or release him on bail (with or without sureties) until
he can be brought or appear before the court of assize or quarter
sessions.

(4) Where the court of summary jurisdiction deals with the case as provided in paragraph (b) of the last foregoing subsection then—

(a) the court shall send to the Crown Court a certificate signed by a
justice of the peace, certifying that the probationer has failed
to comply with such of the requirements of the probation order
as may be specified in the certificate, together with such other
particulars of the case as may be desirable; and a certificate
purporting to be so signed shall be admissible as evidence of the
failure before the court of assize or quarter sessions; and

(b) where the probationer is brought or appears before the Crown
Court and it is proved to the satisfaction of that court that
he has failed to comply with any of the requirements of the
probation order, that court may deal, with him, for the offence
in respect of which the probation order was made, in any
manner in which the court could deal with him if he had just
been convicted before that court of that offence.

(5) A fine imposed under this section in respect of a failure to comply with the requirements of a probation order shall be deemed for the purposes of any enactment to be a sum adjudged to be paid by a conviction.

(6) A probationer who is required by the probation order to submit to treatment for his mental condition shall not be treated for the purposes of this section as having failed to comply with that requirement on the ground only that he has refused to undergo any surgical, electrical or other treatment if, in the opinion of the court, his refusal was reasonable having regard to all the circumstances; and without prejudice to the provisions of section eight of this Act, a probationer who is convicted of an offence committed during the probation period shall not on that account be liable to be dealt with under this section for failing to comply with any requirement of the probation order.

NOTES

This section is printed as amended by the Criminal Justice Act, 1967, s. 54 (5) and the Courts Act, 1971.

" **During the probation period.**"—It is to be noted that the information must be laid during the probation period, or it will be out of time.

Bail on arrest.—A warrant may be endorsed for bail (Magistrates' Courts Act, 1952, s. 93; 21 Halsbury's Statutes, 3rd Edn., 265).

"**The Court.**"—Where the probation order was in force prior to January 1, 1971 a juvenile court can deal with a probationer, although he has attained the age of seventeen years, during the probation period. See the Children and Young Persons Act, 1933, s. 48 (2), and the Children and Young Persons Act, 1969, Scheds. V and VI and Sched. IV, paras. 5 (2) and 18. See also S.I. 1970 No. 1498, p. 614, *post*.

Maximum fine.—The maximum fine which may be imposed by a magistrates' court under sub-s. (3) shall be twenty pounds instead of ten pounds. A fine not exceeding twenty pounds may, without prejudice to the continuance in force of the probation order, be imposed by the Crown Court instead of dealing with a failure to comply with the requirement of a probation order under sub-s. (4) (b) (Criminal Justice Act, 1967, s. 54 (5)).

" **Section nineteen of this Act.**"—See p. 373, *post*.

" **Certificate.**"—The certificate is admissible evidence, but the section does not say in terms that it is conclusive. It must be proved to the satisfaction of the court that the probationer has failed to comply with a requirement of the probation order before that court may deal with him for the original offence. It would therefore appear that the court may give the probationer an opportunity of disputing the certificate and may hear evidence for both prosecution and defence.

See *R.* v. *Chapman and Pidgley*, [1960] 1 All E. R. 452; 124 J. P. 219, in which it was held in the Court of Criminal Appeal that if the prisoner does not admit all the matters, including the alleged breach, the matter not admitted must be strictly proved. In *R.* v. *Tucker* (1967), 111 Sol. Jo. 516, C. A. at quarter sessions there was no trial of the issue whether there was a breach of a condition of a probation order. It was held that the magistrates' certificate was not conclusive and that the proceedings were a nullity. The matter was returned to quarter sessions for further consideration.

Fine.—As to enforcement of a fine, see pp. 314–321.

" **Just been convicted.**".—The powers of the court to deal with an offender after he has reached the age of seventeen are those which would be exercisable if the offence in respect of which the order was made were an offence which could have been tried summarily under s. 19 of the Magistrates' Courts Act, 1952, with the offender's consent, and had been so tried. (See s. 9 of the Criminal Justice Act, 1961, p. 300, *post*, and the operation of this section is not affected by its repeal in relation to probation orders made before January 1, 1971 (S.I. 1970 No. 1498, Sched. III, para. 2, p. 623, *post*).)

" **Power of court.**"—This includes the power to make a fresh probation order See *R.* v. *Havant Justices, Ex parte Jacobs*, [1957] 1 All E. R. 475; 121 J. P. 197. See also *R.* v. *Thompson*, [1969] 1 All E. R. 60; 133 J. P. 71, C. A. A court should only make a fresh probation order after a "proper reflection".

" **Procedure.**"—The alleged breach of requirement should be put clearly to the defendant and if he does not admit it, the case should be tried on that issue. See *R.* v. *Devine*, [1956] 1 All E. R. 548; 120 J. P. 238, C. C. A.

Compensation order.—See note to s. 11 (2), p. 290, *post*, as to the effect of sub-s. (4) on an order for the payment of compensation.

Committal under sub-s. (3) (b).—As to release on bail see Criminal Justice Act, 1967, s. 54 (4).

7. Absolute and conditional discharge.—(1) Where a court by or before which a person is convicted of an offence (not being an offence the sentence for which is fixed by law) is of opinion, having regard to the circumstances including the nature of the offence and the character of the offender, that it is inexpedient to inflict punishment and that a probation order is not appropriate, the court may make an order discharging him absolutely, or, if the court thinks fit, discharging him subject to the condition that he commits no offence during such period, not exceeding three years from the date of the order, as may be specified therein.

(2) An order discharging a person subject to such a condition as aforesaid is in this Act referred to as " an order for conditional discharge," and the period specified in any such order as " the period of conditional discharge."

(3) Before making an order for conditional discharge the court shall explain to the offender in ordinary language that if he commits another offence during the period of conditional discharge he will be liable to be sentenced for the original offence.

(4) Where, under the following provisions of this Part of this Act, a person conditionally discharged under this section is sentenced for the offence in respect of which the order for conditional discharge was made, that order shall cease to have effect.

NOTES

This section is printed as amended by the Criminal Justice Act, 1967, s. 52.

Offence the sentence for which is fixed by law.—See the definition in s. 80 (1) of the Act, p. 293.

Conditional discharge.—There is no need to obtain the defendant's consent to such an order.

8. Commission of further offence.—(1) If it appears to a judge or justice of the peace on whom jurisdiction is hereinafter conferred that a person in whose case a probation order or an order for conditional discharge has been made has been convicted by a court in any part of Great Britain of an offence committed during the probation period or during the period of conditional discharge, and has been dealt with in respect of that offence, the judge or justice may issue a summons requiring that person to appear at the place and time specified therein, or may issue a warrant for his arrest:

Provided that a justice of the peace shall not issue such a summons except on information and shall not issue such a warrant except on information in writing and on oath.

(2) The following persons shall have jurisdiction for the purposes of the foregoing subsection, that is to say—

    (a) if the probation order or order for conditional discharge was made by the Crown Court, that court;

    (b)–(c) [*Repealed by the Courts Act, 1971.*]

    (d) if the order was made by a court of summary jurisdiction, a justice acting for the petty sessional division or place for which that court acts;

    (e) in the case of a probation order, by whatever court it was made, a justice acting for the petty sessional division or place for which the supervising court acts.

(3) A summons or warrant issued under this section shall direct the person so convicted to appear or to be brought before the court by which the probation order or the order for conditional discharge was made:

Provided that—

(a) if that court is a court of summary jurisdiction and the summons or warrant is issued by a justice acting for the petty sessional division for which the supervising court acts, the summons or warrant may direct him to appear or to be brought before the supervising court; and

(b) [*Repealed by the Courts Act, 1971.*]

(4) If a person in whose case a probation order or an order for conditional discharge has been made by the Crown Court is convicted by a court of summary jurisdiction in respect of an offence committed during the probation period or during the period of conditional discharge, the court of summary jurisdiction may commit him to custody or release him on bail (with or without sureties) until he can be brought or appear before the court by which the order was made; and if it does so the court of summary jurisdiction shall send to the Crown Court a copy of the minute or memorandum of the conviction entered in the register required to be kept under section twenty-two of the Summary Jurisdiction Act, 1879, signed by the clerk of the court by whom the register is kept.

(5) Where it is proved to the satisfaction of the court by which a probation order or an order for conditional discharge was made, or, if the order (being a probation order) was made by a court of summary jurisdiction, to the satisfaction of that court or the supervising court, that the person in whose case that order was made has been convicted of an offence committed during the probation period, or during the period of conditional discharge, as the case may be, the court may deal with him, for the offence for which the order was made, in any manner in which the court could deal with him if he had just been convicted by or before that court of that offence.

(6) If a person in whose case a probation order or an order for conditional discharge has been made by a court of summary jurisdiction is convicted before the Crown Court of an offence committed during the probation period or during the period of conditional discharge, or is dealt with by a court of assize or quarter sessions for an offence so committed in respect of which he was committed for sentence to that court, the Crown Court may deal with him, for the offence for which the order was made, in any manner in which the court of summary jurisdiction could deal with him if it had just convicted him of that offence.

(7) If a person in whose case a probation order or an order for conditional discharge has been made by a court of summary jurisdiction is convicted by another court of summary jurisdiction of any offence committed during the probation period, or during the period of conditional discharge, that court may, with the consent of the court which made the order or, in the case of a probation order, with the consent of that court or of the supervising court, deal with him, for the offence for which the order was made, in any manner in which the court could deal with him if it had just convicted him of that offence.

(8) In this section the expression "committing justice," in relation to a person in whose case a probation order or an order for conditional discharge has been made by the Crown Court, includes any justice acting

for the petty sessional division or place for which the justices acted by whom he was committed for trial or for sentence.

NOTES

This section is printed as amended as to England and Wales by the Criminal Justice Act, 1967, ss. 56 (3), 103 and Sched. VII, and the Courts Act, 1971.

Bail on arrest.—A warrant issued under this section by a justice requiring him to be brought before a magistrates' court, may be endorsed for bail by virtue of s. 93 of the Magistrates' Courts Act, 1952; 32 Halsbury's Statutes, 2nd Edn., 495.

Subsection (4).—It is clear that the court is not bound in all circumstances, *e.g.*, if the further offence is trifling, to send the offender to the Crown Court. The word is " may," and is followed by the words " if it does so."

Extract from register.—Section 22 of the Summary Jurisdiction Act, 1879, was repealed by the Magistrates' Courts Act, 1952. See now rule 54 of the Magistrates' Courts Rules, 1968.

Just been convicted.—See note to s. 6, p. 285, *ante.*

Taking original offence into consideration.—The original offence should not be taken into consideration in dealing with the subsequent offence but should be dealt with by a separate adjudication. *R.* v. *Devine*, [1956], I All E. R. 548; 120 J. P. 238; *R.* v. *Webb*, [1953], I All E. R. 1156; 117 J. P. 319; and *R.* v. *Fry*, [1955] I All E. R. 21, 119 J. P. 75; The sentence should in general be made consecutive and should be more than a nominal one. Where, however, the offender is to undergo borstal training for the substantive offence, a consecutive sentence of imprisonment would not be appropriate. In such cases the court could pass a concurrent sentence of imprisonment for six months or less, or a sentence of borstal training. If however, the original order were made by a magistrates' court, then it would be proper to pass a concurrent nominal sentence. (*Per* Hinchcliffe, J., after consultation with Lord Parker, C.J., *R.* v. *Stuart*, [1964] 3 All E. R. 672; 129 J. P. 35 (C. C. A.)).

Breach of two current probation orders.—In the case of *R.* v. *Keeley*, [1960] 2 All E. R. 415, 124 J. P. 325, it was held that although the first probation order might be ineffective for supervision purposes during the currency of the second probation order, nevertheless it remained in full effect to enable a court to impose a punishment for the original offence.

Costs.—The costs of these proceedings are to be treated for the purposes of the Costs in Criminal Cases Act, 1952, as part of the costs of the original proceedings (Criminal Justice Act, 1967, s. 31 (4)).

9. Probation orders relating to persons residing in Scotland.—

(1) Where the court by which a probation order is made under section three of this Act is satisfied that the offender resides or will reside in Scotland, subsection (2) of that section shall not apply to the order, but the order shall specify as the appropriate court for the purposes of this section a court of summary jurisdiction (which, in the case of an offender convicted on indictment, shall be the sheriff court) having jurisdiction in the place in Scotland in which the offender resides or will reside.

(2) Where a probation order has been made under section three of this Act and the supervising court is satisfied that the probationer proposes to reside or is residing in Scotland, the power of that court to amend the order under the First Schedule to this Act shall include power to amend it by substituting for the provisions required by subsection (2) of the said section three the provisions required by subsection (1) of this section; and the court may so amend the order without summoning the probationer and without his consent.

(3) [*Repealed by the Criminal Justice Act, 1967, s. 103 and Sched. VII.*]

(4) Subsection (1) of section five and subsections (1) and (2) of section six of this Act shall not apply to any order made or amended under this section; but the provisions of the Criminal Justice (Scotland) Act, 1949 (except paragraph (b) of subsection (2) of section five and section six of that Act) shall apply to the order as if it were a probation order made under section two of that Act and as if the court specified in the order as the appropriate court had been named as such under subsection (2) of that section.

(5) If in the case of a probation order made or amended under this section the appropriate court (as defined by the Criminal Justice (Scotland) Act, 1949) is satisfied that the probationer has failed to comply with any requirement of the probation order, the court may, instead of dealing with him in any manner authorised by the said Act, commit him to custody or release him on bail until he can be brought or appear before the court in England by which the probation order was made, and, if it so commits him or releases him on bail,—

(a) the court shall send to the said court in England a certificate certifying that the probationer has failed to comply with such of the requirements of the probation order as may be specified in the certificate, together with such other particulars of the case as may be desirable;

(b) that court shall have the same powers as if the probationer had been brought or appeared before it in pursuance of a warrant or summons issued under subsection (1) of section six of this Act;

and a certificate purporting to be signed by the clerk of the appropriate court shall be admissible as evidence of the failure before the court which made the probation order.

(6) In relation to a probation order made or amended under this section, the appropriate court (as defined by the Criminal Justice (Scotland) Act, 1949) shall have jurisdiction for the purposes of subsection (1) of section eight of this Act; and paragraph (a) of the proviso to subsection (3) of that section shall not apply to any summons or warrant issued under that section by that court.

(7) The court by which a probation order is made or amended under this section shall send three copies of the order as made or amended to the clerk of the court specified in the order as the appropriate court, together with such documents and information relating to the case as it considers likely to be of assistance to that court; and subsection (6) of section three of this Act, or paragraph 6 of the First Schedule to this Act, as the case may be, shall not apply to any such order.

(8) Where a probation order which is amended under subsection (2) of this section is an order to which the provisions of this Act apply by virtue of section seven of the Criminal Justice (Scotland) Act, 1949 (which relates to probation orders under that Act relating to persons residing in England), then, notwithstanding anything in that section or this section, the order shall, as from the date of the amendment, have effect in all respects as if it were an order made under section two of that Act in the case of a person residing in Scotland, and as if the court specified as the appropriate court in the order as so amended had been named as such under subsection (2) of the said section two.

(9) *A probation order shall not be made under section 3 of this Act as modified by subsection (1) of this section, or amended under subsection (2) of this section in respect of a person who has not attained the age of sixteen.*

NOTES

This section is printed as substituted by the Criminal Justice (Scotland) Act, 1949, ss. 77, 79 (2) and Sched. XI, and as amended by the Criminal Justice Act, 1967, s. 103 and Sched. VII and the Social Work (Scotland) Act, 1968, ss. 95, 97, 98, and Sched. VIII, para. 21.

From a date to be appointed, the words in italics are added.

Treatment for mental condition.—See Criminal Justice Act, 1967, s. 54 (7).

10. [*Repealed by the Criminal Justice (Scotland) Act,* 1949, *s.* 79 (3) *and Sched. XII, and replaced by s.* 7 *of that Act, pp.* 297, 299.]

11. Supplementary provisions as to probation and discharge.—(1) Any court may, on making a probation order or an order for conditional discharge under this part of this Act, if it thinks it expedient for the purpose of the reformation of the offender, allow any person who consents to do so to give security for the good behaviour of the offender.

(2) A Court, on making a probation order or an order for conditional discharge or on discharging an offender absolutely under this Part of this Act, may, without prejudice to its power of awarding costs against him, order the offender to pay such damages for injury or compensation for loss as the court thinks reasonable; but, in the case of an order made by a court of summary jurisdiction, the damages and compensation together shall not exceed one hundred pounds or such greater sum as may be allowed by any enactment other than this section.

(3) An order for the payment of damages or compensation as aforesaid may be enforced in like manner as an order for the payment of costs by the offender; and where the court, in addition to making such an order for the payment of damages or compensation to any person, orders the offender to pay to that person any costs, the orders for the payment of damages or compensation and for the payment of costs may be enforced as if they constituted a single order for the payment of costs.

(4) In proceedings before the Crown Court under the foregoing provisions of this Act, any question whether a probationer has failed to comply with the requirements of the probation order or has been convicted of an offence committed during the probation period, and any question whether any person in whose case an order for conditional discharge has been made has been convicted of an offence committed during the period of conditional discharge, shall be determined by the court and not by the verdict of a jury.

(5) Section four of the Summary Jurisdiction (Process) Act, 1881, shall apply to any process issued by any judge or justice under the foregoing provisions of this Act, or under section six of the Probation of

Offenders Act, 1907, as it applies to Scotland, as it applies to process issued under the Summary Jurisdiction Acts by a court of summary jurisdiction.

NOTES

This section is printed as amended by the Magistrates' Courts Act, 1952. The Children and Young Persons Act, 1969, s. 72 (4) and Sched. VI, and the Courts Act, 1971.

Payment of money.—The payment of sums for damages or compensation must not be included among the requirements of a probation order (see s. 3 (3) of this Act, p. 279, *ante*). It was held improper to use the probation order made under the Probation of Offenders Act, 1907, as a means of recovering money not the subject of a charge (*R.* v. *Peel*, [1943] 2 All E. R. 99; 107 J. P. 159, C. C. A.).

" Costs."—These are enforceable in summary cases, in the case of an adult, by distress and imprisonment, see Administration of Justice Act, 1970, s. 12, and Sched. IX. In the case of a juvenile enforcement may be by means of a money payment or supervision order but a detention centre or attendance centre order in default of committal to a remand home is no longer possible. As to power to order payment by the parent of a juvenile, see the Children and Young Persons Act, 1933, s. 55, p. 59.

For s. 4 of the Summary Jurisdiction (Process) Act, 1881, see 21 Halsbury's Statutes, 3rd Edn., 56.

Compensation order.—When an offender is sentenced to imprisonment for a breach of probation, an order for compensation continues in force, but the fact that he is still liable to pay compensation may well be a factor to be taken into account by the sentencing court in assessing an appropriate punishment (*R.* v. *Evans*, [1963] 1 Q. B. 979; [1961] 1 All E.R. 313; 125 J.P. 134).

12. Effects of probation and discharge.—(1) Subject as hereinafter provided, a conviction of an offence for which an order is made under this Part of this Act placing the offender on probation or discharging him absolutely or conditionally shall be deemed not to be a conviction for any purpose other than the purposes of the proceedings in which the order is made and of any subsequent proceedings which may be taken against the offender under the foregoing provisions of this Act:

Provided that where an offender, being not less than seventeen years of age at the time of his conviction of an offence for which he is placed on probation or conditionally discharged as aforesaid, is subsequently sentenced under this Part of this Act for that offence, the provisions of this subsection shall cease to apply to the conviction.

(2) Without prejudice to the foregoing provisions of this section, the conviction of an offender who is placed on probation or discharged absolutely or conditionally as aforesaid shall in any event be disregarded for the purposes of any enactment which imposes any disqualification or disability upon convicted persons, or authorises or requires the imposition of any such disqualification or disability.

(3) The foregoing provisions of this section shall not affect—

    (a) any right of any such offender as aforesaid to appeal against his conviction, or to rely thereon in bar of any subsequent proceedings for the same offence;

    (b) the revesting or restoration of any property in consequence of conviction of any such offender; or

(c) the operation, in relation to any such offender, of any enactment in force at the commencement of this Act which is expressed to extend to persons dealt with under subsection (1) of section one of the Probation of Offenders Act, 1907, as well as to convicted persons.

NOTE

Disqualification or disability.—The commonest type of disqualification by magistrates' courts is for certain offences under the Road Traffic Acts.

Notwithstanding the provisions of s. 12 (2), *supra* a court convicting a person of an offence specified in Schedule 1 to the Road Traffic Act, 1962 may order that he shall be disqualified for holding or obtaining a licence and shall make such order of endorsement or disqualification as the court is required to make in accordance with ss. 5 or 7 of the 1962 Act. (Criminal Justice Act, 1967, s. 51 (1).)

Notwithstanding the provisions of s. 12 (1), *supra* a conviction in respect of which a court has ordered a person to be disqualified or of which particulars have been endorsed on any licence held by him shall be taken into account in determining his liability to punishment or disqualification for any offence specified in Sched. 1, to the Road Traffic Act, 1962, committed subsequently (Criminal Justice Act, 1967, s. 51 (2)).

46. Approved probation hostels and homes.—(1) The Secretary of State may approve premises for the reception of persons who may be required to reside therein by a probation order and such premises shall be known—

(a) if the persons so residing are employed outside the premises, or are awaiting such employment, as " approved probation hostels ";
(b) in any other case, as " approved probation homes ".

(2) The Secretary of State may make rules for the regulation, management and inspection of approved probation hostels and of approved probation homes; and such rules may in particular provide that no person shall be appointed to be in charge of an approved probation hostel or home unless the Secretary of State has consented to his appointment:

Provided that the rules shall not prohibit the making of such an appointment in case of emergency without the previous consent of the Secretary of State, but may in that case require notice of the appointment to be given immediately to the Secretary of State and enable him, if he thinks fit, to require the appointment to be terminated.

NOTES

This section is printed as amended by the Children and Young Persons Act, 1969, s. 72 (4) and Sched. VI.

As to the inspection of other institutions used for the residence of probationers, see the next following section.

Rules.—See the Approved Probation Hostel and Home Rules, 1949. As to the future pattern of approved hostels and homes see Home Office Circular 289/1970, p. 687, *post.*

The Administration of Children's Homes Regulations, 1951, p. 979, do not apply to approved probation hostels and approved probation homes within the meaning of this section (*ibid.*, r. 17), but presumably they do apply to other institutions referred to in the next section.

47. Inspection of institutions for residence of probationers.—(1) Any institution, not being an approved probation hostel or an approved probation home, in which a person is required by a probation order to reside otherwise than for the purpose of his submitting to treatment for his mental condition as a resident patient shall, so long as he resides there, be subject to inspection by the Secretary of State unless it is, as a whole, otherwise subject to inspection by a Government department.

(2) A person appointed by the Secretary of State to inspect any such institution as aforesaid shall have power to enter the institution and to make such investigation of the treatment of any persons residing there as he thinks fit; and any person who obstructs him in the exercise of the power aforesaid shall be liable on summary conviction to a fine not exceeding five pounds.

NOTES

This section is printed as amended by the Children and Young Persons Act, 1969, s. 72 (4) and Sched. VI.

Obstructs.—The word " wilfully " is not used here, but no doubt it would be a good defence to show that the obstruction was unintentional.

Powers of inspection.—The occasion of the inspection may be that a single probationer resides on the premises, but the inspector is apparently entitled to investigate the treatment of " any persons residing there " even if not probationers.

80. Interpretation.—(1) In this Act, unless the context otherwise requires, the following expressions have the meaning hereby respectively assigned to them, that is to say:

" Approved probation hostel " and " Approved probation home " have the meaning assigned to them by section forty-six of this Act;

"*Approved school*" *means a school approved under section seventy-nine of the Children and Young Persons Act, 1933;*

*   *   *   *   *

" Court of summary jurisdiction " includes examining justices within the meaning of the Criminal Justice Act, 1925;

" Detention centre " has the meaning assigned to it by section forty-eight of this Act;

" Enactment " includes an enactment contained in a local Act and any order, regulation or other instrument having effect by virtue of an Act;

" England " includes Wales;

" Impose imprisonment " means pass a sentence of imprisonment or commit to prison in default of payment of any sum of money or for failing to do or abstain from doing anything required to be done or left undone;

" Local authority " means, in relation to any probation area, any authority out of whose funds the salary of the clerk to the justices for a petty sessional division or place contained in the probation area is paid;

" Offence the sentence for which is fixed by law " means an offence for which the court is required to sentence the offender to death or imprisonment for life or to detention during His Majesty's pleasure;

" Order for conditional discharge " has the meaning assigned to it by section seven of this Act;

" Period of conditional discharge " has the meaning assigned to it by section seven of this Act;

" Probationer " means a person for the time being under supervision by virtue of a probation order;

" Probation order " has the meaning assigned to it by section three of this Act;

" Probation period " means the period for which a probationer is placed under supervision by a probation order;

" Remand centre " has the meaning assigned to it by section forty-eight of this Act;

"*Remand home*" *means premises established or used by the council of a county or county borough under the provisions of section seventy-seven of the Children and Young Persons Act, 1933;*

"Sentence" includes an order for detention in a detention centre, but does not include a committal in default of payment of any sum of money or failing to do or abstain from doing anything required to be done or left undone;

" The statutory restrictions upon the imprisonment of young offenders " has the same meaning as in the Criminal Justice Act, 1961 ;

" Sum adjudged to be paid by a conviction " includes any costs, damages or compensation adjudged to be paid by the conviction of which the amount is ascertained by the conviction;

" Supervising court " means, in relation to a probation order, a court of summary jurisdiction acting for the petty sessional division or place for the time being named in the order; and where the probationer was a child or young person within the meaning of the Children and Young Persons Act, 1933, when the probation order was made, means a juvenile court for that division or place;

(2) Any reference in this Act to a previous sentence of imprisonment shall be construed as including a reference to a previous sentence of penal servitude; any such reference to a previous sentence of Borstal training shall be construed as including a reference to a previous sentence of detention in a Borstal institution; and any such reference to a previous conviction or sentence shall be construed as a reference to a previous conviction by a court in any part of Great Britain and to a previous sentence passed by any such court.

(3) Where the age of any person at any time is material for the purposes of any provision of this Act, or of any Order in Council made thereunder, regulating the powers of a court, his age at the material time shall be deemed to be or to have been that which appears to the court after considering any available evidence to be or to have been his age at that time.

(4) References in this Act to an offence punishable with imprisonment shall be construed, in relation to any offender, without regard to any prohibition or restriction imposed by or under any enactment upon the

imprisonment of offenders of his age, but shall not be construed as including an offence for which the court is required to impose a sentence of imprisonment for life.

(5) For the purposes of this Act, except subsection (6) of section three thereof, where a probation order or an order for conditional discharge has been made on appeal, the order shall be deemed to have been made by the court from which the appeal was brought.

(6) Where any provision of this Act empowers a court on conviction of an offender to pass a sentence or make an order in lieu of dealing with him in any other manner, the said provision shall not be construed as taking away any power of the court to order the offender to pay costs, damages or compensation.

(7) References in this Act to any enactment shall, unless the context otherwise requires, be construed as references to that enactment as amended by any subsequent enactment including this Act.

NOTES

This section is printed as amended by the Magistrates' Courts Act, 1952, the Mental Health Act, 1959, the Criminal Justice Act, 1961, the Administration of Justice Act, 1964 and the Children and Young Persons Act, 1969. From a date to be appointed the definitions of "Approved school" and "Remand home" are repealed, s. 72 (4) and Sched. VI, *ibid.*

" **Court of summary jurisdiction.**"—There is a wide definition of this term in s. 13 (11) of the Interpretation Act, 1889; 32 Halsbury's Statutes, 3rd Edn., 442. This is generally considered as not including examining justices though opinions are divided on the point. In some enactments the terms " court of summary jurisdiction " and " examining justices " are used in opposition, while in others it is clear that the former includes the latter. The present definition, for the purposes of this Act, prevents ambiguity.

" **Sentence.**"—It is to be noted that this definition does not include an order committing a juvenile to the care of a local authority.

By s. 59 of the Children and Young Persons Act, 1933, p. 62, *ante*, the word " sentence " is not to be used in relation to children and young persons dealt with summarily. References in any enactment to a sentence are to be construed as including an order made upon a finding of guilt; *ibid.*

Probation order on appeal.—The exception made in sub-s. (5) means that the responsibility of the court and of the probation officer for dealing with the copies of the probation order and for transmitting documents and information rest upon the appeal court and the probation officer there.

Section 5   FIRST SCHEDULE

DISCHARGE AND AMENDMENT OF PROBATION ORDERS

Discharge

1. The court by which a probation order was made may, upon application made by the probation officer or by the probationer, discharge the order.

Amendment

2.—(1) If the supervising court is satisfied that a probationer proposes to change, or has changed his residence from the petty sessional division named in the probation order to another petty sessional division, the court may, and if application in that behalf is made by the probation officer, shall, by order amend the probation order by substituting for the petty sessional division named therein the petty sessional division where the probationer proposes to reside or is residing:

Provided that if the probation order contains requirements which, in the opinion of the court, cannot be complied with unless the probationer continues to reside in the division named in the order, the court shall not amend the order as aforesaid unless, in accordance with the following provisions of this Schedule, they cancel those requirements or substitute therefor other requirements which can be so complied with.

(2) Where a probation order is amended under this paragraph, the supervising court shall send to the clerk to the justices for the new division named in the order a copy of the order, together with such documents and information relating to the case as it considers likely to be of assistance to that court.

NOTE

As to the duty of the probation officer to apply to the court if he becomes aware that a probationer has changed his residence, see r. 39 of the Probation Rules, 1965, p. 530, *post.*

3. Without prejudice to the provisions of the last foregoing paragraph, the supervising court may, upon application made by the probation officer or by the probationer, by order amend a probation order by cancelling any of the requirements thereof or by inserting therein (either in addition to or in substitution for any such requirement) any requirement which could be included in the order if it were then being made by that court in accordance with the provisions of sections three and four of this Act:

Provided that—

    (a) the court shall not amend a probation order by reducing the probation period, or by extending that period beyond the end of three years from the date of the original order;

    (b) the court shall not so amend a probation order that the probationer is thereby required to reside in an approved probation hostel or home, or in any other institution, or to submit to treatment for his mental condition, for any period exceeding twelve months in all;

    (c) the court shall not amend a probation order by inserting therein a requirement that the probationer shall submit to treatment for his mental condition unless the amending order is made within three months after the date of the original order.

4. Where the medical practitioner by whom or under whose direction a probationer is being treated for his mental condition in pursuance of any requirement of the probation order is of opinion—

    (a) that the treatment of the probationer should be continued beyond the period specified in that behalf in the order, or

    (b) that the probationer needs different treatment, being treatment of a kind to which he could be required to submit in pursuance of a probation order, or

    (c) that the probationer is not susceptible to treatment, or

    (d) that the probationer does not require further treatment,

or where the practitioner is for any reason unwilling to continue to treat or direct the treatment of the probationer, he shall make a report in writing to that effect to the probationer officer and the probation officer shall apply to the supervising court for the variation or cancellation of the requirement.

General

5. Where the supervising court proposes to amend a probation order under this Schedule, otherwise than on the application of the probationer, it shall summon him to appear before the court; and if the probationer is not less than fourteen years of age, the court shall not amend a probation order unless the probationer expresses his willingness to comply with the requirements of the order as amended:

Provided that this paragraph shall not apply to an order cancelling a requirement of the probation order or reducing the period of any requirement, or substituting a new petty sessional division for the division named in the probation order.

6. On the making of an order discharging or amending a probation order the clerk to the court shall forthwith give copies of the discharging or amending order to the probation officer; and the probation officer shall give a copy to the probationer and to the person in charge of any institution in which the probationer is or was required by the order to reside:

Provided that if the order amends the probation order by substituting a new petty sessional division for the division named in the probation order the copies of the order shall be sent to the clerk to the justices for the new petty sessional division and he shall be responsible for giving copies of the order to the probation officer.

7. Subsection (7) of section three of this Act shall apply to any order made under this Schedule by virtue of which a probationer is required to reside in an institution as it applies to a probation order made under that section.

NOTES

"Discharge and amendment."—Generally, the court which made the order or the supervising court can discharge it, and only the supervising court can amend it, but where the probationer resides in Scotland, "the appropriate court" may, apparently, amend or discharge the order, see Criminal Justice (Scotland) Act, 1949, s. 4 and Second Schedule, read with s. 9 of the English Act.

Notice to Secretary of State.—Section 3 (7), p. 280, *ante*, requires notice of orders containing a requirement to reside in certain institutions, to be given to the Secretary of State.

Application to courts.—As to probation officer's duty to apply to court where person under his supervision changes his residence, see rule 39 of the Probation Rules, 1965, p. 530, *post*, and Home Office letter H.O. 205/52/N dated 15th September, 1952.

CRIMINAL JUSTICE (SCOTLAND) ACT, 1949

[12, 13 & 14 Geo 6, c. 94]

7. Probation orders relating to persons residing in England.— (1) Where the court by which a probation order is made under section two of this Act is satisfied that the offender has attained the age of seventeen and resides or will reside in England, subsection (2) of the said section shall not apply to the order, but the order shall contain a requirement that he be under the supervision of a probation officer appointed for or assigned to the petty sessional division in which the offender resides or will reside; and that division shall be named in the order.

(2) Where a probation order has been made under section two of this Act and the court in Scotland by which the order was made or the appropriate court is satisfied that the probationer has attained the age of seventeen and proposes to reside or is residing in England, the power of that court to amend the order under the Second Schedule to this Act shall include power [to omit therefrom the name of the probation officer named therein and] to insert the provisions required by subsection (1) of this section; and the court may so amend the order without summoning the probationer and without his consent.

(3) [*Repealed as to England and Wales by the Criminal Justice Act, 1967, Sched. VIII.*]

(4) Subsections (1) [to (3)] of section four and subsection (1) of section five of this Act shall not apply to any order made or amended under this section; but subject as hereinafter provided the provisions of the Criminal Justice Act, 1948 (except section eight of that Act) shall apply to the order as if it were a probation order made under section three of that Act:

Provided that in the application to any such order of section six of the said Act (which relates to breach of a requirement of a probation order) paragraph (a) of subsection (2), paragraph (a) of subsection (3) and paragraph (b) of subsection (4) of that section shall not apply, and paragraph (b) of subsection (3) and paragraph (a) of subsection (4) of that section shall have effect as if for references therein to a court of assize or quarter sessions and the court of assize or quarter sessions there were substituted references to a court in Scotland and to the court in Scotland by which the probationer order was made or amended under this section.

(5) If it appears on information to a justice acting for the petty sessional division or place for which the supervising court (as defined in the Criminal Justice Act, 1948) acts that a person in whose case a probation order has been made or amended under this section has been convicted by a court in any part of Great Britain of an offence committed during the period specified in the order, he may issue a summons requiring that person to appear, at the place and time specified therein, before the court in Scotland by which the probation order was made or, if the information is in writing and on oath, may issue a warrant for his arrest, directing that person to be brought before the last-mentioned court.

(6) If a warrant for the arrest of a probationer issued under section six of this Act by a court is executed in England, and the probationer cannot forthwith be brought before that court, the warrant shall have effect as if it directed him to be brought before a court of summary jurisdiction for the place where he is arrested; and the court of summary jurisdiction shall commit him to custody or release him on bail (with or without sureties) until he can be brought or appear before the court in Scotland.

(7) The court by which a probation order is made or amended in accordance with the provisions of this section shall send three copies of the order to the clerk to the justices for the petty sessional division named therein, together with such documents and information relating to the

case as it considers likely to be of assistance to the court acting for that petty sessional division.

(8) Where a probation order which is amended under subsection (2) of this section is an order to which the provisions of this Act apply by virtue of section nine of the Criminal Justice Act, 1948 (which relates to probation orders under that Act relating to persons residing in Scotland) then, notwithstanding anything in that section or this section, the order shall, as from the date of the amendment, have effect in all respects as if it were an order made under section three of that Act in the case of a person residing in England.]

NOTE

This section is printed as amended by the Children and Young Persons Act, 1969, s. 72 (3) and Sched. V. The words in square brackets are repealed as to Scotland only, by the Social Work (Scotland) Act, 1968.

7A. Further provisions as to probation orders relating to persons residing or formerly residing in England.—(1) Where the court by which a probation order is made under section 2 of this Act or subsection (6) of this section is satisfied that the person to whom the order relates is under the age of seventeen and resides or will reside in England, subsection (2) of the said section 2 shall not apply to the order but the order shall name the petty sessions area in which that person resides or will reside and the court shall send notification of the order to the clerk to the justices for that area.

(2) Where a probation order has been made under section 2 of this Act or subsection (6) of this section and the court which made the order or the appropriate court is satisfied that the person to whom the order relates is under the age of seventeen and proposes to reside or is residing in England, the power of that court to amend the order under Schedule 2 to this Act shall include power, without summoning him and without his consent, to insert in the order the name of the petty sessions area aforesaid; and where the court exercises the power conferred on it by virtue of this subsection it shall send notification of the order to the clerk aforesaid.

(3) A court which sends a notification to a clerk in pursuance of the foregoing provisions of this section shall send to him with it three copies of the probation order in question and such other documents and information relating to the case as it considers likely to be of assistance to the juvenile court mentioned in the following subsection.

(4) It shall be the duty of the clerk to whom a notification is sent in pursuance of the foregoing provisions of this section to refer the notification to a juvenile court acting for the petty sessions area named in the order, and on such a reference the court—

    (a) may make a supervision order under the Children and Young Persons Act, 1969 in respect of a person to whom the notification relates; and

    (b) if it does not make such an order, shall dismiss the case.

(5) A supervision order made by virtue of the foregoing subsection shall not include a requirement authorised by section 12 of the said Act of 1969 unless the supervised person is before the court when the supervision

order is made, and in relation to a supervision order made by virtue of that subsection—

    (a) section 15 of that Act shall have effect as if in subsection (4) paragraph (b) and the words following it were omitted; and

    (b) section 17 (a) of that Act shall have effect as if the second reference to the supervision order were a reference to the probation order in consequence of which the supervision order is made;

and when a juvenile court disposes of a case referred to it in pursuance of the foregoing subsection, the probation order in consequence of which the reference was made shall cease to have effect.

(6) The court which, in pursuance of subsection (1) of section 73 of the Social Work (Scotland) Act, 1968, considers a case referred to it in consequence of a notification under paragraph (i) of that subsection (which relates to a case in which a person subject to a supervision order made by virtue of this section moves to Scotland)—

    (a) may, if it is of opinion that the person to whom the notification relates should continue to be under supervision, make a probation order in respect of him for a period specified in the order; and

    (b) if it does not make such an order, shall dismiss the case;

and when the court disposes of a case in pursuance of this subsection the supervision order aforesaid shall cease to have effect.

(7) Notwithstanding any provision to the contrary in section 2 of this Act, a probation order made by virtue of the foregoing subsection which includes only requirements having the like effect as any requirement or provision of the supervision order to which the notification relates may be made without summoning the person to whom the notification relates and without his consent, and shall specify a period of supervision which shall expire not later than the date on which that supervision order would have ceased to have effect by the effluxion of time; and, except as aforesaid, Part I of this Act shall apply to that probation order.

(8) In this section "petty sessions area" has the same meaning as in the said Act of 1969.

NOTE

This section was added by the Children and Young Persons Act, 1969, Sched. V.

CRIMINAL JUSTICE ACT, 1961
[9 & 10 Eliz. 2, c. 39]

9. Breach of probation, etc.—Where an order for conditional discharge under section seven of the Criminal Justice Act, 1948 has been made by a magistrates' court in the case of an offender under seventeen years of age in respect of an offence not being a summary offence or an offence which, in the case of an adult, could have been tried summarily with his consent under section nineteen of the Magistrates' Courts Act, 1952, any powers exercisable by that or any other court in respect of the offender after he has attained the age of seventeen years under any of the following enactments, that is to say—

(a) [*Repealed by the Children and Young Persons Act, 1969, s. 72 (4) and Sched. VI.*]

(b) subsections (5) to (7) of section eight of that Act (which relate to further offences committed during the probation period or during the period of conditional discharge),

shall be those which would be exercisable if that offence were an offence which could have been tried summarily under the said section nineteen with the offender's consent, and had been so tried.

NOTES

This section is printed as amended by the Children and Young Persons Act, 1969, s. 72 (3), (4) and Scheds. V and VI.

" **Age.**"—See note at p. 53, *ante.*

Criminal Justice Act, 1948, ss. 3, 6, 7, 8.—See pp. 279 *et seq., ante.*

Probation order under s. 3 Criminal Justice Act, 1948.—The reference to such probation orders was repealed by the Act of 1969, the operation of the section is not affected however in relation to orders made before January 1, 1971 (S.I. 1970 No. 1498, Sched. III, para. 2).

CRIMINAL JUSTICE ACT, 1967
[1967 c. 80]

53. Substitution of conditional discharge for probation.—(1) Where on an application made by the probationer or the probation officer it appears to the court having power to discharge a probation order made under section 3 of the Criminal Justice Act, 1948, that the order is no longer appropriate in the case of the probationer, the court may make, in substitution for the probation order, an order discharging him in respect of the original offence, subject to the condition that he commits no offence between the making of the order under this section and the expiration of the probation period.

(2) A person in respect of whom an order is made under this section shall so long as the said condition continues in force be treated in all respects and in particular for the purposes of section 8 of the said Act of 1948 (commission of further offence by probationer or person subject to order for conditional discharge) as if the original order made in his case had been an order for conditional discharge made under section 7 of that Act by the court which made the original order and as if the period of conditional discharge were the same as the probation period.

(3) On the making of an order under this section the clerk of the court shall forthwith give copies thereof to the probation officer, who shall give a copy to the person in respect of whom the order is made and to the person

in charge of any institution in which that person was required by the probation order to reside.

NOTES

Notice of order.—See Magistrates' Courts Rules, 1968, r. 25 (3).

"On an application."—Application shall be by complaint. Rule 86, Magistrates' Courts Rules, 1968.

54. Miscellaneous provisions as to probation orders.—(1) The power of discharging a probation order conferred by paragraph 1 of Schedule 1 to the Criminal Justice Act, 1948, on the court by or before which the probationer is convicted shall, except where that court is the Crown Court and includes in the order a direction to the contrary, be exercised instead by the supervising court within the meaning of that Act.

(2) The power of discharging such an order conferred by virtue of section 80(5) of the said Act of 1948, in a case where the order is made on appeal, on the court from which the appeal is brought shall, except where that court is the Crown Court and there is included in the order a direction that the power should be reserved to that court, be exercised instead by the supervising court within the meaning of that Act.

(3) Subsections (2) and (3) of section 5 of the said Act of 1948 (compulsory review of probation orders after six months) shall cease to have effect.

(4) [*Repealed by the Courts Act,* 1971.]

(5) Where a probationer appears or is brought before the Crown Court and the court is satisfied that he has failed to comply with any of the requirements of the probation order the Crown Court may, instead of dealing with him under section 6(4)(b) of the said Act of 1948 for the offence in respect of which the probation order was made, impose on him a fine not exceeding £20, without prejudice, however, to the continuance of the probation order; and the maximum fine which may be imposed by a magistrates' court under section 6(3) of that Act for the like failure shall be £20 instead of £10.

(6) The maximum fine which may be imposed by a court in Scotland under section 5(2)(a) of the Criminal Justice (Scotland) Act, 1949, on a probationer for failure to comply with any of the requirements of a probation order shall be £20 instead of £10.

(7) A probation order made or amended by virtue of section 9 of the Criminal Justice Act, 1948 (probationers residing or intending to reside in Scotland) may, notwithstanding section 4(9) of that Act, include a requirement that the probationer shall submit to treatment for his mental condition, and—

 (a) subsections (1), (3) and (7) of the said section 4 and section 3(2) of the Criminal Justice (Scotland) Act, 1949 (all of which regulate the making of probation orders which include such requirement) shall apply to the making of an order which includes any such requirement by virtue of this subsection as they apply to the making of an order which includes any such requirement by virtue of the said sections 4 and 3 respectively; and

   (b) subsections (4) to (6) of the said section 3 (functions of probation
       officer and medical practitioner where such a requirement has
       been imposed) shall apply in relation to a probationer who is
       undergoing treatment in Scotland in pursuance of a require-
       ment imposed by virtue of this subsection as they apply in
       relation to a probationer undergoing such treatment in pur-
       suance of a requirement imposed by virtue of the said section
       3.

(8) A probation order made or amended by virtue of section 7 of the
Criminal Justice (Scotland) Act, 1949 (Scottish probation orders relating
to persons residing or intending to reside in England) may, notwithstanding
section 3(9) of that Act, include a requirement that the probationer shall
submit to treatment for his mental condition, and—

   (a) subsections (1), (3) and (7) of the said section 3 and section 4(2)
       of the Criminal Justice Act, 1948 (all of which regulate the
       making of probation orders which include any such require-
       ment) shall apply to the making of an order which includes any
       such requirement by virtue of this subsection as they apply to
       the making of an order which includes any such requirement
       by virtue of the said sections 3 and 4 respectively; and
   (b) subsections (4) to (6) of the said section 4 (functions of probation
       officer and medical practitioner where such a requirement has
       been imposed) shall apply in relation to a probationer who is
       undergoing treatment in England or Wales in pursuance of a
       requirement imposed by virtue of this subsection as they apply
       in relation to a probationer undergoing such treatment in
       pursuance of a requirement imposed by virtue of the said
       section 4.

NOTE

This section is printed as amended by the Courts Act, 1971.

55. Selection of probation officers.—A probation officer under whose
supervision a woman or girl is placed in pursuance of an order under
section 3 of the Criminal Justice Act, 1948, may be a man or a woman.

NOTE

This section is printed as amended by the Children and Young Persons Act, 1969,
s. 72 (4) and Sched. VI.

57. Social inquiry report before sentence.—(1) The Secretary of
State may by rules make provision requiring that in any case to which the
rules apply a court of any prescribed class shall before passing on any
person a sentence to which the rules apply consider a social inquiry report,
that is to say a report about him and his circumstances, made by a probation officer or any other person authorised to do so by the rules.

(2) Rules under this section may apply to a sentence of imprisonment or detention of any class prescribed by the rules and may make different provision for different cases.

(3) No sentence shall be invalidated by the failure of a court to consider a social inquiry report in accordance with rules under subsection (1) of this section, but any other court on appeal from that court shall consider such a report in determining whether a different sentence should be passed on the appellant from the sentence passed on him by the court below.

(4) In this section "sentence of imprisonment or detention" means a sentence of imprisonment, borstal training or detention in a detention centre or a sentence of detention passed under section 53 of the Children and Young Persons Act, 1933 (young offenders convicted of grave crimes).

NOTES

This section shall come into force on such day as the Secretary of State may by order appoint (s. 106).

At the time of going to press no day had been appointed for the coming into force of this section. See, however, Home Office Circular No. 188/1968/C1.

SECTION 7.—BORSTAL

INTRODUCTORY NOTE

Borstal institutions are not prisons, and a borstal institution is intended to provide discipline and training rather than to impose punishment. That a young man or woman sentenced to borstal training which may mean a term of years in a borstal institution feels that it is a heavy punishment is beyond doubt, because of the length of the sentence, and such sentences may be taken to have as much deterrent effect as a sentence of imprisonment of the same length. The advantage of borstal treatment over imprisonment is that it provides far greater opportunity for reform, and that there is not the same stigma attaching to a borstal sentence as to a sentence of imprisonment.

The system has many critics, but the results of the system having regard to the material have been such as to justify amply the continuance and development of the borstal system.

It is still necessary for cases to be committed either for trial or for sentence if a borstal sentence is thought desirable. The only exception is contained in s. 31 of the Children and Young Persons Act, 1969, p. 177, *ante*, which provides that in case of behaviour detrimental to others accommodated in a community home, a person may be removed to a borstal institution by order of a juvenile court.

The actual duration of the detention depends upon conduct and progress, and the Secretary of State has adequate powers of early licensing in suitable cases. Within certain limits, a borstal sentence answers the description of an indeterminate sentence, and each case is studied by the institution authorities so that the most beneficial results may follow the training and discipline afforded by the institution.

Sentences of borstal training are dealt with in s. 20 of the Criminal Justice Act, 1948, *infra*, s. 28 of the Magistrates' Courts Act, 1952 and s. 45 of the Prison Act, 1952, pp. 307, 309, *post*.

The period of detention is determined in accordance with the provisions of s. 45 of the Prison Act, 1952, and not by the court. The offender must be at least fifteen and under twenty-one years old at the date of conviction. There is power to raise the minimum age for borstal to seventeen (Children and Young Persons Act, 1969, s. 7 (1)).

CRIMINAL JUSTICE ACT, 1948

[11 & 12 Geo. 6, c. 58]

20. Borstal training.—(1) Where a person is convicted on indictment of an offence punishable with imprisonment, then if on the day of his conviction he is not less than [fifteen] but under twenty-one years of age and a sentence of borstal training is available in his case under subsection (2) of section one of the Criminal Justice Act, 1961, the court may, in lieu of any other sentence, pass a sentence of borstal training.

(2) [*Repealed by the Prison Act, 1952, Sched. IV.*]

(3) [*Repealed by the Magistrates' Courts Act, 1952, Sched. VI.*]

(4) [*Repealed by the Courts Act, 1971, Sched. XI.*]

(5) Where an offender is so committed for sentence as aforesaid, the following provisions shall have effect, that is to say :—

    (a) the Crown Court shall inquire into the circumstances of the case and may—

        (i) if a sentence of borstal training is available in his case under subsection (2) of section one of the Criminal Justice Act, 1961, sentence him to borstal training ; or

        (ii) in any case, deal with him in any manner in which the court of summary jurisdiction might have dealt with him ;

    (b) . . .

    (d) [*Repealed by the Criminal Justice Act, 1967, s. 103 and Sched. VII.*]

(6) . . .

NOTES

Section 20 of the Criminal Justice Act, 1948, as set out above is shown in the form in which it now stands after the operation of the amendments made to it by virtue of the Legal Aid and Advice Act, 1949, ss. 18 (6), 24 (1) and S.I. 1963 No. 432, the Criminal Justice Act, 1961, s. 41, Scheds. IV, V and S.I. 1963 No. 755, the Criminal Justice Administration Act, 1962, s. 20, Sched. V and S.I. 1962 No. 791, the Criminal Justice Act, 1967 and the Courts Act, 1971, s. 56 and Scheds. VIII and XI.

Period of training.—The court does not determine the length of the period of training. This is provided by s. 45 of the Prison Act, 1952 ; see p. 309, *post*.

" Convicted."—See s. 59 of the Children and Young Persons Act, 1933, p. 62, *ante*. The word " conviction " is not to be used in relation to persons under seventeen, dealt with summarily.

" Age."—See s. 39 (3) of the Criminal Justice Act, 1961, p. 420, *post* and note " Attained the age ", at p. 53, *ante*.

"Not less than fifteen."—From a date to be appointed for the word "fifteen" there shall be substituted the word "seventeen" (Children and Young Persons Act, 1969, s. 7 (1)). The object of the amendment is to enable the minimum age for borstal to be raised as and when the system of community homes under the Act of 1969 can make suitable provision.

Magistrates' Courts Act, 1952, s. 28.—See p. 307, *ante*.

"Where an offender is so committed."—This refers to sub-s. (4) which has been repealed. This would appear to be an error in drafting of the Courts Act, 1971, which does not make any consequential amendments to sub-s. (5). For interpretation of statutes so as to modify the language to meet the intention see Maxwell on Interpretation of Statutes; pp. 228–232.

Sentence.—In the case of *R. v. Amos*, [1961] 1 All E. R. 191 ; 125 J. P. 167 (C. C. A.) ; 125 J. P. 169, it was held that the fact that a sentence of borstal training would have the effect of depriving an offender of his liberty for a longer period than the maximum term of imprisonment for the offence was a relevant consideration for the court and no more, and did not have the effect of depriving quarter sessions of the power to pass a sentence of borstal training where such a sentence was, in all the circumstances, appropriate.

Arrangements for supervision and after-care.—See Home Office Circular No. 154/1967 dated August 30, 1967. The arrangements include provision for application for assisted visits.

Forms of commitment.—See Forms Nos. 41, 42 in the Magistrates' Courts (Forms) Rules, 1968, S.I. 1968 No. 1919.

Fines outstanding against persons detained in Borstal Institutions.—See Home Office Circular No. 122/1968, p. 697, *post.*

Jurisdiction of the Crown Court.—In *R.* v. *Hammond,* [1963] 2 Q. B. 450; [1963] 2 All E. R. 475; 127 J. P. 402, it was held that the words "deal with him in any manner in which the court of summary jurisdiction might have dealt with him" in s. 20 (5) did not confer on [quarter sessions] jurisdiction to impose a sentence that could not have been imposed by the court of summary jurisdiction at the time when they decided to commit the appellant to quarter sessions; accordingly quarter sessions had no jurisdiction to sentence the appellant to detention at a detention centre, as the court of summary jurisdiction had not been notified that a detention centre was available to that court for persons of the age of the appellant.

Justices.—In cases committed by a juvenile court under s. 28 Magistrates' Courts Act, 1952, or s. 67 Mental Health Act, 1959, the Crown Court shall consist of a judge sitting with two justices each of whom is a member of a juvenile court panel and who are chosen so that the Court shall include a man and a woman. (Courts Act, 1971, s. 5 and r. 3 Crown Court Rules, 1971, S.I. 1971 No. 1292, p. 654, *post.*)

Ashford Prison.—See Home Office letter 123/61/C.1, as to the use of this prison for male offenders committed under s. 28 of the Magistrates' Courts, Act, 1952, or sentenced to borstal training.

Offence punishable with imprisonment.—See s. 80 (4), p. 294, *ante.*

Documents.—Rule 16 of the Magistrates' Courts Rules, 1968, sets out the documents which the summary court must forward to the higher court.

Committal.—On committal with a view to a borstal sentence an offender even under the age of 17 must be sent to prison unless a remand centre is available. See s. 28 (4) of the Magistrates' Courts Act, 1952, *infra* and s. 23 (4) Children and Young Persons Act, 1969.

Appeal.—It appears that the right of appeal to the Crown Court against conviction by a summary court arises on the day of committal to the Crown Court.

Transfers.—See s. 44 of the Prison Act, 1952, p. 308, *post.*

Committal under s. 29 of the Magistrates' Courts Act, 1952.—In *R.* v. *Dangerfield,* [1959] 3 All E. R. 88, the Court of Criminal Appeal said it was desirable that where an offender under 21 was committed to quarter sessions for sentence he should, in a proper case, be committed under s. 29 in order that wider powers might be open to quarter sessions. See also *R.* v. *Pegg,* [1952] W. N. 52.

It should be noted that s. 29 applies only to persons who are not less than seventeen years old.

Unlawfully at large.—Any person sentenced to borstal training or ordered to be detained in a detention centre who is unlawfully at large, may be arrested by a constable without warrant and taken back, and in calculating the period for which he is liable to be detained no account shall be taken of the time he is absent, unless the Secretary of State directs otherwise (Prison Act, 1952, s. 49, p. 392, *post*).

MAGISTRATES' COURTS ACT, 1952

[15 & 16 Geo. 6 & 1 Eliz. 2, c. 55]

28.—Committal to quarter sessions with a view to a borstal sentence.—(1) Where a person is convicted by a magistrates' court of an offence punishable on summary conviction with imprisonment, then, if on the day of the conviction he is not less than [fifteen] but under twenty-one years old and is a person who, under subsections (2) and (4) of section one of the Criminal Justice Act, 1961, may be committed for a sentence of borstal training, the court may commit him in custody or on bail to the Crown Court for sentence in accordance with the provisions of section twenty of the Criminal Justice Act, 1948.

(4) A person committed in custody under subsection (1) of this section shall be committed—

    (a) if the court has been notified by the Secretary of State that a remand centre is available for the reception, from that court, of persons of the class or description of the person committed, to a remand centre ;

    (b) if the court has not been so notified, to a prison.

NOTES

This section is printed as amended by the Criminal Law Act, 1967, the Criminal Justice Act, 1967, and the Courts Act, 1971.

"**Convicted;**" "**age.**"—See notes to s. 20 of the Criminal Justice Act, 1948, as amended by this Act, p. 306, *ante.*

"**Not less than fifteen.**"—From a date to be appointed for the word "fifteen" there shall be substituted the word "seventeen" (s. 7 (1) Children and Young Persons Act, 1969).

"**Under twenty-one.**"—In *R.* v. *Baxter,* [1969] 3 All E. R. 1290, the accused attained the age of twenty-one years between the date when he was convicted and committed for sentence to [quarter sessions] and the date of the hearing at [quarter sessions].

On appeal it was held that he was lawfully sentenced to borstal training.

Form of commitment.—See Form No. 41 in the Schedule to the Magistrates' Courts (Forms) Rules, 1968.

Second sentence of detention at detention centre.—In the case of *R.* v. *Moore,* [1968] 1 All E. R. 790 it was held, *inter alia,* that only very rarely should a sentence of detention at a detention centre be imposed when an accused had already served one such sentence.

Per curiam, where there is an option to commit an offender to [the Crown Court] for sentence either under s. 28 or under s. 29 it is normally appropriate to commit under s. 29.

PRISON ACT, 1952
[15 & 16 Geo. 6 & 1 Eliz. 2, c. 52]

44. Transfers from prison to Borstal institution and vice versa. —(1) If the Secretary of State is satisfied that a person serving a sentence of imprisonment is under twenty-one years of age and might with advantage be detained in a borstal institution he may, after consultation where practicable with the judge or presiding chairman of the court which passed the sentence, transfer that person to a borstal institution ; and the provision of the next following section shall thereupon apply to him as if he had on the date of the transfer been sentenced to borstal training.

Provided that if on that date the unexpired term of his sentence is less than two years those provisions shall apply to him as if he had been sentenced to borstal training two years before the expiration of that term.

(2) If a person detained in a borstal institution is reported to the Secretary of State by the board of visitors to be incorrigible, or to be exercising a bad influence on the other inmates of the institution, the Secretary of State may commute the unexpired part of the term for which the said person is then liable to be detained in a borstal institution to such term of imprisonment as the Secretary of State may determine, not exceeding the said unexpired part; and for the purpose of this Act and of the Criminal Justice Act, 1961 the said person shall be treated as if he had been sentenced to imprisonment for that term.

NOTES

This section is printed as amended by the Criminal Justice Act, 1961 and the Prison Commissioners Dissolution Order, 1963, S.I. 1963, No. 597.

Borstal institutions are for the detention and training of persons who are at least fifteen years of age on conviction; see s. 43 (1) of the Prison Act, 1952, p. 390, *post*.

45. Release of persons sentenced to borstal training.—(1) A person sentenced to borstal training shall be detained in a borstal institution, and after his release therefrom shall be subject to supervision, in accordance with the following provisions of this section; subject, however, to the power of the Secretary of State under subsection (2) of the last preceding section to commute in certain cases the unexpired part of the term for which a person is liable to be so detained to a term of imprisonment.

(2) A person sentenced to borstal training shall be detained in a borstal institution for such period, not extending beyond two years after the date of his sentence and not being less than six months from that date, as the Secretary of State may determine and shall then be released.

Provided that the Secretary of State may, if he thinks fit, direct that any such person shall be released from a borstal institution before the expiration of the said six months.

(3) A person shall, after his release from a borstal institution and until the expiration of two years from the date of his release, be under the supervision of such society or person as may be specified in a notice to be given to him by the Secretary of State on his release, and shall, while under that supervision, comply with such requirements as may be so specified:

Provided that the Secretary of State may at any time modify or cancel any of the said requirements or order that a person who is under supervision as aforesaid shall cease to be under supervision.

(4) If before the expiration of two years from the date of his release the Secretary of State is satisfied that a person who is under supervision after his release from a borstal institution under subsection (2) of this section has failed to comply with any requirement for the time being specified in the notice given to him under subsection (3) of this section, the Secretary of State may by order recall him to a borstal institution; and thereupon he shall be liable to be detained in the borstal institution until the expiration of two years from the date of his sentence, or the expiration of six months from the date of his being taken into custody under the order, whichever is the later, and, if at large, shall be deemed to be unlawfully at large:

Provided that—

(a) any such order shall, at the expiration of two years from the date of his release, cease to have effect unless the person to whom it relates is then in custody thereunder; and

(b) the Secretary of State may at any time release a person who is detained in a borstal institution under this subsection; and the provisions of subsection (3) of this section and the preceding provisions of this subsection shall apply on his release under this paragraph as they apply in the case of his original release, except that the references to the period of two years from the date of his release shall be construed as references to the period of two years from the date of his original release.

(5) If any person while under supervision, or after his recall to a borstal institution, as aforesaid, or after being ordered to be returned to a borstal institution under section twelve of the Criminal Justice Act, 1961, is sentenced by a court in any part of Great Britain to corrective training or borstal training, his original sentence of borstal training shall cease to have effect.

(6) The Secretary of State in exercising his functions under this section shall consider any report made to him by a board of visitors on the advisability of releasing a person from a borstal institution.

NOTES

Section 45 of the Prison Act, 1952, as set out above is shown in the form in which it now stands after the operation of the amendments made to it by virtue of the Criminal Justice Act, 1961, s. 41, Sched. IV and S.I. 1961 No. 1672 and the Prison Commissioners Dissolution Order 1963, S.I. 1963 No. 597.

Computation of age.—See s. 9 Family Law Reform Act, 1969, p. 1310, *post.*

Supervision and after-care.—See Home Office Circular No. 154/1967 dated August 30, 1967. Probation and after-care committees may spend up to an average of £3 10s. for male borstal inmates discharged to their areas and/or their wives and families. The circular deals with applications for assisted visits, and for pocket money for homeless boys on leave.

Borstal trainees.—As to interviews with officers of the Department of Employment and Productivity see Home Office Circular No. 5/1970 dated January 28, 1970, sent to Secretaries to Probation and After-Care Committee, and copies to probation officers.

CRIMINAL JUSTICE ACT, 1961
[9 & 10 Eliz. 2 c. 39]

PART I

POWERS OF COURTS IN RESPECT OF YOUNG OFFENDERS

Borstal Training and Imprisonment

1. Conditions for and term of sentence of borstal training.—
(1) *The minimum age at conviction which qualifies for a sentence of borstal training under section twenty of the Criminal Justice Act, 1948, shall be fifteen instead of sixteen years.*

(2) The power of a court to pass a sentence of borstal training under the said section twenty in the case of a person convicted as therein mentioned shall be exercisable in any case where the court is of opinion, having regard to the circumstances of the offence and after taking into account the offender's character and previous conduct, that it is expedient that he should be detained for training for not less than six months:

Provided that such a sentence shall not be passed on a person who is under seventeen years of age on the day of his conviction unless the court is of opinion that no other method of dealing with him is appropriate.

(3) Before passing a sentence of borstal training in the case of an offender of any age, the court shall consider any report made in respect of him by or on behalf of the Secretary of State, and section thirty-seven of this Act shall apply accordingly.

(4) The foregoing provisions of this section shall apply in relation to committal for a sentence of borstal training under section twenty-eight of the Magistrates' Courts Act, 1952, as they apply to the passing of such a sentence under section twenty of the Criminal Justice Act, 1948.

(5) Subsections (7) and (8) of section twenty of the Criminal Justice Act, 1948, and subsections (2) and (3) of section twenty-eight of the Magistrates' Courts Act, 1952, shall cease to have effect.

NOTES

This section is printed as amended by the Prison Commissioners Dissolution Order 1963, S.I. 1963, No. 597, para. 3 (2) and Sched. 2, and the Children and Young Persons Act, 1969, s. 72 (4) and Sched. VI; from a date to be appointed the words in italics are repealed (*ibid.*).

"**Age.**"—See s. 39 (3), p. 420, *post*, and note "Attained the Age" at p. 53, *ante*.

"**Expedient.**"—The circumstances in which the court can pass a sentence of borstal training are different from those in s. 20 of the Criminal Justice Act, 1948, as originally enacted. That section is amended by this Act, s. 41 and Sched. IV. See also s. 28 of the Magistrates' Courts Act, 1952, 1951, p. 307, which is similarly amended.

Report of Secretary of State.—The court is not bound by the report, it need only consider it (*R. v. Watkins, R. v. Smallwood, R. v. Jones* (1910), 74 J.P. 382; but see observation by the Court of Criminal Appeal in *R. v. Tarbotton*, [1942] 1 All E. R. 198).

The Secretary of State's report should be handed to the offender with appropriate oral observation. See *Practice Note, Court of Criminal Appeal*, [1959] 2 All E. R. 734 (C. C. A.), where Lord Parker, C.J., is reported as having said, "The court is finding over and over again that it is impossible to tell from the transcript in any particular case whether the Prison Commissioners' report has ever been handed to the offender or his counsel or solicitor, as required by s. 21 (5) and s. 20 (8) of the Criminal Justice Act, 1948. (See now s. 37 Criminal Justice Act, 1961.) Even when subsequent inquiries are made, it is difficult to find out what happened. The court thinks that the handing of a copy should be a routine matter, and that it should be accompanied by some oral observation, such as: ' I now hand you the report,' which will appear on the transcript. The proper time for doing this will be after the notices of previous convictions have been proved, and this, indeed, was stated to be the proper course by Lord Goddard, C.J. *R. v. Dickson*, [1950] 1 K. B. 394 at p. 396; [1949] 2 All E. R. 810, at p. 812."

See also *R. v. Noseda*, [1958] 2 All E. R. 567; 122 J. P. 373.

2. Serious offences by children and young persons.—[*This section amends s. 53 of the Children and Young Persons Act, 1933, p. 57, ante, and s. 17 (1) of the Criminal Justice Act, 1948, p. 372, post. Those sections are there printed as amended.*]

PART II

TREATMENT AND SUPERVISION OF PRISONERS AND OTHER
DETAINED PERSONS

Borstal Institutions and Detention Centres

11. Term of detention and supervision under sentence of borstal training.—(1) The maximum period for which a person sentenced to borstal training after the commencement of this section may be detained under subsection (2) of section forty-five of the Prison Act, 1952, shall be two years instead of three years, and the minimum period for which such a person may be so detained shall (subject to any direction of the Secretary of State under that subsection) be six months instead of nine months.

(2) The period for which a person sentenced to borstal training after the commencement of this section is to be under supervision under subsection (3) of the said section forty-five after his release from a borstal institution shall (subject to any order of the Secretary of State under that subsection) be a period of two years beginning with the date of his release instead of a period beginning with that date and continuing until the expiration of four years from the date of his sentence.

NOTES

This section is printed as amended by the Prison Commissioners Dissolution Order 1963, S.I. 1963, No. 597, para. 3 (2) and Sched. 2.

" **Sentenced to borstal training.**"—See s. 38 (5), p. 419, *post*.

Prison Act, 1952, s. 45.—See p. 309, *ante*.

12. Return to borstal institution on re-conviction.—(1) Where a person sentenced to borstal training—

(a) being under supervision after his release from a borstal institution; or

(b) having become unlawfully at large from a borstal institution and not having returned or been returned thereto,

is convicted, whether on indictment or summarily, of an offence for which the court has power, or would have power but for the statutory restrictions upon the imprisonment of young offenders, to pass sentence of imprisonment, the court may, instead of dealing with him in any other manner, order that he be returned to a borstal institution.

(2) A person ordered under this section to be returned to a borstal institution shall be liable to be detained for the like period, and if under supervision shall be treated for all other purposes, as if he had been recalled to a borstal institution by order of the Secretary of State in pursuance of section forty-five of the Prison Act, 1952, and had been taken into custody in pursuance of that order on the date of the order under this section.

(3) Before making an order under this section in respect of an offender, the court shall consider any report made by or on behalf of the Secretary of State on his response to the training already undergone by him, and section thirty-seven of this Act shall apply accordingly.

(4) Where the offender is under supervision as aforesaid, and the court by which he is convicted is a magistrates' court and has not received such a report as aforesaid, the court shall adjourn the hearing in accordance with subsection (3) of section fourteen of the Magistrates' Courts Act, 1952, and remand the offender in custody to enable such a report to be made.

(5) References in this section to a person under supervision after his release from a borstal institution do not include a person who, being under supervision as aforesaid, is for the time being deemed by virtue of section forty-five of the Prison Act, 1952, to be unlawfully at large.

NOTES

This section is printed as amended by the Prison Commissioners' Dissolution Order, 1963 (S.I. 1963 No. 597).

" Sentenced to borstal training."—See s. 38 (5), p. 419, *post*.

" Court;" " statutory restrictions upon the imprisonment of young offenders."—For definitions, see s. 39, p. 419, *post*.

Prison Act, 1952, s. 45.—See p. 309, *ante*.

Magistrates' Courts Act, 1952, s. 14.—See p. 378, *post*.

Appeal.—An accused, convicted by a magistrates' court of an indictable offence and committed to quarter sessions for sentence, has no right of appeal against sentence where he is ordered, pursuant to this section to be returned to a borstal institution, as distinct from where he is sentenced to a new borstal term (*R. v. Bebbington*, [1969] 3 All E. R. 426; 133 J. P. 689).

16. Removal to borstal institution.—(1) [*Repealed by the Children and Young Persons Act*, 1969, s. 72 (4) *and Sched. VI. See now s.* 31, ibid.]

17. Proceedings for removal under s. 16.—[*Repealed by the Children and Young Persons Act*, 1969.]

INTRODUCTORY NOTE

As to fines outstanding against persons detained in borstal institutions, detention centres and approved schools, see Home Office circulars nos. 122/1968 and 237/1968, pp. 697 *et seq., post.*

MAGISTRATES' COURTS ACT, 1952
[15 & 16 Geo. 6 & 1 Eliz. 2, c. 55]

*   *   *   *

67. Release from custody and reduction of detention on payment. —(1) Where imprisonment or other detention has been imposed on any person by the order of a magistrates' court in default of payment of any sum adjudged to be paid by the conviction or order of a magistrates' court or for want of sufficient distress to satisfy such a sum, then, on the payment of the sum, together with the costs and charges, if any, of the commitment and distress, the order shall cease to have effect; and if the person has been committed to custody he shall be released unless he is in custody for some other cause.

(2) Where, after a period of imprisonment or other detention has been imposed on any person in default of payment of any sum adjudged to be paid by the conviction or order of a magistrates' court or for want of sufficient distress to satisfy such a sum, payment is made in accordance with the rules of part of the sum, the period of detention shall be reduced by such number of days as bears to the total number of days in that period less one day the same proportion as the amount so paid bears to so much of the said sum, and the costs and charges of any distress levied to satisfy that sum, as was due at the time the period of detention was imposed.

(3) In calculating the reduction required under the last preceding subsection any fraction of a day shall be left out of account.

NOTES

Period of detention.—When detention is in default of payment of a fine or other sum of money the limitations governing committal must be observed. See s. 64 and Sched. III of the Magistrates' Courts Act, 1952 (21 Halsbury's Statutes, 3rd Edn., 238, 295). In magistrates' courts committals for doing or failing to do an act are dealt with in *ibid.,* s. 54, which provides a maximum period of two months' imprisonment.

Payment after detention has been imposed.—See rule 45 of the Magistrates' Courts Rules, 1968.

68. Application of money found on defaulter to satisfy sum adjudged.—(1) Where a magistrates' court has adjudged a person to pay a sum by a conviction or has ordered the enforcement of a sum due from a person under an affiliation order or an order enforceable as an affiliation order, the court may order him to be searched.

(2) Any money found on the arrest of a person adjudged to pay such a sum as aforesaid, or on a search as aforesaid, or on his being taken to a prison or other place of detention in default of payment of such a sum or for want of sufficient distress to satisfy such a sum, may, unless the court otherwise directs, be applied towards payment of the said sum; and the balance, if any, shall be returned to him.

(3) A magistrates' court shall not allow the application as aforesaid of any money found on a person if it is satisfied that the money does not belong to him or that the loss of the money would be more injurious to his family than would be his detention.

NOTE
Direction under subsection (2).—See rule 52 of the Magistrates' Courts Rules, 1968.

"Order enforceable as an affiliation order."—This section applies to legal aid contributions orders as if they were enforceable as an affiliation order (Administration of Justice Act, 1970, s. 43 and Sched. X).

Sums adjudged to be paid by a summary conviction

69. Restrictions on power to impose imprisonment on conviction.—(1) [*Repealed by the Criminal Justice Act,* 1967, ss. 44, 103 *and Sched. VII. See now ss.* 44–46, ibid.]

70. Restriction on committal after conviction.—Means inquiry.
[*Repealed by the Criminal Justice Act,* 1967, s. 103 *and Sched. VII.*]

(2) A magistrates' court may, for the purpose of enabling inquiry to be made under section 44 of the Criminal Justice Act, 1967—

(a) issue a summons requiring the offender to appear before the court at the time and place appointed in the summons; or
(b) issue a warrant to arrest him and bring him before the court.

(3) On the failure of the offender to appear before the court in answer to a summons under this section the court may issue a warrant to arrest him and bring him before the court.

(4) A warrant issued under this section may be executed in like manner, and the like proceedings may be taken with a view to its execution, in any part of the United Kingdom, as if it had been issued under section fifteen of this Act.

(5) Notwithstanding anything in section one hundred and two of this Act, a warrant under this section shall cease to have effect when the sum in respect of which the warrant is issued is paid to the police officer holding the warrant.

NOTES
Means inquiry.—Although the reference to a warrant of commitment in s. 44 Criminal Justice Act, 1967, would seem to make it inapplicable to the case of a juvenile, it is submitted that the procedure of means inquiry is appropriate, and indeed there may be cases where attachment of earnings is considered and by s. 46

Criminal Justice Act, 1967, the court must enquire into a defaulter's means. In many cases however, *e.g.* where the defaulter is a schoolboy, it is unrealistic to suppose that a summons or warrant to secure attendance at such an enquiry is anything other than an attempt to enforce a fine by the issue of process itself. It must be doubted whether this is a proper procedure.

The enforcement of fines against adults is materially affected by the provisions of ss. 44–46 of the Criminal Justice Act, 1967 and as regards juveniles, the Children and Young Persons Act, 1969. Committal to remand home, detention centre or attendance centre in default is no longer possible, and there must be few cases where distress or an attachment of earnings order is applicable. If the defaulter attains the age of 17, the "adult" provisions will however apply. If the parent of a juvenile is ordered to pay a fine, damages, compensation or costs, the order may be enforced as if it had been adjudged to be paid on summary conviction by the court which made the order. The sum may alternatively be enforced therefore by committal (see ss. 12, 41 and Sched. IX, Part I, Administration of Justice Act, 1970).

71. Supervision pending payment.—(1) Where any person is adjudged to pay a sum by a summary conviction and the convicting court does not commit him to prison forthwith in default of payment, the court may, either on the occasion of the conviction or on a subsequent occasion, order him to be placed under the supervision of such person as the court may from time to time appoint.

(2) An order placing a person under supervision in respect of any sum shall remain in force so long as he remains liable to pay the sum or any part of it unless the order ceases to have effect or is discharged under the next following subsection.

(3) An order under this section shall cease to have effect on the making of a transfer of fine order under section seventy-two of this Act with respect to the sum adjudged to be paid and may be discharged by the court that made it, without prejudice in either case to the making of a new order.

(4) Where a person under twenty-one years old has been adjudged to pay a sum by a summary conviction and the convicting court does not commit him to prison forthwith in default of payment, the court shall not commit him to prison in default of payment of the sum, or for want of sufficient distress to satisfy the sum, unless he has been placed under supervision in respect of the sum or the court is satisfied that it is undesirable or impracticable to place him under supervision.

(5) Where a court, being satisfied as aforesaid, commits a person under twenty-one years old to prison without an order under this section having been made, the court shall state the grounds on which it is so satisfied in the warrant of commitment.

(6) Where an order placing a person under supervision with respect to a sum is in force, a magistrates' court shall not commit him to prison in default of payment of the sum, or for want of sufficient distress to satisfy the sum, unless the court has before committing him taken such steps as may be reasonably practicable to obtain from the person appointed for his supervision an oral or written report on the offender's conduct and means and has considered any report so obtained, in addition, in a case where an inquiry is required by the last preceding section, to that inquiry.

NOTES

Juvenile.—The provisions of s. 71 apply to a juvenile, and in view of the difficulty that may be experienced in enforcing a fine, it may be good practice to consider such an order in each case.

Order for supervision.—See rule 46 of the Magistrates' Courts Rules, 1968, as to service of an order, and as to the duties of the person appointed to supervise.

Determination of age.—See s. 126 (5), p. 388, *post.*

*   *   *   *

96. Forfeiture of recognizance.—(1) Where a recognizance to keep the peace or to be of good behaviour has been entered into before a magistrates' court or any recognizance is conditioned for the appearance of a person before a magistrates' court or for his doing any other thing connected with a proceeding before a magistrates' court, and the recognizance appears to the court to be forfeited, the court may, subject to the next following subsection, declare the recognizance to be forfeited and adjudge the persons bound thereby, whether as principal or sureties, or any of them, to pay the sum in which they are respectively bound.

(2) Where a recognizance is conditioned to keep the peace or to be of good behaviour, the court shall not declare it forfeited except by order made on complaint.

(3) The court which declares the recognizance to be forfeited may, instead of adjudging any person to pay the whole sum in which he is bound, adjudge him to pay part only of the sum or remit the sum.

(4) Payment of any sum adjudged to be paid under this section, including any costs awarded against the defendant, may be enforced, and any such sum shall be applied, as if it were a fine and as if the adjudication were a summary conviction of an offence not punishable with imprisonment and so much of section 44 (10) of the Criminal Justice Act, 1967, as empowers a court to remit fines shall not apply to the sum but so much thereof as relates to remission after a term of imprisonment has been imposed shall so apply.

Provided that, at any time before the issue of a warrant of commitment to enforce payment of the sum, or before the sale of goods under a warrant of distress to satisfy the sum, the court may remit the whole or any part of the sum either absolutely or on such conditions as the court thinks just.

(5) A recognizance such as is mentioned in this section shall not be enforced otherwise than in accordance with this section, and accordingly shall not be transmitted to the Crown Court nor shall its forfeiture be certified to the Crown Court.

NOTES

This section is printed as amended by the Criminal Justice Act, 1967, s. 103 and Sched. VI and the Courts Act, 1971, 56 and Sched. VIII.

Forfeiture of recognizance.—The court will hear any evidence tendered by the parties before forfeiting the recognizance. See also *R.* v. *Ossett JJ., Ex. parte Tebb,* [1972] Crim. L. R. 39.

No appeal against forfeiture.—There is no appeal (*R.* v. *Durham JJ., Ex parte Laurent,* [1945] K. B. 33; [1944] 2 All E. R. 530; 109 J. P. 21).

" As if . . . . a summary conviction."—Sections 63 to 72 of this Act (21 Halsbury's Statutes, 3rd Edn., 237–245) will apply to the recovery of sums adjudged to be paid.

CRIMINAL JUSTICE ACT, 1961
[9 & 10 Eliz. 2, c. 39]

Fine, Probation and Attendance Centre

8. Fines for young offenders.—(1) *The limit imposed by section thirty-two of the Magistrates' Courts Act, 1952, upon the amount of the fine which may be imposed by a magistrates' court on finding guilty an offender under fourteen years of age shall be raised from forty shillings to ten pounds.*

(2) [*Repealed by the Children and Young Persons Act, 1967, s. 72 (4) and Sched. VI. See now s. 6, ibid.*]

(3) Where a person under seventeen years of age is found guilty by a magistrates' court of an offence for which, apart from this subsection, the court would have power to impose a fine of an amount exceeding fifty pounds, the amount of any fine imposed by the court shall not exceed fifty pounds.

(4) Subsection (1) of section fifty-five of the Children and Young Persons Act, 1933, which provides for the payment by parents or guardians of fines, damages or costs incurred by children or young persons, shall apply in relation to compensation for loss under subsection (2) of section eleven of the Criminal Justice Act, 1948, and to any sums which the court has power to award under section four of the Forfeiture Act, 1870, or section thirty-four of the Magistrates' Courts Act, 1952, as it applies in relation to damages or costs.

NOTES

This section is printed as amended by the Children and Young Persons Act, 1969. From a date to be appointed the words in italics are repealed, s. 72 (4) and Sched. VI, *ibid.* As to fine on child see s. 34 (5), *ibid.*

"**Age.**"—See note to s. 1, p. 311, *ante.*

Magistrates' Courts Act, 1952.—For s. 32, see p. 277, *ante*; for s. 34, see p. 381, *post.*

Children and Young Persons Act, 1933, s. 55.—See p. 59, *ante.*

Criminal Justice Act, 1948, s. 11.—See p. 290, *ante.*

Forfeiture Act, 1870.—See 8 Halsbury's Statutes, 3rd Edn., 179.

CRIMINAL JUSTICE ACT, 1967
[1967 c. 80]

Enforcement of payment of fines, etc.

44. Restriction on magistrates' courts' power to impose imprisonment for default in payment of fines, etc.—(1) The following provisions of this section shall have effect with respect to the issue of a warrant of commitment under Part III of the Magistrates' Courts Act, 1952, for default in paying a sum adjudged to be paid by a conviction of a magistrates' court; and accordingly sections 69 and 70(1) of that Act (existing restrictions on the power of magistrates' courts to issue such warrants) shall cease to have effect.

(2) A magistrates' court shall not on the occasion of convicting an offender of an offence issue a warrant of commitment for a default in paying any such sum unless—

(a) in the case of an offence punishable with imprisonment, he appears to the court to have sufficient means to pay the sum forthwith;

(b) it appears to the court that he is unlikely to remain long enough at a place of abode in the United Kingdom to enable payment of the sum to be enforced by other methods; or

(c) on the occasion of that conviction the court sentences him to immediate imprisonment or detention in a detention centre for that or another offence or he is already serving a term of imprisonment or detention in a detention centre.

(3) A magistrates' court shall not in advance of the issue of a warrant of commitment fix a term of imprisonment which is to be served by an offender in the event of a default in paying a sum adjudged to be paid by a conviction, except where it has power to issue a warrant of commitment forthwith, but postpones issuing the warrant under section 65(2) of the Magistrates' Courts Act, 1952 (power to fix a term and postpone the issue of a warrant).

(4) Where on the occasion of the offender's conviction a magistrates' court does not issue a warrant of commitment for a default in paying any such sum as aforesaid or fix a term of imprisonment under the said section 65(2) which is to be served by him in the event of any such default, it shall not thereafter issue a warrant of commitment for any such default or for want of sufficient distress to satisfy such a sum unless—

(a) he is already serving a term of imprisonment or detention in a detention centre; or

(b) the court has since the conviction inquired into his means in his presence on at least one occasion.

(5) Where a magistrates' court is required by the last foregoing subsection to inquire into a person's means, the court may not on the occasion of the inquiry or at any time thereafter issue a warrant of commitment for a default in paying any such sum unless—

(a) in the case of an offence punishable with imprisonment, the offender appears to the court to have sufficient means to pay the sum forthwith; or

(b) the court has considered or tried all other methods of enforcing payment of the sum and it appears to the court that they are inappropriate or unsuccessful.

(6) After the occasion of an offender's conviction by a magistrates' court, the court shall not, unless—

(a) the court has previously fixed a term of imprisonment under section 65(2) of the Magistrates' Courts Act, 1952 which is to be served by the offender in the event of a default in paying a sum adjudged to be paid by the conviction; or

(b) the offender is serving a term of imprisonment or detention in a detention centre;

issue a warrant of commitment for a default in paying the sum or fix such a term except at a hearing at which the offender is present; and sub-sections (2) to (5) of section 70 of that Act (process for securing appearance of offender at means inquiry) shall apply in relation to a hearing required to be held by this subsection as they apply in relation to an inquiry into a person's means.

(7) Where a magistrates' court issues a warrant of commitment on the ground that one of the conditions mentioned in subsection (2) or (5) of this section is satisfied, it shall state that fact, specifying the ground, in the warrant.

(8) A magistrates' court may, either before or on inquiring into a person's means under this section, and a justice of the peace acting for the same petty sessions area as that court may before any such inquiry, order him to furnish to the court within a period specified in the order such a statement of his means as the court may require.

(9) A person who fails to comply with an order under the last foregoing subsection shall be liable on summary conviction to a fine not exceeding £50.

(10) Where a fine has been imposed on conviction of an offender by a magistrates' court, the court may, on inquiring into his means or at a hearing under subsection (6) of this section, remit the whole or any part of the fine if the court thinks it just to do so having regard to any change in his circumstances since the conviction, and where the court remits the whole or part of the fine after a term of imprisonment has been fixed, it shall also reduce the term by an amount which bears the same proportion to the whole term as the amount remitted bears to the whole fine or, as the case may be, shall remit the whole term.

In calculating the reduction in a term of imprisonment required by this subsection any fraction of a day shall be left out of account.

(11) Notwithstanding the definition of "fine" in the Magistrates' Courts Act, 1952, references in the last foregoing subsection to a fine do not include any other sum adjudged to be paid on conviction, whether as a pecuniary penalty, forfeiture, compensation or otherwise.

NOTE

This section is printed as amended by the Courts Act, 1971, s. 56 and Scheds. VIII and XI.

45. Enforcement of payment of fines by High Court and county court.—(1) Subject to the provisions of the next following subsection, payment of a sum adjudged to be paid by a conviction of a magistrates' court may be enforced by the High Court or a county court (otherwise than by issue of a writ of fieri facias or other process against goods or by imprisonment or attachment of earnings) as if the sum were due to the clerk of the magistrates' court in pursuance of a judgment or order of the High Court or county court, as the case may be.

(2) The foregoing subsection shall not be construed as authorising the enforcement by a county court of payment of a fine exceeding the limit for

the time being in force under section 40 of the County Courts Act, 1959, on the amount of any penalty recoverable by statute in a county court.

(3) The clerk of the magistrates' court shall not take proceedings by virtue of subsection (1) of this section to recover any sum adjudged to be paid by a conviction of the court from any person unless authorised to do so by the court after an inquiry under the last foregoing section into that person's means.

(4) Any expenses incurred by the clerk of a magistrates' court in recovering any such sum shall be treated for the purposes of Part IV of the Justices of the Peace Act, 1949, as expenses of the magistrates' courts committee.

NOTE

This section is printed as amended by the Administration of Justice Act, 1970, s. 42.

46. Enforcement of payment of fines by attachment of earnings orders.—[*Repealed by the Administration of Justice Act*, 1970, *s.* 54 *and Sched. XI. See now Attachment of Earnings Act*, 1971, *s.* 1.]

50. Supplementary provisions as to payment of fines, etc.—Sections 44 to 46 of this Act and Part III of the Magistrates' Courts Act, 1952, shall have effect as if those sections were contained in that Part of that Act and in section 5(5) of the Criminal Justice Act, 1961 (construction of references to terms of imprisonment) the reference to section 14 of the Criminal Justice Act, 1948, shall be construed as including a reference to section 47 of this Act.

ADMINISTRATION OF JUSTICE ACT, 1970

[1970 c. 31]

12. Restriction on magistrates' power of committal for civil debt.—(1) The power of a magistrates' court under section 64 of the Act of 1952 to issue a warrant to commit to prison a person who makes default in paying a sum adjudged to be paid by such a court shall be restricted in accordance with this section.

(2) This section does not affect the court's power to issue such a warrant in the case of default in paying a sum adjudged to be paid by a conviction, or treated (by any enactment relating to the collection or enforcement of fines, costs, compensation or forfeited recognisances) as so adjudged to be paid; but in the case of a sum adjudged to be paid by an order the power shall be exercisable only in respect of default under—

   (a) a magistrates' court maintenance order;
   (b) an order for the payment of any of the taxes, contributions or liabilities specified in Schedule 4 to this Act; or

(c) an order (in this Act referred to as a "legal aid contribution order") under section 76 of the Criminal Justice Act, 1967 (contribution by legally assisted person to cost of his defence in a criminal case).

NOTE

Legal aid contribution order.—See the provisions of the Criminal Justice Act, 1967, p. 330, *post.*

41. Recovery of costs and compensation awarded by magistrates, the Crown Court, etc.—(1) In the cases specified in Part I of Schedule 9 to this Act (being cases where, in criminal proceedings, a court makes an order against the accused for the payment of costs, compensation, etc.) any sum required to be paid by such an order as is there mentioned shall be treated, for the purposes of collection and enforcement, as if it had been adjudged to be paid on a conviction by a magistrates' court, being—

(a) where the order is made by a magistrates' court, that court; and
(b) in any other case, such magistrates' court as may be specified in the order.

(2) In the cases specified in Part II of the said Schedule (being cases where a court makes an order against the prosecutor in criminal proceedings, and certain cases where an order for costs arises out of an appeal to quarter sessions in proceedings which are not criminal) any sum required to be paid by such an order as is there mentioned shall be enforceable as if the order were for the payment of money recoverable summarily as a civil debt.

(3) Without prejudice to the foregoing subsections, but subject to subsection (4) below, in the cases specified in Schedule 9 to this Act any sum required to be paid by such an order as is there mentioned shall be enforceable by the High Court or a county court (otherwise than by issue of a writ of fieri facias or other process against goods or by imprisonment or attachment of earnings) as if the sum were due in pursuance of a judgment or order of the High Court or county court, as the case may be.

(4) Subsection (3) above shall not authorise the enforcement by a county court of payment of any sum exceeding the limit for the time being in force under section 40 of the County Courts Act, 1959 on the amount of any penalty recoverable by statute in a county court.

(5) References in subsections (1) and (2) above to orders mentioned in Schedule 9 to this Act include references to orders made before the day appointed under section 54 of this Act for the coming into force of this section, except an order in the case of which the person entitled to payment has before that day begun proceedings for its enforcement; and in relation to such a case the enactments in force immediately before that day with reference to the enforcement of such an order shall continue to apply notwithstanding any repeal effected by this Act, without prejudice however to section 13 (6) of this Act.

For the purpose of the operation of subsection (1) above with respect to an order made (otherwise than by a magistrates' court) before the day so appointed, the order shall be deemed to specify the magistrates' court for the petty sessions area in which the person subject to the order for the time being resides.

(6) In the Magistrates' Courts Act, 1952—

    (a) in section 72 (1) (transfer of fine order in England and Wales) and in section 72A (1) (the same as between England and Scotland), for the words from the beginning to "the offender" there shall be substituted in each case the words "Where a magistrates' court has, or is treated by any enactment as having, adjudged a person by a conviction to pay a sum and it appears to the court that the person"; and

    (b) in section 72 (2) (enforcement functions on transfer of fine in England and Wales), for the words "the convicting court" there shall be substituted the words "the court which made the order".

(7) In section 32 (2) of the Courts-Martial (Appeals) Act, 1968 (enforcement of order for costs against unsuccessful appellant or applicant for leave to appeal to that court), for paragraph (a) there shall be substituted the following:—

    "(a) in the same manner as an order for costs made by the criminal division of the Court of Appeal under section 25 of the Criminal Appeal Act, 1968; or".

(8) In any of the cases specified in Part I of Schedule 9 to this Act, a court (other than a magistrates' court) which makes such an order as is there mentioned may, if it thinks that the period for which the person subject to the order is liable apart from this subsection to be committed to prison for default under the order is insufficient, specify a longer period for that purpose, but not exceeding twelve months; and then, in the case of default—

    (a) the specified period shall be substituted as the maximum for which the person may be imprisoned under section 64 of the Magistrates' Courts Act, 1952 (distress or committal); and

    (b) paragraph 2 of Schedule 3 to that Act shall apply, with the necessary modifications, for the reduction of the specified period where, at the time of the person's imprisonment, he has made part payment under the order.

(9) Where a magistrates' court has power to commit a person to prison for default in paying a sum due under an order enforceable as mentioned in this section, the court shall not exercise the power unless it is satisfied that all other methods of enforcing payment have been tried or considered and either have proved unsuccessful or are likely to do so.

SCHEDULE 9

Section 41

ENFORCEMENT OF ORDERS FOR COSTS, COMPENSATION, ETC.

PART I

CASES WHERE PAYMENT ENFORCEABLE AS ON SUMMARY CONVICTION

Costs awarded by Magistrates

1. Where a magistrates' court, on the summary trial of an information, makes an order as to costs to be paid by the accused to the prosecutor.

2. Where an appellant to quarter sessions against conviction or sentence by a magistrates' court abandons his appeal and the magistrates' court orders him to pay costs to the other party to the appeal.

Costs awarded by assizes and quarter sessions

3. Where a person appeals to quarter sessions against conviction or sentence by a magistrates' court, and quarter sessions makes an order as to costs to be paid by him.

4. Where a person is prosecuted or tried on indictment or inquisition before a court of assize or quarter sessions and is convicted, and the court orders him to pay the whole or part of the costs incurred in or about the prosecution and conviction.

5. Where the accused is ordered by quarter sessions to pay costs, under powers exercisable by virtue of section 14 of the Costs in Criminal Cases Act, 1952 (committal to quarter sessions for sentence and other purposes; appeal under Vagrancy Act, 1824).

Costs awarded by Court of Appeal (criminal division) or House of Lords

6. Where the criminal division of the Court of Appeal dismisses an appeal or application for leave to appeal and orders the appellant or applicant to pay the whole or part of the costs of the appeal or application.

7. Where the criminal division of the Court of Appeal or the House of Lords dismisses an application for leave to appeal to that House (being an application made by the person who was the appellant before the criminal division) and orders him to pay the whole or part of the costs of the application.

Criminal costs awarded by High Court

8. Where a person is tried at bar in the Queen's Bench Division of the High Court and is convicted, and the High Court orders him to pay the whole or part of the costs incurred in or about the prosecution and conviction.

Miscellaneous orders for costs, compensation, damages etc.

9. Where a court makes an order for the payment of costs by an offender and does so under the Costs in Criminal Cases Act, 1952 as applied by section 31 (1) or (2) of the Criminal Justice Act, 1967 (proceedings in which a person is dealt with for a further offence after being put on probation, conditionally discharged, bound over or given a suspended sentence).

9A. Where under section 8 of the Criminal Damage Act, 1971 a court orders the payment of a sum by way of compensation in respect of the whole or part of any loss of or damage to property.

10. Where under section 4 of the Forfeiture Act, 1870 or section 34 of the Magistrates' Courts Act, 1952 a court awards a sum of money by way of satisfaction or compensation for damage to, or loss of, property suffered through or by means of an indictable offence.

11. Where under section 11 (2) of the Criminal Justice Act, 1948 a court, on making a probation order or an order for conditional discharge, or on discharging an offender absolutely, orders the offender to pay damages for injury or compensation for loss.

12. Where under section 55 of the Children and Young Persons Act, 1933 a court orders any fine, damages, compensation or costs, or any sum awarded by way of satisfaction or compensation to be paid by the parent or guardian of a child or young person.

SECTION 9.—LEGAL AID

This section contains a number of provisions relevant to the making of legal aid orders and the enforcement of legal aid contribution orders. The juvenile court which makes the order is required to enforce contributions against an adult who is an appropriate contributor.

A legal aid contribution order may be enforced by an attachment of earnings order (Attachment of Earnings Act, 1971, s. 1 (3)) or by committal in accordance with the provisions of the Administration of Justice Act, 1970.

LEGAL AID AND ADVICE ACT, 1949
[1949 c. 51]

General note.—"Civil" legal aid is available in certain proceedings before the Crown Court or a magistrates' court. They are set out in the Schedule to the Act and Regulations made under ss. 1 and 2.

1. Scope and general conditions of legal aid in connection with proceedings.—(1) This and the three next following sections provide for, and (save as hereinafter mentioned) relate only to, legal aid in connection with proceedings before courts and tribunals in England and Wales, not being proceedings in which free legal aid may be given under Part IV of the Criminal Justice Act, 1967.

(2) Unless and until regulations otherwise provide, the proceedings in connection with which legal aid may be given are any proceedings of a description mentioned in Part I of the First Schedule to this Act, except proceedings mentioned in Part II of that Schedule.

(3) Subject to the provisions of this section, the proceedings in connection with which legal aid may be given may be varied by regulat ions and the regulations may describe the proceedings to be included or excluded by reference to the court or tribunal, to the issues involved, to the capacity in which the person requiring legal aid is concerned, or otherwise.

FIRST SCHEDULE

Section 1

PROCEEDINGS FOR WHICH LEGAL AID MAY BE GIVEN
UNDER SECTION ONE

PART 1
DESCRIPTION OF PROCEEDINGS

1. Proceedings in any of the following courts—

(a) the House of Lords in the exercise of its jurisdiction in relation to appeals from courts in England or Northern Ireland;

(b) the Judicial Committee of the Privy Council;
(c) the Court of Appeal and the High Court;
(d) any county court;

2. Proceedings before any person to whom a case is referred in whole or in part by any of the said courts.

3. The following proceedings in a court of summary jurisdiction or the Crown court, namely—

(a) proceedings for or relating to an affiliation order within the meaning of the Affiliation Proceedings Act, 1957, or an order under the Matrimonial Proceedings (Magistrates' Courts) Act, 1960;
(b) proceedings under the Guardianship of Minors Act, 1971;
(c) *proceedings under the Small Tenements Recovery Act*, 1838.

4. Proceedings before a coroner.

NOTE

See the Legal Aid (Extension of Proceedings) Regulations, 1969, p. 370, *post.* See also the Legal Aid (General) Regulations, 1971, S.I. 1971 No. 62, and the Legal Aid (Amendment of Resources) Regulations, 1960, S.I. 1960 No. 1471, as amended by S.I. 1969 No. 922, S.I. 1970 No. 1162 and S.I. 1971 Nos. 63 and 103.

The repeal of the Small Tenements Recovery Act, 1838, by the Rent Act, 1965, is not yet operative.

CRIMINAL JUSTICE ACT, 1967

[1967 c. 80]

General note.—These provisions are printed as amended by the Children and Young Persons Act, 1969, the Administration of Justice Act, 1970, and the Courts Act, 1971.

73. Power to order legal aid to be given.—(1) The following provisions of this section have effect with respect to the giving of legal aid in connection with criminal proceedings, and the proceedings mentioned in subsections (3A) and (3B) of this section, but any power conferred by those provisions to give such aid shall be exercisable only in the circumstances mentioned in section 75 (1), and subject to the provisions of section 75 (2) to (4), of this Act.

(2) Where a person is charged with an offence before a magistrates' court or appears or is brought before a magistrates' court to be dealt with, the court may order that he shall be given legal aid for the purpose of the proceedings before the court and any other magistrates' court to which the case is remitted in pursuance of section 56 (1) of the Children and Young Persons Act, 1933.

(3) Where a person convicted or sentenced by a magistrates' court desires to appeal to the Crown Court, either of those courts may order that he shall be given legal aid for the purpose of the appeal and where any such person gives notice of appeal, either of those courts may order that the other party to the appeal shall be given legal aid for the purpose of resisting the appeal.

(3A) Where a person—

(a) is or is to be brought before a juvenile court under section 1 of the Children and Young Persons Act, 1969; or

(b) is the subject of an application to a magistrates' court under section 15 or section 21 of that Act; or

(c) is or is to be brought before a juvenile court under section 31 of that Act,

the court may order that he shall be given legal aid for the purpose of proceedings before the court and, in a case falling within paragraph (a) of this subsection, before any juvenile court to which the case is remitted.

(3B) Where a person desires to appeal to the Crown Court in pursuance of section 2 (12), 3 (8), 16 (8), 21 (4) or 31 (6) of the said Act of 1969, that court or the court from whose decision the appeal lies may order that he be given legal aid for the purpose of the appeal.

(4) Where a person is committed to or appears before the Crown Court for trial or sentence, or appears or is brought before the Crown Court to be dealt with, the court which commits him or to which he is committed, or before which he appears or is brought, may order that he shall be given legal aid for the purpose of the trial or other proceedings before the Crown Court.

(5) Where a person is convicted or sentenced by the Crown Court and desires to appeal to the Court of Appeal against his conviction or sentence, the criminal division of the Court of Appeal may order that he shall be given legal aid for the purpose of the appeal and any proceedings preliminary or incidental thereto.

(6) Where a person is convicted by a court-martial and desires to appeal to the Courts-Martial Appeal Court, the latter court may order that he shall be given legal aid for the purpose of the appeal and any proceedings preliminary or incidental thereto.

(7) Where either party to an appeal to the criminal division of the Court of Appeal or the Courts-Martial Appeal Court desires to appeal to the House of Lords from a decision of one of those Courts, the court which gave the decision may order that the person to whose conviction or sentence the appeal relates shall be given legal aid for the purpose of the appeal and any proceedings preliminary or incidental thereto.

(8) Where the criminal division of the Court of Appeal or the House of Lords orders a person to be retried by the Crown Court under section I of the Criminal Appeal Act, 1964 (new trials in cases of fresh evidence), the former court or the House of Lords, as the case may be, or the latter court may order that he shall be given legal aid for the purpose of the retrial.

(9) In the following provisions of this Part of this Act "legal aid order" means an order made under any provision of this section and "legally assisted person" means a person to whom legal aid is ordered to be given by such an order.

74. Supplementary provisions as to legal aid orders.—(1) For the purposes of this Part of this Act legal aid, in relation to any proceedings to which a person is a party, shall be taken, subject to the following provisions of this section, as consisting of representation by a solicitor and counsel assigned by the court, including advice on the preparation of that person's case for those proceedings.

(2) Notwithstanding anything in the last foregoing subsection legal aid ordered to be given for the purposes of any proceedings before a magistrates' court shall not include representation by counsel except in the case of any indictable offence where the court is of opinion that, because of circumstances which make the case unusually grave or difficult, representation by both counsel and solicitor would be desirable and except in the case of proceedings under section 1 of the Children and Young Persons Act, 1969 where it is alleged that the condition set out in subsection (2) (f) of that section is satisfied in consequence of an indictable offence and where the court is of the opinion aforesaid.

(3) Where the Crown Court makes a legal aid order under subsection (3), (3B) or (4) of the last foregoing section, the court may, in cases of urgency where it appears to the court that there is no time to instruct a solicitor, order that the legal aid to be given shall consist of representation by counsel only, and where a magistrates' court or court of quarter sessions makes a legal aid order under any of those subsections for the purpose of proceedings in the Crown Court, being proceedings at which solicitors have a right of audience, the court may order that the legal aid to be given shall consist of representation by a solicitor only.

(4) Where a court makes a legal aid order under subsection (5) or (6) of the last foregoing section, the court may order that the legal aid to be given shall consist of representation by counsel only.

(5) A legal aid order under subsection (2) or (3A) of the last foregoing section for the purpose of proceedings before a magistrates' court shall be authority for the solicitor assigned by the court to give advice on the question whether there appear to be reasonable grounds of appeal from any determination in those proceedings and assistance by him in the giving of a notice of appeal or making of an application for a case to be stated, being a notice given or application made within the ordinary time for doing so.

(6) Legal aid which may be ordered to be given to any person convicted or sentenced by a magistrates' court for the purpose of an appeal to the Crown Court by a legal aid order under subsection (3) of the last foregoing section or to any person by a legal aid order under subsection (3B) of that section shall be authority for counsel or the solicitor assigned to him to give advice, in the event of the court confirming or varying his conviction or sentence, or, as the case may be, dismissing the appeal mentioned in the said subsection (3B) or otherwise altering the order to which the appeal relates on the question whether there appear to be reasonable grounds of appeal from the decision of the court and, if such grounds appear to exist, assistance in the making of an application for a case to be stated.

(7) Legal aid which may be ordered to be given to any person for the purpose of any proceedings by a legal aid order under subsection (4) of the last foregoing section shall, in the event of his being convicted or sentenced in those proceedings, include advice on the question whether there appear to be reasonable grounds of appeal and—

  (a) if such grounds appear to exist, assistance in the preparation of an application for leave to appeal or in the giving of a notice of appeal;

(b) while that question is being considered, assistance in the making of a provisional application or the giving of a provisional notice.

(8) Legal aid which may be ordered to be given to any person for the purpose of any appeal by a legal aid order under subsection (5) or (6) of the last foregoing section may, without prejudice to subsection (1) of this section, consist in the first instance of advice, by counsel or a solicitor assigned by the court, on the question whether there appear to be reasonable grounds of appeal and assistance by that solicitor in the preparation of an application for leave to appeal or in the giving of a notice of appeal.

(9) A legal aid order under the said subsection (5) or (6) may, if the court thinks fit, include provision that the legal aid ordered to be given shall be deemed to include the like advice and assistance previously given by counsel or a solicitor not then assigned by the court.

(10) The reference in subsection (2) of the last foregoing section to a person charged with an offence before a magistrates' court includes a reference to a person summoned or arrested for an offence and under a duty to appear or a liability to be brought before a magistrates' court in respect of that offence; and the power to make a legal aid order under that subsection shall, in the case of a person arrested for an offence who has not appeared or been brought before a magistrates' court, be exercisable by the magistrates' court to which an application for legal aid is made in pursuance of regulations under this Part of this Act.

(11) Any reference in the said subsection (2) to a person charged with an offence includes a reference to a person against whom proceedings are instituted under section 91 of the Magistrates' Courts Act, 1952 (binding over) in respect of an actual or apprehended breach of the peace or other misbehaviour, and any such reference to a person brought before a magistrates' court to be dealt with includes a reference to a person brought before a metropolitan stipendiary magistrate to be dealt with under section 9 of the Extradition Act, 1870 or section 5 of the Fugitive Offenders Act, 1881 (hearing of extradition and similar proceedings).

(12) In the last foregoing section—

"dealt with" means dealt with under section 6 or 8 of the Criminal Justice Act, 1948 or under section 40 of this Act, or dealt with for a failure to comply with a condition of a recognisance to keep the peace or be of good behaviour;

"sentence" includes an order of a court in respect of which an appeal lies (with or without leave) to another court, and "sentenced" shall be construed accordingly.

75. Circumstances in which legal aid may be given.—(1) Subject to the following provisions of this section, the power to make a legal aid order shall be exercisable by a court having power under section 73 of this Act to do so where it appears to the court desirable to do so in the interests of justice, and a court having power to do so shall make such an order—

(a) where a person is committed for trial on a charge of murder; or
(b) where the prosecutor appeals or applies for leave to appeal from the criminal division of the Court of Appeal or the Courts-Martial Appeal Court to the House of Lords.

(2) A court shall not make a legal aid order for the giving of aid to any person for the purpose of any criminal proceedings or any other purpose unless it appears to the court that his means are such that he requires assistance in meeting the costs which he may incur for that purpose.

(3) A court may refuse to make a legal aid order for the giving of aid to any person unless he first makes a payment on account of any contribution towards costs which he may be liable to make under the next following section, but shall only refuse to do so if it appears to the court from a statement furnished by him under the next following subsection or otherwise that it is likely that he will be required to make such a contribution and that he has the means to make an immediate payment.

(4) Without prejudice to subsection (2) of this section, before a court makes a legal aid order for the giving of aid to any person, the court shall require him to furnish a written statement of his means in a prescribed form.

(4A) Subsections (3) and (4) of this section shall have effect, in their application to a person who has not attained the age of sixteen, as if the words "he", "him" and "his" referred to that person and a person who is an appropriate contributor in relation to him or such of them as the court selects, and as if for the word "shall" in subsection (4) there were substituted the word "may"; and the court may require that a statement furnished by an appropriate contributor in pursuance of subsection (4) shall specify both his means and those of the other person aforesaid.

(5) Where a doubt arises whether a legal aid order should be made for the giving of aid to any person, the doubt shall be resolved in that person's favour.

76. Liability for contributions.—(1) A person to whom legal aid has been ordered to be given for any purpose by a legal aid order may be ordered by a court having power to do so to make such contribution to the appropriate authority in respect of the costs incurred on his behalf for that purpose as appears to the court reasonable having regard to his resources and commitments or, if it so appears, to pay the whole amount of those costs to that authority.

(1A) In a case where a legally assisted person has not attained the age of sixteen, the power conferred by the last foregoing subsection to order him to pay contributions in respect of the relevant costs shall include power to order any person who is an appropriate contributor in relation to him to pay such contributions; and for the purposes of any order proposed to be made by virtue of this subsection in connection with a legal aid order, an appropriate contributor who has failed to furnish a statement which he was required to furnish in pursuance of section 75 (4) of this Act in connection with the legal aid order shall be deemed to have resources and commitments which are such that he may reasonably be ordered to pay the whole amount of the costs in question.

(2) In this Part of this Act any reference to a contribution towards costs shall be construed as including a reference to a payment of the whole amount thereof.

(3) A person may be ordered under this section to make a contribution towards costs in one sum or by instalments.

(4) An order under this section may be made—

(a) where the legal aid was ordered to be given for the purpose of proceedings before a magistrates' court and the legally assisted person is not committed to the Crown Court for trial or sentence, by that magistrates' court, or any other magistrates' court to which the case is remitted in pursuance of section 56 (1) of the Children and Young Persons Act, 1933, after disposing of the case;

(b) where the legal aid was ordered to be given for the purpose of proceedings before a magistrates' court and the legally assisted person is committed to the Crown Court as aforesaid, by the latter court, after disposing of the case;

(c) where the legal aid was ordered to be given for the purpose of an appeal to, or a trial or other proceedings before the Crown Court, by that court, after disposing of the appeal or hearing as the case may be;

(d) where the legal aid was ordered to be given for the purpose of an appeal to the Court of Appeal, the Courts-Martial Appeal Court or the House of Lords, by the Court in question or that House, as the case may be, after disposing of the appeal.

(5) Nothing in subsection (4) of this subsection applies in a case where the legal aid order in question was made by virtue of section 73 (3A) or (3B) of this Act, and in such a case an order under this section may be made—

(a) where the legal aid was ordered to be given for the purpose of proceedings before a magistrates' court, by that court, or any other magistrates' court to which the case is remitted in pursuance of section 2 (11) of the Children and Young Persons Act, 1969, after disposing of the case; and

(b) where the legal aid was ordered to be given for the purposes of an appeal to the Crown Court, by that court after disposing of the appeal.

NOTE

"**Appropriate authority.**"—See Administration of Justice Act, 1970, s. 43, p. 336, *post.*

77. Means inquiry by the Supplementary Benefits Commission.

—(1) At any time after a person has applied for legal aid a court having power to make a legal aid order under section 73 of this Act or an order under the last foregoing section may, and shall on an application made by a legally assisted person, or a person who is an appropriate contributor in relation to him in the prescribed circumstances and within the prescribed time, request the Supplementary Benefits Commission to inquire into the means of that person and any such contributor or of either or any of them and the Commission shall comply with the request and report to the court.

(2) Where the court receives a report under the foregoing subsection before making an order under the last foregoing section, the court shall in determining whether or not to make such an order and in determining the terms of the order have regard to the report.

(3) Where the court receives any such report after making an order under the last foregoing section, it shall reconsider the order and may vary its terms in the light of the report.

78. Computation of resources.—(1) Regulations made by the Secretary of State with the consent of the Treasury may make provision as to the manner in which a person's resources and commitments are to be taken into account for the purpose of determining whether his means are such that he or any other person should be given legal aid under this Part of this Act and for the purpose of determining the amount of the contribution which he may be required to make towards the costs of the legal aid.

(2) Except in so far as regulations under the foregoing subsection otherwise provide, any resources and commitments of a person's wife or husband shall be treated for the purposes aforesaid as that person's resources and commitments, and the regulations may also—

(a) make provision, in relation to infants, for taking into account the resources and commitments of other persons; and

(b) make provision as to the manner in which the resources and commitments of other persons are to be taken into account for those purposes.

79. Supplementary provisions as to payment of contributions.—(1) Where a legally assisted person is given legal aid for the purposes of any proceedings, any sums due under an order for costs made in his favour with respect to those proceedings shall be paid into the fund out of which the costs of legal aid fall to be paid under section 81 (1) of this Act or, in the case of appeals to or from the Courts-Martial Appeal Court, to the Secretary of State.

(2) If the total contribution made by or in respect of a legally assisted person in respect of any costs is more than the difference between the costs incurred on his behalf and the sums due in respect of costs under such an order, the excess shall be repaid—

(a) where the contribution was made by one person only, to him; and

(b) where the contribution was made by two or more persons, to them in proportion to the amounts contributed by them.

(3) to (7) [*Repealed by the Administration of Justice Act, 1970. See now Sched. X, ibid.*]

(8) Any sum paid by way of contribution towards costs to a clerk of a magistrates' court shall be paid by him to the Secretary of State, and section 27 (1) of the Justices of the Peace Act, 1949 (application of fines, fees, etc.) shall not apply to any such sum, but section 27 (9) of that Act (regulations as to accounts) shall apply to any such sum as it applies to a sum payable under the said subsection (1).

80. Amendment and revocation of legal aid orders.—(1) A court having power to make a legal aid order may on the application of the legally assisted person or otherwise amend any such order by substituting for any legal representative or representatives previously assigned to him any legal representative or representatives whom the court could have assigned to him if it had then been making the legal aid order.

(2) A court having power to make a legal aid order may revoke any such order—

(a) on the application of the legally assisted person; or

(b) if the only legal representative or all the legal representatives for the time being assigned to him withdraws or withdraw from the case and it appears to the court that, because of his conduct, it is not desirable to amend the order under the foregoing sub-section.

(3) The amendment or revocation of a legal aid order under this section shall not affect the right of any legal representative previously assigned to the legally assisted person to remuneration for work done before the date of the amendment or revocation as the case may be, but where a court revokes such an order, the court may make an order under section 76 of this Act as if it had disposed of the case.

81. Payment of costs of legal aid.—(1) Where a legal aid order has been made for the giving of aid to a legally assisted person, the costs of the legal aid given to him shall be paid by whichever of the following methods is appropriate, that is to say—

(a) in the case of proceedings in a magistrates' court, they shall be paid out of the legal aid fund;

(b) in the case of any proceedings not falling within paragraph (a) above, they shall be paid by the Secretary of State.

(2) Subject to regulations under section 83 of this Act, the costs of legal aid ordered to be given to a legally assisted person for the purpose of any proceedings shall include sums on account of the fees payable to any counsel or solicitor assigned to him and disbursements reasonably incurred by any such solicitor for or in connection with those proceedings.

(3) Costs required by this section to be paid in respect of any proceedings shall not include any sum in respect of allowances to witnesses attending to give evidence in those proceedings in any case where such allowances are payable under the provisions of any other enactment.

(4) Costs required by this section to be paid out of the legal aid fund shall be paid in like manner as costs which fall to be so paid under Part I of the Legal Aid and Advice Act, 1949, and—

(a) the functions of the Law Society under that Part of that Act shall include securing the payment of costs so required and the recovery of sums due to the legal aid fund under this Part of this Act; and

(b) references to that Part of that Act in sections 8 (3) to (5), 9 (2) to (9) and 11 of that Act (administration and financing of the legal aid scheme under that Part of that Act) shall be construed as including references to this Part of this Act, so far as it relates to the payment of costs and the recovery of sums as aforesaid.

82. Solicitors and Counsel.—(1) Any practising barrister or solicitor may be assigned to act for a legally assisted person unless he is for the time being excluded by virtue of the next following subsection as being unfit so to act by reason of his conduct when acting for legally assisted persons or his professional conduct generally.

(2) The Lord Chancellor may make rules—

(a) empowering a tribunal established under the rules—

(i) to hear and determine complaints against a barrister or solicitor;

(ii) to exclude from acting for legally assisted persons (whether permanently or temporarily) any barrister or solicitor against whom a complaint is proved and, in the case of a member of a firm of solicitors, any other person who is for the time being a member of the same firm;

(iii) to reduce or cancel the remuneration otherwise payable to any such barrister or solicitor or to his firm under a legal aid order;

(iv) to order any such barrister or solicitor to pay all or any of the costs of the proceedings on any such complaint;

(b) regulating the making of complaints to that tribunal and the disposal by the tribunal of complaints so made; and

(c) providing for the notification of the decisions of that tribunal to all courts which have power under section 73 of this Act to make a legal aid order.

(3) Where a barrister or solicitor is aggrieved by any decision of the tribunal excluding him (whether permanently or temporarily) from acting for legally assisted persons, he may appeal against the decision to the High Court, and the High Court (whose decision shall be final) may confirm or quash the decision appealed against or may substitute such other decision as the court thinks fit.

(4) Provision shall be made by rules of court for regulating appeals to the High Court under the last foregoing subsection, and those rules shall provide for limiting the time within which appeals may be brought.

(5) The expenses of any tribunal established by virtue of this section shall be defrayed out of the legal aid fund and—

(a) the functions of the Law Society under Part I of the Legal Aid and Advice Act, 1949 shall include securing the payment of such expenses; and

(b) references to that Part of that Act in sections 8 (3) to (5), 9 (2) to (9) and 11 of that Act (administration and financing of the legal aid scheme under that Part of that Act) shall be construed as including references to this subsection.

83. Regulations.—(1) Without prejudice to any other provision of this Part of this Act authorising the making of regulations or rules, the Secretary of State may make such regulations as appear to him necessary or desirable for giving effect to this Part of this Act or for preventing abuses thereof and, in particular, any such regulations may—

(a) make provision as to the manner of making applications for legal aid under this Part of this Act and the time when such applications may be made and disposed of;

(b) provide for the exercise of the powers of any court under this Part of this Act by a person entitled to sit as a member of the court or any officer of the court;

(c) confer on any person aggrieved by a decision of any such officer exercising those powers a right to have the matter determined by the court or, if it is so prescribed, by a person entitled to sit as a member of the court;

(d) require any officer of a prescribed court to report to the court or any person entitled to sit as a member of the court any case in which it appears to him that, although no application has been made for the purpose, a legal aid order ought to be made under section 73 of this Act;

(e) make provision with respect to the manner in which counsel and solicitors are to be assigned to legally assisted persons in pursuance of legal aid orders;

(f) prescribe rates or scales of payment of any costs payable in accordance with section 81 (1) of this Act and the conditions under which such costs may be allowed;

(g) provide for the assessment and taxation of such costs and for the review of any assessment made or taxation carried out under the regulations;

(h) provide for the giving of information, by courts by which, or officers by whom, legal aid orders or orders for the payment of costs under the Costs in Criminal Cases Act, 1952 are made, to persons responsible for the administration of funds mentioned in section 81 (1) of this Act, and for the giving of information as aforesaid, where an order is made under section 76 (1) of this Act, to the appropriate authority; and

(i) prescribe the forms to be used for the purposes of this Part of this Act.

(2) The Secretary of State in making regulations under this section as to the amounts payable to counsel or a solicitor assigned to give legal aid under this Part of this Act, and any person by whom any such amount falls to be assessed, taxed or reviewed under the regulations, shall have regard to the principle of allowing fair remuneration according to the work actually and reasonably done.

(3) Regulations under this section may make different provision for different cases.

84. Interpretation of Part IV.—(1) In this Part of this Act, except so far as the context otherwise requires—

"appropriate authority" [*Repealed by the Administration of Justice Act,* 1970. *See now s.* 43, *ibid., p.* 336, *post.*]

"appropriate contributor", in relation to a person who has not attained the age of sixteen, means his father, any person who has been adjudged to be his putative father and (whether or not he is legitimate) his mother;

"committed for sentence" means committed under the Vagrancy Act, 1824, section 6 or 8 of the Criminal Justice Act, 1948, section 28 or 29 of the Magistrates' Courts Act, 1952, section 67 of the Mental Health Act, 1959 or section 41 or 62 (6) of this Act;

"legal aid fund" means the legal aid fund established under the Legal Aid and Advice Act, 1949;

"prescribed" means prescribed by regulations made under this Part of this Act.

(2) Any power to make an application in pursuance of this Part of this Act which is exercisable by a person who has not attained the age of seventeen shall also be exercisable by his parent or guardian on his behalf, without prejudice to any powers of the parent or guardian apart from this subsection; and in this subsection "guardian" has the same meaning as in section 70 (2) of the Children and Young Persons Act, 1969.

(3) A person who attains the age of sixteen after a legal aid order is made in respect of him or, in a case where such an order is made in pursuance of an application, after the application is made, shall be treated for the purposes of this Part of this Act, in relation to the order, as not having attained that age.

NOTE

"Appropriate authority."—See s. 43, Administration of Justice Act, 1970.

ADMINISTRATION OF JUSTICE ACT, 1970

[1970 c. 31]

General note.—This section is printed as amended by the Courts Act, 1970.

43. Procedure for recovery of legal aid contributions in criminal cases.—(1) The appropriate authority for the purposes of section 76 of the Criminal Justice Act, 1967 (that is to say, the authority to whom a recipient of legal aid in a criminal case may under that section be ordered to pay a contribution towards the costs) shall be the clerk of a magistrates' court (referred to in this section as "the collecting court") specified in the order; and the court so specified shall be—

(a) in a case where the court making the legal aid contribution order is itself a magistrates' court, that court;

(b) in a case where the order is made on the disposal of an appeal from a magistrates' court, or in respect of a person who was committed (whether for trial or otherwise) by a magistrates' court to the Crown Court, the court from which the appeal is brought or, as the case may be, which committed him; and

(c) in any other case, a magistrates' court nominated by the court making the order.

(2) Subject to subsection (5) below, any sum required to be paid by a legal aid contribution order shall be recoverable as if it had been adjudged to be paid by an order of the collecting court, subject to and in accordance with the provisions of Schedule 10 to this Act (being provisions which mainly apply the same enforcement procedure as for maintenance orders).

(3) Without prejudice to subsection (2) above, but subject to the following subsections, payment of any sum required to be paid by a legal aid contribution order shall be enforceable by the High Court or a county court (otherwise than by issue of a writ of fieri facias or other process against goods or by imprisonment or attachment of earnings) as if the sum were due to the clerk of the collecting court in pursuance of a judgment or order of the High Court or county court, as the case may be.

(4) The last foregoing subsection shall not authorise the enforcement by a county court of payment of any sum exceeding the limit for the time being in force under section 40 of the County Courts Act, 1959 on the amount of any penalty recoverable by statute in a county court.

(5) Where a legal aid contribution order has been made by the Courts-Martial Appeal Court in respect of a member of Her Majesty's armed forces and the Secretary of State notifies the collecting court that any sum payable under the order will be recovered by deductions from the person's pay in pursuance of one of the enactments amended by subsection (6) below, the collecting court shall not enforce payment of any such sum unless and until the Secretary of State subsequently notifies it that the person is no longer a member of those forces, and that the sum has not been fully recovered.

(6) In section 150 (1) of the Army Act, 1955 and section 150 (1) of the Air Force Act, 1955 (enforcement by deduction from service-man's pay of certain orders made by civil courts), after paragraph (c) there shall be inserted—

> "(d) a contribution towards the costs of legal aid ordered for him, under Part IV of the Criminal Justice Act, 1967, for the purpose of, or in connection with, an appeal to or from the Courts-Martial Appeal Court";

and in section 1 (1) of the Naval Forces (Enforcement of Maintenance Liabilities) Act, 1947 (which enables maintenance payments due from a person in naval or marine service to be recovered by deductions from pay), after paragraph (b) there shall be inserted—

> "(c) for the payment of any contribution towards the costs of legal aid ordered for him, under Part IV of the Criminal Justice Act, 1967, for the purpose of, or in connection with, an appeal to or from the Courts-Martial Appeal Court."

(7) The clerk of the collecting court shall not take proceedings by virtue of subsection (3) above to recover any sum required to be paid by a legal aid contribution order unless authorised to do so by the court.

(8) Any expenses incurred by the clerk of a magistrates' court in recovering any sum so required to be paid shall be treated for the purposes of Part IV of the Justices of the Peace Act, 1949, as expenses of the magistrates' court committee.

(9) Nothing in this section applies to a legal aid contribution order made before the day appointed under section 54 of this Act for the coming into force of this section; and in relation to such an order the enactments in force immediately before that day and relating to the enforcement of such an order shall continue to apply notwithstanding any repeal effected by this Act, without prejudice however to section 13 (6) of this Act.

(10) In this section "legal aid contribution order" means an order under section 76 of the Criminal Justice Act, 1967.

* * * * *

SCHEDULE 10

Section 43

ENFORCEMENT BY MAGISTRATES' COURT OF LEGAL AID
CONTRIBUTION ORDER

General provisions as to enforcement

1. In this Schedule "collecting court" and "legal aid contribution order" have the same meaning as in section 43 of this Act.

2. The collecting court may, in relation to a legal aid contribution order, exercise the powers of section 63 of the Magistrates' Courts Act, 1952 (power to dispense with immediate payment); and for the purposes of that section any provision made by the court which made the order as to time for payment, or payment by instalments, shall be treated as made by the collecting court.

3. Sections 74 (complaint for arrears), 75 (effect of committal on arrears) and 76 (power to remit arrears) of the Magistrates' Courts Act, 1952 shall apply as if a legal aid contribution order were enforceable as an affiliation order.

4. Any costs awarded, under section 55 of the Magistrates' Courts Act, 1952, on the hearing of a complaint for the enforcement of a legal aid contribution order shall be enforceable as a sum required to be paid by that order.

5. Sections 17 and 18 of the Maintenance Orders Act, 1958 (not more than one committal for same arrears, and power to review committals) shall apply as if a legal aid contribution order were a maintenance order.

6. Section 68 of the Magistrates' Courts Act, 1952 (application of money found on defaulter to satisfy sum adjudged) shall apply as if a legal aid contribution order were enforceable as an affiliation order.

Transfer of enforcement proceedings to different court

7.—(1) Where it appears to the collecting court that a person subject to a legal aid contribution order is residing in a petty sessions area other than that for which the court acts, the court may make a transfer order under this paragraph, that is to say an order making payment under the legal aid contribution order enforceable in that other petty sessions area (which area shall be specified in the transfer order).

(2) As from the date of a transfer order under this paragraph the court which made the order shall cease to the collecting court for the purposes of the legal aid contribution order and of section 43 of this Act and this Schedule and be replaced as such by a magistrates' court acting for the petty sessions area specified in the transfer order.

LEGAL AID IN CRIMINAL PROCEEDINGS (GENERAL) REGULATIONS, 1968

[S.I. 1968 No. 1231]

General note.—These regulations are printed as amended by the Legal Aid in Criminal Proceedings (General) (Amendment) Regulations, 1970, S.I. 1970 No. 1980.

In any enactment or other instrument (passed or made before the commencement of the Courts Act, 1971, or later) there shall be substituted for the reference to Court of Assize, Court of Quarter Sessions, a reference to the Crown Court, and for Clerk of Assize, Clerk of the Peace, the appropriate officer of the Crown Court (Courts Act, 1971, s. 56 (1) and Sched. VIII, para. 2).

ARRANGEMENT OF REGULATIONS

In pursuance of the powers conferred upon me by section 83 of the Criminal Justice Act, 1967, I hereby make the following Regulations:—

Proceedings in a magistrates' court

1.—(1) An application for a legal aid order in respect of proceedings in a magistrates' court under section 73 (2) or (3A) of the Act (magistrates' court proceedings) may be made to the justices' clerk—

- (a) if the application is made by a parent or guardian on behalf of a person who has not attained the age of seventeen years, in Form 1A in the Schedule to these Regulations,
- (b) if the application is made by any other person, in Form 1 in the Schedule to these Regulations.

(2) An application for a legal aid order may be made orally to the court.

(3) A legal aid order shall not be made until the court, a justice of the peace or the justices' clerk has considered the statement of means of the applicant except where the applicant is not required in pursuance of Regulation 4 (4) of these Regulations to furnish a statement of means.

(4) Subject to the provisions of this Regulation, the powers of the court to determine an application for a legal aid order may be exercised by the justices' clerk or a justice of the peace to whom the clerk has referred the application.

(5) Where an application for a legal aid order is made orally to the court, the court may refer it to the justices' clerk for determination.

(6) The justices' clerk considering an application for a legal aid order shall—

- (a) make an order; or
- (b) refuse to make an order unless the applicant, or where the applicant has not attained the age of sixteen years an appropriate contributor, or both first makes or make, as the case may be, a payment or payments on account of any contribution towards costs which they or either of them may be ordered to make; or
- (c) refer the application to the court or a justice of the peace.

(7) Where the justices' clerk refuses to make a legal aid order unless the applicant, or where the applicant has not attained the age of sixteen years an appropriate contributor, or both makes or make, as the case may be, a payment or payments on account of any contribution towards costs which they or either of them may be ordered to make, the applicant shall be entitled, on request, to have the application determined by the court or a justice of the peace, as the clerk thinks fit.

(8) Where the court or a justice of the peace determines an application for a legal aid order by refusing to make a legal aid order, the justices' clerk shall not make a legal aid order except where the court or justice of the peace refused to make a legal aid order unless the applicant, or where the applicant has not attained the age of sixteen years an appropriate contributor, or both first made a payment or payments as aforesaid and such payment or payments is or are made.

(9) In this Regulation the expression "justice of the peace" means a justice of the peace who is entitled to sit as a member of the magistrates' court and "legal aid order" means a legal aid order within the meaning of paragraph (1) of this Regulation.

Proceedings in the Crown Court

2.—(1) An application for a legal aid order under section 73 (3), (3B) or (4) of the Act (proceedings in the Crown Court) may be made—

(a) (i) to the appropriate officer of the Crown Court [as the case may be], or

  (ii) in the case of an appeal to the Crown Court, to the justices' clerk;

(b) (i) if the application is made by a parent or guardian on behalf of a person who has not attained the age of seventeen years, in Form 2A in the Schedule to these Regulations,

  (ii) if the application is made by any other person, in Form 2 in the Schedule to these Regulations.

(2) An application for a legal aid order may be made orally to the Crown Court, or to the magistrates' court at the conclusion of the proceedings in that court.

(3) (a) An application for a legal aid order under section 73 (8) of the Act (retrial) may be made in Form 2 or Form 2A in the Schedule to these Regulations to the appropriate officer of the Crown Court [as the case may be].

(b) An application for such an order may be made orally to the Court of Appeal or the House of Lords, as the case may be, immediately after the decision of the court.

(4) A legal aid order shall not be made until the court, a judge of the court, the proper officer of the court or, where the application is made to the magistrates' court or justices' clerk, a justice of the peace has considered the statement of means of the applicant, except where the applicant is not required in pursuance of Regulation 4 (4) of these Regulations to furnish a statement of means.

(5) Subject to the provisions of this Regulation, the powers of the court to determine an application for a legal aid order may be exercised by a judge of the court, the proper officer of the court, or, where the application is made to the magistrates' court or justices' clerk, a justice of the peace.

(6) Where an application for a legal aid order is made orally to the court, the court may refer it to the proper officer of the court for determination.

(7) The proper officer of the court considering an application for a legal aid order shall—

(a) make an order; or

(b) refuse to make an order unless the applicant, or where the applicant has not attained the age of sixteen years an appropriate contributor, or both first makes or make, as the case may be, a payment or payments on account of any contribution towards costs which they or either of them may be ordered to make; or

(c) except where the proper officer of the court is a justices' clerk, refer the application to a judge of the court, or, if he is, to the magistrates' court or a justice of the peace.

(8) Where the proper officer of the court refuses to make a legal aid order unless the applicant, or where the applicant has not attained the age of sixteen years, an appropriate contributor, or both first makes or make, as the case may be, a payment or payments on account of any contribution towards costs which they or either of them may be ordered to make, the applicant shall be entitled, on request, to have the application determined by a judge of the court or, if the proper officer of the court is a justices' clerk, the magistrates' court or a justice of the peace, as the justices' clerk thinks fit.

(9) Where the court or a judge of the court or a justice of the peace determines an application for a legal aid order by refusing to make a legal aid order, the proper officer of the court shall not make a legal aid order except where the court, judge or justice refused to make a legal aid order unless the applicant, or where the applicant has not attained the age of sixteen years an appropriate contributor, or both first made a payment or payments as aforesaid and such payment or payments is or are made.

(10) In this Regulation the expression "magistrates' court" means the court which committed or convicted the applicant, "justice of the peace" means a justice of the peace who is entitled to sit as a member of the magistrates' court, "justices' clerk" means the clerk to the magistrates' court, and "legal aid order" means a legal aid order within the meaning of paragraph (1) or (3) of this Regulation, as the case may be.

Proceedings in the House of Lords or Court of Appeal

3.—(1) Notice of application for a legal aid order under section 73 (5) of the Act (appeal to the Court of Appeal) may be given in Form 3, and under section 73 (7) of the Act (appeal to the House of Lords) may be given in Form 3A, in the Schedule to these Regulations and in either case may be given to the Registrar.

(2) An application for a legal aid order may be made orally to the Court of Appeal, a judge of the court or the Registrar.

(3) A legal aid order shall not be made until—

(a) a notice of appeal or application for leave to appeal to the Court of Appeal or the House of Lords, as the case may be, has been given, and
(b) the Court of Appeal, a judge of the court or the Registrar has considered the statement of means of the applicant for legal aid.

(4) Subject to the provisions of this Regulation, the powers of the Court of Appeal to determine an application for a legal aid order may be exercised by a judge of the court or the Registrar.

(5) Where an application for a legal aid order is made orally to the Court of Appeal, the court may refer it to a judge of the court or the Registrar for determination; and where such an application is made orally to a judge of the court, he may refer it to the Registrar for determination.

(6) The Registrar considering an application for a legal aid order shall—

(a) make an order; or
(b) refuse to make an order unless the applicant, or where the applicant has not attained the age of sixteen years an appropriate contributor, or both first makes or make, as the case may be, a payment or payments on account of any contribution towards costs which they or either of them may be ordered to make; or
(c) refer the application to the Court of Appeal or a judge of the court.

(7) Where the Registrar refuses to make a legal aid order unless the applicant or where the applicant has not attained the age of sixteen years an appropriate contributor, or both first makes or make, as the case may be, a payment or payments on account of any contribution towards costs which they or either of them may be ordered to make, the applicant shall be entitled, on request, to have the application determined by a judge of the court.

(8) Where a judge of the court refuses to make a legal aid order or refuses unless the applicant first makes a payment as aforesaid, the applicant shall be entitled, on request, to have the application determined by the Court of Appeal.

(9) Where the Court of Appeal or a judge of the court determines an application for a legal aid order by refusing to make a legal aid order, the Registrar shall not make a legal aid order except where the court or judge refused to make a legal aid order unless the applicant first made a payment as aforesaid and such payment is made.

(10) In this Regulation the expression "legal aid order" means a legal aid order within the meaning of paragraph (1) of this Regulation.

Statement of means

4.—(1) A statement of means submitted by an applicant or an appropriate contributor shall be in Form 4 in the Schedule to these Regulations.

(2) Where the applicant is an infant, a statement of means submitted by a person other than the applicant, being a person who is not an appropriate contributor, shall be in Form 5 in the Schedule to these Regulations.

(3) If an applicant who has attained the age of sixteen years does not furnish a statement of means at the time that he makes an application for legal aid, he shall be required to do so by a proper officer of the court to whom or to whose court he is making the application, unless he has already submitted such a statement in pursuance of a previous application in respect of the same case.

(4) If a statement of means of an applicant who has not attained the age of sixteen years or an appropriate contributor is not furnished at the time that the applicant makes an application for legal aid, either or both may be required to furnish one by the proper officer of the court to whom or to whose court the application is made unless the person who has not furnished a statement of means at that time has already submitted a statement in pursuance of a previous application in respect of the same case.

General powers to make legal aid order

5. Subject to the provisions of Regulation 4 of these Regulations, nothing in Regulation 1, 2 or 3 of these Regulations shall affect the power of a court or a judge of the court or the Registrar (subject to the provisions of section 75 of the Act) to make a legal aid order, whether an application has been made for legal aid or not, or the right of an applicant whose application has been refused to apply to the court at the trial or other proceedings.

Legal aid orders

6.—(1) A legal aid order shall be in Form 6 in the Schedule to these Regulations.

(2) A copy of such order shall be delivered or sent to the solicitor assigned or to counsel (where counsel only is assigned).

(3) When a legal aid order has been made or an application for legal aid has been refused, the proper officer of the court to which the application is made shall forthwith notify the applicant, except where the application was made on behalf of the applicant by his parent or guardian, in which case the proper officer shall notify the parent or guardian, as the case may be.

(4) (a) An order amending a legal aid order under section 80 (1) of the Act shall be in Form 7 in the Schedule to these Regulations.

(b) A copy of the amending order shall be sent or delivered to the solicitor assigned by such order or to counsel (where counsel only is assigned) and to the solicitor and counsel assigned by the order which is amended.

(c) A copy of the order which is amended shall be sent or delivered to the solicitor assigned by the amending order or to counsel (where counsel only is assigned by such order).

(d) The legally assisted person except where the application for legal aid was made on his behalf by his parent or guardian, the parent or guardian, as the case may be, shall be notified that the order has been amended.

(5) (a) An order revoking a legal aid order under section 80 (2) of the Act shall be in Form 8 in the Schedule to these Regulations.

(b) A copy of an order revoking a legal aid order shall be sent or delivered to—

(i) the solicitor and counsel assigned under the order which is revoked, and

(ii) where the application for legal aid was made on behalf of the legally assisted person by his parent or guardian, the parent or guardian making the application, or, in the case of any other application, the legally assisted person.

(6) Where a legal aid order is amended in accordance with paragraph (4) of this Regulation, counsel originally assigned shall send or deliver forthwith to the solicitor who instructed him, or (where counsel only was assigned) to the counsel newly assigned, all papers and other things in his possession relating to the proceedings and the solicitor originally assigned shall send or deliver all papers and other things in his possession relating to the proceedings to the solicitor newly assigned (or to counsel, if counsel only is assigned by the amending order).

(7) Where a legal aid order is revoked in accordance with paragraph (5) of this Regulation, the counsel assigned shall send or deliver all papers and other things in his possession relating to those proceedings to the solicitor assigned or (where no solicitor is assigned) to the legally assisted person and the solicitor assigned shall send or deliver all papers and other things in his possession relating to the proceedings to the legally assisted person.

Exclusion of solicitors and counsel

7.—(1) The proper officer of each court shall keep a list of solicitors and counsel, notified to him by the Secretary of State, who are for the time being excluded from acting for legally assisted persons under section 82 of the Act.

(2) Any reference in these Regulations to solicitors or counsel shall not apply to solicitors or counsel so excluded.

Assignment of solicitor

8. Subject to the provisions of Regulations 11 and 14 of these Regulations, any person in respect of whom a legal aid order is made, entitling him to the services of a solicitor, may select any solicitor who is willing to act and such solicitor shall be assigned to him.

Selection of counsel

9. Where a legal aid order is made in respect of the services of solicitor and counsel, the solicitor may instruct any counsel who is willing to act:
Provided that in the case of proceedings in the Court of Appeal or House of Lords, counsel may be assigned by the court or person making or amending the legal aid order.

Assignment of counsel only

10.—(1) Where a legal aid order in respect of proceedings in the Crown Court is made or amended so as to provide for representation by counsel only, counsel shall be assigned by the court or person making or amending the legal aid order.

(2) Where a legal aid order in respect of proceedings in the Court of Appeal is made or amended so as to provide for representation by counsel only, counsel shall be assigned by the court, a judge of the court or the Registrar.

Assignment of counsel for House of Lords or Court of Appeal

11. In assigning counsel or solicitor to a legally assisted person in respect of an appeal to the House of Lords or Court of Appeal, the court, the judge of the court or the Registrar shall have regard, as far as is reasonably practicable, to the wishes of the legally assisted person, the identity of the solicitor or counsel, if any, who represented him in any earlier proceedings and the nature of the appeal.

Commencement of legal aid order

12. In making a legal aid order in respect of proceedings in the Court of Appeal, the court, a judge of the court or the Registrar, as the case may be, may specify the stage of the proceedings at which the legal aid shall commence.

Assignment of two counsel

13.—(1) Except as provided by paragraph (2) of this Regulation, a legal aid order shall not provide for the services of more than one counsel.

(2) In trials at the Crown Court or appeals to the House of Lords or the Court of Appeal, an order may provide for the services of two counsel—

  (a) on a charge of murder; or
  (b) where it appears to the court or person making the legal aid order that the case is one of exceptional difficulty, gravity or complexity and that the interests of justice require that the legally assisted person shall have the services of two counsel.

(3) Where, in such case as is specified in paragraph (2) of this Regulation, a legal aid order provides for the services of one counsel, it may be amended to provide for the services of two counsel.

Assignment of one solicitor or counsel to more than one legally assisted person

14. A solicitor or counsel may be assigned to two or more legally assisted persons whose cases are heard together, unless the interests of justice require that such persons be separately represented.

Documents

15. Where a notice of application for leave to appeal or a notice of appeal has been given to the Court of Appeal, copies of documents (including transcripts) may be supplied by the Registrar in accordance with rules made under the Criminal Appeal Act, 1968.

Notes of evidence and depositions

16. Where a legal aid order is made in respect of an appeal to quarter sessions, the justices' clerk shall supply, on the application of the solicitor assigned to the appellant or respondent on whose application such an order was made, copies of any notes of evidence or depositions taken in the proceedings in the magistrates' court.

Transfer of documents

17. Where a person is committed by a lower court to a higher court or appeals or applies for leave to appeal from a lower court to a higher court, the proper officer of the lower court shall send to the proper officer of the higher court the following documents (if any):—

  (a) a copy of any legal aid order previously made in the same case;
  (b) a copy of any contribution order previously made;
  (c) a copy of any legal aid application which has been refused;
  (d) any statement of means already submitted.

Payments on account of contributions

18.—(1) Where a person is ordered under section 75 (3) of the Act, to make a payment on account of any contribution towards costs, such payment on account shall be made to the proper officer of the court ordering such payment unless that court directs otherwise.

(2) Where such payment is made otherwise than to the appropriate authority, the person receiving such payment shall forward it to the appropriate authority.

Delivery of contribution orders

19.—(1) Where a contribution order is made, it shall be in Form 9 in the Schedule to these Regulations, a copy shall be sent or delivered to the person ordered to make the contribution and, if the order is made by a court other than a magistrates' court, a copy shall be sent by the proper officer of the court making the order to the appropriate authority.

(2) Where a payment on account has been made and a contribution order is not made by the court or person empowered in that behalf, the proper officer of that court shall notify the appropriate authority and the person who made the payment on account.

Assessment of contribution as proportion of taxed costs

20.—(1) Where a contribution order is made in respect of proceedings in a court other than a magistrates' court on such terms that the amount payable by the legally assisted person or appropriate contributor cannot be assessed without reference to the actual legal aid costs, the proper officer of that court shall send to the appropriate authority particulars of the amount of taxed costs in that court.

(2) Where a contribution order on such terms as aforesaid is made in respect of proceedings in a magistrates' court, the appropriate authority shall notify the Law Society, which shall send the appropriate authority particulars of the legal aid costs payable out of the legal aid fund.

(3) The appropriate authority on receipt of the aforesaid particulars shall notify the legally assisted person or appropriate contributor of the amount of the contribution payable by him.

Reference to Supplementary Benefits Commission

21. Where a legally assisted person or appropriate contributor in respect of whom a contribution order may be or has been made wishes the Supplementary Benefits Commission (hereinafter referred to as "the Commission") to enquire into his means, application may be made to the court having power to make or vary the order, either in court, during or immediately after consideration by the court as to whether such an order should be made, or in writing to the proper officer of the court within one month of the contribution order being made.

Forms and procedure of Supplementary Benefits Commission

22.—(1) A request to the Commission to enquire into the means of any person shall be in Form 10 in the Schedule to these Regulations and be accompanied by—

(a) the statement of means of that person;

(b) the statement of means of a person referred to in Regulation 4 (2) of these Regulations, where one has been submitted.

(2) Where such a request is made, the Commission may require from that person such further information (including any documents) as it may think necessary for a proper inquiry and may require such person to attend at an office of the Ministry of Social Security for this purpose.

Variation of contribution orders

23.—(1) Any power of a court to make a contribution order after receiving a report from the Commission or to revoke or otherwise vary a contribution order made before receiving such a report may be exercised by any person entitled to sit as a member of the court.

(2) Any power of a court to revoke or reduce the amount of a contribution order made before receiving such a report may, if the court so authorises either generally or in a particular case, be exercised by the proper officer.

(3) An order revoking or otherwise varying a contribution order shall be in Form 11 in the Schedule to these Regulations.

(4) A copy of such an order shall be sent to the appropriate authority and the person to whom the order relates.

(5) Where, after such a report as aforesaid has been received, a contribution order is not made, the proper officer shall inform the legally assisted person or appropriate contributor, or both, as the case may be.

(6) Where a contribution order made before receiving such a report is not revoked or otherwise varied, the proper officer shall inform the person to whom the order relates and the appropriate authority.

Stay of enforcement of contribution orders

24. Where a reference is made to the Commission after a contribution order has been made, the proper officer of the court, other than a magistrates' court making the reference, shall inform the appropriate authority and no action shall be taken thereafter to enforce the order, until the appropriate authority has been informed of the result of the reference.

Refund of payments on account

25.—(1) Where a payment on account has been made and a court having power to make a contribution order does not do so or that court or the proper officer or a person entitled to sit as a member of that court revokes a contribution order, the payment made on account shall be refunded by the appropriate authority in accordance with the provisions of section 79 (2) of the Act.

(2) Where a contribution order is made or varied so that the amount ordered to be paid is less than any amount paid on account, the difference between the said amounts shall be refunded by the appropriate authority in accordance with the provisions of section 79 (2) of the Act.

Disposal of sums received from legally assisted persons after conviction

26.—(1) Where a legally assisted person or an appropriate contributor to whom this Regulation applies is ordered to make a contribution in respect of legal aid, any payment on account received by a magistrates' court shall, unless the person paying the money specifically appropriates such payment or any part of it to payment of the contribution, be applied in the first place in accordance with the provisions of section 114 of the Magistrates' Courts Act, 1952 and any sums paid in addition to the sums referred to in paragraphs (a) and (b) above shall be paid to the Secretary of State in accordance with section 79 (8) of the Act.

(2) This Regulation applies to a legally assisted person who is ordered to pay any sum adjudged to be paid by a conviction and to an appropriate contributor who is ordered to pay a fine, damages, compensation or costs under the provisions of section 55 of the Children and Young Persons Act, 1933 or section 3 (6) of the Children and Young Persons Act, 1969.

Recovery of costs

27.—Where a court makes an order that the costs of a legally aided person shall be paid by any other person, the proper officer of that court shall notify the authority from whose funds the costs of legal aid are to be paid, or, in the case of an order made by a magistrates' court, the Law Society, of the order and of the name and address of the person by whom the costs are to be paid.

Enforcement of orders for payment of costs

28. Where a person ordered to pay the costs of a legally aided person does not pay them in accordance with section 79 (1) of the Act, they may be recovered summarily by the aforesaid authority referred to in Regulation 27 of these Regulations or the Law Society, as the case may be, as a sum adjudged to be paid as a civil debt by order of a magistrates' court.

Notification of fund into which costs are to be paid

29. Where any court makes such an order as is referred to in Regulation 27 of these Regulations, the court shall cause the person against whom the order is made to be informed of the fund into which the payment must be made in accordance with section 79 (1) of the Act.

Legal aid records

30.—(1) The proper officer of each court shall keep a record, in the manner and form directed from time to time by the Secretary of State, of all cases in which an application for legal aid was made to the court or a legal aid order was made, under Regulation 5 of these Regulations, by the court without application; and shall send to the Secretary of State such information from such record as the Secretary of State shall from time to time direct.

(2) The proper officer of each court shall send to the Secretary of State a copy of every contribution order made by his court.

Interpretation

31.—(1) In these Regulations, unless the context otherwise requires—

"the Act" means the Criminal Justice Act, 1967;

"applicant" means, in relation to an application for legal aid made on behalf of a person who has not attained the age of seventeen years by his parent or guardian, that person and in the case of any other application for legal aid the person making the application;

"appropriate authority" has the meaning assigned to it by section 84 of the Act;

"appropriate contributor" has the meaning assigned to it by section 84 (1) of the Act;

"contribution" means a sum ordered by a court to be paid in accordance with the provisions of section 76 (1) and (1A) of the Act;

"contribution order" means an order made by a court under section 76 of the Act;

"Court of Appeal" means the criminal division of the Court of Appeal;

"guardian" has the same meaning as in section 70 (2) of the Children and Young Persons Act, 1969;

"judge of the court" means—

(i) in the case of the Court of Appeal, a Lord Justice of Appeal or a judge of the Queen's Bench Division of the High Court;

(ii) in the case of the Crown Court [a judge of the High Court, Circuit judge or Recorder];

"legal aid fund" has the meaning assigned to it by section 84 of the Act;

"legal aid order" means an order made under section 73 of the Act and includes an order made solely for the purpose described in section 74 (8) of the Act;

"legally assisted person" has the meaning assigned to it by section 73 (9) of the Act;

"proper officer" means the Clerk of the Parliaments, the Registrar of Criminal Appeals, the appropriate officer of the Crown Court or the justices' clerk (as the case may be);

"Registrar" means the Registrar of Criminal Appeals;
"statement of means" means a statement of means submitted in accordance with Regulation 4 of these Regulations.

(1A) An applicant who attains the age of sixteen years after the date on which the application is made shall be treated for the purposes of these Regulations as not having attained that age.

(2) The Interpretation Act, 1889, shall apply to the interpretation of these Regulations as it applies to the interpretation of an Act of Parliament.

(3) Any reference in these Regulations to an enactment is a reference thereto as amended.

Determination in private and in absence of legally assisted person

32. Where it is provided by these Regulations that any matter may be determined otherwise than by a court, it may be determined in private and in the absence of the applicant or legally assisted person or appropriate contributor.

Forms

33. The forms set out in the Schedule to these Regulations may be used with such variation as the circumstances may require.

Citation and commencement

34.—(1) These Regulations may be cited as the Legal Aid in Criminal Proceedings (General) Regulations, 1968.

(2) These Regulations shall come into operation on 1 October 1968.

SCHEDULE

FORM 1

Application for legal aid by applicant (magistrates' court)
(Criminal Justice Act, 1967, s. 73; General Reg. 1 (1) (b))

I, (a) ....
apply for legal aid for the purpose of the following proceedings before the...........
.... Magistrates' Court.
(b) ....

My case is due to be heard on (c) ....

Special circumstances (d) ....

My permanent address is ....

My present address (where different from above) is ....

I was born on ....

I attach a statement of my means.

I attach a statement of my parents' means (e)/My parents' name and address is

....

I understand that I (or my parents if I am under 16) may be required by the Supplementary Benefits Commission to supply further information about my means. I also understand that the court may order me to make a contribution

(a) Full name in BLOCK letters. State whether Mr., Mrs., Miss.
(b) State reason for your appearance in the magistrates' court, *e.g.* charge of theft, alleged failure to comply with a requirement of a probation order or a condition of a recognisance.
(c) Insert date if known.
(d) Set out here any special circumstances justifying legal aid.
(e) If you are under 16, either attach a statement of your parents' means or give their name and address.

to the costs of legal aid or to pay the whole costs if it considers that my means enable me to do so and, if I am under 16, may make a similar order with respect to my parents.

The solicitor I wish to act for me is (ᶠ) ....
.... of ....

(Signed) ....

(ᶠ) If you do not give the name of a solicitor, the court will select the solicitor assigned to you.

FORM 1A

Application for legal aid (magistrates' court) by parent or guardian of person who has not attained the age of seventeen

(Criminal Justice Act, 1967, s. 73; General Reg. 1 (1) (a))

I, (ᵃ) ....
the parent/guardian of

(Child's name) (ᵇ) ....

(Child's date of birth) ....
apply on his behalf for legal aid for the purpose of the following proceedings before the ....
Magistrates' Court.

(ᶜ) ....
The case is due to be heard on (ᵈ) ....
Special circumstances (ᵉ) ....
My permanent address is ....
My present address (where different from above) is...

    I attach (i) a statement of my means; and
         (ii) a statement of the child's means.

    I understand that I or the child may be required by the Supplementary Benefits Commission to supply further information about my means. I also understand that the court may order the child and, if he has not attained the age of 16, may order me to make a contribution to the costs of legal aid or to pay the whole costs if it considers that our means enable us to do so.

The solicitor whom I wish to act for the child is (ᶠ)...
.... of ....

(Signed) ....

(ᵃ) Full name in BLOCK letters. State whether Mr., Mrs., Miss.
(ᵇ) Give full name in BLOCK letters of child on whose behalf you are applying for legal aid and child's date of birth.
(ᶜ) State reason for the child's appearance in the magistrates' court, *e.g.* charge of theft, as being in need of care or control.
(ᵈ) Insert date if known.
(ᵉ) Set out here any special circumstances justifying legal aid.
(ᶠ) If you do not give the name of a solicitor, the court will select the solicitor assigned to you.

FORM 2

Application for legal aid by applicant (assizes or quarter sessions)

(Criminal Justice Act, 1967, s. 73; General Reg. 2 (1) (b) (ii))

I, (ᵃ) ....
apply for legal aid for the following purpose:

(ᵃ) Full name in BLOCK letters. State whether Mr., Mrs., Miss.

$\left\{\begin{array}{l}\end{array}\right.$

$(^b)$
- (1) on..........................I was committed for trial and need legal aid for my defence;
- (2) on..........................I was convicted by the..............................
Magistrates' Court and committed to assizes/quarter sessions for sentence or to be otherwise dealt with and need legal aid;
- (3) I need legal aid for an appeal to quarter sessions against my conviction and/or sentence on ....
by the .... Magistrates' Court;
- (4) I need legal aid for ....
....

Special circumstances $(^c)$ ....

My permanent address is ....

My present address (where different from above) is.................................

I was born on ....

I attach a statement of my means $(^d)$/I have already furnished a statement of my means to the clerk to the justices for $(^e)$ ....
and there has been no change in my financial position.

I attach a statement of my parents' means $(^f)$/My parents' name and address is ....

I understand that I (or may parents if I am under 16) may be required by the Supplementary Benefits Commission to supply further information about my means. I also understand that the court may order me to make a contribution to the costs of legal aid or to pay the whole costs if it considers that my means enable me to do so and, if I am under 16, may make a similar order with respect to my parents.

The solicitor whom I wish to act for me is $(^g)$ ....
.... of ....
(Signed) ....

$(^b)$ Delete as necessary. If legal aid is required for a purpose not mentioned at (1), (2) or (3) describe this at (4). Insert date of conviction or committal if known.
$(^c)$ Set out here any special circumstances justifying legal aid.
$(^d)$ Unless you have already furnished a statement of your means and there has been no change in your financial position, you must attach a statement of your means.
$(^e)$ State the name of the magistrates' court.
$(^f)$ If you are under 16, either attach a statement of your parents' means or give their name and address.
$(^g)$ If you do not give the name of a solicitor, the court will select the solicitor assigned to you.

FORM 2A

Application for legal aid (assizes or quarter sessions) by parent or guardian of person who has not attained the age of seventeen

(*Criminal Justice Act*, 1967, s. 73; *General Reg.* 2 (1) (b) (i))

I, $(^a)$ ....
the parent/guardian of

(Child's name) $(^b)$ ....

(Child's date of birth) ....
apply on his behalf for legal aid for the following purpose:

$(^a)$ Full name in BLOCK letters. State whether Mr., Mrs., Miss.
$(^b)$ Give full name in BLOCK letters of child on whose behalf you are applying for legal aid and child's date of birth.

(^{c})

(1) on..............................he was committed for trial and needs legal aid for his defence;

(2) on..............................he was found guilty by the..........................
Magistrates' Court and committed to assizes/quarter sessions for sentence or to be otherwise dealt with and needs legal aid;

(3) he needs legal aid for an appeal to quarter sessions against the finding and/or order on...
by the .... Magistrates' Court

(4) he needs legal aid for...
....

Special circumstances (^{d}) ....

My permanent address is ....

My present address (where different from above) is....................................

I attach a statement of my means/I have already furnished a statement of my means to the clerk to the justices for (^{e}) ....
and there has been no change in my financial position (^{f}).

I attach a statement of the child's means/I have already furnished a statement of the child's means to the clerk to the justices for (^{e}) ....
and there has been no change in his financial position (^{f}) ....

I understand that I or the child may be required by the Supplementary Benefits Commission to supply further information about my means, I also understand that the court may order the child and, if he has not attained the age of 16, may order me to make a contribution to the costs of legal aid or to pay the whole costs if it considers that our means enable us to do so.

The solicitor whom I wish to act for me is (^{g}) ....
.... of ....

(Signed) ....

(^{c}) Delete as necessary. If legal aid is required for a purpose not mentioned at (1), (2) or (3) describe this at (4).   Insert date of conviction or committal if known.

(^{d}) Set out here any special circumstances justifying legal aid.

(^{e}) Fill in the name of the magistrates' court.

(^{f}) Unless you have already furnished a statement of your means and/or the child's means and there has been no change in your/his financial position, you must attach a statement of your/his means.

(^{g}) If you do not give the name of a solicitor, the court will select the solicitor assigned to you.

FORM 3

Notice of application for legal aid in Court of Appeal

(Criminal Justice Act, 1967, s. 73; General Reg. 3)

To the Registrar,
Criminal Appeal Office,
Royal Courts of Justice,
Strand,
London, W.C.2.

PART I

Particulars of appellant:

	Forenames	Surname	Age on conviction
Full names: (Block letters)			
Address: (If detained give address where detained and, if detained in prison, give prison number).			

Court where tried and/or sentenced:

| Dates of appearances at the Court including dates of conviction (if convicted at the Court) and sentence. | Name of Court |
| | Name of Judge |

Particulars of offences of which convicted: whether convicted on indictment or by a magistrates' court: particulars of sentences and orders:

Offences	Convicted on indictment or by magistrates' court	Sentences and orders
....	....	....
....	....	....

Offences taken into consideration when sentenced.

Total sentence.

PART 2

Particulars of application

I wish to apply for legal aid.

Signed ....

Date ....

FORM 3A

Notice of application for legal aid in the House of Lords

(Criminal Justice Act, 1967, s. 73; General Reg. 3)

To the Registrar,
Criminal Appeal Office,
Royal Courts of Justice,
Strand,
London, W.C.2.

Full names of the applicant ....

Criminal appeal reference number ....

Date of decision of the Criminal Division of the Court of Appeal
....

Name and address of place at which applicant detained or, if not detained applicant's address.
....

I apply for legal aid for the purpose of—

*(a) appealing to the House of Lords against the above decision;
*(b) opposing the appeal by the prosecutor.

* Delete as necessary.

Signed ....

Date ....

FORM 4

Statement of means by applicant or appropriate contributor

(Criminal Justice Act, 1967, *s.* 75; *General Reg.* 4 (1))

This form is for use by an applicant for legal aid. If the applicant has not attained the age of sixteen, the applicant's father or mother may also be required to complete the form.

The form requires the person completing it to give particulars of his financial position. This information is needed before legal aid can be granted. Failure to provide the information may lead to delay in considering the application for legal aid. If there is any material change in your financial position after completing this form and before the conclusion of the case you should inform the court.

WARNING—If you knowingly or recklessly make a statement which is false in a material particular or knowingly fail to disclose any material fact, you are liable to be prosecuted and, if convicted, to imprisonment for a term not exceeding four months or a fine not exceeding £100 or both. The Supplementary Benefits Commission may be asked by the court to investigate the accuracy of your statement of means.

PART I

1. Full Name of person completing form ....
     (Block letters)   ....

2. Date of Birth..

3. (ᵃ) Unmarried/Married/Married but living apart/Divorced/Widow/Widower

4. Permanent address ....

5. Present address (where different from above) ....
....

6. Occupation (state normal occupation) ....

7. Have you been unemployed during the last twelve months? YES/NO.
If your answer is "Yes", state periods of unemployment during the last twelve months ....
....

8. If you are under the age of eighteen years, are you being wholly or mainly maintained by a parent or guardian? YES/NO.
If your answer is "Yes", give his address...

9. If legal aid is being sought for your child and he has not yet attained the age of sixteen years, give:
     (a) his full name ....
     (b) his date of birth ....
     (c) your relationship to him ....
     (d) his address (where different from yours) ....

(ᵃ) Delete all but one.

PART 2—INCOME

Give below particulars of your income from all sources for the twelve months immediately preceding the date on which this form is completed. If you are married and living with your wife/husband, particulars of her/his income must also be stated.

The amounts stated should be the net amounts after deduction of income tax and National Insurance contributions.

Instead of giving amounts for the previous twelve months you may express amounts on a weekly or monthly basis if you state the basis in the remarks column.

Description of Income	Amount		Remarks	FOR OFFICIAL USE ONLY
	Your income	Income of wife/husband		
1. Wages or salary including overtime, commission and bonuses.				
2. If in business on your own account, net profit.				
3. Family allowances.				
4. National Insurance benefit– (a) Unemployment (b) Sickness (c) Pension.				
5. Supplementary pension or allowance from the Supplementary Benefits Commission.				
6. Net income from sub-letting house, rooms, etc.				
7. Other income (give details).				

Write "NONE" where appropriate.

If legal aid is being sought for your child, has he any source of income not included above? YES/NO.

If your answer is "Yes", give details below:

Description of Income	Amount	Remarks	FOR OFFICIAL USE ONLY

PART 3—CAPITAL OR SAVINGS

Give below particulars of all your capital or savings. If you are married and living with your wife/husband, give details of her/his capital and savings also.

	Yourself	Wife/husband	FOR OFFICIAL USE ONLY
1. Do you or your wife/husband own house property? (Answer Yes or No). If your answer is "Yes", state:— (a) the value, (*i.e.* approximate selling price) (b) the amount of any outstanding mortgage (c) whether you are living in the house.			
2. Give particulars of all capital or savings belonging to you or your wife/husband. You should state the amount and description (*e.g.* money in the National Savings Bank or other banks, National Savings Certificates, cash, stocks and shares, etc.).			

Write "NONE" where appropriate.

If legal aid is being sought for your child, has he any capital or savings not included above? YES/NO.

If your answer is "Yes", give details below:

Description of capital or savings	Amount	Remarks	FOR OFFICIAL USE ONLY

PART 4—EXPENSES

In assessing your means for legal aid purposes the court will make allowances for your outgoings on the maintenance of your wife/husband, family and other dependent relatives, the cost of your accommodation, reasonable expenses in connection with your employment and other special expenses such as hire purchase payments. To assist the court please give the following particulars of your outgoings.

(1) *Maintenance of dependants.* If you are married and you are living with your wife/husband, you should include her/him and any children or other relatives financially supported by either of you. If you are unmarried or you are married but not living with your wife/husband, you should include only children or other relatives financially supported by you personally.

(a) *Dependants living with you:—*

Name	Age	Relationship	Whether fully dependent on you; if not, state means of dependant
....	....	....	....
....	....	....	....

(b) *Dependants not living with you:—*

Name	Age	Relationship	Weekly amounts of your payments for maintenance
....	....	....	....
....	....	....	....

(2) *Living accommodation (state whether payments are weekly, monthly, quarterly or annual):—*

Rent..

Mortgage repayments...

Ground rent...

Rates ....

Board and lodging ....

Bed and breakfast ....

(3) *Expenses in connection with your employment:—*

Travelling ....

Tools..

Other expenses ....

(4) *Other expenses:—*

    (a) Hire purchase payments..

        Amount outstanding on hire purchase debt(s) ....

        Nature of goods ....

    (b) Insurance premiums ....

        State sum insured and date policy taken out..

        Date policy due to mature...

    (c) Give details of any order of a court under which you are currently required to pay money and of amount involved...

        ....

    (d) Other debts or expenses ....

        ....

Write "NONE" where appropriate.

DIVISION I.—GENERAL

PART 5—ADDITIONAL INFORMATION

Give below any additional information which you think the court should know about your financial circumstances, including any changes which are likely to occur within the next twelve months ....

....

PART 6—DECLARATION

I declare that, to the best of my knowledge and belief, I have given a complete and correct statement of my income, savings and capital (and that of my spouse) (^{c}) (and that of my child) (^{d}).

Signature ....

Date ....

(^{c}) Delete unless you are married and are living with your spouse.
(^{d}) Delete unless legal aid is being sought for your child.

FORM 5

Statement of means of person financially responsible for applicant
(Criminal Justice Act, 1967, s. 78 (2); General Reg. 4 (2))

If you are the parent or guardian of an applicant for legal aid who is under eighteen or you have the care and control of him or you are otherwise liable to maintain him and you are not an appropriate contributor, you are requested to complete this form and return it to the clerk of the court to which the applicant has applied for legal aid.

PART I

1. Name and address of applicant ....
2. Your full name and address ....
3. Your relationship to applicant ....
4. Your occupation (state normal occupation) ....
5. Have you been unemployed during the past twelve months? YES/NO.
   If your answer is "Yes", state periods of unemployment during the last twelve months
   ....

PART 2—INCOME

Give below particulars of your income from all sources for the twelve months immediately preceding the date on which this form is completed. If you are married and living with your wife/husband, particulars of her/his income must also be stated.

The amounts stated should be the net amounts after deduction of income tax and National Insurance contributions.

Instead of giving amounts for the previous twelve months you may express amounts on a weekly or monthly basis if you state the basis in the remarks column.

Description of Income	Amount		Remarks	FOR OFFICIAL USE ONLY
	Your income	Income of wife/husband		
1. Wages or salary including overtime, commission and bonuses.				
2. If in business on your own account, net profit.				
3. Family allowances.				
4. National Insurance bene-fit— (a) Unemployment (b) Sickness (c) Pension.				
5. Supplementary pension or allowance from the Supplementary Benefits Commission.				
6. Net income from sub-letting house, rooms, etc.				
7. Other income (give de-tails).				

Write "NONE" where appropriate.

Has the child any source of income not included above? YES/NO.

If your answer is "Yes", give details below:

Description of Income	Amount	Remarks	FOR OFFICIAL USE ONLY

PART 3—CAPITAL OR SAVINGS

Give below particulars of all your capital or savings. If you are married and living with your wife/husband, give details of her/his capital and savings also.

	Yourself	Wife/husband	FOR OFFICIAL USE ONLY
1. Do you or your wife/husband own house property? (Answer Yes or No). If your answer is "Yes", state:— (a) the value, (*i.e.* approximate selling price) (b) the amount of any outstanding mortgage (c) whether you are living in the house.			
2. Give particulars of all capital or savings belonging to you or your wife/husband. You should state the amount and description (*e.g.* money in the National Savings Bank or other banks, National Savings Certificates, cash, stocks and shares, etc.).			

Write "NONE" where appropriate.

Has the child any capital or savings not included above? YES/NO.

If your answer is "Yes", give details below:

Description of capital or savings	Amount	Remarks	FOR OFFICIAL USE ONLY

PART 4—EXPENSES

In assessing your means for legal aid purposes the court will make allowances for your outgoings on the maintenance of your wife/husband, family and other dependent relatives, the cost of your accommodation, reasonable expenses in connection with your employment and other special expenses such as hire purchase payments. To assist the court please give the following particulars of your outgoings.

(1) *Maintenance of dependants.* If you are married and you are living with your wife/husband, you should include her/him and any children or other relatives financially supported by either of you. If you are unmarried or you are married but not living with your wife/husband, you should include only children or other relatives financially supported by you personally.

(a) *Dependants living with you:—*

Name	Age	Relationship	Whether fully dependent on you; if not, state means of dependant
....	....	....	....
....	....	....	....

(b) *Dependants not living with you:—*

Name	Age	Relationship	Weekly amounts of your payments for maintenance
....	....	....	....
....	....	....	....

(2) *Living accommodation (state whether payments are weekly, monthly, quarterly or annual):—*

Rent ....

Mortgage repayments ....

Ground rent..

Rates ....

Board and lodging ....

Bed and breakfast ....

(3) *Expenses in connection with your employment:—*

Travelling ....

Tools..

Other expenses ....

(4) *Other expenses:—*

(a) Hire purchase payments..
Amount outstanding on hire purchase debt(s) ....
Nature of goods ....

(b) Insurance premiums ....
State sum insured and date policy taken out..
Date policy due to mature..

(c) Give details of any order of a court under which you are currently required to pay money and of amount involved ....
....

(d) Other debts or expenses...
....

Write "NONE" where appropriate.

PART 5—ADDITIONAL INFORMATION

Give below any additional information which you think the court should know about your financial circumstances, including any changes which are likely to occur within the next twelve months ....

....

PART 6—DECLARATION

I declare that, to the best of my knowledge and belief, I have given a complete and correct statement of my income, savings and capital (and that of my spouse) (ᶜ) and that of the child.

Signature ....

Date ....

(ᶜ) Delete unless you are married and are living with your spouse.

FORM 6

Legal aid order (Criminal Justice Act, 1967, ss. 73, 75;
General Reg. 6).

In accordance with the provisions of sections 73 and 75 of the Criminal Justice Act, 1967, the ....
Court hereby grants legal aid to ....
for the following purpose (ᵃ):

(1) Proceedings before a magistrates' court in connection with (ᵇ) ....
....

(2) Appealing to the Crown Court against a decision of the ....
.... Magistrates' Court on....................................

(3) Resisting an appeal to the Crown Court against a decision of the ....
.... Magistrates'
Court on ....

(4) Proceedings before the Crown Court in connection with (ᶜ) ....
....
including, in the event of his being convicted or sentenced in those proceedings, advice and assistance in regard to the making of an appeal to the criminal division of the Court of Appeal as provided in section 74 (7) of the Criminal Justice Act, 1967.

(5) An appeal to the Court of Appeal and any proceedings preliminary or incidental thereto.

(6) Advice by counsel or solicitor assigned by the Court of Appeal on the question whether there appear to be reasonable grounds of appeal and assistance by that counsel or solicitor in the preparation of an application for leave to appeal or the giving of a notice of appeal.

(7) An appeal to the House of Lords and any proceedings preliminary or incidental thereto.

(8) A retrial by the Crown Court ordered by the Court of Appeal or the House of Lords.

Except as otherwise provided above, the legal aid granted shall consist of representation by a solicitor/solicitor and counsel/solicitor and two counsel/counsel only (ᵈ), including advice on the preparation of the case for the proceedings.

(ᵃ) Delete (1) to (8) as necessary.
(ᵇ) State charge etc.
(ᶜ) State nature of proceedings.
(ᵈ) Delete as necessary.

The solicitor assigned is...
of ....
The legally aided person has paid the sum of £   s.   d. to...........................
.... as a payment on account of any contribution which he may be
ordered to make at the conclusion of the case.
The legally assisted person has been committed to ....
...........................prison/released on bail and may be communicated with at (d)
....

Dated this........................... day of .... 19......

(Signed) (e) ....

(e) Signature and designation of clerk to court.

FORM 7

Order amending legal aid order

(*Criminal Justice Act,* 1967, *s.* 80; *General Reg.* 6)

The...court hereby amends the order.........
granting legal aid to ....
of ....
by substituting for the solicitor (a) named in the order another solicitor, namely
....
of ....
/and by authorising the instruction of counsel in place of the counsel already
instructed.(b)

Dated this............................. day of.................. 19......

Signed (c) ....

(a) Where counsel only is assigned by the order, amend accordingly.
(b) Delete as necessary.
(c) Signature and designation of clerk to court.

FORM 8

Order revoking legal aid order

(*Criminal Justice Act,* 1967, *s.* 80, *General Reg.* 6)

The .... court hereby
revokes, as from this date, the order granting legal aid to ....
of ....
.... for the
purpose of ....

Dated this .... day of..................... 19......

Signature (a)...

NOTE TO LEGALLY ASSISTED PERSON

You are no longer entitled to legal aid. Your solicitor and counsel (if any) will
cease to act further for you unless you yourself re-employ them and if you do so
you will be responsible for their costs from the above date. The court has power
to order you to pay a contribution towards any legal aid costs already incurred on
your behalf.

(a) Signature and designation of clerk to court.

FORM 9

Contribution order

(Criminal Justice Act, 1967, *s.* 76, *General Reg.* 19)

TO (ª) ....
of ....

By virtue of the powers contained in section 76 of the Criminal Justice Act, 1967
the ....
.... (name of court) hereby
orders you to pay in respect of the legal aid provided for you under legal aid order(s)
no.(s)...............:—

(ᵇ) ⎰ a contribution of £............towards the costs
    ⎱ the whole costs amounting to £............
    ⎱ *the whole costs, or £............, whichever is less.

This sum should be paid to the Clerk to the Justices, ...
Magistrates' Court...(ᵇ) on or before
.... (ᵇ) in ....
instalments of ...., the first to be paid on or before
...., the
second and subsequent instalments to be paid ....

(ᶜ) Signed..
(Date) ....

* You will be informed of the amount payable as soon as the legal aid costs incurred are
known.

(ª) Name and address of legally assisted person.
(ᵇ) Delete as necessary.
(ᶜ) Signature and designation of clerk to the court.

FORM 10

Reference to Supplementary Benefits Commission

(Criminal Justice Act, 1967, *s.* 77; *General Reg.* 22)

To: The Manager,
　　Legal Aid Assessment
　　Office,
　　Ministry of Social
　　Security

Name and Address of Court

　　............................
　　............................
　　............................
　　............................
　　............................
　　............................
　　............................

Date ....
Reference ....

Dear Sir

Name of legally assisted person ....
　　(or applicant)
Present address (if different from ....
　　that shown in Form 4). ....

Address of wife/husband where known ....

(if different from above). ....

The attached statement(s) of means is/are referred for inquiry and report as to means. This request is made:—

(a) { on the application of the legally assisted person.
{ by the court without application by the legally assisted person.

(b) The legally assisted person's resources were assessed for the purpose of a contribution order on ....(date).

Yours faithfully,

(c) Signed...

(a) Delete as appropriate.
(b) Leave blank if no assessment has yet been made.
(c) Signature and designation of clerk to court.

FORM 11

Variation or revocation of contribution order

(*Criminal Justice Act*, 1967, s. 77; *General Reg.* 23)

To (a) ....
of ....

Having considered a report on your means by the Supplementary Benefits Commission the ....
court hereby revokes/varies as follows (b) contribution order no. ....
made on ....

(b) The total amount which you are required to pay towards the costs of legal aid shall be .... This sum should be paid to the Clerk to the Justices, ...
Magistrates' Court .... on or before
....
in .... instalments of ....
the first to be paid on or before ....
the second and subsequent instalments to be paid ....

(c)Signed ....

(Date) ....

(a) Name and address of legally assisted person.
(b) Delete as necessary.
(c) Signature and designation of clerk to court.

LEGAL AID IN CRIMINAL PROCEEDINGS (ASSESSMENT OF RESOURCES) REGULATIONS, 1968

[S.I. 1968 No. 1265]

General note.—These regulations are printed as amended by the Legal Aid in Criminal Proceedings (Assessment of Resources) (Amendment) Regulations, 1970, S.I. 1970 No. 1994.

ARRANGEMENT OF REGULATIONS

In pursuance of the powers conferred upon me by section 78 of the Criminal Justice Act, 1967, I hereby, with the consent of the Treasury, make the following Regulations:—

General

1. The resources and commitments of any person may be assessed in accordance with the provisions of these Regulations by—

(a) the court empowered to make a legal aid order or a contribution order, as the case may be, in the particular case, by virtue of section 73 or 76 (4) of the Act; or

(b) any person entitled to sit as a member of that court; or

(c) the proper officer of that court,

hereinafter referred to as "the assessor".

Resources of persons other than applicant or legally assisted person

2.—(1) In assessing the resources and commitments of any person for the purpose of deciding whether he is eligible for legal aid or should make any payment or contribution in respect of legal aid ordered or to be ordered, the assessor (without prejudice to the other provisions of these Regulations)—

(a) may treat as the resources or commitments of that person any resources or commitments of his spouse unless it would in the circumstances of the case be unreasonable or impracticable for the spouse to make available his resources to that person;

(b) when the application is made by or on behalf of an infant, may take into account the resources and commitments of all or any of the following persons as the assessor, having regard to the circumstances, including the age and resources of the infant, may decide—

(i) any person who under section 22 of the Ministry of Social Security Act, 1966, is liable to maintain the infant, or would be so liable if the infant were under the age of sixteen;

(ii) any person having the care and control of the infant, not being a person having such care and control by reason of any contract or for some temporary purpose:

Provided that for the purposes of this Regulation the expression "person" shall not include the Minister of Social Security or a local authority or a fit person under the Children and Young Persons Act, 1933.

(2) The resources of an infant shall include any sums payable under an order of the court or under any arrangement to any person for the maintenance of such infant.

Assessment of resources on applications for legal aid

3.—(1) In determining whether the means of an applicant or an appropriate contributor are such that the applicant should be given legal aid under Part IV of the Act, in respect of all or part of the costs which he is likely to incur, or whether the applicant or an appropriate contributor shall be required to make a payment on account of any contribution which may be ordered under section 75 (3) of the Act, the assessor shall assess, in accordance with the provisions of this Regulation, the resources of any person whose resources are to be taken into account.

(2) In making such determination, the assessor shall consider any statement of means submitted by any person and shall have regard to the costs likely to be incurred by such person if legal aid is not ordered and to the resources immediately available to such person at the date of the application which could, and ought reasonably to, be used to meet such costs, after such person has provided for all necessary commitments.

(3) In assessing the resources available to such person, the assessor shall not have regard to any capital which could not be realised, or on the security of which money could not be raised, in time to enable legal representation or advice to be obtained.

(4) Where it appears desirable in the interests of justice to make a legal aid order, such an order shall not be refused if—

   (a) the applicant, or his spouse with whom he is living, is in receipt of a supplementary pension or allowance payable under the Ministry of Social Security Act, 1966; or
   (b) the applicant's resources at the date of the application which are immediately available do not exceed £25, or, where the applicant is married and living with his spouse, the joint resources of the applicant and his spouse which are immediately available do not exceed £40; or
   (c) where the applicant is an infant, any person referred to in Regulation 21 (1) (b) of these Regulations whose resources are taken into account by the assessor is in receipt of such a supplementary pension or allowance, or the resources of such person at the date of the application which are immediately available do no exceed £25, or, where such person is married and living with his spouse, the joint resources of that person and his spouse which are immediately available do not exceed £40.

Assessment of resources for contribution orders

4.—(1) In determining whether a legally assisted person or an appropriate contributor shall be required to make a contribution under section 76 of the Act (whether in respect of the whole or part of the costs incurred) the assessor shall, in making his assessment of the resources of any person, have regard to—

   (a) that person's likely income determined in accordance with Regulation 5 of these Regulations during the period of twelve months from the date of assessment;
   (b) such part, if any, of that person's capital determined in accordance with Regulation 6 of these Regulations as it seems reasonable to the assessor to take into account.

(2) No legally assisted person shall be required to make a contribution as aforesaid if—

    (a) he or an appropriate contributor is in receipt of a supplementary pension or allowance payable under the Ministry of Social Security Act, 1966; or

    (b) the income from all sources during the period of 12 months prior to the date of assessment of the legally assisted person, an appropriate contributor or any other person referred to in Regulation 2 (1) (b) of these Regulations whose resources are taken into account by the assessor after deducting income tax and national insurance contributions amounted to £250 or less and the capital at the date of assessment of the legally assisted person, appropriate contributor or other person, as the case may be, is £25 or less:

Provided that in relation to a legally assisted person, appropriate contributor or other person who is married and living with his wife for the reference to his income amounting to £250 or less there shall be substituted a reference to their joint income amounting to £450 or less and for the reference to his capital being £25 or less there shall be substituted a reference to their joint capital being £40 or less.

Assessment of income

5.—(1) In assessing a person's likely income, the assessor may, where appropriate, have regard to any income received by him at any time during a period between a date twelve months prior to the submission of his statement of means and the date of assessment.

(2) The income of a person from any trade or business or gainful occupation other than employment at a wage or salary shall be deemed to be the profits therefrom which will accrue during the period of twelve months from the date of assessment, and in calculating such profits the assessor may have regard to the profits of the last accounting period for which accounts have been made up.

(3) In assessing the income of any person there shall be deducted reasonable sums in respect of—

    (a) the total amount of tax which it is estimated would be payable by him if his income for the period of assessment were his income for a fiscal year;

    (b) his national insurance contributions for that period;

    (c) expenses incurred in connection with his employment at a wage or salary;

    (d) his annual outgoings in respect of accommodation including—

        (i) the rent, after deducting the proceeds of sub-letting any part of the premises;

        (ii) rates, repairs and insurance;

        (iii) any instalments (whether of interest or capital) payable in respect of a mortgage debt or heritable security charged on the house in which he resides or on any interest therein after deducting the proceeds of sub-letting any part of the premises;

    (e) the maintenance of his spouse or former spouse, children whom he is liable to maintain and his dependent relatives, whether living with him or not;

    (f) any other matter for which he must, or reasonably may, provide.

(4) In assessing income from any source the assessor may disregard such amount as he considers to be reasonable to disregard, having regard to the nature of the income or to any other circumstances.

Assessment of capital

6.—(1) Subject to the provisions of this Regulation, in assessing the capital of any person there shall be included the amount or value of every resource of a capital nature belonging to him on the date of the assessment.

(2) So far as such resource does not consist of money, the amount or value thereof shall be taken to be the amount which that resource would realise if sold in the open market or, if there is only a restricted market for the resource, the amount which it would realise in that market, after deduction of any expenses incurred in the sale, or, if such amount cannot be ascertained, an amount which appears to the assessor to be reasonable.

(3) In assessing such capital, there shall be wholly disregarded—

(a) any death grant paid under the provisions of section 39 of the National Insurance Act, 1965;

(b) any maternity grant which a woman is paid under the provisions of section 23 of the said Act;

(c) save in exceptional cases, the personal clothing of the person, the household furniture and effects of the dwelling-house occupied by him and the personal tools and equipment of his trade.

(4) If account is taken of the value of any dwelling-house in which a person resides, the amount taken into account shall not exceed one half of the amount by which the value of the dwelling-house, after deducting therefrom the amount of any incumbrances charged thereon, exceeds £3,000.

Disclosure of increases in resources

7. Before the assessor determines whether a contribution order should be made, the applicant or legally assisted person or appropriate contributor shall disclose to him any material change in his resources since submission of his statement of means.

Interpretation

8.—(1) In these Regulations—

"the Act" means the Criminal Justice Act, 1967;

"applicant" means in relation to an application made on behalf of a person who has not attained the age of seventeen years by his parent or guardian, that person and in the case of any other application the person making the application;

"application" is used with reference not only to an application for legal aid but also to an offer of legal aid made by a court without any such application;

"date of assessment" means the date on which the court empowered to make the contribution order first assesses the means of the legally assisted person or an appropriate contributor, or, if before such an assessment is made, the Supplementary Benefits Commission is requested to inquire into the means of the legally assisted person or appropriate contributor;

"national insurance contributions" means contributions payable under the National Health Service Contributions Act, 1965, the National Insurance Act, 1965, the National Insurance (Industrial Injuries) Act, 1965, or any scheme made under either of the two last-mentioned Acts;

"proper officer" means the Clerk of the Parliaments, the Registrar of Criminal Appeals, the appropriate officer of the Crown Court or the justices' clerk (as the case may be);

"statement of means" means a statement of means submitted by an applicant for legal aid or an appropriate contributor or, where the applicant is an infant, submitted by a person liable to maintain or having the care and control of the applicant.

(2) The Interpretation Act, 1889, shall apply to the interpretation of these Regulations as it applies to the interpretation of an Act of Parliament.

(3) References in these Regulations to any enactment or subordinate instrument shall include references to such enactment or subordinate instrument as amended from time to time.

Citation and commencement

9. These Regulations may be cited as the Legal Aid in Criminal Proceedings (Assessment of Resources) Regulations, 1968 and shall come into operation on 1st October 1968.

THE LEGAL AID (EXTENSION OF PROCEEDINGS) REGULATIONS, 1969

[S.I. 1969 No. 921]

1.—(1) These Regulations may be cited as the Legal Aid (Extension of Proceedings) Regulations, 1969, and shall come into operation on 1st August 1969.

(2) The Interpretation Act, 1889, shall apply to the interpretation of these Regulations as it applies to the interpretation of an Act of Parliament.

2. Notwithstanding anything in paragraph 1 of Part II of the First Schedule to the Legal Aid and Advice Act, 1949, the making of a counterclaim for defamation in proceedings for which legal aid may be given shall not of itself affect any right of the defendant to the counterclaim to legal aid in the proceedings and legal aid may be granted to enable him to defend such counterclaim.

3. The proceedings in which legal aid may be given shall include the proceedings contained in the Schedule to these Regulations.

SCHEDULE
PROCEEDINGS IN CONNECTION WITH WHICH LEGAL AID MAY BE GIVEN

1. Proceedings in a magistrates' court or a court of quarter sessions under sections 62, 63, 65, 66, 84, 85 (1) and 102 (1) (a) and (b) of the Children and Young Persons Act, 1933, section 40 of the Education Act, 1944, and section 33 of the Children and Young Persons Act, 1963.

2. Proceedings in a magistrates' court under sections 2 and 4 of the Children Act, 1948, section 43 of the National Assistance Act, 1948, section 22 of the Maintenance Orders Act, 1950, section 4 of the Maintenance Orders Act, 1958, section 3 of the Children and Young Persons Act, 1963, and section 23 of the Ministry of Social Security Act, 1966.

3. Proceedings in a magistrates' court in which a parent or guardian opposes the making of an adoption order and the court is asked to dispense with his consent under section 5 of the Adoption Act, 1958.

NOTE
These Regulations were made by the Lord Chancellor under ss. 1 and 12 of the Legal Aid and Advice Act, 1949 and came into operation on August 1, 1969.

SECTION 10.—OTHER PROVISIONS AFFECTING TREATMENT AND DETENTION OF JUVENILES

INTRODUCTORY NOTE

Sections 6 and 7 of this Division of the book deal with probation and borstal training. This section includes certain other statutory provisions which affect juveniles, if not exclusively, at least as well as adults.

The group of sections from 17 to 20 of the Criminal Justice Act, 1948, carried further the policy of keeping young offenders out of prison and of providing other and better means of dealing with them. These provisions were amended or repealed by later legislation, in particular the Criminal Justice Act, 1961. No court may now impose imprisonment on anyone who is under 17 years of age. This restriction on imprisonment calls for alternative methods of punishment or treatment, and the Criminal Justice Act, 1948, created detention centres and attendance centres for this purpose. The provisions relating to the former were repealed and re-enacted with amplifications by the Criminal Justice Act, 1961, while those relating to the latter were amended both by that Act and the Children and Young Persons Act, 1963. Considerable use is being made of these centres by courts to which they are available. In previous editions it was suggested that s. 17 of the Criminal Justice Act, 1948, foreshadowed an attempt to keep out of prison all offenders under 21 who are dealt with summarily. The First Offenders Act, 1958, gave support to that suggestion, and the Criminal Justice Act, 1961, went further, for s. 3 of that Act precludes a court from passing a sentence of imprisonment of more than six months or of less than three years in any case where the offender is within the limits of age qualifying for a sentence of borstal training. The section goes on to make provision for extending this prohibition by Order in Council to terms of imprisonment of less than six months where sufficient accommodation is available in detention centres. The Children and Young Persons Act, 1969, precludes commitment to detention or attendance centre in default and indeed the courts may be precluded from sentencing a juvenile to a detention or attendance centre altogether (s. 7 (3) *ibid.*). It is anticipated that this subsection will be brought into operation when provisions for intermediate treatment within the terms of a supervision order (see s. 12 of the Act of 1969) can afford suitable alternatives.

It is still possible for a non-offender to be removed from a community home or approved school (Children and Young Persons Act, 1969, Sched. III, para. 2) to a borstal institution but the power to do so is confined to cases where behaviour is detrimental to others accommodated in the community home.

The Criminal Justice Act, 1948, also contained provisions for the detention of young people on remand or on committal for trial or sentence. These provisions are now to be found in s. 23 Children and Young Persons Act, 1969, and in s. 26 of the Magistrates' Courts Act, 1952. None of the remand centres envisaged in the former section are yet available, after nearly twenty years of existence on paper. While some of the accommodation necessary is in existence, in law the buildings are prisons, subject to prison rules, and presumably all that is necessary for the transformation is the formulation of Remand Centre Rules. The latter section, as did its predecessor, emphasizes the desirability of remands, on bail or in custody, for the purpose of obtaining medical and other reports before deciding on treatment, where the circumstances point to the usefulness of such information.

Section 40 of the Magistrates' Courts Act, 1952, which empowers a court to order the taking of fingerprints in certain cases, is to be construed together with s. 33 of the Criminal Justice Act, 1967, and s. 8 of the Children and Young Persons Act, 1969.

Also reproduced are ss. 48 and 49 of the 1948 Act, which respectively empower the Secretary of State to establish remand centres, detention centres, attendance centres and borstal institutions and to prohibit the use of premises as a remand home unless approved by him.

CRIMINAL JUSTICE ACT, 1948
[11 & 12 Geo. 6, c. 58]

Powers relating to young offenders

17. Restriction on imprisonment.—The Crown Court shall not impose imprisonment on a person under seventeen years of age.

(2) No court shall impose imprisonment on a person under twenty-one years of age unless the court is of opinion that no other method of dealing with him is appropriate; and for the purpose of determining whether any other method of dealing with any such person is appropriate the court shall obtain and consider information about the circumstances, and shall take into account any information before the court which is relevant to his character and his physical and mental condition.

(3) [*Repealed by the Courts Act, 1971.*]

(4) [*Repealed by the Magistrates' Courts Act, 1952.*]

(5) [*Repealed by the Magistrates' Courts Act, 1952.*]

(6) In this section the expression " court " includes a justice of the peace.

NOTES

This section is printed as amended by the Magistrates' Courts Act, 1952, the Criminal Justice Act, 1961, and the Courts Act, 1971.

" **Impose imprisonment.**"—This is defined in s. 80 (1) as meaning:—

" pass a sentence of imprisonment or commit to prison in default of payment of any sum of money or for failing to do or abstain from doing anything required to be done or left undone." Where an offender under the age of 17, who has previously been subject to probation or conditional discharge orders, is sentenced to a period of borstal training for a substantive offence, the outstanding orders cannot by reason of the offender's age be dealt with by a nominal concurrent sentence of one day's imprisonment. A nominal fine should normally be imposed in respect of them. (*R.* v. *Jones*, [1970] 3 All E. R. 263; 134 J. P. 633).

" Committal to prison."—In the case of a remand or a committal for trial a young person may still be sent to prison in certain circumstances; see s. 23 of the Children and Young Persons Act, 1969, p. 166, *post*. By s. 28 (4) of the Magistrates' Courts Act, 1952, p. 308, *ante*, in the case of committal to the Crown Court with a view to a sentence of borstal training a young person must be sent to prison if a remand centre is not available.

Imprisonment under 18.—Section 120 (2) of the Education Act, 1944, extended to persons under 18 years of age in respect of certain offences the restrictions of the repealed s. 52 (3) and of s. 54 of the Children and Young Persons Act, 1933, which itself is repealed by the Children and Young Persons Act, 1969. The reference in s. 120 (2) to s. 52 (3) of the 1933 Act was repealed by the Criminal Justice Act, 1948; although the reference to s. 54 was not repealed by the Act of 1969. While a remand home is no longer available as a punishment, they may be sent to prison, but subject now to the restrictions in this section, and in s. 107 of the Magistrates' Courts Act, 1952, p. 385, *post*.

First offenders.—Imprisonment of first offenders is restricted by the First Offenders Act, 1958; 21 Halsbury's Statutes, 3rd Edn., 324.

Transfer to borstal of prisoners under 21.—Section 44 of the Prison Act, 1952, p. 308, *ante*, gives power to the Secretary of State to transfer to borstal, subject to certain conditions, persons under 21 who are serving a sentence of imprisonment.

Determination of age.—By s. 80 (3) of the Criminal Justice Act, 1948:—

" Where the age of any person at any time is material for the purposes of any provision of this Act, or of any Order in Council made thereunder, regulating the powers of a court, his age at the material time shall be deemed to be or to have been that which appears to the court after considering any available evidence to be or to have been his age at that time."

The section must be applied having regard to the age of the defendant at the time the court deals with him, not at the date of commission of the offence. Contrast the wording in s. 53 (1) of the Children and Young Persons Act, 1933, p. 57, *ante*.

19. Attendance at an attendance centre.—(1) Where a court of summary jurisdiction has power, or would but for the statutory restrictions upon the imprisonment of young offenders have power, to impose imprisonment on a person who is *not less than seventeen but* under twenty-one years of age, or to deal with any such person under section six of this Act for failure to comply with any of the requirements of a probation order, the court may, if it has been notified by the Secretary of State that an attendance centre is available for the reception from that court of persons of his class or description, order him to attend at such a centre, to be specified in the order, for such number of hours, as may be so specified:

Provided that no such order shall be made in the case of a person who has been previously sentenced to imprisonment, borstal training or detention in a detention centre, or has been ordered to be sent to an approved school.

(2) The times at which an offender is required to attend at an attendance centre by virtue of an order made under this section shall be such as to avoid interference, so far as practicable, with his school hours or working hours, and the first such time shall be specified in the order (being a time at which the centre is available for the attendance of the offender in accordance with the notification of the Secretary of State) and the subsequent times shall be fixed by the officer in charge of the centre, having regard to the offender's circumstances:

Provided that an offender shall not be required under this section to attend at an attendance centre on more than one occasion on any day, or for more than three hours on any occasion.

(3) The court by which an order has been made under subsection (1) of this section, or any justice acting for the petty sessional division or place for which that court acts, may, on the application of the offender or of the officer in charge of the attendance centre specified in the order—

    (a) by order discharge the order; or

    (b) by order vary the day or hour specified therein for the offender's first attendance at the centre;

and where the application is made by the said officer, the court or justice may deal with it without summoning the offender.

(4) Where an order is made under subsection (1) or subsection (3) of this section, the clerk to the justices shall deliver or send a copy of the order to the officer in charge of the attendance centre specified therein, and shall also deliver a copy to the offender or send a copy by registered post addressed to the offender's last or usual place of abode.

(5) Where a person has been ordered to attend at an attendance centre in default of the payment of any sum of money then—

    (a) on payment of the whole sum to any person authorised to receive it, the order shall cease to have effect;

    (b) on the payment of a part of the said sum as aforesaid, the total number of hours for which the offender is required to attend at the centre shall be reduced proportionately, that is to say by such number of complete hours as bears to the said total number the proportion most nearly approximating to, without exceeding, the proportion which the part paid bears to the said sum.

(6) [*Repealed by the Justices of the Peace Act,* 1949.]

(7) Where an order under subsection (1) of this section has been made and it appears on information to a justice acting for the petty sessional division or place for which the court which made the order acts that the person in whose case the order was made—

    (a) has failed without reasonable excuse to attend at the centre in accordance with the order; or

    (b) while attending at the centre has committed a breach of the rules made under section fifty-two of this Act which cannot be adequately dealt with under those rules;

the justice may issue a summons requiring the offender to appear at the place and time specified therein before a court of summary jurisdiction for the petty sessional division or place for which the justice acts, or may, if the information is in writing and on oath, issue a warrant for his arrest requiring him to be brought before such a court.

(8) If it is proved to the satisfaction of the court before which an offender appears or is brought under the last foregoing subsection that he has failed to attend as aforesaid, or has committed such a breach of rules as aforesaid, that court may revoke the order requiring his attendance

at the attendance centre and deal with him in any manner in which he could have been dealt with by the court which made the order if the order had not been made.

NOTES

From a date to be appointed the words in italics are to be inserted (Children and Young Persons Act, 1969, s. 72 (3) and Sched. V.). Presumably this will be complementary to an order under s. 7 (3), *ibid.*

This section is printed as amended by the Justices of the Peace Act, 1949, and the Magistrates' Courts Act, 1952, the Criminal Justice Act, 1961 and the Children and Young Persons Acts, 1963 and 1969.

Rules.—Sub-s. (6), which dealt with the power to make Rules about the receipt and application of fines, etc., was repealed by the Justices of the Peace Act, 1949. See the Attendance Centre Rules, 1958, p. 475, *post*, and the Magistrates' Courts (Attendance Centre) Rules, 1958, S.I. 1958 No. 1991 as to management and discipline, etc.

" **Impose imprisonment.**"—See note to s. 17, p. 373, *ante*.

Breach of probation.—For s. 6 of the Criminal Justice Act, 1948, see p. 283, *ante*.

It is suggested that where a court of summary jurisdiction decides to deal with a failure to comply with a requirement of a probation order without " passing sentence " for the original offence, and without prejudice to the continuance in force of the probation order, it may always exercise its powers under this section, even if the original offence is one for which imprisonment could not have been imposed in the case of an adult. If, however, the court decides to deal with the original offence, it cannot exercise powers under this section unless the original offence could have been dealt with in that way.

Children and Young Persons Act, 1969.—For the purposes of s. 15 (4) (a), *ibid.*, this section is modified by s. 16 (10), *ibid.*, p. 158, *ante*. A magistrates' court may make an attendance centre order on failure to comply with the requirements of a supervision order.

Failure to attend or breach of rules.—The wording of sub-s. (8) makes it clear that the way in which the court deals with the offender in substitution for the attendance order must be such as would have been possible at the time of the making of the attendance order, which may be different, having regard to his age, from that which would be possible at the time of the substitution.

Metropolitan police district.—In a Home Office letter dated June 19, 1958, notification was given that six attendance centres established in the Metropolitan police district were available to each court acting for an area wholly or in part within that district. The view was expressed that courts ordinarily accept 10 miles or a travelling time of 45 minutes as a reasonable maximum for an offender to travel to such an attendance centre.

Appeal.—In Home Office letter CHN 400/4/5 of March, 1956, sent to Clerks of the Peace the opinion is expressed that on an appeal from the decision of a magistrates' court to quarter sessions, as the appeal court may exercise any power the magistrates' court might have exercised, it may make an attendance centre order if the magistrates' court has been notified by the Secretary of State that the attendance centre to which the appeal court proposes to send the offender is available for the reception of boys found guilty by the magistrates' court.

" **Number of hours** ".—See s. 10 of the Criminal Justice Act, 1961, p. 406, *post*, as to restrictions on the aggregate number of hours for which a person may be ordered to attend at an attendance centre.

Service of order, sub-s. (4).—The order may be sent by the recorded delivery service. See the Recorded Delivery Service Act, 1962, and Home Office letter 122/68/C dated July 23, 1962.

27. Remand of persons aged 17 to 20.—(1) Where a court remands a person charged with or convicted of an offence or commits him for

trial or sentence and he is not less than seventeen but under twenty-one years old and is not released on bail, then, if the court has been notified by the Secretary of State that a remand centre is available for the reception from the court of persons of his class or description, it shall commit him to a remand centre and, if it has not been so notified, it shall commit him to a prison.

(2) Where a person is committed to a remand centre in pursuance of this section, the centre shall be specified in the warrant and he shall be detained there for the period for which he is remanded or until he is delivered thence in due course of law.

(3) In this section "court" includes a justice; and nothing in this section affects the provisions of section 105 (5) of the Magistrates' Court Act, 1952 (which provides for remands to the custody of a constable).

NOTES

This section is printed as substituted by the Children and Young Persons Act, 1969, s. 72 (3) and Sched. V.

Remand centre, rules.—See s. 47 of the Prison Act, 1952, p. 391, *post*, as to the power of the Secretary of State to make rules for the regulation and management of remand centres.

Interim orders.—As to the use of remand centres in the case of interim orders made under the Children and Young Persons Act, 1969, see s. 22 (5), *ibid*.

Certificate of unruliness or depravity.—A certificate is specifically required where a juvenile is committed to a remand centre or prison under ss. 22 or 23 Children and Young Persons Act, 1969 see the Magistrates' Courts (Children and Young Persons) Rules, 1970, r. 27, p. 580, *post*.

Probation hostel or home.—Rule 8 of the Approved Probation Hostel and Home Rules, 1949, p. 478, *post*, prohibits the use of such hostels or homes for a person on remand.

Institutions for Offenders

48. Remand centres, detention centres and borstal institutions.—

(1) [*Repealed by the Prison Act*, 1952, *re-enacted in s.* 43 *of that Act, p.* 390, post.]

(2) The Secretary of State may provide attendance centres, that is to say places at which offenders under twenty-one years of age may be required to attend, in pursuance of orders made under section nineteen of this Act, on such occasions and at such times as will avoid interference so far as is practicable with their school hours or working hours, and be given under supervision appropriate occupation or instruction ; and for the purpose aforesaid the Secretary of State may make arrangements with any local authority or police authority for the use of premises of that authority.

(3) [*Repealed by the Prison Act*, 1952, *re-enacted in s.* 43 *of that Act, p.* 390, post.]

(4) [*Repealed by the Children and Young Persons Act*, 1969, *s.* 72 (4) *and Sched. VI.*]

(5)–(7) [*Repealed by the Prison Act, 1952, re-enacted in s. 43 of that Act, p. 390, post.*]

NOTES

This section is printed as amended by the Prison Act, 1952, and the Children and Young Persons Acts, 1963 and 1969.

"**Remand Centres.**"—As to the uses that can be made of remand centres, see s. 27, p. 375, *ante*, and notes thereto.

"**Measurement and photographing of prisoners.**"—See Prison Act, 1952; s. 16, p. 388, *post*. As to taking finger prints, see also s. 40 of the Magistrates Courts Act, 1952, p. 382, *post*.

49. Remand homes.—(1) *As from such date as may be specified in an order made by statutory instrument by the Secretary of State, no premises shall be used as a remand home unless a certificate of approval has been issued by the Secretary of State.*

(2) *The Secretary of State may by rules made under this Act apply to remand homes, with such adaptations and modifications as he thinks fit, the provisions of section seventy-nine and subsection (3) of section one hundred and six of the Children and Young Persons Act, 1933 (which relate to the approval of schools for the purposes of that Act and the evidence of such approval).*

(3) *No person shall be appointed after the commencement of this Act to be in charge of a remand home established by a county council or a county borough council unless his appointment has been approved by the Secretary of State.*

(4) *Councils of counties and county boroughs may provide in remand homes provided for their areas facilities for the observation of any person detained therein on whose physical or mental condition a medical report may be desirable for the assistance of the court in determining the most suitable method of dealing with his case, or may, if facilities for observation are available at any other institution or place, arrange for the use of those facilities for the observation of any such person as aforesaid.*

(5) [*Repealed by the Children and Young Persons Act, 1969, s. 72 (4) and Sched. VI.*]

(6) *Any expenses incurred by the council of a county or county borough in giving effect to arrangements made under subsection (4) of this section, and any sums paid by such a council under subsection (4) of the last foregoing section, shall be treated for the purposes of any grant under section one hundred and four of the Children and Young Persons Act, 1933, as expenses of the council in respect of remand homes.*

NOTES

General note.—From a date to be appointed the remainder of this section is repealed by the Children and Young Persons Act, 1969, s. 72 (4) and Sched. VI. Section 77 (1) of the Act of 1933 (provision of remand homes) continues to apply by virtue of para. 13 (1) (c) Sched. IV Act of 1969. So long as this applies to any particular planning area, it will be necessary for this section to remain in force.

For s. 79 of the Children and Young Persons Act, 1933, see p. 65, *ante*.

For s. 104 of the Children and Young Persons Act, 1933, see p. 79, *ante*.

For s. 106 of the Children and Young Persons Act, 1933, see p. 80, *ante*.

Rules.—See the Remand Home Rules, 1939, pp. 468 *et seq.*, *post.*

Remand for medical report.—See Magistrates' Courts Act, 1952, ss. 14 (3), *infra* and 26, p. 379, *post.*

72. Powers of court in relation to absconders from approved schools, etc.—[*Repealed by the Children and Young Persons Act*, 1969, *s.* 72 (4) *and Sched. VI.*]

75. Power to order detention in a remand centre under s. 67 of the Children and Young Persons Act, 1933.—[*Repealed by the Children and Young Persons Act*, 1969, *s.* 72 (4) *and Sched. VI. See now ss.* 22 *and* 23, ibid.]

MAGISTRATES' COURTS ACT, 1952

[15 & 16 Geo. 6 & 1 Eliz. 2, c. 55]

6. Adjournment of inquiry.—(1) A magistrates' court may, before beginning to inquire into an offence as examining justices, or at any time during the inquiry, adjourn the hearing, and if it does so shall remand the accused.

(2) The court shall when adjourning fix the time and place at which the hearing is to be resumed; and the time fixed shall be that at which the accused is required to appear or be brought before the court in pursuance of the remand.

NOTE

Examining justices hearing evidence in respect of an indictable offence must do so in the physical presence of the accused. Appearance by counsel or solicitor does not suffice. See s. 4 (3), *ibid.*, and the proviso to s. 99, *ibid.*; 21 Halsbury's Statutes, 3rd Edn., 271.

*   *   *   *

14. Adjournment of trial.—(1) A magistrates' court may at any time, whether before or after beginning to try an information, adjourn the trial, and may do so, notwithstanding anything in this Act, when composed of a single justice.

(2) The court may when adjourning either fix the time and place at which the trial is to be resumed, or, unless it remands the accused, leave the time and place to be determined later by the court; but the trial shall not be resumed at that time and place unless the court is satisfied that the parties have had adequate notice thereof.

(3) A magistrates' court may, for the purpose of enabling inquiries to be made or of determining the most suitable method of dealing with the case, exercise its power to adjourn after convicting the accused and before

sentencing him or otherwise dealing with him; but, if it does so, the adjournment shall not be for more than four weeks at a time unless the court remands the accused in custody and where it so remands him the adjournment shall not be for more than three weeks at a time.

(4) On adjourning the trial of an information the court may remand the accused and, where the accused has attained the age of seventeen, shall do so if—

(a) the offence is not a summary one; or

(b) the court has proceeded under subsection (3) of section eighteen of this Act to summary trial after having begun to inquire into the information as examining justices;

and, where the court remands the accused, the time fixed for the resumption of the trial shall be that at which he is required to appear or be brought before the court in pursuance of the remand.

NOTES

This section is printed as amended by the Criminal Justice Act, 1967, ss. 30, 130 and Sched. VI.

The general power to remand in custody or on bail is dealt with in ss. 105 and 106, pp. 383, *et seq., post.*

Magistrates' Courts Act, 1957.—Sub-s. (2) is modified by s. 1 (3) of the Magistrates' Courts Act, 1957. By *ibid.,* s. 1 (1), the modification does not apply to juvenile courts and the section is not reproduced here. (But see s. 46 (1) of the Children and Young Persons Act, 1933, Sched. V. for modification of the Act of 1957 in relation to notification of a plea of guilty by a person who is believed to be over seventeen.)

Forms.—For form of commitment on remand after conviction or for medical examination, see Forms Nos. 14, 15, p. 589, *post.*

Remand.—Where a magistrates' court, sitting in the capacity of examining justices remand an accused person under this section before beginning to enquire into the offence charged, they have a discretion under s. 105 (1) (p. 383, *post*) to remand him in custody or on bail and there is no overriding requirement that bail is to be granted in all cases where sworn evidence connecting him with the crime has not yet been given.

R. v. Guest, Ex parte Metropolitan Police Commissioner, [1961] 3 All E. R. 118; 126 J. P. 21.

Offences triable on indictment or summarily

18. Information for offence triable either on indictment or summarily.—(1) [By the Children and Young Persons Act, 1969, this section applies where the accused has attained the age of seventeen and accordingly it is not reproduced.]

*   *   *   *

Remand for medical examination

26. Remand for medical examination.—(1) If, on the trial by a magistrates' court of an offence punishable on summary conviction with imprisonment, the court is satisfied that the accused did the act or made the omission charged, but is of opinion that an inquiry ought to be made into his physical or mental condition before the method of dealing with him is determined, the court shall adjourn the case to enable a medical examination and report to be made and shall remand him; but the adjournment shall not be for more than three weeks at a time where a court remands him in custody nor for more than four weeks at a time where it remands him on bail.

(2) [*Repealed by the Children and Young Persons Act,* 1969, s. 72 (4) and Sched. VI.]

(3) Where on such an adjournment as aforesaid the accused is remanded on bail, it shall be a condition of the recognisance that he

    (a) undergo medical examination by a duly qualified medical practitioner or, where the inquiry is into his mental condition and the recognizance so specifies, two such practitioners ; and

    (b) for the purpose attend at an institution or place, or on any such practitioner, specified in the recognizance and, where the inquiry is into his mental condition, comply with any directions which may be given to him for the said purpose by any person so specified or by a person of any class so specified.

and, if arrangements have been made for the reception of the accused, it may be a condition of the recognizance that he shall, for the purpose of the examination, reside, until the expiration of such period as may be specified in the recognizance or he is discharged therefrom, whichever occurs first, in an institution or place so specified, not being an institution or place to which he could have been committed.

(4) Where a magistrates' court on committing any person for trial on bail is of opinion that an inquiry ought to be made as aforesaid, the conditions of the recognizance taken for the purpose of his committal may, in addition to the condition for his appearance, include the like conditions as could be included in the conditions of a recognizance with respect to the like inquiry by virtue of the last preceding subsection.

(5) The Costs in Criminal Cases Act, 1952, shall apply to a duly qualified medical practitioner who makes a report otherwise than in writing for the purposes of this section as it applies to a person called to give evidence, and shall so apply notwithstanding that the proceedings for the purposes of which the report is made are not proceedings to which section five of that Act applies.

(6) [*Repealed by the Mental Health Act,* 1959.]

NOTES

    This section is printed as amended by the Mental Health Act, 1959, the Criminal Justice Act, 1967, and the Children and Young Persons Act, 1969.

    Offence punishable with imprisonment.—A magistrates' court cannot impose imprisonment on a juvenile, but for the purposes of this section the expression must be construed as meaning an offence so punishable in the case of an adult, see s. 126 (8), p. 388, *post.*

    Documents and information.—As to the documents and information to be sent to those responsible for the medical examination and report, see rule 23 of the Magistrates' Courts Rules, 1968.

Remand of young person.—See s. 23 of the Children and Young Persons Act, 1969, p. 166, *ante*.

Remand centres.—See note "Committal to Prison," p. 373, *ante*.

Failure to surrender to bail.—See s. 97, Magistrates' Courts Act, 1952, as to the court's power to issue a warrant.

Enforcement of recognisance.—See *ibid.*, s. 96, p. 317, *post*.

Forms.—See note to s. 14, p. 379, *ante*.

"Who makes a report."—*i.e.*, a witness allowance may be paid even if the offence is not indictable. See also s. 32 (3) Criminal Justice Act, 1967.

*   *   *   *

34. Compensation on conviction of indictable offence.—Where a magistrates' court convicts a person of an indictable offence, the court shall have the same power to award a sum of money to any person aggrieved as a court has under section four of the Forfeiture Act, 1870; and any sum so awarded shall be enforceable in the same way as costs ordered to be paid by the offender.

NOTE

This section is printed as amended by the Criminal Law Act, 1967, and the Courts Act, 1971.

Enforcement.—The enforcement of costs in criminal cases is dealt with in the Administration of Justice Act, 1970.

In *R. v. Dorset Quarter Sessions, Ex parte Randall*, [1967] 2 Q. B. 222; [1966] 3 All E. R. 952 a magistrates' court made an order for payment of compensation at the same time as committing for borstal sentence. It was held that although an order for compensation made by a magistrates' court was an order made at the time and in consequence of a conviction, it was not a sentence and accordingly there had been jurisdiction to make the order for borstal training.

Forfeiture Act, 1870.—Section 4 of this Act is amended by the Criminal Law Act, 1967, s. 10 and Sched. 2 to have effect as if the references to felony included any offence tried on indictment, as if the reference to loss of property included damage to property, but did not include loss or damage due to an accident arising out of the presence of a motor vehicle on a road, and as if the reference to £100 were a reference to £400, but an order may only be made on the application of any person aggrieved, immediately after conviction. (*R. v. Forest JJ., Ex parte Coppin*, [1969] 2 All E. R. 668; 133 J. P. 433. *Cf.* the provisions of s. 8 Criminal Damage Act, 1971, where the order may be made "on application or otherwise".)

38. Bail on arrest without warrant.—(1) On a person's being taken into custody for an offence without a warrant, a police officer not below the rank of inspector, or the police officer in charge of the police station to which the person is brought, may, and, if it will not be practicable to bring him before a magistrates' court within twenty-four hours after his being taken into custody, shall, inquire into the case and, unless the offence appears to the officer to be a serious one, release him on his entering into a recognisance, with or without sureties, for a reasonable amount, conditioned for his appearance before a magistrates' court at the time and place named in the recognisance.

(2) Where, on a person's being taken into custody for an offence without a warrant, it appears to any such officer as aforesaid that the inquiry into the case cannot be completed forthwith, he may release that person on his entering into a recognisance, with or without sureties, for a reasonable amount, conditioned for his appearance at such a police station and at such a time as is named in the recognizance unless he previously receives

a notice in writing from the officer in charge of that police station that his attendance is not required; and any such recognizance may be enforced as if it were conditioned for the appearance of that person before a magistrates' court for the petty sessions area in which the police station named in the recognizance is situated.

(3) A recognizance conditioned for the appearance of a person at a police station as mentioned in the last preceding subsection may, where that person is apparently under seventeen years old, be taken from his parent or guardian with or without sureties.

(4) Where a person is taken into custody for an offence without a warrant and is retained in custody, he shall be brought before a magistrates' court as soon as practicable.

NOTES

This section is printed as amended by the Children and Young Persons Act, 1969, s. 72 (4) and Sched. VI, see note to s. 29 (6), *ibid.*

Enforcement of recognizance.—This is dealt with in s. 96, p. 317, *post.*

Guardian.—For definition, see s. 126 (1), p. 387, *post.*

*   *   *   *

40. Taking finger-prints.—(1) Where any person not less than fourteen years old who has been taken into custody is charged with an offence before a magistrates' court, the court may, if it thinks fit, on the application of a police officer not below the rank of inspector, order the finger-prints of that person to be taken by a constable.

(2) Finger-prints taken in pursuance of an order under this section shall be taken either at the place where the court is sitting or, if the person to whom the order relates is remanded in custody, at any place to which he is committed; and a constable may use such reasonable force as may be necessary for that purpose.

(3) The provisions of this section shall be in addition to those of any other enactment under which finger-prints may be taken.

(4) Where the finger-prints of any person have been taken in pursuance of an order under this section, then, if he is acquitted, or the examining justices determine not to commit him for trial, or if the information against him is dismissed, the finger-prints and all copies and records of them shall be destroyed.

NOTES

Taken into custody.—These words limit the power to make an order to cases where the defendant has been arrested, and exclude those in which he has appeared in answer to a summons, but this section is applied to a person not less than fourteen who appears before a magistrates court in answer to a summons for any offence punishable with imprisonment (Criminal Justice Act, 1967, s. 33) by the same section any reference to finger-prints shall be construed as including a reference to palm-prints. See also s. 8 of the Children and Young Persons Act, 1969.

Other enactments.—The other enactments referred to in sub-s. (3) can be found conveniently set out in " Stone's Justices' Manual ".

Form of order.—See Form No. 6 in the Schedule to the Magistrates' Courts (Forms) Rules, 1968.

Remand

105. Remand in custody or on bail.—(1) Where a magistrates' court has power to remand any person, then, subject to any enactment modifying that power, the court may—

(a) remand him in custody, that is to say, commit him to custody to be brought before the court at the end of the period of remand or at such earlier time as the court may require; or

(b) remand him on bail, that is to say, take from him a recognizance, with or without sureties, conditioned as provided in subsection (3) of this section.

and may, instead of taking recognizances in accordance with paragraph (b) of this subsection, fix the amount of the recognizances with a view to their being taken subsequently in accordance with section ninety-five of this Act and in the mean time commit him to custody in accordance with paragraph (a) of this subsection.

(2) Where a person is brought before the court after remand, the court may further remand him.

(3) A recognizance on which a person is remanded on bail as aforesaid may be conditioned—

(a) for his appearance before the court at the end of the period of remand; or

(b) for his appearance at every time and place to which during the course of the proceedings the hearing may be from time to time adjourned;

and, where the recognizance is conditioned as provided in paragraph (b) of this subsection, the fixing at any time of the time for the next appearance shall be deemed to be a remand; but nothing in this subsection shall deprive the court of power at any subsequent hearing to remand him afresh.

(4) Subject to the provisions of the next following section, a magistrates' court shall not remand a person for a period exceeding eight clear days:

Provided that—

(a) if the court remands him on bail, it may remand him for a longer period if he and the other party consent;

(b) where the court adjourns a trial under subsection (3) of section fourteen or section twenty-six of this Act, the court may remand him for the period of the adjournment;

(c) where a person is charged with an offence triable on indictment that is also triable summarily, then, if the court thinks the case proper to be tried summarily but is not at the time so constituted, and sitting in such a place, as will enable it to proceed with the trial, the court may remand him until the next occasion on which it will be practicable for the court to be so constituted, and to sit in such a place, as aforesaid, notwithstanding that the remand is for a period exceeding eight clear days.

(5) A magistrates' court having power to remand a person in custody may, if the remand is for a period not exceeding three clear days, commit him to the custody of a constable.

NOTES

Commit to custody.—See definition in s. 126 (1), p. 386, *post.*

Metropolitan magistrates.—The section deprived metropolitan magistrates of the power to remand for a longer period given by s. 36 of the Metropolitan Police Courts Act, 1839; 21 Halsbury's Statutes, 3rd Edn., 21.

Medical examination.—It may be made a condition of the recognizance for the defendant to undergo medical examination. See s. 26, p. 379, *ante.*

Period of remand.—Formerly there was no statutory limit in summary cases. See the repealed s. 16 of the Summary Jurisdiction Act, 1848.

Bringing up defendant during remand.—The power may be exercised in summary as well as in indictable cases.

When sureties not found.—See Rule 22 of the Magistrates' Courts Rules, 1968 which is as follows:—

" Where the court, with a view to a person's being remanded on bail, under paragraph (a) of the proviso to subsection (4) of section one hundred and five of the Act, for a period exceeding eight days, has fixed the amount of the recognizances to be taken for that purpose but commits that person to custody because the recognizances of the sureties have not yet been taken, the warrant of commitment shall direct the governor or keeper of the prison or place to which he is committed to bring him before the court at the end of eight clear days or at such earlier time as may be specified in the warrant, unless in the meantime the sureties have entered into their recognizances."

Place of remand.—See s. 23 of the Children and Young Persons Act, 1969, p. 166, *ante.*

Remand in absence of child or young person.—See s. 48 (3) of the Children and Young Persons Act, 1933, p. 54, *ante,* and s. 46 (2), *ibid.,* p. 52, *ante.*

Forms.—See note to s. 14, p. 379, *ante.*

Remand before evidence given.—See note " Remand " to s. 14, p. 379, *ante.*

"Custody of a constable."—In relation to a child or young person the reference to three clear days has effect as if there were substituted a reference to twenty-four hours (Children and Young Persons Act, 1969, s. 23.)

106. Further remand.—(1) If a magistrates' court is satisfied that any person who has been remanded is unable by reason of illness or accident to appear or be brought before the court at the expiration of the period for which he was remanded, the court may, in his absence, remand him for a further time; and subsection (4) of the last preceding section shall not apply.

(2) Notwithstanding anything in subsection (1) of the last preceding section, the power of a court under the preceding subsection to remand a person on bail for a further time may be exercised by enlarging his recognizance and those of his sureties, if any, to a later time.

(3) Where a person remanded on bail is bound by the recognizance to appear before a magistrates' court at any time, and the court has no power to remand him under subsection (1) of this section, the court may in his absence enlarge the recognizance, and those of his sureties, if any, to a later time; and the enlargement of the recognizance shall be deemed to be a further remand.

NOTE

See notes to s. 105, *supra.*

*   *   *   *

107. Restrictions on the imposition of imprisonment.—(1) A magistrates' court shall not impose imprisonment for less than five days.

(2) A magistrates' court shall not impose imprisonment on any person under seventeen years old.

(3) Where a magistrates' court imposes imprisonment on a person under twenty-one years old under powers contained in subsection (2) of section seventeen of the Criminal Justice Act, 1948 (which prohibits the imposition of imprisonment on a person under twenty-one years old unless there is no other appropriate method of dealing with him), the court shall state the reason for its opinion that no other method of dealing with him is appropriate, and cause that reason to be specified in the warrant of commitment and to be entered in the register.

(4) [*Repealed.*]

(5) [*Repealed.*]

(6) [*Repealed.*]

NOTES

This section is printed as amended by the Criminal Justice Act, 1961.

Impose imprisonment.—See definition in s. 126, p. 387, *ante*.

Committal to prison on remand, etc.—In the case of a remand or a committal for trial a young person may still be sent to prison in certain circumstances; see s. 23 of the Children and Young Persons Act, 1969, p. 166, *ante*. By s. 28 (4) of the Magistrates' Courts Act, 1952, p. 308, *ante*, in the case of committal to the Crown Court with a view to a sentence of borstal training a young person may be sent to prison if a remand centre is not available.

Detention of offender for one day in court-house or police station.—See s. 110, *infra*.

Imprisonment under eighteen (Education Act, 1944).—See note to s. 17 of the Criminal Justice Act, 1948, p. 372, *ante*.

Transfer to borstal.—S. 44 of the Prison Act, 1952, p. 308, *ante*, gives power to the Secretary of State to transfer to and from borstal. The section fixes no lower age limit and its provisions could possibly be applied therefore to a young person of fifteen years of age who had been ordered to be detained by the Crown Court.

Determination of age.—See s. 126 (5), p. 388, *post*.

First offenders.—Additional restrictions on the imprisonment of first offenders are imposed by the First Offenders Act, 1958, 21 Halsbury's Statutes, 3rd Edn., 324.

*   *   *   *

110. Detention of offender for one day in court-house or police station.—(1) A magistrates' court that has power to commit to prison a person convicted of an offence, or would have that power but for section thirty-nine or forty-four of the Criminal Justice Act, 1967 or section seventy-one of this Act may order him to be detained within the precincts of the courthouse or at any police station until such hour, not later than eight o'clock in the evening of the day on which the order is made, as the court may direct, and, if it does so, shall not, where it has power to commit him to prison, exercise that power.

(2) A court shall not make such an order under this section as will deprive the offender of a reasonable opportunity of returning to his abode on the day of the order.

NOTE

This section is printed as amended by the Criminal Justice Act, 1967, s. 103 and Sched. VI.

Juveniles.—As a magistrates' court cannot impose imprisonment on a child or young person, and s. 107 (2) is not mentioned in s. 110, one day's detention cannot be ordered in the case of a juvenile. See *R.* v. *Jones*, [1970] 3 All E. R. 263.

*   *   *   *

125. " Summary " and " Indictable " offence.—In this Act—

   (a) the expression " summary offence " means an offence which, if committed by an adult, is triable by a magistrates' court (whether or not it is also triable on indictment) except an offence triable by a magistrates' court with the consent of the accused under section nineteen of this Act or section five of the Newspaper Libel and Registration Act, 1881;

   (b) the expression " indictable offence " means an offence which, if committed by an adult, is triable on indictment (whether or not it is also triable by a magistrates' court) except an offence otherwise triable only by a magistrates' court which, under section twenty-five of this Act or any enactment not contained in this Act, is required to be tried on indictment at the instance of the accused or the prosecutor.

NOTE

In this Act, when the intention is to refer to an offence which is purely summary, reference is made to an offence which is not an indictable offence. Conversely, reference is sometimes made to an offence which is not a summary offence.

126. Interpretation of other terms.—(1) In this Act, unless the context otherwise requires, the following expressions have the meaning hereby assigned to them, that is to say—

   " Act " includes local Act;

   " Affiliation order " means an order made under the Bastardy Laws Amendment Act, 1872, adjudging a man to be the putative father of a bastard child and ordering him to pay a sum of money weekly or otherwise to the mother of a bastard child or to any other person who is named in the order;

   " City of London " includes the Inner Temple and the Middle Temple;

   " Commit to custody " means commit to prison or, where any enactment authorises or requires committal to some other place of detention instead of committal to prison, to that other place;

   " County ", means an administrative county exclusive of any borough in which the jurisdiction of county justices is excluded by virtue of subsection (2) of section one hundred and fifty-four of the Municipal Corporations Act, 1882 or subsection (3) of section sixteen of the Justices of the Peace Act 1949, and references to a county include references to the City of London and any London commission area;

   " Domestic proceedings " has the meaning assigned to it by section fifty-six of this Act;

" Enactment " includes an enactment contained in a local Act or in any order, regulation or other instrument having effect by virtue of an Act;

" Fine " except for the purposes of any enactment imposing a limit on the amount of any fine includes any pecuniary penalty or pecuniary forfeiture or pecuniary compensation payable under a conviction;

" Guardian " in relation to any person includes anybody who, in the opinion of the magistrates' court or police officer having cognisance of any proceedings in which that person is concerned, has for the time being charge of or control over that person;

" Impose imprisonment " means pass a sentence of imprisonment or fix a term of imprisonment for failure to pay any sum of money, or for want of sufficient distress to satisfy any sum of money, or for failure to do or abstain from doing anything required to be done or left undone;

" Metropolitan stipendiary magistrate ", " Metropolitan stipendiary court " and " Metropolitan stipendiary court area " mean metropolitan police magistrate, metropolitan police court and metropolitan police court area;

" Petty sessions area " means any of the following areas, that is to say, a borough having a separate commission of the peace, a county not divided into petty-sessional divisions and a petty-sessional division of a county;

" Prescribed " means prescribed by the rules;

" The Register " means the register of proceedings before a magistrates' court required by the rules to be kept by the clerk of the court;

" The Rules " means rules made under section fifteen of the Justices of the Peace Act, 1949;

" Sentence " does not include a committal in default of payment of any sum of money, or for want of sufficient distress to satisfy any sum of money, or for failure to do or abstain from doing anything required to be done or left undone;

" Sum enforceable as a civil debt " means—

(a) any sum recoverable summarily as a civil debt which is adjudged to be paid by the order of a magistrates' court;

(b) any other sum expressed by this or any other Act to be so enforceable.

" Transfer of fine order " has the meaning assigned to it by section seventy-two of this Act.

(2) Except where the contrary is expressed or implied, anything required or authorised by this Act to be done by justices may, where two or more justices are present, be done by one of them on behalf of the others.

(3) Any reference in this Act to a sum adjudged to be paid by a conviction or order of a magistrates' court shall be construed as including a reference to any costs, damages or compensation adjudged to be paid by the conviction or order of which the amount is ascertained by the conviction or order.

(4) In relation to a borough having a separate commission of the peace in which the jurisdiction of the county justices is not excluded, any reference in this Act to a justice for the borough shall be construed as including a reference to a justice for the county when acting for the borough.

(5) Where the age of any person at any time is material for the purposes of any provision of this Act regulating the powers of a magistrates' court, his age at the material time shall be deemed to be or to have been that which appears to the court after considering any available evidence to be or to have been his age at that time.

(6) Except where the context otherwise requires, any reference in this Act to an offence shall be construed as including a reference to an alleged offence; and any reference in this Act to an offence committed, completed or begun anywhere shall be construed as including a reference to an offence alleged to have been committed, completed or begun there.

(7) [Repealed by the Criminal Law Act, 1967, s. 10 and Sched. III.]

(8) References in this Act to an offence punishable on summary conviction with imprisonment shall be construed without regard to any prohibition or restriction imposed by or under this or any other Act on imprisonment of young offenders.

(9) The provisions of this Act authorising a magistrates' court on conviction of an offender to pass a sentence or make an order instead of dealing with him in any other way shall not be construed as taking away any power to order him to pay costs, damages or compensation.

(10) Except where the context otherwise requires, references in this Act to any enactment shall include a reference to that enactment as amended, extended or applied by any other enactment, including this Act.

NOTES

This section is printed as amended by the Matrimonial Proceedings (Magistrates' Court) Act, 1960; the Criminal Justice Act, 1961; the Criminal Justice Administration Act, 1962, and the Administration of Justice Act, 1964, the Criminal Law Act, 1967 and the Courts Act, 1971.

" **Affiliation Order.**"—Orders are now made under the Affiliation Proceedings Act, 1957.

PRISON ACT, 1952
[15 & 16 Geo. 6 & 1 Eliz. 2, c. 52]

16. Photographing and measuring of prisoners.—The Secretary of State may make regulations as to the measuring and photographing of prisoners and such regulations may prescribe the time or times at which and the manner and dress in which prisoners shall be measured and photographed and the number of copies of the measurements and photographs of each prisoner which shall be made and the persons to whom they shall be sent.

NOTE

For power of a magistrates' court to order finger-prints to be taken, see s. 40 of the Magistrates' Courts Act, 1952, p. 382, ante.

*   *   *   *

22. Removal of prisoners for judicial and other purposes.—
(1) Rules made under section forty-seven of this Act may provide in
what manner an appellant within the meaning of the Criminal Appeal
Act, 1907, when in custody, is to be taken to, kept in custody at, and
brought back from, any place at which he is entitled to be present for
the purposes of that Act, or any place to which the Court of Criminal
Appeal or any judge thereof may order him to be taken for the purpose
of any proceedings of that court.

(2) The Secretary of State may—

(a) [*Repealed.*]
(b) if he is satisfied that a person so detained requires medical or
surgical treatment of any description, direct him to be taken
to a hospital or other suitable place for the purpose of the
treatment;

and where any person is directed under this subsection to be taken to
any place he shall, unless the Secretary of State otherwise directs, be
kept in custody while being so taken, while at that place, and while
being taken back to the prison in which he is required in accordance with
law to be detained.

NOTES

This section is printed as amended by the Criminal Justice Act, 1961.   See also
ss. 28, 29 of that Act, p. 413, *post*.

Remand centres, etc.—As to the application of s. 22 to remand centres, detention centres and borstal institutions, see s. 43, p. 390, *post*.

*   *   *   *

**25. Remission for good conduct and release on licence of persons
sentenced to terms of imprisonment.**—(1) Rules made under section
forty-seven of this Act may make provision whereby, in such circumstances as may be prescribed by the rules, a person serving a sentence of
imprisonment for such a term as may be so prescribed may be granted
remission of such part of that sentence as may be so prescribed on the
ground of his industry and good conduct, and on the discharge of a
person from prison in pursuance of any such remission as aforesaid his
sentence shall expire.

*   *   *   *

(7) A person who is committed to prison in default of payment of a sum
adjudged to be paid by a conviction shall be treated for the purposes of
subsection (1) of this section, as undergoing a sentence of imprisonment
for the term for which he is committed, and consecutive terms of imprisonment shall be treated for all the purposes of this section as one term.

NOTES

This section is printed as amended by the Criminal Justice Act, 1961, and the
Courts Act, 1971.

Subsections (2) to (6).—These subsections are repealed by the Criminal Justice
Act, 1967 as to England and Wales.

Subsections (1) and (7).—These subsections do not apply to remand centres or
borstal institutions, but apply to detention centres.   See s. 43 (4) (b), *infra*.

*   *   *   *

Remand centres, detention centres and borstal institutions

43. Remand centres, detention centres and borstal institutions.
—(1) The Secretary of State may provide—

(a) remand centres, that is to say places for the detention of persons not less than fourteen but under twenty-one years of age who are remanded or committed in custody for trial or sentence;

(b) detention centres, that is to say places in which persons not less than fourteen but under twenty-one years of age who are ordered to be detained in such centres under the Criminal Justice Act, 1948, or the Criminal Justice Act, 1961, may be kept for short periods under discipline suitable to persons of their age and description ; and

(c) borstal institutions, that is to say places in which offenders not less than fifteen but under twenty-one years of age may be detained and given such training and instruction as will conduce to their reformation and the prevention of crime.

(2) The Secretary of State shall provide in remand centres facilities for the observation of any person detained therein on whose physical or mental condition a medical report may be desirable for the assistance of the court in determining the most suitable method of dealing with his case.

(3) The following provisions, that is to say—

(a) section six of the Prevention of Crimes Act, 1871 (which relates to the registration of prisoners);

(b) subsections (2) and (3) of section six, section sixteen and sections twenty-two and thirty-six of this Act; and

(c) subject as provided in the next following subsection, the other provisions of this Act preceding this section,

shall apply to remand centres, detention centres and borstal institutions and to persons detained therein as they apply to prisons and prisoners.

(4) The application as aforesaid of the provisions mentioned in paragraph (c) of the preceding subsection shall be subject to the following exceptions, adaptations and modifications:—

(a) subsections (2) to (6) of section eighteen, subsections (2) to (6) of section twenty-five, sections twenty-six to thirty and subsection (2) of section thirty-seven shall not so apply;

(b) subsections (1) and (7) of section twenty-five shall not apply to borstal institutions;

(c) rules made under section 47 of this Act may require the board of visitors appointed for any borstal institution to consider periodically the character, conduct and prospects of each of the persons detained therein and to report to the Secretary of State on the advisability of his release under supervision;

(d) the provisions mentioned in paragraph (c) of the last preceding subsection other than those specified in paragraphs (a) to (c) hereof shall apply as aforesaid subject to such adaptations and modifications as may be made by rules of the Secretary of State.

(5) References in the preceding provisions of this Act to imprisonment shall, so far as those provisions apply to institutions provided under this section, be construed as including detention in those institutions.

NOTES

This section is printed as amended by the Criminal Justice Acts, 1961 and 1967 and the Courts Act, 1971.

Remand centres.—As to the uses that can be made of remand centres, see s. 22 and 23 of the Children and Young Persons Act, 1969, p. 164, *ante*.

Detention centres.—See s. 4 the Criminal Justice Act, 1961, p. 402, *post*.

Borstal institutions.—See s. 20 of the Criminal Justice Act, 1948, as amended by the Magistrates' Courts Act, 1952, p. 305, *ante*, and see s. 28 of the last-named Act, p. 245, *ante*. See also s. 45 of this Act, p. 309, *ante*.

Registration of finger-prints, etc.—See s. 16 of this Act and s. 40 of the Magistrates' Courts Act, 1952, p. 382, *ante*.

44. Transfers from prison to borstal institution and vice versa. —[*This section is reproduced with notes at p.* 308, ante.]

45. Release of persons sentenced to borstal training.—[*This section is reproduced with notes at p.* 309, ante.]

46. Temporary detention of persons liable to detention in a borstal institution.—A person who is required to be taken to a borstal institution may, until arrangements can be made for taking him there, be temporarily detained elsewhere.

NOTES

The section does not indicate places in which such a person may be detained, nor does it state by whom the place is to be determined.   It would seem appropriate that a remand centre should be used where one is available, and that otherwise the place might be a prison.   If the period is quite short, possibly a police station might be used.   The period of detention and supervision dates from the date of the sentence, in accordance with s. 45, p. 309, *ante*.

It is to be noted that the form of commitment in the Schedule to the Summary Jurisdiction (Children and Young Persons) Rules, 1933 (form No. 26), included a direction to detain temporarily in a prison, the form No. 33 in the 1970 rules contains no such direction.   Where a juvenile is before the juvenile court under s. 31 of the Children and Young Persons Act, 1969, he may be detained in a remand centre if the court is not in a position to decide whether or not to order removal to Borstal, but not a prison.

Rules for the management of prisons and other institutions

47. Rules for the management of prisons, remand centres, detention centres and borstal institutions.—(1) The Secretary of State may make rules for the regulation and management of prisons, remand centres, detention centres and borstal institutions respectively, and for the classification, treatment, employment, discipline and control of persons required to be detained therein.

(2) Rules made under this section shall make provision for ensuring that a person who is charged with any offence under the rules shall be given a proper opportunity of presenting his case.

(3) Rules made under this section may provide for the training of particular classes of persons and their allocation for that purpose to any prison or other institution in which they may lawfully be detained.

(4) Rules made under this section shall provide for the special treatment of the following persons whilst required to be detained in a prison, that is to say—

    (a)–(c) [*Repealed by the Criminal Justice Act, 1967 s. 103 and Sched. VII, as to England and Wales.*]

    (d) any person detained in a prison, not being a person serving a sentence or a person imprisoned in default of payment of a sum adjudged to be paid by him on his conviction.

(5) Rules made under this section may provide for the temporary release of persons detained in a prison, borstal institution, or detention centre, not being persons committed in custody for trial before the Crown Court or committed to be sentenced or otherwise dealt with by the Crown Court or remanded in custody by any court.

NOTES

This section is printed as amended by the Criminal Justice Acts, 1961 and 1967 and the Courts Act, 1971.

Rules.—See the Prison Rules, 1964 (S.I. 1964 No. 388), the Borstal Rules, 1964 (S.I. 1964, No. 387), and the Detention Centre Rules, 1952, pp. 482 *et seq., post.*

Any statutory instrument containing rules under this Act shall be subject to annulment in pursuance of a resolution of either House of Parliament (Criminal Justice Act, 1967, s. 66 (4)).

*   *   *   *

49. Persons unlawfully at large.—(1) Any person who, having been sentenced to imprisonment or borstal training or ordered to be detained in a detention centre, or having been committed to a prison or remand centre, is unlawfully at large, may be arrested by a constable without warrant and taken to the place in which he is required in accordance with law to be detained.

(2) Where any person sentenced to imprisonment or borstal training, or ordered to be detained in a detention centre, is unlawfully at large at any time during the period for which he is liable to be detained in pursuance of the sentence or order, then, unless the Secretary of State otherwise directs, no account shall be taken, in calculating the period for which he is liable to be so detained, of any time during which he is absent from the prison, borstal institution, or detention centre, as the case may be:

Provided that—

    (a) this subsection shall not apply to any period during which any such person as aforesaid is detained in pursuance of the sentence or order or in pursuance of any other sentence of any court in the United Kingdom in a prison, borstal institution, or detention centre.

(b) this subsection shall not apply to a person who is unlawfully at large from a borstal institution by reason only that he has been recalled thereto under section forty-five of this Act;

(c) [*Repealed.*]

(3) The provisions of the last preceding subsection shall apply to a person who is detained in custody in default of payment of any sum of money as if he were sentenced to imprisonment.

(4) For the purposes of this section a person who, after being temporarily released in pursuance of rules made under subsection (5) of section forty-seven of this Act, is at large at any time during the period for which he is liable to be detained in pursuance of his sentence shall be deemed to be unlawfully at large if the period for which he was temporarily released has expired or if an order recalling him has been made by the Secretary of State in pursuance of the rules.

NOTES

This section is printed as amended by the Criminal Justice Acts, 1961 and 1967, the Prison Commissioners Dissolution Order, 1963 and the Children and Young Persons Act, 1969.

"Sentenced to imprisonment."—Any reference in this section to a person sentenced to imprisonment shall be construed as including a reference to any such person as is mentioned in s. 69 (1) of the Criminal Justice Act, 1967 (*ibid.*, p. 435, *post*).

Escape from care of a local authority.—See s. 32 of the Children and Young Persons Act, 1969.

Detained in pursuance of the sentence.—This part of the proviso to subsection (2) is intended, apparently, to cover the period between the arrest of the person unlawfully at large and his return in custody to the place from which he escaped.

Detention in default of payment.—Subsection (3) applies the provisions of sub-s. (2) to persons imprisoned not only in default of payment of fines but also for non-payment of civil debts, costs, and sums due under various orders made by justices.

CHILDREN AND YOUNG PERSONS (HARMFUL PUBLICATIONS) ACT, 1955

[3 & 4 Eliz. 2, c. 28]

ARRANGEMENT OF SECTIONS

An Act to prevent the dissemination of certain pictorial publications harmful to children and young persons.   [6th May, 1955.]

1. Works to which this Act applies.—This Act applies to any book, magazine or other like work which is of a kind likely to fall into the hands of children or young persons and consists wholly or mainly of stories told in pictures (with or without the addition of written matter), being stories portraying—

 (a) the commission of crimes; or
 (b) acts of violence or cruelty; or
 (c) incidents of a repulsive or horrible nature;

in such a way that the work as a whole would tend to corrupt a child or young person into whose hands it might fall.

2. Penalty for printing, publishing, selling, &c., works to which this Act applies.—(1) A person who prints, publishes, sells or lets on hire a work to which this Act applies, or has any such work in his possession for the purpose of selling it or letting it on hire, shall be guilty of an offence and liable, on summary conviction, to imprisonment for a term not exceeding four months or to a fine not exceeding one hundred pounds or to both:

Provided that, in any proceedings taken under this subsection against a person in respect of selling or letting on hire a work or of having it in his possession for the purpose of selling it or letting it on hire, it shall be a defence for him to prove that he had not examined the contents of the work and had no reasonable cause to suspect that it was one to which this Act applies.

(2) A prosecution for an offence under this section shall not, in England or Wales, be instituted except by, or with the consent of, the Attorney General.

NOTE

Summary conviction.—The defendant, if he appears personally, is entitled to claim to be tried by a jury (s. 25 of the Magistrates' Courts Act, 1952, p. 276, *ante*).

3. Power to search for, and dispose of, works to which this Act applies and articles for printing them.—(1) Where, upon an information being laid before a justice of the peace that a person has, or is suspected of having, committed an offence under the last foregoing section with respect to a work (hereafter in this subsection referred to as " the relevant work "), the justice issues a summons directed to that person requiring him to answer to the information or issues a warrant to arrest that person, that or any other justice, if satisfied by written information substantiated on oath that there is reasonable ground for suspecting that the said person has in his possession or under his control—

 (a) any copies of the relevant work or any other work to which this Act applies; or
 (b) any plate prepared for the purpose of printing copies of the relevant work or any other work to which this Act applies or any photographic film prepared for that purpose;

may grant a search warrant authorising any constable named therein to enter (if necessary by force) any premises specified in the warrant and any vehicle or stall used by the said person for the purposes of trade or business and to search the premises, vehicle or stall and seize any of the following things which the constable finds therein or thereon, that is to say:—

(i) any copies of the relevant work and any copies of any other work which the constable has reasonable cause to believe to be one to which this Act applies; and

(ii) any plate which the constable has reasonable cause to believe to have been prepared for the purpose of printing copies of any such work as is mentioned in paragraph (i) of this subsection and any photographic film which he has reasonable cause to believe to have been prepared for that purpose.

(2) The court by or before which a person is convicted of an offence under the last foregoing section with respect to a work may order any copies of that work and any plate prepared for the purpose of printing copies of that work or photographic film prepared for that purpose, being copies which have, or a plate or film which has, been found in his possession or under his control, to be forfeited:

Provided that an order made under this section by a magistrates' court or, on appeal from a magistrates' court, by a court of quarter sessions shall not take effect until the expiration of the ordinary time within which an appeal in the matter of the proceedings in which the order was made may be lodged (whether by giving notice of appeal or applying for a case to be stated for the opinion of the High Court) or, where such an appeal is duly lodged, until the appeal is finally decided or abandoned.

(3) In the application of this section to Scotland there shall be substituted in subsection (1) for the words from the beginning of the subsection to " any other justice " the words " Where proceedings have been instituted against a person in respect of an offence under the last foregoing section with respect to a work (hereafter in this subsection referred to as ' the relevant work '), the sheriff "; and for the proviso to subsection (2) there shall be substituted the following proviso:—

" Provided that an order made under this subsection shall not take effect until the expiration of the time within which an appeal under section sixty-two of the Summary Jurisdiction (Scotland) Act, 1954, may be taken in respect of the proceedings in which the order was made or, where such an appeal is taken, until the appeal is finally disposed of or abandoned ".

NOTES

" **Forfeited.**"—See s. 115 of the Magistrates' Courts Act, 1952; 21 Halsbury's Statutes, 3rd Edn., 282.

" **Time within which an appeal ... may be lodged.**"—See Crown Court Rules p. 654, *post*.

4. Prohibition of importation of works to which this Act applies and articles for printing them.—The importation of—

(a) any work to which this Act applies; and

(b) any plate prepared for the purpose of printing copies of any such work and any photographic film prepared for that purpose;

is hereby prohibited.

5. Short title, interpretation, extent, commencement and dura-tion.—(1) This Act may be cited as the Children and Young Persons (Harmful Publications) Act, 1955.

(2) In this Act the expressions " child " and " young person " have the meanings assigned to them respectively by section one hundred and seven of the Children and Young Persons Act, 1933, or, in Scotland, by section one hundred and ten of the Children and Young Persons (Scotland) Act, 1937, the expression " plate " (except where it occurs in the expres-sion " photographic plate ") includes block, mould, matrix and stencil and the expression " photographic film " includes photographic plate.

(3) No provision of this Act, other than the provisions of the last fore-going section, shall extend to Northern Ireland.

(4) This Act shall come into operation at the expiration of one month beginning with the date of its passing.

(5)

NOTES

Section 107 of the Children and Young Persons Act, 1933 is printed at p. 81, *ante*.

Sub-s. (4).—This Act was passed on 6th May, 1955.

Sub-s. (5).—The Act was continued in force till the end of December 1969 by the Expiring Laws Continuance Act, 1968, s. 76. By the Expiring Laws Act, 1969, s. 1 the whole Act becomes permanent and this subsection ceases to have effect.

SEXUAL OFFENCES ACT, 1956

[4 & 5 Eliz. 2, c. 69]

28. Causing or encouraging prostitution of, intercourse with, or indecent assault on, girl under sixteen.—(1) It is an offence for a person to cause or encourage the prostitution of, or the commission of unlawful sexual intercourse with, or of an indecent assault on, a girl under the age of sixteen for whom he is responsible.

(2) Where a girl has become a prostitute, or has had unlawful sexual intercourse, or has been indecently assaulted, a person shall be deemed for the purposes of this section to have caused or encouraged it, if he knowingly allowed her to consort with, or to enter or continue in the employment of, any prostitute or person of known immoral character.

(3) The persons who are to be treated for the purposes of this section as responsible for a girl are (subject to the next following subsection)—

    (a) any person who is her parent or legal guardian; and
    (b) any person who has actual possession or control of her, or to whose charge she has been committed by her parent or legal guardian or by a person having the custody of her; and
    (c) any other person who has the custody, charge or care of her.

(4) In the last foregoing subsection—

(a) " parent " does not include, in relation to any girl, a person deprived of the custody of her by order of a court of competent jurisdiction but (subject to that), in the case of a girl who has been adopted under the Adoption Act, 1950, or any Act thereby repealed, means her adopters and, in the case of a girl who is illegitimate (and has not been so adopted), means her mother and any person who has been adjudged to be her putative father;

(b) " legal guardian " means, in relation to any girl, any person who is for the time being her guardian, having been appointed according to law by deed or will or by order of a court of competent jurisdiction.

(5) If, on a charge of an offence against a girl under this section, the girl appears to the court to have been under the age of sixteen at the time of the offence charged, she shall be presumed for the purposes of this section to have been so, unless the contrary is proved.

NOTES

" **Cause or encourage.**"—In certain circumstances failure to prevent may come within these words (*R.* v. *Ralphs* (1913), 9 Cr. App. Rep. 86, C. C. A.); and see sub-s. (2).

A verdict of " negligence " under this section is a verdict of not guilty, as mere negligence is not an offence; there must be some actual " causing or encouraging " (*R.* v. *Chainey*, [1914] 1 K. B. 137; 78 J. P. 127).

" **Unlawful sexual intercourse.**"—In the case of *R.* v. *Chapman*, [1958] 3 All E. R. 143, C. C. A., it was held by the Court of Criminal Appeal, in dealing with an offence under s. 19 of this Act, that the word " unlawful " did not connote intercourse contrary to some positive enactment. The Court expressed the view that the word was not surplusage, but meant " illicit ", *i.e.* outside the bond of marriage.

Adoption Act, 1950.—See also the Adoption Act, 1958, pp. 1026 *et seq., post.*

Evidence.—Husband or wife of the accused may be called by the prosecution; see s. 39 of the Sexual Offences Act, 1956.

Procedure.—Prosecution must be by indictment.

" **Prostitution.**"—This means offering by a female, for reward, of her body commonly for purposes of lewdness, not necessarily for natural sexual connection; see *R.* v. *De Munck*, [1918] 1 K. B. 635; 82 J. P. 160.

43. Power to search for and remove woman detained for immoral purposes.—(1) Where it is made to appear by information on oath laid before a justice of the peace by a woman's parent, relative or guardian, or by any other person who in the opinion of the justice is acting in the woman's interests, that there is reasonable cause to suspect—

(a) that the woman is detained in any place within the justice's jurisdiction in order that she may have unlawful sexual intercourse with men or with a particular man; and

(b) that either she is so detained against her will, or she is under the age of sixteen or is a defective, or she is under the age of eighteen and is so detained against the will of her parent or guardian;

then the justice may issue a warrant authorising a named constable to search for her and to take her to and detain her in a place of safety until she can be brought before a justice of the peace.

(2) A justice before whom a woman is brought in pursuance of the foregoing subsection may cause her to be delivered up to her parent or guardian, or otherwise dealt with as circumstances may permit and require.

(3) A constable authorised by a warrant under this section to search for a woman may enter (if need be, by force) any premises specified in the warrant, and remove the woman from the premises.

(4) A constable executing a warrant issued under this section shall be accompanied by the person applying for the warrant, if that person so desires, unless the justice issuing it otherwise directs.

(5) In this section " guardian " means any person having the lawful care or charge of the woman.

(6) The powers conferred by this section shall be in addition to and not in derogation of those conferred by section forty of the Children and Young Persons Act, 1933.

NOTES

Unlawful sexual intercourse.—See note to s. 28, p. 397, *ante*.

" Woman."—This word includes " girl ", see s. 46, *ibid*.

Subsection (2).—In the case of a girl under the age of seventeen years proceedings might be taken under s. 1 of the Children and Young Persons Act, 1969, p. 130, *ante*.

INDECENCY WITH CHILDREN ACT, 1960

[8 & 9 Eliz. 2, c. 33]

An Act to make further provision for the punishment of indecent conduct towards young children, and to increase the maximum sentence of imprisonment under the Sexual Offences Act, 1956, for certain existing offences against young girls. [*2nd June,* 1960]

1. Indecent conduct towards young child.—(1) Any person who commits an act of gross indecency with or towards a child under the age of fourteen, or who incites a child under that age to such an act with him or another, shall be liable on conviction on indictment to imprisonment for a term not exceeding two years, or on summary conviction to imprisonment for a term not exceeding six months, to a fine not exceeding four hundred pounds, or to both.

(2) On a charge of an offence under this section, the wife or husband of the accused shall be competent to give evidence at every stage of the proceedings, whether for the defence or for the prosecution, and whether the accused is charged solely or jointly with any other person:

Provided that—

(a) the wife or husband shall not be compellable either to give evidence or, in giving evidence, to disclose any communication made to her or him during the marriage by the accused; and

(b) the failure of the wife or husband of the accused to give evidence shall not be made the subject of any comment by the prosecution.

This subsection shall not affect section one of the Criminal Evidence Act, 1898, or any case where the wife or husband of the accused may at common law be called as a witness without the consent of the accused.

(3) References in the Children and Young Persons Act, 1933, except in section fifteen (which relates to the competence as a witness of the wife or husband of the accused), to the offences mentioned in the First Schedule to that Act shall include offences under this section.

(4) Offences under this section shall be deemed to be offences against the person for the purpose of section three of the Visiting Forces Act, 1952 (which restricts the trial by United Kingdom courts of offenders connected with visiting forces).

NOTES

This section is printed as amended by the Criminal Justice Act, 1967, s. 92 and Sched. 11.

This section fills the gap in the law revealed by the decisions in *Fairclough* v. *Whipp*, [1951] 2 All E. R. 834; 35 Cr. App. Rep. 138; 115 J. P. 612; and *R.* v. *Burrows*, [1952] 1 All E. R. 58; 35 Cr. App. Rep. 180; 116 J. P. 47, where charges of indecent assault failed because there was only an invitation and no assault or hostile act resulting in indecent conduct.

" **Any person.**"—The offence may be committed by a man or a woman. Contrast s. 13 of the Sexual Offences Act, 1956.

" **Gross indecency.**"—There appears to be no decision on the meaning of this expression, but some effect must be given to the use of the word " gross." For an example of what the Court of Criminal Appeal considered to be gross indecency between a man and a boy, see *R.* v. *Burrows, supra.*

" **Incites.**"—The offence may be committed although the incitement has no effect: see *R.* v. *Gregory* (1867), L. R. 1 C. C. R. 77; 31 J. P. 453.

Procedure.—Section 18 of the Magistrates' Courts Act, 1952, p. 379, *ante*, applies. If it is proposed to proceed as for a summary offence the defendant, if present in person, has the right to claim trial by jury, in virtue of s. 25 of that Act. See p. 276, *ante*.

Evidence of child.—As to the exclusion of the public while a child gives evidence, see the Children and Young Persons Act, 1933, s. 37, p. 44, *ante*; as to restriction on newspaper publication, see s. 39, p. 46, *ante*. A child of tender years may, subject to the provisions of s. 38, p. 44, *ante*, give evidence not on oath.

Corroboration.—The unsworn evidence of a child must be corroborated in a material particular implicating the accused, see s. 38, p. 44, *ante*, and the unsworn evidence of other children is not sufficient corroboration; see *R.* v. *Manser* (1934), 25 Cr. App. Rep. 18; 78 Sol. Jo. 769. Although it is clear that on a charge of indecent assault on young children evidence of similar acts of indecency is admissible to enable the jury to decide whether visits of the children to the accused person were in pursuance of a guilty or an innocent association yet, where the evidence of indecency is tenuous to a degree and where, even if the conduct is held to be indecent, it is a different form of indecency, then the trial judge can only exercise his discretion by excluding that evidence, for its prejudicial effect would be overwhelming (*R.* v. *Doughty*, [1965] 1 All E. R. 560; 129 J. P. 172).

Consent of Director of Public Prosecutions.—In the case of *R.* v. *Assistant Recorder of Kingston-upon-Hull, Ex parte Morgan*, [1969] 2 Q. B. 58; [1969] 1 All E. R. 416; 133 J. P. 165, it was held that as the alleged offence was incitement and there was no reference to the word "incites" in s. 8 of the Sexual Offences Act, 1967 (c. 60) the consent of the Director of Public Prosecution was not necessary to institute the proceedings.

2. Length of imprisonment for certain offences against young girls.—(1) The maximum term of imprisonment to which a person is liable under the Sexual Offences Act, 1956, if convicted on indictment of an attempt to have unlawful sexual intercourse with a girl under the age of thirteen, or of an indecent assault on a girl who is stated in the indictment and proved to have been at the time under that age,—

(a) in the case of such an attempt, shall be seven years; and
(b) in the case of an indecent assault, shall be five years.

(2) In the case of a person convicted of attempted incest with a girl who is stated in the indictment and proved to have been at the time under the age of thirteen the foregoing subsection shall apply as it applies in the case of a person convicted of an attempt to have unlawful sexual intercourse with a girl under that age.

(3) Accordingly in the Second Schedule to that Act, for the words " two years " in the third column in items 2 (b), 14 (b) and 17 (i), there shall be substituted—

(a) in item (2) (b) the words " seven years ";
(b) in item 14 (b) the words " if with a girl under thirteen who is stated to have been so in the indictment, seven years; otherwise two years ";
(c) in item 17 (i) the words " if on a girl under thirteen who is stated to have been so in the indictment, five years; otherwise two years ".

(4) This section shall not apply to offences committed on or before the date this Act is passed.

NOTE
Date of Act.—The Act was passed on June 2, 1960.

3. Short title, extent and commencement.—(1) This Act may be cited as the Indecency with Children Act, 1960.

(2) This Act shall not extend to Scotland or Northern Ireland.

(3) This Act shall come into force at the expiration of one month beginning with the date it is passed.

NOTE
The Act was passed on June 2, 1960.

CRIMINAL JUSTICE ACT, 1961

[9 & 10 Eliz. 2, c. 39]

3. Elimination of intermediate and short prison sentences.— (1) Without prejudice to any other enactment prohibiting or restricting the imposition of imprisonment on persons of any age, a sentence of imprisonment shall not be passed by any court on a person within the limits of age which qualify for a sentence of borstal training except—

(a) for a term not exceeding six months ; or

(b) (where the court has power to pass such a sentence) for a term of not less than three years.

(2) Subsection (1) of this section shall not apply in the case of a person who is serving a sentence of imprisonment at the time when the court passes sentence ; and for the purpose of this subsection a person sentenced to imprisonment who has been recalled or returned to prison after being released subject to supervision or on licence, and has not been released again or discharged, shall be treated as serving the sentence.

(3) In relation to a person who has served a previous sentence of imprisonment for a term of not less than six months, or a previous sentence of borstal training, subsection (1) of this section shall have effect as if for the reference to three years there were substituted a reference to eighteen months ; and for the purpose of this subsection a person sentenced to borstal training shall be treated as having served the sentence if he has been released subject to supervision, whether or not he has subsequently been recalled or returned to a borstal institution.

(4) The foregoing provisions of this section, so far as they affect the passing of consecutive sentences by magistrates' courts, shall have effect notwithstanding anything in section one hundred and eight of the Magistrates' Courts Act, 1952 (which authorises such courts in specified circumstances to impose consecutive sentences of imprisonment totalling more than six months).

(5) Her Majesty may by Order in Council direct that paragraph (a) of subsection (1) of this section shall be repealed, either generally or so far as it relates to persons, or male or female persons, of any age described in the Order :

Provided that—

(a) an Order in Council shall not be made under this subsection unless the Secretary of State is satisfied that sufficient accommodation is available in detention centres for the numbers of offenders for whom such accommodation is likely to be required in consequence of the Order ;

(b) no recommendation shall be made to Her Majesty in Council to make an Order under this subsection unless a draft of the Order has been laid before Parliament and has been approved by resolution of each House of Parliament.

NOTES

" **Impose imprisonment.**"—For definition, see note to s. 17, p. 372, *ante*.

It is submitted that the phrase " where the court has power to impose imprisonment " must relate to that stage of the proceedings which the court has then reached.
If an offence is punishable by fine and not imprisonment without the option of a
fine the court cannot, without imposing any fine, order detention as a punishment.

**Consecutive sentences of a year or less in the aggregate exceeding three
years.**—The court can look to s. 38 (4) and in the light of that subsection the court
can impose a sentence which is one of less than six months or one of three years or
more, provided that such a sentence can be properly passed in respect of the offences
the court is dealing with.

In *R. v. Scully*, [1966] 2 All E. R. 953 (C.C.A.) it was argued that the provisions
of s. 38 (4) do not enable a court to pass aggregate sentences so as to bring them
up above the period of three years.

"**Limit of age.**"—See Criminal Justice Act, 1948, s. 20, p. 305, *ante*, and Magistrates' Courts Act, 1952, s. 28, p. 307, *ante*, in each case as amended and ultimately
substituted by this Act, s. 41, and Scheds. IV and VI, *post*.

Subsection (1).—As to removals from prison, see s. 34, p. 416, *post*.

" **Court** "; " **sentence.**"—For definitions see s. 38 (1), p. 418, *post*.

" **Term.**"—See s. 38 (4), p. 419, *post*.

Borstal training.—In *R. v. Lowe*, [1964] 2 All E. R. 116; 128 J. P. 336 on an
appeal to the Court of Criminal Appeal against a sentence of three years imprisonment
for assault occasioning actual bodily harm it was held that " the trial judge having
decided initially that the appropriate sentence would be one of imprisonment and
that the appropriate term would be two years, and being able by this section to pass
sentence on the appellant only for a term not exceeding six months or of three years
or more, should have passed the indeterminate sentence of borstal training.

Detention Centre and Remand Home

4. Detention of offenders aged 14 to 20.—(1) In any case where a
court has power, or would have power but for the statutory restrictions
upon the imprisonment of young offenders, to pass sentence of imprisonment of an offender under twenty-one *but not less than fourteen* years of
age, the court may, subject to the provisions of this section order him to
be detained in a detention centre.

(2) An order for the detention of an offender under this section may be
made for the following term, that is to say—

    (a) where *the offender has attained the age of seventeen or is convicted
    before the Crown Court and* the maximum term of imprisonment
    for which the court could (or could but for any such restriction)
    pass sentence in his case exceeds three months, any term of not
    less than three nor more than six months;

    (b) in any other case, a term of three months.

(3) An order under this section shall not be made in respect of any
person unless the court has been notified by the Secretary of State that
a detention centre is available for the reception from that court of persons
of his class or description, or an Order in Council under subsection (5) of
section three of this Act is in force in respect of persons of his age and sex.

(4) An order under this section shall not be made in respect of a person
who is serving or has served a sentence of imprisonment for a term of not
less than six months or a sentence of borstal training unless it appears to
the court that there are special circumstances (whether relating to the

offence or to the offender) which warrant the making of such an order in his case ; and before making such an order in respect of such an offender the court shall—

(a) in any case, consider any report made in respect of him by or on behalf of the Secretary of State.

(b) if the court is a magistrates' court and has not received any such report, adjourn the hearing under subsection (3) of section fourteen of the Magistrates' Courts Act, 1952, and remand the offender in custody to enable such a report to be made ;

and section thirty-seven of this Act shall apply accordingly.

NOTES

From a date to be appointed the words in italics are repealed by the Children and Young Persons Act, 1969, s. 72 (4) and Sched. VI. See s. 7 (3), *ibid*.

This section is printed as amended by the Prison Commissioners Dissolution Order 1963 (S.I. 1963 No. 597) para. 3 (2) and Sched. 2, and the Courts Act, 1971. By s. 56 and Sched. VIII, *ibid*., the reference to the Crown Court shall cease to have effect when the repeal of the italicised words is brought into force.

" **Age.**"—See note to s. 1, p. 311, *ante*.

" **Detention centre.**"—For meaning, see Prison Act, 1952, s. 43, p. 390, *ante*, as amended by this Act.

When an Order in Council has been made under s. 3 (5), p. 401, *ante*, courts will have power to make detention centre orders in respect of offenders of the age and sex described in the Order without having been notified by the Secretary of State of the availability of a detention centre.

Social inquiry report.—A committal to a detention centre is a sentence to which s. 57 of the Criminal Justice Act, 1967, p. 303, *ante*, applies, and the Secretary of State may by rules provide that before passing such a sentence a court must consider a social inquiry report (s. 57 was not in force at the time of going to press).

See also Home Office Circular No. 226/67.H.2 dated May 7, 1968, which applies the arrangements set out in Home Office Circular No. 226/1967, dated November 30, 1967, to relatives visiting detention centre inmates. Any expenditure incurred by the probation and after-care service in helping parents or close relatives of detention centre inmates to visit them once in a three months' sentence or twice in a six months' sentence where the Ministry of Social Security is unable to help and the expense of a visit would cause financial hardship may be reclaimed.

Assisted visits to prisoners.—The Ministry of Social Security (Supplementary Benefits) Commission may make grants to enable a prisoner's wife (or a close relative) to visit him. See Prison Department Circular Instruction No. 103/67. Para. 7 of that instruction states that it applies to persons serving sentences of detention as to prisoners, and that travelling expenses of parents or close relatives of detention centre inmates will continue to be met once during a three months' sentence and twice during a six months' sentence subject to para. 2 of the Circular.

Availability of detention centres for boys aged 14 and under 17.—See Home Office Circular No. 90/1970 p. 846, *post*.

Notification that detention centre is not available.—See the Children and Young Persons Act, 1969, s. 7 (3), p. 145, *post*.

Girls.—There is now no provision for the detention of girls in detention centres. On the recommendation of the Advisory Council on the penal system, the Home Office have decided not to replace the existing detention centre which closed on January 31, 1969 (see Home Office Circular No. 277/1968).

Physical condition.—In the case of *R. v. Jobes*, [1962] Crim. L. R. 714, the Court of Criminal Appeal ordered the immediate release of the appellant, and felt that because of his physical condition he should never have been sent to a detention centre.

Consecutive terms of detention.—See s. 7, p. 405, *post*.

Supervision after release.—See s. 13 and Sched. 1, pp. 406, 421, *post*.

Determination of age.—See note to s. 17 of the Criminal Justice Act, 1948, p. 373, *ante.*

Commitment.—For form of commitment see form 32 of the Magistrates' Courts (Children and Young Persons) Rules, 1970, p. 598, *post.*

Rules.—See the Detention Centre Rules, 1952, p. 482, *post.*

Unlawfully at large.—Any person sentenced to borstal training or ordered to be detained in a detention centre who is unlawfully at large, may be arrested by a constable without warrant and taken back, and in calculating the period for which he is liable to be detained no account shall be taken of the time he is absent, unless the Secretary of State directs otherwise (Prison Act, 1952, s. 49, p. 392, *ante*).

Young person guilty of indictable offence.—The period of detention in the case of a young person tried summarily for an indictable offence must not exceed 3 months. See s. 4 (2) (b), p. 402, *ante.*

Probation order.—In the case of *R.* v. *Evans,* [1958] 3 All E. R. 673; 123 J. P. 128, the Court of Criminal Appeal held that the making of a probation order for one offence at the same time as the making of a detention centre order for another offence was contrary to the spirit and intention of the Act, and quashed the probation order.

" Court "; " statutory restrictions upon the imprisonment of young offenders "; " term."—For definitions, see s. 39, p. 419, *post.*
By s. 38 (1), p. 418, *post* " sentence " does not include committal for default etc.   The disposal of defaulters is dealt with in ss. 5 and 6, *infra.*

Sentence.—See s. 38, p. 418, *post.*   It does not include committal for default. The disposal of defaulters is dealt with in ss. 5 and 6, *post.*

Magistrates' Courts Act, 1952, s. 14.—See p. 378, *ante.*

Subsection (4)—Reports.—In Home Office circular 138/63/c4 dated June 24, 1963 it is stated that magistrates' courts are being advised that the arrangements set out in paras. 21–24 of that circular should apply in cases under sub-s. (4) and that if they remand an offender after conviction for a prison governor's report they should also call for a social enquiry report, if one is not already available.   The circular further states that they are also being advised that a remand for at least two weeks is desirable, so that the prison governor can receive the social enquiry report a week before his report is required.

Report of the Advisory Council on the Penal System.—See Home Office Circular No. 159/1971, p. 840, *post.*

5. Defaulters already detained in detention centre.—(1) Where a court has power to commit a person to prison for any term for a default, and that person has attained the age of seventeen and is detained in a detention centre under a previous sentence or warrant, the court may, subject to the provisions of this section, commit him to a detention centre for a term not exceeding the term aforesaid or six months, whichever is the shorter.

(2) Except as provided by the following provisions of this Part of this Act, a person shall not be committed under this section to a detention centre—

(a) [*Repealed by the Children and Young Persons Act,* 1969, s. 72 (4) *and Sched. VI.*]
(b) for any term exceeding six months,

(3) [*Repealed by the Children and Young Persons Act*, 1969, *s.* 72 (4) *and Sched. VI.*]

(4) This section applies in relation to the fixing of a term of imprisonment to be served in the event of default of payment of a fine or other sum of money as it applies in relation to committal to prison in default of such payment; and in any such case subsection (2) of this section shall apply in relation to the term fixed by the court, and not to that term as reduced by virtue of any subsequent payment.

(5) Subject to the foregoing provisions of this section Part III of the Magistrates' Courts Act, 1952, and sections fourteen and fifteen of the Criminal Justice Act, 1948, shall have effect as if references to imprisonment included references to detention under this section; and references in those enactments, or in any other enactment relating to the satisfaction and enforcement of fines, recognizances and orders, to a prison or to the governor of a prison shall be construed accordingly.

(6) Where, after a warrant or order has been issued or made by a magistrates' court—

(a) committing a person to prison, for any default; or
(b) fixing a term of imprisonment, to be served by him in the event of any default,

it is made to appear to a justice of the peace that that person is for the time being detained in a detention centre, the justice may amend the warrant or order by substituting that centre for the prison named therein and, where the term of imprisonment specified in the warrant or order exceeds six months, by reducing that term to six months.

NOTES

This section is printed as amended by the Children and Young Persons Act, 1969, s. 72 (3) and (4) and Scheds. V and VI. There is no longer power to commit a young person in default. See s. 7 (4), *ibid.*

Social inquiry report.—See note to s. 4, *supra.*

Assisted visits to prisoners.—See note to s. 4, *supra.*

See notes to s. 4, p. 403, *ante.*

Default.—For definition, see s. 39, p. 419, *post.*

Period of detention.—When the imprisonment is in default of payment of a fine or other sum of money the special limitations governing such committals must be observed. In courts of summary jurisdiction, committals for doing or failing to do an act are dealt with in s. 54 of the Magistrates' Courts Act, 1952, which provides a maximum period of two months' imprisonment. In cases to which s. 91 of that Act applies the period of imprisonment might be as much as six months.

7. Consecutive terms and aggregate periods of detention.—(1) Subject to the provisions of this section, any court which makes an order or issues a warrant for the detention of any person in a detention centre may direct that the term of detention under the order or warrant shall commence on the expiration of any other term for which that person is liable to be detained in a detention centre by virtue of an order or warrant made or issued by that or any other court.

(2) *A direction shall not be given under subsection* (1) *of this section in connection with the making of an order under section four of this Act where the offender is under seventeen years of age.*

(3) Where a direction under subsection (1) of this section is given in connection with the making of an order under section four of this Act, the term of detention specified in that order may, if the court thinks fit, be a term of less than three months.

(4) The aggregate of the terms for which a person may be ordered to be detained in a detention centre by virtue of any two or more orders made by the same court on the same occasion shall not in any case exceed six months.

(5) Without prejudice to subsection (4) of this section, the total term for which a person may be detained in a detention centre shall not exceed nine months at a time ; and accordingly so much of any term for which a person is ordered to be so detained as, together with any other term on which it is wholly or partly consecutive, exceeds nine months shall be treated as remitted.

NOTES

This section is printed as amended by the Children and Young Persons Act, 1969, s. 72 (4) and Sched. VI. From a date to be appointed the words in italics are repealed, s. 72 (4) (*ibid.*). When a notification under s. 7 (3), *ibid.*, is received by a court there will no longer be power to commit to "detention centre". Presumably the repeal of sub-s. (2) will become operative when the notification is to courts generally, and that in turn presupposes that schemes for intermediate treatment provide suitable alternatives.

See notes to s. 4, p. 403, *ante*.

10. Attendance at attendance centres.—(1) [*Repealed.*]

(2) The aggregate number of hours for which a person may be required to attend at an attendance centre by virtue of an order under the said section nineteen—

    (a) shall not be less than twelve *except where he is under fourteen years of age and the court is of opinion, having regard to his age or any other circumstances, that twelve hours would be excessive;* and

    (b) shall not exceed twelve except where the court is of opinion, having regard to all the circumstances, that twelve hours would be inadequate, and in that case shall not exceed twenty-four hours.

(3) An order shall not be made under the said section nineteen unless the court is satisfied that the attendance centre to be specified in the order is reasonably accessible to the person concerned, having regard to his age, the means of access available to him and any other circumstances.

NOTES

From a date to be appointed the words in italics are repealed by the Children and Young Persons Act, 1969, s. 72 (4) and Sched. VI. See notes to s. 7, *ante*.

" Age."—See note to s. 1, p. 311, *ante*.

" Attendance centre."—For definition see s. 48 of the Criminal Justice Act, 1948, p. 376, *ante*, as amended by this Act.

Criminal Justice Act, 1948, s. 19.—See p. 373, *ante*, as amended by this Act.

13. Supervision after release from detention centre.—Every
person who is detained in a detention centre in pursuance of an order

made under section four of this Act, being an order made after the commencement of this section, shall, after his release from the detention centre, be subject to supervision under the First Schedule to this Act.

18. Directions as to management of approved schools.—(1) *If it appears to the Secretary of State that the provision made in any approved school with regard to any matter relating to—*

    (a) *the premises or equipment of the school,*
    (b) *the number or grades of the staff employed in the school, or*
    (c) *the education, training or welfare of persons under the care of the managers,*

is inadequate or unsuitable, he may give to the managers such directions as he thinks necessary for securing that proper provision is made with respect thereto.

(2) *Where it appears to the Secretary of State that the managers of an approved school have failed to give effect to any directions under this section, subsection (2) of section seventy-nine of the Children and Young Persons Act, 1933 (which empowers the Secretary of State in certain circumstances to withdraw his certificate of approval) shall apply as it applies where he is dissatisfied as mentioned in that section.*

NOTE

From a date to be appointed the whole of this section is repealed by the Children and Young Persons Act, 1969, s. 72 (4) and Sched. VI.

Children and Young Persons Act, 1933, s. 79.—See p. 65, *ante*.

"**Under the care of managers.**"—A reference to "the children in the care of local authorities who are accommodated and maintained in those premises" is substituted by para. 3 (2) (b) of Sched. III of the Children and Young Persons Act, 1969.

19. Constitution of managers.—(1) *The Secretary of State may by order make provision for regulating the constitution and proceedings of the managers of any approved school other than a school provided by a local authority or by a joint committee representing two or more local authorities; and any such order shall have effect notwithstanding anything in any trust deed relating to the school.*

(2) *Before making an order under the foregoing subsection in respect of any school, the Secretary of State shall afford to the managers of the school an opportunity for making representations with respect to the proposed order; and in making any such order the Secretary of State shall have regard to all the circumstances of the school, and to the manner in which it has been managed theretofore.*

(3) *If in the case of an approved school, other than a school provided by a local authority or by a joint committee representing two or more local authorities, the Secretary of State is satisfied that by reason of special circumstances it is necessary to do so in the interests of the efficient management of the school, he may appoint one or more persons as additional members of the body constituting the managers of the school; and any person so appointed shall, notwithstanding anything in any trust deed relating to the school or in*

any order made in respect of the school under subsection (1) of this section, be one of the managers of the school until such time as his appointment is terminated by the Secretary of State or under subsection (4) of this section.

(4) Any order or appointment made under this section in respect of an approved school shall cease to have effect if that school ceases to be an approved school; but nothing in this subsection shall effect the validity of anything done while the order or appointment was in force.

(5) In this section "trust deed", in relation to any school, includes any instrument (not being an order under this section) regulating the constitution of the school, or its maintenance, management or conduct, or the constitution or proceedings of its managers.

NOTES

From a date to be appointed the whole of this section is repealed by the Children and Young Persons Act, 1969, s. 72 (4) and Sched. VI.

" **Order.**"—An order may be varied or revoked by a subsequent order. See s. 36 (2), p. 418, *post.*

Miscellaneous

20. Supervision of certain prisoners after release.—[*Repealed by the Criminal Justice Act, 1967 s. 103 and Sched. VII.*]

21. Repeal of provisions for notifying address.—Section twenty-two of the Criminal Justice Act, 1948, section twenty-nine of the Prison Act, 1952, and the First Schedule to the last mentioned Act (which contain provisions requiring certain discharged prisoners to notify their addresses) shall cease to have effect.

22. Penalties for assisting escape from prison, etc.—(1) The maximum term of imprisonment which may be imposed for an offence under section thirty-nine of the Prison Act, 1952 (which relates to assisting prisoners to escape) shall be five years instead of two years.

(2) If any person knowingly harbours a person who has escaped from a prison or other institution to which the said section thirty-nine applies, or who, having been sentenced in any part of the United Kingdom or in any of the Channel Islands or the Isle of Man to imprisonment or detention, is otherwise unlawfully at large, or gives to any such person any assistance with intent to prevent, hinder or interfere with his being taken into custody, he shall be liable—

    (a) on summary conviction, to imprisonment for a term not exceeding six months or to a fine not exceeding one hundred pounds, or to both ;

    (b) on conviction on indictment, to imprisonment for a term not exceeding two years, or to a fine, or to both.

(3) In the following enactments (which make provision for the application of sections thirty-nine to forty-two of the Prison Act, 1952) that is to say, subsection (3) of section one hundred and twenty-two of the Army Act, 1955, subsection (3) of section one hundred and twenty-two of the Air Force Act, 1955, and subsection (3) of section eighty-two of the Naval

Discipline Act, 1957, references to the said section thirty-nine shall be construed as including references to subsection (2) of this section.

(4) [*Repealed by the Children and Young Persons Act, 1969, s. 72 (4) and Sched. VI.*]

NOTES

" **Knowingly.**"—See note to Adoption Act, 1958, s. 44, p. 1074, *post.*

" **Six months.**"—See note to s. 1 of the Children and Young Persons Act, 1933, p. 18, *ante.*

23. Prison Rules.—(1) For the purposes of rules under section forty-seven of the Prison Act, 1952 (which authorises the making of rules for the regulation and management of prisons and the discipline and control of persons required to be detained therein) any offence against the rules committed by a prisoner may be treated as committed in the prison in which he is for the time being confined.

(2) Without prejudice to any power to make provision by rules under the said section forty-seven for the confiscation of money or articles conveyed or deposited in contravention of the said Act or of the rules, provision may be made by such rules for the withholding from prisoners (subject to such exceptions as may be prescribed by the rules) of any money or other article sent to them through the post office, and for the disposal of any such money or article either by returning it to the sender (where the sender's name and address are known) or in such other manner as may be prescribed by or determined under the rules :

Provided that in relation to a prisoner committed to prison in default of payment of any sum of money, the rules shall provide for the application of any money withheld as aforesaid in or towards the satisfaction of the amount due from him unless, upon being informed of the receipt of the money, he objects to its being so applied.

(3) A prisoner who would, apart from this subsection, be discharged on any of the days to which this subsection applies in his case shall be discharged on the next preceding day which is not one of those days.

The days to which this subsection applies are Sunday, Christmas Day, Good Friday and any day which under the Bank Holidays Act, 1871, is a bank holiday in England and Wales and, in the case of a person who is serving a term or more than one month, any Saturday.

(4) In this section the references to prisons and prisoners include references respectively to borstal institutions, detention centres and remand centres and to persons detained therein.

NOTES

" **Detention centre.**"—See note to s. 4, p. 402, *ante.*

" **Remand centre.**"—See ss. 43 and 48 Prison Act, 1952, p. 390 *ante.*

Prison Act, 1952, s. 47.—See p. 391, *ante.*

" **Rules.**"—See the Prison Rules 1964, S.I. 1964 No. 388.

24. Management of prisons, etc.—(1) Subject to the provisions of this section, Her Majesty may by Order in Council make provision for transferring to the Secretary of State any or all of the functions of the Prison Commissioners (in this section referred to as " the Commissioners ").

(2) An Order in Council under this section may contain such incidental, consequential and supplemental provisions as may be necessary or expedient in connection with the transfer effected by that or any previous Order thereunder, including provisions—

(a) for the transfer of any property, rights or liabilities to which the Commissioners are entitled or subject, and for the vesting in the person from time to time holding office as Secretary of State of land or other property transferred by any such Order, or acquired under powers so transferred;

(b) for the carrying on and completion by or under the authority of the Secretary of State of anything begun by or under the authority of the Commissioners before the date of transfer;

(c) for the substitution of the Secretary of State for the Commissioners in any instrument, contract or legal proceedings made or begun before that date;

(d) for the transfer to the Home Department of Commissioners and inspectors, officers or servants of the Commissioners and (in the case of the transfer of the powers and jurisdiction of the Commissioners in respect of all institutions within their superintendence) for the dissolution of the Commissioners.

(3) An Order in Council under this section may make such adaptations or repeals in the enactments relating to the Commissioners, or to institutions within their superintendence, as may be necessary or expedient in consequence of the Order or any previous Order thereunder, and shall in particular make provision for securing that any report which, apart from any such Order, would be required by subsection (1) of section five of the Prison Act, 1952, to be made to the Secretary of State by the commissioners shall be issued by the Secretary of State and laid before Parliament under that section accordingly.

(4) A certificate of the Secretary of State that any property vested in the Commissioners has been transferred to the Secretary of State by virtue of an Order in Council under this section shall be conclusive evidence of the transfer.

(5) No recommendation shall be made to Her Majesty in Council to make an Order under this section unless a draft of the Order has been laid before Parliament and has been approved by resolution of each House of Parliament.

(6) In this section " functions " includes powers and duties, and " the date of transfer " means the date on which an Order in Council under this section transferring functions of the Commissioners comes into force.

NOTE

" **Order in Council.**"—See the Prison Commissioners Dissolution Order 1963, S.I. 1963 No. 597.

25. Reports to Parliament on approved schools, remand homes and attendance centres.—[*Repealed by the Children and Young Persons Act*, 1969, *s.* 72 (4) *and Sched. VI.*]

PART III

TRANSFER, SUPERVISION AND RECALL OF PRISONERS WITHIN THE BRITISH ISLANDS

26. Transfer to serve sentence.—(1) The responsible Minister may, on the application of a person serving a sentence of imprisonment or detention in any part of the United Kingdom, make an order for his transfer to another part of the United Kingdom, there to serve the remainder of his sentence, and for his removal to an appropriate institution in that part of the United Kingdom.

(2) Where a person has been sentenced to imprisonment or detention in any of the Channel Islands or the Isle of Man, the Secretary of State may, without application in that behalf, make an order for his transfer to any part of the United Kingdom, there to serve his sentence or the remainder of his sentence, as the case may be, and for his removal to an appropriate institution in that part of the United Kingdom.

(3) Where a girl or woman has been sentenced to borstal training in Northern Ireland, the Minister of Home Affairs for Northern Ireland may, without application in that behalf, make an order for her transfer to another part of the United Kingdom, there to serve her sentence or the remainder of her sentence, as the case may be, and for her removal to a borstal institution in that part of the United Kingdom.

(4) Subject to the following provisions of this section, a person transferred under this section to any part of the United Kingdom there to serve his sentence or the remainder of his sentence shall be treated for purposes of detention, release, recall and otherwise as if that sentence (and any other sentence to which he may be subject) had been passed by a court in that part of the United Kingdom and, where it is not a sentence which could be so passed, as if it could be so passed.

(5) Where a person sentenced to borstal training is transferred under this section to any part of the United Kingdom, the provisions applicable to him shall be those applicable to a person sentenced to borstal training by a court in that part of the United Kingdom :

Provided that—

(a) where a person so sentenced after the commencement of section eleven of this Act is transferred from England and Wales, the maximum and minimum periods for which he may be detained in a borstal institution shall be those prescribed by subsection (2) of section forty-five of the Prison Act, 1952, as amended by the said section eleven, and not those applicable to the corresponding sentence in Scotland or Northern Ireland ;

(b) where a person so sentenced at any time in Scotland or Northern Ireland is transferred to England and Wales, the period after his release during which, under subsections (3) and (4) of the said section forty-five, he remains under supervision and is liable to be recalled shall end not later than the date on which he would have ceased to be under supervision under the law of the place where he was sentenced if he had been released there.

(6) Where a person sentenced to imprisonment or detention, not being a person sentenced to borstal training, is released and, by reason of his having been transferred under this section, his release occurs otherwise than in his place of sentence (that is to say, the part of the United Kingdom or island in which his sentence was passed)—

> (a) he shall not on his release be subject to supervision under the law of the part of the United Kingdom in which he is at the time of his release unless he would have been subject to supervision if he had been released at that time in his place of sentence without having been transferred from that place ; and

> (b) if in accordance with the foregoing provisions of this section he is on his release subject to supervision under the law of the part of the United Kingdom in which he is at the time of his release, the period after his release for which he is so subject shall not extend beyond the expiration of the maximum period after his release for which he could have continued to be subject to supervision under the law of his place of sentence if he had been released in that place at the said time :

Provided that this subsection shall not apply in the case of a person sentenced in any of the Channel Islands or the Isle of Man to corrective training or preventive detention.

(7) In subsection (6) of this section references to supervision include references to any obligation to comply with requirements or conditions imposed by a licence or otherwise imposed by law on or in connection with release from a prison or other institution, and any liability to be recalled or returned thereto ; and for the purposes of that subsection it shall be assumed that a person who, if released in his place of sentence, could have been placed under supervision, would have been so placed.

NOTES

Definitions.—For " appropriate institution ", " responsible Minister ", " court ". see s. 39 (1), p. 419, *post*; for " imprisonment or detention " and " sentence ", see s. 38, p. 418 *post*.

Prison Act, 1952, s. 45.—See p. 309, *ante*.

27. Temporary transfer.—(1) The responsible Minister may, on the application of a person serving a sentence of imprisonment or detention in any part of the United Kingdom, make an order for his temporary transfer to another part of the United Kingdom or to any of the Channel Islands or the Isle of Man and for his removal to an appropriate institution there.

(2) The Secretary of State may, on the application of a person serving a sentence of imprisonment or detention in any of the Channel Islands or the Isle of Man, make an order for his temporary transfer to any part of the United Kingdom or another of those islands and for his removal to an appropriate institution there.

(3) A person removed in pursuance of any such order from one country or island to another shall while in the country or island to which he is so

removed be kept in custody except so far as the Minister by whom the order was made may in any particular case or class of case otherwise direct.

(4) A person removed in pursuance of any such order from one country or island to another may without further order be returned to the country or island from which he was removed.

NOTE

Definitions.—See note to s. 26, p. 412, *ante*.

28. Transfer for trial.—(1) If it appears to the responsible Minister that a person serving a sentence of imprisonment or detention in any part of the United Kingdom should be transferred to another part of the United Kingdom for the purpose of attending criminal proceedings against him there, that Minister may make an order for his transfer to that other part, and for his removal to a prison or other institution there.

(2) During the period for which a person transferred under subsection (1) of this section remains in the part of the United Kingdom to which he is transferred, the provisions of section twenty-six of this Act relating to the treatment of persons transferred under that section shall apply to him as if he had been transferred to that part under that section.

(3) Where a person has been transferred under subsection (1) of this section for the purpose of any proceedings, the responsible Minister may,—

(a) if that person is sentenced to imprisonment or detention in those proceedings, make an order under section twenty-six of this Act (but without application in that behalf) transferring him back to the country from which he was transferred under subsection (1) of this section ;

(b) if he is not so sentenced, make an order for his return to the said country, and for his removal to an appropriate institution in that country, there to serve the remainder of the sentence referred to in subsection (1) of this section.

NOTE

Definitions.—See note to s. 26, p. 412, *ante*.

29. Removal for other judicial purposes.—(1) If the responsible Minister is satisfied, in the case of a person detained in any part of the United Kingdom in a prison, borstal institution, remand centre, detention centre or place of safety, that the attendance of that person at any place in that or any other part of the United Kingdom is desirable in the interests of justice or for the purposes of any public inquiry, the responsible Minister may direct that person to be taken to that place.

(2) Where any person is directed under this section to be taken to any place he shall, unless the responsible Minister otherwise directs, be kept in custody while being so taken, while at that place, and while being taken back to the prison or other institution or place in which he is required in accordance with law to be detained.

(3) In this section "place of safety" has—

(a) in relation to England and Wales, the same meaning as in the Children and Young Persons Act, 1933; and
(b) in relation to Scotland, the same meaning as in the Children and Young Persons (Scotland) Act, 1937; and
(c) in relation to Northern Ireland, the same meaning as in the Children and Young Persons Act (Northern Ireland) 1950.

NOTES

This section is printed as amended by the Children and Young Persons Acts, 1963 and 1969.

Definitions.—For " prison " and " responsible Minister ", see s. 39 (1), p. 419, *post.*

30. Prisoners unlawfully at large.—(1) The following enactments (relating to the arrest and return of prisoners and other persons unlawfully at large) that is to say—

(a) subsection (1) of section forty-nine of the Prison Act, 1952 ;
(b) subsection (1) of section thirty-seven of the Prisons (Scotland) Act, 1952 ; and
(c) subsection (1) of section thirty-eight of the Prison Act (Northern Ireland) 1953,

shall extend throughout the United Kingdom, the Channel Islands and the Isle of Man ; and any reference in those enactments to a constable shall include a reference to a person being a constable under the law of any part of the United Kingdom or of the Isle of Man, to a member of the police in Jersey, and to an officer of police within the meaning of section forty-three of the Larceny (Guernsey) Law, 1958, or any corresponding law for the time being in force.

(2) The enactments mentioned in subsection (1) of this section shall also apply to persons who, being unlawfully at large under any law of the Channel Islands or of the Isle of Man, are for the time being within the United Kingdom as they apply respectively to persons unlawfully at large under the law of England, Scotland and Northern Ireland ; and any person arrested in the United Kingdom under the said enactments as applied by this subsection may be taken to the place in the Channel Islands or the Isle of Man in which he is required in accordance with the law in force therein to be detained.

(3) Where a person who, having been sentenced to imprisonment or detention, is unlawfully at large during any period during which he is liable to be detained in a prison, borstal institution or detention centre in any part of the United Kingdom is sentenced to imprisonment or detention by a court in another part of the United Kingdom, the provisions of section twenty-six of this Act relating to the treatment of persons transferred under that section shall apply to him, while he remains in that other part of the United Kingdom, as if he had been transferred there under that section immediately before he was so sentenced, and the responsible Minister may, if he thinks fit, make an order under that section (but without application in that behalf) transferring him back to the part of the United Kingdom from which he was unlawfully at large.

(4) In paragraph (a) of the proviso to subsection (2) of section forty-nine of the Prison Act, 1952 (which in effect enables a person who is unlawfully at large during the currency of his original sentence to count towards that sentence any period during which he is detained in pursuance of a sentence of any court) and in the proviso to subsection (2) of section thirty-seven of the Prisons (Scotland) Act, 1952, and in subsection (3) of section thirty-eight of the Prison Act (Northern Ireland), 1953 (which contain corresponding provisions for Scotland and Northern Ireland) references to a court shall include references to any court in the United Kingdom.

NOTES

Definitions.—See note to s. 26, p. 412, *ante*.

Prison Act, 1952, s. 49.—See p. 392, *ante*.

31. Subsequent sentence in case of persons transferred or removed under Part III.—(1) The power of a court in any part of the United Kingdom to order that the term of any sentence of imprisonment or detention passed by the court shall commence at or before the expiration of another term of imprisonment or detention shall include power to make such an order where that other term was imposed by sentence of a court elsewhere in the United Kingdom or in any of the Channel Islands or the Isle of Man if the offender—

(a) is serving that other sentence in that part of the United Kingdom ; or

(b) is for the time being present in that part of the United Kingdom,

by virtue of an order under this Part of this Act, or is unlawfully at large under the law of the country in which that other sentence was passed.

(2) The provisions of this section shall be without prejudice to the powers exercisable by any court apart from those provisions.

NOTE

Definitions.—See note to s. 26, p. 412, *ante*.

32. Supervision and recall.—(1) The enactments mentioned in the next following subsection, so far as they make provision—

(a) for the supervision of persons released from a prison or other institution in any part of the United Kingdom ;

(b) for the imposition upon persons so released of requirements or conditions to be complied with by them ; or

(c) for the recall or return of persons so released to such a prison or institution.

shall apply to a person so released who is for the time being in any other part of the United Kingdom or in the Channel Islands or the Isle of Man ; and for that purpose those enactments shall extend throughout the United Kingdom, the Channel Islands and the Isle of Man.

(2) The following are the enactments extended by this section, that is to say—

(a) section 45 of the Prison Act, 1952 ;

(b) sections 19 and 33 of the Prisons (Scotland) Act, 1952;
(c) section 55 (4) of the Children and Young Persons Act (Northern Ireland), 1950;
(d) sections 20, 21, 22 and 23 of the Prison Act (Northern Ireland), 1953, and Schedules 1, 2 and 3 to that Act;
(e) section 13 of and Schedule 1 to this Act;
(f) sections 11, 12 and 14 of the Criminal Justice (Scotland) Act, 1963, and Schedule 1 to that Act; and
(g) sections 60 to 63 of the Criminal Justice Act, 1967.
(h) section 58A of the Children and Young Persons (Scotland) Act, 1937.

(3) Part II of the Third Schedule to this Act shall have effect for the purposes of that Schedule as extended by this section.

NOTES

This section is printed as amended by the Criminal Justice (Scotland) Act, 1963, s. 52 and Sched. 5, the Criminal Justice Act, 1967, and the Children and Young Persons Act, 1969 as it amends Sched. VIII of the Social Work (Scotland) Act, 1968. At the time of going to press sub-s. (3) had not been brought into force.

Extension of the Criminal Justice (Scotland) Act, 1963 to England, Northern Ireland, the Isle of Man and the Channel Islands.—See s. 53, *ibid.*

33. Orders under Part III.—Any order of a Secretary of State under this Part of this Act shall be given under the hand of the Secretary of State or of an Under-Secretary or Assistant Under-Secretary of State.

PART IV

SUPPLEMENTAL

34. Removals from prison consequential on Part I.—(1) Subject to subsection (2) of this section, the Secretary of State may, if satisfied that it is expedient to do so, remove from a prison to a borstal institution or a detention centre any person who, at or after the commencement of subsection (2) of section two or subsection (1) of section three of this Act, or of an Order in Council under subsection (5) of the said section three, is serving a sentence of imprisonment in a prison in England and Wales, being a sentence which, by virtue of that enactment or of that Order, as the case may be, could not then be passed in his case by a court in England and Wales.

(2) A person shall not be removed under this section to a borstal institution unless his sentence of imprisonment was a sentence for a term exceeding six months, and shall not be removed thereunder to a detention centre if the unexpired period of the term of his sentence exceeds nine months.

(3) Where a person is removed under this section to a borstal institution, he shall thereafter be treated as if his sentence had been a sentence of borstal training except that—

(a) his liability to be detained under section forty-five of the Prison Act, 1952, in a borstal institution shall continue until the expiration of his term of imprisonment, and shall then determine ;

(b) subsections (3) to (5) of section forty-five of the Prison Act, 1952, shall not apply to him on his release, but the Secretary of State may release him on licence at any time before the expiration of the said term, and in that case subsections (3) to (6) of section twenty-five of that Act (which relate to persons released from prison on licence under that section), shall apply as if for references to a prison there were substituted references to a prison or a borstal institution.

(4) Where a person is removed under this section to a detention centre, he shall thereafter be treated as if his sentence had been an order for his detention in a detention centre for a term equal to his term of imprisonment.

(5) Notwithstanding anything in this section, a person transferred thereunder shall, while detained in a borstal institution or detention centre, be treated for the purposes of section three of this Act as if he were serving his sentence of imprisonment.

(6) Where an order has been made under Part III of this Act for the removal to a prison in England and Wales of a person who, under this section, could be removed from that prison to a borstal institution or detention centre, or who, immediately before his removal, was undergoing a sentence of detention in a young offenders institution in Scotland, the Secretary of State may direct that he shall, on his arrival in England and Wales, be taken to a borstal institution or a detention centre instead of that prison and subsections (3) to (5) of this section shall apply to any person in whose case a direction is given as if he had been removed under this section.

NOTES

This section is printed as amended by the Prison Commissioners Dissolution Order 1963, S.I. 1963 No. 597, para. 3 (2) and Sched. 2 and the Criminal Justice (Scotland) Act, 1963, s. 52 and Sched. 5.

Definitions.—For "sentence " and " term ", see s. 38, p. 418, *post*.

Prison Act, 1952, ss. 25, 45.—See pp. 389, 309, *ante*.

35. Legal custody.—(1) Any person required or authorised by or under this Act to be taken to any place or to be kept in custody shall, while being so taken or kept, be deemed to be in legal custody.

(2) A constable, or any other person required or authorised by or under this Act to take any person or to keep him at any place shall, while taking or keeping him there have all the powers, authorities, protection and privileges which a constable has within the area for which he acts as constable.

36. General provisions as to orders.—(1) Any power of the Secretary of State to make orders under this Act (other than orders under subsection (1) of section nineteen or under Part III) shall be exercisable by statutory instrument.

(2) Any Order in Council or order under this Act may be varied or revoked by a subsequent Order in Council or order.

37. Secretary of State's reports.—In any case where a court is required by this Act to consider a report made by or on behalf of the Secretary of State in respect of an offender, the court shall cause a copy of the report to be given to the offender or his counsel or solicitor.

NOTE

This section is printed as amended by the Prison Commissioners Dissolution Order 1963, S.I. 1963 No. 597, para. 3 (2) and Sched. 2.

38. Construction of references to sentence of imprisonment, etc.—(1) Except as provided by subsection (3) of this section, the expression " sentence " in this Act does not include a committal for default or the fixing of a term to be served in the event of default, or a committal or attachment for contempt of court.

(2) For the purposes of any provisions of this Act referring to a person who is serving or has served a sentence of any description, the expression " sentence " includes—

    (a) in any case, a sentence of that description passed by a court in Scotland, Northern Ireland, any of the Channel Islands or the Isle of Man ; and

    (b) in the case of imprisonment, a sentence passed by a court-martial on a person found guilty of a civil offence (within the meaning of the Naval Discipline Act, 1957, the Army Act, 1955, or the Air Force Act, 1955), and a sentence which is treated by virtue of the Colonial Prisoners Removal Act, 1884, as a sentence passed by a court in England and Wales.

(3) For the purposes of Part III and of sections twenty-two and thirty-four of this Act—

    (a) the expression " imprisonment or detention " means imprisonment, corrective training, preventive detention, borstal training or detention in a detention centre ;

    (b) the expression " sentence " includes a sentence passed by a court-martial for any offence, and any order made by any court imposing imprisonment or detention, and " sentenced " shall be construed accordingly.

    (c) any reference to a person serving a sentence of, or sentenced to, imprisonment or detention shall be construed as including a reference to a person who, under any enactment relating to children and young persons in force in any part of the United Kingdom or any of the Channel Islands or the Isle of Man, has been sentenced by a court to be detained for an offence and is liable to be detained in accordance with directions given by the Secretary of State, by the Minister of Home Affairs for Northern Ireland or by the Governor of the Isle of Man with the concurrence of the Secretary of State, and any other reference to a sentence of imprisonment or detention shall be construed accordingly.

(4) For the purposes of any reference in this Act to a term of imprisonment or of detention in a detention centre or to a term of imprisonment or detention, consecutive terms and terms which are wholly or partly concurrent shall be treated as a single term.

(5) For the purposes of this Act (and of any enactment referred to in Part III of this Act)—

(a) a sentence of detention in a young offenders' institution passed in Scotland, and a sentence of penal servitude passed in any of the Channel Islands or the Isle of Man shall be treated as a sentence of imprisonment for the like term ;

(b) a sentence of detention in a borstal institution passed as aforesaid shall be treated as a sentence of borstal training ;

(c) a sentence of death passed by any court (including a court-martial) on a person subsequently pardoned by Her Majesty on condition of his serving a term of imprisonment or penal servitude shall be treated as a sentence of imprisonment or penal servitude passed by that court for that term ; and

(d) without prejudice to paragraph (c) of this subsection, any reference to a person on whom a sentence of any description has been passed includes a reference to a person who under the law of any part of the United Kingdom, any of the Channel Islands or the Isle of Man is treated as a person on whom a sentence of that description has been passed ;

and " sentenced " shall be construed accordingly.

NOTES

This section is printed as amended by the Criminal Justice (Scotland) Act, 1963, s. 52 and Sched. 5, and the Criminal Justice Act, 1967, s. 69.

" **Default.**"—See s. 39 (1), *infra.*

Consecutive sentences.—See note to s. 3, p. 402, *ante.*

39. Interpretation.—(1) In this Act, unless the context otherwise requires, the following expressions have the meanings hereby assigned to them, that is to say :—

" appropriate institution " means—

(a) in relation to a person sentenced to borstal training who is removed under Part III of this Act to any part of the United Kingdom, a borstal institution ;

(b) in relation to a person sentenced to detention in a detention centre who is so removed to England and Wales or Scotland, a detention centre ;

(bb) in relation to a person sentenced to imprisonment when under twenty-one years of age who is so removed to Scotland, a young offenders institution ;

(c) in relation to any other person who is removed under the said Part III, a prison ;

" court-martial " includes the Courts-Martial Appeal Court and any officer exercising jurisdiction under section forty-nine of the Naval Discipline Act, 1957 ;

" default " means failure to pay, or want of sufficient distress to satisfy, any fine or other sum of money, or failure to do or abstain from doing any thing required to be done or left undone ;

" enactment " includes an enactment of the Parliament of Northern Ireland ;

" prison " does not include a naval, military or air force prison ;

" responsible Minister " means—

(a) in relation to persons detained in England and Wales or in Scotland, a Secretary of State ;

(b) in relation to persons detained in Northern Ireland, the Minister of Home Affairs for Northern Ireland ;

" the statutory restrictions upon the imprisonment of young offenders " means subsection (1) of section seventeen of the Criminal Justice Act, 1948, subsection (2) of section one hundred and seven of the Magistrates' Courts Act, 1952, and section three of this Act.

(2) Except as otherwise expressly provided, references in this Act to a court do not include references to a court-martial ; and nothing in this Act shall be construed as affecting the punishment which may be awarded by a court-martial under the Naval Discipline Act, 1957, the Army Act, 1955, or the Air Force Act, 1955, for a civil offence within the meaning of those Acts.

(3) Where the age of any person at any time is material for the purposes of any provision of this Act regulating the powers of a court or justice of the peace, his age at the material time shall be deemed to be or to have been that which appears to the court of justice, after considering any available evidence, to be or to have been his age at that time.

(4) Any reference in this Act to any other enactment is a reference thereto as amended, and includes a reference thereto as extended or applied, by or under any other enactment, including this Act.

NOTES

This section is printed as amended by the Criminal Justice Administration Act, 1962, and the Criminal Justice (Scotland) Act, 1963.

" **Age.**"—See note to s. 1, p. 311, *ante.*

40. (*Applies to Northern Ireland*).

41. Minor and consequential amendments and repeals.—[*The enactments where reproduced are printed as amended.*]

    *   *   *   *   *

43. Expenses.—There shall be paid out of moneys provided by Parliament any increase attributable to the provisions of this Act in the sums which, under any other enactment, are payable out of moneys so provided.

44. Commencement.—(1) The foregoing provisions of this Act (including the Schedules therein referred to) shall come into operation on such date as the Secretary of State may by order appoint.

(2) Different dates may be appointed by order under this section for different purposes of this Act ; and any reference in this Act to the commencement of any provision of this Act shall be construed as a reference to the date appointed for the purposes of that provision.

NOTE

At the time of going to press all of the provisions of this Act except s. 32 (3) and Part II of Sched. III had been brought into force.

45. Short title.—This Act may be cited as the Criminal Justice Act, 1961.

SCHEDULES

Section 13   FIRST SCHEDULE

SUPERVISION OF PERSONS RELEASED FROM DETENTION CENTRES

1. A person detained in a detention centre in pursuance of an order under section four of this Act shall, after his release and until the expiration of the period of twelve months from the date of his release, be under the supervision of such society or person as may be specified in a notice to be given to him by the Secretary of State on his release, and shall, while under that supervision, comply with such requirements as may be so specified:

Provided that the Secretary of State may at any time modify or cancel any of the said requirements or order that a person who is under supervision as aforesaid shall cease to be under supervision.

2. If before the expiration of the said period of twelve months the Secretary of State is satisfied that a person under supervision under the foregoing paragraph has failed to comply with any requirement for the time being specified in the notice given to him under that paragraph, the Secretary of State may by order recall him to a detention centre ; and thereupon he shall be liable to be detained in the detention centre until the expiration of a period equivalent to that part of his term which was unexpired on the date of his release from the detention centre, or until the expiration of the period of fourteen days from the date of his being taken into custody under the order, whichever is the later, and, if at large, shall be deemed to be unlawfully at large :

Provided that—

(a) a person shall not be recalled more than once under this paragraph by virtue of the same order under section four of this Act ; and

(b) an order under this paragraph shall, at the expiration of the said period of twelve months, cease to have effect unless the person to whom it relates is then in custody thereunder.

3. The Secretary of State may at any time release a person who is detained in a detention centre under paragraph 2 of this Schedule.

NOTES

This Schedule is printed as amended by the Prison Commissioners Dissolution Order, 1963, S.I. 1963, No. 597.

Section 14   SECOND SCHEDULE

SUPERVISION OF PERSONS RELEASED FROM APPROVED SCHOOLS

[*Repealed by the Children and Young Persons Act, 1969 s. 72 (4) and Sched. VI.*]

Sections 20 and 32   THIRD SCHEDULE

SUPERVISION OF CERTAIN DISCHARGED PRISONERS

[Repealed as to England and Wales by the Criminal Justice Act, 1967, s. 103 and Sched. VII.]

FOURTH SCHEDULE   Section 41

MINOR AND CONSEQUENTIAL AMENDMENTS

[The enactments where reproduced are printed as amended.]

Section 41   FIFTH SCHEDULE

ENACTMENTS REPEALED

[Not reproduced.   Effect is given to the repeals where enactments are reproduced.]

Section 41   SIXTH SCHEDULE

ENACTMENTS RELATING TO BORSTAL TRAINING AS THEY WILL HAVE EFFECT, SUBJECT TO S. 41 (3) OF THIS ACT AND TO S. 18 (6) OF THE LEGAL AID AND ADVICE ACT, 1949, WHEN ALL AMENDMENTS MADE IN THEM BY THIS ACT OPERATE.

NOTES

Amendments.—This Schedule, as originally enacted was designed to show the provisions of the various statutes reproduced in it in the form in which they would appear when all of the amendments to them contained in the Act of 1961 had become operative.   However, before that Act came fully into force, the provisions of the Criminal Justice Act, 1948, s. 20 and the Prison Act, 1952, s. 45, two of the provisions so printed, were further amended and they are now printed at pp. 305, 309, *et seq., ante.*

BETTING, GAMING AND LOTTERIES ACT, 1963
[1963 c. 2]

Special Provisions with respect to young persons

21. Betting with young persons.—(1) If any person—

(a) has any betting transaction with a young person ; or

(b) employs a young person in the effecting of any betting transaction or in a licensed betting office ; or

(c) receives or negotiates any bet through a young person,

he shall be guilty of an offence :

Provided that a person shall not be guilty of an offence under this subsection by reason of—

(i) the employment of a young person in the effecting of betting transactions by post ; or

(ii) the carriage by a young person of a communication relating to a betting transaction for the purposes of its conveyance by post.

(2) In this section, the expression " young person " means a person—

(a) who is under the age of eighteen years and whom the person committing an offence in relation to him under this section knows, or ought to know, to be under that age ; or

(b) who is apparently under the said age :

Provided that in the case of any proceedings under this section for an offence in respect of a person apparently under the said age it shall be a defence to prove that at the time of the alleged offence he had in fact attained that age.

NOTE

Definitions.—For " betting transaction, licensed betting office ", see s. 55 (1), *post*.

22. Betting circulars not to be sent to young persons.—(1) If any person, for the purpose of earning commission, reward or other profit, sends or causes to be sent to a person whom he knows to be under the age of eighteen years any circular, notice, advertisement, letter, telegram or other document which invites or may reasonably be implied to invite the person receiving it to make any bet, or to enter into or take any share or interest in any betting transaction, or to apply to any person or at any place with a view to obtaining information or advice for the purpose of any bet or for information as to any race, fight, game, sport or other contingency upon which betting is generally carried on, he shall be guilty of an offence.

(2) If any such document as aforesaid names or refers to anyone as a person to whom any payment may be made, or from whom information may be obtained, for the purpose of or relation to betting, the person so named or referred to shall be deemed to have sent that document or caused it to be sent unless he proves that he had not consented to be so named and that he was not in any way a party to, and was wholly ignorant of, the sending of the document.

(3) If any such document as aforesaid is sent to any person at any university, college, school or other place of education and that person is under the age of eighteen years, the person sending the document or causing it to be sent shall be deemed to have known that person to be under that age unless he proves that he had reasonable grounds for believing him to be of full age.

NOTES

This section is printed as amended by the Family Law Reform Act, 1969, s. 1 (3) and Sched. 1.

Definition.—For " betting transaction " see s. 55 (1), *post*.

45. Exemption of certain small lotteries conducted for charitable sporting or other purposes.—(1) . . .

(2) In construing subsection (1) (c) of this section, any purpose for which any society is established and conducted which is calculated to benefit the society as a whole shall not be held to be a purpose of private gain by reason only that action in its fulfilment would result in benefit to any person as an individual ; and for the purposes of this section, the

expression "society" includes a club, institution, organisation or association of persons, by whatever name called, and any separate branch or section of such a club, institution, organisation or association.

51. Search warrants.—(1) If a justice of the peace is satisfied on information on oath that there is reasonable ground for suspecting that an offence under this Act is being, has been or is about to be committed on any premises, he may issue a warrant in writing authorising any constable to enter those premises, if necessary by force, at any time within fourteen days from the time of the issue of the warrant and search them ; and any constable who enters the premises under the authority of the warrant may—

    (a) seize and remove any document, money or valuable thing, instrument or other thing whatsoever found on the premises which he has reasonable cause to believe may be required as evidence for the purposes of proceedings in respect of any such offence ; and

    (b) arrest and search any person found on the premises whom he has reasonable cause to believe to be committing or to have committed any such offence.

In its application to Scotland, the foregoing subsection shall have effect as if for the reference to a justice of the peace there were substituted a reference to the sheriff or a magistrate or justice of the peace having jurisdiction in the place where the premises are situated.

NOTE

" **Premises.**"—See the definition in s. 55 (1), *post.*

52. Penalties and forfeitures.—(1) A person guilty of an offence under any of the following provisions of this Act, that is to say sections 1 (1), 2 (1), 4, 5, 6, 16, 32, (4), 42, 43, 44, 45 and 47, paragraph 29 of Schedule 2 and paragraph 17 of Schedule 5, shall be liable—

    (a) on summary conviction, to a fine not exceeding one hundred pounds or, in the case of a second or any subsequent conviction for an offence under the same provision, to imprisonment for a term not exceeding three months or to a fine not exceeding two hundred pounds or to both ; or

    (b) on conviction on indictment, to a fine not exceeding five hundred pounds or, in the case of a second or any subsequent conviction for an offence under the same provision, to imprisonment for a term not exceeding one year or to a fine not exceeding seven hundred and fifty pounds or to both.

(2) A person guilty of an offence under any provision of this Act not mentioned in the foregoing subsection, being a provision which does not specify any other penalty, shall be liable—

    (a) on summary conviction, to a fine not exceeding fifty pounds or, in the case of a second or any subsequent conviction for an offence under the same provision, to imprisonment for a term not exceeding two months or to a fine not exceeding one hundred pounds or to both ; or

(b) on conviction on indictment, to a fine not exceeding three hundred pounds or, in the case of a second or any subsequent conviction for an offence under the same provision, to imprisonment for a term not exceeding six months or to a fine not exceeding five hundred pounds or to both.

(3) Subject to section 8 (3) of this Act, for the purposes of any provision of this Act with respect to a second or subsequent conviction, a conviction for an offence under any provision repealed by this Act shall be deemed to have been a conviction for the like offence under the corresponding provision of this Act.

(4) The court by or before whom a person is convicted of any offence under this Act may order anything produced to the court and shown to the satisfaction of the court to relate to the offence to be forfeited and either destroyed or dealt with in such other manner as the court may order.

NOTE

" **Second or any subsequent conviction.**"—A second or subsequent conviction is a conviction in respect of an offence committed after the first conviction.

54. Construction of certain references to private gain.—(1) In construing section forty-three or section forty-eight of this Act or section thirty-three or section forty-one of the Gaming Act, 1968, proceeds of any entertainment, lottery, gaming or amusement promoted on behalf of a society to which this subsection extends which are applied for any purpose calculated to benefit the society as a whole shall not be held to be applied for purposes of private gain by reason only that their application for that purpose results in benefit to any person as an individual.

(2) For the purposes of section forty-eight of this Act or section thirty-three or forty-one of that Act, where any payment falls to be made by way of a hiring, maintenance or other charge in respect of a machine to which Part III of that Act applies, or in respect of any equipment for holding a lottery or gaming at any entertainment, then, if, but only if, the amount of that charge falls to be determined wholly or partly by reference to the extent to which that or some other such machine or equipment is used for the purposes of lotteries or gaming that payment shall be held to be an application of the stakes hazarded or proceeds of the entertainment, as the case may require, for purposes of private gain; and accordingly any reference in any of those sections to expenses shall not include a reference to any such charge falling to be so determined.

(3) Subsection (1) of this section extends to any society which is established and conducted either—

(a) wholly for purposes other than purposes of any commercial undertaking ; or

(b) wholly or mainly for the purposes of participation in or support of athletic sports or athletic games ;

and in this section the expression " society " includes any club, institution, organisation or association of persons, by whatever name called, and any separate branch or section of such a club, institution, organisation or association.

NOTES

This section is printed as amended by the Gaming Act, 1968, s. 53 and Sched. II. See now the provisions of that Act particularly ss. 7, 17, p. 440, *post*.

" **Gaming.**"—For meaning, see s. 55 (1), *infra*.

55. Interpretation, etc.—General.—(1) In this Act, except where the context otherwise requires, the following expressions have the following meanings respectively, that is to say—

" betting transaction " includes the collection or payment of winnings on a bet and any transaction in which one or more of the parties is acting as a bookmaker ;

*   *   *   *

" contravention ", in relation to any requirement, includes a failure to comply with that requirement, and cognate expressions shall be construed accordingly ;

*   *   *   *

" game of chance " includes a game of chance and skill combined and a pretended game of change or of chance and skill combined, but does not include any athletic game or sport ;

*   *   *   *

" gaming " means the playing of a game of chance for winnings in money or money's worth ;

*   *   *   *

" licensed betting office " means premises in respect of which a betting office licence is for the time being in force ;

*   *   *   *

" money " includes a cheque, banknote, postal order or money order ;

*   *   *   *

" player ", in relation to a game of chance, includes any person taking part in the game against whom other persons taking part in the game stake, play or bet ;

*   *   *   *

" premises " include any place and, in sections 1, 32 and 33 of this Act, includes any vessel ;

*   *   *   *

" winnings " includes winnings of any kind and any reference to the amount or to the payment of winnings shall be construed accordingly.

*   *   *   *

(5) Save where the context otherwise requires, any reference in this Act to any enactment shall be construed as a reference to that enactment as amended by or under any other enactment.

58. Short title, extent and commencement.—(1) This Act may be cited as the Betting, Gaming and Lotteries Act, 1963.

(2) This Act shall not extend to Northern Ireland.

(3) This Act shall come into force at the expiration of the period of one month beginning with the day on which it is passed.

LICENSING ACT, 1964

[1964, c. 26]

INTRODUCTORY NOTE

Earlier Licensing Acts are repealed by the Licensing Act, 1964, which re-enacts many of their provisions.   Under that Act children under fourteen are prohibited from being in bars of licensed premises, unless they are the children of the licensee, reside on the premises or are passing through the bar to some other part of the premises not otherwise conveniently accessible.   A licensee commits an offence if he sells intoxicants or allows them to be sold to a person under eighteen, or allows such a person to consume drinks in a bar, except that it is permitted to sell beer, porter, cider or perry to such a person if it is to be consumed with a table meal in a part of the premises which is not a bar.   He may deliver intoxicants to such a person for consumption off the premises only if delivery is to that person's residence or place of work, or if that person is a member of the licensee's family or staff.   It is prohibited to send any one under eighteen to buy intoxicants from licensed premises unless the person is employed as a messenger to deliver intoxicants.   The former provision that in such cases intoxicants might be supplied in corked and sealed vessels no longer applies.   It is an offence to employ a person under eighteen to work in a bar even if he receives no wages for his work.

Intoxicants may not be given to children under five, except on medical grounds. See s. 5 of the Children and Young Persons Act, 1933, p. 21, *ante*.

167. Saving for liqueur chocolates.—(1) No provision of this Act as to the sale, supply, purchase, delivery or consumption of intoxicating liquor, except subsection (2) of this section, and no enactment requiring the authority of an excise licence for the sale or supply of intoxicating liquor, shall have effect in relation to intoxicating liquor in confectionery which—

(a) does not contain intoxicating liquor in a proportion greater than one fiftieth of a gallon of liquor (computed as proof spirit) per pound of the confectionery ; and

(b) either consists of separate pieces weighing not more than one and a half ounces or is designed to be broken into such pieces for the purposes of consumption.

(2) Intoxicating liquor in confectionery shall not be sold to a person under sixteen, and if any person knowingly contravenes this subsection he shall be liable on a first conviction to a fine not exceeding ten pounds and on a subsequent conviction to a fine not exceeding twenty-five pounds.

NOTES

Definitions.—For " enactment " and " intoxicating liquor ", see s. 201 (1), p. 431, *post*.

" **Knowingly.**"—This relates to the age of the person to whom the confectionery is sold.   As to the defence of reasonable belief that the person was not under sixteen see *Sherras* v. *De Rutzen*, [1895] 1 Q. B. 918 ; 59 J. P. 440, and *R.* v. *Cohen*, [1951] 1 K. B. 505 ; [1951] 1 All E. R. 203 ; 115 J. P. 91.

" **Subsequent conviction.**"—A conviction that took place more than five years previously is to be disregarded for the purposes of the imposition of an increased penalty; section 194 (2) (14 Halsbury's Statutes, 3rd Edn., 539).

PART XII—PROTECTION OF PERSONS UNDER EIGHTEEN AND OTHER PROVISIONS AS TO CONDUCT OF LICENSED PREMISES AND LICENSED CANTEENS

Persons under eighteen

168. Children prohibited from bars.—(1) The holder of a justices' licence shall not allow a person under fourteen to be in the bar of the licensed premises during the permitted hours.

(2) No person shall cause or procure, or attempt to cause or procure, any person under fourteen to be in the bar of licensed premises during the permitted hours.

(3) Where it is shown that a person under fourteen was in the bar of any licensed premises during the permitted hours, the holder of the justices' licence shall be guilty of an offence under this section unless he proves either—

    (a) that he used due diligence to prevent the person under fourteen from being admitted to the bar, or

    (b) that the person under fourteen had apparently attained that age.

(4) No offence shall be committed under this section if the person under fourteen—

    (a) is the licence-holder's child, or

    (b) resides in the premises, but is not employed there, or

    (c) is in the bar solely for the purpose of passing to or from some part of the premises which is not a bar and to or from which there is no other convenient means of access or egress.

(5) No offence shall be committed under this section if the bar is in any railway refreshment-rooms or other premises constructed, fitted and intended to be used bona fide for any purpose to which the holding of a justices' licence is merely ancillary.

(6) If any person contravenes this section he shall be liable, on a first conviction to a fine not exceeding forty shillings, and on a subsequent conviction to a fine not exceeding five pounds.

(7) A local education authority may institute proceedings for an offence under this section.

(8) Where in any proceedings under this section it is alleged that a person was at any time under fourteen, and he appears to the court to have then been under that age, he shall be deemed for the purposes of the proceedings to have then been under that age, unless the contrary is shown.

NOTES

" **Permitted hours.**"—See ss. 59, 60, *et seq.*; 17 Halsbury's Statutes, 3rd Edn., 1119, 1120.

" **Resides.**"—See s. 201 (2), p. 431, *post.*

Definitions.—For " justices' licence ", see s. 1 (1) ; for " licensed premises ", see s. 200 (1) ; for " bar ", see s. 201, p. 431, *post.*

" **Subsequent conviction.**"—See note to s. 167, *ante.*

" **Due diligence.**"—The appellant held a licence for an inn, and his wife carried on the business of dressmaker on an upper floor.   Two girls, one aged ten, called for a skirt ; the wife then asked them to go into the bar parlour while she fetched it.

It was held that the appellant was not responsible for the action of his wife, and as the justices had found no want of diligence on his part, the sentence must be quashed (*Russon* v. *Dutton (No. 1*), (1911), 75 J. P. 207).

Licence and licensed premises.—For the Licensing Acts and notes thereon, see the current edition of *Paterson's Licensing Acts.*

169. Serving or delivering intoxicating liquor to or for consumption by persons under 18.—(1) Subject to subsection (4) of this section, in licensed premises the holder of the licence or his servant shall not knowingly sell intoxicating liquor to a person under eighteen or knowingly allow a person under eighteen to consume intoxicating liquor in a bar nor shall the holder of the licence knowingly allow any person to sell intoxicating liquor to a person under eighteen.

(2) Subject to subsection (4) of this section, a person under eighteen shall not in licensed premises buy or attempt to buy intoxicating liquor, nor consume intoxicating liquor in a bar.

(3) No person shall buy or attempt to buy intoxicating liquor for consumption in a bar in licensed premises by a person under eighteen.

(4) Subsections (1) and (2) of this section do not prohibit the sale to or purchase by a person who has attained the age of sixteen of beer, porter, cider or perry for consumption at a meal in a part of the premises usually set apart for the service of meals which is not a bar.

(5) Subject to subsection (7) of this section, the holder of the licence or his servant shall not knowingly deliver, nor shall the holder of the licence knowingly allow any person to deliver, to a person under eighteen intoxicating liquor sold in licensed premises for consumption off the premises, except where the delivery is made at the residence or working place of the purchaser.

(6) Subject to subsection (7) of this section, a person shall not knowingly send a person under eighteen for the purpose of obtaining intoxicating liquor sold or to be sold in licensed premises for consumption off the premises, whether the liquor is to be obtained from the licensed premises or other premises from which it is delivered in pursuance of the sale.

(7) Subsections (5) and (6) of this section do not apply where the person under eighteen is a member of the licence holder's family or his servant or apprentice and is employed as a messenger to deliver intoxicating liquor.

(8) A person guilty of an offence under this section, other than an offence under subsection (2), shall be liable, on a first conviction to a fine not exceeding twenty-five pounds, and on a second or subsequent conviction to a fine not exceeding fifty pounds ; and on a person's second or subsequent conviction of such an offence the court may, if the offence was committed by him as the holder of a justices' licence, order that he shall forfeit the licence.

(9) A person guilty of an offence under subsection (2) of this section shall be liable to a fine not exceeding twenty pounds.

NOTES

Definitions.—For " justices' licence ", see s. 1 (1); for " licensed premises " see s. 200 (1); for " bar " and " intoxicating liquor ", see s. 201 (1), p. 431, *post.*

" **Second or subsequent conviction.**"—A conviction that took place more than five years previously is to be disregarded for the purposes of the imposition of an increased penalty. Section 194 (2), *ibid.*

" **Knowingly.**"—See note to s. 167, p. 427, *ante.*

" **Meal.**"—Presumably a " table meal ". See s. 201, p. 431, *post.*

170. Persons under 18 not to be employed in bars.—(1) If any person under eighteen is employed in any bar of licensed premises at a time when the bar is open for the sale or consumption of intoxicating liquor, the holder of the licence shall be liable on a first conviction to a fine not exceeding five pounds and on a subsequent conviction to a fine not exceeding twenty pounds.

(2) For the purposes of this section a person shall not be deemed to be employed in a bar by reason only that in the course of his employment in some other part of the premises he enters the bar for the purpose of giving or receiving any message or of passing to or from some part of the premises which is not a bar and to or from which there is no other convenient means of access or egress.

(3) For the purposes of this section a person shall be deemed to be employed by the person for whom he works notwithstanding that he receives no wages for his work.

(4) Where in any proceedings under this section it is alleged that a person was at any time under eighteen, and he appears to the court to have then been under that age, he shall be deemed for the purposes of the proceedings to have then been under that age unless the contrary is shown.

NOTES

Definitions.—For " licensed premises ", see s. 200 (1); for " bar " and " intoxicating liquor ", see s. 201 (1), p. 336, *post.*

" **Subsequent conviction.**"—See note to s. 167, p. 431, *ante.*

Evidence of age.—There is in this section no deeming section as in s. 168 (8). In *Wallworth* v. *Balmer*, [1965] 3 All E. R. 721, it was held that there should be evidence of the age of the person to whom the intoxicating liquor was sold, but the evidence could be visual evidence from seeing the person himself.

171. Exclusion from sections 168 to 170 of bars while in regular use for service of table meals.—References in the foregoing provisions of this Part of this Act to a bar do not include a bar at any time when it is usual in the premises in question for it to be, and it is,—

(a) set apart for the service of table meals; and

(b) not used for the sale or supply of intoxicating liquor otherwise than to persons having table meals there and for consumption by such a person as an ancillary to his meal.

NOTE

" **Bar, intoxicating liquor, table meal.**"—See s. 201, *infra.*

*   *   *   *

200. Meaning of " licensed premises " in this Act and s. 12 of Licensing Act, 1872.—(1) Any reference in this Act to licensed premises shall, unless the context otherwise requires, be construed as a reference to premises for which a justices' licence is in force and as including a reference to any premises or place, other than a licensed canteen, where intoxicating liquor is sold by retail under a licence and, except in section 103, any premises where the Secretary of State carries on a business of selling liquor by retail in the exercise of powers conferred on him by Part V of this Act.

(2) In section 12 of the Licensing Act, 1872, the expression " licensed premises " shall include any place where intoxicating liquor is sold under an occasional licence.

NOTES

" **Premises.**"—This word is not defined in the Act.

" **Justices' licence.**"—See s. 1 (1), *ibid.*

" **Intoxicating liquor.**"—See s. 201, *infra.*

" **Permitted hours.**"—See s. 60, *ibid.*

201. Interpretation of other expressions.—(1) In this Act, unless the context otherwise requires—

" bar " includes any place exclusively or mainly used for the sale and consumption of intoxicating liquor ;

*　　　　*　　　　*　　　　*

" enactment " includes an enactment contained in any order, regulation or other instrument having effect by virtue of an Act ;

*　　　　*　　　　*　　　　*

" intoxicating liquor " means spirits, wine, beer, porter, cider, perry, and British wine and any fermented, distilled or spirituous liquor that cannot for the time being be sold without an excise licence; but does not include beer or porter for the sale of which an excise licence is not required ;

*　　　　*　　　　*　　　　*

" table meal " means a meal eaten by a person seated at a table, or at a counter or other structure which serves the purpose of a table and is not used for the service of refreshments for consumption by persons not seated at a table or structure serving the purpose of a table.

*　　　　*　　　　*　　　　*

(2) For the purposes of this Act a person shall be treated as residing in any premises, notwithstanding that he occupies sleeping accommodation in a separate building, if he is provided with that accommodation in the course of a business of providing board and lodging for reward at those premises and the building is habitually used for the purpose by way of annexe or overflow in connection with those premises and is occupied and managed with those premises.

*　　　　*　　　　*　　　　*

NOTE

See also s. 171, *ibid.*, p. 430, *ante* and *Donaghue* v. *M'Intyre*, 1911 S. C. (J) 61.

CRIMINAL JUSTICE ACT, 1967

[1967 c. 80]

2. Written statements before examining justices.—(1) In committal proceedings a written statement by any person shall, if the conditions mentioned in the next following subsection are satisfied, be admissible as evidence to the like extent as oral evidence to the like effect by that person.

(2) The said conditions are:—

    (a) the statement purports to be signed by the person who made it;

    (b) the statement contains a declaration by that person to the effect that it is true to the best of his knowledge and belief and that he made the statement knowing that, if it were tendered in evidence, he would be liable to prosecution if he wilfully stated in it anything which he knew to be false or did not believe to be true;

    (c) before the statement is tendered in evidence, a copy of the statement is given, by or on behalf of the party proposing to tender it, to each of the other parties to the proceedings; and

    (d) none of the other parties, before the statement is tendered in evidence at the committal proceedings, objects to the statement being so tendered under this section.

(3) The following provisions shall also have effect in relation to any written statement tendered in evidence under this section, that is to say—

    (a) if the statement is made by a person under the age of twenty-one, it shall give his age;

    (b) if it is made by a person who cannot read it, it shall be read to him before he signs it and shall be accompanied by a declaration by the person who so read the statement to the effect that it was so read; and

    (c) if it refers to any other document as an exhibit, the copy given to any other party to the proceedings under paragraph (c) of the last foregoing subsection shall be accompanied by a copy of that document or by such information as may be necessary in order to enable the party to whom it is given to inspect that document or a copy thereof.

(3A) *In the case of a statement which indicates in pursuance of subsection (3) (a) of this section that the person making it has not attained the age of fourteen, subsection (2) (b) of this section shall have effect as if for the words from "made" onwards there were substituted the words "understands the importance of telling the truth".*

(4) Notwithstanding that a written statement made by any person may be admissible in committal proceedings by virtue of this section, the court before which the proceedings are held may, of its own motion or on the application of any party to the proceedings, require that person to attend before the court and give evidence.

(5) So much of any statement as is admitted in evidence by virtue of this section shall, unless the court commits the defendant for trial by virtue of the last foregoing section or the court otherwise directs, be read

aloud at the hearing, and where the court so directs an account shall be given orally of so much of any statement as is not read aloud.

(6) Any document or object referred to as an exhibit and identified in a written statement tendered in evidence under this section shall be treated as if it had been produced as an exhibit and identified in court by the maker of the statement.

(7) Section 13 (3) of the Criminal Justice Act, 1925 (reading of deposition as evidence at the trial) shall apply to any written statement tendered in evidence in committal proceedings under this section, as it applies to a deposition taken in such proceedings, but in its application to any such statement that subsection shall have effect as if paragraph (b) thereof were omitted.

(8) In s. 2 (2) of the Administration of Justice (Miscellaneous Provisions) Act, 1933 (procedure for preferring bills of indictment) the reference in proviso (i) to facts disclosed in any deposition taken before a justice in the presence of the defendant shall be construed as including a reference to facts disclosed in any such written statement as aforesaid.

(9) Section 23 of the Magistrates' Courts Act, 1952 (use in summary trial of evidence given in committal proceedings) shall not apply to any such statement as aforesaid.

(10) A person whose written statement is tendered in evidence in committal proceedings under this section shall be treated for the purposes of s. 1 of the Criminal Procedure (Attendance of Witnesses) Act, 1965 (witness orders) as a witness who has been examined by the court.

NOTE

Prospective amendment: Children and Young Persons Act, 1969.—From a date to be appointed a new sub-s. (3A) is to be inserted after sub-s. (3) by the Children and Young Persons Act, 1969, s. 72 (3) and Sched. V, para. 55.

9. Proof by written statement.—(1) In any criminal proceedings, other than committal proceedings, a written statement by any person shall, if such of the conditions mentioned in the next following subsection as are applicable are satisfied, be admissible as evidence to the like extent as oral evidence to the like effect by that person.

(2) The said conditions are—

  (a) the statement purports to be signed by the person who made it;
  (b) the statement contains a declaration by that person to the effect that it is true to the best of his knowledge and belief and that he made the statement knowing that, if it were tendered in evidence, he would be liable to prosecution if he wilfully stated in it anything which he knew to be false or did not believe to be true;
  (c) before the hearing at which the statement is tendered in evidence, a copy of the statement is served, by or on behalf of the party proposing to tender it, on each of the other parties to the proceedings; and
  (d) none of the other parties or their solicitors, within seven days from the service of the copy of the statement, serves a notice on the party so proposing objecting to the statement being tendered in evidence under this section:

Provided that the conditions mentioned in paragraphs (c) and (d) of this subsection shall not apply if the parties agree before or during the hearing that the statement shall be so tendered.

(3) The following provisions shall also have effect in relation to any written statement tendered in evidence under this section, that is to say—

(a) if the statement is made by a person under the age of twenty-one, it shall give his age;

(b) if it is made by a person who cannot read it, it shall be read to him before he signs it and shall be accompanied by a declaration by the person who so read the statement to the effect that it was so read; and

(c) if it refers to any other document as an exhibit, the copy served on any other party to the proceedings under paragraph (c) of the last foregoing subsection shall be accompanied by a copy of that document or by such information as may be necessary in order to enable the party on whom it is served to inspect that document or a copy thereof.

(3A) *In the case of a statement which indicates in pursuance of subsection (3) (a) of this section that the person making it has not attained the age of fourteen, subsection (2) (b) of this section shall have effect as if for the words from "made" onwards there were substituted the words "understands the importance of telling the truth".*

(4) Notwithstanding that a written statement made by any person may be admissible as evidence by virtue of this section—

(a) the party by whom or on whose behalf a copy of the statement was served may call that person to give evidence; and

(b) the court may, of its own motion or on the application of any party to the proceedings, require that person to attend before the court and give evidence.

(5) An application under paragraph (b) of the last foregoing subsection to a court other than a magistrates' court may be made before the hearing and on any such application the powers of the court shall be exercisable by a puisne judge of the High Court, a circuit judge or a Recorder sitting alone.

(6) So much of any statement as is admitted in evidence by virtue of this section shall, unless the court otherwise directs, be read aloud at the hearing and where the court so directs an account shall be given orally of so much of any statement as is not read aloud.

(7) Any document or object referred to as an exhibit and identified in a written statement tendered in evidence under this section shall be treated as if it had been produced as an exhibit and identified in court by the maker of the statement.

(8) A document required by this section to be served on any person may be served—

(a) by delivering it to him or to his solicitor; or

(b) by addressing it to him and leaving it at his usual or last known place of abode or place of business or by addressing it to his solicitor and leaving it at his office; or

(c) by sending it in a registered letter or by the recorded delivery service addressed to him at his usual or last known place of abode or place of business or addressed to his solicitor at his office; or

(d) in the case of a body corporate, by delivering it to the secretary or clerk of the body at its registered or principal office or sending it in a registered letter or by the recorded delivery service addressed to the secretary or clerk of that body at that office.

NOTES

This section is printed as amended by the Courts Act, 1971, s. 56 and Sched. VIII.

Prospective amendment: Children and Young Persons Act, 1969. From a date to be appointed a new sub-s. (3A) is to be inserted after sub-s. (3) by the Children and Young Persons Act, 1969, s. 72 (3) and Sched. V, para. 55.

33. Taking and use of finger-prints and palm-prints.—Section 40 of the Magistrates' Courts Act, 1952 (taking of finger-prints from a person not less than fourteen who has been taken into custody and charged with an offence) shall apply to any person of not less than fourteen who appears before a magistrates' court in answer to a summons for any offence punishable with imprisonment, and in that section and in section 39 of the Criminal Justice Act, 1948 (proof of previous convictions by finger-print) any reference to finger-prints shall be construed as including a reference to palm-prints.

NOTE

Form of Order.—See Form No. 6 in the Schedule to the Magistrates' Courts (Forms) Rules, 1968.

69. Extension of enactments relating to persons sentenced to imprisonment or detention to young offenders sentenced to detention.—(1) In section 38(3) of the Criminal Justice Act, 1961 (construction of references to imprisonment or detention and sentence) at the end there shall be added the following paragraph—

" (c) any reference to a person serving a sentence of, or sentenced to, imprisonment or detention shall be construed as including a reference to a person who, under any enactment relating to children and young persons in force in any part of the United Kingdom or any of the Channel Islands or the Isle of Man, has been sentenced by a court to be detained for an offence and is liable to be detained in accordance with directions given by the Secretary of State, by the Minister of Home Affairs for Northern Ireland or by the Governor of the Isle of Man with the concurrence of the Secretary of State, and any other reference to a sentence of imprisonment or detention shall be construed accordingly."

(2) In section 49 of the Prison Act, 1952, section 37 of the Prisons (Scotland) Act, 1952, and section 38(2) of the Prison Act (Northern Ireland), 1953 (persons unlawfully at large) any reference to a person

sentenced to imprisonment shall be construed as including a reference to any such person as is mentioned in the foregoing subsection.

NOTE

This section came into force on October 1, 1967 (S.I. 1967 No. 1234, Scotland S.I. 1967 No. 1289).

71. Exercise of powers of release.—Any power conferred by or under any enactment to release a person from a prison or other institution to which the Prison Act, 1952, applies or from an approved school may be exercised notwithstanding that he is not for the time being detained in that institution or school and a person released by virtue of this section shall, after his release, be treated in all respects as if he had been released from that institution or school.

NOTE

This section came into force on October 1, 1967 (S.I. 1967 No. 1234).

FIREARMS ACT, 1968

[1968 c. 27]

General restrictions on possession and handling of firearms and ammunition

1. Requirement of firearm certificate.—(1) Subject to any exemption under this Act, it is an offence for a person—

(a) to have in his possession, or to purchase or acquire, a firearm to which this section applies without holding a firearm certificate in force at the time, or otherwise than as authorised by such a certificate;

(b) to have in his possession, or to purchase or acquire, any ammunition to which this section applies without holding a firearm certificate in force at the time, or otherwise than as authorised by such a certificate, or in quantities in excess of those so authorised.

(2) It is an offence for a person to fail to comply with a condition subject to which a firearm certificate is held by him.

(3) This section applies to every firearm except—

(a) a shot gun (that is to say a smooth-bore gun with a barrel not less than 24 inches in length, not being an air gun); and

(b) an air weapon (that is to say, an air rifle, air gun or air pistol not of a type declared by rules made by the Secretary of State under section 53 of this Act to be specially dangerous).

(4) This section applies to any ammunition for a firearm, except the following articles, namely:—

(a) cartridges containing five or more shots, none of which exceeds ·36 inch in diameter;

(b) ammunition for an air gun, air rifle or air pistol; and
(c) blank cartridges not more than one inch in diameter measured immediately in front of the rim or cannelure of the base of the cartridge.

22. Acquisition and possession of firearms by minors.—(1) It is an offence for a person under the age of seventeen to purchase or hire any firearm or ammunition.

(2) It is an offence for a person under the age of fourteen to have in his possession any firearm or ammunition to which section 1 of this Act applies, except in circumstances where under section 11(1), (3) or (4) of this Act he is entitled to have possession of it without holding a firearm certificate.

(3) It is an offence for a person under the age of fifteen to have with him an assembled shot gun except while under the supervision of a person of or over the age of twenty-one, or while the shot gun is so covered with a securely fastened gun cover that it cannot be fired.

(4) Subject to section 23 below, it is an offence for a person under the age of fourteen to have with him an air weapon or ammunition for an air weapon.

(5) Subject to section 23 below, it is an offence for a person under the age of seventeen to have an air weapon with him in a public place, except an air gun or air rifle which is so covered with a securely fastened gun cover that it cannot be fired.

NOTES

Offence.—The punishment for an offence under sub-ss. (1) and (2) is 6 months' imprisonment or a fine of £200, or both, imposed on summary conviction; under sub-ss. (3), (4) and (5) the punishment is a fine of £50, imposed on summary conviction (Sched. 6, Part I). See also s. 51 and Sched. 6, Part II, pp. 439, 440, *post*.

Definitions.—See s. 57, p. 439, *post*.

Firearm certificate.—From May 1, 1968, it will be an offence for anyone to have in his possession, purchase or acquire a shot gun without holding a certificate authorising him to possess a shot gun (s. 85 of the Criminal Justice Act, 1967).

23. Exceptions from s. 22 (4) and (5).—(1) It is not an offence under section 22(4) of this Act for a person to have with him an air weapon or ammunition while he is under the supervision of a person of or over the age of twenty-one; but where a person has with him an air weapon on any premises in circumstances where he would be prohibited from having it with him but for this subsection, it is an offence—

(a) for him to use it for firing any missile beyond those premises; or
(b) for the person under whose supervision he is to allow him so to use it.

(2) It is not an offence under section 22(4) or (5) of this Act for a person to have with him an air weapon or ammunition at a time when—

(a) being a member of a rifle club or miniature rifle club for the time being approved by the Secretary of State for the purposes of this section or section 11(3) of this Act, he is engaged as such a member in or in connection with target practice; or

(b) he is using the weapon or ammunition at a shooting gallery where the only firearms used are either air weapons or miniature rifles not exceeding ·23 inch calibre.

NOTES

Offence.—The punishment under sub-s. (1) is a fine of £50 imposed on summary conviction (Sched. 6, Part I). See also s. 51 and Sched. 6, Part II, paras. 7 and 8, pp. 439, 440, *post*.

Definitions.—See s. 57, p. 439, *post*.

24. Supplying firearms to minors.—(1) It is an offence to sell or let on hire any firearm or ammunition to a person under the age of seventeen.

(2) It is an offence—

(a) to make a gift of or lend any firearm or ammunition to which section 1 of this Act applies to a person under the age of fourteen; or

(b) to part with the possession of any such firearm or ammunition to a person under that age, except in circumstances where that person is entitled under section 11(1), (3) or (4) of this Act to have possession thereof without holding a firearm certificate.

(3) It is an offence to make a gift of a shot gun or ammunition for a shot gun to a person under the age of fifteen.

(4) It is an offence—

(a) to make a gift of an air weapon or ammunition for an air weapon to a person under the age of fourteen; or

(b) to part with the possession of an air weapon or ammunition for an air weapon to a person under that age except where by virtue of section 23 of this Act the person is not prohibited from having it with him.

(5) In proceedings for an offence under any provision of this section it is a defence to prove that the person charged with the offence believed the other person to be of or over the age mentioned in that provision and had reasonable ground for the belief.

NOTES

Offence.—The punishment under sub-ss. (1) and (2) is 6 months' imprisonment or a fine of £200; or both, imposed on summary conviction; under sub-ss. (3) and (4) the punishment is a fine of £50 imposed on summary conviction (Sched. 6, Part I). See also s. 51 and Sched. 6, Part II, paras. 7, 8 and 9, *infra*.

Definition.—For definition of firearm see *infra*.

51. Prosecution and punishment of offences.—

(4) Notwithstanding section 104 of the Magistrates' Courts Act, 1952 or section 23 of the Summary Jurisdiction (Scotland) Act, 1954 (limitation of time for taking proceedings) summary proceedings for an offence under this Act, other than an offence under section 22 (3) or an offence relating specifically to air weapons, may be instituted at any time within four years after the commission of the offence:

Provided that no such proceedings shall be instituted in England after the expiration of six months after the commission of the offence unless they are instituted by, or by the direction of, the Director of Public Prosecutions.

NOTE

Penalties.—The penalties provided by s. 51 and Sched. 6 in respect of children and young persons are inconsistent with the provisions of earlier statutes not re- pealed or amended by this statute. The Magistrates' Courts Act, 1952, s. 107, p. 385 provides that a magistrates' court shall not impose imprisonment on any person under the age of seventeen years. The Criminal Justice Act, 1961, s. 8, p. 318, limits the amount of a fine which may be imposed by a magistrates' court on an offender under fourteen, to ten pounds, and that on an offender under seventeen to fifty pounds. The alternative power under s.'7 (7) (a) of the Children and Young Persons Act, 1969, p. 146, does not seem appropriate since the offences under s. 22 cannot be committed by an adult.

57. Interpretation.—(1) In this Act, the expression "firearm" means a lethal barrelled weapon of any description from which any shot, bullet or other missile can be discharged and includes—

(a) any prohibited weapon, whether it is such a lethal weapon as aforesaid or not; and

(b) any component part of such a lethal or prohibited weapon; and

(c) any accessory to any such weapon designed or adapted to diminish the noise or flash caused by firing the weapon;

and so much of section 1 of this Act as excludes any description of firearm from the category of firearms to which that section applies shall be con- strued as also excluding component parts of, and accessories to firearms of, that description.

(2) In this Act, the expression "ammunition" means ammunition for any firearm and includes grenades, bombs and other like missiles, whether capable of use with a firearm or not, and also includes prohibited ammunition.

(4) In this Act—

"acquire" means hire, accept as a gift or borrow and "acquisition" shall be construed accordingly;

"air weapon" has the meaning assigned to it by section 1(3)(b) of this Act;

"shot gun" has the meaning assigned to it by section 1(3)(a) of this Act and in sections 3(1) and 45(2) of this Act and in the definition of "firearms dealer", includes any component part of a shot gun and any accessory to a shot gun designed or adapted to diminish the noise or flash caused by firing the gun;

SCHEDULE 6

PROSECUTION AND PUNISHMENT OF OFFENCES

PART I

TABLE OF PUNISHMENTS

Note.—The provisions in this Table are dealt with in the notes headed "offence" to ss. 22, 23, 24.

PART II

SUPPLEMENTARY PROVISIONS AS TO TRIAL AND PUNISHMENT OF OFFENCES

*   *   *   *   *

7. The court by which a person is convicted of an offence under section 22(4) or (5), 23(1) or 24(4) of this Act may make such order as it thinks fit as to the forfeiture or disposal of the air weapon or ammunition in respect of which the offence was committed.

8. The court by which a person is convicted of an offence under section 22(3), (4) or (5), 23(1) or 24(4) may make such order as it thinks fit as to the forfeiture or disposal of any firearm or ammunition found in his possession.

9. The court by which a person is convicted of an offence under section 24(3) of this Act may make such order as it thinks fit as to the forfeiture or disposal of the shot gun or ammunition in respect of which the offence was committed.

GAMING ACT, 1968

[1968 c. 65]

7. Special provisions as to persons under 18.—(1) No person under eighteen shall take part in gaming to which this Part of this Act applies on any premises to which section 6 of this Act applies.

(2) In the case of any such premises as are mentioned in section 6 (2) (a) of this Act, neither the holder of the licence or certificate nor any person employed by him shall knowingly allow a person under eighteen to take part in any such gaming on the premises.

(3) In the case of any such premises as are mentioned in paragraph (b) or paragraph (c) of section 6 (2) of this Act, neither the manager nor any person employed by him, or employed by the Secretary of State under his supervision, shall knowingly allow a person under eighteen to take part in any such gaming on the premises.

(4) In this section "the manager", in relation to any such premises as are mentioned in paragraph (b) or paragraph (c) of section 6 (2) of this Act, means any person who, in relation to those premises,—

    (a) where they are in England or Wales, is subject to the statutory provisions affecting the holders of licences by virtue of paragraph 8 of Schedule 9 to the Licensing Act, 1964, or

    (b) [*Applies to Scotland.*]

NOTES

Commencement.—See s. 54, *post.*

"Under eighteen".—See note "Computation of age", at p. 310 *ante.*

"Section 6".—This section makes provision as to gaming on premises licensed for retail sale of liquor.

Definitions.—See *ibid.*, s. 55.

Knowingly.—See note at p. 1074.

17. Exclusion of persons under 18.—Except as provided by section 20 or section 21 of this Act, no person under eighteen shall be present in any room while gaming to which this Part of this Act applies takes place in that room.

NOTES

Commencement.—See s. 54, *post.*

Ss. 20, 21.—S. 20 makes special provision for bingo clubs, and s. 21 for gaming for prizes. Ss. 20 (6) and 21 (4) permit the presence of persons under eighteen if they do not take part in the game or gaming respectively.

54. Short title, extent and commencement.—(1) This Act may be cited as the Gaming Act, 1968.

(2) This Act (except section 10 (4)) shall not extend to Northern Ireland.

(3) Sections 10, 43 (1), 48, 51 and 52 of this Act and this section and Schedule 1 to this Act shall come into operation on the passing of this Act.

(4) Subject to the last preceding subsection, the provisions of this Act shall come into operation on such day as the Secretary of State may by order appoint, and different days may be so appointed for different provisions of this Act or for different purposes (including, in the case of any provision of section 53 of this Act, the amendment or repeal of different enactments to which that provision is applicable).

(5) Any order made under this section may make such transitional provision as appears to the Secretary of State to be necessary or expedient in connection with the provisions of this Act which are thereby brought (wholly or in part) into force, including such adaptations of those provisions or any provision of this Act then in force as appear to him to be necessary or expedient in consequence of the partial operation of this Act (whether before, on or after the day appointed by the order).

SECTION 11.—MENTAL DISORDER

MENTAL HEALTH ACT, 1959
[7 & 8 Eliz. 2, c. 72]

General note.—Of the sections reproduced here, s. 10 alone extends to Scotland (see s. 150).

PART I

PRELIMINARY

4. Definition and classification of mental disorder.—(1) In this Act " mental disorder " means mental illness, arrested or incomplete development of mind, psychopathic disorder, and any other disorder or disability of mind; and " mentally disordered " shall be construed accordingly.

(2) In this Act " severe subnormality " means a state of arrested or incomplete development of mind which includes subnormality of intelligence and is of such a nature or degree that the patient is incapable of living an independent life or of guarding himself against serious exploitation, or will be so incapable when of an age to do so.

(3) In this Act " subnormality " means a state of arrested or incomplete development of mind (not amounting to severe subnormality) which includes subnormality of intelligence and is of a nature or degree which requires or is susceptible to medical treatment or other special care or training of the patient.

(4) In this Act " psychopathic disorder " means a persistent disorder or disability of mind (whether or not including subnormality of intelligence) which results in abnormally aggressive or seriously irresponsible conduct on the part of the patient, and requires or is susceptible to medical treatment.

(5) Nothing in this section shall be construed as implying that a person may be dealt with under this Act as suffering from mental disorder, or from any form of mental disorder described in this section, by reason only of promiscuity or other immoral conduct.

NOTES

" Mental illness."—This phrase is not defined.

" Medical treatment."—This includes nursing, and also includes care and training under medical supervision (see s. 147).

*   *   *   *

PART II

LOCAL AUTHORITY SERVICES

General Provisions

9. Functions of children authorities. (1) Any local authority for the purposes of the Children Act, 1948 (in this section referred to as a

442

children authority) may accommodate in homes provided under section thirty-eight of the Children and Young Persons Act, 1969 any child who, not being in their care within the meaning of Part II of the Children Act, 1948, is a person whose care or after-care is for the time being undertaken by that or any other authority as local health authority in pursuance of arrangements made under section twenty-eight of the National Health Service Act, 1946, or under section twenty-seven of the National Health Service (Scotland) Act, 1947, for the care or after-care of persons who are or have been suffering from mental disorder.

(2) Where a child whose care or after-care is for the time being undertaken by a local health authority in pursuance of such arrangements as aforesaid is accommodated in a home provided under the said Section thirty-eight by the same authority as children authority, the authority may make such adjustments as appear to them to be appropriate between the accounts kept by them as local health authority and the accounts kept by them as children authority.

(3) Nothing in this Act, or in any other enactment, shall be construed as preventing a children authority from receiving into their care under section one of the Children Act, 1948, a child who is mentally disordered, nor as preventing a local health authority from accommodating in pursuance of such arrangements as aforesaid any child who is in the care of that or any other authority as a children authority.

(4) In this section " child " has the same meaning as in the Children Act, 1948.

NOTES

This section is printed as amended by the National Health Service (Scotland) Act, 1960, and the Children and Young Persons Act, 1969, s. 72 (3) and Sched. V.

Transitional provisions.—Until the coming into operation of a regional plan for a particular planning area this section shall have effect as if a home provided by the local authority under Children Act, 1948, s. 15 were a community home so provided under the Children and Young Persons Act, 1969 (Sched. IV, para. 13, *ibid.*, and S.I. 1969 No. 1565, Sched. III).

" **Mental disorder.**"—For definition, see s. 4 (1), *ante.*

" **Child.**"—This means a person under the age of eighteen years; see s. 59 of the Children Act, 1948, p. 923, *post.*

" **Local health authority.**"—For definition, see s. 147 (1); see also s. 38 of the Children Act, 1948, p. 914, *post.*

10. Welfare of certain hospital patients.—(1) Subject to the provisions of this section, where a mentally disordered patient being—

(a) a child or young person in respect of whom the rights and powers of a parent are vested in a local authority by virtue of—

(i) section 24 of the Children and Young Persons Act, 1969 (which relates to the powers and duties of local authorities with respect to persons committed to their care in pursuance of that Act);

(ii) [*Repealed by the Social Work (Scotland) Act, 1968.*]

(iii) section three of the Children Act, 1948 (which relates to children in respect of whom parental rights have been assumed by a local authority under section two of that Act); or

(iv) section 17 of the Social Work (Scotland) Act, 1968 (which makes corresponding provision for Scotland).

(b) a person who is subject to the guardianship of a local health authority under the following provisions of this Act; or under the provisions of the Mental Health (Scotland) Act, 1960, or

(c) a person the functions of whose nearest relative under this Act or under the Mental Health (Scotland) Act, 1960, are for the time being transferred to a local health authority,

is admitted to a hospital or nursing home in England and Wales (whether for treatment for mental disorder or for any other reason) then, without prejudice to their duties in relation to the patient apart from the provisions of this section, the authority shall arrange for visits to be made to him on behalf of the authority, and shall take such other steps in relation to the patient while in the hospital or nursing home as would be expected to be taken by his parents.

(2) Section eight of the Children Act, 1948, and subsection (6) of section five of the Matrimonial Proceedings (Children) Act, 1958 (which provide for the removal from the care of local authorities of children who come under control under the enactments relating to mental deficiency or to lunacy and mental treatment) shall cease to have effect.

NOTES

This section is printed as amended by the Mental Health (Scotland) Act, 1960, the Social Work (Scotland) Act, 1968, ss. 95 (2) 98 and Sched. IX, Part II, and the Children and Young Persons Act, 1969, s. 72 (3) and Sched. V.

" Mental disorder"; " Mentally disordered."—See s. 4 (1), *ante*.

S. 24 of the Children and Young Persons Act, 1969.—See p. 167, *ante*.

S. 3 of the Children Act, 1948.—See p. 887, *post*.

" Hospital."—For definition, see s. 147.

" Nursing home."—Mental nursing home is defined in s. 14.

" Local health authority."—See note to s. 9, p. 443, *ante*.

Sub-s. (2).—These repeals enable the local authorities social services departments to keep in touch with children in hospitals.

" Guardianship. "—See ss. 33 *et seq.;* 25 Halsbury's Statutes, 3rd Edn., 70 *et seq.*

" Nearest relative."—See definition in s. 49.

Provision for care and training of children in lieu of education

11. Examination and classification under Education Act, 1944.— [*Sections 11–13 are repealed by the Education (Handicapped Children) Act, 1970, s. 2 and Sched.*]

*   *   *   *

PART IV

COMPULSORY ADMISSION TO HOSPITAL AND GUARDIANSHIP

FUNCTIONS OF RELATIVES OF PATIENTS

50. Children and young persons in care of local authority.—In any case where the rights and powers of a parent of a patient, being a child or young person, are vested in a local authority or other person by virtue of—

(a) section 24 of the Children and Young Persons Act, 1969 (which relates to the powers and duties of local authorities with respect to persons committed to their care in pursuance of that Act).

(b) [*Repealed by the Social Work (Scotland) Act, 1968.*]

(c) section three of the Children Act, 1948 (which relates to children in respect of whom parental rights have been assumed under section two of that Act), or

(d) section 17 of the Social Work (Scotland) Act, 1968 (which makes corresponding provision for Scotland),

that authority or person shall be deemed to be the nearest relative of the patient in preference to any person except the patient's husband or wife (if any) and except, in a case where the said rights and powers are vested in a local authority by virtue of subsection (2) of the said section three, or subsection (2) of the said section 17, any parent of the patient not being the person on whose account the resolution mentioned in that subsection was passed.

NOTES

This section is printed as amended by the Social Work (Scotland) Act, 1968, ss. 95, 97 and 98 and Scheds. VIII and IX, Part II and the Children and Young Persons Act, 1969, s. 72 (3) and Sched. V.

" **Patient.**"—This means a person suffering or appearing to be suffering from mental disorder (see s. 147).

PART V

ADMISSION OF PATIENTS CONCERNED IN CRIMINAL PROCEEDINGS, ETC., AND TRANSFER OF PATIENTS UNDER SENTENCE

Provisions for compulsory admission or guardianship of patients convicted of criminal offences, etc.

60. Powers of courts to order hospital admission or guardianship.—(1) Where a person is convicted before the Crown Court of an offence other than an offence the sentence for which is fixed by law, or is convicted by a magistrates' court of an offence punishable on summary conviction with imprisonment, and the following conditions are satisfied, that is to say—

(a) the court is satisfied, on the written or oral evidence of two medical practitioners (complying with the provisions of section sixty-two of this Act),—

(i) that the offender is suffering from mental illness psychopathic disorder, subnormality or severe subnormality; and

(ii) that the mental disorder is of a nature or degree which warrants the detention of the patient in a hospital for medical treatment, or the reception of the patient into guardianship under this Act; and

(b) the court is of opinion, having regard to all the circumstances including the nature of the offence and the character and antecedents of the offender, and to the other available methods of dealing with him, that the most suitable method of disposing of the case is by means of an order under this section,

the court may by order authorise his admission to and detention in such hospital as may be specified in the order or, as the case may be, place him under the guardianship of a local health authority or of such other person approved by a local health authority as may be so specified.

(2) Where a person is charged before a magistrates' court with any act or omission as an offence and the court would have power, on convicting him of that offence, to make an order under subsection (1) of this section in his case as being a person suffering from mental illness or severe subnormality, then, if the court is satisfied that the accused did the act or made the omission charged, the court may, if it thinks fit, make such an order without convicting him.

(3) An order for the admission of an offender to a hospital (in this Part of this Act referred to as a hospital order) shall not be made under this section unless the court is satisfied that arrangements have been made for the admission of the offender to that hospital in the event of such an order being made by the court, and for his admission thereto within a period of twenty-eight days beginning with the date of the making of such an order.

(4) An order placing an offender under the guardianship of a local health authority or of any other person (in this Part of this Act referred to as a guardianship order) shall not be made under this section unless the court is satisfied that that authority or person is willing to receive the offender into guardianship.

(5) A hospital order or guardianship order shall specify the form or forms of mental disorder referred to in paragraph (a) of subsection (1) of this section from which, upon the evidence taken into account under that paragraph, the offender is found by the court to be suffering; and no such order shall be made unless the offender is described by each of the practitioners whose evidence is taken into account as aforesaid as suffering from the same one of those forms of mental disorder, whether or not he is also described by either of them as suffering from another of those forms.

(6) Where an order is made under this section, the court shall not pass sentence of imprisonment or impose a fine or make a probation order in respect of the offence or make any such order as is mentioned in paragraphs (b) or (c) of section 7 (7) of the Children and Young Persons Act, 1969, in respect of the offender, but may make any other order which the court has power to make apart from this section; and for the purposes of this subsection "sentence of imprisonment" includes any sentence or order for detention.

NOTES

This section is printed as amended by the Children and Young Persons Act, 1969, s. 72 (3), (4) and Scheds. V and VI and the Courts Act, 1971.

"Medical practitioner"; "medical treatment."—For definition, see s. 147 of the Mental Health Act, 1959.

"Local health authority."—See note to s. 9, p. 443, *ante*.

"Mental disorder," etc.—The four forms of disorder are defined in s. 4, p. 442, *ante*.

"Order without convicting him."—The power conferred on magistrates' courts to commit to the Crown Court under s. 67, p. 451, *post*, is restricted to convicted offenders.

"Magistrates' court."—This includes a juvenile court. See s. 124 of the Magistrates' Courts Act, 1952; 21 Halsbury's Statutes, 3rd Edn., 286.

Medical evidence.—As to written reports, see s. 62, *infra*.

Regulations.—See the Mental Health (Hospital and Guardianship) Regulations, 1960, S.I. 1960, No. 1241.

Documents to be sent.—See Rules 27 and 62 of the Magistrates' Courts Rules, 1968, p. 556, *post*.

Forms.—For forms of hospital order and guardianship order see Forms Nos. 34, 42 and 35, 36, pp. 599, 542, *post*.

Offences not punishable with imprisonment.—For the procedure in cases of mentally disordered persons who commit such offences see Home Office circular No. 151/1961, p. 681, *post*.

Medical reports.—See s. 62 (3), (4) *post*.

Care proceedings.—See s. 1 (3), (5) (b) Children and Young Persons Act, 1969.

62. Requirements as to medical evidence.—(1) Of the medical practitioners whose evidence is taken into account under paragraph (a) of subsection (1) of section sixty of this Act, at least one shall be a practitioner approved for the purposes of section twenty-eight of this Act by a local health authority as having special experience in the diagnosis or treatment of mental disorders.

(2) For the purposes of the said paragraph (a) a report in writing purporting to be signed by a medical practitioner may, subject to the provisions of this section, be received in evidence without proof of the signature or qualifications of the practitioner; but the court may in any case require that the practitioner by whom such a report was signed be called to give oral evidence.

(3) Where, in pursuance of directions of the court, any such report as aforesaid is tendered in evidence otherwise than by or on behalf of the accused, then—

(a) if the accused is represented by counsel or solicitor, a copy of the report shall be given to his counsel or solicitor;

(b) if the accused is not so represented, the substance of the report shall be disclosed to the accused or, where he is a child or young person, to his parent or guardian if present in court;

(c) in any case, the accused may require that the practitioner by whom the report was signed be called to give oral evidence, and evidence to rebut the evidence contained in the report may be called by or on behalf of the accused.

(4) In relation to a child or young person brought before a juvenile court under section 1 of the Children and Young Persons Act, 1969, subsection (3) of this section shall have effect as if for references to the accused there were substituted references to the child or young person.

NOTES

This section is printed as amended by the Children and Young Persons Acts, 1963 and 1969. See also s. 26 of the Act of 1963, p. 97, *ante*.

"**Child** "; "**young person** "; "**guardian.**"—For definitions, see s. 80 of the Mental Health Act, 1959, and s. 107 of the Children and Young Persons Act, 1933, p. 81, *ante*.

"**Local health authority.**"—See note to s. 9, p. 443, *ante*.

"**Report in writing.**"—The provisions about disclosure of written reports are slightly different from, and will presumably override, those in Rules 11 and 22 of the Magistrates' Courts (Children and Young Persons) Rules, 1970, pp. 574, 579, *post*.

Documents to be sent.—See Rules 27 and 62 of the Magistrates' Courts Rules, 1968, pp. 556, 559, *post*.

Forms.—For forms of—
  Hospital order in care proceedings, see Form 34, p. 599, *post*;
  Guardianship order in care proceedings, see Form 42, p. 603, *post*.

"**Medical practitioner.**"—For definition, see s. 147.

Mental disorder.—For definition, see s. 4, p. 442, *ante*.

63. Effects of hospital orders and guardianship orders.—(1) A hospital order shall be sufficient authority—

  (a) for a constable, a mental welfare officer or any other person directed to do so by the court to convey the patient to the hospital specified in the order within a period of twenty-eight days; and

  (b) for the managers of the hospital to admit him at any time within that period and thereafter detain him in accordance with the provisions of this Act.

(2) A guardianship order shall confer on the authority or person therein named as guardian the like powers as a guardianship application made and accepted under Part IV of this Act.

(3) A patient who is admitted to a hospital in pursuance of a hospital order, or placed under guardianship by a guardianship order, shall be treated for the purposes of Part IV of this Act (other than sections thirty-one and thirty-two, or section thirty-four, as the case may be) as if he had been so admitted or placed on the date of the order in pursuance of an application for admission for treatment or a guardianship application, as the case may be, duly made under the said Part IV, except that—

  (a) the power to order the discharge of the patient under section forty-seven shall not be exercisable by his nearest relative; and

  (b) the special provisions relating to the expiration and renewal of authority for detention and guardianship in the case of psychopathic and subnormal patients shall not apply;

and accordingly the provisions of the said Part IV specified in the first column of the Third Schedule to this Act shall apply in relation to him subject to the exceptions and modifications set out in the second column of that Schedule and the remaining provisions of the said Part IV shall not apply.

(4) Without prejudice to any provision of Part IV of this Act as applied by this section, an application to a Mental Health Review Tribunal may be made in respect of a patient admitted to a hospital in pursuance of a hospital order, or placed under guardianship by a guardian-h p order, as follows, that is to say—

    (a) by the patient, within the period of six months beginning with the date of the order or with the day on which he attains the age of sixteen years, whichever is the later;

    (b) by the nearest relative of the patient, within the period of twelve months beginning with the date of the order, and in any subsequent period of twelve months.

(5) Where a patient is admitted to a hospital in pursuance of a hospital order, or placed under guardianship by a guardianship order, any previous application, hospital order or guardianship order by virtue of which he was liable to be detained in a hospital or subject to guardianship shall cease to have effect:

Provided that if the first-mentioned order, or the conviction on which it was made, is quashed on appeal, this subsection shall not apply and section forty-six of this Act shall have effect as if during any period for which the patient was liable to be detained or subject to guardianship under the order, he had been detained in custody as mentioned in that section.

NOTES

" **Guardianship order** "; "**hospital order.**"—For definition, see s. 60, p. 445, *ante*; and see also ss. 26 to 34.

" **Nearest relative.**"—See Part IV.

" **Patient.**"—This is defined by s. 147 as a person suffering or appearing to be suffering from mental disorder (see s. 4, p. 442, *ante*).

Psychopathic disorder, subnormality.—For definition, see s. 4, p. 442, *ante*.

Custody, conveyance and detention.—See s. 139.

Application.—For the application of Part IV of the Act to patients admitted to hospital or placed under guardianship under Part V (which relates to criminal proceedings), see Sched. III.

64. Supplementary provisions as to hospital orders.—(1) The court by which a hospital order is made may give such directions as it thinks fit for the conveyance of the patient to a place of safety and his detention therein pending his admission to the hospital within the period of twenty-eight days referred to in subsection (1) of section sixty-three of this Act.

(2) If within the said period of twenty-eight days it appears to the Minister that by reason of an emergency or other special circumstances it is not practicable for the patient to be received into the hospital specified in the order, he may give directions for the admission of the patient to such other hospital as appears to be appropriate in lieu of the hospital so specified; and where such directions are given the Minister

shall cause the person having the custody of the patient to be informed, and the hospital order shall have effect as if the hospital specified in the directions were substituted for the hospital specified in the order.

NOTES

" **Hospital order.**"—See s. 60, p. 445, *ante*.

" **Patient.**"—See note to s. 50, p. 445, *ante*.

" **Place of safety.**"—By s. 80, this is defined in relation to a child or young person as a place of safety within the meaning of the Children and Young Persons Act, 1933. See s. 107 of that Act, p. 81, *ante*.

Custody, conveyance and detention.—See s. 139 of the Mental Health Act, 1959.

" **Minister.**"—This means the Minister of Health (see s. 147).

65. Power of higher courts to restrict discharge from hospital.—(1) Where a hospital order is made in respect of an offender by the Crown Court, and it appears to the court, having regard to the nature of the offence, the antecedents of the offender and the risk of his committing further offences if set at large, that it is necessary for the protection of the public so to do, the court may, subject to the provisions of this section, further order that the offender shall be subject to the special restrictions set out in this section, either without limit of time or during such period as may be specified in the order.

(2) An order under this section (in this Act referred to as an order restricting discharge) shall not be made in the case of any person unless at least one of the medical practitioners whose evidence is taken into account by the court under paragraph (a) of subsection (1) of section sixty of this Act has given evidence orally before the court.

(3) The special restrictions applicable to a patient in respect of whom an order restricting discharge is in force are as follows, that is to say—

> (a) none of the provisions of Part IV of this Act relating to the duration, renewal and expiration of authority for the detention of patients shall apply, and the patient shall continue to be liable to be detained by virtue of the relevant hospital order until he is duly discharged under the said Part IV or absolutely discharged under the next following section ;
>
> (b) no application shall be made to a Mental Health Review Tribunal in respect of the patient under section sixty-three of this Act or under any provision of the said Part IV ;
>
> (c) the following powers shall be exercisable only with the consent of the Secretary of State, that is to say—
>
>> (i) power to grant leave of absence to the patient under section thirty-nine of this Act;
>>
>> (ii) power to transfer the patient in pursuance of regulations under section forty-one of this Act ; and
>>
>> (iii) power to order the discharge of the patient under section forty-seven of this Act ;
>
> and if leave of absence is granted under the said section thirty-nine the power to recall the patient under that section shall be vested in the Secretary of State as well as the responsible medical officer ; and

(d) the power of the Secretary of State to recall the patient under the said section thirty-nine, and the power to take the patient into custody and return him under section forty of this Act, may be exercised at any time;

and in relation to any such patient the provisions of the said Part IV described in the first column of the Third Schedule to this Act shall have effect to the exceptions and modifications set out in the third column of that Schedule in lieu of those set out in the second column of that Schedule.

(4) A hospital order shall not cease to have effect under subsection (5) of section sixty-three of this Act if an order restricting the discharge of the patient is in force at the material time.

(5) Where an order restricting the discharge of a patient ceases to have effect while the relevant hospital order continues in force, the provisions of section sixty-three of this Act and the Third Schedule to this Act shall apply to the patient as if he had been admitted to the hospital in pursuance of a hospital order (without an order restricting his discharge) made on the date on which the order restricting his discharge ceased to have effect.

NOTES

This section is printed as amended by the Courts Act, 1971.

" **Hospital order.**"—See s. 60, p. 445, *ante*, and definition in s. 147.

" **Medical practitioner** "; " **patient.**"—For definition, see s. 147, *ibid.*

" **Responsible medical officer.**"—For definition, see s. 80, *ibid.*

Restriction order.—As to the effect of a restriction order see *R. v. Higginbotham*, [1961] 3 All E. R. 616; 125 J. P. 642, C.C.A. In that case a hospital order had been made in respect of the appellant, coupled with an order restricting the hospital from discharging him without the consent of the Secretary of State, under this section. He walked out of the hospital and committed other offences. On the hearing of his appeal against sentence imposed on him for those offences, Glyn-Jones, J., giving the judgment of the court on dismissing the appeal, said that it might be useful if the court said that it was unsafe for courts to assume that the making of a hospital order coupled with a restrictive order under s. 65 was sufficient by itself to ensure that the convicted person would be kept in safe custody. The only way in which that could be achieved was for the courts to ascertain first, before making the order, which mental hospital could receive the man. That must be done; and, further, the court must find out whether the hospital had facilities for keeping patients in safe custody so that they would not have the opportunity to walk out and commit a crime. There were such institutions; and, if there was no vacancy in them, it must be pointed out that the powers of the court to make a hospital order were permissive and not mandatory. If, for the protection of the public, the court thought it necessary that an accused man should be incarcerated, the ordinary penal jurisdiction should be used, leaving it to the medical authorities to make arrangements for appropriate medical treatment, if it were necessary, in some place where the man would be kept in safe custody, so that the kind of thing which happened in this case could be avoided.

67. Power of magistrates' courts to commit for restriction order.—(1) If in the case of a person of or over the age of fourteen years who is convicted by a magistrates' court of an offence punishable on summary conviction with imprisonment—

(a) the conditions which, under subsection (1) of section sixty of this Act, are required to be satisfied for the making of a hospital order are satisfied in respect of the offender; but

    (b) it appears to the court, having regard to the nature of the offence, the antecedents of the offender and the risk of his committing further offences if set at large, that if a hospital order is made an order restricting his discharge should also be made,

the court may, instead of making a hospital order or dealing with him in any other manner, commit him in custody to the Crown Court to be dealt with in respect of the offence.

    (2) [*Repealed by the Courts Act, 1971, s. 56 and Sched. XI, Part IV.*]

    (3) Where an offender is committed to the Crown Court under this section, the Crown Court shall inquire into the circumstances of the case and may—

    (a) if that court would have power so to do under the foregoing provisions of this Part of this Act upon the conviction of the offender before that court of such an offence as is described in subsection (1) of section sixty of this Act, make a hospital order in his case, with or without an order restricting his discharge;

    (b) if the court does not make such an order, deal with the offender in any other manner in which the magistrates' court might have dealt with him.

    (4) The power of a magistrates' court under section twenty-nine of the Magistrates' Courts Act, 1952 (which enables such a court to commit an offender to the Crown Court where the court is of opinion that greater punishment should be inflicted for the offence than the court has power to inflict) shall also be exercisable by a magistrates' court where it is of opinion that greater punishment should be inflicted as aforesaid on the offender unless a hospital order is made in his case with an order restricting his discharge.

    (5) The power of the Crown Court to make a hospital order, with or without an order restricting discharge, in the case of a person convicted before that court of an offence may, in the like circumstances and subject to the like conditions, be exercised by such a court in the case of a person committed to the court under section five of the Vagrancy Act, 1824 (which provides for the committal to the Crown Court of persons being incorrigible rogues within the meaning of that section).

NOTES

    This section is printed as amended by the Criminal Justice Act, 1967, s. 105 and Sched. VII, and the Courts Act, 1971.

    " Hospital order."—See s. 60, p. 445, *ante*.

    Hospital, committed to.—See s. 68, *infra*.

    " Magistrates' court."—See note to s. 60, p. 445, *ante*.

    Committal to Crown Court for order restricting discharge, etc.—See Rule 17 of the Magistrates' Courts Rules, 1968, p. 555, *post*.

    Forms.—For form of commitment to the Crown Court for restriction order, see Form No. 43, p. 544, *post*.

    For form of commitment to the Crown Court for restriction order or sentence, see Form No. 44, p. 545, *post*.

    Legal Aid.—See Criminal Justice Act, 1967, s. 73 (4), p. 327, *ante*.

"**Duration of sentence.**"—See Criminal Justice Administration Act, 1962, s. 17.

Constitution of Crown Court.—Where the Crown Court deals with the case of a person committed by a juvenile court under this section the judge shall (where practicable) sit with two justices each of whom is a member of a juvenile court panel and also are chosen so that the court shall include a man and a woman (Crown Court Rules, 1971, r. 3).

Protection of public.—In the Court of Appeal, Criminal Division, on an application to abandon an appeal against a sentence of imprisonment the court took the opportunity to deal with general matters which should be borne in mind by courts dealing with prisoners under the Mental Health Act, 1959, in the hope that they would be of some use to courts and particularly to magistrates' courts which cannot make restriction orders but must commit to the Crown Court before such orders can be made (*R.* v. *Gardiner*, [1967] 1 All E. R. 895; 131 J. P. 273).

68. Committal to hospital under s. 67.—(1) Where an offender is committed under subsection (1) of section sixty-seven of this Act and the magistrates' court by which he is committed is satisfied that arrangements have been made for the admission of the offender to a hospital in the event of an order being made under this section, the court may, instead of committing him in custody, by order direct him to be admitted to that hospital, specifying it, and to be detained there until the case is disposed of by the Crown Court, and may give such directions as it thinks fit for his production from the hospital to attend the Crown Court by which his case is to be dealt with.

(2) Subsection (1) of section sixty-three and section sixty-four of this Act shall apply in relation to an order under this section as they apply in relation to a hospital order, but as if references to the period of twenty-eight days mentioned in the said subsection (1) were omitted; and subject as aforesaid an order under this section shall, until the offender's case is disposed of by the Crown Court have the like effect as a hospital order together with an order restricting his discharge, made without limitation of time.

(3) [*Repealed by the Courts Act,* 1971.]

NOTES

This section is printed as amended by the Courts Act, 1971, s. 56 and Sched. XI, Part IV.

"**Hospital order.**"—See s. 60, p. 445, *ante.*

Documents to be sent.—See Rule 27 of the Magistrates' Courts Rules, 1968, p. 556, *post.*

Forms.—For form of order to admission to hospital pending restriction order, see Form 45, p. 545, *post.*

70. Appeals from magistrates' courts.—(1) Where on the trial of an information charging a person with an offence a magistrates' court makes a hospital order or guardianship order in respect of him without convicting him, he shall have the like right of appeal against the order as if it had been made on his conviction; and on any such appeal the Crown Court shall have the like powers as if the appeal had been against both conviction and sentence.

(2) [*Repealed by the Children and Young Persons Act,* 1969.]

(3) An appeal by a child or young person with respect to whom any such order has been made, whether the appeal is against the order or against the finding upon which the order was made, may be brought by him or by his parent or guardian on his behalf.

(4) [*Repealed by the Courts Act,* 1971.]

NOTES

This section is printed as amended by the Children and Young Persons Act, 1963, the Children and Young Persons Act, 1969, s. 72 (4) and Sched. VI and the Courts Act, 1971, s. 56 and Scheds. VIII and XI, Part IV.

" **Child** "; " **young person** "; " **guardian.**"—For definition, see s. 80 of the Mental Health Act, 1959, and s. 107 of the Children and Young Persons Act, 1933, p. 81, *ante.*

" **Hospital order** "; " **guardianship order.**"—See s. 60 of the Mental Health Act, p. 445, *ante.*

Legal Aid.—See s. 73 (3), Criminal Justice Act, 1967.

Transfer to hospital or guardianship of prisoners, etc.

72. Removal to hospital of persons serving sentences of imprisonment, etc.—(1) If in the case of a person serving a sentence of imprisonment the Secretary of State is satisfied, by reports from at least two medical practitioners (complying with the provisions of this section)—

(a) that the said person is suffering from mental illness, psychopathic disorder, subnormality or severe subnormality; and

(b) that the mental disorder is of a nature or degree which warrants the detention of the patient in a hospital for medical treatment;

the Secretary of State may, if he is of opinion having regard to the public interest and all the circumstances that it is expedient so to do, by warrant direct that that person be removed to and detained in such hospital (not being a mental nursing home) as may be specified in the direction.

(2) A direction under this section (in this Act referred to as a transfer direction) shall cease to have effect at the expiration of the period of fourteen days beginning with the date on which it is given unless within that period the person with respect to whom it was given has been received into the hospital specified therein.

(3) A transfer direction with respect to any person shall have the like effect as a hospital order made in his case.

(4) Of the medical practitioners whose reports are taken into account under subsection (1) of this section, at least one shall be a practitioner approved for the purposes of section twenty-eight of this Act by a local health authority as having special experience in the diagnosis or treatment of mental disorders.

(5) A transfer direction shall specify the form or forms of mental disorder referred to in paragraph (a) of subsection (1) of this section from which, upon the reports taken into account under that subsection, the patient is found by the Secretary of State to be suffering; and no such direction shall be given unless the patient is described in each of

those reports as suffering from the same one of those forms, whether or not he is also described in either of them as suffering from another of those forms.

(6) References in this section to a person serving a sentence of imprisonment include references—

(a) to a person detained in pursuance of any sentence or order for detention made by a court in criminal proceedings (other than an order under any enactment to which section seventy-one of this Act applies);

(b) to a person committed to custody under subsection (3) of section ninety-one of the Magistrates' Courts Act, 1952 (which relates to persons who fail to comply with an order to enter into recognisances to keep the peace or be of good behaviour); and

(c) to a person committed by a court to a prison or other institution to which the Prison Act, 1952, applies in default of payment of any sum adjudged to be paid on his conviction.

NOTES

This section is printed as amended by the Children and Young Persons Acts, 1963 and 1969.

" Hospital order."—See s. 60, p. 445, ante.

" Medical practitioners "; " medical treatment "; " patient."—For definitions, see s. 147.

73. Removal to hospital of other prisoners.—(1) If in the case of a person to whom this section applies the Secretary of State is satisfied by the like reports as are required for the purposes of the last foregoing section that that person is suffering from mental illness or severe subnormality of a nature or degree which warrants the detention of the patient in a hospital for medical treatment, the Secretary of State shall have the like power of giving a transfer direction in respect of him under that section as if he were serving a sentence of imprisonment.

(2) This section applies to the following persons, that is to say—

(a) persons committed in custody for trial at the Crown Court or committed in custody to the Crown Court under section six or section eight of the Criminal Justice Act, 1948;

(b) persons committed in custody to the Crown Court under section twenty-eight or section twenty-nine of the Magistrates' Courts Act, 1952, section five of the Vagrancy Act, 1824, or section sixty-seven of this Act;

(c) persons remanded in custody by the Crown Court to await a judgment or sentence which has been respited;

(d) persons remanded in custody by a magistrates' court;

(e) civil prisoners, that is to say, persons committed by a court to prison for a limited term (including persons committed to prison in pursuance of a writ of attachment), not being persons falling to be dealt with under section seventy-two of this Act;

(f) aliens detained in a prison or other institution to which the Prison Act, 1952, applies, in pursuance of the Aliens Order, 1953, or any order amending or replacing that Order.

(3) Subsections (2) to (5) of the last foregoing section shall apply for the purposes of this section and of any transfer direction given by virtue of this section as they apply for the purposes of that section and of any transfer direction thereunder.

NOTES

This section is printed as amended by the Criminal Justice Act, 1961 and the Courts Act, 1971.

" **Medical treatment.**"—For definition, see s. 147.

" **Transfer direction.**"—See s. 72 (2), p. 454, *ante.*

" **Mental illness** "; " **severe subnormality.**"—See s. 4, p. 442, *ante.*

Notice on committal of person subject to transfer direction.—See Rule 9 of the Magistrates' Courts Rules, 1968.

Notice of further remand in certain cases.—See Rule 24, *ibid.*

Forms.—For form of notice on committal for trial of person subject to transfer direction under s. 73, see Form 16, *ibid.*

74. Restriction on discharge of prisoners removed to hospital.—

(1) Where a transfer direction is given in respect of any person, the Secretary of State, if he thinks fit, may by warrant further direct that that person shall be subject to the special restrictions set out in section sixty-five of this Act; and where the Secretary of State gives a transfer direction in respect of any such person as is described in paragraphs (a) to (d) of subsection (2) of the last foregoing section, he shall also give a direction under this section applying the said restrictions to him.

(2) A direction under this section (in this Act referred to as a direction restricting discharge) shall have the like effect as an order restricting the discharge of the patient made under the said section sixty-five.

77. Further provisions as to persons remanded by magistrates' courts.—

(1) A transfer direction given in respect of a person remanded in custody by a magistrates' court shall cease to have effect on the expiration of the period of remand unless, upon his being brought before the magistrates' court, he is committed in custody for trial at the Crown Court.

(2) Where, on the expiration of the period of remand of any such person, he is committed in custody for trial as aforesaid, section seventy-six of this Act shall apply as if the transfer direction given in his case were a direction given in respect of a person so committed.

(3) Where a transfer direction has been given in respect of a person remanded as aforesaid, the power of further remanding him under section one hundred and five of the Magistrates' Courts Act, 1952, may be exercised by the court without his being brought before the court; and if the

court further remands such a person in custody (whether or not he is brought before the court) the period of remand shall, for the purposes of this section, be deemed not to have expired.

(4) Where a transfer direction in respect of any person ceases to have effect under this section, then unless the court before which he is brought on the expiration of the period of remand—

(a) passes a sentence of imprisonment (within the meaning of sub-section (6) of section sixty of this Act) on him; or

(b) makes a hospital order or guardianship order in his case,

he shall continue to be liable to be detained in the hospital in which he was detained under the transfer direction as if he had been admitted thereto, on the date on which that direction ceased to have effect, in pursuance of an application for admission for treatment made under Part IV of this Act, and the provisions of this Act shall apply accordingly.

NOTES

This section is printed as amended by the Courts Act, 1971.

" Hospital order "; **" guardianship order."**—See s. 60, p. 445, *ante.*

" Transfer direction."—See s. 72 (2), p. 454, *ante.*

Section 105 of the Magistrates' Courts Act, 1952.—See p. 383, *ante.*

Section 76.—This refers to persons committed for trial or sentence.

79. Reception into guardianship of persons sent to approved schools.—[*Repealed by the Children and Young Persons Act, 1969, s. 72 (4) and Sched. VI.*]

PART IX

MISCELLANEOUS AND GENERAL

Supplemental

153. Commencement.—(1) This Act (except this section) shall come into operation on such date as the Minister may by order appoint.

(2) Different dates may be appointed by order under this section for different purposes of this Act; and any reference in any provision of this Act to the commencement of this Act shall, unless otherwise provided by any such order, be construed as a reference to the date on which that provision comes into operation.

(3) Without prejudice to section thirty-seven of the Interpretation Act, 1889 (which authorises the exercise of statutory powers between the passing and the commencement of an Act conferring them), the following powers, that is to say—

(a) the power of the Minister to give directions under subsection (1) of section twenty-eight of the National Health Service Act, 1946, for defining the duties of local health authorities under that section as amended by this Act; and

(b) the powers of the Minister and of local health authorities with respect to the submission, approval or making of proposals under section twenty of that Act for modifying in the light of such directions the proposals in force at the passing of this Act for the carrying out of the duties of those authorities under the said section twenty-eight,

may be exercised at any time after the passing of this Act.

NOTES

" **Local health authorities.**"—See note to s. 9, p. 443, *ante.*
" **Minister.**"—This means the Minister of Health (see s. 147).

SECOND SCHEDULE

[Section 11]

[*Repealed by the Education (Handicapped Children) Act,* 1970.]

SECTION 12.—STATUTORY RULES, ORDERS, INSTRUMENTS, BY-LAWS AND OFFICIAL CIRCULARS

I.—STATUTORY RULES, ORDERS AND INSTRUMENTS

CONTENTS   PAGE

THE APPROVED SCHOOL RULES, 1933

[S. R. & O. 1933, No. 774]

[These rules are printed as amended by the Approved School Rules, 1949, 1963 and 1970.]

1. These Rules may be cited as The Approved School Rules, 1933.

2. These Rules shall come into operation on the first day of November, 1933.

3. In these Rules the following expressions have the meanings hereby respectively assigned to them, that is to say—

" the Act " means the Children and Young Persons Act, 1933.

" School " means a school approved by the Secretary of State under section 79 of the Children and Young Persons Act, 1933.

" Managers " in relation to an approved school established or taken over by a local authority or by a joint committee representing two or more local authorities means the local authority or the joint committee, as the case may be, and in relation to any other approved school means the persons for the time being having the management or control thereof.

"Local authority school" means an approved school established or taken over by a local authority or by a joint committee representing two or more local authorities.

"Chief Inspector" means the Chief Inspector appointed by the Secretary of State under section 103 of the Children and Young Persons Act, 1933, for the purposes of the enactments relating to children and young persons.

Management

4. Two at least of the Managers of a boys' school shall be women, and two at least of the Managers of a girls' school shall be men.

5. The Managers shall appoint a Finance Committee and such other Committees as they think necessary for the efficient management of the school. Any Committee so appointed shall have such powers or duties as the Managers may determine.

6. The Managers shall appoint one of their number to be Chairman. They shall also appoint a Correspondent and a Treasurer. No member of the staff of the school shall be eligible for appointment as Correspondent or Treasurer.

7. The Correspondent shall notify to the Secretary of State the names and addresses of the Managers of the school and shall similarly notify any change due to death, retirement or other cause.

8.—(1) The Managers shall meet so far as practicable once a month at the school.

(2) A sufficient number of Managers to ensure adequate supervision shall be resident within a reasonable distance of the school.

9. The Managers and any Committee appointed by them shall keep minutes of their proceedings and these minutes shall be open to inspection by or on behalf of the Chief Inspector and by or on behalf of the District Auditor.

10.—(1) The Managers shall maintain an efficient standard throughout the school and for this purpose they shall take into consideration any report which may be communicated to them by or on behalf of the Secretary of State.

(2) It shall be the duty of the Managers to ensure that the condition of the school and the training, welfare and education of the boys resident in the school are satisfactory, and for this purpose they shall pay frequent visits to the school.

(3) The school shall be visited at least once a month by at least one Manager who shall satisfy himself regarding the care of the boys and the state of the school, or some part of it, and shall enter his conclusions in the Log Book or other convenient record kept at the school.

(4) The Managers shall exercise an effective control over all expenditure.

11. The name of the school shall be chosen by the Managers subject to the approval of the Secretary of State.

12. Rules 4, 5, 6, 7, 8 and 9 shall not apply where supplementary rules to the like effect made by the Managers of a local authority school under paragraph 1 (2) of the Fourth Schedule to the Act, have been approved by the Secretary of State.

Accommodation

13.—(1) The number of boys resident in a school at any time, shall not exceed such number as may be fixed for that school from time to time by the Secretary of State.

(2) Except with the special authority of the Secretary of State the Managers shall not receive or retain in the school any boy otherwise than in accordance with the classification of the school as determined by the Secretary of State in pursuance of section eighty-one of the Act.

Appointment of Staff

14.—(1) The Managers shall be responsible for the appointment, suspension or dismissal of the staff of the school:

Provided that no appointment as Headmaster (which expression in these Rules includes a Principal) shall be made without the prior approval of the Secretary of State.

(2) Any vacancy for a Headmaster shall be advertised unless the Managers obtain the consent of the Secretary of State to dispense with this requirement.

15. The Headmaster, Deputy Headmaster, matron, teachers, housemasters and instructors shall be employed under a written agreement or, in the case of a local authority school, under a minute of the local authority.

16. Except with the consent of the Secretary of State no member of the staff shall be retained after he has reached the age of 65 years.

17. In every school, not being a local authority school, the Managers shall cause to be given to every member of the staff who is not eligible for superannuation under the Teachers Superannuation Acts immediately on his appointment a copy of the superannuation scheme approved by the Secretary of State, and shall take such steps as are necessary to allow any eligible member to enter the scheme.

Headmaster

18. The Headmaster shall be responsible to the Managers for the efficient conduct of the school.

He shall keep a Register of Admissions and Discharges in which shall be recorded all admissions, and discharges; a Log Book in which shall be entered every event of importance connected with the school; a Daily Register of the presence or absence of each boy; and a Punishment Book. These shall be available for inspection by the Managers at all times. The Log Book shall be laid before the Managers at each of their meetings and shall be signed by the Chairman.

The Headmaster shall not incur any expenditure other than petty expenditure within a limit approved by the Managers, without their previous sanction or that of a Manager authorised to act on their behalf.

19. The Headmaster with the approval of the Managers shall determine the duties of the other members of the staff. These duties may include duties connected with the supervision of the boys in the school, and their recreation.

20. The Headmaster shall obtain the authority of the Managers and shall also notify the Chief Inspector before leaving the school for more than two days.

21.—(1) Where there is no Deputy Headmaster, the Managers shall appoint in writing the Principal Teacher or other experienced member of the staff to exercise the functions of the Headmaster during the Headmaster's absence and shall communicate to the Chief Inspector the name of the person so appointed.

(2) The Deputy Headmaster (or, as the case may be, the person appointed under paragraph (1) of this Rule) shall exercise the functions of the Headmaster during the Headmaster's absence and such of these Rules as relate to the powers and duties of the Headmaster shall apply accordingly.

Care of Boys

23. Each boy shall be provided with a separate bed and shall be kept supplied with suitable clothing similar to that worn in ordinary life.

24. The boys shall be supplied with sufficient and varied food based on a dietary scale to be drawn up by the Managers after consultation with the Headmaster and Medical Officer. The dietary scale shall include a list of dishes and a table of quantities to be supplied to each boy.

The dietary scale shall be subject to the approval of the Chief Inspector and, subject to the provisions of Rule 34 (ii), no substantial alteration shall be made in it without his approval.   A copy shall be kept posted in the school kitchen.

School Routine

25. The Daily Routine of the school (including the hours of rising, school-room instruction and practical training, domestic work, meals, recreation and retiring) shall be in accordance with a scheme approved from time to time by the Chief Inspector.

A copy of the Daily Routine shall be kept posted in some conspicuous place in the school.

Any substantial deviation from the Daily Routine shall be entered in the Log Book and a notification shall be sent forthwith to the Chief Inspector.

Education

26.—(1) The education given in the school shall be based on the principles of the Education Act, 1944, so as to secure efficient full-time primary or secondary education suitable to the age, ability and aptitude of each individual boy while of compulsory school age and his further education thereafter as long as he remains in the school.

(2) The schoolroom time table and syllabus shall be subject to the approval of the Chief Inspector and a copy of the time table shall be kept posted in the schoolroom.

26A.—(1) The practical training of all boys shall be in accordance with a scheme approved from time to time by the Chief Inspector.

(2) Any substantial deviation from the scheme shall be recorded in the Log Book and a notification shall be sent forthwith to the Chief Inspector.

(3) The practical training given to boys over compulsory school age shall so far as practicable be directed to their preparation for a particular form of employment: regard shall be had to the capacity and preference of each boy and in all suitable cases the parent or guardian shall be consulted.

27. The attendance of boys in the schoolroom and at all classes of practical training shall be recorded in a form prescribed by the Chief Inspector.

Employment

28. No boy shall be employed in such a way as to impair his capacity for profiting by instruction or to deprive him of reasonable recreation and leisure. Boys under twelve shall not be employed except in light work such as making their own beds or cleaning their own boots.

Religious Instruction

29. Each day shall be begun with simple worship.   So far as practicable arrangements shall be made for the attendance of the boys each Sunday at a place of public worship.

Religious instruction shall be given suited to the age and capacity of the boys.

Where a school for boys of a particular religious persuasion has consented to receive a boy who does not belong to that religious persuasion the Managers shall so far as practicable arrange for him to receive religious assistance and instruction from a minister of the religious persuasion to which he belongs.

Recreation, Visits and Letters

30.—(1) Adequate provision shall be made for free time and recreation, including organised games and walks and visits outside the school boundaries; and except in bad weather at least one hour daily shall be spent in the open air.

(2) If a cadet contingent is maintained at the school, enlistment shall not be compulsory and training or drill shall not be used as a means of enforcing school discipline.

31. Boys shall be encouraged to write to their parents at least once a month and for this purpose postage stamps shall be provided by the Managers.

31A.—Boys shall be allowed to receive letters from their parents, relatives and friends, and, at such reasonable intervals as the Managers may determine, visits from them.

32. Arrangements shall be made for the giving of pocket money each week subject to such conditions as may be approved by the Chief Inspector.

32A. The Headmaster may suspend any of the facilities mentioned in Rules 31A and 32 of these Rules if he is satisfied that they interfere with the discipline of the school: any such suspension shall be recorded in the Log Book.

Discipline and Punishment

33. The discipline of the school shall be maintained by the personal influence of the Headmaster and staff and shall be promoted by a system of rewards and privileges, which shall be subject to the approval of the Chief Inspector.

34. When punishment is necessary for the maintenance of discipline, one of the following methods shall be adopted :—

    (i) Forfeiture of rewards or privileges (including pocket-money) or temporary loss of recreation.

    (ii) Alteration of meals for a period not exceeding three days : provided that any such alteration shall be within the limits of a special dietary scale approved by the Chief Inspector.

    (iii) Separation from other boys : provided that this punishment shall only be used in exceptional cases and subject to the following conditions :—

        (a) No boys under the age of twelve shall be kept in separation.

        (b) The room used for the purpose shall be light and airy and kept lighted after dark.

        (c) Some form of occupation shall be given.

        (d) Means of communication with a member of the staff shall be provided.

        (e) If the separation is to be continued for more than 24 hours the written consent of one of the Managers shall be obtained and the circumstances shall be reported immediately to the Chief Inspector.

    (iv) Corporal punishment. Every effort shall be made to enforce discipline without resort to corporal punishment. Where it is found necessary its application shall be in strict accordance with Rule 35 or 36 as the case may be.

35. Corporal punishment in boys' schools shall be subject to the following conditions :—

    (a) It shall be inflicted only with a cane or tawse of a type approved by the Secretary of State.

    (b) If applied on the hands, the cane shall be used and the number of strokes shall not exceed three on each hand, but no boy over fifteen shall be so punished.

(c) If applied on the posterior with a cane or tawse, it shall be applied
    over the boy's ordinary cloth trousers and the number of strokes
    shall not exceed six for boys under fifteen or eight for boys of
    fifteen and over : provided that in exceptional cases, with the
    special approval of one of the Managers, twelve strokes may be
    administered to boys of fifteen and over.

(d) No boy with any physical or mental disability shall be so punished
    without the sanction of the Medical Officer.

(e) No corporal punishment shall be inflicted except by the Headmaster
    (or during his absence by the officer appointed under Rule 21 to
    exercise the duties of the Headmaster) or by an officer of the school
    in his presence and under his direction.

(f) It shall not be inflicted in the presence of other boys.

(g) Notwithstanding the provisions of paragraphs (e) and (f) of this Rule,
    for minor offences committed in the schoolroom by boys under
    fifteen, the principal teacher may be authorised by the Managers
    to administer with the cane not more than two strokes on each hand.
    Where the principal teacher is so authorised by the Managers to
    administer corporal punishment, he shall keep a book to be known
    as the Schoolroom Punishment Book and he shall at once enter
    therein any corporal punishment inflicted by him under this para-
    graph.

36. Corporal punishment in girls' schools shall be subject to the following
conditions :—

(a) It shall be inflicted only on the hands with a cane of a type approved
    by the Secretary of State and shall not exceed three strokes on each
    hand, but only girls under fifteen shall be so punished.

(b) No girl with any physical or mental disability shall be so punished
    without the sanction of the Medical Officer.

(c) It shall only be inflicted by the Headmistress (or during her absence
    by the officer appointed under Rule 21 to exercise the duties of
    Headmistress) or by an officer of the school in her presence and
    under her direction.

(d) It shall not be inflicted in the presence of other girls.

(e) Notwithstanding the provisions of paragraphs (c) and (d) of this Rule,
    for minor offences committed in the schoolroom by girls under
    fifteen, the principal teacher may be authorised by the Managers
    to administer with the cane not more than two strokes on each hand.
    Where the principal teacher is so authorised by the Managers to
    administer corporal punishment, she shall keep a book to be known
    as the Schoolroom Punishment Book and she shall at once enter
    therein any corporal punishment inflicted by her under this para-
    graph.

37. The Headmaster shall be responsible for the immediate recording of all
corporal and other serious punishment in the Punishment Book which he is
required to keep under Rule 18, except corporal punishment inflicted by the
principal teacher under Rule 35 (g) or 36 (e) as the case may be, and he shall
enter therein such details as may be required by the Chief Inspector.

The Headmaster shall examine the Schoolroom Punishment Book, if any,
at least once a week and shall sign it.

The Punishment Book (and the Schoolroom Punishment Book, if any) shall
be examined at each meeting of the Managers and shall be signed by the Chairman. They shall also be shown to the Medical Officer at least once a quarter.

38. Except as provided by these Rules no member of the staff shall inflict any kind of corporal punishment. The term " corporal punishment " includes striking, cuffing, shaking or any other form of physical violence. Any person who commits a breach of this rule shall render himself liable to instant dismissal.

39. No boy shall be allowed to administer any form of punishment to any other boy.

Medical Officer

44.—(1) The Managers shall appoint a Medical Officer whose duties shall include—

    (a) a thorough examination of each boy on admission and shortly before leaving the school;

    (b) a quarterly inspection of each boy;

    (c) visits to the school at least once a week;

    (d) general inspection of the school from the hygienic point of view and advice as to dietary and general hygiene;

    (e) the examination and treatment of all sick and ailing boys;

    (f) the keeping of medical records in a form approved by the Chief Inspector;

    (g) the furnishing of such reports and certificates as the Managers may require.

(2) Notice of any meeting of the Managers shall be given to the Medical Officer so that he may have an opportunity of attending and presenting a report.

Dentist

45.—(1) The Managers shall appoint a Dentist whose duties shall include an examination of the teeth of each boy shortly after admission to the school (and thereafter at least once every six months) and the undertaking of such fillings, extractions or other dental work as may be necessary.

(2) The Dentist shall keep a record of his work in a form approved by the Chief Inspector.

Notification of Illness

46. The Headmaster shall report at once any death and any case of serious illness, infectious disease or accident to the parent or guardian of the boy, to the Chief Inspector and, unless he is not in such care, to the local authority in whose care the boy is.

Any violent or sudden death shall be notified immediately by the Managers to the Coroner of the district in which the death occurs. A report of the proceedings at any inquest shall be sent without delay to the Chief Inspector by the Headmaster.

Records

47. The Managers shall arrange for the keeping of all registers and records required by the Chief Inspector and shall cause to be sent to him such returns, statements and other information as may be required by him from time to time.

Promulgation of Rules

48. The Managers shall cause a copy of these Rules to be given to each member of the staff and to the Medical Officer and Dentist on appointment.

Inspection

49. The Managers shall arrange that the school shall be open at all times to inspection by or on behalf of the Chief Inspector and they shall give all facilities for the examination of the books and records of the school.

Interpretation

50. The Interpretation Act, 1889, shall apply to the interpretation of these Rules as it applies to the interpretation of an Act of Parliament.

NOTES

These Rules are dated July 28, 1933. They were made by the Secretary of State for the management and discipline of approved schools under para. 1 of Sched. IV to the Children and Young Persons Act, 1933, p. 85, *ante*.

They are printed as amended by the Approved School Rules, 1949 (S.I. 1949 No. 2052), and the Approved School Rules, 1963 (S.I. 1963 No. 1056), and 1970.

The Interpretation Act, 1889.—See 32 Halsbury's Statutes, 3rd Edn., 434.

" Boys " must evidently include " girls " except where the context otherwise requires. See Interpretation Act, 1889, s. 1; 32 Halsbury's Statutes, 3rd Edn., 435.

Para. 31A—Financial assistance for visits to boys and girls at approved schools.— Home Office Circular No. 227/1967, dated November 23, 1967, describes arrangements under which the Supplementary Benefits Commission were prepared to assist parents to visit their children at approved schools at intervals of two months. Home Office Circular No. 217/1969 dated October 27, 1969, states that subject to the conditions in the former letter the Commission will be prepared to assist parents to visit at intervals of one month.

Fines outstanding against persons detained in Approved Schools.—See Home Office Circular No. 237/1968, p. 697, *post*.

THE VOLUNTARY HOMES (REGISTRATION) REGULATIONS, 1948

[S.I. 1948 No. 2408]

See Division 2, p. 867, *post*.

THE VOLUNTARY HOMES (RETURN OF PARTICULARS) REGULATIONS, 1949

[S.I. 1949 No. 2092]

[These Regulations are printed as amended in 1950 and 1955.]

1. The particulars set out in the Schedule to these Regulations shall be the particulars to be sent to the Secretary of State with respect to voluntary homes in accordance with section ninety-three of the Children and Young Persons Act, 1933.

2. The aforesaid particulars shall, in each year subsequent to the year one thousand nine hundred and fifty-five, be sent to the Secretary of State before the thirtieth day of April.

3.—(1) These Regulations may be cited as the Voluntary Homes (Return of Particulars) Regulations, 1949.

(2) The Children and Young Persons (Voluntary Homes) Regulations, 1945, are hereby revoked.

SCHEDULE

1. Name and full postal address of the voluntary home.
2. Full name of the person in charge of the home.
3. Full name and address of the organisation or person carrying on the home.
4. Full name and address of the chairman of the organisation.
5. Full name and address of the secretary of the organisation.
6. If admission to the home is restricted to certain categories of persons under the age of eighteen, particulars of those categories.
7. Religious persuasion or persuasions in which it is undertaken to bring up persons under the age of eighteen in the home.

8. [*Revoked by the Voluntary Homes (Return of Particulars) Regulations, 1950.*]

9. The number of (a) boys and (b) girls under the age of eighteen in the home who—

    (i) have not attained the age of two,

    (ii) have attained the age of two, but have not attained the age of five,

    (iii) have attained the age of five, but have not attained the age of fifteen,

    (iv) have attained the age of fifteen, but have not attained the age of eighteen,

and particulars as to the number in each such class who are (a) boys in respect of whom payment is being made by a local authority for the purposes of the Children Act, 1948, and (b) girls in respect of whom such a payment is being made.

10. The number of (a) boys and (b) girls under the age of eighteen in the home who—

    (i) not being over compulsory school age within the meaning of the Education Acts, 1944 and 1946, are attending school full time,

    (ii) are over compulsory school age within the meaning of the Education Acts, 1944 and 1946, and are receiving full time education or vocational training, and

    (iii) are in employment,

and particulars as to the number of (a) boys and (b) girls in each such class who are, as the case may be, attending school, receiving education or training, or in employment (i) in the home and (ii) outside the home.

11. The number of (a) boys and (b) girls under the age of eighteen in the home, other than persons in respect of whom payment is being made by a local authority for the purposes of the Children Act, 1948, who are judged to be likely to return to their parent or guardian within six months of coming into the care of the organisation or person carrying on the home.

12. The number of (a) boys and (b) girls under the age of eighteen in the home who are defectives within the meaning of the Mental Deficiency Acts, 1913 to 1938—

    (i) who have been reported to the local authority for the purposes of the Mental Deficiency Act, 1913, under section fifty-seven of the Education Act, 1944,

    (ii) who have otherwise been reported to the said authority.

and particulars as to the number in each such class who are (a) boys in respect of whom payment is being made by a local authority for the purposes of the Children Act, 1948, and (b) girls in respect of whom such payment is being made.

13. Amount of weekly charge made to a local authority in respect of each child in the care of that local authority under the Children Act, 1948.

14. The name of any government department or departments, other than the Home Office, which inspect the home, and the date of the last inspection by each such government department.

NOTES

These Regulations were made by the Secretary of State under s. 93 of the Children and Young Persons Act, 1933, p. 74, *ante,* and are dated November 10, 1949. They are printed as amended by the Voluntary Homes (Return of Particulars) Regulations, 1950 (S.I. 1950 No. 1758) and the Voluntary Homes (Return of Particulars) Regulations, 1955 (S.I. 1955 No. 1839) *infra.*

The Children Act, 1948.—See Division 2, pp. 867 *et seq., post.*

THE VOLUNTARY HOMES (RETURN OF PARTICULARS) REGULATIONS, 1955
[S.I. 1955 No. 1839)

1. [*Amends Regulation 2 of the principal Regulations, q.v.,* p. 466, *ante.*]

2. Notwithstanding anything in the principal Regulations, the particulars to be sent to the Secretary of State with respect to voluntary homes in accordance with section ninety-three of the Children and Young Persons Act, 1933, in the year one thousand nine hundred and fifty-five shall be the particulars set out in the Schedule to these Regulations.

3. In these Regulations, the expression " the principal Regulations " means the Voluntary Homes (Return of Particulars) Regulations, 1949, as amended by the Voluntary Homes (Return of Particulars) Regulations, 1950.

4. These Regulations may be cited as the Voluntary Homes (Return of Particulars) Regulations, 1955.

SCHEDULE   Regulation 2

1. Name and full postal address of the voluntary home.

2. Full name and address of the organisation or persons carrying on the home.

3. The number of—
  (a) boys, and
  (b) girls,

under the age of eighteen in the home on the thirtieth day of November, 1955.

4. The number of children under the age of eighteen in the home on the thirtieth day of November, 1955, in respect of whom payment is being made by a local authority for the purposes of the Children Act, 1948.

NOTES

These regulations which were dated December 5, 1955, were made under s. 93 of the Children and Young Persons Act, 1933, p. 74, *ante*, and came into force on that date.

THE CHILDREN AND YOUNG PERSONS (COLLECTION OF PARENTAL CONTRIBUTIONS) REGULATIONS, 1933
[S. R. & O. 1933, No. 1022]

[Lapsed on repeal of enabling powers by Children and Young Persons Act, 1969, s. 72 (4), Sched. VI.]

THE REMAND HOME RULES, 1939
[S. R. & O. 1939, No. 12]

1. A remand home provided under section 77 of the Act may be either a remand home established by a council in a building erected, acquired or leased by the council, or premises used as a remand home by arrangement made with the occupiers by a council. Such premises may include Homes for boys and girls and other similar institutions and private dwelling houses. Public assistance institutions shall not be used as remand homes except with the consent of the Minister of Health.

2. Remand homes shall be open to inspection at all times by or on behalf of the Chief Inspector.

3. Care shall be taken to keep in separation any boy who may be likely to exercise a bad influence over others.

4. Where accommodation is provided in a remand home for boys and girls, arrangements shall be made, so far as practicable, for the separation of boys from girls except while under supervision. The sleeping accommodation for boys shall be separate from that for girls.

5. Each boy shall sleep in a separate bed.

6. The boys shall be supplied with sufficient and varied food.

7. The boys shall wear their own clothing provided that where desirable on sanitary or other grounds suitable clothes and shoes similar to those worn in ordinary life shall be supplied. Suitable outdoor clothing shall be provided if the boys are taken out in cold or wet weather.

8. Each boy shall be thoroughly cleansed on admission ; and shall be medically examined by a doctor within twenty-four hours, or in cases of difficulty within forty-eight hours, after his admission to the remand home, and also at any other time or times that may be considered necessary by the Medical Officer or Superintendent. Such examinations shall include any steps necessary to ascertain whether venereal disease is present in cases where reason exists to suspect its occurrence, and may take place either at the remand home or, if the Medical Officer desires it, at a suitable clinic.

9. Any boy known or suspected to be suffering from an infectious disease in the remand home shall so far as is practicable be isolated from others ; and where such infectious disease occurs in a remand home, any boy subsequently admitted shall so far as is practicable be kept separate for the necessary period from those who have been in contact with the disease.

10. Arrangements shall be made so far as is reasonably possible for suitable schoolroom instruction either on or off the premises to be given to boys of school age. Practical work of a suitable character shall be provided for boys over school age or not receiving schoolroom instruction.

Boys may be occupied within reasonable limits in the work of the remand home, but boys under 12 shall not be so occupied except in light work such as making their own beds or cleaning their own boots.

11. The boys shall be allowed not less than two hours daily for recreation and exercise of which not less than one hour shall be spent in exercise in the open air except in inclement weather. A sufficient supply of suitable reading books and games shall be provided and renewed periodically when necessary.

12. Arrangements shall be made for the attendance of the boys each Sunday at a religious service in the remand home or at a place of public worship. They may be visited at convenient times by a minister of the religious persuasion to which they belong.

13. The discipline of the remand home shall be maintained by the personal influence of the Superintendent.

14. When punishment is necessary for the maintenance of discipline, one of the following methods shall be adopted :—

  (i) temporary loss of recreation or privileges ;

  (ii) reduction in quality or quantity of food ; provided that when a boy is deprived of any regular meal he shall be given in lieu bread and tea or cocoa, and that no boy shall be deprived of two meals in succession ;

  (iii) separation from other boys, subject to the following conditions :—

    (a) no boy under the age of 12 shall be kept in separation ;

    (b) the room used for the purpose shall be light and airy and kept lighted after dark ;

    (c) some form of occupation shall be given ;

    (d) means of communication with a member of the staff shall be provided ;

  (iv) corporal punishment. Every effort shall be made to enforce discipline without resort to corporal punishment. Where it is found necessary its application shall be in strict accordance with the following rules.

15. Corporal punishment for boys shall be subject to the following conditions :—

  (a) it shall be inflicted only with a cane or similar instrument to be approved by the council ;

  (b) it shall be applied either on the hands or on the posterior over the boy's ordinary cloth trousers ;

  (c) it shall be limited in the former case to not more than three strokes on each hand, and in the latter, to not more than six strokes.

16. Corporal punishment shall not be administered to girls.

17. No member of the staff other than the Superintendent or, in his absence, the responsible officer left in charge shall inflict corporal punishment. No other member of the staff may inflict any kind of corporal punishment ; and no form of striking, cuffing, shaking or other corporal punishment not authorised by these Rules shall be inflicted by any person. All punishments (corporal or other) shall be immediately recorded in the log book required to be kept under Rule 23 ; and a return of the corporal punishments administered shall be made quarterly to the Chief Inspector in such form as he may require.

18. (1) A doctor shall be appointed as Medical Officer at every remand home; and necessary medical treatment shall be given to the boys. The duties of a Medical Officer shall include regular attendance at the remand home, general supervision of the hygienic condition of the premises and of the health of the boys and the suitable provision of medical attention. If it becomes necessary to remove a boy from the remand home to a hospital, clinic, or other place of safety for medical treatment or examination, or if the Medical Officer is of opinion that on medical grounds a boy should not be further accommodated in the remand home, the Superintendent shall inform the parent of the boy, and the Council.

(2) Any reference in paragraph (1) of this rule to the parent of a boy shall be construed as including, unless he is not in such care, a reference to the local authority in whose care he is.

19. No operative treatment shall be carried out on a boy without the previous consent of his parent or guardian unless either the parent or guardian cannot be found or the condition of the boy is such that any delay would involve unnecessary suffering or injury to health.

20. (1) The Superintendent shall report at once any death and any case of serious illness, infectious disease or accident, to the parent of the boy, to the council and to the Chief Inspector. Any violent or sudden death shall be notified immediately by the council to the Coroner of the district.

(2) Paragraph 2 of Rule 18 of these Rules shall have effect for the purposes of this Rule as it has effect for the purposes of the said Rule 18.

21. Arrangements shall be made for any premises used as a remand home to be regularly visited by persons appointed for that purpose by the council. The visitors so appointed shall include women, and visits shall be paid at intervals not exceeding three months. At least two such visits shall be paid without notice in every year. The premises shall also be open for visits at all reasonable hours by officers and members of every council making use of the home.

22. Reasonable facilities shall be given for boys to receive visits from their relatives and friends and to send or receive letters.

23. The Superintendent shall keep a register of admissions and discharges in which shall be recorded all admissions and discharges, a daily register in such form as may be required by the Chief Inspector showing the presence or absence of each boy accommodated, and a log book in which shall be entered every event of importance connected with the remand home and all punishments. These books shall be open to inspection by or on behalf of the council or the Chief Inspector and shall be inspected by or on behalf of the council at regular intervals not exceeding three months.

24. Every absconding shall be noted in the log book and in the daily register, and a return of all abscondings shall be made quarterly to the Chief Inspector.

26.—(1) In these Rules the following expressions have the meanings hereby respectively assigned to them, that is to say :—

" the Act " means the Children and Young Persons Act, 1933.

" Council " means the council of a county, a county borough or a London borough or the Common Council of the City of London acting separately or jointly with another such council.

" Chief Inspector " means the Chief Inspector appointed by the Secretary of State under section 103 of the Children and Young Persons Act, 1933, for the purposes of the enactments relating to children and young persons.

" Infectious disease " means :—

Enteric fever (typhoid)	Cerebro-spinal meningitis (spotted
Scarlet fever	fever)
Diphtheria	Encephalitis lethargica
Chicken pox	Influenza
Small pox	German measles
Measles	Mumps
Epidemic conjunctivitis	Whooping cough
Venereal disease	Granular conjunctivitis (trachoma)
Acute rheumatism	Tubercular disease
Chorea	Erysipelas
Scabies	Ringworm

" Superintendent " means the person in charge of a remand home.

(2) The Interpretation Act, 1889, shall apply to the interpretation of these Rules as it applies to the interpretation of an Act of Parliament.

27. The Remand Home Rules, 1933, are hereby revoked.

28.—(1) These Rules may be cited as the Remand Home Rules, 1939.

(2) These Rules shall come into operation on the 1st March, 1939.

(3) These Rules shall apply to all remand homes referred to in Rule 1 above.

Provided that if the Secretary of State is satisfied with regard to any particular remand home or remand homes that owing to the small number of boys received, the nature of the premises or other special circumstances it is desirable so to do, he may from time to time by notice in writing to the council and to the Superintendent suspend the application of any part of these Rules to the remand home specified in the notice for such time and on such conditions as may be specified in the notice.

NOTES

These Rules are dated January 2, 1939, and were made by the Secretary of State under s. 78 (3) of the Children and Young Persons Act, 1933, p. 64, *ante*. They are printed as amended by the London Government Order, 1965, S.I. 1965 No. 654 and the Remand Home Rules, 1970, S.I. 1970 No. 1510.

Interpretation Act, 1889.—See 32 Halsbury's Statutes, 3rd Edn., 434.

Evidently the word " boys " includes " girls " except where the context otherwise requires. See Interpretation Act, 1889, s. 1; 32 Halsbury's Statutes, 3rd Edn., 435.

THE EMPLOYMENT ABROAD OF PERSONS UNDER THE AGE OF EIGHTEEN

FORM OF LICENCE AND REGULATION, 1933

[S. R. & O. 1933, No. 992]

1. I prescribe the annexed form of licence for use under that section.

2. I make the following regulation :—

The particulars to be sent by a police magistrate to the Secretary of State for transmission to the proper consular officer where a licence is granted, renewed or varied for a person under the age of 18 to go out of the United Kingdom for the purpose of singing, playing, performing, or being exhibited, for profit, shall be as follows :—

(a) The name and address of the said person.

(b) The date and place of birth, and, where known, the nationality of the said person.

(c) The name and address of the applicant for the licence.

(d) Where the father, mother, or guardian is not the applicant for the licence, the name and address of the father, mother or guardian.

(e) Particulars of the engagement, with the place or places at which and the period or periods during which the said person is to sing, play, perform, or be exhibited.

(f) Copy of the contract of employment or other document showing the terms and conditions of employment.

(g) Copy of the licence.

3. The Form of Licence prescribed by the Secretary of State and the Regulation dated 27th August, 1913, made under section 2 of the Children (Employment Abroad) Act, 1913, are hereby repealed.

NOTES

The prescribed forms of licence, renewal, variation and revocation of licence are not printed here.

This Regulation is dated October 18, 1933, and was made by the Secretary of State under s. 25 of the Children and Young Persons Act, 1933, p. 35, *ante*.

THE JUVENILE COURTS (CONSTITUTION) RULES, 1954
[S.I. 1954 No. 1711]

NOTE

See the provisions of s. 61 of the Children and Young Persons Act, 1969, p. 207, *ante* No regulations under that section have yet been made.

1.—(1) The justices for each petty sessions area shall at their meeting held in the month of October, 1955, in accordance with rules made under section thirteen of the Justices of the Peace Act, 1949, for the purpose of electing a chairman of the justices, and thereafter at the said meeting in every third year, appoint in accordance with these Rules justices specially qualified for dealing with juvenile cases to form a juvenile court panel for that area.

(2) The panel for a petty sessions area shall, except as provided in paragraph (4) of this Rule, be appointed from amongst the number of the justices for that area who have not attained the age of sixty-five years.

(3) The number of persons appointed to the panel for a petty sessions area shall be such as the said justices at the time of appointment think sufficient for the juvenile courts in the area and the said justices may at any time appoint an additional member to the panel.

(4) If in the case of a petty sessions area being a petty sessional division of a county the justices consider that a sufficient number of persons cannot otherwise be appointed to the panel, they may appoint a justice for the county, who is specially qualified as aforesaid and who has not attained the age of sixty-five years, notwithstanding that he is not a justice for that area.

2. Where a stipendiary magistrate exercises jurisdiction in a petty sessions area he shall be a member of the panel therefor by virtue of his office, whether or not he has attained the age of sixty-five years.

3. A justice shall be eligible for appointment to a panel for a petty sessions area whether or not he is or has been a member of the panel for that or any other area.

4. Subject to Rule 7 of these Rules the members of a panel shall serve thereon from the first day of November next following the date of appointment for a period of three years.

5. A justice who attains the age of sixty-five years shall forthwith cease to be a member of a panel :
Provided that the Lord Chancellor may, if it appears necessary to him in order that there may be a sufficient number of justices on the panel for a petty sessions area, direct in the case of a particular justice that he may continue to be a member of the panel for such period as may be specified in the direction.

6. If a vacancy occurs in the membership of a panel for a petty sessions area the justices for that area shall as soon as practicable, unless they consider that it is not necessary, appoint such a justice to fill the vacancy as might have been appointed to the panel under Rule 1 of these Rules.

7. A justice appointed to a panel to fill a vacancy or as an additional member shall, subject to Rule 5 of these Rules, serve thereon until the end of the period for which the other members of the panel were appointed.

8. The clerk to the justices for each petty sessions area shall forthwith notify the Secretary of State—

(a) of the name, address and age of every member of the panel for that area appointed under Rule 1 or Rule 6, and of every person elected under paragraph (1) or (2) of Rule 9 of these Rules, specifying in each case the provision of these Rules under which he is appointed or, as the case may be, elected ;

(b) of the name of every justice ceasing to be a member of the said panel and of the reason why he ceases to be a member thereof and of every occasion on which the justices consider it unnecessary to fill a vacancy in the said panel.

9.—(1) The members of the panel for each petty sessions area shall on the occasion of their appointment or as soon as practicable thereafter meet and elect from amongst their number by secret ballot a chairman and as many deputy chairmen as will ensure that each juvenile court in the area sits under the chairmanship of a person so elected in accordance with paragraph (1) of Rule 13 of these Rules, and may at any subsequent time elect an additional deputy chairman.

(2) If a vacancy occurs in the chairmanship or a deputy chairmanship, the members of the panel shall elect by secret ballot a chairman or, as the case may be, deputy chairman to hold office for the remainder of the period for which the members serve.

10. The members of a panel shall meet as often as may be necessary but not less often than twice a year to make arrangements connected with the holding of juvenile courts and to discuss questions connected with the work of those courts.

11. The justices to sit in each juvenile court shall be chosen from the panel, in such manner as the panel determine, so as to ensure that paragraph (1) of Rule 12 and paragraph (1) of Rule 13 of these Rules can be complied with.

12.—(1) Each juvenile court shall be constituted of not more than three justices and, subject to the following provisions of this Rule, shall include a man and a woman.

(2) If at any sitting of a juvenile court the only member of the panel present is a stipendiary magistrate who thinks it inexpedient in the interests of justice for there to be an adjournment, he may sit alone.

(3) If at any sitting of a juvenile court no man or no woman is available owing to circumstances unforeseen when the justices to sit were chosen under Rule 11 of these Rules, or if the only man or woman present cannot properly sit as a member of the court, and in any such case the other members of the panel present think it inexpedient in the interests of justice for there to be an adjournment, the court may be constituted without a man or, as the case may be, without a woman.

(4) Nothing in paragraph (1) of this Rule shall be construed as requiring a juvenile court to include both a man and a woman in any case in which a single justice has by law jurisdiction to act.

13.—(1) Except as provided in paragraph (2) of this Rule, each juvenile court shall sit under the chairmanship of the chairman or a deputy chairman elected under Rule 9 of these Rules.

(2) If at any sitting of a juvenile court the chairman or a deputy chairman is not available owing to circumstances unforeseen when the justices to sit were chosen under Rule 11 of these Rules or he cannot properly sit as a member of the court, the members of that court shall choose one of their number to preside.

14.—(1) In these Rules, " panel " means a panel formed in pursuance of Rule 1 of these Rules and, in relation to a petty sessional division of a county, references to the justices for a petty sessions area are references to the justices who ordinarily act in and for that division.

(2) The Interpretation Act, 1889, shall apply to the interpretation of these Rules as it applies to the interpretation of an Act of Parliament.

15.—(1) The Rules specified in the Schedule to these Rules are hereby revoked.

(2) Members of an old panel shall be deemed to have been appointed under these Rules to be members of a panel for a period ending at the expiration of the month of October, 1955, and any chairman selected under the Rules revoked by this Rule shall be deemed to have been elected under paragraph (1) of Rule 9 of these Rules for a term of office ending at the expiration of the said month.

(3) Any direction given by the Lord Chancellor and any other thing done unde rthe Rules revoked by these Rules shall be deemed to have been given or done so far as it could have been so given or done under the corresponding provision of these Rules.

(4) In this Rule the expression " old panel " means a panel appointed under the Rules revoked by this Rule and the expression " member of an old panel " means a member thereof serving as such immediately before the coming into operation of these Rules.

16. These Rules shall not apply in the metropolitan stipendiary court area or in the City of London.

17. These Rules may be cited as the Juvenile Courts (Constitution) Rules, 1954, and shall come into operation on the first day of March, 1955.

SCHEDULE   Rule 15 (1)

The Juvenile Courts (Constitution) Rules, 1933
The Juvenile Courts (Constitution) Rules, 1934
The Juvenile Courts (Constitution) Rules, 1942
The Juvenile Courts (Constitution) (Amendment) Rules, 1950
The Juvenile Courts (Constitution) Rules, 1952

NOTES

These rules were made on December 17, 1954 under s. 15 of the Justices of the Peace Act, 1949 (21 Halsbury's Statutes, 3rd Edn., 120) as extended by s. 14, *ibid.* and by s. 122 of the Magistrate's Courts Act, 1952 (21 Halsbury's Statutes, 3rd Edn., 284).

They came into operation on March 1, 1955.

Rule 5.—In Home Office Circular 205/1964 dated August 26, 1964, it is stated that the Lord Chancellor takes the view that the proviso to r. 5 which allows him to direct that a particular justice shall continue to serve after 65 does not empower him to give such a direction once the justice has reached that age. Any application for such a direction should accordingly be made some time before the justice reaches that age.

See also the Home Office letter as to the Appointment of Juvenile Court Panels from November 1, 1970.

Rule 11.—Constitution of court.—In *Re J. S. an Infant*, [1959] 3 All E. R. 856; 124 J.P. 89, an appeal under the Adoption Act, 1958, was allowed and a new trial ordered on two grounds, one of which was that the court held that to give a woman justice notice to attend without making any inquiry whether she could attend or not was not "ensuring" her attendance within r. 11, and that as there was no evidence as to the circumstances of her absence, the proceedings were null and void.

Rule 12 (3). "**Cannot properly sit as a member of the court.**"—If for instance he is a member of a local authority and that authority is a party to a case and he is thereby disqualified under s. 3 of the Justices of the Peace Act, 1949 (21 Halsbury's Statutes, 3rd Edn., 112).

THE ATTENDANCE CENTRE RULES, 1958
[S.I. 1958 No. 1990]

General

1. These Rules shall apply to any attendance centre (hereinafter called "a centre") provided by the Secretary of State under subsection (2) of section forty-eight of the Act for the reception of male persons.

Occupation and instruction

2.—(1) The occupation and instruction given at a centre shall be such as to occupy the persons attending there during the period of attendance in a manner conducive to health of mind and body.

(2) The occupation and instruction shall be in accordance with a scheme approved by or on behalf of the Secretary of State.

Officer in charge

3.—(1) The officer in charge shall maintain a register in which shall be recorded in respect of each person required to attend—

   (a) every attendance or failure to attend;

   (b) the duration of each attendance; and

   (c) the commission of any breach of these Rules and the manner in which it is dealt with.

(2) Subject to the provisions of Rule 9 of these Rules, it shall be the duty of the officer in charge to ensure that any person attending at the centre who has not completed the period of attendance specified in the order is, before leaving the centre, informed (both orally and in writing) of the day and time when he is next required to attend at the centre unless in any particular case it is impracticable to give this information.

Attendance

4.—(1) Persons required to attend at the centre shall so attend—

    (a) on the first occasion, at the time specified in the order; and

    (b) on any subsequent occasion, at such time as may be notified to them in accordance with paragraph (2) of Rule 3 of these Rules, or, if no such notification has been given, at such time as may be notified to them in writing by or on behalf of the officer in charge;

and on attending shall report to, and place themselves under the direction of, the officer in charge.

(2) The occasions of a person's attendance at a centre and the duration of each attendance shall, so far as practicable and subject to the provisions of Rule 9 of these Rules, be so arranged by the officer in charge that the duration of attendance on any occasion is not less than one hour.

Admission to centre

5. No person, other than a person on an occasion when he is required to attend in pursuance of an order, shall be admitted to, or remain in, a centre except with the permission of the Secretary of State or the officer in charge.

Unfitness for attendance

6.—(1) The officer in charge may at any time require a person attending at the centre to leave it if, in the opinion of the officer, that person is—

    (a) so unwell as to be unfit to remain at the centre on that occasion; or

    (b) infested with vermin or suffering from any infectious disease or otherwise in a condition likely to be detrimental to other persons attending at the centre.

(2) Where a person is so required to leave, he shall be instructed in accordance with paragraph (2) of Rule 3 of these Rules as to his further attendance at the centre.

Discipline

7. The discipline of a centre shall be maintained by the personal influence of the officer in charge and staff.

8. Persons shall while attending at a centre conduct themselves in an orderly manner and shall obey any order given or instruction issued by the officer in charge or any member of the staff.

9.—(1) Any person committing a breach of these Rules may be required to leave the centre at any time.

(2) Where a person is so required to leave, he shall either—

    (a) be instructed in accordance with paragraph (2) of Rule 3 of these Rules as to his further attendance at the centre; or

    (b) be informed (both orally and in writing) that he is not required to attend at the centre again and that it is intended in respect of the said breach to take steps to bring him before a court under subsection (7) of section nineteen of the Act.

10. Without prejudice to the generality of the last foregoing Rule, the officer in charge or any member of the staff may deal with a person committing a breach of these Rules in either or both of the following ways, that is to say:—

    (a) by separating him from other persons attending at the centre;

    (b) by giving him a less attractive form of occupation;

during the whole or any part of the period of attendance specified in the order then remaining uncompleted.

Interpretation

11. In these Rules, unless the context otherwise requires, the following expressions have the meanings hereby respectively assigned to them, that is to say:—

" centre " has the meaning assigned to it in Rule 1 of these Rules;

" member of the staff " means any person, other than the officer in charge, for the time being carrying out any instructional or supervisory duties at a centre;

" officer in charge " means the person for the time being in charge of a centre;

" order " means an order made by a magistrates' court under section nineteen of the Act requiring an offender to attend at a centre;

" the Act " means the Criminal Justice Act, 1948.

Revocation

12. The Attendance Centre Rules, 1950, and the Attendance Centre Rules, 1953, are hereby revoked.

Citation and commencement

13. These Rules may be cited as the Attendance Centre Rules, 1958, and shall come into operation on the first day of December, 1958.

NOTE

These Rules were made November 24, 1958, by the Secretary of State under s. 52 of the Criminal Justice Act, 1948; 25 Halsbury's Statutes, 3rd Edn., 818.

Forms.—See forms Nos. 30 and 47 Magistrates' Courts (Children and Young Persons) Rules, 1970, p. 597, *post*.

THE APPROVED PROBATION HOSTEL AND HOME RULES, 1949
[S.I. 1949 No. 1376]

Management

1.—(1) Every hostel and home shall be managed by a committee which shall be known as the Managing Committee (hereinafter referred to as " the Committee ").

(2) Two at least of the members of the Committee shall be men and two at least shall be women.

(3) No member of the staff of the hostel or home shall be a member of the Committee.

(4) A sufficient number of members of the Committee to ensure adequate supervision shall be resident within a reasonable distance of the hostel or home.

2.—(1) The Committee may appoint a Finance Sub-Committee and such other sub-committees as they think necessary for the efficient management of the hostel or home.

(2) Any sub-committee so appointed shall have such powers and duties as the Committee may determine.

3. The Committee shall appoint one of their number to be Chairman and shall also appoint a Secretary and a Treasurer:

Provided that the same person may be appointed as Secretary and Treasurer but no member of the staff of the hostel or home shall be eligible for appointment to either of those offices.

4. The Secretary shall notify to the Secretary of State the names and addresses of the members of the Committee and any change due to death, retirement or other cause.

5.—(1) The Committee shall meet so far as practicable once a month and shall so arrange their meetings as to ensure that they meet at the hostel or home at least once in every two months.

(2) The Committee and any sub-committee appointed by them shall keep minutes of their proceedings and these minutes shall be open to inspection by or on behalf of the Secretary of State and by the auditor appointed under Rule 33 of these Rules.

6.—(1) It shall be the duty of the Committee to ensure that the condition of the hostel or home and the training and welfare of the residents are satisfactory; and for this purpose the Committee shall take into account any communication which may be made to them by or on behalf of the Secretary of State.

(2) The hostel or home shall be visited at least once a month by at least one member of the Committee who shall satisfy himself regarding the care of the residents and the state of the hostel or home, or some part of it, and shall enter his conclusions in the log book kept under Rule 14 of these Rules.

(3) The Committee shall exercise an effective control over all expenditure.

Admissions and Discharges

7.—(1) The number of residents in a hostel or home at any time shall not exceed such number as may be approved in respect of that hostel or home by the Secretary of State.

(2) Except with the prior authority of the Secretary of State the Committee shall not receive in the hostel or home any person who is outside the limits of age approved by the Secretary of State for that hostel or home.

8.—(1) A person shall not be received in a hostel or home—

    (a) if he is on remand;

    (b) if he is the subject of an interim order under subsection (2) of section sixty-seven of the Children and Young Persons Act, 1933 (which relates to temporary detention in a place of safety);

    (c) if he is a defective within the meaning of section one of the Mental Deficiency Act, 1913;

    (d) if he is suffering from epilepsy to such a degree that he cannot be accommodated therein without detriment to himself or other residents.

(2) A woman or girl who is pregnant shall not be received in a hostel or home unless it is approved for the admission of such cases.

NOTE

This sub-para. is modified by Home Office Circular No. 198/1966, p. 686, *post*. It is now within the Warden's discretion whether or not to allow a pregnant girl to remain.

(3) A person shall not be received in a hostel or home unless his period of residence is intended to be of sufficient duration to enable him to complete the scheme of training provided in the hostel or home.

9. Subject to the foregoing provisions of these Rules, no hostel or home shall, except with the consent of the Secretary of State, refuse to accept a person who is under the supervision of a probation officer and is required by the probation order or supervision order to reside therein and who falls within the category of persons for which the hostel or home is approved.

10. Except with the authority of the Secretary of State—

(a) no person under supervision shall reside in a hostel or home for any period other than the period, if any, for which he is required so to reside by the probation order or supervision order;

(b) no person shall reside in a hostel or home for more than a year.

11.—(1) The Committee shall not, except in case of emergency require a person under supervision to cease to reside in the hostel or home before the expiry of the term of residence specified in the probation order or supervision order.

(2) The Committee shall in any such case of emergency give reasonable notice to the probation officer or other person responsible for supervision, and shall at the same time inform the Secretary of State, of their intention to act under the foregoing paragraph of this Rule together with their reasons therefor.

12. Where a person under supervision absconds from a hostel or home, the Warden shall forthwith notify the probation officer or other person responsible for supervision.

Staff

13.—(1) The Committee shall be responsible for the appointment, suspension or dismissal of the staff of the hostel or home.

(2) Any vacancy for a Warden shall, except in case of emergency, be advertised by the Committee unless the prior consent of the Secretary of State to dispense with this requirement is obtained.

(3) No appointment as Warden shall, except in case of emergency, be made without the consent of the Secretary of State.

(4) Where an appointment as Warden has been made in case of emergency without such consent as aforesaid, the Committee shall forthwith notify the Secretary of State of the appointment and of the circumstances in which it was made, and the Secretary of State may, if he thinks fit, require the Committee to terminate the appointment.

(5) Except with the consent of the Secretary of State no member of the staff shall be retained after he has reached the age of sixty-five years.

Warden

14.—(1) The Warden shall be responsible to the Committee for the efficient conduct of the hostel or home.

(2) The Warden shall keep the following records, which shall at all times be available for inspection by any member of the Committee, that is to say—

(a) a register of admissions and discharges in which shall be recorded all admissions to and discharges from the hostel or home;

(b) a log book in which shall be entered every event of importance connected with the hostel or home;

(c) a daily register of the presence or absence of each resident;

(d) a record of the progress of every person under supervision residing in the hostel or home.

(3) The log book shall be laid before the Committee at each of their meetings and shall be signed by the Chairman.

(4) The Warden shall, on the request of the probation officer or other person responsible for supervision, make a written report on the progress of a person under supervision residing in the hostel or home.

15. The Warden shall not incur any expenditure, other than petty expenditure within a limit approved by the Committee, without the previous sanction either of the Committee or of a member thereof authorised to act on behalf of the Committee.

16. The Warden shall, subject to any directions of the Committee, determine the duties of the other members of the staff.

General Care and Welfare of Residents

17. Each resident shall be provided with a separate bed and shall be kept supplied with such suitable clothing of a type worn in everyday life as may be necessary.

18.—(1) Residents shall be supplied with sufficient and varied food.

(2) Records shall be kept of the dishes that have been served and the weekly quantities of the main foodstuffs used.

19. Every hostel and home shall provide a scheme of training approved by the Secretary of State.

20. Residents in a hostel shall as soon as practicable, and in any case within two weeks of admission, be assisted in finding suitable employment outside the hostel.

21. A probation officer or other person responsible for supervision shall be allowed to see in private at any reasonable time any resident who is under his supervision.

22. Residents shall be given reasonable facilities for the practice of their religion and for attending each Sunday at a place of public worship.

23.—(1) Adequate provision shall be made for free time and recreation which shall include activities outside the grounds of the hostel or home.

(2) Arrangements shall be made for residents in a home to spend at least one hour daily in the open air.

24. Arrangements shall be made for the giving of pocket money each week to residents in a home subject to such conditions as may be approved by the Secretary of State.

25. Residents in a hostel shall be charged for the expenses of their maintenance in accordance with a scale approved by the Secretary of State.

Discipline

26. The discipline of the hostel or home shall be maintained by the personal influence of the Warden and staff.

27.—(1) The Warden shall be responsible for the immediate recording of any disciplinary action in the log book.

(2) No resident shall be allowed to administer any form of punishment to any other resident.

28.—(1) No corporal punishment of any kind shall be inflicted on a resident.

(2) For the purposes of this Rule the term " corporal punishment " includes striking, cuffing or shaking or the intentional infliction of any form of physical pain as a means of punishment.

Medical Care of Residents

29.—(1) The Committee shall appoint a Medical Officer whose duties shall include:—

    (a) an examination of each resident as soon as practicable after admission;
    (b) periodic inspection of the hostel or home from the hygienic point of view;
    (c) advice as to dietary and general hygiene;

(d) the keeping of medical records in which shall be entered particulars of every medical examination carried out under this Rule and case notes relating to any resident receiving medical attention.

(2) Notice of any meeting of the Committee shall be given to the Medical Officer so that he may have an opportunity of attending and presenting a report.

30. The Committee shall ensure that arrangements are made for the provision of any necessary medical and dental treatment.

31. The Committee shall at once notify the Secretary of State of the death of any resident or of any accident which results in serious injury to a resident.

General

32. The Committee shall arrange for the keeping of all registers and records required by the Secretary of State and shall cause to be sent to the Secretary of State such returns, statements, and other information as may be required by him from time to time.

33. The Committee shall make such arrangements as may be approved by the Secretary of State for the appointment of an auditor and for the audit of the accounts of the hostel or home.

34. The Committee shall cause a copy of these Rules to be given on appointment to each member of the staff and to the Medical Officer.

35. The Committee shall arrange for the hostel or home to be open at all times to inspection by or on behalf of the Secretary of State and shall, in connection with any such inspection, give all facilities for the examination of the books and records of the hostel or home.

36.—(1) In these Rules, unless the context otherwise requires, the following expressions have the meanings hereby respectively assigned to them, that is to say:—

" approved probation home " and " approved probation hostel " have the meanings assigned to them in subsection (1) of section forty-six of the Criminal Justice Act, 1948.

" Committee " has the meaning assigned to it in Rule 1 of these Rules;

" home " means an approved probation home;

" hostel " means an approved probation hostel;

" person under supervision " means a person under supervision in pursuance of a requirement of a probation order or supervision order;

" probation order " means an order made under section one of the Probation of Offenders Act, 1907, or section three of the Criminal Justice Act, 1948, whereby an offender is required respectively to be under the supervision of a person named in the order or of a probation officer appointed for or assigned to a petty sessional division or place named in the order;

" requirement of a probation order " includes a condition of a recognisance entered into by an offender under the said Act of 1907, and any reference to a person being required by a probation order shall be construed accordingly;

" resident " means a person residing in a hostel or home, whether in pursuance of a requirement of a probation order or supervision order or not;

" supervision order " means an order made under section sixty-two, section sixty-three, section sixty-four or section eighty-four of the

Children and Young Persons Act, 1933, placing a child or young person under the supervision of a probation officer or some other person appointed for the purpose by the court;

" Warden " means the person in charge of a hostel or home.

(2) The Interpretation Act, 1889, shall apply to the interpretation of these Rules as it applies to the interpretation of an Act of Parliament.

37. These Rules may be cited as the Approved Probation Hostel and Home Rules, 1949, and shall come into operation on the first day of August, 1949.

NOTES

These Rules were made by the Secretary of State under s. 46 (2) of the Criminal Justice Act, 1948, p. 292, *ante*.

Rule 10.—A hostel or home is precluded from receiving a person who is the subject of a supervision order, if, on admission, he would be more than 17 years and 6 months old; Home Office Probation Bulletin No. 6, 2 (b).

Rule 11.   Amendment or variation.—Except in cases of emergency, the usual procedure in the case of a probation order will be for the probation officer to apply to the court for a variation of the requirement; Criminal Justice Act, 1948, Sched. 1, para. 1, p. 295, *ante*.

THE DETENTION CENTRE RULES, 1952

[S.I. 1952 No. 1432]

PRELIMINARY

Interpretation

1.—(1) These Rules apply to Detention Centres (hereinafter referred to as " Centres ") and to persons required to be detained therein (hereinafter referred to as " inmates ").

(2) In these Rules unless the context otherwise requires words and expressions have the meanings respectively assigned to them as follows:—

" Chaplain " means a clergyman appointed under the Prison Acts, 1865 and 1877;

" Commissioners " means the Prison Commissioners, and " Assistant Commissioner " means a person appointed by the Secretary of State to assist the Prison Commissioners and to be an inspector of prisons;

" Compulsory school age " has the meaning assigned to it by subsection (5) of section eighteen of the Criminal Justice Act, 1948;

" Junior Centre " and " Senior Centre " have the meanings assigned to them by rule 3;

" Legal adviser " means, in relation to an inmate, the inmate's counsel or solicitor, and includes a clerk authorised by his counsel or solicitor to interview the inmate;

" Minister " means a person appointed under section three of the Prison Ministers Act, 1863, as amended by the Prison Acts, 1865 to 1898;

" Offence " has the meaning assigned to it by rule 31;

" Officer " means an officer or servant of a Centre;

" Restricted diet " has the meaning assigned to it by sub-paragraph (h) of paragraph (2) of Rule 32;

" Warden " and " Deputy Warden " mean an officer appointed under the Prison Acts, 1865 to 1898, who is assigned by the Commissioners to take charge of a Centre or to act as deputy to an officer so assigned.

(3) References to the Church of England include, in relation to a Centre situated in Wales or an inmate who is a member of the Church in Wales, reference to the Church in Wales.

(4) The Interpretation Act, 1889, shall apply to the interpretation of these Rules as it applies to the interpretation of an Act of Parliament.

Citation and commencement

2. These Rules may be cited as the Detention Centre Rules, 1952, and shall come into operation on the thirty-first day of July, 1952.

CLASSIFICATION AND GRADING

Classification

3.—(1) An inmate shall be detained in that one of the four following types of Centre appropriate to his or her age and sex, namely—

    (a) junior Centre for males under the age of seventeen;
    (b) junior Centre for females under the age of seventeen;
    (c) senior Centre for males aged seventeen or over;
    (d) senior Centre for females aged seventeen or over:

Provided that a person under the age of seventeen may be detained in a senior Centre and a person aged seventeen or over may be detained in a junior Centre if in either case the Prison Commissioners, having regard to the person's mental or physical development, so direct.

(2) A senior and a junior Centre for persons of the same sex may be in the same building.

Grading

4.—(1) On arrival at a Centre an inmate shall be placed in Grade I.

(2) Subject to any general directions by the Commissioners, an inmate may be promoted from Grade I to Grade II—

    (a) after being not less than four weeks in Grade I, or, in the case of an inmate ordered to be detained for a term of one month, such less period in Grade I as the Warden may determine, and
    (b) if in the opinion of the Warden his conduct justifies the promotion.

(3) Inmates promoted to Grade II shall be given such privileges as the Commissioners from time to time determine.

ACCOMMODATION

Sleeping accommodation

5. No sleeping accommodation for inmates shall be used unless it is certified by a Commissioner or Assistant Commissioner to be of such size and to be lighted, warmed, ventilated and fitted in such a manner as is requisite for health, and when such accommodation is locked it shall be furnished with the means of enabling inmates to communicate at any time with an officer. If the certificate is cancelled, that accommodation shall not be so used unless it is again certified. The certificate shall specify the maximum number of inmates to be accommodated at any one time in any room and the number so specified shall not be exceeded without the authority of the Commissioners.

Detention rooms

6. No room shall be used as a detention room for the confinement of an inmate in pursuance of a disciplinary award under rule 32 or rule 33 or for the confinement of a refractory or violent inmate under rule 38, unless it is certified by a Commissioner or Assistant Commissioner to be suitable for the purpose and to be furnished with the means of enabling the inmate so confined to communicate at any time with an officer.

Beds and bedding

7. Every inmate shall be provided with a separate bed and with separate bedding adequate for warmth and health.

RECEPTION AND REMOVAL

(i) *Reception*

Search

8.—(1) Every inmate shall be searched by an officer on reception at a Centre, and at such subsequent times as may be directed, and all unauthorised articles shall be taken from him.

(2) The searching of an inmate shall be conducted in as seemly a manner as is consistent with the necessity of discovering any concealed article.

(3) No inmate shall be stripped and searched in the sight of another inmate.

(4) An inmate shall be searched only by officers of the same sex as the inmate.

Retention of property

9. All money, clothing or other effects belonging to an inmate which he is not allowed to retain shall be placed in the custody of the Warden, who shall keep an inventory thereof, which shall be signed by the inmate.

Recording of particulars

10.—(1) A personal record of each inmate shall be prepared and maintained in such manner as the Commissioners determine.

(2) Every inmate may be photographed on reception and subsequently, but no copy of the photograph shall be given to a person who is not authorised to receive it.

Interview by Warden

11. Every inmate shall as soon as possible after his reception be separately interviewed by the Warden.

Medical examination

12. Every inmate shall, on the day of his reception, as soon as possible after his reception, be separately examined by the Medical Officer, who shall record the state of health of the inmate and such other particulars as may be directed:

    Provided that when an inmate is received too late to be examined on the same day he shall be examined as soon as possible on the next day, and in any case within twenty-four hours of reception.

Babies

13. Subject to such conditions as the Commissioners determine, a girl may have her baby with her in the Centre during the period of lactation and longer if required in special circumstances, and the baby may be supplied with clothing and necessaries at the public expense.

(ii) *Information to inmates*

Providing and explaining information

14. The Warden shall ensure that every inmate receives a careful explanation of so much of these Rules and of any other regulations as should be brought to his knowledge, including those relating to payments, to activities of the Centre, to the proper methods of submitting petitions to the Secretary of State and of making complaints, to food, clothing, bedding, and other necessaries, and to the disciplinary requirements of the Centre so that he may understand both his rights and his obligations.

(iii) *Removal and release*

Custody during removal, etc.

15. An inmate whom the Secretary of State has directed to be taken to any place shall while outside the Centre be kept in the custody of officers of a Centre or of prison officers:

Provided that an inmate directed to be brought before a magistrates' court may while outside the Centre be in the custody of police officers.

Protection from Public view

16. When inmates are removed to or from a Centre, they shall be exposed to public view as little as possible and proper safeguards shall be adopted to protect them from insult or curiosity.

Final interview with Warden and with Medical Officer

17. An inmate shall before release or removal to any other place be interviewed by the Warden, and shall, as short a time as is practicable before release or removal to any other place, be examined by the Medical Officer, and shall not be so removed unless the Medical Officer certifies that he is fit for removal.

Return of clothes

18. On the release of an inmate, his own clothes shall be returned to him unless it has been found necessary to destroy or otherwise dispose of them, in which case proper clothing shall be provided.

(iv) *Deaths of inmates*

Record of death

19. The Medical Officer shall keep a record of the death of an inmate which shall include the following particulars:—

> At what time the deceased was taken ill, when the illness was first notified to the Medical Officer, the nature of the illness, when the inmate died, and an account of the appearance after death (in cases where a *post mortem* examination is made), together with any special remarks that appear to the Medical Officer to be required.

Notice to Coroner, etc.

20. Upon the death of an inmate the Warden shall give immediate notice thereof to the Coroner having jurisdiction, to the Board of Visitors, and to the Commissioners.

DISCIPLINE AND CONTROL

(i) *General*

Inspection

21. Centres shall be open to inspection at all times by and on behalf of the Commissioners and by inspectors designated for the purpose on behalf of the Secretary of State.

Supervision by Warden

22.—(1) The Warden shall exercise a close and constant personal supervision of the whole Centre. He shall visit and inspect daily all parts of the Centre where inmates are working or accommodated, and shall give special attention to every inmate who is sick.

(2) At least twice a fortnight the Warden shall during the night visit the Centre and satisfy himself as to its state.

Performance of Warden's duties by other persons

23.—(1) The Warden may depute any officer to act in his stead in his absence, and that officer shall in the Warden's absence perform all the duties of the Warden.

(2) The Warden may delegate to the Deputy Warden (if any) such duties as from time to time the Commissioners approve.

Supervision, etc., of girls

24. Girls shall be attended only by women officers and if working under a male instructor shall be supervised by a woman officer.

Use of force

25.—(1) No officer in dealing with inmates shall use force unnecessarily and, when the application of force to an inmate is necessary, no more force than is necessary shall be used.

(2) No officer shall deliberately act in a manner calculated to provoke an inmate.

(ii) *Remission*

Conditions of remitting sentence

(1) An inmate ordered to be detained in a detention centre for a term of more than one month may, on the ground of his industry and good conduct, be granted remission not exceeding one-third of that term:
Provided that this Rule shall not permit the reduction of the term to less than 31 days.

(2) For the purposes of this Rule, a period for which an inmate is required to be detained in default of payment of a sum adjudged to be paid by a conviction, or an order made upon a finding of guilt, shall be treated as a term for which he is ordered to be detained.

(3) For the purposes of this Rule, consecutive terms of detention shall be treated as one term.

(4) This Rule shall have effect subject to any disciplinary award of forfeiture of remission.

(iii) *Offences against discipline*

Warden to deal with reports

27. No report against an inmate shall be dealt with by any officer except the Warden, or an officer who by virtue of rule 23 has authority to deal with such reports.

Separation of reported inmates

28. When an inmate has been reported for an offence the Warden may order him to be kept apart from other inmates pending adjudication.

Information to reported inmate

29. An inmate shall, before a report against him is dealt with, be informed of the offence for which he has been reported and shall be given a proper opportunity of hearing the facts alleged against him and of presenting his case.

Unauthorised articles

30. The Warden may deprive an inmate of any unauthorised article found in his room or in his possession.

Offences

31. An inmate whose behaviour is such as to offend against the good order and discipline of the Centre may be punished by the Warden or the Board of Visitors in the manner provided by these rules.

Investigation of offences, and awards, by Warden

32.—(1) Every offence shall be reported forthwith, and the Warden shall investigate the report not later than the following day, unless that day is a Sunday or a public holiday.

(2) If upon investigation the Warden considers that the offence is proved, he shall (subject to the provisions of rule 33) make one or more of the following awards:—

- (a) caution;
- (b) removal for a period not exceeding fourteen days from such activity or activities of the Centre, other than work, as are specified in the award;
- (c) extra work or fatigues outside normal working hours, for not more than two hours on any one day and for a period not exceeding fourteen days;
- (d) stoppage of payments under paragraph (2) of rule 47 for a period not exceeding fourteen days;
- (e) reduction to Grade I;
- (f) removal to a detention room for a period not exceeding fourteen days under such restrictions of activities of the Centre (including work) and with such stoppage of payments under paragraph (2) of rule 47 as the Commissioners shall have determined;
- (g) confinement to a detention room for a period not exceeding twenty-four hours in a junior Centre and three days in a senior Centre;
- (h) restricted diet upon a scale approved by the Commissioners for a period not exceeding three days in a junior Centre and seven days in a senior Centre, provided that the said scale shall not be such as to reduce the offender's diet below a nutritional standard adequate for his health and strength at normal work;
- (i) forfeiture of remission of the term of detention for a period not exceeding seven days.

NOTE

See Home Office Circular No. 159/1971 as to the abolition of dietary punishment and confinement to a detention room.

Investigation of offences, and awards, by Boards of Visitors

33.—(1) Where an inmate is reported for an offence upon which the Warden, having regard to the circumstances of the case, thinks it expedient that the Board of Visitors should adjudicate, the Warden may after investigation refer the case to the Board Visitors.

(2) The Board of Visitors shall inquire into every case referred to them under the foregoing paragraph and, if they find the offence proved, shall make one or more awards authorised under paragraph (2) of rule 32:
Provided that—

    (a) an award lettered (b), (c), (d) or (f) in the said paragraph (2) may be for a period not exceeding twenty-eight days;

    (b) an award of confinement to a detention room may be for a period not exceeding three days in a junior Centre and seven days in a senior Centre;

    (c) an award of forfeiture of remission of the term of detention may be for a period exceeding seven days.

(3) The Warden may, notwithstanding the foregoing provisions of this rule, refer to the Commissioners a case to which paragraph (1) of this rule applies, and thereupon a Commissioner or Assistant Commissioner shall have authority to inquire into the case and deal with it in the same manner as the Board of Visitors.

(4) The functions of the Board of Visitors under this rule shall be exercised by not less than two and not more than five members of the Board.

Medical certificate

34. Confinement to a detention room or restricted diet shall in no case be awarded under rule 32 or rule 33 unless the Medical Officer has certified that the inmate is in a fit condition of health to sustain it.

Visits by Warden and Medical Officer

35. Every inmate undergoing confinement to a detention room or subject to restricted diet in accordance with rule 32 or rule 33 shall be visited at least once a day by both the Warden and the Medical Officer, and if he is undergoing confinement to a detention room he shall be visited by an officer appointed for that purpose at intervals of not more than three hours during the day.

Remission and mitigation of awards

36.—(1) A disciplinary award may be determined or mitigated by the Secretary of State.

(2) A disciplinary award other than an award lettered (a) or (i) in paragraph (2) of rule 32 may be determined or mitigated at any time during the currency thereof by the authority responsible for the award.

(iv) *Restraints*

Mechanical restraints

37.—(1) Mechanical restraints shall not be used in a junior Centre, and shall not be used in a senior Centre as a punishment or for any purpose other than safe custody during removal, except on medical grounds by direction of the Medical Officer, or in the circumstances and under the conditions stated in the following paragraphs of this rule.

(2) When it appears to the Warden that it is necessary to place an inmate of a senior Centre under mechanical restraint in order to prevent his injuring himself or others, or damaging property, or creating a disturbance, the Warden may order him to be placed under mechanical restraint, and notice thereof shall forthwith be given to a member of the Board of Visitors and to the Medical Officer.

(3) The Medical Officer on receipt of the aforesaid notice shall forthwith inform the Warden whether he concurs in the order, and if on medical grounds

he does not concur the Warden shall act in accordance with any recommendations which he makes.

(4) No inmate shall be kept under mechanical restraint longer than is necessary, or for a longer period than twenty-four hours unless an order in writing from a member of the Board of Visitors or a Commissioner or Assistant Commissioner is given, specifying the reason thereof and the time during which the inmate may be so kept, which order shall be preserved by the Warden as his warrant.

(5) Particulars of every case of mechanical restraint shall be forthwith recorded by the Warden.

(6) No mechanical means of restraint shall be used except of such patterns and in such manner and under such conditions as may be approved by the Secretary of State.

Temporary confinement

38.—(1) The Warden may order a refractory or violent inmate to be temporarily confined to a detention room, but no inmate shall be confined under this rule to such a room after he has ceased to be refractory or violent.

(2) An inmate so confined under the foregoing paragraph shall be visited at least once a day by the Warden and the Medical Officer and at intervals of not more than three hours during the day by an officer appointed for that purpose.

(v) *Complaints by inmates*

Complaints to be recorded and put forward

39.—(1) Arrangements shall be made that every request by an inmate to see the Warden, or a Commissioner or Assistant Commissioner, or a member of the Board of Visitors, shall be recorded by the officer to whom it is made and conveyed without delay to the Warden.

(2) The Warden shall at a convenient hour on every day, other than Sundays and public holidays, hear the applications of all inmates who have made a request to see him, and shall inform the next Commissioner or Assistant Commissioner or member of the Board of Visitors who visits the Centre of every such request of an inmate to see such Commissioner or Assistant Commissioner or member.

(vi) *Prohibited articles*

Prohibited articles generally

40. No person shall without authority convey into o throw into or deposit in a Centre, or convey or throw out of a Centre, or convey to an inmate, or deposit in any place with the intent that it shall come into the possession of an inmate, any money, clothing, food, drink, tobacco, letter, paper, book, tool, or other article whatever. Anything so conveyed, thrown or deposited may be confiscated by the Warden.

Drink and Tobacco

41.—(1) No inmate shall be given or allowed to have any intoxicating liquor except in pursuance of a written order of the Medical Officer specifying the quantity to be given and the name of the inmate for whose use it is intended.

(2) No inmate of a junior Centre and, except in accordance with such orders as may be given by the Warden with the approval of the Commissioners, no inmate of a senior Centre shall be allowed to smoke or to have in his possession any tobacco.

(vii) *Control of admission*

General restrictions

42.—(1) All persons and vehicles entering or leaving the Centre may be examined and searched.

(2) A person suspected of bringing any prohibited article into the Centre, or of carrying out a prohibited article or any property belonging to the Centre, or while in a Centre of being in possession of a prohibited article, or in improper possession of any property belonging to the Centre, shall be stopped and immediate notice thereof shall be given to the Warden, who may order that he shall be examined and searched.

(3) The Warden may refuse admission to the Centre of a person who is not willing to be examined and searched.

(4) The Warden may direct the removal from the Centre of a person who while in the Centre is not willing to be examined and searched, or whose conduct is improper.

Visitors viewing Centres

43.—(1) The Warden shall not, except as provided by statute, or as directed by the Secretary of State or the Commissioners, allow any person to view the Centre.

(2) The Warden shall ensure that no person authorised to view the Centre makes a sketch, or takes a photograph or holds communication with an inmate, unless authorised to do so by the Secretary of State or the Commissioners.

EMPLOYMENT OF INMATES

Normal working week

44. The normal working week shall be forty-four hours.

Education

45.—(1) In the case of inmates of compulsory school age, arrangements shall be made for their full-time education within the normal working week.

(2) In the case of inmates not of compulsory school age, arrangements shall be made for their part-time education either within the normal working week or outside it.

Recreation

46. At least one hour a day shall be devoted to physical training or to organised games and such period shall be deemed to form part of the normal working week.

General requirements

47.—(1) The Medical Officer may excuse an inmate from work or from physical training or organised games on medical grounds, and no inmate shall be employed on any work unless he has been certified as fit for that type of work by the Medical Officer.

(2) Inmates may receive payments related to their industry in accordance with rates approved by the Commissioners, and may spend money so received on such articles and subject to such conditions as the Commissioners determine.

(3) No inmate shall be set to any type of work not authorised by the Commissioners.

(4) Except with the authority of the Commissioners, no inmate shall work in the service of another inmate or of an officer or for the private benefit of any person.

Religion and Welfare

(i) *Religion*

Recording of denomination

48. The religious denomination of every inmate shall be ascertained and recorded on his reception and he shall be treated as a member of the denomination then recorded unless and until he satisfies the Board of Visitors that he has good grounds for desiring the record to be altered.

Visits by special ministers

49. Where an inmate is recorded as belonging to a religious denomination other than the Church of England for which no Minister has been appointed to the Centre, the Warden shall if the inmate so requests arrange for him, so far as possible, to be visited by a minister of that denomination, and every such inmate shall be informed of this rule on reception.

Religious services

50.—(1) At least once on every Sunday, Christmas Day and Good Friday and on such other occasions as may be arranged, the Chaplain shall conduct for inmates belonging to the Church of England periods of religious worship or instruction.

(2) Ministers shall conduct for inmates of their denominations periods of religious worship or instruction at such times as may be arranged.

Visits by chaplain or minister

51. Every inmate shall so far as practicable be regularly visited at proper and reasonable times by the Chaplain or, if he is recorded as belonging to a denomination other than the Church of England, by a minister of his own denomination.

Religious books

52. There shall so far as practicable be available for the personal use of every inmate such of the Scriptures and books of religious observance and instruction recognised for his denomination as are accepted by the Commissioners for use in Centres.

Interviews, visits to sick, etc.

53.—(1) The Chaplain or a Minister shall—

(a) interview individually every inmate recorded as belonging to the Church of England or to that Minister's denomination, as the case may be, as soon as possible after the inmate's reception, a short time before his discharge, and from time to time as often as practicable during his detention; and

(b) if no other arrangements are made, read the burial service at the funeral of such an inmate dying in the Centre.

(2) The Chaplain shall daily visit any sick inmate who is recorded as belonging to the Church of England, and a Minister shall so far as possible do the same for any such inmate recorded as belonging to the Minister's denomination.

(3) When an inmate not recorded as belonging to the Church of England is sick and is not regularly visited by a minister of his own denomination, the Chaplain shall visit him if the inmate is willing.

Sunday work, etc.

54. Arrangements shall be made for the avoidance of all unnecessary work by inmates of the Christian religion on Sunday, Christmas Day and Good Friday, and by inmates recorded as belonging to other religions on their recognised days of religious observance.

Substitute for chaplain or minister

55.—(1) Such person as the Commissioners approve may officiate in the Chaplain's absence.

(2) A Minister may with the consent of the Commissioners appoint a substitute to act for him in his absence.

(ii) *Libraries*

Library

56. A library shall be provided in every Centre and, subject to such conditions as the Commissioners determine, every inmate shall be allowed to have library books and to exchange them as often as practicable.

(iii) *Social relations and after-care*

Family relationships, etc.

57.—(1) Special attention shall be paid to the maintenance of such relations between an inmate and his family as are judged to be desirable in the best interests of the inmate.

(2) So far as is practicable and in the opinion of the Warden desirable, an inmate shall be encouraged and assisted to maintain or establish such relations with persons or agencies outside the Centre as may promote his social rehabilitation.

(3) The Warden may at any time communicate to an inmate, or to his family or friends, any matter of importance to such inmate.

After-care

58.—(1) It shall be the duty of the Board of Visitors to make such arrangements as are practicable for the after-care of inmates of the Centre who are willing to accept after-care.

(2) In discharging the said duty the Board of Visitors shall act in consultation with the Warden and with a probation officer.

Information to family of death, etc.

59. Upon the death or serious illness, or certification as insane or mentally defective, of an inmate, or the sustaining by an inmate of a serious accident, the Warden shall at once inform the nearest relative whose address is known, and shall in any event inform any other person whom the inmate has requested may be so informed.

(iv) *Letters and visits*

Normal minimum provision

60.—(1) Every inmate shall be allowed to write and receive a letter on reception and thereafter once in two weeks and to receive a visit once in four weeks:

Provided that in lieu of a visit the Warden may allow an inmate to write a letter and receive a reply.

(2) The Warden may for special reasons allow an inmate to receive or write additional letters or receive additional visits.

Letters and visits generally

61.—(1) Without prejudice to the provisions of rule 60 the Commissioners, notwithstanding any provision of this and the following five rules, may impose such restrictions upon and supervision over letters and visits as they consider necessary for securing discipline and good order, for the prevention of crime and criminal associations, and for the welfare of individuals.

(2) Except as provided in these rules, no person shall be allowed to communicate with an inmate without special authority.

(3) Subject to paragraph (3) of rule 89 every letter to or from an inmate shall be read by the Warden or by a responsible officer deputed by him for the purpose, and it shall be within the discretion of the Warden to stop any letter on the ground that its contents are objectionable or that it is of inordinate length.

(4) The degree of supervision to be exercised during visits to inmates shall, subject to any express provision of these rules, be in the discretion of the Warden.

Deferment

62. When an inmate who is entitled to a letter or visit under any provision of these rules is at the time in a detention room under rule 32, rule 33 or rule 38, the letter or visit may in the Warden's discretion be deferred until the period in the detention room has expired.

(v) *Visits for special purposes*

Visits by police

63. An officer of police may visit any inmate who is willing to see him on production of an order issued by or on behalf of the appropriate chief officer of police.

Visits by legal adviser

64.—(1) Reasonable facilities shall be allowed for the legal adviser of an inmate who is a party to legal proceedings, civil or criminal, to interview the inmate with reference to those proceedings out of the hearing of an officer.

(2) The legal adviser of an inmate may, with the permission of the Commissioners, see such inmate with reference to any other legal business.

Persons detained in default of payment

65. Where a person has been ordered to be detained in a Centre in default of the payment of a sum of money, he shall be allowed to have an interview with his friends on a week-day at any reasonable hour, or to communicate by letter with them for the purpose of providing for a payment which would procure his release from detention, and every such person shall on his reception be informed of this rule.

Special purpose visits not to be forfeited

66. The visits and letters under rules 63, 64 and 65 shall be additional to the visits and letters allowed under any other of the foregoing rules.

PHYSICAL WELFARE

(i) *Medical Services*

Hospital

67.—(1) At every Centre a suitable part of the Centre shall be equipped and furnished as a sick bay for the medical care and treatment of inmates suffering from minor sicknesses.

(2) Any sick inmate for whom adequate treatment cannot be provided in the Centre shall as soon as possible be removed to a hospital.

Medical Officer; general duties

68.—(1) The Medical Officer shall have the care of the mental and physical health of the inmates.

(2) Without prejudice to the duties expressly conferred on the Medical Officer by the foregoing rules and in particular rule 35 and 38 the Medical Officer shall as often as is in his opinion necessary, and normally every day, visit every sick inmate in the Centre, and every other inmate to whom his attention is specially directed.

Immediate attendance and consultations

69.—(1) The Medical Officer shall attend at once on receiving information of the illness of an inmate.

(2) The Medical Officer may at his discretion call into consultation another medical practitioner.

(3) The Medical Officer shall keep a record of occasions on which in accordance with this Rule he consults another medical practitioner.

Duty to report

70. The Medical Officer shall report to the Warden any matter which appears to him to require the consideration of the Commissioners on medical grounds, and the Warden shall send such report to the Commissioners.

Report on danger to health, etc.

71. Whenever the Medical Officer has reason to believe that an inmate's mental or physical health is likely to be injuriously affected by his continued detention or by any conditions of his detention, or that the life of an inmate will be endangered by his detention or that a sick inmate will not survive his sentence or is totally or permanently unfit for Centre discipline, he shall without delay report the case in writing to the Warden with such recommendations as he thinks fit, and the Warden shall forward such report and recommendations to the Commissioners forthwith.

Recommendations on diet, etc.

72. The Medical Officer shall report in writing to the Warden the case of any inmate to which he thinks it necessary on medical grounds to draw attention, and shall make such recommendations as he deems needful for the alteration of the diet or treatment of the inmate or for his separation from other inmates, or for the supply to him of additional clothing, bedding or other articles, and the Warden shall so far as practicable carry such recommendations into effect.

Suicidal inmates

73. The Medical Officer shall draw the attention of the Warden to any inmate who he may have reason to think has suicidal intentions in order that special observation may be kept on such inmate, and the Warden shall, without delay, direct that such inmate be observed at frequent intervals.

Mental illness

74. The Medical Officer shall keep under special observation every inmate whose mental condition appears to require it, and shall take such steps as he considers proper for his segregation, and if necessary his certification under the Acts relating to lunacy or mental deficiency.

Serious illness

75. The Medical Officer shall give notice to the Warden and the Chaplain when an inmate appears to be seriously ill.

(ii) *Hygiene*

Supervision of hygiene

76. The Medical Officer shall oversee and shall advise the Warden upon the hygiene of the Centre and the inmates, including arrangements for cleanliness, sanitation, heating, lighting and ventilation.

Washing, shaving, and hair cutting

77. Arrangements shall be made for every inmate to wash at all proper times, to have a hot bath at least once a week and for male inmates (unless excused or prohibited on medical or other grounds) to shave or be shaved when necessary and to have their hair cut as required. The hair of a male inmate may be cut as short as is necessary for good appearance, but the hair of a female inmate shall not be cut without her consent, except by direction of the Medical Officer for the eradication of vermin, dirt, or disease, which direction shall be given in writing.

Toilet articles

78. Every inmate shall be provided on admission with such toilet articles as are necessary for health and cleanliness and arrangements shall be made for the replacement of those articles when necessary.

(iii) *Food*

Quality of food

79. The food provided for inmates shall be of a nutritional value adequate for health and strength and of wholesome quality, well prepared and served, and reasonably varied.

Inspection of food

80. The Medical Officer shall frequently inspect the food, cooked and un-cooked, provided for inmates, and shall report to the Warden on the state and quality of the food and on any deficiency in the quantity or defect in the quality of the water.

No private food

81. Except as determined by the Commissioners, or on medical grounds, no inmate shall be allowed to have any food other than the normal Centre diet.

Quantity of food

82. Except in the case of inmates on restricted diet, or on the written recommendation of the Medical Officer in the case of an inmate who persistently wastes his food, or on medical grounds by direction of the Medical Officer, no inmate shall have less food than is provided in the normal Centre diet.

(iv) *Clothing*

No private clothing

83. Every inmate shall be provided with an outfit of clothing adequate for warmth and health, in accordance with a scale approved by the Commissioners, and shall, except as approved by the Commissioners, wear such clothing and no other.

Protective clothing

84. The clothing provided shall, where necessary, include suitable protective clothing for use at work.

Appellants

Application of rules

85. The four following rules apply to inmates who are appellants within the meaning of the Criminal Appeal Act, 1907 (hereinafter called " appellants ").

Appellants absent from Centre

86.—(1) An appellant who, when in custody, is to be taken to, kept in custody at, or brought back from, any place at which he is entitled to be present for the purposes of the Criminal Appeal Act, 1907, or any place to which the Court of Criminal Appeal or any Judge thereof may order him to be taken for the purpose of any proceedings of the Court, shall while absent from the Centre be kept in the custody of the officer designated in that behalf by the Warden.

(2) An appellant when absent from the Centre under this rule shall wear his own clothing or, if his own clothing cannot be used, clothing different from Centre dress.

Payments

87. If an appellant is ordered to be released by the Court of Criminal Appeal otherwise than on bail pending the hearing of his appeal, payments related to his industry at a rate fixed by the Commissioners shall be made to him in respect of the time during which he has been treated as subject to this section of these Rules.

Private medical adviser and other visitors

88.—(1) An appellant may for the purposes of his appeal receive a visit from a registered medical practitioner selected by him or by his friends or legal adviser, under the same conditions as apply to a visit by his legal adviser.

(2) An appellant may for the purposes of his appeal receive a visit from any other person.

Letters and other facilities

89.—(1) Writing materials to such extent as the Warden considers reasonable shall be furnished to any appellant who requires them for the purpose of preparing his appeal.

(2) An appellant may write letters to his legal adviser or other persons for the purpose of his appeal.

(3) A confidential written communication prepared as instructions for the legal adviser of an appellant may be delivered personally to such legal adviser, without being examined by an officer, unless the Warden has reason to suppose that it contains matter not relating to such instructions, but all other written communications shall be treated as letters, and shall not be sent out without being previously inspected by the Warden.

Staff

General obligations

90.—(1) Every officer shall conform to these rules and to the regulations of the Centre and shall support the Warden in the maintenance thereof.

(2) Every officer shall obey the lawful instructions of the Warden.

(3) Every officer shall at once communicate to the Warden any abuses or impropriety which may come to his knowledge.

Sick inmates

91. Every officer shall direct the attention of the Warden to any inmate (whether he complains or not) who appears to be out of health or whose state of mind appears to be deserving of special notice and care, and the Warden shall without delay bring such cases to the notice of the Medical Officer.

Business transactions

92.—(1) No officer shall without the authority of the Commissioners carry out any pecuniary or business transaction with or on behalf of an inmate.

(2) No officer shall without authority bring in or carry out, or attempt to bring in or carry out, or knowingly allow to be brought in or carried out, to or for an inmate, or deposit in any place with intent that it shall come into possession of an inmate, any article whatsoever.

Gratuities

93. No officer shall receive any unauthorised fee, gratuity, or other consideration in connexion with his duty.

Ex-inmates, etc.

94. No officer shall knowingly communicate with an ex-inmate or with the friends or relatives of an inmate or ex-inmate except with the knowledge of the Warden.

Search if required

95. Every officer shall submit himself to be searched in the Centre if called upon to do so by the Warden.

Communications to Press, etc.

96.—(1) No officer shall, directly or indirectly, make any unauthorised communication to representatives of the Press or other persons in reference to matters which have become known to him in the course of his duty.

(2) No officer shall without authority publish any matter or make any public pronouncement relating to the administration or the inmates of an institution to which the Prison Acts, 1865 to 1898, apply.

Quarters

97.—(1) Every officer shall occupy such quarters as may be assigned to him and shall at any time vacate them if required to do so.

(2) On the termination of an officer's service he shall give up the quarters he has occupied as soon as he is required to do so; and on the death of an officer his family shall give up the quarters when required to do so.

Code of discipline

98. A code of discipline, setting out the offences against discipline, the procedure for dealing therewith, and the awards therefor, shall be formulated by the Commissioners with the approval of the Secretary of State and shall apply to such classes of officers as are stated in the code.

BOARDS OF VISITORS

Term of office

99. The members of a Board of Visitors appointed by the Secretary of State under subsection (2) of section fifty-three of the Criminal Justice Act, 1948, shall hold office for such a period, not exceeding three years, as he may fix.

Chairman

100.—(1) When a Board of Visitors is initially constituted one of the members shall be appointed by the Secretary of State to be chairman for a period of twelve months.

(2) Except as provided by the foregoing paragraph the Board of Visitors shall at their first meeting in each year of office appoint a chairman and shall, if a casual vacancy occurs in the office of chairman, fill the vacancy as soon as possible.

Meetings and visits

101. The Board shall meet at the Centre at least once a month to discharge their functions under these Rules, and members of the Board shall frequently visit and inspect the Centre.

Rota and quorum

102.—(1) The Board shall at their first meeting arrange a rota of attendance at the Centre and fix a quorum not less than three for the purpose of carrying out their duties, and may at that or a later meeting appoint a vice-chairman, who, unless upon the occurrence of a casual vacancy in the office of chairman he is himself appointed chairman, shall hold office during the term of office for which the chairman has been appointed.

(2) The quorum fixed in pursuance of the foregoing paragraph shall not be required for performing a function which in accordance with an express provision of these Rules may be performed by a smaller number.

Vacancies

103. The powers of the Board shall not be affected by vacancies, so long as the quorum for meetings is sufficient.

Minutes

104. The Board shall keep minutes of their proceedings.

Inquiries, etc.

105. The Board shall co-operate with the Commissioners and with the Warden in promoting the efficiency of the Centre, and shall make inquiry into any matter specially referred to the Board by the Secretary of State or the Commissioners, and report thereon.

Abuses

106. The Board shall bring all abuses in connexion with the Centre which come to their knowledge to the notice of the Commissioners immediately, and in case of urgent necessity may suspend an officer until the decision of the Commissioners is made known.

Adjudication, report, etc.

107.—(1) The Board shall hear and adjudicate on such offences as under rule 33 are referred to them.

(2) They shall furnish such information with respect to the offences reported to them and their awards as may from time to time be required by the Commissioners or the Secretary of State.

Access to Centre

108.—(1) The Board and all members of the Board shall have free access to all parts of the Centre and to all inmates, and may see such inmates as they desire, out of sight and hearing of officers.

(2) They shall hear and investigate any application which an inmate desires to make to them, and if necessary shall report the same, with their opinion, to the Commissioners.

Sick inmates

109. The Board shall attend to any report which they receive that the mind or body of an inmate is likely to be injured by the conditions of his detention, and shall communicate their opinion to the Commissioners. If the case is urgent, they shall give such directions thereon as they deem expedient, communicating the same to the Commissioners.

Restraint

110. If the Warden represents to a member of the Board that he or the Medical Officer has, in pursuance of the provisions of these Rules in that behalf, put an inmate under mechanical restraint, and that it is necessary that the inmate be so kept for more than twenty-four hours, such member may authorise the continuance of that restraint by order in writing, which shall specify the cause thereof and the time during which the inmate is to be so kept.

Diet

111. The Board shall inspect the dietary of inmates and if they find the quality of the food unsatisfactory they shall report the matter to the Commissioners and note the same in their minutes, and the Warden shall immediately take such steps thereupon as may be necessary.

Books

112. The Board may inspect any of the books of the Centre, and a note of any such inspection shall be made in their minutes.

Additional visits or letters

113. The Board may, in any case of special importance or urgency, allow an inmate an additional visit or letter.

Denominational records

114. The Board shall investigate and decide on every application from an inmate to change the record of his religious denomination. Before granting such an application, they shall satisfy themselves that it is made from conscientious motives, and not from caprice or a desire to escape any regulations of the Centre.

Buildings

115. The Board may inquire into the state of the buildings of the Centre, and if any repairs or additions appear to them to be necessary shall report thereon with their advice and suggestions to the Secretary of State or the Commissioners.

Annual and other reports

116. The Board shall make an annual report at the end of each year to the Secretary of State with regard to all or any of the matters referred to in these Rules, with their advice and suggestions upon any such matter, and they may make such other reports to the Secretary of State or to the Commissioners as they consider necessary concerning any matter relating to the Centre to which, in their opinion, attention should be drawn.

Permissions and consultation

117. The Board shall, before granting any permission which they have power to grant under these Rules, satisfy themselves by consultation with the Warden that it can be granted without interfering with the security, good order, and proper government of the Centre and inmates therein, and if after such permission has been granted its continuance seems likely to cause such interference, or an inmate has abused permission granted to him or has been guilty of misconduct, they may suspend or withdraw the permission.

Contracts

118. A member of a Board of Visitors of a Centre shall not have any interest in any contract made in respect of that Centre.

NOTES

These rules were made on July 28, 1952, under s. 52 of the Criminal Justice Act, 1948 (25 Halsbury's Statutes, 3rd Edn., 821). They are printed as amended by S. I. 1968 No. 1014.

"Commissioners, Prison Commissioners, Assistant Commissioners."—Now the Secretary of State; see the Prison Commissioners' Dissolution Order 1963 (S.I. 1963 No. 597).

Fines outstanding against persons detained. See Home Office Circular No. 122/1968, p. 697, *post*.

THE CHILDREN AND YOUNG PERSONS ACT, 1963 (COMMENCEMENT NO. 3) ORDER, 1968
[S.I. 1968 No. 1727]

1. The remaining provisions of the Children and Young Persons Act, 1963, which have not previously come into operation and are specified in the Schedule hereto (which relate to the employment of children and young persons) shall come into operation on 3rd March 1969 except that for the purposes of applying for licences under section 37 of the Act, and granting such licences to have effect on and after the said date, these provisions shall come into operation on 2nd December 1968.

2. This Order may be cited as the Children and Young Persons Act, 1963 (Commencement No. 3) Order, 1968.

SCHEDULE

Provisions of the Act	Subject matter of provisions
Sections 34 to 44	Employment of children and young persons.
In Schedule 3, paragraphs 4 to 10 and 29 to 32	Minor and consequential amendments of the Children and Young Persons Act, 1933 and the Children and Young Persons (Scotland) Act, 1937.
In Schedule 4, paragraphs 3 and 4	Transitional provisions.
So much of Schedule 5 as is set out in the Appendix hereto	Repeals.

APPENDIX

Chapter	Short title	Extent of repeal
23 & 24 Geo. 5. c. 12.	The Children and Young Persons Act, 1933	Section 22. In section 24, subsections (3) and (5). In section 25, in subsection (1), the words "he has attained the age of fourteen years and". In section 26, in subsection (1), the words "or in default of payment of such a fine". In section 29, subsections (1) and (2).
1 Edw. 8 & 1 Geo. 6. c. 37.	The Children and Young Persons (Scotland) Act, 1937	Section 32. In section 34, subsections (3) and (5). In section 37, paragraph (g). In section 38, subsections (1), (2) and (7).

NOTE

This Order was made on October 30, 1968, by the Secretary of State under s. 65(6) of the Children and Young Persons Act, 1963.

THE CHILDREN (PERFORMANCES) REGULATIONS, 1968
[S.I. 1968 No. 1728]

ARRANGEMENT OF REGULATIONS

PART I
APPLICATION FOR LICENCE, ETC.

PART I

APPLICATION FOR LICENCE, ETC.

Application for a licence

1.—(1) An application to a licensing authority for a licence authorising a child to take part in a performance to which section 37 of the Children and Young Persons Act, 1963 applies shall be made in writing in the form set out in Schedule 1 to these Regulations or in a form to the like effect and shall be signed by the applicant and a parent of the child and shall be accompanied by the documents specified therein.

(2) The applicant shall be the person responsible for the production of the performance in which the child is to take part.

(3) The licensing authority may refuse to grant a licence if the application form is not received by them at least twenty-one days before the day on which the first performance for which the licence is required takes place.

Power of licensing authorities to obtain additional information

2.—(1) The licensing authority may make such inquiries as they consider necessary to enable them to be satisfied that they should grant a licence as required by section 37(4) of the Act, and in particular they may request a report from the head teacher in respect of the child, they may request that the child be medically examined in order to ascertain whether he is fit to take part in the performances for which the licence is requested and that his health will not suffer by reason of taking part in such performances and may interview the applicant, the child and his parents and the proposed matron and private teacher (if any).

(2) The licensing authority may make such inquiries as they consider necessary to enable them to consider, if a licence should be granted, whether the licence should be granted subject to a condition relating to the manner in which sums earned by the child in taking part in any performance to which the licence relates should be dealt with.

Form of licence

3.—(1) A licence granted to an applicant by a licensing authority shall be in the form set out in Schedule 2 to these Regulations or in a form to the like effect.

(2) The licence shall specify the names, dates, places and nature of the performances except that in the case of a licence granted to the British Broadcasting Corporation, the Independent Television Authority, a programme contractor within the meaning of section 1(5) of the Television Act, 1964 or a body supplying programmes to such a programme contractor to be broadcast by the Independent Television Authority or a licence authorising a child to take part in a performance to be recorded (by whatever means) with a view to its use in a film intended for public exhibition the licence may, if the applicant so requests in the application form, in lieu of specifying the said dates, specify the number of days on which the child may perform, and the period, not exceeding six months, in which the performances may take place.

(3) One print of the photograph of the child accompanying the application form shall be attached to the licence; the other print shall be retained by the licensing authority.

(4) The licensing authority shall send a copy of the licence to the parent who signed the application form.

Particulars to be sent to a local authority under section 39(3) of the Act

4. Where a place of performance specified in a licence is in the area of another local authority, the licensing authority shall send to that local authority a copy of the application form and the licence and such other information, if any, relating to the child as they think appropriate.

Records to be kept by the holder of a licence under section 39(5) of the Act

5. The holder of a licence shall keep the records specified in Schedule 3 to these Regulations, and shall retain them for six months after the performance or last performance to which the licence relates.

PART II

RESTRICTIONS ON THE GRANT OF LICENCES

Number of performing days

6.—(1) Subject to paragraphs (2) and (3) of this Regulation, a licensing authority shall not grant a licence—

   (a) in respect of a child who has attained the age of thirteen years if, during the twelve months preceding any performance in respect of which a licence is requested, he will have taken part in other performances on more than seventy-nine days;

   (b) in respect of a child who has not attained the age of thirteen years if, during the twelve months preceding any performance in respect of which a licence is requested, he will have taken part in other performances on more than thirty-nine days.

(2) The relevant number of days of other performances specified in paragraph (1) of this Regulation may be increased by four if the licensing authority so determine:

Provided that the licensing authority shall not so determine if the child has taken part in a performance on any of the six days preceding any of the said four additional days of performance.

(3) Where application is made for a licence for a child to take part in a performance to be recorded (by whatever means) with a view to its use in a television broadcast or in a film intended for public exhibition and—

(a) the child will not have taken part in any performance other than such a performance as aforesaid during the twelve months preceding the performance in respect of which the licence is requested, and

(b) the purpose of the performance for which the licence is requested is to continue the recording of a performance which is incomplete,

the relevant number of days of other performances specified in paragraph (1) of this Regulation may be increased by ten if the licensing authority so determine.

(4) In deciding whether or not to grant a licence and, if a licence should be granted, the number of days in respect of which it should be granted, the licensing authority shall take into account—

(a) the arrangements for rehearsals taking place during the fourteen days preceding the day of the first performance for which the licence is requested, and

(b) any other form of employment in which the child is employed during the twenty-eight days preceding the day of the first performance for which the licence is requested.

(5) In this Regulation the expression "other performances" includes an entertainment for which a licence under section 22(1) or (6) of the Children and Young Persons Act, 1933 has been granted, an entertainment for which by section 22(2) of that Act (charitable performance) a licence is not necessary and a performance for which by section 29(1) of that Act (broadcast performance) a licence is not necessary.

Troupe work

7.—(1) Subject to paragraph (2) of this Regulation, a licensing authority shall not grant a licence in respect of a child who has attained the age of thirteen years if the child—

(a) by reason of taking part in any performance for which the licence is requested will have to live elsewhere than at the place where he would otherwise live, and

(b) has during the three months preceding the performance for which the licence is requested or, if the licence is requested for more than one performance, the first performance, lived elsewhere than at the place where he would otherwise have lived by reason of taking part in a performance.

(2) Paragraph (1) of this Regulation shall not apply where—

(a) the licence is for acting and the part the child is to act cannot be taken except by a child of about his age, or

(b) the licence is for dancing in a ballet which does not form part of an entertainment of which anything other than ballet or opera also forms part and the part the child is to dance cannot be taken except by a child of about his age, or

(c) the nature of the child's part in the performance is wholly or mainly musical and either the nature of the performance is also wholly or mainly musical or the performance consists only of opera and ballet.

(3) On the extension of the compulsory school age (or, in Scotland, school age) to sixteen years, that is to say—

(a) in England and Wales, on the coming into force of an Order in Council under section 35 of the Education Act, 1944, and

(b) in Scotland, on the coming into force of regulations under section 32 of the Education (Scotland) Act, 1962, paragraph (1) of this Regulation shall have effect as if for the word "thirteen" there were substituted the word "fourteen".

Medical examinations

8.—(1) Subject to paragraph (2) of this Regulation, a licensing authority shall not grant a licence—

(a) for performances for film or television, or

(b) for broadcast performances, other than performances for television, with respect to which the applicant for the purposes of Regulation 3(2) of these Regulations requests in the application form that the child may perform on more than six days in a period not exceeding six months, or

(c) for other performances if the child would perform on the maximum number of days in a week permitted under Part IV or V of these Regulations, as the case may be, and for a period exceeding one week,

unless the school medical officer, or other medically qualified person approved by them, has examined the child and has certified that he is fit to take part in the performances for which the licence is requested and that his health will not suffer by reason of taking part in such performances.

(2) Where a child has been medically examined under paragraph (1) of this Regulation, he need not be medically examined in order that a further licence may be granted in respect of a performance taking place within a period of six months from the date of the said medical examination unless it appears desirable to the licensing authority that he should be medically examined.

Part III

Restrictions and Conditions Applying to all Licences

Application of Part III

9. The restrictions and conditions specified in this Part of these Regulations shall apply in the case of every licence.

Education

10.—(1) The licensing authority shall not grant a licence unless they are satisfied that the child's education will not suffer by reason of taking part in the performances for which the licence is requested and have approved the arrangements (if any) for the education of the child during the currency of the licence.

(2) The holder of the licence shall ensure that the arrangements for the child's education during the currency of the licence, approved by the licensing authority, are carried out.

(3) The licensing authority shall not approve any arrangements for the education of a child by a private teacher unless they are satisfied that—

(a) the course of study proposed for the child is satisfactory;

(b) the said course of study will be properly taught by the private teacher;

(c) the private teacher is a suitable person to teach the child in question; and

(d) the private teacher will not teach more than five other children at the same time, or, if the other children being taught at the same time have reached a similar standard in the subject to the child in question, eleven.

(4) (a) The licensing authority shall not approve any arrangements for the education of a child by a private teacher unless they are satisfied that the child will, during the currency of the licence, receive education for periods which, when aggregated, total not less than three hours on each day on which the child would be required to attend school if he were a pupil attending a school maintained by the local authority (or, in Scotland, a public school).

(b) The requirements of sub-paragraph (a) of this paragraph shall be deemed to be satisfied if, in a case to which this sub-paragraph applies, the licensing authority are satisfied that the child will receive education—

> (i) for not less than six hours a week,
> (ii) during each complete period of four weeks on location, or, if there is a period on location of less than four weeks, during that period, for periods not less than the aggregate periods of education required by sub-paragraph (a) of this paragraph in respect of the period on location,
> (iii) on days other than days on which the child would not be required to attend school if he were a pupil attending a school maintained by the local authority (or, in Scotland, a public school), and
> (iv) for not more than five hours on any such day.

(c) Sub-paragraph (b) of this paragraph applies—

> (i) if the performances to which the licence relates are to be recorded (by whatever means) with a view to their use in a broadcast or in a film intended for public exhibition,
> (ii) to any period of recording on location exceeding one week.

(d) In calculating any period of education for the purposes of this paragraph there shall be disregarded—

> (i) any period which takes place, in the case of a child taking part in a performance to be recorded (by whatever means) with a view to its use in a broadcast or film intended for public exhibition, other than during the hours when he is permitted to be present at a place of performance or rehearsal under Regulations 27 to 29 of these Regulations, or, in any other case, which takes place other than between the hours of nine in the morning and four in the afternoon,
> (ii) any period which is less than thirty minutes.

(e) In this paragraph the expression "on location" means at a place which is one mile or more from any film or broadcasting studio (including any land adjacent to the studio and occupied and used in connection with it).

(5) Any licence under which a child is to be taught by a private teacher shall be subject to the condition that the local authority approve the schoolroom or other place where the child is to receive education, and the local authority may give their approval subject to such conditions as they consider necessary to ensure that the place is suitable for the child's education.

Earnings

11.—(1) Where the licensing authority think fit, they may grant a licence subject to a condition requiring the holder of the licence to ensure that the sums earned by the child in respect of whom the licence is granted in taking part in a performance to which the licence relates, or such part of those sums as may be required by the condition, shall be dealt with in a manner approved by the licensing authority.

(2) Any such condition shall be set out in the licence.

Matrons

12.—(1) A person, who may be a man or a woman, approved by the licensing authority (in these Regulations referred to as a matron) shall be in charge of the child at all times during the period beginning with the first and ending with the last performance to which the licence relates except while the child is in the charge of a parent or teacher.

(2) The licensing authority shall not approve a matron unless they are satisfied that she is suitable and competent to exercise proper care and control of a child of the age and sex of the child in question and that she will not be prevented from carrying out her duties towards the child by other activities or duties towards other children.

(3) Without prejudice to the last foregoing paragraph, the licensing authority shall not approve a matron if she is to be in charge of more than eleven other children during the time when she would be in charge of the child in question if approval were given.

(4) The licensing authority shall not approve as matron the private teacher of the child in question if she is to be in charge of more than two other children during the time when she would be in charge of the child if approval were given.

(5) A matron while in charge of a child under this Regulation shall have the care and control of the child with a view to securing his health, comfort, kind treatment and moral welfare.

(6) Where a child suffers any injury or illness while in the charge of a matron or teacher, the holder of the licence shall ensure that the parent of the child named in the application form and the local authority are notified immediately of such injury or illness.

Lodgings

13.—(1) Where by reason of taking part in a performance a child has to live elsewhere than at the place where he would otherwise live, that child shall live only in premises which have been approved by the local authority as suitable for occupation by him.

(2) The local authority's approval may be subject to any of the following conditions:—

    (a) that transport for the child from the said premises to the place of performance or rehearsal is provided;

    (b) that suitable arrangements are made for meals for the child;

    (c) any other condition conducive to the welfare of the child in connection with the premises in which the child will live.

Place of performance and place of rehearsal

14.—(1) A child shall not take part in a performance or rehearsal unless the place of performance or rehearsal has been approved by the local authority.

(2) The local authority shall not approve the place of performance or rehearsal unless they are satisfied that, having regard to the age of the child and the nature, time and duration of the performance or rehearsal—

    (a) suitable arrangements have been made for meals for the child, for the child to dress for the performance or rehearsal, and for the child's rest and recreation, when not taking part in a performance or rehearsal;

    (b) the place is provided with suitable and sufficient sanitary conveniences and washing facilities, and

    (c) the child will be adequately protected against inclement weather,

and their approval may be given subject to such conditions as they consider necessary for the purposes of this paragraph.

(3) Arrangements for a child who has attained the age of five years to dress for a performance or rehearsal shall not be deemed to be suitable unless such a child can dress only with children of the same sex as the child in question.

Arrangements for getting home

15. The holder of the licence shall ensure that suitable arrangements (having regard to the child's age) are made for the child to get to his home or other destination after the last performance or rehearsal on any day.

Break in performances

16.—(1) Subject to the provisions of paragraph (2) of this Regulation, a child who takes part in performances, other than performances in a circus, or rehearsals on the maximum number of days in a week permitted under Part IV or V of these Regulations, as the case may be, for a period of eight consecutive weeks, shall not take part in any performance or rehearsal or be employed in any other form of employment during the fourteen days next ensuing.

(2) This Regulation shall not apply if the number of days specified in the licence on which the child may perform is less than sixty.

Further medical examinations

17.—(1) (a) Where a licence specifies the dates of performances and these fall on days in four consecutive weeks or more or where a licence specifies the period in which performances may take place and such period is one month or more, the holder of the licence shall ensure that the child is medically examined within forty-eight hours after the end of each such period of four weeks or each month, as the case may be, in order to ascertain whether he is fit to take part in any further performances for which the licence has been granted and whether his health will suffer by reason of taking part in such performances.

(b) The holder of the licence shall obtain from the person making the medical examination a report stating whether in his opinion the child is fit to take part in any further performances for which the licence has been granted and whether his health will suffer by reason of taking part in such performances.

(c) If the report states that the child is not fit or that his health would suffer as aforesaid, he shall not take part in any further performance until the person making the medical examination has certified that the child is fit to take part and that his health will not suffer thereby.

(2) Where a child has been medically examined under Regulation 8(1) of these Regulations, that child shall be medically examined during the seven days immediately following the day of the last performance to which the licence relates unless the licensing authority are satisfied, having regard to the date of the last medical examination of the child under these Regulations and the number and nature of performances in which the child has taken part, that no such medical examination is necessary.

(3) Where a medical examination is required under this Regulation, it shall be carried out by the school medical officer of the licensing authority or of the local authority or other medically qualified person approved by either of the said authorities; and a copy of the medical report shall be sent to the licensing authority.

Restriction on employment

18.—(1) On the day on which or on the day immediately following the day on which a child takes part in a performance, he shall not be employed in any other form of employment.

(2) On the day on which a child takes part in a performance for which a licence has been granted, he shall not take part in a performance for which a licence is not required.

Production of licence

19. The holder of a licence shall on request produce the licence at all reasonable hours at the place of performance to an authorised officer of the local authority or a constable.

PART IV

PERFORMANCES OTHER THAN BROADCAST OR RECORDED PERFORMANCES

Licences to which Part IV applies

20. The restrictions and conditions specified in this Part of these Regulations shall apply in the case of every licence authorising a child to take part in a performance other than a broadcast performance or a performance to be recorded (by whatever means) with a view to its use in a broadcast or in a film intended for public exhibition.

Maximum number of days in a week on which a child may take part in performances and rehearsals

21.—(1) Subject to the provisions of paragraph (2) of this Regulation, a child shall not take part in performances or rehearsals to which this Part of these Regulations applies on more than six consecutive days.

(2) Where in any period of seven days a child takes part in performances or rehearsals to some of which this Part of these Regulations applies and to others of which Part V of these Regulations applies, he shall not take part in such performances or rehearsals on more than five days in that period.

Maximum number and length of performances and rehearsals daily

22.—(1) A child shall not take part in a performance or rehearsal the duration of which exceeds three and a half hours.

(2) A child shall not take part in a performance or rehearsal if the duration of his appearances in the performance or rehearsal exceeds two and a half hours.

(3) A child shall not take part in more than one performance or rehearsal on any day unless he performs the same part in the performances or rehearsals, except where he takes the place of another performer in the same performance, and the performances or rehearsals are of the same nature.

(4) On any day on which a child is required to attend school after the morning session he shall not take part in more than one performance or rehearsal.

(5) Subject to the provisions of paragraph (3) of this Regulation, a child on any other day shall not take part in more than two performances or rehearsals or more than one performance and one rehearsal.

(6) (a) Subject to the provisions of sub-paragraph (b) of this paragraph, a child shall not take part in more than one performance or rehearsal on any day unless there is an interval of not less than one and a half hours between the end of his part in the first performance or rehearsal and the beginning of his part in the second performance or rehearsal.

(b) On not more than two days in any week a child may take part in more than one performance or rehearsal on any day if—

>> (i) there is an interval of not less than forty-five minutes between the end of his part in the first performance or rehearsal and the beginning of his part in the second performance or rehearsal; and

>> (ii) he is not present at the place of performance or rehearsal on such a day for more than six hours.

(7) Notwithstanding paragraphs (4), (5) and (6) of this Regulation and subject to paragraph (3) of this Regulation, where a child takes part in a performance in a circus—

> (a) on any day on which he is required to attend school after the morning session, he may take part in not more than two performances or rehearsals or not more than one performance and one rehearsal;

> (b) on any other day, he may take part in not more than three performances or rehearsals:

Provided that—

>> (i) he shall not take part in more than one performance or rehearsal unless there is an interval of not less than one and a half hours between the end of his part in one performance or rehearsal and the beginning of his part in the next performance or rehearsal, and

>> (ii) the duration of his appearance in a performance or rehearsal does not exceed thirty minutes.

Earliest and latest hours at place of performance and place of rehearsal

23.—(1) Subject to the provisions of paragraph (2) of this Regulation, a child shall not be present at a place of performance or rehearsal after whichever is the earlier of the two following times:—

> (a) ten in the evening, if he has not attained the age of thirteen years, or half-past ten if he has;

> (b) thirty minutes after the end of his part in the performance or rehearsal or the last performance or rehearsal.

(2) If in order to enable a child to take part in a performance the child's presence at the place of performance is required after the latest permitted time specified in paragraph (1) of this Regulation, he may be present at the place of performance not later than eleven in the evening on not more than three evenings in a week, provided that he is not so present on more than eight evenings in a period of four consecutive weeks.

(3) A child shall not be present at a place of performance or rehearsal before ten in the morning, and on the day immediately following a day on which a child has taken part in a performance or rehearsal he shall not take part in a performance or rehearsal until after the expiration of not less than fourteen hours from the end of his part in the performance or rehearsal in which he last performed on the preceding day.

(4) This Regulation shall not apply with respect to a place of performance or rehearsal where the child lives or receives education in that place.

Part V

Broadcast and Recorded Performances

Licences to which Part V applies

24. The restrictions and conditions specified in this Part of these Regulations shall apply in the case of every licence authorising a child to take part in a broadcast performance or a performance to be recorded (by whatever means) with a view to its use in a broadcast or a film intended for public exhibition.

Maximum number of days in a week on which a child may take part in performances and rehearsals

25. Where in any period of seven days a child takes part in performances or rehearsals to all of which this Part of these Regulations applies or to some of which this Part applies and to others of which Part IV of these Regulations applies, he shall not take part in such performances or rehearsals on more than five days in that period.

Limitation on daily performances

26. On any day a child may take part only in performances or rehearsals which are of the same nature and in which he performs the same part or takes the place of another performer in the same performance.

Children aged thirteen or more

27.—(1) Subject to the provisions of paragraph (2) of this Regulation, a child who has attained the age of thirteen years shall not be present at a place of performance or rehearsal—

    (a) for more than eight hours a day;

    (b) before nine in the morning or after seven in the evening, except that a child may be present after half-past eight in the morning if on the preceding day he was not present after half-past six in the evening.

(2) Notwithstanding the provisions of paragraph (1) of this Regulation, where the holder of the licence is the British Broadcasting Corporation, the Independent Television Authority, a programme contractor within the meaning of section 1(5) of the Television Act, 1964, or a body supplying programmes to such a programme contractor to be broadcast by the Independent Television Authority, a child who has attained the age of thirteen years may—

    (a) be present in any week at a place of performance or rehearsal between the hours of ten in the morning and ten in the evening—

        (i) for not more than twelve hours on any one day, or

        (ii) for not more than ten hours a day on any two days, or

        (iii) for not more than eight hours a day on any three days,

    if he is not present at a place of performance or rehearsal on any other day in that week and has not been present at a place of performance or rehearsal after seven in the evening on more than twenty days during the preceding twelve months; or

    (b) be present on one day in any week at a place of performance or rehearsal for not more than twelve hours between the hours of ten in the morning and ten in the evening, provided that—

        (i) he is not present at the place of performance or rehearsal for more than four hours on any other day in that week;

        (ii) he does not take part in a performance or rehearsal for a total period of more than two hours on any other day in that week;

(iii) he does not take part in a performance or rehearsal on the day immediately following the day on which he has been present at the place of performance or rehearsal after seven in the evening in accordance with this paragraph; and

(iv) he has not been present at a place of performance or rehearsal after seven in the evening in accordance with this paragraph on any day during the six preceding days.

(3) A child who has attained the age of thirteen years shall not take part in a performance or rehearsal on any day—

(a) for a continuous period of more than one hour without an interval for rest;

(b) for a total period of more than three and a half hours.

(4) A child who has attained the age of thirteen years shall not be present at a place of performance or rehearsal—

(a) for more than four consecutive hours without there being two or more intervals of which one shall be for the purpose of a meal and shall be of not less than one hour and the other or others shall be for the purpose of rest and shall not be less than fifteen minutes;

(b) for more than eight consecutive hours without there being three or more intervals of which two shall be for the purposes of meals and shall each be of not less than one hour and the other or others shall be for the purpose of rest and shall not be less than fifteen minutes.

(5) In calculating the number of hours on any day during which a child is present at a place of performance or rehearsal, there shall, in the case of a child for whom arrangements for his education by a private teacher have been approved by the licensing authority, be included any periods of education taken into account for the purpose of complying with the requirements of Regulation 10(4) of these Regulations, whether or not they take place at the place of performance or rehearsal.

Children aged five to twelve

28.—(1) Subject to the provisions of paragraph (2) of this Regulation, a child who has attained the age of five years but has not attained the age of thirteen years shall not be present at a place of performance or rehearsal—

(a) for more than seven and a half hours a day;

(b) before nine in the morning or after half-past four in the afternoon, except that a child who has attained the age of ten years may be present until five in the afternoon.

(2) Notwithstanding the provisions of paragraph (1) of this Regulation, Regulation 27(2) of these Regulations shall apply to a child who has attained the age of twelve years as if for the word "thirteen" there were substituted the word "twelve" and for the words "seven in the evening" wherever they occur there were substituted the words "five in the afternoon".

(3) A child who has attained the age of five years but has not attained the age of thirteen years shall not take part in a performance or rehearsal on any day—

(a) for a continuous period of more than forty-five minutes without an interval for rest;

(b) for a total period of more than three hours.

(4) A child who has attained the age of five years but has not attained the age of thirteen years shall not be present at a place of performance or rehearsal—

    (a) for more than three and a half consecutive hours without there being two or more intervals of which one shall be for the purpose of a meal and shall be of not less than one hour and the other or others shall be for the purpose of rest and shall not be less than fifteen minutes;

    (b) for more than eight consecutive hours without there being three or more intervals of which two shall be for the purposes of meals and shall each be of not less than one hour and the other or others shall be for the purpose of rest and shall not be less than fifteen minutes.

(5) In calculating the number of hours on any day during which a child is present at a place of performance or rehearsal, there shall, in the case of a child for whom arrangements for his education by a private teacher have been approved by the licensing authority, be included any periods of education taken into account for the purpose of complying with the requirements of Regulation 10(4) of these Regulations, whether or not they take place at the place of performance or rehearsal.

Children under five

29.—(1) A child who has not attained the age of five years shall not be present at a place of performance or rehearsal—

    (a) for more than five hours a day;

    (b) before half-past nine in the morning or after half-past four in the afternoon.

(2) Such a child shall not take part in a performance or rehearsal on any day—

    (a) for a continuous period of more than thrity minutes without an interval for rest;

    (b) for a total period of more than two hours.

(3) Any time during which such a child is present at a place of performance or rehearsal, but is not taking part in a performance or rehearsal, shall be used for the purposes of meals, rest and recreation.

Night-work

30.—(1) Notwithstanding anything in Regulations 27 to 29 of these Regulations, but subject to the restrictions and conditions laid down in paragraph (2) of this Regulation, where the local authority are satisfied that a scene must be recorded out of doors and after the latest permitted hour, they may permit a child to take part in a performance after the latest permitted hour, but they shall only permit the child to take part in a performance after midnight and before the earliest permitted hour if they are satisfied that it is impracticable for the recording of the performance to be completed before midnight.

(2) Where the local authority permit a child to take part in a performance after the latest permitted hour, the following restrictions and conditions shall apply:—

    (a) the number of hours during which the child takes part in a performance after the latest permitted hour shall be included in computing the maximum number of hours during which he may take part in a performance or rehearsal on any one day under Regulations 27 to 29 of these Regulations;

    (b) the child shall not take part in any other performance or rehearsal until not less than sixteen hours have elapsed since the end of his part in the performance;

(c) where the child takes part in a performance after the latest permitted hour on two successive days, the local authority shall not permit him to take part in any further performance after the latest permitted hour during the seven days immediately following the said two days.

(3) In this Regulation "latest permitted hour" and "earliest permitted hour" in relation to a particular child mean the latest hour and the earliest hour respectively at which that child may be present at the place of performance or rehearsal under Regulations 27 to 29 of these Regulations.

Exceptions to Regulations 27 to 29

31.—(a) The matron in charge of a child may allow that child to take part in a performance for a period not exceeding thirty minutes immediately following the latest permitted hour if—

(i) the total number of hours during which the child takes part in a performance, including the said period of thirty minutes, does not exceed the maximum number of hours permitted under Regulations 27 to 29 of these Regulations;

(ii) it appears to the matron that the welfare of the child will not be prejudiced, and

(iii) it appears to the matron that the conditions necessitating the child taking part in a performance after the latest permitted hour arose in circumstances outside the control of the holder of the licence.

(b) If a child takes part in a performance after the latest permitted hour under this Regulation, the holder of the licence shall ensure that the matron notifies the local authority not later than the day immediately following the day on which that child takes part in the performance.

(c) In this Regulation "latest permitted hour" in relation to a particular child means the latest hour at which that child may be present at the place of performance or rehearsal under Regulations 27 to 29 of these Regulations.

(2) The matron in charge of a child may allow one of the intervals to be set aside for the purposes of meals under Regulation 27 or 28 of these Regulations, as the case may be, to be reduced where the child is taking part in a performance or rehearsal out of doors, provided that—

(a) the duration of that interval is not less than thirty minutes, and

(b) the maximum number of hours during which he may take part in a performance or rehearsal under the said Regulation 27 or 28 is not exceeded.

PART VI

PERFORMANCES FOR WHICH BY REASON OF SECTION 37(3) (a) OF THE ACT A LICENCE IS NOT REQUIRED

Performances for which a licence is not required, other than broadcast or recorded performances

32. Regulations 33 and 34 of these Regulations shall apply in the case of a child taking part in a performance for which by reason of section 37(3) (a) of the Act a licence is not required, being a performance other than a broadcast performance or a performance to be recorded (by whatever means) with a view to its use in a broadcast or in a film intended for public exhibition.

Maximum number and length of performances daily

33.—(1) A child shall not take part in a performance the duration of which exceeds three and a half hours.

(2) A child shall not take part in a performance if the duration of his appearances in the performance exceeds two and a half hours.

(3) A child shall not take part in more than one performance on any day unless he performs the same part in the performances, except where he takes the place of another performer in the same performance, and the performances are of the same nature.

(4) On any day on which a child is required to attend school after the morning session he shall not take part in more than one performance.

(5) Subject to the provisions of paragraph (3) of this Regulation, a child on any other day shall not take part in more than two performances.

(6) (a) Subject to the provisions of sub-paragraph (b) of this paragraph, a child shall not take part in more than one performance on any day unless there is an interval of not less than one and a half hours between the end of his part in the first performance and the beginning of his part in the second performance.

(b) On not more than two days in any week a child may take part in more than one performance on any day if—

(i) there is an interval of not less than forty-five minutes between the end of his part in the first performance and the beginning of his part in the second performance; and

(ii) he is not present at the place of performance on such a day for more than six hours.

(7) Notwithstanding paragraphs (4), (5) and (6) of this Regulation and subject to paragraph (3) of this Regulation, where a child takes part in a performance in a circus—

(a) on any day on which he is required to attend school after the morning session, he may take part in not more than two performances;

(b) on any other day, he may take part in not more than three performances:

Provided that—

(i) he shall not take part in more than one performance unless there is an interval of not less than one and a half hours between the end of his part in one performance and the beginning of his part in the next performance, and

(ii) the duration of his appearance in a performance does not exceed thirty minutes.

Earliest and latest hours at place of performance

34.—(1) Subject to the provisions of paragraph (2) of this Regulation, a child shall not be present at a place of performance after whichever is the earlier of the two following times:—

(a) ten in the evening, if he has not attained the age of thirteen years, or half-past ten if he has;

(b) thirty minutes after the end of his part in the performance or last performance.

(2) If in order to enable a child to take part in a performance the child's presence at the place of performance is required after the latest permitted time specified in paragraph (1) of this Regulation, he may be present at the place of performance not later than eleven in the evening on not more than three evenings in a week.

(3) A child shall not be present at a place of performance before ten in the morning, and on the day immediately following a day on which a child has taken part in a performance he shall not take part in a performance until after the expiration of not less than fourteen hours from the end of his part in the performance in which he last performed on the preceding day.

(4) This Regulation shall not apply with respect to a place of performance where the child lives or receives education in that place.

Broadcast and recorded performances for which a licence is not required

35. Regulations 36 to 40 of these Regulations shall apply in the case of a child taking part in a performance for which by reason of section 37(3) (a) of the Act a licence is not required, being a broadcast performance or a performance to be recorded (by whatever means) with a view to its use in a broadcast or in a film intended for public exhibition.

Limitation on daily performances

36. On any day a child may take part only in performances which are of the same nature and in which he performs the same part or takes the place of another performer in the same performance.

Children aged thirteen or more

37.—(1) A child who has attained the age of thirteen years shall not be present at a place of performance—

    (a) for more than eight hours a day;
    (b) before nine in the morning or after seven in the evening, except that a child may be present after half-past eight in the morning if on the preceding day he was not present after half-past six in the evening.

(2) Such a child shall not take part in a performance on any day—

    (a) for a continuous period of more than one hour without an interval for rest;
    (b) for a total period of more than three and a half hours.

(3) Such a child shall not be present at a place of performance for more than four consecutive hours without there being two or more intervals of which one shall be for the purpose of a meal and shall be of not less than one hour and the other or others shall be for the purpose of rest and shall not be less than fifteen minutes.

Children aged five to twelve

38.—(1) A child who has attained the age of five years but has not attained the age of thirteen years shall not be present at a place of performance—

    (a) for more than seven and a half hours a day;
    (b) before nine in the morning or after half-past four in the afternoon, except that a child who has attained the age of ten years may be present until five in the afternoon.

(2) Such a child shall not take part in a performance on any day—

    (a) for a continuous period of more than forty-five minutes without an interval for rest;
    (b) for a total period of more than three hours.

(3) Such a child shall not be present at a place of performance for more than three and a half consecutive hours without there being two or more intervals of which one shall be for the purpose of a meal and shall be of not less than one hour and the other or others shall be for the purpose of rest and shall not be less than fifteen minutes.

Children aged two to four

39.—(1) A child who has attained the age of two years but has not attained the age of five years shall not be present at a place of performance—

(a) for more than five hours a day;

(b) before half-past nine in the morning or after half-past four in the afternoon.

(2) Such a child shall not take part in a performance on any day—

(a) for a continuous period of more than thirty minutes without an interval for rest;

(b) for a total period of more than two hours.

(3) Any time during which such a child is present at a place of performance, but is not taking part in a performance, shall be used for the purposes of meals, rest and recreation.

Children under two

40.—(1) A child who has not attained the age of two years shall not be present at a place of performance—

(a) for more than three hours a day;

(b) before half-past nine in the morning or after four in the afternoon.

(2) Such a child shall not take part in a performance on any day—

(a) for a continuous period of more than twenty minutes without an interval for rest;

(b) for a total period of more than one hour.

(3) Any time during which such a child is present at a place of performance, but is not taking part in a performance, shall be used for the purposes of meals, rest and recreation.

Restriction on employment

41.—(1) On the day on which or on the day immediately following the day on which a child takes part in a performance for which by reason of section 37(3) (a) of the Act a licence is not required, he shall not be employed in any other form of employment.

(2) On the day on which a child takes part in a performance for which by reason of section 37(3) (a) of the Act a licence is not required, he shall not take part in a performance for which a licence is required.

Part VII

Interpretation, Citation and Commencement

Interpretation

42.—(1) In these Regulations, unless the context otherwise requires—

"the Act" means the Children and Young Persons Act, 1963;

"day" means a period of twenty-four hours beginning and ending at midnight and, for the purposes of Regulation 30(2) (a) of these Regulations, any performance taking place after midnight and before the earliest permitted hour as defined in Regulation 30(3) of these Regulations shall be deemed to have taken place before midnight;

"licence" means a licence authorising a child to take part in a performance;

"licensing authority" means the local education authority (or, in Scotland, the education authority) to whom an application for a licence is made or by whom a licence is granted;

"local authority" means a local education authority (or, in Scotland, the education authority) in whose area a performance takes place;

"parent" includes a guardian or other person who has for the time being the charge of or control over the child;

"performance" means a performance to which section 37 of the Act applies;

"rehearsal" means any rehearsal for, or preparation for the recording of, a performance to which a licence relates, being a rehearsal which takes place on the day of performance or during the period beginning with the first and ending with the last performance to which the licence relates;

"school medical officer" means the duly qualified medical practitioner employed or engaged by the licensing authority, whether regularly or for the purposes of any particular case, to carry out medical examinations of pupils;

"week" means a period of seven days beginning with the day on which the first performance for which the licence is granted takes place or any seventh day thereafter.

(2) The Interpretation Act, 1889 shall apply to the interpretation of these Regulations as it applies to the interpretation of an Act of Parliament.

Citation and commencement

43.—(1) These Regulations may be cited as the Children (Performances) Regulations, 1968.

(2) These Regulations shall come into operation on 2nd December 1968 for the purposes of applying for licences under section 37 of the Act, and granting such licences to have effect on and after 3rd March 1969.

(3) Subject to paragraph (2) of this Regulation, these Regulations shall come into operation on 3rd March 1969.

Regulation 1   SCHEDULE 1

Form of Application for a Licence

(Note—It is important that this form, duly completed, should be sent so as to reach the licensing authority not less than twenty-one days before the first performance for which the licence is requested, since the licensing authority may otherwise refuse to grant a licence.)

Application to the   Council

Part I

(To be completed by the applicant)

1. I hereby apply for a licence under section 37 of the Children and Young Persons Act, 1963 authorising the child (*insert name of child*)

*(1) to take part in performances on the dates specified in item 4(i) of the Annexe to this Part.

*(2) to take part in performances on the number of days and during the period specified in item 4(ii) of the Annexe to this Part ([a]).

*Delete if inapplicable.

2. I certify that to the best of my knowledge the particulars contained in the Annexe to this Part are correct.

3. I attach the following:—
   (a) the birth certificate of the child or other satisfactory evidence of the child's age;
   (b) two identical prints (unmounted) of a photograph of the child taken during the six months preceding the date of this application;
   (c) a copy of the contract, draft contract or other documents containing particulars of the agreement regulating the child's appearance in the performances for which the licence is requested;
   *(d) a declaration under section 38(1)(a) or (b) of the Children and Young Persons Act, 1963.

*Delete if inapplicable.

4. I understand that if a licence is granted to me it will be granted subject to the restrictions and conditions laid down in the Children (Performances) Regulations, 1968 and to such other conditions as the local authority or the licensing authority may impose under the said Regulations.

Date.................   Signed...
                                                        (Applicant)
             Full name:

             Address:

             Occupation:

NOTE—Any person who fails to observe any condition subject to which a licence is granted or knowingly or recklessly makes any false statement in or in connection with an application for a licence is liable to a fine not exceeding £100 or imprisonment for a term not exceeding three months or both (section 40 of the Children and Young Persons Act, 1963).

([a]) A licence specifying the number of days on which a child may perform and the period, not exceeding six months, in which the performances may take place may be granted only to the British Broadcasting Corporation, the Independent Television Authority, a programme contractor within the meaning of section 1(5) of the Television Act, 1964 or a body supplying programmes to such a programme contractor to be broadcast by the Independent Television Authority or in respect of a child taking part in a performance to be recorded (by whatever means) with a view to its use in a film intended for public exhibition.

ANNEXE TO PART I

PARTICULARS CONNECTED WITH THE PERFORMANCE IN WHICH THE CHILD IS TO TAKE PART

1. Name and nature ([a]) of the performances in respect of which the licence is requested.

2. Description of the child's part.

3. Place of the performances in respect of which the licence is requested ([b]).

4. (i) The dates of performances for which the licence is requested, or
   (ii) The number of days, and the period during which, it is requested that the child may take part in performances (ᶜ).

5. Time and duration of performances in respect of which the licence is requested.

6. Approximate duration of the child's appearances in the performances in respect of which the licence is requested.

7. The amount of night-work (if any) for which approval will be sought from the local authority under Regulation 30 of the Children (Performances) Regulations, 1968, stating—

   (i) the approximate number of days,
   (ii) the approximate duration on each day.

8. The sums to be earned by the child in taking part in the performances in respect of which the licence is requested.

9. Proposed arrangements for rehearsals taking place during the fourteen days preceding the first performance for which the licence is requested, stating in respect of each rehearsal—

   (i) the date,
   (ii) the place,
   (iii) the approximate duration.

10. The days or half days on which leave of absence from school is requested to enable the child to take part in performances for which the licence is requested or in rehearsals.

11. Proposed arrangements (if any) under Regulation 10 of the Children (Performances) Regulations, 1968, for the education of the child during the period for which the licence is requested stating—

    (i) the name and address of the school to be attended, or
    (ii) (a) the name, address and qualification of the proposed private teacher,

    (b) the place where the child will be taught,

    (c) the proposed course of study,

    (d) the number of other children to be taught by the private teacher at the same time as

the child in respect of whom this application is made, and the sex and age of each such child,
    (e) whether the child is to receive the required amount of education in accordance with Regulation 10(4)(a) or Regulation 10(4)(b).

12. The name of the local authority (if any) which has previously approved the appointment of the private teacher for the purposes of a licence.

13. The name, address and description of the proposed matron.

14. The name of the local authority (if any) which has previously approved the appointment of the matron for the purposes of a licence.

15. The number of other children to be in the charge of the matron during the time when she would be in charge of the child in respect of whom this application is made, and the sex and age of each such child.

16. The address of the lodgings where the child will live if a licence is granted by reason of which the child has to live elsewhere than at the place where he would otherwise live, the name of the householder and the number of other children who will live in the same lodgings.

17. Approximate length of time which the child will spend travelling—

    (a) to the place of performance or rehearsal,
    (b) from the place of performance or rehearsal,

and the arrangements (if any) for transport—

    (a) to the place of performance or rehearsal,
    (b) from the place of performance or rehearsal,

18. Name of any other licensing authority to which an application has been made for another child to take part in performances to which this application relates.

(a) Nature of the performances, e.g. theatrical, filming, television, etc.
(b) This includes the places at which work on location is to be done.
(c) A licence specifying the number of days on which a child may perform and the period, not exceeding six months, in which the performances may take place may be granted only to the British Broadcasting Corporation, the Independent Television Authority, a programme contractor within the meaning of section 1(5) of the Television Act, 1964 or a body supplying programmes to such a programme contractor to be broadcast by the Independent Television Authority or in respect of a child taking part in a performance to be recorded (by whatever means) with a view to its use in a film intended for public exhibition.

PART II

(TO BE COMPLETED BY A PARENT)

(Note—Parent includes a guardian or other person who has for the time being the charge of or control over the child.)

Please give the following particulars:—

1. Full name of child.

2. Date of birth of child.

3. Address of child.

4. Name and address of schools attended by the child during the twelve months preceding the date of this application or, if he has not attended school, the name and address of his private teacher.

5. Particulars of each licence granted during the twelve months preceding the date of this application by any local authority other than the licensing authority to whom this application is made, stating in each case—
    (i) the name of the local authority,
    (ii) the date on which the licence was granted,
    (iii) the dates and nature of the performances.

6. Particulars of each application for a licence made during the twelve months preceding the date of this application and refused by any local authority other than the licensing authority to whom this application is made, stating in each case—
    (i) the name of the local authority,
    (ii) the date of the application,
    (iii) the reasons (if known) for the refusal to grant a licence.

7. Particulars of each performance for which a licence was not required in which the child took part during the twelve months preceding the date of this application, stating in each case—
    (i) the date,
    (ii) the place,
    (iii) the nature of the performance
    (iv) the name of the person responsible for the production of the performance in which the child took part.

8. Dates (if any) on which the child has been absent from school during the twelve months preceding the date of this application by reason of his taking part in a performance.

9. Particulars of any other form of employment in which the child is employed during the twenty-eight days preceding the day of the first performance for which the licence is requested stating—

> (i) the nature of the employment,
> (ii) the days on which the child is employed,
> (iii) the times during which the child is employed.

10. Particulars relating to the sums earned by the child during the twelve months preceding the date of this application stating—

> (i) whether the sums earned were in respect of performances for which a licence was granted, performances for which a licence was not required or other forms of employment,
> (ii) the amount of the sums earned,
> (iii) the date on which payment was received,
> (iv) the name, address and description of the person from whom the payment was received.

I support this application for a licence.

I certify that to the best of my knowledge the foregoing particulars are correct and I understand that if a licence is granted it will be granted subject to the restrictions and conditions laid down in the Children (Performances) Regulations, 1968 and to such other conditions as the local authority or the licensing authority may impose under the said Regulations.

Date......................... Signed...............................
                                                        (Parent)
               Full Name:

               Address:

               Relationship to child:*

NOTE—Any person who fails to observe any condition subject to which a licence is granted or knowingly or recklessly makes any false statement in or in connection with an application for a licence is liable to a fine not exceeding £100 or imprisonment for a term not exceeding three months or both (section 40 of the Children and Young Persons Act, 1963).

---

*State whether parent, guardian or other person having for the time being the charge of or control over the child.

SCHEDULE 2   Regulation 3

FORM OF LICENCE

The   Council, on an application relating to
                                (hereinafter called "the child"), whose
photograph is attached hereto, hereby grant to
a licence authorising the child—

*(1) to take part in performances on the dates specified below, or

*(2) to take part in performances on the number of days and during the period specified below (ª),

subject to the restrictions and conditions laid down in the Children (Performances) Regulations, 1968 and to such other conditions as the local authority or the licensing authority may impose under the said Regulations.

The performances in respect of which the licence is granted are (ᵇ)

*The child may be absent from (*insert name of school*) for the purposes authorised by this licence on (ᶜ)

*The holder of the licence shall ensure that (ᵈ)

*Delete if inapplicable.

(ª) A licence specifying the number of days on which a child may perform and the period, not exceeding six months, in which the performances may take place may be granted only to the British Broadcasting Corporation, the Independent Television Authority, a programme contractor within the meaning of section 1(5) of the Television Act, 1964, or a body supplying programmes to such a programme contractor to be broadcast by the Independent Televison Authority or in respect of a child taking part in a performance to be recorded (by whatever means) with a view to its use in a film intended for public exhibition.

(ᵇ) In the case of (1) above state the names, dates, places and nature of the performances and in the case of (2) above state the names, places and nature of the performances, the number of days on which the child may perform and the period in which the performances may take place.

(ᶜ) Set out the days or half days on which the child may be absent from school. If absence from school is granted to enable a child to take part in a rehearsal, this should also be stated.

(ᵈ) Set out the terms of any condition imposed under Regulation 11 of the Children (Performances) Regulations, 1968, in respect of any sums earned by the child in taking part in the performances to which this licence relates.

Regulation 5   SCHEDULE 3

RECORDS TO BE KEPT BY THE HOLDER OF A LICENCE

The holder of a licence shall keep the following records:—

1. The licence.

2. The following particulars in respect of each day (or night) on which the child is present at the place of performance:—

(a) the date,
(b) the time of arrival at the place of performance,
(c) the time of departure from the place of performance,
(d) the times of each period during which the child took part in a performance or rehearsal,
(e) the time of each rest interval,
(f) the time of each meal interval,
(g) the times of any night-work authorised by the local authority under Regulation 30 of the Children (Performances) Regulations, 1968.

3. Where arrangements are made for the education of the child by a private teacher, the date and duration of each lesson and the subject taught.

4. Details of injuries and illnesses (if any) suffered by the child at the place of performance, including the dates on which such injuries occurred and stating whether such injuries or illnesses prevented the child from being present at the place of performance.

5. The dates of medical examinations (if any) of the child carried out under Regulation 17 of the Children (Performances) Regulations, 1968.

6. The dates of the breaks in performances required under Regulation 16 of the Children (Performances) Regulations, 1968.

7. The amount of all sums earned by the child by reason of taking part in the performance and the names, addresses and description of the persons to whom such sums were paid.

8. Where the licensing authority grant a licence subject to the condition that sums earned by the child shall be dealt with in a manner approved by them, the amount of the sums and the manner in which they have been dealt with.

NOTE

These Regulations were made on October 30, 1968, by the Secretary of State under ss. 37 and 39 of the Children and Young Persons Act, 1963.

THE JUVENILE COURTS (LONDON) ORDER, 1965

[S.I. 1965 No. 584]

1. Juvenile courts for the metropolitan area shall sit for the divisions consisting of those parts of that area which are specified in the first column of the Schedule hereto at the places respectively specified in the second column of that Schedule opposite to the description of each division.

2. A juvenile court may sit at any time, in case of need, in a magistrates' room in the magistrates' court at Bow Street for the purpose of hearing cases arising in any part of the metropolitan area.

3. In this Order the expression " the metropolitan area " means the inner London area and the City of London.

4.—(1) The Juvenile Courts (London) Order, 1964 and the Juvenile Courts (London) (No. 2) Order, 1964 are hereby revoked.

(2) Anything done before 1st April 1965 by or in relation to a juvenile court for the Hampstead petty sessional division or a juvenile court specified in an order revoked by this Order shall for the purposes of any subsequent proceedings in relation to that thing or any other thing subsequently done in relation thereto, be deemed to have been done by or in relation to a juvenile court for the metropolitan area.

5. This Order may be cited as the Juvenile Courts (London) Order, 1965 and shall come into operation on 1st April 1965.

Article 1   SCHEDULE

Division	Place of sitting
East Central The London borough of Islington.	163A Seymour Place, W.1.
South Central The London boroughs of Southwark and Lambeth.	4 Kimpton Road, Camberwell Green, S.E.5.
South Eastern The London boroughs of Lewisham and Greenwich.	The part of the magistrates' court for the South Eastern petty sessional division consisting of the premises known as 7 Blackheath Road, Greenwich, S.E.10.
South Western The London borough of Wandsworth.	Anchor Mission, 273, Garratt Lane, Wandsworth, S.W.18. and The Town Hall, Wandsworth
Thames The City of London and the London boroughs of Hackney and Tower Hamlets.	The Court House, 58B, Bow Road, E.3.
West Central The London borough of Camden.	163A, Seymour Place, W.1.
West London The Royal borough of Kensington and Chelsea and the London borough of Hammersmith.	[1A, Walton Street, S.W.3.]
Westminster The City of Westminster.	163A, Seymour Place, W.1.

NOTE

This order was made on March 22, 1965 under Sched. 2 to the Children and Young Persons Act, 1933, as amended, and came into operation on April 1, 1965. It is printed as amended by S.I. 1968 No. 592 and S.I. 1970 No 897 The Schedule to the 1933 Act is to be read with s. 12 (1) Administration of Justice Act, 1964 The juvenile court for the West London Division now sits at 163A, Seymour Place. No amending order has been made; but each juvenile court has jurisdiction over the whole Inner London Area (Administration of Justice Act, 1964)

THE PROBATION RULES, 1965
[S.I. 1965 No. 723]

ARRANGEMENT OF RULES

PART I

1–15. [*Not reproduced.*]

PART II

16–20. [*Not reproduced.*]

PART III

21–28. [*Not reproduced.*]

Part IV
Duties of Probation Officers

Part V
Expenditure on Persons for Whom Probation Officer Responsible

Part VI

Part VII

Part VIII
Miscellaneous

Schedules

Part IV
Duties of Probation Officers

Records

29.—(1) A probation officer shall keep an up-to-date record in accordance with any directions issued by the Secretary of State concerning each person who is under his supervision or in respect of whom he otherwise has duties.

(2) Any such record shall, unless required elsewhere, be retained in the probation office in such manner that it is not readily accessible except to persons authorised by the probation committee or a probation inspector appointed by the Secretary of State.

Supervision etc. of persons released from custody

30.—(1) It shall be part of the duties of a probation officer, if so requested, to undertake directly or on behalf of the Central After-Care Association or the managers of an approved school the supervision (for any period not exceeding three years) of any person who has been released from an institution and is subject to supervision in England and Wales by virtue of any enactment or of a condition or requirement of a licence under which he was so released.

A reference in this paragraph to a person having been released from an institution shall include a reference to a person having been discharged from hospital if he might have been remitted to an institution instead of being so discharged.

In this paragraph " an institution " means an institution to which the Prison Act, 1952, the Prisons (Scotland) Act, 1952 or the Prison Act (Northern Ireland), 1953 applies, or an approved school.

(2) Where a probation officer undertakes the supervision of a person released from an approved school, he shall, if so requested by the managers of the school, discharge on their behalf their obligations under paragraph 12 (2) of Schedule 4 to the Children and Young Persons Act, 1933, or paragraph 12 (2) of Schedule 2 to the Children and Young Persons (Scotland) Act, 1937, or paragraph 12 (2) of Schedule 4 to the Children and Young Persons Act (Northern Ireland), 1950, as the case may be, (which relate to the assistance to be given to such persons).

(3) It shall be part of the duties of a probation officer, if so requested by the managers of an approved school, to visit, advise and befriend any such person as is mentioned in paragraph 7 of Schedule 2 to the Criminal Justice Act, 1961, or paragraph 7 of Schedule 2 to the Criminal Justice (Scotland) Act, 1963, as the case may be, (which relate to certain persons ceasing to be under the supervision of such managers) and, if so requested by the managers, to give him on their behalf such assistance as is there mentioned.

(4) It shall be part of the duties of a probation officer to advise, assist and befriend any person, not subject to supervision as aforesaid, who has been released after serving a period of imprisonment and is willing to be so assisted:

Provided that a probation officer shall not be required to act under this paragraph in relation to any person except during the twelve months following that person's release.

(5) In this Rule " an approved school " means a school approved under section 79 of the Children and Young Persons Act, 1933, or under section 83 of the Children and Young Persons (Scotland) Act, 1937 or under section 106 of the Children and Young Persons Act (Northern Ireland), 1950.

NOTE

Army recruitment.—See Home Office Circular No PBN/62, 280/1/2 dated June 30, and the note setting out the conditions which apply

Duties in connection with adoption, custody, conciliation and consent to marriage

31. A probation officer shall, if so requested by or on behalf of a court—

(a) act as a guardian ad litem in proceedings under the Adoption Act, 1958,

(b) make a report to the court with a view to assisting it in making an order or provision with respect to the custody, maintenance or education of a child under subsection (1) or (2) of section 26 of the Matrimonial Causes Act, 1950, or under Part I of the Matrimonial Proceedings (Children) Act, 1958, or under the Guardianship of Infants Acts, 1886 and 1925,

(c) make a report to the court with respect to the matters specified by the court under section 4 (2) of the Matrimonial Proceedings (Magistrates' Courts) Act, 1960,

(d) attempt to effect a conciliation between the parties to any matrimonial cause or matter or any proceedings under the Matrimonial Proceedings (Magistrates' Courts) Act, 1960.

(e) make enquiries with respect to an application under section 3 of the Marriage Act, 1949, for consent to marriage.

Supervision of children in divorce proceedings

32. Where a court has made an order under section 6 of the Matrimonial Proceedings (Children) Act, 1958, for the supervision of a child by a probation officer, the probation officer responsible for carrying out the order shall be a probation officer appointed for, or assigned to, the petty sessions area in which the child for the time being resides, selected in the same manner as the probation officer who is to be responsible for the supervision of a probationer.

Explaining probation or supervision order

33. A probation officer shall endeavour to ensure that a person under his supervision understands—

    (a) the effect of the order placing him under his supervision ; and

    (b) a court's power to amend or discharge the order.

Visiting school children

34. If a person under the supervision of a probation officer or in respect of whom he otherwise has duties attends a school, the probation officer shall from time to time discuss with the head teacher of the school his behaviour and progress at the school, but shall not visit him there.

Keeping in touch

35.—(1) A probation officer shall, subject to any provision of the probation order, keep in close touch with a probationer, meet him frequently, and, unless there is good reason for not doing so, visit his residence from time to time and require him to report to him at stated intervals.

    (2) The intervals at which in accordance with paragraph (1) of this Rule the probation officer meets the probationer, visits his residence and requires him to report, shall be determined amongst other circumstances by his behaviour and progress and regard shall be had to the importance of frequent meetings during the early part of the probation period.

    (3) Where a probationer normally resides with his family, but has temporarily ceased so to reside, a probation officer appointed for, or assigned to, the petty sessions area in which his family reside shall, unless there is good reason for not doing so, keep in touch with his family.

    (4) So far as is suitable having regard to the circumstances of the case, this Rule shall apply to a person under the supervision of a probation officer, other than a probationer, as it applies to a probationer.

Welfare and employment

36.—(1) A probation officer shall, where appropriate, encourage a person under his supervision or in respect of whom he otherwise has duties to make use of any statutory or voluntary agency which might contribute to his welfare, and to take advantage of any available social, recreational or educational facilities suited to his age, ability and temperament.

    (2) A probation officer shall, where appropriate, endeavour to ensure that such a person is in suitable and regular employment.

NOTE

    Army recruitment.—See note, *supra*

Reports

37.—(1) A probation officer shall from time to time make a confidential report to the case committee concerning the mode of life and progress of persons under his supervision.

    (2) A probation officer shall make a confidential report concerning the mode of life and progress of any person under his supervision to the court which made the order placing the person under his supervision not being the supervising court, if so requested by the first-mentioned court.

(3) A probation officer shall make a confidential report to the supervising court or to a justice acting for the petty sessions area for which the supervising court acts concerning any failure by a probationer to comply with the requirements of the probation order to which the probation officer is aware.

Contents of certain reports

38. A report made by a probation officer in pursuance of section 5 (2) of the Criminal Justice Act, 1948 shall include—

(a) any report made at the request of the probation officer by the person in charge of the institution in which the probationer is required to reside ; and

(b) a report about the suitability of his home or any other place where he proposes to reside, should the requirement of residence be cancelled, by a probation officer appointed for, or assigned to, the petty sessions area in which that home or place is situated.

Applications to court

39.—(1) If a probation officer becomes aware that a person under his supervision has changed his residence from the petty sessions area named in the order placing him under his supervision to another petty sessions area, he shall apply in the case of a probationer to the supervising court to amend the order in accordance with paragraph 2 (1) of Schedule 1 to the Criminal Justice Act, 1948, and in the case of a person placed under his supervision by a supervision order to a juvenile court to amend the order in pursuance of paragraph 4 of Schedule 1 to the Children and Young Persons Act, 1963 unless—

(a) the probation officer has reason to believe that the person under supervision is unlikely to reside there for a reasonable time ; or

(b) the probation officer has ascertained from, in the case of a probationer, the supervising court, or, in the case of a person placed under his supervision by a supervision order, a juvenile court acting for the petty sessions area named in the order, that that court and the court having jurisdiction in the petty sessions area where the person under supervision is residing are satisfied that, having regard to the special circumstances of the case, it is desirable that the person should remain under his supervision.

(2) Where it appears to a probation officer that an application can properly be made for the discharge or amendment (otherwise than as provided by the foregoing paragraph of this Rule) of a probation or supervision order relating to a person under his supervision, the probation officer shall make such application unless the person under supervision or any other person makes the application.

NOTE

Servicemen's dependants; probationers accompanying parents overseas.—It is sometimes possible for the Army authorities to arrange for some form of supervision for a probationer who accompanies or joins his father on the latter's posting to the British Army of the Rhine (see Home Office Circular No 62/68 dated March 21, 1968)

PART V

EXPENDITURE ON PERSONS FOR WHOM PROBATION OFFICER RESPONSIBLE

Maintenance

40. Where a probation or supervision order requires a person to reside in any place, otherwise than for the purpose of his submitting to treatment for his mental condition as a voluntary or resident patient, the probation committee responsible for making the payments described in Schedule 1 to these Rules shall be—

(a) in the case of a probation or supervision order made by a magistrates' court (whether or not the requirement as to residence was imposed in the order as made or subsequently), the committee for the probation area in which the petty sessions area for which that court acted is comprised ;

(b) in the case of a probation order made by a court in Scotland which is amended by a magistrates' court, in pursuance of the powers conferred by section 7 (4) of the Criminal Justice (Scotland) Act, 1949, by the imposition of a requirement as to residence in England, the committee for the probation area in which the petty sessions area for which the magistrates' court acted is comprised :

(c) in any other case, the committee for the probation area from which the person placed under supervision was committed for trial or sentence.

Fares incurred in reporting

41. A probation committee may, in case of hardship, pay fares necessarily incurred by a person under the supervision of a probation officer in reporting to the probation officer.

Financial assistance

42.—(1) Where a probation officer has responsibilities in relation to any person, the probation committee may grant that person financial assistance if this is necessary.

(2) The aggregate expenditure of a probation committee under this Rule in any year shall not exceed an amount approved by the Secretary of State.

*   *   *   *

Part VIII

Miscellaneous

Interpretation

52.—(1) In these Rules unless the context otherwise requires—

*   *   *   *

" person under the supervision of a probation officer " means a person placed under the supervision of a probation officer by a probation or supervision order ;

" single probation area " means a probation area comprising only one petty sessions area ;

" supervision order " means an order made under the Children and Young Persons Act, 1933 placing a child or young person under the supervision of a probation officer.

(2) References in these Rules to an enactment or statutory instrument shall be construed as references to that enactment or statutory instrument as amended by any other enactment ot statutory instrument.

(3) The Interpretation Act, 1889 shall apply to the interpretation of these Rules as it applies to the interpretation of an Act of Parliament.

*   *   *   *

SCHEDULE 1   Rule 40

PAYMENTS IN RESPECT OF PERSONS UNDER SUPERVISION

Maintenance

1.—(1) Where a probation or supervision order requires a person to reside in an approved probation hostel or home, the probation committee responsible shall pay to the body by whom the hostel or home is managed such sum as the Secretary of State has for the time being authorised for that purpose.

(2) Where a probation or supervision order requires a person to reside in an institution other than an approved probation hostel or home, the probation committee may pay to the person or body by whom the institution is managed such contribution towards his maintenance and for such period as the committee, with the approval of the Secretary of State, determines.

(3) Where a probation or supervision order requires a person to reside in a private house other than his home, the probation committee may pay to the person in whose house the person under supervision resides such contribution towards his maintenance, not exceeding the amount which would be payable by the local authority in whose area the house is situate if the person were being boarded out in that house by that authority under section 13 of the Children Act, 1948, and for such period as the committee determines.

Travelling expenses

2. The probation committee responsible shall pay the fare of the person under supervision to and from the place where he is required to reside, together with any incidental expenses reasonably incurred on the journey :

Provided that no sum shall be paid in respect of a journey save to a place approved by the probation officer.

NOTES

These rules were made on March 31, 1965 under Sched. 5 to the Criminal Justice Act, 1948, and come into operation on April 1, 1965.

Rule 32.—Section 6 of the Matrimonial Proceedings (Children) Act, 1958, is repealed by the Matrimonial Causes Act, 1965, and replaced by s. 37 of that Act.

Sched. I, para. 1 (2). Non-approved hostels and homes. See extract from Home Office Probation and After-Care Bulletin No. 17, printed at p. 687, *post*.

PRACTICE DIRECTION

COURT OF CRIMINAL APPEAL

(Lord Parker, C.J., Fenton Atkinson and James, J.J.)

Lord Parker, C.J., at the sitting of the court, read the following statement : The judges of the Queen's Bench Division have considered the Practice Direction of Jan. 31, 1955, in regard to the disclosure to the defence of antecedents (as opposed to convictions) in cases tried on indictment. They are of opinion that provision should be made for the disclosure of such antecedents at an earlier stage than that set out in that Practice Direction. They have resolved that para. (3) of the direction should be amended and that the direction in its amended form should be re-issued. It now will read as follows:

(1) Details of previous convictions must always be supplied by the police to the defending solicitor, or if no solicitor is instructed to defending counsel, on request. The judges are of opinion that there is no obligation on a police officer to satisfy himself that the prisoner has authorised a statement of previous convictions to be given as it is clearly within the ordinary authority of solicitor and counsel to obtain this information. In order that the defence may be properly conducted, the prisoner's advisers must know whether they can safely put the prisoner's character in issue.

(2) There is no need for police officers to supply a list of previous convictions to the court before conviction, because the prisoner's previous convictions are always set out in the confidential calendar with which the judge is supplied by the governor of the gaol, whose duty it is to supply it.   The police will, of course, give any information to the governor that he may require to enable him to perform his duty.

(3) A proof of evidence should be prepared by a police officer containing particulars of the prisoner's age, education and employment, the date of arrest, whether the prisoner has been on bail, and a statement summarising any previous convictions and any previous findings of guilt (including findings of guilt excluded from the details of previous convictions by reason of the Children and Young Persons Act, 1963, s. 16 (2)).   It should also set out the date (if known) of the last discharge from prison or other place of custody. It may also contain a short and concise statement as to the prisoner's domestic and family circumstances, his general reputation and associates.   Attached to the proof of evidence should be a factual statement of any convictions and of any previous findings of guilt which should be supplied in accordance with para. (1) above (except those excluded by operation of the Children and Young Persons Act, 1963, s. 16 (2).

This proof, other than the attachments, should be given either with his brief or at the outset of the case to counsel for the prosecution.   Subject in any particular case to a direction by the presiding judge to the contrary, counsel for the prisoner (or the prisoner if not legally represented) should be entitled to be supplied with a copy of such proof of evidence as relates to his client (or himself if not represented) : (a) in the case of a plea of not guilty as soon as the jury retire to consider their verdict, (b) in the case of a plea of guilty as soon as the plea is entered.

A copy of the proof of evidence shall be given to the shorthand writer when the officer is called to prove the contents.   He may use it to check his note, but must only transcribe so much as is given in evidence.

June 21, 1966   [1966] 2 All E. R. 929.

THE SOCIAL WORK (SCOTLAND) ACT, 1968
(COMMENCEMENT No. 1) ORDER, 1969
[S.I. 1969 No. 430]

1. This order may be cited as the Social Work (Scotland) Act, 1968 (Commencement No. 1) Order, 1969.

2. The provisions of the Social Work (Scotland) Act, 1968 specified in Schedules 1 and 2 to this order shall come into operation on the dates and to the extent specified therein.

SCHEDULE 1

PROVISIONS COMING INTO FORCE ON 1ST APRIL, 1969

Provisions of the Act	Subject matter of provisions
Section 1(1), (2), (3) and (6)	Local authorities for the administration of the Act.
Section 2(1) and (3)	Establishment of social work committee.
Section 5	Powers of Secretary of State.
Section 19	Amendment of Children Act, 1958.

Provisions of the Act	Subject matter of provisions
Section 27(2) to (5)	Probation schemes.
Section 84	Transfer of assets and liabilities.
Section 85	Transfer and compensation of officers.
Section 90	Orders, regulations etc.
Section 94	Interpretation.
Section 95(2)	Repeals.
Section 96	Power of Parliament of Northern Ireland to make consequential amendments of the Act.
Section 97(2) to the extent that it extends to Northern Ireland the application of the provisions of section 96 of the Act.	Extension of certain provisions of the Act to Northern Ireland.
Section 99	Short title.
Schedule 1	Amendment of Children Act, 1958.
Schedule 6	Transfer of assets and liabilities.
Schedule 9 to the extent set out in the Appendix hereto.	Repeals.

APPENDIX TO SCHEDULE 1

Repeals Taking Effect on 1st April, 1969

Chapter	Short title	Extent of repeal
12, 13 & 14 Geo. 6 c. 94.	The Criminal Justice (Scotland) Act, 1949	Section 4(2) and (3).
6 & 7 Eliz. 2 c. 65.	The Children Act, 1958	Section 1. Section 2(6) and (7).

SCHEDULE 2

Provisions Coming into Force on 1st July, 1969

Provision of the Act	Subject matter of provisions
Section 3(1) to (8)	The director of social work.
Section 7	Advisory Council on Social Work.
Section 8	Research
Section 9	Training courses and grants for training in social work.
Section 10	Financial and other assistance to voluntary organisations, etc., for social work.
Section 60	Control of residential and other establishments.
Section 62(2)	Form of application for registration.
Section 63	Special provisions for registration by Secretary of State.
Section 87(5)	Charges for services and accommodation.
Section 91	Expenses.
Schedule 9 to the extent set out in the Appendix hereto.	Repeals.

APPENDIX TO SCHEDULE 2

REPEALS TAKING EFFECT ON 1ST JULY, 1969

Chapter	Short title	Extent of repeal
11 & 12 Geo. 6 c. 43	The Children Act, 1948	Section 44.
15 & 16 Geo. 6 & 1 Eliz. 2 c. 61.	The Prisons (Scotland) Act, 1952	Section 18(1) to (3A).
1963 c. 39.	The Criminal Justice (Scotland) Act, 1963	Section 15(2).

THE SOCIAL WORK (SCOTLAND) ACT, 1968 (COMMENCEMENT No. 2) ORDER, 1969
[S.I. 1969 No. 1274]

1. This Order may be cited as the Social Work (Scotland) Act, 1968 (Commencement No. 2) Order, 1969.

2. The provisions of the Social Work (Scotland) Act, 1968, specified in the Schedule to this Order shall come into operation on 17th November 1969 to the extent specified therein.

SCHEDULE

Provisions Coming Into Force 17th November, 1969

Provisions of the Act	Subject matter of provisions
Section 1(4)	Functions of local authorities.
Section 2(2) and (4)	Functions of social work committee.
Section 3(9)	Repeal of section 41 of Children Act, 1948.
Section 4	Provisions relating to performances of functions by local authorities.
Section 6	Supervision of establishments providing accommodation for persons and inspection of records, etc.
Section 11	Acquisition of land.
Section 12	General social welfare services of local authorities.
Section 13	Power of local authorities to assist persons in need in disposal of produce of their work.
Section 14(4) to the extent that it provides for sections 44 and 45 of the Health Services and Public Health Act, 1968 to cease to have effect.	Repeal of sections 44 and 45 of Health Services and Public Health Act, 1968.
Section 15	Duty of local authority to provide for orphans, deserted children, etc.
Section 16	Assumption by local authority of parental rights.
Section 17	Effect of assumption by local authority of parental rights.
Section 18	Duration and rescission of resolutions under section 16.

Provisions of the Act	Subject matter of provisions
Section 20	Duty of local authority to further the best interests of a child in their care and to afford opportunity for his proper development.
Section 21	Mode of provision of accommodation and maintenance.
Section 22	Removal of children in residential establishments.
Section 23	Power of local authorities and voluntary organisations to arrange for emigration of children.
Section 24	Financial assistance towards expenses of maintenance, education or training of persons over school age.
Section 25	Power of local authority to guarantee indentures and other deeds of apprenticeship, etc., of persons in their care.
Section 26	After-care of children formerly in care of local authorities or voluntary organisations.
Section 27(1), (6) and (7)	Supervision and care of persons put on probation or released from prisons, etc.
Section 28	Burial or cremation of the dead.
Section 29	Power of local authority to defray expenses of parent, etc., visiting persons or attending funerals.
Section 33	Formation of children's panels.
Section 35(4) and (5)	Rules for children's hearings.
Section 36(8)	Rules in relation to the duties of reporter.
Section 45	Rules as respects transmissions of information and conveyance of children to residential establishments, etc.
Section 59	Provision of residential and other establishments by local authorities, and maximum period for repayment of sums borrowed for such provision.
Section 61	Restriction on carrying on of establishments.
Section 62(1) and (3)–(10)	Registration.
Section 64	Appeals against refusal or cancellation of registration.
Section 65	Removal of persons from establishments.
Section 66	Duty to furnish particulars of establishments.
Section 67	Inspection of establishments by local authorities.
Section 68	Visiting of persons in establishments on behalf of local authorities.
Section 86	Adjustments between authority providing accommodation, etc., and authority of area of residence.
Section 87(1)–(4) and (6)	Charges that may be made for services and accommodation.
Section 88	Duty of parents to notify change of address.
Section 89	Application of Tribunals and Inquiries Act, 1958.
Section 93	Transitional provisions.

Provisions of the Act	Subject matter of provisions
Section 95(1) and (3)	Minor and consequential amendments and savings.
Section 97(1) (to the extent that it extends to England and Wales the application of the provisions of sections 86 and 87, and of Schedule 8 and Part II of Schedule 9 insofar as these are brought into operation by this order) and (4).	Extension of certain provisions of the Act to England and Wales.
Schedule 3	Children's Panels.
Schedule 5	Appeal Tribunals.
Paragraphs 1, 3, 8 and 9 of Schedule 7	Transitional provisions.
So much of Schedule 8 as is specified in Appendix A hereto.	Minor and consequential amendments.
So much of Schedule 9 as is specified in Appendix B hereto.	Enactments repealed.

APPENDIX A TO SCHEDULE

Provision of Schedule 8	Enactment amended
Paragraph 2	Section 70(2) of the Children and Young Persons Act, 1933.
Paragraph 3	Section 76(1B) of the Children and Young Persons Act, 1933.
Paragraph 4	Section 90(6) of the Children and Young Persons Act, 1933.
Paragraph 8	Section 101 of the Children and Young Persons (Scotland) Act, 1937.
Paragraph 11	Section 15(1) and (4) of the National Health Service (Scotland) Act, 1947.
Paragraph 12	Section 27 of the National Health Service (Scotland) Act, 1947.
Paragraph 13	Section 63 of the National Health Service (Scotland) Act, 1947.
Paragraph 14	Section 32(1) of the National Assistance Act, 1948.
Paragraph 15	Section 41 of the National Assistance Act, 1948.
Paragraph 16	Section 65 of the National Assistance Act, 1948.
Paragraph 17	Section 1(4) and (5) of the Children Act, 1948.
Paragraph 18	Section 13(1) of the Children Act, 1948.
Paragraph 19	Section 59(1) of the Children Act, 1948.
Paragraph 20	Nurseries and Child-Minders Regulation Act, 1948.
Paragraph 22	Section 2 of the Criminal Justice (Scotland) Act, 1949.

Provisions of Schedule 8	Enactment amended
Paragraph 23	Section 3(4) and (6) of the Criminal Justice (Scotland) Act, 1949.
Paragraph 24	Section 5(1) of the Criminal Justice (Scotland) Act, 1949.
Paragraph 27 in so far as it substitutes the words "an officer of a local authority" for the words "a probation officer".	Section 10 of the Criminal Justice (Scotland) Act, 1949.
Paragraph 30 in so far as it adds a definition of "local authority".	Section 78(1) of the Criminal Justice (Scotland) Act, 1949.
Paragraph 31	Schedule 2 to the Criminal Justice (Scotland) Act, 1949.
Paragraph 36	Section 8(1) of the Valuation and Rating (Scotland) Act, 1956.
Paragraph 37 in so far as it inserts a new paragraph (d).	Section 4(3) of the Adoption Act, 1958.
Paragraph 38	Section 15(4) of the Adoption Act, 1958.
Paragraph 40	Section 43(3) of the Adoption Act, 1958.
Paragraph 41	Section 57 of the Adoption Act, 1958.
Paragraph 42	Section 10(4) of the Matrimonial Proceedings (Children) Act, 1958.
Paragraph 43	Section 11 of the Matrimonial Proceedings (Children) Act, 1958.
Paragraph 44	Section 2(3) and (4) of the Children Act, 1958.
Paragraph 45	Section 6 of the Children Act, 1958.
Paragraph 46	Section 7(4) of the Children Act, 1958.
Paragraph 47	Section 17 of the Children Act, 1958.
Paragraph 48	Section 10(1) of the Mental Health Act, 1959.
Paragraph 49	Section 50 of the Mental Health Act, 1959.
Paragraph 50	Mental Health (Scotland) Act, 1960.
Paragraph 51	Section 7 of the Mental Health (Scotland) Act, 1960.
Paragraph 52	Section 10(1) of the Mental Health (Scotland) Act, 1960.
Paragraph 53	Section 30(2) of the Mental Health (Scotland) Act, 1960.
Paragraph 54	Section 46 of the Mental Health (Scotland) Act, 1960.
Paragraph 56	Section 59(1) of the Mental Health (Scotland) Act, 1960.
Paragraph 58 in so far as it inserts a definition of "residential establishment".	Section 72(1) of the Mental Health (Scotland) Act, 1960.
Paragraph 59	Section 111 of the Mental Health (Scotland) Act, 1960.
Paragraph 60	Section 3(5) of the Health Visiting and Social Work (Training) Act, 1962.
Paragraph 68 in so far as it inserts a reference to section 23 of the Social Work (Scotland) Act, 1968.	Section 55 of the Children and Young Persons Act, 1963.
Paragraph 73	Section 15 of the Registration of Births, Deaths and Marriages (Scotland) Act, 1965.
Paragraph 74(2)	Section 11(3) of the Family Allowances Act, 1965.

APPENDIX B TO SCHEDULE

(Provisions of Schedule 9 to the Act)

PART I

Chapter	Short title	Extent of repeal
1 Edw. 8 & 1 Geo. 6 c. 37.	The Children and Young Persons (Scotland) Act, 1937	Section 96 to 98. Section 106.
11 & 12 Geo. 6 c. 29.	The National Assistance Act, 1948	Section 21. Section 22(1). Sections 23 and 24. Section 26(1) and (5). Section 37. Sections 29 and 30. Section 32. Sections 34 to 40. Section 50(3). Section 58(1) and (4).
11 & 12 Geo. 6 c. 43.	The Children Act, 1948	The Whole Act except sections 5 and 6(3) and (4) and Part III.
12, 13 & 14 Geo. 6 c. 94.	The Criminal Justice (Scotland) Act, 1949	Section 2(3) and (9). In section 7, in subsection (2), the words from "to omit" to "and", and in subsection (4), the words "to (3)". Sections 11 to 13.
12, 13 & 14 Geo. 6 c. 94—*cont.*	The Criminal Justice (Scotland) Act, 1949—*cont.*	In section 75 subsections (1)(a), (3)(d), (4)(a) and (c), insofar as they refer to the training of probation officers or of officers or servants serving in approved probation hostels or homes or of persons for appointment as probation officers or as such officers or servants; subsections (3)(a) to (c), (4)(b) and (5). In section 78(1) the definitions of "Approved probation hostel" and "Approved probation home", "Salaried probation officer", "Voluntary probation officer", "Whole-time probation officer". Schedule 1. Schedule 2 to the extent specified in Schedule 9. Schedule 3.
5 & 6 Eliz. 2 c. 1.	The Police, Fire and Probation Officers Remuneration Act, 1956	In section 1(1)(d), the words from "or" to "1949".
6 & 7 Eliz. 2 c. 40.	The Matrimonial Proceedings (Children) Act, 1958	Section 11(2) and (3). In section 12(1), the words "of a probation officer or", and section 12(3).

Chapter	Short title	Extent of repeal
8 & 9 Eliz. 2 c. 61.	The Mental Health (Scotland) Act, 1960	Sections 8 and 9. Section 12(2). Sections 19 to 21. In section 111(1), the definition of "residential home for persons suffering from mental disorder".
1963 c. 37.	The Children and Young Persons Act, 1963	Section 1. Sections 45 to 50. Section 58.
1963 c. 39.	The Criminal Justice (Scotland) Act, 1963	Section 15(1).
1968 c. 46.	The Health Services and Public Health Act, 1968	Section 44. Section 45.

PART II

Chapter	Short title	Extent of repeal
1963 c. 37.	The Children and Young Persons Act, 1963	In section 45(1) the words "the Children and Young Persons (Scotland) Acts, 1937 and 1956".

THE MAGISTRATES' COURTS (FORMS) RULES, 1968
[S.I. 1968 No. 1919]

These rules were made on November 27, 1968, under s. 15 of the Justices of the Peace Act, 1949, as extended by s. 122 of the Magistrates' Courts Act, 1952

*   *   *   *

SCHEDULE—FORMS

*   *   *   *

6

Order for taking finger-prints and palm-prints of defendant
(M.C. Act, 1952, s. 40; C.J. Act, 1967, s. 33)

In the [county of   . Petty Sessional Division of   ].
Before the Magistrates' Court sitting at   .

A.B. (hereinafter called the defendant) having on the   day of   , 19   , been taken into custody is this day charged that he/she on the   day of   , 19   , at   , in the [county] aforesaid, did (*state shortly particulars of offence*):

[*or* A.B. (hereinafter called the defendant) appearing before this Court in answer to a summons for (*state shortly particulars of offence*) being an offence punishable with imprisonment:]

And application being made to the Court in that behalf by (*insert name and rank*) of the   Police Force:

And it appearing to the Court that the defendant is not less than fourteen years of age:

It is ordered that the finger-prints and palm-prints of the defendant be taken by a constable.

Dated the   day of   , 19   .

J.P.,
Justice of the Peace for the [county] aforesaid.
[*or* By order of the Court,

J.C.,
Clerk of the Court.]

7

Warrant for arrest of defendant on failure to surrender to bail (M.C. *Act*, 1952, ss. 93, 97; M.C. *Rules*, 1968, rr. 78, 79)

In the [county of   .   Petty Sessional Division of
            ].

To each and all of the constables of   [*or* To X.Y. of
            ].

A.B. (hereinafter called the defendant) was on the   day of
        , 19   , charged before [*or* convicted by] the Magistrates' Court sitting at   , [*or* was charged at the   Police Station] (*state shortly particulars of offence*):

And [, the hearing of the case being adjourned,] the defendant was released [in pursuance of section 38 [*or* 93] of the Magistrates' Courts Act, 1952,] upon a recognisance conditioned for his/her appearance this day, at the hour of   in the   noon, before the Magistrates' Court sitting at   :

And, in breach of the said recognisance, the defendant has this day failed to appear:

You are hereby commanded to bring the defendant before the Magistrates' Court sitting at   , or a justice of the peace of the petty sessional division in which the court is situate, forthwith.

Dated the   day of   , 19   .

J.P.,
Justice of the Peace for the [county] aforesaid.
[*or* By order of the Court,

J.C.,
Clerk of the Court.]

(*Endorsement where bail is allowed*)

It is directed that the defendant on arrest be released on bail on entering into a recognisance in the sum of   , with   surety   in the sum of   [each], for his/her appearance before the Magistrates' Court sitting at   , at the hour of   in the   noon of the next day upon which the Court is open [*or* on the   day of   , 19   ]. [The defendant's recognisance shall be subject to the following condition[s] (*specify*)].

J.P.,
Justice of the Peace for the [county] aforesaid.
[*or* By order of the Court,

J.C.,
Clerk of the Court.]

*   *   *   *

15

Notice to governor of prison of person committed on bail for trial
(M.C. Rules, 1968, r. 8)

In the [county of   .   Petty Sessional Division of   ].

To the Governor of Her Majesty's prison [*or* the remand centre] at   .

The undermentioned person has been committed on bail for trial at the Crown Court for the [county] of   to be held at   .

      Name, age, address and
        occupation of accused

Charge

Committing Court

    Bailed this   day of   , 19   .

                             J.C.,
                   Clerk of the Court.

        *   *   *   *

35

Hospital order (M.H. Act, 1959, s. 60; M.C. Rules, 1968, r. 27)

In the [county of   .   Petty Sessional Division of   ].

Before the Magistrates' Court sitting at   .

A.B. is this day charged with (*state shortly particulars of offence*), being an offence punishable on summary conviction with imprisonment:

And the Court has convicted A.B. of the said offence [*or* is satisfied that A.B. did the act or made the omission charged]:

And the Court has heard [*or* considered] the [written] evidence of two medical practitioners, namely (*insert names and addresses*), [each] of whom [the first mentioned] is approved for the purposes of section 28 of the Mental Health Act, 1959, by a local health authority as having special experience in the diagnosis or treatment of mental disorders, and each of the said practitioners has described the said A.B. as suffering from mental illness [*or* psychopathic disorder *or* subnormality *or* severe subnormality]:

And the Court is satisfied that he/she is suffering from the following form(s) of mental disorder within the meaning of the Mental Health Act, 1959, namely mental illness [*or* psychopathic disorder *or* subnormality *or* severe subnormality], and that the disorder is of a nature or degree which warrants his/her detention in a hospital for medical treatment and is satisfied that arrangements have been made for his/her admission to the hospital hereinafter specified within twenty-eight days of this date and that the most suitable method of disposing of the case is by means of a hospital order:

It is ordered that the said A.B. be admitted to and detained in (*insert name and address of hospital*):

[And that he/she be conveyed to the said hospital by E.F.]:

[And it is directed that pending admission to the said hospital within the said period of twenty-eight days the said A.B. shall be detained in a place of safety, namely   ] [and shall be conveyed thither by E.F.].

    Dated the   day of   , 19   .

                             J.P.,
      Justice of the Peace for the [county] first above mentioned.
      [*or* By order of the Court,

                            J.C.,
                 Clerk of the Court.]

36

Guardianship order (M.H. Act, 1959, s. 60; M.C. Rules, 1968, r. 27)

In the [county of   . Petty Sessional Division of   ].

Before the Magistrates' Court sitting at   .

A.B. is this day charged with (*state shortly particulars of offence*), being an offence punishable on summary conviction with imprisonment:

And the Court has convicted A.B. of the said offence [*or* is satisfied that A.B. did the act or made the omission charged]:

And the Court has heard [*or* considered] the [written] evidence of two medical practitioners, namely (*insert names and addresses*), [each] of whom [the first mentioned] is approved for the purposes of section 28 of the Mental Health Act, 1959, by a local health authority as having special experience in the diagnosis or treatment of mental disorders, and each of the said practitioners has described the said A.B. as suffering from mental illness [*or* psychopathic disorder *or* subnormality *or* severe subnormality]:

And the Court is satisfied that he/she is suffering from the following form(s) of mental disorder within the meaning of the Mental Health Act, 1959, namely mental illness [*or* psychopathic disorder *or* subnormality *or* severe subnormality], and that the disorder is of a nature or degree which warrants his/her reception into guardianship under that Act and is satisfied that the authority [*or* person] hereinafter specified is willing to receive him/her into guardianship and that the most suitable method of disposing of the case is by means of a guardianship order:

It is ordered that the said A.B. be placed under guardianship of a local health authority, namely the   County [Borough] Council [*or* of C.D. being a person approved by a local health authority, namely the   County [Borough] Council].

Dated the   day of   , 19   .

J.P.,
Justice of the Peace for the [county] first above mentioned.
[*or* By order of the Court.

J.C.,
Clerk of the Court.]

*   *   *   *

41

*Commitment to the Crown Court: borstal case (M.C. Act, 1952, s. 28; C.J. Act, 1948,
s. 20; C.J. Act, 1961, s. 1; M.C. Rules, 1968, rr, 77, 78, 80)*

In the [county of   . Petty Sessional Division of   ].

To each and all of the constables of   [*or* To X.Y.
of   ] and to the Governor of the remand centre at
          [*or* Her Majesty's prison at   ].

A.B. (hereinafter called the defendant) [, having consented to be tried summarily,] was this day [*or* on the   day of   , 19   ,] convicted by the Magistrates' Court sitting at   , (*state shortly particulars of offence*):

And it appeared to the Court that on the day of his/her said conviction the defendant was not less than fifteen and under twenty-one years of age:

And the Court is of opinion, having regard to the circumstances of the offence and taking into account the defendant's character and previous conduct, that it is expedient that he/she should be detained for training for not less than six months [and, he/she being then under seventeen years of age, that no other method of dealing with him/her is appropriate]:

And it was this day adjudged that the defendant should be committed in custody to the Crown Court for sentence in accordance with the provisions of section 20 of the Criminal Justice Act, 1948:

You, the said constables [*or* X.Y.], are hereby commanded to convey the defendant to the said remand centre [*or* prison] and there deliver him/her to the Governor thereof, together with this warrant; and you, the said Governor, to receive the defendant into your custody and, unless he/she shall have been bailed in the meantime, keep him/her until the next sitting of the Crown Court and to have him/her there, together with this warrant, there to be dealt with according to law.

Dated the   day of   , 19   .

J.P.,
Justice of the Peace for the [county] aforesaid.
[or By order of the Court,

J.C.,
Clerk of the Court.]

(*Endorsement where bail is allowed*)

The Court hereby certifies that the defendant may be bailed by recognisance in the sum of   , with   surety   in the sum of   [each], to appear before the next sitting of the Crown Court, and that the defendant has [not] entered into his/her recognisance. [The defendant's recognisance shall be subject to the following condition[s] (*specify*)].

J.P.,
Justice of the Peace for the [county] aforesaid.
[or By order of the Court,

J.C.,
Clerk of the Court.]

*   *   *   *

43

Commitment to the Crown Court for restriction order (M.H. Act, 1959, s. 67 (1))

In the [county of   . Petty Sessional Division of   ].
To each and all of the constables of   [or To X.Y. of   ]
and to the Governor of Her Majesty's prison [or the remand centre] at   .

A.B. (hereinafter called the defendant) [, having consented to be tried summarily,] was this day [or on the   day of   , 19   ,] convicted by the Magistrates' Court sitting at   , (*state shortly particulars of offence*), being an offence punishable on summary conviction with imprisonment:

And it appeared to the Court that on the day of his/her said conviction the defendant was not less than fourteen years of age:

And the conditions which, under section 60 (1) of the Mental Health Act, 1959, are required to be satisfied for the making of a hospital order are satisfied in respect of the defendant:

And it appeared to the Court, having regard to the nature of the offence, the antecedents of the defendant and the risk of his/her committing further offences if set at large, that if a hospital order is made an order restricting the discharge of the defendant should also be made:

And it was this day adjudged that the defendant should be committed in custody to the Crown Court under the provisions of section 67 (1) of the Mental Health Act, 1959, to be dealt with in respect of the offence:

You, the said constables [or X.Y.], are hereby commanded to convey the defendant to the said prison [or remand centre] and there deliver him/her to the Governor thereof, together with this warrant; and you, the said Governor, to receive the defendant into your custody and to keep him/her until the next sitting of the Crown Court and to have him/her there, together with this warrant, there to be dealt with according to law.

Dated the   day of   , 19   .

J.P.,
Justice of the Peace for the [county] aforesaid.
[or By order of the Court,

J.C.,
Clerk of the Court.]

*   *   *   *

45

Order of admission to hospital pending restriction order
(M.H. Act, 1959, s. 68)

In the [county of   . Petty Sessional Division of   ].

To the Managers of the   Hospital at   .

A.B. (hereinafter called the defendant) [, having consented to be tried summarily,] was this day [*or* on the   day of   , 19   ,] convicted by the Magistrates' Court sitting at   (*state shortly particulars of offence*) being an offence punishable on summary conviction with imprisonment:

And it appeared to the Court that on the day of his/her said conviction the defendant was not less than fourteen years of age:

And the conditions which, under section 60 of the Mental Health Act, 1959, are required to be satisfied for the making of a hospital order are satisfied in respect of the defendant:

And it appeared to the Court, having regard to the nature of the offence, the antecedents of the defendant and the risk of his/her committing further offences if set at large, that if a hospital order is made an order restricting his/her discharge should also be made:

And the Court has committed the defendant to the Crown Court under section 67 (1) of the Mental Health Act, 1959, to be dealt with in respect of the offence:

The Court being satisfied that arrangements have been made for the admission of the defendant to the hospital hereinafter specified:

It was this day directed that the defendant be admitted to the Hospital at   and be detained there until the Crown Court has disposed of the case:

And it was directed that C.D. [*or* you, the said Managers,] should produce the defendant from the said hospital to attend the next sitting of the Crown Court on the day and at the time to be notified by the Clerk of the Peace.

Dated the   day of   , 19   .

> J.P.,
> Justice of the Peace for the [county] aforesaid.
> [*or* By order of the Court,
>
> J.C.,
> Clerk of the Court.]

*   *   *   *

Miscellaneous

95

Commitment to higher court: summary offence, etc. (C.J. Act, 1967, s. 56; M.C. Rules, 1968, rr. 77, 78, 80)

In the [county of   . Petty Sessional Division of   ].

Before the Magistrates' Court sitting at   .

To each and all of the constables of   [*or* To X.Y. of   ] and to the Governor of Her Majesty's prison [*or* the remand centre] at   .

A.B. (hereinafter called the defendant) [, having consented to be tried summarily,] was this day [*or* on the   day of   , 19   ,] convicted by this Court (*state shortly particulars of offence*):

[*or* A.B. (hereinafter called the defendant) was on the   day of 19   , convicted by this Court [*or* the Magistrates' Court sitting at   ], (*state shortly particulars of offence*) and on the said date [*or* on the day of   , 19   ,] the Court sentenced the defendant to imprisonment for (*state period*) but made an order which [, as subsequently amended by the competent court,] provided that the sentence should not take effect unless during the period beginning on the date of the order and ending on the   day of   , 19   , he/she committed in Great Britain another offence punishable with imprisonment:

And [this Court was satisfied that] the defendant was this day [*or* on the   day of   , 19   ,] convicted by this Court [*or* the Magistrates' Court sitting at   ] of a further offence, namely, (*state shortly particulars of offence*), being an offence punishable with imprisonment committed by him/her on the   day of   , 19   , during the said period:]

And this Court has committed the defendant to the Crown Court to be held at   under the Vagrancy Act, 1824 [*or* section 8 (4) of the Criminal Justice Act, 1948] [*or* section 28 [*or* 29] of the Magistrates' Courts Act, 1952] [*or* section 41 (2) [*or* 62 (6)] of the Criminal Justice Act, 1967]:

And it was this day adjudged that the defendant should be committed in custody under section 56 of the Criminal Justice Act, 1967 to the Crown Court to be dealt with in respect of the said offence [*or* suspended sentence]:

You, the said constables [*or* X.Y.], are hereby commanded to convey the defendant to the said prison [*or* remand centre] and there deliver him/her to the Governor thereof, together with this warrant: and you, the said Governor, to receive the defendant into your custody and, unless he/she shall have been bailed in the meantime, keep him/her until the next sitting of the Crown Court and to have him/her there, together with this warrant, there to be dealt with according to law.

Dated the   day of   , 19   .

J.P.,
Justice of the Peace for the [county] aforesaid.
[*or* By order of the Court.

J.C.,
Clerk of the Court.]

(*Endorsement where bail is allowed*)

The Court hereby certifies that the defendant may be bailed by recognisance in the sum of   , with   suret   in the sum of   [each], to appear before the next sitting of the Crown Court and that the defendant has [not] entered into his/her recognisance. [The defendant's recognisance shall be subject to the following condition[s] (*specify*)].

J.P.,
Justice of the Peace for the [county] aforesaid.
[*or* By order of the Court,

J.C.,
Clerk of the Court.]

     *   *   *   *

96

Notice to governor of prison of person committed on bail to higher court otherwise than for trial (M.C. Rules, 1968, r. 16 (3))

In the [county of   . Petty Sessional Division of   ].

To the Governor of Her Majesty's prison [*or* the remand centre] at   .

The undermentioned person has been committed on bail to the next sitting of the Crown Court to be held at   .

Name, age, address and occupation of person committed	
Enactment under which he/she is committed and brief particulars of offence or other circumstance giving rise to committal	
Committing court	

Bailed this   day of   , 19   .

J.C.,
Clerk of the Court.

*   *   *   *

119

Recognisance: general (M.C. Act, 1952, ss. 7, 14, 26, 89, 91; C.J. Act, 1967, ss. 20, 21, 41, 62; M.C. Rules, 1968, rr. 69, 72.)

In the [county of   . Petty Sessional Division of   ].

Recognisance of principal

I acknowledge that I owe to our Sovereign Lady the Queen the sum of   , payment thereof to be enforced against me by due process of law if I fail to comply with any of the conditions endorsed hereon.

(Signed) A.B. of   .
Taken before me the   day of   , 19   .

J.P.,
Justice of the Peace for the [county] aforesaid.
[*or* J.C.,
Clerk of the Magistrates' Court sitting at   .]
[*or* E.F.,
[Inspector] of the   Police.]

Recognisance of surety

I/We acknowledge that I/we owe to our Sovereign Lady the Queen the sum of   [each], payment thereof to be enforced [severally] against me/us by due process of law if the above mentioned principal fails to comply with the condition[s] endorsed hereon [other than the condition[s] requiring him to   ].

(Signed) G.H. of   .
          J.K. of   .

Taken before me the   day of   , 19   .

J.P.,
Justice of the Peace for the [county] aforesaid.
[*or* J.C.,
Clerk of the Magistrates' Court sitting at   .]
[*or* E.F.,
[Inspector] of the   Police.]

(Endorsement)

Condition[s]

The condition[s] of this recognizance is [are] that if the principal—

appears before the Magistrates' Court sitting at   , on   day the   day of   , 19   , at the hour of   in the noon [and appears at every time and place to which during the course of the proceedings against the principal the hearing may be from time to time adjourned, unless the Court otherwise orders in the meantime,] to answer to the charge made against him/her by ,

[or appears before the next sitting of the Crown Court to be held at , and there surrenders himself/herself into custody [and takes his/her trial upon any indictment preferred against him/her],]

[and, subject to the condition for his/her said appearance, undergoes medical examination by a [or two] duly qualified medical practitioner[s] [, of whom one is approved for the purposes of section 28 of the Mental Health Act, 1959,] and for the purpose attends at (insert name and address of institution or place or name and address of doctor) and complies with any directions given to him/her for that purpose by [and resides there until the expiration of from the date of admission or until earlier discharge],]

[and, subject to the condition for his/her appearance, (state any special conditions of bail),]

[or keeps the peace and is of good behaviour towards Her Majesty and all Her liege people, and especially towards for the period of from the date of this recognisance,]

[or appears on such date and at such time and place as may be notified to him/her by the Clerk of the Peace at the hearing of his/her appeal to Crown Court aforesaid from a decision of the Magistrates' Court sitting at , dated the day of , 19 , whereby the principal was convicted (state shortly particulars of offence) [or was sentenced or ordered],]

[or prosecutes without delay his/her appeal to the High Court of Justice from a conviction [or order] of the Magistrates' Court sitting at , dated the day of , 19 , whereby the principal was convicted (state shortly particulars of offence) [or was ordered], and submits to the judgment of the High Court and pays such costs as may be awarded by the High Court [*and, unless the determination appealed against is reversed, appears before the said Magistrates' Court within ten days after the said judgment is given],]

[or (where prosecutor is appealing) prosecutes without delay his/her appeal to the High Court of Justice from a determination of the Magistrates' Court sitting at on the day of , 19 , whereby the said Magistrates' Court dismissed an information laid by the principal alleging that X.Y. had (state shortly particulars of offence) [or (state other determination appealed against)], and pays such costs as may be awarded by the High Court,]

then this recognisance shall be void, but otherwise shall remain in full force.

---

* Delete if the principal is not to be released on bail pending the appeal to the High Court.

* * * *

GENERAL

132

Summons to witness (M.C. Act, 1952, s. 77; M.C. Rules, 1968, r. 81)

In the [county of . Petty Sessional Division of].
To E.F., of .

Information [or complaint] has been laid [or made] by that A.B. (state shortly particulars of offence or complaint):

And I, the undersigned [or state name] Justice of the Peace, being satisfied that you are likely to be able to [give material evidence] [and] [produce the under-mentioned document[s] or thing[s] likely to be material evidence] therein and that you will not voluntarily attend for that purpose:

You are therefore hereby summoned to appear on   day the
day of   , 19   , at the hour of   in the   noon, before
the Magistrates' Court sitting at   , to [give evidence therein] [and]
[produce the following document[s] or thing[s]:—   ].

Dated the   day of   , 19   .

> J.P.,
> Justice of the Peace for the [county] first above mentioned.
> [or This summons was issued by the above named Justice of the Peace.

> J.C.,
> Clerk of the Magistrates' Court sitting at   .]

133

Warrant for arrest of witness on failure to appear to summons (M.C. Act, 1952, ss. 77, 93; M.C. Rules, 1968, rr. 78, 79)

In the [county of   . Petty Sessional Division of   ].

To each and all of the constables of   [or To X.Y. of   ].

E.F. (hereinafter called the witness) was summoned to appear on   day
the   day of   , 19   , at the hour of   in the
          noon, before the Magistrates' Court sitting at   , on the
hearing of an information [or complaint] against A.B., to [give evidence therein]
[and] [produce the following document[s] or thing[s]:—   ].

And the witness has failed to attend in answer to the said summons and it appears
to the Court that there is no just excuse for the failure:

And it is proved to the satisfaction of the Court by evidence on oath [or affirma-
tion] that the witness is likely to be able to [give material evidence] [and] [produce
the document[s] or thing[s] aforesaid] on the said hearing, and [and it is further
proved by declaration [or certificate]] that he/she has been duly served with the
said summons and has been paid [or had tendered to him/her] a reasonable sum for
his/her costs and expenses in that behalf.

You are hereby commanded to bring the witness before the Magistrates' Court
sitting at   , or a justice of the peace of the petty sessional division
in which the court is situate, forthwith.

Dated the   day of   , 19   .

> J.P.,
> Justice of the Peace for the [county] aforesaid.
> [or By order of the Court,

> J.C.,
> Clerk of the Court.]

(Endorsement where bail is allowed)

It is directed that the witness on arrest be released on bail on entering into a
recognisance in the sum of   , with   suret   in the sum
of   [each], for his/her appearance for the purpose above mentioned before
the Magistrates' Court sitting at   , at the hour of   in the
          noon of the next day upon which such Court is open [or on the
day of   , 19   ]. [The witness's recognisance shall be subject to the
following condition[s] (*specify*)].

> J.P.,
> Justice of the Peace for the [county] aforesaid.
> [or By order of the Court,

> J.C.,
> Clerk of the Court.]

134

Warrant for arrest of witness in first instance (M.C. Act, 1952, ss. 77, 93;
M.C. Rules, 1968, rr. 78, 79.)

In the [county of   . Petty Sessional Division of   ].

To each and all of the constables of   [*or* To X.Y. of   ].

Information has been laid by   that A.B. (*state shortly*
particulars of offence):

And I, the undersigned Justice of the Peace, being satisfied by evidence on oath
[*or* affirmation] that E.F. (hereinafter called the witness) is likely to be able to
[give material evidence therein] [and] [produce the undermentioned document[s]
or thing[s] likely to be material evidence therein,] and that he/she will not voluntarily attend for that purpose and that it is probable that a summons would not
procure his/her attendance:

You are hereby commanded to bring the witness before the Magistrates' Court
sitting at   , or a justice of the peace of the petty sessional division
in which the court is situate, forthwith.

Dated the   day of   , 19   .

J.P.,
Justice of the Peace for the [county] first above mentioned.

(*Endorsement where bail is allowed*)

It is directed that the witness on arrest be released on bail on entering into a
recognisance in the sum of   , with   suret   in the sum of
[each], for his/her appearance for the purpose above mentioned before the Magistrates' Court sitting at   , at the hour of   in the   noon
of the next day upon which the court is open [*or* on the   day of
, 19   ]. [The witness's recognisance shall be subject to the following
condition[s] (*specify*)].

J.P.,
Justice of the Peace for the [county] first above mentioned.

THE MAGISTRATES' COURTS RULES, 1968
[S.I. 1968 No. 1920]

These rules were made on November 27, 1968, under s. 15 of the Justices of the Peace Act,
1949, as extended by s. 122 of the Magistrates' Courts Act, 1952

4. Taking depositions of witnesses and statement of accused.—(1) This
Rule does not apply to committal proceedings where under section 1 of the
Criminal Justice Act, 1967, a magistrates' court commits a person for trial
without consideration of the evidence.

(2) A magistrates' court inquiring into an offence as examining justices, shall
cause the evidence of each witness, including the evidence of the accused, but
not including any witness of his merely to his character, to be put into writing;
and as soon as may be after the examination of such a witness shall cause his
deposition to be read to him in the presence and hearing of the accused, and shall
require the witness to sign the deposition.

(3) The depositions shall be authenticated by a certificate signed by one of
the examining justices.

(4) Before a statement made in writing by or taken in writing from a child
is received in evidence under section 27 (1) of the Children and Young Persons
Act, 1963, the court shall cause the effect of that subsection to be explained to
the accused in ordinary language and, if the defence does not object to the
application of that subsection, shall inform him that he may ask questions
about the circumstances in which the statement was made or taken.

(5) Any such statement as aforesaid which is received in evidence shall be made an exhibit.

(6) After the evidence for the prosecution (including any statements tendered under section 2 of the Criminal Justice Act, 1967) has been given, and after hearing any submission, if any is made, the court shall, unless it then decides not to commit for trial, cause the charge to be written down, if this has not already been done, and read to the accused, and shall explain it to him in ordinary language.

(7) The court shall then ask the accused whether he wishes to say anything in answer to the charge and, if he is not represented by counsel or a solicitor, shall before asking the question say to him—

"You will have an opportunity to give evidence on oath before us and to call witnesses. But first I am going to ask you whether you wish to say anything in answer to the charge. You need not say anything unless you wish to do so. Anything you say will be taken down and may be given in evidence at your trial. You should take no notice of any promise or threat which any person may have made to persuade you to say anything,"

or words to that effect.

(8) Whatever the accused says in answer to the charge shall be put into writing, read over to him and signed by one of the examining justices and also, if the accused wishes, by him.

(9) The court shall then say to the accused—

"I must warn you that if this court should commit you for trial you may not be permitted at that trial to give evidence of an alibi or to call witnesses in support of an alibi unless you have earlier given particulars of the alibi and of the witnesses. You may give those particulars now to this court or to the solicitor for the prosecution not later than seven days from the end of these committal proceedings.",

or words to that effect and, if it appears to the court that the accused may not understand the meaning of the term "alibi", the court shall explain it to him:
Provided that the court shall not be required to give this warning in any case where it appears to the court that, having regard to the nature of the offence with which the accused is charged, it is unnecessary to do so.

(10) After complying with the requirements of this Rule relating to the statement of the accused, and whether or not he has made a statement in answer to the charge, the court shall give him an opportunity to give evidence himself and to call witnesses.

(11) Where the accused is represented by counsel or a solicitor, his counsel or solicitor shall be heard on his behalf, either before or after the evidence for the defence is taken, at his discretion, and may, if the accused gives evidence himself and call witnesses, be heard on his behalf with the leave of the court both before and after the evidence is taken:
Provided that, where the court gives leave to counsel or the solicitor for the accused to be heard, after as well as before, the evidence is taken, counsel or the solicitor for the prosecution shall be entitled to be heard immediately before counsel or the solicitor for the accused is heard for the second time.

(12) Where the court determines to commit the accused for trial in respect of a charge which differs from that which was read to him in accordance with the provisions of paragraph (6) of this Rule, the court shall cause the new charge to be read to him.

(13) Where the court has given to the accused the warning required by paragraph (9) of this Rule the clerk of the court shall give to him written notice of

the provisions of section 11 of the Criminal Justice Act, 1967 about giving notice of particulars of alibi to the solicitor for the prosecution and the solicitor's name and address shall be stated in the notice.

*   *   *   *

10. Documents and exhibits to be retained and sent to court of trial.— (1) A magistrates' court that commits a person for trial shall, unless there are reasons for not doing so, retain any documents and articles produced by a witness who is subject to a conditional witness order or in whose case the court has directed that a witness order be treated as a conditional order.

(2) As soon as practicable after the committal of any person for trial, and in any case before the first day of sitting of the court to which he is committed, the clerk of the magistrates' court that committed him shall, subject to the provisions of section 5 of the Prosecution of Offences Act, 1879 (which relates to the sending of documents and things to the Director of Public Prosecutions), send to the proper officer of the court of trial—

(a) the information, if it is in writing;

(b) the depositions and written statements tendered in evidence, together with a certificate authenticating the depositions and statements, and any admission of facts made for the purposes of the committal proceedings under section 10 of the Criminal Justices Act, 1967 and not withdrawn;

(c) all statements made by the accused before the magistrates' court;

(d) a list of the names, addresses and occupations of the witnesses in respect of whom witness orders have been made;

(e) if the accused is committed for trial on bail, the recognisance of the accused;

(f) any recognisance entered into by any person as surety for the accused;

(g) a list of the documents and articles produced in evidence before the justice or treated as so produced;

(h) such of the documents and articles referred to in the last preceding sub-paragraph as have been retained by the justices;

(i) a certificate showing whether the accused was informed at the committal proceedings of the requirements of section 11 of the Criminal Justice Act, 1967 (notice of alibi) and a record of any particulars given by him to the magistrates' court under that section;

(j) if the committal was under section 1 of the Criminal Justice Act, 1967 (committal for trial without consideration of the evidence), a statement to that effect;

(k) if the magistrates' court has made an order under section 3 (2) of the Criminal Justice Act, 1967 (removal of restrictions on reports of committal proceedings), a statement to that effect.

(l) the certificate of the examining justices as to costs of prosecution (Form B in the Schedule to the Costs in Criminal Cases Regulations, 1908);

(m) if any person under 17 is concerned in the committal proceedings, a statement whether the magistrates' court has given a direction under section 39 of the Children and Young Persons Act, 1933 (prohibition of publication of certain matter in newspapers).

(3) Paragraph (2) of this Rule shall apply to the committal of a person under section 12 (2) or (3) of the Act as if sub-paragraphs (b) to (d) and (g) to (m) were omitted.

(4) The clerk shall, in compiling the list mentioned in paragraph (2) (d) of this Rule, indicate the names of the witnesses, if any, to whom he has given any such

notice as is referred to in Rule 6 (1) of these Rules and shall include in the list the date of any such notice.

(5) The clerk shall retain a copy of any list sent in pursuance of paragraph 2 (d) of this Rule.

(6) If after a list has been sent in pursuance of paragraph (2) (d) of this Rule to the proper officer of the court of trial the clerk of the magistrates' court gives any such notice as aforesaid, he shall send written particulars of the notice to the officer.

(7) In the application of this Rule in relation to any committal to the Central Criminal Court, in paragraph (2) for the words "before the first day of sitting of the court to which he is committed" there shall be substituted the words "within four days from the date of his committal (not counting Sundays, Good Friday, Christmas Day or bank holidays)".

(8) In the application of this Rule as aforesaid, the said period of four days may be extended for so long as the clerk of the Central Criminal Court directs, having regard to the length of any document mentioned in paragraph (2) of this Rule or any other relevant circumstances.

(9) Upon the committal of any person to the Central Criminal Court, the clerk of the magistrates' court that committed him shall forthwith in writing notify the clerk of the Central Criminal Court of that committal.

(10) In the application of this Rule in relation to any committal under section 14 of the Criminal Justice Administration Act, 1962, to a court other than the Central Criminal Court, in paragraph (2) the words "and in any case before the first day of sitting of the court to which he is committed" shall be omitted.

11. Supply of copies of depositions and information to accused.—The person having custody of the depositions on which any person has been committed for trial shall, as soon as is practicable after application is made to him by or on behalf of the accused, supply to the accused copies of the depositions, a copy of the list of witnesses mentioned in Rule 10 (2) (d) of these Rules and, if the information is in writing, of the information.

*   *   *   *

13. Order of evidence and speeches: information.—(1) On the summary trial of an information, where the accused does not plead guilty, the prosecutor shall call the evidence for the prosecution, and before doing so may address the court.

(2) At the conclusion of the evidence for the prosecution, the accused may address the court, whether or not he afterwards makes an unsworn statement or calls evidence.

(3) At the conclusion of the evidence, if any, for the defence, the prosecutor may call evidence to rebut that evidence.

(4) At the conclusion of the evidence for the defence and any unsworn statement which the accused may make and the evidence, if any, in rebuttal, the accused may address the court if he has not already done so.

(5) Either party may, with the leave of the court, address the court a second time, but where the court grants leave to one party it shall not refuse leave to the other.

(6) Where both parties address the court twice the prosecutor shall address the court for the second time before the accused does so.

NOTES

This Rule is applied to proceedings under s. 1 (2) (e) of the Children and Young Persons Act, 1969, by r. 16 (2) (c) of the Magistrates' Courts Rules, 1970, p. 577, *post.*

In *Simms* v. *Moore*, [1970] 2 Q. B. 327; [1970] 3 All E. R. 1, the principles which should govern the examination of witnesses by a justices' clerk in criminal cases were set out by Lord Parker, C.J.

1. In general neither the court nor the justices' clerk should take an active part in the proceedings except to clear up ambiguities in the evidence.

2. So far as examining witnesses is concerned this should never be done if the party concerned is legally represented; nor should this be done where a party, although unrepresented is competent to and desires to examine the witness himself.

3. Where the party is not competent, through a lack of knowledge of court procedure or rules of evidence or otherwise, the court can at its discretion permit the clerk to do so.

4. When this is permitted the clerk may do so by reference to a proof of evidence handed in to him provided always an opportunity is given to the other side to see it or have a copy.

5. Generally, the discretion should be so exercised only when there are reasonable grounds for thinking that thereby the interests of justice would be best promoted.

14. Order of evidence and speeches: complaint.—(1) On the hearing of a complaint, except where the court determines under section 45 (3) of the Act to make the order with the consent of the defendant without hearing evidence, the complainant shall call his evidence, and before doing so may address the court.

(2) At the conclusion of the evidence for the complainant the defendant may address the court, whether or not he afterwards calls evidence.

(3) At the conclusion of the evidence, if any, for the defence, the complainant may call evidence to rebut that evidence.

(4) At the conclusion of the evidence for the defence and the evidence, if any, in rebuttal, the defendant may address the court if he has not already done so.

(5) Either party may, with the leave of the court, address the court a second time, but where the court grants leave to one party it shall not refuse leave to the other.

(6) Where the defendant obtains leave to address the court for a second time his second address shall be made before the second address, if any, of the complainant.

NOTES

This Rule is applied to proceedings as set out in r. 13 of the Magistrates' Courts (Children and Young Persons) Rules, 1970, p. 576, *post*, by r. 15 (2), *ibid*.

The opportunity to make an unsworn statement is only given in criminal proceedings (r. 13, *supra*) *Aggas* v. *Aggas*, [1971] 2 All E. R. 1497; 135 J. P. 484.

15. Form of conviction or order.—(1) A form of summary conviction or order made on complaint shall be drawn up if required for an appeal or other legal purpose, and if drawn up shall be in such one of the prescribed forms as is appropriate to the case.

(2) Where the conviction is of an offence that could not have been tried summarily without the consent of the accused, the conviction shall contain a statement that the accused consented to the summary trial.

NOTE

See note to r. 14.

16. Committals for sentence, etc.—(1) Where a magistrates' court commits an offender to the Crown Court under the Vagrancy Act, 1824, section 28 or 29 of the Act or section 41 (2) (a), 56 (1) or 62 (6) of the Criminal Justice Act, 1967, after convicting him of an offence, the clerk of the magistrates' court shall send to the proper officer of the court to which the offender is committed—

(a) a copy signed by the clerk of the magistrates' court of the minute or memorandum of the conviction entered in the register;

(b) a copy of any note of the evidence given at the trial of the offender, any written statement tendered in evidence and any deposition;

(c) such documents and articles produced in evidence before the court as have been retained by the court;

(d) any report relating to the offender considered by the court;

(e) if the offender is committed on bail, his recognisance and any recognisance entered into by any person as his surety; and

(f) if the court imposes under s. 56 (8) of the Criminal Justice Act, 1967, an interim disqualification for holding or obtaining a licence under Part II of the Road Traffic Act, 1960, a statement of the date of birth and sex of the offender.

(2) Where a magistrates' court commits an offender to the Crown Court under the Vagrancy Act, 1824, section 8 (4) of the Criminal Justice Act, 1948, section 28 or 29 of the Act or section 41 (2), 56 (1) or 62 (6) of the Criminal Justice Act, 1967 and the magistrates' court on that occasion imposes, under section 56 (8) of the Criminal Justice Act, 1967, an interim disqualification for holding or obtaining a licence under Part II of the Road Traffic Act, 1960, the clerk of the magistrates' court shall give notice of the interim disqualification to the proper officer of the court to which the offender is committed.

(3) Where a magistrates' court commits a person on bail to a court of assize or quarter sessions under any of the enactments mentioned in paragraph (2) of this Rule or under section 6 (3) (b) or 8 (3) (b) of the Criminal Justice Act, 1948, the clerk of the magistrates' court shall give notice thereof in writing to the governor of the prison to which persons of the sex of the person committed are committed by that court if committed in custody for trial and also, if the person committed is under 21, to the governor of the remand centre to which he would have been committed if the court had refused him bail.

17. Committal to the Crown Court for order restricting discharge, etc.—Where a magistrates' court commits an offender to the Crown Court either—

(a) under section 67 (1) of the Mental Health Act, 1959 with a view to the making of a hospital order with an order restricting his discharge; or

(b) under section 29 of the Act, as modified by subsection (4) of the said section 67, with a view to the passing of a more severe sentence than the magistrates' court has power to inflict if such an order is not made,

the clerk of the court shall send to the clerk of the peace—

(i) the copies, documents and articles specified in Rule 16 of these Rules;

(ii) any written evidence about the offender given by a medical practitioner under section 60 (1) (a) of the Mental Health Act, 1959 or a copy of a note of any oral evidence so given;

(iii) the name and address of the hospital the managers of which have agreed to admit the offender if a hospital order is made; and

(iv) if the offender has been admitted to a hospital under section 68 of that Act, the name and address of that hospital.

*   *   *   *

23. Documents to be sent on remand for medical inquiry.—On exercising the powers conferred by section 26 of the Act a court shall—

(a) where the accused is remanded in custody, send to the institution or place to which he is committed;

(b) where the accused is remanded on bail, send to the institution or place at which, or the person by whom, he is to be examined, a statement of the reasons why the court is of opinion that an inquiry ought to be made into his physical or mental condition and of any information before the court about his physical or mental condition.

* * * *

HOSPITAL ORDER

27. Documents to be sent under Mental Health Act, 1959.—(1) The court by which a hospital order is made under section 60 or 61 of the Mental Health Act, 1959, shall send to the hospital named in the order such information in the possession of the court as it considers likely to be of assistance in dealing with the patient to whom the order relates, and in particular such information about the mental condition, character and antecedents of the patient, and, in the case of an order made under the said section 60, about the nature of the offence.

(2) The court by which a guardianship order is made under the said section 60 or 61 shall send to the local health authority named therein as guardian or, as the case may be, the local health authority for the area in which the person so named resides, such information in the possession of the court as it considers likely to be of assistance in dealing with the patient to whom the order relates and in particular such information about the mental condition, character and antecedents of the patient, and, in the case of an order made under the said section 60, about the nature of the offence.

(3) The court by which an offender is ordered to be admitted to hospital under section 68 of the Mental Health Act, 1959 shall send to the hospital such information in the possession of the court as it considers likely to assist in the treatment of the offender until his case is dealt with by the Crown Court.

* * * *

APPEAL TO MAGISTRATES' COURT

30. Appeal to be by complaint.—Where under any enactment an appeal lies to a magistrates' court against the decision or order of a local authority or other authority, or other body or person, the appeal shall be by way of complaint for an order.

* * * *

36. Service of copy of order.—Where a magistrates' court makes, revokes, discharges, revives, alters or varies an affiliation order or order enforceable as an affiliation order, the court shall cause a copy of its order to be served on the defendant by delivering it to him or by sending it by post in a letter addressed to him at his last known or usual place of abode.

* * * *

SATISFACTION, ENFORCEMENT AND APPLICATION OF PAYMENTS

38. Notice to defendant of fine or forfeited recognisance.—(1) Where under section 47 (3) or 49 of the Criminal Justice Act, 1967 or section 19 (5) of the Coroners Act, 1887, a magistrates' court is required to enforce payment of a fine imposed or recognisance forfeited by the Crown Court or by a coroner or where a magistrates' court allows time for payment of a sum adjudged to be paid by a summary conviction, or directs that the sum be paid by instalments, or where the offender is absent when a sum is adjudged to be paid by a summary conviction, the clerk of the court shall serve on the offender notice in writing stating the amount of the sum and, if it is to be paid by instalments, the amount of the instalments, the date on which the sum, or each of the instalments, is to be paid and the places and times at which payment may be made; and a warrant of distress or commitment shall not be issued until the preceding provisions of this Rule have been complied with.

(2) A notice under this Rule shall be served by delivering it to the offender or by sending it to him by post in a letter addressed to him at his last known or usual place of abode.

39. To whom payments are to be made.—(1) A person adjudged by the conviction or order of a magistrates' court to pay any sum shall, unless the court otherwise directs, pay that sum, or any instalment of that sum, to the clerk of the court.

(2) Where payment of any sum or instalment of any sum adjudged to be paid by the conviction or order of a magistrates' court is made to any person other than the clerk of the court, that person, unless he is the person to whom the court has directed payment to be made, shall, as soon as may be, account for and, if the clerk so requires, pay over the sum or instalment to the clerk of the court.

(3) Where payment of any sum adjudged to be paid by the conviction or order of a magistrates' court, or any instalment of such a sum, is directed to be made to the clerk of some other magistrates' court, the clerk of the court that adjudged the sum to be paid shall pay over any sums received by him on account of the said sum or instalment to the clerk of that other court.

40. Duty of clerk to give receipt.—The clerk of a magistrates' court shall give or send a receipt to any person who makes a payment to him in pursuance of a conviction or order of a magistrates' court and who asks for a receipt.

* * * *

42. Application for further time.—An application under section 63 (2) of the Act may, unless the court requires the applicant to attend, be made in writing.

* * * *

46. Order for supervision.—(1) Unless an order under section 71 (1) of the Act is made in the offender's presence, the clerk of the court making the order shall deliver to the offender, or serve on him by post, notice in writing of the order.

(2) It shall be the duty of any person for the time being appointed under the said section to advise and befriend the offender with a view to inducing him to pay the sum adjudged to be paid and thereby avoid committal to custody and to give any information required by a magistrates' court about the offender's conduct and means.

* * * *

49. Enforcement of affiliation orders, etc.—(1) Subject to the following provisions of this Rule, a complaint for the enforcement of an affiliation order, or an order enforceable as an affiliation order, shall be heard by the court that made the order;
Provided that—
(a) where the complainant is the person in whose favour the order was made and resides in a petty sessions area other than that for which

that court acts, and payment is directed to be made to the complainant or to the clerk of a magistrates' court acting for that petty sessions area, the complaint may be heard by the last-mentioned court;

    (b) where the complainant is the clerk of a magistrates' court, the complaint may be heard by that court.

(2) Where a complaint is made to a justice of the peace for the enforcement of such an order as aforesaid and it appears to him that the defendant is for the time being in some petty sessions area other than that for which the justice is acting and that the order may be more conveniently enforced by a magistrates' court acting for that area, the justice shall cause the clerk of the court to send the complaint by post to the clerk of a magistrates' court acting for that other petty sessions area, and for that purpose shall write down the complaint if this has not already been done.

(3) On receipt by the clerk of a magistrates' court of a complaint sent under the last preceding paragraph, he shall bring it before the court; and the court shall issue a summons or warrant for procuring the appearance of the defendant before it, and shall hear and determine the complaint.

(4) If, after a complaint has been sent to the clerk of a magistrates' court under this Rule, the clerk of the court to which the complaint was made receives any payment under the order, he shall forthwith send by post to the clerk to whom the complaint was sent a certificate of the amount of the payment and of the date when it was made.

(5) If, after a complaint has been sent as aforesaid, payment under the order is made, not to the clerk of the court to which the complaint was originally made, but to the person specified in the order, that person shall forthwith inform the clerk of the amount and date as aforesaid and the clerk shall forthwith send a certificate of the amount and date as required by the last preceding paragraph.

(6) A certificate under this Rule purporting to be signed by the clerk of the court to which the complaint was originally made shall be admissible as evidence on the hearing of the complaint that the amount specified in the certificate was paid on the date so specified.

(7) This Rule shall not apply—

    (a) where jurisdiction is confined by section 88 (2) (a) of the Children and Young Persons Act, 1933, to courts having jurisdiction in the place where the person liable is residing;
    (b) to a contribution order.

NOTE

By Sched. X of the Administration of Justice Act, 1970, ss. 74, 75 and 76 of the Magistrates' Courts Act, 1952, apply as if a legal aid contribution order were enforceable as an affiliation order.

*   *   *   *

EVIDENCE—CRIMINAL PROCEEDINGS

58. Written statements in committal proceedings or summary trial.—
(1) Written statements to be tendered in evidence under section 2 or 9 of the Criminal Justice Act, 1967, shall be in the prescribed form.

(2) When a copy of such a statement is given to or served on any party to the proceedings a copy of the statement and of any exhibit which accompanied it shall be given to the clerk of the magistrates' court as soon as practicable thereafter, and where a copy of any such statement is given or served by or on behalf of the prosecutor, the accused shall be given notice of his right to object to the statement being tendered in evidence.

(3) Where before a magistrates' court enquiring into an offence as examining justices the accused objects to a written statement being tendered in evidence and he has been given a copy of the statement but has not given notice of his intention to object to the statement being tendered in evidence, the court shall, if necessary, adjourn to enable the witness to be called.

(4) Where a written statement to be tendered in evidence under the said section 2 or 9 refers to any document or object as an exhibit, that document or object shall wherever possible be identified by means of a label or other mark of identification signed by the maker of the statement, and before a magistrates' court treats any document or object referred to as an exhibit in such a written statement as an exhibit produced and identified in court by the maker of the statement, the court shall be satisfied that the document or object is sufficiently described in the statement for it to be identified.

(5) If it appears to a magistrates' court that any part of a written statement is inadmissible there shall be written against that part "Treated as inadmissible, J.P., an Examining Justice" if the written statement is tendered in evidence under the said section 2, or "Ruled inadmissible, J.P., Justice of the Peace" if the written statement is tendered in evidence under the said section 9.

(6) Where a written statement is tendered in evidence under the said section 2 or 9 before a magistrates' court the name and address of the maker of the statement shall be read aloud unless the court otherwise directs.

(7) Where under subsection (5) of the said section 2 or subsection (6) of the said section 9 in any proceedings before a magistrates' court any part of a written statement has to be read aloud, or an account has to be given orally of so much of any written statement as is not read aloud, the statement shall be read or the account given by or on behalf of the party which has tendered the statement in evidence.

(8) Written statements tendered in evidence under the said section 2 before a magistrates' court acting as examining justices shall be authenticated by a certificate signed by one of the examining justices.

(9) A written statement tendered in evidence under the said section 2 or 9 before a magistrates' court and not sent to a court of assize or quarter sessions under Rule 10, 16 or 17 of these Rules shall be preserved for a period of three years by the clerk of the magistrates' court.

NOTE

See r. 15 (3) of the Magistrates' Courts (Children and Young Persons) Rules, 1970, p. 577, *ante.*

59. Proof by formal admission.—Where under section 10 of the Criminal Justice Act, 1967, a fact is admitted orally in court by or on behalf of the prosecutor or defendant for the purposes of the summary trial of an offence or proceedings before a magistrates' court acting as examining justices the court shall cause the admission to be written down and signed by or on behalf of the party making the admission.

APPEAL TO THE CROWN COURT

62. Documents to be sent to the Crown Court.—(1) A clerk of a magistrates' court shall as soon as practicable send to the clerk of the peace any notice of appeal to the Crown Court given to the clerk of the court.

(2) The clerk of a magistrates' court shall send to the clerk of the peace, with the notice of appeal, a statement of the decision from which the appeal is brought and of the last known or usual place of abode of the parties to the appeal.

(3) Where any person, having given notice of appeal to the Crown Court has for the purpose of his release from custody entered into a recognisance conditioned for his appearance at the hearing of the appeal, the clerk of the court from whose decision the appeal is brought shall before the day fixed for hearing the appeal send the recognisance to the clerk of the peace.

(4) Where any such recognisance has been entered into otherwise than before the magistrates' court from whose decision the appeal is brought, or the clerk of that court, the person who took the recognisance shall send it forthwith to that clerk.

(5) Where a notice of appeal is given in respect of a hospital order or guardianship order made under section 60 or 61 of the Mental Health Act, 1959, the clerk of the magistrates' court from which the appeal is brought shall send with the notice to the clerk of the peace any written evidence considered by the court under paragraph (a) of subsection (1) of the said section 60.

(6) Where a notice of appeal is given in respect of an appeal against conviction by a magistrates' court the clerk of the court shall send with the notice to the clerk of the peace any admission of facts made for the purposes of the summary trial under section 10 of the Criminal Justice Act, 1967.

63. Notice for purpose of appeal.—(1) A notice of appeal for the purposes of section 84 of the Act shall be in writing and signed by or on behalf of the appellant and shall state the general grounds of appeal.

(2) Any notice of appeal required by the Act to be given to any person may be sent by post in a registered letter or by recorded delivery service addressed to him at his last known or usual place of abode or, if he is the clerk of a court or an officer of the Crown or a local authority, at his office.

64. Abandonment of appeal.—(1) Service on any person of a notice under section 85 of the Act may be effected by delivering it to him or by sending it by post in a registered letter or by recorded delivery service addressed to him at his last known or usual place of abode or, if he is the clerk of a court or an officer of the Crown or a local authority, at his office.

(2) Where notice to abandon an appeal has been given by the appellant, any recognisance conditioned for the appearance of the appellant at the hearing of the appeal shall have effect as if conditioned for the appearance of the appellant before the court from whose decision the appeal was brought at a time and place to be notified to the appellant by the clerk of that court.

*   *   *   *

Miscellaneous

84. Application for, and notice to be given of, order under s. 106 of Road Traffic Act, 1960.—(1) An application under section 106 of the Road Traffic Act, 1960, or section 2 of the Road Traffic (Disqualification) Act, 1970, for an order removing a disqualification or disqualifications for holding or obtaining a licence shall be by complaint.

(2) The justice to whom the complaint is made shall issue a summons directed to the chief officer of police, requiring him to appear before a magistrates' court acting for the petty sessions area for which the justice is acting to show cause why an order should not be made on the complaint.

(3) Where a magistrates' court makes an order under either of the aforesaid sections the court shall cause notice of the making of the order and a copy of the

particulars of the order endorsed on the licence, if any, previously held by the applicant for the order to be sent to the council of the county or county borough to which notice of the applicant's disqualification was sent.

*   *   *   *

88. Application for summons to witness or warrant for his arrest.— (1) An application for the issue of a summons or warrant under section 77 of the Act may be made by the applicant in person or by his counsel or solicitor.

(2) An application for the issue of such a summons may be made by delivering or sending the application in writing to the clerk to the magistrates' court for submission to a justice of the peace.

*   *   *   *

90. Saving for the Summary Jurisdiction (Children and Young Persons) Rules, 1933.—The provisions of these Rules shall have effect subject to the Summary Jurisdiction (Children and Young Persons) Rules, 1933.

*   *   *   *

92. Construction of references to registered post in rules made before 1961 under justices of the Peace Act, 1949.—Any references in rules made before 13th February 1961 and made or having effect as if made under section 15 of the Justices of the Peace Act, 1949, to registered post, a registered letter or the registration of a letter shall be construed as including a reference to the recorded delivery service, a letter sent by that service and the acceptance by an officer of the Post Office of a letter for recorded delivery, respectively.

93. Signature of forms prescribed by rules made under Justices of the Peace Act, 1949.—(1) Subject to paragraph (2) of this Rule, where any form prescribed by rules made or having effect as if made under section 15 of the Justices of the Peace Act, 1949 contains provision for signature by a justice of the peace only, the form shall have effect as if it contained provision in the alternative for signature by the clerk of a magistrates' court.

(2) This Rule shall not apply to any form of warrant, other than a warrant of commitment or of distress, or to any form prescribed in the Magistrates' Courts (Forms) Rules, 1968.

94. Interpretation.—(1) In these Rules "the Act" means the Magistrates' Courts Act, 1952, "contribution order" has the meaning assigned to it by section 87 of the Children and Young Persons Act, 1933, "judgment summons" has the meaning assigned to it by Rule 48 and other expressions have the same meaning as in the Act.

(2) The Interpretation Act, 1889 shall apply to the interpretation of these Rules as it applies to the interpretation of an Act of Parliament.

THE CHILDREN AND YOUNG PERSONS ACT, 1969 (COMMENCEMENT No. 1) ORDER, 1969
[S.I. 1969 No. 1552]

Citation

1. This Order may be cited as the Children and Young Persons Act, 1969 (Commencement No. 1) Order, 1969.

Interpretation

2. In this Order "the Act" means the Children and Young Persons Act, 1969.

Day appointed for coming into force of certain provisions of the Act

3. The provisions of the Act specified in column 1 of the Schedule to this Order (which relate to the matters specified in column 2 thereof) shall come into operation on 16th November 1969.

SCHEDULE

PROVISIONS COMING INTO FORCE ON 16TH NOVEMBER, 1969

Provisions of the Act	Subject matter of provisions
Section 69	Orders and regulations etc.
Section 70	Interpretation and ancillary provisions.
Section 72(3), so far as it relates to paragraphs 63, 64(1), 69, 73, 75 and 76 of Schedule 5	Minor and consequential amendments.
Section 72(4), so far as it relates to the repeal set out in the Appendix to this Schedule	Repeals.
Section 73	Citation, commencement and extent.
Paragraphs 63, 64(1), 69, 73, 75 and 76 of Schedule 5	Amendment of sections 90(1) and 94(1) of the Social Work (Scotland) Act, 1968 and of paragraph 1(1)(a) of Schedule 7 and paragraphs 17(1), 51(1) and 54 of Schedule 8 thereto.
Schedule 6, so far as it relates to the repeal set out in the Appendix to this Schedule	Repeals.

APPENDIX TO SCHEDULE

REPEAL TAKING EFFECT FROM 16TH NOVEMBER, 1969

Chapter	Short title	Extent of repeal
1968 c. 49.	The Social Work (Scotland) Act, 1968	In section 90(1) the words "or to prescribe any matter".

NOTE

This Order was made under s. 73(2) of the Children and Young Persons Act, 1969, and brought into operation on November 16, 1969, the provisions specified.

THE CHILDREN AND YOUNG PERSONS ACT, 1969
(COMMENCEMENT No. 2) ORDER, 1969
[S.I. 1969 No. 1565]

Citation

1. This Order may be cited as the Children and Young Persons Act, 1969 (Commencement No. 2) Order, 1969.

Interpretation and extent

2.—(1) In this Order "the Act" means the Children and Young Persons Act, 1969.

(2) Nothing in this Order shall bring into force, in their application to Scotland, any provisions of paragraph 54 of Schedule 5 to the Act and, accordingly, the references to the said provisions in Schedule 1 to this Order shall not include references thereto in their application to Scotland.

Days appointed for coming into force of certain provisions of the Act

3. The provisions of the Act specified in column 1 of each of the first two Schedules to this Order (which relate to the matters specified in column 2 thereof) shall, subject to Article 2(2) of this Order, come into force on the day specified in the heading to that Schedule.

Transitional provisions

4. The transitional provisions contained in Schedule 3 to this Order shall have effect in connection with the provisions brought into force by this Order which are referred to in that Schedule.

SCHEDULE 1

Provisions Coming into Force on 1st December, 1969

Provisions of the Act	Subject matter of provisions
Section 33(1), so far as it relates to paragraph 6 of Schedule 1.	Legal aid.
Section 35	Regional planning of accommodation for children in care.
Section 36	Regional plans for community homes.
Section 37	Approval and variation of regional plans.
Section 38	Provision of community homes by local authorities.
Section 39	Instruments of management for assisted and controlled community homes.
Section 40	Supplementary provisions as to instruments of management and trust deeds.
Section 41	Management of controlled community homes.
Section 42	Management of assisted community homes.
Section 43	Control of premises used for, and conduct of, community homes.
Section 44	Controlled and assisted community homes exempted from certain provisions as to voluntary homes.

Provisions of the Act	Subject matter of provisions
Section 45	Determination of disputes relating to controlled and assisted community homes.
Section 46, except subsection (2) so far as it relates to paragraphs 3, 4 and 8 of Schedule 3.	Discontinuance of approved schools etc. on establishment of community homes.
Section 47	Discontinuance by voluntary organisation of controlled or assisted community home.
Section 48	Financial provisions applicable on cessation of controlled or assisted community home.
Section 49	Provision of accommodation and maintenance for children in care.
Section 50	Accommodation of persons over school age in convenient community home.
Section 58	Inspection of children's homes etc. by persons authorised by Secretary of State.
Section 59	Powers of entry supplemental to section 58.
Section 60	Extradition offences.
Section 62(2)	Contributions in respect of children and young persons in care.
Section 63	Returns of information and presentation of reports etc. to Parliament.
Section 64	Expenses of Secretary of State in providing homes offering specialised facilities.
Section 65	Grants to voluntary organisations etc.
Section 66	Increase of rate support grants.
Section 67	Administrative expenses.
Section 68	Compulsory acquisition of land.
Section 71	Application to Isles of Scilly.
Section 72(1), so far as it relates to graphs 13 and 14 of Schedule 4.	Transitional provisions.
Section 72(3), so far as it relates to the provisions of Schedule 5 specified in Appendix A to this Schedule.	Minor and consequential amendments.
Section 72(4), so far as it relates to the repeals set out in Appendix B to this Schedule.	Repeals.
In Schedule 1, paragraph 6	Modifications of Part IV of Criminal Justice Act, 1967.
Schedule 2	Children's regional planning committees.
Schedule 3, except paragraphs 3, 4 and 8	Approved schools and other institutions.
In Schedule 4, paragraphs 13 and 14	Transitional provisions and savings.
In Schedule 5, the provisions specified in Appendix A to this Schedule.	Minor and consequential amendments of enactments.
Schedule 6, so far as it relates to the repeals set out in Appendix B to this Schedule.	Repeals.

Appendix A to Schedule 1

Amendments Taking Effect From 1st December, 1969

Provisions of Schedule 5	Enactments amended
Paragraph 4	Section 46 of the Children and Young Persons Act, 1933.
Paragraphs 14, 15, 18, 19, 20(2), 21(1) and 21(3).	Sections 4(3), 20(1), 39(1), 43(1), 51(3) and 54(3) and (5) of the Children Act, 1948.
In paragraph 20(1), the following provision:— "In subsection (1) of section 51 of the said Act of 1948, for the words from 'homes' to 'this Act' there shall be substituted the words 'community homes provided by them or in controlled community homes'."	Section 51(1) of the Children Act, 1948.
Paragraph 37	Section 9 of the Mental Health Act, 1959.
Paragraphs 51 and 52	Sections 45(1) and 49(1) of the Children and Young Persons Act, 1963.
In paragraph 54(2), the following provision:— "for the words from '5(1)' to '1956' there shall be substituted the words '13(2) of the Children Act, 1948'."	Section 11(2) of the Family Allowances Act, 1965.
Paragraph 54(3)	Section 11(3) of the Family Allowances Act, 1965.
Paragraphs 65(2) and 66	Sections 97(1) and 98 of the Social Work (Scotland) Act, 1968.

Appendix B to Schedule 1

Repeals Taking Effect From 1st December, 1969

Chapter	Short title	Extent of repeal
1894 c. 60.	The Merchant Shipping Act, 1894.	In section 183(3), the proviso.
1918 c. 57.	The War Pensions (Administrative Provisions) Act, 1918.	Section 9(4).
1920 c. 23.	The War Pensions Act, 1920.	Section 9.
1933 c. 12.	The Children and Young Persons Act, 1933.	Sections 76(2) and 77(1). Section 94.
1948 c. 43.	The Children Act, 1948	Section 3(3) to (5). In section 4(3), the proviso. Sections 7, 15 and 16. Section 39(1)(e). Section 51(2). Section 54(1) and (2).
1956 c. 50.	The Family Allowances and National Insurance Act, 1956.	Section 5.

Chapter	Short title	Extent of repeal
1958 c. 65.	The Children Act, 1958.	In Schedule 2 the entry relating to section 54 of the Children Act, 1948.
1963 c. 37.	The Children and Young Persons Act, 1963.	Section 1(4).
1968 c. 49.	The Social Work (Scotland) Act, 1968.	In Schedule 8, paragraph 18.

SCHEDULE 2

PROVISIONS COMING INTO FORCE ON 1ST JANUARY, 1970

Provisions of the Act	Subject matter of provisions
Section 51	Modification of general duty of local authorities with respect to foster children.
Section 52	Amendments of definitions of "foster child" and "protected child".
Section 53	Modification of duty of persons maintaining foster children to notify local authority.
Section 54	Inspection of premises in which foster children are kept.
Section 55	Imposition of requirements and prohibitions relating to the keeping of foster children.
Section 56, except subsection (1)(a).	Extension of disqualification for keeping foster children.
Section 57	Modifications of provisions as to offences.
Section 72(3), so far as it relates to the provisions of Schedule 5 specified in Appendix A to this Schedule.	Minor and consequential amendments.
Section 72(4), so far as it relates to the repeals set out in Appendix B to this Schedule.	Repeals.
Section 72(5), except so far as it relates to sections 2(4) and 6(1)(b) of the Children Act, 1958.	Sections 1 to 6 and 14 of the Children Act, 1958, as amended.
In Schedule 5, the provisons specified in Appendix A to this Schedule.	Minor and consequential amendments.
Schedule 6, so far as it relates to the repeals set out in Appendix B to this Schedule.	Repeals.
Schedule 7, except so far as it relates to sections 2(4) and 6(1)(b) of the Children Act, 1958.	Sections 1 to 6 and 14 of the Children Act, 1958, as amended.

APPENDIX A TO SCHEDULE 2

AMENDMENTS TAKING EFFECT FROM 1ST JANUARY, 1970

Provisions of Schedule 5	Enactments amended
Paragraphs 30 and 31	Section 9 and 12(1) of the Children Act, 1958.
Paragraph 35	Section 37(2) of the Adoption Act, 1958.

APPENDIX B TO SCHEDULE 2

REPEALS TAKING EFFECT FROM 1ST JANUARY, 1970

Chapter	Short title	Extent of repeal
1958 c. 65.	The Children Act, 1958.	In section 2, in subsection (1) the words from "for reward" to "one month", in subsection (2) the words from "by" in the first place where it occurs to "or" where that word first subsequently occurs, and subsections (6) and (7). In section 3, in subsection (4), the words from "or is removed" to "maintaining him" and the words from "or removal" onwards, in subsection (5) the words "need not give a notice under subsection (4) of this section but", and subsection (6).
1958 c. 5 (7 & 8 Eliz. 2)	The Adoption Act, 1958.	In section 37, in subsection (1) the words "but is not a foster child within the meaning of Part 1 of the Children Act, 1958", in subsection (2) the words from "by reason" to "subsection nor".

SCHEDULE 3

TRANSITIONAL MODIFICATIONS OF PARAGRAPHS 20 AND 37 OF SCHEDULE 5 TO THE ACT

So long as section 15 of the Children Act, 1948 continues to apply to a local authority by virtue of paragraph 13 of Schedule 4 to the Act then, in relation to that authority, paragraphs 20 and 37 of Schedule 5 to the Act shall have effect as if they provided that section 51 of the said Act of 1948, as amended by the said paragraph 20, and section 9 of the Mental Health Act, 1959, as amended by the said paragraph 37, should have effect as if a home provided by the local authority under the said section 15 were a community home so provided under the Act.

NOTE

This Order was made under s. 73(2) and (3) of the Children and Young Persons Act, 1969, and brought into operation on the dates specified the provisions of the Act referred to in the Order.

THE SOCIAL WORK (SCOTLAND) ACT, 1968 (COMMENCE-MENT NO. 3) ORDER, 1970
[S.I. 1970 No. 196 (C. 6) (S. 13)]

1. This order may be cited as the Social Work (Scotland) Act, 1968 (Commencement No. 3) Order, 1970.

2. Section 92 (effect of Act on rate support grant) of the Social Work (Scotland) Act, 1968 shall come into operation on 9th February 1970.

THE JUSTICES' CLERKS RULES, 1970
[S.I. 1970 No. 231 (L. 12)]

1. These Rules may be cited as the Justices' Clerks Rules, 1970, and shall come into operation on 1st April 1970.

2. The Interpretation Act, 1889, shall apply for the interpretation of these Rules as it applies for the interpretation of an Act of Parliament.

3. The things specified in the Schedule to these Rules, being things authorised to be done by, to or before a single justice of the peace for a petty sessions area, may be done by, to or before the justices' clerk for that area.

SCHEDULE

1. The laying of an information or the making of a complaint, other than an information or complaint substantiated on oath.

2. The issue of any summons, including a witness summons.

3. The adjournment of the hearing of a complaint if the parties to the complaint consent to the complaint being adjourned.

4.—(1) The further adjournment of criminal proceedings with the consent of the prosecutor and the accused if, but only if,

    (a) the accused, not having been remanded on the previous adjournment, is not remanded on the further adjournment; or

    (b) the accused, having been remanded on bail on the previous adjournment, is remanded on bail on the like terms and conditions.

(2) The remand of the accused on bail at the time of further adjourning the proceedings in pursuance of sub-paragraph (1) (b) above.

5. The determination that a complaint for the revocation, discharge, revival, alteration, variation or enforcement of an affiliation order or an order enforceable as an affiliation order be dealt with by a magistrates' court acting for another petty sessions area in accordance with the provisions of Rule 34 or 49 of the Magistrates' Courts Rules, 1968.

6. The allowing of further time for payment of a sum enforceable by a magistrates' court.

7. The making of a transfer of fine order, that is to say, an order making payment by a person of a sum adjudged to be paid by a conviction enforceable in the petty sessions area in which he is residing.

8. The making of an order before an inquiry into the means of a person under section 44 of the Criminal Justice Act, 1967, that that person shall furnish to the court a statement of his means in accordance with section 44 (8).

9. The making of an order, where proceedings relating to an attachment of earnings order are brought in a magistrates' court, before the hearing of those proceedings

that the defendant and any person appearing to the justices' clerk to be an employer of the defendant shall give to the magistrates' court within such period as may be specified by the order such particulars as may be so specified.

10. The giving of consent for another magistrates' court to deal with an offender for an earlier offence in respect of which, after the offender had attained the age of seventeen years, a court had made a probation order or an order for conditional discharge, where the justices' clerk is the clerk of the court which made the order or, in the case of a probation order, of that court or of the supervising court.

11. The amending, in accordance with paragraph 2 (1) of Schedule 1 to the Criminal Justice Act, 1948, of a probation order made after the probationer had attained the age of seventeen years by substituting for the petty sessions area named in the order the area in which the probationer proposes to reside or is residing.

THE CHILDREN AND YOUNG PERSONS (PLANNING AREAS) ORDER, 1970
[S.I. 1970 No. 335]

Citation and operation
1. This Order may be cited as the Children and Young Persons (Planning Areas) Order, 1970 and shall come into operation on 1st April 1970.

Interpretation
2.—(1) In this Order the expression "the Act" means the Children and Young Persons Act, 1969.

(2) The Interpretation Act, 1889, shall apply to the interpretation of this Order as it applies to the interpretation of an Act of Parliament.

Planning areas
3. For the purposes of Part II of the Act there shall be the twelve planning areas designated in column 1 of the Schedule to this Order comprising, respectively, the local authority areas specified opposite thereto in column 2 of that Schedule.

Period for the establishment of children's regional planning committees
4. The period first mentioned in section 35 (3) of the Act (which provides that it shall be the duty of the local authorities whose areas are included in a planning area to establish a children's regional planning committee for that area within such period as may be provided by the order specifying the planning area or such longer period as the Secretary of State may allow) shall be the period ending on 30th June 1970.

Article 3.   SCHEDULE
PLANNING AREAS

Planning Area	Areas comprised in planning area
Area No. 1	The counties of Cumberland, Durham, Northumberland and Westmorland and the county boroughs of Carlisle, Darlington, Gateshead, Hartlepool, Newcastle upon Tyne, South Shields, Sunderland, Teesside and Tynemouth.
Area No. 2	The counties of the East Riding, the North Riding and the West Riding of Yorkshire and the county boroughs of Barnsley, Bradford, Dewsbury, Doncaster, Halifax, Huddersfield, Kingston upon Hull, Leeds, Rotherham, Sheffield, Wakefield and York.

Planning Area	Areas comprised in planning area
Area No. 3	The counties of Chester and Lancaster and the county boroughs of Barrow-in-Furness, Birkenhead, Blackburn, Blackpool, Bolton, Bootle, Burnley, Bury, Chester, Liverpool, Manchester, Oldham, Preston, Rochdale, St. Helens, Salford, Southport, Stockport, Wallasey, Warrington and Wigan.
Area No. 4	The counties of Herefordshire, Salop, Staffordshire, Warwickshire and Worcestershire and the county boroughs of Birmingham, Burton upon Trent, Coventry, Dudley, Solihull, Stoke-on-Trent, Walsall, Warley, West Bromwich, Wolverhampton and Worcester.
Area No. 5	The counties of Derbyshire, Leicester, Lincoln—Parts of Holland, Lincoln—Parts of Kesteven, Lincoln—Parts of Lindsey, Northamptonshire, Nottinghamshire and Rutland and the county boroughs of Derby, Grimsby, Leicester, Lincoln, Northampton and Nottingham.
Area No. 6	The counties of Cambridgeshire and Isle of Ely, Essex, Huntingdon and Peterborough, Norfolk, East Suffolk and West Suffolk and the county boroughs of Great Yarmouth, Ipswich, Norwich and Southend-on-Sea.
Area No. 7	The counties of Bedford, Berkshire, Buckingham, Hertfordshire and Oxford and the county boroughs of Luton, Oxford and Reading.
Area No. 8	The City of London and all the London boroughs.
Area No. 9	The counties of Kent, Surrey, East Sussex and West Sussex and the county boroughs of Brighton, Canterbury, Eastbourne and Hastings.
Area No. 10	The counties of Dorset, Hampshire, Isle of Wight and Wiltshire and the county boroughs of Bournemouth, Portsmouth and Southampton.
Area No. 11	The counties of Cornwall, Devon, Gloucestershire and Somerset and the county boroughs of Bath, Bristol, Exeter, Gloucester, Plymouth and Torbay.
Area No. 12	All the counties and county boroughs in Wales, the county of Monmouthshire and the county borough of Newport.

THE SOCIAL WORK (SCOTLAND) ACT, 1968 (COMMENCEMENT NO. 4) ORDER, 1970
[S.I. 1970 No. 846 (C. 20) (S. 65)]

1. This order may be cited as the Social Work (Scotland) Act, 1968 (Commencement No. 4) Order, 1970.

2. Subsection (3) (accommodation for children's hearings) of section 34 and subsections (1) to (7) of section 36 (the reporter and deputies) of the Social Work (Scotland) Act, 1968 shall come into operation on 1st July 1970.

THE CHILDREN AND YOUNG PERSONS ACT, 1969 (ABOLITION OF APPROVED SCHOOL ORDERS) ORDER, 1970
[S.I. 1970 No. 1499]

1. This Order may be cited as the Children and Young Persons Act, 1969 (Abolition of Approved School Orders) Order, 1970 and shall come into operation on 31st December 1970.

2. The day specified for the purposes of section 7 (5) of the Children and Young Persons Act, 1969 (which provides that an order sending a person to an approved school shall not be made after such day as the Secretary of State may by order specify) shall be 31st December 1970.

THE CHILDREN AND YOUNG PERSONS ACT, 1969 (AUTHORISA-TION FOR THE PURPOSES OF SECTION 1) ORDER, 1970
[S.I. 1970 No. 1500]

1. This Order may be cited as the Children and Young Persons Act, 1969 (Authorisation for the purposes of Section 1) Order, 1970, and shall come into operation on 1st January 1971.

2. The National Society for the Prevention of Cruelty to Children are hereby authorised to bring proceedings in pursuance of section 1 of the Children and Young Persons Act, 1969 (care proceedings in juvenile courts).

THE MAGISTRATES' COURTS (CHILDREN AND YOUNG PERSONS) RULES, 1970
[S.I. 1970 No. 1792 (L. 32)]

PART I
GENERAL

Citation and operation
1. These Rules may be cited as the Magistrates' Courts (Children and Young Persons) Rules 1970 and shall come into operation on 1st January 1971.

Interpretation
2.—(1) In these Rules the following expressions have the meanings hereby repectively assigned to them, that is to say:—

"the Act of 1933" means the Children and Young Persons Act, 1933;
"the Act of 1963" means the Children and Young Persons Act, 1963;
"the Act of 1969" means the Children and Young Persons Act, 1969;
"child" means a person under the age of fourteen;
"court" means a juvenile court except that in Part VI it means a magistrates' court, whether a juvenile court or not;
"register" means the separate register kept for the juvenile court pursuant to Rule 23 of these Rules;
"young person" means a person who has attained the age of fourteen and is under the age of seventeen.

(2) In these Rules, unless the context otherwise requires, any reference to a Rule, Part or Schedule shall be construed as a reference to a Rule contained in these Rules, a Part thereof or a Schedule thereto, and any reference in a Rule to a paragraph shall be construed as a reference to a paragraph of that Rule.

(3) In these Rules, unless the context otherwise requires, any reference to any enactment shall be construed as a reference to that enactment as amended, extended or applied by any subsequent enactment.

(4) The Interpretation Act, 1889, shall apply to the interpretation of these Rules as it applies to the interpretation of an Act of Parliament.

Revocations, savings etc.

3.—(1) Subject to paragraph (3), the Rules specified in Schedule 1 are hereby revoked.

(2) Subject to paragraph (3), the provisions of the Magistrates' Courts Rules, 1968, as amended, shall have effect subject to these Rules.

(3) Nothing in these Rules shall apply in connection with any proceedings begun before the coming into operation thereof.

PART II
JUVENILE OFFENDERS

Application of Part II

4. This Part shall apply in the case of a child or young person brought before a court charged with an offence except that only Rules 5 and 8 (2) shall apply where the court is inquiring into the offence as examining justices.

Assistance in conducting defence

5.—(1) The court shall, except in any case where the child or young person is legally represented, allow his parent or guardian to assist him in conducting his defence, including the cross-examination of witnesses for the prosecution.

(2) Where the parent or guardian cannot be found or cannot in the opinion of the court reasonably be required to attend, the court may allow any relative or other responsible person to take the place of the parent or guardian for the purposes of this Part.

Duty of court to explain charge in simple language

6. The court shall explain to the child or young person the substance of the charge in simple language suitable to his age and understanding.

NOTE

"Plea of guilty."—Where an accused who is charged before a magistrates' court is not represented or is of tender age, or where for any other reason there must necessarily be doubts as to his ability finally to decide whether he is guilty or not, the court ought to defer final acceptance of a plea of guilty from the accused, until they have had a chance to learn more of the matter and to see whether there is some undisclosed factor which may render the unequivocal plea of guilty a misleading one; and if, having waited until the facts are outlined and something has been heard of what the accused has to say, the magistrates' court find that there are elements which indicate that the accused really means a plea of "not guilty" that plea must be entered.

In *R.* v. *Blandford Justices, Ex parte G. (an infant)*, [1967] 1 Q. B. 82; [1966] 1 All E. R. 1021: (i) the magistrates should have directed a plea of "not guilty" to be entered, and certiorari would be granted; (ii) r. 6 did not impose on a juvenile court the duty in all cases where a young person was charged with stealing to explain to the accused in detail the legal elements of the offence of larceny.

See also *S. (an infant)* v. *Manchester City Recorder*, [1971] A. C. 481; [1969] 3 All E. R. 1230; 134 J. P. 3. In this case the Divisional Court granted leave to appeal certifying that points of law of general public importance were involved. In the House of Lords it was held that in summary proceedings, as in cases tried on indictment, the accused may apply at any time before sentence to change his plea and it is for the court then to decide whether justice requires that that should be permitted.

Duty of court to ask child or young person whether he admits charge

7. The court shall then ask the child or young person whether he admits the charge.

Evidence in support of charge and cross-examination

8.—(1) If the child or young person does not admit the charge the court shall hear the evidence of the witnesses in support of the charge. At the close of the evidence-in-chief of each witness the witness may be cross-examined by or on behalf of the child or young person.

(2) If in any case where the child or young person is not legally represented or assisted in his defence as provided by Rule 5, the child or young person, instead of asking questions by way of cross-examination, makes assertions, the court shall then put to the witness such questions as it thinks necessary on behalf of the child or young person and may for this purpose question the child or young person in order to bring out or clear up any point arising out of any such assertions.

Evidence for defence

9. If it appears to the court that a *prima facie* case is made out, the child or young person shall be told that he may give evidence or make a statement, and the evidence of any witnesses for the defence shall be heard.

Procedure after finding of guilt

10.—(1) Where the child or young person is found guilty of an offence, whether after a plea of guilty or otherwise—

(a) he and his parent or guardian, if present, shall be given an opportunity of making a statement;

(b) the court shall take into consideration such information as to the general conduct, home surroundings, school record and medical history of the child or young person as may be necessary to enable it to deal with the case in his best interests and, in particular, shall take into consideration such information as aforesaid which is provided in pursuance of section 9 of the Act of 1969;

(c) if such information as aforesaid is not fully available, the court shall consider the desirability of remanding the child or young person for such inquiry as may be necessary;

(d) any written report of a probation officer, local authority or registered medical practitioner may be received and considered by the court without being read aloud, and

(e) if the court considers it necessary in the interests of the child or young person, it may require him or his parent or guardian, if present, to withdraw from the court.

(2) Where, in pursuance of paragraph (1) (d), a report has been considered without being read aloud or where the child or young person, his parent or guardian has been required to withdraw from the court in pursuance of paragraph (1) (e), then—

(a) the child or young person shall be told the substance of any part of the information given to the court bearing on his character or conduct which the court considers to be material to the manner in which the case should be dealt with unless it appears to it impracticable so to do having regard to his age and understanding, and

(b) the parent or guardian of the child or young person, if present, shall be told the substance of any part of such information which the court considers to be material as aforesaid and which has references to his character or conduct or to the character, conduct, home surroundings or health of the child or young person;

and, if such a person, having been told the substance of any part of such information desires to produce further evidence with reference thereto, the court, if it thinks the further evidence would be material, shall adjourn the proceedings for the production thereof and shall, if necessary in the case of a report, require the attendance at the adjourned hearing of the person who made the report.

NOTE

See the Report of the Committee on Children and Young Persons (Ingleby Report) Cmnd. 1191, which concludes that skilful summarizing of the contents of the report is, on balance to be preferred to handing a copy to the defendant or parents. The emphasis must be on "skilful", as the court has a duty to disclose any part bearing on character or conduct which the court considers material.

Duty of court to explain manner in which it proposes to deal with case and effect of order

11.—(1) Before finally disposing of the case or before remitting the case to another court in pursuance of section 56 of the Act of 1933, the court shall inform the child or young person and his parent or guardian, if present, or any person assisting him in his defence, of the manner in which it proposes to deal with the case and allow any of those persons so informed to make representations:

Provided that the child or young person shall not be informed as aforesaid if the court considers it undesirable so to do.

(2) On making any order, the court shall explain to the child or young person the general nature and effect of the order unless, in the case of an order requiring his parent or guardian to enter into a recognisance, it appears to it undesirable so to do.

NOTE

These provisions take account of the recommendations of the Inglebey Committee. See Home Office circular No. 17/1964, p. 677, *post.*

Notice to be given where remand is extended in absence of child or young person

12. Where a child or young person has been remanded, and the period of remand is extended in his absence in accordance with section 48 of the Act of 1933, notice shall be given to him and his sureties (if any) of the date at which he will be required to appear before the court.

NOTE

Forms.—See forms Nos. 18, 19, p. 591, *post.*

PART III

CARE PROCEEDINGS AND PROCEEDINGS RELATING TO CARE, SUPERVISION OR FIT PERSON ORDERS

Application and interpretation of Part III

13.—(1) This Part shall apply in connection with proceedings in a court in the case of any person in relation to whom proceedings are brought or proposed to be brought under—

(a) any of the following provisions of the Act of 1969, namely:—

    (i) section 1 (care proceedings),
    (ii) section 15 (variation and discharge of supervision orders),
    (iii) section 21 (variation and discharge of care orders),
    (iv) section 31 (removal of person in care to Borstal), and
    (v) paragraph 22 of Schedule 4 (supervised person resident in Scotland);

(b) section 72 of the Social Work (Scotland) Act, 1968 (persons subject to Scottish supervision requirement resident in England or Wales);

(c) paragraph 3 or 5 of Schedule 1 to the Act of 1963 (variation and discharge of supervision order under the Act of 1933);

(d) section 7A of the Criminal Justice (Scotland) Act, 1949 (person subject to Scottish probation order resident in England or Wales), or
(e) either of the following provisions of the Act of 1933, namely—

(i) section 66 (discharge of supervision order under the Act of 1933 and substitution of care order), and
(ii) section 84 (discharge of fit person order and substitution of care order),

except that Rules 14, 15 (2), 19 and 20 shall not apply in connection with proceedings under the enactments mentioned in sub-paragraphs (b) and (d) above.

(2) In this Part of the Rules the following expressions have the meanings hereby respectively assigned to them, that is to say:—

"the applicant" means the person by whom proceedings are brought or proposed to be brought;
"the appropriate local authority" means—

(a) in relation to proceedings under section 1 of the Act of 1969, the local authority to whom notice of the proceedings falls to be given under section 2 (3) of that Act,
(b) in relation to proceedings under section 15 of the Act of 1969 or under paragraph 22 of Schedule 4 thereto, the local authority whose area is named in the supervision order in pursuance of section 18 (2) (a) of that Act,
(c) in relation to proceedings under section 21 of the Act of 1969, the local authority to whose care the relevant infant is committed by the care order, and
(d) in relation to proceedings under paragraph 3 or 5 of Schedule 1 to the Act of 1963 or under section 66 or 84 of the Act of 1933, the local authority in whose area the relevant infant appears to reside;

"guardian" has the same meaning as in section 70 (2) of the Act of 1969;
"the offence condition" means the condition set out in section 1 (2) (f) of the Act of 1969;
"the relevant infant" means a person in relation to whom proceedings are brought or proposed to be brought as mentioned in paragraph (1);
"reside" has the meaning assigned to it by section 70 (1) of the Act of 1969;
"the respondent" means the relevant infant except that—

(a) in relation to proceedings under section 84 of the Act of 1933 in which the appropriate local authority is not the applicant, it means that authority,
(b) in relation to other proceedings in which the relevant infant is the applicant it means—

(i) in the case of proceedings under section 15 of the Act of 1969 or paragraph 22 of Schedule 4 thereto or under paragraph 3 or 5 of Schedule 1 to the Act of 1963, the supervisor of the relevant infant,
(ii) in the case of proceedings under section 21 of the Act of 1969, the local authority to whose care the relevant infant is committed.

NOTES

"Section 72 of the Social Work (Scotland) Act, 1968."—The Act of 1969 does not make provision for an English juvenile court to issue a summons to secure the attendance of a juvenile before the court which is considering under sub-section 1A making a supervision order. The order may be made in his absence, but no requirement authorised by s. 12 Children and Young Persons Act, 1969, shall be included unless the juvenile is present. As notice of the proceedings is required (see r. 14, *infra*) the juvenile will be able to attend if he disputes the need for an order. The same remarks apply to a reference under 7A (4) Criminal Justice (Scotland) Act, 1949.

"**The respondent.**"—It would appear that the only respondent in care proceedings is the juvenile himself. Although the rules allow for the conduct of the case by a parent or legal representation of the juvenile or parent (r. 17) there is no provision for the appointment of a guardian *ad litem*. If there is a conflict of interest the relevant infant may request the court not to allow the parent to conduct the case on his behalf (r. 17), but this presupposes that the infant is capable of expressing an independent opinion. In cases of neglect, where the infant is of tender years, the infant may be effectively unrepresented.

Notice by person proposing to bring care etc. proceedings

14.—(1) An applicant proposing to bring proceedings shall send a notice to the clerk of the court specifying the grounds for the proceedings and the persons to whom a copy of the notice is sent in pursuance of paragraph (2).

(2) Without prejudice to sections 2 (3) and 34 (2) of the Act of 1969, the applicant shall—

 (a) send to each of the persons mentioned in paragraph (3) a copy of the said notice, and

 (b) notify each of the those persons of the date, time and place appointed for the hearing unless a summons is issued for the purpose of securing his attendance thereat.

(3) The persons referred to in paragraph (2) are the following persons other than the person who is the applicant:—

 (a) the relevant infant, unless it appears to the applicant inappropriate to notify him in pursuance of paragraph (2), having regard to his age and understanding;

 (b) the parent or guardian of the relevant infant if the whereabouts of such parent or guardian is known to the applicant;

 (c) the appropriate local authority;

 (d) where the proceedings are care proceedings brought under section 1 of the Act of 1969 and notice thereof falls to be given to a probation officer in pursuance of section 34 (2) of the Act of 1969, that probation officer, and

 (e) where the proceedings are for the variation or discharge of a supervision order which names a person other than the appropriate authority as the supervisor, that supervisor.

NOTE

"**Unless a summons is issued.**"—See ss. 2 (4) and 16 (2) Children and Young Persons Act, 1969. It is submitted that in the ordinary case a summons is preferable to a notice of the grounds and the time etc. appointed for the hearing. As legal aid is available in many of the proceedings to which this part of the rule applies a summons will allow sufficient time for legal representation to be obtained.

Adjournment of proceedings and procedure at hearing

15.—(1) The court may, at any time, whether before or after the beginning of the hearing, adjourn the hearing, and, when so doing, may either fix the date, time and place at which the hearing is to be resumed or, unless it makes an interim order in respect of the relevant infant in pursuance of section 2 (10) or 16 (4) of the Act of 1969, leave the date, time and place to be determined later by the court; but the hearing shall not be resumed at that date, time and place unless the court is satisfied that the applicant and the respondent have had adequate notice thereof.

(2) Subject to the provisions of the Act of 1969 or, as the case may be, the Act of 1933, sections 48, 49 and 100 of the Magistrates' Courts Act, 1952 (non-appearance of parties and defects in process) and, subject to Rule 16 (2) (c) of these Rules, Rules 14 and 15 (1) of the Magistrates' Courts Rules, 1968 (order of evidence and speeches and form of order) shall apply to the proceedings as

if they were by way of complaint and as if any references therein to the complainant, to the defendant and to the defence were, respectively, references to the applicant, to the respondent and to his case.

(3) Where the proceedings are brought under section 1 of the Act of 1969 and it is alleged that the offence condition is satisfied then, in relation to any written statement tendered in evidence under section 9 of the Criminal Justice Act, 1967, to substantiate or refute that allegation, Rule 58 of the Magistrates' Courts Rules, 1968, shall apply as if any references therein to the prosecutor and to the accused were, respectively, references to the applicant and to the relevant infant.

Duty of court to explain nature of proceedings; evidence and order of speeches

16.—(1) Except where the relevant infant is the applicant or where, by virtue of any enactment, the court may proceed in his absence, before proceeding with the hearing the court shall inform him of the general nature both of the proceedings and of the grounds on which they are brought, in terms suitable to his age and understanding, or if by reason of his age and understanding or his absence it is impracticable so to do, shall so inform any parent or guardian who is present at the hearing.

(2) Where the proceedings are brought under section 1 of the 1969 Act and it is alleged that the offence condition is satisfied, then, unless the case falls to be remitted to another court in pursuance of section 2 (11) of the Act of 1969 and it does not appear to the court appropriate to determine under section 3 (5) of that Act whether the offence condition is satisfied before remitting the case—

(a) the court shall explain to the relevant infant the substance of the alleged offence in simple language suitable to his age and understanding and ask him whether or not he admits to being guilty of that offence and, before considering any other matter relevant to the proceedings, shall consider and determine whether or not the offence condition is satisfied;

(b) in relation to the proceedings by way of such consideration Rules 8 and 9 shall apply subject to any necessary modifications and, in particular, as if any reference therein to the charge were a reference to the allegation;

(c) in relation to proceedings by way of such consideration Rules 15 (2), 18 (2) and 19 of these Rules shall not apply but Rule 13 of the Magistrates' Courts Rules, 1968 (order of evidence and speeches) shall apply to the proceedings as if they were criminal proceedings to which that Rule applies and as if any references therein to the accused, to the defence, to the prosecutor and to the prosecution were, respectively, references to the relevant infant, to his case, to the applicant and to his case, and

(d) on determining whether or not the offence condition is satisfied, the court shall inform the relevant infant of their finding.

Conduct of case on behalf of relevant infant

17.—(1) Except where—

(a) the relevant infant or his parent or guardian is legally represented, or

(b) the proceedings are brought under section 1 of the Act of 1969 in pursuance of a request made by his parent or guardian for the purposes of section 3 (1) of the Act of 1963 or in pursuance of an order thereunder,

the court shall, unless the relevant infant otherwise requests, allow his parent or guardian to conduct the case on his behalf, subject however, to the provisions of Rule 18 (2).

(2) If the court thinks it appropriate to do so it may, unless the relevant infant otherwise requests, allow a relative of his or some other responsible person to conduct the case on his behalf and any person so allowed is hereafter referred to as "his friend".

NOTE

See note to r. 13.

Power of court to hear evidence in absence of relevant infant and to require parent or guardian to withdraw

18.—(1) Where, in the case of proceedings under section 1 of the Act of 1969, the ground on which the proceedings are brought or, in the case of any proceedings, the evidence likely to be given, is such that in the opinion of the court it is in the interests of the relevant infant that the whole, or any part, of the evidence should not be given in his presence, then, unless the relevant infant is conducting his own case, the court may hear the whole or part of the evidence, as it thinks appropriate, in his absence:

Provided that evidence relating to the character or conduct of the relevant infant (including, in the case of proceedings under section 1 of the Act of 1969, evidence that the offence condition is satisfied) shall be heard in his presence.

(2) Subject to Rule 16 (2) (c), if the court is satisfied that in the special circumstances it is appropriate so to do, it may require a parent or guardian of the relevant infant to withdraw from the court while the relevant infant gives evidence or makes a statement:

Provided that the court shall inform the person so excluded of the substance of any allegations made against him by the relevant infant and shall give the person an opportunity of meeting it by calling evidence or otherwise.

Duty of court to explain procedure to respondent at end of applicant's case

19. Subject to Rule 16 (2) (c), if it appears to the court after hearing the evidence in support of the applicant's case that he has made out a *prima facie* case it shall tell the respondent or the person conducting the case on his behalf under Rule 17 that he may give evidence or make a statement and call witnesses.

Procedure after applicant's case has been proved

20.—(1) Where the court is satisfied that the applicant's case has been proved—

    (a) the court shall take into consideration such information as to the relevant infant's general conduct, home surroundings, school record and medical history as may be necessary to enable it to deal with the case in his best interests and, in particular, shall take into consideration such information as aforesaid which is provided in pursuance of section 9 of the Act of 1969;

    (b) if such information as aforesaid is not fully available, the court shall consider the desirability of adjourning the case for such inquiry as may be necessary;

    (c) any written report of a probation officer, local authority, local education authority or registered medical practitioner may be received and considered by the court without being read aloud, and

    (d) if the court considers it necessary in the interests of the relevant infant, it may require him or his parent or guardian, if present, to withdraw from the court.

(2) Where, in pursuance of paragraph (1) (c), a report has been considered without being read aloud or where the relevant infant, his parent or guardian

has been required to withdraw from the court in pursuance of paragraph (1) (d), then—

    (a) the relevant infant shall be told the substance of any part of the information given to the court bearing on his character or conduct which the court considers to be material to the manner in which the case should be dealt with unless it appears to it impracticable so to do having regard to his age and understanding, and

    (b) the relevant infant's parent or guardian, if present, shall be told the substance of any part of such information which the court considers to be material as aforesaid and which has references to his character or conduct or to the character, conduct, home surroundings or health of the relevant infant;

and, if such a person, having been told the substance of any part of such information desires to produce further evidence with reference thereto, the court, if it thinks the further evidence would be material, shall adjourn the proceedings for the production thereof and shall, if necessary in the case of a report, require the attendance at the adjourned hearing of the person who made the report.

NOTE

"Without being read aloud."—See note to rule 10.

Duty of court to explain manner in which it proposes to deal with case and effect of order

21.—(1) Before finally disposing of the case or before remitting the case to another court in pursuance of section 2 (11) of the Act of 1969, the court shall inform the relevant infant, any person conducting the case on his behalf, and his parent or guardian, if present, of the manner in which it proposes to deal with the case and allow any of those persons so informed to make representations:

Provided that the relevant infant shall not be informed as aforesaid if the court considers it undesirable or, having regard to his age and understanding, impracticable so to inform him.

(2) On making any order, the court shall explain to the relevant infant the general nature and effect of the order unless it appears to it impracticable so to do having regard to his age and understanding or, in the case of an order requiring his parent or guardian to enter into a recognisance, it appears to it undesirable so to do.

NOTE

The former requirement for service of a notice of the effect of a supervision order is replaced by this compendious provision, which follows the recommendations of the Ingleby Committee (see note to r. 11).

Part IV

Proceedings under Section 3 of the Children and Young Persons Act, 1963

Notice of complaint and restrictions on adjudicating justice

22.—(1) A parent or guardian who applies by complaint to a juvenile court under section 3 of the Act of 1963 after the failure or refusal of the local authority to bring a person before the court, shall send a notice specifying the time and place fixed for the hearing of the complaint to any other person who, being a parent of that child or young person, lives apart from the applicant and if any such person appears at the hearing he shall be entitled to be heard.

(2) A justice who sits as a member of a juvenile court which hears such a complaint as aforesaid shall not sit as a member of the court before which that child or young person appears or is brought as a result of an order directed to the local authority in respect of him under the said section 3.

Part V

Register

Register of proceedings in juvenile courts

23. Such part of the register kept in pursuance of rules made under the Magistrates' Courts Act, 1952, as relates to proceedings in a juvenile court, other than proceedings under the Adoption Act, 1958, shall be kept in a separate book.

Part VI

Miscellaneous

Service of contribution orders etc.

24. A contribution order, an order attaching an affiliation order or an arrears order made on a parent or other person liable to make contributions in respect of, or to maintain, a child or young person, may be served by any constable or officer of a local authority by delivering a copy of the order to the person on whom it is made, or by leaving the same at that person's last known or usual place of abode with some other person for him, or by sending the same by registered post or by recorded delivery service to him at his last known or usual place of abode.

Notice of order made under section 88 of the Children and Young Persons Act, 1933

25. Where an order is made under section 88 (1) of the Act of 1933 in respect of an affiliation order, payments under which have been ordered to be made to a collecting officer, notice of the making of the order shall be given by the clerk of the court to the collecting officer, either personally or by written notice sent or delivered to his address by post or otherwise.

Issue of summons or warrant to enforce attendance of parent or guardian

26. Where a child or young person is charged with an offence, or is for any other reason brought before a court, a summons or warrant may be issued by a court to enforce the attendance of a parent or guardian under section 34 of the Act of 1933, in the same manner as if an information were laid upon which a summons or warrant could be issued against a defendant under the Magistrates' Courts Act, 1952 and a summons to the child or young person may include a summons to the parent or guardian to enforce his attendance for the said purpose.

Form of warrant where young person is committed to remand centre or prison

27. Where a young person is committed to a remand centre under section 22 (5) or section 23 (2) of the Act of 1969 or is committed to a prison under the said section 23 (2), the court shall include in the order of committal a certificate that the young person is of so unruly a character that he cannot safely be committed to the care of a local authority.

Forms

28.—(1) The forms in Schedule 2, or forms to the like effect, may be used with such variation as the circumstances may require, and may be so used in lieu of forms contained in the Schedule to the Magistrates' Courts (Forms) Rules, 1968, as amended.

(2) For the purpose of facilitating the performance by supervisors of their functions under section 14 of the Act of 1969 of advising, assisting and befriending persons subject to supervision orders, the additional requirements set out at the end of Forms 43, 44 and 45 contained in the said Schedule 2 are hereby prescribed for the purposes of section 18 (2) (b) of the Act of 1969.

NOTES

Prescribed provisions.—Section 18 (2) (b) of the Children and Young Persons Act, 1969, provides that a supervision order may contain requirements prescribed by rules under s. 15 of the Justices of the Peace Act, 1949—the requirements set out at the end of these forms are the only additional ones so far prescribed.

These rules were made in accordance with s. 15 Justices of the Peace Act, 1949, as amended by the Magistrates' Courts Act, 1952, and extended by s. 18 (2) (b) of the Children and Young Persons Act, 1969.

Appeals from Juvenile Court.—By rule 2, Court means a juvenile court and these rules would therefore have no application to proceedings on appeal before the Crown Court, nor to proceedings before a magistrates' court that is not a juvenile court (except in relation to Part VI). The effect is that s. 43 of the Criminal Justice Act, 1948, which requires a copy of a probation report to be given to the defendant or his parent will apply.

Interpretation Act, 1889.—See 32 Halsbury's Statutes, 3rd Edn., 434.

Magistrates' Courts Act, 1952; saving for juvenile courts.—See note to s. 45 Children and Young Persons Act, 1933, p. 51, *ante*.

SCHEDULE OF FORMS

[Provision is made by the Summary Jurisdiction (Children and Young Persons) (Welsh Forms) Rules, 1969, S.I. 1969 No. 259, for the use of Welsh forms in connection with proceedings in magistrates' courts in Wales and Monmouthshire involving children and young persons. The Rules include provision authorising the use of bilingual forms in connection with such proceedings and provide that in certain cases a person served with a form in one language may require the form in the other language.

The provisions are operative from June 1, 1969.]

1

Summons: offence
(M.C. Act, 1952, s. 1; C. & Y.P. Act, 1933, s. 34)

In the [county of   . Petty Sessional Division of   ].

To A.B. (hereinafter called the defendant) [and E.F. his/her parent/guardian] of   .

Information has this day been laid before [me, the undersigned] [*or state name*] [Justice of the Peace] [Clerk to the Justices] by C.D. that you the defendant, who are believed to be a child/young person, on the   day of   , 19   , at   in the [county] aforesaid [*or* of   ] (*state briefly particulars of offence*):

[And information has further been laid by C.D. that you E.F. are the parent [*or* guardian] of the defendant.]

You are therefore hereby summoned [each of you] to appear on   day the   day of   , 19   , at the hour of   in the noon before the [Juvenile] [Magistrates'] Court sitting at   to answer to the said information.

Dated the   day of   , 19   .

J.P.,
Justice of the Peace for the [county] first above mentioned.
[*or* This summons was issued by the above-named justice of the peace.

J.C.,
Clerk of the Magistrates' Court sitting at   .]
[*or* J.C.,
Clerk to the Justices for the Petty
Sessional Division aforesaid.]

2

Summons for attendance of parent or guardian of child or young person: offence
(C. & Y.P. Act, 1933, s. 34)

In the [county of   . Petty Sessional Division of   ].
To C.D. of   .

A.B., who is believed to be a child/young person, of whom you are stated to be the parent/guardian, is charged for that he/she on the   day of   , 19   , at   in the [county] aforesaid [*or* of   ], (*state briefly particulars of offence*):

You are therefore hereby summoned to appear before the [Juvenile] [Magistrates'] Court sitting at   on   day, the   day of   , 19   , at the hour of   in the   noon and during all the stages of the proceedings.

Dated the   day of   , 19   .

J.P.,
Justice of the Peace for the [county] first above mentioned.
[*or* This summons was issued by the above-named justice of the peace.

J.C.,
Clerk of the Magistrates' Court sitting at   .]
[*or* J.C.,
Clerk to the Justices for the Petty
Sessional Division aforesaid.]

3

Warrant for arrest of child or young person: offence
(M.C. Act, 1952, ss. 1, 93)

In the [county of   . Petty Sessional Division of   ].
To each and all the constables of   .

Information on oath [*or* affirmation] has this day been laid before me, the undersigned Justice of the Peace, by C.D. that A.B. (hereinafter called the defendant),

who is believed to be a child/young person on the   day of   ,
19   , at   in the [county] aforesaid [*or* of   ], (*state
briefly particulars of offence*):

You are therefore hereby commanded forthwith to arrest the defendant and
bring him/her before the [Juvenile] [Magistrates'] Court sitting at
              to answer to the said information.

Dated the   day of   , 19   .

                                        J.P.,
          Justice of the Peace for the [county] first above mentioned.

Endorsement where bail is allowed

It is directed that the defendant on arrest be released on bail on entering into a
recognisance in the sum of   , with suret   in the sum of   [each]
for his/her appearance before the said [Juvenile] [Magistrates'] Court at the hour
of   in the   noon, at the next sitting [*or* on the   day of
                    , 19   ].

[The defendant's recognisance shall be subject to the following condition[s]
(*specify*).]

                                        J.P.,
          Justice of the Peace for the [county] first above mentioned.

4

Summons: care proceedings and proceedings in respect of supervision order
    (*C. & Y.P. Act*, 1969, ss. 2 (4), 16 (2); *C. & Y.P. Act*, 1933, s. 34)

In the [county of   . Petty Sessional Division of   ].
To A.B. (hereinafter called the relevant infant) [and E.F. his/her parent/guardian]
of   .

[The council of the county/county borough of   ]
[C.D. a constable/an authorised person] [C.D. the relevant infant's supervisor]
having given notice that the relevant infant is to be brought before the court under
section [1] [15] of the Children and Young Persons Act, 1969 on grounds specified
in the notice:

And application having been duly made in that behalf to [me the undersigned]
[*or state name*] [Justice of the Peace] [Clerk to the Justices]:

You are hereby summoned [each of you] to appear on   . day, the
          day of   , 19   , at the hour of   in the   noon
before the Juvenile Court sitting at   to attend proceedings brought
in pursuance of the said notice.

Dated the   day of   , 19   .

                                        J.P.,
          Justice of the Peace for the [county] first above mentioned.
[*or* This summons was issued by the above-named justice of the peace.

                                        J.C.,
          Clerk of the Magistrates' Court sitting at   .]
                              [*or* J.C.,
          Clerk to the Justices for the Petty
                                        Sessional Division aforesaid.]

5

Summons for attendance of parent or guardian of child or young person: care proceedings and proceedings in respect of supervision order
(C. & Y.P. Act, 1933, s. 34)

In the [county of   . Petty Sessional Division of   ].

To E.F. being a parent/guardian of A.B. (hereinafter called the relevant infant), who is believed to be a child/young person, of   .

[The council of the   county/county borough of   ]
[C.D. a constable/an authorised person] [C.D. the relevant infant's supervisor] having given notice that the relevant infant is to be brought before the court under section [1] [15] of the Children and Young Persons Act, 1969 on grounds specified in the notice:

And application having been duly made in that behalf to [me the undersigned] [*or state name*] [Justice of the Peace] [Clerk to the Justices]:

You are hereby summoned to appear on   day, the   day of   , 19   , at the hour of   in the   noon before the Juvenile Court sitting at   to attend proceedings brought in pursuance of the said notice.

Dated the   day of   , 19   .

J.P.,
Justice of the Peace for the [county] first above mentioned.
[*or* This summons was issued by the above-named justice of the peace.

J.C.,
Clerk of the Magistrates' Court sitting at   .]
[*or* J.C.,
Clerk to the Justices for the Petty
                    Sessional Division aforesaid.]

6

Warrant for arrest: care proceedings and proceedings in respect of supervision order
(C. & Y.P. Act, 1969, ss. 2 (4), 16 (2); M.C. Act, 1952, s. 47 (3)
and (4))

In the [county of   . Petty Sessional Division of   ].

[Before the [Juvenile] [Magistrates'] Court sitting at   .]

To each and all the constables of   .

[The council of the county/county borough of   ] [C.D. a constable/an authorised person] [C.D. the supervisor of the relevant infant hereinafter mentioned] having given notice that A.B. of   (hereinafter called the relevant infant) is to be brought before the court under section [1] [15] of the Children and Young Persons Act, 1969 on grounds specified in the notice:

[And the relevant infant having been summoned to appear on   day, the day of   , 19   , at the hour of   in the noon before the [Juvenile] [Magistrates'] Court sitting at   to attend proceedings brought in pursuance of the said notice:]

[And I, the undersigned Justice of the Peace, being satisfied by evidence on oath/affirmation that the said summons cannot be served:]

[And the Court being satisfied by evidence on oath/affirmation that the relevant infant having failed to attend in answer to the said summons was served therewith within what appears to them to be a reasonable time before the hearing/adjourned hearing:]

[And the Court being satisfied by evidence on oath/affirmation that the relevant infant having on a previous occasion attended proceedings brought in pursuance of the said notice has failed to attend the adjourned hearing thereof and has had adequate notice of the time and place of the adjourned hearing:]

You are hereby commanded to bring the relevant infant before the [Juvenile] [Magistrates'] Court sitting at   , or a justice of the peace immediately or, in any case, within seventy-two hours.

J.P.,

Justice of the Peace for the [county] first above mentioned.

[*or* By order of the Court,

J.C.,

Clerk of the Court.]

(*Endorsement where bail is allowed*)

It is directed that the relevant infant on arrest be released on bail on entering into a recognisance in the sum of   , with   suret   in the sum of   [each] for his/her appearance before the [Juvenile] [Magistrates'] Court sitting at   , at the hour of   in the   noon, at the next sitting of the said Court [*or* on the   day of   , 19   ]. [The relevant infant's recognisance shall be subject to the following condition[s] (*specify*).]

J.P.,

Justice of the Peace for the [county] aforesaid.

[*or* By order of the Court,

J.C.,

Clerk of the Court.]

7

Notice of care proceedings

(*C. & Y.P. Act*, 1969, *s.* 1; *M.C.* (*C. & Y.P.*) *Rules*, 1970, *r.* 14)

To the Clerk of the Juvenile Court sitting at   .

Take notice that A.B. of   (hereinafter called the relevant infant), who is believed to be a child/young person, is to be brought before the Court under section 1 of the Children and Young Persons Act, 1969 on the grounds hereinafter mentioned.

It is alleged that the following condition is satisfied with respect to the relevant infant, that is to say, (*specify in the terms of section* 1 (2) (a) *to* (f) *identifying, in the case of paragraph* (f), *the offence*).

It is further alleged that the relevant infant is in need of care or control which he is unlikely to receive unless an order is made under the said section 1.

In pursuance of Rule 14 of the Magistrates' Courts (Children and Young Persons) Rules, 1970 a copy of this notice is being sent to each of the following persons, that is to say, to:—

Dated the   day of   , 19 .

C.D.,

[On behalf of the council of the county/county borough of   ].

[A constable].

[An authorised person].

8

Notice to parent under rule 22

(*C. & Y.P. Act*, 1963, *s.* 3; *M.C.* (*C. & Y.P.*) *Rules*, 1970, *r.* 22)

To C.B. of   .

Take notice that I have complained to the Juvenile Court sitting at   for an order against the council of the county/county borough of   , directing them to bring A.B. before the court on the ground that I am unable to control him/her.

The complaint will be heard by the Court on   day, the   day of   , 19 , at the hour of   in the   noon.

You may if you wish speak to the Court about him/her before the Court reaches a decision upon the complaint.

(*Signed*) B.B.

9

Authority to remove to a place of safety
(C. & Y.P. Act, 1969, s. 28 (1))

In the [county of   . Petty Sessional Division of   ].

C.D. of   (hereinafter called the applicant) has this day applied under section 28 (1) of the Children and Young Persons Act, 1969, for authority to detain and take to a place of safety A.B. of   , a child or young person (hereinafter called the relevant infant):

And I, the undersigned Justice of the Peace, am satisfied that the applicant has reasonable cause to believe (*specify belief in terms of section* 28 (1) (a), (b) *or* (c)) and hereby grant the said application:

And the relevant infant may be detained in a place of safety by virtue of this authorisation for a period of   days beginning with the date hereof.

Dated the   day of   , 19   .

J.P.,
Justice of the Peace for the [county] aforesaid.

10

Warrant to search for or remove a child or young person
(C. & Y.P. Act, 1933, s. 40; C. & Y.P. Act, 1963, s. 23 (1))

In the [county of   . Petty Sessional Division of   ].

To each and all the constables of   .

Information on oath [*or* affirmation] has this day been laid before me, the under-signed Justice of the Peace, by C.D. of   , a person acting in the interests of a child or young person, namely (*insert name and address or other iden-tifying particulars*) (hereinafter called the relevant infant) that there is reasonable cause to suspect (*specify in the terms of section* 40 (1) (a) *or* (b) *of the Children and Young Persons Act,* 1933):

[You are hereby authorised to search for the relevant infant and, if it is found that (*specify in the terms of section* 40 (1)), to take him to a place of safety:]

[You are hereby authorised to remove the relevant infant with or without search to a place of safety:]

[And for the purposes hereof you are hereby authorised to enter (*specify house etc.*):]

[It is hereby directed that when executing this warrant you shall not be accom-panied by the said C.D./shall be accompanied by a duly qualified medical prac-titioner:]

And the relevant infant may be detained in a place of safety by virtue of this warrant until he can be brought before a juvenile court, except that the relevant infant shall not be so detained for a period exceeding   days.

Dated the   day of   , 19   .

J.P.,
Justice of the Peace for the [county] aforesaid.

11

Order for removal of foster child or protected child to a place of safety
(C. Act, 1958, s. 7; A. Act, 1958, s. 43; C. & Y.P. Act, 1963, s. 23 (1))

In the [county of   . Petty Sessional Division of   ].

[Before the Juvenile Court sitting at   ].

To each and all the constables of   [and to C.D. of   , a person authorised to visit foster/protected children].

[Complaint having this day been made by the council of the county/county borough of   ] [Application having this day been duly made to me, the undersigned Justice of the Peace, by C.D. of   , a person authorised to visit foster/protected children], on the ground that A.B. of   , a foster/protected child (hereinafter called the child) is (*state briefly grounds of complaint or application*):

[Proof having been given that there is imminent danger to the health or well-being of the child:]

It is hereby ordered that the child [and all other foster children kept at (*specify premises*)] be removed to a place of safety:

And the child [and any other foster child so removed] may be detained in a place of safety by virtue of this order until restored to a parent, relative or guardian or until other arrangements can be made, except that the child [and any other foster child so removed] shall not be so detained for a period exceeding   days.

Dated the   day of   , 19 .

           J.P.,
Justice of the Peace for the [county] first above mentioned.
[*or* By order of the Court,

           J.C.,
       Clerk of the Court.]

12

Warrant of commitment to care of local authority: remand on adjournment
(*M.C. Act*, 1952, ss. 6, 14, 105; *C. & Y.P. Act*, 1969, ss. 20, 23)

In the [county of   . Petty Sessional Division of   ].
Before the [Juvenile] [Magistrates'] Court sitting at   .

To each and all the constables of   and to the council of the county/county borough of   .

A.B. of   (hereinafter called the defendant), who is believed to have been born on   , appeared this day before the Court charged with (*state briefly particulars of offence*):

And the Court decided to adjourn the hearing and remand the defendant:

It is hereby ordered that the defendant be committed to the care of the said council, in whose area it appears that [the defendant resides] [the offence was committed], and that the said council shall, unless he/she is bailed in the meantime, keep the defendant in their care, until the   day of   ,
19 , and on that day the said council shall convey the defendant at the hour of   in the   noon before the [Juvenile] [Magistrates'] Court sitting at   to be further dealt with according to law unless otherwise ordered in the meantime:

And you the said constables are hereby required, unless the defendant is forthwith received into the care of a person authorised by, and acting on behalf of, the said council, to deliver the defendant, together with this warrant, into the care of a person authorised and acting as aforesaid.

Dated the   day of   , 19 .

           J.P.,
Justice of the Peace for the [county] first above mentioned.
[*or* By order of the Court,

           J.C.,
       Clerk of the Court.]

(*Endorsement where bail is allowed to be as in Form 16.*)

13

Warrant of commitment to remand centre or prison: remand on adjournment
(*M.C. Act*, 1952, ss. 6, 14, 105; *C. & Y.P. Act*, 1969, s. 23)

In the [county of   . Petty Sessional Division of   ].
Before the [Juvenile] [Magistrates'] Court sitting at   .

To each and all the constables of   and to the Governor of the remand centre/Her Majesty's prison at   .

A.B. of   (hereinafter called the defendant), who is believed to have been born on   , appeared this day before the Court charged with (*state briefly particulars of offence*):

And the Court decided to adjourn the hearing and remand the defendant:

It is hereby certified that the defendant is of so unruly a character that he/she cannot safely be committed to the care of a local authority:

[The Court having been notified by the Secretary of State that the said remand centre is available for the reception from the Court of persons of the defendant's class or description:]

It is hereby ordered that the defendant be committed to the custody of the said Governor who shall receive and keep the defendant in his custody (unless bailed in the meantime) until the   day of   , 19   , and on that day the said Governor shall convey the defendant at the hour of   in the   noon before the [Juvenile] [Magistrates'] Court sitting at to be further dealt with according to law unless otherwise ordered in the meantime:

And you the said constables are hereby required to deliver the defendant, together with this warrant, into the custody of the said Governor.

Dated the   day of   , 19   .

J.P.,
Justice of the Peace for the [county] aforesaid.
[*or* By order of the Court,

J.C.,
Clerk of the Court.]

(*Endorsement where bail is allowed to be as in Form 16.*)

14

Warrant of commitment to care of local authority: remand for enquiries
(*M.C. Act*, 1952, *ss.* 14, 26, 105; *C. & Y.P. Act*, 1969, *ss.* 20, 23)

In the [county of   . Petty Sessional Division of   ].

Before the Juvenile Court sitting at   .

To each and all the constables of   and to the council of the county/county borough of   .

A.B. of   (hereinafter called the defendant), who is believed to have been born on   , appeared this day before the Court charged with (*state briefly particulars of offence*):

The Court, having found the defendant guilty of the said offence, decided to adjourn the hearing and remand the defendant for the purpose of [enabling enquiries to be made] [and] [of determining the most suitable method of dealing with the case]:

[*or* The Court, being satisfied that the defendant did the act/made the omission charged but, being of the opinion that an inquiry ought to be made into the defendant's [physical] [and] [mental] condition before the method of dealing with the case was determined, decided to adjourn the hearing and remand the defendant:]

It is hereby ordered that the defendant be committed to the care of the said council, in whose area it appears that [the defendant resides] [the offence was committed] and that the said council shall, unless he/she is bailed in the meantime, keep the defendant in their care until the   day of   , 19   , and on that day the said council convey the defendant at the hour of   in the   noon before the Juvenile Court sitting at   to be further dealt with according to law unless otherwise ordered in the meantime:

[And the said council are hereby requested to arrange for such an inquiry as aforesaid to be made by a duly qualified medical practitioner [*or* by two duly qualified medical practitioners of whom one is approved for the purposes of section 28 of the Mental Health Act, 1959 by a local health authority as having special experience in the diagnosis or treatment of mental disorders], who shall report the result of such inquiry to the Court:]

And you the said constables are hereby required, unless the defendant is forth-with received into the care of a person authorised by, and acting on behalf of, the said council, to deliver the defendant, together with this warrant, into the care of a person authorised and acting as aforesaid.

Dated the   day of   , 19   .

J.P.,

Justice of the Peace for the [county] first above mentioned.
[*or* By order of the Court,

J.C.,
Clerk of the Court.]

(*Endorsement where bail is allowed to be as in Form* 16.)

15

Warrant of commitment to remand centre or prison: remand for enquiries
(*M.C. Act*, 1952, *ss.* 14, 26, 105; *C. & Y.P. Act*, 1969, *s.* 23)

In the [county of   .   Petty Sessional Division of   ].
Before the Juvenile Court sitting at   .

To each and all the constables of   and to the Governor of the remand centre/Her Majesty's prison at   .

A.B. of   (hereinafter called the defendant), who is believed to have been born on   , appeared this day before the Court charged with (*state briefly particulars of offence*):

The Court, having found the defendant guilty of the said offence, decided to adjourn the hearing and remand the defendant for the purpose of [enabling enquiries to be made] [and] [of determining the most suitable method of dealing with the case]:

[*or* The Court, being satisfied that the defendant did the act/made the omission charged but, being of the opinion that an inquiry ought to be made into the defendant's [physical] [and] [mental] condition before the method of dealing with the case was determined, decided to adjourn the hearing and remand the defendant:]

It is hereby certified that the defendant is of so unruly a character that he/she cannot safely be committed to the care of a local authority:

[The Court having been notified by the Secretary of State that the said remand centre is available for the reception from the Court of persons of the defendant's class or description:]

It is hereby ordered that the defendant be committed to the custody of the said Governor who shall receive and keep the defendant in his custody (unless bailed in the meantime) until the   day of   , 19   , and on that day the said Governor shall convey the defendant at the hour of   in the   noon before the Juvenile Court sitting at   to be further dealt with according to law unless otherwise ordered in the meantime:

[And you, the said Governor, are hereby requested to arrange for such an inquiry as aforesaid to be made by a duly qualified medical practitioner [*or* by two duly qualified medical practitioners of whom one is approved for the purposes of section 28 of the Mental Health Act, 1959 by a local health authority as having special experience in the diagnosis or treatment of mental disorders], who shall report the result of such inquiry to the Court:]

And you the said constables are hereby required to deliver the defendant, together with this warrant, into the custody of the said Governor.

Dated the   day of   , 19   .

J.P.,
Justice of the Peace for the [county] aforesaid.
[*or* By order of the Court,

J.C.,
Clerk of the Court.]

(*Endorsement where bail is allowed to be as in Form* 16.]

16

Endorsement of warrant of commitment where bail is allowed

The Court hereby certifies that the defendant may be bailed by recognisance in the sum of   , with   suret   in the sum of [each], to appear [on the day and at the hour above mentioned before the said Juvenile/Magistrates' Court [before the said Court of Assize/Quarter Sessions]:

And that the defendant has [not] entered into the said recognisance.

[The defendant's recognisance shall be subject to the following condition[s] (*specify*).]

J.P.,
Justice of the Peace for the [county] first above mentioned.
[*or* By order of the Court,

J.C.,
Clerk of the Court.]

17

Warrant of commitment to remand centre or prison in substitution for commitment to care of local authority
(*C. & Y.P. Act*, 1969, s. 23 (2), (3))

In the [county of   . Petty Sessional Division of   ].

Before the [Juvenile] [Magistrates'] Court sitting at   .

To each and all the constables of   and to the Governor of the remand centre/Her Majesty's prison at   .

A.B. of   (hereinafter called the defendant), who is believed to have been born on   , was committed to the care of the council of the county/county borough of   by a warrant issued on the   day of   , 19   , by the Juvenile Court sitting at   :

It is hereby certified that the defendant is of so unruly a character that he cannot safely remain committed to the care of a local authority:

[The Court having been notified by the Secretary of State that the said remand centre is available for the reception from the Court of persons of the defendant's class or description:]

On the application of the said council it is hereby ordered (*continue as in Form* 13, *Form* 15 *or Form* 26, *as appropriate*).

18

Order for extended remand
(*C. & Y.P. Act*, 1933, s. 48 (3); *C. & Y.P. Act*, 1969, s. 23)

In the [county of   . Petty Sessional Division of   ].

Before the Juvenile Court sitting at   .

To [the council of the county/county borough of   ] [each and all the constables of   and the Governor of the remand centre/Her Majesty's prison at   ].

A.B. (hereinafter called the defendant) having been committed to the care/ custody of the said council/Governor under a warrant of commitment dated the   day of   , 19   , and the Court having deemed it expedient to extend the period of the defendant's remand:

It is hereby ordered that unless the defendant is bailed in the meantime the defendant remain committed to the care/custody of the said council/Governor until the   day of   , 19   , and on the said day the said council/the said constables shall convey the defendant at the hour of   in the noon before the Juvenile Court sitting at   to be further dealt with according to law, unless otherwise ordered in the meantime.

Dated the   day of   , 19   .

J.P.,
Justice of the Peace for the [county] first above mentioned.
[or By order of the Court,

J.C.,
Clerk of the Court.]

(Endorsement where bail is allowed to be as in Form 16.)

19
Notice of extended remand

To A.B. (hereinafter called the defendant) of   and to C.D. of and to E.F. of   (suret   for the defendant).

Take notice that you, the defendant, were remanded by the Juvenile Court sitting at   to appear before the said Court on the   day of   , 19   , and that the Juvenile Court sitting at   has this day in your absence remanded you, the defendant, to appear before the juvenile Court sitting at   on   day the   day of   , 19   , at the hour of   in the   noon.

Dated the   day of   , 19   .

J.C.,
Clerk of the Juvenile Court sitting at   .

20
Interim care order : care proceedings
(C. & Y.P. Act, 1969, ss. 2 (10), 20, 22)

In the [county of   . Petty Sessional Division of   ].

Before the Juvenile Court sitting at   .

To each and all the constables of   and to the council of the county/ county borough of   .

[A.B. of   (hereinafter called the relevant infant), who is believed to have been born on   , was this day [or was on the   day of   , 19   ,] brought before the Court under section 1 of the Children and Young Persons Act, 1969:]

[or The Court having made a direction under section 2 (9) of the Children and Young Persons Act, 1969, A.B. of   (hereinafter called the relevant infant), who is believed to have been born on   was this day [or on the   day of   , 19   ] deemed to have been brought before the Court under section 1 of the said Act of 1969:]

[And the Court is not in a position to decide what order, if any, ought to be made under the said section 1 :]

[And the Court has directed that the relevant infant be brought before a Juvenile Court acting for the   petty sessional area:]

It is hereby ordered that the relevant infant be committed for a period of days to the care of the said council in whose area it appears that [the relevant infant resides] [the circumstances in consequence of which this order is made arose]:

It is further ordered [, subject to the direction hereinafter given,] that the said council shall bring the relevant infant before [the Court] [a Juvenile Court acting for the   petty sessional area (hereinafter called the specified Court)] on the expiration of this order or at such earlier time as the [specified] Court may require:

[By reason of the relevant infant being under the age of five years/of the illness of/of an accident to the relevant infant, it is hereby directed that the relevant infant shall only be brought before the [specified] Court as aforesaid if the [specified] Court so requires.]

And you the said constables are hereby required, unless the relevant infant is forthwith received into the care of a person authorised by, and acting on behalf of, the said council, to deliver the relevant infant, together with this Order, into the care of a person authorised and acting as aforesaid.

J.P.,
Justice of the Peace for the [county] first above mentioned.

[or By order of the Court,

J.C.,
Clerk of the Court.]

21

Interim care order: proceedings in respect of supervision order
(C. & Y.P. Act, 1969, ss. 16 (4), 20, 22)

In the [county of   .   Petty Sessional Division of   ].

Before the Juvenile Court sitting at   .

To each and all the constables of   and to the council of the county/ county borough of   .

A.B. of   (hereinafter called the relevant infant) who is believed to have been born on   , was this day [or was on the   day of   , 19   ,] on an application under section 15 (1) of the Children and Young Persons Act, 1969, brought before the Court under [a warrant issued under section 16 (2)] [an interim care order made under section 16 (3)] of that Act:

[The Court considers that it is likely to exercise its powers under the said section 15 (1) to make an order in respect of the relevant infant but seeks information which it considers is unlikely to be obtained unless an interim care order is made:]

And the relevant infant [being present] [not being present, the Court is satisfied that the relevant infant is under the age of five/cannot be present by reason of illness/accident]:

It is hereby ordered (*continue as in Form* 20).

22

Interim care order by justice following arrest on warrant
(C. & Y.P. Act, 1969, ss. 2 (5), 16 (3), 20, 22)

In the [county of   .   Petty Sessional Division of   ].

To each and all the constables of   and to the council of the county/ county borough of   .

A.B. of   (hereinafter called the relevant infant), who is believed to have been born on   , is detained in pursuance of a warrant issued in pursuance of section [2 (4)] [16 (2)] of the Children and Young Persons Act, 1969:

In pursuance of the said warrant the relevant infant was this day brought before me, the undersigned Justice of the Peace.

It is hereby ordered (*continue as in Form* 20).

J.P.,
Justice of the Peace for the [county] first above mentioned.

23

Interim care order following detention in place of safety
(C. & Y.P. Act, 1933, s. 40; C. Act, 1958, s. 7; A. Act, 1958, s. 43; C. & Y.P.
Act, 1963, s. 23; C. & Y.P. Act, 1969, ss. 20, 22, 28.)

In the [county of   .   Petty Sessional Division of   ].

[Before the Juvenile Court sitting at   .]

To each and all the constables of   and to the council of the county/county borough of   .

A.B. of   (hereinafter called the relevant infant), who is believed to have been born on   , is detained in pursuance of [section 40 of the

Children and Young Persons Act, 1933] [section 7 of the Children Act, 1958] [section 43 of the Adoption Act, 1958] [section 28 of the Children and Young Persons Act, 1969]:

Application has been duly made to [the Court] [me, the undersigned Justice of the Peace,] for an interim care order in respect of the relevant infant:

And the relevant infant [being present] [not being present, the Court is/I am satisfied that the relevant infant is under the age of five/cannot be present by reason of illness/accident]:

It is hereby ordered (*continue as in Form* 20).

24
Further interim order
(*C. & Y.P. Act*, 1969, *s.* 22)

In the [county of   . Petty Sessional Division of   ].
Before the Juvenile Court sitting at   .
To each and all the constables of   and to the council of the county/county borough of   .
A.B. of   (hereinafter called the relevant infant), who is believed to have been born on   , was committed to the care of a local authority by an interim care order made on the   day of   , 19   , and the said order has not yet expired:

And the relevant infant [being present] [not being present, the Court is satisfied that the relevant infant is under the age of five/cannot be present by reason of illness/accident]:

It is hereby ordered (*continue as in Form* 20).

25
Warrant of commitment to care of local authority: committal for trial
(*C. & Y.P. Act*, 1969, *ss.* 20, 23)

In the [county of   . Petty Sessional Division of   ].
Before the [Juvenile] [Magistrates'] Court sitting at   .
To each and all the constables of   and to the council of the county/county borough of   .
A.B. of   (hereinafter called the defendant), who is believed to have been born on   , having been charged this day before the Court sitting as Examining Justices with (*state briefly particulars of offence*):

And the Court after inquiring into the said offence having committed the defendant for trial at the next sitting of the Crown Court to be held at
      :

It is hereby ordered that the defendant be committed to the care of the said council, in whose area it appears [the accused resides] [the offence was committed], and that the said council shall, unless he/she is bailed in the meantime, keep the defendant in their care until the defendant is delivered in due course of law:

And you the said constables are hereby required, unless the defendant is forth-with received into the care of a person authorised by, and acting on behalf of, the said council, to deliver the defendant, together with this warrant, into the care of a person authorised and acting as aforesaid.

Dated the   day of   , 19   .
                  J.P.,
Justice of the Peace for the [county] first above mentioned.
[*or* By order of the Court,
                          J.C.,
                  Clerk of the Court.]

(*Endorsement where bail is allowed to be as in Form* 16.)

26

Warrant of commitment to remand centre or prison: committal for trial
(M.C. Act, 1952, ss. 7, 105; C. & Y.P. Act, 1969, s. 23)

In the [county of   . Petty Sessional Division of   ].
Before the [Juvenile] [Magistrates'] Court sitting at   .

To each and all the constables of   and to the Governor of the
remand centre/Her Majesty's prison at   .

A.B. of   (hereinafter called the defendant), who is believed to
have been born on   , having been charged this day before the Court
sitting as Examining Justices with (*state briefly particulars of offence*):

And the Court after inquiring into the said offence having committed the defendant for trial at the next sitting of the Crown Court to be held at
          :

It is hereby certified that the defendant is of so unruly a character that he/she
cannot safely be committed to the care of a local authority:

[The Court having been notified by the Secretary of State that the said remand
centre is available for the reception from the Court of persons of the defendant's
class or description:]

It is hereby ordered that the defendant be committed to the custody of the said
Governor who shall receive and keep the defendant in his custody [, unless bailed
in the meantime,] until the defendant is delivered in due course of law.

And you the said constables are hereby required to deliver the defendant, together with this warrant, into the custody of the said Governor.

Dated the   day of   , 19   .

J.P.,
Justice of the Peace for the [county] first above mentioned.
[*or* By order of the Court,

J.C.,
Clerk of the Court.]

(*Endorsement where bail is allowed to be as in Form* 16.)

27

Notice of fine etc.: criminal proceedings
(M.C. Rules, 1968, r. 38)

In the [county of   . Petty Sessional Division of   ].
Before the [Juvenile] [Magistrates'] Court sitting at   .
To A.B., of

ADJUDICATION		
Fine		
Compensation		
Costs		
Total		

C.D. of   , who is believed
to have been born on   , was
this day [*or* on the   day of
          , 19   ,] found guilty of an of-
fence, namely, (*state briefly particulars of the
offence*), and you, being the parent/guardian
of the said C.D. were ordered to pay the
sum of   , as shown in the margin
hereof the sum to be paid forthwith [*or* on
or before the   day of
          , 19   ] [*or* by weekly [*or* monthly] instalments of   , the first instal-
ment to be paid on or before the   day of   , 19   ]. Payment
should be made either by post to me, the Clerk of the Court at (*insert address*) or
made personally at (*insert the address and also days and hours when payment can
be made*). Failure to pay forthwith [*or* on or before the appointed day[s]] will
render you liable to [*imprisonment for (*state period*)] [arrest] or your money and
goods liable to distraint without further notice [, unless you have applied for and

been granted before that day further time for payment. Application for the grant of further time may be made either in person to the Court or by letter addressed to me, the Clerk of the Court at (*insert address*) and stating fully the grounds on which the application is made].

Dated the   day of   , 19   .

                                        J.P.,
                            Clerk of the Court.

NOTE. Any communication sent by post must be properly stamped. Cash should not be sent in unregistered envelopes.

---

* Delete unless magistrates' court on occasion of conviction has, under section 65 (2) of the Magistrates' Courts Act, 1952, fixed a term of imprisonment in default and postponed the issue of the warrant of commitment.

28

Offence condition finding: care proceedings
(*C. & Y.P. Act,* 1969, *s.* 1; *M.C.* (*C. & Y.P. Rules, r.* 16 (2))

In the [county of   . Petty Sessional Division of   ].
Before the Juvenile Court sitting at   .

A.B. of   (hereinafter called the relevant infant), who is believed to have been born on   , was this day [*or* was on the   day of   , 19   ,] brought before the Court under section 1 of the Children and Young Persons Act, 1969:

And it was alleged that the following condition was satisfied with respect to the relevant infant, that is to say, that he/she was guilty of an offence, namely, (*state briefly particulars of offence*):

It is hereby adjudged that the relevant infant is [not] guilty of the said offence.

Dated the   day of   , 19   .

                                        J.P.,
                    Justice of the Peace for the [county] aforesaid.
                    [*or* By order of the Court,

                                        J.C.,
                            Clerk of the Court.]

29

Compensation order: care proceedings
(*C. & Y.P. Act,* 1969, *s.* 3 (6))

In the [county of   . Petty Sessional Division of   ].
Before the Juvenile Court sitting at   .

A.B. of   (hereinafter called the relevant infant), who is believed to have been born on   , was this day [*or* was on the   day of   , 19   ,] brought before the Court under section 1 of the Children and Young Persons Act, 1969:

Upon the Court being satisfied that the following condition was satisfied with respect to the relevant infant, that is to say, that he/she was guilty of an [indictable offence] [offence under section 14 (1) of the Criminal Justice Administration Act, 1914], namely, (*state briefly particulars of offence*) application for compensation was made by G.H. of   (hereinafter called the person aggrieved):

It is hereby ordered that [the relevant infant] [C.D. of   ,
a parent/guardian of the relevant infant,] shall pay, by way of satisfaction or compensation to the person aggrieved, the sum of   , [by weekly/ monthly instalments of   , the first instalment of] the said sum to be paid [forthwith] [not later than the   day of   , 19   ]:

[And it is ordered that the said parent/guardian of the relevant infant, in default of payment, be imprisoned in Her Majesty's prison at for (*state period*) unless payment be sooner made.]

Dated the   day of   , 19   .

J.P.,
Justice of the Peace for the [county] aforesaid.
[*or* By order of the Court,

J.C.
Clerk of the Court.]

30

Attendance centre order : offence
(*C.J. Act,* 1948, *s.* 19; *C.J. Act,* 1961, *s.* 10)

In the [county of   . Petty Sessional Division of   ].
Before the Juvenile Court sitting at   .

A.B. of   (hereinafter called the defendant) who is believed to have been born on   , was this day [*or* was on the   day of   , 19   ,] found guilty of an offence which is punishable on summary conviction in the case of an adult with imprisonment in that he on the day of   , 19   , (*state briefly particulars of offence*):

And the Court having been notified by the Secretary of State that the attendance centre specified herein is available for the reception from the Court of persons of the defendant's class or description:

And the Court being satisfied that the attendance centre is reasonably accessible to the defendant, having regard to his age, the means of access available to him and any other circumstances:

[And the Court being of the opinion that twelve hours attendance would be [excessive, having regard to the defendant's age *or* the following circumstances, namely, (*specify*), the defendant being under the age of fourteen years,] [inadequate, having regard to all the circumstances]:]

It is hereby ordered that the defendant do attend at the attendance centre at (*here insert address of centre*) on the first occasion on the   day of   , 19   , at the hour of   in the   noon, and subsequently at such times as shall be fixed by the officer in charge of the said centre, until he shall have completed a period of attendance of   hours.

Dated the   day of   , 19   .

J.P.,
Justice of the Peace for the [county] aforesaid.
[*or* By order of the Court,

J.C.,
Clerk of the Court.]

31

Order on failure to comply with attendance centre order or on breach of Attendance Centre Rules
(*C.J. Act,* 1948, *s.* 19)

In the [county of   . Petty Sessional Division of   ].
Before the Juvenile Court sitting at   .

On the   day of   , 19   , the Court ordered that A.B. (hereinafter called the defendant) should attend at the attendance centre at (*here insert address of centre*).

The defendant has this day appeared [*or* been brought] before this Court under section 19 (7) of the Criminal Justice Act, 1948, and the Court is satisfied that on the day of   , 19   , he failed without reasonable excuse to attend at the said centre in accordance with the said order [*or* while attending at the said centre he committed a breach of the Attendance Centre Rules, 1958, which could not be adequately dealt with under those Rules, namely, (*here set out particulars of breach*)].

The said attendance centre order is hereby revoked and it is hereby ordered that the defendant for the offence in respect of which that order was made (*set out terns of new order*).

Dated the   day of   , 19   .

                J.P.,
         Justice of the Peace for the [county] aforesaid.
         [*or* By order of the Court,

                           J.C.,
                     Clerk of the Court.]

32
Commitment to detention centre: offence
(C.J. Act, 1961, s. 4)

In the [county of   . Petty Sessional Division of   ].

To each and all of the constables of   and to the Warden of the detention centre at   .

Before the Juvenile Court sitting at   .

A.B. (hereinafter called the defendant) who appears to the Court to have attained the age of fourteen years and to be under the age of seventeen years, having been born, so far as has been ascertained, on the   day of   , 19   , is this day [*or* was on the   day of   , 19   ,] found guilty of an offence for which the Court has or would but for the statutory restrictions upon the imprisonment of young offenders have power to impose imprisonment on him/her in that he/she on the   day of   , 19   , did (*state briefly particulars of offence*):

And the Court having been notified by the Secretary of State that the detention centre specified herein is available for the reception from the Court of persons of his/her class or description:

It is ordered that the defendant be detained in the detention centre at   for a period of three months:

You, the said constables, are hereby commanded to convey the defendant to the said detention centre, and there deliver him/her to the Warden thereof, together with this warrant; and you, the Warden of the said detention centre, to receive the defendant into your custody and keep him/her for a period of three months.

Dated the   day of   , 19   .

                J.P.,
         Justice of the Peace for the [county] aforesaid.
         [*or* By order of the Court,

                           J.C.,
                     Clerk of the Court.]

33
Commitment to borstal institution in substitution for care order
(C. & Y.P. Act, 1969, s. 31)

In the [county of   . Petty Sessional Division of   ].

Before the Juvenile Court sitting at   .

To each and all the constables of   and to the Governor of the borstal institution at   .

A.B. of   (hereinafter called the defendant), who is believed to have been born on   , was committed to the care of the council of the county/county borough of   by a care order, other than an interim order, made on the   day of   , 19   , by the Juvenile Court sitting at   :

The defendant was this day [*or* was on the   day of   , 19 ,] brought before the Court by the said council, with the consent of the Secretary of State, under section 31 (1) of the Children and Young Persons Act, 1969:

The Court is satisfied that the defendant's behaviour is such that it will be detrimental to the persons accommodated in any community home or premises treated as such a home by paragraph 3 (2) (a) of Schedule 3 to the said Act for him to be accommodated there:

It is hereby ordered that the defendant be removed to the borstal institution at
:

You, the said constables, are hereby required to deliver the defendant, together with this order, into the custody of the Governor of the said borstal institution; and you the said Governor are required to receive and keep the defendant in your custody in accordance with section 31 (3) of the said Act of 1969.

Dated the   day of   , 19 .

J.P.,
Justice of the Peace for the [county] first above mentioned.
[*or* By order of the Court,

J.C.,
Clerk of the Court.]

34

Hospital order: care proceedings
(*C. & Y.P. Act*, 1969, s. 1 (3): *M.H. Act*, 1959, s. 63)

In the [county of   . Petty Sessional Division of   ].

Before the Juvenile Court sitting at   .

A.B. of   (hereinafter called the relevant infant), who is believed to have been born on   , was this day [*or* was on the   day of   , 19 ,] brought before the Court under section 1 of the Children and Young Persons Act, 1969:

And the Court is satisfied that the following condition is satisfied with respect to the relevant infant, that is to say, (*specify in the terms of section* 1 (2) (a) *to* (f) *identifying, in the case of paragraph* (f), *the offence*) and also that he is in need of care or control which he is unlikely to receive unless an order under the said section is made in respect of him:

And the Court has heard [*or* considered] the [written] evidence of two medical practitioners (*insert names and addresses*), [each] of whom [the first-mentioned] is approved, for the purposes of section 28 of the Mental Health Act, 1959, by a local health authority as having special experience in the diagnosis or treatment of mental disorders, and each of the said practitioners has described the relevant infant as suffering from mental illness [*or* psychopathic disorder *or* subnormality *or* severe subnormality]:

And the Court is satisfied that the relevant infant is suffering from the following forms of mental disorder within the meaning of the said Act of 1959, namely, mental illness [*or* psychopathic disorder *or* subnormality *or* severe subnormality] and that the disorder is of a nature or degree which warrants the relevant infant's detention in a hospital for mental treatment and is satisfied that arrangements have been made for the relevant infant's admission to the hospital hereinafter specified within twenty-eight days of this date and that the most suitable method of disposing of the case is by means of a hospital order:

It is hereby ordered that the relevant infant be admitted to and detained in (*insert name and address of hospital*):

[And that the relevant infant be conveyed to the said hospital by E.F.:]

[And it is directed that pending admission to the said hospital the relevant infant shall be detained in a place of safety, namely,   ] [and shall be conveyed there by E.F.].

Dated the   day of   , 19   .

J.P.,
Justice of the Peace for the [county] aforesaid.
[or By order of the Court,

J.C.,
Clerk of the Court.]

NOTE

For form of Hospital Order in criminal proceedings see form No. 35, p. 542, *ante*.

35

Care order: criminal proceedings
(C. & Y.P. Act, 1969, *ss.* 7 (7), 20)

In the [county of   . Petty Sessional Division of   ].

Before the Juvenile Court sitting at   .

To each and all the constables of   and to the council of the county/ county borough of   .

A.B. of   (hereinafter called the defendant), who is believed to have been born on   , is this day [or was on the   day of , 19   ,] found guilty of an offence punishable in the case of an adult with imprisonment, namely, (*state briefly particulars of offence*):

It is hereby ordered that the defendant be committed to the care of the said council in whose area it appears that [the defendant resides] [the offence was committed, it not appearing that the defendant resides in the area of any local authority in England or Wales]:

And you the said constables are hereby required, unless the defendant is forthwith received into the care of a person authorised by, and acting on behalf of, the said council, to deliver the defendant, together with this order, into the care of a person authorised and acting as aforesaid.

Dated the   day of   , 19   .

J.P.,
Justice of the Peace for the [county] first above mentioned.
[or By order of the Court,

J.C.,
Clerk of the Court.]

36

Care order: care proceedings
(C. & Y.P. Act, 1969, *ss.* 1 (3), 20)

In the [county of   . Petty Sessional Division of   ].

Before the Juvenile Court sitting at   .

To each and all the constables of   and to the council of the county/ county borough of   .

A.B. of   (hereinafter called the relevant infant), who is believed to have been born on   , was this day [or was on the   day of , 19   ,] brought before the Court under section 1 of the Children and Young Persons Act, 1969:

And the Court is satisfied that the following condition is satisfied with respect to the relevant infant, that is to say, (*specify in the terms of section* 1 (2) (a) *to* (f) *identifying, in the case of paragraph* (f), *the offence*) and also that he is in need of care or control which he is unlikely to receive unless an order under the said section is made in respect of him:

It is hereby ordered that the relevant infant be committed to the care of the said council in whose area it appears that [the relevant infant resides] [circumstances in consequence of which this order is made arose, it not appearing that the relevant infant resides in the area of any local authority in England or Wales]:

And you the said constables are hereby required, unless the relevant infant is forthwith received into the care of a person authorised by, and acting on behalf of, the said council, to deliver the relevant infant, together with this order, into the care of a person authorised and acting as aforesaid.

Dated the   day of   , 19   .

J.P.,

Justice of the Peace for the [county] first above mentioned.
[or By order of the Court,

J.C.,
Clerk of the Court.]

37

Care order made on discharge of supervision order
(C. & Y.P. Act, 1969, ss. 15 (1), 20)

In the [county of   . Petty Sessional Division of   ].

Before the Juvenile Court sitting at   .

To each and all the constables of   and to the council of the county/ county borough of   .

The Juvenile Court sitting at   on the   day of   , 19   , made a supervision order within the meaning of the Children and Young Persons Act, 1969, in respect of A.B. of   (hereinafter called the supervised person) who is believed to have been born on   :

[The said supervision order was varied by an order made by the Juvenile Court sitting at   on the   day of   , 19   :]

The said supervision order [as so varied] names the county/county borough of   and the   petty sessional area as the areas in which it appears the supervised person resides or will reside and places him under the supervision of [the council of the said county/county borough] [a probation officer appointed for, or assigned to, the said petty sessional area] (hereinafter called the supervisor) and, unless previously discharged, ceases to have effect on (*specify the date*):

[The supervised person] [E.F. a parent/guardian of the supervised person on his behalf] [The supervisor] has applied for the discharge of the said supervision order:]

And the Court is satisfied that the supervised person is unlikely to receive the care and control that he needs unless this order is made:

It is hereby ordered that the said supervision order be discharged but that the supervised person be committed to the care of the council first above mentioned in whose area it appears that [the supervised person resides] [circumstances in consequence of which this order is made arose, it not appearing that the supervised person resides in the area of any local authority in England or Wales]:

And you the said constables are hereby required, unless the supervised person is forthwith received into the care of a person authorised by, and acting on behalf of, the council first above mentioned, to deliver the supervised person, together with this order, into the care of a person authorised and acting as aforesaid.

Dated the   day of   , 19   .

J.P.,
Justice of the Peace for the [county] first above mentioned.
[or By order of the Court,

J.C.,
Clerk of the Court.]

38

Order of recognisance to keep proper care, etc.: criminal proceedings
(C. & Y.P. Act, 1969, s. 7 (7))

In the [county of   .   Petty Sessional Division of   ].
Before the [Juvenile] [Magistrates'] Court sitting at   .
    A.B. of   (hereinafter called the defendant), who is believed to have been born on   , is this day [*or* was on the   day of   , 19   ,] found guilty of an offence, namely, (*state briefly particulars of offence*):

It is hereby ordered that E.F. of   , a parent/guardian of the defendant who has consented to the making of this order, do forthwith enter into a recognisance in the sum of   to take proper care of, and exercise proper control over, the defendant [for the period of   ] [until the defendant attains the age of eighteen].

     Dated the   day of   , 19   .

                     J.P.,
       Justice of the Peace for the [county] aforesaid.
       [*or* By order of the Court,

                               J.C.,
                       Clerk of the Court.]

39

Order of recognisance to keep proper care, etc.: care proceedings
(C. & Y.P. Act, 1969, s. 1 (3))

In the [county of   .   Petty Sessional Division of   ].
Before the Juvenile Court sitting at   .
    A.B. of   (hereinafter called the relevant infant), who is believed to have been born on   , was this day [*or* was on the   day of   , 19   ,] brought before the Court under section 1 of the Children and Young Persons Act, 1969:

And the Court is satisfied that the following condition is satisfied with respect to the relevant infant, that is to say, (*specify in the terms of section 1 (2) (a) to (f) identifying, in the case of paragraph* (f), *the offence*) and also that he is in need of care or control which he is unlikely to receive unless an order under the said section is made in respect of him:

It is hereby ordered that E.F. of   , a parent/guardian of the relevant infant who has consented to the making of this order, do forthwith enter into a recognisance in the sum of   to take proper care of, and exercise proper control over, the relevant infant [for a period of   ] [until the relevant infant attains the age of eighteen].

     Dated the   day of   , 19   .

                     J.P.,
       Justice of the Peace for the [county] aforesaid.
       [*or* By order of the Court,

                               J.C.,
                       Clerk of the Court.]

40

Order of recognisance to keep the peace, etc.: care proceedings
(C. & Y.P. Act, 1969, s. 3 (7))

In the [county of   .   Petty Sessional Division of   ].
Before the Juvenile Court sitting at   .
    A.B. of   , a young person who is believed to have been born on   , was this day [*or* was on the   day of   , 19   ,]

brought before the Court under section 1 of the Children and Young Persons Act, 1969:

And the Court is satisfied that the following condition is satisfied with respect to the said young person, that is to say, he is guilty of an offence, namely, (*state briefly particulars of offence*) and also that he is in need of care or control which he is unlikely to receive unless an order under the said section is made in respect of him:

It is ordered that the said young person, who has consented to the making of this order, do forthwith enter into a recognisance in the sum of   to [keep the peace] [and] [be of good behaviour] for the period of   from the date of this order.

Dated the   day of   , 19   .

J.P.,
Justice of the Peace for the [county] aforesaid.
[*or* By order of the Court,

J.C.,
Clerk of the Court.]

41

Order extending or discharging care order
C. & Y.P. Act, 1969, s. 21)

In the [county of   .   Petty Sessional Division of   ].
Before the Juvenile Court sitting at   .

The Juvenile Court sitting at   on the   day of
, 19   , made a care order in respect of A.B. of   (hereinafter called the relevant infant), who is believed to have been born on   :

The said order commits the relevant infant to the care of the council of the county/county borough of   :

[The said order, unless extended or discharged, would, in pursuance of section 20 (3) (b) of the Children and Young Persons Act, 1969, cease to have effect when the relevant infant attains the age of eighteen years:

The relevant infant is accommodated in a community home/a home provided by the Secretary of State and it appears to the Court that by reason of his/her mental condition or behaviour it is in his/her/the public interest for him/her to continue to be so accommodated after attaining the age of eighteen years:]

[The said council] [The relevant infant] [E.F., a parent or guardian of the relevant infant on his/her behalf] has applied for the [extension] [discharge] of the said order:

It is hereby ordered that the said order shall [continue in force until the relevant infant attains the age of nineteen years] [be discharged].

Dated the   day of   , 19   .

J.P.,
Justice of the Peace for the [county] first above mentioned.
[*or* By order of the Court,

J.C.,
Clerk of the Court.]

42

Guardianship order: care proceedings
(C. & Y.P. Act, 1969, s. 1 (3); M.H. Act, 1959, s. 63)

In the [county of   .   Petty Sessional Division of   ].
Before the Juvenile Court sitting at   .

A.B. of   (hereinafter called the relevant infant), who is believed to have been born on   , was this day [*or* was on the   day of
, 19   ,] brought before the Court under section 1 of the Children and Young Persons Act, 1969:

And the Court is satisfied that the following condition is satisfied with respect to the relevant infant, that is to say, (*specify in the terms of section* 1 (2) (a) *to* (f) *identifying, in the case of paragraph* (f), *the offence*) and also that he is in need of care or control which he is unlikely to receive unless an order under the said section is made in respect of him:

And the Court has heard [*or* considered] the [written] evidence of two medical practitioners (*insert names and addresses*), [each] of whom [the first-mentioned] is approved, for the purposes of section 28 of the Mental Health Act, 1959, by a local health authority as having special experience in the diagnosis or treatment of mental disorders, and each of the said practitioners has described the relevant infant as suffering from mental illness [*or* psychopathic disorder *or* subnormality *or* severe subnormality]:

And the Court is satisfied that the relevant infant is suffering from the following forms of mental disorder within the meaning of the said Act of 1959, namely, mental illness [*or* psychopathic disorder *or* subnormality *or* severe subnormality] and that the disorder is of a nature or degree which warrants the relevant infant's reception into guardianship under that Act and is satisfied that the authority [*or* person] hereinafter specified is willing to receive the relevant infant into guardianship and that the most suitable method of disposing of the case is by means of a guardianship order:

It is hereby ordered that the relevant infant be placed under the guardianship of a local health authority, namely, the council of the county/county borough of [*or* of C.D., being a person approved by a local health authority, namely, the council of the county/county borough of   ].

Dated the   day of   , 19   .

J.P.,
Justice of the Peace for the [county] first above mentioned.
[*or* By order of the Court,

J.C.,
Clerk of the Court.]

NOTE

For form of Guardianship Order in criminal proceedings see form 36, p. 600, *ante*.

43
Supervision order: criminal proceedings
(C. & Y.P. Act, 1969, ss. 7 (7), 11, 12, 13, 17, 18)

In the [county of   . Petty Sessional Division of   ].
Before the Juvenile Court sitting at   .

A.B. of   (hereinafter called the defendant), who is believed to have been born on   , is this day [*or* was on the   day of   , 19   ,] found guilty of an offence, namely, (*state briefly particulars of offence*):

It appears to the Court that the defendant resides/will reside in the county/county borough of   and in the   petty sessional area:

It is hereby ordered that the defendant be placed under the supervision of [the council of the said county/county borough] [the council of the county/county borough of   who have agreed to be designated as the supervisor] [a probation officer appointed for, or assigned to the said petty sessional area] (hereinafter called the supervisor) [for the period of   ]:

[It is further ordered that the defendant reside with G.H. of   who has agreed to this requirement:]

[It is further ordered that the defendant shall comply with such directions as may be given by the supervisor in pursuance of section 12 of the Children and Young Persons Act, 1969 requiring him (*specify in the terms of section* 12 (2))] [and in relation to such directions and this order section 12 (3) (a)/(b)/(c) of the said Act of 1969 shall have effect as if for the reference to ninety/thirty days there were substituted a reference to   days:]

[It is further ordered that the defendant shall for the following period, namely, submit to treatment (*specify treatment in the terms of section* 12 (4)) the Court being satisfied, on the evidence of a medical practitioner approved for the purposes of section 28 of the Mental Health Act, 1959, that his/her mental condition is such as requires and may be susceptible of treatment but is not such as to warrant his/her detention in pursuance of a hospital order under Part V of the said Act of 1959] [and the defendant, being over age of fourteen years, having consented to this requirement:]

[It is further ordered that, for the purpose of facilitating the performance by the supervisor of his duty to advise, assist and befriend the defendant, the defendant shall comply with the following additional requirements:—

1. that he/she shall inform the supervisor at once of any change of his/her residence or employment;
2. that he/she shall keep in touch with the supervisor in accordance with such instructions as may from time to time be given by the supervisor and, in particular, that he/she shall, if the supervisor so requires, receive visits from the supervisor at his/her home:

(*either or both the above further requirements may be included*)].

Dated the   day of   , 19   .

J.P.,

Justice of the Peace for the [county] first above mentioned.
[*or* By order of the Court,

J.C.,

Clerk of the Court.]

44

Supervision order: care proceedings
(*C. & Y.P. Act*, 1969, ss. 1 (3), 11, 12, 13, 17, 18)

In the [county of   .   Petty Sessional Division of   ].

Before the Juvenile Court sitting at   .

A.B. of   (hereinafter called the relevant infant), who is believed to have been born on   , was this day [*or* was on the   day of   , 19   ,] brought before the Court under section 1 of the Children and Young Persons Act, 1969:

And the Court is satisfied that the following condition is satisfied with respect to the relevant infant, that is to say, (*specify in the terms of section* 1 (2) (a) *to* (f) *identifying, in the case of paragraph* (f), *the offence*) and also that he is in need of care or control which he is unlikely to receive unless an order under the said section is made in respect of him:

It appears to the Court that the relevant infant resides/will reside in the county/county borough of   and in the   petty sessional area:

It is hereby ordered that the relevant infant be placed under the supervision of [the council of the said county/county borough] [the council of the county/county borough of   , who have agreed to be designated as the supervisor] [a probation officer appointed for, or assigned to the said petty sessional area] (hereinafter called the supervisor) [for the period of   ] [until the relevant infant attains the age of eighteen years]:

[It is further ordered that the relevant infant reside with G.H. of   who has agreed to this requirement:]

[It is further ordered that the relevant infant shall comply with such directions as may be given by the supervisor in pursuance of section 12 of the Children and Young Persons Act, 1969 requiring him (*specify in the terms of section* 12 (2))] [and in relation to such directions and this order section 12 (3) (a)/(b)/(c) of the said Act of 1969 shall have effect as if for the reference to ninety/thirty days there were substituted a reference to   days:]

[It is further ordered that the relevant infant shall for the following period, namely,   submit to treatment (*specify treatment in the terms of section* 12 (4)), the Court being satisfied, on the evidence of a medical practitioner approved for the purposes of section 28 of the Mental Health Act, 1959, that his/her mental condition is such as requires and may be susceptible of treatment but is not such as to warrant his/her detention in pursuance of a hospital order under Part V of the said Act of 1959] [and the relevant infant, being over the age of fourteen years, having consented to this requirement:]

[It is further ordered that, for the purpose of facilitating the performance by the supervisor of his duty to advise, assist and befriend the relevant infant, the relevant infant shall comply with the following additional requirements:—

1.   that he/she shall inform the supervisor at once of any change of his/her residence or employment;
2.   that he/she shall keep in touch with the supervisor in accordance with such instructions as may from time to time be given by the supervisor and, in particular, that he/she shall, if the supervisor so requires, receive visits from the supervisor at his/her home:

(*either or both of the above further requirements may be included*)].

Dated the   day of   , 19   .

J.P.,
Justice of the Peace for the [county] first above mentioned.
[*or* By order of the Court,

J.C.,
Clerk of the Court.]

45

Supervision order made on discharge of care order
(*C. & Y.P. Act*, 1969, *ss.* 11, 12, 13, 17, 18, 21 (2))

In the [county of   .   Petty Sessional Division of   ].
Before the Juvenile Court sitting at   .

The Juvenile Court sitting at   on the   day of   , 19   , made a care order committing A.B. of   (hereinafter called the relevant infant), who is believed to have been born on   , to the care of the council of the county/county borough of   :

[The relevant infant] [E.F. a parent/guardian of the relevant infant on his behalf] [The said council] has applied for the discharge of the said order:

It appears to the Court that the relevant infant resides/will reside in the county/ county borough of   and in the   petty sessional area:

It is hereby ordered that the said care order be discharged but that the relevant infant be placed under the supervision of [the council of the last-mentioned county/ county borough] [the council of the county/county borough of   , who have agreed to be designated as the supervisor] [a probation officer appointed for, or assigned to, the said petty sessional area] (hereinafter called the supervisor) [for the period of   ] [until the relevant infant attains the age of eighteen years]:

[It is further ordered that the relevant infant reside with G.H. of   who has agreed to this requirement:]

[It is further ordered that the relevant infant shall comply with such directions as may be given by the supervisor in pursuance of section 12 of the Children and Young Persons Act, 1969 requiring him (*specify in the terms of section* 12 (2))] [and in relation to such directions and this order section 12 (3) (a)/(b)/(c) of the said Act of 1969 shall have effect as if for the reference to ninety/thirty days there were substituted a reference to   days:]

[It is further ordered that, for the purpose of facilitating the performance by the supervisor of his duty to advise, assist and befriend the relevant infant, the relevant infant shall comply with the following additional requirements:—

1.   that he/she shall inform the supervisor at once of any change of his/her residence or employment;

2. that he/she shall keep in touch with the supervisor in accordance with such instructions as may from time to time be given by the supervisor and, in particular, that he/she shall, if the supervisor so requires, receive visits from the supervisor at his/her home:

(*either or both of the above further requirements may be included*)].

Dated the   day of   , 19   .

J.P.,

Justice of the Peace for the [county] first above mentioned.
[*or* By order of the Court,

J.C.,

Clerk of the Court.]

46

Order varying or discharging supervision order
(*C. & Y.P. Act,* 1969, *ss.* 15, 16)

In the [county of   .   Petty Sessional Division of   ].
Before the [Juvenile] [Magistrates'] Court sitting at   .
The Juvenile Court sitting at   on the   day of
, 19   , made a supervision order within the meaning of the Children and Young Persons Act, 1969 in respect of A.B. of   (hereinafter called the supervised person), who is believed to have been born on   .

[The said supervision order was varied by an order made by the Juvenile Court sitting at   on the   day of   , 19   :]

The said supervision order [as so varied] names the county/county borough of   and the   petty sessional area as the areas in which it appears the supervised person resides or will reside and places him under the supervision of [the council of the said county/county borough] [the council of the county/county borough of   ] [a probation officer appointed for, or assigned to, the said petty sessional area] and, unless previously discharged, ceases to have effect on (*specify the date*).

The said supervision order [as so varied] in pursuance of sections 12 and 18 (2) of the said Act of 1969 contains certain requirements including the following requirement[s] (*specify requirement[s] proposed to be varied*):]

[The supervised person] [E.F. a parent/guardian of the supervised person on his behalf] [The supervisor] has applied for the [variation] [discharge] of the said supervision order:

[The supervisor has referred to the Court a report from a medical practitioner in pursuance of section 15 (5) of the said Act of 1969 proposing that a mental health treatment requirement should be [cancelled] [varied] for the following reasons (*specify in the terms of section* 15 (5)):]

It is hereby ordered that the said supervision order [varied as aforesaid] shall be [discharged] [varied/further varied as follows:—

].

Dated the   day of   , 19   .

J.P.,

Justice of the Peace for the [county] first above mentioned.
[*or* By order of the Court,

J.C.,

Clerk of the Court.]

47

Attendance centre order on failure to comply with requirement of supervision order
(*C. & Y.P. Act,* 1969, *ss.* 15 (2), (4), 16)

In the [county of   .   Petty Sessional Division of   ].
Before the [Magistrates'] [Juvenile] Court sitting at   .
The Juvenile Court sitting at   on the   day of
, 19   , made a supervision order within the meaning of the Children and

Young Persons Act, 1969 in respect of A.B. of   (hereinafter called the supervised person), who is believed to have been born on   :

The said supervision order was not made by virtue of section 1 of the said Act or on the discharge of a care order:

[The said supervision order was varied by an order made by the Juvenile Court sitting at   on the   day of   , 19   :]

The said supervision order [as so varied] names the county/county borough of   and the   petty sessional area as the areas in which it appears the supervised person resides or will reside and places him/her under the supervision of [the council of the said county/county borough] [the council of the county/county borough of   ] [a probation officer appointed for, or assigned to, the said petty sessional area] (hereinafter called the supervisor):

The said supervision order [as so varied] in pursuance of sections 12 and 18 (2) of the said Act of 1969 contains certain requirements including the following requirement[s] (*specify requirement[s] contravened or proposed to be varied*):

On the application of the supervisor the Court is satisfied that the supervised person has failed to comply with the [said] [mentioned] requirement[s]:

[It is hereby ordered that the said supervision order [varied as aforesaid] shall be [discharged] [varied/further varied as follows:—

                                                                                    :]

And the Court having been notified by the Secretary of State that the attendance centre specified herein is available for the reception from the Court of persons of the supervised person's class or description:

And the Court being satisfied that the attendance centre is reasonably accessible to the supervised person, having regard to the means of access available to the relevant infant and any other circumstances:

[And the Court being satisfied that twelve hours attendance would be inadequate having regard to all the circumstances:]

It is [further] ordered that the supervised person, in respect of the said failure, do attend at the attendance centre at   , on the first occasion on the   day of   , 19   , at the hour of   in the   noon, and subsequently at such times as shall be fixed by the officer in charge of the said centre until a period of attendance of   hours has been completed.]

Dated the   day of   , 19   .

                                        J.P.,
            Justice of the Peace for the [county] first above mentioned.
            [*or* By order of the Court,

                                                        J.C.,
                                            Clerk of the Court.]

48

Fine on failure to comply with requirement of supervision order
(C. & Y.P. Act, 1969, ss. 15 (2), (4), 16)

In the [county of   . Petty Sessional Division of   ].

Before the [Magistrates'] [Juvenile] Court sitting at   .

The Juvenile Court sitting at   on the   day of   , 19   , made a supervision order within the meaning of the Children and Young Persons Act, 1969 in respect of A.B. of   (hereinafter called the supervised person), who is believed to have been born on   :

The said supervision order was not made by virtue of section 1 of the said Act or on the discharge of a care order:

[The said supervision order was varied by an order made by the Juvenile Court sitting at   on the   day of   , 19   :]

The said supervision order [as so varied] names the county/county borough of   and the   petty sessional area as the areas in which it appears the supervised person resides or will reside and places him/her under the supervision of [the council of the said county/county borough] [the council of the county/county borough of   ] [a probation officer appointed for, or assigned to, the said petty sessional area] (hereinafter called the supervisor):

The said supervision order [as so varied] in pursuance of sections 12 and 18 (2) of the said Act of 1969 contains certain requirements including the following require-ment[s] (*specify requirement[s] contravened or proposed to be varied*):

On the application of the supervisor the Court is satisfied that the supervised person has failed to comply with the [said] [mentioned] requirement[s]:

[It is hereby ordered that the said supervision order [varied as aforesaid] shall be [discharged] [varied/further varied as follows:—

                                                                               :]

It is [further] ordered that the supervised person, in respect of the said failure, shall pay a fine of   [by weekly/monthly instalments of   , the first instalment of] the said sum to be paid [forthwith] [not later than the day of   , 19   ].

Dated the   day of   , 19   .

                                   J.P.,
          Justice of the Peace for the [county] first above mentioned.
          [*or* By order of the Court,

                                             J.C.,
                              Clerk of the Court.]

49

Detention centre order on failure to comply with requirement of supervision order
(*C. & Y.P. Act,* 1969, *s.* 15 (2), (4))

In the [county of   . Petty Sessional Division of   ].
Before the [Magistrates'] [Juvenile] Court sitting at   .

To each and all the constables of   and to the Warden of the detention centre at   .

The Juvenile Court sitting at   on the   day of   , 19   , made a supervision order within the meaning of the Children and Young Persons Act, 1969 in respect of A.B. of   (hereinafter called the supervised person), who is believed to have been born on   :

The said supervision order was not made by virtue of section 1 of the said Act or on the discharge of a care order:

[The said supervision order was varied by an order made by the Juvenile Court sitting at   on the   day of   , 19   :]

The said supervision order [as so varied] names the county/county borough of   and the   petty sessional area as the areas in which it appears the supervised person resides or will reside and places him/her under the supervision of [the council of the said county/county borough] [the council of the county/county borough of   ] [a probation officer appointed for, or assigned to, the said petty sessional area] (hereinafter called the supervisor):

The said supervision order [as so varied] in pursuance of sections 12 and 18 (2) of the said Act of 1969 contains certain requirements including the following require-ment[s] (*specify requirement[s] contravened*):

On the application of the supervisor the Court is satisfied that the supervised person has failed to comply with the [said] [mentioned] requirement[s]:

It is hereby ordered that the said supervision order [varied as aforesaid] shall be discharged:

And the Court having been notified by the Secretary of State that the detention centre specified herein is available for the reception from the Court of persons of the supervised person's class or description:

It is further ordered that the supervised person, in respect of the said failure, be detained in the detention centre at   for a period of (*state period of detention*):

You, the said constables, are hereby commanded to convey the supervised person to the said detention centre, and there deliver him/her to the Warden thereof, together with this warrant; and you, the Warden of the said detention centre, to receive the supervised person into your custody and keep him/her for (*state period*).

Dated the　　　　　　　　　day of　　　　　　　, 19　　.

J.P.,
Justice of the Peace for the [county] first above mentioned.
[*or* By order of the Court,

J.C.,
Clerk of the Court.]

50

Imprisonment on failure to comply with requirement of supervision order
(*C. & Y.P. Act*, 1969, s. 15 (2), (4), 16)

In the [county of　　　　　　. Petty Sessional Division of　　　　　].

Before the [Magistrates'] [Juvenile] Court sitting at　　　　　　　.

[To each and all the constables of　　　　　　and to the Governor of Her Majesty's prison at　　　　　.]

The Juvenile Court sitting at　　　　　on the　　　　day of , 19　, made a supervision order within the meaning of the Children and Young Persons Act, 1969 in respect of A.B. of　　　　　(hereinafter called the supervised person) who is believed to have been born on　　　　:

[The said supervision order was not made by virtue of section 1 of the said Act or on the discharge of a care order:]

[The said supervision order was varied by an order made by the Juvenile Court sitting at　　　　on the　　　　day of　　　, 19　:]

The said supervision order [as so varied] names the county/county borough of　　　　and the　　　　petty sessional area as the areas in which it appears the supervised person resides or will reside and places him/her under the supervision of [the council of the said county/county borough] [the council of the county/county borough of　　　　] [a probation officer appointed for, or assigned to, the said petty sessional area] (hereinafter called the supervisor):

The said supervision order [as so varied] in pursuance of sections 12 and 18 (2) of the said Act of 1969 contains certain requirements including the following requirement[s] (*specify requirement[s] contravened*):

On the application of the supervisor the Court is satisfied that the supervised person has failed to comply with the [said] [　　　　mentioned] requirement[s]:

It is hereby ordered that the said supervision order [varied as aforesaid] shall be discharged:

And the Court is of opinion that no method of dealing with the supervised person, other than the imposition of imprisonment, is appropriate because (*state reason*):

[And the Court sentences the supervised person, in respect of the said failure, to imprisonment for (*state period*):

And it is ordered that the said sentence of imprisonment shall not take effect unless during the period of　　　　years from today the supervised person commits in Great Britain another offence punishable with imprisonment and thereafter an order is made under section 40 of the Criminal Justice Act, 1967, that the sentence shall take effect:]

[And it is adjudged that the supervised person, in respect of the said failure, be imprisoned in Her Majesty's prison aforesaid for (*state period*):

And the Court is not required to suspend the sentence because paragraph　　　　of section 39 (3) of the Criminal Justice Act, 1967, applies:]

You, the said constables are hereby commanded to convey the supervised person to the said prison and there deliver him/her to the Governor thereof, together with this warrant; and you, the Governor of the said prison, to receive the supervised person into your custody and keep him/her for (*state period*).]

Dated the   day of   , 19   .

J.P.,
Justice of the Peace for the [county] first above mentioned.
[*or* By order of the Court,

J.C.,
Clerk of the Court.]

51

Remittal order: criminal proceedings
(C. & Y.P. Act, 1933, s. 56; C. & Y.P. Act, 1969, s. 7 (8))

In the [county of   . Petty Sessional Division of   ].

Before the Magistrates' Court sitting at   .

A.B. (hereinafter called the defendant) of   has this day been found guilty by the said Court of (*state the offence*):

The defendant is a child [*or* young person] who is believed to have been born on the   day of   , 19   :

It is hereby ordered that the case be remitted to the Juvenile Court sitting at   acting for the same place as the Court [*or* for the place where the defendant resides]:

And it is directed that the defendant be committed to   until brought before the Juvenile Court [*or* be released upon entering into a recognisance in the sum of £   , with   suret   in the sum of £   [each] to appear at that Juvenile Court on   day the   day of   , 19   , at the hour of   in the   noon].

Dated the   day of   , 19   .

J.P.,
Justice of the Peace for the [county] aforesaid.
[*or* By order of the Court,

J.C.,
Clerk of the Court.]

52

Remittal order: care proceedings
(C. & Y.P. Act, 1969, s. 2 (11))

In the [county of   . Petty Sessional Division of   ].

Before the Juvenile Court sitting at   .

A.B. of   (hereinafter called the relevant infant), who is believed to have been born on   , was this day [*or* was on the   day of   , 19   ,] brought before the Court under section 1 of the Children and Young Persons Act, 1969:

And it was alleged that the following condition was satisfied with respect to the relevant infant, that is to say, (*specify in the terms of section* 1 (2) (a) *to* (f) *identifying, in the case of paragraph* (f), *the offence*):

[It is hereby adjudged that the relevant infant is guilty of the said offence:]

It appearing to the Court that the relevant infant resides in the county/county borough of   and in the   petty sessional area, it is hereby directed that the relevant infant be brought before a Juvenile Court acting for that petty sessional area:

[*Omit in cases where interim order is made.*

Accordingly, it shall be the duty of the council of the said county/county borough to give effect within twenty-one days to the aforesaid direction.]

Dated the   day of   , 19   .

J.P.,
Justice of the Peace for the [county] first above mentioned.
[*or* By order of the Court,

J.C.,
Clerk of the Court.]

53

Summons to parent, etc.: contribution order
(C. & Y.P. Act, 1933, ss. 86, 87; C. & Y.P. Act, 1969, s. 62)

In the [county of   . Petty Sessional Division of   ].
To C.D. of   .

Complaint has been made this day to [me the undersigned] [*or state name*] [Justice of the Peace] [Clerk to the Justices] by the council of the county/county borough of   that you are liable to make contributions under section 86 of the Children and Young Persons Act, 1933, in respect of A.B. being a person in the care of the said council:

You are therefore summoned to appear on   day, the   day of   , 19   , at the hour of   in the   noon before the Magistrates' Court sitting at   to show cause why an order should not be made requiring you to contribute such weekly sum as the Court, having regard to your means and subject to section 62 of the Children and Young Persons Act, 1969, thinks fit.

Dated the   day of   , 19   .

J.P.,
Justice of the Peace for the [county] first above mentioned.
[*or* This summons was issued by the above-named Justice of the
Peace.

J.C.,
Clerk of the Magistrates' Court sitting at   .]
[*or* J.C.,
Clerk to the Justices for the Petty Sessional Division
aforesaid.]

54

Contribution order
(C. & Y.P. Act, 1933, ss. 86, 87; C. & Y.P. Act, 1969, s. 62)

In the [county of   . Petty Sessional Division of   ].
Before the Magistrates' Court sitting at   .

Complaint has been made by the council of the county/county borough of   that E.F. of   (hereinafter called the contributory) is liable to make contributions under section 86 of the Children and Young Persons Act 1933 as the father/mother of A.B., believed to have been born on   , who is in the care of the said council (hereinafter called the relevant infant):

The said council, by notice in writing given to the contributory on the day of   , 19   , proposed a weekly contribution of   [but the said council and the contributory have not within one month of that date agreed on the amount of the contribution] [and the contributory agreed the amount of the contribution but has defaulted in making the contribution due for (*specify week*):]

It is hereby ordered in pursuance of section 87 of the said Act of 1933 that the contributory do pay to the said council a weekly sum of   until the relevant infant ceases to be in the care of the said council or sooner attains the age of sixteen years, except in respect of such periods, if any, as the relevant infant is allowed by the said council to be under the charge and control of a parent, guardian, relative or friend:

[And it is further ordered that the contributory do pay the sum of   for costs.]

Dated the   day of   , 19   .

J.P.,
Justice of the Peace for the [county] first above mentioned.
[*or* By order of the Court,

J.C.,
Clerk of the Court.]

55

Arrears order
(*C. & Y.P. Act*, 1963, *s.* 30)

In the [county of   . Petty Sessional Division of   ].

Before the Magistrates' Court sitting at   .

Complaint has been made by the council of the county/county borough of   that E.F. of   (hereinafter called the contributory) was liable to make contributions under section 86 of the Children and Young Persons Act, 1933 as the father/mother of A.B., believed to have been born on   , who is in the care of the said council, in respect of a period of default during which no order was in force under section 87 of the said Act of 1933 requiring the contributory to make such contributions and the said council has applied for an arrears order:

The said council, by notice in writing given to the contributory on the day of   , 19   , proposed a weekly contribution of   [but the said council and the contributory have not within one month of that date agreed on the amount of the contribution] [and the contributory agreed the amount of the contribution but has defaulted in making the contribution due for (*specify week*):]

The Court finds that the period of default is   :

It is hereby ordered in pursuance of section 30 of the Children and Young Persons Act, 1963, that the contributory do pay to the said council a weekly sum of   for a period of   weeks.

Dated the   day of   , 19   .

J.P.,
Justice of the Peace for the [county] first above mentioned.
[*or* By order of the Court,

J.C.,
Clerk of the Court.]

56

Register of the Juvenile Court
(M.C. (C. & Y.P.) Rules, 1970, r. 23)

In the [County of   .
Petty Sessional Division of   ].
Register of the Juvenile Court sitting at   .
The   day of   , 19   .

I	2	3	4	5	6	7
Number	Name of Informant, Complainant or Applicant	Name of child or young person and date of birth	Nature of offence, matter of complaint or ground of application with date (of offence, etc.)	Plea, admission or consent to order	Minute of adjudication	Whether parents ordered to pay fine, compensation or costs

(Signature)
Justice of the Peace for the [county] of
A Justice adjudicating.
[*or* Clerk of the Court present during these proceedings.]

THE CHILDREN AND YOUNG PERSONS ACT, 1969 (COMMENCEMENT NO. 3) ORDER, 1970
[S.I. 1970 No. 1498]

Citation

1. This Order may be cited as the Children and Young Persons Act, 1969 (Commencement No. 3) Order, 1970.

Interpretation

2.—(1) In this Order "the Act" means the Children and Young Persons Act, 1969.

(2) The Interpretation Act, 1889 shall apply to the interpretation of this Order as it applies to the interpretation of an Act of Parliament.

Days appointed for coming into force of certain provisions of the Act

3. The provisions of the Act specified in column I of each of the first two Schedules to this Order (which relate to the matters specified in column 2 thereof) shall come into force on the day specified in the heading to that Schedule.

Transitional provisions

4. The transitional provisions contained in Schedule 3 to this Order shall have effect in connection with the provisions brought into force by this Order.

SCHEDULE 1

PROVISIONS COMING INTO FORCE ON 1ST JANUARY 1971

Provisions of the Act	Subject matter of provisions
Section 1	Care proceedings in juvenile courts.
Section 2	Provisions supplementary to section 1.
Section 3	Further supplementary provisions relating to section 1 (2) (f).
Section 5 (8) and section 5 (9), so far as it relates to the definition of "the appropriate local authority".	Local authority to be notified of decision to lay information against young person.
Section 6	Summary trial of young persons.
Section 7, except subsections (1) and (3).	Alterations in treatment of young offenders etc.
Section 9	Investigations by local authorities.
Section 10	Further limitations on publication of particulars of children and young persons etc.
Section 11	Supervision orders.
Section 12	Power to include requirements in supervision orders.
Section 13	Selection of supervisor.
Section 14	Duty of supervisor.
Section 15	Variation and discharge of supervision orders.
Section 16	Provisions supplementary to section 15.
Section 17	Termination of supervision.
Section 18	Supplementary provisions relating to supervision orders.
Section 19	Facilities for the carrying out of supervisors' directions.
Section 20	Orders for committal to care of local authorities.
Section 21	Variation and discharge of care orders.
Section 22	Special provisions relating to interim orders.
Section 23	Remand to care of local authorities etc.
Section 24, except subsections (5) and (6).	Powers and duties of local authorities etc. with respect to persons committed to their care.
Section 25	Transfers between England or Wales and Northern Ireland.
Section 26	Transfers between England or Wales and the Channel Islands or Isle of Man.
Section 27	Consequential modifications of 1948 c. 43 sections 11 and 12.
Section 28	Detention of child or young person in place of safety.
Section 29, except subsection (4).	Release or further detention of arrested child or young person.
Section 30	Detention of young offenders in community homes.
Section 31	Removal to borstal institutions of persons committed to care of local authorities.
Section 32	Detention of absentees.
Section 33, except subsection (1) so far as it relates to paragraph 6 of Schedule 1.	Legal aid.

Provisions of the Act	Subject matter of provisions
Section 34	Transitional modifications of Part I for persons of specified ages.
Section 46 (2), so far as it relates to paragraphs 3, 4 and 8 of Schedule 3.	Discontinuance of approved schools etc. on establishment of community homes.
Section 56 (1) (a)	Extension of disqualification for keeping foster children.
Section 61	Rules relating to juvenile court panels and composition of juvenile courts.
Section 62, except subsection (2).	Contributions in respect of children and young persons in care.
Section 72 (1), so far as it relates to paragraphs 1, 1A, 4, 5 (2), 6 to 12 and 15 to 18 of Schedule 4 and section 72 (2).	Transitional provisions.
Section 72 (3), so far as it relates to the provisions of Schedule 5 specified in Appendix A to this Schedule.	Minor and consequential amendments.
Section 72 (4), so far as it relates to the repeals set out in Appendix B to this Schedule.	Repeals.
Section 72 (5), so far as it relates to sections 2 (4) and 6 (1) (b) of the Children Act, 1958.	Sections 1 to 6 and 14 of the Children Act, 1958, as amended.
Schedule 1, except paragraph 6.	Modifications of Part IV of the Criminal Justice Act, 1967.
In Schedule 3, paragraphs 3, 4 and 8.	Approved schools and other institutions.
In Schedule 4, paragraphs 1, 1A, 4, 5 (2), 6 to 12 and 15 to 24.	Transitional provisions and savings.
In Schedule 5, the provisions specified in Appendix A to this Schedule.	Minor and consequential amendments of enactments.
Schedule 6, so far as it relates to the repeals set out in Appendix B to this Schedule.	Repeals.
Schedule 7, so far as it relates to sections 2 (4) and 6 (1) (b) of the Children Act, 1958.	Sections 1 to 6 and 14 of the Children Act, 1958, as amended.

Appendix A to Schedule 1

Amendments taking effect from 1st January 1971

Provisions of Schedule 5	Enactments amended
Paragraph 1	The Police (Property) Act, 1897.
Paragraphs 2, 3, 5 to 10 and 12.	Sections 10, 34 (2), 55 (1), 56 (1), 63, 86 (1), 87 (1) to (3), 88 (1), (2) (c) and (4) and 107 (1) and (2) of the Children and Young Persons Act, 1933.
Paragraph 13	Section 40 of the Education Act, 1944.
Paragraphs 16, 17, 21 (2) and 22.	Sections 23 (1), 26 (1), (3) and (4) (b), 54 (4) and 59 (1) of the Children Act, 1948.

Provisions of Schedule 5	Enactments amended
In paragraph 20 (1), the following provision:— "and at the end of that subsection there shall be added the words "or sections 2 (5), 16 (3) or 28 of the Children and Young Persons Act, 1969 and of children detained by them in pursuance of arrangements under section 29 (3) of that Act"."."	Section 51 (1) of the Children Act, 1948.
Paragraph 24.	Section 27 of the Criminal Justice Act, 1948.
Paragraphs 25 and 26.	Section 7 of the Criminal Justice (Scotland) Act, 1949.
Paragraph 27.	Section 37 (7) of the Sexual Offences Act, 1956.
Paragraph 28.	Sections 5 (2) (a) and 7 (4) (a) and (6) of the Affiliation Proceedings Act, 1957.
Paragraphs 29 and 32.	Sections 2 (4) and 17 of the Children Act, 1958.
Paragraphs 33, 34 and 36.	Sections 4 (3) (a), 15 (3) and 57 (1) of the Adoption Act, 1958.
Paragraphs 38 to 41.	Sections 10 (1) (a) (i), 50 (a), 60 (6) and 62 (4) of the Mental Health Act, 1959.
Paragraphs 42 and 43.	Sections 10 (1) (a) (ii) and 46 (b) of the Mental Health (Scotland) Act, 1960.
Paragraphs 44 to 46.	Sections 5 (1) and 6 (3), 9 and 29 (3) (a) of the Criminal Justice Act, 1961.
Paragraphs 47 to 50 and 53.	Sections 3 (1), 23 (1) (b) and (5), 29, 30 (1) and (3) to (5) and 57 (3) of the Children and Young Persons Act, 1963.
Paragraph 54 (1) and in paragraph 54 (2), the following provision:— "In subsection (2) of that section for the words "said Act of 1933" there shall be substituted the words "Children and Young Persons Act, 1969 (other than an interim order)" and".	Section 11 (1) (b) and (2) of the Family Allowances Act, 1965.
Paragraph 56.	Section 3 (3) of the Criminal Justice Act, 1967.
Paragraphs 57 to 62, 64 (2), 65 (1), 67 and 68, 70 to 72, 74 and 77 to 83.	Sections 44, 72, 73, 74, 75, 76 (4), 94 (1) and 97 (1) of the Social Work (Scotland) Act, 1968, and Schedules 2, 8 and 9 thereto.

Appendix B to Schedule 1
Repeals taking effect from 1st January 1971

Chapter	Short title	Extent of repeal
1933 c. 12.	The Children and Young Persons Act, 1933.	In section 10 (2) the words from "and may" onwards. Section 26 (6), 29 (3) and 32. In section 34 (2) the words "or taken to a place of safety". Section 35.

Chapter	Short title	Extent of repeal
1933 c. 12 (*cont.*)	The Children and Young Persons Act, 1933.—(*cont.*)	In section 44, in subsection (1) the words from "being" to "as", and subsection (2). In section 48 (2) the words "a probationer or" and "any failure to comply with the requirements of the probation order or" and the words from "or to amend" onwards. Section 54. In section 55 subsection (2), and in subsection (4) the words "or on forfeiture of any such security as aforesaid". Section 57. Sections 62 to 75, 76 (1), 1A and 1B, 77 (3) and (4), 78, 79 (4), 81 (2) and 82 to 85. In section 86, subsection (2), in subsection (3) the words "or ordered to be sent to an approved school" and the words from "and", in the first place where it occurs to the end of the subsection, and subsection (4). Sections 89 (1), 90 and 91. In section 102, paragraphs (a) and (b) of subsection (1), and in subsection (2) the words from "the rights" to "Act or". In section 107 (1) the definitions of "approved school order", and "special reception centre". Section 107 (2). Section 108 (2) and (3). In Schedule 4, paragraphs 4, 5, 7, 8, 9, 11, 12 and 13.
1937 c. 37.	The Children and Young Persons (Scotland) Act, 1937.	Sections 82, 86, 87 and 89.
1938 c. 40.	The Children and Young Persons Act, 1938.	In Schedule 2, paragraph 13. The whole Act.
1944 c. 31.	The Education Act, 1944.	Section 40A.
1948 c. 40.	The Education (Miscellaneous Provisions) Act, 1948.	In Schedule 1, the entries relating to section 40 of the Education Act, 1944.
1948 c. 43.	The Children Act, 1948.	Sections 5 and 6 (3) and (4). In section 23, in subsection (1), the words from "(which" to "aliment)" and subsection (3). Section 25. In section 26 (1), paragraph (c), and in paragraph (ii) the words "or (c)" and the words from "or", in the second place where it occurs, onwards. In section 59, in subsection (1), the definition of "approved school order".

Chapter	Short title	Extent of repeal
1948 c. 43 (*cont.*)	The Children Act 1948— (*cont.*)	In Schedule 3, the entries relating to sections 70, 82, 84, 90 and 107 of the Act of 1933.
1948 c. 58.	The Criminal Justice Act, 1948.	In section 3 (5) the words from "if the" to "age". In section 11 (1) the words from the beginning to "behaviour" in the first place where it occurs. In sections 46 (1) and 47 (1) the words "or a supervision order". Sections 48 (4), 49 (5), 71, 72 and 75. In section 80 (1), the definition of "supervision order" and in the definition of "sentence" the words from "an", in the second place where it occurs, to "school". In Schedule 9, the entries relating to sections 54, 70, 78, 82 and 90 of the Act of 1933, in the entry relating to section 48 (2) of the Act of 1933 the words "a probationer or" and "any failure to comply with the requirements of the probation order or" and the words from "or to amend" to the end of the entry, and the entry relating to the Children and Young Persons Act, 1938.
1949 c. 101.	The Justices of the Peace Act, 1949.	Section 14.
1950 c. 37.	The Maintenance Orders Act, 1950.	In Schedule 1, in the entry relating to section 86 of the Act of 1933, the words from "or as" onwards.
1952 c. 50.	The Children and Young Persons (Amendment) Act, 1952.	Sections 2 to 5. In the Schedule, paragraphs 2, 3, 5, 8, 9 and 11 to 16.
1952 c. 52.	The Prison Act, 1952.	In section 49 (2) the words "remand home or", where they first occur, and the words "remand home" wherever else they occur. In section 50, the words from "and subsection" onwards. In section 53 (1) the definition of "remand home".
1952 c. 55.	The Magistrates' Courts Act, 1952.	Sections 20, 21 and 26 (2). In section 38 (1), the words from "The provisions of this" onwards.
1953 c. 33.	The Education (Miscellaneous Provisions) Act, 1953.	Section 11.
1956 c. 24.	The Children and Young Persons Act, 1956.	The whole Act.
1957 c. 55.	The Affiliation Proceedings Act, 1957.	In section 5 (2) (d) the words from "or" onwards. In section 7 (5) the words "Sub-paragraph (ii) of".

Chapter	Short title	Extent of repeal
1958 c. 55.	The Local Government Act, 1958.	In Schedule 8, in paragraph 2, sub-paragraph (3), in sub-paragraph (4) the words "paragraph (b) of", and sub-paragraph (5).
1958 c. 65.	The Children Act, 1958.	In section 2, in subsection (4) the words "the Children and Young Persons Act, 1933 or of". In section 17, in the definition of "fit person order" the words "the Children and Young Persons Act, 1933 or".
1958 c. 5 (7 & 8 Eliz. 2).	The Adoption Act, 1958.	In section 15 (3) the words from "fit person by" to "care of a" and the words "fit person order or" and "as the case may be". In section 37, in subsection (3) the words "in an approved school or".
1959 c. 72.	The Mental Health Act, 1959.	In section 60 (6) the words from "including" onwards. Section 61. Section 70 (2). In section 72 (6) (a) the words from "or made" to "Act 1933" and from "or an order" onwards. In section 75 (1), the words "(other than a person detained in a remand home)" and in paragraph (b) the words from "or as" to "have been remitted", and in section 75 (2) the words from "including" to "1963". Section 79. In section 80 (1), the definitions of "approved school" and "remand home".
1961 c. 39.	The Criminal Justice Act, 1961.	In section 5 (2), paragraph (a) and the words following paragraph (b), and section 5 (3). In section 6, subsections (1) and (2), and in subsection (3) the words from "or ordering" to "home" in paragraph (a), the words from "or" to "home" in paragraph (b) and the words "or remand home" and "a prison is so named and". In section 7, in subsection (3) the words from "and where" onwards. Section 8 (2). In section 9, paragraph (a). Sections 14 to 17, 22 (4) and 25. In section 29 (1), the words "remand home" and "special reception centre or other" and in section 29 (3) the words from "special" to "1933 and".

Chapter	Short title	Extent of repeal
1961 c. 39. (*cont.*)	The Criminal Justice Act, 1961—(*cont.*)	Schedule 2. In Schedule 4 the entries relating to sections 54, 72, 78, 82, 83 and 88 of the Act of 1933 and to Schedule 4 to that Act and the entries relating to the Children and Young Persons Act, 1938, section 72 and the change in the definition of "sentence" in section 80 (1) of the Criminal Justice Act, 1948, sections 20 and 32 of the Magistrates' Courts Act, 1952 and section 79 of the Mental Health Act, 1959.
1963 c. 33.	The London Government Act, 1963.	In Schedule 17, paragraph 18 (c).
1963 c. 37.	The Children and Young Persons Act, 1963.	Sections 2 and 4 to 15. Section 22. In section 23, in subsection (1), paragraph (a) and the word "authority", subsection (2), in subsection (3) the words "or subsection (2)" in both places and the words "takes refuge there or", and subsections (6) to (8). Section 24. In section 25 (1) the words "or taken to a place of safety", and section 25 (2). In section 29, in subsection (1) the words "continue to" and subsection (2). Section 33. Section 53 (1) and (2). In section 55 the words from "section 84 (5)" to "principal Act", the word "or" immediately preceding the words "section 17" and the words from "(which relate" onwards. Sections 59 and 61. In section 65 (5), the words "subsections (1) and (2) of section 10 and", "and 53 (1)" and "27" and "34". Schedule 1. In Schedule 3, paragraphs 10, 16 to 23, 25 to 27, 33, 34, 35, 36, 44, 46, 48 and 49, and in paragraph 50 the words "special reception centre or other", and "'special reception centre' has the same meaning as in the Children and Young Persons Act, 1933 and".

Chapter	Short title	Extent of repeal
1963 c. 39.	The Criminal Justice (Scotland) Act, 1963.	In Schedule 5, the entry relating to the Children Act, 1948.
1965 c. 53.	The Family Allowances Act, 1965.	In section 11 (1), sub-paragraph (i) of paragraph (a) and in paragraph (c) the words from "made" to "order".
1967 c. 80.	The Criminal Justice Act, 1967	In section 55, the words "or any provision of the Children and Young Persons Act, 1933" and the words from "and accordingly" onwards.
		In section 77 (1), the words "on his means".
		In Part I of Schedule 3, the entries relating to sections 72 (5) and 82 (5) of the Act of 1933 and section 14 of the Act of 1963.
1968 c. 49.	The Social Work (Scotland) Act, 1968.	In section 72 (2), the words "of the Children and Young Persons Acts, 1933 to 1963 or, as the case may be", the word "respectively" and the words "to a supervision order within the meaning of section 5 of the Children and Young Persons Act, 1963 or".
		In section 73 (2) the word "juvenile".
		In section 74, in subsection (3) the words "in England or Wales or" and "if he thinks fit" and the words from "an approved" to "be" where it first occurs, in subsection (4) the words from "the Children" to "be of", the words "an approved school or" in the first, second and third places where they occur, the word "of" and "in" following those words in the first and third of those places respectively and the words "section 71 of the said Act of 1933 or" and "section 90 of the said Act of 1933 or under", and in subsection (5) the words "of the Acts of 1933 to 1963 or, as the case may be", the words "of a local authority or, as the case may be" and the words "those Acts or".
		In section 75, in subsection (1) the words "the Secretary of State or" and "approved school or", and in subsection (3) the words "approved school or".

Chapter	Short title	Extent of repeal
1968 c. 49. —(cont.)	The Social Work (Scotland) Act, 1968—(cont.)	In section 76, in subsections (1) and (2), the word "juvenile" wherever it occurs, and in subsection (4) the words "approved school or" and "of the approved school or". Section 77 (1) (b). In Schedule 2, in paragraph 10 the words from "and" to "1933". In Schedule 8, paragraphs 2 to 5, 21 and 35.

SCHEDULE 2

PROVISIONS COMING INTO FORCE ON 1ST APRIL 1971

Provisions of the Act	Subject matter of provisions
Section 24 (5) and (6)	Duty of local authority to appoint visitor for persons committed to their care.

SCHEDULE 3

TRANSITIONAL PROVISIONS

1.—(1) In this Schedule the following expressions have the meanings hereby respectively assigned to them, that is to say:—

"the Act of 1933" means the Children and Young Persons Act, 1933;
"the Act of 1937" means the Children and Young Persons (Scotland) Act, 1937;
"the Act of 1961" means the Criminal Justice Act, 1961; and
"the Act of 1968" means the Social Work (Scotland) Act, 1968.

(2) In this Schedule, except where the context otherwise requires, any reference to an enactment shall be construed as a reference to that enactment as amended, extended or applied by or under any other enactment.

2. Without prejudice to the operation of paragraphs 5 (2) and 18 of Schedule 4 to the Act nothing in any provision of Schedule 5 or 6 thereto brought into force by this Order shall affect the operation of section 48 of the Act of 1933 or section 9 of the Act of 1961 in relation to a person subject to a probation order which continues in force by virtue of the said paragraph 5 (2).

3. Without prejudice to the operation of paragraphs 15 and 18 of Schedule 4 to the Act nothing in any provision of the Act brought into force by this Order shall affect—

(a) any order of a court for the detention of any person in a remand home, special reception centre or other place of safety in England and Wales (other than a person subject to an approved school order or detained by virtue of a warrant under section 15 of the Act of 1961) and in force immediately before 1st January 1971; or

(b) the operation of any enactment relating to a person subject to such an order until he is brought before a court in pursuance of the order or released;

and, accordingly, any such enactment shall have effect in relation to such a person, until he is brought before a court as aforesaid or released, as if this Order had not been made.

4.—(1) Until the date of the coming into force of section 44 of the Act of 1968 nothing in any provision of the Act brought into force by this Order shall affect the operation of any enactment relating to persons sent or transferred to an approved school in Scotland or committed to the care of a fit person under the Act of 1937 or to custody in a remand home provided under that Act and, accordingly, until that date, any such enactment shall have effect in relation to such a person as if this Order had not been made.

(2) In relation to a person who is subject to an approved school or fit person order within the meaning of the Act of 1937 or an order of committal to custody in a remand home provided under that Act immediately before the date mentioned in the preceding sub-paragraph and continues to be so subject on and after that date by virtue of paragraph 4 of Schedule 7 to the Act of 1968 the preceding sub-paragraph shall have effect as if for references to that date there were substituted references to the date on which the order ceases to have effect.

5. So long as section 77 (1) of the Act of 1933 (provision of remand homes) applies to a local authority by virtue of paragraph 13 (1) (c) of Schedule 4 to the Act, section 78 (3) of the Act of 1933 shall, notwithstanding the repeal of that section contained in Schedule 6 to the Act, continue to apply in relation to remand homes provided by that authority as if for the words "detained in custody" there were substituted the word "accommodated".

6. Any contribution order made under section 87 of the Act of 1933 or any affiliation order made by virtue of or revived under section 26 of the Children Act, 1948 and in force immediately before 1st January 1971 shall have effect from that date as if made under the said section 87 or, as the case may be, made by virtue of or revived under the said section 26, as modified by the Act.

7. Any rules made by virtue of section 14 of the Justices of the Peace Act, 1949 shall have effect from 1st January 1971 as if they were made by virtue of section 61 of the Act.

THE CHILDREN AND YOUNG PERSONS ACT, 1969 (TRANSITIONAL MODIFICATIONS OF PART I) ORDER, 1970

[S.I. 1970 No. 1882]

1. This Order may be cited as the Children and Young Persons Act, 1969 (Transitional Modifications of Part I) Order, 1970 and shall come into operation on 1st January 1971.

2. In this Order "the Act" means the Children and Young Persons Act, 1969.

3. Any reference to a child in section 13 (2) (selection of supervisor) or 28 (4) or (5) (detention of children and young persons by constables) of the Act shall be construed as excluding a child who has attained the age of 10 years.

4.—(1) Any reference to a young person in any provision of the Act specified in paragraph (2) of this Article shall be construed as including a child who has attained the age of 10 years.

(2) The provisions of the Act referred to in paragraph (1) of this Article are sections 5 (8) (decision to lay an information against a young person to be

notified to the appropriate local authority), 7 (7) (orders in criminal proceedings against young persons), 7 (8) (remittals), 9 (1) (investigations by local authorities), 23 (1) (remand to care of local authorities) and 29 (1) (release or further detention of arrested children and young persons).

5. The age of 10 years is hereby specified for the purposes of section 34 (2) and (3) of the Act (which, in relation to proceedings against persons who have attained an age to be specified, provide for notice of the proceedings to be given to a probation officer and for the modification of a local authority's duty under section 9 to make investigations and provide the court with information).

THE CHILDREN AND YOUNG PERSONS ACT, 1969 (COMMENCEMENT NO. 3) (AMENDMENT) ORDER, 1970

[S.I. 1970 No. 1883]

1. This Order may be cited as the Children and Young Persons Act, 1969 (Commencement No. 3) (Amendment) Order, 1970.

2. In Schedule 3 to the Children and Young Persons Act, 1969 (Commencement No. 3) Order, 1970 (transitional provisions) there shall be inserted after paragraph 2 the following paragraph:—

"2A. Without prejudice to the operation of sub-paragraph (1) of paragraph 12 of Schedule 4 to the Act, nothing in any provision of the Act brought into force by this Order shall affect the operation of section 102 (1) (a) of the Act of 1933 in relation to such proceedings as are mentioned in sub-paragraph (2) of the said paragraph 12; but the said section 102 (1) (a) shall have effect in relation to such proceedings as if a care order were among the orders mentioned therein.".

THE APPROVED SCHOOLS AND CLASSIFYING CENTRES (CONTRIBUTIONS BY LOCAL AUTHORITIES) REGULATIONS, 1971

[S.I. 1971 No. 222]

1. These Regulations may be cited as the Approved Schools and Classifying Centres (Contributions by Local Authorities) Regulations, 1971 and shall come into operation on 1st April 1971.

2. The Interpretation Act, 1889 shall apply to the interpretation of these Regulations as it applies to the interpretation of an Act of Parliament.

3. The contributions which, under paragraph 8 (1) of Schedule 3 to the Children and Young Persons Act, 1969 (financial provisions in respect of approved schools and certain classifying centres), are payable by local authorities in respect of children in their care who are accommodated and maintained in the premises of an approved school or in a classifying centre falling within paragraph 4 (3) (a) of the said Schedule 3 to the managers of the school or, as the case may be, to the local authority providing the centre, shall be at the rate of £18·55 a week.

4. The Approved Schools and Classifying Centres (Contributions by Local Authorities) Regulations, 1970 are hereby revoked.

THE SOCIAL WORK (SCOTLAND) ACT, 1968 (COMMENCEMENT No. 5) ORDER, 1971

[S.I. 1971 No. 184 (C. 1) (S. 20)]

1. This order may be cited as the Social Work (Scotland) Act, 1968 (Commencement No. 5) Order, 1971.

2. The provisions of the Social Work (Scotland) Act, 1968 (hereinafter referred to as "the Act") specified in Schedules 1 and 2 to this order shall come into operation on the dates and to the extent specified therein.

3. The transitional provisions contained in Schedule 3 to this order shall have effect in connection with the provisions brought into force by this order which are referred to in that Schedule.

SCHEDULE 1
PROVISIONS COMING INTO FORCE ON 1ST MARCH 1971

Provisions of the Act	Subject matter of provisions
Paragraph 4 of Schedule 7	Transitional provisions relating to certain court orders.

SCHEDULE 2
PROVISIONS COMING INTO FORCE ON 15TH APRIL 1971

Provisions of the Act	Subject matter of provisions
Section 1 (5)	Transfer of functions from education authorities to local authorities.
Section 30	Definition of child and parent for Part III.
Section 31	Restriction on prosecution of children for offences.
Section 32	Children in need of compulsory measures of care.
Section 34 (1) and (2)	Children's hearings.
Section 35 (1) to (3)	Provisions as to privacy of children's hearings.
Section 37	Reports of cases of children who may require compulsory measures of care and the interim detention of such children in places of safety.
Section 38	Initial investigation of cases by reporter.
Section 39	Action on initial investigation by reporter.
Section 40	Attendance of child at children's hearing.
Section 41	Attendance of parent at children's hearing.
Section 42	Conduct of children's hearing and application to sheriff for findings.
Section 43	Discharge of referral and power of children's hearing to order further investigation after consideration of the facts.
Section 44	Disposal of case by children's hearing other than by discharge of referral.
Section 46	Children to whom Part IV of the Mental Health (Scotland) Act, 1960 may apply.
Section 47	Duration of supervision requirements and their variation.
Section 48	Review of requirement of children's hearing.

Provisions of the Act	Subject matter of provisions
Section 49	Appeal against decision of a children's hearing.
Section 50	Appeal to Court of Session.
Section 51	Reconsideration by hearing after appeal, and subsequent appeal.
Section 52	Power of Secretary of State to terminate a supervision requirement.
Section 53	Legal aid in proceedings before the sheriff and any appeals to the Court of Session.
Section 54	Transfer of case to another children's hearing.
Section 55	Presumption and determination of age.
Section 56	Reference and remit of children's cases by courts to children's hearings.
Section 57	Reference and remit of cases of certain young persons by courts to children's hearings.
Section 58	Prohibition or publication of proceedings.
Part V (Sections 69 to 77)	Return and removal of children within United Kingdom.
Part VI (Sections 78 to 83)	Contributions in respect of children in care, etc.
Section 97 insofar as not already brought into operation.	Extension of certain provisions to England and Wales, Northern Ireland and the Channel Islands.
Schedule 2	Amendment of Part IV of the Children and Young Persons (Scotland) Act, 1937.
Schedule 4	Amendment of Legal Aid (Scotland) Act, 1967.
Paragraphs 2, 5, 6 and 7 of Schedule 7.	Transitional provisions.
Schedule 8 to the extent set out in Appendix A hereto.	Minor and consequential amendments.
Schedule 9 to the extent set out in Appendix B hereto.	Enactments repealed.

APPENDIX A TO SCHEDULE 2

Provision of Schedule 8	Enactment amended
Paragraph 1	Section 9 (4) of the Criminal Appeal (Scotland) Act, 1926.
Paragraph 6	Section 38 (3) of the Children and Young Persons (Scotland) Act, 1937.
Paragraph 7	Section 87 of the Children and Young Persons (Scotland) Act, 1937.
Paragraph 9	Section 103 of the Children and Young Persons (Scotland) Act, 1937.
Paragraph 10	Section 110 (1) of the Children and Young Persons (Scotland) Act, 1937.
Paragraph 25	Section 8 (1) of the Criminal Justice (Scotland) Act, 1949.
Paragraph 26	Section 9 (1) of the Criminal Justice (Scotland) Act, 1949.
Paragraph 27 insofar as not already brought into operation.	Section 10 of the Criminal Justice (Scotland) Act, 1949.
Paragraph 28	Section 28 of the Criminal Justice (Scotland) Act, 1949.
Paragraph 29	Section 30 (1) of the Criminal Justice (Scotland) Act, 1949.

Provision of Schedule 8	Enactment amended
Paragraph 30 insofar as not already brought into operation.	Section 78 (1) of the Criminal Justice (Scotland) Act, 1949.
Paragraph 32	Section 8 (1) of the Maintenance Orders Act, 1950.
Paragraph 33	Section 9 of the Maintenance Orders Act, 1950.
Paragraph 34	Section 16 (2) of the Maintenance Orders Act, 1950.
Paragraph 37 insofar as not already brought into operation.	Section 4 (3) of the Adoption Act, 1958.
Paragraph 39	Section 36 (2) of the Adoption Act, 1958.
Paragraph 55	Section 57 (3) of the Mental Health (Scotland) Act, 1960.
Paragraph 57	Section 66 (7) of the Mental Health (Scotland) Act, 1960.
Paragraph 58 insofar as not already brought into operation.	Section 72 (1) of the Mental Health (Scotland) Act, 1960.
Paragraph 59A	Section 32 (2) of the Criminal Justice Act, 1961.
Paragraph 61	Section 36 (3) of the Education (Scotland) Act, 1962.
Paragraph 62	Section 44 of the Education (Scotland) Act, 1962.
Paragraph 65	Section 85 (5) of the Education (Scotland) Act, 1962.
Paragraph 66	Section 141 (2) of the Education (Scotland) Act, 1962.
Paragraph 67	Section 145 of the Education (Scotland) Act, 1962.
Paragraph 68 insofar as not already brought into operation.	Section 55 of the Children and Young Persons Act, 1963.
Paragraph 69 (1)	Section 57 (2) of the Children and Young Persons Act, 1963.
Paragraph 70	Section 1 (4) of the Criminal Justice (Scotland) Act, 1963.
Paragraph 71	Section 7 (1) of the Criminal Justice (Scotland) Act, 1963.
Paragraph 72	Section 29 of the Criminal Justice (Scotland) Act, 1963.
Paragraph 74 (1) and (3)	Section 11 of the Family Allowances Act, 1965.

APPENDIX B TO SCHEDULE 2
(*Provisions of Schedule 9 to the Act*)

PART I

Chapter	Short title	Extent of Repeal
1 Edw. 8 & 1 Geo. 6 c. 37.	The Children and Young Persons (Scotland) Act, 1937.	In section 21 (2), the words from "may take" to the end of the subsection. In section 42 (1), the words "or is for any other reason brought before a court" and in subsection (2) the words "or taken to a place of safety" and the words "or the person by whom he is taken to the place of safety, as the case may be". In section 47 (1) the words "until he can be brought before a juvenile court", wherever occurring.

Chapter	Short title	Extent of Repeal
1 Edw. 8 & 1 Geo. 6 c. 37 —(cont.)	The Children and Young Persons (Scotland) Act, 1937—(cont.)	In section 49 (1) the words "either as being in need of care or protection or", the words "or otherwise", and the words "and for securing that proper provision is made for his education and training". Section 49 (2). Section 51. Section 53 (2) and (3). Section 59 (1) and in subsection (4), the words "under this section, or". Sections 60 and 61. In section 63 (3) the words "under the Probation of Offenders Act, 1907". Sections 65 and 66. Sections 68 and 86. In section 87 (2) and (4) the words "England or" wherever they occur, in subsection (5) the words "in relation to England, the Secretary of State, and" and subsection (6). Sections 88 to 95. Section 101 (5) and (6). Section 107 (1) (a) and (2). Section 109. In section 110 (1)— the following definitions— "Approved school" "Approved school order"; "Headmaster"; "In need of care or protection"; in the definition of "Justice" the words "(except in section 51 of this Act)"; and the definition of "Managers". In section 110, in subsection (3) (a) (ii) the words "and the juvenile court for any area" and subsection (3) (a) (iv). Section 111. Section 112. Schedule 2. Schedule 3.
11 & 12 Geo. 6 c. 43.	The Children Act, 1948.	Sections 5 and 6 (3) and (4) and Part III.
12, 13 & 14 Geo. 6 c. 94.	The Criminal Justice (Scotland) Act, 1949.	Section 5 (3). In section 28, subsection (2), and in subsection (3), the words "a remand home or" and the words "home or". Sections 50 and 51. Sections 69 to 73. Section 75 to the extent specified in Schedule 9 insofar as not already brought into operation.

Chapter	Short title	Extent of Repeal
12, 13 & 14 Geo. 6 c. 94 —(*cont.*)	The Criminal Justice (Scotland) Act, 1949—(*cont.*)	Section 78 (1) to the extent specified in Schedule 9 insofar as not already brought into operation.
14 Geo. 6 c. 37.	The Maintenance Orders Act, 1950.	Schedule 1, insofar as relating to the modification of the Children and Young Persons (Scotland) Act, 1937.
15 & 16 Geo. 6 & 1 Eliz. 2 c. 61.	The Prisons (Scotland) Act, 1952.	In section 32, in subsection (3), the words "who is not less than seventeen years of age", and subsection (4).
4 & 5 Eliz. 2 c. 24.	The Children and Young Persons Act, 1956.	The whole Act.
4 & 5 Eliz. 2 c. 50.	The Family Allowances and National Insurance Act, 1956	The whole Act.
6 & 7 Eliz. 2 c. 65.	The Children Act, 1958.	In section 2, in subsection (4) the words from "or by virtue of" to "of an approved school".
7 & 8 Eliz. 2 c. 5.	The Adoption Act, 1958.	Section 4 (3) (b). In section 11 (1), the words "or juvenile court". In section 15 (3), the words from "fit person by" to "care of a" and the words "fit person order or" and "as the case may be". In section 37 (3), the words "in an approved school or".
8 & 9 Eliz. 2 c. 61.	The Mental Health (Scotland) Act, 1960.	In section 10, in subsection (1), in paragraph (a), head (i), and at the end of head (ii) the word "or". Section 46 (a). In section 55 (10) the words from "including" to the word "school". Section 56. In section 57, in subsection 3 (b), the words "or young person"; and subsection (5). Section 69 (1) (b). Section 71. In section 72, the definitions of "approved school" and "remand home" and in the definition of "place of safety" the words "or young person" first occurring.
10 & 11 Eliz. 2 c. 47.	The Education (Scotland) Act, 1962.	Section 36 (4) and (5). Section 44 (3) and (4).
1963 c. 39.	The Criminal Justice (Scotland) Act, 1963.	In section 11, in subsection (2), the words from "if the offender" to the words "detention centre", and subsection (3) and (5). Part II. Schedule 2.

PART II

Chapter	Short title	Extent of Repeal
6 & 7 Eliz. 2 c. 65.	The Children Act, 1958.	In section 2 (4) the words from "or of" to "1937".
7 & 8 Eliz. 2 c. 72.	The Mental Health Act, 1959.	In section 10 (1), in sub-paragraph (a), head (ii). In section 50, sub-paragraph (b).
1963 c. 37.	The Children and Young Persons Act, 1963.	Sections 51 and 52.
1965 c. 53.	The Family Allowances Act, 1965.	In section 11 (2), the words "or the said Act of 1937".

SCHEDULE 3

TRANSITIONAL PROVISIONS

1.—(1) Paragraph 4 of Schedule 7 to the Act shall have effect as if there was included among the classes of children specified in sub-paragraph (1) of that paragraph any child who immediately before the commencement of Part III of the Act was subject to—

(a) an order transferring him to an approved school made under subsection (1) or subsection (3) of section 87 of the Children and Young Persons (Scotland) Act, 1937 (power to send children and young persons from England and Wales, Northern Ireland, Isle of Man and Channel Islands to approved schools in Scotland); or

(b) an order under paragraph 23 of Schedule 4 to the Children and Young Persons Act, 1969 (interim power to send persons subject to care orders from England and Wales to approved schools in Scotland); or

(c) an order made either under section 51 of the Children and Young Persons Act, 1963 (supervision of persons moving from England and Wales to Scotland) as originally enacted or under that section as amended by paragraphs 20 and 21 of Schedule 4 to the said Act of 1969,

and any reference in the said paragraph 4 to a child to whom that paragraph applies shall be construed accordingly.

(2) Sub-paragraph (2) of the said paragraph 4 shall have effect as if at the end of that sub-paragraph there were inserted the following words:—

"with the substitution for any reference to an approved school of a reference to an establishment which was immediately before the coming into operation of the said Part III an approved school, and with any other necessary modifications.".

2.—(1) Where by virtue of paragraph 5 of Schedule 7 to the Act a court exercises jurisdiction in respect of a child or young person charged with an offence before the commencement of Part III of the Act, the powers conferred on certain courts by sections 56 and 57 of the Act (which relate to the reference and remit of the cases of children and certain young persons by courts to children's hearings, being children and young persons charged with an offence after the said commencement) shall, subject to sub-paragraph (2) below, be available to and exercisable by the said court in relation to the said child or young person.

(2) In the case of any juvenile court constituted under section 51 of the Children and Young Persons (Scotland) Act, 1937, the provisions of sub-paragraph (1) above shall apply until such time as the Secretary of State makes a direction in relation to that court under sub-paragraph (2) of the said paragraph 5, and on any such direction being made any question arising from any remit or reference by the said court under section 56 or section 57 of the Act shall be dealt with by the sheriff having jurisdiction in the former area of that court as if the said remit or, as the case may be, the said reference had been made by him.

3. Where by virtue of paragraph 5 of Schedule 7 to the Act a sheriff exercises jurisdiction in respect of a child or young person charged with an offence before the commencement of Part III of the Act, the powers conferred on the sheriff by section 58A of the Children and Young Persons (Scotland) Act, 1937 set out in paragraph 16 of Schedule 2 to the Act (committal for residential training of children charged with an offence after the said commencement) shall be available to and exercisable by the said sheriff in relation to the said child or young person.

THE CHILDREN AND YOUNG PERSONS (DESIGNATION OF GUERNSEY ORDER) ORDER, 1971
[S.I. 1971 No. 348]

1. This Order may be cited as the Children and Young Persons (Designation of Guernsey Order) Order, 1971 and shall come into operation on 22nd March 1971.

2. A special care order within the meaning of the Children and Young Persons (Guernsey) Law, 1967, as amended by the Children and Young Persons (Amendment) (Guernsey) Law, 1971, being an order which satisfies the conditions set out in section 26 (1) of the Children and Young Persons Act, 1969 (transfers between England or Wales and the Channel Islands or Isle of Man), is hereby designated for the purposes of the said section 26.

THE CHILDREN AND YOUNG PERSONS (DEFINITION OF INDEPENDENT PERSONS) REGULATIONS, 1971
[S.I. 1971 No. 486]

1. These regulations may be cited as the Children and Young Persons (Definition of Independent Persons) Regulations, 1971 and shall come into operation on 1st April 1971.

2.—(1) In these regulations "the Act" means the Children and Young Persons Act, 1969.

(2) The Interpretation Act, 1889, shall apply to the interpretation of these regulations as it applies to the interpretation of an Act of Parliament.

3. For the purposes of section 24 (5) of the Act a local authority to whose care a person is committed by a care order may appoint as an independent person to be a visitor to that person any person other than the following:

(1) Any person having any connection with that authority by reason of

    (a) being a member, or a member of a committee or sub-committee, whether elected or co-opted; or
    (b) being an officer or person appointed; or
    (c) holding a paid office or appointment for profit; or
    (d) being employed under a contract to supply goods or services to that authority; or
    (e) being a spouse of any such person.

(2) Any person having a connection with a community home managed by a local authority under the provisions of the Act by reason of

    (a) being a member, or a member of a social services committee or sub-committee, whether elected or co-opted; or
    (b) being an officer or person appointed to perform services for the benefit of the authority in respect of the functions of its social services committee; or

(c) holding a paid office or appointment for profit, the object of which is the performance of services for the benefit of the authority in respect of the functions of its social services committee; or

(d) providing services, whether paid or unpaid, in or in connection with any community home; or

(e) being employed under a contract to supply goods or services to a community home managed by the authority; or

(f) being the spouse of any such person.

(3) Any person having any connection with a community home provided by a voluntary organisation under the provisions of the Act by reason of

(a) being a member of any body of management of such a voluntary organisation; or

(b) holding any paid office or appointment for profit which is in the gift of any such organisation, the object of which is the performance of services for the benefit of that organisation in respect of a community home; or

(c) providing services, whether paid or unpaid, in or in connection with any community home provided by such an organisation; or

(d) being a member of a body of management or any community home constituted under section 39 of the Act; or

(e) being employed under a contract to supply goods or services to a community home managed by such an organisation; or

(f) being a spouse of any such person.

THE SOCIAL WORK (SCOTLAND) ACT, 1968 (COMMENCEMENT NO. 6) ORDER, 1971
[S.I. 1971 No. 556 (C. 14) (S. 78)]

1. This order may be cited as the Social Work (Scotland) Act, 1968 (Commencement No. 6) Order, 1971.

2. Section 14 (home help and laundry facilities) of the Social Work (Scotland) Act, 1968 and the entry in Schedule 9 of the said Act relating to the repeal of section 13 of the Health Services and Public Health Act, 1968, shall come into operation on 1st April 1971.

THE CHILDREN AND YOUNG PERSONS ACT, 1969 (COMMENCEMENT NO. 4) ORDER, 1971
[S.I. 1971 No. 588 (C. 15)]

Citation
1. This Order may be cited as the Children and Young Persons Act, 1969 (Commencement No. 4) Order, 1971.

Interpretation
2. In this Order "the Act" means the Children and Young Persons Act, 1969.

Day appointed for coming into force of certain provisions of the Act
3. The provisions of Schedule 5 to the Act specified in column 1 of the Schedule to this Order (which relate to the matters specified in column 2 thereof and which, in their application to England and Wales, were brought

into force on 1st December 1969) and, so far as it relates to those provisions, section 72 (3) thereof, shall, in their application to Scotland, come into force on 15th April 1971.

SCHEDULE
PROVISIONS OF SCHEDULE 5 COMING INTO FORCE ON 15TH APRIL 1971

Provisions of Schedule 5	Subject matter of provisions
In paragraph 54 (2), the following provision:— "for the words from "5 (1)" to "1956" there shall be substitued the words "13 (2) of the Children Act 1948"".	Amendment of section 11 (2) of the Family Allowances Act, 1965.
Paragraph 54 (3).	Amendment of section 11 (3) of the Family Allowances Act, 1965.

THE CHILDREN AND YOUNG PERSONS (TERMINATION OF TRANSITIONAL PROVISIONS) ORDER, 1971
[S.I. 1971 No. 589]

1. This Order may be cited as the Children and Young Persons (Termination of Transitional Provisions) Order, 1971 and shall come into operation on 15th April 1971.

2. The day specified for the purposes of section 72 (2) of the Children and Young Persons Act, 1969 (transitional provisions) shall be 15th April 1971, being the day on and after which the transitional provisions set out in Part II of Schedule 4 to the said Act of 1969 will, in the opinion of the Secretary of State, be unnecessary in consequence of the coming into force of provisions of the Social Work (Scotland) Act, 1968.

THE CROWN COURT RULES, 1971
[S.I. 1971 No. 1292]

General note.—The time limit for appeal is now 21 days and not 14 as under the repealed s. 84 Magistrates' Courts Act, 1952. (There are exceptions in Sched. I.) As regards the qualifications of justices it should be noted that r. 3 (4) speaks of an appeal or committal from a *juvenile court* and the person appealing or committed need not therefore be a juvenile at the time of the proceedings before the Crown Court.

ARRANGEMENT OF RULES
PART I
1–2. [*Not reproduced.*]

PART II
JUSTICES AS JUDGES OF CROWN COURT

Part II
Justices as Judges of Crown Court

Number and qualification of justices

3.—(1) Subject to the provisions of Rule 4 and to any directions under section 5 (5) of the Courts Act, 1971, on any proceedings to which a subsequent paragraph of this Rule applies, the number of justices sitting to hear the proceedings and the qualification of those justices shall be as specified in that paragraph.

(2) On the hearing of an appeal against a decision of licensing justices under the Licensing Act, 1964, the Crown Court shall consist of a judge sitting with four justices, each of whom is a member of a licensing committee appointed under Schedule 1 to that Act and two (but not more than two) of whom are justices for the petty sessions area comprising the premises to which the appeal relates.

(3) On the hearing of an appeal against a decision of any authority under the Betting, Gaming and Lotteries Act, 1963, or the Gaming Act, 1968, the Crown Court shall consist of a judge sitting with four justices, two (but not more than two) of whom are justices for the petty sessions area comprising the premises to which the appeal relates.

(4) On the hearing of an appeal from a juvenile court or of proceedings on committal by a juvenile court to the Crown Court under section 28 of the Magistrates' Courts Act, 1952, or section 67 of the Mental Health Act, 1959, the Crown Court shall consist of a judge sitting with two justices each of whom is a member of a juvenile court panel who are chosen so that the Court shall include a man and a woman.

Dispensations for special circumstances

4.—(1) The Crown Court may enter on any appeal or any proceedings on committal to the Court for sentence notwithstanding that the Court is not constituted as required by section 5 (1) of the Courts Act, 1971, or Rule 3 if it appears to the judge that the Court could not be so constituted without unreasonable delay and the Court includes—

    (a) in a case to which paragraph (2) of that Rule applies, at least two justices each of whom is a member of a committee specified in that paragraph, provided that the Court includes a justice for the petty sessions area so specified and a justice for some other area;

    (b) in a case to which paragraph (3) of that Rule applies, at least two justices including a justice for the petty sessions area so specified and a justice for some other area;

    (c) in a case to which paragraph (4) of that Rule applies, one justice who is a member of a juvenile court panel;

    (d) in any other case, one justice:

Provided that the judge may sit without one or both of the justices required by sub-paragraphs (a) and (b) above if the parties appearing at the hearing of the appeal agree.

(2) The Crown Court may at any stage continue with any proceedings with a Court from which any one or more of the justices initially comprising the Court has withdrawn, or is absent for any reason.

Disqualifications

5. A justice of the peace shall not sit in the Crown Court on the hearing of an appeal in a matter on which he adjudicated or of proceedings on committal of a person to the Court for sentence under section 28 or 29 of the Magistrates' Courts Act, 1952 by a court of which he was a member.

PART III

APPEALS TO THE CROWN COURT

Application of Part III

6.—(1) Subject to the following provisions of this Rule, this Part of these Rules shall apply to every appeal which by or under any enactment lies to the Crown Court from any court, tribunal or person.

(2) This Part of these Rules shall have effect subject to the provisions of the enactments listed in Part I of Schedule 1 (being enactments which make special procedural provisions in respect of certain appeals) which enactments shall be amended in accordance with Part II of that Schedule.

Notice of appeal

7.—(1) An appeal shall be commenced by the appellant's giving notice of appeal in accordance with the following provisions of this Rule.

(2) The notice required by the preceding paragraph shall be in writing and shall be given—

    (a) in a case where the appeal is against a decision of a magistrates' court, to the clerk of the magistrates' court;

    (b) in any other case, to the appropriate officer of the Crown Court; and

    (c) in any case, to any other party to the appeal.

(3) Notice of appeal shall be given within 21 days after the day on which the decision appealed against is given and, in the case of an appeal arising out of a conviction by a magistrates' court, shall state whether the appeal is against conviction or sentence or both.

(4) For the purposes of the preceding paragraph, the day on which a decision of a magistrates' court is given shall, where the court has adjourned the trial

of an information after conviction, be the day on which the court sentences or otherwise deals with the offender.

(5) The time for giving notice of appeal may be extended, either before or after it expires, by the Crown Court, on an application made in accordance with paragraph (6).

(6) An application for an extension of time shall be made in writing, specifying the grounds of the application and sent to the appropriate officer of the Crown Court.

(7) Where the Crown Court extends the time for giving notice of appeal, the appropriate officer of the Crown Court shall give notice of the extension to the appellant and, in the case of an appeal from the decision of a magistrates' court, to the clerk of that court; and the appellant shall give notice of the extension to any other party to the appeal.

Entry of appeal and notice of hearing
8. On receiving notice of appeal, the appropriate officer of the Crown Court shall enter the appeal and give notice of the time and place of the hearing to the appellant, any other party to the appeal and, where the appeal is against a decision of a magistrates' court, to the clerk of the magistrates' court.

Abandonment of appeal
9.—(1) Without prejudice to the power of the Crown Court to give leave for an appeal to be abandoned, an appellant may abandon an appeal by giving notice in writing, in accordance with the following provisions of this Rule, not later than the third day before the day fixed for hearing the appeal.

(2) The notice required by the preceding paragraph shall be given—

(a) in a case where the appeal is against a decision of a magistrates' court, to the clerk of the magistrates' court;
(b) in the case of an appeal under section 21 of the Licensing Act, 1964, to the clerk to the licensing justices;
(c) in any other case, to the appropriate officer of the Crown Court; and
(d) in any case, to any other party to the appeal;

and, in the case of an appeal mentioned in sub-paragraph (a) or (b), the appellant shall send a copy of the notice to the appropriate officer of the Crown Court.

(3) For the purposes of determining whether notice of abandonment was given in time there shall be disregarded any Saturday, Sunday and any day which is, or is to be observed as, a bank holiday, or a holiday under the Bank Holidays Act, 1871, or the Holidays Extension Act, 1875, in England and Wales.

PART V

MISCELLANEOUS

Applications to Crown Court for bail
17.—(1) This Rule applies where an application to the Crown Court for bail is made otherwise than during the hearing of proceedings in the Crown Court.

(2) Subject to paragraph (8), notice in writing of intention to apply to the Crown Court for bail shall be given to the prosecutor and to the Director of Public Prosecutions, if the prosecution is being carried on by him, at least 24 hours before the application is made.

(3) On receiving notice under paragraph (2), the prosecutor or Director of Public Prosecutions shall—

(a) notify the appropriate officer of the Crown Court and the applicant that he wishes to be represented at the hearing of the application; or

(b) notify the appropriate officer and the applicant that he does not oppose the application; or

(c) give to the appropriate officer, for the consideration of the Crown Court, a written statement of his reasons for opposing the application, at the same time sending a copy of the statement to the applicant.

(4) A notice under paragraph (2) shall be in the form prescribed in Schedule 2 or a form to the like effect, and the applicant shall give a copy of the notice to the appropriate officer of the Crown Court.

(5) The applicant shall not be entitled to be present on the hearing of his application unless the Crown Court gives him leave to be present.

(6) Where a person who desires to apply for bail has not been able to instruct a solicitor to apply on his behalf under the preceding paragraphs of this Rule, he may give notice in writing to the Crown Court of his desire to apply for bail, requesting that the Official Solicitor shall act for him in the application, and the Court may, if it thinks fit, assign the Official Solicitor to act for the applicant accordingly.

(7) Where the Official Solicitor has been so assigned the Crown Court may, if it thinks fit, dispense with the requirements of paragraph (2) and deal with the application in a summary manner.

Supplementary provisions about bail

18.—(1) Every applicant to the Crown Court for bail shall inform the Court of any earlier application to the High Court or the Crown Court for bail in the course of the same proceedings.

(2) On hearing an application for bail the Crown Court may order that the applicant shall be released from custody on entering into a recogniasnce, with or without sureties, or giving other security before—

(a) an officer of the Crown Court;

(b) a justice; or

(c) any other person authorised by virtue of section 95 (1) of the Magistrates' Courts Act, 1952, to take a recognisance where a magistrates' court having power to take the recognisance has, instead of taking it, fixed the amount in which the principal and his sureties, if any, are to be bound.

(3) A person who, in pursuance of an order made by the Crown Court under this Rule, proposes to enter into a recognisance or give other security before a justice or other person must, unless the Crown Court otherwise directs, give notice to the prosecutor at least 24 hours before he enters into the recognisance or gives security as aforesaid.

(4) Where, in pursuance of an order of the Crown Court, a recognisance is entered into or other security given before a justice or other person, it shall be his duty to cause the recognisance or, as the case may be, a statement of the other security given, to be transmitted forthwith to the appropriate officer of the Crown Court and, unless the recognisance is entered into at a prison, a copy of such recognisance or statement shall at the same time be sent to the governor of the prison in which the applicant is detained.

Time limits for beginning of trials

19. The periods prescribed for the purposes of paragraphs (a) and (b) of section 7 (4) of the Courts Act, 1971, shall be 14 days and 8 weeks respectively and accordingly the trial of a person committed by a magistrates' court—

    (a) shall not begin until the expiration of 14 days beginning with the date of his committal except with his consent and the consent of the prosecution, and

    (b) shall, unless the Crown Court has otherwise ordered, begin not later than the expiration of 8 weeks beginning with the date of his committal.

Appeal against refusal to excuse from jury service

20.—(1) A person summoned under Part V of the Courts Act, 1971, for jury service may appeal in accordance with the provisions of this Rule against any refusal of the appropriate officer to excuse him under section 34 (2) of that Act.

(2) Subject to paragraph (3), an appeal under this Rule shall be heard by the Crown Court.

(3) Where the appellant is summoned under the said Part V to attend before the High Court or a county court and the appeal has not been decided by the Crown Court before the day on which the appellant is required by the summons to attend, the appeal shall be heard by the court before which he is summoned to attend.

(4) An appeal under this Rule shall be commenced by the appellant's giving notice of appeal to the appropriate officer of the Crown Court and such notice shall be in writing and shall specify the matters upon which the appellant relies as providing good reason why he should be excused from attending in pursuance of the summons.

(5) The Court shall not dismiss an appeal under this Rule unless the appellant has been given an opportunity of making representations.

(6) Where an appeal under this Rule is decided in the absence of the appellant, the appropriate officer of the Crown Court shall notify him of the decision without delay.

Application to Crown Court to state case

21.—(1) An application under section 10 (3) of the Courts Act, 1971, to the Crown Court to state a case for the opinion of the High Court shall be made in writing to the appropriate officer of the Crown Court within 14 days after the date of the decision in respect of which the application is made.

(2) The time for making such an application may be extended, either before or after it expires, by the Crown Court.

(3) If the Crown Court considers that the application is frivolous, it may refuse to state a case, and shall in that case, if the applicant so requires, cause a certificate stating the reasons for the refusal to be given to him.

(4) If the Crown Court so orders, the applicant shall, before the case is stated and delivered to him, enter before an officer of the Crown Court into a recognisance, with or without sureties and in such sum as the Crown Court considers proper, having regard to the means of the applicant, conditioned to prosecute the appeal without delay.

Business in chambers

22.—(1) The jurisdiction of the Crown Court specified in the following paragraph may be exercised by a judge of the Crown Court sitting in chambers.

(2) The said jurisdiction is—

(a) hearing applications for bail;

(b) issuing a summons or warrant;

(c) hearing any application relating to procedural matters preliminary or incidental to proceedings in the Crown Court, including applications relating to legal aid but not including an application under section 7 (3) of the Courts Act, 1971 (application for direction varying the place of trial on indictment);

(d) jurisdiction under Rule 7 (7), 20 or 21.

Service of documents

23. Any notice or other document which is required by these Rules to be given to any person may be served personally on that person or sent to him by post at his usual or last known residence or place of business in England or Wales or, in the case of a company, at the company's registered office in England or Wales.

Repeal of enactments

24. The enactments specified in Schedule 3 (being enactments about appeals to the Crown Court or costs between party and party in the Crown Court which are superseded by the provisions of these Rules) are hereby repealed to the extent specified in the third column of that Schedule in their application to England and Wales.

SCHEDULE 1   Rule 6

ENACTMENTS RELATING TO APPEALS TO CROWN COURT

PART I

ENACTMENTS MAKING SPECIAL PROVISIONS ABOUT PROCEDURE ON APPEALS TO CROWN COURT

Chapter	Act	Section or Schedule
1930 c. 44.	The Land Drainage Act, 1930	Section 30.
1952 c. 68.	The Cinematograph Act, 1952	Section 6.
1957 c. 56.	The Housing Act, 1957	Section 14 (5).
1963 c. 2.	The Betting, Gaming and Lotteries Act, 1963	Schedule 1, paragraphs 21, 28. Schedule 2, paragraph 6. Schedule 3, paragraph 13. Schedule 6, paragraph 8. Schedule 7, paragraph 5.
1963 c. 33.	The London Government Act, 1963	Schedule 12, paragraph 19 (4).
1964 c. 26.	The Licensing Act, 1964	Sections 22, 50, 146, 154.
1967 c. 9.	The General Rate Act, 1967	Section 7 (1).
1968 c. 27.	The Firearms Act, 1968	Section 44. Schedule 5 Part II.
1968 c. 54.	The Theatres Act, 1968	Section 14 (4).
1968 c. 65.	The Gaming Act, 1968	Schedule 2, paragraphs 29, 31, 45, 46, 50, 61. Schedule 3, paragraphs 12, 13, 15, 16. Schedule 7, paragraphs 11, 20. Schedule 9, paragraph 11.
1969 c. 54.	The Children and Young Persons Act, 1969	Section 21 (5).

Part II

Amendments

1. In section 14 (5) of the Housing Act, 1957 for the words "one month" there shall be substituted the words "twenty-one days".

2.—(1) In paragraph 21 (1) of Schedule 1 to the Betting, Gaming and Lotteries Act, 1963, for the words "fourteen days" there shall be substituted the words "twenty-one days".

(2) In paragraph 6 of Schedule 2 to that Act for the words "and he may appeal" to the end of the paragraph there shall be substituted the words "and within twenty-one days of being so notified he may by notice to the appropriate officer of the Crown Court and to the registering authority appeal against the refusal or revocation to the Crown Court".

(3) In paragraph 13 (2) of Schedule 3 to that Act, for the words from "to the next" to the end of the paragraph there shall be substituted the words "to the Crown Court, and such appeal shall be commenced by giving notice to the appropriate officer of the Crown Court and to the licensing authority within twenty-one days of the holder's being notified of the revocation by the licensing authority".

(4) In paragraph 5 of Schedule 7 to that Act, for the words from "to the next practicable" to the end of the paragraph there shall be substituted the words "to the Crown Court and such appeal shall be commenced by giving notice to the appropriate officer of the Crown Court and to the local authority within twenty-one days of the day on which notice of the refusal or revocation is given to the society".

3. In section 22 (1) of the Licensing Act, 1964, for the words "fourteen days" there shall be substituted the words "twenty-one days".

4. In section 7 (1) of the General Rate Act, 1967, for the words "to the next practicable court of quarter sessions" there shall be substituted the words "to the Crown Court and such appeal shall be commenced by giving notice to the appropriate officer of the Crown Court within twenty-one days of—

    (a) the date of publication of the rate under section 4 of this Act; or
    (b) the act or thing done by the rating authority; or
    (c) the giving of notice for the purposes of this section to the rating authority as to the neglect or omission concerned,

whichever is the latest".

5. In the Gaming Act, 1968, for the words "fourteen days" where they occur in paragraph 29 (1) of Schedule 2, paragraphs 12 and 15 of Schedule 3 and paragraphs 11 and 20 of Schedule 7 there shall be substituted the words "twenty-one days".

6. In section 3 (8) of the Children and Young Persons Act, 1969, for the words "fourteen days" there shall be substituted the words "twenty-one days".

Rule 17 (4)   SCHEDULE 2

Form of Notice of Application for Bail
In the Crown Court

Application for Bail

Take notice that an application for bail will be made to the Crown Court at
        on   at   a.m./p.m.
(*see note below*) on behalf of

Full name: Forenames   Surname
(block letters)

Crown Court reference number:—

place of detention:—
(if detained in prison,
give prison number)

Particulars of proceedings
during which applicant was
committed to custody:—

Details of any relevant previous
application for bail:—

Grounds of application for bail.
(State fully facts relied upon and list
previous convictions (if any). Give
details of any proposed sureties and
answer   any   objections   raised
previously.):—

Notes
     The appropriate officer of the Crown Court should be consulted about the time and place
of the hearing before this Notice is sent to the prosecutor. A copy of this Notice should be
sent to the Crown Court.

SCHEDULE 3   Rule 24
REPEAL OF ENACTMENTS

Chapter	Short title	Extent of repeal
35 & 36 Vict. c. 93.	The Pawnbrokers Act, 1872	In section 52 the words from "for the county or place" to the end of the section.
53 & 54 Vict. c. 59.	The Public Health Acts Amendment Act, 1890.	In section 7 the words "in manner provided by the Summary Jurisdiction Acts".
61 & 62 Vict. c. 16.	The Canals Protection (London) Act, 1898.	In section 5 the words "in manner provided by the Summary Jurisdiction Acts".
7 Edw. 7 c. 53.	The Public Health Acts (Amendment) Act, 1907.	In section 7 the words "in manner provided by the Summary Jurisdiction Acts".
15 & 16 Geo. 5 c. 38.	The Performing Animals (Regulation) Act, 1925.	In section 2 (2) the words "in manner provided by the Summary Jurisdiction Acts".
15 & 16 Geo. 5 c. 50.	The Theatrical Employers Registration Act, 1925.	In section 6 (1) the words "in the manner prescribed by the Summary Jurisdiction Acts".
17 & 18 Geo. 5 c. 21.	The Moneylenders Act, 1927.	In section 2 (7) the words from "in manner" to the end of the subsection.
23 & 24 Geo. 5 c. 25.	The Pharmacy and Poisons Act, 1933.	In section 21 (2) the words "in accordance with rules made for the purposes of this section by the Secretary of State".

Chapter	Short title	Extent of repeal
7 & 8 Eliz. 2 c. 25.	The Highways Act, 1959.	Section 276.
1963 c. 2.	The Betting, Gaming and Lotteries Act, 1963.	In Schedule 1, paragraph 22 and in paragraph 28 (2) the words "22 or as the case may be".
1964 c. 26.	The Licensing Act, 1964.	In section 22 (3) the words from "but no order" to the end of the subsection. Section 24. In section 25 (1) the words "under section 24 (2) of this Act".
1968 c. 27.	The Firearms Act, 1968.	In Schedule 5, in paragraph 4 the words "and if he does so" to the end of the paragraph, and paragraphs 6 and 8.
1968 c. 65.	The Gaming Act, 1968.	In Schedule 2, paragraph 30 (1) and in paragraph 30 (2) the words "under the preceding sub-paragraph". In Schedule 9, paragraph 14 (1) and in paragraph 14 (2) the words "under the preceding sub-paragraph".

PRACTICE DIRECTION

Directions given on October 14, 1971, by the Lord Chief Justice with the concurrence of the Lord Chancellor under ss. 4 (5) and 5 (4) of the Courts Act, 1971, and Sched. 10 to the Act.

Classification of offences

1. For the purposes of trial in the Crown Court, offences are to be classified as follows:

Class 1
The following offences, which are to be tried by a High Court judge:

(1) Any offences for which a person may be sentenced to death.
(2) Misprision of treason and treason felony.
(3) Murder.
(4) Genocide.
(5) An offence under the Official Secrets Act, 1911, s. 1.
(6) Incitement, attempt or conspiracy to commit any of the above offences.

Class 2
The following offences, which are to be tried by a High Court judge unless a particular case is released by or on the authority of a presiding judge, that is to say, a High Court judge assigned to have special responsibility for a particular circuit: Manslaughter; infanticide; child destruction; abortion (Offences against the Person Act, 1861, s. 58); rape; sexual intercourse with girl under 13; incest with girl under 13; sedition; an offence under the Geneva Conventions Act, 1957, s. 1; mutiny; piracy; incitement, attempt or conspiracy to commit any of the above offences.

Class 3

All indictable offences other than those in classes 1, 2 and 4. They may be listed for trial by a High Court judge or by a circuit judge or recorder.

Class 4

(1) All offences which may, in appropriate circumstances, be tried either on indictment or summarily. They include—

- (a) indictable offences which may be tried summarily (Magistrates' Courts Act, 1952, s. 19, Sched. 1);
- (b) offences which are both indictable and summary (Magistrates' Courts Act, 1952, s. 18);
- (c) offences punishable on summary conviction with more than three months' imprisonment where the accused may claim to be tried on indictment (Magistrates' Courts Act, 1952, s. 25).

(2) Conspiracy to commit any of the above offences.

(3) The following offences:

- (a) Causing death by reckless or dangerous driving (Road Traffic Act, 1960, s. 1).
- (b) Wounding or causing grievous bodily harm with intent (Offences Against the Person Act, 1861, s. 18).
- (c) Burglary (Theft Act, 1968, s. 9) in a dwelling in circumstances set out in Sched. 1, para. 11 (c) of the Magistrates' Courts Act, 1952.
- (d) Robbery, or assault with intent to rob (Theft Act, 1968, s. 8).
- (e) Offences under Forgery Act, 1913 (being offences under that Act which are not triable summarily, *i.e.*, other than offences under s. 2 (2) (a) or s. 7 where the value of the property does not exceed £100).
- (f) Incitement, attempt or conspiracy to commit any of the above offences.
- (g) Conspiracy to commit an offence which is in no circumstances triable on indictment or an act which is not an offence.

(4) Any offence in class 3, if included in class 4 in accordance with directions, which may be either general or particular, given by a presiding judge or on his authority.

When tried on indictment offences in class 4 may be tried by a High Court judge, circuit judge or recorder but will normally be listed for trial by a circuit judge or recorder.

Committals for trial

2. (i) A magistrates' court, on committing a person for trial under the Magistrates' Courts Act, 1952, s. 7 (1), shall, if the offence, or any of the offences is included in classes 1 to 3, specify the most convenient location of the Crown Court where a High Court judge regularly sits, and if the offence is in class 4 shall, subject to para. 2 (ii), specify the most convenient location of the Crown Court.

(ii) If in the view of the justices, when committing a person for trial for an offence in class 4, the case should be tried by a High Court judge, they shall indicate that view, giving reasons, in a notice to be included with the papers sent to the Crown Court, and shall commit to the most convenient location of the Crown Court where a High Court judge regularly sits.

The following considerations should influence the justices in favour of trial by a High Court judge, namely where:—

- (i) the case involves death or serious risk to life (excluding cases of dangerous driving, or causing death by dangerous driving, having no aggravating features);

    (ii) widespread public concern is involved;

    (iii) the case involves violence of a serious nature;

    (iv) the offence involves dishonesty in respect of a substantial sum of money;

    (v) the accused holds a public position or is a professional or other person owing a duty to the public;

    (vi) the circumstances are of unusual gravity in some respect other than those indicated above;

    (vii) a novel or difficult issue of law is likely to be involved, or a prosecution for the offence is rare or novel.

3. In selecting the most convenient location of the Crown Court, the justices shall have regard to the considerations referred to in paragraphs (a) and (b) of section 7 (1) of the Courts Act, 1971 and to the location or locations of the Crown Court designated by a Presiding judge as the location or locations to which cases should normally be committed from their petty sessions area.

4. Where on one occasion a person is committed in respect of a number of offences, all the committals shall be to the same location of the Crown Court and that location shall be one where a High Court judge regularly sits if such a location is appropriate for any of the offences.

Committals for sentence or to be dealt with

5. Where a probation order or order for conditional discharge has been made, or suspended sentence passed, and the offender is committed to be dealt with for the original offence or in respect of the suspended sentence, he shall be committed in accordance with paras. 6 to 9 below.

6. If the order was made or the sentence was passed by the Crown Court, he shall be committed to the location of the Crown Court where the order was made or suspended sentence passed, unless it is inconvenient or impracticable to do so.

7. If he is not so committed and the order was made by a High Court judge or, before the appointed day, by a court of assize, he shall be committed to the most convenient location of the Crown Court where a High Court judge regularly sits.

8. In all other cases where a person is committed for sentence or to be dealt with he shall be committed to the most convenient location of the Crown Court.

9. In selecting the most convenient location of the Crown Court, the justices shall have regard to the location or locations of the Crown Court designated by a Presiding judge as the location or locations to which cases should normally be committed from their petty sessions area.

Appeals, etc. under Crown Court's original civil jurisdiction

10. The hearing of an appeal or of proceedings under the civil jurisdiction of the Crown Court, shall take place at the location of the Crown Court designated by a Presiding judge as the appropriate location for such proceedings originating in the areas concerned.

Removal of driving disqualification

11. Application should be made to the location of the Crown Court where the order of disqualification was made, or, if it was made by a court of assize or quarter sessions, to the location of the Crown Court which is most convenient to the place where the order was made.

Allocation of proceedings to Crown Court

12. (i) Class 1 and class 2 offences shall be tried by a High Court judge, unless in the case of a class 2 offence the case is released by or under the authority of a presiding judge having regard to all the circumstances. Where the prosecution of such an offence has been undertaken by the Director of Public Prosecutions, the Director's views shall, where practicable, be obtained before the case is considered for release.

(ii) Class 3 offences shall be listed for trial by a High Court judge unless, after having regard to the considerations set out in paragraph 2 above, the officer responsible for listing decides that the case should be listed for trial by a circuit judge or recorder. Such a decision shall only be taken after consultation with a Presiding judge (or a judge acting for him) or in accordance with directions, which may be either general or particular, given by a presiding judge.

(iii) Class 4 offences shall be listed for trial by a circuit judge or recorder unless, bearing in mind the considerations set out in para. 2 above and the views, if any, put forward by justices, the officer responsible for listing decides that the case should be tried by a High Court judge. Such a decision shall only be taken after consultation with a presiding judge (or a judge acting for him) or in accordance with directions, either general or particular, given by a presiding judge.

(iv) Where a probation order, case order or order for conditional discharge has been made, or a suspended sentence passed, by a High Court judge, and the offender is committed to or brought before the Crown Court, his case should be listed for hearing by a High Court judge unless, in accordance with the decision of the officer responsible for listing, his case is listed for hearing by a circuit judge or recorder. Such a decision shall only be taken after consultation with a presiding judge (or a judge acting for him) or in accordance with directions, either general or particular, given by a presiding judge.

(v) All other proceedings before the Crown Court (excluding an application under s. 7 (3) of the Courts Act, 1971 for a direction, or further direction, varying the place of trial) including appeals, committals for sentence or to be dealt with, and proceedings under the original civil jurisdiction of the Crown Court shall normally be listed for hearing by a court presided over by a circuit judge or recorder.

Allocation of proceedings to lay justices

13. In addition to the classes of case specified in the Courts Act, 1971, s. 5 (1) (appeals and proceedings on committals for sentence) any other proceedings which, in accordance with these directions, are listed for hearing by a circuit judge or recorder are suitable for allocation to a court comprising justices of the peace.

Transfer between locations of Crown Court

14. Without prejudice to the provisions of the Courts Act, 1971, ss. 7 (2) and (3) (transfer of trials on indictment), the Crown Court may give directions for the transfer from one location of the Crown Court to another of:—

(i) appeals;
(ii) proceedings on committal for sentence, or to be dealt with;
(iii) proceedings under the original civil jurisdiction of the Crown Court where this appears desirable for the expediting of the hearing or the convenience of the parties.

Such directions may be given in a particular case by an officer of the Crown Court, or generally, in relation to a class or classes of case, by the presiding judge or a judge acting on his behalf.

If dissatisfied with such directions given by an officer of the Crown Court, any party to the proceedings may apply to a judge of the Crown Court who may hear the application in chambers.

Application to Crown Court for bail

15. (i) Where a person gives notice in writing to the Crown Court that he wishes to apply for bail, and requests that the Official Solicitor shall act for him in the application, the application shall be heard by a Crown Court judge in London.

(ii) All other applications shall be heard at the location of the Crown Court where the proceedings in respect of which the application for bail arises, took place or are due to take place.

Transitional arrangements

16. Without prejudice to the provisions of the Courts Act, 1971, Sched. 10, Pt. 1, para. 2 (1) (part heard proceedings to be continued and disposed of as if the Act had not been passed) any cases before a court of Assize or quarter sessions which are not begun before the appointed day shall be heard by the Crown Court in accordance with paragraph 12 of these directions and shall where necessary be transferred accordingly.

NOTE

In para. 2 (i) immediately before the word "shall" in the first place where it occurs, insert the words "or order the Criminal Justice Act, 1967, s. 1 (Directions of the Lord Chief Justice, November 24, 1971).

THE CHILDREN AND YOUNG PERSONS (DESIGNATION OF ISLE OF MAN ORDER) ORDER, 1971

[S. I. 1971 No. 1288]

1. This Order may be cited as the Children and Young Persons (Designation of Isle of Man Order) Order, 1971 and shall come into operation on 16th August 1971.

2. A care order made for the purpose of section 2 of the Children and Young Persons Act, 1971 (an Act of Tynwald), being an order which satisfies the conditions set out in section 26(1) of the Children and Young Persons Act, 1969 (transfers between England or Wales and the Channel Islands or Isle of Man), is hereby designated for the purposes of the said section 26.

II.—BYE-LAWS

INNER LONDON EDUCATION AUTHORITY

Employment of children

Bye-laws made by the Inner London Education Authority on 9 September 1968 under Section 18 of the Children and Young Persons Acts, 1933 to 1963 (as amended by the Education Acts, 1944 to 1962) with respect to the employment of children in the Inner London Education Area (exclusive of the City of London). The bye-laws were confirmed by the Secretary of State for the Home Department on 29 November 1968 who decided they should come into force on 1 January 1969. By Section 18 (1) (f) of the Children and Young Persons Act, 1933, no child may be employed to lift, carry or move anything so heavy as to be likely to cause injury to him. The employment of children in factories, mines or quarries, or in any industrial undertaking other than one in which only members of the same family are employed is prohibited by other statutes.

Employment of children

1. No child shall be employed in any of the following occupations:

    (a) In the kitchen of any hotel, cook shop, fried fish shop, eating house or refreshment room.

    (b) As a marker, attendant or assistant in any billiard or bagatelle saloon, or other place used or licensed for games, or in any registered club.

    (c) In or in connection with the sale of intoxicating liquors, except in places where such liquors are sold exclusively in sealed vessels.

    (d) In collecting or sorting rags, scrap metal or refuse.

    (e) As an attendant or assistant in any premises or fairground used for the purpose of public amusement by means of automatic machines, mutoscopes, shooting ranges, games of chance or skill, or similar devices.

    (f) In any slaughterhouse.

    (g) In or in connection with any racing course or track or other place where any like sport is carried on or as an assistant in any business conducted therein.

    (h) In any agricultural work involving heavy strain.

    (i) In or in connection with the sale or delivery of paraffin, turpentine or turpentine substitute (also known as white spirit), methylated spirit or petroleum spirit.

    (j) In touting or selling from door to door.

    (k) In window cleaning, except as part of an incidental to light housework.

Regulation of employment

2. No child under the age of 13 shall be employed provided that subject to the provisions of these bye-laws a child who has attained the age of 12 years may be employed by his parent or guardian in light agricultural or horticultural work.

3. Subject to the provisions of bye-law 4, no child shall be employed on any school day except between 5 p.m. and 7 p.m. "School day" means any day on which a child is required to attend school.

4. A child who has attained the age of 13 may be employed before school between 7 a.m. and 8 a.m. in the delivery of milk and other goods carried by a milk roundsman or newspapers but if so employed shall not also be employed

after school hours except in an employment not prohibited in bye-law 1 for a period of not more than one hour which shall be between 5 p.m. and 7 p.m.

5. No child shall be employed on any Saturday or other school holiday for more than four hours or before 7 a.m. or after 7 p.m. "School holiday" means a day on which the school at which the child should attend is not open for the purposes for which he is required to attend.

6. No child shall be employed on Sunday except in the delivery of milk or newspapers, and then for not more than two hours between 7 a.m. and 10 a.m.

7. No child shall be employed for more than 20 hours in any week. The expression "week" means the period between midnight on Saturday night and midnight on the succeeding Saturday night.

8. The following conditions (a) to (e) inclusive shall be observed in relation to the employment of any child:

(a) The employer of any child shall forthwith on the engagement of the child in his employment send a written notification to the Inner London Education Authority at the education divisional office for the area in which the child lives stating his name and address, the name, address and date of birth of the child, the occupation in which, and the place at which the child is or is to be employed and the times at which the employment begins and ends. The employer shall send to the said Authority, on the first day of November and the first day of May in every year, a similar notification in respect of each child employed by him on those dates.

(b) No child shall be employed unless he has an Employment Card (issued by the said Authority) with him. He shall produce the Employment Card for inspection when required to do so by any authorised officer of the said Authority or a police officer and shall return it to the said Authority when the employment ceases or when he ceases to be a child.

(c) Within fourteen days from the date when the employment begins, and thereafter at the expiration of every period of twelve months during the course of such employment, the child shall obtain from the Principal School Medical Officer a certificate (for which no charge shall be made) that such employment of the class referred to in the certificate will not be prejudicial to the health or physical development of the child and will not render him unfit to obtain proper benefit from his education, and the employer shall be so informed by the said Authority.

A certificate shall cease to be valid if there is issued subsequently by the Principal School Medical Officer and served upon the employer a further certificate that the employment of the child will be prejudicial to his health or physical development or education.

(d) A child to whom an Employment Card has been issued in accordance with the provisions of these bye-laws shall be employed only within the times entered thereon by the said Authority.

(e) The employer shall keep affixed in a conspicuous position in the place in, or in connection with which, the child is employed, a notice showing the name, address and date of birth of the child, the occupation in which, and the times within which, the child may be employed.

9. Any person who employs a child in any work out of doors shall ensure that he is provided during the course of his employment with footwear and clothing sufficient to protect him from inclement weather.

10. Bye-laws 1 to 6 inclusive with respect to the employment of children made by the London County Council and except as regards bye-law 1 (i), confirmed

by the Secretary of State on 8 October 1952 and as regards bye-law 1 (i) so confirmed on 26 February 1963 in so far as they apply to the area of the Inner London Education Authority are hereby revoked.

Explanatory notes

1. For the purposes of these bye-laws:

    (a) The expression "child" means a person who is not over compulsory school age.

        (i) A child whose fifteenth birthday (or sixteenth birthday for a child attending a special school) occurs between the first day of September and the last day of January (both dates inclusive) is of compulsory school age until the end of the Spring term which includes such month of February.

        (ii) A child whose fifteenth birthday (or sixteenth birthday for a child attending a special school) occurs between the first day of February and the last day of August (both dates inclusive) is of compulsory school age until the end of the Summer term in that year.

    (b) The expression "guardian" in relation to a child includes any person who, in the opinion of the Court having cognisance of any case in relation to the child or in which the child is concerned, has for the time being the charge of or control over the child.

    (c) A person who assists in a trade or occupation carried on for profit shall be deemed to be employed notwithstanding that he receives no reward for his labour.

2. No child taking part in any entertainment, in pursuance of a licence under section 37 of the Children and Young Persons Act, 1963, may under the terms of the Children (Performances) Regulations, 1968 be employed on the day or days of, or the day following such entertainment, in any other employment.

Penalties

3. Section 21 of the Children and Young Persons Act, 1933, provides as follows:

"If a person is employed in contravention of any of the provisions of Section 18 of the Act or the provisions of any bye-laws made thereunder, the employer and any person (other than the person employed) to whose act or default the contravention is attributable shall be liable on summary conviction to a fine not exceeding £20, or, in the case of a second or subsequent offence, not exceeding £50".

Street trading

Bye-laws made by the London County Council on 20 February 1951 and amended on 27 May 1952, and 15 December 1953. The bye-laws, except for bye-law 7, were confirmed by the Secretary of State for the Home Department on 8 October 1952, who fixed the date on which such bye-laws should come into operation as 1 December 1952, and, as regard bye-law 7, were confirmed by the Secretary of State for the Home Department on 17 June 1954, who fixed the date on which that bye-law should come into operation as 1 August 1954. In accordance with Article 9 (3) of the London Government Order 1965, the following bye-laws made by the London County Council as local education authority apply to the Inner London Education Area (exclusive of the City of London).

1. No person under the age of 18 years shall engage in street trading and except as provided in bye-law 2 no person under the age of 18 years shall be employed in street trading.

2. Subject to the provisions of bye-laws 3–8 (inclusive) hereof a boy who has attained the age of 16 years, if he holds a licence from the London County Council permitting him so to be employed (hereinafter referred to as the "licensed person"), may be employed by his parent or guardian to assist in the business of a costermonger carried on at a fixed stall or pitch by such parent or guardian. In this bye-law the expression "costermonger" means and includes a person who sells in any street or public place at a fixed stall or pitch any fruit, vegetables or other articles of food or articles of general merchandise.

3. An application by a boy as referred to in the last preceding bye-law for a licence permitting him to be employed as therein referred to may only be refused by the London County Council on the following grounds:

    (a) That the applicant is by reason of physical or mental deficiency unfit to trade in the streets, or

    (b) that his licence has been previously revoked, or

    (c) that he is not regularly attending a course of instruction he is required by law to attend, or

    (d) that he is regularly engaged or employed in some other full-time occupation.

4. Licences referred to in the last but one preceding bye-law shall expire on 31 December in each year.

5. Every licensed person shall obtain a badge, for which no charge shall be made, from the London County Council which he shall wear in a conspicuous manner while employed in street trading.

6. No licensed person shall be employed in street trading before 8 a.m. or after 7 p.m. on any weekday or at any time on a Sunday; nor shall he be employed for more than 8 hours on any day or for more than 45 hours in any one week.

7. No licensed person shall in any street or public place tout or importune to the annoyance or obstruction of any passenger.

8. No licensed person shall whilst employed in street trading be assisted by any unlicensed person under the age of 18 years.

9. The London County Council may suspend or revoke any licence if the holder:

    (a) is found guilty or convicted of any offence; or

    (b) commits a breach of any of these bye-laws; or

    (c) uses the licence as a cloak for begging, immorality, imposition, or other improper purpose; or

    (d) alters, defaces, lends, sells, pawns, transfers or disposes of his badge; or

    (e) fails to notify the London County Council within one week of any change of his address; or

    (f) fails to attend regularly a course of instruction he is required by law to attend.

10. The bye-laws made by the London County Council and confirmed by the Secretary of State on 5 May 1921, 13 May 1924, and 17 May 1934, are hereby revoked.

Explanatory notes

Statutory interpretation of terms

    1. (a) "Public place" includes any public park, garden, sea beach or railway station, and any ground to which the public for the time being have or are permitted to have access, whether on payment or otherwise.

(b) "Street" includes any highway and any public bridge, road, lane, foot-way, square, court, alley or passage, whether a thoroughfare or not.

(c) The expression "street trading" includes the hawking of newspapers, matches, flowers and other articles, playing, singing or performing for profit, shoe-blacking and other like occupations carried on in streets or public places.

2. The restrictions on street trading imposed by the bye-laws do not apply to persons employed at established open air markets, or in any other place where it is customary for a retail trade or business (within the meaning of the Shops Act, 1950) to be carried on, but restrictions imposed by the Employment Bye-laws apply to persons not over compulsory school age.

3. No person under 18 may engage or be employed in street trading on Sun-day, except (a) where the employment is at a place where the occupier is allowed to trade up to 2 p.m. on Sunday subject to a requirement to close on Saturday; or (b) in any specified area in London, on any other day fixed by the local authority for that purpose, but restrictions imposed by the Employment Bye-laws apply to persons not over compulsory school age.

Penalties

4. If a person illegally engages in street trading he is liable to a fine not exceeding £10 for the first offence and not exceeding £20 for a subsequent offence.

III.—OFFICIAL CIRCULARS

CONTENTS

Home Office Circular No. 18/1956.   *Dated February* 14, 1956.

PUBLICATION OF PARTICULARS OF JUVENILE WITNESSES IN PROCEEDINGS ARISING OUT OF ANY OFFENCE AGAINST OR ANY CONDUCT CONTRARY TO DECENCY OR MORALITY

1. I am directed by the Secretary of State to say that he has received representations from the General Council of the Press about a number of cases in which newspapers have published the names and addresses of children or young persons who have given evidence in proceedings for sexual offences. Section 39 of the Children and Young Persons Act, 1933, provides that in any proceedings arising out of any offence against or any conduct contrary to decency or morality the court may direct that no newspaper shall reveal the name or other identifying particulars of any child or young person concerned in the proceedings. There is thus a means of preventing publication whenever it is considered undesirable in the interests of the young witness. The Press Council are of the opinion, however, that this provision is not operating effectively because the attention of the court is not expressly drawn to its powers at the outset of every such case in which a child or young person is concerned. In some cases it would appear that the matter is not brought to the notice of the court at all; in other cases it is dealt with too late to prevent publication of particulars of the witness in the first reports of the proceedings.

2. The Secretary of State agrees with the Council that all practicable steps should be taken to ensure that full advantage is taken of the powers available, so that juvenile witnesses are protected where necessary and so that newspapers are in no doubt whether they may or may not publish identifying particulars. He accordingly suggests that, in all proceedings to which section 39 of the Children and Young Persons Act applies, the clerk to the justices should inform the court at the beginning of the case that a child or young person is concerned in the proceedings and remind the court that it may give a direction prohibiting the publication of identifying particulars. In order that the clerk may be aware in advance of those criminal cases to which the section is likely to apply, chief officers of police have been asked to inform him before the proceedings if it is intended to call juvenile witnesses to give evidence for the prosecution.

3. As regards proceedings for an indictable offence in which the accused person is committed for trial, the Secretary of State considers that it would be helpful to the superior court to be aware in advance of cases to which section 39 may apply. He would therefore also suggest that, when forwarding the depositions in this type of case to the proper officer of the court of trial, the clerk to the justices should as a matter of course enclose a statement showing that the attention of the examining justices had been drawn to the provisions of section 39 and that they did or did not give a direction prohibiting publication.

4. Similar considerations apply to proceedings on appeal from the decision of a magistrates' court and the Secretary of State has suggested to the police that in cases in which they are the respondents, they should inform the appeal committee or the court of quarter sessions at the beginning of the hearing whether a direction under section 39 was given in the proceedings before the magistrates' court.

NOTE

This letter was sent to all Clerks to Justices.

The scope of this circular is extended by circulars 17/1964, 14/1965 and 15/1965 pp. 675, *et seq., post.*

Home Office Circular No. 19/1964   *Dated January* 21, 1964 *(Extract).*

CHILDREN AND YOUNG PERSONS ACT, 1963: PARTS I AND III

Section 27—Evidence of children in committal proceedings for sexual offences

8. Subsection (1) of section 27 provides that, subject to the exceptions mentioned in subsection (2), where examining justices are inquiring into a sexual offence (as defined in subsection (4), a child under the age of 14 is not to be called as a witness for the prosecution, but a statement made by or taken from, the child in writing is to be admissible in evidence instead. The purpose of section 27 is to save the child, where possible, from having to give oral evidence about the offence on two separate occasions. The Magistrates' Courts Rules, 1963 provides for any statement admitted under section 27 to be treated as an exhibit. The Secretary of State has suggested to clerks to justices that if a child is called to give oral evidence at the committal proceedings a note should be made on the papers sent forward to the court of trial of the provision that excluded the operation of subsection (1).

NOTE

This circular was sent to clerks of assize.

Home Office Circular No. 14/1965   *Dated January* 28, 1965.

PROTECTION FROM PUBLICITY OF JUVENILES CONCERNED IN PROCEEDINGS RELATING TO OFFENCES AGAINST OR CONDUCT CONTRARY TO DECENCY OR MORALITY

1. I am directed by the Secretary of State to refer to the procedure recommended in Home Office Circular No. 21/56 by which Chief Constables were asked to ensure that, if a juvenile was to be called as a prosecution witness in any case arising out of offences against or conduct contrary to decency or morality, the clerk to the court was informed of the prosecution's intentions so that he might remind the court of its power under section 39 of the Children and Young Persons Act, 1933 to direct that no newspaper should reveal the name or any other identifying particulars of any child or young person concerned in the proceedings.

2. These arrangements have worked well, but experience has shown that there is a gap in them, and it is desirable in order that full advantage may be taken of the powers given by section 39, that clerks to courts should be informed beforehand not only of cases in which juveniles are to be called as witnesses in cases concerning offences against decency or morality, but also of all such cases where a juvenile is the person in respect of whom an offence is alleged to have been committed. This extension of the existing procedure would help to ensure that identifying particulars are not inadvertently published of children concerned, for example, in a case in which they would have appeared as witnesses had it not been known in advance that the accused would plead guilty or where statements made by children are to be given in evidence instead of their oral testimony under section 27 of the Children and Young Persons Act, 1963.

3. The Secretary of State would be grateful if arrangements could be made to inform clerks to justices accordingly. He would also be glad if the existing arrangements for informing Courts of Quarter Sessions in appeals to which the police are respondents, whether Magistrates' Courts have given directions under section 39 of the Act of 1933 could be extended to the class of case referred to in the preceding paragraph.

NOTE

This circular was sent to chief constables.

Home Office Circular No. 15/1965   *Dated January* 28, 1965.

PROTECTION FROM PUBLICITY OF JUVENILES CONCERNED IN PROCEEDINGS RELATING TO OFFENCES AGAINST OR CON-DUCT CONTRARY TO DECENCY OR MORALITY

1. I am directed by the Secretary of State to enclose for your information a copy of a circular which has been sent to chief officers of police about the protection from publicity of juveniles concerned in proceedings relating to offences against or conduct contrary to decency or morality.

2. The Secretary of State would be glad if you would treat the suggestions made in Home Office Circular No. 18/56 and paragraph 6 of Circular No. 17/64 as applying to the extended classes of case in which the police have now been asked to take action in the same way as they apply to proceedings relating to offences against or conduct contrary to decency or morality in which juvenile witnesses appear for the prosecution.

NOTE
This circular was sent to the clerks to the justices.

Home Office Circular No. 208/1964.   *Dated September* 9, 1964.

TREATMENT OF CHILD WITNESSES IN PROCEEDINGS IN RESPECT OF SEXUAL OFFENCES

1. I am directed by the Secretary of State to refer to section 27 of the Children and Young Persons Act, 1963, which makes it generally unnecessary, where a sexual offence is to be tried on indictment, for a child under the age of fourteen to give oral evidence in the committal proceedings unless the defence require it. Otherwise (apart from the special provisions of sections 42 and 43 of the Children and Young Persons Act, 1933) a child's evidence about an alleged sexual offence must be given orally.

2. In the debates in Parliament on the Children and Young Persons Act, 1963, a general wish was expressed that the treatment of child witnesses should be such as to reduce to a minimum the strain involved in appearing in court. The need of children for special treatment will, of course, vary according to their intelligence and maturity, which are not always directly related to their age. The term " child " is therefore used in this circular without reference to any specific limit of age and, because most child witnesses in sexual cases are likely to be girls, it is treated as feminine; but the advice given applies equally to witnesses who are boys.

Date and time of trial

3. It adds considerably to the strain if a child has to attend court for several hours or on more than one day before her evidence is called. It would therefore be helpful if a sexual case in which a child has to give evidence could be taken on a fixed date and as early as possible on the day's list; if the child's evidence could be heard early in the proceedings; and if she could then be released from attendance.

Waiting arrangements

4. Section 31 of the Children and Young Persons Act, 1933, provides that, while waiting in a court, a child under the age of seventeen shall not associate with adult defendants and that a girl shall be under the care of a woman.

It is desirable that a child witness should be able to wait in privacy and comfort —if possible, in a separate room—and should have a trusted adult close at hand at all times, especially when giving her evidence.

Protection from publicity

5. The effect of the arrangements suggested in previous Home Office Circulars is that in any proceedings in respect of a sexual offence the court will be warned in advance if a witness under the age of seventeen is to be called for the prosecution, and so will be able to consider whether to exercise its powers under sections 37 and 39 of the Children and Young Persons Act, 1933. Section 37 enables the public to be excluded while a witness under seventeen is giving evidence. The use of this provision saves the child from the embarrassment of telling her story in public; and this object is more likely to be attained if the court is cleared before she enters. Section 39 empowers the court to prohibit the publication of the child's name or school or other identifying particulars, or any photograph of her.

6. This circular is issued with the approval of the Lord Chief Justice who hopes that all criminal courts will have regard to it.

NOTE

This circular was sent to Clerks of Assize, Clerks of the Peace and Clerks to Justices.

Home Office Circular No. 17/1964 *Dated January* 22, 1964.

CHILDREN AND YOUNG PERSONS ACT, 1963: PARTS I AND III

1, 2. [*Not reproduced.*]

Child witnesses of sexual offences

3. Clerks to justices may like to know that, in connection with section 27 of the new Act, chief officers of police have been given the following advice:

(a) It is desirable to ensure that evidence of the child's age is available to the court.

(b) The officer who took the statement should be called as a witness to produce it (and to prove that it was made by the child in question); he should be prepared to answer questions relating to the child's capacity to give evidence on oath. A copy of the statement should be made ready to be handed to the defence at the time at which it is tendered in evidence, and after the accused has signified that he does not object to the application of the section. It is expected that the child's statement, if admitted in evidence, will normally be read aloud to the court.

(c) Where the prosecution is not legally represented the officer should produce the statement as taken, in so far as it refers to any charge before the court, and should not seek to amend it by striking out matters that he thinks inadmissible.

(d) Where the prosecution require the attendance of the child to establish the identity of any person, or where it has not been possible to obtain a statement, the court should be so informed at the commencement of the proceedings. In the latter event the prosecution must be ready with evidence to satisfy the court of the circumstances that made it impossible to obtain a statement.

(e) Particular attention should be paid to proceedings that are imminent on 1st February 1964 so that steps may be taken before the inquiry to obtain a statement for use in the proceedings.

4. The Secretary of State suggests that when a child is called to give oral evidence by reason of the operation of subsection (2) or subsection (3) a note should be made on the documents sent to the court of trial, if the accused is committed, stating the provision that excluded the operation of subsection (1).

5. In proceedings for offences to which section 27 relates the Secretary of State suggests that the justices will wish to bear in mind the desirability of the accused person's being legally represented.

Protection from publicity for juvenile defendants and witnesses

6. In Home Office Circular No. 18/1956 the Secretary of State suggested that, in all cases to which section 39 of the Children and Young Persons Act, 1933 applied, the clerk to the justices should remind the court of its powers under that section and, in a case committed for trial, include with the depositions a statement that the examining justices, having had their attention drawn to those powers, did or did not exercise them. Section 39, as extended by section 57 (1) of the new Act, will apply in any proceedings against or in respect of a person under 17, or in which such a person is a witness. The Secretary of State thinks that it would be sufficient to draw the court's attention especially to its powers under that section only in cases where:

(a) one of the defendants before an ordinary magistrates' court is under the age of 17, or

(b) the proceedings arise (in the current phrase) " out of an offence against or conduct contrary to decency or morality."

In the second class of case the justices' attention might also be drawn to their power under section 37 of the Act of 1933 to exclude the public while a witness under 17 gives evidence. If in a case of the kinds mentioned at (a) and (b) above (or in any other case in which the justices have given a direction under section 37 or section 39) the defendant is committed to a superior court for trial or for sentence, it would be helpful if the statement suggested in Home Office Circular No. 18/1956 could be included with the depositions or other documents sent to the clerk of that court.

Recommendations of the Ingleby Committee

7. The following paragraphs deal with matters of interest to justices on which the Ingleby Committee expressed an opinion, although they did not recommend any change in the law. Quotations are from the Committee's report (Cmd. 1191).

Reports by local authorities and probation officers

10. The Ingleby Committee recommended that the attention of justices who serve in juvenile courts should be drawn to the considerations set out in the following paragraphs of their report, which relate to the way in which juvenile courts deal with reports submitted by local authorities or probation officers.

" 209. Many witnesses have pointed to the undesirability of indiscriminately reading aloud these reports in the presence of the child. It is obvious that harm and distress may often be caused to a child when he hears spoken in public an analysis of his character, the causes of his behaviour and commentaries on his background and inter-family relationships. If, for example, a child hears for the first time in court that he is illegitimate, or that his mother is a prostitute, or that his father is in prison, the effect upon him may well be disastrous.

210. Apart from the effect on the child, the disclosure to parents of certain matters properly referred to in reports may sometimes be undesirable, for example, when one parent learns for the first time in court of some circumstance which the other had kept secret. Disclosures made in this way may prejudice the maintenance or the restoration of marital harmony, and therefore the interests of the child.

211. Another disadvantage of revealing indiscriminately the contents of reports is that it may deter reporting agents, for example schoolmasters, from producing full and frank reports.

212. On the other hand, if nothing in the reports is disclosed, or if material parts of them are not disclosed, the parents and the child are denied the opportunity of refuting allegations which may affect the court's decision on the appropriate method of treatment for the child, and even where no injustice results there may often be the appearance of injustice ".

The Committee concluded that the difficulties could be met only by the skilled summarising of reports by the chairman, as permitted under the existing Rules. They asked that courts reminded that :

" while relevant information in reports should not be withheld from parents and children, reports will often contain confidential matter over which the court will need to exercise great care "

and suggested that

" the courts might encourage reporting agents to submit such confidential matter, where necessary, in a separate section appropriately marked, and to state their reasons why they considered that any particular items of information should not be disclosed, or should be disclosed only with circumspection (para. 217)."

Legal aid

11. " We . . . think that the existing power to allow free legal aid should be readily exercised in criminal cases in juvenile courts . . . " (para. 251).

The Lord Chancellor has under consideration the Committee's further recommendation that legal aid should be extended to civil proceedings in juvenile courts.

Cruelty to children

12. " While it is imperative that the power to impose imprisonment in cases of child cruelty or neglect should be retained, courts should, in applying the law, make full use of the facilities available for the rehabilitation of the family through residential training or skilled social help." (para. 550 (125)).

NOTE

This circular was sent to clerks to justices.

Legal Aid.—This is now available in civil proceedings in juvenile courts.

Home Office Circular No. 118/1961.   *Dated July* 13, 1961.

STAMFORD HOUSE REMAND HOME—SECURE ACCOMMODATION

1. I am directed by the Secretary of State to say that, as you will be aware, much public concern has been expressed about the need to remand to prison, under the provisions of section 27 (1) of the Criminal Justice Act, 1948, some young persons who, having attained the age of fourteen years and being under

the age of seventeen years, are certified by a court to be so unruly that they cannot safely be detained in a remand home or so depraved that they are not fit to be so detained. Most of these juveniles are boys, and the problem they present will not be wholly solved by the provision of remand centres which is at present in hand, because it is likely that the greater part of the population of remand centres will be the more mature and criminally sophisticated youths of seventeen to twenty-one years of age with whom it is undesirable that boys of fourteen and fifteen should be allowed to mix. Accordingly, the Secretary of State has had under consideration the question of providing secure accommodation for these unruly or depraved younger boys in a few selected remand homes in suitable parts of the country.

2. At his invitation, the London County Council has been good enough to provide in Stamford House remand home secure accommodation for the custody, at any one time, of up to seven boys *who have attained the age of fourteen but not sixteen years* and who would otherwise, because of their unruly or depraved behaviour, need to be remanded to prison. These facilities will be brought into use on Monday, 24th July next and will be available, primarily, for boys resident in the administrative county of London; although it may be possible for boys from the area of the geographical counties adjoining London (Middlesex, Essex, Kent and Surrey) to be received in the secure unit at the discretion of the London County Council and if there is room for them at the time of their remand.

3. It is proposed that the Remand Home Superintendent shall have discretion as to which boys remanded to Stamford House shall be placed in the secure provision and as to when (if at all) they shall be moved to the open part of the remand home. He will of course find it most helpful when exercising this discretion to receive at the time of the admission an expression of the court's opinion as to the boy's likely behaviour. If the court considers that a boy may possibly require to be placed in the secure unit, it will be helpful if the clerk of the court (or an officer on his behalf) will telephone Stamford House (Shepherd's Bush 9461) at once to make sure that a vacancy can if necessary be found for the boy in the unit.

4. It will be feasible to accommodate these additional boys at Stamford House only if some reduction is made in the number and age-range of other boys at the remand home. It is considered that this reduction might best be achieved by arranging that boys under the age of twelve years should no longer be sent to this remand home as a place of safety, on remand, or for classification for approved school purposes. The Secretary of State therefore suggests that, subject to vacancies being available, such boys should be sent to a reception centre or children's home, if they require to be lodged in a place of safety, or to a special reception centre if on remand; and the managers of the Royal Philanthropic Society's Classifying School at Redhill have agreed that non-Roman Catholic boys under the age of twelve with respect to whom an approved school order is made by a court in the county of London should in future be classified at their school instead of, as hitherto, at Stamford House. The Secretary of State hereby gives notice, under section 6 of the Children and Young Persons (Amendment) Act, 1952, that the Royal Philanthropic Society's Classifying School, Redhill, is available from 24th July, 1961, to the magistrates' courts for the metropolitan stipendiary court area and the petty sessional division of Hampstead for the reception of boys, other than Roman Catholics, under the age of twelve years. From this date, these courts should specify the Royal Philanthropic Society's Classifying School in approved school orders made in relation to such boys unless, in a particular case, the court considers that for some special reason it is undesirable that a boy should be sent to the classifying school; in such a particular case, it is open to the court to specify some other approved school, provided that (a) the special reason for so doing is stated

in the approved school order, and (b) the managers of the school selected are willing and able to receive the boy. Arrangements for the admission of boys to the classifying school should be made direct with the school (Telephone No. Redhill 2128). All applications for vacancies in approved schools for Roman Catholic boys under the age of twelve years committed to approved schools by courts in the County of London should, from 24th July, 1961, be made to the Central Vacancies Pool at the Home Office Children's Department, Horseferry House, Thorney Street, London, S.W.1.

NOTE

This circular was sent to chief clerks, metropolitan magistrates courts; the chief clerk, metropolitan juvenile courts; the clerk to the justices for the petty sessional division of Hampstead; the clerk of the London County Council; clerks to justices and clerks of county and county borough councils in the geographical counties of Middlesex, Essex, Kent and Surrey, and to Town Clerks.

Home Office Circular No. 151/1961.   *Dated August 25, 1961.*

ADMISSION OF OFFENDERS TO HOSPITAL UNDER PART IV OF THE MENTAL HEALTH ACT, 1959

1. I am directed by the Secretary of State to say that, in the light of experience since the Mental Health Act, 1959, came into force on 1st November, 1960, he thinks that it may be helpful to magistrates' courts to have some guidance on procedure in the case of mentally disordered persons who commit offences not punishable with imprisonment and who cannot therefore be admitted to hospital in pursuance of a hospital order under section 60 of the Act.

2. In some cases the offender will be in such obvious need of mental treatment that he will be dealt with by the police under section 136 of the Act, and it will then be unnecessary for him to be charged and brought before the court at all. This section enables a police constable to remove to a place of safety, for the purpose of medical examination and the making of arrangements for treatment, a person found in a public place who appears to be suffering from mental disorder and to be in immediate need of care and control.

3. In other cases an offender who has been charged but not yet brought before the court may be found to be in urgent need of treatment for mental disorder. If the police can then obtain the services of a medical practitioner and, on his making the necessary recommendation, get into touch with a mental welfare officer, it may be possible for the mental welfare officer, on the basis of the practitioner's recommendation, to make an emergency application, under section 29 of the Act, for the offender's admission to hospital. In such circumstances it will probably be desirable for the mental welfare officer to attend the court, so that when the court has disposed of the case he can escort the offender to hospital. The admission of the offender to hospital is unlikely to interfere with whatever method of disposing of the case is adopted by the court, since the court itself has no power either to sentence the offender to imprisonment or to order his detention in hospital.

4. If mental disorder is not detected until the offender appears in court, the court may decide to remand him for a medical report, in accordance with the provisions of sections 14 and 105 of the Magistrates' Courts Act, 1952. If the court decides to remand for a medical report, it is important that it should be made clear that the object of the remand is to enable the possibility of the offender's admission to hospital under Part IV of the Mental Health Act to be considered. Since the offence is not punishable with imprisonment, no doubt

the court will in many cases consider it appropriate to remand the offender on bail, provided that he agrees to attend for examination at a named psychiatric hospital. If, on examination, it appears to the hospital that compulsory detention for treatment is required, arrangements for admission to hospital can have been made by the time the offender is due to appear in court again.

5. Where the court sees no alternative to a remand in custody, and the prison medical officer comes to the conclusion, after examining the offender, that compulsory detention in hospital is required, he will be prepared to notify the mental welfare officer for the area in which the court is situated that he intends to report to the court to that effect and that he presumes that the mental welfare officer will be required to attend the court. This should ensure that the offender is admitted to hospital as soon as possible after the court has dealt with the offence.

6. A copy of this circular is being sent to Chief Officers of Police for their information.

NOTE

This circular was sent to Clerks to the Justices.

Home Office Circular No. 186/1960   *Dated November* 25, 1960.

PROBATIONERS AND PERSONS SUBJECT TO SUPERVISION ORDERS WHO ARE REQUIRED TO RESIDE IN PRIVATE HOUSES

RULES 70 AND 71 OF THE PROBATION RULES, 1949

1. I am directed by the Secretary of State to refer to paragraph 2 (b) of Home Office Circular No. 176/1953, and to say that he has had under review the rates at which he has authorised payments by probation committees under the above Rules towards the maintenance and clothing of probationers and persons subject to supervision orders (hereinafter described collectively as " persons under supervision ") who are required by their probation or supervision orders to reside in private houses.

2. The changes described below have been made with a view to facilitating the use of lodgings for wage-earners under supervision who are homeless or who (for one reason or another) must or should live away from home, and who need some help with the cost for a limited period.

3. From the date of this circular, the maximum payments that may be made by a probation committee under Rule 70 in respect of a wage earner will (like those in respect of a non-wage earner) be governed by the boarding-out allowance that would be paid in respect of a person in care by the local authority for the area in which the person under supervision will live. Expenditure under Rule 71 on clothing for a person under supervision (whether or not a wage earner) to whom Rule 70 applies will be governed by the same considerations.

4. The maximum rates of payment that may now be made under Rule 70 (and under Rule 71) as regards persons under supervision to whom Rule 70 applies) are set out in full in the Appendix to this circular. This circular replaces paragraph 2 (b) of Home Office Circular No. 176/1953; and in Home Office Circular No. 216/1949 it replaces the last sentence of paragraph 82, the last sentence of paragraph 83 in its application to Rule 70, and paragraph 3 of Appendix II.

APPENDIX

PERSONS UNDER SUPERVISION REQUIRED TO RESIDE IN PRIVATE HOUSES

Rule 70

    (a) A probation committee may make payments for maximum periods of
         (i) for a person under 21, twelve months;
         (ii) for a person aged 21 and over, six weeks;
       or such longer period as the Secretary of State may approve in the partic-
       ular case.

    (b) The payments may be of an amount not greater that that which would be
       made, in the same circumstances, by the local authority for the area
       where the person under supervision will live, if he were in the care of that
       local authority.

Rule 71

    (c) Expenditure on clothing for persons under supervision to whom Rule 70
       applies may be at a rate not greater than that which would be paid in
       the same circumstances by the local authority for the area, in respect
       of a person in their care.

NOTES

This circular was sent to:—

The Secretary of the Probation Committee,
(Extra copy enclosed for the Committee's Treasurer),
The Clerk of the County Council,⎫ for information
The Town Clerk,⎭
(Copies to all probation officers for information)

    The Probation Rules, 1949, are revoked by the Probation Rules, 1965, but the general authority contained in this circular for payment towards the cost of residence in private lodgings is continued in force.

Home Office Circular No. 80/1965   *Dated April* 13, 1965 *(Extract).*

THE PROBATION RULES, 1965

Duties of Probation Officers (Part IV)

    29. Part IV supplements the prescription of duties of probation officers given in general terms in paragraph 3 (5) of Schedule 5 to the Criminal Justice Act, 1948. In view of recommendation 78 made by the Departmental Committee on the Probation Service, the duties of a senior and a principal probation officer are not prescribed in the new Rules.

    30. Rule 29 repeats provisions for the keeping and safeguarding by probation officers of current records and for their inspection.

    31. Rule 30 repeats, with certain modifications, provisions prescribing the duties to be performed by probation officers in relation to the after-care of persons released from custody. Paragraph (1) relates to statutory after-care of persons released from prisons, borstals, detention centres and approved schools. For the present, the Central After-Care Association remains respon- sible for the statutory after-care of persons released from prisons and borstals, but the paragraph is so worded as to enable effect to be given in due course to the recommendation of the Advisory Council on the Treatment of Offenders (in their report " The Organisation of After-Care ") that this responsibility should fall directly on the probation and after-care service, as does responsibility for detention centre after-care.

    32. Paragraphs (2) and (3) of Rule 30 contain further provisions relating to approved school after-care and paragraph (5) extends the Rule to cover the provision of after-care for persons released from approved schools in Scotland and Northern Ireland who are to reside in England or Wales. Paragraph (4)

relates to "voluntary" after-care—that is, the after-care of persons not subject to statutory supervision on release. (The duty is a general one and no longer depends upon a request from the Central After-Care Association or the National Association of Discharged Prisoners' Aid Societies.) Though the probation officer's obligation under paragraph (4) ends twelve months after a person's release, it is open to the officer, in exceptional cases and with the approval of the probation committee, to continue after-care beyond that period.

33. A person subject to after-care, whether statutory or voluntary, is not a " person under the supervision of a probation officer " as defined in rule 52 (1). Nevertheless, Rules 16 and 17 (which relate to the general duties of probation and case committees) apply to after-care, as to other work of probation officers. In particular, Rule 17 requires a case committee to review the work of probation officers in individual cases, without distinction as to the type of case, whether after-care or otherwise. To comply with this rule a case committee will in the ordinary course expect a probation officer to report to them on these after-care cases about which either the committee or the officer judges it desirable that the committee should be informed. Rule 36 (which relates to welfare and employment) and Rule 42 (which relates to befriending funds) also apply to after-care. (Information and guidance to probation committees on various aspects of after-care will be given in a circular on this subject which is in course of preparation and will be issued shortly.)

34. Rule 31 repeats provisions in the Probation Rules, 1949 relating to adoption and custody proceedings and newly requires a probation officer, when so requested by or on behalf of a court, to make reports under section 4 (2) of the Matrimonial Proceedings (Magistrates' Courts) Act, 1960, to attempt conciliation in matrimonial cases and to make enquiries in connection with applications for consent to marriage. It is open to a probation committee to direct that a probation officer should attempt conciliation in cases not referred by a court.

35. Rule 32 repeats provisions relating to supervision of children in divorce proceedings.

36. Rule 33 restates a probation officer's duty to explain a probation or supervision order.

37. Rule 34 repeats provisions relating to visiting school children. Rule 35 repeats provisions relating to keeping in touch with probationers, extending their application, so far as is suitable, to persons placed under supervision by an order made under the Children and Young Persons Act, 1933.

38. Rule 36 repeats provisions relating to the welfare and employment of persons in respect of whom a probation officer has responsibilities.

39. Rule 37 repeats provisions relating to confidential reports on persons placed under supervision by order of a court, (see paragraph 33 above as regards reports to case-committees on after-care cases).

40. Rule 38 repeats provisions relating to reports made to assist the supervising court in reviewing after six months requirements of residence in institutions as required by section 5 of the Criminal Justice Act, 1948. (Recommendation 15 in the second report of the Departmental Committee on the Probation Service that such a review should no longer be required, will be considered when opportunity offers for amending legislation.)

41. Rule 39 repeats provisions relating to applications to court by probation officers (unless the probationer makes application) for amendment or discharge of probation orders, and extends them to apply also to supervision orders (unless the person under supervision or any other person makes application under the provisions of Schedule 1 to the Childrens and Young Persons Act, 1963).

Expenditure on persons for whom probation officer responsible (Part V)

42. Rules 40 to 42 prescribe the conditions governing payments by probation committees in pursuance of paragraph 3 (1) (d) and (2) of Schedule 5 to the Criminal Justice Act, 1948.

43. Rule 40 gives effect to the recommendation made in paragraph 207 of the report of the Departmental Committee on the Probation Service that the liability for maintenance of a person under supervision who is subject to a requirement of residence should rest, whether or not the residence requirement is inserted in the probation or supervision order when it is first made, on the committee for the area of the court which makes the original order. There is an exception, provided by paragraph (d) of the Rule, where the original order was made in Scotland: in this case the liability falls on the probation committee for the area of the court which amends the order by imposing a requirement as to residence in England. The payments to be made under Rule 40 are prescribed in Schedule 1 as follows:

> Paragraph 1 (1) preserves the obligation on probation committees to pay a weekly flat rate (as authorised by the Secretary of State from time to time) for each person required to reside in an approved hostel or home. As hitherto, flat rate contributions (which cover clothing and all other necessary expenditure) do not attract Exchequer grant: a grant equal to the sum required to cover the balance of the cost of each hostel or home is paid direct to the hostel or home in pursuance of section 77 (3) of the Criminal Justice Act, 1948.

> Paragraph 1 (2) repeats the provision empowering probation committees, with the prior approval of the Secretary of State, to contribute towards the maintenance of persons required to reside in institutions other than approved probation hostels and homes. The general authority given in Home Office Circular No. 89/1964 for specified contributions towards maintenance of mothers with children at the Elizabeth Fry Home and Crowley House continues in force by virtue of Rule 53 (2). Individual application should be made for the Secretary of State's approval in any other case.

> Paragraph 1 (3) gives statutory force to existing arrangements (set out in Home Office Circular No. 186/1960) for payment towards maintenance of persons required to reside in lodgings. The period of maintenance is newly left to the discretion of the probation committee. The term " maintenance " includes necessary clothing.

> Paragraph 2 requires a probation committee to pay travelling expenses to and from the place where a person is required to reside.

44. Rule 41 repeats the provision enabling a probation committee, in case of hardship to pay the fares necessarily incurred by a person under supervision (as defined in Rule 52 (1)) in reporting to the probation officer.

45. Rule 42 repeats provisions enabling a probation committee, with the approval of the Secretary of State, to maintain a befriending fund from which assistance can be given to persons in relation to whom a probation officer has responsibilities. Only the amount actually expended in any year can rank for grant. The fund is intended to be used for small items of emergency expenditure and only when provision is not available from any other public or voluntary source. Assistance may be given from a befriending fund to persons for whose after-care a probation officer is responsible under Rule 30; when the after-care is voluntary, payment should not in general be made after twelve months (see paragraph 32 above). Subject to what is said above about the nature of expenditure appropriate to the befriending fund, assistance may be given from such a fund to the family of a prisoner for whose after-care on his release a

probation officer has assumed responsibility. The Secretary of State is ready to consider any application from a probation committee for an increase in the maximum annual amount to be expended from a befriending fund, where this is considered necessary upon the assumption by the committee of responsibility for work previously undertaken by after-care organisations. (Probation committees are empowered by Rule 50 (1) to delegate authority to make such emergency payments from a befriending fund as they think fit.)

NOTES

This circular was sent to secretaries to probation committees, clerks to justices and county councils, town clerks and probation officers.

Home Office Circular No. 198/1966   *Dated November 11, 1966.*

APPROVED PROBATION HOSTELS AND HOMES FOR GIRLS—PREGNANCY

1. I am directed by the Secretary of State to refer to Rule 8 (2) of the Approved Probation Hostel and Home Rules, 1949, which precludes the admission of a pregnant girl to a hostel or home unless it is approved for the admission of such cases.

2. Pregnancy is frequently not confirmed until some time after a girl has been admitted, or may occur during a girl's stay, and it has been the practice to require such girls to leave the hostel or home as soon as the liaison probation officer can make suitable arrangements. It has been represented to the Secretary of State than when girls have to leave in advance of admission to a mother and baby home the several changes involved have an unsettling effect. He has accordingly decided where a girl has settled satisfactorily in a hostel or home before pregnancy is established she may, at the discretion of the Warden in consultation with the liaison officer, be allowed to remain as long as she is fit enough to continue work or participate in training without detriment to her health, that is to say usually until the twenty-eighth week of pregnancy. This should enable a girl to pass directly from the hostel or home to the mother and baby home.

3. Where pregnancy is discovered shortly after arrival, or the girl has shown no sign of settling down, it will be reasonable to continue the practice of making suitable alternative arrangements without delay.

4. It will be for the liaison probation officer to apply to the court for the cancellation of the requirement of residence when the girl leaves, since it is not to be expected that she will return to the hostel or home after the birth of her baby. While a baby should not be received into a hostel or home, circumstances may arise (e.g. where the child is still-born or is placed immediately for adoption) in which it will be reasonable for the girl herself to return alone and if the court requires her to do so she may be accepted. The periods covered by requirements of residence should not total more than twelve months.

5. An additional copy of the circular is enclosed for the information of the Warden.

NOTE

This circular was sent to Secretaries of the Managing Committees and to Principal Probation Officers in areas where hostels and homes for girls are situated.

HOME OFFICE PROBATION AND AFTER-CARE BULLETIN NO. 17. (EXTRACT)

*   *   *   *

11. Non-approved Hostels and Homes

If a person under the supervision of a probation officer is required, as a condition of the probation or supervision order, to reside in a non-approved hostel or home it is possible for contributions to be made from probation funds towards the cost of his or her maintenance (Schedule 1, paragraph 1 (2) of the Probation Rules 1965). The consent of the Secretary of State is required in all cases, unless the requirement is for residence in certain training homes for neglectful mothers where general authority has been delegated to Probation Committees to approve the cost of maintenance (see paragraph 13 of Bulletin No. 13 and paragraph 11 of Bulletin No. 16). Applications for the Secretary of State's approval must be made before the requirement of residence is inserted in the order and should be accompanied by a full report on the case, including the reason why residence in a particular hostel or home is desirable.

Applications will be considered on their merits but, in general, approval will only be given where:

(a) the person is not eligible for admission to an approved probation hostel or home;

(b) a person otherwise eligible for admission to an approved hostel or home cannot be found a place;

(c) the person is likely to benefit from a stay in the institution within the maximum period of residence allowed under a probation or supervision order (12 months) and he or she will be ready to assume normal living by the end of that time.

In the case of persons admitted to special institutions, other than hospitals, because they are alcoholics or drug addicts, the application should be accompanied by a medical opinion.

In the case of unmarried mothers and pregnant girls approval will only be given in respect of girls of 17 years of age and over who are in need of a period of training and supervision away from home. Approval will not be given in cases where the primary need is accommodation and medical care for a short period before and after confinement. An assurance will be required that financial support cannot be provided by the local authority Health and Welfare Services. Payments from probation funds can only be approved in respect of the mother and no payment can be made specifically for the maintenance of the child. See also paragraph 12 of Bulletin No. 13.

All persons will be expected to make contributions towards their maintenance from any earnings or other income, including maternity benefit or family allowances during the period of residence.

Approval, if given, will be for a maximum period of 6 months in the first instance. If it is considered desirable that payment should be continued for a further period application should be made to the Home Office before the end of the initial six months and should be accompanied by a progress report and a statement of reasons why an extension of stay is necessary.

Home Office Circular No. 289/1970.   *Dated 30th December, 1970.*

FUTURE PATTERN OF APPROVED PROBATION HOSTELS AND HOMES

1. Section 7 (2) of the Children and Young Persons Act, 1969 will come into operation on 1 January 1971. From that date courts will no longer have power

to make probation orders in respect of persons aged under 17 years or to include in a supervision order a requirement to reside in an approved probation hostel or home. Requirements to reside in probation hostels and homes included in probation or supervision orders in respect of young persons aged 15 and 16 years made before 1 January 1971 will not be affected and the existing law will continue to apply.

2. Since a large number of the existing probation hostels and homes have been catering for the age group 15–18 years the opportunity is being taken to re-allocate most of those wishing to remain in the probation field to meet the shortage of places in the age range 17–21 years. The opportunity is also being taken to provide a more even geographical spread of the two age groups into which the hostels will generally be divided within the age range of 17–21 years. Although it is not proposed that each of these hostels and homes should serve a specific catchment area the new arrangements will assist the placing of offenders in hostels nearer to the community in which they have roots than has usually been possible in the past.

3. The new pattern of probation hostels and homes which will come into effect on 1 January 1971 is shown at Appendix A. To assist those hostels and homes changing to an older age group it is proposed that they will initially concentrate on offenders whose age is nearest to that of their present residents, phasing in the remainder of the higher age group as younger residents are discharged. It is envisaged that this process might take some six to nine months and it is hoped that courts and probation officers will co-operate with wardens to achieve a smooth change-over to the higher age groups. Probation hostels for adult male offenders are also shown for convenience in Appendix A. These hostels are not, of course, affected by the Children and Young Persons Act and they will continue to be available only to the courts in the probation and after-care areas detailed in Home Office Circulars 19, 64, 96 and 146/1970.

4. A small number of the existing probation hostels and homes (shown in Appendix B) may not be remaining in the longer term in the probation field. Some are seeking a place in the new system of community homes provided for in the Children and Young Persons Act while others may operate in other fields or close. These hostels and homes will not admit any further residents on probation from 1 January; they will however continue as approved probation hostels and homes until all the present residents have been discharged. Where the hostel or home is seeking to become a community home it may be possible for arrangements to be made with local authorities for persons subject to care orders to be accommodated in the hostel or home during this interim period.

APPENDIX A

Pattern of Approved Probation Hostels and Homes after 1 January 1971

Revised Age Groups

Approved Probation Hostels for Young Men

County	Hostel or Home	Age on reception as from 1 January 1971
Berkshire	Manor Lodge Hostel, 8 Straight Road, Old Windsor	From 17 to under 19
	St. Leonard's Reading Hostel, 2 Southcote Road, Reading, RG3 2AA	From 17 to under 19

County	Hostel or Home	Age on reception as from 1 January 1971
Cheshire	Parkfield Hostel, 62 Wood Lane, Timperley, Altringham	From 18 to under 21
Gloucestershire	Ashley House Hostel, 14 Somerset Street, Kingsdown, Bristol, BS2 8NB	From 17 to under 19
Lancashire	St. Josephs Hostel (Roman Catholic) Millers Street, Patricroft, Eccles, Manchester, M30 8PF	From 17 to under 21
	Southwood Hostel, 24 Southwood Road, Liverpool, L17 7 BQ	From 17 to under 19
Leicestershire	Kirk Lodge, 322 London Road, Leicester, LE2 2PJ	From 18 to under 21
London	Ellison House, 134 Camberwell Road, London, S.E.5	From 17 to under 19
	MacGregor House, 127 Tulse Hill, S.W.2	From 17 to under 20
	St. Edmund's, 298 Leigham Court Road, Streatham, S.W.16	From 17 to under 21 (catholics and non-catholics accepted)
Northamptonshire	Stone House, 125 Harlestone Road, Dallington, Northampton, NN5 6AA	From 17 to under 19
Northumberland	Ozanam House, 79 Dunholme Road, Newcastle-upon-Tyne, NE4 6XD	From 17 to under 21
Nottinghamshire	Trent House, Woodborough Road, Alexandra Park, Nottingham, NG3 4JB	From 17 to under 19
Suffolk	Lightfoot House, 37 Fuchsia Lane, Ipswich	From 18 to under 21
Warwickshire	McIntyre House, 125 Edward Street, Nuneaton	From 17 to under 19

County	Hostel or Home	Age on reception as from 1 January 1971
Worcestershire	Upper Norgrove Hostel, Church Road, Webheath, Redditch	From 18 to under 21
Yorkshire	Spooner House 365 Killinghall Road Bradford	From 17 to under 19

APPROVED PROBATION HOSTELS FOR ADULT MEN

County	Hostel	Age on reception
Kent	Fleming House, 32 Tonbridge Road, Maidstone	From 19 to under 25
Oxfordshire	Maudsley House, 112 Abingdon Road, Oxford, OX1 4PY	From 21 to under 30
Warwickshire	Elliott House, 96 Edgbaston Road, Birmingham, 12	From 21 to under 30
Yorkshire	Cardigan House, 84 Cardigan Road, Leeds, LS6 3BJ	From 19 to under 25

APPENDIX B

EXISTING APPROVED PROBATION HOSTELS AND HOMES WHICH MAY NOT CONTINUE IN THE PROBATION FIELD AFTER 1 JANUARY 1971

APPROVED PROBATION HOSTELS FOR BOYS

County	Hostel
London	Howard House, 30 Belsize Avenue, Haverstock Hill, N.W.3
	St. Vincents Hostel, 21 Breakspears Road, Brockley, S.E.4
	West Ham Hostel, 199 Romford Road, Forest Gate, E.7
Sussex	Diplock House, 37 Vernon Terrace, Brighton, BN1 3JH
Yorkshire	Osborn House, 138 Burngreave Road, Sheffield, S3 3DH
	St. John's Hostel (Bishop Poskitt Memorial), 263 Hyde Park Road, Leeds, LS6 1AG

APPROVED PROBATION HOMES FOR BOYS

County	Home
Surrey	High Beech, Coopers Hill, Nutfield, Nr. Redhill
Wales	House O' The Trees, Penygraig, Tonypandy, Glamorgan

APPROVED PROBATION HOSTELS FOR GIRLS

County	Hostel
London	Burford House, 104 West Hill, Putney, S.W.15
	Newhaven House, 272 Colney Hatch Lane, New Southgate, N.11
Warwickshire	Carpenter House, 33 Portland Road, Edgbaston, Birmingham, 16
Yorkshire	Longden House, 29–31 Kenwood Park Road, Sheffield, S7 1NE

APPROVED PROBATION HOMES FOR GIRLS

County	Home
Gloucester	Charlton Court, Charlton Kings, Cheltenham, GL52 6JD
London	St. Margarets, 6 Sydenham Hill, London, S.E.26

APPROVED PROBATION HOSTELS FOR WOMEN

County	Hostel or Home	Age on reception from 1 January 1971
Berkshire	Elizabeth Fry House, 6 Coley Avenue, Reading, RG1 6LQ	From 18 to under 21
Lancashire	Adelaide House, 115 Edge Lane, Liverpool, L7 2PF	From 17 to under 19
London	Katherine Price Hughes Hostel, 28 Highbury Grove, N.5	From 18 to under 21

County	Hostel or Home	Age on reception from 1 *January* 1971
Nottinghamshire	Southwell House, 106 Raleigh Street, Nottingham, NG7 4DJ	From 17 to under 19
Somerset	Rocklands, Weston Lane, Bath, BA1 4AB	From 17 to under 19
Worcestershire	Braley House, 89 Ombersley Road, Worcester	From 18 to under 21
Yorkshire	Ripon House, 63 Clarendon Road, Leeds, LS2 9NE	From 18 to under 21

APPROVED PROBATION HOMES FOR YOUNG MEN

County	Hostel or Home	Age group on reception from 1 *January* 1971
Essex	Windyridge, Nayland, Nr. Colchester	From 18 to under 21
Kent	Hollywood Manor, West Kingsdown, Nr. Sevenoaks	From 17 to under 19

Note Although High Beech, Coopers Hill Road, Nutfield, Nr. Redhill, Surrey will become a voluntary home it will continue to provide a limited number of places for young men between 17 and 19 years of age on probation. Prior authority under para. 1 (2) of Sched. 1 to the Probation Rules, 1965, should be obtained for contributions towards the cost of maintenance.

APPROVED PROBATION HOMES FOR YOUNG WOMEN

County	Hostel or Home	Age group on reception from 1 *January* 1971
Hampshire	St. Barbara's, 145 Stakes Road, Purbrook, Hants., PO7 5PL	From 17 to under 21

NOTE

This circular was sent to Clerks of Assize, Clerks of the Peace, Clerks to the Justices, Secretary of the Probation and After-Care Committee and to all probation officers (for information).

Home Office Circular No. 41/1971.   *Dated 2nd February, 1971.*

APPROVED PROBATION HOSTELS AND HOMES FLAT RATES AND MAINTENANCE CHARGE TO RESIDENTS IN HOSTELS

FINANCIAL YEAR 1971/72

1. Home Office Circular No. 42/1970 of 11 March 1970 informed you of the weekly flat rates for approved probation hostels and homes and the weekly maintenance charge to hostel residents, for the financial year 1970/71.

2. It has been decided after consultation with the local authorities' associations to adopt in future one flat rate for Hostels and Homes. Consequent upon the provisions of Part 1 of the Children and Young Persons Act, 1969, the number of probation homes will be reduced from the present seven to four only, and a separate flat rate applied to this small number of establishments would not be possible to predict accurately in advance.

3. The flat rate for Hostels and Homes for the financial year beginning 1 April 1971 will be £13·86. This amount was determined in consultation with the local authorities' associations to take account of an estimated reduction in the numbers of residents for whom it will be necessary to provide accommodation following the full effect of the provisions of the Children and Young Persons Act, 1969 when young persons under the age of 17 are no longer resident. It also reflects the costs of re-building and modernisation of some hostels and one home.

4. A further circular notifying the weekly charge to residents will be issued shortly.

NOTE

This circular was sent to the Secretary of the Probation Committee (extra copy enclosed for the Committee's Treasurer), the Clerk to the Justices and the Clerk of the County Council (for information), the Town Clerk, copies, for information, to principal probation officers and senior probation officers in charge of areas.

Home Office Circular No. 63/1968.   *Dated 5th March, 1968.*

REFUSAL OF PARENTAL CONSENT TO A LIFE-SAVING BLOOD TRANSFUSION OR OPERATION FOR A CHILD

1. Last year the Ministry of Health issued a circular letter on this subject to the Secretaries of Regional Hospital Boards and Boards of Governors. The issue of this letter arose out of correspondence with local authority associations, and we understand that the associations gave it and the associated correspondence a wide circulation among their membership. It has, however, since been suggested that it would nevertheless be useful if we were to circulate the letter to all authorities. With the agreement of the Ministry of Health I am accordingly enclosing a copy of their circular letter which was issued after consultation with the Home Office. We share the Ministry's view that the use of care, protection or control proceedings is not the best way of dealing with situations in which parents refuse their consent to operations or blood transfusions and a child's life is thereby endangered.

2. The Ministry of Health circular dealt solely with life-saving transfusions or operations, and was sent to hospital authorities for the purpose of explaining why it should not be necessary to resort to the care, protection or control procedure in such cases. The advice in it in no way seeks to restrict the statutory duty of local authorities or the powers of the courts, but it is hoped that, as a result of its being issued, occasions for local authorities to consider the possibility of court proceedings in such circumstances will become much less likely to arise.

NOTE

This circular was sent to the Clerks to the County Councils, County Borough Councils and to the London Borough Council, with copies for the Medical Officer of Health and the Children's Officer.

Ministry of Health Circular F/P9/1B dated April 14, 1967

REFUSAL OF PARENTAL CONSENT TO BLOOD TRANSFUSIONS AND OPERATIONS

Representations have been received from local authority associations about the difficulties that may arise when parents refuse consent to a life-saving blood transfusion or operation for a child. Hospitals are still on occasion asking the local authority to bring the child before a juvenile court as being in need of care, protection or control with a view to a fit person order being made under the Children and Young Persons Acts.

It appears that the departmental advice circulated to Board Secretaries and S.A.M.O.s in 1961 and referred to in Ministerial replies to Parliamentary Questions on 27th March, 1961, and 14th February, 1966, may not have been sufficiently widely known in hospitals.

This advice is that hospital authorities should not in such cases resort to this procedure for the purpose of obtaining a consent to life-saving blood transfusion or operation. This procedure was not devised with this purpose in mind and there are a number of legal and practical difficulties about its use for this purpose. In particular, it has not been established in the higher courts whether the consent of a fit person to whose care a child has been committed by order of a court provides any added protection to a doctor who carries out a life-saving operation or blood transfusion in the face of continued parental opposition. Moreover, it may not be possible to complete the procedure in time.

Hospital authorities should therefore rely on the clinical judgment of the consultants concerned after full discussion with the parents. If in such a case the consultant obtains a written supporting opinion from a colleague that the patient's life is in danger if operation or transfusion is withheld, and an acknowledgment (preferably in writing) from the parent or guardian that despite the explanation of the danger he refuses consent, then the consultant would run little risk in a court of law if he acts with due professional competence and according to his own professional conscience, and operates on the child or gives the child a transfusion.

I should be glad if you would ensure that this advice, in which the Joint Consultants Committee concur, is brought to the attention of staff who may be concerned at hospital level with this situation.

NOTE
This circular was sent to Secretaries of Regional Hospital Boards and Board of Governors.

Home Office Circular No. 131/1968.   *Dated 20th May, 1968.*

TRANSFERS OF SUPERVISION UNDER SECTION 37 OF THE MATRIMONIAL CAUSES ACT, 1965

I am directed by the Secretary of State to refer to children who are under the supervision of a local authority in pursuance of a court order under section 37(1) of the Matrimonial Causes Act, 1965, and to say that he has had under consideration, in consultation with the Lord Chancellor and the Associations of local authorities, the introduction of a uniform procedure for securing consideration by the court of a variation of the court order in cases of a change of residence. He would be grateful if local authorities would be good enough to adopt, with effect from the date of this circular, the following procedure in cases where the parent having custody of the child moves to an address outside the area of the authority specified in the order in pursuance of section 37(2) of the Act.

2. Where the new address is in the area of another authority in England or Wales, the supervising authority, if they consider that, having regard to the

child's interests, a transfer of supervision is desirable, should send to the other authority concerned and to the Registrar of the court which made the order (in London Divorce Registry cases, the Senior Registrar) written particulars of:

    (a) the parent's new address, and

    (b) the reasons why the authority seek a variation in the supervision order.

3. On receipt of these particulars the court will consider whether to vary the order by specifying the new local authority. Notification of any such variation will be sent to both local authorities concerned.

4. Where the parent's new address is not in England or Wales, the supervising authority should inform the Registrar (in London Divorce Registry cases, the Senior Registrar) only. The court will then consider whether to discharge the order.

5. A copy of this circular is enclosed for the Children's Officer.

NOTES

This circular was sent to Clerks of County, County Borough and London Borough Councils.

Matrimonial Causes Act, 1965, s. 37.—See p. 835 of the main volume.

Home Office Circular No. 188/1968.   *Dated 14th August, 1968.*

SOCIAL ENQUIRY REPORTS BEFORE SENTENCE

I am directed by the Secretary of State to refer to section 57 of the Criminal Justice Act, 1967, which enables him to make rules requiring a court to consider a social enquiry report prepared by a probation officer before passing a custodial sentence on an offender. As was foreshadowed when this provision was before Parliament, the Secretary of State sees advantage in seeking to achieve its object, at least in the first instance, informally by making recommendations to the courts rather than by exercising the rule-making power.

2. The Secretary of State is accordingly recommending to all courts that they should, as a normal practice, consider a social enquiry report before imposing on an offender aged 17 or over (as regards offenders under 17, see paragraph 9 below) a sentence in any of the following categories:

    (a) detention in a detention centre;

    (b) borstal training;

    (c) a sentence of imprisonment (including a suspended sentence) of two years or less where the offender has not received a previous sentence of imprisonment (including a suspended sentence) or borstal training;

    (d) any sentence of imprisonment on a woman.

He also recommends that a magistrates' court should consider a report before committing an offender to quarter sessions for sentence under section 28 or 29 of the Magistrates' Courts Act, 1952.

3. The courts will also wish to bear in mind, in this context, the view expressed by the Departmental Committee on the Probation Service (Cmnd. 1650) that a social enquiry report should normally be obtained before a probation order is made.

4. As regards category (a) in paragraph 2 above, the higher courts receive a pre-trial report in nearly all cases where a detention centre order is made, and experience at the centres suggests that it is desirable that magistrates' courts also should consider a report before making a detention centre order. As regards category (c), the Secretary of State suggests that it is desirable, on

general penal and social grounds, that a court should have the means of considering an offender's background in some detail before sentencing him to imprisonment for the first time. In cases of a suspended sentence the Secretary of State's
recommendation is that a report should be considered before such a sentence
is passed; but this is not intended to discourage a court from obtaining a further
report, should it so wish, if a person subject to a suspended sentence is convicted
of a further charge and the suspended sentence falls to take effect under section
40(1) of the Criminal Justice Act, 1967. Category (d) includes any woman on
whom a sentence of imprisonment may be passed, since it is widely recognised
that the social consequences of imprisoning women tend to be more severe and
background inquiries are therefore particularly valuable. As regards the
recommendation that magistrates' courts should obtain a report before committing an offender to quarter sessions for sentence, inquiries show that in a substantial proportion of cases committed for sentence, the sentence passed by the
superior court is one within the powers of the committing court: in some of
these cases consideration of a social enquiry report might have disposed the
magistrates' court to pass sentence instead of committing the offender. Where
the court decides to commit, it will no doubt arrange for the report to be forwarded to quarter sessions.

5. The Secretary of State recognises that the recommendations set out in
paragraph 2 above will call for some flexibility in application: there may from
time to time be exceptional cases where it is clearly unnecessary or inappropriate
to call for a report—for example, where a previous report has recently been
submitted.

6. The Secretary of State recognizes that it is already the practice of many
magistrates' courts to ask for social enquiry reports in a wide range of cases,
as a result of the adoption by magistrates' courts of arrangements for the provision of reports in the light of those recommended for the superior courts by
the Departmental Committee on the Business of the Criminal Courts (Cmnd.
1289; see Home Office Circular No. 83/1963); and he would not wish the present
recommendations to be regarded as in any way restricting the range of cases in
which such reports are already received.

7. The reports prepared by probation officers under the arrangements
suggested in this circular will include information of the kind already provided
in their reports to courts, and will describe the character, personality and social
and domestic background of the accused; his record while at any educational,
training or residential establishment (other than Home Office establishments)
which he has recently attended, or while receiving after-care; his employment
prospects and, where appropriate, his attitudes and habits as known to his
recent employer. The court's attention will also be drawn to any information
obtained in the course of a social enquiry which suggests that a medical report
would be helpful.

8. The extensive enquiries that are necessary to enable a report of this kind
to be compiled make it important that adequate time should be allowed: a
remand for a week at least is likely to be needed. In some cases the provisions
of section 18 of the Criminal Justice Act, 1967 will require a remand on bail;
in others, the courts will no doubt have in mind the desirability of remanding
on bail where appropriate, particularly where a custodial sentence may not
eventually be imposed.

9. What is said above (apart from paragraph 3) applies only to offenders
aged 17 and over. In the cases of offenders under that age section 35 of the
Children and Young Persons Act, 1933 already provides for social enquiry
reports to be made by the local authority or a probation officer, except in
cases of a trivial nature, on children and young persons who appear before the
courts; and the Summary Jurisdiction (Children and Young Persons) Rules,

1933 require a juvenile court, except in cases which appear to it to be of a trivial nature, to obtain such information as to the general conduct, home surroundings, school record and medical history of the child or young person as may enable it to deal with the case in his best interests and, if such information is not fully available, to consider the desirability of adjourning the case for such enquiry as may be necessary. Thus such information is normally available to a court before making an order removing a child or young person from home. In the Secretary of State's view full information should always be considered by a court before such an order is made, and he recommends that courts should follow the practice of not making an approved school order, a fit person order or a detention centre order except after consideration of a social enquiry report, and should if necessary adjourn the case for this purpose.

10. The reports furnished to the court under the arrangements recommended in this circular may also be expected to be of value, in a number of ways, after sentence has been passed. The practice of making social enquiries after sentence has developed considerably in recent years. Social enquiry reports often enable much-needed help to be given urgently to a prisoner's wife and family; they alert the prison welfare officer to any special needs and provide a point of contact; and recently such reports when available have proved a valuable source of information when parole has been under consideration.

11. The Secretary of State recognises that the adoption of the recommendations made in this circular will involve some additional work for the probation service in preparing reports, with a particular increase in the service provided to the magistrates' courts; and he has consulted the representative bodies concerned about this aspect of the arrangements.

12. The Secretary of State wishes to keep under review the working of the new arrangements. Some statistical information is currently collected about the numbers of social enquiry reports prepared, but this would not be adequate for the purpose, and he therefore proposes to consult probation and after-care committees on the working of the new scheme. He would also be glad to receive any comments which courts may wish to make when some experience has been gained of its working.

13. The Secretary of State suggests that the new arrangements should apply from 1st October 1968.

NOTE

This circular was sent to Clerks to Justices, and a similar circular to Clerks of Assize and Clerks of the Peace, and copies to Secretaries to Probation Committees and to Probation Officers for information.

Home Office Circular No. 122/1968.   *Dated 8th November, 1968.*

FINES OUTSTANDING AGAINST PERSONS DETAINED IN BORSTAL INSTITUTIONS, DETENTION CENTRES AND APPROVED SCHOOLS

Borstals and approved schools

I am directed by the Secretary of State to say that clerks to justices may find it useful to have the following information about his practice when his attention is called to the fact that an offender who has been sentenced to borstal training or ordered to be sent to an approved school has recorded against him fines which were imposed by a magistrates' court and have not been paid. The primary object of borstal or approved school training is the reformation of the person concerned and it is desirable for him to be able to undergo his training in the knowledge that, when it is completed he will have the opportunity to make a fresh start. In the case of an offender serving a sentence of imprisonment or of detention in a detention centre, courts can, and commonly do, lodge warrants of commitment in default of payment of outstanding fines so that the term in default will run out concurrently with the later sentence and the offender can be released in due course without any outstanding liability. This method of disposal is not available in the case of a person detained in a borstal institution or an approved school because a warrant of commitment in default of payment of a fine cannot be lodged. The beneficial effect of his training may, however, be seriously impaired if after release he is faced with a continuing obligation to pay a fine imposed a considerable time before and a liability to be sent to prison or a detention centre if he fails to do so.

2. For these reasons the Secretary of State has for a number of years adopted the practice of asking whether the justices agree that outstanding fines, and any sums ordered to be forfeited as recognizances (if not already remitted by the court), should be written off the books of the courts as irrecoverable. Similarly, he has suggested that the justices might consider taking no action to enforce payment of any costs outstanding. Where there is an amount due under an order for compensation or damages, the Secretary of State has suggested that the position of the offender might be explained to the person to whom the money is due, and his agreement sought to a proposal that no further steps should be taken to enforce payment.

3. Many courts are already familiar with the views of the Secretary of State on these matters, and normally seek authority for writing-off outstanding fines on learning of the defaulter's admission to borstal or approved school. Others are not; and the Secretary of State would be glad if you would draw the attention of the justices to the views set out above and, if they concur, suggest that they should agree that authority to write off outstanding fines be sought in future cases as they come to notice.

4. Section 44(10) of the Criminal Justice Act, 1967, empowers a magistrates' court to remit the whole or part of an outstanding fine if the court thinks it just to do so having regard to any change in the offender's circumstances since his conviction, but this power can be used only where the offender is present in court. In the Secretary of State's view the production under escort of numbers of borstal inmates to attend court for such proceedings would involve an undesirable interruption of training and an undue strain upon the borstal administration, and he will not therefore normally be prepared to authorise production for this purpose. Similar considerations apply in the case of approved school children. In these circumstances it is suggested that where, in the light of the considerations mentioned in paragraph 1 above, the justices think it right to dispose of a fine outstanding against a borstal or approved school inmate who is not to be brought before the court for some other reason, it will generally be more convenient to seek authority for the fine to be written off.

Detention Centres

5. Sections 5 and 6 of the Criminal Justice Act, 1961, enable courts in the case of defaulters who are already detained in a detention centre to lodge a warrant of commitment in default. The question of seeking authority to write-off fines imposed on offenders detained in a detention centre will not therefore normally arise. It will be appreciated that warrants should be lodged without delay if the court does not wish the term which the defaulter is already serving to be extended.

General

6. Where authority is sought to write off a fine in any case where payment of costs is also outstanding it would be helpful if the intention of the justices to

enforce or not to enforce payment could be indicated. Similarly in any case where, as suggested above, an approach has been made to a person to whom a sum is due by way of compensation, the Secretary of State would be glad to know the result in order that he can arrange for the inmate to be informed.

7. Borstal institutions, detention centres and approved schools have been asked to notify courts of the admission of persons who have fines, or other sums of money ordered to be paid, still outstanding against them and for this purpose forms will be used as in the specimens attached as Appendices A and B to this circular. There is, of course, no objection to courts taking the initiative in applying for write-off as suggested in this circular and, indeed, such initiative would often be welcome since inmates are sometimes unable to recall with accuracy when and where a fine was imposed on them or for how much.

8. It would be of great assistance and simplify the work involved if requests for authority to write off fines recorded against borstal inmates or approved school children could be forwarded in the form annexed as Appendix C.

9. The original copies of the forms referred to in paragraphs 7 and 8 will be returned after authorisation to the courts, where they should be retained for production to visiting auditors when requested. It would be helpful if all other authorities received for the writing off of fines could be similarly retained for production to the auditors when needed.

NOTE

This circular was sent to Clerks to Justices.

APPENDIX A

Date		
day	month	year

Home Office

Report of Defaulter Committed to a Detention Centre
Home Office Circular No. 122/1968, Paragraph 5

This form is to be sent direct to the Court by the Detention Centre.

To. The Clerk to the Justices,	From. The Warden,

The person named below was committed to the above-named Detention Centre on
.... (date) at................................. (court)

and he has reported that the following fines etc., (or balances thereof) which were imposed at your court have not been paid. His earliest date of release is..........
....

Name   ....

Date of conviction or finding of guilt   ....

Offence   ....

Fine   (or balance) outstanding   ....

Costs   „   „   ....

Compensation   „   „   ....

Damages   „   „   ....

                                   Warden

APPENDIX B

	Date		For H.O. use CSJ.
day	month	year	

HOME OFFICE

REQUEST TO WRITE OFF FINES ETC.
HOME OFFICE CIRCULAR No. 122/1968

This form is to be sent direct to the Court by the borstal or approved school.

To. The Clerk to the Justices,	From. Governor/Headmaster,

The person named below was sentenced to borstal training/committed to an approved school on................... (date) at...................... (court) and he has reported that the following fines etc., (or balances thereof) which were imposed at your court have not been paid.

Name   ....

Date of conviction or finding of guilt   ....

Offence   ....

Fine   (or balance) outstanding   ....

Costs   „   „   ....

Compensation   „   „   ....

Damages   „   „   ....

He has......in cash and from this he has agreed to pay......towards the sum outstanding. A remittance is duly enclosed. Please complete the reply section below and send the whole form to Home Office, Accounts Branch, who will reply to you direct. If the amounts reported above do not agree with those shown in the court records then please amend this form accordingly.

Governor/Headmaster.

Reply from Court

The justices agree/do not agree that this fine may be written off. The information provided (as amended) agrees with the court records.

The justices do/do not intend to enforce the payment of costs.

The persons entitled to receive compensation or damages have/have not agreed that payment should not be enforced.

To.
  Home Office
  Accounts Branch
  Courts Section
  Tolworth Tower
  SURBITON, Surrey
	Clerk to the Justices.
	
	Date.
	    Form No. 1446

APPENDIX C

Form of application for authority to write off fines or balances of fines outstanding against persons ordered to be detained in borstal institutions or approved schools.

Fining Court: ....

Name of defendant: ....

Date of conviction or finding of guilt: ....

Amount of fine outstanding: ....

Amount of costs outstanding: ....

    Do the Justices intend to enforce payment of costs? ....

Amount of compensation/damages outstanding: ....

    Does the person or body entitled to receive compensation/damages agree that payment should not be enforced? ....

Name of borstal institution or approved school in which detained, if known

....

    It is requested that authority be given to write off from the books of the Court the fines or balances of fines shown above which the Justices consider should not be enforced.

....
(Clerk to the Justices)

Date: ....

This form should be sent to:

Home Office
Accounts Branch
Courts Section
Tolworth Tower
SURBITON
Surrey

Home Office Circular No. 237/1968   *Dated 8th November, 1968.*

FINES OUTSTANDING AGAINST APPROVED SCHOOL BOYS AND GIRLS

A copy is enclosed of Home Office Circular No. 122/1968 which describes the Home Secretary's practice where there are outstanding against boys in borstal institutions, detention centres and approved schools fines or other monies that have been ordered by a magistrates' court to be paid. In addition, justices and their clerks are informed that approved schools (in addition to borstal institutions and detention centres) have been asked to notify courts of the admission of boys against whom fines or other such monies are outstanding. In general, the procedures described in the circular should not be initiated while a boy is in a classifying school or centre, since it may take some weeks to complete, but classifying schools and centres may be able to assist training schools by drawing to their attention boys against whom there are fines or other monies outstanding.

2. The managers of training schools should, if they agree, arrange for particulars to be sent to the justices' clerk concerned in any case in which there are outstanding against a boy in the school monies that he has been ordered by a magistrates' court to pay. For convenience, reports made for this purpose should be in the form shown at Appendix B to Home Office Circular No. 122/1968: supplies of this form can be obtained from this Department (Room 135) on request.

3. Where the justices' clerk to whom a school has sent particulars in accordance with paragraph 2 above forwards to the Home Office an application for the fine to be written off and the authority is duly given, the Home Office will ask the school to inform the boy concerned.

4. Some boys may be unable to give the correct name and address of the courts by which they have been ordered to make payments. Managers of schools at which experience indicates that there are likely to be some boys with fines outstanding against them may find it helpful therefore to obtain from the Home Office a copy of the booklet listing the addresses of magistrates' courts in England and Wales to assist them in identifying the courts concerned.

5. This circular and the enclosure relate only to fines and other monies ordered to be paid by magistrates' courts. Schools should consult the Home Office about any fines or other monies that higher courts have ordered to be paid and which are outstanding against boys detained in an approved school.

6. For convenience, reference is made in this circular to boys, but the principles and procedure described apply equally in cases in which there are fines or other monies outstanding against girls.

NOTE

This circular was issued to correspondents of approved schools in England and Wales. Copies sent to headmasters and headmistresses for information.

Home Office Circular No. 255/1968   *Dated 8th November, 1968.*

CHILDREN AND YOUNG PERSONS ACT, 1963, PART III— LICENSING FOR PERFORMING ABROAD

APPENDIX TO HOME OFFICE CIRCULAR NO. 255/1968
CHILDREN AND YOUNG PERSONS ACT, 1933

Restrictions on persons under 18 going abroad for the purpose of performing for profit: licensing of children and young persons performing abroad

1. Section 25 of the Children and Young Persons Act, 1933, as amended (which, with section 26 extends to Scotland and Northern Ireland) prohibits

any person under 18 from going abroad for the purposes of singing, playing, performing, or being exhibited for profit unless a licence has been granted in respect of him (subsection (1)). "Abroad" means outside the United Kingdom and the Irish Republic and, by virtue of section 42(1) of the Children and Young Persons Act, 1963, the words "singing, playing, performing or being exhibited" include taking part in any broadcast performance or any performance recorded with a view to its use in a broadcast or in a film intended for public exhibition. Licences may only be granted by the Chief Magistrate or any magistrate sitting at Bow Street (subsection (9)).

2. A licence may be granted in respect of a child under 14 only if the engagement is for acting, or for dancing in a ballet in a performance of ballet or opera, and the application is accompanied by a declaration that the part cannot be taken except by a person of about his age; or for taking a musical part in a performance that is wholly or mainly musical—that is the same kinds of performance as those permitted under section 38(1) of the Children and Young Persons Act, 1963, for a child under 13.

3. A magistrate may grant a licence subject to such restrictions and conditions as he thinks fit to ensure the welfare of the person concerned, provided he is satisfied that the parent or guardian consents; that the person is going abroad to fulfil a particular engagement; that he is fit for the purpose and that arrangements have been made to secure his health, kind treatment and adequate supervision while abroad and his return from abroad when the licence expires; and that he has been furnished with a copy of the contract of employment or other document showing the terms and conditions of employment drawn up in a language understood by him (subsection (2)).

4. The applicant for the licence, who is the person responsible for the person going abroad must, at least seven days before making the application, give notice to the police for the district in which the person under 18 lives of his intention to apply for a licence, together with a copy of the contract of employment. The police are required to send the copy contract to the magistrate and may also make a report on the case and show cause why a licence should not be granted. A licence cannot be granted unless the magistrate is satisfied that notice has been properly given, but if the notice was given less than seven days before the application was made the magistrate may grant a licence if he is satisfied that the officer to whom notice was given has made sufficient enquiries about the case and does not oppose the application (subsection (3)).

5. A licence may not be granted for more than three months, but may be renewed from time to time for the same period and may be revoked or varied (subsections (4) and (5)).

6. Unless he is satisfied that in the circumstances it is unnecessary, the magistrate must require the applicant to enter into a recognisance for the observance of the restrictions and conditions in the licence (subsection (6)).

7. In any case where the magistrate is satisfied that it is not in the interests of the person to whom the licence relates to require him to return from abroad when the licence expires the magistrate may by order release all persons concerned from any obligation to cause him to return (subsection (7)).

8. On receiving notice of an intended application for a licence the police should immediately make enquiries about the applicant and the person to whom the application relates and, if that person is under the compulsory school leaving age, the local education authority should be asked to comment on the application, in particular on

    (a) the number of days in the 12 months preceding the first day for which the section 25 licence is required on which the child has taken part in performances to which section 37(2) of the Children and Young Persons Act, 1963, applies;

(b) the nature of the performances, *e.g.* films, television, etc., and

(c) whether they are satisfied that, having regard to the arrangements (if any) that have been or will be made therefor, the child's education will not suffer by reason of going abroad for the purpose for which the licence is requested.

The copy contract should then be sent to the magistrate, together with a report on the case. The report should indicate any reasons there may be for or against the grant of a licence and whether the surety proposed would be able to pay the amount fixed (usually £100) if required to do so.

9. In urgent cases the police should if possible report to the magistrate in time for the application to be heard in under seven days. In most cases a written report is sufficient, but if they wish the police may attend or be repre sented at the hearing.

10. An applicant for renewal of a licence need not notify the police of the application but, unless he is the parent or guardian of the person concerned, he must satisfy the magistrate that the person's parent or guardian consents to renewal. If any material information comes to the notice of the police at any time during the currency of a licence it should be reported to the Chief Magistrate at Bow Street, who may revoke or vary the licence.

11. When a licence is granted or renewed the police are informed. One of the conditions of the licence is that when the licence, as originally granted or as renewed, expires or the person to whom it relates returns to the U.K. the applicant should forthwith inform the police of the address at which the person is living. Another condition is that within seven days of the expiration of the licence or the person's return to the U.K. the applicant should produce the person to whom the licence relates to the magistrate then sitting at Bow Street. If the police are not notified of the person's return they should so inform the magistrate who may be able to confirm the person's return or advise the police of the action to be taken.

12. Section 26(6) of the Act provides that where there is any reason to believe that any person under 17 is about to go abroad in contravention of the licensing provisions he may be taken to a place of safety by a constable or any person authorised by a justice of the peace and detained there until he can be restored to his relatives or until other arrangements have been made for him.

13. All correspondence about applications for licenses or persons to whom or in respect of whom a licence relates should be addressed to the Chief Clerk, Bow Street Magistrates Court, London W.C.2.

NOTE

This is the Appendix to Home Office Circular No. 255/1968 dated November 8, 1968 which was sent to Chief Officers of Police.

Home Office Circular No. 19/1969   *Dated 28th January,* 1969.

ABSCONDERS FROM APPROVED SCHOOLS AND FROM SUPERVISION:
INFORMING THE POLICE AND PARENTS

The present procedure for informing the police about boys and girls who abscond from approved schools or from supervision is described in paragraph 10 of Home Office Circular No. 29/1949, Appendix I to that circular and Item 3 of Approved Schools Bulletin No. 108 (issued in December 1967). The importance of notifying the parents or guardians of a boy (or girl) who absconds is self-evident, and no formal advice has hitherto been issued on how this should be done. There is now a need, however, to supplement the present advice about notifying the police; and, in view of some misunderstandings and complaints that have come to notice, schools may also find it helpful to have the following further guidance on procedure for notifying parents and guardians. For convenience, only boys are mentioned, but the advice applies equally to girls.

Information for the police

2. Where a boy absconds from a school, or from supervision, the school now notifies the police in the area from which the absconding has occurred, the boy's home area and any other area to which it is thought he may go. In future, schools should instead

(a) telephone to the local police, giving them the absonder's full name, date of birth, description, home address. details of his absconding, his Criminal Record Office number (if any) and any information that is available about his intentions (*e.g.* names and addresses of relations or friends to whom he may go);

(b) confirm this information to the local police in writing (unless the absconder has already been recovered or other circumstances make it unnecessary to do so); and

(c) send the Criminal Record Office, New Scotland Yard, London, S.W.1 a copy of any written notification sent to the local police.

The local police will immediately send particulars of the absconder to the police for his home area and other areas to which it is thought he might go. If he is still at large after ten days, the Criminal Record Office will publish details in the Police Gazette, which is sent to all police forces in England and Wales.

3. It is important that the police should always be informed promptly when an absconder has been recovered or his apprehension is no longer desired. In such circumstances schools should therefore notify both the local police (who will notify all the police forces to whom they notified the absconding) and the Criminal Record Office (who will cancel the entry in the Police Gazette, if one has been made).

4. In replying to letters from the police, their reference number should always be quoted.

Information for parents and guardians

5. It is common practice for the school from which a boy absconds to inform his parents (or guardians) and seek their co-operation in securing his safe return. Parents have, however, sometimes complained to the Home Office that they have not been informed in good time that their son has absconded or, alternatively, that they have suffered unnecessary anxiety because of a failure to inform them promptly that he has been safely recovered. This has usually been found to have been due to some misunderstanding.

6. The action to be taken in a particular case depends mainly on the circumstances and on the school's knowledge of the boy concerned and his parents. Managers are asked, however, to review the practice followed at their school in the light of the following suggestions, which are based on a study of complaints received by the Home Office.

(a) *Interval between absconding and notification*

Where a boy's absence comes to notice immediately, or almost immediately, it is reasonable to defer notification while there is hope that he may be quickly recovered. Where, however, the boy is known to have left the neighbourhood, or has had enough time to do so, notification should not be deferred, especially if it is to be made by letter (see sub-paragraph (d) below) and delay would entail missing the latest collection of letters on the day in question.

(b) *Notification where an absconder is recovered before his absence has been notified*

There is no need to inform the parents on each occasion on which a boy breaks bounds briefly, has come to no harm and is not known to have committed any offence. Where, however, a boy is known to have committed offences or there are other unusual circumstances (*e.g.* he has been found a long way from the school) the parents should be informed. (A girl's parents should always be informed if she is known, or thought, to have had sexual intercourse.) Failure to keep parents informed of such matters is likely to impair their confidence in the school and their relationship with the staff.

(c) *Notification of return*

Information that an absconder has been safely returned to the school, or is known to have been apprehended and to be safe, should be sent to the parents as soon as possible.

(d) *Means of communication*

Most parents of boys in approved schools are not accessible by telephone but if they are, news about absconders should be conveyed by telephone and confirmed by letter. In other cases the parents should be informed by letter that their son has absconded. Letters about the recovery of an absconder should be sent as quickly as possible, but if reliance on the post is likely to result in undue delay (*e.g.* at week-ends or holiday periods) it may be advisable to send a telegram, especially where the parents have shown anxiety and concern.

(e) *Importance of direct communication*

Some complaints of failure to notify parents about absconders have arisen because arrangements made by schools for a message to be passed by a third party have miscarried. Schools should notify the parents direct in all cases. In particular, they should not expect the police to make special arrangements to notify the parents of an absconder's recovery.

7. Most of the suggestions made in paragraph 6 are unlikely to be relevant where a boy absconds from supervision (except where he has been placed away from home), but schools should do what they can to keep the parents informed.

8. Item 3 of Approved Schools Bulletin No. 108 is cancelled; and schools may find it convenient to add a reference to this circular to paragraph 10 of their copies of Home Office Circular No. 29/1949, the remainder of which is still applicable.

NOTE

This circular was issued to correspondents of all approved schools in England and Wales. Copies sent to headmasters and headmistresses for information.

Home Office Circular No. 178/1969   *Dated 5th September, 1969.*

FINES OUTSTANDING AGAINST APPROVED PROBATION HOSTEL AND HOME RESIDENTS

Home Office Circular No. 122/1968 drew attention to the Secretary of State's wish that, in general, clerks to justices should seek authority for fines or other monies which have been ordered by a magistrates' court to be paid by residents in borstal institutions, detention centres, and approved schools to be written off as irrecoverable.

2. The Secretary of State hopes that the same practice may be extended to boys and girls who are required by the court under the terms of a probation or supervision order to reside in approved probation homes and the wardens of these homes have been asked to notify courts of the admission of persons who have fines or other monies still outstanding against them.

3. Should the court wish to take the initiative in applying for write off of fines outstanding against residents in approved probation homes it would be helpful if the application could be made in the form of Appendix C to Home Office Circular 122/1968 suitably amended.

4. In the case of residents in approved probation hostels, who are normally in full time employment, the Secretary of State continues to hold the view that they should, as far as possible, contribute from their earnings towards paying off the fine.

NOTE

This circular was sent to the Clerks to the Justices.

Home Office Circular No. 239/1969   *Dated 18th November, 1969.*

CHILDREN AND YOUNG PERSONS ACT, 1969

Introduction

The Children and Young Persons Act, 1969, received the Royal Assent on October 22, 1969. Under section 73, the Act will come into force by stages and this circular is concerned with the first three stages. Further circulars will be issued from time to time as more sections of the Act are brought into force. Additional copies of the circular are attached for the Children's Officer and the Financial Officer.

2. Commencement No. 1 Order brought into operation on November 16, 1969, sections 69, 70 and 73 and also certain minor provisions relating to the Social Work (Scotland) Act, 1968.

3. To enable a start to be made on the establishment of the system of community homes, the provisions of sections 35 to 50, 58 and 59 in Part II of the Act are brought into force on 1 December 1969 (Commencement No. 2 Order, copy enclosed) together with certain general provisions in Part III and related provisions in Schedules 2 to 6.

4. Modifications to the Children Act, 1958, contained in sections 51 to 57 in Part II of the Act and related provisions in Schedules 5 to 7 are by the same No. 2 Order brought into force on 1 January 1970. A separate circular will be issued shortly.

Part I—Care and other Treatment of Juveniles through Court Proceedings

5. The bringing into force of paragraph 6 of Schedule 1 will enable regulations under Part IV of the Criminal Justice Act, 1967, to be made about legal aid. A circular will be issued shortly about the intended initial timetable for bringing Part I of the Act into operation.

PART II—COMMUNITY HOMES

Planning areas and committees

6. Section 35 enables the Secretary of State, by order, to divide England and Wales into planning areas. Before doing so, he is required to consult each local authority, whose area or part of whose area is included in a planning area, and such other local authorities as he thinks fit. All local authorities will be addressed separately on the proposals to establish about 12 planning areas, which the Secretary of State intends to create as soon as the consultations are complete. These proposals do not involve the partitioning of any one authority's area. Subsections (3) and (4) place a duty upon local authorities within each planning area to establish for that area a children's regional planning committee in accordance with the provisions of Schedule 2 to the Act. A period of 3 months is proposed for this purpose, after the planning area has, by order, been specified. A guidance circular on the establishment of these committees will issue shortly.

Regional plans

7. Section 36 requires a children's regional planning committee to prepare and submit to the Secretary of State a regional plan for the provision and maintenance of community homes, whose prime purpose is the accommodation and maintenance of children in the care of the authorities in that planning area.

8. Community homes may be provided either by local authorities or by voluntary organisations. If the latter, then one local authority will participate in the management of the voluntary home in accordance with an instrument of management to be made in respect of that home (section 36(2)).

9. Voluntary community homes are of two kinds and the regional plan will designate which it is to be. A controlled community home is one in which the ultimate responsibility for its management, equipment and maintenance vests in a local authority and as assisted home is one where this responsibility vests in the voluntary organisation providing the home (section 36(3)).

10. It is further provided in section 36 that every regional plan shall contain proposals with regard to the nature and purpose of the community homes in it and for the provision of facilities for the observation and assessment of children in care. The actual form and content of the first plan will be the subject of a direction by the Secretary of State, which will be issued, with an explanatory circular, shortly before the committees are established (subsections (4) and (6)).

11. Children's regional planning committees are required to obtain the consent of voluntary organisations who are providing voluntary community homes and of local authorities who are either providing their own community homes or participating in the management of a voluntary home, before any such provisions are included in the regional plan (section 36(5)).

12. Section 37 enables the Secretary of State, after considering a plan submitted to him, to approve it wholly or in part. If approved in part, the planning committee has to submit a further plan to supplement that part already approved. A committee of its own motion may submit a further plan to vary or replace an existing plan (or where part only of a plan has been approved, that part) and this may take the form either of amendments to the existing plan (or part of a plan) or a new plan. Notice of the Secretary of State's approval will be given in writing to the committee and the committee are required to notify the local authorities and voluntary organisations concerned.

Local authority community homes

13. Section 38 places a duty upon the local authority to provide and run the homes, which it has consented so to do in an approved plan. This provision

eventually replaces the existing duty to provide children's homes under section 15 of the Children Act, 1948. As to transitional arrangements, attention is drawn to paragraph 38 below.

Instruments of management for voluntary homes

14. Sections 39 to 42 contain sundry provisions relating to the instruments of management for controlled and assisted homes. A separate circular will issue in due course setting out general guidance on the matters which might be expected to be included in such instruments and on the procedure for reaching agreement between the voluntary organisation and the local authority on their provisions.

15. It should perhaps be stressed that the Act provides that nothing in an instrument of management shall affect the purposes (usually governed by the provisions of a trust deed) for which the premises of a voluntary home are held. If the purposes for which a community home is intended to be used run contrary to the provisions of a trust deed (which is defined to include the memorandum and articles of association of a company) then, if the voluntary organisation so wish, it may, in accordance with the law relating to charities, seek to amend the deed. Subject to this very important exception, the instrument of management shall contain the necessary provisions as to the purpose and management of the community home and shall prevail over the trust deed in the event of any inconsistency between them (section 40).

16. Section 41 contains those management provisions which are peculiar to a controlled community home and section 42 those which relate only to an assisted home.

Community home regulations

17. The Secretary of State is empowered by section 43 to make regulations with respect to the conduct of community homes and for securing the welfare of children in them. It is intended to exercise this power in 1970 after the usual consultations. It is not expected that these initial regulations would deal with matters affecting equipment, standards of building or accommodation and matters requiring the Secretary of State's approval to the use of buildings as community homes, mentioned in section 43(2)(a), (f) or (g).

Exemption of voluntary community homes from provisions applicable to other voluntary homes

18. A voluntary community home may, before becoming a community home, have been a voluntary home registered under Part IV of the Children Act, 1948. It will not be removed from the register on account of this change of status. Other voluntary community homes may have previously enjoyed some other status, for example, as a school or a hostel in which case there will be no additional requirement to register as a voluntary home. In both instances, the regulations relating to the conduct of voluntary homes, and to the annual return of particulars will not apply so long as they are community homes (section 44).

Disputes in voluntary community homes

19. Section 45 empowers the Secretary of State to determine disputes relating to a controlled or an assisted home, which are referred to him either by a local authority or a voluntary organisation. The arrangements for the joint management of voluntary community homes by voluntary organisations and local authorities are designed to provide a forum in which matters between the parties can be resolved locally. The power in section 45 is regarded by the Secretary of State as a reserve power for use when settlement by negotiation, both locally in the management body and between the organisation and any

local authority concerned, proves impossible and the future status of the voluntary home as a community home is thereby seriously imperilled. The Secretary of State's power to determine disputes does not extend to questions relating to religious instruction given in a home, where the trust deed for that home provides for such questions to be determined by an ecclesiastical authority (section 45(5)).

Discontinuance of approved schools, remand homes etc.

20. Section 46 empowers the Secretary of State to make orders terminating the status of an institution as an approved school, remand home, approved probation hostel or approved probation home (referred to as "an approved institution") when it is no longer required *as such* in consequence of the establishment of community homes for a planning area. On these orders depend the various transitional provisions in Schedule 3 relating to change of status, staff safeguards and the transfer of assets and liabilities. Further guidance will be issued to all local authorities who may be concerned in assuming responsibility for an approved institution.

Discontinuance of voluntary community homes

21. Section 47 enables voluntary organisations, on giving 2 years' notice, to withdraw a controlled or assisted home provided by them from the community home system. When necessary, interim arrangements can be made for the management of the home by a local authority during the period of notice. If a voluntary home ceases to be a community home, the financial consequences of this cessation are governed by the provisions of section 48.

MODIFICATIONS OF THE CHILDREN ACT, 1948

Provision of accommodation

22. Section 49 substitutes a new section 13 for the one enacted in 1948. The new section omits certain obsolete provisions and enables local authorities to maintain children in care in community homes. The requirement in the old section 13(6) to obtain the Secretary of State's authorisation to the use of residential facilities in premises other than children's homes is repealed. The effect of the new section 13 on the placement in an approved school of a child in the authority's care, while the court retains power to make approved school orders, is the subject of a separate circular.

23. The new section 13(2) in the 1948 Act, together with the repeal (in Schedule 6) of section 3(3) to (5) of that Act and of section 5 of the Family Allowances and National Insurance Act, 1956, brings together in one subsection the discretionary power of a local authority to allow a child in their care to be under the charge and control of a parent, guardian, relative or friend. The child remains legally in care; it is only the charge and control which passes to the parent, guardian, relative or friend. (See also paragraph 40 below.)

24. The new section 13(3) of the 1948 Act enables the Secretary of State to determine the terms and conditions under which a child in the care of a local authority is accommodated in a home provided by him under section 64 of the 1969 Act. (See paragraph 31 below.)

Hostel accommodation

25. Consequent upon the inclusion within the term "community homes" of hostels provided by local children's authorities under the previous provisions of the 1948 Act, it was necessary to recast section 19 of that Act. Section 50 substitutes a new section 19 and similarly enables a local authority to provide

accommodation for persons not in care who are over compulsory school age but under 21 in a community home which is provided for children over compulsory school age.

Inspection

26. Section 58 enables the Secretary of State to cause to be inspected by persons who are authorised by him, the range of premises used for the accommodation of children in care, children boarded out by voluntary organisations, foster children and protected children within the meaning of Part IV of the Adoption Act, 1958. Section 59 constitutes the authority for a person, who is so authorised to inspect, to have a right of entry to the premises. This provision replaces, in terms appropriate to the new system of community homes, the provisions of section 94 of the 1933 Act and section 54(1) and (2) of the 1948 Act, which are repealed.

Miscellaneous Provisions

Extradition

27. Section 60 extends the range of offences for which accused or convicted persons may be surrendered from this country to foreign States under the Extradition Acts and to other Commonwealth countries under the Fugitive Offenders Act, 1967, so as to include offences of the following descriptions: cruelty to a person under 16 (as in section 1 of the Children and Young Persons Act, 1933) and indecent conduct towards a child (as in section 1 of the Indecency with Children Act, 1960).

Parental contributions

28. Only section 62(2) is brought into force at this stage and this is consequential upon the new section 13(2) of the 1948 Act (section 49 of this Act, see paragraph 23 above) and the repeal of section 5 of the Family Allowances and National Insurance Act, 1956 and of section 3(3) to (5) of the 1948 Act. Children who are subject to resolutions under section 2 of the 1948 Act and those who are subject to fit person orders will now be subject to uniform provisions as to the power of the authority to allow them to be under the charge and control of a parent, guardian, relative or friend while remaining in care. No contribution is payable by the parent when the local authority have so relinquished the charge and control of the child.

Returns and reports

29. The provisions of section 63 place a duty upon local authorities, voluntary organisations and the clerks of juvenile courts to transmit information to the Secretary of State at such times and in such form as he may direct, with respect to the local authority performance of their statutory functions, children in their care, children cared for by voluntary organisations and the court proceedings respectively.

30. Section 63(4) and (5) require the Secretary of State to lay before Parliament an annual abstract, which will be primarily statistical, and a descriptive triennial report.

Secretary of State's homes

31. By section 64 the Secretary of State is empowered to incur expenditure in providing equipping and maintaining homes for the accommodation of children who are in the care of local authorities and need facilities which, in his opinion, are unlikely to be available in community homes. Three such homes

are contemplated for seriously disturbed children and the first home should be in use early in 1970. Further guidance will be issued later on the nature of the facilities, conditions of admission and the charges to be paid by local authorities (see paragraph 24).

Grants to voluntary organisations

32. Section 65(1) enables the Secretary of State to make grants to voluntary organisations towards expenditure incurred by them on assisted community homes. It is intended that these grants should be made only for capital expenditure incurred in the establishment or improvement or adaptation of assisted homes. Grants may reimburse all or part of the capital cost or of the cost of borrowing. They will not be available to meet the general running costs of assisted homes.

33. The power in section 46(1) of the 1948 Act to make grants to voluntary organisations in respect of registered voluntary homes will continue in being but will not apply to such homes which are either controlled or assisted homes, or which are designated as such in a regional plan which was then in operation, at the time when the expenditure was incurred (section 65(2) and see also paragraph 18 above).

34. Section 65(3) and (4) contain provision linked to an order under section 46 for the making of grants in respect of certain financial obligations incurred when an institution was an approved school (or an approved probation home or hostel) where the premises concerned are to be used for purposes approved by the Secretary of State as being for the benefit of children—instead of being used as a community home. These provisions thus complement the provisions of paragraph 11 of Schedule 3 which enable certain contingent liabilities as to the repayment of grant for capital works to be "transferred" to the voluntary organisation in the same circumstances (see paragraph 20).

Rate support grants

35. Expenditure by local authorities in discharging new duties under this Act will generally be relevant expenditure for the purposes of rate support grants. If the new duties should be prescribed before the grants for an ensuing period are settled by a main rate support grant order a forecast of the expenditure arising from those duties would figure in the settlement. Where expenditure arises from any provisions of the Act which may be brought into operation during a rate support grant period, that is to say, after the settlement of the main order for that period, the Minister of Housing and Local Government is enabled, by virtue of section 66, to take it into account in preparing a rate support grant increase order.

36. Special financial arrangements governing expenditure on old functions such as the provision and use of approved schools and remand homes are not altered, until those establishments cease to function in those categories.

Acquisition of land

37. Section 68 enables county borough and London borough councils and the Common Council of the City of London compulsorily to purchase land on the authority of the Secretary of State, for the purpose of this Act and of section 1 of the Act of 1963. Similar but general provisions relating to the compulsory acquisition by county councils, acting under the authority of the Secretary of State, are contained in section 159(1) of the Local Government Act, 1933, as modified by section 68(3) of this Act.

Schedule 4. Transitional Savings

38. Attention is drawn to the important transitional savings in paragraph 13 of Schedule 4. Starting on December 1, 1969, and continuing until a comprehensive regional plan for a particular planning area is in force (this may be on different days for different planning areas), local authorities in a planning area will continue to provide equip and maintain homes for the accommodation of children in their care, and to accommodate children in voluntary homes under the provisions of sections 15 and 16 respectively of the 1948 Act, notwithstanding the coming into force of section 38 of this Act and the repeal in Schedule 6 of those two sections of the 1948 Act. Similar savings apply in relation to accommodation in hostels provided under section 19 of the 1948 Act, notwithstanding the coming into force of section 50 of this Act (paragraph 13(1)(a) and (b)).

39. Section 77(1) of the Act of 1933 placed a duty on a local authority to provide for their area remand homes. Starting on December 1, 1969 and again continuing until a complete regional plan is in force, this subsection shall continue to apply as if the statutory duty were replaced by a permissive power (paragraph 13(1)(c)).

40. A change occurs in the legal status of children, who were at home "on trial" under the provisions of section 3(3) of the 1948 Act on the eve of December 1, 1969. Paragraph 14 of Schedule 4 provides that such children shall again be in the care of the local authority on December 1, 1969, but shall be deemed to be under the charge and control of the parent, guardian, relative or friend under the same terms as were applicable prior to that day. (See also paragraph 23 above.)

Amendments to the Children and Young Persons Act, 1933, the Children Act, 1948 and the Mental Health Act, 1959

41. Attention is drawn to a number of minor or consequential amendments to the Act of 1933 and the Act of 1948, set out in paragraphs 4, 14, 15, 18, 19, 21(1) and 21(3) of Schedule 5 to this Act.

42. Amendments relating to section 51(1) and (3) of the Children Act, 1948 and to section 9(1) of the Mental Health Act, 1959, set out in the first part of paragraph 20(1), paragraph 20(2) and paragraph 37 of Schedule 5 are also brought into force but will not fully apply until such time as the local authorities in a particular planning area cease to provide homes under section 15 of the 1948 Act. Until that time, by virtue of the transitional provisions in Schedule 3 to the Commencement No. 2 Order, these Amendments in paragraphs 20 and 37 shall have effect as if a home provided under section 15 were a community home provided by a local authority. (See also paragraph 38 above.)

Amendments to the Children and Young Persons Act, 1963

43. Two consequential amendments are made by paragraphs 51 and 52 of Schedule 5 to section 45 and 49 respectively of the Act of 1963.

Amendments to the Family Allowances Act, 1965

44. These amendments in the latter half of paragraph 54(2) and in paragraph 54(3) of Schedule 5 are consequential upon the coming into force of section 49 of this Act and the repeal of section 3(3) to (5) of the 1948 Act and section 5 of the Family Allowances and National Insurance Act, 1956.

Repeals

45. Various obsolete or redundant provisions, together with those which are consequential on the coming into force of the parts of the Act already referred to in this circular, are repealed in Schedule 6.

NOTE

This circular was sent to the Clerks of County, County Borough and London Borough Councils and the Common Council of the City of London.

Home Office Circular No. 240/1969   *Dated 18th November,* 1969.

CHILDREN AND YOUNG PERSONS ACT, 1969

1. I am directed by the Secretary of State to forward the enclosed copies of the Children and Young Persons Act, 1969 (Commencement No. 1) Order and the Children and Young Persons Act, 1969 (Commencement No. 2) Order which bring certain provisions of the Act into force on November 16, 1969, December 1, 1969 and January 1, 1970.

2. The provisions brought into force on November 16, 1969 concern amendments to the Social Work (Scotland) Act, 1968 and some related provisions. They were brought into force in preparation for the bringing into force of part of that Act later in November.

3. A separate circular will be issued later on the provisions to be brought into force on January 1, 1970, which relate to the law on private fostering

4. With the exception of the minor amendment to the law described in paragraph 11 below, the provisions to be brought into force on November 16, and December 1 do not directly alter the powers or the procedure of the courts. Apart from the purely Scottish provisions referred to in paragraph 2, they comprise the provisions on children's regional planning committees and the new system of community homes and most of the general and supplementary provisions in Part III of the Act. This will enable planning of the community home system to start as soon as possible.

5. The Secretary of State recently announced in Parliament his intention to bring into force on October 1, 1970, most of the remaining provisions of the Act. These will include the introduction of care proceedings, the new code of supervision and the replacement of approved school and fit person orders by care orders, but will not initially include the provisions of sections 4, 5 and 7(1) of the Act affecting the prosecution of children and young persons and the minimum age for borstal training. On the same date the tenth birthday will be specified as the age below which the local authority will normally be responsible for supervising a child under a supervision order and for providing the courts with information on a child's home surroundings. Further circulars will be issued about these provisions in due course.

6. Section 49 of the Act, which comes into force on December 1, 1969, substitutes a new section 13 of the Children Act, 1948. At present, a child in the care of a local authority may be accommodated in an approved school only if the school is provided by that local authority and the Secretary of State approves. The new section 13 contains no comparable restriction, since under the 1969 Act the separate approved school order will be abolished and approved schools will cease to form a separate system of residential establishments for children and young persons. The provision in the new section 13 of the 1948 Act for a local authority to discharge their duty to provide accommodation and maintenance for a child in their care by "making such other arrangements as seem appropriate to the local authority" will cover the accommodation of such a child in an

approved school while approved schools as such remain. This applies to children already in the care of a local authority as well as those who come into care after December 1.

7. When subsections (5) and (6) of section 7 of the Act (which abolish approved school and fit person orders) come into effect (which is intended on October 1, 1970) children and young persons subject to approved school orders or in the care of local authorities under fit person orders will be deemed, by paragraphs 7 and 8 of Schedule 4, to be subject to care orders. In the meantime, it will remain the statutory duty of a court which, after that date, would make a care order to decide whether to make an approved school order or a fit person order. On the other hand, it will become the statutory duty of the local authority to take account of the possibility of an approved school placement in the case of any child in their care for whom they consider that such a placement is likely to prove the most suitable of those available. In the case of fit person orders made from now on the court will have been aware of the possibility of such a placement when making the order.

8. The attention of the local authorities has been drawn to these considerations and the Secretary of State has expressed the hope that each authority will make arrangements for consultation with courts committing children to their care so as to avoid any misunderstanding in these cases.

9. It will be for the local authority to decide whether to seek an approved school placement in the light of their statutory duty to do what is best for the child, and for the managers of the school to decide whether to accept the child. Local authorities have been asked not to seek to place a child in their care in an approved school except through the existing approved school classifying agencies. This should assist in assessing whether such a placement best meets the child's needs and, if so, where these needs can best be met. In this connection, local authorities and approved schools have been reminded that the primary function of the schools, during this interim period, is to meet the needs of the courts in respect of children subject to approved school orders.

10. These arrangements apply to the accommodation of a child in care in an approved school. Where such a placement is made it will be open to the authority to return the child to other accommodation. It will also remain open to a local authority to bring a child before the juvenile court with a view to the making of an approved school order in which case he could be accommodated, until October 1, 1970, only in an approved school and thereafter, if still subject to the order on that date, in whatever manner the authority considered most appropriate.

11. Paragraph 4 of Schedule 5 to the Act amends section 46 of the Children and Young Persons Act, 1963. This amendment deals with the situation where, owing to a mistake as to his age, a young person is summoned to appear before an adult magistrates' court and pleads guilty by post under the Magistrates' Courts Act 1957 and the court does not discover that he is, in fact, under the age of seventeen until the proceedings are completed. In these circumstances there is nothing in the existing law to prevent the court's decision being invalidated by the subsequent discovery that the accused was a young person. The amendment provides that if in the case of a child or young person who pleads guilty by post the court has no reason to believe that he is a child or young person he should be deemed to have attained the age of seventeen. It does not enable an adult court to deal with a young person who pleads guilty by post if they have some reason to believe that he is under the age of seventeen, but operates only where the court deals with the case, in good faith, on the footing that the accused is aged seventeen or over.

NOTE

This circular was sent to the Clerks to the Justices.

Home Office Circular No. 246/1969   *Dated 25th November, 1969.*

CHILDREN AND YOUNG PERSONS ACT, 1969

The Children and Young Persons Act, 1969 received the Royal Assent on 22nd October, 1969 and will be brought into force by stages. Sections 69, 70 and 73 and some provisions relating to the Social Work (Scotland) Act, 1968 came into operation on 16th November, 1969 (Commencement No. 1 Order, S.I. 1969 No. 1552 of 3rd November, 1969). The main stage affecting England and Wales is 1st December, 1969 for those provisions in Part II of the Act concerned with the regional planning of a system of community homes and powers of inspection. Other miscellaneous provisions in Part III and in the Schedules are also brought into force on this day.

2. The next stage is 1st January, 1970 for the remaining provisions of Part II relating to private fostering. Provisions which come into force on 1st December, 1969 and 1st January, 1970 are set out in the Commencement No. 2 Order, S.I. 1969 No. 1565 of 6th November, 1969.

3. Provisions in Part I of the Act which concern voluntary organisations are not being brought into force in these first two stages and further circulars will be issued in due course to those organisations who are affected.

4. No immediate action on the part of voluntary organisations is required by virtue of the coming into force of those provisions of the Act listed in the Commencement No. 1 and No. 2 Orders. Nevertheless they may wish to consider what role they would like to play in the provision of voluntary community homes. When a children's regional planning committee is established for a particular planning area, an organisation may approach a committee or a relevant local authority in that area (irrespective of whether the voluntary home is located within that area) in order to open negotiations on the future status of the home as a community home. The committee or a relevant local authority may also approach a voluntary organisation with proposals.

5. I am to emphasise that there is nothing in the Act which prevents a voluntary home from remaining outside the community home system, if the organisation operating a home does not wish its premises to form part of such a system. On the other hand, if a voluntary home caters or intends to cater regularly for a significant number of children, who are legally in the care of local authorities, then the Secretary of State hopes that the organisation will give careful consideration to the advantages which accrue from controlled and assisted status of voluntary community homes under sections 39 to 42 of the Act.

6. I am also to point out that the formal consent of the voluntary organisation is required under section 36(5) and 37(5)(c) before any proposals are included in a regional plan or further regional plan relating to a community home by a voluntary organisation provided or proposed to be provided. Guidance will follow on the contents of instruments of management for voluntary community homes.

7. While the timetable for the subsequent action under the various provisions in Part II of the Act, from the making of planning area orders through to the making of instruments of management following the approval of a regional plan, must be speculative, the following guide may be of assistance to voluntary organisations in the timing of their own deliberations:

December 1969	Consultations by the Secretary of State with local authorities on planning areas.
January 1970	Planning area orders made.
March/April 1970	Children's regional planning committees established by local authorities.

| April 1970 to December 1971 | Planning committees prepare and submit regional plans. |
| April 1971 to April 1972 | Regional plans approved and brought into force. |

NOTE

This circular was sent to the Secretaries of Voluntary Organisations.

Home Office Circular No. 261/1969   *Dated 9th December, 1969.*

CHILDREN AND YOUNG PERSONS ACT, 1969— FOSTER CHILDREN

1. I am directed by the Secretary of State to refer to paragraph 3 of Home Office Circular No. 240/1969 and to send you the enclosed notes on those provisions of the Children and Young Persons Act, 1969, principally sections 51–57, which relate to private fostering. With certain minor exceptions, these provisions, which amend the Children Act, 1958, will come into force on 1st January, 1970.

2. These notes have also been sent to local authorities, and cover all the amendments to the Act of 1958, including those which do not directly affect the courts. Most of the amendments, however, are such that they may be relevant in proceedings brought under the 1958 Act.

3. Arrangements are being made for publicity to be given to these changes in the law on private fostering by the display of posters and by broadcast Government announcements.

NOTE

This circular was sent to the Clerks to the Justices.

NOTES ON THE CHILDREN ACT, 1958, AS AMENDED BY THE
CHILDREN AND YOUNG PERSONS ACT, 1969

For some time local authorities have been experiencing difficulty in carrying out their duties under the Children Act, 1958, to supervise children placed privately with foster parents. The amendments to the Act made by the Children and Young Persons Act, 1969, are designed to strengthen the powers of local authorities to supervise foster children and result from discussions between the Home Office and the local authority associations. (Somewhat similar amendments to the Nurseries and Child Minders Regulation Act, 1948, were made in the Health Services and Public Health Act, 1968.)

2. The principal amendments of the Children Act, 1958, are contained in sections 51–57 of the Children and Young Persons Act, 1969. Minor and consequential amendments and repeals are set out in Schedules 5 and 6 of the 1969 Act. Schedule 7 sets out sections 1–6 and 14 of the Children Act, 1958, as amended; it should however be noted that there are also minor amendments to sections of the Act other than those which appear in this Schedule.

3. All the amendments mentioned in paragraph 2, with the exception of section 56(1)(a), and of certain minor amendments in the Schedules relating to provisions of the 1969 Act which are not yet in operation, come into force on 1st January, 1970.

SECTION 51—MODIFICATION OF GENERAL DUTY OF LOCAL AUTHORITY
WITH RESPECT TO FOSTER CHILDREN

4. This substitutes a new section for section 1 of the Children Act, 1958. Under the new section it remains the duty of the local authority to satisfy themselves as to the well-being of foster children in their area. In place of the present requirement to visit all foster children from time to time, irrespective of the degree of supervision required, the new section substitutes a duty to secure that, so far as it appears

to the authority to be appropriate, the foster children are visited from time to time by officers of the authority and that such advice is given as to the care and maintenance of the children as appears to be needed.

5. This amendment is designed to make the duty of local authorities more flexible. It established clearly in the law the principle that the nature and degree of supervision given should be related to the authority's assessment of the needs of each individual case. While it is likely that an initial visit will normally be necessary, local authorities will not be obliged to make or continue visits where they are satisfied that visiting is not necessary to safeguard the welfare of the child or children in that home. For example, older children who are from time to time left with friends of the family for a few months while their parents are abroad may not need as much supervision as young children of overseas students who have come from a different climate and culture and have been placed with strangers.

SECTION 52—AMENDMENTS TO THE DEFINITION OF "FOSTER CHILD" AND "PROTECTED CHILD"

6. Subsection (1) amends the definition of foster child in section 2 of the Act by omitting the words "for reward for a period exceeding one month". The amended basic definition of a foster child is therefore "a child below the upper limit of compulsory school age whose care and maintenance are undertaken by a person who is not a relative or guardian of his". This definition is qualified by the subsequent subsections of section 2, as amended; in particular, children looked after for not more than six days are excluded—see paragraph 9.

7. The omission of the reference to reward will bring within the scope of the Children Act, 1958, fostering undertaken without reward, which has not hitherto been covered, including long term arrangements which amount to de facto adoptions. Some of these arrangements may prove quite satisfactory and regular visits to the home may not be necessary. There are, however, cases in which a person, or a couple, who would not be considered suitable adopters, obtain possession of a child, and, since they receive no payment, the child has not previously come within the definition of a foster child. If no notice of intention to apply for an adoption order is given, such a child has not hitherto been protected by either the Children Act, 1958, or the Adoption Act, 1958. From 1st January, 1970, authorities will have the power and the duty to supervise such children under the Children Act, 1958, irrespective of the date of placement.

8. The change in the definition of "foster child" will mean that the receipt or the promise of payment for looking after a foster child will cease to be relevant. Difficulties which authorities have experienced in establishing whether a particular fostering arrangement is "for reward" will no longer arise.

9. The omission of the words "for a period of one month" means that with certain exceptions (see paragraphs 11 and 12) anyone other than a relative or guardian who undertakes the care and maintenance of a child for more than six days is a foster parent and must comply with the requirements of the Children Act, 1958. This closes the gap which has existed between the Nurseries and Child-Minders Regulation Act, 1948, which protects only those children who are looked after for periods not exceeding six days, and the Children Act, 1958, which did not previously protect children who were looked after for periods of less than one month. The period was originally fixed at one month so as to exempt those who only took children occasionally, e.g., for short holidays, or in an emergency. This has now been achieved in another way by exempting those who are not "regular foster parents" (see paragraphs 12–14).

10. Subsection (2) narrows the exception from the definition of a foster child in section 2(3)(c) of the 1958 Act which at present covers children accommodated in any school within the meaning of the Education Acts, 1944–1953, or the Education (Scotland) Acts, 1939–1956. This amendment limits the exception to children who are "receiving full time education" in such schools, and is designed to bring within the protection of the 1958 Act children under school age who live on school premises, the children of school age who live on school premises but are being educated at day schools in the area. (See paragraph 47 for children at boarding schools in school holidays.)

11. Subsection (3) inserts a new subsection, (3A), in section 2 of the 1958 Act. Paragraph (a) of the new subsection exempts from the definition of a foster child a child whose care and maintenance are undertaken by a person other than a relative or guardian who does not intend to, and does not in fact, undertake his care and maintenance for a period of more than six days. Such children are protected by the Nurseries and Child-Minders Regulation Act, 1948, as amended (see paragraph 9).

12. Paragraph (b) of the new subsection (3A) exempts, from the definition of a foster child, children whose care and maintenance are undertaken for less than a month by those who are not regular foster parents (as defined by this subsection). This preserves the position whereby those who occasionally take children for a short holiday or in an emergency are exempt from the requirements of the Act (see paragraph 9).

13. The question whether a person is a "regular foster parent" is relevant only where a child is being looked after for not more than 27 days. The Children Act, 1958 (as amended) will apply on all occasions where a foster child is looked after for more than 27 days, irrespective of whether the foster parent comes within the definition of a "regular foster parent". The definition of a regular foster parent is a person (other than a relative or guardian) who during the period of twelve months immediately preceding the day on which he begins to undertake the care and maintenance of a child, has cared for one or more children either for a period of not less than three months (or periods amounting in the aggregate to not less than three months) or for at least three continuous periods each of which was of more than six days. The effect will be that all those who look after children at all regularly for periods not exceeding 27 days will either be "regular foster parents" or covered by the Nurseries and Child-Minders Regulation Act, 1948. The exemption is intended to cover, for instance the good neighbour who takes a child for two or three weeks on an isolated occasion when the child's mother is ill, or the friend who has a child for a fortnight's holiday once or twice a year.

14. In the case of the *Surrey County Council* v. *Battersby*, [1965] 2 Q. B. 194; [1965] 1 All E. R. 273; 129 J.P. 116, it was held that a period does not cease to be a continuous period simply because a child occasionally at a weekend goes to the home of its parent.

15. Subsection (4) amends section 37 of the Adoption Act, 1958, which defines a protected child for the purpose of Part IV of that Act. These amendments are consequential on the omission from the definition of a foster parent of the words "for reward". Section 50 of the Adoption Act, 1958, prohibits any payment or reward in respect of a child placed for adoption, and it has previously been possible to distinguish a "protected child" under the Adoption Act, 1958, from a foster child under the Children Act, 1958, by the absence of reward. Now that non-reward cases are to be included in the definition of a foster child it has been necessary to clarify the position by amending the definition of a protected child in section 37 of the Adoption Act, 1958 as follows:—

   (a) Subsection 1(a) is amended so that a child is only a protected child if he is placed with a person (other than a parent guardian or relative) "who proposes to adopt him".
   (b) In subsection (1) the words excluding those who are foster children within the meaning of the Children Act, 1958, are omitted because they are no longer necessary. (See (a) above.)
   (c) In subsection (2) the words referring to a child only temporarily in the care and possession of a person are omitted because as a result of (a) above they are no longer relevant.

The references to the Minister of Pensions and National Insurance have been omitted from section 37 of the Adoption Act, 1958, and from section 2(2) of the Children Act, 1958, because they are no longer relevant.

16. Subsection (5) adds a new subsection (4A) to section 2 of the Children Act, 1958. This is consequential on the amended definition of "protected child" in section 37 of the Adoption Act, 1958. It provides that a child is not a foster child while he is placed in the care of a person who proposes to adopt him under arrangements made by a local authority or registered adoption society, nor while he is a protected child within the meaning of Part IV of the Adoption Act, 1958.

17. The combined effect of subsections (4) and (5) is that in future the Adoption Act provisions will apply to all children placed with a view to adoption, and only to such children, and all other cases will be covered by the Children Act, 1958.

SECTION 53—MODIFICATION OF DUTY OF PERSONS MAINTAINING FOSTER CHILDREN TO NOTIFY LOCAL AUTHORITY

18. The principal effect of this section is to amend section 3 of the Children Act, 1958, so that the present requirement on a person to notify the local authority of each child whom he proposes to maintain as a foster child, and each foster child who is removed from his care, is replaced by a requirement to give notice only when a person becomes, or ceases to be, a foster parent. The object is to relieve local authorities and foster parents of some of the work of giving and dealing with notifications in cases where the authority is satisfied with the general quality of care foster parents provide and there is no need to require particulars of every arrival and departure. Section 3, as amended, is intended to ensure that authorities are aware which homes are being used for private fostering; and section 4(2), as extended, will cover any requirements needed in relation to particular foster homes, including requirements to give notifications in respect of individual children (see paragraphs 30–33).

19. Subsection (1) sets out the general intention of section 53, which is to modify section 3 of the Children Act, 1958.

20. Subsection (2) amends section 3(1) of the Act *firstly* by requiring notice to be given not less than two weeks and not more than four weeks before the date on which it is proposed that a foster child shall be received instead of the existing requirement to give at least two weeks' notice. Now that notices will relate not to the reception of particular children, but to the intention to begin private fostering, it is necessary to define the period more precisely so that notifications are not given, and local authorities do not have to investigate homes, in cases where there is no more than a general intention to take foster children at some date in the future if the opportunity should arise. Where such a notice is given it is hoped that every effort will be made to investigate the home before the first child is received.

21. Secondly, subsection (2) amends section 3(1) of the Act so as to require notifications of the reception of a child in an emergency, or of a foster child who becomes a foster child while in a person's care, to be given within forty-eight hours instead of one week as at present. This will enable local authorities to follow up such notifications as expeditiously as possible and to act quickly where a child is placed in an unsuitable home without prior notification. It should be particularly noted that, on 1st January, 1970, section 3(1) of the 1958 Act (as amended) will apply for the first time to all children, already living with foster parents, who come within the extended definition of "foster child" in section 2 but not within the present definition. Unless the foster parents in question have already notified the local authority of another child still in their care who comes within the present definition, they will then be required to give notification within forty eight hours. In making arrangements to publicise the extended scope of the Act of 1958, and in considering questions of enforcement, authorities will no doubt bear in mind that some foster parents, *e.g.*, those who have been looking after a child without reward for a long time, may nevertheless not immediately become aware that the provisions of the Act now apply in their case.

22. Subsection (3) amends section 3(2) of the Act by adding, to the details which the notice must give, the date on which it is intended that the child should be received or, as the case may be, the date on which the child was in fact received or became a foster child. This is intended to avoid local authorities receiving notifications in vague terms, and to assist them in the timing of initial visits. (A child does not necessarily become a foster child on the date on which he is received; for example, if a parent, relative or guardian also lives in the foster home for a time, the child does not become a foster child until the date the parent, relative or guardian leaves.)

23. Subsection (4) inserts a new subsection (3A) in section 3 of the Act. The effect of the new subsection is that separate notices will no longer be required in respect of individual foster children. In future, notice must be given when a

person intends to become a foster parent. This is achieved by relieving a foster parent of the obligation to give notice in respect of a child if he has given notice on a previous occasion and if he has not, since that notice was given, ceased to maintain a foster child on those premises in circumstances in which he was required to give notice of this under the new subsection (5A) (see paragraph 26). (Local authorities will have power to require particulars of individual children received by a foster parent or a person who proposes to keep foster children, in cases where they consider this necessary—see paragraph 31.)

24. Subsection (5) makes consequential amendments to section 3(3) of the Act, which requires notice to be given of a change of address on the part of the foster parent or a change in the premises in which a foster child is kept. The amendments make it clear that notice of such a change may be given in respect of one or more children, and requires between two and four weeks' advance notice to be given in normal circumstances, and notice within forty-eight hours after a change made in an emergency.

25. Subsection (6) removes from section 3(4) of the Act the requirement to notify the removal of every foster child from the care of the person maintaining him and leaves only the requirement to notify the death of any foster child. It also makes consequential amendments to section 3(5) of the Act by omitting the reference to circumstances in which notice of removal need not be given (since this is now superfluous) and requiring the person who was maintaining a foster child who is removed or removes himself from his care, at the request of the local authority, the name and address, if known, of the person (if any) into whose care the child has been removed.

26. Subsection (7) adds to new subsections (5A) and (5B) to section 3 of the Act. Subsection (5A) requires a person who has been maintaining one or more foster children at any premises and who ceases to maintain foster children at those premises to give notice to the local authority within forty-eight hours, unless notice so required under subsection (3) or (4); this replaces the requirement to notify the removal of individual foster children. Subsection (5B) clarifies the position of a person who ceases to maintain foster children temporarily but expects to receive them back within twenty-seven days; its effect is that such a person will not be required to notify the local authority that he had ceased to maintain foster children unless he abandons his intention to have the child or children back within that period, or the period expires without their returning, in which case he must give notice within forty-eight hours.

SECTION 54—INSPECTION OF PREMISES IN WHICH FOSTER CHILDREN ARE KEPT

27. Subsection (1) amends section 4(1) of the Children Act, 1958, to make it clear that an officer of a local authority may inspect the whole or any part of premises in which foster children are kept. For example, the kitchen may be inspected even though foster children may not be "kept" in that part of the premises.

28. Subsection (2) adds to section 4 of the 1958 Act a new subsection (1A) which authorises a justice of the peace to issue a warrant for an officer of a local authority to enter premises, if need be by force, and search for a foster child at any reasonable time within forty-eight hours of the issue of the warrant. Such a warrant may be issued only if the justice of the peace is satisfied, on sworn information in writing, that there is reasonable cause to believe that a foster child is in the premises, or part of them, and that admission to those premises has been refused to an authorised officer of the local authority, or that such refusal is thought to be likely or that the occupier is temporarily absent. This brings the Children Act, 1958, into line with the Nurseries and Child-Minders Act, 1948 (section 7(2)) under which there is power to issue a warrant for inspection.

Only an officer of the local authority is qualified to inspect premises in which foster children are kept and the warrant will therefore authorise an officer of the local authority to enter the premises. If, however, there is any reason to expect that a breach of the peace may ensue, the police should be asked to co-operate by sending a constable to accompany the local authority's officer to the premises concerned.

29. Subsection (3) adds, to the list of offences in section 14(1) of the 1958 Act, that of wilfully obstructing a person entitled to enter any premises by virtue of a warrant to carry out an inspection under section 4(1A).

SECTION 55—IMPOSITION OF REQUIREMENTS AND PROHIBITIONS
RELATING TO THE KEEPING OF FOSTER CHILDREN

30. Subsection (1) amends section 4(2) of the Children Act, 1958, by extending the local authority's power to impose requirements on foster parents so as to include those who use premises only partly for keeping foster children. This means that in future conditions can be imposed on *any* home in which foster children are kept, instead of, as hitherto, only those used wholly or mainly for keeping foster children; and in each case where notice of intention to begin keeping foster children is given the question will arise what conditions, if any, should be imposed. It will also become possible to impose conditions as respects existing foster homes where the premises are not used wholly or mainly for keeping foster children. (Although section 4(2) of the Act refers to foster children in the plural, the Interpretation Act, 1889, provides that the plural includes the singular, and conditions may be imposed even if only one foster child is kept in the premises.) It is for each local authority to decide to what extent, if any, some or all of the various types of condition may be imposed by the Children's Committee or by an appropriate officer of the Council acting under the authority of that committee.

31. Subsection (2) adds two new requirements to those which may be imposed under section 4(2) of the Act. The new paragraph (g) will enable requirements to be imposed in respect of the fire precautions to be taken in the premises; this may be particularly important where young children are kept. The new paragraph (h) will enable the local authority to require the giving of particulars of any foster child received in the premises or of any change in the number or identity of the foster children kept there. Foster parents in general have been relieved of the obligation to notify the reception of every child (see paragraph 23) and the new paragraph (h) enables the local authority to impose comparable requirements to the extent that seems necessary in relation to particular foster homes, or to particular categories of children (see also paragraph 33).

32. The suggestion was made, during the Parliamentary proceedings on the Bill, that section 4(2) of the 1958 Act should expressly provide for requirements to be imposed in respect of such matters as window-bars and fencing in the interests of safety. No amendment was made for this purpose because it was considered that the matter was already covered by paragraph (b), which relates to the accommodation and equipment to be provided for the children.

33. Subsection (3) makes an addition to the final paragraph of section 4(2) of the Act so as to permit any of the requirements listed to be limited to a particular class of foster children. For example, the local authority might wish to impose a requirement under the new paragraph (h) that the reception of, say, every child under the age of twelve months or every handicapped child, should be notified. (The substitution of (b) to (h) for (b) to (f) is a consequence of the addition of the two new requirements—see paragraph 31.)

34. Subsection (4) deals with prohibitions, and replaces section 4 (3) of the Act by the three new subsections 4(3), 4(3A) and 4(3B). Doubt had been expressed whether a prohibition could be imposed under the original section 4(3) if the premises were suitable but the person was not. It was the clear intention of Parliament in 1958 that this should be possible. The new provisions remove any possible doubts by setting out separately the three distinct grounds on which a prohibition may be imposed, which are (a) if the premises are unsuitable for foster children; or (b) if the person is not a suitable person to have the care of foster children; or (c) if it would be detrimental to a particular child to be kept by that person in those premises. The latter prohibition might be applied if, for example, the premises were generally suitable for keeping foster children but would not be suitable for a child with a particular handicap, or if a foster parent was regarded as suitable for keeping older children but not for looking after a very young baby.

35. The new subsection (3A) of section 4 sets out the three forms the prohibition may take. If particular premises are unsuitable a prohibition as at (a) may prevent

the person from keeping any foster child in those premises. If the person is unsuitable, a prohibition as at (b) may prevent him for keeping foster children in any premises in the area of the local authority imposing it. If the premises or the person are unsuitable only in respect of a particular child, a prohibition as at (c) may relate to the keeping by him of a particular child specified in the prohibition in specified premises.

36. The new subsection (3B) of section 4 enables a local authority to cancel a prohibition if they think fit, either of their own motion (e.g., if they are aware that the premises have been suitably improved) or on an application made by the prospective foster parent on the grounds of a change in the circumstances in which a foster child would be kept by him.

37. Subsection (5) makes an addition to section 5(1) of the 1958 Act (which confers a right to appeal to a juvenile court, within fourteen days, against the imposition of a prohibition or requirement) by conferring a similar right of appeal to a juvenile court against the refusal of a local authority to grant an application for the cancellation of a prohibition imposed under subsection (3A) of section 4. For example, if a person claims to have improved the premises the local authority considered unsuitable, and the local authority refuse to grant his application for cancellation of the prohibition on the grounds that they are still not suitable, that person could appeal to a juvenile court within fourteen days of the refusal.

SECTION 56—EXTENSION OF DISQUALIFICATION FOR KEEPING FOSTER CHILDREN

38. Subsection (1) amends the list of orders in section 6 of the 1958 Act (which disqualify a person from maintaining foster children unless he has disclosed the existence of the order to the local authority and obtained their consent. The amendment at (a), to section 6(b) of the 1958 Act, will not come into force on 1st January, 1970; it will be brought into operation at the same time as the relevant sections of the Children and Young Persons Act, 1969 and the Social Work (Scotland) Act, 1968.

39. The amendment at (b), to section 6 (c) of the Act, disqualifies a person who had been placed on probation or given an absolute or conditional discharge in respect of any offence against children referred to in that paragraph unless he has disclosed that fact to the local authority and obtained their consent. For other purposes a conviction followed by probation or discharge does not count as a conviction.

40. The amendment at (c), to section 6(e) of the 1958 Act, rectifies a minor omission. It will disqualify a person who has been refused registration of any premises under section 1(3) of the Nurseries and Child-Minders Regulation Act, 1948 (as well as those who have had the registration of the premises cancelled).

41. The amendment at (d) makes an addition (f) to the list of orders in section 6 of the 1958 Act. In future a person against whom an order has been made under section 43 of the Adoption Act, 1958, for the removal of a protected child who was being kept or was about to be kept by him will be disqualified from keeping foster children unless he has disclosed that fact to the local authority and obtained their consent.

42. Subsection (2) adds a new subsection (2) to section 6 of the 1958 Act, relating to persons who live or are employed on premises in which it is proposed to keep foster children. In future if a person residing in or employed at the premises, for example, a son, lodger or cook of the intending foster parent, has been convicted of an offence against children or has had an order made against him removing a foster child from his care, the employer will not be able to keep foster children unless he has disclosed this fact to the local authority and obtained their consent. There is, however, protection for the person who is not aware of the fact of the other person's conviction or order (see paragraph 43).

SECTION 57—MODIFICATIONS OF PROVISIONS AS TO OFFENCES

43. Subsection (1) adds to section 14 of the Act (which deals with offences) a new subsection (1A) which protects from conviction a person who keeps a foster child in contravention of section 6 of the Act if he proves that he did not know, and had no

reasonable ground for believing, that a person living or employed in the premises had a disqualification from keeping foster children. For example, a foster parent could be expected to know whether a member of his family had such a disqualification, but he might not know in the case of an employee or a lodger, and he will not be guilty of an offence if he can establish that he did not know and had no reason to know of the other person's disqualification.

44. Subsection (2) adds a new subsection (2A) to section 14(2) of the Act. It has not previously been possible to bring a prosecution for failure to give a notification required by the Act unless the failure has been discovered within six months, which is the time limit for bringing summary proceedings laid down in section 194 of the Magistrates' Courts Act, 1952. The new subsection (2A) will permit proceedings for the offence to be brought at any time within six months from the date on which the local authority became aware of it.

SCHEDULE 5—MINOR AND CONSEQUENTIAL AMENDMENTS OF ENACTMENTS

45. Paragraph 29, which amends section 2(4) of the 1958 Act, will not come into force on 1st January, 1970. It will be brought into operation when the powers to make supervision orders under the Children and Young Persons Act, 1969, comes into force. The reference in the amended section 2(4) to a "supervision requirement" is to a supervision requirement under the Social Work (Scotland) Act, 1968.

46. Paragraph 30 amends section 9 of the 1958 Act, which relates to insurances on the lives of foster children, and is a consequence of the amended definitition of a foster child (see paragraph 6). It preserves the position whereby a person who maintains a foster child *for reward* shall be deemed for the purposes of the Life Assurance Act, 1774, to have no interest in the life of the child.

47. Paragraph 31 amends section 12(1) of the 1958 Act and reduces from one month to two weeks the period for which a child below the upper limit of compulsory school age can reside in a school during the school holidays without coming within the definition of a foster child. This was considered desirable because in some cases the staff available to look after such children in boarding schools during the holidays has not been adequate, particularly in the case of schools which take in for the holidays children from other schools which have closed.

48. Paragraph 32, which amends certain definitions in section 17 of the 1958 Act, will not come into operation on 1st January, 1970 but at a later date.

49. Paragraph 35 amends section 37(2) of the Adoption Act, 1958, by omitting the reference to section 2(5) of the Children Act, 1958, which is repealed by Schedule 6 of the Children and Young Persons Act, 1969 (see paragraph 53).

SCHEDULE 6—REPEALS: CHILDREN ACT, 1958

50. In section 2(1) the words "for reward for a period exceeding one month" are repealed as a consequence of the amended definition of a foster child resulting from section 52(1) (see paragraph 6).

51. In section 2(2) the words "by the Minister of Pensions and National Insurance or" are repealed because no children below the upper limit of compulsory school age are now boarded out by the Department of Health and Social Security and no more children will come into the care of that Department.

52. In section 2(4) the words "the Children and Young Persons Act, 1933, or of" will not be repealed on 1st January, 1970 but at a later date (see paragraph 45).

53. Section 2(5) and (6) dealt with the meaning of "reward" and are repealed as redundant as a consequence of the amended definition of a foster child (see paragraph 6).

54. In section 3(4) the reference to notification of the removal of a child is repealed as a consequence of section 53(6) of the Children and Young Persons Act, 1969, (see paragraph 25) but if a child dies the person who was maintaining him is still required to notify, within forty-eight hours, both the local authority and the person from whom the child was received.

55. In section 3(5) the reference to notice of removal is repealed as a further consequence of section 53(6) of the 1969 Act.

56. Section 3(6), which gave the local authority power to exempt any person from the duty of giving notices under this section is repealed, again in consequence of section 53 of the 1969 Act.

57. In section 17, the reference in the definition of a fit person order to the Children and Young Persons Act, 1933, will be repealed at a later date.

58. In Schedule 2 of the Children Act, 1958 the reference to section 54 of the Children Act, 1948, is repealed with effect from 1st December, 1969, the date of the repeal of that section by the 1969 Act.

Adoption Act, 1958

59. In the Adoption Act, 1958, section 15(3) the reference to fit person orders will not be repealed on 1st January, 1970, but on the abolition of fit person orders.

60. In section 37(1) the words "but is not a foster child within the meaning of Part I of the Children Act, 1958" are repealed as a consequence of section 52(4)(b) of the 1969 Act.

61. In section 37(2) the words from "by reason" to "that subsection" are repealed as a consequence of section 52(4)(c) of the 1969 Act.

62. In section 37(3) the reference to an approved school is not repealed on 1st January, 1970, but will be repealed at a later date.

Schedule 7—Sections 1 to 6 and 14 of the Children Act, 1948 as Amended

63. Schedule 7 sets out sections 1–6 and 14 of the Children Act, 1958, as amended. It should be noted that amendments to section 2(4) (see paragraph 45) and section 6(b) (see paragraph 38) do not come into force on 1st January, 1970, and that amendments to sections 9 and 12 which are not shown in Schedule 7 do come into force on 1st January, 1970 (see paragraphs 46 and 47).

Home Office Circular No. 184/1970.   *Dated* 21 *August,* 1970

CHILDREN AND YOUNG PERSONS ACT, 1969: ADMISSION OF CHILDREN IN CARE TO APPROVED SCHOOLS AFTER 1 JANUARY 1971 AND POSITION OF SCHOOLS DURING THE TRANSITIONAL PERIOD

Abolition of the approved school order

As indicated in Home Office Circulars No. 180/1970 (issued to Correspondents of approved schools) and No. 182/1970 (issued to local authorities) the Secretary of State intends to make a commencement order bringing into force most of Part I of the Children and Young Persons Act, 1969, on 1 January 1971; and an order under section 7 (5) specifying the same date for the purposes of that subsection and accordingly for the purposes of paragraphs 3–7 of Schedule 3. From that date the courts will no longer have power to make approved school orders (section 7) and the boys and girls who are already subject to approved school orders will be deemed instead to be in the care of the appropriate local authority (paragraph 7 of Schedule 4). Guidance will be issued in a separate circular on the formal and administrative implications of this change in status of the boys and girls already in the schools or who may be admitted after 1 January 1971 and on the necessary consequential amendments to the approved school rules and on the other consequential changes in the law relating to approved schools for which the Act provides.

2. The object of this circular is to deal (in accordance with the undertaking given in paragraph 14 of the Home Office Circular 238/1969) with the question of procedures for the admission of boys and girls in care to approved schools

after 1 January, 1971, during the transitional period before regional plans are approved and implemented, *i.e.* the period during which all the children whom the schools will be taking will be in the care of a local authority but the schools will still be operating as approved schools, and will not have acquired community home status.

Position of the schools

3. Until regional plans for the accommodation of children in care are approved by the Secretary of State and, in the case of each particular school, an order has been made under section 46 formally terminating its status as an approved school, with a view to acquisition of a new status as a community home (or whatever other future may have been chosen for the establishment in accordance with the options open to the school—see Home Office Circular No. 47/1970) approved schools will continue to operate within the provisions of the Children and Young Persons Act, 1933, subject only to such necessary amendments as have been made in schedule 4 to the Children and Young Persons Act, 1969 to take account of the abolition of the approved school order itself. Paragraph 3 of Schedule 3, which will also be brought into operation on 1 January, 1971, enables approved schools to be used for the accommodation of children in care and when read with paragraph 7 has the effect of ensuring that such accommodation of children will not conflict with the terms of any trust deed. The combined effect of these provisions is that approved schools will be added to the range of facilities available to local authorities for the accommodation of children in their care.

4. The Secretary of State will however retain his overall responsibility for approved schools and to this end will be concerned to ensure that their general character as establishments structured and staffed to provide care, control and treatment for boys and girls whose needs can best be met only in a residential setting with most or all of the education provided on the premises, remains unchanged. In this connection it will accordingly be noted that the regulatory provisions of the existing law in relation to the classification of schools (certified numbers, religious persuasion, age and sex of those admitted), approval of staffing structures and control of expenditure generally will continue to apply.

5. The abolition of the approved school order on 1 January 1971 will however necessarily bring about a fundamental change in one aspect of the operation of the approved school service as a whole, namely, the procedures for securing the admission of boys and girls to particular schools. For while it is intended that the service provided by the classifying schools (and remand homes) should continue during this transitional period, both as being of value on child care grounds and as being integral to the proper functioning of the service as a whole, the statutory framework within which they have hitherto operated will have been abolished—namely, the selection by the courts of the children who are in need of approved school training (by their power to make approved school orders), the power of the Secretary of State to determine to which school the child is to be sent (section 8 of the 1963 Act) which is exercised mainly through the medium of the classifying schools and remand homes, and the obligation on the part of managers to accept the boys and girls allocated to them in this way (section 81 (2) of the 1933 Act). These provisions, linked specifically as they are to the approved school order will be amongst those repealed on 1 January 1971.

6. The position after 1 January 1971 will accordingly be that in the kind of case where the courts would have made an approved school order, there will instead be power to make a care order committing the child to the care of a local authority. Once a child has been made the subject of a care order, the local authority will have the responsibility of deciding what kind of care is needed. As already stated, the range of facilities available to local authorities

for all children in care will include approved schools; and there will continue to be children for whom the kind of treatment that only the approved schools can provide is wanted. It is expected that the schools generally will eventually be integrated into the community home system, but in the meantime it is necessary to ensure that the facilities of the existing nationally structured and centrally financed approved school service are made available in the most productive way to individual local authorities for children in their care. At the same time, it is recognised that for their part the local authorities have and will retain full responsibility for the treatment of each individual child, and that the managers of the schools will be under no statutory obligation to admit any particular child.

The problem

7. The problem is twofold: on the one hand to identify the minority of children coming into care whose treatment needs can best be met only within the kind of total living situation which approved schools provide, and on the other hand to identify and secure a place in an appropriate school. These twin problems of assessment and allocation are very closely inter-related. For while the responsibility for deciding what kind of care, control and treatment the child needs and where the child is to be sent to get it, will rest with the local authority in whose care the child is, there will be no statutory obligation on the managers of an approved school to accept placements of children in care by local authorities. It is clearly therefore essential that whatever method of assessment be adopted by local authorities it should be such as to satisfy the approved school to which it is desired that the child in question should be allocated. The selection and allocation of children to approved schools is a two-way transaction in which it is as needful for the *receiving* establishment to be assured of the appropriateness of the placement as it is for the *placing* authority. With this general principle as the starting point, the following factors should be taken into account.

(a) *Standard of assessment*

8. The essence of the provision made by approved schools is that they provide care, control, education and treatment in a total living situation. Removal of a child from his familiar environment (which is what care in a total living situation implies) is a step that should be taken only if clearly unavoidable. It is children who are found after diagnosis and assessment to need a period in a structured environment who should receive treatment of this kind. By the same token it is more than ever important that the treatment decision is right: an inappropriate placement can be damaging to the child. It is therefore of the first importance that a child should not be placed in an approved school unless that child's needs really can best be met there, and conversely that the child who does need such a placement is identified.

9. Thorough and reliable assessment of the child's needs in the way of care and control, is crucial to proper treatment. By definition, these are children with serious and complex problems. It will be recognised that to this extent the proper assessment of their needs will necessarily entail a fairly lengthy and penetrating analysis of what has gone wrong and what form of care, control and treatment is needed in order to put it right.

(b) *Allocation*

10. Hitherto the courts have taken care of the selection of children for approved schools, so that the assessment machinery has been concerned with determining only which school best meets the child's needs and providing a diagnosis as a basis for treatment. Once the approved school order has been abolished it will be for the local authority in whose care the child is to decide whether residential treatment is appropriate and where. But whereas local

authorities will be familiar with the range and scope of residential provision within the existing child care services, the character and potential of the approved school system will not necessarily be equally familiar to all local authorities, and even those with expertise derived from running their own approved schools will not always have any very detailed knowledge of other schools. During this period when approved schools will continue to exist as a separate system, structured moreover to operate on a national and not a regional basis, it is desirable that the procedures for allocation to approved schools should link as closely as possible into the existing machinery within the approved school service, if full use is to be made of their considerable range of facilities.

Inter-relationship of assessment and allocation

11. It is clearly not impracticable for assessment and allocation to be treated as distinct and separate exercises. To some extent this occurs already in those cases where allocation to an approved school is carried out by the Vacancies Pool at the Home Office on the basis of case papers submitted direct by the local authority. But it has always been recognised that this arrangement (it applies only to those classes of child which for geographical or other reasons cannot practicably be fitted into the normal classifying system) is less than perfect in its operation, and workable at best only if (a) the case papers are in sufficient detail and cover the necessary range of reports, *i.e.* provide the material on which a reasoned judgment can properly be based; and (b) there are in the last resort facilities for running further tests in an assessment situation if the case is particularly difficult or complex. It is desirable therefore that whatever allocation system is adopted, it should be closely integrated into the assessment system.

The problems of disruptive children

12. Many if not most of the children who pass through the approved school system are not only disturbed and difficult to treat, but are potentially and often actually disruptive of the environment in which they are placed. This may be manifested in physical violence, but can be no less a problem when found in the form of disaffection and incitement of misbehaviour by others. This is a problem which there is no reason to suppose will disappear and it raises a special problem over placement. For these are often the kind of child for whom there is the most need to find places in approved schools (they are often the ones for whom other forms of residential provision have been tried without success). But they are also the kind of child whom, understandably, the individual schools are likely to be the most reluctant to admit or to keep if trouble develops after admission. There will be no statutory obligation upon the schools to accept these difficult youngsters. On the other hand the schools recognise and have always recognised that their role in the child care field is precisely to deal with children who need more constant support, attention and control than can be provided in the conditions prevailing in most children's homes (which are not ordinarily structured to handle this kind of situation), and that their expertise includes the handling of children who are anti-social or disruptive and have special needs, as well as those whose problems can be relatively peacefully contained.

13. There should accordingly be no reason to doubt the continued willingness of the schools generally, and of the individual school in each case, to handle these difficult children provided that the schools are satisfied that the initial assessment is adequate and the allocation appropriate; and that they could count on arrangements being made for securing transfer of the child elsewhere (if necessary after re-assessment) if it transpires that the school cannot handle him or that his treatment needs are not such as can best be met at that school.

Attitude of the family

14. Approved schools provide treatment in a setting that provides a substantial degree of control, coupled with care and education. It is a setting, however, which inevitably—even if no significant physical distance is involved—entails a degree of separation from the child's home, his home neighbourhood and friends. In carrying out their first duty to do what is best for the child, local authorities will wish to satisfy themselves and be able to demonstrate to parents and others who may be apprehensive about an approved school placement that this form of treatment is appropriate for a particular child. This is a field in which the approved school classifying establishments have proven expertise; and where their recommendations as to placement and advice as to treatment needs may be expected to carry deserved weight both within the family and in the wider context of the public at large.

Recommended procedure

15. The following procedure which has the support of the local authority and approved school representative associations is accordingly recommended to local authorities and schools.

16. *Local authorities* seeking an approved school placement (under section 13 (1) of the Children Act, 1948) for a child in their care should, in the interests of ensuring (a) that the facilities provided by approved schools should be readily available to them for the accommodation of children in care (including the more socially disruptive), and (b) that they are in a position to make the best use of these facilities—seek the advice of the appropriate approved school classifying establishment or of the Home Office Vacancies Pool (in accordance with the arrangements set out in Annex A to this circular) before attempting to negotiate a placement with an individual school. This need not necessitate in every case the actual referral of the child to the classifying school or remand home, as the case may be. In a straightforward case where full assessment has already been carried out, it should be possible for the classifying establishment to make a recommendation on the basis of scrutiny of the case papers alone, supplemented as necessary by consultation with the local authority (for details of the range of reports that should normally be supplied—see Annex B).

17. *Managers of schools* should likewise in the interests of (a) securing a fair and appropriate distribution of placements within the service as a whole, and (b) safeguarding the general character of the facilities which approved schools exist to provide, not accept placements other than in accordance with this procedure.

18. The basic principle underlying this recommended rule of practice is thus that the local authority should not seek nor the schools be expected to accept a proposed placement without the reassurance of a recommendation from the recognised approved school classifying agency from whom they have been accustomed to accept placements, that the particular placement is in fact appropriate in the context of the existing approved school system in relation to the child's needs, to the school's facilities and resources and to the overall demands on the approved school service as a whole. For as indicated in paragraph 4 above the approved school service as a whole is structured, regulated and financed by the Secretary of State on the basis of providing what are recognised as specialised facilities for the care, control and treatment of a minority of children whose needs cannot be met otherwise than in the supportive setting of a structured environment capable of providing a total living situation. So long therefore as the schools continue to operate as such, during this transitional period, the Secretary of State will be concerned to ensure that facilities thus provided from public funds, and subject to his control, should not cease to be available for the purpose for which these funds continue to be provided. While therefore it is recognised that in a period of transition a flexible approach

to assessment and allocation is desirable and necessary, and while local authorities and managers are not therefore required to regard the procedures recommended in paragraph 16 above as necessarily mandatory in all circumstances,
the proposed rule of practice is strongly commended as a very desirable safeguard
in the interests of the child, the local authority and the school.

Charges

19. Flat rate contributions will continue to be payable during the transitional
period and any local authority placing a child in care in an approved school
will be liable to pay them. For the present rate see Home Office Circular
22/1970. Any remand home designated under section 11 (1) of the Children and
Young Persons Act, 1963 will be treated as an approved school for financial
purposes if a direction has been made under section 11 (3).

Transfer to other accommodation

30. Sometimes it will be found that a child is not making satisfactory progress
in the school in which he has been placed and it might be felt that it would be
in the child's best interests to move him to some other form of establishment or
perhaps to another approved school. The initiative for such a move may come
from the "care" authority or from the school, who advise the authority. The
"care" authority may consider it necessary to consult a classifying agency in
respect of a transfer to another approved school in which case the general procedure recommended in relation to admission to approved schools should apply.
In cases of this kind, however, the Home Office Inspectorate might well be able
to assist authorities in view of their knowledge of all the schools concerned, by
suggesting a more suitable placement for a child who is making poor progress
in the school in which he has been placed. Transfers to establishments other
than approved schools will be a matter for the local authority in whose care the
child is.

Special units

21. There are special units providing secure accommodation at 3 of the boys'
classifying schools (Kingswood, Red Bank and Redhill). There are about 70
places for boys in the units, and the unit at Red Bank School provides secure
accommodation also for up to 6 girls. The question whether a child can be
accepted in one of these units rests, ultimately, with the managers of the schools
concerned, but since places are so restricted, and since treatment in these units
is only suitable for a small group of children with very severe behaviour problems, it has been the rule that admission is made to the special units only after
consultation with the Home Office Inspectorate. This procedure will continue.
Where, therefore, a "care" authority is seeking a placement in one of the units,
the authority should consult the Regional Inspectorate before a final decision
is taken. The schools should not accept a boy or girl for admission to a special
unit unless this clearance has been obtained.

General

22. It will be noted that—even with a recognised element of pre-selection by
local authorities—the task of the classifying schools and remand homes will
include a dual responsibility: not only to recommend what approved school is
best suited to the needs of the children whose cases are referred to them (whether
or not the school carries out the assessment itself) but also to advise on whether
approved school placement is appropriate at all. If the system is to work
satisfactorily there will be a need for local authorities and the classifying

establishments respectively to familiarise themselves with the general scope of one another's facilities for the residential (and other) care of these difficult and disturbed children.

Position of schools during the transitional period

23. This circular is not concerned with the long term arrangements for the assessment and allocation of children in care after the community home system has been brought into effect. This will be a matter for regional planning committees to determine within the broad framework of the community home system as a whole. But to the extent that former approved schools will be part of that system, account has been taken in the framing of the suggested transitional procedure for assessment and allocation of "care" children to approved schools, of the fact that identification of the treatment needs of this group of particularly difficult children will remain a problem to which a solution will have to be found within the wider framework of the assessment and allocation of all children in care under the community home system. The procedure outlined in paragraph 16 above has accordingly been framed so as to avoid, as far as possible, imposing any rigid pattern such as would either fetter regional planning committees in the development of flexible systems of assessment that drew upon a broad variety of sources of expertise, or inhibit the existing approved schools including the classifying establishments from demonstrating the facilities which they will be in a position to offer to regional planning committees.

24. It must however be emphasised that while, in the consideration of proposals from schools for authority to introduce modifications or changes in their structure or functions, the Secretary of State will always be prepared to take account as far as possible of an assured future regional role within the community home system, the approved school service is structured, operated and financed as a national, not regional, service, and must therefore so remain during the transitional period, until such time as the new and regionally structured role of the schools has been worked out by regional planning committees and incorporated in approved regional plans. For as managers and local authorities will be aware, approved school expenditure is financed under a system by which the local authority contribute towards half of the cost of maintenance of the schools. Community homes on the other hand will be financed either by a voluntary organisation (assisted homes) or by a particular local authority (controlled and local authority homes). For an approved school therefore to incur expenditure as a charge against approved school funds, before it had become a community home, on activities which related solely to its future role and which did not arise from its function as an approved school would be inappropriate since it would amount to anticipating community home expenditure that ought properly to fall upon which ever local authority or voluntary organisation was eventually to be responsible for the home, at the expense of all the other local authorities. This need not be regarded as implying that no change in the function of individual schools can be contemplated during the transitional period. Within the framework of the approved school system modification in role and structure has always been possible. But so long as an establishment remains an approved school and financed from approved school funds, any changes would have to be such as to be justifiable for approved school purposes and on the basis of a service that is, and must continue to be, structured on a national, not a regional basis.

NOTE

This circular was sent to correspondents of approved schools in England and Wales (copies for information to heads of schools) and to Councils of counties, county boroughs and London boroughs in England and Wales (copy for information of Chief Financial Officer and Children's Officer).

ANNEX A

CLASSIFYING APPROVED SCHOOLS AND REMAND HOMES

The local authority in whose care the child is should apply for a place in an approved school to the classifying school, remand/classifying centre that serves their area as set out below.   Where there is no classifying establishment, application should be made to the Home Office Vacancies Pool, Room 136, Horseferry House, Dean Ryle Street, London, S.W.1.   Telephone: 01–834 6655 Ext. 695.

Boys

I. *London* (*i.e.* the Inner London boroughs, the Common Council of the City of London and the Inner London Education Authority).

(a) 12 and over (including Roman Catholics)	Stamford House, Hammersmith
(b) Under 12	
(I) Non-Roman Catholics	Royal Philanthropic Society's School, Redhill
(II) Roman Catholics	Vacancies Pool

II. *Others*

(a) Non-Roman Catholics

(I) Durham, Lincolnshire, Northumberland, Nottinghamshire, Yorkshire	Aycliffe School, Co. Durham
(II) Berkshire, Breconshire, Cardiganshire, Carmarthenshire, Cornwall, Devonshire, Dorset, Glamorgan, Gloucestershire, Hampshire, Herefordshire, Isle of Wight, Monmouthshire, Oxfordshire, Pembrokeshire, Radnorshire, Somerset, Warwickshire, Wiltshire, Worcestershire	Kingswood School, Bristol
(III) Anglesy, Caernarvonshire, Cheshire, Cumberland, Denbighshire, Derbyshire, Flintshire, Lancashire, Merionethshire, Montgomeryshire, Shropshire, Staffordshire, Westmorland	Red Bank School, Newton-le-Willows
(IV) Bedfordshire, Buckinghamshire, Cambridgeshire, Essex, Hertfordshire, Huntingdonshire, Kent, Leicestershire, Norfolk, Northamptonshire, Rutland, Suffolk, Surrey, Sussex, Ely, Soke of Peterborough and the Outer London Boroughs	Royal Philanthropic Society's School, Redhill

(b) Roman Catholic

(I) Kingswood geographical area (as in (a) (II) above)	Kingswood School, Bristol
(II) Buckinghamshire, Essex, Hertfordshire, Kent, Surrey, Sussex and the Outer London Boroughs	Royal Philanthropic Society's School, Redhill
(III) Others	Vacancies Pool

Girls

I. *London* (*i.e.* the Greater London Council area with Kent, Surrey and Sussex)

(a) 15 and over (including Roman Catholics)	Cumberlow Lodge, Lambeth
(b) Age 14 (including Roman Catholics)	Middlesex Lodge, Hillingdon
(c) Under 14 (including Roman Catholics)	Vacancies Pool

II. *Others* (including Roman Catholics)

(a) Age 14 from Bedfordshire, Berkshire, Buckinghamshire, Cambridgeshire, Ely, Dorset, Essex, Hampshire, Hertfordshire, Isle of Wight, Norfolk, Oxfordshire and Suffolk	Middlesex Lodge, Hillingdon
(b) 14 and over	
(I) Cumberland, Durham Northumberland, Westmorland, Yorkshire	The Moss, Sheffield
(II) Cornwall, Devon, Gloucestershire, Somerset, Wiltshire, and South, Central Wales and Monmouthshire	Horfield Lodge, Bristol
(III) Lancashire and Cheshire	Alder House, Manchester. Derwent House, Liverpool
(c) Others (*i.e.* all girls under 14 and those aged 14 and over not mentioned above).	Vacancies Pool

ANNEX B

ASSESSMENT: RANGE OF REPORTS REQUIRED BY THE CLASSIFYING CENTRES IF A "PAPER" ALLOCATION IS TO BE CONSIDERED

1. Background report:
   a pen picture,
   personal history (in chronological order),
   social worker's report (including family background).
2. Report from present/past school.
3. School and/or employment record.
4. Medical report.
5. Psychiatric report.
6. Educational psychologist's report.

Note. Where a full report has recently been supplied to a court on any of the aspects mentioned above, there would be no need to duplicate them.

Home Office Circular No. 7/1971.   *Dated February 2,* 1971

CHILDREN AND YOUNG PERSONS ACT, 1969: ADMISSION OF BOYS IN CARE TO APPROVED SCHOOLS AFTER 1 JANUARY 1971

Tennal classifying school

1. Home Office Circular No. 184/1970 which was issued on 21 August 1970 set out the procedures for the admission to approved schools of boys and girls

in the care of local authorities during the transitional period until the community home system is established. Paragraph 16 of that circular recommended that local authorities seeking a place in an approved school should seek the advice of the appropriate classifying agency.

2. The object of this circular is to inform you that an additional classifying agency will become available on 15 February 1971, arrangements having been made with the managers of Tennal School, Balden Road, Harborne, Birmingham, B32 2EW (Telephone 021 427 5241) to open a classifying school in addition to the existing training school.

Catchment area to be served by Tennal School

3. It is intended that the new classifying school will in due course classify all boys from regional planning areas 4 and 5; but initially only one of the 3 units will be functioning and admissions will be restricted to boys (including Roman Catholics) WHO HAVE NOT REACHED THEIR 14TH BIRTHDAY, who are in the care of the local authorities in the following administrative counties including the county boroughs within those counties:

Derbyshire
Herefordshire
Leicestershire
Lincolnshire (parts of Holland)
Lincolnshire (parts of Kesteven)
Lincolnshire (parts of Lindsey)
Northamptonshire
Nottinghamshire
Rutland
Shropshire
Staffordshire
Warwickshire
Worcestershire

Applications for assessment should be made in the usual way to the Principal of Tennal School.

4. In the case of a boy from these areas who IS AGED 14 OR OVER, application should continue to be made to the appropriate classifying agency as set out in Home Office Circular No. 184/1970. A further circular will be issued as soon as Tennal School is in a position to extend classifying facilities to the higher age ranges.

Consequential changes in the catchment areas for assessment by the other classifying schools

5. The opening of the first classifying unit at Tennal School will have the effect of making additional facilities for assessment available at some of the other classifying schools for other boys; and with the agreement of the schools concerned, the following further arrangements have been made and will also come into operation on 15 February 1971.

6. RED BANK Classifying School, Newton-le-Willows will accept Roman Catholic boys WHO HAVE NOT REACHED THEIR 14TH BIRTHDAY and who are in the care of Lancashire County Council in addition to boys of all ages from that area of other religious persuasion.

7. AYCLIFFE Classifying School, near Darlington, will accept boys of all ages (including Roman Catholic boys) from the Counties of Cumberland and West-

morland and the City of Carlisle who were formerly classified by Red Bank School or the Vacancies Pool.

NOTE

This circular was sent to correspondents of approved schools in England and Wales (copies for the information of heads of schools) and to councils of counties, county boroughs and London boroughs in England and Wales (copies for information of Chief Financial Officer and Children's Officer).

Home Office Circular No. 32/1971.   *Dated June 11, 1971*

CHILDREN AND YOUNG PERSONS ACT, 1969: ADMISSION OF GIRLS IN CARE TO APPROVED SCHOOLS

The Cedars classifying centre

1. Home Office Circular No. 184/1970 which was issued on 21 August 1970 set out the procedures for the admission to approved schools of boys and girls in the care of local authorities during the transitional period until the community home system is established. Paragraph 16 of that circular recommended that local authorities seeking a place in an approved school should seek the advice of the appropriate classifying agency.

2. With the agreement of the Breadsall Remand Home Joint Committee an additional classifying agency is to become available, arrangements having been made for The Cedars Remand Home, Hilltop, Breadsall, near Derby (Tel.: Derby 831273 STD.: 0332) to classify all girls from regional planning area 5. Accordingly, from 21 June next, The Cedars will be the central classifying agency for girls of all ages and of whatever religion who are in the care of local authorities in the following administrative counties, including the county boroughs within those counties:—

Derbyshire
Leicestershire
Lincolnshire (Parts of Holland)
Lincolnshire (Parts of Kesteven)
Lincolnshire (Parts of Lindsey)
Northamptonshire
Nottinghamshire
Rutland

Associated centres

3. To avoid building up pressure on places at The Cedars, additional facilities are being provided at the following "associated centres". These "associated centres" are existing residential child care establishments which the local authorities who provide them have agreed may assist in the process of classification:

Responsible Local Authority	*Associated Centre*
Derbyshire	Springhill Reception Centre, Duffield, near Derby
Grimsby, CB	The Cedars Reception Centre, Grimsby
Leicestershire	The Holt Reception Centre, Birstall, near Leicester
Nottinghamshire	South Collingham Hall Reception Centre, Near Newark
Nottingham CB	Enderleigh Remand Home for Girls, Nottingham

Applications

4. In all cases where admission to an approved school is thought to be desirable application should be made through the central classifying agency at The Cedars and addressed to The Superintendent. It follows that applications for a place in an approved school in the circumstances described in the circular should no longer be addressed to the Vacancies Pool.

Amendments to Home Office Circular No. 184/1970

5. Item II (Others) of Appendix A to Circular No. 184/1970 should be amended to include these new facilities. They should be inserted in Item IIb after the entry for Lancashire and Cheshire as follows:

> IV   *All ages*
> Derbyshire
> Leicestershire
> Lincolnshire   The Cedars,
> Northamptonshire   Breadsall,
> Nottinghamshire   Near Derby
> Rutland

Alder House remand home classifying centre

6. You will wish to note that Alder House Remand Home Classifying Centre, Manchester has removed to another building. References to Alder House in Circulars Nos. 48/1970, 184/1970 and 10/1971 should be amended to read: Burford Remand Home Classifying Centre, Clarendon Road, Whalley Range, Manchester, M16 8LD. (Tel.: 061–881 9293).

NOTE

This circular was sent to correspondents of approved schools in England and Wales (copies for the information of heads of schools) and to councils of counties, county boroughs and London boroughs in England and Wales (copies for information of Directors of Social Services and Treasurers).

Home Office Circular No. 222/1970.   *Dated October 8,* 1970

CHILDREN IN CARE: NOTIFICATIONS TO THE DEPARTMENT OF HEALTH AND SOCIAL SECURITY

1. We are directed by the Secretary of State for the Home Department and the Secretary of State for Social Services to advise you of the effect of the Children and Young Persons Act, 1969, on the position, in relation to family allowances, of children in care, and of the new arrangements which, as from the date of coming into force of Part I of the Act, will replace those set out in Home Office Circular 224/1968. As explained in Home Office Circular 182/1970, the Secretary of State for the Home Department has decided that this date shall be 1 January 1971.

2. For the purposes of the Family Allowances Act, 1965, a boy or girl is regarded as a child if he or she is:

> (1) under the upper limit of compulsory school age;
> (2) under 16 and incapacitated for regular employment;
> (3) under 19 and in full-time education or low-paid apprenticeship.

3. Under section 11 of the Family Allowances Act, regardless of the amount of any contributions towards maintenance, a child cannot be counted as in a family for allowances purposes during any period:—

> (1) while liable to be detained by virtue of section 53 of the Children and Young Persons Act, 1933, and not discharged on licence;

(2) while there is in force an order (other than an interim order) made under the Children and Young Persons Act, 1969, committing the child to the care of a local authority, unless the child:—

    (a) is allowed by the authority under the provisions of section 13 (2) of the Children Act, 1948, as amended by section 49 of the 1969 Act, to be under the control of a parent, guardian, relative or friend of the child, or

    (b) has been taken for adoption (see paragraph 4 below);

(3) while there is in force a resolution of a local authority passed under section 2 (1) of the Children Act, 1948, unless the child:—

    (a) is allowed by the authority under the provisions of section 13 (2) of the Children Act, 1948, as amended, to be under the control of a parent, guardian, relative or friend, or

    (b) has been taken for adoption (see paragraph 4).

4. For the purposes of this Circular, "taken for adoption" means that the child is in the care and possession of a person who has given notice of intention to apply for an adoption order in respect of him, unless 12 weeks have elapsed since the giving of the notice without the application being made or the application has been refused by the court or withdrawn.

5. A child living away from his parents in circumstances other than those indicated in paragraph 3 is not automatically excluded from family allowances, but it is normally a condition of his inclusion in his parents' family if he has been away from them for more than 4 weeks that a parent is contributing at least 18s. (90p) a week towards his maintenance. Temporary interruptions of contributions may be disregarded for up to 4 weeks. If the conditions are not satisfied for his inclusion in the parents' family, the child may be counted as in the family of another private person who is providing for him in that person's own home or contributing at least 18s. (90p) a week towards his support elsewhere. The effect of these rules in the case of a child received into care under the Children Act, 1948, or committed to care under the provisions of the Acts dealing with matrimonial causes or proceedings or wardship proceedings, is that the parents (or guardian) will cease to be entitled to allowances in respect of the child when he has been in care for a period of 4 weeks unless and until they start to maintain him to the extent of 18s. (90p) a week or more: and a boarded-out child who does not count as in his parents' family may be counted as in the family of the foster-parents for the time being.

6. Where the right to allowances is lost because the conditions of entitlement have ceased to be satisfied for any reason it is important that the award is terminated; otherwise, if allowance orders continue to be cashed, the parents will incur an overpayment which they may be required to repay, and if it appears that they have acted fraudulently in obtaining the money proceedings may have to be instituted. *It is therefore essential that the Department of Health and Social Security is made aware as quickly as possible:*

    (a) of any occurrence which causes a child's statutory exclusion from his family or allows him again to be included after a period of disqualification;
    and,
    (b) in the case of a child living away from home for other reasons, of the absence of maintenance payments over certain periods.

7. It is accordingly requested that the procedures set out in the following appendices to this Circular should be followed with effect from 1 January 1971:

Appendix I   Children committed or deemed to be committed to the care of the local authority or made the subject of a resolution assuming parental rights.

    Appendix II   Children in care under section 1 of the Children Act, 1948.

    Appendix III   Children committed to the care of the local authority under provisions of the Matrimonial Proceedings (Magistrates' Courts) Act, 1960, the Matrimonial Causes Act, 1965, or the Family Law Reform Act, 1969.

(*Note.* From 1 January 1971 the responsibility for notifying the Department of Health and Social Security of a child committed to the care of a local authority but placed in an approved school will rest with the local authority concerned. The special notification procedure whereby forms FAM 190A were completed by Headmasters will be discontinued.)

8. In order to reduce to a minimum the clerical work involved the Department of Health and Social Security has, wherever possible, prepared pre-addressed code cards which can be sent by post without cover or payment of postage. The abbreviations on the cards have been adopted to avoid disclosing the position to the casual reader. Code cards should be completed and despatched to the Department at the address given below as soon as possible after the event which is being notified.

    Department of Health and Social Security,
    Family Allowances Branch (Index),
    Newcastle-upon-Tyne, NE98 1YX

(If old stocks of code cards are held showing "Ministry of Pensions and National Insurance" or "Ministry of Social Security" in the address they should be corrected before posting to read as above.)

9. Further supplies of code cards may be obtained on request from Family Allowances Branch, Newcastle, to which any queries on the application of this Circular should be addressed.

Cancellation of earlier Circular

10. Home Office Circular No. 224/1968 has been replaced by this Circular and should be cancelled with effect from 1 January 1971.

NOTE

This circular was sent to the Clerks of County, County Borough and London Borough Councils, with additional copies for Children's Officers and County and Borough Treasurers.

APPENDIX I

CHILDREN COMMITTED OR DEEMED TO BE COMMITTED TO THE CARE OF THE LOCAL AUTHORITY UNDER A "CARE ORDER" OR MADE THE SUBJECT OF A RESOLUTION ASSUMING PARENTAL RIGHTS

1. Local authorities are asked to complete code cards, form FAM 192, for children in their care who are the subject of an order or resolution as in paragraph 3 (2) and (3) of this Circular. A card should be completed in each of the following circumstances:

    (1) when a child comes into the care of a local authority under a care order (other than an interim order) made under the Children and Young Persons Act, 1969;

    (2) when a child in care or deemed to be in care under a care order is allowed by the authority under section 13 (2) of the Children Act, 1948, as amended, to be under the charge and control of a parent or other person;

    (3) when a child as in (2) returns to the control of the authority;

    (4) when a care order ceases to have effect;

    (5) when a child becomes the subject of a resolution passed by the authority under section 2 of the Children Act;

(6) when a child who is the subject of a section 2 resolution is allowed by the local authority (under section 4 (3) or 13 (2) of the Children Act) to be under control of a parent or other person;

(7) when a child (as in (6)) returns to the care of the authority; and

(8) when a resolution lapses or is rescinded or determined.

2. The key to form FAM 192 is given below

DB	Date of birth
NAP	Name and address of parents or guardian
CNLA	Code number of local authority
DR	Date of local authority's resolution
DC	Date of court order
DPGRF	Date child permitted to be in care of parent, guardian, relative or friend
NAPGRF	Name and address of the parent, guardian, relative or friend
DRB	Date child received back into care of local authority
DRR	Date of lapse, rescission or determination of local authority's resolution
DRO	Date care order ceases to have effect
NAPCC	Name and address of the person having care of child after cessation of care order or parental resolution.

3. Where a child is the subject of an "internal order" under the Children and Young Persons Act, 1969, and a further order is made resulting in the child's being in care for a total period of more than 28 days, the local authority is asked to advise the Department of Health and Social Security (address as in paragraph 8) by letter.

APPENDIX II

CHILDREN IN CARE UNDER SECTION I OF THE CHILDREN ACT, 1948

1. For children in care under section 1 of the Children Act, 1948 who are not the subject of a resolution passed under Section 2, local authorities are asked, in cases where there is at least one other child in the family, to notify the absence or break-down of parental contributions as indicated below, using code card, form FAM 193:

FIRST, as soon as possible after a period of TWO consecutive weeks in respect of which the parent or guardian has not contributed at the rate of at least 18s. a week; and

AGAIN, immediately after a period of FIVE consecutive weeks not covered by contributions at that rate.

2. Subject to what is said in paragraph 3, notifications should be sent whether or not the parent has been assessed for maintenance. If no assessment can be made because the parent cannot be traced, the FAM 193 should indicate that the address given is the last known address by the addition of the symbol "LKA".

3. The two-week notification need not be sent in cases where the child's stay in care is not expected to exceed four weeks in all or, in longer-stay cases, where the child is expected to be released to his parent or guardian within four weeks of the date when the last contribution was made. A five-week notification should, however, be sent wherever the situation requires it, regardless of the expected duration of the child's stay.

4. On receipt of a two-week notification the Department of Health and Social Security will write to the parent or guardian reminding him (if they have not already done so in recent months) that the absence of contributions at the required rate over a period of more than four weeks will lead to loss of title to Family allowances. By this means it is hoped to secure that the necessary payments will be started or resumed within four weeks and that title to the allowances will thus be maintained. If payments are not started or resumed, however, on receipt of a five-week notification the Department will take steps to reduce or terminate the allowances, as necessary, and will be unable to reinstate them unless, as the result of a fresh claim, it is subsequently established that the conditions of entitlement are again being

satisfied. If the allowances are reinstated while the child is still in care the Department will notify the authority and will wish to be advised of any subsequent breakdown of maintenance payments in accordance with paragraph 1.

5. The key to form FAM 193 is as follows:

DB	Date of birth of child
NA/P	Name and address of parent(s) or guardian
CNLA	Code number of local authority
DA	Date of child's last admission to care
NC2	No contribution* for two weeks
NC5 since . . .	No contribution* for five weeks; date of last contribution* received.

6. If, while in care of a local authority as in paragraph 1, a child is committed under a "care" order or is made the subject of a resolution assuming parental rights, the FAM 193 procedure will no longer be appropriate. Action should proceed as in Appendix I.

APPENDIX III

CHILDREN COMMITTED TO CARE UNDER

(a) s. 2 (1) (e) of the *Matrimonial Proceedings (Magistrates' Courts) Act*, 1960
(b) *The Matrimonial Causes Act*, 1965, or
(c) s. 7 of the *Family Law Reform Act*, 1969

Like those in care as in Appendix II, children who are committed to the care of a local authority under any of the provisions listed above are eligible for inclusion in a family for allowances purposes if the maintenance conditions for them are satisfied. The Family Allowances position may have to be reviewed if what had been a single family unit has become two for allowances purposes. The Department therefore needs to have early notification of all such committals, and local authorities are asked to complete forms FAM 193 (adapted as necessary) in respect of them, whether or not any payments have been made. If, following such a notification, entitlement to family allowances in respect of the child(ren) still continues, the Department will inform the local authority accordingly, and the normal procedure set out in Appendix II to this Circular should be applied thereafter, as and when appropriate.

Home Office Circular No. 195/1970.   *Dated September* 4, 1970

DISTRIBUTION OF APPROVED SCHOOLS BETWEEN PLAN-NING AREAS

I am directed by the Secretary of State to say that in the course of discussions with the local authority associations and the approved school representative organisations on arrangements for the implementation of the Children and Young Persons Act, 1969, it has been recognised that one of the most complex tasks confronting Regional Planning Committees, local authorities, and the managers of approved schools will be that of settling how best to distribute the existing *nationally* structured system of approved schools between *regional* planning areas. While this is a matter for determination by Regional Planning Committees in the light of their examination of all the needs and facilities of their areas, and on the basis of discussion between all the local authorities and voluntary organisations concerned, it has been agreed by the local authority associations and approved school representative bodies that it might be useful if the Home Office were to offer some general help, based on a review of the whole

* As defined in paragraph 1.

national system, on how the existing facilities provided by approved schools might be shared out between regional planning areas in drawing up initial regional plans.

2. On this basis the Home Office has examined the present pattern of provision and is circulating herewith—

> in *Appendix A* details of the existing pattern of use of approved schools showing the numbers of boys and girls, where they came from and how they are distributed in approved schools now. Appendix A also contains brief notes on the main factors taken into account in making placements under the existing system; and

> in *Appendix B* a "model" distribution of approved schools as between planning areas showing how existing facilities might be shared between planning areas.

3. It is emphasised that the model in Appendix B is *not* intended to serve as a blue-print for regional plans. It represents no more than a suggestion how needs of the order indicated in the tables in Appendix A could be met from approved school facilities as they now exist. It is recognised that neither of these factors is constant. But a model of the kind provided in Appendix B may be a useful starting point for regional planning committees and local authorities in their consideration both of their own regional needs and of the possible needs of other regions. Such a model may also help voluntary organisations who are seeking a role for their establishments in the community home system, by indicating—however roughly—the pattern of need which Regional Planning Committess are likely to have to meet.

4. In the suggested distribution of approved schools in Appendix B a proportion of schools have been shown as providing shared use between 2 or more planning areas. This reflects the implications both of the present geographical distribution of approved schools, and of the present pattern of need, which for certain minority groups (*e.g.* girls) has not justified establishments other than on a widely-shared basis. The approved school system as a whole has existed to meet specialised needs, *i.e.* those of boys and girls considered by the courts to be unsuitable for treatment in children's homes or other settings, and to require removal from home for residential treatment. Regional Planning Committees will no doubt wish to consider in the long term how far they can meet these specialised needs independently. But it may be found that some at least of these needs can most suitably be met by community homes serving 2 or more planning areas.

Superintending Inspectors

5. The Superintending Inspectors will be glad to assist in any way they can in discussions between Regional Planning Committees, children's authorities and approved school managers about any matter arising from this circular.

NOTE

This circular was sent to the Secretaries of Children's Regional Planning Committees, Councils of Counties, County Boroughs and London Boroughs with additional copies for the Children's Officer, and the Correspondents of approved schools in England and Wales, with copies to the Heads.

APPENDIX A

EXISTING PATTERN OF USE OF APPROVED SCHOOLS

1. *Location of schools*

In assessing how the places available at existing approved schools can best serve the needs of the planning areas, the first factor to consider is the location of the existing schools. As is evident from the following table, these schools are geographically very unevenly distributed over the country as a whole and their distribution which is the product of over a century of growth and change does not accord at all well with the boundaries of the planning areas:

Category of School	Planning Area												Total
	1	2	3	4	5	6	7	8	9	10	11	12	
Boys													
Senior	3	4	2	3	1	2	3	1	4	1	2	1	27
Intermediate	3	3	5	3	2	4	0	0	3	2	2	2	29
Junior	4	3	5	2	3	0	2	0	6	1	2	2	30
Girls													
Senior	1	3	2	2	0	0	0	1	5	1	4	0	19
Intermediate	1	1	1	1	0	0	0	0	0	1	2	1	8
Junior	1	0	1	1	0	0	0	1	1	0	1	0	6
	13	14	16	12	6	6	5	3	19	6	13	6	119

(*Note :* the purpose of this table is to show the distribution of what have traditionally been known as training schools and, accordingly, the 4 classifying schools for boys (but not their attached training schools) have been omitted from this table together with the 3 special (secure) units and Meadowcroft (in Area 3) which provides for approved school girls who are pregnant.)

2. *Location of children*

Although the present policy is to arrange for a child's admission to the school nearest his home that can satisfactorily meet his needs, the uneven distribution of the schools themselves and variations as between different parts of the country in the numbers of children committed to approved schools, and the specialist needs of the children themselves (see paragraph 3 (iii) below), make it inevitable that many children are placed in schools some distance away from their homes (an acute example of this is the London Planning Area which has only 3 approved schools within its boundaries and one of the biggest needs in terms of places). The problem is well illustrated in the following table which analyses the approved school population as it was at 30 June 1969 and shows that 2,459 (or about 42%) of the boys and 749 (or about 27%) of the girls were then in schools outside the boundaries of what are now the planning areas in which their homes are situated:

Position at 30/6/1969

Planning area	Boys			Girls		
	In schools in own area	In schools outside own area	Total	In schools in own area	In schools outside own area	Total
1	384	78	462	31	30	61
2	559	139	698	47	79	126
3	808	357	1165	70	121	191
4	408	299	707	42	75	117
5	229	229	458	—	71	71
6	139	85	224	—	37	37
7	82	130	212	—	55	55
8	49	811	860	31	171	202
9	229	35	264	20	28	48
10	86	121	207	7	37	44
11	135	65	200	33	7	40
12	218	110	328	3	38	41
	3326	2459	5785	284	749	1033

(*Note.* This Table does not include figures for children in the establishments to which the note at paragraph 1 above relates.)

3. *Factors that have affected allocation to approved schools*

Apart from the location of the schools and the simple question of the availability of vacancies, the factors that have resulted in the pattern of allocation indicated in paragraph 2 include:

(i) *Category of school.* There are 3 categories of schools for boys and 3 for girls, based on age at entry. In practice a school may, with authority, have admitted individual boys (or girls) slightly older or younger than the normal age range for the school but each school has been equipped and staffed to provide for the category of boys (or girls) for which it has been classified and has not been able to provide suitably for boys (or girls) significantly outside that age range. While a formal variation of the age ranges has from time to time been introduced in particular schools to meet changing needs, there has been a limit to the extent to which this has been possible, since any major shift to a different age group has meant major changes in regime, staffing and physical provision.

(ii) *Religion.* A child has been sent, where practicable, to a school for persons of the religious denomination to which he belonged (section 8 (2) of the Children and Young Persons Act, 1963). Normally a Roman Catholic child has been sent to a Roman Catholic school. There are 18 schools for Roman Catholic boys and 7 for Roman Catholic girls.

(iii) *Specialised needs.* Some children have been sent, not to the nearest appropriate school for their age, sex and religion, but to a school providing specialised treatment or training—*e.g.* a particularly disturbed youngster may have been sent to a school at which special emphasis is given to psychiatric help or a boy suitable for nautical training may have been sent to a nautical school. Some schools have catered primarily for the problems of the dull child while others conversely have concentrated on facilities for the children with relatively high scholastic potential.

(iv) *Associates.* Where it has been necessary, both in the interests of the schools and of the children, to separate a group of boys or girls who have been associated together, either in the circumstances leading to their committal, or in disruptive behaviour at a school, arrangements to disperse them may have resulted in some boys and girls being sent to schools a long way from their homes.

(v) *Transfer: re-committal.* In some cases a boy or girl who has been making poor progress at one school may have been helped by being given an opportunity to make a fresh start at another school which is likely (if the first school was the school nearest his home) to have been further away from his home. Again, if a boy or girl has been recommitted to an approved school, a fresh start at another school may have been desirable and may have resulted in the choice of a school further from the home area.

APPENDIX B

Model of possible distribution of approved schools between planning areas

1. The tables attached—as indicated in the covering note to this Appendix—constitute a suggested model for the distribution of approved schools between planning areas which it is hoped may provide a useful basis for discussion by planning committees, local authorities and voluntary organisations. As already explained this is intended only as a working model to show how—on the basis of a known demand (the figures for the approved school population in June 1969*)—the existing facilities available within the approved school system might reasonably be shared out between planning areas. To the extent that the estimated future needs of particular categories of child, estimated future functions and treatment patterns of particular establishments and estimated inter related facilities in other fields of child care in a planning area may emerge in the course of planning discussions these will of course directly affect the final pattern of use of former approved schools

* *Note.* At the time when this exercise was begun these figures were the most recently available comprehensive figures for the approved school population. In recent months the number of committals to approved schools has risen.

within the regional plan. This model is therefore in no sense intended as a blueprint, but rather as a useful starting point for discussion which shows the kind of problems that the existing pattern of approved schools presents and the kind of solution that such a pattern of residential establishments would seem to imply.

2. The suggested distribution of approved schools in the tables below has accordingly been prepared on the following basis:

(a) Wherever possible it has been suggested that the needs of a planning area should be met by schools situated within its boundaries. (Exceptions from this principle have been introduced where one planning area is asked to make use of places in a second planning area in order to make places in some of its own schools available for a third planning area that is itself badly situated to use places in the second area).

(b) No account has been taken of the existing pattern of denominational usage.

(c) The existing certified number for the school has been taken as the number of places that might be available under community home status, except where plans for changes have been approved.

(d) The existing divisions of the schools into categories based on age and sex have been used. (In the short term, schools equipped and staffed to provide for a particular age group cannot readily or quickly be modified to provide for a different or an extended age group).

(e) It has been assumed that (i) during the transitional period approved schools in general will continue to function as such, and (ii) their managers will wish to seek for them a place in the community home system.

3. It will be noted that for some planning areas the usage suggested shows a deficiency of places for girls, even after account has been taken of the suggested use of a number of places in neighbouring planning areas. For these areas the only places likely to be available are a long way from the home area: schools shown with a likely surplus of available places are in some cases at a considerable distance from the areas with net deficiencies; and on the whole it has seemed better not to make specific proposals for the allocation of places in a distant school. But the accommodation available in each planning area is shown and the planning committees concerned may wish to consider whether to negotiate for places at one of the distant schools or whether the need can be met locally in provision that is outside the approved school system.

4. It will be noted that in some cases schools are shown as wholly or mainly available to planning areas other than the one in which the school is geographically situated. In such cases it would be reasonable for the local authority associated with it under its new status as a community home to come from one of the planning areas which the home predominantly serves rather than from the one in which it is actually situated.

5. It will also be noted that the tables do not include any reference either to the classifying schools or to the special closed units at Red Bank, Redhill and Kingswood or to Meadowcroft School for pregnant girls. For a variety of reasons, these 2 categories of establishment raise special questions, and are accordingly dealt with separately in the following paragraphs.

Classifying schools

6. The provision of assessment facilities will be a matter to which each regional planning committee will wish to give special attention. On the hypothesis that each classifying school will find an assessment role within an appropriate planning area, the position might be as follows:

Region	School
I	Aycliffe
II	Kingswood
4	Tennal
8	Redhill
3	Red Bank.

It may well be found, however, that planning committees whose areas do not contain classifying schools or centres will continue for some time to come to need access to the classifying facilities at present used for boys and girls from their areas.

Special (secure) units

7. In the short term it seems probable that each planning committee will need access to the special (secure) unit that now serves the committee's area. In the longer term, all or most planning committees may make fresh provision, either individually or in agreement with neighbouring planning committees. On this basis the short term use might be:

Red Bank Special Unit: Areas 1, 2, 3. Area 4 (geographical counties of Salop and Staffordshire only). Area 5 (geographical counties of Derbyshire, Nottinghamshire and Lincolnshire only) and Area 12 (geographical counties of Anglesey, Caernarvonshire, Denbighshire, Flintshire, Merioneth and Montgomeryshire only).

Kingswood Special Unit: Areas 7, 10, 11. In Areas 4 and 12 the parts not served by Red Bank.

Redhill Special Unit: Areas 6, 8, 9 and 5 (parts not served by Red Bank).

Meadowcroft

8. This school for girls who are pregnant has facilities for the care of the girls and their babies. It is intended to serve primarily Areas 3, 2 and 1 but, subject to the needs of those Areas it is understood that places will be available for girls from other Areas.

APPROVED SCHOOLS—SUGGESTED USE BY PLANNING AREAS
PLANNING AREA I

I. *Children from Area 1 in approved schools*
   Summary of position at 30 June 1969

	In Schools		Total	No. of Approved School places then in Area 1	Balance
	In Area 1	In other Areas			
Boys					
Senior	63	51	114	305	191
Intermediate	139	26	165	320	155
Junior	182	1	183	339	156
	384	78	462	964	502
Girls					
Senior	14	20	34	32	−2
Intermediate	13	10	23	40	21
Junior	4	—	4	60	56
	31	30	61	136	75

(These figures do not include boys and girls at Classifying Schools or Centres or at the Special (Secure) Units attached to 3 of the former.)

II. *Suggested use of schools*

	Management	Certified Number	Suggested allocation of places	
			Area 1	Other Areas
Boys—Senior				
(a) *In Area 1*				
Edmond Castle, Wetheral, Carlisle	Local Committee	80	20	3: 60
Netherton, Morpeth, Northumberland	Local Committee	105	105	Nil
Wellesley Nautical School, Blyth, Northumberland	Local Committee	120	120	Nil
(b) *In other Areas*				
Richmond Hill, Richmond, Yorks	Local Committee	80	30	2: 50
			275	
		Need (1969)	114	
		Balance	161	
Boys—Intermediate				
(a) *In Area 1*				
Axwell Park, Blaydon-on-Tyne, Co. Durham	Local Committee	120	120	Nil
Aycliffe TS, Copelaw, Aycliffe, Nr. Darlington	Local Committee	120	105	2: 15
Pelham House, Calderbridge, Seascale, Cumberland	Local Committee	80	45	3: 35
(b) *In other Areas* Nil				
			270	
		Need (1969)	165	
		Balance	105	
Boys—Junior				
(a) *In Area 1*				
The Castle, Stanhope, Bishop Auckland, Co. Durham	Local Committee	107	107	Nil
Longhirst Hall, Morpeth, Northumberland	Local Committee	72	72	Nil
St. Peter's, Gainford, Darlington	Hexham and Newcastle Diocesan Rescue Society (Roman Catholic)	100	60	2: 40

| | Management | Certified Number | Suggested allocation of places | |
			Area 1	Other Areas
Boys—Junior—cont.				
Starnthwaite Ghyll, Crosthwaite, Kendal, Westmorland	Local Committee	60	10	3: 50
(b) *In other Areas* Nil				
		249		
Need (1969)		183		
Balance		66		
Girls—Senior				
(a) *In Area 1*				
St. Hilda's, Gosforth, Newcastle-on-Tyne 3	Local Committee	32 (including 6 hostel places)	32	Nil
(b) *In other Areas*				
St. John's Home, Wakefield	Local Committee	30	6	2: 10 3: 10 5: 4
		38		
Need (1969)		34		
Balance		4		
Girls—Intermediate				
(a) *In Area 1*				
Benton Grange School, Newcastle-on-Tyne 7	Local Committee (Roman Catholic)	44 (including 8 hostel places)	24	2: 20
(b) *In other Areas*				
Springhead Park School, Rothwell, Nr. Leeds	National Assocn. for Mental Health	32 (including 8 hostel places)	4	2: 20 3: 4 5: 4
		28		
Need (1969)		23		
Balance		5		
Girls—Junior				
(a) *In Area 1*				
Northumberland Village Homes, Whitley Bay, Northumberland	Local Committee	60 (including 6 hostel places)	18	2: 24 3: 18
(b) *In other Areas* Nil				
		18		
Need (1969)		4		
Balance		14		

Approved schools—suggested use by planning areas

Planning area 2

I. *Children from Area 2 in approved schools*
Summary of position at 30 June 1969

	In Schools		Total	No. of Approved School places then in Area 2	Balance
	In Area 2	In other Areas			
Boys					
Senior	145	13	158	362	204
Intermediate	243	44	287	356	69
Junior	171	82	253	217	− 36
	559	139	698	935	237
Girls					
Senior	34	28	62	129	67
Intermediate	13	21	34	32	− 2
Junior	Nil	30	30	Nil	− 30
	47	79	126	161	35

(These figures do not include boys and girls at Classifying Schools or Centres or at the Special (Secure) Units attached to 3 of the former.)

II. *Suggested use of schools*

	Management	Certified Number	Suggested allocation of places	
			Area 2	Other Areas
Boys—Senior				
(a) *In Area 2*				
Dobroyd Castle, Todmorden, Lancashire (but situated in Area 2)	Local Committee	71	31	3: 40
East Moor, Adel, Leeds	Local Committee	121	61	5: 60
Richmond Hill, Richmond, Yorks	Local Committee	80	50	1: 30
St. Camillus', Scarthingwell, Tadcaster, Yorkshire	Local Committee (Roman Catholic)	90	63	3: 15 / 5: 12
(b) *In other Areas*				
Nil			205	
		Need (1969)	158	
		Balance	47	

Management	Certified Number	Suggested allocation of places	
		Area 2	Other Areas

Boys—Intermediate

(a) *In Area 2*

Castle Howard, Welburn, York	Kingston-upon-Hull City Council	120	120	Nil
St. William's, Market Weighton, York	Local Committee (Roman Catholic)	116	116	Nil
Shadwell, Moortown, Leeds, 17	Leeds City Council	120	120	Nil

(b) *In other Areas*

Aycliffe TS, Copelaw, Aycliffe, Nr. Darlington	Local Committee	120	15	1: 105
	Need (1969)		371 287	
	Balance		84	

Boys—Junior

(a) *In Area 2*

Morland House, Ilkley, Yorkshire	Bradford City Council	80	80	Nil
Stockton Hall, Stockton-on-Forest, York	York City Council	100	100	Nil
Thorparch Grange, Boston Spa, Yorkshire	Leeds City Council	110	110	Nil

(b) *In other Areas*

St. Peter's School, Gainford, Darlington	Hexham and Newcastle Diocesan Rescue Society (Roman Catholic)	100	40	1: 60
	Need (1969)		330 253	
	Balance		77	

Girls—Senior

(a) *In Area 2*

Hyrstlands, Batley, Yorkshire	Salvation Army	29	19	3: 10
Moorside, Blackbrook Road, Sheffield, 10	Sheffield City Council	70 (including 12 hostel places)	40	3: 20 5: 10

	Management	Certified Number	Suggested allocation of places	
			Area 2	Other Areas

Girls—Senior—cont.

St. John's Home, Wakefield, Yorkshire	Local Committee	30	10	1: 60 3: 10 5: 4

(b) *In other Areas*
Nil

		Need (1969)	60 62	
		Balance	7	

Girls—Intermediate

(a) *In Area 2*

Springfield Park, Rothwell, Nr. Leeds	National Assocn. for Mental Health	32 (including 8 hostel places)	20	1: 4 3: 4 5: 4

(b) *In other Areas*

Benton Grange, Benton Park Road, Newcastle-upon-Tyne, 7	Local Committee (Roman Catholic)	44 (including 8 hostel places)	20	1: 24
		Need (1969)	40 34	
		Balance	6	

Girls—Junior

(a) *In Area 2*
Nil

(b) *In other Areas*

Northumberland Village Homes, Whitley Bay, Northumberland	Local Committee	60 (including 6 hostel places)	24	1: 18 3: 18
Blackbrook House, St. Helen's, Lancashire	Liverpool Catholic Training Schools Association	50 (including 10 hostel places)	6	3: 38 5: 6
		Need (1969)	30 30	
		Balance	Nil	

Approved schools—suggested use by planning areas

Planning area 3

I. *Children from Area 3 in approved schools*
Summary of position at 30 June 1969

| | In Schools | | Total | No. of Approved School places then in Area 3 | Balance |
	In Area 3	In other Areas			
Boys					
Senior	163	149	312	215	−97
Intermediate	376	139	515	530	15
Junior	269	69	338	393	55
	808	357	1165	1138	−27
Girls					
Senior	27	72	99	58	−41
Intermediate	10	29	39	20	−19
Junior	27	20	47	50	3
	64	121	185	128	−57

(These figures do not include boys and girls at Classifying Schools or Centres or at the Special (Secure) Units attached to 3 of the former.)

II. *Suggested use of schools*

| | Management | Certified Number | Suggested allocation of places | |
			Area 3	Other Areas
Boys—Senior				
(a) *In Area 3*				
The Fylde, Poulton-le-Fylde, Blackpool	Local Committee	120	120	Nil
St. Thomas More, Birkdale, Southport	Liverpool Catholic Training Schools Association (Roman Catholic)	95	95	Nil
(b) *In other Areas*				
Edmond Castle, Wetheral, Carlisle	Local Committee	80	60	1: 20
(b) *Boys—Senior*				
Dobroyd Castle, Todmorden, Lancashire (but situated in Area 2)	Local Committee	71	40	2: 31

Management	Certified Number	Suggested allocation of places	
		Area 3	Other Areas

Boys Senior—cont.

	Management	Certified Number	Area 3	Other Areas
St. Camillus', Scarthingwell, Tadcaster, Yorkshire	Local Committee (Roman Catholic)	90	15	2: 63 5: 12
	Need (1969)		330 312	
	Balance		18	

Boys—Intermediate

(a) *In Area 3*

	Management	Certified Number	Area 3	Other Areas
Farnworth St. Aidans, Widnes, Lancs	Liverpool Catholic Training Schools Association (Roman Catholic)	111	111	Nil
Greenfield House, Billinge, Nr. Wigan Lancs	Liverpool Catholic Training Schools Association (Roman Catholic)	50	50	Nil
Mobberley, Knutsford, Cheshire	Manchester City Council	120	120	Nil
Red Bank TS, Newton-le-Willows, Lancs	Red Bank Schools Limited	120	120	Nil
St. Joseph's, Nantwich, Cheshire	Brothers of the Christian Schools (Roman Catholic)	125	115	4: 10

(b) *In other Areas*

	Management	Certified Number	Area 3	Other Areas
Pelham House, Calderbridge, Seascale, Cumberland	Local Committee	80	35	1: 45
	Need		551 515	
	Balance		36	

Boys—Junior

(a) *In Area 3*

	Management	Certified Number	Area 3	Other Areas
Blackburn House,* Blackburn	Blackburn County Borough Council	90	90	Nil
Danesford, Congleton, Cheshire	National Children's Homes	100 (including 14 hostel places)	50	4: 30 5: 20
Greystone Heath, Penketh, Nr. Warrington	Liverpool City Council	104	104	Nil

* Expected to become available in the autumn of 1970.

	Management	Certified Number	Suggested allocation of places Area 3	Other Areas
Boys—Junior—cont.				
St. George's, Freshfield, Formby, Liverpool	Liverpool Catholic Children's Protection Society (Roman Catholic)	120	120	Nil
St. Vincent's, Formby, Liverpool	Liverpool Catholic Training Schools Association (Roman Catholic)	47	47	Nil
West Bank, Heaton Mersey, Stockport, Cheshire	Salford Catholic Protection and Rescue Society Inc. (Roman Catholic)	22	22	Nil
Boys—Junior				
(b) *In other Areas*				
Starnthwaite Ghyll, Crosthwaite, Kendal, Westmorland	Local Committee	60	50	1: 10
		Need (1969)	483 338	
		Balance	145	
Girls—Senior				
(a) *In Area 3*				
Poplar Bank, Huyton, Liverpool	Local Committee	30 (including 8 hostel places)	30	Nil
St. Christopher's Home, Great Crosby, Liverpool	Local Committee affiliated to Liverpool Diocesan Board of Moral Welfare	28 (including 5 hostel places)	28	Nil
(b) *In other Areas*				
Hyrstlands, Batley, Yorkshire	Salvation Army	29	10	2: 19
Moorside, Blackbrook Road, Sheffield, 10	Sheffield City Council	70 (including 12 hostel places)	20	2: 40 5: 10

	Management	Certified Number	Suggested allocation of places	
			Area 4	Other Areas
Girls—Senior—cont.				
St. John's Home, Wakefield, Yorkshire	Local Committee	30	10	1: 6 2: 10 5: 4
St. John's Home, 18 Gravelly Hill North, Birmingham, 23	Sisters of Charity of St. Vincent de Paul (Roman Catholic)	54 (including 9 hostel places)	10	4: 21 5: 9 6: 7 7: 7
		108		
	Need (1969)	99		
	Balance	9		
Girls—Intermediate				
(a) *Inside Area 3*				
Northenden Road, Sale, Cheshire	Local Committee	20[a]	20	Nil
(b) *In other Areas*				
Springhead Park, Rothwell, Nr. Leeds	National Assocn. for Mental Health	32 (including 8 hostel places)	4	1: 4 2: 20 5: 4
		24		
	Need (1969)	45		
	Balance	−21		
Girls—Junior				
(a) *In Area 3*				
Blackbrook House, St. Helen's, Lancashire	Sisters of Charity of St. Vincent de Paul (Roman Catholic)	50 (including 10 hostel places)	38	2: 6 5: 6
(b) *In other Areas*				
Northumberland Village Homes, Whitley Bay, Northumberland	Local Committee	60 (including 6 hostel places)	18	1: 18 2: 24
		56		
	Need (1969)	47		
	Balance	9		

Note

[a] The Certified Number for Northenden Road was formerly 48 but a return to that figure depends upon the outcome of building proposals.

Meadowcroft, at Hutton, Preston, a school for 20 pregnant girls, managed by Lancashire County Council, is omitted from these proposals because of its specialised role, but may serve Planning Areas 1 and 2 as well as Area 3.

Approved schools—suggested use by planning areas

Planning area 4

I. *Children from Area 4 in approved schools*
Summary of position at 30 June 1969

	In Schools		Total	No. of Approved School places then in Area 4	Balance
	In Area 4	In other Areas			
Boys					
Senior	134	72	206	309	103
Intermediate	158	149	307	296	− 11
Junior	116	78	194	174	− 20
	408	299	707	779	72
Girls					
Senior	17	44	61	94	33
Intermediate	12	25	37	36	− 1
Junior	13	6	19	30	11
	42	75	117	160	43

(These figures do not include boys and girls at Classifying Schools or Centres or at the Special (Secure) Units attached to 3 of the former.)

II. *Suggested use of schools*

	Management	Certified Number	Suggested allocation of places	
			Area 4	Other Areas
Boys—Senior				
(a) *In Area 4*				
Boreatton Park, Baschurch, Nr. Shrewsbury, Salop	Local Committee	111	101	12: 10
Norton, Kineton, Warwickshire	Local Committee	110	60	5: 50
Shawbury, Shustoke, Nr. Coleshill, Warwickshire	Birmingham City Council	88	88	Nil
(b) *In other Areas*				
St. John's, Apethorpe, Peterborough, Northants	Northampton Diocesan Catholic Child Protection and Welfare Society (Roman Catholic)	81	30	5: 40 6: 11
			279	
	Need (1969)		206	
	Balance		73	

	Management	Certified Number	Suggested allocation of places	
			Area 4	Other Areas
Boys—Intermediate				
(a) *In Area 4*				
Quinta, Weston Rhyn, Nr. Oswestry, Salop	Dr. Barnardo's	97	97	Nil
St. Gilbert's, Hartlebury, Nr. Kidderminster, Worcestershire	Brothers of the Christian Schools (Roman Catholic)	95	80	5 : 15
Werrington, Rocester, Nr. Uttoxeter, Staffs	Staffordshire County Council	104	84	5 : 20
(b) *In other Areas*				
Sedbury Park, Chepstow, Monmouthshire (but situated in Gloucester)	Local Committee	120 (including 20 hostel places)	40	11 : 20 12 : 60
Ty Mawr, Gilwern, Nr. Abergavenny, Monmouthshire	Breconshire County Council	119	40	12 : 60 others : 19
St. Joseph's, Nantwich, Cheshire	Brothers of the Christian Schools (Roman Catholic)	125	10	3 : 115
		Need (1969)	351 315	
		Balance	36	
Boys—Junior				
(a) *In Area 4*				
Druids Heath, Aldridge, Walsall, Staffs	Dr. Barnardo's	90	90	Nil
Tennal, Balden Road, Harborne, Birmingham, 32	Local Committee	60	60	Nil
(b) *In other Areas*				
Danesford, Congleton, Cheshire	National Children's Homes	100 (including 14 hostel places)	30	3 : 50 5 : 20
Desford, Nr. Leicester	Leicester City Council	139	30	5 : 109
		Need (1969)	210 194	
		Balance	16	

	Management	Certified Number	Suggested allocation of places		
			Area 4	Other Areas	

Girls—Senior					
(a) *In Area 4*					
Rowley Hall, Stafford	Local Committee	40	34	5:	6
St. John's, 18 Gravelly Hill North, Birmingham, 23	Sisters of Charity of St. Vincent de Paul (Roman Catholic)	54 (including 9 hostel places)	21	3: 5: 6: 7:	10 9 7 7
(b) *In other Areas*					
Jordan's Brook House	Gloucestershire County Council	24 (all hostel places)	10	11:	14
Farringdon House, Clyst Honiton, Nr. Exeter	Local Committee	60 (including 6 hostel places)	20	8: 11:	30 10
			85		
		Need (1969)	61		
		Balance	24		
Girls—Intermediate					
(a) *In Area 4*					
Knowle Hill, Kenilworth, Warwickshire	Local Committee	36	30	5:	6
(b) *In other Areas*					
St. Euphrasia's, Troy, Monmouth	Sisters of the Good Shepherd (Roman Catholic)	52 (including 10 hostel places)	17	12:	35
			47		
		Need (1969)	37		
		Balance	10		
Girls—Junior					
(a) *In Area 4*					
Newfield, Cash's Lane, Coventry	Local Committee	30	25	5:	5
(b) *In other Areas* Nil					
			25		
		Need (1969)	19		
		Balance	6		

Approved schools—suggested use by planning areas

Planning area 5

I. *Children from Area 5 in approved schools*
Summary of position at 30 June 1969

	In Schools		Total	No. of Approved School places then in Area 5	Balance
	In Area 5	In other Areas			
Boys					
Senior	15	144	159	81	−78
Intermediate	95	73	168	210	42
Junior	119	12	131	226	95
	229	229	458	517	59
Girls					
Senior	Nil	41	41	Nil	−41
Intermediate	,,	15	15	,,	−15
Junior	,,	15	15	,,	−15
	Nil	71	71	Nil	−71

(These figures do not include boys and girls at Classifying Schools or Centres or at the Special (Secure) Units attached to 3 of the former.)

II. *Suggested use of schools*

	Management	Certified Number	Suggested allocation of places	
			Area 5	Other Areas
Boys—Senior				
(a) *In Area 5*				
St. John's School, Apethorpe, Peterborough, Northants	Northampton Diocesan Catholic Child Protection and Welfare Society (Roman Catholic)	81	40	4: 30 6: 11
(b) *In other Areas*				
East Moor School, Tile Lane, Adel, Leeds, 16	Local Committee	121	60	2: 61
Norton School, Kineton, Warwicks	Local Committee	110	50	4: 60
Carlton School, Carlton, Nr. Bedford	Local Committee	80	10	6: 10 7: 60
(b) *In other Areas*				
St. Camillus' School, Scarthingwell, Tadcaster, Yorks	Local Committee (Roman Catholic)	90	12	2: 63 3: 15
			172	
		Need (1969)	159	
		Balance	13	

	Management	Certified Number	Suggested allocation of places	
			Area 5	Other Areas
Boys—Intermediate				
(a) *In Area 5*				
Risley Hall School, Risley, Derby	Nottinghamshire County Council	90	90	Nil
St. John's School, Tiffield, Towcester, Northants	Local Committee	120	100	7: 20
(b) *In other Areas*				
St. Gilbert's School, Hartlebury, Nr. Kidderminster, Worcs	Brothers of the Christian Schools (Roman Catholic)	95	15	4: 80
Werrington School, Rocester, Nr. Uttoxeter, Staffs	Staffordshire County Council	104	20	4: 84
			225	
		Need (1969)	168	
		Balance	57	
Boys—Junior				
(a) *In Area 5*				
Desford School, Desford, Nr. Leicester	Leicester City Council	139	109	4: 30
Egerton House, Old Town, Brackley, Northants	Local Committee	31	21	7: 10
Skegby Hall, Skegby, Sutton-in-Ashfield, Notts	Nottinghamshire County Council	56	56	Nil
(b) *In other Areas*				
Danesford School, West Street, Congleton, Cheshire	National Children's Home	100 (including 14 hostel places)	20	3: 50 / 4: 30
			206	
		Need (1969)	131	
		Balance	75	
Girls—Senior				
(a) *No school in Area 5*				
(b) *In other Areas*				
Moorside School, Blackbrook Road, Sheffield	Sheffield City Council	70 (including 12 hostel places)	10	2: 40 / 3: 20

	Management	Certified Number	Suggested allocation of places	
			Area 5	Other Areas
Girls—Senior—cont.				
St. John's Home, Training School, St. John's Square, Wakefield, Yorks	Local Committee	30	4	1: 6 2: 10 3: 10
Rowley Hall School, Stafford	Local Committee	40	6	4: 34
St. John's Home, 18 Gravelly Hill North, Birmingham, 23	Sisters of Charity of St. Vincent de Paul (Roman Catholic)	54 (including 9 hostel places)	9	3: 10 4: 21 6: 7 7: 7
St. Joseph's School, Ashwicke Hall, Marshfield, Nr. Chippenham, Wilts	Sisters of the Good Shepherd (Roman Catholic)	68 (including 8 hostel places)	20	8: 18 11: 15 12: 15
		Need (1969)	49 41	
		Balance	8	
Girls—Intermediate				
(a) *No schools in Area 5*				
(b) *In other places*				
Springhead Park School, Park Lane, Rothwell, Nr. Leeds	National Assocn. for Mental Health	32 (including 8 hostel places)	4	1: 4 2: 20 3: 4
Knowle Hill School, Kenilworth, Warwicks	Local Committee	36	6	4: 30
		Need (1969)	10 15	
		Balance	− 5	
Girls—Junior				
(a) *No schools in Area 5*				
(b) *In other Areas*				
Blackbrook House, St. Helen's, Lancs	Liverpool Catholic Training Schools Assocn. (Roman Catholic)	50 (including 10 hostel places)	6	2: 6 3: 38
Newfield School, Cash's Lane, Coventry	Local Committee	30	5	4: 25
		Need (1969)	11 15	
		Balance	− 4	

Note. Unless and until fresh provision is made for girls in this Area, it may be necessary to look to Area 11 for placements.

Approved schools—suggested use by planning areas

Planning area 6

I. *Children from Area 6 in approved schools*
Summary of position at 30 June 1969

	In Schools		Total	No. of Approved School places then in Area 6	Balance
	In Area 6	In other Areas			
Boys					
Senior	72	23	95	217	122
Intermediate	67	18	85	325	240
Junior	Nil	44	44	Nil	−44
	139	85	224	542	318
Girls					
Senior	Nil	25	25	Nil	−25
Intermediate	,,	10	10	,,	−10
Junior	,,	2	2	,,	−2
	Nil	37	37	Nil	−37

(These figures do not include boys and girls at Classifying Schools or Centres or at the Special (Secure) Units attached to 3 of the former.)

II. *Suggested use of schools*

	Management	Certified Number	Suggested allocation of places	
			Area 6	Other Areas
(a) *In Area 6*				
Ardale School, Stifford, Nr. Grays, Essex	Essex County Council	100	Nil	8: 100
Kerrison School, Thorndon, Eye, Suffolk	Local Committee	110	110	Nil
(b) *In other Areas*				
St. John's School, Apethorpe, Peterborough, Northants	Northampton Diocesan Catholic Children's Protection and Welfare Society (Roman Catholic)	81	11	4: 30 / 5: 40
Carlton School, Carlton,	Local Committee	80	10	5: 10 / 7: 60
(b) *In other Areas*				
Herts TS, Chapmore End, Ware, Herts	Herts Training School Ltd.	132 (including 14 hostel places)	12	7: 40 / 8: 80
			143	
		Need (1969)	95	
		Balance	48	

	Management	Certified Number	Suggested allocation of places	
			Area 6	Other Areas
Boys—Intermediate				
(a) *In Area 6*				
Chafford School, Michaelstowe Hall, Ramsay, Harwich, Essex	Essex County Council	91	70	8: 21
Essex Home School, Rainsford Road, Chelmsford, Essex	Local Committee	84	Nil	8: 84
Red House School, Buxton, Norwich, Norfolk	Local Committee	90	50	8: 40
Kneesworth House School, Kneesworth, Royston, Herts	Cambs and Isle of Ely County Council	48	10	7: 38
(b) *In other Areas* Nil				
		Need (1969)	130 85	
		Balance	45	
Boys—Junior				
(a) *No schools in Area 6*				
(b) *In other Areas*				
Pishiobury School, Sawbridgeworth, Herts	Herts County Council	70	50	8: 20
Knotley House School, Chiddingstone Causeway, Tonbridge, Kent	Dr. Barnardo's	64	14	8: 50
		Need (1969)	64 44	
		Balance	20	
Girls—Senior				
(a) *No schools in Area 6*				
(b) *In other areas*				
Chaworth School, Ottershaw, Chertsey, Surrey	Local Committee	28	6	7: 7 8: 15
St. Lawrence's School, Frant, Tunbridge Wells, Kent	The Sisters of the Sacred Hearts of Jesus and Mary (Roman Catholic)	36 (including 6 hostel places)	8	7: 8 8: 20

	Management	Certified Number	Suggested allocation of places	
			Area 6	Other Areas
Girls—Senior—cont.				
Woodlands School, London Road, East Grinstead, Sussex	Salvation Army	26 (including 6 hostel places)	6	7: 8 9: 12
Avalon School, Summerhill, Chislehurst, Kent	Salvation Army	27	4	7: 4 8: 19
St. John's School, 18 Gravelly Hill North, Birmingham, 23	Sisters of Charity of St. Vincent de Paul (Roman Catholic)	54 (including 9 hostel places	7	3: 10 4: 21 5: 9 7: 7
			31	
		Need (1969)	25	
			—	
		Balance	6	

Girls—Intermediate

(a) *No schools in Area 6*

(b) *In other Areas*

Note. The need in 1969 was for 5 places. Until fresh provision is made girls may have to be sent to intermediate schools in Area 11 (Avonside or Longfords) or Area 10 (Greenacres).

Girls—Junior

(a) *No schools in Area 6*

	Management	Certified Number	Area 6	Other Areas
(b) *In other Areas*				
Princess Mary Village Homes, Addlestone, Weybridge, Surrey	Local Committee	56	8	7: 8 8: 16 9: 20 10: 4
Ave Maria School, Glenure Road, Eltham Park, London, S.E.9	Local Committee (Roman Catholic)	40 (including 6 hostel places)	5	7: 7 8: 28
			13	
		Need (1969)	7	
			—	
		Balance	6	

APPROVED SCHOOLS—SUGGESTED USE BY PLANNING AREAS

PLANNING AREA 7

I. *Children from Area 7 in approved schools*
Summary of position at 30 June 1969

	In Schools		Total	No. of Approved School places then in Area 7	Balance
	In Area 7	*In other Areas*			
Boys					
Senior	55	33	88	316	228
Intermediate	Nil	80	80	Nil	− 80
Junior	27	17	44	133	89
	82	130	212	449	237
Girls					
Senior	Nil	36	36	Nil	− 36
Intermediate	,,	9	9	,,	− 9
Junior	,,	10	10	,,	− 10
	Nil	55	55	Nil	− 55

(These figures do not include boys and girls at Classifying Schools or Centres or at the Special (Secure) Units attached to 3 of the former.)

II. *Suggested use of schools*

	Management	Certified Number	Suggested allocation of places	
			Area 7	*Other Areas*
Boys—Senior				
(a) *In Area 7*				
Carlton School, Carlton, Nr. Bedford	Local Committee	80	60	5: 10 6: 10
Herts TS, Chapmore End, Ware, Herts	Herts Training School Ltd.	132 (including 14 hostel places)	40	6: 12 8: 80
St. Benedict's School, Wokefield Park, Mortimer, Reading, Berks	Brothers of the Christian Schools (Roman Catholic)	104	20	8: 60 10: 24
(b) *In other Areas*				
Nil				

Need (1969)   120
 88

Balance   32

	Management	Certified Number	Suggested allocation of places	
			Area 7	Other Areas
Boys—Intermediate				
(a) *No schools in Area 7*				
(b) *In other Areas*				
Kneesworth House School, Kneesworth, Royston, Herts	Cambridgeshire and Isle of Ely County Council	48	38	6: 10
St. Edward's School, Sherfield English, Nr. Romsey, Hants	Local Committee (Roman Catholic)	100	10	8: 70 / 10: 20
Cotswold Community, Ashton Keynes, Nr. Swindon, Wilts	The Rainer Foundation	60	10	8: 15 / 10: 35
St. John's School, Tiffield, Towcester, Northants	Local Committee	120	20	5: 100
		Need (1969)	78 80	
		Balance	−2	
Boys—Junior				
(a) *In Area 7*				
Danesbury School, Warren Park Road, Hertford	Herts County Council	60	60	Nil
Pishiobury School, Sawbridgeworth, Herts	Herts County Council	70	Nil	6: 50 / 8: 20
(b) *In other Areas*				
Egerton House School, Old Town, Brackley, Northants	Local Committee	31	10	5: 21
		Need (1969)	70 44	
		Balance	26	
Girls—Senior				
(a) *No schools in Area 7*				
(b) *In other Areas*				
Chaworth School, Ottershaw, Chertsey, Surrey	Local Committee	28	7	6: 6 / 8: 15
St. Lawrence's School, Frant, Tunbridge Wells, Kent	The Sisters of the Sacred Hearts of Jesus and Mary (Roman Catholic)	36 (including 6 hostel places)	8	6: 8 / 8: 20

	Management	Certified Number	Suggested allocation of places	
			Area 7	Other Areas
Girls—Senior—cont.				
Woodlands School, London Road, East Grinstead, Sussex	Salvation Army	26 (including 6 hostel places)	8	6: 6 9: 12
Duncroft School, Moor Lane, Staines, Middx	National Assocn. for Mental Health	40 (including 8 hostel places)	8	8: 24 9: 24 10: 4
Avalon School, Summerhill, Chislehurst, Kent	Salvation Army	27	4	6: 4 8: 19
St. John's Home, 18 Gravelly Hill North, Birmingham, 23	Sisters of Charity of St. Vincent de Paul (Roman Catholic)	54 (including 9 hostel places)	7	3: 10 4: 21 5: 9 6: 7
			42	
		Need (1969)	36	
			—	
		Balance	6	

Girls—Intermediate

(a) *No schools in Area 7*

(b) *In other Areas*

	Management	Certified Number	Area 7	Other Areas
Longfords School, Minchinhampton, Stroud, Glos	Church Moral Aid Association	32	10	9: 12 11: 10
			10	
		Need (1969)	7	
			—	
		Balance	3	

Girls—Junior

(a) *No schools in Area 7*

(b) *In other Areas*

	Management	Certified Number	Area 7	Other Areas
Princess Mary Village Homes, Addlestone, Weybridge, Surrey	Local Committee	56	8	6: 8 8: 16 9: 20 10: 4
Ave Maria School, Glenure Road, Eltham Park, London, S.E.9	Local Committee (Roman Catholic)	40 (including 6 hostel places)	7	6: 5 8: 28
			15	
		Need (1969)	12	
			—	
		Balance	3	

Approved schools—suggested use by planning areas

Planning area 8

I. *Children from Area 8 in approved schools*
Summary of position at 30 June 69

	In Schools		Total	No. of Approved School places then in Area 8	Balance
	In Area 8	In other Areas			
Boys					
Senior	49	277	326	70	−256
Intermediate	Nil	328	328	Nil	−328
Junior	,,	206	206	,,	−206
	49	811	860	70	−790
Girls					
Senior	5	112	117	27	−90
Intermediate	Nil	47	47	Nil	−47
Junior	26	12	38	40	2
	31	171	202	67	−135

(These figures do not include boys and girls at Classifying Schools or Centres or at the Special (Secure) Units attached to 3 of the former.)

II. *Suggested use of schools*

	Management	Certified Number	Suggested allocation of places	
			Area 8	Other Areas
Boys—Senior				
(a) *In Area 8*				
St. Christopher's School, 201 Uxbridge Road, Hayes, Middlesex	Hillingdon London Borough Council	60	60	Nil
(b) *In other Areas*				
Ardale School Stifford, Nr. Grays, Essex	Essex County Council	100	100	Nil
Herts TS, Chapmore End, Ware, Herts	Herts Training School Limited	132 (including 14 hostel places)	80	6: 12 7: 40
St. Benedict's School, Wokefield Park, Mortimer, Reading, Berks	Brothers of The Christian Schools (Roman Catholic)	104	60	7: 20 10: 24

Management	Certified Number	Suggested allocation of places	
		Area 8	Other Areas

Boys—Senior—cont.

Banstead Hall School, Brighton Road, Banstead, Surrey	Surrey County Council	75	50	9: 25
Royal Philanthropic Society's School, Redhill, Surrey	Royal Philanthropic Society	80 (including 22 hostel places)	50	9: 30
		Need (1969)	400 326	
		Balance	74	

Boys—Intermediate

(a) *No schools in Area 8*

(b) *In other Areas*

Chafford School, Michaelstowe Hall, Ramsay, Harwich, Essex	Essex County Council	91	21	6: 70
Essex Home School, Rainsford Road, Chelmsford, Essex	Local Committee	84	84	Nil
Red House School, Buxton, Norwich, Norfolk	Local Committee	90	40	6: 50
Hays Bridge School, Brick House Lane, South Godstone, Surrey	Surrey County Council	75 (including 10 hostel places)	15	9: 60
St. Vincent's School, Temple Hill, Dartford, Kent	Southwark Catholic Children's Society (Roman Catholic)	96	96	Nil
St. Edward's School, Sherfield English, Nr. Romsey, Hants	Local Committee (Roman Catholic)	100	70	7: 10 / 10: 20
Cotswold Community, Ashton Keynes, Nr. Swindon, Wilts	The Rainer Foundation	60	15	7: 10 / 10: 35
		Need (1969)	341 328	
		Balance	13	

	Management	Certified Number	Suggested allocation of places	
			Area 8	Other Areas
Boys—Junior				
(a) *No schools in Area 8*				
b) *In other Areas*				
Pishiobury School, Sawbridgeworth, Herts	Herts County Council	70	20	6: 50
Finnart House School, Oatlands Drive, Weybridge, Surrey	Local Committee	69	49	10: 20
Knotley House School, Chiddingstone Causeway, Tonbridge, Kent	Dr. Barnardo's	64	50	6: 14
St. Thomas More School, West Grinstead, Nr. Horsham, Sussex	Southwark Catholic Children's Society (Roman Catholic)	86	81	9: 5
St. Vincent's School, Castle Road, Tankerton, Kent	Southwark Catholic Children's Society (Roman Catholic)	52	47	9: 5
			247	
		Need (1969)	206	
		Balance	41	
Girls—Senior				
(a) *In Area 8*				
Avalon School, Summerhill, Chislehurst, Kent	Salvation Army	27	19	6: 4 7: 4
(b) *In other Areas*				
Chaworth School, Ottershaw, Chertsey, Surrey	Local Committee	28	15	6: 6 7: 7
The Crescent School, Frenchay Road, Downend, Bristol	Bristol City Council	72 (including 8 hostel places)	12	10: 15 11: 30 12: 15
St. Lawrence's School, Frant, Tunbridge Wells, Kent	Sisters of the Sacred Hearts of Jesus and Mary (Roman Catholic)	36 (including 6 hostel places)	20	6: 8 7: 8

	Management	Certified Number	Suggested allocation of places	
			Area 8	Other Areas
Girls—Senior—cont.				
St. Joseph's School, Ashwicke Hall, Marshfield, Nr. Chippenham, Wilts	Sisters of the Good Shepherd (Roman Catholic)	68 (including 8 hostel places)	18	5: 20 11: 15 12: 15
Duncroft School, Moor Lane, Staines, Middx	National Association for Mental Health	40 (including 8 hostel places)	24	8: 8 9: 4 10: 4
Farringdon House School, Farringdon, Clyst Honiton, Nr. Exeter, Devon	Local Committee	60 (including 6 hostel places)	30	4: 20 11: 10
		Need (1969)	138 117	
		Balance	21	
Girls—Intermediate				
(a) *No Schools in Area* 8				
(b) *In other Areas*				
Greenacres School, Curzon Street, Calne, Wilts	Local Committee	51	26 (including 8 hostel places)	10: 25
Avonside School, 17 Walcot Parade, Bath	Local Committee	34	14	9: 10 11: 10
		Need (1969)	40 47	
		Balance	−7	
Girls—Junior				
(a) *In Area* 8				
Ave Maria School, Glenure Road, Eltham Park, London, S.E.9	Local Committee (Roman Catholic)	40 (including 6 hostel places)	28	6: 5 7: 7
(b) *In other Areas*				
Princess Mary Village Homes, Addlestone, Weybridge, Surrey	Local Committee	56	16	6: 8 7: 8 9: 20 10: 4
		Need (1969)	44 38	
		Balance	6	

APPROVED SCHOOLS—SUGGESTED USE BY PLANNING AREA
PLANNING AREA 9

I. *Children from Area 9 in approved schools*
 Summary of position at 30 June 69

	In Schools		Total	No. of Approved School places then in Area 9	Balance
	In Area 9	*In other Areas*			
Boys					
Senior	105	23	128	331	203
Intermediate	66	11	77	261	184
Junior	58	1	59	369	310
	229	35	264	961	697
Girls					
Senior	17	13	30	162	132
Intermediate	Nil	10	10	Nil	−10
Junior	3	5	8	48	40
	20	28	48	210	162

(These figures do not include boys and girls at Classifying Schools or Centres or at the Special (Secure) Units attached to 3 of the former.)

II. *Suggested use of schools*

	Management	Certified Number	Suggested allocation of places	
			Area 9	Other Areas
Boys—Senior				
(a) *In Area 9*				
Banstead Hall School, Brighton Road, Banstead, Surrey	Surrey County Council	75	25	8: 50
North Downs School, South Darenth, Dartford, Kent	Kent County Council	100	100	Nil
Park House School, Peper Harrow, Nr. Godalming, Surrey	Local Committee	96	96	—
Royal Philanthropic Society's School, Redhill, Surrey	The Royal Philanthropic Society	80 (including 22 hostel places)	30	8: 50
(b) *In other Areas* Nil				
			251	
		Need (1969)	128	
		Balance	123	

Note. The Managers of Park House are understood to be considering the possibility of a specialised role, under which places might be widely available to other Areas.

	Management	Certified Number	Suggested allocation of places Area 9	Other Areas

Boys—Intermediate

(a) *In Area 9*

Hays Bridge School, Brick House Lane, South Godstone, Surrey	Surrey County Council	75 (including 10 hostel places)	70	8: 15
Mayford School, Mayford Green, Woking, Surrey	Surrey County Council	90	90	Nil
St. Vincent's School, Castle Road, Tankerton, Kent	Southwark Catholic Children's Society (Roman Catholic)	52	5	8: 47

(b) *In other Areas*
Nil

			150
	Need (1969)		77
	Balance		73

Boys—Junior

(a) *In Area 9*

Finnart House School, Oatlands Drive, Weybridge, Surrey	Local Committee	69	Nil	8: 49 / 10: 20
Knotley House School, Chiddingstone Causeway, Tonbridge, Kent	Dr. Barnardo's	64	Nil	8: 50 / 6: 14
Mile Oak School, Portslade, Sussex	E. Sussex County Council	80	80	Nil
St. Thomas More School, West Grinstead, Nr. Horsham, Sussex	Southwark Catholic Children's Society (Roman Catholic)	86	5	8: 81
Walsh Manor School, Crowborough, Sussex	E. Sussex County Council	18	18	Nil
St. Vincent's School, Temple Hill, Dartford, Kent	Southwark Catholic Children's Society (Roman Catholic)	96	Nil	8: 96

(b) *In other Areas*
Nil

			108
	Need (1969)		59
	Balance		49

| | Management | Certified Number | Suggested allocation of places | |
			Area 9	Other Areas

Girls—Senior

(a) *In Area* 9

Chaworth School, Ottershaw, Chertsey, Surrey	Local Committee	28	Nil	6 :6 7: 7 8: 15
Duncroft School, Moor Lane, Staines, Middlesex	National Association for Mental Health	40 (including 8 hostel places)	4	7: 8 8: 24 10: 4
St. Lawrence's School, Frant, Tunbridge Wells, Kent	Sisters of the Sacred Hearts of Jesus and Mary (Roman Catholic)	36 (including 6 hostel places)	Nil	6: 8 7: 8 8: 20
Shermanbury Grange, Shermanbury, Horsham, Sussex	W. Sussex County Council	32	32	Nil
Woodlands School, London Road, E. Grinstead, Sussex	Salvation Army	26 (including 6 hostel places)	12	6: 6 7: 8

(b) *In other Areas*
Nil

		48
Need (1969)		30
		—
Balance		18

Girls—Intermediate

(a) *No Schools in Area* 9

(b) *In other Areas*

Avonside School, 17 Walcot Parade, Bath, Somerset	Local Committee	34	10	8: 14 11: 10
Longfords School, Minchinhampton, Stroud, Glos	Church Moral Aid Association	32	12	7: 10 11: 10

		22
Need (1969)		13
		—
Balance		9

Girls—Junior

(a) *In Area* 9

Princess Mary Village Homes, Addlestone, Weybridge, Surrey	Local Committee	56	20	6: 8 7: 8 8: 16 10: 4

(b) *In other Areas*
Nil

		20
Need (1969)		8
		—
Balance		12

APPROVED SCHOOLS—SUGGESTED USE BY PLANNING AREAS

PLANNING AREA 10

I. *Children from Area 10 in approved schools*
Summary of position at 30 June 69

	In Schools		Total	No. of Approved School places then in Area 10	Balance
	In Area 10	In other Areas			
Boys					
Senior	3	71	74	88	14
Intermediate	46	27	73	190	117
Junior	37	23	60	56	−4
	86	121	207	334	127
Girls					
Senior	3	19	22	17	−5
Intermediate	4	10	14	45	31
Junior	Nil	8	8	Nil	−8
	7	37	44	62	18

(These figures do not include boys and girls at Classifying Schools or Centres or at the Special (Secure) Units attached to 3 of the former.)

II. *Suggested use of schools*

	Management	Certified Number	Suggested allocation of places	
			Area 10	Other Areas
Boys—Senior				
(a) *In Area 10*				
St. Swithin's Nautical School, Yarmouth, Isle of Wight	Brothers of the Christian Schools (Roman Catholic)	88	88	Nil
(b) *In other Areas*				
St. Benedict's School, Wokefield Park, Mortimer, Reading, Berks	Brothers of the Christian Schools (Roman Catholic)	104	24	7: 20 8: 60
National Nautical School, Nore Road, Portishead, Bristol	Incorporated National Nautical School, Somerset	116 (including 20 hostel places)	20	11: 50 12: 20 others: 26
(b) *In other Areas*				
Northbrook School, Beacon Lane, Whipton, Exeter	Local Committee	75	20	11: 40 others: 15
			152	
	Need (1969)		74	
	Balance		78	

	Management	Certified Number	Suggested allocation of places	
			Area 10	Other Areas

Boys—Intermediate

(a) *In Area* 10

| Cotswold Community, Ashton Keynes, Nr. Swindon, Wilts | The Rainer Foundation | 60 | 35 | 7: 10
8: 15 |
| St. Edward's School, Sherfield English, Nr. Romsey, Hants | Local Committee (Roman Catholic) | 100 | 20 | 7: 10
8: 70 |

(b) *In other Areas*

Kingswood School, Britannia Road, Kingswood, Bristol	Local Committee	105	40	11: 65
		Need (1969)	95 73	
		Balance	22	

Boys—Junior

(a) *In Area* 10

| Winton House School, Andover Road, Winchester, Hants | Hants County Council | 56 | 56 | Nil |

(b) *In other Areas*

Finnart House School, Oatlands Drive, Weybridge, Surrey	Local Committee	69	20	8: 49
		Need (1969)	76 60	
		Balance	16	

Girls—Senior

(a) *In Area* 10

| St. Michael's School, 29 Churchfields, Salisbury, Wilts | Wilts County Council | 17 | 17 | Nil |

	Management	Certified Number	Suggested allocation of places	
			Area 10	Other Areas

Girls—Senior—cont.

(b) *In other Areas*

The Crescent School, Frenchay Road, Downend, Bristol	Bristol City Council	72 (including 8 hostel places)	15	8: 12 11: 30 12: 15
Duncroft School, Moor Lane, Staines, Middlesex	National Association for Mental Health	40 (including 8 hostel places)	4	7: 8 8: 24 9: 4
		Need (1969)	36 22	
		Balance	— 14	

Girls—Intermediate

(a) *In Area 10*

Greenacres School, Curzon Street, Calne, Wilts	Local Committee	51 (including 8 hostel places)	25	8: 26

(b) *In other Areas*
Nil

		Need (1969)	25 14	
		Balance	— 11	

Girls—Junior

(a) *No schools in Area 10*

(b) *In other Areas*

Ryalls Court School, Marlpit Lane, Seaton, Devon	National Children's Home	52 (including 8 hostel places)	15	11: 20 12: 17
Princess Mary Village Homes, Addlestone, Weybridge, Surrey	Local Committee	56	4	6: 8 7: 8 8: 16 9: 20
		Need (1969)	19 8	
		Balance	— 11	

Approved schools—suggested use by planning areas

Planning area 11

I. *Children from Area 11 in approved schools*
   Summary of position at 30 *June* 69

	In Schools		Total	No. of Approved School places then in Area 11	Balance
	In Area 11	*In other Areas*			
Boys					
Senior	39	19	58	191	133
Intermediate	37	20	57	225	168
Junior	59	26	85	103	18
	135	65	200	519	319
Girls					
Senior	18	4	22	224	202
Intermediate	7	2	9	66	57
Junior	8	1	9	52	43
	33	7	40	342	302

(These figures do not include boys and girls at Classifying Schools or Centres or at the Special (Secure) Units attached to 3 of the former.)

II. *Suggested use of schools*

	Management	Certified Number	Suggested allocation of places	
			Area 11	*Other Areas*
Boys—senior				
(a) *In Area 11*				
National Nautical School, Nore Road, Portishead, Bristol, Somerset	Incorporated National Nautical School, Somerset	116 (including 20 hostel places)	50 10: 20 12: 20 others: 26	
Northbrook School, Beacon Lane, Whipton, Exeter, Devon	Local Committee	75	40 10: 20 others: 15	
(b) *In other Areas*				
Nil				

Need (1969)   90
                   58
                   ──
Balance   32

Note. There would appear to be some spare capacity in the senior boys schools in this Area which might be available to Areas other than those specifically mentioned.

	Management	Certified Number	Suggested allocation of places	
			Area 11	Other Areas
Boys—Intermediate				
(a) *In Area* 11				
Kingswood School, Britannia Road, Kingswood, Bristol	Local Committee	105	65	10: 40
Sedbury Park School, Chepstow, Mon	Local Committee	120 (including 20 hostel places)	20	4: 40 12: 60
(b) *In other Areas* Nil				
		Need (1969)	85 57	
		Balance	28	
Boys—Junior				
(a) *In Area* 11				
Eagle House School, Church Street, Bathford, Bath, Somerset	Local Committee	28	28	Nil
Forde Park School, College Road, Newton Abbot, Devon	Local Committee	75	75	Nil
(b) *In other Areas* Nil				
		Need (1969)	103 85	
		Balance	18	
Girls—Senior				
(a) *In Area* 11				
The Crescent School, Frenchay Road, Downend, Bristol	Bristol City Council	72 (including 8 hostel places)	30	8: 12 10: 15 12: 15
Farringdon House School, Farringdon, Clyst Honiton, Nr. Exeter, Devon	Local Committee	60 (including 6 hostel places)	10	4: 20 8: 30
Jordan's Brook House School, Upton Lane, Barnwood, Glos	Gloucestershire County Council	24 (all hostel places)	14	4: 10

	Management	Certified Number	Suggested allocation of places	
			Area 11	Other Areas

Girls—Senior—cont.

St. Joseph's School, Ashwicke Hall, Marshfield, Nr. Chippenham, Wilts	Sisters of the Good Shepherd (Roman Catholic)	68 (including 8 hostel places)	15	8: 18 12: 15 5: 20

(b) *In other Areas*
Nil

	Certified Number	Area 11
Need (1969)		69 18
Balance		51

Girls—Intermediate

(a) *In Area 11*

	Management	Certified Number	Area 11	Other Areas
Avonside School, 17 Walcot Parade, Bath, Somerset	Local Committee	34	10	8: 14 9: 10
Longfords School, Minchinhampton, Stroud, Glos	Church Moral Aid Association Incorporated	32	10	7: 10 9: 12

(b) *In other Areas*
Nil

		Area 11
Need (1969)		20 9
Balance		11

Girls—Junior

(a) *In Area 11*

	Management	Certified Number	Area 11	Other Areas
Ryalls Court School, Marlpit Lane, Seaton, Devon	National Children's Home	52 (including 8 hostel places)	20	10: 15 12: 17

(b) *In other Areas*
Nil

		Area 11
Need (1969)		20 9
Balance		11

Note. The balance of places for girls in relation to the 1969 need would appear to show spare capacity in this Area that might be available to other Areas on a wider scale that is indicated above.

APPROVED SCHOOLS—SUGGESTED USE BY PLANNING AREAS

PLANNING AREA 12

I. *Children from Area 12 in approved schools*
Summary of position at 30 *June* 1969

	In Schools			No of Approved School places then in Area 12	Balance
	In Area 12	In other Areas	Total		
Boys					
Senior	32	34	66	76	10
Intermediate	64	68	132	218	86
Junior	122	8	130	180	50
	218	110	328	474	146
Girls					
Senior	—	19	19	—	− 19
Intermediate	3	9	12	52	40
Junior	—	10	10	—	− 10
	3	38	41	52	11

(These figures do not include boys and girls at Classifying Schools or Centres or at the Special (Secure) Units attached to 3 of the former.)

II. *Suggested use of schools*

	Management	Certified Number	Suggested allocation of places	
			Area 12	Other Areas
Boys—Senior				
(a) *In Area* 12				
Glamorgan Farm School, Neath, Glamorgan	Glamorgan County Council	76 (including 16 hostel places)	76	Nil
(b) *In other Areas*				
National Nautical School, Nore Road, Portishead, Bristol, Somerset	Incorporated National Nautical School, Som.	116 (including 20 hostel places)	20	10: 20 11: 50 others: 26
Boreatton Park School, Baschurch, Nr. Shrewsbury, Salop	Local Committee	111	10	4: 101
			106	
	Need (1969)		66	
	Balance		40	

	Management	Certified Number	Suggested allocation of places	
			Area 12	Other Areas

Boys—Intermediate

(a) *In Area* 12

| Bryn Estyn School, Bryn Estyn Road, Rhosnessney, Wrexham, Denbighshire | Local Committee | 99 (including 14 hostel places) | 99 | Nil |
| Ty Mawr School, Gilwern, Nr. Abergavenny, Mon | Breconshire County Council | 119 | 60 | 4: 40 others: 19 |

(b) *In other Areas*

| Sedbury Park School, Chepstow, Mon | Local Committee | 120 (including 20 hostel places) | 60 | 4: 40 11: 20 |

			219	
		Need (1969)	132	
		Balance	87	

Boys—Junior

(a) *In Area* 12

| Bryn-y-don School, Dinas Powis, Glamorgan | Cardiff City Council and Glamorgan County Council | 125 | 125 | Nil |
| Headlands School, Paget Place, Penarth, Glamorgan | National Children's Home | 55 (including 15 hostel places) | 55 | Nil |

(b) *In other Areas*

Nil

			180	
		Need (1969)	130	
		Balance	50	

Note. The balance of intermediate places for boys in relation to the 1969 need would appear to show spare capacity in this Area that might be available to other Areas on a wider scale than is indicated here.

Girls—Senior

(a) *No Schools in Area* 12

(b) *In other Areas*

| The Crescent School, Frenchay Road, Downend, Bristol | Bristol City Council | 72 (including 8 hostel places) | 15 | 11: 30 8: 12 10: 15 |

	Management	Certified Number	Suggested allocation of places	
			Area 12	Other Areas
Girls—Senior—cont.				
St. Joseph's School, Ashwicke Hall, Marshfield, Nr. Chippenham, Wilts	Sisters of the Good Shepherd (Roman Catholic)	68 (including 8 hostel places)	15	5: 20 8: 18 11: 15
		Need (1969)	30 19	
		Balance	11	
Girls—Intermediate				
(a) *In Area 12*				
St. Euphrasia's School, Troy House, Troy, Monmouth	Sisters of the Good Shepherd (Roman Catholic)	52 (including 10 hostel places)	35	4: 17
(b) *In other Areas* Nil				
		Need (1969)	35 10	
		Balance	25	
Girls—Junior				
(a) *No Schools in Area 12*				
(b) *In other Areas*				
Ryalls Court School, Marlpit Lane, Seaton, Devon	National Children's Home	52 (including 8 hostel places)	17	10: 15 11: 20
		Need (1969)	17 10	
		Balance	7	

Home Office Circular No. 255/1970.   *Dated November 17, 1970*

CHILDREN AND YOUNG PERSONS ACT, 1969: THE CONSEQUENCES OF ABOLISHING THE APPROVED SCHOOL ORDER

1. In accordance with the undertaking given in the first paragraph of Home Office Circular No. 184/1970, this circular deals with the formal and administrative implications of the abolition of the approved school order and the resultant change in status of boys and girls already in approved schools, or in remand homes awaiting admission to approved schools, on 1 January 1971, the necessary consequential amendments to the Remand Home and Approved School Rules, and certain other consequential changes in the law relating to approved schools for which the Act provides.

2. These matters are dealt with in the attached memorandum which, for ease of reference, has been divided into 3 parts, as follows:—

Part I deals with the legal effects of the abolition of the approved school order for children who are subject to such orders on 31 December 1970. Attention is drawn particularly to paragraph 13 which deals with the position of children who are absconders on the specified day from establishments other than approved schools, or from supervision. It will be important for the local authority concerned to take the appropriate action as indicated to ensure that there is no doubt that such an absconder is required by them to live at the premises where he was living before he absconded. The nomination of care authorities (paragraphs 10, 11 and 18) will be the subject of a circular letter to Correspondents of approved schools towards the end of the year.

Part II suggests the working administrative arrangements which might be adopted as between care authorities and managers of schools to deal with transitional problems of practice and procedure following the abolition of the approved school order.

Part III deals with the amendments necessary to the Approved School Rules and Remand Home Rules to take account of the change in status of the children accommodated in these establishments and of the consequential changes in the statutory responsibilities of the managers of approved schools, and of the local authorities providing remand homes, in relation to these children. Copies of the Approved School Rules, 1970, and Remand Home Rules, 1970, are attached.

3. It is desirable that the parents or guardian of each child subject to an approved school order on 31 December 1970 should be told in advance how their child's position will be altered by the statutory changes taking effect on that date. Attached at Annexes A and B are suggestions for a letter and an accompanying leaflet which might be sent by each school (or, suitably amended, by remand homes) to all the parents and guardians concerned. It will also be important that the children subject to approved school orders who will pass into care on 1 January should be told of their changed status and future prospects. This, it is suggested, is a matter for personal explanation by staff to each child. It may be possible in some cases to use the leaflet at Annex B for this purpose. But for most children some direct verbal explanation of what is inevitably a complicated matter will probably be desirable. The set of notes at Annex C has been attached to this circular in the hope that it may assist staff who have to undertake this task by indicating the main points requiring explanation. Communication with parents, guardians and children is likely to lead to requests for further information or explanation; schools and local authorities are asked to deal with them as sympathetically and reassuringly as possible.

4. This circular does not attempt to give guidance on the consequential changes in detailed practice and procedure in the field covered by existing Approved School Bulletins and Home Office Circulars. These documents are being reviewed and amended bulletins and circulars appropriate to the transitional period, and revised indexes, will be issued in due course.

NOTE

This circular was sent to correspondents of approved schools in England and Wales (copies for information to heads of schools), Superintendents of Remand Homes, and to councils of counties, county boroughs and London boroughs in England and Wales. (Copies for information of Financial Officer and Children's Officer.)

PART I—LEGAL EFFECTS

1. The abolition of the approved school order has been brought about by the Secretary of State's specifying, in pursuance of section 7 (5) of the Act, the day after which orders sending persons to approved schools will not be made. The day specified is 31 December 1970 (see Home Office Circular No. 236/1970 and accompanying Commencement No. 3 Order 1970). At the same time the transitional provisions and savings in Part I of Schedule 4 will be brought into force under section 72 (1) of the Act.

Substitution of care orders

2. Paragraph 7 (1) of Schedule 4 provides that all existing approved school orders in force on the specified day shall cease to have effect at the end of that day. Under sub-paragraph 7 (2), any person under the age of 19 who is subject to an approved school order will be deemed from the end of the specified day to be the subject of a care order (within the meaning of section 20) made on the same day and by the same court as the approved school order. Sub-paragraph 7 (2) (a) has the effect of placing the person concerned under the care of the local authority named in the approved school order, or of a local authority nominated by the Secretary of State if none was named in the order (see paragraphs 10 and 11 below); and sub-paragraph 7 (2) (b) provides for a person released on supervision before the specified day to be regarded as having been allowed by the local authority concerned to remain under the charge and control of whoever was last nominated in relation to him under paragraph 1 (1) of Schedule 2 of the Criminal Justice Act, 1961. The local authority which will become responsible for a child or young person under these provisions is referred to in this memorandum as the "care authority".

3. Under paragraph 7 (1) (a), children in approved schools will, from the specified day, no longer be liable to be detained under the following provisions of the existing law (which, in effect, supplement the powers of detention conferred by the approved school order itself):—

(a) section 73 of the Children and Young Persons Act, 1933, which empowers the managers of an approved school, with the consent of the Secretary of State, to extend the period of detention of a person in the school for up to 6 months beyond the expiry of his normal period of detention (but not beyond the age of 19) if the managers are satisfied that he is in need of further care or training;

(b) section 82 of the same Act which provides that if a person subject to an approved school order absconds and is brought to his school, his period of detention shall be increased by a period equal to that during which he was unlawfully at large; and

(c) paragraph 2 of Schedule 2 to the Criminal Justice Act, 1961, which provides for the recall and further detention, on the written order of the managers, of a person subject to an approved school order who has been released under supervision.

These provisions will be repealed as from the specified day. Any child detained under these provisions on the specified day will be deemed to be the subject of a care order unless he is eligible for immediate release on grounds of age (see paragraph 7 below).

4. Under paragraph 7 (1) (b), a person who has attained the age of 19 will not be liable after the specified day to be detained under section 15 of the Criminal Justice Act, 1961. This section provides for the removal for a period of up to 28 days of a seriously unruly or disruptive boy or girl over 15 from an approved school to another approved school or to a remand home. Paragraph 7 (2), however, provides that where a person who is under 19 is subject to detention

under section 15 of the 1961 Act on the specified day, the warrant issued under section 15 remains valid. Where the person concerned is over 19, the effect of sub-paragraph 7 (1) (b) is that he should automatically be released.

5. Paragraph 7 (2) of Schedule 4, also provides that where a person is simultaneously subject to more than one approved school order on the specified day, it is the most recent order that will be taken into account.

Duration of Care Orders

6. The effect of the provisions of sub-paragraph 7 (2) read with section 20 (3) of the Act is that all persons who are the subject of an approved school order at the end of the specified day will (unless the new care order is discharged sooner under section 21 of the Act) remain in care until the age of 18 or, if the person concerned was 16 or over when the approved school order was made, or if there is an application to extend the order under section 21 (1), until the age of 19. The effect this will have, by comparison with the provisions previously in force, will vary according to the age of the person concerned at the time the approved school order was made:

(a) If he was then aged 16 or over, the new care order may last as long as the maximum period for which he could have been detained under the original approved school order (*i.e.* up to the age of 19).

(b) If he was then aged 15 but under 16, he may be in care for a slightly shorter period than that for which he could have been detained under the approved school order (because the care order will, unless discharged earlier, expire at the 18th birthday, whereas detention under the approved school order could have lasted for 3 years).

(c) If he was then under 15, the care order may remain effective until he is 18, which will be longer than the three-year period for which he could have been detained under the approved school order.

7. Where a person subject to an approved school order on the specified day is 19 or over, or is 18 and was under 16 when the order was made, he will not thereafter be subject to a care order and he will be free to leave the school on 1 January. In practice it will perhaps be more convenient for the managers of approved schools to allow such children to leave the school shortly before the specified day under paragraph 5 of Schedule 4 of the 1933 Act. Similarly, persons in either of these categories who are under the supervision of the managers of an approved school on the specified day will not be subject to a care order from 1 January 1971 and should be so informed by the managers (see also paragraph 16).

8. In reaching decisions about the length of time that an individual child will remain in residence in an approved school after the specified day, or remain under the charge and control of the person with whom he lived whilst under supervision, care authorities will no doubt take account of the period for which he might reasonably have been expected to remain at the school, or under supervision, under the original approved school order. Nevertheless, it will in all cases be entirely within the discretion of care authorities to decide how long particular children should remain in care; and it will be for them to consider, in appropriate cases, whether to apply to the court under section 21 (1) of the Act (as applied by paragraph 3 (2) of Schedule 3) for a care order to continue in force after the age of 18 (see paragraphs 168 and 169 of the Guide to Part I of the Act (issued with Home Office Circular No. 236/1970).

9. The provisions of the Act relating to the review and discharge of care orders, and to appeals, are dealt with in paragraphs 161–163 of the Guide to Part I of the Act.

Nomination of Care Authorities

10. Paragraph 7 (2) (a) of Schedule 4 empowers the Secretary of State in certain cases to nominate the local authority who is to become the care authority (see paragraph 2 above). These will be cases where no local authority is named in the approved school order, *i.e.* where the child has been certified by the court, under section 70 (2) (b) of the Children and Young Persons Act, 1933, as resident outside England and Wales, or the order has been made under section 40A of the Education Act, 1944, in respect of a vagrant child not receiving efficient full time education. Under paragraph 7 (3) of Schedule 4 the Secretary of State will be able to vary the nomination he has made.

11. Where under section 70 (2) of the 1933 Act a local authority is named in the approved school order, it is either the authority in whose district the person named in the order was resident or, if that is not known, the authority in whose district the offence was committed or the circumstances leading to committal to an approved school arose. Similar criteria will govern the selection of the local authority to whose care a person is committed by a care order after 1 January 1971 under section 20 (2) of the 1969 Act. To ensure consistency, the nomination of a care authority under paragraph 7 (2) (a) of Schedule 4 in cases where no local authority has been named in the order will, so far as possible, follow the same principles. Where, therefore, the parents or guardian of an "outside England" case have settled in this country since the making of the order the authority in whose area they habitually reside will be nominated as the care authority. Where the test of parental residence cannot be applied, the local authority in whose area the offence was committed will be nominated. In the case of vagrant children subject to orders made under section 40A of the Education Act, 1944, the criterion of parental residence will be applied where possible, although it seems more likely that it will be necessary to nominate the authority in whose area the child was found. If for any reason neither criterion can be applied, the local authority in whose area the school in which the child is detained is situated will be nominated. Nomination will be subject to review under paragraph 7 (3) of Schedule 4 at the request of a local authority and another authority may be nominated in respect of a child deemed to be in care if in the opinion of the Secretary of State it would be right to do so. The identification of children for whom no local authority has been named in the approved school order and the nomination of authorities in respect of them will be undertaken by the Home Office before the specified day.

Absconders

12. Paragraph 7 (4) of Schedule 4 provides that a person who becomes subject to a care order under sub-paragraph (2) and is unlawfully absent from an approved school on the specified day will be regarded as required by the care authority to return to that school to live.

13. Sub-paragraph (4), as worded, does not specifically cover cases of children subject to an approved school order who on the specified day are absconders not from an approved school but from a hospital (or other institution) to which they have been transferred, or from the place where, or person with whom, they had been required to live. To ensure that there is no doubt that the transitional provisions of paragraph 7 (4) will apply, it is desirable that care authorities should notify hospitals, parents, supervisors etc. in any such case where the child is an absconder on 1 January 1971 that from that date onwards he is subject to a requirement by the care authority to live at the place from which he absconded. Otherwise, the provision of section 32 as to the recovery of absentees may not be effective in such cases.

14. A child under supervision under sub-paragraph 7 (2) (b) who becomes an absentee *after the specified day* would appear to be subject to the provisions of

section 32 of the Act even though there may have been no express requirement by the local authority as to where he should live.

After-care

15. Under section 20 of the Children Act, 1948, and section 58 of the Children and Young Persons Act, 1963, a local authority is empowered to provide financial and other assistance to persons who were formerly in their care and are under the age of 21. Paragraph 7 of Schedule 2 to the Criminal Justice Act, 1961 (which will be repealed from the specified day) currently confers a similar power on managers of an approved school to assist persons who have formerly been under their supervision.

16. Paragraph 7 (5) of Schedule 4 provides that a person who on the specified day is subject to an approved school order, or is subject to supervision under Schedule 2 to the 1961 Act, or is eligible for assistance under paragraph 7 of that Schedule and who (because of his age) is not deemed to be the subject of a care order under sub-paragraph (2), shall be eligible for assistance under section 20 of the 1948 Act and section 58 of the 1963 Act as if he had been in the care of a local authority on the specified day, notwithstanding that he may have attained the age of 18.

Mental Health Act, 1959

17. Paragraph 7 (7) provides that where on the specified day a direction under section 74 of the Mental Health Act, 1959, is in force in respect of a child subject to an approved school order who has been transferred to hospital under section 72 of the Mental Health Act, any restrictions imposed by virtue of the direction shall cease to have effect. The effect of sub-paragraph (7) therefore is that after the specified day the section 74 direction will be treated as if it had never been made; and the child regarded as if he was simply subject to a transfer direction under section 72. Such children will be deemed to be in care from 1 January 1971.

Scotland, Northern Ireland, Channel Isles and Isle of Man

18. Under paragraph 7 (8), a child detained in an English approved school on the specified day by virtue of a Scottish approved school order or a Northern Ireland training school order and the existing "cross border" provisions (section 83 (1) of the 1933 Act) or a child from the Channel Isles or the Isle of Man detained in an English approved school under section 83 (3) of the 1933 Act, will be deemed to be subject to a care order made by a court in England on the day when the original order was made and committed to the care of such local authority as the Secretary of State may designate in his case. In any case where the parents of such a child have taken up residence in this country, the local authority in whose area the parents are resident will be nominated; in all other cases, the local authority in whose area the school in which the child is detained is situated will be nominated. The identification of such children and the nomination of authorities in respect of them will be carried out, and the local authority (and the school) informed, shortly before the specified day.

Sections 16 *and* 17 *of the Criminal Justice Act,* 1961 *(removal to borstal)*

19. There may be on the specified day persons detained in approved schools who are the subject of uncompleted proceedings under section 16 of the Criminal Justice Act, 1961. As from 1 January 1971 section 16 will be repealed and it will not be possible for such proceedings to be continued under that section. Such persons will, however, become subject to a care order under paragraph 7 of Schedule 4 of the 1969 Act and it will be possible to bring them before a juvenile court after the specified day under section 31 of the 1969 Act (a applied by paragraph 3 (2) of Schedule 3 to the Act). Where, however, a person subject to such proceedings is detained in a remand home on the specified day

under an interim order under section 17 (2) of the 1961 Act, neither section 31 (which relates specifically to community homes) nor paragraph 3 (2) of Schedule 3 (which applies the provisions of section 31 to persons accommodated in approved schools) will apply. It will be necessary, therefore, with the court's agreement, to return the person to the approved school and to bring the person again before the court after the specified day under fresh proceedings under section 31 of the 1969 Act. Administrative arrangements will be made to ensure that in both cases the Secretary of State's authority to bring the person before a court will permit the court to proceed under the legal provisions appropriate to the date of the hearing.

Part II—The relationship between local authorities and approved schools in the transitional period

20. During the transitional period the schools will continue to operate as approved schools until they acquire their new status as community homes or, alternatively, become schools under the Education Act or cease to be approved institutions (see Home Office Circular No. 47/1970). It is clearly desirable in the interest of the children that the impending legislative changes, so far as they affect the responsibilities of managers and care authorities, should not be allowed to disrupt or significantly alter the course of treatment and education now being provided by the schools. It is with this concept of a continuing service in mind that the following suggestions for establishing and maintaining effective working relationships between care authorities and the schools in the transitional period are made.

The responsibility of managers for running the schools

21. The basic change brought about by the abolition of the approved school order is that responsibility for the long-term treatment of children will rest with the local authority in whose care they are. Managers will continue to be responsible for the running of their school in the sense that it will be they who will regulate the conduct of school business and set the pattern of activities within it.

22. There will clearly be a need for close co-operation and consultation between care authorities and the managers and staffs of the schools when the needs and problems of individual children are being considered. It is the staff of the schools who will be in day to day contact with the children, and they will consequently be in a position to assist care authorities with professional opinions and advice on the developing needs of each child and bring to their attention any cases where a change in treatment seems to be desirable.

Treatment of the child whilst in the school

23. The division of responsibility between the managers, with their concern with the day to day running of the school, and the care authorities with their ultimate responsibility for the welfare of the individual child will call for close and continuous co-operation between them on questions relating to the treatment of children whom authorities have placed in the schools. It is suggested that as a general working rule a care authority should be content to leave the day to day handling of the child while in the school to the discretion of the staff and managers once it has been decided that a particular school can provide for a child the kind of treatment that he needs. It is nevertheless clearly desirable that in accordance with normal child care practice the general strategy of the treatment of the child should be worked out in co-operation with the local authority children's department concerned and due account taken of assessment reports obtained before admission to the school, and this treatment plan should be kept under regular review in consultation with the children's department.

The appropriate machinery for this will depend to some extent on the particular circumstances of each case, but it is to be hoped that arrangements will be made for at least some joint case conferences to be held regularly either at the children's department offices or at the school.

Home leave
24. Rule 30A of the Approved School Rules, which limits the amount of home leave which may be granted to a child in an approved school, will be revoked when the approved school order is abolished (see paragraph 51). Visits home will become part of the general treatment strategy and it will be for care authorities to decide how long a child should spend at home and when home visits should take place. But home leave may affect the organisation of school activities and staffing arrangements, and managers will wish to retain a measure of discretion in this respect. It is hoped, therefore, that subject to normal safeguards as to consultation in difficult cases, care authorities will allow schools some latitude in the granting of home leave.

25. While the revocation of Rule 30A will mean that local authorities will assume a general responsibility for matters connected with home leave, it has been decided that so long as flat-rate arrangements continue the managers of schools should retain responsibility for the payment of weekly allowances to parents (in accordance with Home Office Circulars Nos. 244/1967 and 176/1970) towards the maintenance of children home on leave from approved schools.

Parental visits and correspondence
26. Rule 31A of the Approved School Rules provides for children to receive letters from their parents and friends, and also visits at such reasonable intervals as the managers may determine. Rule 32A provides that the headmaster may suspend these facilities (and also pocket money) if he is satisfied that they interfere with the discipline of the school. But in view of the treatment implications, and the ultimate responsibility of the care authority, headmasters are asked, where practicable, to consult the care authority before deciding to suspend any of these facilities in any individual case. (This would not preclude a school from reaching an agreement with care authorities on a general scheme for the administration of rewards and privileges and obtaining discretion to act over a wide field without prior consultation.)

Pocket money
27. Pocket money is at present provided for as part of the general scheme of financing approved schools; and the cost is covered by the flat-rate. Since the flat-rate will continue to operate during the transitional period, schools are authorised to continue to pay pocket money at the rate approved by the Home Office. Any payments that a care authority wish to make over and above the approved rate would be a matter for the care authority to bear as a charge against local authority child care funds.

Contributions by young people who go out to work
28. When the approved school order is abolished, section 13 of the Children and Young Persons Act, 1963 (which requires a young person who goes out to work from an approved school to pay to the school managers a weekly sum fixed by the Secretary of State) will be repealed and the position of such young people will in future be regulated by section 62 of the Children and Young Persons Act, 1969, and section 24 of the Children Act, 1948, which provide that contributions shall be made *to the local authority in whose care the child is*. By virtue of the operation of section 62 (3) and (4) of the 1969 Act, the level of contribution cannot be standardised, and it will be for care authorities to fix individual contributions in accordance with the provisions of that section.

Absentees

29. At present the position of a child who absconds from an approved school is regulated by section 82 of the Children and Young Persons Act, 1933, but this will be repealed when the approved school order is abolished and replaced by section 32 of the 1969 Act (see also paragraphs 12–14 above). This section provides that if a person in the care of a local authority is absent from any premises where he is at that time required by the authority to live, he may be arrested anywhere in the United Kingdom and returned either to the place from which he absented himself or to some other place specified by the local authority. It will not, in future, be possible to bring a child before a court on the grounds that he is an absentee (as it is under section 82) although there will still be provision under section 31 of the 1969 Act for children in care who have attained the age of 15 to be brought before a court with a view to their removal to borstal (see paragraphs 33 and 34 below).

30. Under section 82 of the 1933 Act, school managers must at present bear the expense of recovering an absconder, but after the abolition of the approved school order such expense will fall under section 32 of the 1969 Act to be met by the care authority concerned. School staff are at present responsible for escorting an absconder back to the school (although in cases of difficulty the police may be asked to assist). From 1 January 1971 this also will become the responsibility of the care authority. It will remain open to care authorities to seek the co-operation of the schools in this matter, and in appropriate cases (for instance where the child in question may need the reassurance of a familiar face) school staff will no doubt be prepared to undertake this work as they do at present, acting on behalf of the care authority. Care authorities should recognise, however, that the work of escorting absconders often causes very great problems for the schools, especially the girls' schools, because of shortages of staff and because of the unruliness and disturbed behaviour of the children concerned.

Charges for recovery of absentees

31. Where school staff undertake the escorting of absentees, the care authority should reimburse the actual expenditure incurred on travelling and subsistence. Schools are not, however, required to make a charge for the time of the staff concerned.

Appearances in court

32. The local authority will normally be represented in court when a child in its care appears there on further charges, but this should not preclude a member of the school staff from attending on behalf of the care authority or in addition to their representative, if this is agreed to be appropriate.

Removal to borstal

33. Under the existing law there are three procedures whereby a child subject to an approved school order can be brought before a court with a view to his removal to borstal (section 82 and paragraph 8 of Schedule 4 of the Children and Young Persons Act, 1933, and section 16 of the Criminal Justice Act, 1961). All of these provisions will be repealed in consequence of the abolition of the approved school order. Section 31 of the 1969 Act, however, provides that a care authority may, subject to the Secretary of State's consent, bring a person over the age of 15 who has been committed to their care by a care order before the court; and the court may then order him to be removed to borstal if they are satisfied that his behaviour is such that it will be detrimental to the other persons accommodated in the same community home for him to remain there. This section is applied to approved schools during the transitional period by virtue of paragraph 3 (2) (a) of Schedule 3 of the 1969 Act.

34. This change means that in future it will be the care authority, instead of the school managers, who take the decision to bring the child before a court and the care authority will be responsible for presenting the case in court. Before a child can be brought to court in this way, the authority will first have to obtain the Secretary of State's consent, as the managers do at present. It has been found in the past that cases of this kind have usually arisen out of a particular crisis in a child's behaviour and action has to be taken swiftly. If a crisis of this kind develops, the school staff should contact the care authority concerned as quickly as possible, preferably by telephone.

Temporary removal from an approved school
35. Section 15 of the Criminal Justice Act, 1961, authorises the managers of an approved school to apply to a justice of the peace for a warrant directing that a child should be removed from the school to a remand home or other approved school, pending enquiry as to the best means of dealing with him, on the grounds that he is so seriously unruly or subversive that it is necessary to remove him immediately from his present school. (Section 15 also provides for removal to a remand centre, but since remand centres have not yet been formally established this provision has remained inoperative). This section will be repealed when the approved school order is abolished. It will then be possible for a care authority to remove a child in their care to another school, or some other residential establishment, if this becomes necessary in circumstances of this kind, without reference to a court (see paragraphs 12 and 13 of Home Office Circular No. 184/1970). It should also be noted that if a child is brought before a court under section 31 of the Act, and the court is unable to make a decision in his case, there is provision for the person concerned to be detained in a remand centre for a period of up to 21 days. This provision, however, will not be operative until remand centres are formally established.

Transfer to other accommodation
36. See paragraph 20 of Home Office Circular No. 184/1970.

Hospital treatment
37. Under the existing system the managers of a school have powers under paragraph 4 of Schedule 4 to the Children and Young Persons Act, 1933, to place a child in hospital including, where necessary, a mental hospital; and the Secretary of State has power under the procedure laid down in section 72 of the Mental Health Act, 1959, to direct that a child should be removed to a mental hospital. Both of these powers will be abolished at the same time as the approved school order. From 1 January 1971, it will be for the local authority in consultation, as necessary, with the schools to make appropriate arrangements under the provisions of section 12 of the Children Act, 1948, and Part 2 of the Mental Health Act, 1959.

Special Units
38. See paragraph 21 of Home Office Circular No. 184/1970.

Review of readiness for leaving the school
39. Under section 14 of the Criminal Justice Act, 1961, it is at present the responsibility of school managers to decide when a child subject to an approved school order is ready for release from detention in an approved school. After the abolition of the approved school order, the statutory position will be different in that a child may be allowed to leave the school to return to his home or live in the community on his own, or be transferred to a different kind of establishment (*e.g.* a children's home or hostel) at the discretion of the local authority in whose care he is, without this affecting the care order to which he remains subject. "Release" from the school will not necessarily mean release

from the care order; this order, unless discharged by the court under section 21 of the Children and Young Persons Act, 1969, on the application of either the local authority or the child, will automatically run until the appropriate expiry date as laid down in section 20 of the Act. But the importance of any such decision from the point of view of the treatment needs and interests of the child will be no less in future than it is at present, and in reaching their decision it may be expected that the care authority concerned will wish to draw upon the advice of the school staff and managers.

40. Under section 27 (4) of the 1969 Act it will be the duty of local authorities to review the case of each child in their care at intervals of not more than 6 months and, if there is a care order in force, to consider whether they should apply to the court to have it discharged. Where the child is at, or has recently left, an approved school it may again be expected that the care authority will wish to draw on the advice of the schools in connection with these regular reviews. (Rule 40 of the Approved School Rules under which managers are required to review the progress of each boy towards the end of his first year in the school and subsequently at quarterly intervals will be revoked when the approved school order is abolished (see paragraph 51).)

Leaving arrangements

41. Children leaving approved schools after the approved school order has been abolished will in most cases continue in the care of local authorities (see paragraph 43 below) and Approved School Rules 40 to 43A, which deal with the placing out and after care responsibilities of managers, will be revoked from 1 January 1971. But while the statutory obligations of managers for the after care of such children will disappear, there may still be a useful part for them to play in the arrangements immediately before the child's departure from the school. In particular, the provision of any necessary "going home" clothing will continue, as in the past, to be covered by flat-rate and to be properly chargeable to the school account. It might also be convenient for the managers, by agreement with the authorities concerned, to notify the parents of the proposed date of a child's return to his home (though not the *decision* to allow him home which will be a matter for the care authority), and to undertake any arrangements that may be necessary to ensure the child's safe return. In this connection it is desirable that in future schools should avoid the use of the term "release", which is no longer appropriate in relation to children who will not be subject to an order as to their detention, but will be in the care of a local authority.

42. From the specified day, the care authorities concerned will assume financial responsibility for any existing after-care arrangements made by managers. There may be cases also where (but for the abolition of the approved school order) there would be a prospect of a child's eventual return to the school and to the care of the managers after a temporary period of placement outside the school under paragraph 4 or 5 of Schedule 4 of the Children and Young Persons Act, 1933. In all cases where a child is released from or placed out of a school under special arrangements which are likely to continue after 31 December 1970, managers should inform the care authority concerned in advance of the specified day to enable them to consider the financial implications of the arrangements and whether they would wish to continue them, or make others, after 1 January.

Supervision

43. Under the present law, when a child is released from an approved school he remains under the supervision of the managers for a period (usually 2 years) after the date of his release. Supervision on behalf of the managers is customarily undertaken either by a local authority or by the probation service. After

the abolition of the approved school order the statutory responsibility of the managers for the supervision of any child who had been released before that date will cease, and there will be no new responsibility imposed upon them in respect of children in care. Overall responsibility for children in care, wherever they may be, will rest with the authority concerned throughout the period of the care order. Any support given to the child or his family after the discharge or expiry of the care order is similarly a matter for the care authority. As far as children released from approved schools before the date of abolition of the approved school order are concerned, or children who, though not yet released, had already been assigned to a particular probation officer, it is expected that in the interest of the child the local authority will wish him to continue to be supervised, or to be supervised on leaving the school—as the case may be—by the probation officer concerned. The extension of supervision arrangements by probation officers after 1 January 1971 will, however, be a matter for specific request by the care authority and subject to acceptance by the probation officer concerned. The Probation and After-Care Service have agreed to co-operate in this respect. Any expenditure incurred by probation officers on children under supervision will be subject to authorisation and reimbursement by the appropriate care authority, but probation and after-care committees have been asked that no charge should be made for the time of the probation staff concerned.

Identification and location of children

44. In the course of day to day correspondence with child care and finance departments, school managers will no doubt have kept local authorities named in approved school orders generally informed of the progress made by "their" children and of such matters as abscondings, release to supervision and placing out. It nevertheless seems important that action should be taken shortly before the specified day to ensure that local authorities are in no doubt as to the identity and whereabouts of each child for whom they will become responsible on 1 January. Managers are asked, therefore, to review the cases of *all* children in their care on 1 December who are not expected to be discharged on or before 1 January, and who will become subject to care orders on that date. They should notify the authorities concerned of the name and current location of each child, and should subsequently inform the local authorities concerned of any changes in the position during December, including new committals and abscondings. Local authorities may wish to supplement the information available to them in their records of particular children, and managers are asked to co-operate with child care departments by providing the information requested as expeditiously as possible.

Exchange of information between schools and local authorities

45. Although under the new system of care orders the managers of approved schools will have no continuing responsibility for the children once they have left the school, there will still be ample scope for them to assist with the continued welfare of the children through co-operation with care authorities. They will no doubt be willing to advise a care authority on such a child's problems in the light of their experience and knowledge of the child. They will also be able to give friendly support to the child himself if the need arises, although it would be for the care authority to provide any financial support that might be necessary. The schools may also be able to help in making arrangements in preparation for a child's leaving by, for example, making use of the contacts which many of them have already made with the Youth Employment Service and with employers who have in the past been willing to take youngsters from the school. It would be helpful to the schools in their turn if care authorities would, from time to time, inform each school concerned of the progress of children still in care who have been accommodated and treated there.

PART III—THE REVISION OF THE REMAND HOME AND APPROVED SCHOOL
RULES

46. The Approved School Rules, 1970 and Remand Home Rules, 1970 (copies attached) amend the Approved School Rules, 1933, as amended, and the Remand Home Rules, 1939 (the principal rules) and will come into operation on 1 January 1971. During the transitional period from 1 January until such time as each approved school or remand home comes into the community home system or is otherwise discontinued by an order made by the Secretary of State under section 46 of the Act, approved schools and remand homes will continue to exist as such, but the children in them will not be detained by virtue of approved school orders or court orders committing them to a remand home but with a few exceptions (notably children detained under section 53 of the Children and Young Persons Act, 1933) will be in the care of local authorities. In consequence certain responsibilities at present vested in the managers of approved schools and remand home superintendents will be transferred to the local authority in whose care the boy or girl is. The Approved School and Remand Home Rules have been amended accordingly to take account of (a) the changes in the status of the children accommodated in these establishments and (b) the consequential changes in the statutory responsibilities of the managers of approved schools, and of local authorities providing remand homes, in relation to these children.

Approved school rules

47. Rule 3 amends Rule 10 (2) of the principal Rules to take account of the fact that during the transitional period boys in approved schools will be formally in the care of local authorities.

48. Rule 4 (1) amends Rule 13 (1) of the principal Rules of which the present wording would not be appropriate after the abolition of the approved school order.

49. Rule 5, paragraph 4 amends Rule 18 of the principal Rules to remove the obligation on headmasters and headmistresses to record in the Register of Admissions and Discharges licences, revocation of licences, recalls and releases. The words "licences, revocation of licences" ceased to have any effect when the relevant provision of the Criminal Justice Act, 1961, came into operation, and the terms "recalls" and "releases" will cease to have effect as from 1 January.

50. Rule 6 provides for the omission of the reference to after-care in Rule 19 of the principal Rules. On the abolition of approved school orders it will be for the local authority having the care of a child to provide for his care after he leaves the school.

51. Rule 7 revoked Rules 22, 30A, and 40 to 43A of the principal Rules which relates to holidays, home leave, placing out and after-care. After 1 January these will be matters within the responsibility of the local authority in whose care the child is (see paragraphs 24 and 40 to 42).

52. Rule 8. The effect of this Rule is to add to Rule 46 of the principal Rules a requirement for headmasters to report the death, or any case of serious illness, infectious disease, or accident, to the local authority responsible for the care of the boy concerned.

Remand home rules

53. Rule 3 omits from Rule 8 of the principal Rules the references to boys awaiting removal to approved schools. Boys will still be moved to approved schools from remand homes but they will be in the care of local authorities and these references will not be appropriate.

54. Rule 4 amends Rule 18 of the principal Rules. The effect is that where a boy is removed from a remand home for medical treatment or examination or

the medical officer is of the opinion that he should not be further accommodated in the home, the superintendent should inform the parent of the boy, the council which maintains the home and the local authority in whose care the boy is; but not the clerk of the committing court. Under paragraph (2) the new Rule will not apply to boys committed to remand homes before 1 January 1971: in these cases superintendents should inform the parent of the boy, the council, the clerk of the committing court and also where the boy is committed under section 54 of the Children and Young Persons Act, 1933, the Secretary of State.

55. Rule 5 adds to Rule 20 of the principal Rules a requirement for superintendents to report at once the death, or any case of serious illness, infectious disease, or accident, to the local authority in whose care the boy is.

56. Rule 6 omits from Rule 21 of the principal Rules words relating to visits of justices of juvenile court panels and officers of remanding courts. Courts will no longer remand to particular homes and these words will not be appropriate.

57. Rule 7 amends Rule 23 of the principal Rules to take account of the fact that boys in remand homes after 1 January 1971 will be in the care of local authorities.

58. Rule 8 abolishes the requirement in Rule 24 of the principal Rules to notify the Secretary of State of a boy who absconds and is not recovered before the end of the period for which he is liable to be detained; such notification will not be appropriate when boys are in the care of local authorities. The remaining provisions of the Rule, however, continue unaltered; in particular, it will still be necessary for a return of all absconders (absentees) to be sent quarterly to the Chief Inspector.

59. Rule 9 revokes Rule 25 of the principal Rules which will be superfluous after 1 January.

ANNEX A

Dear [Name of parent or guardian]

I am writing to let you know that on 1 January 1971 there will be some changes in the law which will affect your son/daughter [   ]. He/she became our responsibility because a court made an Approved School Order, but from 1 January next this order will be abolished, and children will be placed in local authority care instead. I enclose a note about this change. The effect varies according to the age and circumstances of each child, but in [   ]'s case it means that [complete sentence by insertion of phrase appropriate to circumstances of individual boy or girl]

1. he/she will be in the care of [local authority] until not later than his/her 18th birthday, but it will be for the local authority to decide for how long he/she remains here, whether he/she would be better placed somewhere else, and when he/she may be allowed to return home.
2. he/she will be in the care of [local authority] until not later than his/her 19th birthday, but it will be for the local authority to decide for how long he/she remains here, whether he/she would be better placed somewhere else, and when he/she may be allowed to return home.
3. he/she will come under the care of [local authority] and will continue for the time being under the existing arrangements made for his supervision.
4. he/she is old enough to be discharged when the approved school order lapses on 1 January [and arrangements will be made for him/her to leave the school on or by that day—or—and his/her supervision will automatically cease on that day]

The fact that local authorities will become responsible for the children in our care after 1 January does not mean that I or the school managers are any less interested in you or your son/daughter and I shall be very pleased to discuss matters with you if you so wish. Alternatively, you may if you prefer discuss your problems with a representative of the Children's Department of your local authority, the address of which is [address].

Yours sincerely

Principal/Headmaster/Headmistress

ANNEX B

Introduction

1. A number of changes in the law concerning the treatment of children and young persons will be brought into force on 1 January 1971. They are intended to lead to better arrangements for helping children who come before the courts or who need to be taken into the care of local authorities. The new laws will alter the powers of the courts and increase the responsibilities of the local child care services. One of the most important changes will be that approved schools, together with children's homes and hostels, remand homes, reception centres and similar places will gradually be absorbed into a comprehensive "community home" system in which children in the care of local authorities will be able to receive the training and treatment appropriate for their individual needs.

Abolition of the approved school order

2. On 1 January 1971 the approved school order will be abolished. From then courts will not have power to make approved school orders, but will instead have power simply to commit a child to the care of a local authority. The decision where a child should then be placed, and how he should be dealt with for as long as the care order is in force, will be a matter for the local authority concerned. This will be the position of a child who comes before the courts *after* 1 January 1971. The position of those who are *already* subject to an approved school order is much the same: a child who was subject to an approved school order before 1 January will be treated from 1 January onwards as if he had been committed to the care of a local authority. This means that responsibility for making decisions about the children already in approved schools on 1 January will pass to the local authorities concerned, but the managers will continue to be responsible for the day-to-day running of their schools and for the care, control and treatment of the children in them.

3. Some older children in approved schools will not become the responsibility of local authorities on 1 January but will be discharged. This applies to any boy or girl who is 19 by that date. It also applies to any boy or girl of 18 who was under 16 when the approved school order was made.

Duration of care orders

4. A child subject to an approved school order at the end of 31 December 1970 who was under 16 when the order was made will remain in local authority care until not later than his 18th birthday. If he was 16 or over when the approved school order was made he will remain in care until not later than his 19th birthday. But it will be open to the local authority to allow him to leave the school, to return to his home, or to live somewhere else, or to go to a different kind of establishment, as soon as they think this right for him.

Children under supervision on 1 January 1971

5. A child released from an approved school to supervision before 1 January 1971 will be transferred on that date to the care of the local authority named in the approved school order. It is expected that the local authority will wish the supervision arrangements to continue, at least for the time being. Any young person under supervision on 1 January 1971 who is 19 on that date, or is 18 and was under 16 when the approved school order was made, will become free of supervision on that date, but may continue, if he wishes, to be advised and befriended (and if necessary assisted financially) by his local authority.

Discharge of the care order: rights of appeal

6. After 1 January local authorities will have to review the case of every child in their care at intervals of not more than 6 months and to consider at each review

whether to apply to a juvenile court for discharge of the care order. It will also be open to every child, and to his parents or guardians acting on his behalf, to apply at any time for discharge of a care order. Application has to be made to the juvenile court acting either for the area of the local authority having the child in their care or for the area where the child normally lives. The court may dismiss the application; or they may discharge the care order; or they may discharge the care order and make a supervision order under which the child would be under the supervision of a local authority or a probation officer. Application may also be made to a juvenile court for the discharge of a supervision order.

7. If an application for the discharge of a care order is unsuccessful, no further application may be made within 3 months except with the consent of the juvenile court. But there will be a right of appeal to quarter sessions against dismissal of the application.

Parental contributions
8. Any existing legal obligation to contribute towards the cost of a child's maintenance at an approved school will remain, and contributions should continue to be forwarded to the local authority to whom payment is normally made.

Home leave
9. From 1 January, local authorities will become responsible for deciding how long a child should be allowed to spend at home on leave from an approved school and when home visits should take place. It is unlikely that this will mean any great change in the present arrangements. Allowances paid by the managers of an approved school towards the cost of maintenance of a child home on leave will still be paid after 1 January provided the parent or guardian continues to qualify for it either on grounds of hardship or because he is in receipt of an allowance from the Supplementary Benefits Commission.

Visits to approved schools
10. The arrangements for visits to schools by parents are not affected by the new law. There is, however, one change resulting from the abolition of the approved school order which will affect parents who are being helped by the Supplementary Benefits Commission to meet the cost of visiting their child. After 1 January, local authorities will have the power to assist any parent or guardian with travelling, subsistence or other expenses incurred in visiting a child in an approved school. From 1 January any parent or guardian who is unable to meet the expense of visiting a child in an approved school should apply for help to the Child Care Department of the local authority responsible for the child, and *not* to the Supplementary Benefits Commission.

Conclusion
11. Decisions affecting the needs and interests of children in approved schools will rest primarily with the local authority and child care services after 1 January. Local authorities will keep in close contact with the managers and staff of schools and draw upon their advice in considering the needs of particular children, but it will be the local authority's responsibility to make the major decisions about a child's future; and in any case of doubt or difficulty, an approach should be made to the Child Care Department of the local authority in whose care the child is. Matters directly concerned with the activities at an approved school, its domestic arrangements, or the care, control and treatment which a child is receiving there, should be discussed with the headmaster.

ANNEX C

NOTE OF POINTS TO BE EXPLAINED TO CHILDREN AND YOUNG PERSONS SUBJECT TO
APPROVED SCHOOL ORDERS ON 1 JANUARY 1971

1. A new law comes into force on 1 January 1971 which affects all those who have been sent to the school under an approved school order.

2. From 1 January the approved school order will be abolished and the courts will instead commit children to the care of a local authority (usually the local

authority for the area in which they live). It will then be for the local authority to decide whether children should go to an approved school or receive some other form of training.

3. Your approved school order will be treated as a care order from 1 January onwards, and you will be in the care of the local authority named in your approved school order. (But see 8 below about some older children of 18 or above.)

4. The managers of this school will still be responsible for your training and education, but any decision about your future will be made by your local authority. We shall, of course, have to help your local authority to make these decisions, and the way in which we look after you here will not change. It will depend on your progress with us, as it always has done, when you are thought to be ready to leave this school.

5. The new law says that you may remain in the care of the local authority until you are 18 or, if you were over 16 when your approved school order was made, until you are 19. This does not necessarily mean that you will have to remain here as long as that. Your local authority will be looking every 6 months at the reports that have been made on your progress and if they think that you are ready to return home or go to live outside the school and start a job, or if they think that you should have some other form of training, then you will be transferred from the school.

6. When you do leave the school you will probably still be in your local authority's care, and they will continue to decide where you will live and what you should do until you are 18 (or 19) unless the care order is cancelled earlier.

7. Cancellation of a care order before it runs out at 18 (or 19) is a matter for a juvenile court. If you or your parents (or guardians) wish to have your care order cancelled after 1 January, this can only be done by applying to the court, who will have to consider carefully whether this is the right course. If the court decide not to cancel the order (or decide to substitute some other kind of order) there will be a right of appeal to quarter sessions.

8. Some who are older will be over the age for a care order on 1 January, and so will be discharged on or before that date. These are (a) those who will be over 19 on 1 January; and (b) those who will be over 18 on 1 January and who were under 16 when their approved school orders were made.

9. All of this is being explained to your parents (guardians) by letter; and we can tell you how it affects each one of you.

Home Office Circular No. 280/1970.   *Dated December 15, 1970*

MAINTENANCE ALLOWANCE FOR APPROVED SCHOOL CHILDREN ON HOME LEAVE

1. Home Office Circular No. 176/1970 (which amended paragraph 4 of Circular No. 244/1967) set out a scale of maximum weekly allowances that might be paid towards the maintenance of children home on leave from approved schools in cases in which the parents were in receipt of an allowance from the Supplementary Benefits Commission of the Department of Health and Social Security or, although not in receipt of such an allowance, were likely to suffer hardship if no assistance was given.

2. The allowances paid by the Supplementary Benefits Commission have again been revised and from the date of this circular the following scale should be substituted for that set out in Home Office Circular No. 244/1967:

Children	*Maximum allowance per week*
Under 11 years of age	£1 16s. 0d.
Aged 11 but under 13	£2 4s. 0d.
Aged 13 but under 16	£2 8s. 0d.
Over 16	£3 1s. 0d.

3. Home Office Circular No. 176/1970 is cancelled.

NOTE

This circular was sent to correspondents of all approved schools in England and Wales.
Copies sent to heads for information.

Home Office Circular No. 44/1970.   *Dated March* 13, 1970

ESTABLISHMENT OF CHILDREN'S REGIONAL PLANNING COMMITTEES

1. I am directed by the Secretary of State to enclose a copy of the Children and Young Persons (Planning Areas) Order, 1970 (S.I. 1970 No. 335) which he has made under section 35 of the Children and Young Persons Act, 1969. The Order prescribes in pursuance of subsection (3) of that section that it shall be the duty of the relevant local authorities in each planning area to establish a children's regional planning committee for the area within the period ending on 30 June 1970. The purpose of this Circular is to give general guidance on this process and to advise the relevant authorities of the matters which they may wish to consider in setting up these committees.

Duties of the committee

2. The primary duties of the planning committees are first, to formulate a comprehensive regional plan under section 36 for the provision and maintenance of community homes: and second, to make arrangements under section 19 for the provision by such persons as they think fit of facilities for enabling the supervisor's directions under section 12 (2) ("intermediate treatment" directions) to be carried out effectively. The first duty will be imposed upon the Committee as soon as it has been established and, to this end, the Secretary of State will at the appropriate time make a general direction under section 36 (6) on the form and content of the plan and issue a further circular. The second duty will come into effect later and will be the subject of separate advice.

Constitution of a committee

3. The committee is to be set up in accordance with the provisions of Schedule 2 to the Act (section 35 (4)). The committee is asked to notify the Under Secretary of State of the date on which it becomes established. The Schedule places responsibility upon the relevant authorities, in each area, acting together, to determine the number of persons, called nominated members, to represent the authorities and to approve the manner of their selection and appointment, subject to the general provisions of section 59 of the Local Government Act, 1933 relating to persons who are disqualified from being members of a local authority or a committee of an authority. The relevant authorities may also determine other matters in relation to the committee (but see paragraphs 5 and 6 below).

4. In view of the provisions of sections 36 (5) and 37 (5) (c), which require, *inter alia*, the formal consent of individual authorities to particular matters relating to the provision or management by them of a community home, it may not be thought necessary to have representation on the committee proportionate to such factors as population, rateable value, or number of children in care. It may be thought sufficient, and desirable, if the committee is not to become too unwieldy, for each authority to be represented by one or two nominated members. Provision for alternate members may be helpful in order to ensure that an authority's views can be presented to the committee in the unavoidable absence of regular members.

5. Although it is open to the relevant authorities acting together to deal with the question of co-opted members, it is suggested that this is better left to the committee itself to decide in the light of experience in carrying out its duties. In this context, there are four points which, perhaps, should be made:—

(a) Subject to any direction given by the relevant authorities acting together under paragraph 1 (1) of Schedule 2, the power of co-option is vested in the nominated members of the committee (paragraph 3 (1) of Schedule 2).

(b) Co-option may be a general one or restricted to particular matters. For example, the Health Service may have a special interest in observation and assessment facilities both outside and inside community homes; the probation and after-care service and juvenile court magistrates may have particular concern for the intermediate treatment schemes and probation hostels; education authorities may have a particular contribution to make on the provision not only of facilities for observation and assessment but also of education in establishments where children of compulsory school age cannot, for whatever reason, use the public educational system. Representatives of voluntary interests may be co-opted on similar grounds (see also paragraph 15 below). These examples of particular interests should not be read as precluding co-option in a more general role of persons from the fields mentioned. Among those with such a general role may be persons of standing in the social work profession in universities and establishments of higher or further education.

(c) The nominated members in committee may determine the extent to which a co-opted member may attend, speak or vote, if such a member has been co-opted for limited specified matters. This power, like the power of co-option itself, is subject to any directions which the relevant authorities acting together may have given (paragraph 3 (2)). It may, however, be prudent to leave these questions of attending, speaking and voting for determination by the nominated members in the light of their experience in operating the planning committee, rather than to rely on directions from the body of relevant authorities.

(d) Both the relevant authorities, in exercising their powers under paragraph 1 (1), and the nominated members, in acting under paragraph 3 (1), are required to ensure that at all times a majority of the members are members of relevant authorities (paragraph 4). Nothing in the Schedule restricts the Committee's powers to invite officials and other persons to attend, address and advise the Committee.

Committee procedure

6. It is provided that the nominated members, subject to any directions from the relevant authorities, should determine the procedure and the quorum of the committee. It is suggested that a quorum of, say, half of the nominated members should suffice. The constitution should provide for the election of a Chairman, perhaps by the nominated members from among their number and for a deputy or for an *ad hoc* appointment in the Chairman's absence. In general, standing orders governing the procedure of local government committees will provide suitable models for adaptation to the procedure of the planning committee (paragraph 5). The relevant authorities or the committee may adopt an appropriate geographical title for the committee.

7. It will be necessary for one authority to take the initiative in convening a meeting of all the relevant authorities in order to take decisions about the initial composition of the committee and about such other matters as they are not prepared to leave to the nominated members in committee to decide. It is

hoped that the prompt choice of the convening authority can be left to the relevant authorities. The convening authority are asked to notify the Under Secretary of State of their selection. It will also be necessary for one authority to assume responsibility for calling the first meeting of the nominated members, for drawing up an agenda for that meeting, for providing a venue and a temporary secretariat for the first meeting. It is understood that meetings have been held in some areas for consultation about planning areas and it may be that similar procedures can be followed to arrange meetings of relevant authorities and the first meetings of the planning committees. In the event of difficulty, the Home Office would be prepared to arrange a neutral venue.

Secretariat

8. It is not envisaged that planning committees would need, in the long run, a permanent full-time secretariat. On the other hand, the volume and complexity of the initial work spread over, say, three or four years will be such that a full-time committee clerk, with access to adequate clerical and typing facilities will be needed. It may be that such a post could be filled either by secondment from a relevant authority or by recruitment by an authority on contract. It may be appropriate to designate a particular Officer of one of the relevant authorities as the secretary of the committee, even though the secretarial duties are performed in the main by a committee clerk.

9. On the professional side of the secretariat, the basic information and advice necessary for the committee's work will come mainly from Children's Officers and Children's Departments. It is recognised that some Children's Officers or members of their staff will need, in addition to their normal duties, to spend time on the collation of information and the preparation and presentation of papers to the committee. It may even be necessary for some professional staff to be engaged on behalf of or seconded to the committee for these purposes in this initial stage.

Finance

10. It is provided in paragraph 6 of Schedule 2 that the general local government law on the financing of joint committees shall apply to the expenses of the planning committee. It is hoped that the relevant authorities will be able to reach early agreement on the basis for sharing the cost. Should this not be possible, the Secretary of State, on reference to him, would be likely to apportion the cost very roughly *pro-rata* to each authority's estimated population under 18 (as last published by the GRO before his decision). If the populations were not too disparate, a simple division based on equal shares would be considered.

11. Provisions as to the accounts and audit are governed by Part X and section 219 (c) of the Local Government Act, 1933. When one relevant authority assumes responsibility for staffing the secretariat, the same authority might conveniently undertake the keeping of the accounts and the preparation of financial statements for submission to the district auditor.

Accommodation and venue of meetings

12. The committee may decide where to hold its meetings, whether at the headquarters of its secretariat or elsewhere and may wish to arrange the venues for the meetings of any working groups (see the following paragraph). The secretariat, permanent and temporary, will need adequate office accommodation.

Appointment of sub-committees, working parties, study groups, etc.

13. At one end of the scale, it is expected that in every planning area there will be found a need for certain types of special facility of which one or two units will be adequate for the whole area; for the purpose of planning the provision

of such facilities the committee will have to meet as one body. For other purposes, where provision may have to be duplicated in several parts of the same planning area, it may be convenient to form smaller working groups within the planning committee to deal initially with a particular aspect of a plan or a scheme of arrangements. The Secretary of State considers that the formation of internal working groups is a matter best left to each committee and he would merely draw attention to the importance of the committee's co-ordinating the work of smaller groups on a consistent basis into a coherent plan for the whole area. It might be helpful to the committee if nominated members, if they so wished, were enabled to visit facilities of special interest located in parts of the planning area other than their own local authority areas.

14. The importance of examining the relevance to one planning area of experiments and projects in other planning areas cannot be over-emphasised. To this end, joint study groups of members and officials or of officials only may be desirable.

15. In all the detailed work of the committee and of any groups appointed by the committee, the Secretary of State wishes to stress the contribution which can be made by voluntary organisations experienced in the general field of child care and in the more specialised area of residential establishments now operating as registered voluntary homes, approved schools or probation homes and hostels. The committee will wish to develop methods by which this experience and the resources which voluntary organisations are prepared to offer for incorporation into the public system can best be utilised.

Relations with the Home Office

16. In order to ensure the closest liaison between the planning committee, the relevant authorities, other public and voluntary bodies in the planning area and his Inspectors, the Secretary of State has re-arranged the grouping of the Regional Inspectorate to coincide with the boundaries of planning areas. Full details of the changes made have been communicated separately to the authorities and organisations affected. As regards regional planning, responsibilities in relation to the planning areas have been allocated to the Superintending Inspectors at the following offices:

Area	*Superintending Inspector*
1 (North) and 2 (Yorks)	Leeds
3 (North-west)	Manchester
4 (West Midlands) and 5 (East Midlands)	Birmingham
6 (East Anglia) and 7 (Home Counties—North)	London (North)
8 (Greater London)	London (Central)
9 (South-east) and 10 (Wessex)	London (South)
11 (South-west) and 12 (Wales)	Cardiff

17. It is these officers or their representatives who will represent the Secretary of State in all the work of regional planning, leading to the formal submission of the regional plan under section 37. Further advice on this will be issued in connection with a general direction under section 36 (6); meanwhile, Superintending Inspectors will be available to advise on and to facilitate in any way they can the early establishment of planning committees.

Relations with other departments

18. Similarly the Department of Education and Science and the Department of Health and Social Security or the Welsh Office will notify planning committees, when established, of H.M. Inspectors and Regional or Departmental Officers to whom matters affecting education, health and welfare services for children in care can be referred for advice.

General

19. Any general queries about this Circular should be addressed to the Under Secretary of State, except insofar as they concern the problems peculiar to a particular region, when they should be addressed in the first instance to the Superintending Inspector referred to in paragraph 16 above. Two additional copies of this Circular are enclosed for the use of the Financial Officer and the Children's Officer.

NOTE

This circular was sent to the Clerks of county, county borough and London borough councils and the Common Council of the City of London.

Home Office Circular No. 137/1970.   *Dated August 12, 1970*

CHILDREN AND YOUNG PERSONS ACT, 1969: FORM AND CONTENT OF REGIONAL PLAN

1. I am directed by the Secretary of State to enclose a copy of a direction made by him under section 36 (6) of the Children and Young Persons Act, 1969 (which empowers the Secretary of State to specify that a regional plan shall be prepared in such form and shall contain such information as he may direct) and a copy of a memorandum of guidance on the preparation of certain estimates which the direction requires.

2. The direction, which applies to the submission of the first comprehensive regional plans, requires plans to be submitted to the Secretary of State on or before 31 December 1971. It is suggested that because of the financial implications the most convenient date for a plan to come into operation is 1 April or 1 October next following its approval by the Secretary of State.

3. Superintending Inspectors of the Home Office together with the regional representatives of the Department of Health and Social Security, H.M. Inspectors of Schools on behalf of the Department of Education and Science and representatives of the Health Department of the Welsh Office will, as indicated in paragraphs 17 and 18 of Home Office Circular No. 44/1970, be available to advise planning committees and relevant local authorities, at their request, on the content of regional plans. It is the Secretary of State's hope, by means of informal consultation during the preparation of a plan, to reduce the period, after the plan's submission to him, required for consideration and any further formal consultation which might be necessary.

4. The attached memorandum of guidance makes suggestions which may be found helpful by committees and their constituent authorities in preparing the estimates of need required in Part I of the plan. It is recognised that estimates of future needs cannot be based on past experience alone. Full weight must be given to factors, such as those mentioned in item 5 of the direction, and to changes of practice and of felt needs so far as they can be foreseen, regionally or locally, and quantified. The estimates in this part of the plan should be regarded as the best attainable approximation to the Planning Area's needs: subsequent reviews of the plan will make the approximation progressively more accurate.

5. The purpose of Note B (see page 7 of the direction) is to make possible, without prior reference to the Regional Planning Committee or the Secretary of State, variations in the use of a particular local authority community home, or its improvement or replacement, when the home is normally used only by

the local authority concerned and the change could have no serious repercussions on the plan as a whole. Any consequential amendment to an approved plan would be made subsequently at a convenient time.

6. An additional copy of this circular and its enclosures is enclosed for the Children's Officer. Further copies can be obtained on application to the Home Office Children's Department (D3).

NOTE

This circular was sent to secretaries of Children's Regional Planning Committees, the Clerks of county, county borough and London borough councils, and the Common Council of the City of London.

PREAMBLE

All regional plans shall be in the following form, shall contain the following information and shall be submitted to the Secretary of State on or before 31 December 1971 or such later date as he may allow. A regional plan shall comprise six Parts. Part I shall set out the regional planning committee's assessment of the residential needs of the planning area and the criteria on which the assessment is based. Part II, III and IV shall each deal with a special aspect of the regional plan as described below and Part V with the remainder of the community home system. Part VI shall deal with any arrangements proposed for the use of homes which are not community homes.

PART I—ASSESSMENT OF RESIDENTIAL NEEDS

1. Estimates of
   (a) the number of children expected to come into the care of the relevant authorities
      (i) in the 12 months ending 31 March 1972;
      (ii) in the 12 months ending 31 March 1975;
   (b) the number of children expected to be in the care of the relevant authorities
      (i) on 31 March 1972
      (ii) on 31 March 1975.

2. Estimates of
   (a) the use, if any, expected to be made for child in care of observation and assessment facilities available outside the community home system or of non-residential observation and assessment facilities within the community home system (with details of the facilities)
      (i) in the 12 months ending 31 March 1972;
      (ii) in the 12 months ending 31 March 1975;
   (b) the expected *number of admissions* of children in care to residential facilities in community homes for the observation of their physical and mental condition and the assessment of their accommodation and treatment needs
      (i) in the 12 months ending 31 March 1972
      (ii) in the 12 months ending 31 March 1975.

3. Estimates of
   (a) the maximum number of children in care likely to require accommodation at any one time in the period from 31 March 1972 to 31 March 1975 in community homes, including those accommodated at the

relevant time in residential observation and assessment centres; in arriving at this estimate due allowance should be made for contingencies, emergency placements and seasonal fluctuations in demand, particularly during school holidays;

(b) the number of children in care at the relevant time whose needs are assumed, in arriving at the estimate in (a) above, to be likely to be better met, and to be capable of being met, by their being

(i) boarded out with foster-parents as members of their families;

(ii) accommodated in lodgings or in residential employment;

(iii) on trial at home under section 13 (2) of the 1948 Act (as amended by the 1969 Act);

(iv) in special boarding schools, hospitals or accommodation provided under the Mental Health Act, 1959;

(v) in section 64 Secretary of State homes; or

(vi) otherwise accommodated outside the community home system.

4. Subdivisions of the estimate at item 3 (a) above in the following groups (further subdivisions may be made at the Committee's discretion):—

(a) by the following age groups:—

(i) children under 2 years;

(ii) other pre-school-age children;

(iii) children of compulsory school age (assuming that the leaving age has been raised to 16) sub-divided into boys and girls; and

(iv) children over compulsory school-age sub-divided into boys and girls;

(b) by residential requirements:—

(i) requiring places in observation and assessment centres;

(ii) requiring places in homes providing wholly or mainly for a particular need, type of treatment, age group or sex: particulars should be given (e.g. 270 boys and girls under school age requiring residential nursery places; 24 girls over compulsory school age requiring hostel places; 120 boys requiring places in homes providing educational facilities on the premises; 12 pregnant girls and mothers with babies requiring places in homes with appropriate facilities);

(iii) requiring places in homes generally, not providing for particular needs; and

(c) to show the need for secure accommodation:—

requiring places in accommodation approved for the purpose of restricting liberty in accordance with regulations to be made under section 43 (2) (c) of the 1969 Act.

5. Any other information which the Committee consider relevant to the general assessment of needs, such as population movements, the effect of preventive measures and the growth of non-residential care facilities.

Part II.—Provision of observation and assessment facilities

6. The following details for each existing home (see, however, note B below) which will be comprised in the community homes system and will provide residential observation and assessment facilities for children in care:

(a) (i) Present and proposed status (see note A below).
     (ii) Proposed responsible (or, for an assisted home, specified) local
          authority.
     (iii) For voluntary homes only, the voluntary organisation providing
          the premises.
(b) Name and address of the home.
(c) Proposed maximum number to be accommodated at any one time, and
     estimated annual number of admissions.
(d) Proposed restrictions, if any, on types or age of children to be observed
     and assessed. The associated educational and medical facilities on
     and off the premises should be described.
(e) Local authorities (other than the proposed responsible or specified
     authority) who will use the facilities on a regular formal basis (*i.e.*
     by instrument of management, contract or reservation of places).
     Full details should be given.
(f) Local authorities who will use the facilities only under *ad hoc* arrange-
     ments. Full details should be given.

7. The following details for each new home (see, however, note B below) under
construction or to be constructed, or to be opened in converted premises, by
31 March 1975 to provide residential observation and assessment facilities for
children in care:

(a) Proposed responsible or specified authority and, if appropriate, pro-
     viding organisation, and status.
(b) Name and address of home (if decided) or approximate location (if no
     site has been agreed). Estimated or probable cost (but excluding
     the cost of any approved accommodation for the purpose of restricting
     liberty (see Part IV) which is to form a part of any home listed in
     this Part), estimated period for completion of works and estimated
     date of occupation.
(c) Proposed maximum number to be accommodated at any one time and
     estimated annual number of admissions.
(d) Proposed restrictions, if any, on types or age of children to be observed
     and assessed. The proposed educational and medical facilities on and
     off the premises should be described.
(e) Local authorities (other than the proposed responsible or specified
     authority) who will use the facilities on a regular formal basis (*i.e.* by
     instrument of management, contract or reservation of places). Full
     details should be given.
(f) Local authorities who will use the facilities only under *ad hoc* arrange-
     ments. Full details should be given.

PART III—PROVISION OF SPECIAL HOMES

8. The following details for each existing home (see, however, note B below)
which is to provide special facilities, *e.g.* for children with particular physical
or mental handicaps or requiring particular forms of treatment:

(a) (i) Present and proposed status (see note A below).
     (ii) Proposed responsible (or, for an assisted home, specified) local
          authority.
     (iii) For voluntary homes only, the voluntary organisation providing
          the premises.
(b) Name and address of home.
(c) Nature, capacity and purpose of the home and special facilities,
     including educational and medical facilities, provided.

(d) Local authorities (other than the proposed responsible or specified authority) who will use the facilities on a regular formal basis (*i.e.* by instrument of management, contract or reservation of places). Full details should be given.

(e) Local authorities who will use the facilities only under *ad hoc* arrangements. Full details should be given.

9. The following details of each new home (see, however, note B below) under construction or to be constructed, or to be opened in converted premises by 31 March 1975 to provide special facilities, *e.g.* for children with particular physical or mental handicaps or requiring particular forms of treatment:

(a) Proposed responsible or specified authority, and, if appropriate, providing organisation, and status.

(b) Name and address of home (if decided) or approximate location (if no site has been agreed). Estimated or probable cost (but excluding the cost of any approved accommodation for the purpose of restricting liberty (see Part IV) which is to form a part of any home listed in this Part), estimated period for completion of works and date of occupation.

(c) Proposed nature, capacity and purpose of the home and special facilities, including educational and medical facilities, to be provided.

(d) Local authorities (other than the proposed responsible or specified authority) who will use the facilities on a regular formal basis (*i.e.* by instrument of management, contract or reservation of places). Full details should be given.

(e) Local authorities who will use the facilities only under *ad hoc* arrangements. Full details should be given.

PART IV—PROVISION OF ACCOMMODATION FOR THE PURPOSE OF RESTRICTING LIBERTY

10. The following details for each home, existing or proposed (see, however, note B below), the whole or part of which is intended to provide, or already provides, accommodation for which approval would need to be sought under Regulations contemplated by section 43 (2) (c) of the 1969 Act (in this Part referred to as "secure accommodation"):

(a) Proposed responsible, or specified authority, and, if appropriate, providing organisation, and status.

(b) Name and address of home (if decided) or approximate location (if no site has been agreed). Estimated or probable cost of new or converted approved accommodation. Estimated period for completion of works and date of occupation.

(c) Proposed capacity of secure accommodation and restrictions, if any, as to use; whether all or part of the home is to be used as approved accommodation.

(d) If approved prior to the submission of the plan, date of Secretary of State's approval; if applicable, date of any direction given, prior to the submission of the plan, under paragraph 3 (3) (b) of Schedule 3 to the 1969 Act.

(e) Local authorities (other than the proposed responsible or specified authority) who will use the facilities on a regular formal basis (*i.e.* by instrument of management, contract or reservation of places). Full details should be given.

(f) Local authorities who will use the facilities under *ad hoc* arrangements. Full details should be given.

PART V—PROVISION OF OTHER HOMES

11. The following details for each other existing home (see, however, note B below) which is to be a community home but is not included in Part II or III or wholly in Part IV:

- (a)   (i) Present and proposed status (see note A below).
  - (ii) Proposed responsible (or, for an assisted home, specified) local authority.
  - (iii) For voluntary homes only, the voluntary organisation providing the premises.
- (b) Name and address of home.
- (c) Proposed nature, capacity and purpose of the home.
- (d) Local authorities (other than the proposed responsible or specified authority) who will use the facilities on a regular formal basis (*i.e.* by instrument of management, contract or reservation of places). Full details should be given.
- (e) Local authorities who will use the facilities under *ad hoc* arrangements. Full details should be given.

12. The following details for each new home (see, however, note B below) under construction or to be constructed, or to be opened in converted premises, by 31 March 1975, as a community home which is not included in Part II or III or wholly in Part IV:

- (a) Responsible authority or organisation and status.
- (b) Name and location of home (if decided) or approximate location (if no site has been agreed). Estimated or probable cost, estimated period for completion of works and probable date of occupation.
- (c) Nature, capacity and purpose of home.
- (d) Local authorities (other than the proposed responsible or specified authority) who will use the facilities on a regular formal basis (*i.e.* by instrument of management, contract or reservation of places). Full details should be given.
- (e) Local authorities who will use the facilities under *ad hoc* arrangements. Full details should be given.

PART VI—OTHER RESIDENTIAL ARRANGEMENTS

13. Details of other places for children in care expected to be available, under arrangements which are in force or are likely to be made by relevant authorities, outside the community home system, for example, in registered voluntary homes or private unregistered establishments or in hospitals (for long-term illnesses) or boarding-schools (provided no alternative arrangements for accommodation in community homes are needed in school holidays).

Notes applicable to Parts II, III, IV and V

A. Where a proposed community home is at present an approved institution, as defined in section 46 of the 1969 Act, there should be recorded in the appropriate place:

- (i) the proposed status as a community home (*i.e.* local authority, controlled or assisted); and
- (ii) the present status as an approved institution (*i.e.* local authority or voluntary approved school or remand home or approved probation home or approved probation hostel).

B. Where a proposed local authority community home is listed in Part II, Part III, wholly in Part IV or Part V and no formal sharing arrangements are contemplated by the plan (see items 6 (e), 7 (e), 8 (d), 9 (d), 10 (e), 11 (d) and 12 (d)), the plan will be deemed to provide for the provision of the home particularised in the Part in question or, in its place, of such other home maintained by the same local authority as includes accommodation of a similar nature, capacity and purpose, whether or not it is of the same name or address and whether or not it includes accommodation, or is used for a purpose, additional to that particularised.

MEMORANDUM OF GUIDANCE ON PART I OF THE REGIONAL PLAN

Introduction

1. The Direction on the Form and Content of Regional Plans provides that the first Part of a plan shall set out the Regional Planning Committee's general assessment of the residential needs of the planning area and the criteria on which the assessment is based. This memorandum is concerned with the task of assessing these needs on a reasonably objective basis. It is not the intention to inhibit in any way a Planning Committee's developing, in consultation with Home Office Regional Inspectors, their own method of assessing needs. The aim is to suggest one way in which a reasonable degree of objectivity might be achieved.

2. References in this memorandum are to the numbered items in the Direction made under section 36 (6) of the Children and Young Persons Act, 1969.

Numbers coming into care

3. Item 1 requires estimates of the numbers of children coming into care during the 13 months ending 31 March 1972 and the 12 months ending 31 March 1975, that is, 3 years later. Estimates must start from a base year, which would naturally be the latest for which statistics are available. 1971/72 will be the first complete year (on the assumption that the main provisions of Part I of the 1969 Act are brought into force in the year 1970/71) in which the new definition of the child care population will apply. It is expected that Regional Planning Committees will start their assessment of needs when the latest statistics available are those for 1969/70, but some Committees, before submitting their plans for approval, may have the 1970/71 figures.

4. A reasonable approximation to the number of children who would have come into care in the base year, say 1969/70, if the main provisions of Part I of the 1969 Act had already been in force may be derived by adding together the following items:—

(a) the number actually received into care under the 1948 Act, committal and fit person orders under the 1933 Act, matrimonial legislation etc.; and

(b) the number admitted, as a result of a court order, to remand homes from residence in the planning area.

It is recognised that there will be an element of double-counting in that, for example, some children who were admitted to remand homes will subsequently have been the subject of fit person orders or reception into care. On the other hand, the number admitted to remand homes, owing to shortage of remand facilities and/or changes in the legal procedures under Part I of the 1969 Act, have been lower than the number who would have been received into care under the 1969 Act provisions for remand or interim care. The adjustment, if any, required, in the total of items (a) and (b) above will vary from area to area.

Numbers in care

5. Item 1 also requires an estimate of the numbers in care on 31 March 1972 and 1975. A reasonable approximation to the equivalent number for 31 March 1970 can be derived by adding together:—

   (a) the number actually in care under existing legislation on that date;
   (b) the number in approved schools for whom local authorities in the planning area were financially responsible;
   (c) the number under 19 subject to after-care on release from approved schools; and
   (d) the number in approved probation hostels and homes, or on probation and residing under a requirement of a probation order in non-approved establishments.

6. If, before the estimate is prepared, figures for a date after the implementation of Part I of the 1969 Act are available, (b) and (c) in the previous paragraph will have been absorbed into (a).

Annual variations

7. To eliminate the possibility that the base year, say 1969/70, may have been exceptional, the figures for that year should be checked against the average and the trend over, say, 3 years from 1967/68.

Projections for 1971/72 and 1974/75

8. Subject to adjustments which the Planning Committee may consider it necessary to make (*e.g.* to take account of the provision of section 20 (3) of the Children and Young Persons Act, 1969 that a care order made when the subject is 16 has effect until the age of 19), estimates for 1971/72 and 1974/75 can be made by adjusting the figures for 1969/70 in proportion to the estimated size of the population of the planning area under the age of 18 in each of these years. In addition to the population projections made by the General Register Office, local authorities themselves may have relevant information.

Observation and assessment

9. Item 2 calls for estimates of the demand for observation and assessment facilities. Among the considerations to be taken into account are the following:—

   (a) the process of assessment is not confined to any particular limits of age—the exclusion of very young children for example, simply because of their age, is not appropriate;
   (b) some of the children received into care will not require assessment, because of the particular circumstances of their reception, the shortness of the time for which it is known that they will be in care or the amount of information already available to the local authority;
   (c) similar reassessment while in care will not be necessary for some children and the frequency with which it will be needed by the remainder will vary;
   (d) assessment will sometimes be preparatory to a court's decision, sometimes following upon initial reception into care under section 1 of the 1948 Act or section 1 of the 1969 Act.

10. The most straightforward method of estimating the demand would seem to be to take the number of all long-stay children admitted to care in 1969/70, to add to it the number of children not in care admitted to remand homes in that year, and to adjust the total to allow for assessment, increasingly found to be desirable, of children with whose families preventive work is being carried out and for the reassessment, because of *e.g.* foster-home breakdown, handicap,

proposed adoption, of children already in care. Annual variations should be checked and projections for 1971/72 and 1974/75 should be made, as described in paragraphs 7 and 8 above.

11. The present shortfall is such that it is not expected that facilities outside the community home system on which children authorities can regularly depend for observation and assessment will materially affect the position in the short term. Nevertheless estimates of these facilities should be made in consultation with and with the agreement of the providing agency. Estimates should cover both day and residential facilities, the number of children who will be assessed annually and the average length of stay or number of available day sessions. Sufficient information should be included to identify the establishments. Undertakings by the providing agency to increase these outside facilities in the period under review should be included.

Number of children needing accommodation in community homes

12. The compilation of item 3 may most conveniently start with a series of estimates of the total number of children who will be in care at intervals during the period 31 March 1972 to 31 March 1975 and of how many children at each point of time are not likely to need accommodation in community homes, because arrangements will appropriately be made elsewhere. From these estimates an approximate estimate may be derived of the maximum number of children in care likely at any one time in the three year period to need accommodation in community homes. Figures to be inserted under item 3 (b) will be those for this same date.

13. Estimates under items 3 (b) (i) to (iv) and (vi) may be derived from the last known figures, say, for 31 March 1970 or 1971, and an examination of figures for the 2 or 3 preceding years, projected forward, but in arriving at projections for the period between 31 March 1972 and 31 March 1975 it must be assumed that some of the arrangements leading to the figures recorded for the base date under items 3 (b) (i) to (iv) and (vi) were made not because they were ideal, but because other facilities were not available. An allowance will therefore need to be made in arriving at estimates of the number of children in care whose needs are likely to be better met, and to be capable of being met, by their accommodation outside the community home system and the maximum number likely to require accommodation within it.

14. Care should be taken in estimating the number likely to be on trial at home (item 3 (b) (iii)) to take into account the statistical effect of the change in the law on 1 December 1969 when children subject to resolutions under section 2 of the 1948 Act but allowed to be at home were deemed once more to be in care, and, if a figure for 31 March 1970 is used as the base, the possibility that some children then subject to after-care following release from approved school might, if the new legislation had been in force, have been in this category.

15. The number under item 3 (b) (v) should be related to a reasonable share of the available facilities and not to any estimate of the number of seriously disturbed children in care. Forty-five places for England and Wales may be assumed to be available by March 1972 and 120 more by 1975. The number of places available to any one planning area will not significantly affect the scale of the other provision required, but it is thought best to include this item for completeness.

16. When, by the process described in paragraph 12 above, an approximate estimate has been derived of the maximum number of children in care likely at any one time in the period 31 March 1972 to 31 March 1975 to need accommodation in community homes, an allowance should be added to cover emergency placements, fluctuations in demand at different times of the year, and similar contingencies. The total thus obtained is the figure to be inserted under item 3 (a).

Categories of age and type of accommodation

17. Item 4 (a) should contain a breakdown of the number recorded at item 3 (a) by certain age groups and, for the groups aged 5 and over, sub-divided into boys and girls. It is suggested that this breakdown and that in item 4 (b) could both be made by analysing the ages and sex of children in care, in remand homes, in approved schools and in probation hostels and homes at two or more points in the past and by projecting the average proportions thus obtained with any adjustments required by the considerations taken into account as suggested in paragraph 8 above. Committees may wish to consider whether there is any basis for adjustment in the light of foreseen social or demographic changes.

18. Item 4 (b) (i) relates back to item 2 which was expressed in terms of the annual number of admissions. Assumptions need to be made about the average length of stay in a community home for observation and assessment, since the actual length of stay may vary from a few days to a few months. A figure of 8 weeks, equivalent, say, to a place utilisation of 6 times each year, may be appropriate. On this basis, the highest annual admissions figure between 1972 and 1975 should be divided by 6 to determine the number of children likely to need to be in observation and assessment centres.

19. Committees will need to consider how far particular treatment facilities and particular types of accommodation for different age groups and for boys or girls can be identified and itemised. Nurseries are an obvious example. Much will depend upon local practice and there are no firm guide-lines of general application which it would be appropriate to suggest for the breakdown of item 4 (b) (ii). Superintending Inspectors will be available to discuss with Committees, if they so wish, the basis which they propose to adopt.

20. Item 4 (b) (iii) is, of course, the remainder which, added to the numbers under item 4 (b) (i) and (ii), makes up the maximum number recorded under item 3 (a). Similarly, the total of the four sub-items (i) to (iv) in item 4 (a) should equal the maximum number recorded under item 3 (a).

Secure accommodation

21. In estimating item 4 (c), experience in the special units of approved schools, in separation in remand homes and approved schools, and in the handling of persistent absconders from children's homes may be relevant. Not all establishments will need even the smallest unit of secure accommodation, although in each region there may be a need for one or more homes devoted to the treatment of children in relatively secure conditions, where approved secure accommodation will comprise a large part of the facilities (see Part IV of the Plan).

22. The requirement, based on approved school experience, might be expressed as a percentage of the present approved school population. A figure of something over 5% is proposed as a basis, which would mean about 500 places in England and Wales. Committees may regard this as an appropriate basis for pro rata estimates covering all categories of secure accommodation.

Other relevant information

23. Item 5 enables Committees to describe the factors taken into account in assessing the need for various residential facilities and in determining the numbers likely to come into or be in care. Explanatory material about population trends in the region, the development of preventive and supportive services with families in their own homes, the growth of non-residential forms of care or treatment and the development of relevant services by other agencies should be included here. It would seem prudent, in preparing these initial plans, to take a cautious view of the effect of these developments in reducing the number of children in care.

Home Office Circular No. 196/1970. *Dated September* 1, 1970.

CHILDREN AND YOUNG PERSONS ACT, 1969: VOLUNTARY COMMUNITY HOMES—INSTRUMENTS OF MANAGEMENT

1. I am directed by the Secretary of State to say that he is required, before a particular voluntary home, or approved institution within the meaning of section 46 of the Children and Young Persons Act, 1969, can acquire the status of a controlled or an assisted community home, to make an instrument of management under the provisions of sections 39 to 42 of the Act. The purpose of this circular is to indicate the general scope of such instruments for both controlled and assisted homes.

The model instruments

2. To this end, model instruments have been prepared (Annexes A and B). The main purposes of an instrument are two: first, to constitute a body of managers and, secondly, to give effect to the provisions of a regional plan by which the home has been designated as a controlled or an assisted community home. The instruments appended to this Circular are only models and the articles they contain are merely indicative of the general scope. Initially the provisions to be included in the articles of a particular instrument must be a matter for negotiation between the voluntary organisation and the local authority which will be responsible for appointing the representative managers. When agreement on the provisions has been reached the procedures outlined in paragraphs 14 and 15 below should be followed.

The managers

3. As regards the number of managers (Article 4 (1)), it is considered that nine will generally be appropriate: the appointment of, for example, twelve or fifteen managers should only be contemplated where there are special circumstances; for their term of office (Article 6 (2)), there are two main choices: either to provide for the term of all managers, or all foundation managers, or all representative managers, to expire on one date and to maintain some continuity by reappointment; or to stagger individual appointments of both foundation and representative managers. The arrangements for local authority elections may have some bearing on the choice. There is, of course, nothing to prevent either the local authority or the voluntary organisation appointing, if they so wish, as one of their managers the nominee of another local authority or other body which will make substantial use of the home.

Staff

4. In the model instrument for controlled homes, no attempt has been made to provide a form of words for Article 22 because the use, under section 41 (4) of the Act, of staff employed by the organisation and the arrangements, if any, for reimbursement of the cost of such staff may be very varied. Such arrangements could include the use, full-time or part-time, of professional staff whom the local authority would otherwise have had to employ or the use of the organisation's staff to supplement religious, educational or recreational provision at the home.

5. Article 23 in the model instrument for assisted homes extends to the staff of such homes the safeguard that their employment shall not be terminated except on retirement, after due notice, or for misconduct. Safeguards, which would apply to staff employed in controlled community homes, already exist under the provisions of the local authorities' code of conditions of service. Article 23 should be read in conjunction with section 42 (4) (a) of the Act, under which, subject to any exemption afforded by the local authority under section

42 (5) (a), the responsible organisation may neither engage any person to work at an assisted home nor terminate his employment without notice, save after consultation with the local authority and, if the authority so directs, with their consent.

6. Examples of the use of the power in section 42 (5) (a) might be the local authority's informing the voluntary organisation that they did not require to be consulted about the engagement or dismissal without notice of any person employed in certain specified occupations or posts in the home or on temporary terms or on certain conditions of service or below a certain level of pay.

7. Nothing has been included in the model instrument for assisted homes about the possible exclusion under section 42 (5) (b) of the Act of the application of section 42 (4) (a) and (b). Section 42 (4) (b) empowers the local authority, after consultation, to require the organisation to terminate the employment of any person at the home (but not, of course, to terminate the employment of that person by the organisation otherwise than at that assisted home). An example of the use of section 42 (5) (b) might be an agreement between the local authority and the voluntary organisation to include in the instrument of management a provision excluding the application of section 42 (4) (a) and (b) in relation to members of a religious order. It is stressed that the examples in this and the preceding paragraph are purely illustrative and in no way imply that such provisions would be appropriate in relation to any particular home.

The role of the managers

8. The responsible authority, or the responsible organisation, are required to exercise their functions (other than functions expressly reserved) in relation to a controlled, or assisted, community home through the body of managers (sections 41 (2) and 42 (2)). The relevant functions are, as laid down in sections 41 (1) and 42 (1), the "management, equipment and maintenance" of the home.

9. The only function reserved to the responsible authority or organisation by the Act is the employment of staff (sections 41 (4) and 42 (4)). The effect of Articles 19, 20 and 21 of the model instruments is that it would be for the responsible authority or organisation to take responsibility for the maintenance of premises and, in agreement with the providing organisation or the specified local authority, for settling arrangements for the admission and discharge of children and fixing charges for children accommodated in the home. The Secretary of State attaches considerable importance to the managers' having a sufficient and a proper role and is of the opinion that use of the power to reserve other matters by the instrument of management or by notice given by the responsible authority, or organisation (sections 41 (3) and 42 (3)) will not generally be justified.

10. The Secretary of State attaches importance also to the principle that accountability for the care and discipline of children in a community home should be firmly placed on the person in charge of the home (and the staff to whom he may delegate particular responsibilities). But the managers' functions will include that of advising and supporting the person in charge and assisting him in the consideration of problems affecting the running of the home. The accountability of the person in charge, and the supporting responsibility of the managers, are provided for by Article 22 (2) of the model instrument for assisted homes (Article 23 (2) of the model for controlled homes).

11. Under the Act, final decisions on the accommodation and treatment of children in the statutory care of a local authority are matters for that authority (and a voluntary organisation will similarly have to take decisions about the accommodation and treatment of children for whom they are responsible). But subject to any understandings reached between the local authority, or the voluntary organisation, and the person in charge of the home, the day to day

care and discipline of a child in a community home in accordance with the Act, regulations to be made under it and any other relevant provisions is the responsibility of the person in charge of the home. Major decisions about a child's treatment in the home will naturally be a matter for consultation between the person in charge and the local authority or voluntary organisation, but the decision in any particular circumstance will be for the person in charge (the local authority or voluntary organisation having the remedy, if they do not concur, of withdrawing the child).

12. The responsibilities of managers will therefore generally include

(a) ensuring the efficient administration of the home in accordance with the Act, and the regulations to be made under it, and with the arrangements laid down in the instrument of management or made under the provisions of Articles 20 and 21 of the model instruments;

(b) advising, supporting and assisting the person in charge of the home as regards its organisation and the care and discipline of children accommodated in it and, where appropriate, giving to him general directions on these matters (Article 22 (2), model for assisted homes; Article 23 (2), model for controlled homes);

(c) inspecting the buildings and grounds and representing to the responsible authority, or organisation, the need for maintenance (Article 19);

(d) fostering good relations between the home and the local community in which it is set;

(e) advising the responsible authority, or organisation, on the appointment of the secretary to the managers (Article 11) and of the person to be in charge of the home (Article 22 (1), model for assisted homes; Article 23 (1), model for controlled homes);

(f) specific functions laid upon the managers by regulations to be made under section 43 (1) and (2) of the Act: such functions may, for example, include

(i) visiting the home regularly by rota and reporting on visits to the body of managers;

(ii) ensuring that staff and children are familiar with fire and safety precautions;

(iii) ensuring that every child has opportunity to attend services and receive instruction, as may be appropriate to any religious persuasion to which he may belong and practicable in the circumstances;

(iv) ensuring that satisfactory arrangements are in effect for visits by relatives and friends to children in the home.

(Foundation managers will have a specific function, imposed by Article 5 of the model instruments, of securing that the character of the home as a voluntary home is preserved and that the terms of any trust deed are observed.) In carrying out their functions managers will recognise the importance of looking to the person in charge of the home, the senior staff of the home and the professional staff of the responsible authority, or organisation, for professional advice.

13. The managers will have a specific responsibility under sections 41 (5) and (6) and 42 (6) and (7) to prepare, and submit to the responsible authority, or organisation, annual estimates of expenditure and receipts, and to keep proper accounts and proper records in relation to the accounts of the home.

Planning procedure, negotiations and submission of draft instrument

14. Once the children's regional planning committee has accepted, in principle, that a particular home would be suitable for incorporation in the regional plan as a voluntary community home and (unless the voluntary organisation and a

relevant authority have already agreed arrangements for their joint management of the home) once the voluntary organisation has indicated that, subject to satisfactory terms being negotiated, it would welcome such an arrangement, it will be for the regional planning committee to obtain the provisional consent of one of the relevant authorities to participate in the management of the home. The terms under which the home is to operate and the provisions which need to be incorporated in the instrument of management should be settled between that relevant authority and the voluntary organisation. In the event of difficulty, it is expected that the secretariat of a regional planning committee would wish to help and the advice of the Home Office would, of course, be readily available. A draft of the provisions for incorporation in the instrument for a controlled home would be prepared by the relevant authority and agreed with the voluntary organisation; for an assisted home, the roles would be reversed.

15. Completion of negotiations should be reported to the regional planning committee, who would then obtain final formal consents under section 36 (5) of the Act from the voluntary organisation and the relevant authority, as a necessary pre-requisite to the submission of the regional plan. Draft instruments of management or provisions for insertion in instruments may be submitted to the Secretary of State with the regional plan or separately in advance. Action to clarify points of doubt could be taken before the regional plan is submitted but it is emphasised that no instrument can be made before the Secretary of State has decided to approve the whole or the relevant part of the regional plan in which the home is designated as a controlled or an assisted home. An instrument comes into force on the date specified in the instrument (section 39 (5)).

16. Queries about this circular may be addressed to the Under Secretary of State or to the Superintending Inspector for the planning area in question. But insofar as a query may relate to any change in the status of a particular establishment, this is a matter initially for the appropriate regional planning committee and the local authority and voluntary organisation who are to participate in its management.

NOTE

Copies of this circular were sent to clerks of county, county borough and London borough councils and of the Common Council of City of London. All voluntary organisations having homes registered under Part IV of the Children Act, 1948, the correspondent (approved schools), the Secretary of the Managing Committee (approved probation homes and hostels), Secretaries of Regional Planning Committees.

ANNEX A

INSTRUMENTS OF MANAGEMENT

No.........

CONTROLLED COMMUNITY HOMES

The [Blackacre] Instrument of Management Order, 19..

Made	............19..
Coming into force	............19..

Whereas the voluntary home known as [Blackacre] and situate at...............
has been designated as a controlled community home by the...................
regional plan which was approved by me on .... 19..:

Now, therefore, in exercise of the powers conferred on me by sections 39 and 40 of the Children and Young Persons Act, 1969, I hereby make the following Order:—

Citation and operation

1. This Order may be cited as the [Blackacre] Instrument of Management Order, 19.. and shall come into force on .... 19.. without prejudice, however, to the making before that date of appointments taking effect from that date.

Interpretation

2. (1) In this Order the following expressions have the meanings hereby respectively assigned to them, that is to say—

"the Act" means the Children and Young Persons Act, 1969;

"the home" means the [Blackacre] voluntary home;

"local authority" has the same meaning as in the Children and Young Persons Act, 1969, except that "the Local Authority" means the council of the county/county borough/London borough of..............;

"the managers" means the body of managers for the home constituted in accordance with this Order except that "the foundation managers" and "the Local Authority managers" mean the managers appointed, respectively, in accordance with Article 4 (2) and Article 4 (3);

"the Organisation" means the organisation by whom the home is provided, namely, the.............. [Society].

(2) The Interpretation Act, 1889, shall apply to the interpretation of this Order as it applies to the interpretation of an Act of Parliament.

(3) Nothing in this Order shall affect the purposes for which the premises comprising the home are held.

Purpose and nature of home

3. (1) The purpose of the home shall be the accommodation of [20 children between the ages of 5 and 18 years] who are in the care either of a local authority or of the Organisation.

(2) The home shall be of such a nature that facilities are provided for........

Body of managers

4. (1) The body of managers for the home shall consist of [nine] persons.

(2) [Three] of the managers shall be foundation managers appointed by [the executive committee of] the Organisation to represent their interests.

(3) [Six] of the managers shall be Local Authority managers appointed by the Local Authority.

5. The foundation managers shall secure that, as far as practicable, the character of the home as a voluntary home is preserved and, subject to section 40 (3) of the Act, that the terms of any trust deed relating to the home are observed.

6. (1) Without prejudice to any power to make appointments before the date on which this Order comes into force taking effect from that date, the managers first appointed under Article 4 of this Order shall be appointed as soon as practicable after that date.

(2) Each manager shall, subject to Article 7 of this Order, be appointed for a term of [three years].

(3) Upon the appointment of a foundation manager the Organisation shall give notice in writing to the Local Authority of the name of the manager.

7. (1) The appointment of a manager may be terminated by [the executive committee of] the Organisation or by the Local Authority, as the case may be, at any time by notice in writing served on the manager, specifying the date on which his appointment is to cease to have effect.

(2) A manager may resign his appointment by giving notice in writing of his intention so to do to the Local Authority and if he is a foundation manager he shall at the same time send a copy of the notice to the Organisation.

8. (1) If a casual vacancy occurs on the body of managers, whether through the termination of the appointment of a manager, the resignation or disqualification of a manager or otherwise [the executive committee of] the Organisation or the Local Authority, as the case may be, shall as soon as practicable appoint a person to fill the vacancy.

(2) A person appointed to the body of managers in accordance with this Article, shall, subject to Article 7 of this Order, serve thereon for the period for which the member he replaced would have served had the vacancy not occurred.

(3) Article 6 (3) shall apply to the appointment of a foundation manager to fill a casual vacancy as it applies to an appointment under that Article.

Qualifications and other provisions as to managers

9. (1) A person shall be disqualified from becoming or being a manager if he is employed by the Local Authority [or the Organisation—see Article 22] in any capacity for the purposes of the home.

    (2) No person shall be eligible for appointment as a manager if he has attained the age of [sixty-five], and a manager shall, upon attaining that age, thereupon cease to be a manager.

    (3) A manager whose term of office has expired or who has at any time been a manager and who is not disqualified under paragraph (1) or ineligible under paragraph (2) of this Article may be reappointed to the body of managers.

10. (1) A manger shall not receive any payment or other remuneration for his services.

    (2) Except so far as the Local Authority may in writing approve, a manager shall not own any interest (otherwise than as a trustee) in any property held for the purposes of the home.

    (3) If a manager has any pecuniary interest, direct or indirect, in any contract or proposed contract for the supply of goods or services to the home and is present at a meeting of the managers at which the contract or proposed contract is the subject of consideration, he shall, as soon as practicable after the commencement of the meeting, disclose the fact, and shall not take part in the consideration or discussion of, or vote on any question with respect to the contract or proposed contract.

Secretary

11. The Local Authority shall, after consultation with the managers, appoint a person to be secretary to the managers.

12. (1) The first meeting of the managers shall be convened by the Local Authority as soon as practicable after all the managers have been appointed in accordance with Article 4.

    (2) Subsequent meetings shall be convened in accordance with Article 13 of this Order, provided that there shall be at least three meetings in any year [except the year in which the first meeting is held], and such other meetings as may be necessary for the efficient discharge of the functions of the managers.

    (3) The managers shall at their first meeting and thereafter at the first meeting in every year elect two of their number to be respectively chairman and vice-chairman for that year.

    (4) If a vacancy occurs in the office of chairman or vice-chairman, the managers shall at their next meeting elect a person to fill the vacancy, and any person so elected shall hold office for the remainder of that year.

    (5) The chairman, if present, shall preside at meetings of the managers, provided that if the chairman is absent the vice-chairman, if present, shall preside and if the chairman and vice-chairman are absent the managers shall, before proceeding to discuss any other business, elect one of their number to preside at the meeting.

    (6) In this Article "year" means a period of twelve months beginning with [date].

13. (1) The Chairman or any two or more managers may at any time convene a meeting of the managers.

    (2) Except in an emergency, the secretary shall, at least seven clear days before a meeting of the managers, give notice in writing of the intended place and time of the meeting, specifying the business to be transacted thereat to:—

        (a) every manager,
        (b) the Local Authority,
        (c) the Organisation:

    Provided that the meeting or any proceedings thereof shall not be invalidated by failure to comply with any provision contained in this paragraph.

14. At a meeting of the managers one third of the total number of managers specified in Article 4 (1) of this Order shall constitute a quorum, provided that at

least one manager shall be a foundation manager and at least one shall be a Local Authority manager.

15. Any matter falling to be determined at a meeting of the managers shall be determined by a majority of the managers present and voting thereon, provided that in the case of an equality of votes the person presiding at the meeting shall have a second or casting vote.

16. (1) The secretary shall cause to be drawn up and kept in a suitable form minutes of the proceedings of meetings of the managers.
 (2) The names of the persons present at a meeting shall be recorded in the minutes.
 (3) The secretary shall send copies of the minutes of every meeting to the Local Authority and the Organisation.

17. No proceedings of the managers shall be invalidated by reason of the fact that at the time of the proceedings there was a vacancy on the body of managers or a defect in the appointment of any of the managers or any of the managers who took part in the proceedings was disqualified from being or ineligible for appointment as a manager.

Finance
18. (1) The secretary shall send to the Organisation a copy of the estimates of expenditure and receipts of the home which, in accordance with section 41 (5) of the Act, are required to be submitted to the Local Authority.
 (2) The Local Authority shall notify the secretary in writing of their approval of the estimates or of any modification thereof which they propose to make and shall send a copy of the notification to the Organisation.

Premises of the home
19. The managers shall regularly inspect any premises belonging to the home for the purpose of ascertaining the condition thereof and shall inform the Local Authority of any measures which in their opinion are necessary for the proper maintenance of the premises.

Admission and discharge of children in the care of the organisation
20. (1) Subject to the following provisions of this Article and to Article 3 of this Order the number and type of children in the care of the Organisation who are to be admitted to the home and the arrangements for their admission and discharge shall be such as may be agreed between the Local Authority and the Organisation.
 (2) The arrangements for admitting a child in the care of the Organisation to the home made in pursuance of paragraph (1) of this Article, shall include provision for taking into account the physical and mental condition of the child and any report thereon which may have been made and his suitability for admission to the home having regard to the facilities provided thereat.
 (3) The Organisation may within [insert period] after the coming into force of this Order, or thereafter on giving six months notice to the Local Authority, require not more than 10 per cent. of the total number of places in the home to be reserved for the accommodation of children in the care of the Organisation.

Charges for children in the care of the Organisation accommodated, and places reserved for them, in the home
21. (1) In respect of a child in their care who is accommodated in the home, the Organisation shall pay to the Local Authority fees on such scale as may be agreed between them for the purpose of this sub-paragraph.
 (2) In respect of any place in the home which is reserved under Article 20 (3) but is unoccupied, the Organisation shall pay to the Local Authority .... per cent. of the fees which would be payable under the preceding sub-paragraph if, throughout the period for which the place is continuously unoccupied, a child in the care of the Organisation were accommodated therein, except that no fees shall be payable under this sub-paragraph where the said period is three months or less.

Staff

22. [Include any arrangements made between the Local Authority and the Organisation in pursuance of section 41 (4) of the Act whereby persons who are not employed by the Local Authority may undertake duties at the home.]

23. (1) The Local Authority shall, after consultation with the managers, appoint a person to be in charge of the home.

(2) The said person shall, subject to any general directions which may be given to him by the managers, be responsible for all matters relating to the organisation of the home and the care and discipline of children accommodated in the home.

(3) The said person shall, except so far as the managers otherwise direct, attend all meetings of the managers.

(4) The Local Authority [may] [shall] appoint a deputy to the person in charge and for any period for which that person is absent or otherwise unable to act or the post of person in charge is vacant, the provisions of paragraphs (2) and (3) of this Article shall apply in relation to the deputy as though he had been appointed to be in charge of the home.

ANNEX B

INSTRUMENTS OF MANAGEMENT

No...........

ASSISTED COMMUNITY HOMES

The [Blackacre] Instrument of Management Order, 19..

Made	............19..
Coming into force	............19..

Whereas the voluntary home known as [Blackacre] and situate at .... has been designated as an assisted community home by the .... regional plan which was approved by me on .... 19..:

Now, therefore, in exercise of the power conferred on me by sections 39 and 40 of the Children and Young Persons Act, 1969, I hereby make the following Order:—

Citation and operation

1. This Order may be cited as the [Blackacre] Instrument of Management Order, 19.. and shall come into force on .... 19.., without prejudice, however, to the making before that date of appointments taking effect from that date.

Interpretation

2. (1) In this Order the following expressions have the meanings hereby respectively assigned to them, that is to say—

"the Act" means the Children and Young Persons Act, 1969;

"the home" means the [Blackacre] voluntary home;

"local authority" has the same meaning as in the Children and Young Persons Act, 1969, except that "the Local Authority" means the council of the county/county borough/London Borough of ....;

"the managers" means the body of managers for the home constituted in accordance with this Order except that "the foundation managers" and "the Local Authority managers" mean the managers appointed, respectively, in accordance with Article 4 (2) and Article 4 (3);

"the Organisation" means the organisation by whom the home is provided, namely, the .... [Society];

(2) The Interpretation Act, 1889, shall apply to the interpretation of this Order as it applies to the interpretation of an Act of Parliament.

(3) Nothing in this Order shall affect the purposes for which the premises comprising the home are held.

Purpose and nature of home

3. (1) The purpose of the home shall be the accommodation of [20 children between the ages of 5 and 18 years] who are in the care either of the Organisation or of a local authority.

    (2) The home shall be of such a nature that facilities are provided for........

Body of managers

4. (1) The body of managers for the home shall consist of [nine] persons.

    (2) [Six] of the managers shall be foundation managers appointed by [the executive committee of] the Organisation to represent their interests.

    (3) [Three] of the managers shall be Local Authority managers appointed by the Local Authority.

5. The foundation managers shall secure that, as far as practicable, the character of the home as a voluntary home is preserved and, subject to section 40 (3) of the Act, that the terms of any trust deed relating to the home are observed.

6. (1) Without prejudice to any power to make appointments before the date on which this Order comes into force taking effect from that date, the managers first appointed under Article 4 of this Order shall be appointed as soon as practicable after that date.

    (2) Each manager shall, subject to Article 7 of this Order, be appointed for a term of [three years].

    (3) Upon the appointment of a Local Authority manager the Local Authority shall give notice in writing to the Organisation of the name of the manager.

7. (1) The appointment of a manager may be terminated by [the executive committee of] the Organisation or the Local Authority, as the case may be, at any time by notice in writing served on the manager, specifying the date on which his appointment is to cease to have effect.

    (2) A manager may resign his appointment by giving notice in writing of his intention so to do to the Organisation; and if he is a Local Authority manager he shall at the same time send a copy of the notice to the Local Authority.

8. (1) If a casual vacancy occurs on the body of managers, whether through the termination of the appointment of a manager, the resignation or disqualification of a manager or otherwise, [the executive committee of] the Organisation or the Local Authority, as the case may be, shall as soon as practicable appoint a person to fill the vacancy.

    (2) A person appointed to the body of managers in accordance with this Article, shall, subject to Article 7 of this Order, serve thereon for the period for which the member he replaced would have served had the vacancy not occurred.

    (3) Article 6 (3) shall apply to the appointment of a Local Authority manager to fill a casual vacancy as it applies to an appointment under that Article.

Qualifications and other provisions as to managers

9. (1) A person shall be disqualified from becoming or being a manager if he is employed by the Organisation in any capacity for the purposes of the home.

    (2) No person shall be eligible for appointment as a manager if he has attained the age of [sixty-five], and a manager shall, upon attaining that age, thereupon cease to be a manager.

    (3) A manager whose term of office has expired or who has at any time been a manager and who is not disqualified under paragraph (1) or ineligible under paragraph (2) of this Article may be reappointed to the body of managers.

10. (1) A manager shall not receive any payment or other remuneration for his services.

    (2) Except so far as the Local Authority may in writing approve, a manager shall not own any interest (otherwise than as a trustee) in any property held for the purposes of the home.

    (3) If a manager has any pecuniary interest, direct or indirect, in any contract or proposed contract for the supply of goods or services to the home and is present at a meeting of the managers at which the contract or proposed

contract is the subject of consideration, he shall, as soon as practicable after the commencement of the meeting, disclose the fact, and shall not take part in the consideration or discussion of, or vote on any question with respect to, the contract or proposed contract.

Secretary

11. The Organisation shall, after consultation with the managers, appoint a person to be secretary to the managers.

Meetings of the managers

12. (1) The first meeting of the managers shall be convened by the Organisation as soon as practicable after all the managers have been appointed in accordance with Article 4.

(2) Subsequent meetings shall be convened in accordance with Article 13 of this Order, provided that there shall be at least three meetings in any year [except the year in which the first meeting is held], and such other meetings as may be necessary for the efficient discharge of the functions of the managers.

(3) The managers shall at their first meeting and thereafter at the first meeting in every year elect two of their number to be respectively chairman and vice-chairman for that year.

(4) If a vacancy occurs in the office of chairman or vice-chairman, the managers shall at their next meeting elect a person to fill the vacancy, and any person so elected shall hold office for the remainder of that year.

(5) The chairman, if present, shall preside at meetings of managers, provided that if the chairman is absent the vice-chairman, if present, shall preside and if the chairman and vice-chairman are absent the managers shall, before proceeding to discuss any other business, elect one of their number to preside at the meeting.

(6) In this Article "year" means a period of twelve months beginning with [date].

13. (1) The chairman or any two or more managers may at any time convene a meeting of the managers.

(2) Except in an emergency, the secretary shall, at least seven clear days before a meeting of the managers, give notice in writing of the intended place and time of the meeting, specifying the business to be transacted thereat to:—

(a) every manager,
(b) the Organisation, and
(c) the Local Authority:

Provided that the meeting or any proceedings thereof shall not be invalidated by a failure to comply with any provision contained in this paragraph.

14. At a meeting of the managers one third of the total number of managers specified in Article 4 (1) of this Order shall constitute a quorum, provided that at least one manager shall be a foundation manager and at least one shall be a Local Authority manager.

15. Any matter falling to be determined at a meeting of the managers shall be determined by a majority of the managers present and voting thereon, provided that in the case of an equality of votes the person presiding at the meeting shall have a second or casting vote.

16. (1) The Secretary shall cause to be drawn up and kept in a suitable form minutes of the proceedings of meetings of the managers.

(2) The names of the persons present at a meeting shall be recorded in the minutes.

(3) The secretary shall send copies of the minutes of every meeting to the Organisation and the Local Authority.

17. No proceedings of the managers shall be invalidated by reason of the fact that at the time of the proceedings there was a vacancy on the body of managers or a defect in the appointment of any of the managers or any of the managers who took part in the proceedings was disqualified from being, or ineligible for appointment as, a manager.

Finance

18. (1) The secretary shall send to the Local Authority a copy of the estimates of expenditure and receipts of the home which, in accordance with section 42 (6) of the Act, are required to be submitted to the Organisation.

(2) The Organisation shall notify the secretary in writing of their approval of the estimates or of any modification thereof which they propose to make and shall send a copy of the notification to the Local Authority.

Premises of the home

19. The managers shall regularly inspect any premises belonging to the home for the purpose of ascertaining the condition thereof and shall inform the Organisation of any measures which in their opinion are necessary for the proper maintenance of the premises.

Admission and discharge of children in the care of local authorities

20. (1) Subject to the following provisions of this Article and to Article 3 of this Order the number and type of children in the care of local authorities who are to be admitted to the home and the arrangements for their admission and discharge shall be such as may be agreed between the Organisation and the Local Authority.

(2) The arrangements for admitting a child in the care of a local authority to the home, made in pursuance of paragraph (1) of this Article, shall include provision for taking into account the physical and mental condition of the child and any report thereon which may have been made and his suitability for admission to the home having regard to the facilities provided thereat.

(3) Not less than half of the total number of places in the home shall be reserved for the accommodation of children in the care of the Local Authority or other local authorities.

(4) The Local Authority may, on giving six months' notice to the Organisation, require such further places to be reserved for the accommodation of children in their care or in the care of other local authorities as they think fit, provided that the number of places so reserved under this and the preceding paragraph shall not exceed three-quarters of the total number of places available in the home.

Charges for children in the care of local authorities accommodated, and places reserved for them, in the home

21. (1) In respect of a child in their care who is accommodated in the home, a local authority shall pay to the Organisation fees on such scale as may be agreed between the Organisation and the Local Authority for the purposes of this sub-paragraph.

(2) In respect of any place in the home which is reserved under Article 20 (3) or (4) but is unoccupied, the Local Authority shall pay to the Organisation .... per cent. of the fees which would be payable under the preceding sub-paragraph if, throughout the period for which the place is continuously unoccupied, a child in the care of a local authority were accommodated therein, except that no fees shall be payable under this sub-paragraph when the said period is three months or less.

Staff

22. (1) The Organisation shall, after consultation with the managers, appoint a person to be in charge of the home.

(2) The said person shall, subject to any general directions which may be given to him by the managers, be responsible for all matters relating to the organisation of the home and the care and discipline of children accommodated in the home.

(3) The said person shall, except so far as the managers otherwise direct, attend all meetings of the managers.

(4) The Organisation [may] [shall] appoint a deputy to the person in charge and for any period for which that person is absent or otherwise unable to act or the post of person in charge is vacant, the provisions of paragraphs (2) and (3) of this Article shall apply in relation to the deputy as though he had been appointed to be in charge of the home.

23. The employment of any person employed in pursuance of section 42 (4) of the Act by the Organisation for the purposes of the home otherwise than for a specified period shall not be terminated except—

(a) on the retirement of the employee,
(b) in the case of the person in charge [or deputy to the person in charge or
............], by three months' notice, and in any other case by one month's notice, or, if the terms of service of the employee specify a greater period of notice than three months or one month as the case may be, by that period of notice, given by the employee or the Organisation, or
(c) on account of misconduct by the employee.

Home Office Circular No. 242/1970.   *Dated October 28, 1970.*

CONVEYING TO AND FROM COURTS OF CHILDREN COMMITTED AND REMANDED TO THE CARE OF LOCAL AUTHORITIES

1. This circular deals with the arrangements for conveying children and young persons to and from court when the relevant provisions of the Children and Young Persons Act, 1969, come into force on 1 January 1971. In the rest of this circular "child" includes "young person". The 1969 Act in no way limits the powers of the courts to remand a child on bail or to adjourn a case and allow the child to go home until the next hearing. This circular is concerned only with cases where a court makes an order involving removal from home.

2. Hitherto local authorities have been responsible for conveying children subject to fit person orders and interim fit person orders; the work of conveying children sent to approved schools has been shared between local authorities, the probation and after-care service and the police; and the police have been responsible for conveying to and from courts in other circumstances. On 1 January 1971 approved school orders and fit person orders will be replaced by care orders; place of safety orders will be replaced by interim care orders; and remand to a named remand home or special reception centre will be replaced by remand to the care of a local authority. This circular suggests what arrangements should be made following these changes in the law. The suggested arrangements, so far as they affect local authorities and the police, have been agreed with the Association of Municipal Corporations and the County Councils Association.

Detention centres, remand centres, borstals and prisons
3. The arrangements for conveying to and from these establishments are not affected by the changes in the law which take place on 1 January 1971. The responsibility will remain with the police and it is proposed that the forms scheduled to the statutory rules should continue to provide accordingly.

Children committed to the care of local authorities—general principles
4. From 1 January 1971 a child may be committed to the care of a local authority by:

(a) a care order;
(b) an interim order;
(c) a warrant issued under section 23 of the 1969 Act when a child is remanded, or committed for trial or sentence, and is not released on bail or committed to a remand centre or prison as unruly.

5. In all these circumstances the order or warrant places responsibility for the child on the local authority; this responsibility includes taking the child from the court and, where the order so requires, taking him back to a court. On 1 January 1971, however, it will not be practicable for all local authorities to take on all the additional work involved, and for a time the help of the police

will be needed. The help of the police will also be needed, on a long-term basis, for the conveyance of some children so as to prevent breaches of the peace or absconding. Subject to these two exceptions, the first of which will be temporary, it is agreed that the local authorities are responsible for the conveyance to and from courts of children subject to the orders listed in paragraph 4, and should, so far as practicable, arrange to take over the care of each child at the court premises. It is hoped that local authorities will make the necessary arrangements to assume this responsibility as soon as possible after 1 January 1971 and that, in the meantime, chief officers of police will co-operate in giving the local authorities such assistance as they may require.

6. The number of cases where the assistance of the police will be needed by local authorities to control a child form only a small proportion of the total. They are likely to be confined to children whose history suggests that they may be violent or may attempt to abscond. It is hoped that chief officers of police will continue to respond to requests for such assistance, which has been generally recognised as a proper function of the police.

Conveying children from a juvenile court

7. In many cases the child will be appearing in a court acting for the area of the local authority where he lives. It is expected that a representative of this local authority will be present at the court and will be able either to take over the care of the child at the court or to arrange for another person to do so on behalf of the authority. Until a local authority is able to assume responsibility in this way for all children appearing in juvenile courts in its area, it may wish to make arrangements with the police for their assistance. It is suggested, however, that the first priority should be for each local authority to make arrangements enabling it to assume responsibility at the court for all children (apart from those referred to in paragraph 6) appearing in juvenile courts in its own area and made subject to one of the orders mentioned in paragraph 4, and to convey the children from the court.

8. A child appearing before a juvenile court acting for an area other than that of the local authority where he lives will occasionally be committed to the care of the local authority for the area of the court (*e.g.* in the case of a remand before a finding of guilt) but it is expected that committals in such cases will normally be to the care of the authority for the area where the child lives (*e.g.* where the court remits the case to the court for the child's home area and does not allow the child to go home in the meantime). In such cases it is suggested that the police should get into touch with the care authority as soon as possible after the order is made so that the latter may decide what arrangements are to be made for the child, *e.g.* whether to ask the authority for the court area to accommodate the child until he can be collected (which might be necessary where the court was a considerable distance away) or whether to arrange for him to be collected or taken direct to the place where the care authority propose to accommodate him initially (which would be desirable where the court was near enough for this to be practicable). Alternatively, a representative of another local authority present at the court may be ready to make enquiries of the care authority.

9. The prescribed forms for the court orders listed in paragraph 4 will have to be in sufficiently flexible terms to cover these various possibilities, and it is proposed that these forms, which will be scheduled to the statutory rules relating to the procedure of juvenile courts, shall provide that, unless the child is forthwith received into the care of a person authorised by, and acting on behalf of, the local authority to whose care he is committed, he shall be delivered by a constable to such a person. The words relating to the duty of the constable are required in order to provide authority for the child's custody, or conveyance by the police in cases where this is necessary, while avoiding the

need for the court to draw up different forms of order depending on the precise arrangements made in each individual case. These words convey no implication that it is a continuing general duty of the police to convey children from juvenile court premises to the care of the local authority.

Conveying children from other courts

10. An adult magistrates' court has no power to make a care order (section 7 (8) of the Act) but may remand to the care of a local authority, for instance where it remits a case to a juvenile court and decides to remand the child otherwise than on bail. The Crown Court, when dealing with children has power to make care orders and to remand, *e.g.* for enquiries or until a sitting on the following day.

11. The arrangements suggested in paragraphs 7 and 8 above cover all these cases. In adult magistrates' courts it is, however, less likely that any local authority representative will be present, and it will normally be for the police to get into touch with the care authority, so that it may decide what arrangements are to be made for the child. At the Crown Court, a probation officer may be ready to make the necessary enquiries of the local authority, although he has no responsibility under the court's order.

Conveying children to courts

12. It is the responsibility of the local authority to whose care a child is committed to arrange for his further appearance in court in pursuance of an interim order, remand warrant or committal for trial or sentence. Where a community home (or a remand home while remand homes continue to exist as such) accommodates children from a number of local authorities the responsibility in relation to each child will rest with the authority in whose care he is; this in no way precludes authorities from making collective arrangements for the conveyance of groups of children by one authority (*e.g.* the authority responsible for the home) where this is convenient. Insofar as local authorities wish for the assistance of the police in the interim period before they are able to take on all this work, or in the case of children who may be violent or may attempt to abscond, this will be a matter for local arrangement.

Children subject to care orders

13. Where a child subject to a care order is moved from one establishment to another, or is required to attend court (*e.g.* in connection with an appeal or an application to discharge the order), it will be the responsibility of the care authority to arrange this. Similarly, when an absentee is arrested, it will be for the care authority to arrange for him to be taken back to the place from which he is absent or to such other place as they direct. The power of arrest conferred on a constable by section 32 (1) of the 1969 Act conveys no implication that the subsequent conveyance of an absentee to such a place is a responsibility of the police, although it will be open to the authority to ask them to undertake it in individual cases *e.g.* where the child is unruly.

Taking children to a place of safety

14. Nothing in this circular affects the conveying to a place of safety of a child:

    (a) whose detention is authorised by a justice under section 28 (1) of the 1969 Act or section 40 of the Children and Young Persons Act, 1933;

    (b) who is detained by a constable under section 28 (2) of the 1969 Act and whose detention in a place of safety is arranged under section 28 (4);

    (c) who is arrested and whose detention in a place of safety is arranged in pursuance of section 29 (3).

In all these cases the responsibility for arranging for the child's conveyance to the place of safety will rest with the police or the person authorised by the justice to detain him, as the case may be.

Probation and After-Care Service
15. With the repeal of section 73 (3) of the 1933 Act, the probation and after-care service ceases to have any statutory responsibility for conveying children from court, although, as suggested in paragraph 11, it may be helpful if probation officers inform local authorities of cases in which children are committed or remanded to care by the Crown Court.

Financial arrangements
16. The 1969 Act and the statutory rules do not deal expressly with financial responsibility, except that section 32 provides that the conveyance of an absentee shall be at the expense of the care authority. In other situations where the police convey a child on behalf of a local authority or assist an authority, or one authority conveys or accommodates a child for another authority, it will be a matter for agreement between those concerned how far financial adjustments are thought desirable and worthwhile. Once the care of a child has been assumed by a local authority in accordance with a court order it seems clear that, in principle, financial responsibility for conveyance as well as accommodation then rests with that authority, so long as it remains legally responsible for the child under the order. In relation to the initial conveyance *from* courts, however, it has been agreed to suggest that, on grounds of practical convenience, it would be appropriate to work on the basis of letting the cost lie where it falls.

Review of arrangements
17. It is proposed to review the arrangements suggested in this circular, including the financial arrangements suggested in paragraph 16, in twelve months time in the light of experience of their operation.

Accommodation of children at juvenile courts
18. A separate circular is being issued on the accommodation need at juvenile courts. The circular will have particular reference to the provision to be included in new buildings, or in modifications which are made to existing buildings, but will deal also with the need for, and use of, waiting rooms, detention rooms and cells.

19. Extra copies of this circular are being sent to clerks of childrens' authorities for the Children's Officer and the Finance Officer.

NOTE
Copies of this circular were sent to the Clerks of county, county borough and London borough councils and the Common Council of the City of London, the Chief Constable, the Clerk to the Justices, the Clerk of Assize, the Clerk of the Peace, the Secretary of Probation and After-Care Committees.

Home Office Circular No. 270/1970.   *Dated December 1, 1970.*

STATISTICS OF PROCEEDINGS UNDER PART I OF THE CHILDREN AND YOUNG PERSONS ACT, 1969

1. Clerks were informed in Home Office Circular No. 192/1970 of the intention to introduce new arrangements for the collection of statistics of these proceedings on 1 January 1971. This circular sets out the particulars which the Secretary of State requires to be transmitted to him, and the times at which

and the form in which he directs them to be submitted, under section 63 (3) of the 1969 Act.

2. The particulars may be transmitted, at the discretion of the Clerk, by sending either

    (a) copies of the relevant orders with a covering form, copies of which are enclosed; or

    (b) a copy of the court register.

Supply of information by copies of court orders
3. The particulars required are as follows:

    (a) *Care proceedings under section 1 of the 1969 Act.* If the proceedings result in an order, a copy of the order should be forwarded. If no order is made, particulars of the proceedings should be entered on the reverse of the covering form.

    (b) *Supervision proceedings.* If a care order is made, under section 15 (1) of the 1969 Act, on the discharge of a supervision order, a copy should be forwarded. Copies of other orders varying or discharging supervision orders are not required.

    (c) *Applications under section 21 of the Act for the extension or discharge of a care order.* Where an application is granted, a copy of the court's order should be forwarded. If the application is refused, particulars of the proceedings should be entered on the reverse of the covering form.

    (d) *Proceedings under section 31 of the Act.* If an order for removal to borstal is made, a copy of the order should be forwarded. If no order is made, particulars of the proceedings should be entered on the reverse of the covering form.

4. Copies of interim orders need not be sent. All that is required is a copy of the order made on the final disposal of the case or, where no order is made, an entry giving relevant particulars on the reverse of the covering form.

Supply of information by copies of the register
5. The Statistical Division will extract the relevant information, ignoring other entries. Entries relating to care proceedings should show the relevant paragraph of section 1 (2) of the 1969 Act in column 4.

Care proceedings in which an offence is alleged
6. Where an offence is alleged in care proceedings, the relevant Act and section should be quoted in the order, in the entry on the reverse of the covering form, or in the entry in the register, as the case may be.

Supervision orders
7. When it becomes possible to include requirements under section 12 (2) of the 1969 Act in supervision orders, the entry in the register or the order should show for each such requirement whether it was included in pursuance of paragraph (a) or (b) (i) or (b) (ii) or (b) (iii) of section 12 (2), or a combination of these, and the number of days for which directions may be given.

Sex of the child
8. The name of the child may not always identify his sex. Where this is not clear from the child's name, M or F should be added in brackets after the name in the register; the order or the entry on the reverse of the covering forms. Clerks may find it simpler to include this in all cases.

Forwarding of returns

9. Copies of the register, or copies of orders with the covering form, should be sent, at the end of each month or quarter, at the option of the clerk to

> Home Office
> Statistical Division
> Tolworth Tower
> SURBITON
> Surrey

from whom further supplies of the covering form may be obtained. Unless notification to the contrary is received before 10 December it will be assumed that those clerks who have not returned the form enclosed with Home Office Circular No. 192/1970 will supply the information by means of copies of court orders. If a clerk wishes to change from one method of providing the information to the other, the Statistical Division should be informed in advance.

NOTE

Copies of this circular were sent to the Clerks to the Justices.

Home Office Circular No. 20/1971.   *Dated March* 31, 1971.

CHILDREN AND YOUNG PERSONS ACT, 1969: SECTION 24 (5) THE CHILDREN AND YOUNG PERSONS (DEFINITION OF INDEPENDENT PERSONS) REGULATIONS, 1971

1. I enclose a copy of the Children and Young Persons (Definition of Independent Persons) Regulations, 1971, which come into effect on 1 April 1971. Printed copies of the Regulations will be distributed as soon as they are available.

Circumstances in which a visitor is required to be appointed

2. A local authority is required by section 24 (5) of the Children and Young Persons Act, 1969 (which comes into effect on 1 April 1971) to appoint an "independent person" to be a visitor to a person in the authority's care in the circumstances defined in the sub-section. These are when the person in care is

    (a) subject to a care order;
    (b) aged five or over;
    (c) accommodated in an establishment which he has not been allowed to leave during the preceding three months for ordinary attendance at school or work;

and it appears to the authority that

    (d) communication between him and his parent or guardian has been so infrequent that it is appropriate to appoint a visitor for him; or

(e) he has not lived with, visited or been visited by either of his parents or his guardian at any time during the preceding 12 months.

As explained in paragraph 164 of the Guide to Part I of the Children and Young Persons Act, 1969 (H.M.S.O. 1970), the provision applies only to children who spend virtually all their time in the home where they are accommodated (but it does not cease to apply if they make occasional outings, *e.g.* for educational purposes), and of these children it applies only to those who have had little or no recent contact with their parents or guardians. It should be noted that under (d) above it is for the local authority to decide whether communication has been so infrequent that it is appropriate to appoint a visitor. A visitor must be appointed, however, if conditions (a) to (c) are fulfilled and it appears to the local authority that there has been no contact for twelve months as provided under (e).

The visitor's role

3. One object of section 24 (5) of the Act is to secure that the safeguard against a child's remaining in care under a care order unnecessarily (*viz.* the child's right to apply under section 21 (2) for the discharge of the care order or the right of his parent or guardian to apply on his behalf) should not be ineffective if the child has no parent, or has parents who are not interested in whether or not he remains in care. This is why the visitor is empowered to exercise, on behalf of the child, the right to apply for discharge of the order.

4. But the visitor is not solely concerned with making an application to the court if he thinks this desirable. He has also the duty of "visiting, advising and befriending" the child. This implies an active, supportive role in which the visitor undertakes much the same sort of work as the voluntary workers used by some authorities to visit, *e.g.* children in long stay hospitals. It should be the aim of the local authorities to appoint persons who are willing and able to undertake this task.

The purpose of the Regulations

5. The purpose of the Regulations is not to define criteria by which a local authority may decide who is, and who is not, a suitable person to undertake a visitor's role, but solely to prescribe the conditions a person must satisfy to be an "independent person" and therefore eligible for consideration by the local authority. The Regulations will thus limit the local authority's field of choice: but they will leave it to the discretion of the local authority to decide in each case whether a person who is not disqualified by the Regulations is in other respects suitable for appointment.

6. The Regulations, and section 24 (5) of the Act, refer to a connection with a community home as a disqualification. The Act does not refer to a connection with a local authority or voluntary children's home or approved school or with a remand home. During the period up to the establishment of the community home system, however, local authorities are asked to take note of the future effect of the Regulations in this respect and to avoid appointing any person who has a connection with any one of these present establishments and who will therefore cease to be eligible for appointment when the establishment becomes a community home.

The effect of the Regulations

7. The Regulations distinguish three categories of persons who are not "independent" for the purposes of section 24 (5) of the Act and so are excluded from appointment. The categories, which are not mutually exclusive, are as follows:

(a) *those connected with the care authority*

   i.e. elected or co-opted members of the authority, or of any of its committees or sub-committees, including, *e.g.* any house committee appointed for a community home, officers of, and persons appointed by, the authority (Regulation 3 (1) (a) and (b)); all staff of the authority (Regulation 3 (1) (b), (c) and (d)); contractors (but not employees of contractors) to the authority (Regulation 3 (1) (d)); and their husbands or wives (Regulation 3 (1) (e)); voluntary workers providing services in or in respect of any community home managed by the care authority, and their husbands or wives, are excluded by Regulation 3 (2) (d) and (f); and local authority managers of any voluntary community home appointed by the care authority, and their husbands or wives, by Regulation 3 (3) (d) and (f);

(b) *those connected, through a local authority, with any community home*

   i.e. elected or co-opted members of any authority which manages one or more community homes, whether local authority homes or controlled voluntary homes, officers of, and persons appointed by, any such authority, and co-opted members of the social services committee of any such authority or of any sub-committee of the social services committee, including, *e.g.* any house committee appointed for a local authority community home (Regulation 3 (2) (a) and (b)); staff providing services in or in respect of any controlled or local authority community home or with social services duties or responsibilities generally (but not other staff) of any local authority which manages one or more local authority or controlled community homes (Regulation 3 (2) (c) and (d)); voluntary workers providing services in or in respect of any controlled or local authority community home (Regulation 3 (2) (d)); contractors (but not employees of contractors) to any controlled or local authority community home (Regulation 3 (2) (e)); and their husbands or wives (Regulation 3 (2) (f)); local authority managers of controlled or assisted homes, and their husbands or wives, are excluded by Regulation 3 (3) (d) and (f);

(c) *those connected, through a voluntary organisation, with any controlled or assisted community home*

   i.e. members of the controlling body of a voluntary organisation which provides one or more controlled or assisted community homes (Regulation 3 (3) (a)); staff of any such organisation, or voluntary workers, with duties or responsibilities in or in respect of any voluntary community home (but not other staff or voluntary workers) (Regulation 3 (3) (d)); contractors (but not employees of contractors) to any assisted community home (Regulation 3 (3) (e)); and their husbands or wives (Regulation 3 (3) (f)).

Selection of visitors

8. Local authorities may consider it appropriate to seek suitable persons to be visitors through the channels they already use to find volunteers for other work in connection with their social services, including their contacts with voluntary organisations of all kinds, whether primarily concerned with the social services or not. Men and women who have experience of work with children, and particularly with children in trouble (perhaps, *e.g.* as teachers, youth leaders, juvenile court magistrates, social workers) may, provided they are not, under the Regulations, disqualified by their current commitments, be thought most suitable and most likely to be ready to accept appointment. But it may be thought generally inappropriate to appoint a person who has been concerned in any way with the proceedings leading to the making of the care order in respect of the child he is to visit. Authorities may wish to consider whether older boys and girls should themselves be consulted about who should be appointed as their visitors.

Appointment of visitors

9. It is desirable that a visitor should receive a formal letter of appointment setting out his responsibilities and the changes in circumstances which he ought to bring to the attention of the appointing authority (since they may affect his "independence") and offering some guidance on how he should carry out his duties. A model which it is hoped local authorities will find helpful is attached to this circular.

10. The visitor's appointment ceases when the care order ceases to be in force, or if he gives notice of resignation in writing to the care authority; or if the authority gives him notice in writing terminating his appointment. If an appointment is terminated, the authority is required to appoint another visitor if the conditions requiring a visitor remain satisfied. An appointment is not, however, automatically terminated if those conditions cease to be satisfied while the care order remains in force.

Expenses of visitors

11. A visitor is entitled to have refunded to him by the care authority any expenses he reasonably incurs in visiting, advising and befriending a child or in applying to the court for the discharge of the care order.

General

12. Additional copies of this circular can be obtained from L.A.S.S. 2 Division, Department of Health and Social Security, Room 251, Horseferry House, Dean Ryle Street, London S.W.1. Copies are enclosed for the Directors of Social Services of local authorities and for the Heads of approved schools and Superintendents of remand homes.

NOTE

This circular was sent to the Clerks of county, county borough and London borough councils and the Common Council of the City of London, Clerks to the Justices, secretaries of voluntary organisations and correspondents of approved schools.

Model letter of appointment of a visitor under section 24 (5) of the children and young persons act, 1969

Dear Mr./Mrs./Miss

The Council are glad that you have agreed to accept appointment as a visitor, under section 24 (5) of the Children and Young Persons Act, 1969, to............ who is in the care of the Council under a care order and is accommodated at .... The care order was made on .... 19.. and, unless previously discharged [or extended], will cease to have effect on............ 19...

As you may know, the duty of a visitor appointed in this way is to visit, assist and befriend the child for whom he is appointed, thus providing for the child support of the kind a parent might give and exercising the active concern for his well-being a parent might show. The visitor's one formal power is his right to apply, if this seems to him desirable, to the juvenile court on behalf of the child for the discharge of the care order.

In visiting ...., you will be going into the establishment where we have placed him/her as a member of the outside community. You will not, of course, have any authority to influence the way in which the establishment generally is conducted or the treatment and education that is provided for .... Such matters are regulated by the law. But the staff of the establishment will be pleased to discuss with you ....'s progress and response to the education and treatment he/she receives within the establishment and to make mutually convenient arrangements for your visits to him/her. In your dealings with the staff you are asked to remember that many of the children in their charge may be extremely disturbed and disruptive and may make very heavy demands upon them. It will therefore be appreciated if you will try to arrange your visits to as not to interfere with the normal routine of the establishment.

The staff of my department will be glad to discuss with you our plans for...... ......'s care and his/her future, any questions you may wish to raise about his/her welfare and any matters which may arise during or from your visits to him/her which give you any cause for concern. We shall welcome your comments at any time and particularly in connection with the reviews of his/her care which the Act requires us to undertake at least once every six months.

Your appointment will continue until the care order ceases to have effect unless before then you give the Council written notice of resignation or the Council gives you notice in writing terminating it. It is an essential feature of these arrangements that you should be independent of this authority and of any community home (or, before the establishment of the community home system, of any approved school, remand home or children's home). If through any change of circumstances you cease to be an independent person, as the law requires an appointed visitor to be, it will be proper for you to resign. If, for example, a visitor (or a visitor's wife or husband) becomes a member, or enters the service, of the appointing authority or any authority or voluntary organisation which provides or manages a community home or enters personally into any contract with the appointing authority or to supply any community home, the appointing local authority should be consulted. The full definition of the circumstances in which a person is not regarded as inde- dent is set out in the Children and Young Persons (Definition of Independent Persons) Regulations, 1971. I hope you will feel free to consult me at any time should you have any doubts about any change that may occur in your circumstances.

All reasonable expenses you may incur as visitor to .... will be re- imbursed by the Council. Again, if you are in any doubt whether a particular expense would be regarded as reasonable, please feel free to consult me or one of my officers about it.

I am sending a copy of this letter to Mr./Mrs./Miss ...., who is in charge of .... where .... has been placed.

Home Office Circular No. 47/1971   *Dated September 14, 1971.*

CHILDREN AND YOUNG PERSONS ACT, 1969: SECTION 24 (5) THE CHILDREN AND YOUNG PERSONS (DEFINITION OF INDEPENDENT PERSONS) REGULATIONS, 1971

1. In D.H.S.S. Circular No. 20/1971, issued on 31 March 1971, local authorities were advised of the circumstances in which they are required by section 24 (5) of the Children and Young Persons Act, 1969, to appoint an "independent person" to be a visitor to a person in the authority's care. It was suggested, in paragraph 8 of the circular, that "men and women who have experience of work with children and particularly with children in trouble (perhaps, *e.g.* as teachers, youth leaders, juvenile court magistrates, social workers) may, provided they are not, under the Regulations, disqualified by their current commitments, be thought most suitable and most likely to be ready to accept appointment. But it may be thought generally inappropriate to appoint a person who has been concerned in any way with the proceedings leading to the making of the care order in respect of the child he is to visit."

2. It was not the intention of this circular to suggest that a juvenile court magistrate on the active list should be asked to accept appointment as a visitor where this might conflict with his judicial responsibilities. Plainly such a conflict might arise in cases where, having acted as visitor, he was called in to deal judicially with any matters subsequently arising in relation to the visited person, or where it became necessary for him to appear in his capacity as visitor either before his own or a neighbouring panel.

3. Local authorities are therefore advised that it will not generally be appropriate for them to approach, with a view to appointment as a visitor in terms of section 24 (5) of the Act, a juvenile court magistrate who is currently on the active list and whose court acts either for their own or a neighbouring local authority's area. Paragraph 8 of circular No. 20/1971 should be noted accordingly.

NOTE

Copies of this circular were sent to Clerks of county, county borough and London borough councils and the Common Council of the City of London, Clerks to Justices, secretaries of voluntary organisations, correspondents of approved schools.

Home Office Circular No. 78/1971   *Dated April 7, 1971.*

COMING INTO FORCE OF PARTS III AND V OF THE SOCIAL WORK (SCOTLAND) ACT, 1968—CROSS-BORDER ARRANGEMENTS CONCERNING CHILDREN

1. Parts III and V of the Social Work (Scotland) Act, 1968, will come into force on 15 April 1971 and the cross-border arrangements described in this circular will come into effect from that date. The Home Secretary has made an order, under section 72 (2) of the Children and Young Persons Act, 1969, specifying 15 April 1971 as the day on which the transitional provisions set out in Part II of Schedule 4 to that Act (described in Home Office Circular No. 295/1970) shall be deemed to have been repealed. Circular No. 295/1970 is accordingly cancelled with effect from 15 April 1971.

2. In this circular

"the 1968 Act" means the Social Work (Scotland) Act, 1968;
"the 1969 Act" means the Children and Young Persons Act, 1969:
"child" means a person who has not attained the age of 18, unless otherwise
   stated.

The 1968 Act—general

3. The 1968 Act establishes children's hearings which will, broadly speaking, replace juvenile courts, and provides for the appointment of officials known as reporters who will be responsible for deciding whether to refer children to hearings, for arranging such hearings and for the performance of other functions in relation to them. A child who has not attained the age of 16 may be referred to a children's hearing if there is satisfied one or more of a number of grounds, including the commission of an offence, which suggest that he may be in need of compulsory measures of care (broadly equivalent to the grounds for care proceedings in England or Wales) and it appears to the reporter that the child is in need of compulsory measures of care. A child under 16 may not be prosecuted except on the instructions of the Lord Advocate or at his instance.

4. A child over the age of 16 who has not attained the age of 18 may be referred to a children's hearing if

   (a) a supervision requirement of a hearing is already in force; or
   (b) his case has been referred to the hearing in pursuance of Part V of the
        1968 Act, which deals with the cross-border arrangements which are
        the subject of this circular.

5. A child referred to a children's hearing under the provisions of Part V of the 1968 Act is included in the definition of a child who may be in need of compulsory measures of care.

6. If a children's hearing decides that a child is in need of compulsory measures of care, they may make a supervision requirement, requiring him

   (a) to submit to supervision in accordance with such conditions as they
        may impose; or
   (b) requiring him to reside in a residential establishment. (Section 44 (1)
        of the 1968 Act which is set out in the Annex to this circular).

Supervision requirements may be varied or terminated by a children's hearing and, in any event, cease to have effect when a child attains the age of 18.

7. The remainder of this circular deals with the cross-border arrangements between Scotland and England or Wales. The relevant statutory provisions are in sections 72 to 77 of the 1968 Act (which, as amended by the 1969 Act, are set out in the Annex to this circular) and section 7A of the Criminal Justice (Scotland) Act, 1949, which was inserted by paragraph 26 of Schedule 5 to the 1969 Act.

Children subject to care orders whose parents reside or propose to reside in Scotland

8. This situation is dealt with in section 75 (2) of the 1968 Act, which applies to children subject to a care order made by a court in England or Wales and also to children committed to the care of a local authority under section 74 (3) of the 1968 Act (see paragraph 24 below) and whose parents return to Scotland. If the

child has not attained the age of 18, the local authority may refer the matter to the appropriate reporter who is required to arrange a children's hearing. (There is no power to refer the case of a person of 18 or over because Scottish supervision requirements cease at 18.) Section 76 (4) places on the local authority a duty to ensure the transfer of the child to the place notified to them by the reporter.

9. As explained in paragraph 5 above, a child so referred to the hearing is included in the definition of children who may be in need of compulsory measures of care and the children's hearing therefore has power to make a supervision requirement. Section 75 (4) provides that when a children's hearing have disposed of a case so referred to them the care order shall cease to have effect.

10. This provision of the law is not mandatory on local authorities. They retain discretion to board a child out in Scotland or to arrange for his accommodation in a residential establishment in Scotland, the child remaining in their care.

Children subject to supervision orders who reside or propose to reside in Scotland

11. This situation is dealt with in section 73 of the 1968 Act. The juvenile court is given power to

    (a) discharge the supervision order; or
    (b) send a notification to the appropriate reporter.

Section 76 (2) places on the clerk to the juvenile court a duty to ensure that all documents relating to the case, or certified copies thereof, are transmitted to the reporter.

12. On receiving such a notification the reporter is required to arrange a children's hearing (unless the supervision order was made on the occasion of a child subject to a Scottish probation order moving to England or Wales (see paragraphs 27–33 below) in which case, if the child returns to Scotland, the reporter will refer the case to the appropriate Scottish court).

13. A child whose case is so referred to the hearing is within the definition of children who may be in need of compulsory measures of care and the children's hearing may make a supervision requirement. Section 73 (3) provides that when a children's hearing have disposed of a case so referred to them the supervision order made in England or Wales shall cease to have effect.

14. Section 73 (1) enables a juvenile court to follow the same procedure in respect of a child subject to a probation order made before 1 January 1971.

15. There is no power to take any action in relation to a person of 18 or over who is subject to a supervision order and who moves to Scotland.

Children resident in, or about to move to Scotland who appear before an English court

16. Section 73 (1A) of the 1968 Act enables a court in England or Wales, if satisfied that a child in respect of whom the court proposes to make a supervision order is residing or proposes to reside in Scotland, to make the order notwithstanding the fact that the child is not habitually resident in the area of a local authority in England or Wales. The order may require the supervised person to comply with directions of the supervisor with respect to his departure to Scotland. The court is required to send notification of the order to the appropriate reporter, who is required to arrange a children's hearing. The procedure is then the same as in paragraphs 12 and 13 above.

17. The effect of the provisions described in paragraphs 8 to 16 above is that whether the child is subject to a care order, or a supervision order, or an order

of a court in England or Wales making a supervision order requiring him to comply with directions with regard to his departure to Scotland, the result is that the child appears before a children's hearing, which has discretion whether to make a supervision requirement and, if it does so, whether that requirement shall require the child to reside in a residential establishment. In these circumstances it is suggested that where a child who is resident in, or about to move to, Scotland and who has not attained the age of 17 is before a court in England or Wales and the court is of opinion that treatment in Scotland is desirable, it should consider which is the most appropriate way by which to ensure the child's appearance before a children's hearing. If the court consider that the child is likely to return to Scotland without being taken there, perhaps with the assistance of the supervisor, a supervision order under section 73 (1A) of the 1968 Act may be appropriate. If the court considers that the child should be temporarily accommodated in England or Wales and taken to Scotland, a care order may be appropriate so that the local authority may refer the case to the reporter under section 75 (2) of the Scottish Act—see paragraph 8 above.

Children subject to Scottish supervision requirements who reside or propose to reside in England or Wales

18. The procedure varies according to whether the Scottish supervision requirement includes a requirement to reside in a residential establishment. If it does not the situation is dealt with in section 72 of the 1968 Act. The children's hearing may either discharge the supervision requirement or send notification of the requirement to a juvenile court acting for the petty sessions area in which the child proposes to reside or is residing.

19. Section 76 (2) of the 1968 Act requires the reporter to ensure that all documents relating to the case or certified copies thereof are transmitted to the court.

20. The juvenile court to which such a notification is sent is given power to make a supervision order. It may do this in the child's absence (section 76 (1) of the 1968 Act) but it may not include in the supervision order a requirement under section 12 of the 1969 Act unless the child is before the court when the supervision order is made. When the case has been disposed of by the juvenile court, whether or not it makes a supervision order, the Scottish supervision requirement ceases to have effect.

21. The supervision order will cease to have effect on the expiration of one year from the date of the notification, or such shorter period as may be specified in the order, and in any case will expire when the child attains the age of 18.

22. A child subject to such a supervision order may not be dealt with under section 15 (2) of the 1969 Act *i.e.* if he attained the age of 18 he cannot be dealt with under section 15 (4) of that Act for failure to comply with any requirement of the order. This is because that subsection provides for the imposition of a fine and other punishment to which a child subject to a Scottish supervision requirement is not liable.

23. Where the Scottish supervision requirement includes a requirement to reside in a residential establishment, the children's hearing, if satisfied that his parent resides or proposes to reside in England or Wales, are required by section 74 (1) of the 1968 Act to review the requirement. On such review they may discharge or continue the requirement; vary it by removing the requirement to reside in a residential establishment and then send notification of the amended requirement to the juvenile court as in paragraph 18 above; or report the case to the Secretary of State with a recommendation for the transfer of the child to the care of a local authority in England or Wales.

23. Where such a recommendation is made the Secretary of State has power to make an order under section 74 (3) of the 1968 Act committing the child to the care of the local authority in whose area the parents of the child proposes to reside or is residing. The Department of Health and Social Security or the Welsh Office will consult the local authority before such an order is made.

25. Where such an order is made, section 74 (6) of the 1968 Act provides that it shall have effect as if it were a care order made under the 1969 Act, but shall expire when the child attains the age of 18, irrespective of whether he had attained the age of 16 when the order was made.

26. This procedure does not affect the power of a children's hearing under section 44 (1) of the 1968 Act to require a child subject to a supervision requirement to reside in a place in England or Wales while remaining subject to the Scottish supervision requirement.

Children under 17 subject to Scottish probation orders who move to England

27. As explained in paragraph 3, children of 16 and over remain liable to prosecution in Scotland and children under 16 may be prosecuted on the instructions of the Lord Advocate or at his instance. Such children may be made subject to a probation order in Scotland. Section 7A of the Criminal Justice (Scotland) Act, 1949, inserted by paragraph 26 of Schedule 5 to the 1969 Act, enables a probation order in force in relation to a child who has not attained the age of 17 to be replaced by a supervision order under the 1969 Act if the child resides or will reside in England or Wales.

28. Subsections (1) to (3) provide for notification of the order to be sent to the clerk to the justices for the petty sessions area in England or Wales in which the child resides or will reside, together with copies of the probation order and other documents and information relating to the case.

29. Subsection (4) requires the clerk to the justices to refer the notification to a juvenile court and gives the court power to make a supervision order under the 1969 Act or dismiss the case. Subsection (5) provides that when the court disposes of the case the Scottish probation order ceases to have effect.

30. The juvenile court may deal with the case in the absence of the child, but, under subsection (5), the court may not include in a supervision order a requirement under section 12 of the 1969 Act unless the child is before the court when the supervision order is made.

31. A supervision order made under this section expires at the expiration of three years, or such shorter period as may be specified in the order, beginning with the date on which the Scottish probation order was made. It may extend beyond the age of 18. In the case of a supervision order made under this section, the powers of a magistrates' court under section 15 (4) of the 1969 Act do not include the power, under paragraph (b) of that subsection, to impose any punishment which the court could have imposed for the offence in consequence of which the supervision order was made.

32. Subsections (6) and (7) deal with the powers of a Scottish court where a person subject to a supervision order made under section 7A (4) of the 1949 Act returns to Scotland and the case is notified to the Scottish court by the reporter —see paragraph 12 above.

Absconders

33. Section 70 of the 1968 Act provides for the arrest in any part of the United Kingdom and the Channel Islands of a child who is required by a supervision requirement to reside in a residential establishment and who absconds.

Addresses of reporters

34. A list of the addresses of reporters will be enclosed with this circular if it is available in time or will be forwarded as soon as possible.

33. Additional copies of this circular are being sent to clerks to local authorities for the director of social services and the financial officer.

NOTE

This circular was sent to the Clerk of Assize, the Clerk of the Peace, the Clerk to the Justices, the clerks of county, county borough and London borough councils and the Common Council of the City of London, the Secretary of Probation and After-Care Committees, the Chief Constable.

Home Office Circular No. 28/1971.   *Dated May 24, 1971.*

TRANSFERS BETWEEN ENGLAND AND NORTHERN IRELAND

1. Section 25 (1) of the 1969 Act provides for the transfer to England of a person in a training school in Northern Ireland or committed to the care of a welfare authority in Northern Ireland. If it appears to the Secretary of State, on the application of the welfare authority or the managers of the training school, that the person's parent or guardian resides or will reside in the area of a local authority in England the Secretary of State may make an order committing him to the care of that local authority. A local authority will be consulted before such an order is made.

2. Such an order will expire in accordance with the provisions of section 25 (3) (a) of the 1969 Act. Since the date on which the Northern Ireland order would have expired is a relevant factor, guidance on this will be given on each individual case when an order is made.

3. An order made under section 25 (1) cannot be extended under section 21 (1).

4. Section 25 (2) makes provision for the transfer to Northern Ireland of a person subject to a care order (other than an interim order). If it appears to the Minister of Home Affairs for Northern Ireland, on the application of the care authority, that the person's parent or guardian resides or will reside in Northern Ireland, the Minister may make an order committing him to the care of the managers of a training school or to the care of a welfare authority in whose area his parent or guardian resides or will reside. Any application by a local authority should be forwarded to the Minister of Home Affairs for Northern Ireland through this office. The application should state the address of the parent or guardian in Northern Ireland and should include full information about the child, with particular relevance to the question whether, if the Minister of Home Affairs for Northern Ireland makes an order, it should commit the child to the care of the managers of a training school or to the care of the welfare authority.

5. The Welsh Office are issuing a similar circular to local authorities in Wales.

6. Additional copies of this circular are enclosed for the director of social services and the financial officer.

NOTE

This circular was sent to the Clerk to the Authority, county councils, county borough councils, London borough councils and the Common Council of the City of London.

Home Office Circular No. 159/1971.   *Dated August 11, 1971.*

DETENTION CENTRES—REPORT OF THE ADVISORY COUNCIL ON THE PENAL SYSTEM

1. I am directed by the Secretary of State to say that he has had under consideration the report on detention centres by the Advisory Council on the Penal System ("Detention Centres", published in February 1970 by H.M. Stationery Office). The purpose of this circular is to indicate his general acceptance of the Advisory Council's recommendations and to draw the attention of the courts to a number of them, in particular those on sentencing matters.

2. The general review of the treatment of young offenders which was the subject of the first recommendation of the report is now being undertaken by the Advisory Council, who have invited evidence from organisations and individuals concerned. Pending the outcome of that review, the Secretary of State accepts the Council's view that the present powers to order detention in a detention centre should be retained. He also accepts the related recommendation that for the present the power (under section 3 of the Criminal Justice Act, 1961) to eliminate imprisonment of young offenders for six months or less should not be exercised.

3. As already announced (see the annex to Home Office Circular No. 236/1970) the Government have decided to wait until alternative facilities are available before considering whether to bring into effect the provision in the Children and Young Persons Act, 1969, which enables the power to commit boys aged 14 to 17 to detention centres to be withdrawn from the courts. Although the Council's recommendations were directed primarily to senior detention centres, they indicated that most of their recommendations could with advantage be applied to junior centres while they continue to operate. This circular may therefore be regarded as applying in general to junior as well as senior detention centres.

4. The Secretary of State endorses the Council's re-definition of the aims and philosophy of detention centres. The Council regarded the phrase "short, sharp shock", which has often been used to describe the centres, as inappropriate and open to misinterpretation. They indicated that in their view "the punitive function of detention centres should be regarded as fulfilled by the deprivation of an offender's liberty", and that treatment within the centres should be aimed at bringing about a change in the young offender's behaviour; "this requires, in short, that all aspects of the regime should be as constructive as possible". The Council recognised that "the shortness of the period in custody . . . places limitations on what can be done by way of reformation, but we are convinced that with young offenders an attempt must be made to help them towards a change of behaviour. This is perhaps most likely to be achieved by making it the aim of the staff of each centre to seek to understand each detainee, to prepare him for life in the community and to instil in him an appreciation of some of the disciplines that a populous society is bound to impose on its members. We consider that in many instances, this approach should make it possible, even within a period of a few weeks, to go at least some way towards helping a young offender to change direction".

The Regime

5. The report examined the regime of detention centres in detail and made a number of recommendations for change designed to make it more effective and consistent with the philosophy summarised above. The report recommended "that the discipline in detention centres should remain firm but that it should in general be less rigid than at present and based to a larger extent on the establishment of mutual respect. Firm discipline can be constructive". The aim will therefore be to eliminate any remaining elements of a merely punitive

approach and to move towards an understanding regime. The report noted with approval that detention centres "demand a high standard of effort". Centres will, as the report recommends, "continue to provide a full and brisk day"; but Wardens are being informed that, as the report also recommends, "individual effort should always be directed towards a constructive purpose and related to the needs, abilities and weaknesses of the particular offender".

6. The report included a number of recommendations reflecting the Council's view that "the biggest contribution towards meeting the needs of the offenders who are sent to detention centres could be made by increased provision for education". Much of what the report recommended in the educational field is already in operation at some centres; and advice is being sent to centres about the development of their educational programme to help young men develop confidence in themselves and their resources in relation to life generally on their release. Remedial education will have priority in the educational programme.

7. The report made the point "that it is noticeable that one of the greatest benefits detainees derive from detention in a detention centre is a marked increase in physical fitness", and included recommendations for a greater emphasis on physical education. These form an integral part of the proposals for the continued development of detention centres on positive lines.

8. As the report recognised, the recommendations made in it have staffing and other financial implications. There is great pressure on the resources of the penal system generally. It will not be practicable to give detention centres a larger share of the Department's resources; and it will be possible to implement the recommendations for an increase in the staffing scale only as resources permit. However, the recommendation for a full-time tutor organiser at each centre will be implemented during the current financial year.

Length of sentence and sentencing questions

9. The sections of the Advisory Council's report which deal with length of sentence and questions of selection are reproduced in Appendix A to this circular. The Secretary of State's views on these recommendations have been formed in the light of consultation with the Lord Chief Justice.

10. The Secretary of State accepts the Council's recommendation that, pending the outcome of the wider review of the treatment of young offenders, there should be no change in the powers of the courts to order detention in a detention centre (Criminal Justice Act, 1961, section 4). The Advisory Council considered (paragraph 105 of report) that the three month sentence will remain the most effective under the regime which they envisaged and which is being developed in the centres. The Secretary of State endorses this view, while recognising that cases may arise where the court will consider, in the light of the circumstances of the offence or the offender, that a longer sentence is necessary. The Secretary of State also commends to the attention of the courts the recommendation that aggregate sentences exceeding 6 months in total should be avoided.

11. The Secretary of State accepts the recommendation that there should be no further statutory limitations on the categories of offender for whom detention centres are available; at the same time, he wishes to draw particular attention to the remarks in paragraph 143 of the Council's report (in Appendix A attached). The Secretary of State takes this opportunity of reminding the courts of the recommendation made in 1968 (Home Office Circular No. 188 or 189/1968, now in Home Office Circular No. 28, 29 or 30/1971) that, before making a detention centre order, a court should, as a normal practice, consider a social enquiry report by a probation officer. The Council stressed the importance of a report

as a means of assisting the court in identifying any offender who may be unsuitable for detention centre training. Where it appears to the court that an offender may be unsuitable for detention centre training on account of physical or
mental handicap, but the information in a social enquiry report is insufficient
to enable the court to reach a decision, the court may wish to obtain a medical
report also before passing sentence. Arrangements are being negotiated to
enable medical examinations to establish physical suitability to be carried out
without delay by police surgeons at the court or in suitable accommodation
elsewhere, so as to avoid the need for a remand in custody solely for this
purpose.

12. The courts no doubt consider with particular care the question whether
an offender appearing to be mentally disturbed should be sent to a detention
centre. The view of the Sub-Committee of the Council which carried out the
review was that, while detention centres do not provide the ideal solution to the
problems of the mentally disturbed young offender, in present circumstances (*i.e.*
pending the outcome of the current young offender inquiry) disturbed young
people who are not medically or psychiatrically ill can be adequately catered
for in detention centres. The Secretary of State accepts this view. In cases of
doubt the courts will no doubt, as indicated above, obtain a medical report.

13. Another difficult problem for the courts, which the Council considered in
some detail (paragraphs 127–8 of report), is how to deal with the young offender
who has already a history of delinquent behaviour and consequent institutional
experience. The Council recognised that young people with this kind of previous
history were unlikely to derive benefit from a short spell in a detention centre,
and that they might blunt the impact of the training on others. The Council
were nevertheless reluctant to recommend that, as a matter of course, committal
of such young offenders to a detention centre should be ruled out in favour of
longer-term custodial training. They concluded, however, that in such cases
the court would be well advised to consider whether borstal training might be
more appropriate than detention in a detention centre. The Secretary of State
concurs in this approach. The Council also expressed the view that if detention
in a detention centre is to be effective it needs to be applied before the offender
has a long string of previous convictions. The Secretary of State, while not
dissenting from this view, suggests that acceptance of it should not in any way
derogate from the existing practice of the courts of considering the available
measures short of custodial treatment before passing a detention centre sentence.

After-Care
14. The Council found that on the whole detention centre after-care worked
satisfactorily, and their only recommendation for change was that steps should
be taken to effect earlier termination of the supervision, after 6 months in
most cases and earlier where this can be justified by the offender's progress
(although a maximum period of supervision of one year will continue to be
available). The Secretary of State accepts this recommendation in principle
and proposes to discuss its implementation with the Probation and After-Care
Service: a separate circular on this question will in due course be sent to
probation and after-care committees.

15. The Secretary of State wishes to draw to the attention of the courts the
Council's views on the importance of the detainee's understanding that the
sentence comprises a period in custody followed by a period under supervision.
The Council found that, while this was explained to an offender as a matter of
practice at an early stage of the period in custody, it was not always explained
when sentence was passed. They considered that "this is unfortunate: if the
offender becomes aware only subsequently of what he may regard as an additional penalty, he may harbour a feeling of resentment harmful to his treatment".

They therefore recommended "that courts, when making a detention centre order, should draw attention to the supervision provisions, with a reference to their purpose and to the possibility of early termination where this is justified by conduct and circumstances". The Secretary of State commends this practice to the courts. It will be necessary, in explaining the supervision requirements, to take into account any circumstances peculiar to the particular offender: for example, if the available information showed that the offender was still in the care of the local authority, it would be unfortunate to give him the impression that he would be liable only to the supervision requirements of a detention centre order.

Committal arrangements

16. The Secretary of State accepts the view that there is no scope for allocation procedures within the detention centre system; and detention centres will continue to receive committals direct from the courts in their areas and to deal with the widest possible range of offenders. The Secretary of State believes that implementation of the helpful recommendations in the Advisory Council's report will enable them better to achieve that aim. The existing committal areas will remain unchanged. While recently the supply of places in senior centres has, in general, been equal to the demand it remains necessary to ask courts to ascertain from the Warden in each case that there is a vacancy in the centre before passing a sentence of detention.

Visits to centres

17. The Secretary of State is aware that many of those who pass sentence already make a point of visiting establishments within the penal system; and he takes this opportunity to endorse the views of the Council on the desirability of those who sit in the courts visiting centres from time to time. Those magistrates who are members of Boards of Visitors of centres will already be in close touch with their operation; and it is hoped that others who wish to visit will approach the Warden concerned.

Detention centre rules

18. The Secretary of State proposes to lay before Parliament rules to amend the Detention Centre Rules, 1952, to provide, among other things, for the abolition of dietary punishment and of confinement to a detention room, as recommended in the Advisory Council's report.

The sentence of the court

19. The information relating to detention centres published in "The Sentence of the Court" has been revised, and a copy is attached at Appendix B. A supply of printed copies will shortly be sent for distribution on the usual basis.

20. Additional copies of this circular and its appendices are enclosed so that they may be available for the information of those who pass sentence in the courts which you serve. A limited supply of further copies may be obtained on application to the Home Office, CI Division.

NOTE

This circular was sent to the Clerk to the Justices, the Clerk of the Peace and the Clerk of Assize.

Home Office Circular No. 86/1971. *Dated April 16, 1971.*

APPEALS TO THE COURT OF APPEAL (CRIMINAL DIVISION)

A recent case suggests that there may be some misunderstanding about the procedure when application for leave to appeal is made to the Court of Appeal (Criminal Division) against an order made by the Crown Court.

An application for leave to appeal may be refused by a single judge of the Court of Appeal, in which case a notification of refusal will be sent to the appellant in the form attached to this circular. As explained on the reverse of the notification, the application may be renewed before a court of three judges if the necessary form is returned to the Registrar within 14 days. If this is not done the effect is that the application is deemed to have been refused by the full court.

Where application for leave to appeal against a care order is refused by a single judge of the Court of Appeal the right to renew the application to the full court should be explained to the child or young person and he should be given an opportunity of consulting his parents before coming to a decision. The warning in Part 6 of the notification about loss of time may be disregarded in the case of care orders because there can be no loss of time where the order terminates on the attainment of a certain age.

If a child or young person wishes to consult his parents before coming to a decision and there is difficulty about doing this within the period of 14 days, the Registrar of the Court of Appeal (Criminal Division) should be informed of the difficulty at once so that consideration can be given to asking a judge whether he will exercise his power to fix a longer period than 14 days within which the decision to renew or abandon the appeal may be taken.

NOTE

This circular was sent to the Clerks of the county, county borough and London borough councils and the Common Council of the City of London, correspondents of approved schools in England and Wales (copies sent to headmasters and headmistresses for information).

COURT OF APPEAL CRIMINAL DIVISION

Criminal Appeal Act, 1968
Form of Judge's Order under section 31   **SJ**

APPELLANT Forename(s)	Surname	Reference No.
		/ /

WHERE DETAINED	INDEX NUMBER	ADDRESS IF NOT DETAINED

ORDER by the Hon. Mr. Justice

(1) APPLICATIONS considered

    (a) EXTENSION of time   (e) Leave to be present
    (b) Leave to appeal against CONVICTION   (f) BAIL
    (c) Leave to appeal against SENTENCE   (g) WITNESS ORDER
    (d) LEGAL AID

(2) decision

direction under Criminal Appeal Act, 1968, section 29
.... days of the time spent in custody as an appellant shall not count towards sentence

/---

(3) observations to the Appellant (if leave refused).

I have considered a transcript of the relevant proceedings at the trial together with documents obtained from the Court of trial and grounds of application submitted by you or on your behalf.

Signed .... Date ....

PART 4	Form SJ sent by Registrar	PART 5	Form SJ was handed to appellant today (Signed (Officer))	Date

PART 6.   RENEWAL

loss of time. A renewal to the Court after refusal by the judge may well result in a direction for the loss of time should the court come to the conclusion that there was no justification for the renewal. If the judge has already directed that you lose time the court might direct that you lose more time.

notice to the registrar. The following applications are renewed:

Date			FOR USE IN THE CRIMINAL APPEAL OFFICE
(Signed)	(Appellant)	SJ	Received

Note

Applications refused by a judge may be renewed for consideration by the full court, or may be abandoned.

RENEWAL

Part 6 of form SJ must be used for the renewal of applications.

The form must be returned to the Registrar to reach him within 14 days of the date shown in part 4 if the appellant is not in custody or part 5 if the appellant is in custody. The appellant will receive two copies of Form SJ and should retain one. An application not renewed will be treated as if refused by the full court.

The court cannot extend the period in which you may renew. If you wish to obtain advice (not from the court), you should do so at once.

ABANDONMENT

Form "A" is required for an abandonment of an application for leave to appeal or of an application for extension of time.

Home Office Circular No. 90/1970.   *Dated August* 19, 1970.

DETENTION CENTRES FOR BOYS AGED 14 AND UNDER 17

1. I am directed by the Secretary of State to inform you that, in consequence of a sharp increase in recent months in the demands on custodial establishments administered by the Prison Department, he has been obliged to consider measures for relieving acute overcrowding at certain establishments. The pressure on Ashford Remand Centre is particularly severe and the Visiting Committee and the London Magistrates have expressed deep concern, which the Secretary of State shares, about conditions at the centre. After full consideration of the resources available to meet the urgent need for relief facilities elsewhere, the Secretary of State has come to the conclusion that this can only be provided by a rearrangement which will lead to a reduction in the number of junior detention centre places available to courts.

2. From 7 September 1970, the detention centre at Send, Woking, Surrey, will accordingly cease to be available for boys between 14 and 17 years of age and will be converted to a senior detention centre to replace Latchmere House, which will be withdrawn as a detention centre and will be used to relieve Ashford Remand Centre. The catchment areas of the junior detention centres at Campsfield House, Kidlington, Oxfordshire and Eastwood Park, Falfield, Gloucester have been re-drawn so as to make them available to the courts which at present commit to Send. The opportunity has been taken also to ease slightly the pressure on the junior detention centre at Foston Hall, Derbyshire by making an adjustment to committal areas in the Midlands. The area served by the junior centre at Kirklevington Grange, Yarm, Yorkshire is not affected.

3. The Secretary of State regrets the necessity to reduce the number of places available in junior detention centres but has been reluctantly forced to conclude that there is no feasible alternative means of meeting the overriding need to relieve the pressure on Ashford Remand Centre. The new arrangements will inevitably mean that there will be occasions when places in junior detention centres are not available to courts, particularly those in the South. The Secretary of State would be grateful for the continued co-operation of the courts in enquiring from the warden of the centre whether a vacancy is available before making an order.

4. For general convenience, the remaining junior detention centres and the courts to which each is available are set out in the annex to this circular. The Secretary of State hereby notifies you, in pursuance of section 4 (3) of the Criminal Justice Act, 1961, that each of the centres listed in the annex will be available from 7 September 1970 to the courts listed below the name of that centre for the reception of boys who have reached the age of 14 but not 17 at the time of committal. With effect from the same date he hereby cancels previous notification of availability of centres for boys of this age.

5. Separate notification has been sent to the courts concerned in the rearrangement of senior detention centre facilities which will result from the withdrawal of Latchmere House from the system.

NOTE

This circular was sent to the Clerk of Assize, the Clerk of the Peace, the Clerk to the Justices, the Chief Constable (for information), the Clerk of the County Council (for information), the Town Clerk (for information), the Children's Officer (for information).

ANNEX

Courts to which junior detention centres for boys aged 14 and under 17 are available

H.M. DETENTION CENTRE
KIRKLEVINGTON GRANGE
Yarm
Yorkshire
Tel. No. Eaglescliff 3491

All courts in the geographical counties of:
Cumberland
Durham
Northumberland
Westmorland
Yorkshire

Courts of Assize
Lancaster

Courts of quarter sessions
For the county of Lancaster, held at Lancaster and Preston
Barrow-in-Furness Borough
Blackburn Borough
Blackpool Borough
Burnley Borough

Magistrates' courts in the petty sessions areas of:
Accrington Borough
Amounderness psd
Barrow-in-Furness Borough
Blackburn Borough
Blackburn and Church psd
Blackpool Borough
Burnley Borough
Burnley and Colne psd
Clitheroe psd
Darwen psd
Fylde psd
Garstang psd
Hawkshead psd
Lancaster Borough
Leyland psd
Leyland Hundred psd
Morecambe and Heysham Borough
Nelson Borough
North Lonsdale psd
Ormskirk psd
Preston Borough
Rossendale psd
South Lonsdale and Hornby psd
Southport Borough
Southport psd
Walton-le-Dale psd

H.M. DETENTION CENTRE
FOSTON HALL
Foston
Derby
Tel. No.: Sudbury 354

All courts in the geographical counties of:
Cheshire
Derby

Lincoln
Nottingham
Anglesey
Caernarvon
Denbigh
Flint

Crown Courts
Liverpool
Manchester

Courts of quarter sessions
For the county of Lancaster, held at Liverpool and Manchester
Bolton Borough
Liverpool City
Manchester City
Oldham Borough
Salford City
Wigan Borough

Magistrates' courts in the petty sessions areas of:
Ashton-under-Lyne Borough
Ashton-under-Lyne psd
Bolton Borough
Bolton psd
Bootle Borough
Bury Borough
Bury psd
Eccles Borough
Leigh Borough
Leigh psd
Liverpool Borough
Liverpool County psd
Manchester Borough
Manchester psd
Middleton Borough psd
Oldham Borough
Oldham psd
Prescot psd
Rochdale Borough
Rochdale County psd
St. Helen's Borough
Salford Borough
Warrington Borough
Warrington psd
Widnes psd
Wigan Borough
Wigan psd

H.M. DETENTION CENTRE
CAMPSFIELD HOUSE
Kidlington
Oxford
Tel. No.: Kidlington 4113

All courts in the geographical counties of:
Buckingham
Essex

Kent
Norfolk
Oxford
Suffolk

All courts in the London Commission Areas of:
Inner London
Middlesex
North East London
South East London
South West London

All courts in the City of London

H.M. DETENTION CENTRE
EASTWOOD PARK
Falfield
Gloucestershire
Tel. No.: Falfield 445/6

All courts in the geographical counties of:
Bedford
Berkshire
Cambridge and Isle of Ely
Cornwall
Devon
Dorset
Gloucester
Hampshire
Hereford
Hertford
Huntingdon and Peterborough
Leicester
Monmouth
Northampton
Rutland
Shropshire
Somerset
Staffordshire
Surrey
Sussex
Warwick
Wiltshire
Worcester
Brecon
Cardigan
Carmarthen
Glamorgan
Merioneth
Montgomery
Pembroke
Radnor

Home Office Circular No. 40/1971.　　　　　　　*Dated February* 10, 1971.

ACCOMMODATION AT JUVENILE COURTS

1. A copy is enclosed of a circular on accommodation needs at juvenile courts which has been issued to local authorities responsible for providing court accommodation, magistrates' courts committees and probation and after-care committees. The circular sets out considerations to be borne in mind when plans for new court buildings, or for modifications to existing buildings, are being prepared.

2. It is suggested that courts using buildings which do not provide all the accommodation recommended in the circular should review their present arrangements for the accommodation of children. The object of the review would be to make arrangements according as closely as possible with those recommended in the circular and in particular, if cells or detention rooms are at present used for children who are not unruly and not likely to abscond, to explore the possibility of using other accommodation for these children.

3. Courts carrying out such a review may wish to consult the local authority social services department, the police and the probation and after-care service, in the same way as it is suggested that these services should be consulted about plans for new accommodation.

4. Extra copies of this circular are being sent to clerks of local authorities for the Director of Social Services (where he has been appointed) or Children's Officer and the Financial Officer.

NOTE

This circular was sent to the Clerk to the Justices, the Clerk of county, county borough and London borough councils and the Common Council of the City of London, the Chief Constable, the Secretary of Probation and After-Care Committees.

Home Office Circular No. 39/1971.　　　　　　　*Dated February* 10, 1971.

COURT AND PROBATION OFFICE BUILDING WORK

1. *The design of new juvenile courts*

Local authorities and magistrates' courts committees will wish to take account of the Children and Young Persons Act, 1969 in relation to the design of new courts and, so far as practicable, in the use of existing accommodation. Paragraph 8 of Home Office Circular No. 221/1970 accordingly said that a further circular would be issued about the effect of the 1969 Act on the accommodation requirements of juvenile courts. It is proposed to revise the current general guidance on juvenile court accommodation, in consultation with representatives of those who provide and use juvenile courts. In the meantime the following paragraphs set out some relevant considerations.

2. All remands, otherwise than on bail, of children and young persons in criminal proceedings, and all interim orders made in care proceedings under Part I of the 1969 Act, place the child or young person temporarily in the care of a local authority, except where a young person of 14 or over is remanded to a prison or remand centre because he is unruly. The local authority are responsible for arranging for a child or young person remanded to their care to be taken from the court and for bringing the child to the court at the expiration of the remand. Local authorities will not be able to take over at once all of the work of escorting children and young persons from courts. In cases where an appropriate representative of the local authority is not present at the court premises at the time the court makes its order, the police will be responsible for the child

or young person until the local authority receive him into their care. Arrangements for the custody and conveyance of children and young persons committed to prisons, remand centres and detention centres are not affected.

3. *Waiting accommodation at juvenile courts*
The requirements for waiting accommodation at a juvenile court are
  (a) a waiting room or area for those children who are not in custody and their parents;
  (b) a waiting room for children who are to appear before the court who are in the care of the local authority or otherwise in custody, and their escorts, or who have appeared before the court and have been committed to local authority care or made subject to some other form of order involving their detention;
  (c) a secure detention room for unruly children.

4. Rooms for purposes (a) and (b) should be ordinary rooms, preferably with windows, furnished with ordinary furniture and located convenient to the court room. If it is not practicable to provide separately for purposes (a) and (b), consideration might be given to using the same accommodation for both purposes if the only alternative would be the use of a secure detention room for children who are not unruly and not likely to abscond. At least two rooms should therefore be provided in any plans for new courts. Where the volume of juvenile court business justifies, the provision made for those in the care of the local authority or otherwise in custody may with advantage be increased to allow separation of those who have appeared before the court and are waiting conveyance, from those waiting to appear. In very busy courts some separation of boys and girls may be desirable.

5. The use of cells should be avoided except where there is no other accommodation for children whose behaviour makes the use of ordinary waiting accommodation out of the question.

6. *Accommodation for local authority officers; consultations*
The 1969 Act also enlarges the responsibilities of local authorities to provide information for juvenile courts, and provides for care orders, committing to local authority care, to replace approved school orders. Some accommodation will accordingly be needed for local authority officers attending the court.

7. The social services department of the local authority, the probation and after-care committee and the police should be consulted about any current plans for the construction of new juvenile courts or modifications to existing courts, including projects the plans for which have already been approved by the Home Office.

8. *Variation of approved plans and minor works*
Where, following consultation with the social services department and the Magistrates' Courts Committee, local authorities decide to make variations in approved plans for new courts, or to undertake minor works at existing court-houses, the work may be put in hand without prior reference to the Home Office in cases where the cost implications are small. Where such action is taken, the Home Office should be informed of the cost, or additional cost involved. Where the cost implications are more substantial, prior approval to the works or variations proposed should be sought before they are put in hand.

9. Extra copies of this circular are enclosed for the information of the Chief Financial Officer and the Architect.

NOTE
This circular was sent to the Clerk of the county council, the Town Clerk (boroughs with a separate Commission of the Peace), the Secretary of the Probation and After-Care Committee, the Clerk of the Magistrates' Courts Committee.

Home Office Circular No. 193/1970.   *Dated September 3, 1970.*

APPOINTMENT OF JUVENILE COURT PANELS

1. I am directed by the Secretary of State to inform you that the period of office of the existing panels of justices appointed to sit in the juvenile courts will end on 31 October 1970. In accordance with the Juvenile Courts (Constitution) Rules, 1954, it will be necessary for the justices, when they meet in October 1970 to elect a chairman of the justices, to appoint a new juvenile court panel to serve for 3 years from 1 November 1970.

2. Section 61 of the Children and Young Persons Act, 1969, which relates to the Lord Chancellor's powers to make rules relating to juvenile court panels and the composition of juvenile courts, has not yet been brought into force and will not affect the procedure for appointing juvenile court panels in October 1970.

3. In deciding on the size of the new panel the justices will wish to take account that, although most of the remaining provisions of the 1969 Act will come into force on 1 January 1971, these provisions will not include sections 4 and 5 of the Act, which relate to the prosecution of children and young persons. At least during the first part of the 3 year period starting on 1 November 1970, it will remain possible to prosecute children aged 10 upwards in the same way as now.

4. Every justice who is to serve on the new panel must be appointed to that panel in accordance with Rule 1 whether or not he is a member of the panel whose period of office ends on 31 October 1970.

Qualifications for appointment to the panel
Experience
5. Rule 1 (1) of the Juvenile Courts (Constitution) Rules, 1954, provides that the justices appointed to the panel shall be especially qualified for dealing with juveniles, but does not specify what special qualifications are required. The Secretary of State suggests that these include direct practical experience of dealing with young persons (*e.g.* through working with youth organisations, teaching, or welfare or similar work) and a real appreciation of the surroundings and way of life of the type of children who are likely to get into trouble.

Age
6. Rule 1 (2) requires that justices appointed to the panel shall be under 65. It is generally accepted as desirable to appoint younger justices for juvenile court work, the most suitable age for first appointment being between 30 and 40 years of age.

Size of panel
7. If a juvenile court panel is unduly large, individual members, and especially new appointments, are unable to obtain sufficient practical experience of this important and specialised work. Rule 1 (3) provides that the size of the panel shall be such as the justices think sufficient for the work, and the intention is that the number of persons appointed shall be no more than is strictly necessary, allowing each member to sit regularly. The rule allows additional members to be appointed at any time, should this prove necessary.

Combination of panels
8. In areas where the number of cases is few, and a very small panel would not enable its members to sit regularly or would make for practical difficulties in arranging juvenile courts, the justices are requested to consider the possibility of combining their panel with that of one or more neighbouring divisions. A

combination order provides greater flexibility in the arrangements for juvenile courts, enables the justices to acquire the necessary experience, facilitates the appointment to the panel of justices whose age and personal qualities make them particularly suited to the juvenile court, and makes it possible for juvenile courts to sit more often than they are able to do in many rural areas at present. The effect of a combination order is limited to providing that, for the purpose of the 1954 Rules, the petty sessional divisions concerned are deemed to be one and that the justices for these areas are deemed to be justices for a single area. In all other respects the petty sessional divisions continue to exist as separate areas. Any Bench which considers that it would be desirable to combine its panel with that of one or more neighbouring divisions should approach the Magistrates' Courts Committee with a view to their recommending a combination order.

Election of chairman and deputy chairman

9. Rule 9 (1) requires members of the panel, on the occasion of their appointment or soon afterwards, to meet and elect from among their number, by secret ballot, a chairman and as many deputy chairmen as may be necessary to ensure that each juvenile court in the area sits under the chairmanship of such a person. The Secretary of State understands that in some areas justices appoint as many deputy chairmen as there are courts in the area. In view of the importance of having skilled and experienced chairmen and deputy chairmen, the number elected should be related to the volume of work rather than to the number of courts, which may mean that a chairman or deputy chairman will hear cases in more than one court.

Notification to the Secretary of State

10. When the new appointments have been made, the Secretary of State would be glad if, in accordance witn Rule 8, you would send on the attached form the names, addresses and ages of the justices appointed to the panel and, if any should be appointed from another petty sessional division under Rule 1 (4), the name of that division. The justices elected as chairmen or deputy chairmen should be indicated on the form. Similar information should be supplied for any subsequent appointment to the panel. If, after appointment, a justice ceases to be a member of the panel, the Secretary of State should be informed of his name and of the reason why he ceases to be a member in accordance with Rule 8 (b).

NOTE

This circular was sent to the Clerk to the Justices, the Clerk of the Peace (for information), the Clerk of the Magistrates' Court Committee (for information).

Home Office Circular No. 294/1970.   *Dated December 22, 1970.*

HOME OFFICE CHILDREN'S DEPARTMENT—CHANGES IN MINISTERIAL RESPONSIBILITY

1. I am directed by the Secretary of State to refer to Home Office Circular No. 238/1970 about the Government's decision that responsibility for the child care services should be transferred from the Home Secretary to the Secretary of State for Social Services and the Secretary of State for Wales on 1 January 1971. This circular gives further particulars of the allocation of Ministerial responsibilities from that date for work previously carried out by the children's Department of the Home Office.

2. The division of functions is set out in detail in the Annex to this circular. In outline, the responsibilities of the three Secretaries of State will be as follows:

(i) *The Secretary of State for Social Services*
In England and Wales:

(a) approved schools ⎫   (pending their integration into the
(b) remand homes ⎭   system of community homes to be established under Part II of the Children and Young Persons Act, 1969)
(c) youth treatment centres   (section 64, Children and Young Persons Act, 1969)

In England alone:
(d) the child care functions of local authority social services departments
(e) the work of voluntary bodies in the field of child care
(f) the employment of children of compulsory school age

(ii) *The Secretary of State for Wales*
Items (d), (e), and (f) above in relation to Wales.

(iii) *The Home Secretary*
(g) the functions of the courts, the police and the probation and after-care service in relation to children and young persons, and the law on these matters.
(h) adoption, guardianship and legitimacy (subject to review after the Departmental Committee on the Adoption of Children has reported).

On matters which are the concern of the three Secretaries of State (*e.g.* liaison between the police and local authorities, functions under Part I of the 1969 Act) the three Departments will act in concert, and action will be taken jointly, or by one Department after consultation with the others. The three Secretaries of State, with the Secretaries of State for Education and Science and for Scotland, and the appropriate Ministers of the Northern Ireland Government, will be jointly concerned with the work of the new Central Council for Education and Training in Social Work.

3. The Children's Department Inspectorate will transfer to the Department of Health and Social Security (the Inspectorate serving Wales will transfer to the Welsh Office), but will continue to give professional advice to, and act on behalf of, the Home Office in matters which are to remain the responsibility of the Home Secretary.

4. In consequence of these changes communications to the central Government—

(a) (i) from courts, chief officers of police and representatives of the probation and after-care service on matters relating to children; and
(ii) from other correspondents on the work of the courts, the police or the probation and after-care service in relation to children
should continue to be addressed to the Home Office for both England and Wales:
(b) from all correspondents on matters relating to approved schools, remand homes and youth treatment centres, and on child care training should be addressed to the Department of Health and Social

Security for both England and Wales (further advice about communications on training will be issued in connection with the establishment of the new Council);

  (c)   (i) from local authorities in relation to the child care functions of their social services departments;

       (ii) from voluntary organisations in relation to their child care activities;

     (iii) from local education authorities in relation to the employment of children of or under compulsory school age; and

     (iv) from other correspondents in relation to any of the matters in (i), (ii) or (iii) above

should be addressed to the Department of Health and Social Security for England and to the Welsh Office for Wales.

5. The operation of the arrangements outlined in this circular will be kept under review, and further guidance will be issued if necessary.

6. These changes in Ministerial responsibility will take effect on 1 January 1971, but the staff concerned will not move to new locations for some time thereafter. From the same date the functions at present carried out jointly for the three Secretaries of State by the Interdepartmental Social Work Group will become the sole responsibility of the Secretaries of State for Social Services and for Wales in England and Wales respectively. Particulars of the administrative arrangements that will operate from 1 January will be the subject of further circulars.

7. Extra copies of this circular are being sent to clerks to Children's Authorities for the Director-designate of Social Services, the Children's Officer and the Finance Officer, and to secretaries of probation and after-care committees for principal probation officers and senior probation officers in charge of areas.

NOTE

This circular was sent to the Clerk of Assize, the Clerk of the Peace, the Clerk to the Justices, the Clerk of county, county borough and London borough councils and the Common Council of the City of London, the Chief Constable, the Secretary of Probation and After-Care Committees, the correspondent (approved schools), the secretaries of voluntary organisations.

ANNEX

1. This annex sets out in more detail the division of functions described in paragraph 2 of the circular. There will be close consultation between the three Departments on matters of common concern, and communications on these matters should be addressed in accordance with the advice given in paragraph 4 of the circular.

2. The descriptions and statutory references in the following lists are not exhaustive, but indicate the main functions and relevant provisions. In particular, the inclusion of an enactment under a particular heading does not necessarily mean that *all* its provisions are relevant to the functions described under that heading, but only that it contains some relevant provisions.

A. *Matters for which D.H.S.S. will be responsible in England and the Welsh Office in Wales*

Description of function	*Main statutes containing relevant provisions*
Duty of local authority to assume care of children. Assumption by local authority of parental rights. Treatment, accommodation and maintenance of children in care. Contributions by parents towards the cost of maintaining children in care. Registration of voluntary children's homes. Planning and provision of community homes.	Children and Young Persons Act, 1933, Part II and sections 86–89. Children Act, 1948. Children and Young Persons Act, 1969, Parts II and III, Schedule 2.

Description of function	*Main statutes containing relevant provisions*
Promotion of welfare of children.	Children and Young Persons Act, 1963, section 1.
Grants to voluntary child care organisations.	Children Act, 1948, section 46.
Advisory Council on Child Care.	Children Act, 1948, section 43.
Capital Investment control over child care projects (other than approved school and remand home projects).	Local Government Act, 1933, Part IX.
Authorisation of compulsory purchase.	Local Government Act, 1933 Children Act, 1948. Children and Young Persons Act, 1969, section 68.
Protection of privately placed foster children.	Children Act, 1958 (as amended by the 1969 Act).
Employment of children of or under compulsory school age.	Children and Young Persons Act, 1933, Part II. Children and Young Persons Act, 1963, Part II.
Transfer of children to and from Scotland and Northern Ireland; accommodation of children from Channel Islands and Isle of Man by local authorities.	Children and Young Persons Act, 1969, section 25 and 26. Social Work (Scotland) Act, 1968, sections 74 and 75.
Child care research.	Children and Young Persons Act, 1963, section 45.
Returns of statistical and other information on child care.	Children and Young Persons Act, 1969, section 63.
(*Note.* Circulars requesting returns will continue to give the address to which they should be submitted.)	

B. *Matters for which D.H.S.S. will be responsible in both England and Wales*

Description of function	*Main statutes containing relevant provisions*
Provision, management and discontinuance of approved schools and remand homes (including capital investment control).	Children and Young Persons Act, 1933, Part IV. Children and Young Persons Act, 1969, section 46 and Schedule 3.
Youth treatment centres.	Children and Young Persons Act, 1969, section 64.
Child care training.	Children Act, 1948.

C. *Matters for which the Home Office will remain responsible*

Description of function	*Main enactments containing relevant provisions*
Constitution, powers and procedure of juvenile courts. Appeals from juvenile courts. Statistics of proceedings in juvenile courts.	Children and Young Persons Act, 1933, Part III. Children and Young Persons Act, 1963, Part I (section 16 onwards), Schedule 2. Children and Young Persons Act, 1969, section 33 and Schedule 1, section 63 so far as it relates to juvenile courts.
Provisions in Criminal Justice Acts and magistrates' courts' legislation relating to children and young persons.	
Exercise of the Royal prerogative of mercy in relation to persons under 17.	
The criminal law in relation to offences by, or against, children.	Children and Young Persons Act, 1933, Part I.

Description of function	*Main enactments containing relevant provisions*
Junior attendance centres.	Criminal Justice Act, 1948, section 19.
Action to prevent removal from the jurisdiction of children who are wards of court or whose removal is prohibited by a court order or injunction.	
Research into delinquency and the work of the courts.	Criminal Justice Act, 1948, section 77.
The Community Development Project.	

Note. The Prison Department of the Home Office remains responsible for borstals, detention centres and remand centres in which young persons under 17 are detained.

D. *Matters which will remain of joint departmental concern*

For functions listed under this heading the Home Office will retain overall responsibility for the law, and responsibility for the work of the courts, the police and the probation and after-care service. D.H.S.S. and the Welsh Office will be responsible for the work of local authorities and voluntary organisations in these fields. These two aspects are closely inter-related, and the three Departments will act jointly or, where the necessary action falls to one or two of the Depratments, after consultation with the other(s).

Description of function	*Main enactments containing relevant provisions*
Care proceedings in juvenile courts. Powers and duties of the police, local authorities and the probation and after-care service in relation to court proceedings affecting children under 17, and to children in trouble, whether offenders or not. Care and supervision of children in accordance with court orders.	Children and Young Persons Act, 1969, Part I.
Accommodation of children ordered to be detained under section 53 of the Children and Young Persons Act, 1933.	Section 53 of the 1933 Act.
Discontinuance of probation homes and hostels for persons under 17.	Children and Young Persons Act, 1969, section 46 and Schedule 3.
*Adoption.	Adoption Act, 1958.
*Guardianship.	Guardianship of Infants Acts, 1886–1925.
*Legitimacy.	Legitimacy Acts, 1926 and 1959.

* Subject to later review—see paragraph 2 (h) of the circular.

Home Office Circular No. 26/1971.   *Dated May 4, 1971.*

YOUTH TREATMENT CENTRES

1. I enclose a copy of the booklet about Youth Treatment Centres which has recently been published by Her Majesty's Stationery Office as a guide to the facilities that these new establishments will provide.

2. Youth Treatment Centres are a new and experimental form of child care establishments that are to be directly provided and run by the Secretary of State for Social Services for severely disturbed and damaged children. They are the establishments referred to in paragraph 23 of Home Office Circular No. 237/1969 and in respect of which Home Office Circulars Nos. 81/1970 (in the case of Clerks to local authorities) and 82/1970 (in the case of Correspondents of

approved schools) were issued. They are intended primarily for children in the care of local authorities (but may also accommodate children convicted of grave crimes and ordered to be detained under section 53 of the Children and Young Persons Act, 1933).

3. It is planned that there should eventually be 3 Youth Treatment Centres, offering a total of 200 places. The first, St. Charles, Brentwood, Essex, which is an adaptation of existing buildings is now completed. The other 2 centres will be purpose built, one in the Midlands and the other in the North: it is not expected that these will be ready until 1974–75.

Qualifications for admission
4. The booklet covers in detail the type, age range and treatment needs of the kind of child for whom these Centres are intended (Chapters I and VI and Annex III), together with the scope and basis of the treatment which will be provided (Chapters II and III). The information in these chapters should be regarded as providing a frame of reference for the guidance of local authorities when considering whether to seek a placement for a child in their care at a Youth Treatment Centre. In addition further background information is given in the later chapters on such matters as design and buildings, staffing and re-search, all of which will help in filling out the picture of what these establish-ments will be trying to do for this minority of severely disturbed and anti-social children.

St. Charles youth treatment centre, Brentwood
5. The first of the three proposed Centres is now ready to receive children. There are places at St. Charles for 48 boys and girls. The full address of St. Charles is Weald Road, Brentwood, Essex (telephone no. Brentwood 225684) and the Medical Director is Dr. F. P. Stephens, M.B., B.S., L.R.C.P., M.R.C.S., D.P.M. (But applications for places should *not* be made direct to the Centre, but in accordance with the procedure set out in paragraph 7 below.)

Age range for St. Charles
6. As stated in paragraph 57 of the booklet, the normal minimum age for admission to the Centres will be 12. Children may continue to be accommo-dated in the Centres up to the maximum limit of duration of the care order to which the boy or girl is subject (either the 18th or 19th birthday depending on the age at which the child came into care), but for the present it is not intended that St. Charles should accommodate children after the 16th birthday.

Admission procedure
7. Admission of children in local authority care will be on the basis of applications made to this Department by the local authority's Director of Social Services. Applications should be addressed to the Under Secretary of State, Department of Health and Social Security, Local Authority Social Services Division, Horseferry House, Dean Ryle Street, London, S.W.1. (As already indicated above, applications should not be made direct to St. Charles.) It should be noted that the number of places will be very limited. The maximum number planned at present is 200, and for some years only 48 will be available (at St. Charles, Brentwood). Admission will therefore have to be limited to children for whom there is clearly a critical need for the specialised treatment the Centres will aim to provide.

8. To assist the Department in the difficult task of allocating places to the children most in need of this treatment, it will be necessary that each application should be accompanied by comprehensive information about the child, in the form set out in the Annex to this circular. In addition to *current* reports obtained specifically for the application, it would be helpful if copies could be

provided of any previous school, case conference, psychologist's and psychiatrist's reports which are available. (Since it will be necessary to copy within the Department all papers submitted in connection with an application it would be appreciated if the papers could, wherever possible, be in suitable form for photocopying, *i.e.* originals, sharp carbons or bold photocopies. All papers submitted with an application will be returned afterwards.)

9. Attention is drawn to Part II of the annexed form. Because of the risk of possible embarrassment or distress to the family it is not intended that special enquiries should be made for the purpose of completing this part of the form. There should be included only such information as is already available on the child's case papers.

10. Where an application is urgent submission need not be delayed only because some items of information are not immediately available; advice may be obtained from Mr. B. A. E. Harrold or Mr. G. M. Rix at this office (telephone number 01–834 6655 extensions 754 and 231 respectively). In such cases however any outstanding items should be supplied as soon as possible later.

11. After an application has been submitted the Director of Social Services will be informed as soon as practicable whether admission has been approved. At the same time all papers submitted in connection with the application will be returned.

Charges

12. The charge payable by a local authority for a child in its care accommodated at a Youth Treatment Centre will be £40 per week for the years 1971/72 and 1972/73. This is less than the estimated full economic cost, which will be high because of the high staffing ratio and intensive care facilities necessary for this severely disturbed group of children. But the charge has been fixed at this level for the remainder of the current rate support grant period in view of the fact that it was not taken into account as relevant expenditure for the purpose of calculating grant for this period. The position will be reviewed before the end of the period, and after 1972/73, when the cost of accommodating children in Youth Treatment Centres will have been taken into account as relevant expenditure for the purposes of calculating rate support grant, it is envisaged that an amount approximating to the full economic cost will be charged.

13. The weekly charge should be regarded as all-inclusive, to broadly the same extent as flat rate covers a child accommodated at an approved school: that is it will cover diet, accommodation, an adequate and reasonable wardrobe, educational, therapeutic and recreational facilities and pocket money. If the care authority wishes to have provision made for anything over and above what is covered by the weekly charge, and the extra items or facilities are regarded as acceptable to the Medical Director in the interests of the treatment needs of the child, the cost will be a matter for the care authority to bear. Weekly allowances to parents towards the maintenance of children on home leave (Home Office Circulars Nos. 244/1967 and 176/1970 refer) will be met by the Centre: but charges incurred in transporting a child to or from the Centre or recovering an absentee will fall to be borne by the care authority.

Accounts

14. The care authority will be sent an account at intervals by the Centre. Payment should be remitted direct to the Centre, not to this Department.

Parental contributions

15. Parental contributions in respect of a child in care accommodated at a Centre will fall to be paid to the care authority in the normal way. Similarly in the case of a child in care at a Centre who is allowed to take employment outside the Centre, the care authority may require a contribution from the child's

earnings—see paragraph 28 of Home Office Circular No. 255/1970 about the consequences of the abolition of the approved school order—and this contribution will be payable to the care authority.

Responsibilities of local authority

16. Attention is drawn to the fact that a child who is in the care of a local authority and who is admitted to a Centre will remain formally in the care of that authority, in the same way as he would if placed by the authority in any other establishment; and the care authority will retain all its existing statutory rights and obligations in relation to the child, as for instance the "visitor provisions" of section 24 of the 1969 Act—see D.H.S.S. Circular 20/1971 of 31 March 1971.

Other interested bodies

17. While, as indicated above, applications for admission to Youth Treatment Centres should be made by local authority Directors of Social Services for the children in their care, arrangements are being made for this booklet to be brought to the notice of hospitals (including psychiatric hospitals), special schools for maladjusted children and child guidance clinics, since these establishments may be concerned with the treatment of children in care who might benefit from this new facility, and it is desirable that they should be aware of it.

18. While the courts will have no power to commit a child to a Youth Treatment Centre, their attention is being drawn to the facilities potentially available at these Centres for children in care and for children subject to orders under section 53 of the Children and Young Persons Act, 1933.

Research

19. As indicated in Chapter VIII of the booklet, research will form an important element of the work of the Centres. At this stage it is too early to give any indication of the specific areas or directions which research will take. But as a basic common requirement for any future research project related to the children at the Centres and their treatment, it will be essential from the outset for comprehensive and planned records to be kept not only on each child's progress but also on all material factors relating to his family and home background. In this connection the particulars submitted with the original application for admission will be of considerable relevance. It may be however that further particulars will be found to be needed to provide adequate material for research purposes, not only on cases of children admitted to the Centres, but also—for control purposes—in respect of a cross section of children not accepted for admission. It is hoped that in these circumstances local authorities will feel able to make facilities available from time to time for research workers associated with the Centres to have access to relevant local authority data.

20. Copies of this circular and the booklet are enclosed for the Director of Social Services and the Treasurer.

NOTE

This circular was sent to councils of counties, county boroughs and London boroughs in England and Wales (copies for the information of the Director of Social Services and the Treasurer), and correspondents of approved schools in England and Wales (copies for information to heads of schools).

I. Form of application for admission of a child in care to St. Charles
Youth Treatment Centre

Name . . . .

Address . . . .

Date of birth . . . .

Religion .... Place of birth........................
Local authority responsible ....
Child's present placement...
Brief description of physical appearance ....

II. Home circumstances

Including (where known without having to make special enquiries) family history of physical and mental illness, alcoholism, drug abuse and criminality.

Mother ....
Father ....
Siblings ....
Others in house or involved ....
Description of home...
Neighbourhood ....
Socio-economic background ....
Social class ....

III. Family relationships

Including reference to relationship with mother, father, siblings, grandparents and significant others; and also relationship of father with mother.

IV. Personal history

Chronological account from birth, including major events, traumas, accidents, changes, separations, moves, court appearances and agencies involved and placements away from home.

V. School history

Including factual account and also reference to relationship with staff, with peers, attendance, attitudes, application, specific difficulties. Description of special education if any.

VI. Medical and psychological history

Including physical illness and psychological disorders, with reference to clinic and hospital attendance and admissions, and also including reference to specialist examination such as EEG.

VII. Current situation

This will include a description of difficult, disturbed and deviant behaviour and symptoms of emotional disturbance which may have led up to current presenting picture. Where there has been absenteeism from a residential establishment even if only overnight or shorter, full details should be given, including the name and type of the establishment and the length of absence.

VIII. Observed behaviour (in present residential setting)

(a) Group response ....
(b) Individual response...
(c) Attitude to staff and authority.....................................
(d) Attitude to family ....
(e) Attitude to peers ....

(f) Attitude to school work ....

(g) Leisure...

(h) General picture ....

IX. PSYCHOLOGIST'S REPORT

1. Intellectual assessment (Test result date) ....

2. Educational tests ....

3. Personality tests ....

4. Special tests. *E.g.* for brain damage, perceptual difficulties research ....
....

5. Observations ....

X. PSYCHIATRIST'S REPORT

XI. ANY FURTHER INFORMATION OR OBSERVATIONS

Home Office Circular No. 285/1970.   *Dated December 30, 1970.*

CHILDREN AND YOUNG PERSONS ACT, 1969: PARENTAL CONTRIBUTIONS

1. This circular deals with the changes in the law on parental contributions which will be made when most of Part I of the Children and Young Persons Act, 1969, comes into force on 1 January 1971. In this circular the term "child" includes "young persons", "the 1933 Act" means the Children and Young Persons Act, 1933, and "the 1969 Act" means the Children and Young Persons Act, 1969.

2. The two main changes are as follows:

(a) The provisions of the existing law which impose a duty to contribute in respect of children subject to fit person orders and approved school orders are amended so that they apply to children subject to care orders.

(b) A limit to the amount of the weekly contribution is introduced by section 62 of the 1969 Act which also lays down a new procedure which must be followed before a contribution order can be made.

Accordingly, from 1 January 1971, the duty to make contributions applies in respect of a child received into care under section 1 of the Children Act, 1948 or a child subject to a care order which is not an interim order. The persons liable to make contributions are specified in section 24 of the Children Act, 1948, which is unchanged.

Contributions

3. Section 86 of the 1933 Act and section 23 of the Children Act, 1948, are amended by paragraphs 8 and 16 of Schedule 5 to the 1969 Act and are subject to the repeals in Schedule 6 to that Act.

4. The local authority to which contributions are payable by the person required to make them is the council of the county or county borough within

which that person is for the time being residing (section 86 (3) of the 1933 Act). Where that authority is not responsible for the child's maintenance the provisions of paragraph 2 of Schedule VIII to the Local Government Act, 1958 (which require contributions to be paid over to the authority responsible for maintenance) will apply. Local authorities will not be required to pay over to the Secretary of State payments made in respect of children accommodated in approved schools if these payments relate to a period after 1 January 1971.

5. Section 62 (3) of the 1969 Act provides that the amount of a contribution shall be such as may be proposed by the care authority and agreed by the contributory or, in default of agreement, as may be determined in court proceedings. Subsection (4) provides that the maximum contribution which may be proposed shall be a weekly amount equal to the weekly amount which, in the opinion of the care authority, they would normally be prepared to pay if a child of the same age were boarded out by them (whether or not the child in respect of whom the contribution is proposed is in fact so boarded out and, if he is, whether or not the local authority are in fact paying that amount). The amount is that which the authority would "normally" be prepared to pay. This disregards exceptional cases where the local authority may pay a foster parent less than the normal amount (because the foster parent is prepared to accept this) or more than the normal amount in the case of a particular child.

6. Section 87 of the 1933 Act, as amended by paragraph 9 of Schedule 5 to the 1969 Act, empowers a magistrates' court, on the application of the local authority to which contributions are payable, and subject to section 62 of the 1969 Act, to make a contribution order on any person who is liable to make contributions in respect of the child. The court may make an order requiring that person to contribute such weekly sum as the court having regard to his means thinks fit, subject to section 62 (6) of the 1969 Act (see paragraph 8 below).

7. Section 62 (5) provides that no contribution order shall be made unless the care authority have, by notice in writing to the contributory, proposed an amount and, either the contributory and the local authority have not, within the period of one month beginning with the day on which the notice was given, agreed on the amount of the contribution or the contributory has defaulted in making one or more contributions of an amount which has been agreed. It is suggested that where the care authority is not the authority to which contributions are payable, the care authority should send the other authority a copy of the notice and should notify that authority of any agreement or failure to agree. Alternatively the care authority might arrange for the other authority to give notice on their behalf, in which case the notice should state that it is given on behalf of the care authority.

8. Section 62 (6) provides that in proceedings for a contribution order, the court shall not order a contributory to pay a contribution greater than that proposed in the notice. It will be necessary for an authority which applies for a contribution order (where it is not the care authority) to inform the court of the amount proposed by the care authority. The court may order the contribution of a lesser sum if, having regard to the contributory's means, it thinks fit. Section 62 (7) similarly provides that in proceedings for the variation of a contribution order the care authority shall specify (to the court) the amount which they propose and the court shall not vary the order so as to require a contribution greater than that amount. Where the authority which appears in the proceedings is not the care authority it will again be for it to inform the court of the amount proposed by the care authority.

9. A contribution order remains in force for as long as the child is in the care of the local authority concerned (section 87 (3) of the 1933 Act as amended by paragraph 9 (3) of Schedule 5 to the 1969 Act), subject to the provisions of section 24 of the Children Act, 1948. Section 62 (2) of the 1969 Act, which is already in force, provides that, whether or not a contribution order has been

made, no contribution shall be payable in respect of a child for any period during which he is allowed by the local authority, under the provisions of section 13 (2) of the 1948 Act as substituted by section 49 of the 1969 Act, to be under the charge and control of a parent, guardian, relative or friend, although remaining in the care of the local authority. This replaces a similar provision in section 5 of the Family Allowances and National Insurance Act, 1956, applying to children subject to fit person orders. The circumstances to which it relates are to be distinguished from those in which a child is boarded out, under the provisions of section 13 (1) (a) of the 1948 Act and the Boarding-Out of Children Regulations, 1955, with a relative.

Jurisdiction
10. Application for a contribution order may be made to a magistrates' court acting for the area in which the proposed contributory resides (section 87 (1) of the 1933 Act) or, where he resides in Scotland or Northern Ireland, to a magistrates' court having jurisdiction in the area of the local authority which is entitled to receive the contributions, which in these cases is the care authority (Schedule 1 to the Maintenance Orders Act, 1950).

Affiliation orders
11. Section 88 of the 1933 Act is amended by paragraph 10 of Schedule 5 to the 1969 Act. The effect of the section as so amended, together with section 23 of the Children Act, 1948 (as amended), is that where a child is in the care of a local authority under section 1 of the Children Act, 1948, or under a care order which is not an interim order, a magistrates' court may order payments under an affiliation order for the child's maintenance which is already in force to be made to the local authority entitled to receive contributions. Subsection (4) of section 88, as amended by paragraph 10 (3) of Schedule 5 to the 1969 Act, provides that such an order shall not remain in force (except for the purpose of recovery of arrears) after the child or young person to whom that order relates has ceased to be subject to the care order, or ceased to be in the care of a local authority under section 1 of the Children Act, 1948, as the case may be, or, in either case, while he is allowed by the local authority to be under the charge and control of a parent, guardian, relative or friend although remaining in the care of the local authority.

12. Section 26 of the Children Act, 1948 (which enables a local authority to apply for an affiliation order in certain circumstances) is amended by paragraph 17 of Schedule 5 to the 1969 Act and is subject to the repeals in Schedule 6. The section as amended enables a local authority to apply for an affiliation order where an illegitimate child is in the care of the authority under section 1 of the Children Act, 1948 or by virtue of a care order which is not an interim order.

Transitional provisions—children who on 1 January 1971 are the subject of fit person orders naming a fit person who is not a local authority
13. Paragraph 9 of Schedule 4 to the 1969 Act provides that nothing in that Act shall affect the operation of any enactment in relation to an order committing the child to the care of a fit person other than a local authority and in force on 1 January 1971. The existing law in sections 86, 87 and 88 of the 1933 Act will continue to apply to such cases and to any contribution orders made in respect of them. Section 62 of the 1969 Act does not apply.

Transitional provisions—children who are deemed to be subject to care orders on 1 January 1971
14. Where a parent is voluntarily paying a contribution which is in excess of the amount which the local authority could propose under section 62 (3) of the 1969 Act, the local authority should propose a fresh contribution which does not

exceed the maximum prescribed by that subsection. Where the parent is paying voluntarily a contribution which is less than this maximum no action will be required unless subsequently it is decided that a higher amount should be requested, when an amount should be proposed in accordance with section 62 (5).

Transitional provisions—children who are deemed to be the subject of care orders on 1 January 1971 and in respect of whom a contribution order is in force

15. The effect of the transitional provision in paragraph 6 of Schedule 3 to the Children and Young Persons Act, 1969 (Commencement No. 3) Order, 1970 (a copy of which was enclosed with Home Office Circular No. 236/1970) is that the contribution order remains in force. This is so even if the amount of the contribution specified in the order exceeds the maximum which could be proposed by the local authority under section 62 (4) of the 1969 Act. It will be open to a contributory, after 1 January 1971, to apply for the variation of the order, when the local authority would be required, by section 62 (7), to specify the weekly amount which, having regard to subsection (4), they propose should be the amount of the contribution. It is suggested that, in cases where the amount of the contribution specified in a contribution order is in excess of the maximum which may be proposed under section 62 (4), the local authority should not leave it to the parents to apply for a variation of the order but should themselves propose a new contribution not exceeding the maximum.

Transitional provisions—orders under section 88 of the 1933 Act, or affiliation orders made by virtue of section 26 of the Children Act, 1948, which are in force on 1 January in respect of children who are deemed to be subject to care orders

16. Any order made under section 88 of the 1933 Act is preserved by paragraph 7 (6) of Schedule 4 (where the order was made in respect of a child formerly subject to an approved school order) and paragraph 8 (2) of Schedule 4 (where the order was made in respect of a child previously subject to a fit person order committing him to the care of a local authority). The orders are deemed to have been made, by virtue of the care order, under section 88 as modified by the 1969 Act.

17. Where an affiliation order has been made on the application of the local authority under section 26 of the Children Act, 1948, or where an affiliation order has been revived under subsection (4) of that section, the order is preserved by paragraph 6 of Schedule 3 to the Children and Young Persons Act, 1969 (Commencement No. 3) Order, 1970. The order will have effect as if made by virtue of, or revived under, section 26 as modified by the 1969 Act.

Arrears

18. Paragraph 50 of Schedule 5 to the 1969 Act makes consequential amendments to section 30 of the Children and Young Persons Act, 1963, the principal effect of which is that arrears orders under that section are treated as contribution orders, and payments made under them as contributions, for the purposes of section 62 of the 1969 Act.

Form of contribution order

19. Form 54 in Schedule 2 to the Magistrates' Courts (Children and Young Persons) Rules, 1970 is designed for the majority of cases, where the care authority is also the authority to whom contributions are payable. Where this is not the case the form should be adapted accordingly.

20. Additional copies are enclosed for the Children's Officer and Financial Officer of local authorities.

NOTE

This circular was sent to the Clerk of county, county borough and London borough councils and the Common Council of the City of London, the Clerk to the Justices.

DIVISION 2

CHILD PROTECTION

CONTENTS

SECTION 1.—INTRODUCTORY NOTE

All children brought up by others than their parents are to a greater or lesser extent unfortunate. Some of the most unfortunate of these have been neglected in their foster-homes, some actively ill-treated and caused to suffer mentally as well as physically. Many women have handed their children to others to bring up, and it would be undesirable to prohibit a mother who is unable to care for her own child from choosing its foster home and making her own arrangements for maintaining contact with it; the child must however be protected from serious neglect and cruelty. Women who are willing, for a variety of reasons and often for very small payments, to provide accommodation for children, may do so from widely differing motives, some good and some not so good.

It is possible to afford some measure of protection to the children involved in these transactions. Child Protection aims at a degree of oversight without actually taking the child into care. The provisions of the Public Health Act, 1936, as extended by s. 35 of the Children Act, 1948, required the notification to the welfare authority of the reception of children of compulsory school age who are maintained for reward and laid down the duty of this authority to " make enquiry whether there are any persons residing in their area who undertake the nursing and maintenance of foster children " for reward.

Welfare authorities exercised supervision over such foster children taken by foster parents for reward. Persons receiving foster children had to give notice to the welfare authority of the receipt of foster children, and of removal or death. Certain exemptions were provided for, such as, to give only one instance, children boarded out under the Children Act, 1948, s. 13, p. 893, *post*, where the local authority was a "fit person," in which case its own officers were accustomed to visit the foster parents and to keep in touch with the foster child.

The welfare authority can take steps to prevent over-crowding where there are foster children and to prevent their being kept in places or by persons unsuitable for them. Child protection visitors have the right to visit, and magistrates' courts may make orders that children be removed.

These provisions were administered under the Children Act, 1948.

An enquiry undertaken in 1946 revealed that there were about a quarter of a million children in this country deprived of a normal home life, living either in foster homes or in institutions. Many foster parents and institutions were doing excellent work, but some very disturbing conditions were revealed. The Curtis Committee was appointed and reported in 1946.

The Children Act, 1948, implemented the principal recommendations of the Curtis Report (Report of the Care of Children Committee) and the Scottish Committee on Homeless Children. The Act replaced the provisions of the former Poor Law which dealt with children who were destitute, abandoned, neglected, or living in such conditions as to require the local authority to take action. The Poor Law was abolished by the National Assistance Act, 1948, which came into force simultaneously with the Children Act, on July 5, 1948.

The Children Act laid down the administrative arrangements which the local authority were to adopt for discharging their functions under this Act, together with similar functions for the care or welfare of children under certain other Acts, especially the Children and Young Persons Act, 1933, and it concentrated under the Home Office the central control over the maintenance and care of children in England and Wales, which was previously divided between the Home Office and the Ministry of Health.

A new department of local government was created, the administrative head of which was known as the Children's Officer. All councils of county boroughs and counties appointed children's committees, with the power to co-opt interested, informed people, to administer the Act. The appointment of a Children's Officer would be made only after consultation with the Home Office.

The Act provides " for the care or welfare, up to the age of eighteen and, in certain cases, for further periods, of boys and girls when they are without parents or have been lost or abandoned by, or are living away from their parents, or when their parents are unfit or unable to take care of them . . ." The first section places upon a local authority the duty to receive such children into care. Here there is no compulsory power, no forcible taking of the child, but a reception into care not against the wish of the parent, guardian, or other person having charge of him. Nor, once having received the child, does an authority under this section have any power to keep him should his parent or guardian wish to remove him from care. Indeed it is laid down that an authority shall endeavour to find a friend or relative willing to give him a home.

Should the home conditions of the child be so bad that a local authority is of the opinion that he should be removed, despite opposition from those having care of him, an order of the court must be obtained under the Children and Young Persons Act, 1969, and even if the child is already in the care of the authority under s. 1, he can only be retained against the parents' wishes if this retention is upheld by the Court. Subject to the provisions of s. 2, a local authority may pass a resolution in respect of a child in care assuming parental rights and powers. If the parent serves notice of objection, the resolution lapses unless the local authority applies by way of complaint to a juvenile court for the resolution to be upheld. In such case, therefore, it is the juvenile court which decides between the local authority and the parent, and the court will regard the welfare of the child as the first and paramount consideration. Normally a resolution remains in force until the child becomes eighteen years of age, but at any time application may be made to a juvenile court for its rescission or the local authority may rescind it if that will be for the benefit of the child.

Irrespective of whether a child came into care voluntarily or under a Court order, it is the duty of the authority having a child in its care " to exercise their powers with respect to him so as to further his best interests, and to afford him opportunity for the proper development of his character and abilities " and to " make such use of facilities and services available for children in care of their own parents as appears to the local authority reasonable in his case " (Children Act, 1948, s. 12).

Where a local authority lacks suitable accommodation for a particular case, the help of voluntary associations may be enlisted to supply the special needs and environment. The importance of the contribution which voluntary homes and associations can make to the welfare of the deprived child is recognized, and Part IV of the Act is devoted to them. The homes are to be registered and inspected by the Home Office, and the local authority will cause the children to be visited. Grants may be made by the central authority for the improvement of their premises and the recruitment of better-qualified staffs (s. 46).

The Act set up " a council, to be known as the Advisory Council on Child Care, for the purpose of advising the Secretary of State," and also laid down that money shall be provided for the training of persons in child care.

The Children Act, 1958, which came into force on April 1, 1959, repealed and re-enacted with modifications the child life protection provisions in the Public Health Acts and the Children Act, 1948. Section 1 of the 1958 Act requires a local authority to ensure the well-being of foster children as defined in s. 2 by causing officers of the authority to visit the children and advise on their care. A person proposing to maintain a foster child must give fourteen days' notice instead of seven days' as previously required by s. 3. Section 4 gives power to officers of the local authority to visit foster children, and to the local authority to impose requirements as to, or to prohibit, the keeping of foster children. By s. 5 a person aggrieved by such a requirement or prohibition may appeal to a juvenile court. The power of a court to order the removal of a foster child from unsuitable surroundings is to be exercised by a juvenile court, and not, as previously, by an ordinary magistrates' court. On proof of imminent danger to the health or well-being of the child the power may be exercised by a justice of the peace (s. 7). A child so removed may be received into care by a local authority under s. 1 of the Children Act, 1948, p. 880, *post*, whether or not his circumstances fall within paras. (a) to (c), and notwithstanding that he may appear to be over the age of seventeen. Refusal to allow a foster child to be visited, or premises to be inspected, is to be treated as giving reasonable cause for suspicion of unnecessary suffering to, or the commission of certain offences against, the child so as to enable a warrant to be issued to search for and remove him under s. 40 of the Children and Young Persons Act, 1933, p. 47, *ante*. Section 11 gives the right of appeal to the Crown Court from a removal order under s. 7, and from any other order made under Part I of the Act.

Part II of the Act, and the First Schedule, amended the provisions of the Adoption Act, 1950, but before the Act came into force, Part II and the First Schedule were repealed and substantially re-enacted by the Adoption Act, 1958, pp. 1026 *et seq.*, *post*, which came into force on the same date.

The Nurseries and Child-Minders Regulation Act, 1948, is intended to ensure that children are well cared for when at nurseries of a particular class, the scope of which is roughly indicated by the description " day nurseries," or when in the care of a child-minder. Nurseries are within the Act if they are places where children below the upper limit of compulsory school age are looked after by the day or for an aggregate period of two hours or more or for longer periods up to six days, whether for reward or not, and are premises which are not wholly or mainly used as private dwellings, nor within the exemptions in respect of hospitals and schools, etc. The distinction between nurseries on the one hand and child-minders on the other is kept throughout the Act and is emphasised by registration being in respect of the premises in the former case, and in

respect of the person in the latter case: other principal distinctions between the two classes of cases are the different age limits of the children
concerned, and the condition of taking reward which is only material to
the case of the child-minder.

The general method of regulation and supervision is by requiring
registration with the local health authority, and by conferring on that
authority powers of entry and inspection and of imposing requirements by
order, and of prosecuting for non-compliance.

It is an offence under the Act to carry on a nursery within the scope
of the Act unless the premises are registered, or for a person to act as a
child-minder of three or more children, to whom he is not related, from
more than one household unless he is registered. A registered child-
minder who acquires a new home must give notice to the local authority
and until he does so is treated as unregistered in relation to the reception
of children in the new home.

Where a local authority propose to refuse or cancel a registration or
to impose requirements the applicant, occupier or person registered,
must be given an opportunity of being heard by the authority and, if
aggrieved by the authority's decision, may appeal to a magistrates' court.
A further right of appeal lies from that court to quarter sessions.

The local health authority's authorised inspector may enter a nursery
at any reasonable time and carry out an inspection of the children, the
arrangements for their welfare and the records kept concerning them.
There is no such unqualified power to enter the home of a registered
child-minder, but if the inspector is refused admission, or if he reasonably
suspects that children are received in the home of a person who is not
but ought to be registered, or in any other premises in breach of the Act,
he may obtain a warrant from a justice of the peace, authorising him to
enter and carry out an inspection. Obstructing an inspector is an
offence leading to penalties.

Hospitals and certain other institutions which are subject to supervision under other statutes or which are provided by public authorities,
are exempt from registration as nurseries.

Prosecutions for offences under the Act may be instituted by the local
health authority.

A Home Office Memorandum dated September 20, 1955, deals generally
with the care of children under five.

Following upon recommendations made by the Ingleby Committee
(Cmnd. 1191) s. 1 of the Children and Young Persons Act, 1963, (p. 91,
ante) extended the power of local authorities to promote the welfare of
children by making available advice, guidance and assistance, and in
other respects. See the Introductory Note to that Act, (pp. 87, et seq.,
ante).

The duty of local authorities to make provision for homes for children
in care under the Children Act, 1948, has needed substantial revision in
view of the comprehensive system of community homes envisaged in the
Children and Young Persons Act, 1969. Local authorities are required to
give effect to regional plans for the provision of homes and ss. 13 and 19
are re-enacted to take account of the changes. Children remanded in
care and children subject to a care order may be accommodated in community homes, they may also be allowed to be in the care of their parents.
The duty to further a child's best interest is modified so that where

necessary the interests of the public may be taken into account. Complex transitional provisions in respect of existing establishments are necessary and at present approved schools and remand homes still exist although the definition of community homes is modified as regards the transitional period.

Substantial changes have been brought about by the Local Authority Social Services Act, 1970, and the Children and Young Persons Act, 1969. The former Act, following the recommendations of the Report of the Committee on Local Authority and Allied Personal Social Services, Cmnd. 3703 (The Seebohm Report) transfers functions under the Acts of 1948 and 1958 to a social services committee, and the director of social services replaces the children's officer.

The Act of 1969 recognised that weaknesses had become apparent as the demand for foster homes increased. The amendment of s. 1 of the Children Act, 1958, relieves local authorities of the heavy burden of visiting irrespective of whether supervision is needed or not. The amendments to s. 2, in particular the omission of the words "for reward for a period exceeding one month" are extremely important. The absence of reward is not evidence that a person is suitable as a foster parent. Similarly *de facto* adoptions are brought into the scope of the Act. Since no payment was received the child was not protected by the Act, and in many cases no adoption application was made and the protection afforded by the provisions of the Adoption Act did not apply either. It is sometimes difficult to prove the receipt of payment especially where the child's parents are unwilling to give evidence. The repeal of the words "for a period of one month" means that any person other than a relative or guardian or proposed adoptive parent (with some exceptions) who undertakes the care and maintenance of a child becomes a foster parent. Children whose care and maintenance were undertaken for a period of seven days to a month, were not protected by either the 1948 or 1958 Acts.

PUBLIC HEALTH ACT, 1936
[26 Geo. 5 & 1 Edw. 8, c. 49]

Notification of births

203. Provision for early notification of births.—(1) In the case of every child born it shall be the duty of the father of the child, if at the time of the birth he is actually residing on the premises where the birth takes place, and of any person in attendance upon the mother at the time of, or within six hours after, the birth, to give notice of the birth in manner provided by this section to the medical officer of health of the welfare authority for the area in which the birth takes place.

(2) Notice under this section shall be given either by posting within thirty-six hours after the birth a pre-paid letter or postcard addressed to the medical officer of health at his office or residence and containing the required information, or by delivering within the said period at that officer's office or residence a written notice containing the required information, and a welfare authority shall, upon application being made to them, supply without charge to any medical practitioner or midwife residing or practising within their area prepaid addressed envelopes together with the forms of notice.

(3) Any person who fails to give notice of a birth in accordance with this section shall be liable to a fine not exceeding twenty shillings, unless he satisfies the court that he believed, and had reasonable grounds for believing, that notice had been duly given by some other person.

(4) [*Repealed by the National Health Service Act,* 1946.]

(5) The requirements of this section with respect to the notification of births shall be in addition to, and not in substitution for, the requirements of any Act relating to the registration of births.

(6) A registrar of births and deaths shall, for the purpose of obtaining information concerning births which have occurred in his sub-district, have access at all reasonable times to notices of births received by a medical officer of health under this section, or to any book in which those notices may be recorded.

(7) This section shall apply to any child which has issued forth from its mother after the expiration of the twenty-eighth week of pregnancy, whether alive or dead.

NOTES

This section is printed as amended by the National Health Service Act, 1946, and the Public Health (Notification of Births) Act, 1965.

" **Premises.**"—By s. 343; 26 Halsbury's Statutes, 3rd Edn., 379, premises include messuages, buildings, lands, easements and hereditaments of any tenure.

" **Welfare authority.**"—See the National Health Service Act, 1946, ss. 19 and 22.

" **Required information.**"—Presumably this means the particulars of the birth.

PART XII

285. Service of notices, etc.—Any notice, order, consent, demand or other document which is required or authorised by or under this Act to be given to or served on any person may, in any case for which no other provision is made by this Act, be given or served either—

(a) by delivering it to that person ; or

(b) in the case of a coroner, or a medical officer of health, by leaving it or sending it in a prepaid letter addressed to him, at either his residence or his office and, in the case of any other officer of a council, by leaving it or sending it in a prepaid letter addressed to him, at his office ; or

(c) in the case of any other person, by leaving it or sending it in a prepaid letter addressed to him, at his usual or last known residence ; or

(d) in the case of an incorporated company or body, by delivering it to their secretary or clerk at their registered or principal office, or by sending it in a prepaid letter addressed to him at that office ; or

(e) in the case of a document to be given to or served on a person as being the owner of any premises by virtue of the fact that he receives the rackrent thereof as agent for another, or would so receive it if the premises were let at a rackrent, by leaving it, or sending it in a prepaid letter addressed to him, at his place of business ; or

(f) in the case of a document to be given to or served on the owner or the occupier of any premises, if it is not practicable after reasonable inquiry to ascertain the name and address of the person to or on whom it should be given or served, or if the premises are unoccupied, by addressing it to the person concerned by the description of " owner " or " occupier " of the premises (naming them) to which it relates, and delivering it to some person on the premises, or, if there is no person on the premises to whom it can be delivered, by affixing it, or a copy of it, to some conspicuous part of the premises.

NOTES

" **Proof of service.**"—In proceedings before justices service of process may be proved by declaration or certificate in the form prescribed by the Magistrates' Courts Rules, 1968, rule 55, and the Magistrates' Courts (Forms) Rules, 1968, forms 140 to 143.

"**Residence.**"—In *R.* v. *Braithwaite*, [1918] 2 K. B. 319; 82 J. P. 242, it was held by the Court of Appeal that, under a somewhat similar section of the Public Health Act, 1875; 26 Halsbury's Statutes, 3rd Edn., 38, authorising service of documents at the residence of the person, a summons for rates was properly served at the defendant's place of business. This must be considered doubtful authority in the ordinary case. Although the section does not require service by recorded delivery, it may be better practice to serve a summons by that method.

Prosecution of offences, etc.

296. Summary proceedings for offences.—All offences under this Act may be prosecuted under the Summary Jurisdiction Acts.

NOTE

The Summary Jurisdiction Acts were almost entirely repealed by the Magistrates' Courts Act, 1952; 21 Halsbury's Statutes, 3rd Edn., 181. Proceedings are now governed by that Act and the Magistrates' Courts Rules, 1968 (S.I. 1968 No. 1919 p. 540, *ante*).

298. Restriction on right to prosecute.—Proceedings in respect of an offence created by or under this Act shall not, without the written consent of the Attorney-General, be taken by any person other than a party aggrieved, or a council or a body whose function it is to enforce the provisions or byelaws in question, or by whom or by whose predecessors the byelaw in question was made.

NOTE

In England and Wales a local authority may institute proceedings for any offence under the provisions relating to child life protection in Part VII of the Children Act, 1948, s. 55 (1), p. 920, *post*.

Appeals and other applications to courts of summary jurisdiction, and appeals to the Crown Court

300. Appeals and applications to courts of summary jurisdiction. —(1) Where any enactment in this Act provides—

(a) for an appeal to a court of summary jurisdiction against a requirement, refusal or other decision of a council; or

(b) for any matter to be determined by, or an application in respect of any matter to be made to, a court of summary jurisdiction,

the procedure shall be by way of complaint for an order, and the Summary Jurisdiction Acts shall apply to the proceedings.

(2) The time within which any such appeal may be brought shall be twenty-one days from the date on which notice of the council's requirement, refusal or other decision was served upon the person desiring to appeal, and for the purposes of this subsection the making of the complaint shall be deemed to be the bringing of the appeal.

(3) In any case where such an appeal lies, the document notifying to the person concerned the decision of the council in the matter shall state the right of appeal to a court of summary jurisdiction and the time within which such an appeal may be brought.

NOTES

Nurseries and Child-Minders Regulation Act, 1948.—This section applies for the purposes of s. 6 of that Act, p. 945, *post*, which relates to appeals, as if the provisions of that Act were contained in this Act (the Public Health Act, 1936) and the last mentioned Act extended to London.

" Enactment."—This includes any enactment in a provisional order confirmed by Parliament (Public Health Act, 1936, s. 343; 26 Halsbury's Statutes, 3rd Edn., 379).

Summary Jurisdiction Acts.—Now the Magistrates' Courts Act, 1952 and 1952 Rules (S.I. 1952 No. 2190).

Appeal to court of summary jurisdiction.—See also Magistrates' Courts Rules, 1968, rule 30, and Magistrates' Courts Act, 1952, ss. 43 *et seq.*; 32 Halsbury's Statutes, 2nd Edn., 456.

301. Appeals to the Crown Court against decisions of justices.— Subject as hereinafter provided, where a person aggrieved by any order, determination or other decision of a court of summary jurisdiction under this Act is not by any other enactment authorised to appeal to the Crown Court, he may appeal to such a court:

Provided that nothing in this section shall be construed as conferring a right of appeal from the decision of a court of summary jurisdiction in any case if each of the parties concerned might under this Act have required that the dispute should be determined by arbitration instead of by such a court.

NOTES

This section is printed as amended by the Courts Act, 1971, s. 56 and Sched. IX.

Nurseries and Child-Minders Regulation Act, 1948.—This section applies for the purposes of s. 6 of that Act, p. 945, *post*, which relates to appeals, as if the provisions of that Act were contained in this Act (the Public Health Act, 1936) and the last mentioned Act extended to London.

Appeals.—There is a general right of appeal to the Crown Court from convictions and sentences of courts of summary jurisdiction, under s. 83 of the Magistrates' Courts Act, 1952; 21 Halsbury's Statutes, 3rd Edn., 254, but no such general right of appeal against orders. This section, however, confers a right of appeal against orders under the Public Health Act, 1936.

For procedure on appeal, see the Crown Court Rules, p. 654, and Magistrates' Courts Rules, 1968, rule 62, p. 559, *ante*.

" **Enactment.**"—See note to s. 300, p. 874, *ante*.

302. Effect of decision of court upon an appeal.—Where upon an appeal under this Act a court varies or reverses any decision of a council, it shall be the duty of the council to give effect to the order of the court and, in particular, to grant or issue any necessary consent, certificate or other document, and to make any necessary entry in any register.

NOTE

Nurseries and Child-Minders Regulation Act, 1948.—This section applies for the purposes of s. 6 of that Act, p. 945, *post*, which relates to appeals, as if the provisions of that Act were contained in this Act (the Public Health Act, 1936) and the last mentioned Act extended to London.

347. Short title, date of commencement, and extent.—(1) This Act may be cited as the Public Health Act, 1936,

(2) This Act shall not extend to Scotland nor, except as otherwise expressly provided, to Northern Ireland.

NOTE

This section is printed as amended by the S.L.R. Act, 1950, and the London Government Act, 1963; 20 Halsbury's Statutes, 3rd Edn., 448.

NATIONAL HEALTH SERVICE ACT, 1946

[9 & 10 Geo. 6, c. 81]

Part III

Health Services Provided by Local Health Authorities

19. Local health authorities.—(1) Subject to the provisions of this section, the local authority for the purposes of this Part of this Act, who shall be called the "local health authority", shall for each county be the council of the county and for each county borough be the council of the county borough.

(2) Where it appears to the Minister to be expedient in the interests of the efficiency of any services provided by local health authorities, whether under this Part of this Act or under any other enactment conferring functions on any local health authority in their capacity as such an authority, that a joint board should be established for the areas of two or more local health authorities for the purpose of performing all or any of the functions of those authorities, the Minister may by order constitute a joint board consisting of members appointed by those authorities and provide for the exercise by the board, in lieu of the authorities, of such of the said functions as may be specified in the order:

Provided that the Minister shall not make such an order except after a local inquiry, unless all the authorities for the areas concerned have consented to the making of the order.

(3) The provisions of Part I of the Fourth Schedule to this Act shall have effect with respect to joint boards constituted under this section, and to orders constituting such joint boards and the provisions of Part II of the Fourth Schedule to this Act shall have effect with respect to health committees of local health authorities.

22. Care of mothers and young children.—(1) It shall be the duty of every local health authority to make arrangements for the care, including in particular dental care, of expectant and nursing mothers and of children who have not attained the age of five years and are not attending primary schools maintained by a local education authority.

(2) The local health authority may, with the approval of the Minister, make and recover from persons availing themselves of the services provided under this section such charges (if any) in respect of residential accommodation, food or articles provided as the authority consider reasonable, having regard to the means of those persons.

(3) The local health authority shall be the welfare authority for the purposes of section two hundred and three of the Public Health Act, 1936.

(4) Regulations may provide, in the case of areas where, under Part III of the First Schedule to the Education Act, 1944, schemes of divisional administration relating to the functions of local education authorities with respect to school health services are in force, for the making, variation and revocation of corresponding schemes of divisional administration relating to the functions of local health authorities under subsection (1) of this section with respect to the care of children who have not attained the age of five years and are not attending primary schools maintained by a local education authority, and the functions of such authorities under subsection (3) of this section.

(5) A local health authority may, with the approval of the Minister, contribute to any voluntary organisation formed for any of the purposes mentioned in subsection (1) of this section.

NOTES

This section is printed as amended by the Children Act, 1948, the National Health Service (Amendment) Act, 1949 and the London Government Act, 1963.

" Local health authority."—As to the meaning of local health authority, see s. 19, p. 876, *ante.*

" Charges."—These may be recovered summarily as a civil debt (s. 71; 23 Halsbury's Statutes, 3rd Edn., 77).

" Welfare authority."—For s. 203 of the Public Health Act, 1936, see p. 872, *ante.*

Education Act, 1944, Sched. I, Part III.—11 Halsbury's Statutes, 3rd Edn., 268.

" Voluntary."—This means not carried on for profit and not provided by a local or public authority (s. 79 (1); 23 Halsbury's Statutes, 3rd Edn., 80).

24. Health visiting.—(1) It shall be the duty of every local health authority to make provision in their area for the visiting of persons in their homes by visitors, to be called " health visitors," for the purpose of giving advice as to the care of young children, persons suffering from illness and expectant or nursing mothers, and as to the measures necessary to prevent the spread of infection.

(2) The duty of a local health authority under this section may be discharged by making arrangements with voluntary organisations for the employment by those organisations of health visitors or by themselves employing health visitors.

NOTES

" Local health authority."—As to the meaning of local health authority, see s. 19, p. 876, *ante.*

" Voluntary."—This means not carried on for profit and not provided by a local or public authority (s. 79 (1); 23 Halsbury's Statutes, 3rd Edn., 80).

SECTION 4.—CHILDREN ACT, 1948

CHILDREN ACT, 1948
[11 & 12 Geo. 6, c. 43]

ARRANGEMENT OF SECTIONS

Part I

Duty of Local Authorities to assume Care of Children

Part II

Treatment of Children in care of Local Authorities

Part III

Contributions towards Maintenance of Children

PART IV

VOLUNTARY HOMES AND VOLUNTARY ORGANISATIONS

PART V

CHILD LIFE PROTECTION

35–37. [*Repealed by the Children Act,* 1958]

PART VI

ADMINISTRATIVE AND FINANCIAL PROVISIONS

PART VII

MISCELLANEOUS AND GENERAL

An Act to make further provision for the care or welfare, up to the age of eighteen and, in certain cases, for further periods, of boys and girls when they are without parents or have been lost or abandoned by, or are living away from, their parents, or when their parents are unfit or unable to take care of them, and in certain other circumstances; to amend the Children and Young Persons Act, 1933, the Children and Young Persons (Scotland) Act, 1937, the Guardianship of Infants Act, 1925, and certain other enactments relating to children; and for purposes connected with the matters aforesaid. [*30th June*, 1948.]

NOTE

Scotland.—The whole of this Act is repealed as to Scotland (Social Work (Scotland) Act, 1968, s. 95 (2) and Sched. IX, Part 1).

Local authorities.—The council of each London borough shall as respects the borough, and the Common Council shall as respects the City, have the functions of the council of a county borough under this Act and be the local authority for such purposes of this Act as refer to a local authority. London Government Act, 1963; s. 47; 20 Halsbury's Statutes, 3rd Edn., 504.

PART I

DUTY OF LOCAL AUTHORITIES TO ASSUME CARE OF CHILDREN

1. Duty of local authority to provide for orphans, deserted children, etc.—(1) Where it appears to a local authority with respect to a child in their area appearing to them to be under the age of seventeen—

- (a) that he has neither parent nor guardian or has been and remains abandoned by his parents or guardian or is lost; or
- (b) that his parents or guardian are, for the time being or permanently, prevented by reason of mental or bodily disease or infirmity or other incapacity or any other circumstances from providing for his proper accommodation, maintenance and upbringing; and
- (c) in either case, that the intervention of the local authority under this section is necessary in the interests of the welfare of the child,

it shall be the duty of the local authority to receive the child into their care under this section.

(2) Where a local authority have received a child into their care under this section, it shall, subject to the provisions of this Part of this Act, be their duty to keep the child in their care so long as the welfare of the child appears to them to require it and the child has not attained the age of eighteen.

(3) Nothing in this section shall authorise a local authority to keep a child in their care under this section if any parent or guardian desires to take over the care of the child, and the local authority, shall, in all cases where it appears to them consistent with the welfare of the child so to do, endeavour to secure that the care of the child is taken over either—

- (a) by a parent or guardian of his, or

(b) by a relative or friend of his, being, where possible, a person of the same religious persuasion as the child or who gives an undertaking that the child will be brought up in that religious persuasion.

(4) Where a local authority receive a child into their care under this section who is then ordinarily resident in the area of another local authority,—

(a) that other local authority may at any time not later than three months after the determination (whether by agreement between the authorities or in accordance with the following provisions of this subsection) of the ordinary residence of the child, or with the concurrence of the first-mentioned authority at any subsequent time, take over the care of the child; and

(b) the first-mentioned authority may recover from the other authority any expenses duly incurred by them under Part II of this Act in respect of him (including any expenses so incurred after he has ceased to be a child and, if the other authority take over the care of him, including also any travelling or other expenses incurred in connection with the taking-over).

Any question arising under this subsection as to the ordinary residence of a child shall be determined by the Secretary of State and in this section any reference to another local authority includes a reference to a local authority in Scotland.

(5) In determining for the purposes of the last foregoing subsection the ordinary residence of any child, any period during which he resided in any place as an inmate of a school or other institution, or in accordance with the requirements of a supervision order or probation order or supervision requirement or the conditions of a recognisance, or while boarded out under this Act, the Poor Law Act, 1930, the Children and Young Persons Act, 1933, the Poor Law (Scotland) Act, 1934, or the Children and Young Persons (Scotland) Act, 1937 or Part II of the Social Work (Scotland) Act, 1968 by a local authority or education authority shall be disregarded.

NOTES

This section is printed as amended by the Social Work (Scotland) Act, 1968, ss. 95, 97, 98 and Sched. VIII.

As to the duty of the local authority to provide temporary accommodation under the National Assistance Act, 1948, see s. 21 (1) (b) of that Act; 23 Halsbury's Statutes, 3rd Edn., 638.

As to the allocation of functions between local authority and local education authority, see Rules made under s. 21 of this Act (S.I. 1951 No. 472), p. 977, *post*.

"**Local authority.**"—See s. 38, *post*. The Local Government Grants (Social Need) Act, 1969, s. 1, provides for grants to local authorities who in the exercise of any of their functions are required to incur expenditure by reason of the existence in any urban area of any social need.

Authorise a local authority to keep a child.—There is no absolute duty on a local authority to return a child placed by them with foster parents, pursuant to s. 1 (1) (b), to its father (*Krishnan* v. *London Borough of Sutton*, [1970] Ch. 181; [1969] 3 All E. R. 1367; 134 J. P. 75).

"**Education authority.**"—See definition of local education authority in s. 59, p. 923, *post*.

"**Child.**"—By s. 59 (1), *post*, " child " is defined as meaning a person under the age of eighteen and any person who has attained that age and is the subject of a care order within the meaning of the Children and Young Persons Act, 1969. The duty to receive a child into care imposed by the present subsection (except in the case of children received on the closing of a voluntary home (s. 29 (6), *post*)) is restricted to persons appearing to be under seventeen, but once a person has been so received he may be retained in the local authority's care until he is eighteen or later if he is the subject of a care order.

" **Parent or guardian.**"—For definition, see ss. 9 and 59 (1), *post*. See also s. 6 (2), *post*.

Rights of parent.—In *Re A. B. (an Infant)*, [1954] 2 All E. R. 287, an illegitimate child in care of the local authority had been boarded out. The putative father, who had married, wished to take over the child and this was the wish of the mother. The foster parents objected, and ultimately the case came before the Divisional Court. The court held that as the child was to be returned to the local authority if they demanded it, and as the council was satisfied that the mother desired to take over the care of the child, the mother should be given the care, the manner in which she would take care of the child being a matter for her. In *Krishnan v. London Borough of Sutton*, [1970] Ch. 181; [1969] 3 All E. R. 1367; 134 J. P. 75 the father of a child received into care and placed with foster parents applied for interim injunctions, *inter alia*, ordering the local authority to remove the child from the foster parents and return her to him. The application was dismissed and the father applied for an injunction restraining the local authority from harbouring the child at the residence of the foster parents. This application was dismissed and the father appealed against the dismissal of both applications.

Both appeals were dismissed and it was held:

(i) as s. 1 (3) imposed no absolute duty on the local authority to retain the child the court could not order the local authority to hand over the child regardless of circumstances;

(ii) even if the court had a discretion to make such an order, it should not be made because it would or might be practicably impossible, as the foster parents were not parties to the proceedings, for the local authority to carry it out, as it might well involve the use of force on unwilling and resistant foster parents and also because of a wardship decision;

(iii) the father had not made out a sufficient case of harbouring by the local authority;

(iv) an order to the local authority not to continue to harbour the child would be nugatory as she was living with the foster parents, and

(v) even if the court had a discretion to make such an order, it could not possibly do so in the circumstances of the case.

" **Abandoned.**"—This implies " leaving the child to its fate " (*Mitchell v. Wright* (1905), 7 F. (Ct. of Sess.) 568, *per* the Lord President, at p. 574 : and see *Re O'Hara*, [1900] 2 I. R. 232, C. A. See also observations in *Watson v. Nikolaisen*, [1955] 2 Q. B. 286 ; [1955] 2 All E. R. 427, a case under the Adoption Act, 1950. See also note " Abandoned " to s. 2, p. 885, *post*.

" **Welfare.**"—The child's welfare is an overriding consideration in all cases. As to the meaning of " welfare " in relation to a child, see *Re McGrath (Infants)*, [1893] 1 Ch. 143, where LINDLEY, L. J., said that " the welfare of a child is not to be measured by money only or by physical comfort only. The word " welfare " must be taken in its widest sense. The moral and religious welfare of the child must be considered as well as its physical well-being. Nor can the ties of affection be disregarded."

" **Receive.**"—It is to be noted that the duty of the local authority is to receive a child into care, not to take it. Where it is considered necessary to take a child, *e.g.* from a bad home or neglectful parents, action must be taken under some statutory authority such as s. 1 of the Children and Young Persons Act, 1969, p. 130, *ante*.

" **Care.**"—This word is not defined in the Act, but would appear to connote actual physical control or possession. Cf. s. 17 of the Children and Young Persons Act, 1933, where it is distinguished from " custody " and " charge "; and see *Brooks v. Blount*, [1923] 1 K. B. 257.

Attainment of age.—See note at p. 53, *ante*.

" **Relative.**"—For definition, see s. 59 (1), *post*.

" **Ordinarily resident.**"—Volition is, in general, an essential of residence, but this is apparently not so in the case of an infant of tender years who is incapable of the necessary volition. See *Re X. Y.*, [1937] Ch. 337, C. A., where it was held that in relation to a pauper lunatic "residence" must mean residence in fact even though the pauper in question was incapable of any volition. Whether the decision is applicable to the case of a child of tender years under the Children Act, 1948, is a matter which only the High Court can decide.

Residence in another area.—The duty to receive a child into care rests with the authority in whose area the child is found, irrespective of his ordinary residence; if he is to be transferred to the authority in whose area he normally resides he should be removed within three months.

Expenses incurred after he has ceased to be a child.—*I.e.*, normally after he has attained the age of eighteen; see s. 59 (1), p. 923, *post*. The expenses which a local authority may incur under Part II of the Act in respect of persons over eighteen are the cost of hostel accommodation provided under s. 19, *post*, and of financial assistance towards the cost of maintenance, education and training under s. 20, *post*.

Protected child.—See s. 43 (3) of the Adoption Act, 1958, p. 1073, *post*, as to receiving a " protected child " into care.

Mental Health Act, 1959.—See s. 9, *ibid.*, p. 442, *ante*, as to the functions of local authorities with reference to children who are or have been suffering from mental disorder.

High Court.—Where a local authority had received a child into care under this section, and was acting within the authority's powers under this Act, it was held that the Court had no right to review the decisions of the authority on what was for the benefit of the child, notwithstanding that the Act was not expressed to bind the Crown. *Re M. (an infant)*, [1961] Ch. 81, [1961] 1 All E. R. 201 ; 125 J. P. 163.

In *Re G. (Infants)*, (1963), 3 All E. R. 370 ; 127 J. P. 549 an order was made for access by both parents at the discretion of the local authority, this order being made under the prerogative jurisdiction of the court in supplementation of the local authority's statutory discretion under this section. Where a child is in the care of a local authority and is to continue in care under this section, and is also a ward of court, the court should exercise its prerogative jurisdiction consistently with the local authority's continuing to have the statutory care of the child with the discretion which this Act confers unimpaired, and should ensure that the limitation to which the local authority's care and discretion were subjected by the Act did not operate to the prejudice of the child, and that, if the local authority's care were terminated, then the court's power and discretion should immediately be brought to bear on the situation (as e.g. by means of an undertaking by the local authority to apply to the court for directions before a change of care is made) ; see p. 374, letters C to E.

In the case of *Re P. (infants)*, [1967] 2 All E. R. 229 a magistrates' court made an order under the Guardianship of Infants Acts giving the custody of two infants to the father. Prior to this order a fit person order had been made placing the children in the care of the local authority. This order was revoked, and the mother and the local authority appealed against the revocation, and also issued summonses making the children wards of court. On the dismissal of the appeal against the revocation of the fit person order the wardship proceedings were reconstituted. It was held:

(i) The exercise by the magistrates' court of its limited statutory jurisdiction over children did not, in the absence of express words in the statute, fetter the power of the Chancery Division in exercising the jurisdiction of the Crown as *parens patriae* over wards of court, though the wardship jurisdiction was most usefully exercised by way of supplement to the magistrates' court order where the court had not the necessary power.

(ii) When magistrates, in exercise of their jurisdiction under the Guardianship of Infants Acts, 1886 and 1925, had made an order for custody, then, unless relief was sought which magistrates could not give, the *forum conveniens* for reconsidering that order was *prima facie* that magistrates' court; and to decide whether to entertain a wardship application the judge should enquire into the case to the extent necessary to determine whether relief was genuinely sought which the magistrates were unable to give, or whether there was some very special reason for invoking the wardship jurisdiction.

In *Re R. M. (an infant)*, [1966] 3 All E. R. 58 an illegitimate child had been received into care and boarded out with foster parents. The mother took no positive action to get the child back. The foster parents applied to make the child a ward of court. It was held that the mother had not disentitled herself by neglect or abandonment from saying she wanted the child back. Wardship was confirmed and care and control given to the mother.

In *Re K. R. (An Infant)*, [1964] Ch. 455; [1963] 3 All E. R. 337; 128 J. P. 7 it was held that: (i) on the mother's notice being given to a local authority that she desired to assume the care of a child received into care under s. 1, the rights of the local authority to keep the child ended, and not only her common law rights revived but also the jurisdiction of the court in relation to the infant became fully effective; accordingly it was open to anyone interested to apply for an order concerning the care and control of the infant and the court could make an interim order placing the infant in the charge of any person whom it thought proper;

(ii) in the circumstances the court would not grant the application that the infant cease to be a ward of court but would continue the wardship and leave the child with the foster parents until the final determination of the matter.

This case was distinguished and *Re A. B. (An Infant)*, [1954] 2 Q. B. 385; [1954] 2 All E. R. 287; 118 J. P. 318, followed in *Re S. (An Infant)*, [1965] 1 All E. R. 33 when Pennycuick, J., held that on an application by the foster parents of a child received into care to make the child a ward of court the court was precluded by authority from reviewing the decision of a local authority, and dismissed the application. On appeal from that decision to the Court of Appeal it was held that the jurisdiction of the Chancery Court over the boy as a ward of court was not ousted by the fact that the local authority had received him into care; [1965] 1 All E. R. 865; 129 J. P. 228).

In *Re C (A) (an infant)*, [1966] 1 All E. R. 560; 130 J. P. 146, it was held that the scope of the proper exercise of the prerogative jurisdiction of the court (*i.e.*, the Family Division of the High Court) over infants was restricted in the case of an infant taken into care under the Children Act, 1948 to circumstances in which the jurisdiction could usefully be employed without conflicting with or encroaching on the local authority's statutory sphere of discretion.

Dicta of Pearson L. J., in *Re Baker (infants)*, [1961] 3 All E. R. 286 and Donovan, J., in *Re A. B. (an infant)*, [1954] 2 All E. R. 293, applied.

Powers of local authority to visit and assist persons formerly in their care.—Where a person was at or after the time when he attained the age of seventeen, in the care of a local authority under the Children Act, 1948, or the Children and Young Persons Act, 1933, but has ceased to be in their care, then, while he is under the age of twenty-one, the local authority, if so requested by him, may cause him to be visited, advised and befriended and, in exceptional circumstances, to be given financial assistance (Children and Young Persons Act, 1963, ss. 58, 65, pp. 115, 117, *ante*.

Family allowance.—See leaflet at p. 1006, *post*.

Poor Law Acts.—The Poor Law Act, 1930 and the Poor Law (Scotland) Act, 1934 were repealed by the National Assistance Act, 1948.

2. Assumption by local authority of parental rights.—(1) Subject to the provisions of this Part of this Act, a local authority may resolve with respect to any child in their care under the foregoing section in whose case it appears to them—

(a) that his parents are dead and that he has no guardian; or

(b) that a parent or guardian of his (hereinafter referred to as the person on whose account the resolution was passed) has abandoned him or suffers from some permanent disability rendering the said person incapable of caring for the child, or is of such habits or mode of life as to be unfit to have the care of the child,

that all the rights and powers which the deceased parents would have if they were still living, or, as the case may be, all the rights and powers of the person on whose account the resolution was passed, shall vest in the local authority.

(2) In the case of a resolution passed by virtue of paragraph (b) of the last foregoing subsection, unless the person on whose account the resolution was passed has consented in writing to the passing of the resolution, the local authority, if the whereabouts of the said person are known to them, shall forthwith after the passing of the resolution serve on him notice in writing of the passing thereof; and if, not later than one month after such a notice is served on him, the person on whose account the resolution was passed serves a notice in writing on the local authority objecting to the resolution, the resolution shall, subject to the provisions of subsection (3) of this section, lapse on the expiration of fourteen days from the service of the notice of objection.

Every notice served by a local authority under this subsection shall inform the person on whom the notice is served of his right to object to the resolution and of the effect of any objection made by him.

(3) Where a notice has been served on a local authority under subsection (2) of this section, the authority may not later than fourteen days from the receipt by them of the notice complain to a juvenile court, or in Scotland the sheriff, having jurisdiction in the area of the authority, and in that event the resolution shall not lapse by reason of the service of the notice until the determination of the complaint, and the court or sheriff may, on the hearing of the complaint, order that the resolution shall not lapse by reason of the service of the notice:

Provided that the court or sheriff shall not so order unless satisfied that the child had been, and at the time when the resolution was passed remained, abandoned by the person who made the objection or that that person is unfit to have the care of the child by reason of mental disorder within the meaning of the Mental Health Act, 1959, or by reason of his habits or mode of life.

(4) Any notice under this section may be served by post, so however that a notice served by a local authority under subsection (2) of this section shall not be duly served by post unless it is sent in a registered letter.

NOTES

This section is printed as amended by the Mental Health Act, 1959.

Social Services Committee.—Unless the matter is urgent the local authority will first consider a report of their social services committee, if one is appointed.

Subject to the provisions, etc.—See particularly s. 6 (2), (children subject to existing orders of court), p. 890, *post.*

" **Local authority.**"—*I.e.*, councils of counties or county boroughs (see s. 38, *post*).

" **Child.**"—For definition, see s. 59 (1), *post.*

Parent or guardian.—This seems to refer to all parents or guardians (see ss. 9, 59 (1), *post*); as to children in respect of whom custody orders are in force, see s. 6 (2), *post.*

" **Abandoned.**"—If the whereabouts of any parent or guardian have remained unknown for not less than twelve months he is deemed to have abandoned a child received into care for the purposes of this section (Children and Young Persons Act, 1963, s. 48, p. 111, *ante*).

Extension of power of local authority.—The power of a local authority to resolve under s. 2 (1) (b) may be exercised if it appears to them that the parent or guardian suffers from mental disorder which renders him unfit to have the care of the child or that he has so persistently failed without reasonable cause to discharge his obligation as to be unfit to have the care of the child. See s. 48 of the Children and Young Persons Act, 1963, p. 111, *ante*.

Guardian.—A court may entertain an application under s. 5 of the Guardianship of Minors Act, 1971, p. 1198, *post*, notwithstanding that a resolution under this section is in force. If the court appoints a guardian the resolution ceases to have effect (s. 50 (2), *ibid.*).

Adoption.—If the child is subsequently adopted the resolution ceases to have effect (s. 15 (4) of the Adoption Act, 1958, p. 1049, *post*).

" Habits or mode of life."—These are very comprehensive words sufficient to include, amongst others, such divers matters as vagrancy, habitual inebriety, immoral, vicious or criminal conduct. On the other hand, the court has held that a distinction must be drawn between the words " act " and " habit," " the one pointing to a single thing done, the other to a usage resulting from repeated action." See *Ely (Bishop)* v. *Close*, [1913] P. 184.

In *Barker* v. *Westmorland County Council* (1958), 56 L. G. R. 267, it was held that evidence of a parent's past life was admissible in deciding whether he was a proper person to have the care of a child.

" Resolution."—A resolution under sub-s. (1) can only be passed in respect of a child already in care under s. 1, *ante*.

" Whereabouts of the said person."—See s. 10, *post*, which imposes on the parents of a child in the care of a local authority a duty to keep the authority informed as to his address.

" Complain."—The procedure is by complaint upon which an order may be made by a court of summary jurisdiction, and will therefore be governed by the Magistrates' Courts Act, 1952 and the Magistrates' Courts Rules, 1968. As the complaint is to be made to a juvenile court it cannot be made to one justice.

Parental rights.—See note to s. 3, *post*, and see also *Re T. (AJJ) (an infant)*, [1970] Ch. 688; [1970] 2 All E. R. 865; 134 J. P. 611 where the High Court declined to interfere in the exercise of a local authority's discretion to remove a child from foster parents and return the child to the mother. In these respects it was said there was no difference between the case of a child committed to the care of a local authority under a Fit Person Order (now Care Order) and that of a child in respect of whom a resolution had been passed.

Legal aid.—Legal aid may be given in connection with proceedings under this section: see Legal Aid (Extension of Proceedings) Regulations, 1969, S.I. 1969 No. 921, p. 370, *ante*.

Family allowance.—A child cannot be treated as included in any family for the purpose of the Family Allowances Act, 1965, whilst a resolution under this section is in force, except as respects periods where he is allowed to be under the control of a parent, guardian, relative or friend. See Department of Health and Social Security leaflet, p. 1006, *post*, and see *Hill* v. *Minister of Pensions and National Insurance*, [1955] 2 All E. R. 890. Family Allowances Act, 1965, s. 11 provides:

11.—(1) A child shall not, for the purposes of this Act, be treated as included in any family as respects any period—

(a) during which his or her residence in a residential establishment is required by a supervision requirement made under s. 44 of the Social Work (Scotland) Act, 1968, and the child is not absent from the residential establishment under supervision;

(b) during which the child is liable to be detained by virtue of s. 53 of the Children and Young Persons Act, 1933, or s. 57 of the Children and Young Persons (Scotland) Act, 1937, and is not discharged on licence;

(bb) during which the child is liable to undergo residential training under commital by virtue of section 58A of the said Act of 1937 and is not released under that section;

(c) during which the child is accommodated by virtue of rules made by the Secretary of State under s. 45 of the Social Work (Scotland) Act, 1968;

(2) A child shall not, for the purposes of this Act, be treated as included in any family as respects any period during which there is in force an order under the Children and

Young Persons Act, 1969 (other than an interim order) committing the child to the care of the local authority, not being a period during which, under the provisions of s. 13 (2) of the Children Act, 1948, the child is allowed by the authority to be under the control of a parent, guardian, relative or friend of the child.

(3) A child in respect of whom there is in force a resolution of a local authority passed under s. 2 (1) of the Children Act, 1948, or under s. 16 (1) of the Social Work (Scotland) Act, 1968, shall not, for the purposes of this Act, be treated as included in any family.

Provided that this subsection shall not have effect as respects any period during which under the provisions of s. 4 or s. 13 (2) of the said Act of 1948, or of ss. 17 or 18 of the said Act of 1968, the child is allowed by the local authority to be, either for a fixed period or otherwise, under the control of a parent, guardian, relative or friend of the child.

(4) Subsections (2) and (3) of this section shall not apply to a child in the care and possession of a person who has given in respect of that child such a notice of intention to apply for an adoption order as is mentioned in s. 36 (1) of the Adoption Act, 1958, unless twelve weeks have elapsed since the giving of the notice without the application being made or the application has been refused by the court or withdrawn.

(5) Any reference in the foregoing provisions of this section to an order made or resolution passed under any enactment includes a reference to an order or resolution which by virtue of any other provision is deemed to be made or passed under that enactment.

(6) Where a person is entitled in respect of a child to a guardian's allowance under s. 29 of the Insurance Act, any allowances payable under this Act for his family shall be such only as would be payable if that child were not included in the family.

(7) In subsection (1) of this section as amended by the Social Work (Scotland) Act, 1968, the expressions "residential establishment" and "supervision requirement" have the meanings assigned to them by section 94 of that Act.

This section is printed as amended by the Social Work (Scotland) Act, 1968, and the Children and Young Persons Act, 1969. See s. 12 of the National Insurance Act, 1971 as to regulations which may be made regarding the children of polygamous marriages.

Determination of resolution by order of juvenile court.—See s. 4, *post.*

3. Effect of assumption by local authority of parental rights.—

(1) While a resolution passed by virtue of paragraph (a) of subsection (1) of section two of this Act is in force with respect to a child, all rights and powers which the deceased parents would have if they were still living shall, in respect of the child, be vested in the local authority in accordance with the resolution.

(2) While a resolution passed by virtue of paragraph (b) of the said subsection (1) is in force with respect to a child, all rights and powers of the person on whose account the resolution was passed shall, in respect of the child, be vested in the local authority in accordance with the resolution, and subsection (3) of section one of this Act shall not in respect of the child apply in relation to the person on whose account the resolution was passed.

[Subsections (3)–(5) are repealed by the Children and Young Persons Act, 1969, s. 72 (4) and Sched. VI. For power to allow a child to be under the charge and control of a parent see s. 13, post, as substituted by s. 49 Children and Young Persons Act, 1969.]

(6) A resolution under the said section two shall not relieve any person from any liability to maintain, or contribute to the maintenance of, the child.

(7) A resolution under the said section two shall not authorise a local authority to cause a child to be brought up in any religious creed other than that in which he would have been brought up but for the resolution.

(8) Any person who—

    (a) knowingly assists or induces or persistently attempts to induce a child to whom this subsection applies to run away, or

    (b) without lawful authority takes away such a child, or

    (c) knowingly harbours or conceals such a child who has run away or who has been taken away or prevents him from returning,

shall be liable on summary conviction to a fine not exceeding twenty pounds or to imprisonment for a term not exceeding two months or to both.

This subsection applies to any child in the care of a local authority under section 1 of this Act with respect to whom a resolution is in force under section 2 thereof and for whom accommodation (whether in a home or otherwise) is being provided by the local authority in pursuance of Part II of this Act ; and references in this subsection to running away or taking away or to returning are references to running away or taking away from, or to returning to, a place where accommodation is or was being so provided.

NOTES

This section is printed as amended by the Children and Young Persons Acts, 1963 and 1969.

" **Local authority.**"—See s. 38, *post.*

" **Parental rights.**"—The parental rights of a father include those of custody of the child, control over the child's actions and correction, right to the child's services, and control of the child's religious education; of these the last is substantially preserved by sub-s. (7). It seems that the word " powers," *supra,* will extend to the giving of consent to marriage of an infant, as to which, see the Marriage Act, 1949, s. 3, p. 1215, *post.* See also note to s. 1.

Upon the death of the child's father the mother has a right to custody and guardianship of the child (Guardianship of Minors Act, 1971, s. 3, p. 1199, *post*).

Rights and powers under this section do not include power to consent to adoption. See the Adoption Act, 1958, s. 4 (3), p. 1031, *post.*

" **Child.**"—For definition, see s. 59 (1), p. 564, *post.*

Offence.—As to prosecutions, see s. 55, p. 561, *post.*

Parent or guardian.—For definition, see ss. 9, 59 (1), *post.* See also s. 6 (2), *post.*

"**Liability to maintain, etc.**"—An enforceable liability to maintain children was unknown at common law and was first created by the old poor law. Now, under the National Assistance Act, 1948, s. 42, the only persons liable to maintain a child are the parents, and their liability ceases when the child attains the age of sixteen. Liability to contribute to the maintenance of children under the Children and Young Persons Act, 1933, s. 86 (p. 67, *ante*), is also now confined to parents. See s. 24, *post,* and notes thereto.

" **Religious creed.**"—Generally the religion in which a child " would have been brought up but for the resolution " is that of the father, who in the absence of a good reason to the contrary, has at common law the absolute right to determine in what religion his child should be brought up (*Re Agar-Ellis, Agar-Ellis* v. *Lascelles* (1878), 10 Ch. D. 49 ; *Re Scanlan (Infants)* (1888), 40 Ch. D. 200). This right is unaffected by ante-nuptial or other agreement (*Re Agar-Ellis, Agar-Ellis* v. *Lascelles, supra*), but it may be lost by immoral conduct (*Shelley* v. *Westbrooke* (1817), Jac. 266), or may be waived or abdicated, as where the father has acquiesced for a long period in the child being brought up in a religion other than his own (*Lyons* v. *Blenkin* (1821), Jac. 245 ; *Hill* v. *Hill* (1862), 31 L. J. Ch. 505), or where he has altogether neglected the religious education of the child (*Davis* v. *Davis* (1862), 26 J. P. 260). Save where the father's right has been lost during his lifetime it continues after his death, and, where he has left no express directions on the subject, the court will, in appropriate cases, direct the child to be brought up in his father's religion (*Re Newbery* (1866), 1 Ch. App. 263; *Re North* (1846), 8 L. T. (O. S.) 313; *Re Austin, Austin* v. *Austin* (1865), 4 De G. J. & Sm. 716).

The effect of s. 1 of the Guardianship of Minors Act, 1971 (p. 1198, *post*), however, appears to be to give the mother equal rights with the father as to the child's religion. In the case of dispute the court has to decide between them, the child's welfare being the first and paramount consideration.

" **Harbours or conceals.**"—It is thought that in order to " harbour " a person it is necessary to give him actual physical shelter. " Conceal " is a wider word and might include failing to reveal knowledge of the child's whereabouts without giving him physical shelter. Where a local authority has allowed any person to take over the care of a child in respect of whom a resolution is in force, and has by notice in writing required that person to return the child, see s. 49 of the Children and Young Persons Act, 1963, p. 112, *ante*.

4. Duration and rescission of resolutions under section two.—

(1) Subject to the provisions of this Part of this Act, a resolution under section two of this Act shall continue in force until the child with respect to whom it was passed attains the age of eighteen.

(2) A resolution under the said section two may be rescinded by resolution of the local authority if it appears to them that the rescinding of the resolution will be for the benefit of the child.

(3) On complaint being made—

    (a) in the case of a resolution passed by virtue of paragraph (a) of subsection (1) of the said section two, by a person claiming to be a parent or guardian of the child;

    (b) in the case of a resolution passed by virtue of paragraph (b) thereof, by the person on whose account the resolution was passed,

a juvenile court, or in Scotland the sheriff, having jurisdiction where the complainant resides, if satisfied that there was no ground for the making of the resolution or that the resolution should in the interests of the child be determined, may by order determine the resolution, and the resolution shall thereupon cease to have effect:

NOTES

This section is printed as amended by the Children and Young Persons Act, 1969, s. 72 (3), (4) and Scheds. V and VI.

" **Child.**"—For definition, see s. 59 (1), *post*.

Complaint.—As the procedure is by way of complaint for an order, the Magistrates' Courts Act, and Rules, 1968, will apply. If the complaint is made on the ground that there was no ground for making the resolution it must be made within six months after the date the resolution was made (s. 104 of the Magistrates' Courts Act, 1952). If it is made on the ground that the resolution should in the interests of the child be determined it may be made at any time.

" **Local authority.**"—See s. 38, *post*.

" **Parent or guardian.**"—For definition, see ss. 9, 59 (1), *post*. In relation to children, see s. 6 (2), *post*.

" **Resides.**"—See note " Residence ", p. 162, *ante*.

Effect of adoption order.—See s. 15 (4) of the Adoption Act, 1958, p. 1049, *post*.

Legal aid.—Legal aid may be given in connection with proceedings under this section, see the Legal Aid (Extension of Proceedings) Regulations, 1969, p. 370, *ante*.

5. Duty of local authority to act as fit person under the Children and Young Persons Acts.—[*Repealed by the Children and Young Persons Act, 1969, s. 72 (4) and Sched. VI.*]

6. Application of preceding provisions to children already subject, or becoming subject, to orders of court.—(1) The reception of a child into their care by a local authority under section one of this Act, and the passing of a resolution with respect to him under section two of this Act, shall not affect any supervision order or probation order previously made with respect to him by any court.

(2) Where an order of any court is in force giving the custody of a child to any person, the foregoing provisions of this Part of this Act shall have effect in relation to the child as if for references to the parents or guardian of the child or to a parent or guardian of his there were substituted references to that person.

[*Subsections (3) and (4) are repealed by the Children and Young Persons Act, 1969, s. 72 (4) and Sched. VI.*]

NOTES

This section is printed as amended by the Criminal Justice Act, 1961, and the Children and Young Persons Act, 1969.

" **Child.**"—For definition, see s. 59 (1), *post*.

" **Local authority.**"—See s. 38, *post*.

Probation order and supervision order.—A probation order may be made in respect of a person over the age of seventeen convicted of an offence; see s. 3 of the Criminal Justice Act, 1948, p. 279, *ante*. The word "convicted" is not used in connection with a juvenile dealt with summarily, the words "found guilty" being substituted, see s. 59 of the Children and Young Persons Act, 1933, p. 62, *ante*. A supervision order may be made in respect of a person under seventeen (in some circumstances eighteen) years of age who is before a juvenile court, under the Children and Young Persons Acts, 1933 to 1969 as being in need of care, or control, upon the revocation of a care order, or in cognate proceedings. A probation order may be for a period of not less than one nor more than three years, and a supervision order for any period not exceeding three years.

Order of any court giving the custody of the child to any person.—Orders for custody may be made—

    (a) Under the inherent jurisdiction of the former Court of Chancery, representing the sovereign as *parens patriae*, which is now vested in the Family Law Division of the High Court (Supreme Court of Judicature (Consolidation) Act, 1925, ss. 18 (1), 56 (1) and the Administration of Justice Act, 1970; 7 Halsbury's Statutes, 3rd Edn., 573; 25 Halsbury's Statutes, 3rd Edn., 708). As to the foundation of this jurisdiction, see *Re D. (an infant)*, [1943] Ch. 305; [1943] 2 All E. R. 411.

    (b) Under s. 9 of the Guardianship of Minors Act, 1971 (p. 1201, *post*). Under this Act an order for custody may be made either by the High Court, a County Court or a magistrates' court, except that a magistrates' court is not competent to make an original order in the case of an infant over the age of sixteen unless he is physically or mentally incapable of self-support. Although this Act is usually invoked in the case of disputes between the parents the discretion thereby given to the court is wide enough to enable it to give the custody to a third party. In *D'Alton* v. *D'Alton* (1878), 4 P. D. 87, custody was given to the mistress of a school.

    (c) By the High Court in any proceedings for divorce or nullity of marriage or judicial separation (Matrimonial Proceedings and Property Act, 1970, s. 18).

(d) By a magistrates' court on an application under s. 2, of the Matrimonial Proceedings (Magistrates' Courts) Act, 1960, p. 1226 *post*.

(e) Under s. 8 of the Adoption Act, 1958, (p. 1042, *post*), which enables the court to which an application for an adoption order is made to make an interim order giving the applicant the custody of the child for not more than two years by way of a probationary period.

" **Parent or guardian.**"—For definition, see ss. 9, 59 (1), *post*. See also sub-s. (2), *supra*.

7. Children in care of Minister of Pensions.—[*Repealed by the Children and Young Persons Act*, 1969, *s. 72 (4) and Sched. VI.*]

8. Children becoming subject to Mental Deficiency or Lunacy and Mental Treatment Acts.—[*Repealed by the Mental Health Act*, 1959.]

9. Meaning of " parents or guardian."—Save as expressly provided in section six of this Act, any reference in this Part of this Act to the parents or guardian of a child shall be construed as a reference to all the persons who are parents of the child or who are guardians of the child.

NOTES

" **Parent or guardian.**"—For definition, see s. 59 (1), *post*. See also s. 6 (2), *ante*.
" **Child.**"—For definition, see s. 59 (1), *post*.

10. Duty of parents to maintain contact with local authorities having their children in care.—(1) The parent of a child who is in the care of a local authority under section one of this Act shall secure that the appropriate local authority are informed of the parent's address for the time being.

(2) Where under subsection (4) of section one of this Act a local authority take over the care of a child from another local authority, that other authority shall where possible inform the parent of the child that the care of the child has been so taken over.

(3) For the purposes of subsection (1) of this section, the appropriate local authority shall be the authority in whose care the child is for the time being:

Provided that where under subsection (4) of section one of this Act a local authority have taken over the care of a child from another authority, then unless and until a parent is informed that the care of a child has been so taken over the appropriate local authority shall in relation to that parent continue to be the authority from whom the care of the child was taken over.

(4) Any parent who knowingly fails to comply with subsection (1) of this section shall be liable on summary conviction to a fine not exceeding ten pounds:

Provided that it shall be a defence in any proceedings under this sub-section to prove that the defendant was residing at the same address as the other parent of the child, and had reasonable cause to believe that the other parent had informed the appropriate authority that both parents were residing at that address.

NOTES

This section is printed as amended by the Children and Young Persons Act, 1963, and the Criminal Justice Act, 1967.

" Parent."—For definition, see s. 9, *ante,* and s. 59 (1), *post.* See also s. 6 (2), *ante.*

" Child."—For definition, see s. 59 (1), *post.*

Child under sixteen.—Even after the child attains sixteen the general policy of the Act is to maintain contact between the child and his parents with a view to his being returned to them (see ss. 1 (3) and 3 (3), *ante*), and to this end a local authority is empowered to pay the expenses of parents visiting children while they are in the authority's care (s. 22, *post*).

" Local authority."—See s. 38, *post.*

PART II

TREATMENT OF CHILDREN IN CARE OF LOCAL AUTHORITIES

11. Children to whom Part II applies.—Except where the contrary intention appears, any reference in this Part of this Act to a child who is or was in the care of the authority is a reference to a child who is or was in the care of the local authority under section 1 of this Act or by virtue of a care order within the meaning of the Children and Young Persons Act, 1969 or a warrant under section 23 (1) of that Act (which relates to remands in the care of local authorities).

NOTES

This section is printed as substituted by s. 27 (1) Children and Young Persons Act, 1969, but nothing in this section as substituted prejudices the application of any provision of Part II of this Act to any person by virtue of an enactment passed after this Act and before the Act of 1969 (s. 27 (1), *ibid.*) (*e.g.* s. 36 Matrimonial Causes Act, 1965).

Local authority.—See s. 38, *post.*

Child.—For definition, see s. 59 (1), *post.*

Matrimonial proceedings.—Part II applies to a child in respect of whom, a court has made an order committing the care of the child to a council of a county or county borough on it appearing to the court that there are exceptional circumstances making it impracticable or undesirable for the child to be entrusted to either of the parties to the marriage or to any other individual. See s. 36 of the Matrimonial Causes Act, 1965, s. 3 (2) of the Matrimonial Proceedings (Magistrates' Courts) Act, 1960, p. 1230, *post,* and the Magistrates' Courts (Matrimonial Proceedings) Rules, 1960, pp. 1268, *et seq., post.*

12. General duty of local authority.—(1) Where a child is in the care of a local authority, it shall be the duty of that authority to exercise their powers with respect to him so as to further his best interests, and to afford him opportunity for the proper development of his character and abilities.

(2) In providing for a child in their care, a local authority shall make such use of facilities and services available for children in the care of their own parents as appears to the local authority reasonable in his case.

NOTES

Child in the care of a local authority.—See s. 11, *supra.*

' Child."—For definition, see s. 59 (1), *post.*

" **Local authority.**"—See s. 38, *post.*

" **Facilities and services.**"—The expression " facilities and services " available to children in the care of their own parents (sub-s. (2), *supra*) includes, presumably, schools, residential and otherwise, and the ancillary services provided therein, nursery schools, youth clubs and youth centres, hospitals, child guidance clinics, infant welfare clinics, etc.

Any overlapping which might otherwise result between the functions of the local authority and the functions of the local education authority as such is to be avoided by regulations under s. 21, p. 901, *post.*

Of particular interest and value in this respect will be the Youth Employment service; see the Employment and Training Act, 1948; 12 Halsbury's Statutes 3rd Edn., 131.

Expenses.—As to contributions towards the expenses of local authorities under this section, see the Local Government Act, 1958.

Parent.—For definition, see ss. 9, *ante,* and 59 (1), *post.* See also s. 6 (2), *ante.*

"**Further his best interests.**"—But see s. 27 (2) Children and Young Persons Act, 1969, for the duty, notwithstanding, to have regard to the protection of the public.

13. Provision of accommodation and maintenance for children in care.—(1) A local authority shall discharge their duty to provide accommodation and maintenance for a child in their care in such one of the following ways as they think fit, namely,—

    (a) by boarding him out on such terms as to payment by the authority and otherwise as the authority may, subject to the provisions of this Act and regulations thereunder, determine; or

    (b) by maintaining him in a community home or in any such home as is referred to in section 64 of the Children and Young Persons Act, 1969; or

    (c) by maintaining him in a voluntary home (other than a community home) the managers of which are willing to receive him;

or by making such other arrangements as seem appropriate to the only authority.

(2) Without prejudice to the generality of sub-section (1) of this section, a local authority may allow a child in their care, either for a fixed period or until the local authority otherwise determine, to be under the charge and control of a parent, guardian, relative or friend.

(3) The terms, as to payment and other matters, on which a child may be accommodated and maintained in any such home as is referred to in section 64 of that Act shall be such as the Secretary of State may from time to time determine."

NOTES

This section is printed as substituted by s. 49 of the Children and Young Persons Act, 1969.

Exchequer grant on expenditure.—See Home Office Circulars Nos. 15/50/D2 and 16/50/D4, dealing with exchequer grant on expenditure in respect of children boarded out, etc., and of persons being assisted under s. 20 of the Act; and maintenance payments by local authorities in respect of children in their care who are placed in voluntary homes.

See also the memorandum by the Home Office for the guidance of Local Authorities on the Provision and Conduct of Residential Nurseries.

" **Local authority.**"—See s. 38, *post.*

"**Accommodation and maintenance.**"—This is not defined in the Act. It seems therefore that it should be given its ordinary colloquial meaning of " an adequate supply of house-room, food and clothing." *Cf. Re G. (Infants),* [1899] 1 Ch. 719.

"**Child.**"—For definition, see s. 59 (1), *post.*

"**Boarding out.**"—The Boarding Out of Children Regulations, 1955, S.I. 1955 No. 1377, made under the Children Act, 1948, s. 14, have not yet been revoked, see p. 984, *post.*

Voluntary home (other than a community home).—*I.e.* a home registered under ss. 29 and 30 of the Children Act, 1948.

"**Such other arrangements.**"—By virtue of para. 3 (1) of Sched. III, in any interim period as defined in that paragraph, children in care may be accommodated in the premises of an approved school but this power is in addition to the schedule.

"**A local authority may**" (s. 13 (2)).—But see s. 22 (4) of this Act for restriction on the exercise of this power. Subsection (2) applies to all children in care and unlike the previous position under s. 5 of the Family Allowance and National Insurance Act, 1956, a child received into care under s. 1 of the Children Act, 1948, may be allowed home on trial. Subsections (3) and (4) of s. 3 of the Children Act, 1948, are redundant in view of the subsection and are repealed. (See Home Office Circular Nos. 239/1969, pp. 707 *et seq., ante,* and 240/1969, pp. 714 *et seq., ante.*)

"**Terms as to payment.**"—By s. 62 (2) no contribution is payable in respect of a period during which a child is "allowed home".

"**Relative or friend.**"—In a number of cases it has been held that the expressions "relations" and "friends" are synonymous. See *Gower* v. *Mainwaring* (1750), 2 Ves. Sen. 87; *Re Caplin's Will* (1865), 2 Drew. & Sm. 527. It seems, however, exceedingly unlikely that such a narrow construction would be put on the word "friend" where it appears in the present section, and that it ought, rather, to be given its ordinary colloquial meaning of a person attached to the child by bonds of affection only.

For definition of "relative," see s. 59 (1), *post.*

"**Compulsory school age.**"—For definition, see s. 59 (1), *post.*

Community home.—As to the power of the local authority to provide accommodation for persons over compulsory school age in a community home see s. 19, p. 899, *post.*

14. Regulations as to boarding-out.—(1) The Secretary of State may by regulations make provision for the welfare of children boarded out by local authorities under paragraph (a) of subsection (1) of the last foregoing section.

(2) Without prejudice to the generality of the last foregoing subsection, regulations under this section may provide—

> (a) for the recording by local authorities of information relating to persons with whom children are boarded out as aforesaid and persons who are willing to have children so boarded out with them;
>
> (b) for securing that children shall not be boarded out in any household unless that household is for the time being approved by such local authority as may be prescribed by the regulations;
>
> (c) for securing that where possible the person with whom any child is to be boarded out is either of the same religious persuasion as the child or gives an undertaking that the child will be brought up in that religious persuasion;

(d) for securing that children boarded out as aforesaid, and the premises in which they are boarded out, will be supervised and inspected by a local authority and that the children will be removed from those premises if their welfare appears to require it.

NOTES

Regulations.—See the Boarding-Out of Children Regulations 1955.

As to Scotland, see the Boarding-out of Children (Scotland) Regulations, 1959 (S.I. 1959 No. 835) (S. 44).

For the method of exercise of the regulation-making power, see s. 58, p. 923, *post*.

" **Welfare.**"—See note to s. 1, p. 881, *ante*.

Child.—For definition, see s. 59 (1), *post*.

Local authority.—See s. 38, *post*.

" **Religious persuasion.**"—Generally the child's religion will be that of his parent. See note to s. 3, p. 887, *ante*. *Cf.* the Children and Young Persons Act, 1969, s. 24 (3), p. 167, *ante*. If the child is of sufficient age he may be consulted as to his religious persuasion, and the court may direct him to be brought up in some religion other than that of his father (*Re W., W.* v. *M.,* [1907] 2 Ch. 557). For a case where the infant desired to be brought up in some faith which is neither Christian nor Jewish see *Skinner* v. *Orde* (1871), L. R. 4 P. C. 60, where the court refused to accede to the desire of an infant to be brought up as a Mohammedan. The age at which an infant will be allowed to choose his own religion is a matter of some doubt. The Poor Law Act, 1930 (now repealed), s. 73 (1) recognised that infants might have definite religious views as young as twelve years of age. This is to some extent in conflict with the common law rule that until a child attains his majority the father has the right to control the child's person, education and conduct (*Re Agar-Ellis, Agar-Ellis* v. *Lascelles* (1883), 24 Ch. D. 317).

In regard to the child's religion, however, as in all other matters concerning him the dominant factor to be considered by the local authority in performing their duties under the present Act, as by the court in the exercise of its jurisdiction, is the welfare of the child. It can seldom be for the welfare of a child to disturb established religious beliefs, even if they have been acquired at a comparatively early age, and it is thought, therefore, that there are many cases in which the authority ought to ensure that a child in its care will continue to be brought up in the faith which he has acquired before coming into their care even though this faith is not that of his father. See *Re Kellers* (1856), 5 I. Ch. R. 328; *Re Browne* (1858), 8 I. Ch. R. 172).

See Regulation 4 of the Administration of Children's Homes Regulations, 1951, p. 980, *post*, and Regulation 19 of the Boarding-Out of Children Regulations, 1955, p. 991, *post*, and clause 2 of the Form of Undertaking, p. 996, *post*.

Inspection.—See s. 54, p. 919, *post*.

15. Duty of local authorities to provide homes.—(1) *A local authority may, and shall in so far as the Secretary of State so requires, provide, equip and maintain, either within or without their area, homes for the accommodation of children in their care.*

(2) *The accommodation provided under the last foregoing subsection by a local authority shall include separate accommodation for the temporary reception of children, with, in particular, the necessary facilities for observation of their physical and mental condition.*

(3) *A local authority may discharge their functions under the foregoing provisions of this section by making arrangements with another local authority for the provision in homes provided by that other local authority of accommodation for children in the care of the first-mentioned local authority; and*

arrangements under this subsection may contain provisions as to payment by the first-mentioned local authority and other terms upon which the accommodation is to be provided.

(4) *The Secretary of State may make regulations as to the exercise by local authorities of their functions under this section and the conduct of homes provided thereunder and for securing the welfare of the children in the homes, and regulations under this subsection may in particular—*

(a) *impose requirements as to the accommodation and equipment to be provided in homes and as to the medical arrangements to be made for protecting the health of the children in the homes;*

(b) *impose requirements as to the facilities which are to be given for the children to receive a religious upbringing appropriate to the persuasion to which they belong;*

(c) *require the approval of the Secretary of State to the construction, acquisition or appropriation of buildings with a view to the use thereof for the purposes of homes, or to the doing of anything (whether by way of addition, diminution or alteration) which materially affects the buildings or grounds or other facilities or amenities available for children in the homes;*

(d) *provide for consultation with the Secretary of State as to applicants for appointment to the charge of a home and empower the Secretary of State to prohibit the appointment of any particular applicant therefor except in the cases (if any) in which the regulations dispense with such consultation by reason that the person to be appointed possesses such qualifications as may be prescribed by the regulations;*

(e) *contain provisions for limiting the period during which children may remain in accommodation provided for the temporary reception of children,*

and may contain different provisions for different descriptions of cases and as respects different descriptions of homes.

(5) *Where it appears to the Secretary of State that any premises used for the purposes of a home provided under this section are unsuitable therefor, or that the conduct of any such home is not in accordance with regulations made by him under the last foregoing subsection or is otherwise unsatisfactory, he may by notice in writing served on the local authority direct that as from such date as may be specified in the notice the premises shall not be used for the said purpose.*

(6) *A direction given under the last foregoing subsection may at any time by revoked by the Secretary of State.*

NOTES

This section is repealed by the Children and Young Persons Act, 1969, s. 72 (4) and Sched. VI. However by para. 13, Sched. IV, *ibid.*, this section and s. 16 continue to apply to local authorities until the coming into operation of a regional plan for a particular planning area. By Sched. III, Children and Young Persons Act, 1969 (Commencement No. 2) Order, 1969 (S.I. 1969 No. 1565) so long as s. 15 continues to apply to a local authority then s. 51 of the Children Act, 1948, and s. 9 Mental Health Act, 1959, as amended have effect as if a home provided by the local authority under this section were a community home so provided under the Act of 1969.

" **Local authority.**"—See s. 38, *post.*

Children in the care of a local authority.—See s. 11, *ante.*

" Functions."—For definition, see s. 59 (1), *post.*

Welfare.—See note to s. 1, p. 881, *ante.*

Regulations.—See notes to s. 14, p. 895, *ante.*
The Administration of Children's Homes Regulations, 1951 (S.I. 1951 No. 1217), are printed p. 979, *post.* See also Home Office Circular No. 193/49, as to consultations with Medical Officer of Health.
As to Scotland, see the Administration of Children's Homes (Scotland) Regulations, 1959 (S.I. 1959 No. 834) (s. 43).

Residential nurseries.—See Home Office memorandum dated June, 1950.

" A religious upbringing appropriate to the persuasion to which they belong."—This phrase is more comprehensive than the words " religious instruction." It would appear to connote something more than the mere teaching of religious doctrine, and to involve constant association with some adult who is a practising member of the child's religious denomination who will see that he attends the appropriate place of worship, and encourage him generally in religious observance. This will be most easily achieved where children can be placed in such homes under foster mothers of their own denomination.

" Appears to the Secretary of State."—The effect of these words is to make the Secretary of State the judge on the question whether or not a particular home is satisfactory. What is material is the opinion of the Secretary of State and not the fact of satisfactoriness or unsatisfactoriness (*Robinson* v. *Sunderland Corporation,* [1899] 1 Q. B. 751). Provided that the Secretary of State comes to a decision in good faith the court has no power to investigate the grounds or reasonableness of his decision or otherwise to interfere (*Point of Ayr Collieries, Ltd.* v. *Lloyd-George,* [1943] 2 All E. R. 546 ; *Carltona, Ltd.* v. *Works Commissioners,* [1943] 2 All E. R. 560). While constitutionally the decision will be the Minister's the multifarious character of his functions will generally necessitate his delegating his powers of ordering the closing of specific homes to responsible officials (*Carltona, Ltd.* v. *Works Commissioners, supra*).

Mental Health Act, 1959.—See s. 9, *ibid.*, p. 442, *ante,* as to the functions of local authorities in respect of persons who are or have been suffering from mental disorder.

16. Accommodation of children in voluntary homes.—(1) *Notwithstanding any agreement made in connection with the placing of a child in a voluntary home under this Part of this Act by a local authority, the authority may at any time, and shall if required so to do by the Secretary of State or the managers of the home, remove the child from the home.*

(2) *No child in the care of a local authority shall be placed in a voluntary home which does not afford facilities for him to receive a religious upbringing appropriate to the persuasion to which he belongs.*

NOTES

This section is repealed by the Children and Young Persons Act, 1969, s. 72 (4) and Sched. VI but is continued in force by para. 13, Sched. IV, *ibid.*, until the coming into operation of a regional plan for a particular planning area.

Local authorities' children in voluntary homes.—S. 13, (1) (c), *ante,* authorises a local authority to place children in its care who cannot, for the time being, be boarded out, either in a home provided by itself or some other local authority or, with the consent of the managers of a voluntary home, in that home.
The welfare of the child so placed in a voluntary home remains the responsibility of the local authority, and he must be visited; see s. 54 (3), p. 919, *post.*

" Child."—For definition, see s. 59 (1), *post.*

" Voluntary home."—See s. 59 (1), *post,* and the Children and Young Persons Act, 1933, s. 92, p. 74, *ante.*

"**Local authority.**"—See s. 38, *post*.

"**Religious upbringing.**"—See note to s. 15 (4), p. 897, *ante*. Regulations have now been made imposing requirements as to facilities for religious upbringing; see Regulation 4 of the Administration of Children's Homes Regulations, 1951, p. 980, *post*.

17. Power of local authorities to arrange for emigration of children.

—(1) A local authority may, with the consent of the Secretary of State, procure or assist in procuring the emigration of any child in their care.

(2) The Secretary of State shall not give his consent under this section unless he is satisfied that emigration would benefit the child, and that suitable arrangements have been or will be made for the child's reception and welfare in the country to which he is going, that the parents or guardian of the child have been consulted or that it is not practicable to consult them, and that the child consents:

Provided that where a child is too young to form or express a proper opinion on the matter, the Secretary of State may consent to his emigration notwithstanding that the child is unable to consent thereto in any case where the child is to emigrate in company with a parent, guardian or relative of his, or is to emigrate for the purpose of joining a parent, guardian, relative or friend.

(3) In the last foregoing subsection the expression "parents or guardian" shall be construed in accordance with the provisions of section nine of this Act.

NOTES

Regulations.—Power to make regulations is conferred on the Secretary of State by s. 33 (1), *post*.

Child in the care of a local authority.—See s. 11, *ante*.

"**Parent or guardian.**"—For definition, see ss. 9, *ante*, and 59 (1), p. 923, *post*. See also s. 6 (2), *ante*.

"**Relative.**"—For definition, see s. 59 (1), *post*.

Adoption Act, 1958.—A provisional adoption order is not required in the case of an infant who is a British subject emigrating under the authority of the Secretary of State under this section (s. 55 of the Children and Young Persons Act, 1963, p. 114, *ante*).

18. Burial or cremation of deceased children.

—(1) A local authority may cause to be buried or cremated the body of any deceased child who immediately before his death was in the care of the authority:

Provided that the authority shall not cause the body to be cremated where cremation is not in accordance with the practice of the child's religious persuasion.

(2) Where a local authority exercise the powers referred to in subsection (1) of this section, they may if at the time of his death the child had not attained the age of sixteen years recover from any parent of the child any expenses incurred by them under the said subsection (1) less any amount received by the authority by way of death grant in respect of that death under section twenty-two of the National Insurance Act, 1946.

(3) Any sums recoverable by a local authority under subsection (2) of this section shall, without prejudice to any other method for the recovery thereof, be recoverable summarily as a civil debt.

(4) Nothing in this section shall affect any enactment regulating or authorising the burial, cremation or anatomical examination of the body of a deceased person.

NOTES

This section is printed as amended by the National Insurance Act, 1957.

Expenses of persons attending funeral.—Local authorities are authorised by s. 22, *post*, to pay in cases of hardship the expenses of persons attending the funerals of such children.

" Local authority."—See s. 38, *post*.

Child in the care of a local authority.—See s. 11, *ante*.

Attainment of age.—See note at p. 53, *ante*.
Under the National Assistance Act, 1948, ss. 42, 64 (1), the obligation of a parent to maintain his child continues until the child is sixteen years of age; in the case of a woman it extends to her illegitimate children and in the case of a man to children of whom he is adjudged to be the putative father. Liability of a parent under a contribution order is similarly limited to the period before the child attains sixteen (s. 24 (2), p. 903, *post*).

Parent.—In relation to an illegitimate child this expression is defined by s. 59 (1), *post*, as meaning the mother only, and accordingly the putative father has, under this section, no liability with regard to the child's funeral expenses. Under s. 4 (2) of the Affiliation Proceedings Act, 1957, he may be ordered to pay the funeral expenses if the child has died before the making of the affiliation order.

Section 22 of the National Insurance Act, 1946.—See now s. 39, National Insurance Act, 1965.

" Recoverable summarily as a civil debt."—The procedure is laid down in the Magistrates' Courts Act, 1952, ss. 47 (8), 50, 64, 73 and 77 (21 Halsbury's Statutes, 3rd Edn., 226, 227, 238, 246, 250).

Enactments regulating or authorising burial, cremation or anatomical examination.—See 3 Halsbury's Statutes, 3rd Edn., 434 *et seq.* (burial and cremation), and 21 Halsbury's Statutes, 3rd Edn., 553, 566 (anatomical examination of bodies).

19. Accommodation of persons over school age in convenient community home.—A local authority may provide accommodation in a community home for any person who is over compulsory school age but has not attained the age of twenty-one if the community home is provided for children who are over compulsory school age and is near the place where that person is employed or seeking employment or receiving education or training.

NOTES

This section is printed as substituted by the Children and Young Persons Act, 1969.

" Local authority."—See s. 38, *post*.

After-care.—As to the duty of local authorities to advise and befriend children over compulsory school age but under eighteen who are no longer in their care, see s. 34, p. 912, *post*.

" Compulsory school age."—For definition, see s. 59 (1), *post*.

" In the care of a local authority."—See s. 11, *ante*.

" Community home."—See s. 36 of the Children and Young Persons Act, 1969.

20. Financial assistance towards expenses of maintenance, education or training of persons over eighteen.—(1) A local authority may make contributions to the cost of the accommodation and maintenance of any person over compulsory school age but under the age of twenty-one who is, or has at any time after ceasing to be of compulsory school age been, in the care of a local authority, being either a person who has attained the age of seventeen but has ceased to be in the care of a local authority, or a person who has attained the age of eighteen, in any place near the place where he may be employed, or seeking employment, or in receipt of education or training.

(2) A local authority may make grants to persons who have attained the age of seventeen, but have not attained the age of twenty-one and who at or after the time when they attained the age of seventeen were in the care of a local authority to enable them to meet expenses connected with their receiving suitable education or training.

(3) Where a person—

(a) is engaged in a course of education or training at the time when he attains the age of twenty-one; or

(b) having previously been engaged in a course of education or training which has been interrupted by any circumstances, resumes the course as soon as practicable,

then if a local authority are at the said time, or were at the time when the course was interrupted, as the case may be, making any contributions or grants in respect of him under any of the foregoing provisions of this section, their powers under those provisions shall continue with respect to him until the completion of the course.

NOTES

This section is printed as amended by the Children and Young Persons Acts, 1963, and 1969.

"**Local authority.**"—See s. 38, *post.*

Financial assistance for persons over eighteen.—They may obtain assistance towards the cost of further education from the local education authority under the Education Act, 1944, s. 81 (11 Halsbury's Statutes, 3rd Edn., 237), and towards the cost of training courses from the Minister of Labour under the Employment and Training Act, 1948, s. 3; 12 Halsbury's Statutes, 3rd Edn., 134.

Where the local authority is assisting under the present section a person who is engaged on an educational or training course when he attains twenty-one they can continue to assist him until the end of the course (sub-s. (3)).

In the case of a child engaged in a course of education or training after the age of sixteen, an order in respect of his maintenance made under the Matrimonial Proceedings (Magistrates' Courts) Act, 1960, the Guardianship of Minors Act, or the Affiliation Proceedings Act, 1957 may extend beyond the age of sixteen.

"**Accommodation.**"—This may be provided in community homes established pursuant to s. 19, p. 899, *ante.*

Attainment of age.—See note at p. 53, *ante.*

"**In the care of a local authority.**"—See s. 11, *ante.*

Expenses connected with education.—The allocation of concurrent functions between the local authority and local education authority is the subject of regulations under s. 21, *infra.*

"**Interrupted by any circumstances.**"—The most frequent cause of interruption of a course of education or training was calling up for full-time training under the National Service Act, 1948. Another cause might be prolonged illness.

21. Allocation of functions as between local authority and local education authority.—The Secretary of State and the Minister of Education, or in Scotland the Secretary of State, may make regulations for providing, where a local authority under this Part of this Act and a local education authority as such have concurrent functions, by which authority the functions are to be exercised, and for determining as respects any functions of a local education authority specified in the regulations whether a child in the care of a local authority is to be treated as a child of parents of sufficient resources or a child of parents without resources.

NOTES

Avoidance of overlapping of functions.—The local education authority for every county is the County Council, and for every county borough is the County Borough Council (Education Act, 1944, s. 6, p. 248, *ante*), except where the Minister of Education constitutes a joint board as the local education authority for the area of two or more councils (*ibid.*, Sched. I, Part I). By s. 38, *post*, the local authorities for the purposes of the present Act are county councils and county borough councils. Except, therefore, in the case of a joint board, the local authority for the purpose of the present Act is the same body as the local education authority. Its functions under the present Act are to be discharged by a Social Services committee set up under s. 2 Local Authority Social Services Act, 1970, while its functions as a local education authority are discharged by an education committee established pursuant to Sched. I, Part II to the Education Act, 1944. A joint social services committee for two or more local authorities may be set up under s. 4 of the 1970 Act, and a joint education committee for two or more local education authorities may be set up pursuant to the Education Act, 1944, Sched. I, Part II, para. 2.

" **Local authority.**"—See s. 38, *post*.

" **Local education authority.**"—For definition, see s. 59 (1), *post*.

" **Functions.**"—For definition, see s. 59 (1), *post*.

" **Child.**"—For definition, see s. 59 (1), *post*.

" **Child of parents of sufficient resources.**"—This expression is not defined in the Education Acts, 1944 to 1953, or in the present Act. It is, however, an underlying principle of the Education Acts that no sums are to be recoverable in respect of benefits provided for a child if to do so would involve the parents in " financial hardship "; for the use of this term see the Education Act, 1944, s. 52 (the recovery of the costs of boarding accommodation); *cf.* the Education (Miscellaneous Provisions) Act, 1948, s. 5 (6) (recovery of cost of clothing), and the Regulations for Scholarships and other Benefits, 1945 (S. R. & O. 1945, No. 666), as amended by subsequent Regulations. Presumably a parent from whom sums are not to be recoverable on the ground that to recover them would involve him in financial hardship would be regarded as being a parent without resources.

Regulations.—See the Local Authorities and Local Education Authorities (Allocation of Functions) Regulations, 1951 (S.I. 1951 No. 472), p. 977, *post*.

22. Power of local authority to defray expenses of parents, etc., visiting children or attending funerals.—A local authority may make payments to any parent or guardian of, or other person connected with, a child in their care in respect of travelling, subsistence or other expenses incurred by the parent, guardian or other person in visiting the child or attending his funeral, if it appears to the authority that the parent, guardian or other person would not otherwise be able to visit the child or attend the funeral without undue hardship and that the circumstances warrant the making of the payments.

NOTES

This section now gives power to the local authority to help with expenses involved in visiting a child who is the subject of a care order, and who is accommodated in an approved school.

" **Local authority.**"—See s. 38, *post.*

" **Parent or guardian.**"—For definition, see ss. 9, *ante,* and 59 (1), *post.* See also s. 6 (2), *ante.*

Child in the care of a local authority.—See s. 11, *ante.*

" **Child.**"—For definition, see s. 59 (1), *post.*

" **Funeral.**"—By s. 18, *ante,* a local authority is empowered to cause the body of any child dying in their care to be buried or, where this is in accordance with the tenets of the child's religious denomination, cremated.

PART III

CONTRIBUTIONS TOWARDS MAINTENANCE OF CHILDREN

23. Contributions in respect of children in care of local authority. —(1) Subject to the provisions of this Part of this Act, sections eighty-six to eighty-eight of the Children and Young Persons Act, 1933, and sections ninety to ninety-two of the Children and Young Persons (Scotland) Act, 1937 shall apply to children received into the care of a local authority under section one of this Act as they apply to children in the care of a local authority by virtue of such an order as is mentioned in subsection (1) of the said section eighty-six.

(2) Subject to the provisions of this Part of this Act, to the provisions of the said Acts of 1933 and 1937 as to appeals and to the provisions of the said Act of 1937 as to revocation or variation, a contribution order in respect of a child in the care of a local authority under section one of this Act shall remain in force so long as he remains in the care of a local authority under the said section one.

NOTES

This section is printed as amended by the Children and Young Persons Act, 1969, s. 72 (3), (4) and Scheds. V and VI.

Maintenance contributions.—For ss. 86 to 88 of the Children and Young Persons Act, 1933, see pp. 67 *et seq., ante,* The only persons now liable to make contributions are the father and mother until the child attains the age of sixteen, and the child himself after he attains that age if he is in remunerative full-time work; see s. 24, *post.*

S. 86 of the 1933 Act, as amended, imposes a duty on the persons specified in s. 24, *infra,* to contribute, apart from any court order.

It should be noted that the fact that a local authority have the right to enforce payments of contributions by applying for and obtaining a contribution order, does not preclude them from making an agreement with the person liable to contribute, which will render an application for such an order unnecessary. (See s. 62 (3) of the Children and Young Persons Act, 1969).

" **Local authority.**"—See s. 38, *post.*

Child.—For definition, see s. 59 (1), *post.*

" **Appeals.**"—The Children and Young Persons Act, 1933, s. 102 (1) (p. 78, *ante*), confers a right of appeal to the Crown Court in, amongst others, the following cases and by the following persons:

" (c) in the case of an order requiring a person to contribute in respect of himself or any other person, by the person required to contribute; "

The paragraph quoted above is printed as amended by s. 60 and Sched. III of this Act, *post.* Para. (d) of sub-s. (1) of s. 102 of the 1933 Act confers a right of appeal, in the case of an order requiring all or any part of the payments accruing due under an affiliation order to be paid to some other person, on the person who would but for the order be entitled to the payments.

" **Contribution order.**"—For definition, see s. 59 (1), *post.*

24. Persons liable to make contributions.—(1) The persons liable under section eighty-six of the said Act of 1933 or section ninety of the said Act of 1937 to make contributions shall be the persons specified in that behalf in the following provisions of this section, and no others.

(2) The father and the mother of a child shall be liable to make contributions in respect of the child, but only so long as the child has not attained the age of sixteen; and no payments shall be required to be made under a contribution order made on the father or mother of a child in respect of any period after the child has attained that age.

(3) A person who has attained the age of sixteen and is engaged in remunerative full-time work shall be liable to make contributions in respect of himself.

NOTES

Liability for maintenance contributions.—This section follows the principle adopted in the National Assistance Act, 1948; see ss. 42, 64 (1) thereof.

Step-parents are no longer liable to make contributions. In the absence of statutory provision to the contrary, "father" is to be taken as the lawful father, and does not include a putative father who may be dealt with by the making or variation of an affiliation order; see s. 26, *infra.* The term "mother" includes the mother of an illegitimate child.

Adopters.—As to the liabilities of adopters, see s. 13 of the Adoption Act, 1958, p. 1047, *post.*

Parental contributions.—Section 62 (4) Children and Young Persons Act, 1969 p. 208, *ante,* provides that the basis of calculation shall be "a boarding out fee", *i.e.* what a local authority would normally be prepared to pay (whether or not the child is in fact boarded out.)

" **Child.**"—For definition, see s. 59 (1), *post.*

25. Repeal of limit to amount of contributions.—[*Repealed by the Children and Young Persons Act, 1969, s. 72 (4) and Sched. VI.*]

26. Affiliation orders.—(1) In England or Wales, where—
  (a) an illegitimate child is in the care of a local authority under section one of this Act, or
  (b) an illegitimate child is in the care of a local authority by virtue of such an order as is mentioned in section 86 (1) of the Children and Young Persons Act, 1933 [or]

and no affiliation order has been made in respect of the child, the local authority whose area includes the place where the mother of the child resides may make application to a court of summary jurisdiction having jurisdiction in that place for a summons to be served under section [one of the Affiliation Proceedings Act, 1957].

Provided that no application shall be made under this subsection—

  (i) in a case falling within paragraph (a) of this subsection, after the expiration of three years from the time when the child was received or last received into the care of the local authority or of another local authority from whom the care of the child was taken over by the first-mentioned authority;

(ii) in a case falling within paragraph (b) of this subsection, after the expiration of three years from the coming into force of the order mentioned in the said paragraph (b).

(2) In any proceedings on an application under the last foregoing subsection the court shall hear such evidence as the local authority may produce, in addition to the evidence required to be heard by section four of the said Act of 1957, and shall in all other respects, but subject to the provisions of the next following subsection, proceed as on an application made by the mother under the said section [one].

(3) An order made under section [four of the said Act of 1957] on an application under subsection (1) of this section shall provide that the payments to be made under the order shall, in lieu of being made to the mother or a person appointed to have the custody of the child, be made to the local authority who are from time to time entitled under section eighty-six of the said Act of 1933 to receive contributions in respect of the child.

(4) Where in accordance with subsection (4) of section eighty-eight of the Children and Young Persons Act, 1933 (which limits the duration of affiliation orders) an affiliation order has ceased to be in force, and but for that subsection the order would still be in force, then if the condition specified in paragraph (a), (b) [or (c)] of subsection (1) of this section is fulfilled, the local authority whose area includes the place where the putative father of the child resides may make application to a court of summary jurisdiction having jurisdiction in that place—

(a) for the affiliation order to be revived, and
(b) for payments thereunder to be made to the local authority who are from time to time entitled under section eighty-six of the said Act of 1933 to receive contributions in respect of the child,

and the court may make an order accordingly.

(5) Part IV of the said Act of 1933 shall apply in relation to an order made on an application under subsection (1) of this section or to an affiliation order revived under the last foregoing subsection as if it were an affiliation order in respect of which an order had been made under subsection (1) of section eighty-eight of that Act.

(6) [*Repealed by the Magistrates' Courts Act,* 1952.]

(7) [*Repealed by the Justices of the Peace Act,* 1949.]

(8) [*This subsection related to Scotland and the whole of this Act is repealed as regards Scotland by the Social Work (Scotland) Act,* 1968.]

NOTES

This section is printed as amended by the Justice of the Peace Act, 1949, the Magistrates' Courts Act, 1952, and the Children and Young Persons Act, 1969, s. 72 (3), (4) and Scheds. V and VI, the inclusion of the word "or" at the end of sub-s. (1) (b) is apparently a legislative slip, as is the inclusion of "or (c)" in sub-s. (4), as para. (c) which followed has been repealed.

Proceedings under this section are " domestic proceedings ". See ss. 56–62 of the Magistrates' Courts Act, 1952, and s. 5 of the Legitimacy Act, 1959, p. 1220, *post.*

For s. 88 of the Children and Young Persons Act, 1933, see p. 70, *ante.*

Scotland and Northern Ireland.—An English court has jurisdiction in proceedings under this section for an affiliation order against a putative father who resides in Scotland or Northern Ireland, and to make, revoke, revive or vary the order, if the act of intercourse resulting in the birth of the child or any act of intercourse between the parties which may have resulted therein took place in England; see s. 3 of the Maintenance Orders Act, 1950. The jurisdiction is exercisable although the child was not born in England; see *ibid.*, s. 27 (2). This section is modified by the Maintenance Orders Act, 1950, s. 14 and First Schedule as follows: Where the putative father of a child in respect of whom an order has been made under s. 88 of the Children and Young Persons Act, 1933, is for the time being residing in Scotland or Northern Ireland, sub-s. (4) shall have effect as if for reference to the local authority whose area includes the place where the putative father of the child resides, and to a court of summary jurisdiction having jurisdiction in that place, there were substituted references to the local authority who, if the affiliation order were still in force, would be entitled to payments thereunder, and to a court of summary jurisdiction having jurisdiction within the area of that authority.

Revival of Order.—The power to obtain a revival of a lapsed affiliation order, which, it seems, applies both where the affiliation order was made on the application of the mother and varied at the instance of the local authority, and where it was originally made on the application of the local authority (see sub-s. (5)), will chiefly be of use where a local authority have allowed a child in their care to return to a relative or guardian and subsequently find it necessary in the interests of the child to receive him back into their care pursuant to s. 3 (4), p. 519, *ante*. As to the procedure for the revival of orders generally, see the Magistrates' Courts Act, 1952, s. 53 (21 Halsbury's Statutes, 3rd Edn., 187).

National assistance.—The present section is complementary to s. 44 of the National Assistance Act, 1948, which gives a similar power of applying for affiliation orders to local authorities for the purposes of that Act.

In the case of *Clapham* v. *National Assistance Board*, [1961] 2 Q. B. 77; [1961] 2 All E. R. 50; 125 J. P. 373, an affiliation order made on the mother's complaint had been set aside on appeal to quarter sessions. It was held that the National Assistance Board had an independent and separable right not only to apply for a summons but also to obtain an affiliation order, and at no stage did the Board step into the shoes of the mother; accordingly the justices had jurisdiction to make an affiliation order on the complaint of the Board.

In *Payne* v. *Critchley and National Assistance Board*, [1962] 2 Q. B. 83; [1962] 1 All E. R. 619; 126 J. P. 162, it was held that s. 44 (1) (a) created a precedent whereby the National Assistance Board could not apply for an affiliation order unless and until they had given assistance in respect of an illegitimate child, but once an order was made, its operation was not limited to the period during which assistance was being given, and there was no difference in its force and effect from one originally obtained by the mother.

" Child."—For definition, see s. 59 (1), *post*.

" Local authority."—See s. 38, *post*.

Time for application.—It is only the application that must be made within the three year period. If it is so made the summons may be issued after the period has expired (*Potts* v. *Cambridge* (1858), 8 E. & B. 847).

" Evidence."—The justices must hear the evidence of the mother and such other evidence as she may produce and must also hear any evidence tendered by or on behalf of the alleged father. It is essential that the mother's evidence is corroborated in a material particular (s. 4 of the Affiliation Proceedings Act, 1957).

Terms of order.—If the court adjudges the man to be the putative father it may make an affiliation order with payment of a weekly sum. Generally as to affiliation procedure, see the current edition of Stone's Justices' Manual, title "Affiliation Proceedings."

Duration of order.—See note "Amount and Duration" at p. 72, and Affiliation Proceedings Act, 1957.

Appeals.—An appeal against the making or refusal of an order, or variation, revocation or revival, lies to the Crown Court. There is also an appeal by case stated to the High Court and in some cases application for *certiorari*.

"**Contributions.**"—Contributions under this section are payable in the case of a child committed to the care of a local authority, or received into the care of a local authority under s. 1, *ante* (see ss. 23 (1), 24, *ante*), to the council of the county or county borough within which the person liable for such contributions is residing (s. 86 (3) of the Children and Young Persons Act, 1933, p. 67, *ante*).

For transitional provisions in relation to an order committing a child to the care of a fit person other than a local authority and in force on January 1, 1971, see Sched. 4, para. 9 Children and Young Persons Act, 1969.

Enforcement of Orders.—Para. (a) of s. 88 (2) of the Children and Young Persons Act, 1933 (p. 70, *ante*) provides that where an order directing that payments under an affiliation order be made to the local authority entitled to receive contributions in respect of a child or young person is in force, powers of enforcing and varying the affiliation order shall only be exercisable by justices and courts of summary jurisdiction having jurisdiction in the place where the putative father is for the time being residing. The paragraph is applied by sub-s. (5) of the present section to an affiliation order made or revived on the application of a local authority as well as to an affiliation order varied on its application.

Enforcement of affiliation orders is by way of complaint for an order in accordance with the provisions of the Magistrates' Courts Act, 1952, see s. 74 of that Act (21 Halsbury's Statutes, 3rd Edn., 247). See note to s. 87 of the Children and Young Persons Act, 1933, p. 70, *ante*.

Attachment of earnings.—See note to s. 87 of the Children and Young Persons Act, 1933, p. 70, *ante*.

Domestic proceedings.—Proceedings under this section are " domestic proceedings ". See ss. 56–62 of the Magistrates' Courts Act, 1952, pp. 1220, *et seq.*, *post*,

PART IV

VOLUNTARY HOMES AND VOLUNTARY ORGANISATIONS

NOTE

A residential home for mentally disordered persons shall be deemed not to be a voluntary home within Part IV of the Children Act, 1948 (Mental Health Act, 1959, s. 19 (3)).

27. Provisions as to voluntary homes to extend to homes supported wholly or partly by endowments.—Section ninety-two of the Children and Young Persons Act, 1933, and section ninety-six of the Children and Young Persons (Scotland) Act, 1937 (which define the expression "voluntary home") shall have effect as if to the reference therein to a home or other institution supported wholly or partly by voluntary contributions there were added a reference to a home or other institution supported wholly or partly by endowments, not being a school within the meaning of the Education Act, 1944, or the Education (Scotland) Act, 1946.

NOTES

Endowed homes.—S. 92 of the Children and Young Persons Act, 1933 (p. 74, *ante*), defines voluntary home as meaning "any home or other institution for the boarding, care and maintenance of poor children or young persons, being a home or other institution supported wholly or partly by voluntary contributions" other than any mental nursing home or residential home for mentally disordered persons within the meaning of Part III of the Mental Health Act, 1959.

Schools.—S. 114 (1) of the Education Act, 1944 defines " school " as meaning " an institution for providing primary or secondary education, or both primary and secondary education, being a school maintained by a local education authority, an independent school, or a school in respect of which grants are made by the Minister to the proprietor of the school."

Scotland.—See note to s. 26 (8), *ante.*

28. Extension of age limits in provisions relating to voluntary homes.

—A person shall not be deemed for the purposes of Part V of the Children and Young Persons Act, 1933, or Part VI of the Children and Young Persons (Scotland) Act, 1937, to cease to be a young person until he attains the age of eighteen, and accordingly references to young persons in the said Part V or the said Part VI, or any other enactment in so far as it relates to the said Part V or the said Part VI, shall be construed as including references to all persons over the age of fourteen who have not attained the age of eighteen.

NOTE

Extension of definition of " young person."—Part V of the Children and Young Persons Act, 1933, being ss. 92–94 (pp. 74 *et seq., ante*), contains provisions for the protection of children or young persons in voluntary homes. By *ibid.*, s. 107 (p. 81, *ante*), " child " is defined as a person under the age of fourteen years, and " young person " as a person who has attained the age of fourteen years but is under the age of seventeen years. Persons who had attained the age of seventeen years were, therefore, outside the protection of Part V as originally enacted. The present section extends the definition of " young persons " for the purpose of Part V of the 1933 Act to include persons up to the age of eighteen.

Scotland.—See note, *supra.*

29. Registration of voluntary homes.

—(1) After the end of the year nineteen hundred and forty-eight no voluntary home shall be carried on unless it is for the time being registered in a register to be kept for the purposes of this section by the Secretary of State.

(2) Application for registration under this section shall be made by the persons carrying on or intending to carry on the home to which the application relates, and shall be made in such manner, and accompanied by such particulars, as the Secretary of State may by regulations prescribe

(3) On an application duly made under the last foregoing subsection, the Secretary of State may either grant or refuse the application, as he thinks fit, but where he refuses the application he shall give the applicant notice in writing of the refusal.

(4) Where at any time after the end of the year nineteen hundred and forty-eight it appears to the Secretary of State that the conduct of any voluntary home is not in accordance with regulations made or directions given under section thirty-one of this Act or is otherwise unsatisfactory, he may, after giving to the persons carrying on the home not less than twenty-eight days' notice in writing of his proposal so to do, remove the home from the register.

(5) Any person who carries on a voluntary home in contravention of the provisions of subsection (1) of this section shall be guilty of an offence and liable on summary conviction to a fine not exceeding fifty pounds and to a further fine not exceeding two pounds in respect of each day during which the offence continues after conviction.

(6) Where—

  (a) a voluntary home is carried on in contravention of the provisions of subsection (1) of this section; or

  (b) notice of a proposal to remove a voluntary home from the register is given under subsection (4) thereof,

the Secretary of State may, notwithstanding that the time for any appeal under the next following section has not expired or that such an appeal is pending, notify the local authority in whose area the home is situated, and require them forthwith to remove from the home and receive into their care under section one of this Act all or any of the children for whom accommodation is being provided in the home; and the local authority shall comply with the requirement whether or not the circumstances of the children are such that they fall within paragraphs (a) to (c) of subsection (1) of the said section one and notwithstanding that any of the children may appear to the local authority to be over the age of seventeen.

For the purpose of carrying out the duty of the local authority under this subsection, any person authorised in that behalf by the local authority may enter any premises in which the home in question is being carried on.

(7) Where the Secretary of State registers a home under this section or removes a home from the register, he shall notify the local authority in whose area the home is situated.

(8) Any notice under this section required to be given by the Secretary of State to the persons carrying on, or intending to carry on, a voluntary home may be given to those persons by being delivered personally to any one of them, or being sent by post in a registered letter to them or any one of them.

For the purposes of section twenty-six of the Interpretation Act, 1889, (which defines " service by post ") a letter enclosing a notice under this section to the persons carrying on a voluntary home or any one of them shall be deemed to be properly addressed if it is addressed to them or him at the home.

(9) Section ninety-five of the Children and Young Persons Act, 1933, and section ninety-nine of the Children and Young Persons (Scotland) Act, 1937, are hereby repealed as from the first day of January, nineteen hundred and forty-nine.

NOTES

This section is printed as amended by the Statute Law Revision Act, 1953.

" **Voluntary home.**"—For definition, see s. 59 (1), *post*.

Regulations.—See s. 58, p. 923, *post*, the Voluntary Homes (Registration) Regulations, 1948 (S.I. 1948 No. 2408), p. 972, *post*, and the Memorandum by the Home Office on the main provisions of the Act affecting Voluntary Homes and Voluntary Organisations in England and Wales issued in November, 1948.

" **Local authority.**"—See s. 38, *post*.

" **Child.**"—For definition, see s. 59 (1), *post*.

Appear to be over the age of seventeen.—It is only children who appear to be under the age of seventeen who may be received into the care of a local authority under s. 1 (1), *ante*, although once a child has been received into care the local authority's duty to him may continue until he is eighteen. See s. 1 (2), p. 880, *ante*, and note thereto.

" **May enter any premises.**"—The power of entry conferred by this subsection is a power to enter for a particular purpose only, that is to say for the purpose of removing children from the home.   Power to enter for the purpose of visiting children in the home is conferred by s. 54 (3), *post*.   It is desirable that all persons entering voluntary homes as agents of a local authority should carry with them a written authorisation, and particularly is this so when they enter for the purpose of removing children.

" **Service by post.**"—S. 26 of the Interpretation Act, 1889, provides that service by post shall be deemed to be effected " by properly addressing, prepaying and posting a letter containing the document, and unless the contrary is proved to have been effected at the time at which the letter would be delivered in the ordinary course of post."

Appeal.—As to the right of appeal against a refusal to register a voluntary home or against removal from the register see s. 30, *post*.

Controlled or assisted community home.—This section does not apply to a voluntary home while it is a controlled or assisted community home (s. 44 of the Children and Young Persons Act, 1969).

30. Appeals.—(1) Where under the last foregoing section application for the registration of a voluntary home is refused, or it is proposed to remove a voluntary home from the register, the persons intending to carry on or carrying on the home, as the case may be, may within fourteen days from the giving of the notice under subsection (3) or subsection (4) of that section appeal against the refusal or proposal; and where the appeal is brought against a proposal to remove a home from the register, the home shall not be removed therefrom before the determination of the appeal.

(2) An appeal under this section shall be brought by notice in writing addressed to the Secretary of State requiring him to refer the refusal or proposal to an appeal tribunal constituted in accordance with the provisions of Part I of the First Schedule to this Act.

(3) On an appeal under this section the appeal tribunal may confirm the refusal or proposal of the Secretary of State or may direct that the home shall be registered or, as the case may be, shall not be removed from the register, and the Secretary of State shall comply with the direction.

(4) The Lord Chancellor may with the concurrence of the Lord President of the Council make rules as to the practice and procedure to be followed with respect to the constitution of appeal tribunals for the purposes of this section, as to the manner of making appeals to such tribunals, and as to proceedings before such tribunals and matters incidental to or consequential on such proceedings; and without prejudice to the generality of the foregoing provisions of this subsection such rules may make provision as to the particulars to be supplied by or to the Secretary of State of matters relevant to the determination of the appeal, and as to representation before such tribunals, whether by counsel or solicitor or otherwise.

(5) The Secretary of State may out of moneys provided by Parliament—

(a) pay to members of tribunals constituted for the purposes of this section such fees and allowances as he may with the consent of the Treasury determine.

(b) defray the expenses of such tribunals up to such amount as he may with the like consent determine.

(6) The provisions of the Arbitration Acts, 1889 to 1934, shall not apply to any proceedings before a tribunal constituted for the purposes of this section except so far as any provisions thereof may be applied thereto with or without modifications by rules made under this section.

(7) [Application to Scotland.]

NOTES

Community home.—See note to s. 29, p. 908, *ante.*

Scotland.—The whole Act is repealed as to Scotland by the Social Work (Scotland) Act, 1968.

" **Appeal tribunal.**"—For Part I of Sched. I, see p. 925, *post.*

Arbitration Acts, 1889 to 1934.—See now the Arbitration Act, 1950.

Rules.—See the Children Act (Appeal Tribunal) Rules, 1949, p. 975, *post.*

31. Regulations as to conduct of voluntary homes.—(1) The Secretary of State may make regulations as to the conduct of voluntary homes and for securing the welfare of the children therein, and regulations under this section may in particular—

    (a) impose requirements as to the accommodation and equipment to be provided in homes, authorise the Secretary of State to give directions prohibiting the provision for the children in any home of clothing of any description specified in the directions, and impose requirements as to the medical arrangements to be made for protecting the health of the children in the homes;

    (b) require the furnishing to the Secretary of State of information as to the facilities provided for the parents and guardians of children in the homes to visit and communicate with the children, and authorise the Secretary of State to give directions as to the provisions of such facilities;

    (c) authorise the Secretary of State to give directions limiting the number of children who may at any one time be accommodated in any particular home;

    (d) provide for consultation with the Secretary of State as to applicants for appointment to the charge of a home and empower the Secretary of State to prohibit the appointment of any particular applicant therefor except in the cases (if any) in which the regulations dispense with such consultation by reason that the person to be appointed possesses such qualifications as may be prescribed by the regulations;

    (e) require notice to be given to the Secretary of State of any change of the person in charge of a home; and

    (f) impose requirements as to the facilities which are to be given for children to receive a religious upbringing appropriate to the persuasion to which they belong,

and may contain different provisions for different descriptions of cases and as respects different descriptions of homes.

(2) Where any regulation under this section provides that this subsection shall have effect in relation thereto, any person who contravenes

or fails to comply with the regulation or any requirement or direction thereunder shall be liable on summary conviction to a fine not exceeding fifty pounds.

NOTES

As to making the regulations, see s. 58, p. 923, *post*.

" **Voluntary home.**"—For definition, see s. 59 (1), *post*.

Person in charge of a home.—This, it is thought, must mean the master, matron, superintendent, etc., not necessarily the proprietor of the home.

" **Religious upbringing.**"—See s. 16 (2), *ante*, which provides that no child in the care of a local authority shall be placed in a voluntary home which does not afford facilities for him to receive a religious upbringing appropriate to his persuasion, and see note to s. 15, p. 895, *ante*.

Regulations.—Regs. 12–14 of the Administration of Children's Homes Regulations, 1951, p. 982, provide that sub-s. (2), *supra*, shall have effect in relation to them.

Community home.—See note to s. 29, p. 909, *ante*.

32. Provisions where particulars to be sent of voluntary homes are varied.—(1) Where the Secretary of State by regulations made under section ninety-three of the Children and Young Persons Act, 1933, or section ninety-seven of the Children and Young Persons (Scotland) Act, 1937, varies the particulars which are to be sent by persons in charge of voluntary homes—

(a) the person in charge of such a home shall send the prescribed particulars to the Secretary of State within three months from the date of the making of the regulations;

(b) where any such home was established before, but not more than three months before, the making of the regulations, compliance with the last foregoing paragraph shall be sufficient compliance with the requirement of the said section ninety-three or ninety-seven to send the prescribed particulars within three months from the establishment of the home;

(c) in the year in which the particulars are varied, compliance with paragraph (a) of this subsection by the person in charge of any voluntary home shall be sufficient compliance with the requirement of the said section ninety-three or ninety-seven to send the prescribed particulars before the prescribed date in that year.

(2) Any default in complying with the requirements of paragraph (a) of the last foregoing subsection shall be deemed to be such a default as is mentioned in subsection (2) of the said section ninety-three or in subsection (3) of the said section ninety-seven, as the case may be.

NOTES

Children and Young Persons Act, 1933, s. 93.—See p. 74, *ante*.

Regulations.—The regulations under this section at present in force are the Voluntary Homes (Return of Particulars) Regulations, 1949, as amended by the Voluntary Homes (Return of Particulars) Regulations, 1950 and 1955, p. 466, *ante*.

" **Voluntary home.**"—For definition, see s. 59 (1), *post*.

" **Person in charge.**"—Who is the person in charge is a question of fact to be determined by the magistrates in the case of default. Presumably, it means the master, matron, superintendent, etc.

" Prescribed."—See the Children and Young Persons Act, 1933, s. 107 (1), p. 81, *ante*.

Community home.—See note to s. 29, p. 909, *ante*.

Scotland.—See note to s. 26, p. 904, *ante*.

33. Powers of Secretary of State as to voluntary organisations.—(1) The Secretary of State may by regulations control the making and carrying out by voluntary organisations of arrangements for the emigration of children.

(2) Any such regulations may contain such consequential and incidental provisions as appear to the Secretary of State to be necessary or expedient, including, in particular, provisions for requiring information to be given to the Secretary of State as to the operations or intended operations of the organisation and for enabling the Secretary of State to be satisfied that suitable arrangements have been or will be made for the children's reception and welfare in the country to which they are going.

(3) The power conferred by Part II of this Act on the Secretary of State to make regulations as to the boarding-out of children by local authorities shall extend also to the boarding-out of children by voluntary organisations:

Provided that in the provisions of the said Part II conferring that power any reference to the supervision and inspection by a local authority of boarded-out children and the premises in which they are boarded out shall, in relation to children boarded out by voluntary organisations, be deemed to be a reference to supervision and inspection either by a local authority or, where it is so provided by or under the regulations, by a voluntary organisation.

(4) Where any regulation under this section provides that this subsection shall have effect in relation thereto, any person who contravenes or fails to comply with the regulation shall be liable on summary conviction to a fine not exceeding fifty pounds.

NOTES

Regulations.—See the Boarding-Out of Children Regulations, 1955, p. 984, *post*.

Prosecutions.—See s. 55, p. 920, *post*.

" Voluntary organisation."—For definition, see s. 59 (1), *post*.

Child emigration.—As to arrangements for child emigration made by local authorities, see s. 17, p. 898, *ante*.

" Child."—For definition, see s. 59 (1), *post*.

" Local authority."—See s. 38, *post*.

Boarding-out regulations.—See s. 14, p. 894, *ante*, and notes thereto.

" Supervision and inspection."—See the Boarding-Out of Children Regulations, 1955, p. 984, *post*.

34. After-care of children formerly in care of local authorities or voluntary organisations.—(1) Where it comes to the knowledge of a local authority that there is in their area any child over compulsory school age who at the time when he ceased to be of that age or at any subsequent time was, but is no longer,—

(a) in the care of a local authority under section one of this Act, or

(b) in the care of a voluntary organisation,

then, unless the authority are satisfied that the welfare of the child does not require it, they shall be under a duty so long as he has not attained the age of eighteen to advise and befriend him:

Provided that where in a case falling within paragraph (b) of this subsection the local authority are satisfied that the voluntary organisation have the necessary facilities for advising and befriending him, the local authority may make arrangements whereby, while the arrangements continue in force, he shall be advised and befriended by the voluntary organisation instead of by the local authority.

(2) Where a child over compulsory school age—

(a) ceases to be in the care of a local authority under section one of this Act and proposes to reside in the area of another local authority, or

(b) ceases to be in the care of a voluntary organisation,

the authority or organisation shall inform the local authority for the area in which the child proposes to reside.

(3) Where it comes to the knowledge of a local authority or a voluntary organisation that a child whom they have been advising and befriending in pursuance of this section proposes to transfer or has transferred his residence to the area of another local authority, the first-mentioned local authority or, as the case may be, the voluntary organisation, shall inform the said other local authority.

NOTES

It may be found that a parent, whose child has been in care under s. 1, removes him from care when he is able to leave school, even should the circumstances otherwise be unchanged. If his parent finds him lodgings, for example, he will be without the safeguard of the Child Life Protection provisions. This section provides some safeguard for such a child.

" **Local authority.**"—See s. 38, *post.*

" **Child.**"—For definition, see s. 59 (1), *post.*

" **Compulsory school age.**"—For definition, see s. 59 (1), *post.*

" **Voluntary organisation.**"—For definition, see s. 59 (1), *post.*

" **Welfare.**"—See notes to s. 1, p. 882, *ante.*

" **Shall inform.**"—These words impose an absolute obligation, but it is one which may, it seems, be impossible to fulfil, unless the information is forthcoming from the child or his parents, etc.

" **Where it comes to the knowledge . . . shall inform.**"—Here the obligation, in contrast to that imposed by sub-s. (2), *supra,* is qualified, and is imposed only where the local authority or voluntary organisation knows of the transfer or proposed transfer.

PART V

CHILD LIFE PROTECTION

35–37.—[*These sections were repealed by the Children Act, 1958, Schedule III. See the corresponding provisions of that Act, pp. 956 et. seq., post.*]

PART VI

ADMINISTRATIVE AND FINANCIAL PROVISIONS

38. Local authorities.—(1) In England and Wales, the local authorities for the purposes of this Act and of Parts III and IV of the Children and Young Persons Act, 1933, and of Part I of the Children Act, 1958, and of Parts I and III of the Children and Young Persons Act, 1963 shall be the councils of counties and county boroughs.

NOTES

This section is printed as amended by the Children Act, 1958, and the Children and Young Persons Act, 1963.

" **Local authorities.**"—The effect of this section is that county councils (including the Greater London Council) and county borough councils become the local authorities not only for the purposes of the present Act, but also for the purposes of the provisions of the Children and Young Persons Acts, 1933 to 1963, and the Children Act, 1958. The same authorities are welfare authorities for the purposes of Part IV of the Adoption Act, 1958. As to London see the note at the commencement of Part VI of the Children and Young Persons Act, 1933, p. 75, *ante*.

Every local authority is, by s. 2 of the Local Authority Social Services Act, 1970, required to appoint a special social services committee, and to appoint a director of social services; see s. 6, p. 930, *post*.

Isles of Scilly.—Sub-s. (1) shall have effect from April 1, 1959, as if amongst the authorities there specified there were included the council of the Isles of Scilly.

See the Isles of Scilly (Children Act, 1948) Order, 1959, S.I. 1959 No. 432, p. 619, *post*.

Parts III and IV of the Children and Young Persons Act, 1933.—See pp. 42 *et seq., ante.*

[*Sections* 39–42 *are repealed by the Local Authority Social Services Act,* 1970, s. 14 *and Sched. III, p.* 933, post. *See now s.* 2 *and Sched. I*, ibid.]

43. Advisory Council on Child Care.—(1) There shall be a council, to be known as the Advisory Council on Child Care, for the purpose of advising the Secretary of State on matters connected with the discharge of his functions in England and Wales under this Act, the Children and Young Persons Acts, 1933 to 1969, the Adoption Act, 1958 and the Adoption Act, 1968.

(2) The said council shall consist of such persons, to be appointed by the Secretary of State, as the Secretary of State may think fit, being persons specially qualified to deal with matters affecting the welfare of children and persons having such other qualifications as the Secretary of State considers requisite.

Among the persons appointed under this subsection there shall be persons having experience in local government.

(3) The Secretary of State shall appoint a person to be chairman, and a person to be the secretary, of the said council.

(4) It shall be the duty of the said council to advise the Secretary of State on any matter which the Secretary of State may refer to them, being such a matter as is mentioned in subsection (1) of this section, and they may also, of their own motion, make representations to the Secretary of State as respects any such matter as is mentioned in that subsection.

(5) The Secretary of State may make out of moneys provided by Parliament such payments to the members of the said council in respect of travelling, subsistence and other expenses as he may with the consent of the Treasury determine.

NOTES

This section is printed as amended by the Adoption Act, 1958, Sched. IV, and the Children and Young Persons Acts, 1963 and 1969.

Advisory Council for England.—It is a common feature of recent social legislation to provide that the Minister responsible for the administration of a statute introducing major reforms shall be given the assistance of a standing body of experts, and the present section follows a familiar pattern. See, for example, the Education Act, 1944, s. 4, constituting the Central Councils for Education; the National Insurance (Industrial Injuries) Act, 1946, s. 61 (23 Halsbury's Statutes, 3rd Edn., 55), constituting the Industrial Injuries Advisory Council, and the National Insurance Act, 1946, s. 41 (23 Halsbury's Statutes, 3rd Edn., 68), constituting the National Insurance Advisory Committee.

44. Advisory Council on child care for Scotland.—[See introductory note, p. 880, *ante*, and also s. 7 Social Work (Scotland) Act, 1968.]

45. Grants for training in child care.—(1) The Secretary of State with the consent of the Treasury may out of moneys provided by Parliament defray or contribute towards any fees or expenses incurred by persons undergoing training approved by the Secretary of State with a view to, or in the course of, their employment for the purposes of any of the enactments specified in subsection (1A) of this section of this Act, or their employment by a voluntary organisation for similar purposes, and may defray or contribute towards the cost of maintenance of persons undergoing such training.

(1A) The enactments referred to in subsection (1) of this section are:—

(a) Parts III and IV of the Children and Young Persons Act, 1933;
(b) this Act;
(c) the Children Act, 1958;
(d) the Adoption Act, 1958;
(e) section 2 (1) (f) of the Matrimonial Proceedings (Magistrates' Courts) Act, 1960, section 38 of the Matrimonial Causes Act, 1965 and section 7 (4) of the Family Law Reform Act, 1969;
(f) the Children and Young Persons Act, 1963, except Part II and section 56; and
(g) the Children and Young Persons Act, 1969.

(2) The Secretary of State may out of moneys provided by Parliament make grants of such amounts, and subject to such conditions, as he may with the consent of the Treasury determine towards expenses incurred by any body of persons in providing courses suitable for persons undergoing training as aforesaid.

NOTE

This section is printed as amended by the Local Authority Social Services Act, 1970.

46. Grants to voluntary organisations.—(1) The Secretary of State may make out of moneys provided by Parliament grants of such amounts, and subject to such conditions, as he may with the consent of the Treasury determine towards expenses incurred or to be incurred by voluntary organisations, in circumstances such that it appears to the Secretary of State requisite that the grants should be made, for improving premises in which voluntary homes are being carried on or the equipment of voluntary homes, or for securing that voluntary homes will be better provided with qualified staff.

(2) A local authority may make contributions to any voluntary organisation the object or primary object of which is to promote the welfare of children.

NOTES

This section is printed as amended by the Local Government Act, 1958, Sched. VIII.

Controlled or assisted community home.—A grant may not be made in connection with a voluntary home which at the time the expenditure was incurred was a controlled or assisted community home or was designated as such in a regional plan which was then in operation (s. 65 (2) Children and Young Persons Act, 1969).

Sub-s. (2) of the present section empowers local authorities to make contributions to voluntary organisations concerned with child welfare.

" **Voluntary organisation.**"—For definition, see s. 59 (1), p. 923, *post.*

" **Voluntary home.**"—For definition, see s. 59 (1), *post.* See also the Children and Young Persons Act, 1933, s. 92, p. 74, *ante.*

" **Local authority.**"—See s. 38, p. 914, *ante.*

47. Grants to local authorities.—[*Repealed by the Local Government Act,* 1958.]

48. Administrative expenses of Secretary of State.—The administrative expenses incurred by the Secretary of State under this Act shall be defrayed out of moneys provided by Parliament.

49. Accounts of councils of county boroughs.—(1) The council of every county borough shall keep separate accounts of the sums received and expended by them in the exercise of their functions under any of the enactments mentioned in subsection (1A) of this section, *other than sums received or expended by them as managers of an approved school or in respect of children sent to an approved school or in respect of remand homes.*

(1A) The enactments referred to in the subsection (1) of this section are:—

(a) the enactments specified in section 45 (1A) of this Act;
(b) section 9 of the Mental Health Act, 1959, and section 10 of that Act so far as it relates to children and young persons in respect of whom the rights and powers of a parent are vested in a local authority as mentioned in subsection (1) (a) of that section; and
(c) section 10 of the Mental Health (Scotland) Act, 1960, so far as it relates to children and young persons in respect of whom the rights and powers of a parent are vested in a local authority as mentioned in subsection (1) (a) of that section.

(2) The accounts to be kept under this section shall be made up and audited in like manner as the accounts of a county council.

(3) The enactments relating to the audit of accounts by a district auditor and to the matters incidental to such audit and consequential thereon shall have effect in relation to the accounts which the council of a county borough are required to keep under this section as they have effect in relation to the accounts of a county council.

NOTES

This section is printed as amended by the Children and Young Persons Act, 1969, and the Local Authority Social Services Act, 1970. From a date to be appointed the words in italics are repealed (Act of 1969, s. 72 (4) and Sched. VI).

The necessity for this section arises from the fact that although by s. 219 of the Local Government Act, 1933 (19 Halsbury's Statutes, 3rd Edn., 393), all the accounts of a county council are automatically subject to district audit, yet by ss. 237–240 of that Act, the accounts of a borough council are not so subject in the absence of a statutory provision to that effect, or unless the council so determines.

" **County borough.**"—The councils of county boroughs are by s. 38, p. 914, *ante,* local authorities for the purposes of the Act. If accounts are kept under s. 8 of the Local Authority Social Services Act, 1970, this section will not apply (s. 8 (5), *ibid.*).

" **Separate accounts.**"—The necessity for keeping separate accounts arises from the fact that the majority of the other accounts of a county borough council are not necessarily subject to district audit.

" **In like manner as the accounts of a county council.**"—See Part X (ss. 219–242, inclusive), of the Local Government Act, 1933 (19 Halsbury's Statutes, 3rd Edn., 523–537). By s. 235 of that Act (19 Halsbury's Statutes, 3rd Edn., 533), the Minister of Health is enabled to make regulations generally with regard to the preparation and audit of accounts which are subject to audit by the district auditor.

London boroughs.—This section does not apply to the accounts kept by a London borough (s. 8 (6), Local Authority Social Services Act, 1970).

PART VII

MISCELLANEOUS AND GENERAL

50. [*Added a new sub-s.* (2A) *to s.* 4 *of the Guardianship of Infants Act,* 1925, *which is now repealed. Accordingly this section is repealed and replaced by s.* 5 *of the Guardianship of Minors Act,* 1971, p. 1200, post.]

51. Provisions as to places of safety.—(1) Local authorities shall make provision, in community homes provided by them or in controlled community homes, for the reception and maintenance of children removed to a place of safety under the Children and Young Persons Act, 1933, the Children and Young Persons (Scotland) Act, 1937, Part I of the Children Act, 1958, or Part IV of the Adoption Act, 1958 or sections 2 (5), 16 (3) or 28 of the Children and Young Persons Act, 1969 and of children detained by them in pursuance of arrangements under s. 29 (3) of that Act.

(2) [*Repealed by the Children and Young Persons Act,* 1969, *s.* 72 (4) *and Sched. VI and S.I.* 1969 *No.* 1565.]

(3) Where under any of the enactments mentioned in subsection (1) of this section a child is removed to a place of safety not being a community home provided by a local authority or a controlled community home and

not being a hospital vested in the Minister of Health or the Secretary of State, the expenses of the child's maintenance there shall be recoverable from the local authority within whose area the child was immediately before his removal.

NOTES

This section is printed as amended by the Adoption Act, 1958, Sched. IV, and the Children and Young Persons Act, 1969, s. 72 (3), (4) and Scheds. V and VI.

Transitional provisions.—So long as s. 15 of this Act continues to apply to a local authority by virtue of para. 13, Sched. IV, Children and Young Persons Act, 1969, p. 229, ante, then the section, as amended by para. 20, Sched. V, ibid., has effect as if a home provided under s. 15 were a community home so provided under the Act of 1969.

"Places of safety."—Provision for the removal of a child to a place of safety is made by the statutes referred to in sub-s. (1), supra, in the following cases:

(i)   By any person authorised by a justice when there is reason to believe that a child or young person is about to leave the United Kingdom in contravention of s. 25 Children and Young Persons Act, 1933, which regulates the sending abroad of juvenile entertainers (note that a constable must now be authorised) (Children and Young Persons Act, 1969, s. 28, p. 173, ante).

(ii) On a justice's warrant where there is reasonable cause to suspect that a child has been ill treated, etc. or that any of certain specified offences has been or is being committed against him.   (Children and Young Persons Act, 1933, s. 40, p. 47, ante.

(iii) By a constable who has reasonable cause to believe that any of the conditions set out in s. 1 (2) (a) to (d) Children and Young Persons Act, 1969, p. 130, ante, is satisfied or that an offence under s. 10 (1) of the Children and Young Persons Act, 1933, p. 23, ante, is being committed.

(iv) By any person authorised by a justice where the applicant has reasonable cause to believe that any of the conditions set out in s. 1 (2) (a) to (e) of the Children and Young Persons Act, 1969, p. 130, ante, is satisfied.

(v)   On an order of a juvenile court, or in cases of urgency, a justice where a protected child is about to be received or is being kept in overcrowded etc. premises, or by a person who is unfit to have the care of him etc. (Adoption Act, 1958, s. 43, p. 1073, post.)   A similar provision as to foster children is s. 7 of the Children Act, 1958, p. 964, post.

A juvenile court before whom a child or young person is brought in care proceedings under s. 15 of the Children and Young Persons Act, 1969, may also make an "interim care order" (Children and Young Persons Act, 1969, ss. 2 (1) and 16 (4), pp. 134, 156, ante).

For definition of community home and place of safety see the Children and Young Persons Act, 1969, s. 36, p. 183, ante, and the Children and Young Persons Act, 1933, s. 107, as amended (p. 81, ante.

Sub-s. (3) makes the expenses of maintaining a child in a place of safety (other than a local authority's community home or a controlled community home or a State hospital) recoverable from the authority in whose area the child was immediately before removal to a place of safety.   It should be noted that there is no obligation on such authority to pay these expenses until they are demanded, and it may be that sometimes where a child is placed in a voluntary home the managers will be prepared to maintain him without seeking to recover the cost.

" Local authority."—See s. 38, p. 914, ante.

" Child."—For definition, see s. 59 (1), post.

52. Amendment of Family Allowances Act, 1945, ss. 11 and 26.
—[*Repealed by S.L.R. (Consequential Repeals) Act, 1965.*]

NOTE

The position as to family allowances and the assumption of parental rights is the subject of Department of Health and Social Security, Leaflet FAM. 33, p. 1006, *post*.

53. Enforcement of orders for payment of money under Guardianship of Infants Acts.—[*Repealed by the Guardianship of Minors Act, 1971. See now s.* 13, *ibid.*]

NOTE

For the Guardianship of Minors Act, 1971, see pp. 1198 *et seq., post*.

54. Provisions as to entry and inspection.—[*Subsections* (1) *and* (2) *are repealed by the Children and Young Persons Act,* 1969, *s.* 72 (4) *and Sched. VI.*]

(3) It shall be the duty of local authorities from time to time to cause children in voluntary homes in their area other than community homes to be visited in the interests of the well-being of the children, and any person authorised in that behalf by a local authority may enter any such voluntary home in the area of the authority for the purpose of visiting the children in the home.

(4) Any person authorised in that behalf by a local authority may enter any voluntary home outside the area of the authority for the purpose of visiting children in the home who are in the care of the authority under section one of this Act or are for the time being committed to the care of the authority by a care order within the meaning of the Children and Young Persons Act, 1969, or by a warrant under s. 23 (1) of that Act.

(5) Nothing in the two last foregoing subsections shall apply to a voluntary home which, otherwise than by virtue of section fifty-eight of the Children and Young Persons Act, 1969 or section ninety-eight of the said Act of 1937, is as a whole subject to inspection by, or under the authority of, a Government department.

(6) A person who proposes to exercise any power of entry or inspection conferred by this Act shall if so required produce some duly authenticated document showing his authority to exercise the power.

(7) Any person who obstructs the exercise of any such power as aforesaid shall be guilty of an offence and liable on summary conviction to a fine not exceeding five pounds in the case of a first offence or twenty pounds in the case of a second or any subsequent offence.

NOTES

This section is printed as amended by the Children Act, 1958, Sched. II, the Adoption Act, 1958, Sched. IV, and the Children and Young Persons Act, 1969, s. 72 (3), (4) and Scheds. V and VI.

Children and Young Persons Act, 1969, s. 58.—See p. 205, *ante.*

Second offence.—As to the meaning of " second offence," see *R.* v. *South Shields Licensing Justices*, [1911] 2 K. B. 1.

"The said Act of 1937."—*I.e.* the Children and Young Persons (Scotland) Act, 1937, which was referred to in sub-s. (4) before amendment by the Act of 1969. Section 98 of the Act of 1937 was repealed as to Scotland by the Social Work (Scotland) Act, 1968.

55. Prosecution of offences.—(1) In England and Wales, a local authority may institute proceedings for any offence under this Act, the provisions of the Children and Young Persons Act, 1933, other than the provisions of Parts I and II thereof.

(2) [*Repealed by the Statute Law Revision Act*, 1953.]

NOTES

This section is printed as amended by the Children Act, 1958, Sched. III.

Prosecutions.—Under s. 98 (1) of the Children and Young Persons Act, 1933, as originally enacted, a local education authority or a poor law authority could institute proceedings for an offence under that Act. By s. 60 (2) of, and Sched. III to, this Act, a new subsection was substituted which empowers the local education authority to prosecute for offences under Parts I and II of the 1933 Act, which deal with matters not directly relating to the care of deprived children. By the present section offences under the other Parts of the 1933 Act as well as under the present Act and the enactments relating to child protection (as to which see s. 14 of the Children Act, 1958, p. 967, *post*), may be prosecuted by the local authority for the purposes of the present Act (see s. 38, p. 914, *ante*). For s. 98 of the Act of 1933, see p. 76, *ante*.

The local authority will doubtless generally authorise the director of social services to institute on its behalf proceedings before a court of summary jurisdiction for the offences to which the present subsection applies, and in that case the director will be able to conduct such proceedings although he is not a certificated solicitor; see the Local Government Act, 1933, s. 277.

Conduct of proceedings.—Section 277 of the Local Government Act, 1933, is as follows:

" **Appearance of local authorities in legal proceedings.**—A local authority may by resolution authorise any member or officer of the authority, either generally or in respect of any particular matter, to institute or defend on their behalf proceedings before any court of summary jurisdiction or to appear on their behalf before a court of summary jurisdiction in any proceedings instituted by them or on their behalf or against them, and any member or officer so authorised shall be entitled to institute or defend any such proceedings and, notwithstanding anything contained in the Solicitors Act, 1957, to conduct any such proceedings although he is not a certificated solicitor."

It is desirable that the authority be in writing, and available for production in court if asked for.

Disqualification of justice.—A justice who is a member of a local authority may not take part in the hearing of any case to which that authority is a party, or to which any committee or officer of that authority is a party (Justices of the Peace Act, 1949, s. 3; 19 Halsbury's Statutes, 3rd Edn., 112).

56. Acquisition of land.—(1) The council of a county borough may be authorised by the Minister of Health to purchase compulsorily any land, whether situated within or outside the area of the council, for the purpose of any of their functions under this Act; and the council of a county or large burgh in Scotland may be authorised by the Secretary of State to purchase compulsorily any land, whether situated within or outside the county or burgh, for the purpose of any of their functions under this Act.

(2) The Acquisition of Land (Authorisation Procedure) Act, 1946, shall apply in relation to the compulsory purchase of land under this section by the council of a county borough as, by virtue of subsection (1) of section one hundred and fifty-nine of the Local Government Act, 1933, it applies to the compulsory purchase of land by a county council for the purpose of their functions under this Act; and accordingly for the purposes of the said Act of 1946 subsection (1) of this section shall be deemed to have been in force immediately before the commencement of that Act.

(3) Section two of the said Act of 1946 (which confers temporary powers for the speedy acquisition of land in urgent cases) shall not apply to the acquisition of land for the purposes of this Act, whether by a county council or by a county borough council.

(4) The Acquisition of Land (Authorisation Procedure) (Scotland) Act, 1947 (other than section two thereof) shall apply in relation to the compulsory purchase of land under this section as if subsection (1) thereof had been in force immediately before the commencement of the said Act.

NOTES

" **Functions.**"—For definition, see s. 59 (1), *post*.

Procedure.—S. 1 (1) of the Acquisition of Land (Authorisation Procedure) Act, 1946 (3 Halsbury's Statutes, 2nd Edn., 1065), provides that the uniform procedure prescribed by that Act shall apply to compulsory purchases under public general Acts in force immediately before the commencement of that Act, other than certain specified Acts.

Acquisition of land (Authorisation Procedure) Act, 1946, s. 2.—This section is repealed by the Statute Law Revision Act, 1953.

Minister of Health.—The powers of the Minister of Health were transferred to the Minister of Housing and Local Government by the Transfer of Functions (Minister of Health and Minister of Local Government and Planning) (No. 2) Order, 1951, S.I. 1951 No. 53, and the Minister of Local Government and Planning (Change of Style and Title) Order, 1952, S.I. 1952 No. 1900. That ministry has now been dissolved and its function in this respect transferred to the Secretary of State by the Secretary of State for the Environment Order, 1970 (S.I. 1970 No. 1681).

57. Transfer, superannuation and compensation of officers.— (1) The Secretary of State may by regulations provide—

(a) for the transfer to a local authority of officers employed immediately before the commencement of this Act by the Common Council of the City of London or the council of a metropolitan borough or county district solely or mainly for the purposes of functions transferred by this Act from that council to the said local authority;

(b) for enabling the Common Council of the City of London and the council of any metropolitan borough or county district in the case of any officer of the council who is a contributory employee or local Act contributor within the meaning of the Local Government Superannuation Act, 1937, and is transferred under the regulations to secure, by resolution passed in respect of him not later than three months after his transfer under the regulations, that for the purposes of the said Act of 1937 any non-contributing service of his shall be reckonable as contributing service and, in the case of any such officer on whom if he had remained in their employment a similar benefit could have been conferred by the council on his becoming entitled to a superannuation allowance, that the length of his service shall be deemed for the purposes of the said Act of 1937 or, as the case may be, the local Act in question, to be increased by such period as may be specified in the resolution;

(c) for granting to persons who immediately before being transferred under the regulations were, by virtue of the employment from which they are so transferred, entitled to participate in superannuation benefits, an option either to participate, by virtue of their employment by the local authority to which they are transferred under the regulations, in superannuation benefits under a superannuation scheme of the local authority specified in the regulations or to retain rights corresponding with those previously enjoyed by them;

(d) for the payment by local authorities, subject to such exceptions or conditions (if any) as may be prescribed by the regulations, of compensation to persons of such descriptions as may be so prescribed who immediately before such date as may be so prescribed were employed by the Common Council of the City of London, the council of a metropolitan borough or the council of a county district in such full-time work as may be prescribed by the regulations and who suffer loss of employment or loss or diminution of emoluments which is attributable to the passing of this Act;

(e) for extending any provision made under paragraph (d) of this subsection to persons of such descriptions as may be prescribed by the regulations who, having before such date as aforesaid been employed as aforesaid and being persons who would have been so employed immediately before that date but for any national service (as defined in the regulations) in which they have been engaged, lose the prospect of their re-employment in any such work as a consequence of the passing of this Act;

(f) for such matters supplementary to and consequential on the matters aforesaid as appear to the Secretary of State to be necessary.

(2) Regulations under this section may provide for the determination by the Secretary of State of all questions arising under the regulations and may make different provisions for different classes of cases.

NOTES

Transfer of officers.—The amendment of s. 22 (3) of the National Health Service Act, 1946, effected by s. 60 and Sched. III, necessitated the passing of the present section in order that child life protection officers formerly employed by the Common Council, the Metropolitan borough councils and county district councils should not be prejudiced.

Regulations.—See the Children Act (Compensation of Officers) Regulations, 1948 (S.I. 1948 No. 1501), and the Children Act (Transfer and Superannuation of Officers) Regulations, 1948 (S.I. 1948 No. 1502).

Local Government Superannuation Act, 1937.—See 19 Halsbury's Statutes, 3rd Edn., 599.

58. Regulations and orders.—(1) Any power to make regulations or orders conferred on a Minister by this Act shall be exercisable by statutory instrument.

(2) Any statutory instrument made in the exercise of any power to make regulations conferred by this Act shall be subject to annulment in pursuance of resolution of either House of Parliament.

NOTE

Statutory Instruments.—See the Statutory Instruments Act, 1946 (32 Halsbury's Statutes, 3rd Edn., 668). S. 5 thereof prescribes a standard period of forty days from the laying of a statutory instrument before Parliament as the period within which action must be taken by way of negative resolution (as under sub-s. (2) of the present section) to annul the instrument. S. 4 provides for copies of statutory instruments required to be laid before Parliament being laid before the instruments are brought into operation, save in exceptional urgent cases. See also the Laying of Documents before Parliament (Interpretation) Act, 1948.

59. Interpretation.—(1) In this Act, except where the context otherwise requires, the following expressions have the meanings hereby assigned to them respectively:—

"child" means a person under the age of eighteen years and any person who has attained that age and is the subject of a care order within the meaning of the Children and Young Persons Act, 1969;

" complain " in relation to Scotland means to make an application, and the expressions " complaint " and " complainant " shall be construed accordingly;

" compulsory school age " has in England and Wales the same meaning as in the Education Act, 1944, and in Scotland means school age as defined in the Education (Scotland) Act, 1946 ;

" contribution order " means in England or Wales a contribution order under section eighty-seven of the Children and Young Persons Act, 1933, and in Scotland a contribution order under section ninety-one of the Children and Young Persons (Scotland) Act, 1937;

" functions " includes powers and duties;

" guardian " means a person appointed by deed or will or by order of a court of competent jurisdiction to be the guardian of a child;

" hospital " has the meaning assigned to it by section seventy-nine of the National Health Service Act, 1946, or, as respects Scotland, section eighty of the National Health Service (Scotland) Act, 1947;

" Large burgh " has the same meaning as in the Local Government (Scotland) Act, 1947;

" local education authority " means a local education authority for the purposes of the Education Act, 1944, or in Scotland an education authority for the purposes of the Education (Scotland) Act, 1946;

" parent "—

     (a) in relation to a child adopted in pursuance of any enactment, means the person or persons by whom he was adopted, to the exclusion of his natural parents;

     (b) in relation to a child who is illegitimate, means his mother, to the exclusion of his father;

" precept for a rate ", in relation to Scotland, means requisition for a rate;

" recognisance ", in relation to Scotland, means bond;

" recoverable summarily as a civil debt ", in relation to Scotland, means recoverable as a civil debt;

" relative " in relation to an infant, means a grandparent, brother, sister, uncle or aunt, whether of the full blood, of the half-blood or by affinity, and includes—

     (a) where an adoption order has been made in respect of the infant or any other person, any person who would be a relative of the infant within the meaning of this definition if the adopted person were the child of the adopter born in lawful wedlock;

     (b) where the infant is illegitimate, the father of the infant and any person who would be a relative of the infant within the meaning of this definition if the infant were the legitimate child of its mother and father.

"supervision requirement" has the same meaning as in the Social Work (Scotland) Act, 1968;

" voluntary home " has the same meaning as in Part V of the Children and Young Persons Act, 1933, or, as respects Scotland, Part VI of the Children and Young Persons (Scotland) Act, 1937;

" voluntary organisation " means a body the activities of which are carried on otherwise than for profit, but does not include any public or local authority.

(2) *Any reference in this Act to the functions of a local authority under the Children and Young Persons Act, 1933, shall be construed as including a reference to the functions of the council of a county or county borough with respect to remand homes.*

(3) References in this Act to any enactment shall, except where the context otherwise requires, be construed as references to the enactment as amended by or under any other enactment, including this Act.

(4) As respects Scotland any reference in this Act to a county or to the council thereof shall be construed, in relation to counties combined for the purposes mentioned in subsection (1) of section one hundred and eighteen of the Local Government (Scotland) Act, 1947, as a reference to the combined county or the joint county council.

(5) A small burgh, as defined in the said Act of 1947, shall for the purposes of this Act be deemed to be included in the county in the area of which it is situated.

NOTES

This section is printed as amended by the Adoption of Children Act, 1949, the Social Work (Scotland) Act, 1968, and the Children and Young Persons Act, 1969, s. 72 (3), (4) and Scheds. V and VI. From a date to be appointed sub-s. (2) is repealed (s. 72 (3) and Sched. V, *ibid.*).

Care order.—See the Children and Young Persons Act, 1969, s. 20 (2), p. 162, *ante*.

" Compulsory school age."—See the Education Act, 1944, s. 35, p. 252, *ante*. The phrase is defined to mean any age between five and fifteen years and the upper limit of compulsory school leaving age became fifteen on April 1, 1947. There is power by Order in Council to raise it to sixteen. As to school leaving dates see s. 9 of the Education Act, 1962, p. 273, *ante*. The provisions of this section have effect for the purposes of any enactment whereby the definition of compulsory school age in the Education Act, 1944 is applied or incorporated.

Where a child is registered at a special school, the compulsory school age extends to sixteen (Education Act, 1944, s. 38, p. 255, *ante*).

" Parents or guardians."—References in Part I, save as expressly provided in s. 6, are to be construed as references to all persons who are parents or guardians of the child (s. 9, of the Children Act, 1948, p. 891, *ante*).

" Contribution order."—For s. 87 of the Children and Young Persons Act, 1933, see p. 255, *ante*.

" Hospital."—For the National Health Service Act, 1946, s. 79, see 23 Halsbury's Statutes, 3rd Edn., 80.

" Local education authority."—See the notes to s. 21, p. 901, *ante*.

" Voluntary home."—This expression is defined in the Children and Young Persons Act, 1933, s. 92, p. 74, *ante*. The application of this section is extended by s. 27 of this Act, p. 906, *ante*.

" Remand homes."—The Children and Young Persons Act, 1933, s. 77 (p. 64, *ante*), makes it lawful for county councils and county borough councils to provide remand homes. (The section has been repealed but continues to apply by virtue of para. 13 (1) (c) Sched. IV Children and Young Persons Act, 1969.

60. Transitional provisions, minor amendments and repeals.— [*Not reproduced.*]

61. Application to Isles of Scilly.—This Act shall, in its application to the Isles of Scilly, have effect subject to such exceptions, adaptations and modifications as may be prescribed by order of the Secretary of State, and any such order may be revoked or varied by a subsequent order.

NOTES

See the Isles of Scilly (Children Act, 1948) Order, 1959, p. 997, *post*.

Generally as to the Isles of Scilly, *cf.* the Local Government Act, 1933, s. 292 (19 Halsbury's Statutes, 3rd Edn., 568).

62. Short title, commencement and extent.—(1) This Act may be cited as the Children Act, 1948.

(2) [*Repealed by the Statute Law Revision Act, 1950.*]

(3) This Act shall not extend to Northern Ireland.

SCHEDULES
FIRST SCHEDULE
[SECTION 30]
APPEAL TRIBUNALS
PART I
CONSTITUTION OF APPEAL TRIBUNALS FOR ENGLAND AND WALES

1. For the purpose of enabling appeal tribunals to be constituted as occasion may require, there shall be appointed two panels, that is to say—

(a) a panel (hereinafter referred to as the "legal panel") appointed by the Lord Chancellor, of persons who will be available to act when required as chairman of any such tribunal; and

(b) a panel (hereinafter referred to as the "welfare panel") appointed by the Lord President of the Council, of persons who will be available to act when required as members of any such tribunal.

2.—(1) No person shall be qualified to be appointed to the legal panel unless he possesses such legal qualifications as the Lord Chancellor considers suitable, and no person shall be qualified to be appointed to the welfare panel unless he has had such experience in children's welfare work as the Lord President of the Council considers suitable.

(2) An officer of any Government department shall be disqualified from being appointed to either of the said panels.

3. Any person appointed to be a member of either of the said panels shall hold office as such subject to such conditions as to the period of his membership and otherwise as may be determined by the Lord Chancellor or the Lord President of the Council, as the case may be.

4. Where any appeal is required to be determined by a tribunal constituted in accordance with this Part of this Schedule, the tribunal shall consist of a chairman being a member of the legal panel and two other members being members of the welfare panel, and the chairman and other members of the tribunal shall be impartial persons appointed from those panels by the Lord Chancellor and the Lord President of the Council respectively.

Part II

Constitution of Appeal Tribunals for Scotland

[*This Act has been repealed* in toto *as to Scotland by the Social Work (Scotland) Act,* 1968.]

NOTES

Where the Secretary of State has refused an application for the registration of a voluntary home in England or Wales, pursuant to s. 29 (3) (b), *ante*, or has given notice that he proposes to remove such a home from the register pursuant to s. 29 (4), *ante*, a right of appeal is conferred by s. 30 (1), *ante*. The appeal is to be brought by notice in writing addressed to the Secretary of State requiring him to refer the refusal or proposal to an appeal tribunal constituted in accordance with Part I of this Schedule (s. 30 (2), *ante*), and the tribunal may either confirm the refusal or proposal, or may direct that the home be registered or not removed from the register, as the case may be (s. 30 (3), *ante*). The Lord Chancellor, with the concurrence of the Lord President of the Council, may make rules as to the practice and procedure to be followed with regard to the constitution of tribunals and as to proceedings before them and, in particular, as to the right of audience before tribunals (s. 30 (4), *ante*). Members of the tribunals may be paid such fees and allowances as the Secretary of State may, with the consent of the Treasury, determine (s. 30 (5), *ante*). See the Children Act (Appeal Tribunal) Rules, 1949, p. 975, *post*.

Part I of the Schedule is modelled on Sched. VI to the Education Act, 1944 (11 Halsbury's Statutes, 3rd Edn., 277), providing for the constitution of independent schools tribunals for England and Wales.

SECOND SCHEDULE

[Section 60]

Transitional Provisions

[*Not reproduced.*]

THIRD SCHEDULE

[SECTION 60]

MINOR AND CONSEQUENTIAL AMENDMENTS

[*This Schedule made minor and consequential amendments to,* inter alia, *the Children and Young Persons Act,* 1933, *the Public Health Act,* 1936, *the Public Health (London) Act,* 1936, *and the National Health Service Act,* 1946. *In so far as these amendments affect the Acts printed in this book they have been incorporated in the texts of the provisions affected.*]

FOURTH SCHEDULE

[*Repealed by the Statute Law Revision Act,* 1950.]

LOCAL AUTHORITY SOCIAL SERVICES ACT, 1970

[1970 c. 42]

1. Local authorities.—The local authorities for the purposes of this Act shall be the councils of counties, county boroughs and London boroughs and the Common Council of the City of London.

NOTE

"**Functions.**"—See s. 15 (2), *post.*

2. Local authority to establish social services committee.—(1) Every local authority shall establish a social services committee and, subject to subsection (3) below, there shall stand referred to that committee all matters relating to the discharge by the authority of—

(a) their functions under the enactments specified in the first column of Schedule 1 to this Act (being the functions which are described in general terms in the second column of that Schedule); and

(b) such other of their functions as, by virtue of the following subsection, fall within the responsibility of the committee.

(2) The Secretary of State may by order designate functions of local authorities under any other enactment for the time being in force as being appropriate for discharge through a local authority's social services committee other than functions which by virtue of that or any other enactment are required to be discharged through some other committee of a local authority; and any functions designated by an order under this section which is for the time being in force shall accordingly fall within the responsibility of the social services committee.

(3) Matters relating to the discharge by a local authority of the following functions of the authority, that is to say—

(a) functions under section 22 of the National Health Service Act, 1946 (care of certain mothers and young children) relating to the dental care of such mothers and children as are mentioned in subsection (1) of that section; and

(b) any other functions under subsection (1) or (2) of the said section 22 specified in a direction given under subsection (4) below and for the time being in force, and any functions under section 12 of the Health Services and Public Health Act, 1968 (prevention of illness and care and after-care of the sick) so specified,

shall not stand referred to a local authority's social services committee.

(4) The Secretary of State may direct that such of the functions mentioned in subsection (3) (b) above as are specified in the direction, being functions which appear to him to be mainly medical in nature, shall stand referred to the health committee of a local authority.

(5) A direction given under subsection (4) above may apply either to local authorities generally or to particular local authorities specified in the direction and may be revoked or varied by a subsequent direction so given.

(6) A matter which by this section stands referred to a local authority's social services committee shall not be included among the matters which stand referred to the authority's health committee under Part II of Schedule 4 to the National Health Services Act, 1946.

(7) Section 33 (2) of the National Assistance Act, 1948 and Schedule 3 to that Act (establishment of committees or joint boards for the purposes of the functions of local authorities under Part III of that Act) and section 39 of the Children Act, 1948 (establishment of children's committees of local authorities), shall cease to have effect.

3. Business of social services committee.—(1) Except with the consent of the Secretary of State (which may be given either generally or with respect to a particular authority) or as provided by this section, no matter, other than a matter which by virtue of section 2 of this Act stands referred to a local authority's social services committee, shall be referred to, or dealt with by, the committee.

(2) A local authority may refer to their social services committee a matter arising in connection with the authority's functions under—

(a) section 5 (1) (c) of the Health Visiting and Social Work (Training) Act, 1962 (research into matters relating to functions of local health authorities), or
(b) section 65 of the Health Services and Public Health Act, 1968 (financial and other assistance to voluntary organisations),

and appearing to the authority to relate to their social services; and a matter which by virtue of paragraph (a) above is referred to a local authority's social services committee shall not stand referred to the authority's health committed under Part II of Schedule 4 to the National Health Service Act, 1946.

(3) A local authority may delegate to their social services committee any of their functions matters relating to which stand referred to the committee by virtue of section 2 of this Act or this section (hereinafter in this Act referred to as "social services functions") and, before exercising any of those functions themselves, the authority shall (unless the matter is urgent) consider a report of the committee with respect to the matter in question.

(4) Nothing in section 2 of this Act or this section prevents a local authority from referring to a committee other than their social services committee a matter which by virtue of either of those sections stands referred to the social services committee and which in the authority's opinion ought to be referred to the other committee on the ground that it relates to a general service of the authority; but before referring any such matter the authority shall receive and consider a report of the social services committee with respect to the subject matter of the proposed reference.

4. Joint committees and sub-committees.—(1) Two or more local authorities may, instead of establishing social services committees for themselves, concur in establishing a joint social services committee; and references in this Act to a local authority's social services committee shall, in relation to an authority which has so concurred with another or others, be construed as references to the joint committee, except where the context otherwise requires.

(2) A social services committee may, subject to any restrictions imposed by the local authority or, as the case may be, the local authorities concurring in the establishment of the committee, establish sub-committees and delegate to them any of the functions of the committee.

(3) The social services committees of two or more local authorities may concur in the establishment of joint sub-committees and may, subject to any restrictions imposed by the local authorities concerned, delegate to them any of the functions of either or any of the committees.

5. Membership of committees and sub-committees.—(1) Subject to subsection (3) below, the members of a local authority's social services committee may include persons who are not members of the authority or, as the case may be, of any authority concurring in the establishment of the committee, provided that they are not disqualified from being members of that authority or any such authority.

(2) Subject to subsection (3) below, a social services committee may, if authorised to do so by the local authority or, as the case may be, the local authorities concurring in the establishment of the committee and subject to any restrictions imposed by that authority or those authorities, co-opt persons to serve as members of the committee, provided that they are not disqualified from being members of that authority or any of the said authorities.

(3) At least a majority of the members of a local authority's social services committee shall be members of that authority or, as the case may be, of the authorities concurring in the establishment of the committee.

(4) The members of a sub-committee established under section 4 (2) of this Act—

   (a) shall include at least one member of the local authority or, as the case may be, of each of the local authorities concerned; and

(b) may include persons who are not members of the social services committee, provided that they are not disqualified from being members of the local authority or, as the case may be, of any of the said authorities.

(5) The members of a joint sub-committee established under section 4 (3) of this Act—

(a) shall include at least one member of each of the local authorities concerned; and

(b) may include persons who are not members of any social services committee concurring in the establishment of the sub-committee, provided that they are not disqualified from being members of any of the said authorities.

(6) In this section "disqualified" means disqualified under section 59 of the Local Government Act, 1933 (which relates to office-holders under local authorities, bankrupts, persons who have been convicted, etc.).

6. The director of social services.—(1) A local authority shall appoint an officer, to be known as the director of social services, for the purposes of their social services functions.

(2) Two or more local authorities may, if they consider that the same person can efficiently discharge, for both or all of them, the functions of director of social services, concur in the appointment of a person as director of social services for both or all of those authorities.

(3) The Secretary of State may make regulations prescribing the qualifications requisite for a person's appointment as a local authority's director of social services.

(4) Until the first coming into force of regulations made under subsection (3) above, a local authority shall not appoint, nor concur in the appointment of, a director of social services except after consultation with the Secretary of State; and—

(a) for the purpose of such consultation an authority shall send to the Secretary of State particulars of the name, age, experience and qualifications of each of the persons from whom a selection is proposed to be made; and

(b) if the Secretary of State is of opinion that any of those persons is not a fit person to be the director of social services, he may give directions prohibiting his appointment.

(5) The director of social services of a local authority shall not, without the approval of the Secretary of State (which may be given either generally or in relation to a particular authority), be employed by that authority in connection with the discharge of any of the authority's functions other than their social services functions.

(6) A local authority which have appointed, or concurred in the appointment of, a director of social services, shall secure the provisions of adequate staff for assisting him in the exercise of his functions.

(7) The authority or authorities appointing a director of social services may pay to him such reasonable remuneration as they may determine; and he shall hold office during their pleasure.

(8) Section 41 of the Children Act, 1948 (appointment of children's officer) shall cease to have effect.

NOTES

Director ... for both or all.—This is so even though the authorities are not combined in appointing a joint committee under s. 4.

Regulations.—No such regulations have yet been made.

7. Local authorities to exercise social services functions under guidance of Secretary of State.—(1) Local authorities shall, in the exercise of their social services functions, including the exercise of any discretion conferred by any relevant enactment, act under the general guidance of the Secretary of State.

(2) Subsection (1) above shall not affect a local authority's duty to exercise their functions under—

    (a) sections 21 and 24 of the National Assistance Act, 1948 (provision of residential or temporary accommodation for the aged, infirm, etc.), or

    (b) section 29 of that Act (welfare of the handicapped), or

    (c) section 3 of the Disabled Persons (Employment) Act, 1958 (provision for employment and training of persons who are seriously disabled),

in accordance with any scheme under any of those sections which is in force with the approval of a Minister of the Crown given under section 34 of the said Act of 1948 or in accordance with a scheme made by a Minister of the Crown under the said section 34.

The foregoing provision is without prejudice to subsection (2) of section 2 of the Chronically Sick and Disabled Persons Act, 1970 (which excludes arrangements made in pursuance of subsection (1) of the said section 2 and certain other arrangements from the requirement that arrangements made by a local authority under section 29 of the said Act of 1948 shall be carried into effect in accordance with a scheme made thereunder).

(3) Subsection (1) above shall not affect a local authority's duty to carry out their duties under—

    (a) section 22 of the National Health Service Act, 1946 (care of certain mothers and young children), or

    (b) section 12 of the Health Services and Public Health Act, 1968 (prevention of illness and care and after-care of the sick),

in accordance with proposals approved or made by a Minister of the Crown under section 20 of the said Act of 1946.

NOTE

Advisory Councils.—In exercising the power of guidance conferred by sub-s. (1), the Secretary of State will have the assistance of the Advisory Council constituted under s. 43 of the Children Act, 1948, p. 914, *ante*.

8. Accounts of certain local authorities.—(1) The council of a county borough may, if they think it convenient so to do, keep separate accounts of the sums received and expended by them in the exercise of their social services functions.

(2) Accounts kept under this section shall be made up and audited in like manner as the accounts of a county council.

(3) The enactments relating to the audit of accounts by a district auditor and to the matters incidental to such audit and consequential thereon shall have effect in relation to the accounts which the council of a county borough keep under this section as they have effect in relation to the accounts of a county council.

(4) The foregoing provisions of this section shall apply to the Common Council of the City of London and to accounts kept by that council under this section as they apply to the council of a county borough and to accounts kept by such a council thereunder.

(5) Section 49 of the Children Act, 1948 (certain councils required to keep separate accounts of sums received and expended by them in exercising functions under the enactments relating to children and young persons) and, in so far as they relate to social services functions, section 55 (1) of the National Health Service Act, 1946 (similar provision relating to functions of certain local health authorities) and section 59 of the National Assistance Act, 1948 (similar provision relating to functions of certain councils under that Act) shall not apply to the council of a county borough who keep accounts under this section or, if the Common Council of the City of London keep accounts thereunder, to that council.

(6) Section 49 of the Children Act, 1948 shall cease to apply to London borough councils.

10. Delegation schemes to be revoked, so far as they relate to social services functions.—(1) After the date of the coming into force of this section no delegation scheme shall be made under section 46 of the Local Government Act, 1958 (certain functions of a county council, so far as they relate to a county district for which a delegation scheme under that section is in force, to be exercisable by the council of that district on behalf of the county council) and no steps shall be taken under section 47 of that Act (procedure for bringing a delegation scheme into operation) to bring into operation any scheme which is not in operation on that date.

(2) The council of a county district for which a delegation scheme is in force immediately before the said date shall, within such period as the Secretary of State may direct, make in accordance with section 48 (1) of the said Act of 1958 a subsequent scheme varying the delegation scheme by revoking it in so far as it relates to functions which at the time when the scheme is made are social services functions of the county council by virtue of section 2 of this Act.

(3) Subsection (2) above shall not be taken as affecting the power of the council of a county district under the said section 48 (1) to revoke a delegation scheme, whether such a delegation scheme as is referred to in subsection (2) above or that scheme as varied in accordance with that subsection.

(4) A direction given under subsection (2) above may prescribe different periods for different counties or for different county districts in a county and may be varied by a subsequent direction so given.

(5) Section 47 (3) of the said Act of 1958 (which, as applied by section 48 (1) of that Act, specifies the times at which subsequent schemes under section 48 (1) may be made), and section 51 of that Act (which enables delegation schemes to be made by certain joint boards), shall cease to have effect.

(6) In section 46 (5) of the said Act of 1958 (which provides that the power of a county council, in the exercise of functions to which a delegation scheme relates, to make contributions to voluntary organisations may be exercised by the county council as well as by the council of the county district for which the scheme is in force) for the words "make contributions to voluntary organisations" there shall be substituted the words "assist voluntary organisations in any manner mentioned in subsection (1) or (2) of section 65 of the Health Services and Public Health Act, 1968".

12. Isles of Scilly.—(1) The Secretary of State may by order direct that this Act shall have effect as if the Council of the Isles of Scilly were a local authority for the purposes of this Act.

(2) In its application to the Isles of Scilly by virtue of an order made under this section, this Act shall have effect with such modifications as may be specified in the order.

13. Orders and regulations.—(1) Orders and regulations of the Secretary of State under this Act shall be made by statutory instrument.

(2) Any order made under any provision of this Act, except an order under section 14 (3), may be varied or revoked by a subsequent order so made.

(3) In the case of a statutory instrument containing an order under section 2 (2) or 14 (3) of this Act or regulations under section 6 (3) thereof, a draft of the instrument shall be laid before Parliament, and an instrument containing an order under the said section 2 (2) shall not be made unless the draft has been approved by a resolution of each House of Parliament.

(4) A statutory instrument containing an order under section 9 (1) or 12 of this Act shall be subject to annulment in pursuance of a resolution of either House of Parliament.

(5) Any order or regulations under this Act may be made so as to apply to England only or to Wales only.
For the purposes of this subsection, Monmouthshire shall be deemed to be part of Wales and not of England.

14. Minor and consequential amendments, repeals and saving for certain schemes.—(1) The enactments specified in Schedule 2 to this Act shall have effect subject to the amendments specified in relation thereto in that Schedule, being minor amendments and amendments consequential on the provisions of this Act.

(2) The enactments specified in Schedule 3 to this Act are hereby repealed to the extent specified in column 3 of that Schedule.

(3) The Secretary of State may by order repeal or amend any provision in any local Act, including an Act confirming a provisional order, or in an instrument in the nature of a local enactment under any Act, where it appears to him that that provision is inconsistent with, or has become unnecessary or requires modification in consequence of, any provision of this Act or corresponds to any provision repealed by this Act.

(4) Nothing in paragraph 7 of Schedule 2 to this Act or in any provision of Schedule 3 thereto shall affect any delegation scheme made under section 46 of the Local Government Act, 1958 and in force immediately before the coming into force of section 10 of this Act until the date on which a scheme made in pursuance of subsection (2) of the said section 10 and varying that delegation scheme comes into operation, and until that date the delegation scheme shall have effect, and the functions to which it relates shall be exercisable in accordance with it, as if this Act had not passed.

15. Citation, interpretation, commencement and extent. —(1) This Act may be cited as the Local Authority Social Services Act, 1970.

(2) In this Act "functions" includes powers and duties and "social services functions" has the meaning given by section 3 (3) of this Act.

(3) Any reference in this Act to an enactment shall be construed as including a reference to that enactment as amended, applied or extended by or under any other enactment, including this Act.

(4) This Act shall come into force on a day appointed by the Secretary of State by order; and different days may be so appointed for different provisions of this Act.

(5) If it appears to the Secretary of State desirable in the interest of the efficient discharge of the functions of a particular local authority to postpone the coming into force of any provision of this Act in the area of that authority, the Secretary of State may by an order under subsection (4) above relating to that provision either appoint a different day later in date for the coming into force of that provision in the area of that authority or except that area from the operation of the order and make a subsequent order under that subsection appointing a day for the coming into force of that provision in that area.

(6) This Act, except section 11, shall not extend to Scotland.

(7) This Act, except section 11 and this subsection, shall not extend to Northern Ireland; the amendments of the Health Visiting and Social Work (Training) Act, 1962 made by section 11 shall be treated for the purposes of section 6 of the Government of Ireland Act, 1920 (which restricts the power of the Parliament of Northern Ireland to alter Acts of the Parliament of the United Kingdom passed after the day appointed for the purposes of that section) as having been made by an Act passed before that day.

SCHEDULE 1

Section 2.

ENACTMENTS CONFERRING FUNCTIONS ASSIGNED TO
SOCIAL SERVICES COMMITTEE

Enactment	Nature of functions
Children and Young Persons Act, 1933 (c. 12) Part III	Protection of the young in relation to criminal and summary proceedings; children appearing before court as in need of care, protection or control; committal of children to approved school or care of fit person, etc.
Part IV	Remand homes, approved schools and children in care of fit persons.
National Health Service Act, 1946 (c. 81) Section 22 (1) and (2)	Care of expectant and nursing mothers and young children.
Section 29	Provision of domestic help for certain households.
The following sections, so far as they apply in relation to any function under the said section 22 or 29 or section 12 or 13 of the Health Services and Public Health Act, 1968 (c. 46), being a social services function:— Section 20	Submission of proposals for provision of certain services.
Section 58 (2)	Acquisition of land.
Section 63	Use of certain premises and equipment.
Section 65	Provision of accommodation for staff.
National Assistance Act, 1948 (c. 29) Sections 21 to 27	Provision of residential accommodation for the aged, infirm, needy, etc.
Sections 29 and 30	Welfare of persons who are blind, deaf, dumb or otherwise handicapped or are suffering from mental disorder; use of voluntary organisations for administration of welfare schemes.
Sections 37 to 41	Registration of disabled or old persons' homes, residential homes for mentally disordered persons and charities for disabled.
Sections 43 to 45	Recovery of costs of providing certain services.
Section 48	Temporary protection of property belonging to persons in hospital or accommodation provided under Part III of the Act, etc.
Section 49	Defraying expenses of local authority officer applying for appointment as receiver for certain patients.
Section 50 (3) and (4)	Burial or cremation of person dying in accommodation provided under the said Part III; recovery of funeral expenses from his estate.
Section 56 (3) except so far as it relates to an offence under section 47 (11)	Prosecution of offences.
Section 58	Acquisition of land.

Enactment	Nature of functions
Children Act, 1948 (c. 43)	Provision for orphans, deserted children, children suffering from mental disorder, etc.; assumption by local authority of parental rights; local authority as fit person under Act of 1933; children in care; financing of children's maintenance and education, etc.; registration of voluntary children's homes and use of voluntary organisations.
Nurseries and Child-Minders Regulation Act, 1948 (c. 53)	Regulation of nurseries and child-minders.
Disabled Persons (Employment) Act, 1958 (c. 33) Section 3	Provision of facilities for enabling disabled persons to be employed or work under special conditions.
Children Act, 1958 (c. 65)	Protection of children living away from their parents; prosecution of offences.
Adoption Act, 1958 (7 & 8 Eliz. 2. c. 5)	Making, etc. arrangements for the adoption of children; regulation of adoption societies; care, possession and supervision of children awaiting adoption; prosecution of offences.
Mental Health Act, 1959 (c. 72) Parts II to VI and IX except— (a) [Repealed by the Education (Handicapped Children) Act, 1970] (b) sections 14 to 18 and section 23 so far as it relates to offences under those sections or any enactment thereby applied; (c) sections 28 (2), 37, 47 (3) and 56 (2) (d); (d) section 131 in its application to offences relating to a mental nursing home or a patient admissible to, or receiving treatment in or at, such a home.	Welfare of the mentally disordered while in hospital or mental nursing home; guardianship of persons suffering from mental disorder including such persons removed to England and Wales from Scotland or Northern Ireland; exercise of functions of nearest relative of person so suffering.
Matrimonial Proceedings (Magistrates' Courts) Act, 1960 (c. 48) Section 2 (1) (f)	Supervision of child subject to court order in matrimonial proceedings.
Mental Health (Scotland) Act, 1960 (c. 61) Section 10	Welfare of certain persons while in hospital in Scotland.
Health Visiting and Social Work (Training) Act, 1962 (c. 33) Section 5 (1) (b), and as extended by section 45 (9) of the Health Services and Public Health Act, 1968 (c. 46).	Research into matters relating to local authority welfare services.

Enactment	Nature of functions
Children and Young Persons Act, 1963 (c. 37)	
Part I	Promotion of welfare of children; powers relating to young persons in need of care, protection or control; further provisions for protection of the young in relation to criminal proceedings; recovery of contributions in respect of child.
Part III, except section 56	Research into matters connected with functions under enactments relating to children and young persons; provisions relating to children in respect of whom parental rights assumed by local authority; assistance of persons formerly in care.
Matrimonial Causes Act, 1925 (c. 72)	
Section 37	Supervision of child subject to court order in matrimonial proceedings.
Ministry of Social Security Act, 1966 (c. 20)	
Schedule 4	Provision and maintenance of reception centres persons without a settled way of living.
Health Services and Public Health Act, 1968 (c. 46)	
Section 12	Prevention of illness and care and after-care of the sick.
Section 13	Provision of home help and laundry facilities for certain households.
Section 45	Promotion of welfare of old people.
Social Work (Scotland) Act, 1968 (c. 49)	
Sections 75 (2) and 76 (4)	Reference for consideration, etc. of case of child in care whose parent moves to Scotland and transfer of child.
Family Law Reform Act, 1969 (c. 46)	
Section 7 (4)	Supervision of ward of court.
Children and Young Persons Act, 1969 (c. 54) The whole Act except sections 1, 2 and 9 in so far as they assign functions to a local authority in their capacity of a local education authority.	Care and other treatment of children and young persons through court proceedings; accommodation for children in care; welfare, etc. of foster children.
Chronically Sick and Disabled Persons Act, 1970 (c. 44)	
Section 1	Obtaining information as to need for, and publishing information as to existence of, certain welfare services.
Section 2	Provision of certain welfare services.
Section 18	Provision of certain information required by Secretary of State.
Section 6 of this Act	Appointment of director of social services, etc.

SCHEDULE II

Minor and Consequential Amendments of Enactments

[The effect of amendments are noted in the sections as printed.]

SCHEDULE III

Repeals

[The effect of the repeals are noted in the sections as printed.]

NURSERIES AND CHILD-MINDERS REGULATION ACT, 1948

[11 & 12 Geo. 6, c. 53]

ARRANGEMENT OF SECTIONS

An Act to provide for the regulation of certain nurseries and of persons who for reward receive children into their homes to look after them; and for purposes connected with the matters aforesaid.

[30th July, 1948.]

General note.—In relation to Scotland any reference to a local health authority wherever occurring shall be construed as a reference to a local authority within the meaning of the Social Work (Scotland) Act, 1968 (ss. 95, 97, 98 and Sched. VIII, *ibid.*).

1. Registration of nurseries and child-minders.—(1) Every local health authority shall keep registers—

(a) of premises in their area, other than premises wholly or mainly used as private dwellings, where children are received to be looked after for the day or for a part or parts thereof of a duration, or an aggregate duration, of two hours or longer or for any longer period not exceeding six days;

(b) of persons in their area who for reward receive into their homes children under the age of five to be looked after as aforesaid.

The registers kept under this subsection shall be open to inspection at all reasonable times.

(2) Any person receiving or proposing to receive children as mentioned in paragraph (a) or (b) of the foregoing subsection may make application to the local health authority for registration thereunder, and on receipt of such an application the local health authority shall, subject to the provisions of this section, register the premises to which or person to whom the application relates.

(3) The local health authority may by order refuse to register any premises if they are satisfied that any person employed or proposed to be employed in looking after children at the premises is not a fit person to look after children, or, where the premises were not at the commencement of this Act in use for the reception of children as mentioned in paragraph (a) of subsection (1) of this section, if the local authority are satisfied that the premises are not fit (whether because of the condition thereof or of the equipment thereof or for any reason connected with the situation, construction or size thereof or with other persons therein) to be used for that purpose.

(4) The local health authority may by order refuse to register any person if they are satisfied that that person, or any person employed or proposed to be employed by him in looking after children, is not a fit person to look after children or that the premises in which the children are received or proposed to be received are not fit (whether because of the condition thereof or of the equipment thereof or for any reason connected with the situation, construction or size thereof or with other persons therein) to be used for the purpose.

NOTES

This section is printed as amended by the Health Services and Public Health Act, 1968.

Registration of premises and of persons.—County and county borough councils, as local health authorities (see *infra*), are required by sub-s. (1) to keep registers; but this section does not make application for registration compulsory, though the penalties provided by s. 4, *post*, in effect oblige occupiers of nurseries within the Act and child-minders to apply for registration. Two registers, which are to be available for public inspection, are to be kept, namely:

    (i) *A register of premises.*—This will be a register of actual buildings or parts of buildings used as nurseries, that is to say, where children under the upper limit of compulsory school age (see s. 13 (2), p. 950, *post*), are received to be looked after for the day or for an aggregate of two hours or longer or for any longer period not exceeding six days at a time. There are three main categories of exception from registration in this register: they are (a) premises used wholly or mainly as private dwellings (see *infra*), (b) institutions, *e.g.*, schools, in respect of which exemption is conferred by s. 8, *post*, and (c) premises used mainly for the reception of children for periods exceeding six days and to which the child life protection enactments (defined in s. 13 (2), *post*) apply (see s. 9 (1), p. 949, *post*). By the Children Act, 1958, s. 3, p. 958, *post*, provision is made for notice to be given to the local authority before the reception of children under the upper limit of compulsory school age for care and maintenance apart from their parents.

    (ii) *A register of persons.*—This will be a register including the names and addresses (see s. 3 (1), p. 943, *post*) of persons, who for reward receive into their homes children under the age of five years to be looked after for the day, or for an aggregate of two hours or longer, or for any longer period not exceeding six days. Exception is made in respect of homes within the Children Act, 1958, s. 2 (p. 956, *post*), by s. 8 (1) of this Act, p. 948, *post*;

in addition, registration is not in effect obligatory on the child-minder, unless failure to register would bring him within the penal scope of s. 4 (2) taken in conjunction with s. 9 (2) of this Act. Registration may be required in respect of more than one home, if a new home is acquired by a person whose name is already registered (s. 4 (3), p. 944, *post*).

The consequences of registration include liability to the imposition of requirements under s. 2, and inspection of premises (ss. 7 (1), 9, 10, pp. 576, 578, 579, *post*).

As to the issue of a certificate of registration, see s. 3, p. 943, *post*; as to cancellation of registration, see s. 5, p. 945, *post*.

" Local health authority."—S. 19 (1) of the National Health Service Act, 1946 (p. 876, *ante*), provides that county councils and county borough councils shall be local health authorities.

" Child."—For definition, see s. 13 (2), *post*.

" Wholly or mainly used as private dwellings."—Premises of this nature are not themselves to be registered under the Act but such one of the occupants (who will not necessarily be the occupier in the legal sense) as carries on upon such premises the business of looking after children is to be registered as a child-minder if the children received by him are under five years of age. Whether premises are mainly used as a private dwelling-house is a question of fact in each case, in answering which it is thought that the word " mainly " should be given its ordinary dictionary meaning of " for the most part; chiefly; principally " (*Miller* v. *Ottilie (Owners)*, [1944] K. B. 188; [1944] 1 All E. R. 277. C. A.) ; and " private dwelling-house " should be construed as meaning a private residence (*Bristol Guardians* v. *Bristol Waterworks Co.*, [1912] 1 Ch. 111 ; affirmed, [1914] A. C. 379) ; and see *Barnes* v. *Shore* (1846), 1 Rob. Eccl. 382) : although the acts of sleeping upon premises at night and having meals in them by day are facts that are residential in character, they are not conclusive evidence of the use of a house as a dwelling-house ; see *Macmillan & Co. Ltd.*, v. *Rees*, [1946] 1 All E. R. 675, C. A.

Application for registration.—By s. 60 (7) Health Services and Public Health Act, 1968, an application for the registration of any premises shall be of no effect unless it contains a statement with respect to each person employed or proposed to be employed in looking after children at the premises and each person who has attained the age of sixteen years and (though not so employed or proposed to be so employed) is normally resident at the premises, whether or not—

  (a) there has been made against him any such order as is mentioned in paragraph (a), (b) or (e) of s. 6 of the Children Act, 1958 (disqualification for keeping foster children);
  (b) he has been convicted as mentioned in paragraph (c) thereof;
  (c) his rights and powers with respect to a child have been vested as mentioned in paragraph (d) thereof; or
  (d) an order has been made under s. 43 of the Adoption Act, 1958 (removal of protected children from unsuitable surroundings) for the removal of a child from his care;

and an application for the registration of a person shall be of no effect unless it contains a similar statement with respect to him, each person employed or proposed to be employed by him in looking after children and each person other than himself who has attained the age of sixteen years and (though not so employed or proposed to be so employed) is normally resident at the premises in which the children are received or proposed to be received; and a person who, in any such application as aforesaid makes, with respect to himself or another any such statement as aforesaid which is false and is known to him to be false or recklessly makes, with respect to himself or another, such a statement which is false shall be guilty of an offence and liable on summary conviction to a fine not exceeding £100 or to imprisonment for a term not exceeding six months or to both.

Refusal of registration.—As to giving notice of intention to make an order of refusal, and as to the right of appeal, see s. 6, p. 945, *post*. Apprehension of a change in circumstances likely to render premises unsuitable for registration would not, in general, it is submitted, be a proper ground for refusing registration in view of the power of cancellation conferred by s. 5, p. 945, *post*.

Imposition of requirements.—See s. 2 (5), (7), *infra*; save for requirements made under para. (c) of sub-s. (4) of s. 2, the order may be made on registration, or at any time thereafter.

2. Power to impose requirements in connection with registration.—(1) The local health authority may by order require that no greater number of children shall be received in premises registered under the foregoing section than may be specified in the order.

(2) The local health authority may by order require in the case of a person registered under the foregoing section that the number of children received in his home as mentioned in paragraph (b) of subsection (1) of that section, shall not at any time exceed such number as may be specified in the order, and in making any order under this subsection, an authority shall have regards to the number of any other children who may be from time to time in the home.

(3) The local health authority may by order made as respects any premises or person registered under the foregoing section require the taking of precautions against the exposure of the children received in the premises to infectious diseases.

(4) The local health authority may by order made as respects any premises registered under the foregoing section impose requirements for securing—

(a) that a person with such qualifications as may be specified by the authority shall be in charge of the premises and of the persons employed thereat;

(b) that the premises shall be adequately staffed, both as respects the number and as respects the qualifications or experience of the persons employed thereat, and adequately equipped;

(c) in the case of premises which at the commencement of this Act were in use for the reception of children as mentioned in paragraph (a) of subsection (1) of section one of this Act, that such repairs shall be carried out on the premises, or such alterations thereof or additions thereto shall be made, as may be specified in the order;

(d) that the premises shall be kept safe and adequately maintained and the equipment thereof shall be adequately maintained;

(e) that there shall be adequate arrangements for feeding the children received in the premises and that an adequate and suitable diet shall be provided for them;

(f) that the children received in the premises shall be under medical supervision;

(g) that records shall be kept in relation to the children received at the premises containing such particulars as may be specified by the authority.

(5) An order under paragraph (c) of the last foregoing subsection may be made either on registration or at any time within one month thereafter, and any other order under this section may be made either on registration or at any subsequent time.

(6) An order under this section may be varied or revoked by a subsequent order of the local health authority.

(7) In the case of premises which at the commencement of this Act were in use for the reception of children as mentioned in paragraph (a) of subsection (1) of section one of this Act, no requirement shall be imposed under paragraphs (a) to (c) of subsection (4) of this section so as to require anything to be done before the expiration of a reasonable time from the commencement of this Act.

NOTES

This section is printed as amended by s. 60 of the Health Services and Public Health Act, 1968.

Procedure.—Powers of imposing requirements must in all cases be exercised by order of the local health authority. Orders cannot be made under this section before registration under s. 1 is effected; in the case of an order under sub-s. (4) (c), *supra*, the power can only be exercised on registration or within one month after registration (sub-s. (5), *supra*). Orders may only be made upon notice in accordance with the provisions of s. 6, *post*, and subject to the right of appeal thereby conferred, save that an order merely varying or revoking a previous order (*cf.* sub-s. (6), *supra*), and not imposing any new requirement or increasing any existing requirement does not, it seems, come within the scope of s. 6, p. 945, *post*.

Requirements imposed under the above section are to be specified in the certificate of registration (s. 3 (1), *infra*).

Sanctions.—Failure to observe the requirements imposed by an order may have penal consequences (see s. 4, *infra*), or lead to cancellation of the registration (see s. 5, p. 945, *post*). Prosecutions in England and Wales may be undertaken by the local health authority (see s. 11, p. 950, *post*). As to entry and inspection, see s. 7, p. 947, *post*.

" **Local health authority.**"—As to meaning, see notes to s. 1, p. 939, *ante*.

" **Children.**"—For definition, see s. 13 (2), p. 950, *post*.

" **Reasonable time.**"—What is a reasonable time must depend on the particular circumstances of each case; *cf. Alexiadi* v. *Robinson* (1861), 2 F. & F. 679. The time within which the requirement is to be fulfilled should, it is suggested, be stated in the order both for practical convenience and in view of the terms of the proviso to s. 5, *post*. If the time is thought by the applicant or the occupier to be too short, the proper course will be to raise the matter by so informing the authority in writing, pursuant to sub-s. (2) of s. 6, p. 945, *post*.

Shall not at any time exceed (sub-s. (2)).—But see Health Services and Public Health Act, 1968, s. 60 (9), p. 953, *post*, for further requirements that may be imposed.

3. Certificates of registration.—(1) The local health authority shall issue certificates of registration under section one of this Act, and any such certificate shall specify the situation of the premises to which, or the name and address of the person to whom, the registration relates and any requirements imposed under the last foregoing section.

(2) On any change occurring in the circumstances particulars of which are stated in a certificate issued under this section, the local health authority shall issue an amended certificate.

(3) Where the local health authority are satisfied that any certificate under this section has been lost or destroyed, the authority shall, on payment of such fee (if any) not exceeding twenty-five pence as the authority may determine, issue a copy of the certificate.

NOTES

This section is printed as amended by the Health Services and Public Health Act, 1968.

Contents of certificate.—The address of a child-minder will generally be that of his home in which he receives children (*cf.* s. 1 (1) (b), p. 939, *ante*).

" Local health authority."—See the National Health Service Act, 1946, s. 19 (1), p. 876, *ante*.

Change of circumstances.—The Act does not contain any provision requiring a certificate to be delivered up on cancellation of a registration; nor, save indirectly through the sanctions provided by s. 4, *post*, does it require any person to inform the local health authority of a change in circumstances, other than the acquisition by a child-minder of a new home (see s. 4 (3), *infra*). The local health authority's means of knowledge, so far as they rest on this statute, are substantially those provided by ss. 7, 9, 10, *post*, and consist of their powers of entry and inspection.

4. Penalties for failure to register and for breach of requirements under section two.—(1) If at any time after the expiration of three months from the commencement of this Act a child is received in any premises as mentioned in paragraph (a) of subsection (1) of section one of this Act and the premises are not registered under that section or any requirement imposed under section two of this Act is contravened or not complied with, the occupier of the premises shall be guilty of an offence.

(2) Where at any such time as aforesaid a person receives as mentioned in paragraph (b) of subsection (1) of section one of this Act a child of whom his is not a relative. Then if he is not registered under section one of this Act, or if he contravenes or fails to comply with any requirement imposed under section two thereof, he shall be guilty of an offence.

(3) Where a person has been registered under section one of this Act and while he is so registered he acquires a new home, then until he has given notice thereof to the local health authority he shall not for the purposes of the last foregoing subsection be treated as being so registered in relation to the reception of children in the new home.

(4) A person guilty of an offence under this section shall be liable on summary conviction to a fine not exceeding fifty pounds or, in the case of a second or subsequent offence, to imprisonment for a term not exceeding three months or to a fine not exceeding one hundred pounds or to both such imprisonment and such fine.

NOTES

This section is printed as amended by the Health Services and Public Health Act, 1968.

See generally the initial note to s. 1 of this Act, p. 940, *ante*; as to powers of entry and inspection, *cf.* s. 7, p. 947, *post*. As to the exclusion of this section where child life protection provisions apply, see s. 9, p. 949, *post*.

Subsection (1).—This subsection applies only in respect of nurseries within the Act, *i.e.* premises as distinct from child-minders. The *occupier* of the premises may not necessarily be the same person as the applicant for registration who may be " any person receiving or proposing to receive children, *etc.*" (see sub-s. (2) of s. 1. p. 940, *ante*). " Occupier " means, it is submitted, the person in legal occupation and control of the premises (*Bruce* v. *McManus*, [1915] 3 K. B. 1), and not the manager or other person, by whatever name called, in charge of day to day running. That the occupier and the applicant for registration need not be the same person is shown by the requirement of notifying both of them contained in sub-s. (1) of s. 6, *infra*.

" **Child.**"—For definition, see s. 13 (2), *post*, but note that the effect of s. 1 (1) (b), *ante*, is to limit the meaning of " Children " in sub-s. (2), *supra*, to children under five years of age.

" **Relative.**"—For definition, see s. 13 (2), p. 950, *post*.

"**Requirement imposed under section two.**"—The requirements which can be imposed by s. 2, p. 940, *ante*, in relation to a child-minder are those limiting the number of children to be received or requiring the taking of precautions against exposure to infectious diseases together with the requirements set out in s. 60 (9) of the Health Services and Public Health Act, 1968, p. 953, *post*.

Second offence.—See *R. v. South Shields Licensing Justices*, [1911] 2 K. B. 1, p. 26, *ante*.

5. Cancellation of registration.—Where—

(a) there has been a contravention of, or non-compliance with, any requirement imposed under section two of this Act in relation to any premises or person registered under section one thereof, or

(b) it appears to the local health authority as respects any premises or person registered under the said section one, that circumstances exist which would justify a refusal under subsection (3) or subsection (4) of that section to register the premises or person,

the local health authority may by order cancel the registration:

Provided that where a requirement to carry out repairs or make alterations or additions has been imposed under paragraph (c) of subsection (4) of section two of this Act, the registration of the premises shall not be cancelled by virtue of paragraph (b) of this section on the grounds that the premises are not fit to be used for the reception of children if—

(i) the time limited by subsection (7) of the said section two for complying with the requirement has not expired, and

(ii) it is shown that the condition of the premises is due to the repairs not having been carried out or the alterations or additions not having been made.

NOTES

Procedure.—If the local health authority propose to cancel a registration they must follow the procedure laid down in s. 6 (1)–(3), *infra*, and a right of appeal against the cancellation is conferred on any person aggrieved thereby; see s. 6 (4), *infra*.

Time of cancellation.—The order for cancellation does not take effect before the time of appealing against it has expired or the appeal is determined (s. 6 (4), *infra*).

" **Local health authority.**"—See the National Health Service Act, 1946, s. 19 (1)' p. 876, *ante*.

" **Child.**"—For definition, see s. 13 (2), p. 950, *post*.

6. Appeals.—(1) Not less than fourteen days before making an order under this Act refusing an application for registration, cancelling any registration, or imposing any requirement under section two of this Act,

the local health authority shall send to the applicant, to the occupier of the premises to which the registration relates, or to the person registered, as the case may be, notice of their intention to make such an order.

(2) Every such notice shall state the grounds on which the authority intend to make the order and shall contain an intimation that if within fourteen days after the receipt of the notice the said applicant, occupier or person informs the authority in writing of his desire to show cause, in person or by a representative, why the order should not be made, the authority shall before making the order afford him an opportunity so to do.

(3) If the local authority, after giving the said applicant, occupier or person such an opportunity as aforesaid, decide to refuse the application, cancel the registration, or impose the requirement, as the case may be, they shall make an order to that effect and shall send him a copy of the order.

(4) A person aggrieved by an order under this Act refusing an application for registration or cancelling any registration, or imposing any requirement under section two of this Act, may appeal to a court of summary jurisdiction, or in Scotland the sheriff, having jurisdiction in the place where the premises in question are situated if the order relates to the registration of premises, or in the place where the person in question resides if the order relates to the registration of a person; and an order cancelling any registration shall not take effect until the expiration of the time within which an appeal may be brought under this section or, where such an appeal is brought, before the determination of the appeal.

(5) Sections three hundred to three hundred and two of the Public Health Act, 1936 (which relate to appeals) shall apply for the purposes of this section as if the provisions of this Act were contained in that Act.

(6) Any notice required to be sent under subsection (1) of this section, and any copy of an order required to be sent under subsection (3) thereof, may be sent by post in a registered letter.

(7) In the application of this section to Scotland, subsection (5) shall be omitted, and any appeal under subsection (4) shall be brought within twenty-one days from the date of the order to which the appeal relates.

NOTES

This section is printed as amended by the London Government Act, 1963.

" Local health authority."—See the National Health Service Act, 1946, s. 19 (1), p. 876, *ante*.

" Occupier."—See the note to s. 4, sub-s. (1), p. 944, *ante*.

" A representative."—No professional qualifications are required for a representative who may, therefore, be any person nominated for the purpose.

" Person aggrieved."—A person aggrieved is a man who has suffered a legal grievance, a man against whom a decision has been pronounced which has wrongfully deprived him of something, or wrongfully refused him something, or wrongfully affected his title to something; see *Re Baron, Ex parte Debtor* v. *Official Receiver*, [1943] Ch. 177, at p. 179; [1943] 2 All E. R. 662, at p. 664, citing *per* James, L.J., in *Re Sidebotham, Ex parte Sidebotham* (1880), 14 Ch. D. 458, at p. 485. *Cf. R.* v. *Surrey Quarter Sessions, Ex parte Lilley*, [1951] 2 K. B. 749; [1951] 2 All E. R. 659; 115 J. P. 507; *R.* v. *Lancashire Quarter Sessions Appeal Committee, Ex parte Huyton-with-Roby Urban District Council* [1954] 3 All E. R. 225; 118 J. P. 526.

Appeal to court of summary jurisdiction.—The procedure is by complaint for an order (Public Health Act, 1936, s. 300, p. 874, *ante*; Magistrates' Courts Rules, 1968, rule 30).

Appeal to the Crown Court.—There is a right of appeal to the Crown Court from the decision of the justices (see s. 301 of the Public Health Act, 1936, p. 874, *ante*). The procedure on appeal to the Crown Court will be under the Magistrates' Courts Act, 1952, ss. 83 *et seq.* and the Magistrates' Courts Rules, 1968 (S.I. 1952 No. 2190 (L. 18)), rules 62, 63, 64, and the Crown Court Rules, p. 654, *ante*.

" May be sent by post in a registered letter."—These words are permissive only and would appear not to exclude personal service or service by ordinary letter; see *Sharpley* v. *Manby*, [1942] 1 K. B. 217; [1942] 1 All E. R. 66, C. A., and compare the provisions of the Interpretation Act, 1889, s. 26; 32 Halsbury's Statutes, 3rd Edn., 452.   It will, however, in all cases be safer to serve all notices under sub-s. (1), *supra*, and all orders under sub-s. (5), *supra*, by registered post or recorded delivery.

7. Inspection.—(1) Any person authorised in that behalf by a local health authority may at all reasonable times enter any premises in the area of the authority which are used for the reception of children as mentioned in paragraph (a) of subsection (1) of section one of this Act, and may inspect the premises and the children so received therein, the arrangements for their welfare, and any records relating to them kept in pursuance of this Act, and may at all reasonable times enter the home of a person registered under section one of this Act by the Authority, and may inspect it and any children received there as mentioned in paragraph (b) of subsection (1) of section one of this Act, the arrangements for their welfare and any records relating to them kept in pursuance of this Act.

(2) If any person authorised as aforesaid has reasonable cause to believe that children are being received in a person's home or in any other premises in contravention of section four of this Act, he may apply to a justice of the peace or in Scotland to the sheriff, and if the justice or sheriff is satisfied on sworn information in writing that there is reasonable cause to believe that children are being received as aforesaid, the justice or sheriff may grant a warrant authorising the applicant to enter the home or other premises and carry out any such inspection as is mentioned in subsection (1) of this section.

(3) A person who proposes to exercise any power of entry or inspection conferred by or under this section shall if so required produce some duly authenticated document showing his authority to exercise the power.

(4) Any person who obstructs the exercise of any such power as aforesaid shall be guilty of an offence and liable on summary conviction to a fine not exceeding five pounds in the case of a first offence or twenty pounds in the case of a second or any subsequent offence.

NOTES

This section is printed as amended by the Health Services and Public Health Act, 1968.

As to the prevention of overlap between these provisions, and those of child life protection enactments, see ss. 9, 10, pp. 949 *et seq.*, *post*.

Powers of entry and inspection.—An inspector should have documentary authority which he should produce on request (sub-s. (3)); his title to enter and inspect them rests on two conditions being satisfied, namely, (i) that the premises are in fact used for the reception of children " to be looked after for the day or for

---

an aggregate of two hours or longer or for any longer period not exceeding six days," and are not exempt either as being wholly or mainly used as a private dwelling (s. 1 (1) (a), *ante*) or under ss. 8 or 9 (1), *post*. A mere opinion or belief, or reasonable suspicion, that premises are so used will not legally justify an entry, if the fact is that they are not. In doubtful cases, therefore, the better course will be not to insist on being allowed to enter, if the right of entry is disputed, but to apply under sub-s. (2) for a warrant, so that there may be no risk of entry being a trespass.

Sub-s. (1) does *not* confer power to enter the home of a person registered as a child-minder: it extends only to premises, as distinct from persons, registered under s. 1, *ante*. To enter and inspect as of right the home of a registered child-minder, a warrant under sub-s. (2), *supra*, is requisite.

The power of inspection extends not only to the premises but also to (i) the children, (ii) the arrangements for their welfare (*cf.* s. 2 (4) (e), (f), p. 942, *ante*), and (iii) any records relating to them kept in pursuance of a requirement under s. 2 (4) (g), *ante*, or otherwise in pursuance of the Act. The Act does *not*, however, confer any power to require the furnishing of oral information.

Entry pursuant to warrant.—Clearly a warrant is unnecessary in any case where admission is voluntarily allowed; in other cases a warrant will be needed to entitle a person to inspect as of right (i) the home of a registered child-minder, and (ii) premises (whether nurseries or homes of child-minders) as to which there is reasonable cause to believe that children are being received in contravention of s. 4, *ante*, although if they were nurseries that in fact were being used as mentioned in sub-s. (1), *supra*, there would be a right to inspect them without warrant. Resistance to a warrant may amount to an offence under sub-s. (4); as to any right to force an entry, *cf.*, *e.g.*, the Children and Young Persons Act, 1933, s. 40 (3), p. 47, *ante*, where the words " if need be by force," which are absent from this section, are expressly included, and consider the Forcible Entry Act, 1381; 18 Halsbury's Statutes, 3rd Edn., 405. As to the mode of executing a warrant, *cf. Launock* v. *Brown* (1819) 2 B. & Ald. 592; (entry to arrest for misdemeanour); the cause of coming should be signified and a request for admittance should be made, and in addition the document showing authority to enter should be produced if required (sub-s. (3), *supra*).

" **Local health authority.**"—See the National Health Service Act, 1946, s. 19 (1), p. 876, *ante*.

Child.—For definition, see s. 13 (2), *post*.

" **Reasonable cause.**"—*Prima facie* the words " if any person . . . has reasonable cause to believe " mean " if there is reasonable cause for believing and the person in question in fact believes "; but they may also mean " if the person acting on what he thinks is reasonable cause (and, of course, acting in good faith) believes ": *Liversidge* v. *Anderson*, [1942] A. C. 206, at p. 220; [1941] 3 All E. R. 338, at p. 345, *per* Lord Maugham.

The person applying for the warrant should state the grounds of his belief fully and fairly.

Granting a warrant.—It would seem that the action of granting such a warrant is a judicial one. See *Hope* v. *Evered* (1886), 17 Q. B. D. 338. The person named in the warrant must observe its directions strictly, and cannot delegate its execution to another.

Prosecutions.—The local health authority is empowered to prosecute (s. 11, p. 950, *post*).

Second offence.—See note at p. 26, *ante*.

8. Exemption of certain institutions from provisions of Act.—

(1) Nothing in this Act shall apply to the reception of children in any hospital, or in any such home or other institution as is mentioned in section two of the Children Act, 1958.

(2) Nothing in this Act shall apply to the reception of children in any school, notwithstanding that they are received to be looked after and not for the purpose of education.

(3) Nothing in this Act shall apply to the reception of children in a

nursery school maintained or assisted by a local education authority or in respect of which payments are made by the Minister of Education under section one hundred of the Education Act, 1944, or by the Secretary of State under section seventy of the Education (Scotland) Act, 1946, or which is recognised as efficient by the Minister of Education or included in a scheme submitted under section seven and approved by the Secretary of State under section sixty-five of the said Act of 1946, or to the reception of children in any play centre maintained or assisted by a local education authority under section fifty-three of the said Act of 1944, or by an education authority under section three of the said Act of 1946.

NOTES

This section is printed as amended by the Children Act, 1958, Sched. II, and the Local Government Act, 1958, Sched. VIII.

Child.—For definition, see s. 13 (2), *post*.

" Hospital."—For definition, see s. 13 (2), *post*.

Children Act, 1958, s. 2.—See p. 956, *post*.

Schools.—The cases of school buildings which are open in the holidays for organised games or other activities and where children are admitted to spend the day, as well as nursery classes in schools, as to which see the Education Act, 1944, s. 8 (2) (b); 11 Halsbury's Statutes, 3rd Edn., 162, are covered by sub-s. (2) of this section. For the definition of school, see s. 13 (2), *post*.

Education Acts.—Section 100 of the Education Act, 1944 (11 Halsbury's Statutes, 3rd Edn., 249), gives the Secretary of State for Education and Science power to make grants to local education authorities and to other persons providing educational services. Section 53 empowers a local education authority with the approval of the Secretary of State to maintain or assist the maintenance of facilities for recreation and physical training including play centres.

9. Exclusion of sections four and seven of Act where child life protection enactments apply.—(1) Where premises falling within paragraph (a) of subsection (1) of section one of this Act are used mainly for the reception of children for periods exceeding six days and in such circumstances that the child life protection enactments apply, sections four and seven of this Act shall not apply to the premises and the provisions of the child life protection enactments as to entry and inspection shall extend to all children received in the premises.

(2) Where a person receives children into his home in such circumstances that apart from this subsection he would be required by subsection (2) of section four of this Act to be registered under section one thereof, then so long as provision for entry and inspection as respects any child received into his home is made by or under the child life protection enactments or any enactment relating to the boarding-out of children,—

(a) sections four and seven of this Act shall not apply,

(b) the said provision for entry and inspection shall apply in relation to all the children aforesaid.

NOTES

This section is printed as amended by the Children Act, 1958, Sched. III.

Exclusion of dual control.—This section and s. 10, *infra*, prevent nurseries and child-minders from being subject to control both under the present Act and under the child life protection provisions of other statutes, which give powers of supervision over persons undertaking the care of foster children, the principle being that the code applicable to the main user of the premises shall be the one to be applied. Thus, in the case of a nursery which is mainly used for the reception of children for more than six days at a time, the child life protection enactments will apply and sub-s. (1) of the present section will exempt the occupier of premises from the penalties for non-registration imposed by s. 4, *ante*, and the premises from inspection under s. 7, *ante*. Inspection will be un 1er the child life protection enactments. On the other hand, where the main use of the nursery is for the reception of children for periods of less than six days at a time, s. 10, *infra*, provides that all the children shall be inspected under s. 7, *ante*, although it will be necessary to comply with the child life protection enactments as to notification in the case of children received for longer periods.

So far as child-minders are concerned, sub-s. (2), *supra*, provides that where any children received are subject to inspection under the child life protection enactments, or any boarding-out enactments, all the children will be subject to inspection under those enactments, and the minder will be exempt from the penal scope of s. 4, *ante*, and his home will be exempt from entry and inspection under s. 7, *ante*.

" **Child.**"—For definition, see s. 13 (2), *post*.

" **Child life protection enactments.**"—For definition, see s. 13 (2), *post*.

" **Boarding-out.**"—See s. 54 (2) of the Children Act, 1948, p. 919, *ante*, as to the inspection of children boarded-out either by a local authority or a voluntary organisation.

10. Exclusion of child life protection enactments where premises registered under Act.—Where premises registered under section one of this Act are used wholly or mainly for the reception of children as mentioned in paragraph (a) of subsection (1) of that section, the provisions of the child life protection enactments as to entry and inspection shall not apply in relation to any children received at the premises, and the provisions of section seven of this Act shall apply in relation to all children received thereat.

NOTE
See the notes to s. 9, *supra*.

11. Prosecution of offences.—In England and Wales, the local health authority may prosecute for any offence under this Act.

NOTES
As to offences under the Act, see ss. 4 and 7 (4), pp. 944, 947, *ante*.

" **Local health authority.**"—See the National Health Service Act, 1946, s. 19 (1), p. 876, *ante*.

12. Payments out of moneys provided by Parliament.—[*Repealed by the Health Services and Public Health Act, 1968, s. 78, and Sched. IV.*]

13. Short title, interpretation and extent.—(1) This Act may be cited as the Nurseries and Child-Minders Regulation Act, 1948.

(2) In this Act the following expressions have the meanings hereby assigned to them respectively, that is to say:—

    " child " means a person who has not attained the upper limit of compulsory school age;

    " child life protection enactments " means the provisions of Part I of the Children Act, 1958;

"compulsory school age", in England and Wales, has the same meaning as in the Education Act, 1944, and in Scotland means school age as defined in the Education (Scotland) Act, 1946;

"hospital" has the same meaning as in section seventy nine of the National Health Service Act, 1946, or, as respects Scotland, section eighty of the National Health Service (Scotland) Act, 1947;

"relative" in relation to an infant means a grandparent, brother, sister, uncle or aunt, whether of the full blood, of the half-blood, or by affinity, and includes—

(a) where an adoption order has been made in respect of the infant or any other person who would be a relative of the infant within the meaning of this definition if the adopted person were the child of the adopter born in lawful wedlock;

(b) where the infant is illegitimate, the father of the infant and any person who would be a relative of the infant within the meaning of this definition if the infant were the legitimate child of its mother and father;

"school", except in the expression "nursery school", means an institution of which the sole or main purpose is the provision of education for children of compulsory school age.

(3) References in this Act to any enactment shall be construed as references to that enactment as amended by any subsequent enactment.

(4) This Act shall not extend to Northern Ireland.

NOTES

This section is printed as amended by the Adoption of Children Act, 1949, s. 13 (*now repealed*), and by the Children Act, 1958, Sched. II.

"**Compulsory school age.**"—By the Education Act, 1944, s. 35 (p. 252, *ante*), compulsory school age is defined as being any age between five and fifteen years, but provision is made for raising the upper limit to sixteen by Order in Council at some later date. As to a child attaining a particular age during a school term, see s. 9 of the Education Act, 1962, p. 273, *ante*.

"**Hospital.**"—For s. 79 of the National Health Service Act, 1946, see 23 Halsbury's Statutes, 3rd Edn., 80.

HEALTH SERVICES AND PUBLIC HEALTH ACT, 1968
[1968 c. 46]

Provisions applicable to England and Wales and Scotland

60. Amendment of Nurseries and Child-Minders Regulation Act, 1948.— The Nurseries and Child-Minders Regulation Act, 1948 shall be amended as follows.

(2) Section 1 (1) (a) (by virtue whereof local health authorities are required to keep registers of premises in their areas, other than premises wholly or mainly used as private dwellings, where children are received

to be looked after for the day or a substantial part thereof or for any longer period not exceeding six days) shall have effect with the substitution, for the words " a substantial part thereof", of the words "for a part or parts thereof of a duration, or an aggregate duration, of two hours or longer"; but the reception, before the expiration of the period of three months beginning with the day on which this section comes into operation, of a child in any premises as mentioned in section 1 (1) (a) or by any person as mentioned in section 1 (1) (b) shall not constitute an offence under section 4 (1) or (2), as the case may be, if it would not have constituted an offence thereunder if this subsection had not been enacted.

(3) Section 4 (2) (which penalises, amongst other things, the reception by a person as mentioned in section 1 (1) (b) of children exceeding two in number and coming from more than one household without his being a relative of theirs and registered under section 1) shall, as from the expiration of the period aforesaid, have effect with the substitution, for the words "children of whom he is not a relative, and (a) the number of the children exceeds two, and (b) the children come from more than one household", of the words "a child of whom he is not a relative".

(4) The punishment that may be imposed on a person guilty of an offence under section 4, being an offence committed after the coming into operation of this section, shall, instead of being a fine not exceeding £25 or, in the case of a second or subsequent offence, imprisonment for a term not exceeding one month or a fine not exceeding £25 or both, be a fine not exceeding £50 or, in the case of a second or subsequent offence, imprisonment for a term not exceeding three months or a fine not exceeding £100 or both, and the proviso to subsection (4) of that section (which limits to £5 the punishment that may be imposed in the case of a first offence under subsection (5) of that section), shall, except in relation to an offence committed before the coming into operation of this section, cease to have effect.

(5) In section 1 (3) (by virtue whereof a local health authority may refuse to register premises if, inter alia, they are satisfied that the premises are not fit to be used for the reception of children), after the word "fit" (where last occurring), there shall be inserted the words "(whether because of the condition thereof or of the equipment thereof or for any reason connected with the situation, construction or size thereof or with other persons therein)".

(6) In section 1 (4) (by virtue whereof a local health authority may refuse to register a person if, *inter alia*, they are satisfied that the premises in which the children are received or are proposed to be received are not fit, whether because of the condition thereof or for any reason connected with other persons therein, to be used for the purpose), after the word "thereof", there shall be inserted the words "or of the equipment thereof" and after the words "connected with" there shall be inserted the words "the situation, construction or size thereof or with".

(7) An application for the registration under section 1 of any premises shall be of no effect unless it contains a statement with respect to each person employed or proposed to be employed in looking after children at the premises and each person who has attained the age of sixteen years and

(though not so employed or proposed to be so employed) is normally resident at the premises, whether or not—

    (a) there has been made against him any such order as is mentioned in paragraph (a), (b) or (e) of section 6 of the Children Act, 1958 (disqualification for keeping foster children);
    (b) he has been convicted as mentioned in paragraph (c) thereof;
    (c) his rights and powers with respect to a child have been vested as mentioned in paragraph (d) thereof; or
    (d) an order has been made under section 43 of the Adoption Act, 1958 (removal of protected children from unsuitable surroundings) for the removal of a child from his care;

and an application for the registration under section 1 of a person shall be of no effect unless it contains a similar statement with respect to him, each person employed or proposed to be employed by him in looking after children and each person other than himself who has attained the age of sixteen years and (though not so employed or proposed to be so employed) is normally resident at the premises in which the children are received or proposed to be received; and a person who, in any such application as aforesaid makes, with respect to himself or another any such statement as aforesaid which is false and is known to him to be false or recklessly makes, with respect to himself or another, such a statement which is false shall be guilty of an offence and liable on summary conviction to a fine not exceeding £100 or to imprisonment for a term not exceeding six months or to both.

(8) Section 2 (2) (which empowers a local health authority to order that the number of children that may be received by a person in his home as mentioned in section 1 (1) (b), together with any other children therein, shall not exceed such number as may be specified) shall have effect with the omission of the words "together with any other children in his home" and the addition at the end thereof of the words "and in making an order under this subsection an authority shall have regard to the number of any other children who may from time to time be in the home".

(9) The power of the local health authority under the said section 2 (2) to limit the number of children that may be received by a person in his home as mentioned in section 1 (1) (b) shall include power by order to impose requirements for securing—

    (a) that there shall be available, for looking after the children received by him as so mentioned, persons adequate in number and in qualifications or experience;
    (b) that the premises in which the children are received shall be kept safe and adequately maintained and the equipment thereof shall be adequately maintained;
    (c) that there shall be adequate arrangements for feeding the children so received and that an adequate and suitable diet shall be provided for them;
    (d) that records shall be kept in relation to the children so received containing such particulars as may be specified by the authority.

(10) In paragraph (d) of section 2 (4) (which specifies, as one of the objects for the securing of which, as respects registered premises, requirements may be imposed by a local health authority, that the premises and

the equipment thereof shall be adequately maintained), after the word "premises", there shall be inserted the words "shall be kept safe and adequately maintained".

(11) Section 7 (inspection) shall have effect—

    (a) as if, at the end of subsection (1) there were added the words "and may at all reasonable times enter the home of a person registered under section one of this Act by the authority, and may inspect it and any children received there as mentioned in paragraph (b) of subsection (1) of section one of this Act, the arrangements for their welfare and any records relating to them kept in pursuance of this Act"; and

    (b) as if, in subsection (2), the words "is refused admission to the home of a person registered under section one of this Act, or" and the words "admission has been refused, or, as the case may be, that" were omitted.

(12) The maximum amount of the fee that, under section 3 (3), may be demanded by a local health authority for the issue of a copy of a certificate of registration under section 1 shall be increased from two shillings and sixpence to five shillings, and accordingly, in that subsection, for the words "two shillings and sixpence" there shall be substituted the words "five shillings".

(13) Section 12 (which authorises the payment out of moneys provided by Parliament of any increase attributable to the Act in grants payable under any other Act and is spent) shall cease to have effect.

CHILDREN ACT, 1958

[6 & 7 Eliz. 2, c. 65]

ARRANGEMENT OF SECTIONS

PART I

CHILD PROTECTION

SECTION		PAGE
1.	Duty of local authorities to ensure well-being of foster children	956
1A.	Scotland	956
2.	Meaning of " foster child "	956
3.	Duty of persons maintaining foster children to notify local authority	958
4.	Power to inspect premises, impose conditions, or prohibit the keeping of foster children	960
5.	Appeal to juvenile court against requirement or prohibition imposed under section four	962
6.	Disqualification for keeping foster children	963
7.	Removal of foster children kept in unsuitable surroundings	964
8.	Extension of power to issue warrants to search for and remove a child	965
9.	Avoidance of insurances on lives of foster children	965
10.	Sittings of juvenile courts in proceedings under Part I	965
11.	Appeal to Crown Crown	966
12.	Extension of Part I to certain school children during holidays	966
13.	Extension of Part I to certain children above compulsory school age	967
14.	Offences	967
15.	Service of notices by post	968
16.	Authentication of documents	968
17.	Interpretation of Part I	968

PART II

AMENDMENTS OF ADOPTION ACT, 1950

[*Repealed by the Adoption Act*, 1958, *s.* 59 *and Sched. VI.*]

PART III

MISCELLANEOUS AND GENERAL

SECTION		PAGE
37.	Prohibition of anonymous advertisements offering to undertake care of children	969
38.	Repeal of obsolete enactments [*Not reproduced.*]	
39.	Expenses	970
40.	Minor and consequential amendments and repeals [*Not reproduced.*]	
41.	Short title, construction, commencement and extent	970

SCHEDULES:

First Schedule—[*Not reproduced.*]
Second Schedule—[*Not reproduced.*]
Third Schedule—[*Not reproduced.*]

An Act to make fresh provision for the protection of children living away from their parents; to amend the law relating to the adoption of children; and for purposes connected with the matters aforesaid. [1st August, 1958]

Part I

Local authorities.—The council of each London borough shall as respects the borough, and the Common Council shall as respects the City have the functions of the council of a county borough under Part I of this Act and be the local authority for such purposes of this Part as refer to a local authority (London Government Act, 1963, s. 47; 20 Halsbury's Statutes, 3rd Edn., 504). Sections 1 to 6 and 14 have effect and are printed as set out in Sched. VII of the Children and Young Persons Act, 1969 (*ibid.*, 72 (5), p. 215, *ante*).

Child Protection

1. Duty of local authorities to ensure well-being of foster children.—It shall be the duty of every local authority to satisfy themselves as to the well-being of children within their area who are foster children within the meaning of this Part of this Act and, for that purpose, to secure that, so far as appears to the authority to be appropriate, the children are visited from time to time by officers of the authority and that such advice is given as to the care and maintenance of the children as appears to be needed.

NOTES

Child and local authority.—For definitions of these words, see s. 17, p. 968, *post*.

Foster child.—For definition, see s. 2, *infra*.

Care and maintenance.—See note to s. 2, *infra*.

So far as appears ... appropriate.—This contrasts with the former provisions to visit irrespective of whether supervision was really necessary or not.

Scotland.—This section is repealed as to Scotland by the Social Work (Scotland) Act, 1968, s. 95 (2), 98 and Sched. IX, Part I and the following section inserted:—

1A. In Scotland, without prejudice to the provisions of the Social Work (Scotland) Act, 1968, it shall be the duty of every local authority to secure the welfare of children within their area who are foster children within the meaning of this Part of this Act and, where the local authority consider such a course to be necessary or expedient for the purposes of this section, they shall cause the children to be visited from time to time by their officers, who shall give such advice as to the care and maintenance of the children as may appear to be necessary.

2. Meaning of "foster child".—(1) In this Part of this Act "foster child" means, subject to the following provisions of this section, a child below the upper limit of the compulsory school age whose care and maintenance are undertaken by a person who is not a relative or guardian of his.

(2) A child is not a foster child within the meaning of this Part of this Act while he is in the care of a local authority or a voluntary organisation or is boarded out by a local health authority or a local education authority (or, in Scotland, an education authority).

(3) A child is not a foster child within the meaning of this Part of this Act while he is in the care of any person—

    (a) in premises in which any parent, adult relative or guardian of his is for the time being residing;

    (b) in any voluntary home within the meaning of Part V of the Children and Young Persons Act, 1933, or in any residential establishment within the meaning of the Social Work (Scotland) Act, 1968;

    (c) in any school within the meaning of the Education Acts, 1944 to 1953, or the Education (Scotland) Acts, 1939 to 1956, in which he is receiving full-time education;

    (d) in any hospital or in any nursing home registered or exempted from registration under Part VI of the Public Health Act, 1936, Part XI of the Public Health (London) Act, 1936, or the Nursing Homes Registration (Scotland) Act, 1938; or

    (e) in any home or institution not specified in this section but maintained by a public or local authority.

(3A) A child is not a foster child within the meaning of this Part of this Act at any time while his care and maintenance are undertaken by a person, other than a relative or guardian of his, if at that time—

    (a) that person does not intend to, and does not in fact, undertake his care and maintenance for a continuous period of more than six days; or

    (b) that person is not a regular foster parent and does not intend to, and does not in fact, undertake his care and maintenance for a continuous period of more than twenty-seven days;

and for the purposes of this subsection a person is a regular foster parent if, during the period of twelve months immediately preceding the date on which he begins to undertake the care and maintenance of the child in question, he had, otherwise than as a relative or guardian, the care and maintenance of one or more children either for a period of, or periods amounting in the aggregate to, not less than three months or for at least three continuous periods each of which was of more than six days.

(4) A child is not a foster child within the meaning of this Part of this Act while he is in the care of any person in compliance with a supervision order within the meaning of the Children and Young Persons Act, 1969, or a probation order or supervision requirement or by virtue of a fit person order or while he is in an approved school or is deemed for the purposes of the Children and Young Persons (Scotland) Act, 1937, to be under the care of the managers of an approved school or while he is liable to be detained or subject to guardianship under the Mental Health Act, 1959, or the Mental Health (Scotland) Act, 1960, or is resident in a residential home for mentally disordered persons within the meaning of Part III of the Mental Health Act, 1959, or in a residential home for persons suffering from mental disorder within the meaning of Part III of the Mental Health (Scotland) Act, 1960.

(4A) A child is not a foster child for the purposes of this Part of this Act while he is placed in the care and possession of a person who proposes to adopt him under arrangements made by such a local authority or registered adoption society as is referred to in Part II of the Adoption Act, 1958, or while he is a protected child within the meaning of Part IV of that Act.

NOTES

"**Compulsory school age.**"—See s. 17, p. 968, *post*, and s. 35 of the Education Act, 1944, at p. 252, *ante*. By s. 13, p. 967, *post*, Part I of this Act is extended to apply to certain children above compulsory school age.

Voluntary home.—For Part V of the Children and Young Persons Act, 1933, see pp. 74 *et seq.*, *ante*. See s. 94 Social Work (Scotland) Act, 1968, for meaning of residential establishment.

Care of a local authority.—See s. 1 of the Children Act, 1948, p. 880, *ante*.

School holidays.—See s. 12, p. 966, *post*, as to the extension of Part I to certain school children during holidays.

Care and maintenance.—*Cf. Wallbridge* v. *Dorset County Council*, [1954] 2 All E. R. 201; 118 J. P. 304; decided under the (repealed) s. 206 of the Public Health Act, 1936, the words of which were not the same as those used in the present section.

"**Undertaken.**"—In *Surrey County Council* v. *Battersby*, [1965] 2 Q. B. 194; [1965] 1 All E. R. 273; 129 J. P. 116, it was held that the word "undertaken" meant "in fact provided care and maintenance" and the test of infraction of s. 2 (1) was, therefore, whether care and maintenance was in fact provided for a period of more than one month. See also note "Proposes" to s. 3, p., 960, *post*.

Definitions.—"Child", "local authority", "parent", "relative" and "voluntary organisations" are defined in s. 17, p. 968, *post*. "Guardian" is not defined in this Act.

Effect of amendments.—The Act of 1969 repealed the words "for reward for a period exceeding one month" in sub-s. (1). The effect of this amendment is to bring within the ambit of the Act those placements where no payment is made and which because there is no application to adopt do not fall within the Adoption Act, 1958. A local authority may supervise whether or not foster parents receive payment. Further any private person other than a relative or guardian or proposed adopter who undertakes the care and maintenance of a child becomes a foster parent unless either the period of care is six days or less (such children being protected by the Nurseries and Child-minders Regulation Act, 1948, as amended), or he is not a regular foster parent as defined by subsection (3A).

In which he is receiving full time education (sub-s. (2)).—Children under school age and children living on school premises and receiving education elsewhere are not excluded from the definition of a foster child.

Transitional provisions.—A person who is subject to an order committing him to the care of a fit person other than a local authority is not a foster child within the meaning of s. 2 of the Children Act, 1958 (Sched. IV, para. 10 Children and Young Persons Act, 1969).

Scotland.—For s. 2 as amended in relation to Scotland see Social Work (Scotland) Act, 1968, s. 19 and Sched. I.

3. Duty of persons maintaining foster children to notify local authority.—(1) Subject to the following provisions of this section, a person who proposes to maintain as a foster child a child not already in his care shall give written notice thereof to the local authority not less than two weeks and not more than four weeks before he receives the child, unless he receives him in an emergency; and a person who maintains a foster child whom he received in an emergency or who became a foster child while in his care shall give written notice thereof to the local authority not later than forty-eight hours after he receives the child or, as the case may be, after the child becomes a foster child.

(2) Every such notice shall specify the date on which it is intended that the child should be received or, as the case may be, on which the child was in fact received or became a foster child and the premises in which the child is to be or is being kept and shall be given to the local authority for the area in which those premises are situated.

(2A) A person shall not be required to give notice under subsection (1) of this section in relation to a child if—

  (a) he has on a previous occasion given notice under that subsection in respect of that or any other child, specifying the premises at which he proposes to keep the child in question; and
  (b) he has not, at any time since that notice was given, ceased to maintain at least one foster child at those premises and been required by virtue of the following provisions of this section to give notice under subsection (5A) of this section in respect of those premises.

(3) Where a person who is maintaining one or more foster children changes his permanent address or the premises in which the child is, or the children are, kept he shall, not less than two weeks and not more than four weeks before the change or, if the change is made in an emergency, not later than forty-eight hours after the change, give written notice to the said local authority, specifying the new address or premises, and if the new premises are in the area of another local authority, the authority to whom the notice is given shall inform that other local authority and give them such of the particulars mentioned in subsection (7) of this section as are known to them.

(4) If a foster child dies the person who was maintaining him shall, within forty-eight hours thereof, give to the local authority and to the person from whom the child was received notice in writing of the death.

(5) Where a foster child is removed or removes himself from the care of the person maintaining him, that person shall at the request of the local authority give them the name and address, if known, of the person (if any) into whose care the child has been removed.

(5A) Subject to the provisions of the following subsection, where a person who has been maintaining one or more foster children at any premises ceases to maintain foster children at those premises and the circumstances are such that no notice is required to be given under subsection (3) or subsection (4) of this section, that person shall, within forty-eight hours after he ceases to maintain any foster child at those premises, give notice in writing thereof to the local authority.

(5B) A person need not give the notice required by the preceding subsection in consequence of his ceasing to maintain foster children at any premises if, at the time he so ceases, he intends within twenty-seven days again to maintain any of them as a foster child at those premises; but if he subsequently abandons that intention or the said period expires without his having given effect to it he shall give the said notice within forty-eight hours of that event.

(7) A person maintaining or proposing to maintain a foster child shall at the request of the local authority give them the following particulars, so far as known to him, that is to say, the name, sex, and date and place

of birth of the child, and the name and address of every person who is a parent or guardian or acts as a guardian of the child or from whom the child has been or is to be received.

NOTES

" Foster child."—For definition, see s. 2, *ante*.

"Notice."—By s. 15, p. 968, *post*, this may be given by post. Notice is required not of the reception of each foster child but of the intention to receive a foster child for the first time.

Definitions.—" Child ", " local authority " and " parent " are defined in s. 17, p. 968, *post*.

In respect of that or any other child.—*I.e.* separate notices are not required in respect of individual foster children but see s. 4 (2) which allows a local authority to require particulars in cases where this is considered necessary.

Death of foster child.—The provision in the (repealed) s. 213 of the Public Health Act, 1936, requiring the death of a foster child to be notified to the coroner, has not been re-enacted.

School child during holidays.—See s. 12, *post*.

" Proposes."—In *Surrey County Council* v. *Battersby*, [1965] 2 Q. B. 194 ; [1965] 1 All E. R. 273 ; 129 J. P. 116, it was held that the requirement in s. 3 (1) was imposed on a person who " proposed " to maintain a foster child, and the word " proposed " referred to the real intention, which in that case was an intention to take the children for a period which might well exceed a month, and in fact did exceed a month, since a period did not cease to be continuous merely because the children returned from time to time to their parents (this case was decided on the wording of s. 2 which defined a foster child as one whose care etc. was undertaken for a period exceeding one month).

4. Power to inspect premises, impose conditions, or prohibit the keeping of foster children.—(1) Any officer of a local authority authorised to visit foster children may, after producing, if asked to do so, some duly authenticated document showing that he is so authorised, inspect any premises in the area of the authority in the whole or any part of which foster children are to be or are being kept.

(1A) If it is shown to the satisfaction of a justice of the peace on sworn information in writing—

    (a) that there is reasonable cause to believe that a foster child is being kept in any premises, or in any part thereof; and

    (b) that admission to those premises or that part thereof has been refused to a duly authorised officer of the local authority or that such a refusal is apprehended or that the occupier is temporarily absent,

the justice may by warrant under his hand authorise an officer of the local authority to enter the premises if need be by force, at any reasonable time within forty-eight hours of the issue of the warrant, for the purpose of inspecting the premises.

(2) Where a person is keeping or proposes to keep foster children in premises used (while foster children are kept therein) wholly or partly for that purpose, the local authority may impose on him requirements, to be complied with, after such time as the authority may specify, whenever a foster child is kept in the premises, as to—

    (a) the number, age and sex of the foster children who may be kept at any one time in the premises or any part thereof;

    (b) the accommodation and equipment to be provided for the children;

    (c) the medical arrangements to be made for protecting the health of the children;

    (d) the giving of particulars of the person for the time being in charge of the children;

    (e) the number, qualifications or experience of the persons employed in looking after the children;

    (f) the keeping of records;

    (g) the fire precautions to be taken in the premises;

    (h) the giving of particulars of any foster child received in the premises and of any change in the number or identity of the foster children kept therein;

but any such requirement may be limited to a particular class of foster children kept in the premises and any requirement imposed under paragraphs (b) to (h) of this subsection may be limited by the authority so as to apply only when the number of foster children kept in the premises exceeds a specified number.

    (3) Where a person proposes to keep a foster child in any premises and the local authority are of the opinion that—

    (a) the premises are not suitable premises in which to keep foster children; or

    (b) that person is not a suitable person to have the care and maintenance of foster children; or

    (c) it would be detrimental to that child to be kept by that person in those premises;

the local authority may impose a prohibition on that person under subsection (3A) of this section.

    (3A) A prohibition imposed on any person under this subsection may—

    (a) prohibit him from keeping any foster child in premises specified in the prohibition; or

    (b) prohibit him from keeping any foster child in any premises in the area of the local authority; or

    (c) prohibit him from keeping a particular child specified in the prohibition in premises so specified.

    (3B) Where a local authority have imposed a prohibition on any person under subsection (3A) of this section, the local authority may, if they think fit, cancel the prohibition, either of their own motion or on an application made by that person on the ground of a change in the circumstances in which a foster child would be kept by him.

    (4) Where a local authority impose a requirement on any person under subsection (2) of this section as respects any premises, they may prohibit him from keeping foster children in the premises after the time specified for compliance with the requirement unless the requirement is complied with.

    (5) Any requirement or prohibition imposed under this section shall be imposed by notice in writing addressed to the person on whom it is imposed.

NOTES

Section 4 (1A) introduces a new power to issue a warrant. Formerly cases arose where there were good grounds for suspecting that foster children were kept in particular premises but, where admission was refused, nothing could be done. There is similar power in respect of daily minded children under s. 7 (2) of the Nurseries and Child-Minders Regulation Act, 1948. As to extension of power to issue warrants to search for and remove a child see s. 8 of the Children Act, 1958, at p. 965 *post*.

"**Partly**" **(sub-s. (2)).**—This amendment clarifies previous law. Private fostering in an ordinary home is now subject to inspection as to any part of the premises, whether children are kept in that part or not, and requirements may also be imposed as to, for example, the maximum number of foster children to be kept at the premises. See s. 57 for modifications of this provision.

" **Foster children.**"—For definition, see s. 2, p. 956, *ante*.

" **Notice.**"—By s. 15, p. 968, *post*, this may be given by post.

" **Duly authenticated document.**"—Section 16, p. 968, provides for the authentication of notices, and in the absence of any express provision for the authentication of documents showing authority to visit foster children, a similar method of authentication might be used.

" **Appeal.**"—For appeal against requirements or prohibitions, see s. 5 and notes thereto, *infra*.

Nurseries and Child-Minders Regulation Act, 1948.—See s. 9 of that Act, p. 949, *ante*, as to the exclusion of the operation of the provisions of the child-life protection enactments as to entry and inspection in respect of certain premises. See s. 10 of that Act (p. 950, *ante*) as to the exclusion of those provisions where premises are registered under that Act.

Local authority.—This is defined in s. 17, p. 968, *post*.

School child during holidays.—See s. 12, *post*.

5. Appeal to juvenile court against requirement or prohibition imposed under section four.—(1) Any person aggrieved by any requirement or prohibition imposed under section four of this Act may, within fourteen days from the date on which he is notified of the requirement or prohibition, or, in the case of a prohibition imposed under subsection (3A) of that section, within fourteen days from the refusal by the local authority to accede to an application by him for the cancellation of the prohibition, appeal to a juvenile court, and where the appeal is against such a requirement the requirement shall not have effect while appeal is pending.

(2) Where the court allows such an appeal it may, instead of cancelling the requirement or prohibition, vary the requirement or allow more time for compliance with it or, where an absolute prohibition has been imposed, substitute for it a prohibition to use the premises after such time as the court may specify unless such specified requirements as the local authority had power to impose under section four of this Act are complied with.

(3) Any notice by which a requirement or prohibition is imposed on any person under section four of this Act shall contain a statement informing him of his right to appeal against the requirement or prohibition and of the time within which he may do so.

(4) Any requirement or prohibition specified or substituted under this section by the court shall be deemed for the purposes of this Part of this Act other than this section to have been imposed by the local authority under section four of this Act.

(5) In the application of this section to Scotland, for references to a juvenile court there shall be substituted references to the sheriff.

NOTES

" **Appeal.** "—This will be by way of complaint for an order and Rule 30 of the Magistrates' Courts Rules, 1968, will apply. It is to be noted that a prohibition takes effect at once but a requirement does not have effect while an appeal is pending.

" **Notice.**"—This may be served by post. See s. 15, p. 968, *post*.

" **Person aggrieved.** "—See *R.* v. *London Quarter Sessions, Ex parte Westminster Corporation*, [1951] 1 All E. R. 1032 ; 115 J. P. 350 ; *R.* v. *Surrey Quarter Sessions, Ex parte Lilley*, [1951] 2 All E. R. 659 ; 115 J. P. 507, and *R.* v. *Lancashire Quarter Sessions Appeal Committee, Ex parte Huyton-with-Roby U.D.C.*, [1954] 3 All E. R. 225 ; 118 J.P. 526.

" **Juvenile court.**"—This will be the juvenile court acting for the area in which the matter of complaint arose and where the requirement or prohibition is imposed. See s. 44 of the Magistrates' Courts Act, 1952. The provisions of the Children and Young Persons Act, 1933, s. 47 (2), p. 53, *ante*, do not apply to sittings of a juvenile court in these proceedings. See s. 10, p. 965, *post*.

Appeal to the Crown Court.—See s. 11, p. 966, *post*.

6. Disqualification for keeping foster children.—(1) A person shall not maintain a foster child if—

   (a) an order has been made against him under this Part of this Act removing a child from his care;

   (b) an order has been made under the Children and Young Persons Act, 1933, the Children and Young Persons Act, 1969, or the Children and Young Persons (Scotland) Act, 1937, or a supervision requirement has been made under the Social Work (Scotland) Act, 1968, and by virtue of the order or requirement a child was removed from his care;

   (c) he has been convicted of any offence specified in the First Schedule to the said Act of 1933 or the First Schedule to the said Act of 1937 or has been placed on probation or discharged absolutely or conditionally for any such offence;

   (d) his rights and powers with respect to a child have been vested in a local authority under section two of the Children Act, 1948, or under section 16 of the Social Work (Scotland) Act, 1968;

   (e) a local health authority or in Scotland a local authority have made an order under subsection (3) or (4) of section one of the Nurseries and Child-Minders Regulation Act, 1948, refusing, or an order under section five of that Act cancelling, the registration of any premises occupied by him or his registration;

   (f) an order has been made under section 43 of the Adoption Act, 1958, for the removal of a protected child who was being kept or was about to be received by him,

unless he has disclosed that fact to the local authority and obtained their consent.

(2) Where this section applies to any person, otherwise than by virtue of this subsection, it shall apply also to any other person who lives in the same premises as he does or who lives in premises at which he is employed.

NOTES

"**Foster child.**"—For definition, see s. 2, p. 956, *ante*.

Paragraph (b).—See s. 1 of the Children and Young Persons Act, 1969, p. 130, *ante*.

Paragraph (c).—For the First Schedule of the 1933 Act, see p. 83, *ante*.

Paragraph (d).—For the Children Act, 1948, s. 2, see p. 884, *ante*.

Paragraph (e).—See pp. 940 and 945, *ante*, for ss. 1 (3), (4) and 5 of the Nurseries and Child-Minders Regulation Act, 1948.

Definitions.—" Child " and " local authority " are defined in s. 17, p. 968, *post*.

"**Or has been placed on probation**" (sub-s. (1) (c)).—A conviction followed by probation is not a conviction for the purposes of any enactment other than the Criminal Justice Act, 1948 (Criminal Justice Act, 1948, s. 12) and the inclusion of these words is necessary to give a local authority an opportunity to consider the case.

Section 43 of the Adoption Act, 1958 (sub-s. (1) (a)).—This fills a gap in previous law. For s. 43 of the Adoption Act, 1958, see p. 1073, *post*.

"**Any other person**" (sub-s. (2)).—Up to now the disqualification attached solely to the foster parent. The disqualification will apparently cover any employee living in the premises, or a lodger.

7. Removal of foster children kept in unsuitable surroundings.— (1) If a juvenile court is satisfied, on the complaint of a local authority, that a foster child is being kept or is about to be received by any person who is unfit to have his care, or in contravention of the last foregoing section or of any prohibition imposed by a local authority under section four of this Act, or in any premises or any environment detrimental or likely to be detrimental to him, the court may make an order for his removal to a place of safety until he can be restored to a parent, relative or guardian of his, or until other arrangements can be made with respect to him; and on proof that there is imminent danger to the health or well-being of the child the power to make an order under this section may be exercised by a justice of the peace acting on the application of a person authorised to visit foster children.

(2) An order under this section may be executed by any person authorised to visit foster children or by any constable, and may be executed on a Sunday.

(3) An order under this section made on the ground that a prohibition of a local authority under section four of this Act has been contravened may require the removal from the premises of all the foster children kept there.

(4) A local authority may receive into their care under section one of the Children Act, 1948, or, as the case may be, Part II of the Social Work (Scotland) Act, 1968, any child removed under this section, whether or not the circumstances of the child are such that they fall within paragraphs (a) to (c) of subsection (1) of the said section one and notwithstanding that he may appear to the local authority to be over the age of seventeen.

(5) Where a child is removed under this section the local authority shall, if practicable, inform a parent or guardian of the child, or any person who acts as his guardian.

(6) In the application of this section to Scotland, for references to a juvenile court there shall be substituted references to the sheriff.

NOTES

This section is printed as amended by the Social Work (Scotland) Act, 1968, and the Statute Law (Repeals) Act, 1969.

"**Foster child.**"—For the meaning of foster child, see s. 2, p. 956, *ante.*

"**Order for his removal.**"—In the absence of imminent danger the appropriate procedure may well be by way of summons to the persons keeping the child to show cause why the order should not be made.

Period of detention.—The order must specify a period, not exceeding twenty-eight days, beyond which the child must not be detained in a place of safety without being brought before a juvenile court (Children and Young Persons Act, 1963, s. 23, p. 95, *ante*).

Children Act, 1948.—For s. 1, see p. 880, *ante.*

Definitions.—" Local authority ", " parent ", " place of safety " and " relative " are defined in s. 17, p. 968, *post.* " Guardian " is not defined in this Act.

Place of safety.—For further provisions, see s. 23 of the Children and Young Persons Act, 1963, p. 95, *ante.*

8. Extension of power to issue warrants to search for and remove a child.

—For the purposes of section forty of the Children and Young Persons Act, 1933, or section forty-seven of the Children and Young Persons (Scotland) Act, 1937 (which enable a warrant authorising the search for and removal of a child to be issued on suspicion of unnecessary suffering caused to, or certain offences committed against, the child), any refusal to allow the visiting of a foster child or the inspection of any premises by a person authorised to do so under this Part of this Act shall be treated as giving reasonable cause for such a suspicion.

NOTES

Children and Young Persons Act, 1933, s. 40.—See p. 47, *ante.*

"**Authority to visit.**"—See s. 1, p. 956, *ante*, as to the duty of local authorities to secure that foster children are visited so far as appears appropriate by officers of the authority, and s. 4, p. 960, *ante*, as to the production by such officers of duly authenticated documents showing that they are so authorised.

Foster child.—See s. 2, p. 956, *ante.*

9. Avoidance of insurances on lives of foster children.

—A person who maintains a foster child for reward shall be deemed for the purposes of the Life Assurance Act, 1774, to have no interest in the life of the child.

NOTE

This section is printed as amended by the Children and Young Persons Act, 1969.

"Foster child."—See s. 2, p. 956, *ante.*

10. Sittings of juvenile courts in proceedings under Part I.—

Subsection (2) of section forty-seven of the Children and Young Persons Act, 1933 (which restricts the time and place at which a sitting of a juvenile court may be held and the persons who may be present at such a sitting) shall not apply to any sitting of a juvenile court in any proceedings under this Part of this Act.

NOTE

For s. 47 (2) of the Children and Young Persons Act, 1933, see p. 53, *ante*.

11. Appeal to the Crown Court.—An appeal shall lie to the Crown Court from any order made under this Part of this Act by a juvenile court or any other magistrates' court within the meaning of the Magistrates' Courts Act, 1952.

NOTES

See Part V of the Magistrates' Courts Act, 1952, and Rules 62–64 of the Magistrates' Courts Rules, 1968 and the Crown Court Rules, 1971, p. 654, *ante*.

Juvenile court or other magistrates' court.—The definition of magistrates' court in s. 124 (1) of the Magistrates' Courts Act, 1952, will include a justice of the peace acting alone in emergency proceedings under this Act and consequently there is a right of appeal from an order made by one justice.

12. Extension of Part I to certain school children during holidays.
—(1) Where a child below the upper limit of the compulsory school age resides during school holidays in a school to which this section applies, then, if he so resides for a period exceeding two weeks, the provisions of this Part of this Act shall apply in relation to him as if paragraph (c) of subsection (3) of section two of this Act were omitted, but subject to the modifications specified in the next following subsection.

(2) Where this Part of this Act applies to a child by virtue of the foregoing subsection—

(a) subsections (1) to (6) of section three, subsections (2) to (5) of section four, and section thirteen of this Act shall not apply; but

(b) the person undertaking the care and maintenance of children in the school during the school holidays shall, not less than two weeks before this Part of this Act first applies to a child in that school during those holidays, give written notice to the local authority that children to whom this Part of this Act applies will reside in the school during those holidays, and any such notice shall state the estimated number of the children.

(3) A local authority may exempt any person from the duty of giving notices under this section, and any such exemption may be granted for a specified period or indefinitely and may be revoked at any time by notice in writing served on that person.

(4) This section applies to any school within the meaning of the Education Acts, 1944 to 1953, which is not a school maintained by a local education authority.

NOTES

This section is printed as amended by the Children and Young Persons Act, 1969, s. 72 (3) and Sched. V.

" **Compulsory school age.**"—See the Education Act, 1944, s. 35, p. 252, *ante*.

" **Notice.**"—This may be given by post, see s. 15, p. 968, *post*.

Definitions.—" Child ", " compulsory school age " and " local authority " are defined in s. 17, p. 968, *post*.

13. Extension of Part I to certain children above compulsory school age.—Where a child is a foster child on attaining the upper limit of the compulsory school age this Part of this Act shall apply in relation to him as it applies in relation to a foster child, until the earliest of the following events, that is to say, until—

(a) he would, apart from that limit, have ceased to be a foster child;

(b) he reaches the age of eighteen; or

(c) he lives elsewhere than with the person with whom he was living when he attained the said limit.

NOTES

" **Foster child.**"—See s. 2, p. 956, *ante*.

" **Compulsory school age.**"—See the Education Act, 1944, s. 35, p. 252, *ante*.

" **Age of eighteen.**"—See note " Attained the age " at p. 53, *ante*.

Definitions.—" Child " and " compulsory school age " are defined in s. 17, p. 968, *post*.

School child during holidays.—See s. 12, *supra*.

14. Offences.—(1) A person shall be guilty of an offence if—

(a) being required, under any provision of this Part of this Act, to give any notice or information, he fails to give the notice within the time specified in that provision or fails to give the information within a reasonable time, or knowingly makes or causes or procures another person to make any false or misleading statement in the notice or information;

(b) he refuses to allow the visiting of any foster child by a duly authorised officer of a local authority or the inspection, under the power conferred by subsection (1) of section four of this Act, of any premises or wilfully obstructs a person entitled to enter any premises by virtue of a warrant under subsection (1A) of that section;

(c) he fails to comply with any requirement imposed by a local authority under this Part of this Act or keeps any foster child in any premises in contravention of a prohibition so imposed;

(d) he maintains a foster child in contravention of section six of this Act; or

(e) he refuses to comply with an order under this Part of this Act for the removal of any child or obstructs any person in the execution of such an order.

(1A) Where section 6 of this Act applies to any person by virtue only of subsection (2) of that section, he shall not be guilty of an offence under paragraph (d) of subsection (1) of this section if he proves that he did not know, and had no reasonable ground for believing, that a person living or employed in the premises in which he lives was a person to whom that section applies.

(2) A person guilty of an offence under this section shall be liable on summary conviction to imprisonment for a term not exceeding six months or a fine not exceeding one hundred pounds or both.

(2A) If any person who is required, under any provision of this Part of this Act, to give a notice fails to give the notice within the time specified in that provision, then, notwithstanding anything in section 104 of the Magistrates' Courts Act, 1952 (time limit for proceedings) proceedings for the offence may be brought at any time within six months from the date when evidence of the offence came to the knowledge of the local authority.

(3) In England and Wales, a local authority may institute proceedings for an offence under this section.

NOTES

Subsection (2).—The defendant, if he appears personally, must be informed of his right to claim trial by jury as he is liable to be sentenced to imprisonment for more than three months. See s. 25 of the Magistrates' Courts Act, 1952, p. 276, *ante.*

" **Local authority may institute proceedings.**"—See notes to s. 55 of the Children Act, 1948, p. 920, *ante.* " Local authority " is defined in s. 17, *infra.*

Requirements, prohibitions.—See s. 5 (4), p. 962, *ante,* as to the decisions of a juvenile court on an appeal.

" **Foster child.**"—See s. 2, p. 956, *ante.*

Applies . . . by virtue of subsection (2).—A person other than the foster parent may be disqualified by virtue of s. 6 (2).

15. Service of notices by post.—Any notice or information required to be given under this Part of this Act may be given by post.

NOTE

" **Post.**"—Service by post is permissive and other effective methods of giving notice may be used. As to service by post, see the Interpretation Act, 1889, s. 25, and as to non-delivery, see *R.* v. *London Quarter Sessions, Ex parte Rossi,* [1956] 1 All E. R. 670; 120 J. P. 239; *Beer* v. *Davies,* [1958] 2 All E. R. 255; 122 J. P. 344; and *Layton* v. *Shires,* [1959] 3 All E. R. 587; 124 J. P. 46.

16. Authentication of documents.—(1) Any notice by a local authority under this Part of this Act may be signed on behalf of the authority by the clerk of the authority or by any other officer of the authority authorised in writing to sign such a notice.

(2) Any notice purporting to bear the signature of the clerk of a local authority or any officer stated therein to be authorised by the authority to sign notices under this Part of this Act shall be deemed, until the contrary is proved, to have been duly given by the authority.

NOTES

See note " Duly authenticated document " to s. 4, p. 962, *ante.*

" **Local authority.**"—This is defined in s. 17, *infra.*

17. Interpretation of Part I.—In this Part of this Act the following expressions have the meanings hereby respectively assigned to them, that is to say,—

"approved school" has the same meaning as in the Children and Young Persons (Scotland) Act, 1937.

" child " means a person under the age of eighteen;

" compulsory school age " has, in England and Wales, the same meaning as in the Education Acts, 1944 to 1953 and, in Scotland, means school age within the meaning of the Education (Scotland) Acts, 1939 to 1956;

"fit person order" means an order under the Children and Young Persons (Scotland) Act, 1937, committing a child to the care of a fit person;

" local authority " means, in England and Wales, the council of a county or county borough and, in Scotland, the council of a county or large burgh;

" parent ", in relation to a child adopted in pursuance of any enactment (including any enactment of the Parliament of Northern Ireland), means the person or one of the persons by whom he was adopted;

"place of safety" means a community home provided by a local authority, a controlled community home, police station, or any hospital, surgery or other suitable place the occupier of which is willing temporarily to receive a child; and in Scotland has the same meaning as in the Social Work (Scotland) Act, 1968;

" relative " has the same meaning as in the Adoption Act, 1958;

"residential establishment" has the same meaning as in the Social Work (Scotland) Act, 1968;

"supervision requirement" has the same meaning as in the Social Work (Scotland) Act, 1968;

" voluntary organisation " means a body the activities of which are carried on otherwise than for profit.

NOTES

This section is printed as amended by the Adoption Act, 1958, the Social Work (Scotland) Act, 1968, and the Children and Young Persons Act, 1969.

Relative.—For definition, see s. 57 of the Adoption Act, 1958, p. 1080, *post*.

Scotland.—See s. 93, Social Work (Scotland) Act, 1968.

PART II

AMENDMENTS OF ADOPTION ACT, 1950

Part II of this Act, which comprises ss. 18 to 36, was repealed and substantially re-enacted from April 1, 1959, by the Adoption Act, 1958, pp. 1026 *et seq., post*. These sections are, accordingly, not reproduced.

PART III

MISCELLANEOUS AND GENERAL

37. Prohibition of anonymous advertisements offering to undertake care of children.—(1) No advertisement indicating that a person will undertake, or will arrange for, the care and maintenance of a child shall be published, unless it truly states that person's name and address.

(2) A person who causes to be published or knowingly publishes an advertisement in contravention of this section shall be guilty of an offence, and liable on summary conviction to imprisonment for a term not exceeding six months or a fine not exceeding one hundred pounds or both.

(3) In England and Wales, a local authority may institute proceedings for an offence under this section.

NOTES

" **Child.**"—By s. 17, p. 968, *ante*, in Part I of this Act "child" means a person under the age of eighteen, but there is no general definition of child for the purposes of Part III.

" **Offence.**"—See note headed "Subsection (2)" to s. 14, p. 968, *ante*.

" **Local authority may institute proceedings** " and " **local authority.**"— See note to s. 14, p. 968, *ante*.

Adoption.—As to restrictions on advertisements in connection with adoption, see the Adoption Act, 1958, s. 51, p. 1077, *post*.

38. Repeal of obsolete enactments.—[*Not reproduced.*]

39. Expenses.—There shall be paid out of moneys provided by Parliament any increase attributable to this Act in the sums payable out of moneys so provided—

    (a) under section forty-seven of the Children Act, 1948; or

    (b) under Part I of the Local Government Act, 1948, or the Local Government (Financial Provisions) (Scotland) Act, 1954, as amended by the Valuation and Rating (Scotland) Act, 1956.

NOTE

Children Act, 1948, s. 47.—This section was repealed by the Local Government Act, 1958, except as respects periods before April 1, 1959. See s. 1 of that Act and Sched. I, para. 4.

40. Minor and consequential amendments and repeals.—[*The enactments affected are reproduced as amended.*]

41. Short title, construction, commencement and extent.—(1) This Act may be cited as the Children Act, 1958.

(2) Any reference in this Act to any other enactment is a reference thereto as amended, and includes a reference thereto as applied, by or under any subsequent enactment, including, except where the context otherwise requires, this Act.

(3) This Act shall come into force on the first day of April, nineteen hundred and fifty-nine.

(4) This Act does not extend to Northern Ireland.

SCHEDULES

FIRST SCHEDULE   Section 35

PROVISIONS AS TO CHILDREN AWAITING ADOPTION OR PLACED WITH STRANGERS

NOTE

The First Schedule was repealed from April 1, 1959, by the Adoption Act, 1958, s. 59 and Sched. VI, and replaced by Part IV of that Act, pp. 1069 *et seq.*, *post*. It is accordingly not reproduced.

SECOND SCHEDULE

Minor and consequential amendments

[The enactments are reproduced as amended.]

THIRD SCHEDULE

Enactments repealed

[Effect has been given to these repeals.]

SECTION 7.—STATUTORY INSTRUMENTS AND OFFICIAL CIRCULARS

CONTENTS

I.—STATUTORY INSTRUMENTS

THE VOLUNTARY HOMES (REGISTRATION) REGULATIONS, 1948
[S.I. 1948 No. 2408]

1. Application for registration of a voluntary home under section twenty-nine of the Children Act, 1948, shall—

(a) if the home was open for the reception of children on the fourth day of July, 1948, be made in the form contained in the First Schedule to these Regulations,

(b) if the home was not open for the reception of children on the said date, but has been opened for the said purpose since the said date or is intended to be opened for that purpose before the first day of January, 1949, be made in the form contained in the Second Schedule to these Regulations,

(c) in the case of a home intended to be opened for the reception of children on or after the first day of January, 1949, be made in the form contained in the Third Schedule to these Regulations,

and the form shall be completed by furnishing the particulars set out therein.

2.—(1) These Regulations may be cited as the Voluntary Homes (Registration) Regulations, 1948, and shall come into operation on the fifteenth day of November, 1948.

(2) These Regulations shall not extend to Scotland.

NOTE

These Regulations, which were made on November 4, 1948, and came into operation on November 15, 1948, were made under s. 29 of the Children Act, 1948, p. 544, *ante*.

FIRST SCHEDULE

Children Act, 1948

Registration of Voluntary Homes

Application for registration under section 29 of the Children Act, 1948, of a voluntary home which was open for the reception of children on 4th July, 1948.

1. Name and full postal address of the voluntary home.	
2. Full name of the person in charge of the home.	
3. Name of the organisation or person carrying on the home.	

4. The home * $\frac{\text{was}}{\text{was not}}$ on 4th July, 1948, one with respect to which particulars were required under section 93 of the Children and Young Persons Act, 1933, to be sent to the Secretary of State.

* Delete whichever is inapplicable.

I hereby declare that the above-mentioned voluntary home was open for the reception of children on 4th July, 1948, and I apply for its registration under section 29 of the Children Act, 1948.

Signature...

Designation.......................................

Full postal address..

....

Date...............................

SECOND SCHEDULE

Children Act, 1948

Registration of Voluntary Homes

Application for registration under section 29 of the Children Act, 1948, of a voluntary home which was not open for the reception of children on 4th July, 1948, but has since opened or is intended to be opened before 1st January, 1949.

1. Full postal address of the voluntary home.	
2. Full name and address of the person in charge of the home.	
3. Name of the organisation or person carrying on, or intending to carry on, the home.	

4. Full name and address of the chairman of the organisation.	
5. Full name and address of the secretary of the organisation.	
6. Date on which the home was opened, or on which it is intended to be opened, for the reception of children.	
7. Number of children (that is, persons under the age of 18) of each sex, and age limits of the children for whom accommodation is, or is intended to be, provided in the home.	
8. Number of persons, other than staff, aged 18 or over for whom accommodation is, or is intended to be, provided in the home.	

9. The home *$\dfrac{\text{is}}{\text{will be}}$

   * (a) supported wholly or partly by voluntary contributions;

     (b) a home (not being a school within the meaning of the Education Act 1944) which is not supported wholly or partly by voluntary contributions but is supported wholly or partly by endowments.

* Delete whichever is inapplicable.

I hereby make application for registration of the above-mentioned voluntary home under section 29 of the Children Act, 1948.

Signature of applicant..

Designation..

Full postal address...

....

Date.............................

THIRD SCHEDULE

CHILDREN ACT, 1948

REGISTRATION OF VOLUNTARY HOMES

Application for registration under section 29 of the Children Act, 1948, of a voluntary home intended to be opened for the reception of children on or after 1st January, 1949.

1. Full postal address of the voluntary home.	
2. Name of the organisation or person intending to carry on the home.	

3. Full name and address of the chairman of the organisation.	
4. Full name and address of the secretary of the organisation.	
5. Date on which it is intended to open the home for the reception of children if application for registration is granted by the Secretary of State.	
6. Number of children (that is, persons under the age of 18) of each sex, and age limits of the children whom it is intended to accommodate in the home.	
7. Number of persons, other than staff, aged 18 or over whom it is intended to accommodate in the home.	

8. If application for registration is granted by the Secretary of State the home will be—

    * (a) supported wholly or partly by voluntary contributions;
       (b) a home (not being a school within the meaning of the Education Act, 1944) which is not supported wholly or partly by voluntary contributions but is supported wholly or partly by endowments.

           * Delete whichever is inapplicable.

    I hereby make application for registration of the above-mentioned voluntary home under section 29 of the Children Act, 1948.

           Signature of applicant......................................

           Designation..

Full postal address..

....

Date...........................

THE CHILDREN ACT (APPEAL TRIBUNAL) RULES, 1949

1. These rules may be cited as the Children Act (Appeal Tribunal) Rules, 1949, and shall come into operation on the first day of January, 1950.

2.—(1) In these Rules, unless the context otherwise requires, the following expressions have the meaning hereby assigned to them respectively :—

    " The Act " means the Children Act, 1948 ;

    " The Tribunal " means the appeal tribunal constituted in accordance with Part I of the First Schedule to the Act ;

    " Voluntary home " has the same meaning as in Part V of the Children and Young Persons Act, 1933, as modified by Part IV of the Act.

(2) The Interpretation Act, 1889, shall apply to the interpretation of these Rules as it applies to the interpretation of an Act of Parliament.

3. Any person desiring to appeal against a refusal to register a voluntary home or a proposal to remove a voluntary home from the register shall state in his notice of appeal an address at which any notice, order, or other document may be served upon him.

4.—(1) On receipt of the notice of appeal the Secretary of State shall forthwith request the Lord Chancellor and the Lord President of the Council respectively to appoint the chairman and members of the tribunal.

(2) The Lord Chancellor shall appoint a person to act as secretary of the tribunal for the purposes of the appeal.

5. The chairman of the tribunal shall fix a date, time and place for the hearing of the appeal and shall cause to be served upon the appellant, not less than twenty-eight days before the date so fixed, a notice in the form set out in the Schedule hereto and shall at the same time send a copy of the notice to the Secretary of State.

6. Not less than twenty-one days before the date fixed for the hearing of the appeal the Secretary of State shall send to the secretary of the tribunal four copies of a statement of the reasons for which registration of the voluntary home has been refused, or for the proposal to remove the voluntary home from the register, and shall at the same time serve a copy of the statement upon the appellant.

7. Not less than seven days before the date fixed for the hearing of the appeal the appellant shall send to the secretary of the tribunal four copies of a statement, signed by or on behalf of the appellant, of the grounds of the appeal, and shall at the same time serve a copy of the statement upon the Secretary of State.

8. The appellant may at any time before the hearing give notice in writing to the secretary of the tribunal that he desires to withdraw his appeal and thereupon the appeal shall be deemed to be dismissed.

9.—(1) The appellant may appear and be heard before the tribunal by counsel or solicitor or in person, or (if the appellant is a partnership) by a partner or (if the appellant is a company) by a duly authorised director or officer of the company.

(2) The Secretary of State may appear and be heard before the tribunal by counsel or solicitor or by any officer of his Department.

10. If either the appellant or the Secretary of State fails to appear at the time fixed for the hearing of the appeal, the tribunal may take such action, whether by proceeding with or adjourning the hearing or otherwise, as may appear to the tribunal to be just and expedient.

11. The hearing of an appeal shall be in public, unless for any reason the tribunal determines that the hearing or any part of it should be in private.

12.—(1) The appellant and the Secretary of State shall have the right to address the tribunal and call witnesses, who shall be subject to cross-examination and to re-examination.

(2) After the evidence has been concluded, the Secretary of State and the appellant shall have the right to address the tribunal if they so desire.

13.—(1) The tribunal may require the attendance of further witnesses in addition to those called by or on behalf of the appellant and the Secretary of State.

(2) The tribunal may permit evidence to be given by affidavit, but may at any stage of the proceedings require the personal attendance of any deponent for examination and cross-examination.

(3) The tribunal shall not reject any evidence on the ground only that such evidence would be inadmissible in a court of law.

14. The provisions of the Arbitration Acts, 1889 to 1934, with respect to the administration of oaths and the taking of affirmations, the summoning, attendance and examination of witnesses, and the production of documents shall apply to proceedings before the tribunal.

15. The decision of the tribunal on the appeal shall, in the event of disagreement, be the decision of the majority and shall be notified in writing by the chairman to the appellant and the Secretary of State as soon as may be after the hearing, together with a brief statement of the reasons for the decision.

16.—(1) The time appointed by these Rules for doing any act in connection with the appeal may be extended by the tribunal or by the chairman upon such terms (if any) as may seem just, notwithstanding that the time appointed has expired before an application for extension is made.

(2) Subject to the provisions of the Act and of these Rules, the tribunal may regulate its own procedure.

SCHEDULE

The Children Act, 1948

Take Notice that your appeal against the Secretary of State's refusal to register (*here insert description of premises*) as a voluntary home (*or*, against the Secretary of State's proposal to remove (*here insert description of premises*) from the register of voluntary homes) will be heard by the Appeal Tribunal sitting at   on the day of   19   , at   o'clock.

If for any reason you do not wish, or are unable, to attend at the above time and place, you should Immediately inform me in writing at the address mentioned at the head of this notice, stating the reasons for your inability to attend.

(Signed)

Chairman.

NOTE

These Rules were made on December 1, 1949 by the Lord Chancellor under s. 30 (4) of the Children Act, 1948, p. 909, *ante*.

THE LOCAL AUTHORITIES AND LOCAL EDUCATION AUTHORITIES (ALLOCATION OF FUNCTIONS) REGULATIONS, 1951

[S.I. 1951 No. 472]

General note.—References to the "Minister of Education" should be read as "Secretary of State for Education and Science". See Secretary of State for Education and Science Order, 1964, S.I. 1964 No. 490.

1. These Regulations may be cited as the Local Authorities and Local Education Authorities (Allocation of Functions) Regulations, 1951, and shall come into operation on the first day of May, 1951.

2.—(1) The Interpretation Act, 1889, shall apply to the interpretation of these Regulations as it applies to the interpretation of an Act of Parliament.

(2) In these Regulations, unless the context requires:—

" The Act " means the Children Act, 1948;

" child " has the meaning assigned to that expression by subsection (1) of Section 59 of the Act, and the expression " child who is in the care of a local authority under the Act " means any child in relation to whom the provisions of Part II of the Act apply;

" compulsory school age " has, subject to the provisions of Section 8 of the Education Act, 1946, the meaning assigned to that expression by Section 35 of the Education Act, 1944, or, in relation to registered pupils at special schools, by subsection (1) of Section 38 of the said last mentioned Act;

" local authority " means the council of a county or county borough in England or Wales, the council of a London borough or the Common Council of the City of London ;

" local education authority " has the meaning assigned to that expression by subsection (1) of Section 114 of the Education Act, 1944;

" school " has the meaning assigned to that expression by subsection (1) of Section 114 of the Education Act, 1944;

" special educational treatment " has the meaning assigned to that expression by paragraph (c) of subsection (2) of Section 8 of the Education Act, 1944.

3. As respects the functions of the local education authority under Regulation 10 of the Provision of Milk and Meals Regulations, 1945, as amended by the Provision of Free Milk Regulations, 1946, the Milk and Meals (Amending) Regulations, 1949, and the Milk and Meals (Amending) Regulations, 1951, made by the Minister of Education under Section 49 of the Education Act, 1944 (which Regulation relates to payment for meals or other refreshment), a child who is in the care of a local authority under the Act shall be treated as a child of parents of sufficient resources to pay the whole of any sum payable under the said Regulation.

4. Where the local education authority are of opinion that a child who is in the care of a local authority under the Act should be provided with board and lodging to enable him to attend a particular county school, voluntary school or special school, or to receive special educational treatment, they shall inform the local authority accordingly, and where the child attends any such school as aforesaid or receives such special educational treatment, the function of providing any such board and lodging shall be exercised by the local authority under the Act, and not by the local education authority under Section 50 of the Education Act, 1944, as amended by the Education Act, 1946, and by the Education (Miscellaneous Provisions) Act, 1948.

5. Where it is necessary for payment to be made of the reasonable travelling expenses of a child who is in the care of a local authority under the Act to enable him to attend school or any establishment for further education, such payments shall be made by the local authority under the Act, and accordingly the local education authority shall not exercise their functions under subsection (2) of Section 55 of the Education Act, 1944, in respect of such child.

6. Where a child who is in the care of a local authority under the Act is provided under subsection (2) of Section 61 of the Education Act, 1944, by the local education authority with board and lodging at a school maintained by a local education authority, the child shall be treated as a child of parents without resources, and accordingly the local education authority shall remit the whole of the boarding fees.

7.—(1) As respects the functions of the local education authority under the Regulations for Scholarships and Other Benefits, 1945, made by the Minister of Education under Section 81 of the Education Act, 1944, a child who is in the care of a local authority under the Act shall be treated—

(a) for the purposes of paragraph (a) of the said Section 81, as a child of parents of sufficient resources, and accordingly the local education authority shall not exercise their functions under the said paragraph in respect of such a child;

(b) for the purposes of paragraph (b) of the said Section 81, as a child of parents without resources, and accordingly the local education authority shall pay the whole of the fees and expenses of such a child;

(c) for the purposes of paragraph (c) of the said Section 81, as a child of parents without resources, and accordingly the local education authority shall pay the whole of the cost of any such scholarships, exhibitions, bursaries or other allowances as are mentioned in the said paragraph (c):

> Provided that the Local Education Authority shall not exercise their functions under the said paragraph (c) so far as those functions relate to the payment of maintenance allowances to parents in respect of pupils over compulsory school age attending school.

(2) The functions of a local authority under Section 20 of the Act in relation to a person who has attained the age of eighteen, and who is in receipt of education or training, shall only be exercised to the extent that the exercise of the functions of the local education authority under paragraph (c) of the said Section 81 does not meet the needs of such a person.

8. As respects the functions of the local education authority under Section 5 of the Education (Miscellaneous Provisions) Act, 1948, a child who is in the care of a local authority under the Act, shall, for the purposes of the Provision of Clothing Regulations, 1948, made by the Minister of Education under sub-section (6) of the said Section 5, be treated as a child of parents of sufficient resources to pay the whole of any sums which under the Regulations the local education authority either shall be obliged to require, or may require, a parent to pay.

NOTES

These Regulations, which were made March 20, 1951, and came into operation May 1, 1951, were made jointly by the Secretary of State and the Minister of Education under s. 21 of the Children Act, 1948, p. 536, *ante*. They are printed as amended by the London Government Order, 1965, S.I. 1965 No. 654.

Education Act, 1946, s. 8.—Repealed by the Education Act, 1962.

Education Act, 1944, s. 35.—See p. 252, *ante*.

Provision of Milk and Meal Regulations, 1945.—S. R. & O. 1945, No. 698, as amended by S. R. & O. 1946, No. 1293, S.I. 1949 No. 2280 and S.I. 1949 No. 340. The reference to reg. 10, is now to be construed as a reference to reg. 10, of the Provision of Milk and Meal Regulations 1969, S.I. 1969 No. 483. The latter are amended by S.I. 1971 No. 1368, made to give effect to S.I. of the Education (Milk) Act, 1971.

Education (Miscellaneous Provisions) Act, 1948.—11 Halsbury's Statutes, 3rd Edn. 294, 372.

Regulations for Scholarships and other Benefits, 1945.—S. R. & O. 1945, No. 666.

Provision of Clothing Regulations, 1948.—S.I. 1948 No. 2222.

THE ADMINISTRATION OF CHILDREN'S HOMES REGULATIONS, 1951

[S.I. 1951 No. 1217]

PART I

LOCAL AUTHORITY HOMES AND VOLUNTARY HOMES

General principles of administration

1. The administering authority shall make arrangements for every home provided, or as the case may be, carried on by them to be conducted in such a manner and on such principles as are calculated to secure the well-being of the children in the home.

Visits by administering authority

2.—(1) The administering authority shall make arrangements for the home to be visited at least once in every month by a person who shall satisfy himself whether the home is conducted in the interests of the well-being of the children and shall report to the administering authority upon his visit and shall enter in the record book referred to in paragraph 3 of the Schedule hereto his name and the date of his visit.

(2) Where the administering authority is a local authority the arrangements shall secure that the person visiting is a member of the children's committee of the local authority, a member of a sub-committee established by that committee or such officer or one of such officers of the local authority as may be designated by the arrangements.

Person in charge of home

3.—(1) The administering authority shall appoint a person to be in charge of the home:

Provided that where a person is in charge of the home immediately before these Regulations come into force that person shall be deemed to have been appointed to be in charge of the home under this paragraph.

(2) The person in charge of the home shall compile the records referred to in the Schedule to these Regulations and shall keep them at all times available for inspection by any person visiting the home under Regulation 2 of these Regulations and by any inspector appointed by the Secretary of State.

(3) The person in charge of the home shall be responsible for the custody of the medical record of each child and shall at all times keep them available to the medical officer, to any inspector appointed by the Secretary of State and to any person specifically authorised to inspect them by the administering authority.

Religious instruction

4. The administering authority shall secure that each child attends such religious services and receives such religious instruction as are appropriate to the religious persuasion to which he belongs and are practicable in all the circumstances of the case.

Medical care

5.—(1) The administering authority for each home which they provide or, as the case may be, carry on shall appoint a medical officer.

(2) The duties of the medical officer shall include—

  (i) the general supervision of the health of the children (excluding their dental health);

 (ii) the general supervision of the hygienic condition of the premises;

(iii) attendance at the home at regular intervals and with sufficient frequency to ensure that he is closely acquainted with the health of the children;

 (iv) the examination of the children at regular intervals;

  (v) the provision of such medical attention as may be necessary other than dental treatment;

 (vi) the giving of advice to the person in charge of the home on any matters affecting the health of any of the children therein or the hygienic condition of the premises;

(vii) the supervision of the compilation of a medical record for each child accommodated in the home containing particulars of the medical history of the child before admission, so far as it is known, his physical and mental condition on admission, his medical history while accommodated in the home and his condition on discharge from the home.

(3) Notwithstanding anything in the preceding provisions of this Regulation the administering authority may appoint more than one medical officer and may divide the preceding duties among them as they see fit.

Dental care

6. The administering authority shall make suitable arrangements for the dental care of the children in the home.

Notification of death, illness or accident

7.—(1) Where the administering authority is a local authority that local authority, and in any other case the person in charge of the home, shall forthwith notify the Secretary of State—

(i) of the death of any child in the home and of the relevant circumstances;
(ii) if known to the local authority or, as the case may be, the person in charge, of the death of any child formerly in the home who dies within two months of ceasing to be in the home and of the relevant circumstances in so far as they can by reasonable enquiry be ascertained;
(iii) of any outbreak among the children in the home under five years of age of infective gastro-enteritis and of any outbreak of any infectious disease among such children which the medical officer states to the person in charge of the home to be sufficiently serious to be so notified.

(2) Where the administering authority is a local authority that local authority, and in any other case the person in charge of the home, shall forthwith notify—

(i) the death of any child in the home and the relevant circumstances;
(ii) any accident to any child in the home or illness from which such a child suffers which the medical officer states to the person in charge of the home as sufficiently serious to be so notified,

to the parent or guardian of the child and, if the child is in the care of a local authority, being a child as respects whom Part II of the Act applies, and that local authority is not the administering authority of the home, to the said local authority.

Consultation with fire authority

8. If the administering authority is not the fire authority within the meaning of the Fire Services Act, 1947, of the area in which the home is situated they shall consult the fire authority on fire precautions in the home.

Fire drill

9. The administering authority shall make arrangements to secure by means of fire drills and practices that the staff in the home, and so far as practicable the children, are well versed in the procedure for saving life in case of fire.

Notification of outbreaks of fire

10. The administering authority shall notify the Secretary of State forthwith of any outbreak of fire in the home necessitating the removal of any children from the home or that part of it in which fire breaks out.

Punishment

11.—(1) No corporal punishment except that authorised by paragraph (3) of this Regulation shall be administered by any person except the person in charge of the home or in his illness or absence his duly authorised deputy.

(2) No corporal punishment shall be administered to a girl who has attained the age of ten years or to a boy who has attained the age at which he is no longer required by law to attend school (hereafter referred to as " school leaving age ").

(3) No corporal punishment shall be administered to a child under ten years of age except by smacking his hands with the bare hand of the person administering the punishment.

(4) No corporal punishment shall be administered to a boy who has attained the age of ten years but has not attained school leaving age except the caning of the posterior of the boy with a cane of a type approved by the Secretary of State applied over the boy's ordinary clothing to the extent of six strokes or less.

(5) No caning shall be administered in the presence of another child.

(6) No corporal punishment shall be administered, without the sanction of the medical officer for the home, to any child known to have any physical or mental disability.

PART II
ADDITIONAL PROVISIONS RELATING ONLY TO VOLUNTARY HOMES

Limitation of numbers to be accommodated

12.—(1) The Secretary of State may give directions to the persons carrying on a voluntary home limiting the number of children who may at any one time be accommodated in that home.

(2) Subsection (2) of section thirty-one of the Act (which provides for penalties for contravention or failure to comply with a Regulation) shall have effect in relation to this Regulation.

Prohibition of certain clothing

13.—(1) The Secretary of State may give directions to the persons carrying on a voluntary home prohibiting the provision for the children in that home or any of them of clothing specified in the directions.

(2) Subsection (2) of section thirty-one of the Act shall have effect in relation to this Regulation.

Visits by parents or guardians

14.—(1) The persons carrying on a voluntary home shall furnish to the Secretary of State on demand such information as he may from time to time require as to the facilities provided by them for the parents and guardians of children in the home to visit and communicate with those children, and shall comply with any directions given by the Secretary of State as to the provision of such facilities.

(2) Subsection (2) of section thirty-one of the Act shall have effect in relation to this Regulation.

Change of persons in charge

15. The persons carrying on a voluntary home shall forthwith give notice to the Secretary of State when a person in charge of a home ceases to be in charge of that home and of any new appointment after such cessation.

PART III
MISCELLANEOUS: EXTENT, INTERPRETATION, CITATION

Exemptions for schools

16. Where a school is established or maintained within a home by a local education authority under the Education Act, 1944, neither the function of inspection under Regulation 2 nor the duties of the person in charge of the home under Regulations 3 and 7, of the medical officer under Regulation 5, of the administering authority under Regulation 6 nor the provisions of Regulation 11 of these Regulations shall apply to the part of the home used as a school during that part of a day in which it is being so used or to any child during that part of a day in which he is attending the school.

Application

17. These Regulations apply to all homes provided by local authorities under section fifteen of the Act and voluntary homes except—

    (i) remand homes within the meaning of Part IV of the Children and Young Persons, Act, 1933 ;

    (ii) approved probation hostels and approved probation homes within the meaning of section forty-six of the Criminal Justice Act, 1948; and

    (iii) any voluntary home which is, as a whole, subject to inspection by or under the authority of a government department otherwise than under the Children and Young Persons Act, 1933.

Interpretation

18.—(1) In these Regulations the following expressions have the meanings hereby respectively assigned to them, that is to say:—

    " the Act " means the Children Act, 1948;

    " administering authority " means the local authority providing or the persons carrying on a home, as the case may be;

    " voluntary home " has the same meaning as in section ninety-two of the Children and Young Persons Act, 1933, as amended by section twenty-seven of the Act.

(2) The Interpretation Act, 1889, shall apply to the interpretation of these Regulations as it applies to the interpretation of an Act of Parliament.

Citation and Commencement

19. These Regulations may be cited as the Administration of Children's Homes Regulations, 1951, and shall come into force on the first day of September, 1951.

SCHEDULE   Regulation 3 (2)

The records to be kept under the provisions of paragraph (2) of Regulation 3 shall be—

    1. A register in which shall be entered the date of admission and the date of discharge of every child accommodated in the home.

    2. In homes accommodating more than twenty children a register indicating every day every child present in the home on that day.

    3. A record book in which shall be recorded events of importance connected with the home.

    4. A record of every fire practice or drill conducted in the home.

    5. Records of the food provided for the children accommodated in the home in sufficient detail to enable any person inspecting the record to judge whether the dietary is satisfactory.

    6. Where consultation under Regulation 8 has taken place a record of fire precautions agreed upon by the administering authority and the fire authority after such consultation as being practicable in and suitable to the circumstances of the home.

    7. A punishment book in which shall be entered a record of all corporal punishment administered.

NOTE

These Regulations were made by the Secretary of State under s. 15 (4) of the Children Act, 1948, p. 530, *ante*, on July 5, 1951, and came into operation on September 1, 1951.

THE BOARDING-OUT OF CHILDREN REGULATIONS, 1955
[S.I. 1955 No. 1377]

TABLE OF CONTENTS
Part I
General

Part II
Provisions Applicable to Boarding-Out for a Period Exceeding Eight Weeks

Part III
Provisions Applicable to Boarding-Out for a Period Expected not to Exceed Eight Weeks in all

Part IV
Supplementary

Schedule

PART I.—GENERAL

Scope of the Regulations

1.—(1) Subject to the provisions of paragraphs (2) and (3) of this Regulation, these Regulations shall apply to the boarding of a child—

(a) by a local authority in whose care the child is, or

(b) by a voluntary organisation in whose charge the child is otherwise than under an approved school order,

with foster parents to live in their dwelling as a member of their family, and the boarding of a child to which these Regulations apply as aforesaid is hereinafter referred to as " boarding-out ", and " board out " and " boarded out " shall be construed accordingly.

(2) For the purposes of these Regulations a child who is delivered into the care and possession of persons or a person proposing to adopt him under the Adoption Act, 1950, shall not be regarded as boarded out.

(3) For the purposes of these Regulations a child shall not be regarded as boarded out by reason only that he stays in the dwelling of any person for a holiday if—

(a) the period of his stay does not exceed twenty-one days, or

(b) he is sent there by a voluntary organisation in whose charge he temporarily is for the sole purpose of the arrangement of that holiday.

(4) Nothing in these Regulations shall require, for the purpose only of complying with any provision thereof relating to a child before he is boarded out, his temporary removal from a household in which he is already living.

NOTES

Local authority in whose care the child is.—That is under s. 1, or s. 6 (4) of the Children Act, 1948, pp. 880, 890, *ante*, or by virtue of para. 1 of the Second Schedule to that Act, or under a fit person order made under the Children and Young Persons Act, 1933, *ante*.

" Local authority " does not include a local education authority or a local health authority as such and a child placed by such an authority is not " placed by a local authority in whose care he is ".

Voluntary organisations.—The revoked Children and Young Persons (Boarding Out) Rules, 1946, did not apply to children boarded-out by a voluntary organisation.

Foster parents.—See definition in Regulation 32 (1). It includes prospective foster parents but not the child's parents.

Boarding-out.—If a child under school leaving age is placed in a manner other than boarding-out, Part I of the Children Act, 1958, may apply if his maintenance is undertaken for reward. See pp. 956 *et seq.*, *ante*.

Approved schools.—See general note to regulations, p. 996, *post*.

Persons with whom children may be boarded out

2. A child shall not be boarded out except with—

(a) a husband and wife jointly, or

(b) a woman, or

(c) a man who is a grandfather, uncle or elder brother of the child:

Provided that if while a child is boarded out his foster parent dies or a woman being his foster parent ceases to live in the household where the child is, nothing in this Regulation shall require the child's removal therefrom and he may be boarded out with the other spouse or with another suitable member of the same household, as the case may be.

NOTES

There is no longer a statutory limitation of the number of foster children who may be in a foster home, *cf.* rule 6 of the revoked Children and Young Persons (Boarding-Out) Rules, 1946. See also note 5 of the Home Office Memorandum on these Regulations.

Insurance.—A foster parent, unless he is a child's legal heir, cannot on the child's death benefit under an insurance policy taken out on or after July 5, 1948. See the Industrial Assurance and Friendly Societies Act, 1948, 14 Halsbury's Statutes, 3rd Edn., 382.

Restriction on boarding-out outside England and Wales

3. A child shall not be boarded out outside England and Wales unless the special circumstances of his case make such boarding-out desirable, and if a child is boarded out outside England and Wales, steps shall be taken to ensure that the like requirements as are specified in Regulations 2, 7 and 8 and, as the case may be, Regulations 19, 21, 22 and 23 or Regulation 28 or Regulation 29 of these Regulations are observed in relation to that child as would have had to be observed under these Regulations if he were boarded out in England or Wales.

Duty of placing authority to terminate boarding-out

4. A care authority or voluntary organisation who have arranged the boarding-out of a child shall not allow him to remain boarded out with any foster-parents if it appears that the boarding-out is no longer in his best interests.

Power of supervising visitor to remove child

5.—(1) Where a visitor whose duty it is under these Regulations to supervise the welfare of a child considers that the conditions in which he is boarded out endanger his health, safety or morals, that visitor may remove him from the foster parents forthwith.

(2) Where a child who is boarded out by a local authority with foster parents whose dwelling is outside the area of that authority is removed under paragraph (1) of this Regulation by a visitor of the care authority, the area authority shall forthwith be notified by the care authority of the reason why he was removed and, if the child is so removed by a visitor of the area authority who are performing any of the supervisory duties in respect of him under Regulation 13 of these Regulations, the care authority shall forthwith be given the like notification by the area authority.

(3) Where a child who is boarded out by a voluntary organisation is removed from foster parents under paragraph (1) of this Regulation by a visitor of the voluntary organisation, the area authority shall forthwith be notified by the organisation of the reason why he was removed and, if the child is so removed by a visitor of the area authority who are performing the supervisory duties in the place of that organisation under Regulation 14 of these Regulations, the voluntary organisation shall forthwith be given the like notification by the area authority.

NOTE

Visitor.—See definition in Regulation 32 (1). The Home Office Memorandum points out that it is not necessary always to visit the child in its foster home, but that if the child is seen elsewhere the foster home must be visited as prescribed by the Regulations. See Regulations 17, 21, 25 and 28.

Medical examination before boarding-out

6. Except in a case of emergency, a child shall not be boarded out with foster parents unless he has within three months before being placed with them been examined by a duly qualified medical practitioner and the practitioner has made a written report on the physical health and mental condition of the child.

NOTE

The doctor is no longer required to report on the child's suitability for boarding-out, as he was in the revoked Children and Young Persons (Boarding-Out) Rules, 1946, rule 7.

Medical examination during boarding-out

7.—(1) A local authority or voluntary organisation who arrange the boarding-out of a child shall ensure that he is examined by a duly qualified medical practitioner—

(a) within one month after being boarded out unless the child has attained the age of two years and has, under Regulation 6 of these Regulations, been so examined within three months before being boarded out; and

(b) at least once in every six months if he has not attained the age of two years or at least once a year if he has attained that age.

(2) Arrangements shall be made for a written report on the physical health and mental condition of the child to be made by the practitioner after each such examination as aforesaid.

Arrangements for medical and dental attention

8. Adequate arrangements shall be made for a child who is boarded out to receive medical and dental attention as required.

Reports by visitors

9. Whenever, in pursuance of these Regulations, a visitor sees a child who is boarded out, he shall after considering the welfare, health, conduct and progress of the child and any complaint made by or concerning him, make a written report about the child, and whenever a visitor so visits the dwelling of foster parents he shall make a written report about its condition.

NOTE
It should be noted that a report in writing must be made on each occasion.

Case records to be kept by local authorities and voluntary organisations

10.—(1) A local authority shall compile a case record in respect of—

(a) every child boarded out by them;

(b) every child boarded out by another local authority in respect of whom they perform any of the supervisory duties under Regulation 13 of these Regulations; and

(c) every child boarded out by a voluntary organisation in relation to whom they perform the supervisory duties;

and the said record shall be kept up-to-date.

(2) A voluntary organisation shall compile a case record in respect of every child boarded out by them and the said record shall be kept up-to-date.

(3) Every case record compiled under this Regulation shall be preserved for at least three years after the child to whom it relates has attained the age of eighteen years or has died before attaining that age, and shall be open to inspection at all reasonable times by any person duly authorised in that behalf by the Secretary of State.

NOTE

Privileged documents.—In the case of *Re D. (Infants)*, [1970] 1 All E. R. 1088; 134 J. P. 387, C. A., the local authority appealed from a Judge's order, in the course of wardship proceedings to produce records relating to two children who were in their care. It was held that the children were in the care of the council and the case records ordered to be discovered were those kept under the Regulations. These were statutory records, confidential and privileged, and it was contrary to wardship proceedings and to public policy for them to be produced. The appeal was allowed.

Registers to be kept by local authorities

11.—(1) A local authority shall, in respect of every child boarded out in their area, whether by them or by another local authority or by a voluntary organisation, enter in a register to be kept for the purpose the particulars specified in paragraph (2) of this Regulation, and so much of the particulars specified in paragraph (3) of this Regulation as may be appropriate.

(2) The particulars to be so entered in the case of every such child are his name, sex, date of birth and religious persuasion, the name and religious persuasion of each foster parent and their address, the name of the authority or organisation by whom he is boarded out, the dates on which boarding-out on each occasion begins and ceases, and the reason why it ceases.

(3) There shall also be so entered—

(a) in the case of a child in respect of whom arrangements have been made under Regulation 13 of these Regulations, a note of those arrangements;

(b) in the case of a child in the care of a local authority boarded out by a voluntary organisation, the name of the care authority; and

(c) in the case of a child boarded out by a voluntary organisation in relation to whom the area authority are, under Regulation 14 of these Regulations, performing the supervisory duties, a note of that fact.

(4) Every register kept under this Regulation shall be preserved for at least five years after every child particulars about whom are entered therein has or would have attained the age of eighteen years, and shall be open to inspection at all reasonable times by any person duly authorised in that behalf by the Secretary of State.

Information to be given to or by area authorities in certain circumstances

12.—(1) Where a child who is boarded out with foster parents in the area of a local authority by another local authority or a voluntary organisation ceases to be boarded out in a household, the authority or organisation by whom the boarding-out was arranged shall inform the area authority thereof and of the date on which the boarding-out ceased, the reason why it ceased and whether it is intended to board out another child in that household.

(2) If, while a child is boarded out with foster parents in the area of a local authority by another local authority or a voluntary organisation, any reason becomes known to the area authority whereby it appears that boarding-out with those foster parents may have ceased to be in the best interests of the child, the care authority, or, as the case may be, the voluntary organisation shall be informed thereof forthwith.

Arrangements in certain cases as regards children boarded out by one local authority in the area of another

13. A care authority may make arrangements with an area authority, either in respect of a child boarded out by the one in the area of the other or generally in respect of all children who may from time to time be so boarded out, for the area authority to perform any of the supervisory duties and to furnish a report as often as may have been agreed on the welfare, health, conduct and progress of each child in respect of whom such arrangements have effect.

Duty of local authority as regards children boarded out by voluntary organisations

14.—(1) In this Regulation and in Regulation 15 of these Regulations a reference in relation to a voluntary organisation to the supervisory duties is a reference to those duties in respect of children boarded out by that voluntary organisation in the area of a particular local authority, and a reference to the voluntary organisation being in a position to discharge the supervisory duties is a reference to that organisation having the requisite facilities, and having made adequate arrangements, for the discharge of those duties in that area.

(2) It shall be the general duty of an area authority to satisfy themselves as regards any voluntary organisation having children boarded out in their area whether or not that organisation are in a position to discharge the supervisory duties, and if satisfied that they are not, the area authority shall, except as otherwise provided in these Regulations, perform the said duties and that organisation shall be relieved of those duties.

(3) As soon as may be after a voluntary organisation board out a child in the area of a local authority in which there is not already a child boarded out by that organisation the area authority shall, for the purpose of carrying out their duty under paragraph (2) of this Regulation, cause investigation to be made into, and shall consider, the question whether that organisation are in a position to discharge the supervisory duties, and for the said purpose, in any period during which that organisation continuously have any children boarded out in the area of that authority, shall cause investigation to be made into, and shall consider, the said question at least once in every three years.

(4) If while an area authority are performing the supervisory duties in the place of a voluntary organisation, they are satisfied that that organisation are in a position to discharge those duties, the area authority shall be relieved thereof as from such date as the organisation have notified the area authority as that upon which they will resume the discharge of those duties.

(5) Notwithstanding anything in paragraph (2) of this Regulation, an area authority shall not except with the written consent of a voluntary organisation take over from that organisation the supervisory duties until one month has elapsed after notice of their intention so to do has been sent to that organisation, and if within that period the area authority receive from that organisation a copy of representations made by them to the Secretary of State under the next following paragraph, they shall not take over the said duties unless the Secretary of State so directs under that paragraph.

(6) If a notice has under the last preceding paragraph been sent by an area authority to a voluntary organisation and that organisation are of opinion that they are in a position to discharge the supervisory duties, they may within the said period of one month make representations to that effect to the Secretary of State, and the Secretary of State, after considering those representations and any representations made to him on behalf of the area authority, may direct either that the organisation shall continue to discharge those duties or that the area authority shall, from such date as may be indicated in the direction, take them over, and the said duties shall continue to be discharged or be so taken over accordingly.

(7) If, after an area authority have under this Regulation performed the supervisory duties in the place of a voluntary organisation for a continuous period of not less than one year, that organisation are of opinion that they are then in a position to discharge those duties, and the area authority, after representations to that effect have been made to them on behalf of that organisation, are not satisfied that that organisation are in such a position, the organisation may make representations to the Secretary of State accordingly; and if the Secretary of State, after considering those representations and any representations made to him on behalf of the area authority, so directs, the organisation shall, from such date as may be indicated in the direction, resume the discharge of those duties and the area authority shall cease to perform them.

(8) Where an area authority take over the supervisory duties from a voluntary organisation, that organisation shall supply to the area authority full information about every child boarded out by them in the area of that authority.

(9) While an area authority perform the supervisory duties in the place of a voluntary organisation, the area authority shall supply to the organisation the information in every relevant case record compiled by them.

Children in the care of a local authority who are boarded out by a voluntary organisation

15.—(1) As soon as may be after a child who is in the care of a local authority and in the charge of a voluntary organisation is boarded out, the organisation shall notify that authority of the boarding-out and of the names and address of the foster parents, and as soon as may be after that child ceases to be boarded out with those foster parents, the organisation shall notify the authority of the reason therefor.

(2) Where such a child is boarded out with foster parents whose dwelling is outside the area of the care authority, and the area authority either—

    (a) are, under Regulation 14 of these Regulations, for the time being performing the supervisory duties in the place of the organisation by whom he is boarded out; or

    (b) subsequently, while the child is so boarded out, take over those duties from that organisation,

notice of the facts shall forthwith after the boarding-out, or, as the case may be, when the area authority take over those duties, be sent by the area authority to the care authority.

(3) Where notice under the last preceding paragraph is received by a care authority, then, notwithstanding anything in paragraph (2) of Regulation 14 of these Regulations, so long as the area authority continue to perform the supervisory duties in the place of the organisation by whom the child is boarded out, these Regulations shall have effect as if he were boarded out by the care authority.

PART II.—PROVISIONS APPLICABLE TO BOARDING-OUT FOR A PERIOD EXCEEDING EIGHT WEEKS

Application of Part II

16. This Part of these Regulations shall have effect only with regard to the boarding-out of a child as a member of a household wherein he is expected to remain for a period exceeding eight weeks, or, as the case may require and subject to the proviso to Regulation 30 of these Regulations, he has remained for a period exceeding eight weeks.

Prior visits to and reports about foster homes

17.—(1) A child shall not be boarded out unless—

    (a) the foster parents and the dwelling where the child will live have been visited by a visitor who is personally acquainted with the child and his needs, or, when that is not practicable, by a visitor who has been fully informed thereof, and the visitor has reported in writing that the sleeping and living accommodation and other domestic conditions at the dwelling are satisfactory and that the household of the foster parents is likely to suit the particular needs of the child;

    (b) information has been obtained by a visitor and a written report made by him—

        (i) on the reputation and religious persuasion of the foster parents and their suitability in age, character, temperament and health to have the charge of the child,

        (ii) as to whether any member of the foster parents' household is believed to be suffering from any physical or mental illness which might adversely affect the child or to have been convicted of any offence which would render it undesirable that the child should associate with him, and

        (iii) on the number, sex and approximate age of the persons in that household;

(c) where a local authority propose to board out a child with foster parents whose dwelling is outside the area of that authority, and where a voluntary organisation propose to board out a child (except in either case if it is a matter of urgency or if within the preceding three months another child has been boarded out by them with those foster parents in that dwelling), the area authority have been asked to report within fourteen days if any reason is known to them why boarding-out with those foster parents might be detrimental to the child's welfare; and

(d) the available history of the child and the relevant reports indicate that boarding-out in that household would be in the best interests of the child.

(2) For the purposes of sub-paragraph (c) of paragraph (1) of this Regulation the area authority shall be notified of the name, sex, date of birth and religious persuasion of the child and the names and address of the foster parents.

NOTES

Area authority.—The area authority is not required to visit the foster home—nor to approve it.

See Regulation 12 as to notifying the care authority or voluntary organisation where the area authority become aware of any reason for removing the child.

Religious persuasion.—See notes at p. 168, *ante.*

Particulars to be given to a local authority about children boarded out in their area

18. Where—

(a) a local authority board out a child with foster parents whose dwelling is outside the area of that authority; or

(b) where a voluntary organisation board out a child,

the authority or organisation, as the case may be, shall notify the area authority, as soon as may be, of any particulars not already sent to them which are required under Regulation 11 of these Regulations to be entered in a register.

Religious persuasion

19. Where possible a child shall be boarded out with foster parents who either are of the same religious persuasion as the child or give an undertaking that he will be brought up in that religious persuasion.

NOTE

See notes at p. 168, *ante.*

Undertaking to be given by foster parents

20.—(1) A local authority or voluntary organisation shall require foster parents to sign an undertaking in respect of any child boarded out with them in the form set out in the Schedule to these Regulations, or in a form to the like effect.

(2) The said undertaking shall be kept by the care authority or, as the case may be, the voluntary organisation, and a copy thereof shall be left with the foster parents.

Visits during boarding-out

21. A local authority or voluntary organisation who have arranged the boarding-out of a child shall ensure that a visitor sees the child and visits the dwelling of the foster parents—

(a) within one month after the commencement of the boarding-out;

(b) thereafter as often as the welfare of the child requires, but not less often than—

    (i) in the case of a child boarded out with foster parents in whose household he has been less than two years, if the child has not attained the age of five years, once in every six weeks, or, if he has attained that age, once in every two months, or

    (ii) in the case of a child who has been in the household of the foster parents more than two years, once in every three months;

(c) within one month after any change of dwelling by the foster parents; and

(d) forthwith after the receipt of a complaint by or concerning the child, unless it appears that action thereon is unnecessary.

Review of welfare, health, conduct and progress

22.—(1) A local authority or voluntary organisation shall ensure that a review of the welfare, health, conduct and progress of every child who is boarded out by them is made in the light of the reports written about him in pursuance of these Regulations—

(a) within three months after the child is placed with any foster parents; and

(b) thereafter, so long as he remains boarded out with those foster parents, as often as is expedient in the particular case, but not less often than once in every six months.

(2) The said review shall be made, so far as is practicable, by persons who do not usually act as visitors, and a note thereof shall be entered in the case record relating to the child, and particulars of any action recommended as a result.

Special provisions as to children who have ceased to be of compulsory school age

23.—(1) Nothing in Regulation 20 or 21 of these Regulations shall apply in relation to the boarding-out of a child who has ceased to be of compulsory school age.

(2) Where a child has already ceased to be of compulsory school age when boarded out with foster parents with whom he was not boarded out when he so ceased, the local authority or voluntary organisation who arrange the boarding-out shall require them to sign an undertaking in respect of him containing such parts of the form of undertaking set out in the Schedule to these Regulations, with or without modifications, as appear appropriate to his case.

(3) Where a child over compulsory school age is boarded out the local authority or voluntary organisation who have arranged the boarding-out shall ensure that a visitor sees the child—

(a) (i) in the case of a child who is already boarded out when he ceases to be of compulsory school age, within three months after so ceasing, or

    (ii) in the case of a child who is already over that age when boarded out with foster parents, within one month after the commencement of the boarding-out;

(b) thereafter not less often than once in every three months;

(c) within one month after any change of dwelling by the foster parents; and

(d) forthwith after the receipt of a complaint by or concerning the child, unless it appears that action thereon is unnecessary.

NOTES

Over compulsory school age.—See also Regulation 28 (2).   Compulsory school age is defined in ss. 35, 114 of the Education Act, 1944, pp. 252, 270, *ante.*

By or concerning the child.—This will no doubt be interpreted as including a complaint made by anyone which relates to the foster parents as well as a complaint about the child.

PART III. PROVISIONS APPLICABLE TO BOARDING-OUT FOR A PERIOD EXPECTED NOT TO EXCEED EIGHT WEEKS IN ALL

Application of Part III

24. This Part of these Regulations shall have effect only with regard to the boarding-out of a child as a member of a household wherein he is expected not to remain for a period exceeding eight weeks in all.

Prior visits to and reports about foster homes

25. A child shall not be boarded out unless the foster parents and the dwelling where the child will live have been visited by a visitor who has reported in writing that the boarding-out of the child with those foster parents would be suitable to the needs of the child for a period not exceeding eight weeks.

Particulars to be given to a local authority about children boarded out in their area

26. Where—

(a) a local authority board out a child with foster parents whose dwelling is outside the area of that authority, or

(b) a voluntary organisation board out a child,

the authority or organisation, as the case may be, shall notify the area authority as soon as may be of the fact that the child has been so boarded out and of the particulars required under Regulation 11 of these Regulations to be entered in a register.

Undertaking to be given by foster parents or notification in lieu

27. In the case of a child who is not over compulsory school age, a local authority or voluntary organisation shall either—

(a) comply with the provisions of Regulation 20 of these Regulations as if that Regulation were included in this Part of these Regulations; or

(b) send a letter to the foster parents stating the religious persuasion of the child and specifying the obligations which they would have been required to undertake in respect of the child if the provisions of the said Regulation 20 had applied to the case.

NOTE

Religious persuasion.—See notes at p. 168, *ante.*

Visits during boarding-out

28.—(1) A local authority or voluntary organisation who have arranged the boarding-out of a child who is not over compulsory school age shall ensure that a visitor sees the child and visits the dwelling of the foster parents—

(a) within two weeks after the commencement of the boarding-out, and

(b) thereafter not less often than once in every four weeks, and

(c) forthwith after the receipt of a complaint by or concerning the child, unless it appears that action thereon is unnecessary.

(2) A local authority or voluntary organisation who have arranged the boarding-out of a child who is over compulsory school age shall ensure that a visitor sees the child—

(a) within one month after the commencement of the boarding-out, and

(b) forthwith after the receipt of a complaint by or concerning him, unless it appears that action thereon is unnecessary.

NOTES

Over compulsory school age.—See also Regulation 23.

By or concerning the child.—See note to Regulation 23.

Boarding-out at intervals with the same foster parents

29. Where a child who is receiving full-time education has been boarded out with foster parents and within four months of ceasing to be boarded out with them is again boarded out with them, Regulations 6, 7, 25, 27 and 28 of these Regulations shall not apply to that boarding-out, but the local authority or voluntary organisation who arranged it shall ensure that a visitor sees the child and visits the dwelling of the foster parents—

(a) within one month after the commencement of the boarding-out, and

(b) forthwith after the receipt of a complaint by or concerning the child, unless it appears that action thereon is unnecessary.

NOTE

This regulation covers the case of a child receiving full-time education who is boarded out, *e.g.*, during school holidays with foster parents with whom he has previously been boarded out.

Provisions where boarding-out extends beyond eight weeks

30. If while this Part of these Regulations has effect with regard to a boarding-out, it becomes expedient that the child boarded out should remain for a period longer than eight weeks in all in the household of which he is already a member, then at the expiration of the said period this Part of these Regulations shall cease to have effect with regard thereto and the provisions of Part II thereof shall have effect as if the child were about to be, or, as the case may require, were, boarded out in that household in such circumstances that the said Part II applied, so however that anything done under this Part of these Regulations which satisfies any requirement of the said Part II shall be deemed to have been done thereunder:

Provided that, if it appears to the care authority, or, in the case of a child boarded out by a voluntary organisation, to the organisation, that the period in excess of eight weeks during which the child will remain boarded out as aforesaid will not exceed four weeks, then this Regulation shall not take effect until the expiration of that further period of four weeks.

PART IV

SUPPLEMENTARY

Transitional provisions

31.—(1) Nothing in Regulation 2, in paragraph (1) of Regulation 15 or in Regulation 20 of these Regulations shall have effect in relation to the boarding-out of a child with foster parents with whom he is boarded out at the date when these Regulations come into operation, so long as he remains boarded out with them.

(2) Where at the date when these Regulations come into operation—

(a) a child is boarded out by a local authority with foster parents whose dwelling is in the area of another local authority and there are in force immediately before the said date administrative arrangements between those authorities made under Rule 18 of the Children and

Young Persons (Boarding-Out) Rules, 1946, in respect of that child, those arrangements shall, so far as they are consistent with these Regulations, continue in force and have effect as if they were arrangements made under Regulation 13 of these Regulations

(b) a child is boarded out—

    (i) by a local authority with foster parents whose dwelling is outside the area of that authority, or

    (ii) by a voluntary organisation,

the authority or organisation, as the case may be, shall within one month of the said date notify the area authority of the fact that the child is so boarded out and of the particulars required under Regulation 11 of these Regulations to be entered in a register.

(3) Notwithstanding anything in Regulation 14 of these Regulations, a local authority shall not take over from a voluntary organisation the supervisory duties except with the written consent of that organisation until the expiration of one year from the date when these Regulations come into operation, but, save as aforesaid, the said Regulation shall have effect as if any child boarded out by a voluntary organisation immediately before the said date had been first so boarded out on that date.

(4) Where, before the date when these Regulations come into operation anything has been done under the Children and Young Persons (Boarding-Out) Rules, 1946, or is deemed by virtue of sub-paragraph (3) of paragraph 4 of the Second Schedule to the Children Act, 1948, to have been done under those Rules, it shall be deemed to have been done, so far as it could have been so done, under the corresponding provisions of these Regulations.

NOTES

1946 Rules.—The revoked Rule 18 was as follows:—

" **18.** Before the local authority boards out a foster child at a home outside the authority's area, the authority shall notify to the local authority in whose area the home is situated—

    (a) the address of the proposed home at which the child will be boarded out, and

    (b) unless they have made administrative arrangements with that other authority, that they will exercise supervision over the child;

and any such administrative arrangements shall include arrangements for visiting the child, exercising supervision over the boarding out arrangements and over the welfare of the child, medical examination and medical care and the furnishing of all reports upon the child."

Interpretation

32.—(1) In these Regulations—

" area authority ", in relation to a child, means the local authority within whose area is the dwelling of the foster parents of that child;

" care authority ", in relation to a child, means a local authority—

    (a) in whose care the child is under section one of the Children Act, 1948, either because he has been received into their care under that section or under subsection (4) of section six of that Act or by virtue of paragraph 1 of the Second Schedule to that Act, or

    (b) to whose care as a fit person the child is committed under the Children and Young Persons Act, 1933,

and references to a child in the care of a local authority shall be construed accordingly;

" child " means a person under the age of eighteen years;

" foster parents " means persons or a person with whom a child is for the time being or is proposed to be boarded out;

" local authority " means the council of a county, a county borough, or a London borough or the Common Council of the City of London ;

" supervisory duties " means the duties imposed by Regulations 7 and 8 and, as the case may be, Regulations 21, 22 and 23 or Regulation 28 or Regulation 29 of these Regulations;

" visitor " means a person carrying out on behalf of a local authority or voluntary organisation any of the duties under these Regulations to see children who are boarded out and to visit the homes of foster parents;

" voluntary organisation " means a body whose activities are carried on otherwise than for profit, but does not include a public or local authority.

(2) The Interpretation Act, 1889, shall apply to the interpretation of these Regulations as it applies to the interpretation of an Act of Parliament.

Revocation

33. The Children and Young Persons (Boarding-Out) Rules, 1946, are hereby revoked.

Extent

34. These Regulations shall not apply to Scotland.

Citation and commencement

35. These Regulations may be cited as the Boarding-Out of Children Regulations, 1955, and shall come into operation on the first day of January, 1956.

NOTES

These Regulations were made by the Secretary of State under s. 14 and sub-s. (3) of s. 33 (pp. 894, 912, *ante*), and sub-para. (4) of the Second Schedule, to the Children Act, 1948; 17 Halsbury's Statutes, 3rd Edn., 581, and are dated September 1, 1955. They are based on the recommendations of the Advisory Council on Child Care. They are printed as amended by the London Government Order, 1965, S.I. 1965 No. 654, which refers, presumably in error, to regulation 33 (1) instead of 32 (1). The amendment has been made to the latter section.

The Regulations came into operation on January 1, 1956. They prescribe what are considered to be the minimum standards, but as pointed out in the Home Office Memorandum, to which reference should be made, there is nothing in the Regulations to prevent a local authority or a voluntary organisation from doing more than is prescribed according to the needs in particular cases.

The Children and Young Persons (Boarding-Out) Rules, 1946, applied only to the boarding-out of children with foster parents by local authorities; these Regulations apply also to the boarding-out of children with foster parents by voluntary organisations. They do not apply to children boarded-out with persons proposing to adopt them under the Adoption Act, 1958, (Reg. 1 (2)), but nothing in the Regulations brings boarding-out to an end when foster parents give notice of their intention to apply for an adoption order. They do not apply to children boarded-out for a short holiday only.

Regulations, 20, 23 and 27   SCHEDULE

FORM OF UNDERTAKING TO BE SIGNED BY FOSTER PARENTS

We/I, A.B. [and B.B.], of   having on the   day of   , 19   , received from [the council of the county/county borough of London borough/City of London hereinafter called " the council ")] [*name of voluntary organisation* (hereinafter called " the organisation ")] C.D., who was born on the   day of   19   , and whose religious persuasion is   , into our/my home as a member of our/my family undertake that—

1. We/I will care for C.D. and bring him/her up as we/I would a child of our/my own.

2. He/she will be brought up in, and will be encouraged to practise, his/her religion.

3. We/I will look after his/her health and consult a doctor whenever he/she is ill and will allow him/her to be medically examined at such times and places as [the council] [the organisation] may require.

4. We/I will inform [the council] [the organisation] immediately of any serious occurrence affecting the child.

5. We/I will at all times permit any person so authorised by the Secretary of State or by [the council] [the organisation] [or by the council of the county/county borough where we/I live] to see him/her and visit our/my home.

6. We/I will allow him/her to be removed from our/my home when so requested by a person authorised by [the council] [the organisation] [or by the council of the county/county borough where we/I live].

7. If we/I decide to move, we/I will notify the new address to [the council] [the organisation] before we/I go.

(Sgd.) ....

(Sgd.) ....

Dated...........................

NOTES

School attendance.—There is no express requirement to send the child to school. Section 39 of the Education Act, 1944, p. 256, *ante*, provides that it is the duty of the parent of a child to secure his regular attendance at school. By s. 114, *ibid.*, parent includes a guardian and every person who has the actual custody of the child. The child's conduct, including his conduct at school, would be one of the subjects of the report of the visitor under Regulation 9.

Religious persuasion.—See p. 168, *ante*.

THE ISLES OF SCILLY (CHILDREN ACT, 1948) ORDER, 1959

[S.I. 1959 No. 432]

1. In its application to the Isles of Scilly the Children Act, 1948 (in this Order referred to as " the Act "), shall have effect subject to the exceptions, adaptations and modifications hereafter prescribed in this Order.

2. Subsection (1) of section thirty-eight of the Act (which, as amended by the Children Act, 1958, specifies the local authorities for the purposes of the Act, of Parts III and IV of the Children and Young Persons Act, 1933, and of Part I of the Children Act, 1958), shall have effect as if amongst the authorities there specified there included the council of the Isles of Scilly.

3. For section thirty-nine of the Act (which requires every local authority to establish a children's committee for the purposes of their functions under the Act and certain other enactments relating to children, and contains other provisions relating to the said committee) there shall be substituted the following section, that is to say:—

" 39. The council of the Isles of Scilly may, if they think fit, delegate to the committee established by them under section thirty-three of, and the Third Schedule to, the National Assistance Act, 1948, their functions under the following enactments, that is to say:—

(a) Parts III and IV of the Children and Young Persons Act, 1933,
(b) section five of the Family Allowances and National Insurance Act, 1956,
(c) Part I of the Children Act, 1958,
(d) Parts II and IV of the Adoption Act, 1958, and
(e) this Act.".

4. Section forty of the Act (which provides for the modification in certain cases of the requirement of section thirty-nine regarding the establishment of a children's committee) shall be omitted.

5. The Interpretation Act, 1889, shall apply to the interpretation of this Order as it applies to the interpretation of an Act of Parliament.

6. This Order may be cited as the Isles of Scilly (Children Act, 1948) Order, 1959, and shall come into operation on the first day of April, 1959.

NOTE

This Order was made under s. 61 of the Children Act, 1948, p. 925, ante, on March 1, 1959.

THE LONDON AUTHORITIES (CHILDREN) ORDER, 1965
[S.I. 1965 No. 554]

1. Subject to the provisions of Article 15 of this Order, a person in the care of the Middlesex County Council immediately before 1st April 1965 in pursuance of an enactment specified in column 1 of the subjoined Table shall, on 1st April 1965, be transferred to the care of the successor authority specified opposite thereto in column 2 of the said table.

TABLE

1 Enactment under which person received into care	2 Successor authority to whom person is transferred
Section 1 (1) of the Children Act, 1948.	The authority in whose area the place from which the person was received into care is on 1st April 1965 situate.
Section 1 (4) of the said Act of 1948.	The authority in whose area the place of ordinary residence of the person as determined for the purpose of the said section 1 (4) is on 1st April 1965 situate.
Section 1 of the said Act of 1948 as applied by section 7 (4) of the Children Act, 1958, or by section 43 (3) of the Adoption Act, 1958.	The authority in whose area the premises from which the person under the said section 7 or section 43 was removed are on 1st April 1965 situate.
Section 6 (4) of the said Act of 1948.	The authority in whose area the person is on 1st April 1965 living or, if there is no such authority, the authority selected by the Middlesex County Council.
Section 3 (4) of the said Act of 1948.	The authority who would have been the successor authority under the foregoing provision if the enactment under which he was last received into care before he was received into care under the said section 3 (4) applied.

2. Subject to the provisions of Article 15 of this Order, a person committed to the care of the Middlesex County Council by an order made by a court under the Children and Young Persons Acts, 1933 to 1963, section 5 (1) of the Matrimonial Proceedings (Children) Act, 1958 or section 2 (1) (*e*) of the Matrimonial Proceedings (Magistrates' Courts) Act, 1960 and in their care in pursuance of such an order immediately before 1st April 1965 shall, on 1st April 1965, be transferred to the care of the successor authority in whose area the place where the person was resident or the offence was committed or the circumstances arose, as the case may be, as determined for the purposes of the order, is then situate.

3. Subject to the provision of Article 15 of this Order, functions, powers, rights or liabilities vested in or attaching to the Middlesex County Council immediately before 1st April 1965 by virtue of a resolution under section 2 of the Children Act, 1948 as respects a person who is not at that time in their care or under section 15 or 47 of the Children and Young Persons Act, 1963 shall, on 1st April 1965, be transferred to and vested in or attached to the successor authority to which he would have been transferred under Article 1 of this Order had he not ceased to be in their care.

4. Subject to the provisions of Article 15 of this Order, a person under the supervision of the Middlesex County Council immediately before 1st April 1965 by virtue of a supervision order shall, on 1st April 1965, be transferred to the supervision of the successor authority in whose area the place where the person was resident when the person was placed under their supervision is on 1st April 1965 situate.

5. Subject to the provisions of Article 15 of this Order, where the children's officer of the Middlesex County Council is immediately before 1st April 1965 acting as the guardian *ad litem* for the purpose of an application for an adoption order under the Adoption Act, 1958, the children's officer of the successor authority in whose area the place where the child who is the subject of the application was residing when the children's officer was appointed guardian *ad litem* shall, on and after 1st April 1965, be deemed to have been duly appointed guardian *ad litem* for that purpose.

6.—(1) Subject to the provisions of Article 15 of this Order, a person in the care of the London County Council immediately before 1st April 1965 in pursuance of an enactment specified in Article 1 or 2 of this Order or under the supervision of the council at that time by virtue of a supervision order shall, on 1st April 1965, be transferred to the care or supervision, as the case may be, of the appropriate successor authority.

(2) Subject to the provisions of Article 15 of this Order, functions, powers, rights and liabilities vested in or attaching to the London County Council immediately before 1st April 1965—

(a) by virtue of a resolution under section 2 of the Children Act, 1948 as respects a person who was not at that time in their care, or

(b) by virtue of making or participating in arrangements for the adoption of an infant under the Adoption Agencies Regulations, 1959, or

(c) under section 15 or 47 of the Children and Young Persons Act, 1963.

shall, on 1st April 1965, be transferred to and vested in or attached to the appropriate successor authority.

(3) Subject to the provisions of Article 15 of this Order, where the children's officer of the London County Council is immediately before 1st April 1965 acting as the guardian *ad litem* for the purpose of an application for an adoption order under the Adoption Act, 1958, the children's officer of the appropriate successor authority shall, on and after 1st April 1965, be deemed to have been duly appointed guardian *ad litem* for that purpose.

(4) For the purposes of this Article the expression " appropriate successor authority " means the successor authority determined in accordance with a scheme made by the London County Council before 1st April 1965 after consultation with the successor authorities and with the approval of the Secretary of State or, if no such scheme has been made, in accordance with a scheme made before 1st April 1965 by the Secretary of State.

7.—(1) A person in the care of the council of a dissolved county borough immediately before 1st April 1965 in pursuance of an enactment specified in Article 1 or 2 of this Order or under the supervision of the council at that time by virtue of a supervision order shall, on 1st April 1965, be transferred to the care or supervision, as the case may be, of the successor authority.

(2) Functions, powers, rights and liabilities vested in or attaching to such a council immediately before 1st April 1965—

    (a) by virtue of a resolution under section 2 of the Children Act, 1948 as respects a person who was not at that time in their care, or

    (b) by virtue of making or participating in arrangements for the adoption of an infant under the Adoption Agencies Regulations, 1959, or

    (c) under section 15 or 47 of the Children and Young Persons Act, 1963,

shall, on 1st April 1965, be transferred to and vested in or attached to the successor authority.

(3) Where the children's officer of such a council is, immediately before 1st April 1965, acting as the guardian *ad litem* for the purposes of an application for an adoption order under the Adoption Act, 1958, the children's officer of the successor authority shall, on and after that date, be deemed to have been duly appointed guardian *ad litem* for that purpose.

8.—(1) Where a person is in the care of the council of an altered county immediately before 1st April 1965 in pursuance of an enactment specified in column 1 of the subjoined Table and the place specified in relation to such a person in column 2 of the said Table is on 1st April 1965 situate in the area of a successor authority, the council shall, unless they decide otherwise, notify before 1st June 1965 that successor authority that that person is in their care.

TABLE

1 Enactment	2 Place
Section 1 (1) of the Children Act, 1948.	The place from which the person was received into care.
Section 1 (4) of the said Act of 1948.	The place or ordinary residence of the person as determined for the purpose of the said section 1 (4).
Section 1 of the said Act of 1948 as applied by section 7 (4) of the Children Act, 1958 or by section 43 (3) of the Adoption Act, 1958.	The place from which the person was removed under the said section 7 or 43.
Section 6 (4) of the said Act of 1948.	The place in which the person is living on 1st April 1965.

(2) Where a person is in the care of the council of an altered county immediately before 1st April 1965 in pursuance of section 3 (4) of the Act of 1948, paragraph (1) of this Article shall apply as if the enactment under which he was last received into their care before he was received into care under the said section 3 (4) were the enactment in pursuance of which he is in the care of the council.

9. Where a person committed to the care of the council of an altered county by an order made by a court under the Children and Young Persons Acts, 1933 to 1963, section 5 (1) of the Matrimonial Proceedings (Children) Act, 1958 or section 2 (1) (e) of the Matrimonial Proceedings (Magistrates' Courts) Act, 1960, is in their care in pursuance of such an order immediately before 1st April 1965 and the place of that person's residence or, as the case may be, the place where the offence was committed or the circumstances arose, as determined for the purposes of the order, is on 1st April 1965 situate in the area of a successor authority, the council shall, unless they decide otherwise, notify before 1st June 1965 that successor authority that that person is in their care.

10. Where functions, powers, rights or liabilities are vested in or attached to the council of an altered county immediately before 1st April 1965, by virtue of a resolution under section 2 of the Children Act, 1948 or under section 15 or 47 of the Children and Young Persons Act, 1963, as respects a person who at that time is not in their care but who had he not ceased to be in their care would be a person described in Article 8 or 9 of this Order, the council shall, unless they decide otherwise, notify before 1st June 1965 the successor authority which would have been notified had the said Article 8 or 9 applied that those functions, powers, rights or liabilities are vested in or attached to them.

11.—(1) Subject to the provisions of Article 15 of this Order, any right or liability vested in or attaching to the council of a dissolved county or county borough under section 1 (4) of the Children Act, 1948 immediately before 1st April 1965 in respect of a person who is or was in the care of another local authority shall, on 1st April 1965, be transferred to and vested in or attached to the successor authority in whose area the place of ordinary residence of that person, as determined for the purposes of the said subsection, is on 1st April 1965 situate.

(2) Where any right or liability is, immediately before 1st April 1965, vested in or attached to the council of an altered county under the said section 1 (4) in respect of a person who is or was in the care of another local authority and whose place of ordinary residence, as so determined, is on 1st April 1965 situate in the area of a successor authority, the council shall, unless they decide otherwise, notify before 1st June 1965 that successor authority that that right or liability is vested in or attached to them.

(3) Any power which would have been exercisable by the council of a dissolved county or county borough, had the London Government Act, 1963 not been enacted, to recover expenses under the said section 1 (4) (b) from another local authority, in respect of a person who had been in their care but is not a person to whom Article 1 or 7 (1) of this Order applies, shall after 1st April 1965 be exercisable by a successor authority incurring expenses to which the said section 1 (4) (b) applies.

12.—(1) Subject to the provisions of Article 15 of this Order, functions, powers, rights or liabilities vested in or attaching to the council of a dissolved county by virtue of being named as local authority in an approved school order, shall after 31st March 1965 be transferred to and vested in or attached to the successor authority in whose area the place where the person was resident or, as the case may be, the offence was committed or the circumstances arose, as determined for the purposes of section 70 (2) of the Children and Young Persons Act, 1933, is on 1st April 1965 situate.

(2) Functions, powers, rights or liabilities vested in or attaching to the council of a dissolved county borough by virtue of being named as local authority in an approved school order, shall after 31st March 1965 be transferred to and vested in or attached to the successor authority.

(3) Where functions, powers, rights or liabilities are vested in or attaching to the council of an altered county by virtue of being named as local authority in an approved school order and the place of residence of the person with respect to whom it is made, as determined for the purposes of the said section 70 (2), or in relation to whom the place where the offence was committed or

the circumstances arose as so determined, as the case may be, is on 1st April 1965 situate in the area of a successor authority, the council shall, unless they decide otherwise, notify before 1st June 1965 that successor authority of the functions, powers, rights or liabilities vested in or attaching to them under the order.

13.—(1) A successor authority which is notified by the council of an altered county that immediately before 1st April 1965—

    (a) a person of a description specified in Article 8 or 9 of this Order was in the care of that council, or

    (b) functions, powers, rights or liabilities of a description specified in Article 10, 11 (2) or 12 (3) of this Order were vested in or attaching to that council,

may, not later than 31st March 1966, take over the care of that person or any of those functions, powers, rights or liabilities.

(2) Any expenses duly incurred after 31st March 1965 by the council of an altered county—

    (a) in respect of a person who is or has been in their care of whom notice has been given to a successor authority under the foregoing Articles of this Order, including any travelling or other expenses incurred in connection with the transfer of his care to a successor authority under paragraph (1) of this Article, or

    (b) otherwise in connection with any functions, powers, rights or liabilities of which notice has been given to a successor authority under the foregoing Articles of this Order.

may be recovered from the notified successor authority.

(3) Where, before a person, function, power, right or liability mentioned in paragraph (1) of this Article is taken over in accordance with that paragraph, the person ceases to be in care or the function, power, right or liability is varied, including variation by reason of the reception back into care of a person to whom such a function, power, right or liability relates, the said paragraph shall apply as if the changed circumstances had existed immediately before 1st April 1965 and the successor authority had been notified thereof.

14. The council of a dissolved county shall before 1st April 1965 notify each successor authority of—

    (a) the persons who will, in accordance with the foregoing provisions of this Order, be transferred to their care or supervision on 1st April 1965, and

    (b) the functions, powers, rights and liabilities which will on that date vest in or attach to that authority in accordance with those provisions, and

    (c) the applications for adoption orders under the Adoption Act, 1958 in which their children's officer will be deemed to have been appointed guardian *ad litem* in accordance wth those provisions.

15.—(1) A successor authority which has been notified by the council of a dissolved county or of an altered county under the foregoing provisions of this Order and which is of opinion that another successor authority should have been notified in accordance with the foregoing provisions of this Order or that, in the case of notification by the council of an altered county, no successor authority should have been notified may, within two months of being so notified, apply to the Secretary of State, to determine whether that other successor authority or, as the case may be, no successor authority should have been notified in accordance with the said provisions :

Provided that this paragraph shall not apply as respects any matter which has been dealt with under Article 5, 6 (3) or 13 (1) of this Order.

(2) A successor authority notified as aforesaid may, within two months of being notified, agree with any other successor authority that—

(a) any person transferred to their care or supervision or whose care may be taken over by them in pursuance of the foregoing provisions of this Order, or

(b) any function, power, right or liability vested in or attaching to them or which may be vested in or attached to them in pursuance of the foregoing provisions of this Order, or

(c) any appointment of their children's officer as guardian *ad litem* in an application for an adoption order under the Adoption Act, 1958 in pursuance of the foregoing provisions of this Order.

be transferred to, vested in or attached to that other successor authority or their children's officer, as the case may be :

Provided that this paragraph shall not apply as respects any matter which has been dealt with under Article 13 (1) of this Order.

(3) Where the Secretary of State determines that another successor authority should have been notified by the council of a dissolved county or where a successor authority notified by the county of a dissolved county agrees with any other successor authority under paragraph (2) of this Article—

(a) that other successor authority may, not later than 31st March 1966, take over the person, function, power, right or liability that is the subject of the determination or agreement.

(b) any expenses duly incurred after 31st March 1965 by the council notified as aforesaid in connection with that person, function, power, right or liability, including any travelling or other expenses incurred in connection with the transfer of his care to that other successor authority, may be recovered from that other successor authority.

(4) Where, before a person, function, power, right or liability mentioned in paragraph (3) (a) of this Article is taken over in accordance with that sub-paragraph, the person ceases to be in care or the function, power, right or liability is varied, including variation by reason of the reception back into care of a person to whom such a function, power, right or liability relates, the said sub-paragraph shall apply as if the changed circumstances had existed immediately before the determination or agreement and had been dealt with in the same way as the matters which were the subject of the determination or agreement.

(5) Where the Secretary of State determines that another successor authority should have been notified by the council of an altered county, or where a successor authority notified by the council of an altered county agrees with any other successor authority under paragraph (2) of this Article, that other successor authority and no other shall be deemed to have been for the purposes of this Order the successor authority that was notified.

(6) Where the Secretary of State determines that no successor authority should have been notified, it shall be deemed that no successor authority has been notified for the purposes of this Order.

(7) Subject to the foregoing provisions of this Article, where a successor authority has been notified by a dissolved county council concerning the appointment of their children's officer as guardian *ad litem* for the purposes of an application for an adoption order under the Adoption Act, 1958, that children's officer shall, for the purposes of the foregoing provisions of this Order, be deemed to have been duly appointed guardian *ad litem* for the purposes of that application.

(8) Subject to the foregoing provisions of this Article, a successor authority which has been notified by a dissolving county council shall be deemed to be

the authority to which for the purposes of the foregoing provisions of this Order, the persons, functions, powers, rights and liabilities therein mentioned are, on 1st April 1965, transferred.

16.—(1) Any functions, powers, rights or liabilities vested in or attaching to a council with respect to a person transferred to the care of a successor authority by or under this Order and subsisting immediately before the transfer shall thereafter vest in or attach to the successor authority; and any order of a court committing such a person to such a council shall after the transfer have effect with the substitution for the name of the council of the name of the successor authority.

(2) Where functions, powers, rights or liabilities vested in or attaching to a council with respect to a person to whom an approved school order, a supervision order or an order made under the proviso to section 4 (3) of the Children Act, 1948 relates, are transferred by or under this Order to a successor authority, the order shall thereafter have effect with the substitution for the name of the council of the name of the successor authority.

(3) Without prejudice to the provisions of paragraph (1) of this Article, where functions, powers, rights or liabilities under a resolution passed under section 2 of the Children Act, 1948 are transferred by or under this Order to a successor authority, the resolution shall thereafter be deemed to have been passed by the successor authority.

17.—(1) Any successor authority may on and after 1st April 1965 exercise the powers conferred by section 58 of the Children and Young Persons Act, 1963 in respect of a person who before that date had been in the care of the council of a dissolved county or county borough.

(2) As respects a person who before 1st April 1965 had been in the care of the council of an altered county, any successor authority may with the consent of that Council exercise on and after that date the powers conferred by the said section 58, without prejudice to the exercise of those powers by that council.

18.—(1) Where any legal proceedings are pending on 1st April 1965 to which the council of a dissolved county or county borough is a party and the matters which are the subject of the proceedings have been transferred by or under this Order, those proceedings may be continued by or against the council of the authority to which those matters have been so transferred and may be amended in such manner as may be necessary or proper in consequence of this Order.

(2) Any determination, requirement, consent, permission, exemption, notice or other thing made, imposed, given, served or done by, to or on a dissolved county or county borough council or the children's officer of such a council which relates to a person, function, power, right or liability transferred by or under this Order shall, if it has effect immediately before the transfer, have the like effect thereafter as if it had been made, imposed, given, served or done by, to or on the council or children's officer of the successor authority.

(3) Any legal proceedings to which the council of an altered county is a party and which are pending when the matters which are the subject of the proceedings are transferred by or under this Order to a successor authority, may be continued by or against the successor authority, and may be amended in such manner as may be necessary or proper in consequence of this Order.

(4) Any determination, requirement, consent, permission, exemption, notice or other thing made, imposed, given, served or done by, to or on the council of an altered county which relates to a person, function, power, right or liability transferred by or under this Order to a successor authority, shall, if it has

effect immediately before the transfer, have the like effect thereafter as if it had been made, imposed, given, served or done by, to or on the successor authority.

19.—(1) In this Order, the expression—

" altered county   means the county of Surrey, Kent, Essex or Hertfordshire :

" approved school order " means an approved school order as defined in the Children and Young Persons Act, 1933 ;

" dissolved county " means the county of London or Middlesex ;

" dissolved county borough " means the county borough of Croydon, East Ham or West Ham ;

" successor authority " means the council of—

(a) in the case of the London County Council, an inner London borough, the City of London or the London borough of Newham ;

(b) in the case of the Middlesex County Council, the London borough of Barnet, Brent, Ealing, Enfield, Haringey, Harrow, Hillingdon, Hounslow or Richmond upon Thames or the county of Hertfordshire or Surrey ;

(c) in the case of the Essex County Council, the London borough of Barking, Havering, Newham, Redbridge or Waltham Forest ;

(d) in the case of the Hertfordshire County Council, the London borough of Barnet ;

(e) in the case of the Kent County Council, the London borough of Bexley or Bromley ;

(f) in the case of the Surrey County Council, the London borough of Croydon, Kingston upon Thames, Merton, Richmond upon Thames or Sutton ;

(g) in the case of the council of the county borough of Croydon, the London borough of Croydon ;

(h) in the case of the councils of the county boroughs of East Ham and West Ham, the London borough of Newham ;

" supervision order " means an order made by a court under any provision of the Children and Young Persons Act, 1933 or under section 6 of the Matrimonial Proceedings (Children) Act, 1958 or under section 2 of the Matrimonial Proceedings (Magistrates' Courts) Act, 1960 placing a person under the supervision of a local authority.

(2) Any reference in this Order to an enactment is a reference to that enactment as amended by or under any other enactment.

(3) The Interpretation Act, 1889 shall apply to the interpretation of this Order as it applies to the interpretation of an Act of Parliament.

20. This Order may be cited as the London Authorities (Children) Order, 1965 and shall come into operation on 30th March 1965.

NOTE

This order was made on 22nd March, 1965, under s. 84 of the London Government Act, 1963 ; 20 Halsbury's Statutes, 3rd Edn., 531. See Home Office Circular No. 59/1965, 1009, *et seq., post.*

II.—OFFICIAL CIRCULARS

Department of Health and Social Security, FAM. 33   *October,* 1971

CHILDREN ABSENT FROM THEIR FAMILIES

FAMILY ALLOWANCES ACTS

This leaflet explains the position under the Family Allowances Acts of children who are living away from the family to whom allowances have been awarded on their behalf.

1. The position of children living away from home varies according to the circumstances of their absence. In some circumstances a child will not be eligible to count for family allowances purposes at all while living away from home but where he is eligible it will normally be a condition for his inclusion in the family that the parent, foster-parent or guardian, as the case may be, is contributing at least 90p a week towards his support. Certain absences from home are normally disregarded, for example, where a child is living away from his parents' home to attend school, temporary absences of short duration, and short periods during which provision for the child is temporarily interrupted.

2. Before a person can be regarded for allowances purposes as contributing towards the cost of providing for a child his/her contributions as mentioned in the leaflet must actually have been received by the person having care of the child; a mere obligation or liability to contribute (for example, under a court order or agreement) or an intention to contribute which has not yet been carried out cannot establish or preserve entitlement to family allowances. Contributions may be in cash or kind or both.

CHILDREN AT SCHOOL OR IN HOSPITAL

At school

3. A child who is living away from his parents' home to attend school and who normally returns home for the holidays is regarded as living at home, and can be counted in the family for allowances purposes whether or not contributions are being made to his support.

4. Where a child does not normally live with his parents, however, and his parents do not contribute at least 90p a week to his support, he is included for family allowances in the family of the person who contributes most towards his support. If the child does not live with this family during school holidays, the contribution must be at least 90p a week.

In hospital

5. A child included in his parents' family who goes into hospital is normally regarded as still living with his parents and may continue to be included in their family whether or not they are contributing towards his support.

6. If before going into hospital the child was included in the family of someone other than his parents, he will remain included in that family, so long as, after the child's first four weeks in hospital, the person concerned contributes at least 90p a week in cash or kind and no one else contributes more.

Children away from Home under Voluntary Arrangements

With relatives or friends

7. When a child leaves his parents temporarily to stay with relatives or friends under a voluntary arrangement he continues to be included in his parents' family for up to 12 weeks from the date on which he leaves them. If he goes to live permanently with relatives or friends, or if he has been away temporarily for longer than 12 weeks, he will remain in his parents' family so long as they are providing at least 90p a week in cash or kind towards his support. A temporary interruption or reduction of such contributions for up to four weeks may be disregarded.

8. If the conditions for the child's inclusion in his parents' family are not satisfied the child may be included in the family of the person who is making the major contribution towards his support. The first four weeks of any temporary absence of the child from that person or of any temporary interruption or reduction in that person's contributions may be disregarded but otherwise, if the child is not living with the person concerned, the amount contributed must be at least 90p a week (but see paragraphs 3 and 4 where the child is away at school).

In the care of a voluntary organisation or local authority

9. A child in the care of a voluntary organisation or in the care of a local authority under voluntary arrangements, including a child in care under Section 1 of the Children Act, 1948, or section 15 (1) of the Social Work (Scotland) Act, 1968 (see paragraph 10, where a child is taken into care by an order of the Court or other official directive), may be placed in a Home or may be boarded out with foster parents. The authority or organisation may require the parent to contribute towards the child's support. A child who is placed in a Home or boarded out may be included in a family in the same way as a child who is away from home in the circumstances dealt with in paragraphs 7 and 8 except that only the first four weeks of the child's absence from his parents can be disregarded. The rights of foster parents are explained in paragraph 11.

Children Removed from the Control of their Parents

10. Special rules apply to the following groups of children. Except as otherwise stated, these children cannot be counted as in any family, including that of a foster parent, regardless of the amount of any maintenance payments made by the parents.

   (a) Children committed to the care of a local authority by an order (other than an interim order) under the Children and Young Persons Acts.
   (b) Children over whom a local authority has assumed parental rights by resolution under the Children Act, 1948, or the Social Work (Scotland) Act, 1968.

Note.—A child in group (a) or (b) may sometimes be allowed by the local authority to be under the control of a parent, guardian, relative or friend. While such an arrangement lasts the child may count for family allowances in the ordinary way. If he is not living with his parents the rules in paragraphs 7 and 8 apply.

(c) Children whose residence in a residential establishment is required by a supervision requirement under section 44 of the Social Work (Scotland) Act, 1968, except when absent from the establishment under supervision.

(d) Children liable to be detained by virtue of section 53 of the Children and Young Persons Act, 1933, or section 57 of the Children and Young Persons (Scotland) Act, 1937, and not discharged on licence.

(e) Children liable to undergo residential training under committal by virtue of section 58A of the Children and Young Persons (Scotland) Act, 1937, and not released under that section.

(f) Children subject to an approved school or fit person order made by a court in Scotland before 15 April 1971.

Special Cases

Position of foster parents

11. A child who is living with foster parents cannot be included in their family for family allowances purposes if the conditions are satisfied for his inclusion in his parents' family. If these conditions are not satisfied the child can be included in the family of the foster parents so long as they contribute more than anyone else towards the cost of providing for the child. In this respect, the payment of a boarding-out allowance by the local authority does not prevent the child from being included in the foster parents' family. The local authority, in determining the amount of boarding-out allowance to be paid to foster parents, may take into account their income, including any family allowances received in respect of fostered children in the care of the authority.

Prospective adopters

12. A child taken into a family with a view to adoption may normally be included in the prospective adopters' family provided the natural parents do not maintain the child at the rate of 90p or more a week in cash or kind. Claims to allowances should be made as soon as possible after the child is taken for adoption and should NOT be delayed until the adoption formalities are completed.

13. Where a person gives notice of intention to apply for an adoption order for a child mentioned in paragraph 10 (a) or (b), the child may be included in a family so long as he remains in the care of the person who gave the notice, unless the application is refused by the Court or withdrawn or the prospective adopter fails to make an application within 12 weeks of the notice of intention. In exceptional cases where the application is delayed, or where it is refused by the Court or withdrawn, the alternative conditions explained in the note below paragraph 10 (b) may assist the claimant.

Changes which must be Reported

14. This leaflet is intended only to give general guidance. Details of changes of circumstances which must be reported are included in the coloured instruction pages at the back of every family allowances order book. Any such changes should be reported immediately to the local office of the Department of Health and Social Security. The local office also give any further advice or information required on this subject.

NOTE

This leaflet gives general guidance on the subject. It must not be treated as a complete and authoritative statement of the law on any particular case.

Home Office Circular No. 59/1965 *Dated March 18, 1965.*

LONDON GOVERNMENT RE-ORGANISATION

TRANSITIONAL ARRANGEMENTS RELATING TO CHILDREN

1. I am directed by the Secretary of State to say that he thinks that courts within the area affected by the London Government changes taking place on 1st April will wish to know of the arrangements made to transfer, from local authorities being dissolved or altered, responsibilities connected with children placed upon them by orders of courts.

2. A Statutory Order being made under section 84 of the London Government Act, 1963 will, among others, have the following effects.

Children in care

3. Children committed to the care of the London County Council or Middlesex County Council by virtue of orders made under the Children and Young Persons Acts 1933–63, section 5 (1) of the Matrimonial Proceedings (Children) Act, 1958 or section 2 (1) (e) of the Matrimonial Proceedings (Magistrates' Courts) Act, 1960 will be transferred to an appropriate successor authority. Children so committed to the care of Croydon County Borough will be transferred to Croydon London Borough and children so committed to East Ham or West Ham County Boroughs to Newham London Borough. Children so committed to one of the counties whose boundaries are being altered—that is, Kent, Surrey, Hertfordshire and Essex—may in certain circumstances be transferred to a London Borough. When a child is transferred, all functions, powers, rights or liabilities vested in the authority named in the court order will be transferred by virtue of the Statutory Order to the successor authority and the court order will be deemed to have been amended by the substitution of the name of the new authority for the old.

Supervision orders

4. The supervision of children by the London County Council or Middlesex County Council by virtue of an order made under the Children and Young Persons Acts, 1933–63 or under section 6 of the Matrimonial Proceedings (Children) Act, 1958 or under section 2 of the Matrimonial Proceedings (Magistrates' Courts) Act, 1960 will be transferred to an appropriate successor authority. The supervision of children by Croydon, East Ham or West Ham County Boroughs will be transferred to Croydon or Newham London Boroughs as the case may be. Court orders will be deemed to have been amended accordingly.

Approved school orders

5. An approved school order naming as local authority the London County Council, Middlesex County Council, or Croydon or East Ham or West Ham County Boroughs will have effect as if the appropriate successor authority were substituted. In certain circumstances an order naming Kent, Hertfordshire, Essex or Sussey County Councils may have effect as if the name of a London Borough were substituted.

Appointment of children's officers as guardians ad litem in adoption cases

6. Where the Children's Officer of the London County Council or the Middlesex County Council is acting as guardian *ad litem* immediately before 1st April for the purpose of an application for an adoption order under the Adoption Act, 1958, the children's officer of the appropriate successor authority will be deemed to have been duly appointed. There will be no need for the court to change the appointment. Where the Children's Officer of the Croydon or the

East Ham or the West Ham County Borough Council is acting as guardian *ad litem*, the appointment will be deemed to have been changed automatically to the Children's Officer of the Croydon or the Newham London Borough Council as the case may be.

Applications to courts for the variation of orders or appointments

7. These arrangements should result in the automatic transfer in appropriate cases of all but a few responsibilities connected with children laid by the courts on authorities being dissolved or changed. It may nevertheless be necessary for officers of an authority to apply to a court in one of the following matters :

(a) The Statutory Order will not provide for the automatic transfer of supervision of a child from an altered county to a London borough. Few children are involved ; and in some cases the county council may be willing to continue supervision even though the child will reside in a London borough after 1st April. It will be open to a county council that does not wish to continue supervision in such circumstances to apply to the court in the normal way for a variation of the supervision order.

(b) The children's officer or a child-care officer of an altered county may be willing to continue to act as guardian *ad litem* despite the transfer to a London borough of the area in which the court has jurisdiction or the applicants for an adoption order reside. The Statutory Order will not, therefore, provide for the automatic change of appointment in such cases. If, however, the officer takes the view that the duties would be carried out more appropriately by another officer, it will be open to him to ask the court to change the appointment.

(c) The Statutory Order will not provide for the automatic change of appointment as guardian *ad litem* of a child-care officer of one of the dissolved or altered authorities who has been appointed by name. It will be open to the officer to ask the court to appoint another person if it is inappropriate for him to continue to perform the duties of guardian *ad litem*.

Continuation of legal proceedings involving a local authority

8. The Statutory Order will ensure that pending proceedings to which the council of a dissolved county or county borough is a party may, if the proceedings are affected by the Order, be continued by or against the council of the successor authority. Similar provisions covering other pending proceedings not affected by the Order are contained in the London Authorities (Property etc.) Order, 1964 (Statutory Instrument 1964 No. 1464). The Secretary of State is confident that the courts will co-operate with the officers of the old and new authorities in reducing to a minimum the inconveniences that could be caused by the appearance of a different local authority in cases that continue beyond 1st April.

9. He would also ask courts to avoid, as far as is possible, in the few days remaining before the London and Middlesex County Councils cease to exist, committing children to their custody under section 9 (1) (b) of the Children and Young Persons Act, 1963.

(Issued to courts of assize and quarter sessions and magistrates' courts within the Greater London Area)

Home Office Circular CHN/64 62/14/4   *Dated March 23, 1965.*

LONDON CHILDREN'S SERVICE

An order has now been made under section 84 of the London Government Act, 1963 to give effect to the arrangements outlined in this department's letter of 10th February for the transfer of children in the care of the existing county and county borough councils, and of other forms of responsibility in respect of individual children attaching to those councils as children authorities.

2. We regret that copies of the order (which will come into operation on 30th March) are not yet available for distribution, but we hope to send you copies on 29th March ; copies should also be on sale by that date.   In the meantime, the accompanying explanatory notes, read in conjunction with appendix A (1) of the letter of 10th February, and the comments below, should enable final arrangements to be made in advance of publication of the order.

3. For Middlesex County Council cases in the categories mentioned in paragraph 1 of the notes, and for transferable altered county cases within such of those categories as are to be dealt with under the order (see paragraph 6 of the notes), the basis for the selection of the new authority, *which must always be one of the successor authorities to the particular county council*, is to be the same as that set out in appendix A (1) to the letter of 10th February, subject to the following points :

(a) if a child in the care of the Middlesex County Council under section 6 (4) of the Children Act, 1948 is not living in the area of one of that council's successor authorities, the council may select any one of those authorities ;

(b) a child in the care of the Middlesex County Council or the council of an altered county under section 3 (4) of the 1948 Act is to be assumed to be in his original " care " category ((i), (ii), (iii) or (iv) of appendix A (1)) ;

(c) for all the county councils, the new authority for any liability or right in category (f) of paragraph 1 of the notes will be selected on the same basis as the new authority for category (iv) in appendix A (1).

4. The scheme referred to in paragraph 2 of the notes, for the transfer of certain London County Council cases, will give effect to the agreed " case-load " scheme.

5. Where, in a county council case—

(a) the council's liability to pay contribution under an approved school order ;

(b) a person in care under section 6 (4) of the Children Act 1948 ; or

(c) after-care responsibility under paragraph 12 (3) of the Fourth Schedule to the Children and Young Persons Act, 1933 (see paragraph 14 (e) of appendix B to the letter of 10th February, and paragraph 14 of the notes) ;

is transferred, the county council are requested to advise the managers of the approved school accordingly, or to arrange for the new authority to do so ; if, in the case of (a), the person to whom the approved school order relates has not been admitted to a school when the liability is transferred, this department should be informed of the transfer.

6. The transfer of a child who is in care or under supervision under the Matrimonial Proceedings (Children) Act, 1958 should be notified to the Divorce Registry or the appropriate divisional registry ; a suitable form of notification is suggested below.

7. We feel sure that, in operating these statutory procedures, authorities will make every effort to ensure that the best interests of each child are safeguarded.   In altered county cases (and in dissolved county council cases where the first authority are replaced by another—see paragraph 5 of the notes) the question whether transfer should take place, and, if so, when, will no doubt be considered in this light.   It will be appreciated that the transfer of statutory

responsibility for a child in care should not in itself necessitate his removal from one children's home or foster home to another and, as far as practicable, continuity of care should be preserved.

8. Additional copies of this letter are enclosed for the Children's Officer and the Treasurer. Further copies will be supplied on request to extension 1616.

Suggested form of notification about Matrimonial Proceedings (Children) Act, (1958) cases—see paragraph 6, above

Please note that, by reason of the London Authorities (Children) Order 1965, made under section 84 of the London Government Act, 1963, the undermentioned child(ren), who were [committed to the care] [placed under the supervision] of the council by order dated   made under the Matrimonial Proceedings (Children) Act 1958, has(ve) been transferred to [care] [supervision] of the   council on (date) and the reference in the said order to the council is to be deemed to be a reference to the   council.

(name of child(ren)—title of proceedings)

THE LONDON AUTHORITIES (CHILDREN) ORDER 1965

EXPLANATORY NOTES

I. Dissolved County and County Borough Councils

1. The order deals with the following responsibilities of each of the dissolved county and county borough councils immediately before 1st April 1965 :

(a) children in the council's care ;
(b) persons no longer in the council's care but
    (i) in respect of whom a resolution of the council under section 2 of the Children Act, 1948 is in force,
    (ii) to whom section 15 of the Children and Young Persons Act, 1963 (committal to an approved school of a child in care) applies, or
    (iii) to whom section 47 of that Act (apprenticeship guarantees) applies ;
(c) children placed under the council's supervision by a court order ;
(d) appointments of the council's children's officer as guardian *ad litem* ;
(e) cases in which the council are making or participating in arrangements for adoption under the Adoption Agencies Regulations, 1959 (this applies to the London County Council and county borough councils only ; it is understood that the Middlesex County Council have no such cases) ;
(f) liability of the council, as the authority of ordinary residence, to pay the expenses of another authority, or right to take over the care of a child, under section 1 (4) of the Children Act, 1948 ; and
(g) flat-rate contributions and conveyance duties under approved school orders.

2. Each of the dissolved council's cases is transferred on 1st April to one of the respective council's successor authorities as defined in article 19 (1). Articles 1 to 5 transfer Middlesex County Council cases in categories (a) to (d) ; article 6 transfers London County Council cases in categories (a) to (e) in accordance with a scheme made under the article ; article 7 transfers county borough council cases in categories (a) to (e) ; articles 11 (1), and 12 (1) and (2), transfer all the dissolved councils' cases in categories (f) and (g).

Procedure for London County Council and Middlesex County Council cases

3. Article 14 lays a duty on the London County Council and the Middlesex County Council to notify each of their successor authorities of the cases that

fall to be transferred to them under the articles mentioned above. Each successor authority will have a duty, under article 15 (8), to take over, on 1st April, cases notified to them, but, under article 15 (1), if they consider, having regard to the relevant provisions of article 1 to 7, 11 or 12, that another successor authority should have been notified in any particular case, they may (while remaining responsible for the case) apply to the Secretary of State for that other authority to be substituted for them (this procedure does not apply to guardian *ad litem* appointments, which are normally only of short duration and may, in any event, be varied on application to a court) ; or, under article 15 (2), another successor authority may agree that the case should be transferable to them.

4. An application to the Secretary of State under article 15 (1), or an agreement under article 15 (2), must be made within two months of the notification by the London County Council or the Middlesex County Council.

5. Where a second authority are substituted for the first (i.e. notified) authority following application to the Secretary of State, or agree under article 15 (2), the second authority, under article 15 (3) have discretion until 31st March 1966 to take over the case, and, whether or not they exercise that discretion, they are liable for the expenses from 1st April 1965 of the first authority. If, while the case remains the responsibility of the first authority, the form of responsibilities change, the liability of the second authority to pay expenses is not affected, and their discretion is a discretion to take over the case in its changed form (article 15 (4)). The most likely examples are of a child going out of the care of the first authority, and becoming one in the category described in (b) of paragraph 1 of these notes, or a child in category (b) (i) having to be received back into the care under section 3 (4) of the Children Act, 1948.

II. COUNCILS OF THE ALTERED COUNTIES

6. Articles 8, 9, 10, 11 (2) and 12 (3) define those cases, within the categories described in (a), (b), (f) and (g) of paragraph 1 of these notes, for which the councils of the altered counties are responsible immediately before 1st April 1965, and which are transferable to those councils' successor authorities under the order. (Cases in categories (c) and (d) are not dealt with as it is considered unnecessary to make special provision for transfer otherwise than by application to a court ; cases in category (e) are not dealt with as they are so few in number and the responsibilities are of limited duration.)

7. Under the above-mentioned articles, it is for the council of each altered county to identify those cases which may be transferred under the order, and to decide which of them should be " offered " to their successor authorities ; the council must notify the selected cases to the appropriate successor authority before 1st June 1965.

8. The authority notified in any particular case have, under article 13 (1), discretion until 31st March 1966 to take over the case and, whether or not they exercise that discretion, are liable under article 13 (2) to pay any expenses incurred by the council of the altered county after 31st March 1965. The discretion of the notified authority to take over a case, and their liability to pay expenses, are not affected by any change in the form of the county council's responsibilities (see examples in paragraph 5 of these notes).

9. Where, having regard to the relevant provisions of articles 8 to 12, an authority notified in any particular case consider that another successor authority should have been notified, or that the case is not transferable under the order, they may, under article 15 (1), apply to the Secretary of State to determine accordingly ; or, under article 15 (2), another successor authority may agree that the case is transferable to them. An application to the Secretary of State, or an agreement, must be made within two months of the notification,

and before the notified authority have taken over the case. Where a second authority are substituted for the first (notified) authority by the Secretary of State, or by agreement, the discretion and liability of the first are transferred to the second (article 15 (5)).

III. GENERAL

10. *Section* 58 *of the Children and Young Persons Act,* 1963.—Under article 17, any successor authority may (subject to the agreement of the county council in altered county cases) exercise the powers of a former care authority under section 58 in respect of a person who had ceased to be in the care of a dissolved council, or the council of an altered county, before 1st April 1965.

11. *Sections* 19 *and* 20 *of the Children Act* 1948.—For the reasons mentioned in paragraph 10 of Appendix B to the Home Office letter of 10th February, no provision is made for the transfer of persons not in care who are being accommodated or assisted under section 19 or 20 of the 1948 Act, and such cases are left to be dealt with by agreement. Under article 11 (3), where a dissolved council are accommodating or assisting a person formerly in their care, and responsibility for the case is taken over by a new authority on 1st April, any right of the dissolved council to recover expenses from another authority under section 1 (4) of the 1948 Act is transferred to the new authority ; similar provision has not been considered necessary for altered county cases.

12. Articles 16 and 18 make general transitional provision relating to cases transferred under the order, so that the new authority are placed in the same position as the old as respects any transferred case. Among the matters dealt with is a resolution of the former authority under section 2 of the Children Act in any particular case ; such a resolution continues in force as though it had been passed by the new authority. Where the care of a child is transferred under the order, any right of the former authority under section 1 (4) of the 1948 Act to recover expenses from another authority is transferred with the case.

13. If the ordinary residence of a child has not been determined before his care is transferred under the order, and the new authority consider that he was ordinarily resident, at the time he was received into the care of the former authority, outside that authority's area (as constituted before 1st April), section 1 (4) applies in the normal way. Similar considerations apply to the right of appeal under section 90 of the Children and Young Persons Act (as modified by section 33 (2) of the Children and Young Persons Act, 1963) in the case of approved school orders.

14. No provision is made in respect of the matters referred to in paragraph 14 of appendix B of the Home Office letter of 10th February. All these matters relate to functions which are exercised by a local authority in respect of the authority's area, and it is considered that articles 12 (3) to (7) (county councils) and 16 (2) (county borough councils), with article 36, of the London Authorities (Property etc.) Order 1964, make adequate transitional provision.

15. On 1st April there will be persons on remand in remand homes or special reception centres, or in places of safety, in respect of whom the authority managing the establishment may wish to recover expenses after that date from another authority, viz. the authority of the area from which the person was removed. It is considered that financial adjustments of this kind can be made without any special provision being made in the order.

16. *No case is transferable under the order to an authority other than one taking over part of the existing responsible authority's area on 1st April.*

NOTE

This circular was sent to the Clerks of the County Councils of Essex, Hertfordshire, Kent, London, Middlesex and Surrey, and the Town Clerks of the London boroughs and the City of London ; and to local authority associations.

DIVISION 3
ADOPTION

ADOPTION

CONTENTS

SECTION 1.—INTRODUCTORY NOTE

The idea of the adoption of a child is quite modern in English juris-prudence. Before the passing of the Adoption of Children Act, 1926, the law of this country decreed that, not only were the rights, liabilities, and duties of the parents of legitimate children inalienable by any act of the parents themselves, but that those of the mothers of illegitimate children were similarly inalienable.

Two cases make this proposition abundantly clear. In that of *Brooks* v. *Blount*, [1923] 1 K. B. 257 ; 87 J. P. 64, the question arose as to the liability of the father of a legitimate child, separated by deed from his wife, to whom he had purported to transfer the custody of the child. " In my opinion," said Lord Hewart, C.J., " it is not possible for parents by their own act to get rid of this legal presumption," *i.e.* that the custody of the child remained with the father. " The person who has the custody of a child," added Salter, J. (*ibid*, p. 267), " cannot be heard to say that he has not the custody of the child, unless he is deprived of the custody by the order of a competent court."

In the case of *Humphrys* v. *Polak*, [1901] 2 K. B. 385; 70 L. J. K. B. 752, the defendants covenanted to maintain and bring up the plaintiff's illegitimate child, as though she were their own, and " for ever to relieve the plaintiff of all liability " towards the child. The defendants after having maintained the child for a month refused to continue to carry out the agreement, whereupon the mother brought an action for damages for breach of contract. It was held that such an action was not maintainable, for " the law does not permit such a trans-ference of the mother's rights and liabilities " (*per* Stirling, L.J., *ibid.*).

It will be seen, therefore, that for all persons who have already taken charge of a child, or who desire to do so, and who wish to secure complete control over such child, it is essential to take advantage of the provisions of the Adoption Act. If they fail to do this they are liable to have the child taken from them at any time by its parents.

The Roman law favoured the idea of adoption and made many elaborate provisions for carrying it out. The underlying idea of these provisions, however, was not the succour of children unwanted by their parents, but the strengthening of the family of the adopter. Thus not only was it legal to adopt children, as it now is in England, but also to adopt adults (Justinian Lib. 1, Tit. xi). Adoption in such cases was made use of for the purpose of handing on honours and estates to adopted children deemed more fitted to make good use of them than the natural children.

By Roman law it was necessary that the adopter should be at least eighteen years older than the person adopted. English law at first fixed the difference in age as twenty-one, subject to exceptions, but the Adop-tion Acts, 1958 to 1964, make no requirement as to difference of age.

The passing of the Adoption of Children Act, 1926, introduced a principle so entirely new, it is of the greatest importance that the consequences of this change should be fully realised and understood.

The motive that brought about this new legislation was not, as in Roman law, the strengthening of the family, or the giving of increased facilities for the bequest of property to persons of alien blood, but the idea of conferring the privileges of parents upon the childless and the advantages of having parents upon the parentless.   The relationship of parent and child is firmly secured to the benefit of both.

In certain instances children whose parents are unable, or unwilling, for some reason to fulfil their duties can, through an adoption order, become part of the family of adoptive parents.   While enormous sums of money have been, and are being, spent in this country upon the provision of orphanages and children's homes, comparatively few people choose to take upon themselves the responsibility of maintaining in their own homes orphan and destitute children.   The principal reason for this is obvious.   Until the passing of the Adoption of Children Act kind-hearted people might accept a child of the tenderest years, bring it up exactly as their own, spend considerable sums upon its education, and lavish their best affections upon it, and yet, at any moment, or at any age up to sixteen, the natural parents retained the legal right to come and remove the child and prevent those who had hitherto maintained him from ever seeing him again.   There was, it is true, some measure of protection for the child and the foster parents in s. 3 of the Custody of Children Act, 1891, p. 1213, *post.* Even when the natural parents had no real desire to recover the child they might demand money from the actual guardians, who might well be willing to pay rather than part with a child whom they had grown to love.

It is not to be wondered at that people, however anxious to take charge of a child, should hesitate to incur such risks from which the most carefully drawn legal document could not protect them.

From the point of view of the child the position was almost equally unfortunate.   The prospect of a happy home, with parents to love and protect him, was denied, and he was sent instead to be brought up by a Board of Guardians, or to grow up in an orphanage.   It is a truism to say that home surroundings are infinitely better for the rearing of children than the life that the very best of institutions can provide.   Legal adoption provides security for the adopter and the adopted alike.

Many applications under the Act are made to a juvenile court, and since this book is intended primarily for those who are concerned in the work of the juvenile courts, it has been thought well to deal with the subject with special attention in relation to those courts.   An attempt has been made to deal with difficulties that have arisen in practice, and to suggest what may be the true view of the law.

The Adoption of Children (Regulation) Act, 1939, was passed for the purpose of regulating the transactions of adoption societies and persons undertaking the arrangement of adoptions, of securing supervision of certain adopted children by welfare authorities, of restricting the sending of children abroad for the purpose of adoption, and of amending the Adoption of Children Act, 1926.

The Adoption of Children Act, 1949, made a number of important changes in the law, and the Rules which were made in consequence made equally important changes in procedure.   The statutes were consolidated, with minor amendments, in the Adoption Act, 1950, which repealed almost entirely the earlier statutes, and consolidation and amendment again took place in 1958.   The law can now usually be ascertained by reference to the Adoption Acts 1958 to 1964.

In the light of experience, and no doubt also in response to representations made by social workers and societies, the facilities for adoption have been somewhat enlarged, the necessity that the infant should be a British subject has been removed, and the supervision by welfare authorities of children in respect of whom arrangements for adoption are being made has been extended.   Further, consent to a proposed adoption may be given without disclosure of the name of the proposed adopter, and in the actual proceedings in such cases the applicant and the parent will not meet.   Individual respondents are not, as a general rule, to be required to attend the hearing, but will be notified of the result.   These arrangements are undoubtedly appreciated by adopters who fear that the natural parent may prove a source of trouble in later years.   The Rules, however, contemplate that difficulties may arise as to proving the identity of the infant in the absence of the mother, who is the best and sometimes the only witness able to prove it, and by the Act of 1958 and the Rules of 1959 evidence of identity may be given by affidavit.

Opportunity was also taken, in the Act of 1949, to enact that where the actual date of birth of the infant is not known the court is to determine the probable date and to insert it in the order as if it were the actual date.   Existing orders can be amended in this and other respects, so that the Adopted Children Register will not give any clue to the fact that a child was a foundling or refugee.   In fact, everything possible has been done to place an adopted child in the same position as a child born to the adopters, even to the extent of succession to property.

The Adoption Act, 1958 made important changes in the law and these are summarised below.   The references are to the sections of that Act, and to the Rules made under or by virtue of s. 9, *ibid.*

It is no longer necessary for an applicant who is not the mother or father or a relative of the infant to be at least 21 years older than the infant (s. 2).

No period before an infant is six weeks old counts towards the minimum period of three months during which the infant must live with the applicant under supervision.   Notice to the local authority need not be given if the applicant, or one of joint applicants, is a parent of the infant or if the infant is over compulsory school age.

The consent of a person or body liable to maintain the infant is no longer required (s. 4), but the person or body must be notified of the hearing and made a respondent (Rules).

The words relating to religious persuasion in s. 4 (2) are altered.

The consent of a parent or guardian can be dispensed with expressly on the ground that the person has persistently failed without reasonable cause to discharge his obligations (s. 5).

The written consent of a parent or guardian can be attested by certain officers as well as by justices of the peace (s. 6).   These include duly authorised county court officers and justices' clerks (Rules).

Unless the applicant, or one of joint applicants, is the father or mother of the infant or the infant is over compulsory school age a medical certificate as to the health of the applicant is required (s. 7 and Rules).

A " body " can no longer be appointed guardian *ad litem* (s. 9).   The Rules prescribe the persons who may be appointed, and provide that the

Director of Social Services of a local authority can be appointed only with the consent of the authority.

There is now a right of appeal to the High Court from a decision of a magistrates' court to grant or refuse an adoption order (s. 10). The Rules of the Supreme Court have been amended by the insertion of a new Rule which provides that such an appeal shall lie to a single judge of the Family Division.

An applicant not ordinarily resident in Great Britain can now apply to the High Court or the county court (but not to a juvenile court) for an adoption order (s. 12).

The provision that an affiliation order in respect of an infant, who is adopted by his mother when a single woman shall cease if she subsequently marries is not re-enacted (see s. 15).

After an adoption order has been made in respect of an illegitimate infant no affiliation order can be made unless the adoption order was made on the application of the mother of the infant alone (s. 15 (2)).

An adopted child will be deemed to be the child of the adopter for the purposes of a will of a person dying after the date of the adoption even if the will was made before that date, unless the contrary intention appears (ss. 16 and 17).

The courts are given additional powers to amend adoption orders (s. 24), and to revoke an adoption order where the person adopted by his father or mother alone becomes a legitimated person on the marriage of his father and mother (s. 26).

Local authorities have now power to make and participate in arrangements for the adoption of children whether or not the child is in the care of the authority (s. 28). The Adoption Agencies Regulations, 1959 (p. 1100, *post*), revoke and replace the Adoption Societies Regulations, and relate to local authorities as well as to adoption societies.

New provisions are made for dealing with offences in respect of making arrangements for adoption, and for proceedings to be taken against individuals (s. 29).

Where an application has been made for adoption, an adoption society or a local authority that has placed the infant with a view to adoption may not remove the infant except with the leave of the court. New provisions are made with regard to the return of the infant by the applicant (s. 35). That section applies, with modifications, where the child is in the care of the local authority, and is placed with someone but not with a view to adoption (s. 36). In such cases parental contributions cease to be payable, and there is a modification as to the provisions in respect of the payment of family allowance (s. 36 (2)).

Part IV of the Act replaces Part III of the 1950 Act. The words " Protected child " are applied to children to whom Part IV applies. Provision is made for their supervision, etc., by ss. 38 to 49. Amendments have been made by the Children and Young Persons Act, 1969, to secure that the Adoption Act applies to all children who are placed with a view to adoption and only such children.

A local authority may prohibit a person from taking over the care and possession of a child if it considers that it would be detrimental to the child to be kept by that person in certain premises, but not if a registered adoption society or another local authority took part in the arrangement (s. 41).

The system of granting licences to send children abroad for adoption is replaced partly by s. 12, which enables adoption orders to be made where the applicant is not ordinarily resident in Great Britain, and partly by s. 53 which permits the High Court or a county court but not a juvenile court to make provisional adoption orders upon the application of persons not domiciled in England or Scotland.

The forms of application for an adoption order prescribed by the Rules recommend applicants to provide a medical certificate as to the health of the infant unless one of the applicants is the mother or father of the infant, or the infant is over compulsory school age.

A juvenile court is no longer absolutely precluded from entertaining an application where the applicant has previously applied to the High Court or a county court to adopt the infant, but there must be a substantial change in the circumstances (Rule 6).

The duties of the guardian *ad litem* have been altered and extended. Provision is made for interim reports. It is no longer the duty of the guardian *ad litem* to serve notices. In a juvenile court any fact tending to establish the identity of an infant with an infant to whom a document relates may be proved by affidavit, and where this is done the power of the court to require the attendance of the witness is restricted. The court is empowered to fix a date for a further hearing when an interim order is made. The court is required to serve notices of the hearing, or further hearings, and of the orders made.

An abridged copy of the adoption order must be sent to the applicant and he is entitled to a full copy if he requires one. A justices' clerk is required to notify the court which made an affiliation order which is still in force, where an adoption order is made in respect of an illegitimate infant in favour of an applicant who is not his mother and a single woman. New forms are prescribed, including a new form of Register. Notices may be served personally or by post, not necessarily by registered post. No provision is made for service by leaving the document with some person other than the individual for him at his last known or usual place of abode. The guardian *ad litem* must be served with a copy of any notice (Rules.).

The Adoption Act, 1960 made provision for the revocation of an adoption order in respect of a person legitimated and adopted by his father and mother before the commencement of that Act on 29th July, 1960.

The Adoption Act, 1964 provided for effect to be given to adoption orders made in Northern Ireland, the Isle of Man or the Channel Islands, and for extracts from adoption registers to be received as evidence in different parts of the United Kingdom. The Adoption Act, 1968, has not yet been brought into operation; it follows the Hague Convention on the adoption of children, 1965 (Cmnd. 2613). The Act confers additional powers to make orders on the High Court or Court of Session in respect of "qualified" applicants (s. 11); the basis is responsibility and residence. The effect of such an order is the same as that of an order under the Act of 1958 (s. 2). The Secretary of State will be able to specify that foreign adoption orders shall have the same effect as an English order for certain purposes (s. 4). English courts will normally have to recognise the determination of the appropriate authority in a convention country, although in certain cases these may be annulled by the English courts (s. 6).

The problems created by the conflicting rights of natural and foster parents have led to the House of Lords in *Re W.*, [1971] A. C. 682; [1971] 2 All E. R. 49, laying down what many have regarded as a "welfare test" in determining whether a parent's consent may be dispensed with on the ground that it is being unreasonably withheld. However, this is an over-statement, and particular attention must be paid to the judgment which has far reaching complications for social workers as well as lawyers. The judgment is important also when one considers the recommendations of the Houghton Committee in the working paper "Adoption of Children" (H.M.S.O. 1970). Apart from the recommendations that the welfare of the child should be the first and prominent consideration, in applications to dispense with parental consent comprehensive charges are envisaged— the creation of a nationally available adoption service as an integral part of a comprehensive social work service; the extension of existing rights to apply for custody under the Guardianship of Minors Act to be made available to relations and foster parents; and a "consent hearing" so that a child can be considered legally free and eligible for adoption.

ADOPTION OF CHILDREN ACT, 1926
[16 & 17 Geo. 5, c. 29]
Unrepealed provisions

5. Effect of an adoption order.—(3) Where an adopted child or the spouse or issue of an adopted child takes any interest in real or personal property under a disposition by the adopter, or where an adopter takes any interest in real or personal property under a disposition by an adopted child or the spouse or issue of an adopted child, any duty which becomes leviable in respect thereof shall be payable at the same rate as if the adopted child had been a child born to the adopter in lawful wedlock.

(4) For the purposes of this section " disposition " means an assurance of any interest in property by any instrument whether *inter vivos* or by will including codicil.

NOTE
This section is printed as amended by the Finance Act, 1949.

" **Child.**"—For a decision in respect of a will made in 1947 to which the Adoption of Children Act, 1926, s. 5 (2) (now repealed) applied that by reason of the contrary intention appearing the expression " child " included an adopted child, see *Re Jebb (deceased) Ward-Smith* v. *Jebb*, [1965] 3 All E. R. 358.

ADOPTION OF CHILDREN ACT, 1949
[12, 13 & 14 Geo. 6, c. 98]
Unrepealed provisions

13. Definition of " relative."—(1) For the purposes of this Act, the expression " relative ", in relation to an infant, means a grandparent, brother, sister, uncle or aunt, whether of the full blood, of the half-blood or by affinity, and includes—

(a) where an adoption order has been made in respect of the infant or any other person, any person who would be a relative of the infant within the meaning of this definition if the adopted person were the child of the adopter born in lawful wedlock;

(b) where the infant is illegitimate, the father of the infant and any person who would be a relative of the infant within the meaning of this definition if the infant were the legitimate child of its mother and father.

(2) The definition contained in the last foregoing subsection shall be substituted for the definition of " relative " in the following enactments, that is to say, subsection (1) of section fifty-nine of the Children Act, 1948, and subsection (2) of section thirteen of the Nurseries and Child-Minders Regulation Act, 1948.

NOTE
This section is printed as amended by the Adoption Act, 1950, and the Adoption Act, 1958.

SECTION 3.—ADOPTION ACTS, 1958 to 1964

ADOPTION ACT, 1958

[7 Eliz. 2, c. 5]

ARRANGEMENT OF SECTIONS

PART I

ADOPTION ORDERS

Making of adoption orders

An Act to consolidate the enactments relating to the adoption of children.

[*18th December*, 1958]

NOTE

Local authorities.—The council of each London borough shall as respects the borough, and the Common Council shall as respects the City have the functions of the council of a county borough under this Act and be the local authority for such purposes of this Act as refer to a local authority (London Government Act, 1963, s. 47; 20 Halsbury's Statutes, 3rd Edn., 504).

PART I

ADOPTION ORDERS

Making of adoption orders

1. Power to make adoption orders.—(1) Subject to the provisions of this Act, the court may, upon an application made in the prescribed manner by a person domiciled in England or Scotland, make an order (in this Act referred to as an adoption order) authorising the applicant to adopt an infant.

(2) An adoption order may be made on the application of two spouses authorising them jointly to adopt an infant; but an adoption order shall not in any other case be made authorising more than one person to adopt an infant.

(3) An adoption order may be made authorising the adoption of an infant by the mother or father of the infant, either alone or jointly with her or his spouse.

(4) An adoption order may be made in respect of an infant who has already been the subject of an adoption order under this Act or the Adoption Act, 1950, or any enactment repealed by that Act, and in relation to an application for an adoption order in respect of such an infant, the adopter or adopters under the previous or last previous adoption order shall be deemed to be the parent or parents of the infant for all the purposes of this Act.

(5) An adoption order shall not be made in England unless the applicant and the infant reside in England and shall not be made in Scotland unless the applicant and the infant reside in Scotland, subject however to section twelve of this Act.

NOTES

Application.—Subject to the Adoption (Juvenile Court) Rules, 1959, the Magistrates' Courts Act, 1952, and Rules apply as if the application were a complaint, as if the respondents were defendants, and as if any notice served were a summons, but a warrant of arrest may not be issued for failure to appear in answer to such a notice. See Rule 33, *ibid.*, p. 1115, *post.* Where a previous application has been dismissed, see Rule 6, *ibid.*, p. 1109, *post.* " Application " is defined in Rule 37.

British Nationality.—See note to s. 19, *post.*

Health of infant.—The forms of application prescribed by the Rules require the applicants to attach to them a report as to the health of the infant.

" Prescribed."—See ss. 9 and 57 (1), *post*, and Rules, pp. 1109 *et seq.*, *post.*

" Domiciled in England or Scotland."—For the law relating to domicile, see 7 Halsbury's Laws (3rd Edn.) 14 *et seq.*

Domicile is largely a question of intention, and a man's domicile may be either his permanent home or the place he intends to make his home.   Many Englishmen earning their living in other parts of the Empire are domiciled in England, to which country they intend to return, and in which they wish to make their homes; though they may be resident abroad for the time being their families and their real home may be in England.

A person on leave in England from abroad may possibly be resident in England, but this would depend on the particular facts of the case.   It may be thought undesirable to make an adoption order under which a child who is a British subject would be taken abroad by foreigners.   The child might even, according to foreign law, acquire a foreign nationality.   See an article at 101 J. P. N. 211.

A married woman takes her husband's domicile.   A man may retain his domicile of choice even after he has been recommended for deportation (*Cruh* v. *Cruh*, [1945] 2 All E. R. 545).

In *Garthwaite* v. *Garthwaite*, [1964] P. 370; [1964] 2 All E. R. 233 it was held *per curiam* that a person can have only one domicile at any time.

Domiciled outside Great Britain.—See note to s. 12, p. 1046, *post*.

"England."—This includes Wales, see s. 57 (1), *post*.

"Adoption order."—An interim order under s. 8, *post*, is not an adoption order within the meaning of the Act; see s. 8 (5), *post*.   The provisions of the Act apply, with certain exceptions, to provisional adoption orders made under s. 53, *post*; see s. 53 (4), *post*.

" Infant."—An adoption order cannot be made after the person to be adopted has attained majority or is or has been married; see s. 57 (1), *post*.   A person ceases to be an infant at the commencement of the relevant anniversary of the date of his birth (s. 9, Family Law Reform Act, 1969).

Infant the subject of High Court Order as to custody.—Where the application is in respect of an infant who has been the subject of an order as to custody in divorce proceedings, it is not necessary to take proceedings to set aside the order of custody, and a county court or a juvenile court may entertain the application for an adoption order in the ordinary way (*Crossley* v. *Crossley*, [1953] 1 All E. R. 891; 117 J. P. 216).

Jewish adoptive parents.—Copies of a letter from the President of the Board of Deputies of British Jews to the secretary of the Association of Municipal Corporations were sent to Town Clerks, with a copy for the Children's Officer.   The letter is reproduced at p. 1176, *post*, with the permission of both those officers, and a knowledgment is made to them for this permission.

Joint adoption.—Except in the case of husband and wife, orders can only be made in the name of one person (see s. 1 (2)).   A corporation, *e.g.*, a charitable society, cannot apparently adopt a child.   The Act throughout seems clearly to indicate adoption by real persons.

In a case where an adoption order had been made on the application of two spouses whose marriage was subsequently found to be bigamous, the Court of Appeal held that the order was valid until set aside by a competent court, to the extent that an order made under the Guardianship of Infants Acts, based on the validity of the adoption order would be upheld: *Skinner* v. *Carter*, [1948] Ch. 387; [1948] 1 All E. R. 917.

Mother of the infant.—An order may be made under sub-s. (3) authorising an unmarried mother to adopt her illegitimate child (*Re D. (an Infant)*, [1958] 3 All E. R. 716; 123 J. P. 112, and in *Re U. (an Infant)*, Times, January 24, 1958).

"Previously adopted."—See s. 10 (3) Adoption Act, 1968, p. 1096, *post*. The power to make a second order may prove useful where an adoption order has not proved a success and the adopters wish to part with the child.   It has even happened that the real parents would like to have the child back, and with the consent of the adopters the real parents have adopted their own child under the second adoption order.

No right of appeal to the Crown Court against an adoption order made by a juvenile court is conferred by the statute.   Appeal lies to the Family Division of the High Court; see s. 10, p. 1045, *post*.

" Parent."—This word is not defined for the purpose of the Act, but *prima facie* it means the legitimate father or mother of the infant, and does not include the natural or putative father of an illegitimate child; see *Butler* v. *Gregory* (1902), 18 T. L. R. 370, and *Re M. (an Infant)*, [1955] 2 All E. R. 911 ; [1955] 2 Q. B. 479.   A resolution under s. 2 (1) of the Children Act, 1948, p. 884, *ante*, ceases to have effect on the making of an adoption order under this Act ; see s. 15 (4), *post*.

" **Reside.**"—Residence denotes some degree of permanency; see notes at p. 162, *ante*.

A person resides where, in common parlance, he lives, and a temporary absence is immaterial provided there is an intention to return; see *R.* v. *St. Leonard, Shoreditch (Inhabitants)* (1865), L. R. 1 Q. B. 21 ; *R.* v. *Glossop Union* (1866), L. R. 1 Q. B. 227 ; and *cf. Levene* v. *Inland Revenue Comrs.*, [1928] A. C. 217, at pp. 222, 223, *per* Viscount Cave ; and *Inland Revenue Comrs.* v. *Lysaght*, [1928] All E. R. Rep. 575 ; [1928] A. C. 234.   An application to adopt was made by applicants who lived in Nigeria but returned to England for periods of three months' leave every fifteen months.   Harman, J., did not accept the submission that they were resident here for the time being whilst on leave and held there was no jurisdiction to make an adoption order.   Residence denotes some degree of permanence, it does not necessarily mean that the applicant has a home of his own, but that he has a settled headquarters in this country (*Re Adoption Application* 52/1951, [1951] 2 All E. R. 931 ; 115 J. P. 625).

As to applicants not ordinarily resident in Great Britain, see now s. 12, *post*.

Venue in magistrates' courts.—Application is to be made to the juvenile court for the petty sessions area in which the applicant or the infant resides at the date of the application.   See Rule 1 of the Adoption (Juvenile Court) Rules, 1959, p. 1109, *post*.

Confidential.—If the applicant desires that his identity be kept confidential, he may, before making the application apply for a serial number to be assigned to him for the purposes of the application, and the proceedings must be conducted with a view to the applicant not being seen by, or made known to, any respondent who is not already aware of his identity, without his consent.   See Rules 3 and 18 of the Adoption (High Court) Rules, 1971, pp. 1156, 1159, *post*; Rules 2 and 14 of the Adoption (County Court) Rules, 1959, pp. 1128, 1131, *post*, and Rules 2 and 15 of the Adoption (Juvenile Court) Rules, 1959, pp. 1109, 1112, *post*.

High Court.—A juvenile court may, at any stage of the proceedings, refuse to proceed on the ground expressly that owing to special circumstances the application appears to the court more fit to be dealt with by the High Court.   See Rule 7 of the Adoption (Juvenile Court) Rules, 1959, p. 1110, *post*.   Proceedings in the High Court are assigned to the Family Division (Administration of Justice Act, 1970, s. 1 and Sched. I).

Definitions.—For " court ", " England ", " infant " and " father ", see s. 57 (1), p. 1080, *post*.

Adoption Act, 1950.—That Act is repealed by s. 59 (2) and Sched. VI of this Act.   The enactments repealed by that Act are specified in Sched. IV, *ibid*.

Infant domiciled abroad.—The High Court has jurisdiction to make an adoption order in respect of an infant domiciled abroad, and such an order will have in England its full operation under the Adoption Act, 1958 (*Re B. (S.) (an infant)*, [1968] 1 Ch. 204; [1967] 3 All E. R. 629).

2. Age and sex of applicant.—(1) Subject to subsection (2) of this section, an adoption order shall not be made in respect of an infant unless the applicant—

    (a) is the mother or father of the infant;

    (b) is a relative of the infant, and has attained the age of twenty-one years; or

    (c) has attained the age of twenty-five years.

(2) An adoption order may be made in respect of an infant on the joint application of two spouses—

    (a) if either of the applicants is the mother or father of the infant; or

(b) if the condition set out in paragraph (b) or paragraph (c) of sub-section (1) of this section is satisfied in the case of one of the applicants, and the other of them has attained the age of twenty-one years.

(3) An adoption order shall not be made in respect of an infant who is a female in favour of a sole applicant who is a male, unless the court is satisfied that there are special circumstances which justify as an exceptional measure the making of an adoption order.

NOTES

" **Mother or father of the infant.**"—See s. 1 (3), *ante*. The word " father " includes the putative father; see s. 57, p. 1080, *post*.

Evidence relating to illegitimacy.—As to the position of an illegitimate child born during the subsistence of a marriage, see s. 43 of the Matrimonial Causes Act, 1965 (17 Halsbury's Statutes, 3rd Edn., 218), which permits evidence to be given by husband or wife as to marital intercourse. The husband or wife is now a compellable witness in respect of such matters, except in relation to criminal proceedings (Civil Evidence Act, 1968, s. 16 (4)).

As to rebuttal of presumption of legitimacy see s. 26 Family Law Reform Act, 1969, p. 1317.

Age of adopter.—The former provision that in certain circumstances the adopter must be at least 21 years older than the infant is not reproduced.

" **Attained the age.**"—See note at p. 53, *ante*.

" **Joint application of two spouses.**"—See s. 1 (2), (3), *ante*. If one applicant is the mother or father the question of age of either spouse does not arise. If one spouse is a relative and at least twenty-one the other spouse must be at least twenty-one. If neither is a relative and one is at least twenty-five the other must be at least twenty-one.

Adoption by natural grandparents.—In *Re D. X.*, [1949] Ch. 320; *sub nom. Re A. B.*, [1949] 1 All E. R. 709, Vaisey, J., made an order in favour of grandparents where the infant was the illegitimate child of their own daughter and made observations as to the need for caution is such cases.

" **Special circumstances.**"—The fact that the applicant is the putative father is not alone sufficient to justify the making of an order under sub-s. (3); see *Re R. M. (an Infant)*, [1941] W. N. 244, C. A. In view of the decision of the Divisional Court in the case of *R. v. City of Liverpool Justices*, [1959] 1 All E. R. 337; 123 J. P. 152, it may be considered advisable to include in the adoption order a statement that the court had found special circumstances and what they were. It is suggested that a near degree of relationship might also be a proper ground for finding special circumstances. Another ground might be the death of the wife where the infant has been living with the husband and wife in suitable circumstances.

See *H., Petitioner*, [1960] S. L. T. Sh. Ct. Rep. 3 (February 6, 1960) Sheriff Ct., where an adoption order was made in respect of a female infant aged one month in favour of a sole male applicant living with his late wife's mother, his wife having died before the application was heard.

Definitions.—For "adoption order ", see s. 1 (1), *ante*, and s. 57 (1), *post*, in conjunction with s. 53 (4), *post*; and for " father ", " relative " and " court ", see s. 57 (1), *post*.

3. Care and possession of infants before adoption, and notification of local authority.—(1) An adoption order shall not be made in respect of any infant unless he has been continuously in the care and possession of the applicant for at least three consecutive months immediately

preceding the date of the order, not counting any time before the date which appears to the court to be the date on which the infant attained the age of six weeks.

(2) Except where the applicant or one of the applicants is a parent of the infant, an adoption order shall not be made in respect of an infant who at the hearing of the application is below the upper limit of the compulsory school age unless the applicant has, at least three months before the date of the order, given notice in writing to the local authority within whose area he was then resident of his intention to apply for an adoption order in respect of the infant.

NOTES

"**Continuously in the care and possession.**"—This, it is suggested, means the kind of care and possession usually exercised by a parent. Thus, if the infant were at boarding school, and never at home continuously for three months, but being cared for by the applicants as if he were their child, spending his holidays with them, it would seem unreasonable to hold that they could not apply for an adoption order. *Cf.* Children and Young Persons Act, 1933, s. 17, p. 28, *ante.*

In the Scottish case of *A., Petitioners*, 1953, S. L. T. (Sh. Ct.) 45, the infant then aged eighteen had been in the custody of the petitioners since she was a few weeks old, but for over two years had been away from home as a probationer nurse, returning only for week-ends and holidays. It was held that she had been continuously in the care and possession of the petitioners. See also *G., Petitioner*, 1955, S. L. T. (Sh. Ct.) 27.

In *Re C. S. C. (an Infant)*, [1960] 1 All E. R. 711; 124 J. P. 260, where the applicants had during the three months allowed the mother to have the child for three nights (two consecutive nights and another night) Roxburgh, J., held that on the facts of this case the child could not be said to have been continuously in the care and possession of the applicants.

In the case of *Re B. (G.A.) (An Infant)*, [1964] Ch. 1; [1963] 3 All E. R. 125; 127 J. P. 492, the infant was with the applicant, a nurse, on an average for three days and two nights in each week whilst she was off duty, and also throughout her holidays. He spent the remainder of his time with a married couple, whom the applicant paid for their services. It was held that the applicant, during the relevant period, had been in effective and parental control of the child's life, for, although the married couple had physical care and control of the child while the applicant was on duty, they were acting on her behalf, under her directions and in accordance with her wishes in the manner of a privately employed children's nurse; accordingly the child had been " continuously in the care and possession of the applicant " as required by this section.

See also the note " One of the three months ", to s. 12, p. 1046, *post.*

"**Parent.**"—See s. 1 (4), *ante*, and the note to that section.

"**Notice.**"—This may be given by post; see s. 55, *post.* As to notice under the subsection in respect of an infant in the care of a local authority, see s. 36, *post*, and as to protected children, see s. 37, *post.* Notice is not required under this section if the infant is above compulsory school age at the hearing of the application or if the applicant or one of joint applicants is a parent of the infant.

Provisional order.—In relation to a provisional adoption order under s. 53, *post*, this section has effect as modified in accordance with s. 53 (5), *post.*

Applicant not ordinarily resident in Great Britain.—For modifications to this section where an applicant is not ordinarily resident in Great Britain; see s. 12 (1), (3), (4), *post.*

In the case of *Re W. (An Infant)*, [1962] Ch. 918; [1962] 2 All E. R. 875; 126 J. P. 445, it was held that the prior care and possession need not, if the applicants are not ordinarily resident in Great Britain be care and possession in England or Scotland. It was stated that s. 12 (3) p. 665, *post*, provides an alternative to s. 3 (1), and need not be called in aid if s. 3 (1) is satisfied without so doing.

Definitions.—For " adoption order ", see s. 1 (1), *ante*, and s. 57 (1), *post*, in conjunction with s. 53 (4), *post*; for " infant ", " court " and " compulsory school age ", see s. 57 (1), *post*, and p. 190, *ante*; and for " local authority ", see s. 28 (1), *post*.

4. Consents.—(1) Subject to section five of this Act, an adoption order shall not be made—

    (a) in any case, except with the consent of every person who is a parent or guardian of the infant;

    (b) on the application of one of two spouses, except with the consent of the other spouse;

and shall not be made in Scotland in respect of an infant who is a minor except with the consent of the infant.

(2) The consent of any person to the making of an adoption order in pursuance of an application (not being the consent of the infant) may be given (either unconditionally or subject to conditions with respect to the religious persuasion in which the infant is proposed to be brought up) without knowing the identity of the applicant for the order.

(3) The reference in paragraph (a) of subsection (1) of this section to a parent of an infant does not include a reference to any person having the rights and powers of a parent of the infant by virtue of any of the following enactments, that is to say—

    (a) section 24 of the Children and Young Persons Act, 1969 (which relates to the powers and duties of local authorities with respect to persons committed to their care in pursuance of that Act);

    (b) [*Repealed by the Social Work (Scotland) Act,* 1968.]

    (c) section three of the Children Act, 1948 (which applies to children in respect of whom the local authority have assumed parental rights by resolution under section two of that Act);

    (d) section seventeen of the Social Work (Scotland) Act, 1968 (which makes corresponding provision for Scotland).

NOTES

This section is printed as amended by the Social Work (Scotland) Act, 1968, ss. 95, 97, 98, and Scheds. VIII and IX, and the Children and Young Persons Act, 1969, s. 72 (3) and Sched. V.

" **Consent.**"—Consent may be in writing and must be operative at the time when the order is made, but may be withdrawn until the time when the order is made (*Re Hollyman*, [1945] 1 All E. R. 290; 109 J. P. 95, C. A.; *Re F. (an Infant)*, [1957] 1 All E. R. 819; 121 J. P. 270), and it must be freely and voluntarily given (*Re P. (an Infant)* (1954), 118 J. P. 139, C. A.). The consent of a natural father is not required; see note " Parent ", p. 1027, *ante*.

For provisions as to evidence of consent, see s. 6, *post*. Consent may be dispensed with in accordance with s. 5, *infra*.

All such consents as are required to an adoption order are necessary to an interim order; see s. 8 (2), *post*.

Payments or rewards in consideration of the grant of any requisite consent are restricted by s. 50, *post*.

The consent is no longer required of any person who is liable by virtue of an order or agreement to contribute to the maintenance of the infant. Notice of the hearing of the application must be served on any such person; Rule 17 and form 7 Adoption (High Court) Rules, 1971; Rule 10 and form 2, Adoption (County Court) Rules, 1959; Rule 12 and form 6, Adoption (Juvenile Court) Rules, 1959.

In the case of *Re E. (an Infant)*, [1963] 3 All E. R. 874 an application by proposed adopters who were not Roman Catholics was refused on the ground that the consent of the mother of the infant could not be dispensed with, she having withdrawn her consent because she wished the infant to be brought up by a Roman Catholic family. The Court of Appeal refused leave to appeal. On an application by the applicants asking that the infant be made a ward of court and that its care and control be committed to them the wardship was continued and the care and control was given to the applicants on their undertaking that the infant should be brought up in the Roman Catholic faith. It was held that in wardship proceedings the paramount consideration was the welfare of the infant, and in considering this the element of religious upbringing was of great importance and the wishes of the mother of an illegitimate child must be very seriously regarded by the court, but the court was not bound to give effect to them if satisfied that the infant's welfare required otherwise.

For forms of consent, see Forms 3, 5 and 4 respectively.

"Parent."—See s. 1 (4), *ante*, and the note to that section. See also the note " Evidence relating to illegitimacy " to s. 2, p. 1029, *ante*.

Definitions.—For " adoption order ", see s. 1 (1), *ante*, and s. 57 (1), *post*, in conjunction with s. 53 (4), *post*; and for " guardian " and " infant ", see s. 57 (1), *post*.

Children and Young Persons Act, 1969, s. 24.—See p. 167, *ante*.

Children Act, 1948, s. 3.—See p. 887, *ante*.

Putative father.—In an interlocutory appeal, for an adoption order in respect of an illegitimate infant, against the decision of Wilberforce, J., dated May, 29, 1962 (reported [1962] 2 All E. R. 833 ; 126 J.P. 403), adjourning the application generally to give the putative father of the infant, who had applied to a magistrates' court for custody of the infant, the opportunity, which he took before the hearing of the appeal, to bring custody proceedings in the High Court, it was held (Diplock, L.J., dissenting) : the court would not interfere with the order made at first instance, but, as the Legitimacy Act, 1959, s. 3, had given a putative father the right to apply for custody of his illegitimate child, would continue the adjournment of the application for adoption, so that the putative father's application for custody of the infant could be brought on for hearing on the same occasion. Decision of Wilberforce, J., affirmed, but not as regards any recognition of pre-eminence of the rights of a putative father.

Although s. 3 (1) of the Legitimacy Act, 1959, does not confer directly on a putative father any rights in relation to adoption, as distinct from custody proceedings, if, indeed, it confers any rights at all, yet in adoption proceedings the welfare of the infant is a paramount consideration and in custody proceedings (to which s. 3 (1) of the Legitimacy Act, 1959, does relate) it is the paramount consideration, the desire of a parent to have the child being subordinate to that paramount consideration ; accordingly in relation to the custody of infants the position of a parent or parents is not pre-eminent, nor are their rights, to 'custody exclusive. *Re Adoption Application No. 41/61*, [1963] Ch. 315 ; [1962] 3 All E. R. 553 ; 126 J.P. 511.

In May 1963, the adoption application was heard in the Chancery Division, together with the putative father's application for the custody of the infant.

It was held that, although under the Adoption Act, 1958, the consent of the putative father was not required for the making of an adoption order, yet both under that Act (s. 7 (1) (b)) and under the Guardianship of Infants Acts (under which the putative father was applying for custody) the welfare of the infant was the guiding consideration ; in the present case the proposals of the mother were more for the welfare of the child than the putative father's proposals, and an adoption order would be made.

Per curiam (i) under para. 9 of Sched. 2 to the Adoption (High Court) Rules, 1959 (now the 1971 Rules), the guardian *ad litem* of an illegitimate child in respect of whom adoption proceedings are pending is not under obligation to seek out the putative father, but if it comes to the guardian's notice that the putative father wishes to be heard by the court on the question whether the adoption order should be made, the guardian should inform the court so that the court may consider whether notice of the hearing should be served on him under the Rules.

(ii) in directing that the adoption proceedings in the present case should be stood over until the putative father had issued a summons for custody the court was merely recognising that he had already taken this step in a magistrates' court, but ordinarily there would be no reason why a putative father should not put his case in adoption proceedings under the rules. *Re Adoption Application No.* 41/61 *(No.* 2), [1964] Ch. 48 ; [1963] 2 All E. R. 1082 ; 127 J.P. 440.

In *Re O. (an Infant)*, [1965] Ch. 23 ; [1964] 1 All E. R. 786, it was held : (i) on the true construction of s. 3 of the Legitimacy Act, 1959, a putative father was not placed in the same position as a legitimate father, although the section gave the putative father *locus standi* to apply for custody of the illegitimate child ; on such an application the fatherhood was a ground to which regard should be had in determining what course was best for the child's welfare, but the fatherhood was not an overriding consideration ; (ii) the better course, where one application is made for custody and another application is made for adoption, is to defer decision on either until both have been heard. The first *dictum* on this case was approved in the case of *Re C. (A.) (an infant)*, C. v. C., [1970] 1 All E. R. 309 where it was held that there is no "principle" in custody cases that a boy of eight should, other things being equal, be with his father, and *cf. W.* v. *W. and C.*, [1968] 3 All E. R. 408.

See also *Re M. (an Infant) (No.* 2), (1964), 108 Sol. Jo. 1031, where the Court of Appeal approved the course indicated in (ii) *supra.*

In the case of In *Re C. (M.A.) (an Infant)*, [1966] 1 All E. R. 838 ; 130 J. P. 217, the putative father applied for custody of the infant in respect of whom an application had been made to adopt, in the county court. The county court proceedings were stayed, and the applicants applied in the High Court for an adoption order. Both applications were heard together and the trial judge said that he found himself compelled to the conclusion that it was best for the boy to be brought up in his father's home. He awarded custody to the father and dismissed the adoption application. The applicants for the adoption order appealed to the Court of Appeal where it was held that in these applications under the Guardianship of Infants Acts, as in wardship cases the welfare of the child was the paramount consideration and (Willmer, L. J., dissenting) the court would not interfere with the exercise of discretion by the trial judge in this case, particularly because :

(a) (*per* Harman L.J.) the directions of the judge in such a case should be interfered with only in the case of some fundamental error and
(b) (*per* Russell, L.J.) great weight was to be attached to the blood tie:

moreover (Willmer, L.J. concurring on this point) it would be wrong, as the child was to go to the father, to insist on the requirement that the child should be brought up a Catholic.

The appeal was dismissed, and leave to appeal to the House of Lords was refused. It should be noted that this case does not change the law in any respect.

As a juvenile court cannot consider an application under the Guardianship of Minors Act, 1971 it would appear that in similar cases a juvenile court should refuse to proceed with an application to adopt on the grounds expressly that the application appeared to the court to be more fit to be dealt with by the High Court (see Rule 7 of the Adoption (Juvenile Court) Rules, 1959. In *Re E. (P.) (an infant)*, [1969] 1 All E. R. 323; 133 J. P. 137, C. A., it was held in the Court of Appeal, Civil Division, that the advantages for a child being adopted, and thereby ceasing to be a bastard, outweighed the loss of his connection with his real father. See also *Re C. (an infant), P. and P.* v. *C.* (1969), 113 Sol. Jo. 721, C. A., where it was held that if the effect of a final order of adoption is to legitimate an illegitimate child and the natural father has nothing to offer in comparison, then such an order should be affirmed.

5. Power to dispense with consent.—(1) The court may dispense with any consent required by paragraph (a) of subsection (1) of section four of this Act if it is satisfied that the person whose consent is to be dispensed with—

(a) has abandoned, neglected or persistently ill-treated the infant; or
(b) cannot be found or is incapable of giving his consent or is withholding his consent unreasonably.

(2) If the court is satisfied that any person whose consent is required by the said paragraph (a) has persistently failed without reasonable cause to

discharge the obligations of a parent or guardian of the infant, the court may dispense with his consent whether or not it is satisfied of the matters mentioned in subsection (1) of this section.

(3) Where a person who has given his consent to the making of an adoption order without knowing the identity of the applicant thereafter subsequently withdraws his consent on the ground only that he does not know the identity of the applicant, his consent shall be deemed for the purposes of this section to be unreasonably withheld.

(4) The court may dispense with the consent of the spouse of an applicant for an adoption order if it is satisfied that the person whose consent is to be dispensed with cannot be found or is incapable of giving his consent or that the spouses have separated and are living apart and that the separation is likely to be permanent.

NOTES

Dispense with any consent.—See *Z. v. Z.*, 1954 S. L. T. (Sh. Ct.) 47 (consent of father when prospective adopters are mother and second husband); *Re C. (an Infant)* (1957), *Times*, April 2, C. A. (mother's consent dispensed with—leave to appeal out of time refused); *Re B. (an Infant)*, [1957] 3 All E. R. 193, C. A. (mother's consent dispensed with—leave to appeal out of time granted). In this last case the mother's consent was dispensed with in the county court, and she was not made a party though her address in Australia was known. The Court of Appeal held that she should have been made a party and that in those circumstances she had a right of appeal.

" Cannot be found."—It will be noticed that although this section dispenses with consent it does not dispense with the service of the notice. It is therefore necessary to serve a notice at the last known place of abode of a respondent who cannot be found. If there is no address at which service can be attempted, it seems reasonable that the court would be justified in dispensing with the consent of a respondent who cannot be found, even though notice had not been served at all. The court would, however, have to be satisfied by evidence that genuine efforts to find the respondent had failed. Service of notices may be by post; see Rule 32 of the Juvenile Court Rules, p. 1115, *post*, Rule 28 of the County Court Rules, p. 1134, *post*, and Rule 28 of the High Court Rules, p. 1161, *post*.

In *R. v. London Quarter Sessions Appeals Committee, Ex parte Rossi*, [1956] 1 All E. R. 670; 120 J. P. 239, the Court of Appeal quashed an affiliation order made at quarter sessions on appeal in the absence of the respondent, holding that as a notice of the resumed hearing of the appeal sent by the clerk of the peace to the respondent by registered post had been returned unopened and undelivered, the respondent could not be said to have been given the notice of hearing required by s. 3 of the Summary Jurisdiction (Appeals) Act, 1933 (21 Halsbury's Statutes, 3rd Edn., 89).

It is submitted that this decision does not affect the right of a court in adoption proceedings to dispense with the consent of a respondent who cannot be found and who, in consequence, cannot be served with the notice prescribed by the Rules. The Adoption Act expressly provides for the case of a respondent who cannot be found and who cannot, therefore, be served with notice, by providing that his consent can be dispensed with. If in spite of this a rule had the effect that consent could not be dispensed with unless notice had been served the rule would be in conflict with the statute and defeat its intention. The law does not require the impossible to be done, and it is submitted that it is satisfied by evidence that notwithstanding all efforts the respondent cannot be found and therefore notice cannot be served. It is not, as in affiliation proceedings, a matter of making an order against a person and of putting him under a liability without his having been given an opportunity of being heard. In the case of *Re R. (Adoption)*, [1966] 3 All E. R. 613, Mr. Justice Buckley having heard the proceedings in chambers delivered judgment in open Court and said that if the circumstances were such that by no practical means could a person whose consent was necessary be communicated with in such a way as to secure his consent, then that person "cannot be found" within the meaning of s. 5. Moreover for similar reasons it could truly be said that the parents were "incapable of giving" their consent for how could a man consent to a proposal of which he was ignorant and could not, as a practical matter, be made aware.

In that case R, who was a national of a country with a totalitarian regime had escaped to this country illegally. His parents were still there, and any attempt to communicate with them would involve danger to them.

Where every reasonable step is not taken to find the mother of a child in respect of whom an adoption order is made the court will grant leave to appeal out of time to a mother who comes forward in such circumstances. The words "cannot be found" in s. 5 of the Act must mean cannot be found by taking all reasonable steps. (Re F. (R.) (an infant), [1970] 1 Q. B. 385; [1969] 3 All E. R. 1101; 133 J. P. 743, C. A.) In this case a county court dispensed with the consent of the mother as she could not be found and made an adoption order. When the mother heard of the order she appealed out of time.

It was held: (i) leave to appeal would be granted in the circumstances; (ii) the court had inherent jurisdiction to remit a case for reconsideration in the circumstances. Per Salmon, L.J.: in adoption proceedings the matter should not be decided on affidavit, it being vital for the court to see the adoptive parents and the natural parent who was objecting and to have reports from the welfare officer in relation to both the respective homes.

" Unreasonably withheld."—As to a particular instance of this, see sub-s. (3), p. 1034, *ante*.

In *Hitchcock* v. *W. B.*, [1952] 2 All E. R. 119; 116 J. P. 401, justices held that the father of an infant had acted unreasonably in withholding his consent to its adoption, and made an adoption order. On appeal to the Divisional Court, it was held that different considerations applied on the making of an adoption order from those which applied on the decision of a question of custody, and that the mere fact that an adoption order would be for the benefit of the child did not answer the question which the justices had to decide, namely, whether consent was unreasonably withheld; and that on the facts found by the justices it could not be said that the father was acting unreasonably. The appeal was allowed.

Material advantage to the infant is one element which the court should take into consideration. In the case of *Re Adoption Act* (1958), *Times*, August 29, 1958, it was held that the mother had vacillated to an extraordinary extent, and that her reasons for her consent or refusal seemed inconsistent with a genuine desire to keep her child for its own sake. The Court of Appeal held that her consent should be held to be unreasonably withheld and that the adoption order ought to be made.

Re K. (an Infant), Rogers v. *Kuzmicz*, [1952] 2 All E. R. 877; 117 J. P. 9, was an appeal to the Court of Appeal by the mother of an infant against an adoption order in respect of which a county court judge had dispensed with her consent as unreasonably withheld. It was held that *prima facie* it would seem eminently reasonable for a parent to withhold consent to an order completely and irrevocably destroying the parental relationship. The withholding of a parent's consent could not be held to be unreasonable merely because the order, if made, would conduce to the child's welfare. It was also held that the withholding of consent could not be held to be unreasonable merely because a documentary consent had been given and subsequently withdrawn. The appeal was allowed.

See also *Watson* v. *Nikolaisen, infra*.

The question whether consent is unreasonably withheld is essentially a question of fact and where the justices have applied the right principles the High Court will not interfere with their decision (*W.* v. *D.* (1955). 120 J. P. 119). See also *L.* v. *M.* (1955), 120 J. P. 27; *Re F.*, [1957] 1 All E. R. 819; 121 J. P. 270; *Re D. (an Infant)*, [1958] 1 All E. R. 427; 122 J. P. 156; *Z.* v. *Z.*, 1954, S. L. T. (Sh. Ct.) 47; *Y. Z. Petitioners*, 1954, S. L. T. (Sh. Ct.) 98.

In *Re L. (An Infant)* ((1962), 106 Sol. Jo. 611) it was held in the Court of Appeal on an appeal against an adoption order made in a county court that owing to the lapse of time and to the fact that the mother had at one time consented, and taking into account the interests of all the parties, that the mother's consent was unreasonably withheld, and her appeal was dismissed.

These cases were considered in the Court of Appeal at the hearing of an appeal by the mother of an infant child from a decision of the Oxford County Court dispensing with her consent to its adoption. It was held that the mother's consent was being unreasonably withheld and had been rightly dispensed with for the following reasons :—

   (a) (*per* Pearson L. J.) the primary consideration was the reasonableness of the mother's attitude in relation to the child, though the effect of her decision on others was also relevant, or (*per* Diplock, L. J.) the relevant consideration was the conduct of the mother as a parent towards the child, though the court's decision was preferably to be based on all the facts of the case and

   (b) considering the totality of the evidence including the strong medical evidence, and having regard, as important factors, to the serious risk of adverse psychological effects on the child if she were taken from the applicants, her foster-parents, to the uncertainty of her future with her natural mother, and to the fact that the mother's conduct and indecision had brought about the present situation, the court could not interfere with the decision that the mother's consent was being unreasonably withheld.

In delivering the judgment of the court, Pearson, L. J., said that he would state briefly the principle involved, that the court was not concerned in this case, where the question was simply whether the mother's consent was being unreasonably withheld, with, in itself, the question which course would be in the best interests of the child. It was not enough to show—indeed it was not strictly a relevant consideration in itself—that, in the interests of the child it would be better that the child should remain with its foster-parents, or that the child should be taken by the mother. What was relevant was the mother's attitude concerning the welfare of the child. *Re C. (an Infant)*, [1965] 2 Q. B. 449; [1964] 3 All E. R. 483; 129 J. P. 62. Leave to appeal to the House of Lords was refused ; (1966), *Times*, January 12.

See an article at 128 J. P. N. 601 where these cases are examined.

In *Re W. (Infants)*, [1965] 3 All E. R. 231 ; 129 J. P. 550, the adoption application was heard more than four years after the adopters had received the children. The father of the infants remarried but concealed the remarriage from the adoption society. He withdrew his consent within three months of giving it and wanted the children back. There was medical evidence that it would be bad for the infants to return to the father.

It was held that although if the application had come before the court much earlier the father could in all probability have been considered not to have acted unreasonably in withholding his consent yet by his conduct the father was largely to blame for the situation that had arisen, and to delay adoption further would be cruel to the children ; accordingly his consent was unreasonably withheld.

The House of Lords has now considered the position in *Re W. (an infant)*, [1971] A. C. 682; [1971] 2 All E. R. 49, H. L., and *O'Connor* v. *A. and B.*, [1971] 2 All E. R. 1230. in the former case the infant had resided with foster parents since a few days after his birth. It was held that in custody cases the welfare of the child is the first and foremost consideration, but in adoption proceedings the child's welfare is only one of three separate conditions as to each of which the court has to be separately satisfied *Per* Hailsham, L.C.: There was no reason for interpreting unreasonably as importing necessarily any element of culpability, callous or self-indulgent indifference or of failure or probable failure of parental duty. The Lord Chancellor referred to the speech of Lord Denning, M.R. in *Re L. (An Infant)* (1962), 106 Sol. Jo. 611 where Lord Denning had said: " . . . I quite agree that (1) the question whether she is unreasonably withholding her consent is to be judged at the date of the hearing ; and (2) the welfare of the child is not the sole consideration; and (3) the one question is whether she is unreasonably withholding her consent. But I must say that in considering whether she is reasonable or unreasonable we must take into account the welfare of the child. A reasonable mother surely gives great weight to what is better for the child. Her anguish of mind is quite understandable; but still it may be unreasonable for her to withhold consent. We must look and see whether it is reasonable or unreasonable according to what a reasonable woman in her place would do in all the circumstances of the case."

That passage might now be considered authoritative. Although welfare per se was not the test, the fact that a reasonable parent did pay regard to his child's welfare must enter into the question of reasonableness as a relevant factor. It was relevant in all cases if and to the extent that a reasonable parent would take it into account. It was decisive in those cases where a reasonable parent must so regard it.

The test of reasonableness or its opposite was to be judged by an objective test. It was normally a question of fact and degree and not of law so long as there was evidence to support the findings of the court. Besides culpability, unreasonableness could include anything which could objectively be adjudged to be unreasonable. It was not confined to culpability or callous indifference. It could include, where carried to excess, sentimentality, romanticism, bigotry, wild prejudice, caprice, fatuousness or excessive lack of common sense. The dictum of Lord Denning, M.R. in *Re L.* (cited in *Re C.,* 1965, *supra*) must now be considered as authoritative.

In the latter case the mother of a child placed for adoption subsequently married the father. The child was then three months old. The appeal against the adoption order was heard by the House three years after the mother withdrew her consent. *Per* Lord Guest, "the claims of the natural parents and the marriage of the parents is of supreme importance in considering the reasonableness or otherwise of the parents on withholding consent. However the instability of the natural parents and the disruption which may be caused by removal of a child who had been in the care of adopters for two and a half years were reasons for not interfering with the decision of the court below."

In *Re P. A. (an Infant)*, [1971] 3 All E. R. 522, C. A. the infant had been with proposed adopters since a month after birth. Lord Denning, M.R. said (applying *Re W., supra*) if the child's welfare were paramount, much could be said for his remaining with the proposed adopters but that was not the sole consideration. Whether consent was unreasonably withheld must be judged by asking what a reasonable mother would do in all the circumstances.

In *Re F. (an Infant)*, [1970] 1 All E. R. 344 the father of a child had pleaded guilty to the manslaughter of the mother, and objected to the appellants' proposal to adopt although considering adoption by his own relatives. His conduct, it was said, although not a dereliction of duty falling exactly within the meaning of the words in subsection (1) in fact far exceeded in gravity that usually encountered in such cases and he had small right to be heard in the matter of adoption. The court in wardship proceedings awarded care and control to the appellants. *Per* Harman, L. J. "I think it may well be that his refusal to approve the proposed adoption by those to whom the court commits the care of the infant may be held unreasonable, and ought to be dispensed with."

" **Abandoned.**"—This must, it would seem, refer to a state of things existing at the time of the application, and not to some past abandonment which has ceased. Cases on abandonment are cited at p. 17, *ante*. These were decided in relation to criminal offences involving suffering, injury or danger to life or health. In *Watson v. Nikolaisen*, [1955] 2 All E. R. 427; 119 J. P. 419, it was held that a parent " abandoned " an infant within the meaning of this section, only if the abandonment was of such a kind as that which rendered a parent liable under the criminal law.

Parental obligations.—In *Re P. (An Infant)* [1962] 3 All E. R. 789; 127 J. P. 18, in making an adoption order, Pennycuick, J., held that he had a discretion to dispense with the consent of the mother of infants whom he said had neglected to visit them except infrequently and had not contributed towards their maintenance even the full amount of the family allowance she had received in respect of them. He examined her failure to discharge her duties as parent under the natural and moral duty of a parent to show affection, care and interest towards the child and also the common law and statutory duty of a parent to maintain the child financially.

See however *Re M. (An Infant)* (1965), 109 Sol. Jo. 574, where the Court of Appeal set aside an adoption order made in a county court by which the mother's consent had been dispensed with on the ground that she had persistently failed without reasonable cause to discharge her obligations to the infant.

" **Likely to be permanent.**"—Where there is a separation order or deed, the court will have little difficulty, but in other cases it will be well to make close inquiry into the circumstances since the adoption of a child by one party to the marriage without the consent of the other might give rise to difficulties, especially with regard to the question of maintaining the child. The other spouse would not be legally bound to maintain it; see s. 13, p. 1047, *post*.

" **Parent.**"—See s. 1 (4), *ante*, and the note to that section.

High Court.—See Practice Direction dated November 13, 1967, at p. 1172, *post*.

Definitions.—For " court ", " infant " and " guardian ", see s. 57 (1), *post*; and for " adoption order ", see s. 1 (1), *ante*, and s. 57 (1), *post*, in conjunction with s. 53 (4), *post*.

Legal aid.—Legal aid may be given in connection with an adoption application where a parent or parents are opposing, and the court is asked to dispense with their consent. See the Legal Aid (Extension of Proceedings) Regulations, 1969, S.I. 1969 No. 921, p. 370, *ante*.

6. Evidence of consent of parent or guardian.—(1) Where a parent or guardian of an infant does not attend in the proceedings on an application for an adoption order for the purpose of giving his consent to the making of the order, then, subject to subsection (2) of this section, a document signifying his consent to the making of such an order shall, if the person in whose favour the order is to be made is named in the document or (where the identity of that person is not known to the consenting party) is distinguished therein in the prescribed manner, be admissible as evidence of that consent, whether the document is executed before or after the commencement of the proceedings; and where any such document is attested as mentioned in subsection (3) of this section, it shall be admissible as aforesaid without further proof of the signature of the person by whom it is executed.

(2) A document signifying the consent of the mother of an infant shall not be admissible under this section unless—

  (a) the infant is at least six weeks old on the date of the execution of the document; and
  (b) the document is attested on that date as mentioned in subsection (3) of this section.

(3) Any reference in this section to a document being attested as mentioned in this subsection is, if the document is executed in the United Kingdom, a reference to its being attested by either a justice of the peace or—

  (a) if it is executed in England, an officer of a county court appointed for the purposes of section eighty-four of the County Courts Act, 1934, or a justices' clerk within the meaning of section twenty-one of the Justices of the Peace Act, 1949;
  (b) (*applies to Scotland.*)

and, if it is executed outside the United Kingdom, a reference to its being attested by a person of any such class as may be prescribed.

(4) For the purposes of this section a document purporting to be attested as mentioned in subsection (3) of this section shall be deemed to be so attested, and to be executed and attested on the date and at the place specified in the document, unless the contrary is proved.

(5) (*Applies to Scotland.*)

NOTES
"Parent."—See s. 1 (4), *ante*, and the note to that section.

General consent to adoption.—It is clear that a consent to adoption, when no actual application by particular adopters is being made, is not valid. In *Re Carroll*, [1931] 1 K. B. 317; 95 J. P. 25, decided under the Adoption of Children Act, 1926, Scrutton L.J., expressed the opinion that the consent of the mother to adoption by anyone nominated by a society without knowing whom, should not be acted upon by any court.

At the time of this decision the act in force did not permit identification of the proposed adopter otherwise than by name and address, but it is submitted that this case is authority for the principle that a general consent to adoption by anyone who might subsequently be willing to adopt is irregular.

" **Evidence.**"—A document which conforms to sub-s. (2) is *prima facie*, but not conclusive, evidence, on mere production.

" **Consent of the mother.**"—In many cases a mother who has given consent will not know the date of the hearing and will have no opportunity of attending unless she alters her mind and wishes to oppose the making of an order. Strict compliance with the provisions of sub-s. (3) is therefore essential.

Signature of consent form.—The form should be signed in the presence of the justice or other person attesting it.

See Form 4 in the Juvenile Court Rules, p. 1120, *post*, and Form 5 in the County Court Rules, p. 1140, *post*, and Form 3 in the High Court Rules, p. 1165, *post*.

Other spouse.—This section does not relate to the consent of the other spouse, unless a parent, and if a document signifying such consent is to be used it must be proved in some other manner, *e.g.*, by identification of handwriting, or the evidence of a witness to the signature. In some circumstances it may be proper to admit the document in evidence without proof, in accordance with the Civil Evidence Act, 1968.

" **Prescribed manner.**"—*I.e.*, manner prescribed by the Adoption Rules; see ss. 9 and 57 (1), *post*. A person proposing to apply for an adoption order and wishing to keep his identity confidential may obtain in advance of making his application a serial number to be assigned to him for the purposes of the application, and the form of consent will then identify the applicant by the serial number only; see the Rules, pp. 1100 *et seq.*, *post*.

" **Justices' clerk.**"—By s. 21 of the Justices of the Peace Act, 1949; 21 Halsbury's Statutes, 3rd Edn., 128, this includes a clerk to a stipendiary magistrate, a clerk to a metropolitan stipendiary court and a clerk at either of the justice rooms of the City of London.

"**United Kingdom.**"—This means Great Britain and Northern Ireland; see the Royal and Parliamentary Titles Act, 1927, s. 2 (2).

"**Such class as may be prescribed.**"—*I.e.*, by the Adoption Rules; see ss. 9 and 57 (1), *post*, and the Rules pp. 1100 *et seq.*, *post*.

Definitions.—For " guardian ", " infant " and " England ", see s. 57 (1), *post*; and for " adoption order ", see s. 1 (1), *ante*, and s. 57 (1), *post*, in conjunction with s. 53 (4), *post*.

County Court officer.—By virtue of s. 205 (5) of the County Courts Act, 1959, the reference in s. 6 (3) of the Adoption Act, 1958, to s. 84 of the County Courts Act, 1934 (repealed by the County Courts Act, 1959) is to be construed as a reference to the corresponding enactment in the 1959 Act (*i.e.*, s. 87).

We are of opinion that a document signifying the consent of a parent or guardian may if it is executed in England be attested by an officer of a county court appointed for the purposes of s. 84 of the County Courts Act, 1934, or s. 87 of the County Courts Act, 1959.

7. Functions of court as to adoption orders.—(1) The court before making an adoption order shall be satisfied—

(a) that every person whose consent is necessary under this Act, and whose consent is not dispensed with, has consented to and understands the nature and effect of the adoption order for which application is made, and in particular in the case of any parent understands that the effect of the adoption order will be permanently to deprive him or her of his or her parental rights;

(b) that the order if made will be for the welfare of the infant; and

(c) that the applicant has not received or agreed to receive, and that no person has made or given or agreed to make or give to the applicant, any payment or other reward in consideration of the adoption except such as the court may sanction.

(2) In determining whether an adoption order if made will be for the welfare of the infant, the court shall have regard (among other things) to the health of the applicant, as evidenced, in such cases as may be prescribed, by the certificate of a fully registered medical practitioner, and shall give due consideration to the wishes of the infant, having regard to his age and understanding.

(3) The court in an adoption order may impose such terms and conditions as the court may think fit, and in particular may require the adopter by bond or otherwise to make for the infant such provision (if any) as in the opinion of the court is just and expedient.

NOTES

" **Infant.**"—If the guardian *ad litem* reports to a county court or juvenile court that in his opinion the infant is able to understand the nature of an adoption order the court must inform the applicant that the personal attendance of the infant is required at the hearing and shall not make an adoption order or interim order unless satisfied that the infant has been informed of the nature of the order.

Rules 11 and 13 and Form 6 of the Adoption (County Court) Rules, 1959, pp. 1130, 1131, 1142, *post.*

Rules 11 and 14 and Form 5 of the Adoption (Juvenile Court) Rules, 1959, pp. 1111, 1112, 1121, *post.*

There are no corresponding provisions in the Adoption (High Court) Rules, 1959.

" **Consent.**"—For persons whose consent is necessary, see s. 4 (1), (3), *ante,* and for cases in which consent may be dispensed with, see s. 5, *ante.* See also note to s. 4, p. 652, *ante.*

" **Parent.**"—See s. 1 (4), *ante,* and the note to that section.

" **Satisfied.**"—Rule 33 of the Adoption (Juvenile Court) Rules, p. 1115, *post,* applies the procedure of the Magistrates' Courts Act and Rules, 1952, to proceedings under the Adoption Act, and under s. 78 of the Magistrates' Courts Act, 1952 (21 Halsbury's Statutes, 3rd Edn., 251) evidence on oath is generally necessary. The applicants may be asked to swear to the truth of the statements contained in their written application, and any witnesses to consents to swear to the handwriting of the respondent in question in any case where there has not been proper attestation. Further, there should be evidence to identify the birth certificate as that of the infant.

Facts tending to establish the identity of an infant may be proved by affidavit in a magistrates' court as well as in the High Court and county courts. See s. 9 (6), *ibid.,* and Rule 17 of the Adoption (Juvenile Court) Rules, 1959, p. 1112, *post.*

" **Welfare of the infant.**"—Where there is a possibility of legitimation, this is a factor to be taken into consideration as an alternative to adoption, *per* Roxburgh, J., in *Re C. S. C. (an Infant),* [1960] 1 All E. R. 711; 124 J. P. 260.

See note to s. 44 of the Children and Young Persons Act, 1933, p. 50, *ante.* See also *Re G. (D.M.) (an Infant)* referred to in notes to s. 10, p. 1046, *post.*

" **Wishes of the infant.**"—Usually the infant is much too young to take any part in the proceedings, but it is necessary that where the child is old enough to understand, the court shall not make an order without being satisfied that he has been told the nature of the application and the effect of an adoption order. The duty of the guardian *ad litem* in this matter is laid down in Rule 9 and Sched. II of the Adoption (Juvenile Court) Rules, 1959. If the infant is not considered too young to understand he must be given notice of the proceedings; Rule 11, p. 1111, *post.*

On the dismissal by the Court of Appeal of an appeal against the refusal of a county court judge to make an adoption order it was held that the county court judge had not exercised his discretion improperly, and the appeal must be dismissed because :—

(i) there was no statutory obligation on the county court judge to see the boy and, as the guardian's final report dealt with the position immediately before the hearing date, the judge was entitled to rely on this report and had not failed to give the " due consideration to the wishes of the " boy required by s. 7 (2) ;

(ii) (per Ormerod and Pearson, L.JJ.) in the circumstances the judge was not in error in refusing to make an adoption order subject to conditions as to access, under s. 7 (3), particularly as the Act contained no provision for the enforcement of such conditions ;

(iii) (per Ormerod and Donovan, L.JJ.) in considering whether to dispense with the mother's consent it was right to have regard to all the circumstances of the case.

Semble (per Pearson and Ormerod, L.JJ.) the parties to a contested application in the county court for adoption of an infant have no right to see the confidential report of the guardian *ad litem*, except in so far as the judge sees fit to disclose its contents at the hearing.

(Per Donovan, L.J.) where the confidential report of the guardian *ad litem* contains allegations against one party having a direct bearing on whether he or she should be allowed to adopt the child or to resist its adoption, it would be unjust not to allow that party an opportunity to meet the allegations and I would regard it as falling within the proper execution of a judge's duty if he disclosed to a party any allegation made against him in the confidential report, and relevant to the question of adoption, so that he might have an opportunity of dealing with it (*Re G. (T.J.) (An Infant)*, [1963] 2 Q. B. 73; [1963] 1 All E. R. 20; 127 J. P. 144) see also *Re P. A. (an Infant)*, [1971] 3 All E. R. 522, *supra*.

" Terms and conditions."—Conditions might relate to the child's education, secular and religious. The suggestion of the First Report of the Committee on Child Adoption, 1925, was—

> " There are many forms which such a provision might take, including *e.g.* a covenant secured by a bond to the tribunal whereby the adopting parent covenants to make testamentary provision for the child up to a given amount or to the extent of a particular proportion of his estate."

With regard to religious persuasion the Act provides in s. 4 (2) that the consent can be given subject to a condition as to religious upbringing, but apart from this it does not appear incumbent on the court to inquire into the question. It may be assumed that a parent or other respondent will satisfy himself as to the religious upbringing of the infant if he attaches importance to this before consenting to the proposed order. It would, no doubt, be proper to insert a condition in an adoption order dealing with the question of religion if the parties so desired. Generally, however, adoption orders contain no special terms and conditions.

As to the absence of provisions for enforcing conditions, see *Re G. (T.J.) (An Infant)*, [1963] 2 Q. B. 73; [1963] 1 All E. R. 20; 127 J. P. 144.

Health of applicants.—See Rule 10 and Form 4 of the Adoption (High Court) Rules, 1971, pp. 1158, 1167, *post*; Rule 3 and Form 3 of the Adoption (County Court) Rules, 1959, pp. 1128, 1139, *post*, and Rule 3 and Form 2 of the Adoption (Juvenile Court) Rules, 1959, pp. 1109, 1119, *post*.

Copy of adoption order.—See Rules 20–22 and Form 10 of the Adoption (County Court) Rules, 1959, pp. 1132, 1145, *post*, and Rules 19–23 and Form 10 of the Adoption (Juvenile Court) Rules, 1959, pp. 1112, 1125, *post*, as to abridged copy of order and as to restriction on the supplying of copies.

See Rule 22 of the Adoption (High Court) Rules, 1971, p. 1160, *post*, as to restriction on the supplying of copies of orders made in the High Court.

" Deprive . . . parental rights."—The deprivation of parental rights results from s. 13 (1), *post*.

" Payment or other reward."—For restriction on the making of payments or other rewards in consideration of adoption, see s. 50, *post*.

" Prescribed."—*I.e.*, by Adoption Rules; see ss. 9 and 57 (1), *post*, and Rule 10 of the Adoption (High Court) Rules, 1971, p. 1158, *post*, and Rule 3 of the Adoption (County Court) Rules, 1959, p. 1128, *post*, and of the Adoption (Juvenile Court) Rules, 1959, p. 1109, *post*.

"**Fully registered medical practitioner.**"—For the meaning of this expression, see the Medical Act, 1956 (c. 76), s. 52 (2), in conjunction with ss. 54 (1) and 57 (2) thereof; 21 Halsbury's Statutes, 3rd Edn. 665, 667.

Definitions.—For " court " and " infant ", see s. 57 (1), *post*; and for " adoption order ", see s. 1 (1), *ante*, and s. 57 (1), *post*, in conjunction with s. 53 (4), *post*.

8. Interim orders.—(1) Subject to the provisions of this section, the court may, upon any application for an adoption order, postpone the determination of the application and make an interim order giving the custody of the infant to the applicant for a period not exceeding two years by way of a probationary period upon such terms as regards provision for the maintenance and education and supervision of the welfare of the infant and otherwise as the court may think fit.

(2) All such consents as are required to an adoption order shall be necessary to an interim order but subject to a like power on the part of the court to dispense with any such consent.

(3) An interim order shall not be made in any case where the making of an adoption order would be unlawful by virtue of section three of this Act.

(4) Where an interim order has been made giving the custody of an infant to the applicant for a period of less than two years, the court may by order extend that period, but the total period for which the custody of the infant is given to the applicant under the order as varied under this subsection shall not exceed two years.

(5) An interim order shall not be deemed to be an adoption order within the meaning of this Act.

NOTES

Interim orders are appropriate where the Court is in some doubt about making the adoption order, and wishes to arrange for an experimental period during which the applicants and the infant can be supervised by the guardian *ad litem* or some other suitable person.

"**Welfare.**"—See the note to s. 7, *supra*. See also cases cited in connection with consent unreasonably withheld, in particular *Hitchcock* v. *W. B.* at p. 1035, *ante*.

"**Determination of application.**"—See the definition in Rule 37 of the Adoption (Juvenile Court) Rules, 1959, p. 1115, *post*.

Appeal against interim order.—An interim order is not an adoption order and therefore it does not appear from the wording of the section that an appeal lies against the making or refusal of an interim order. It is true that in *Re K. (an Infant)*, *Rogers and another* v. *Kuzmicz*, [1952] 2 All E. R. 877; 117 J. P. 9, the Court of Appeal heard and determined an appeal from an interim order made under the Adoption Act, 1950, by a county court, but different considerations from those applicable to cases heard by juvenile courts apply to orders made by county courts.

Further hearing.—Where an interim order is made in the High Court the applicant must obtain an appointment for further hearing at least two months before the expiration of the period of the interim order, and if he fails the guardian *ad litem* must apply. The juvenile court, or in the county court the registrar, must fix a time for the further hearing at any time not less than a month before the expiration of the period of the interim order. See Rule 20 of the Adoption (High Court) Rules, 1971, p. 1159, *post*, and of the Adoption (County Court) Rules, 1959, p. 1132, *post*, and Rule 18 of the Adoption (Juvenile Court) Rules, 1959, p. 1112, *post*.

Notice of the hearing must be served, see respectively Rule 20 and Form 8, Rule 19 and Forms 7 and 8, and Rule 18 and Forms 7 and 8, *post*.

Such an order being made on the adjournment of an application, it is not unreasonable that an end should be put to the order at any time by consent of the parties and upon their request to have the application finally determined, as for instance when the applicants wish to withdraw it.

"**Consents.**"—For the consents required to an adoption order, see s. 4 (1), (3), *ante*, and for the power of the court to dispense with consent, see s. 5, *ante*. See also note to s. 4, p. 1031, *ante*.

As to return of infants placed by adoption societies or local authorities, where the period specified in an interim order expires without an adoption order having been made, see s. 35 (4), *post*.

Service of interim order.—See Rule 23 of the Adoption (High Court) Rules, 1971, p. 1160, *post*; Rules 21 and 23 of the Adoption (County Court) Rules, 1959, p. 1132, *post*, and Rules 22 and 25 of the Adoption (Juvenile Court) Rules, 1959, p. 1113, *post*.

As an interim order is not an adoption order no copy or duplicate should be sent to the Registrar-General.

Definitions.—For " court " and " infant ", see s. 57 (1), *post*; and for " adoption order ", see s. 1 (1), *ante*, and s. 57 (1), *post*, in conjunction with s. 53 (4), *post*.

9. Jurisdiction and procedure in England.—(1) An application for

an adoption order may be made in England to the High Court or, at the option of the applicant but subject to Adoption Rules, to any county court or magistrates' court within the jurisdiction of which the applicant or the infant resides at the date of the application.

(2) In this Act " Adoption Rules " means rules made under subsection (3) of this section or made by virtue of this section under section fifteen of the Justices of the Peace Act, 1949.

(3) Rules in regard to any matter to be prescribed under this Part of this Act and dealing generally with all matters of procedure and incidental matters arising out of this Part of this Act and for carrying this Part of this Act into effect shall be made in England by the Lord Chancellor.

(4) Subsection (3) of this section does not apply in relation to proceedings before magistrates' courts, but the power to make rules conferred by section fifteen of the Justices of the Peace Act, 1949, shall include power to make provision as to any of the matters mentioned in that subsection.

(5) Adoption Rules may provide for applications for adoption orders being heard and determined otherwise than in open court and, where the application is made to a magistrates' court, for the hearing and determination of the application in a juvenile court, and may make provision for excluding or restricting the jurisdiction of any court where a previous application made by the same applicant in respect of the same infant has been refused by that or any other court.

(6) Adoption Rules made as respects magistrates' courts may provide for enabling any fact tending to establish the identity of an infant with an infant to whom a document relates to be proved by affidavit and for excluding or restricting in relation to any facts that may be so proved the power of a justice of the peace to compel the attendance of witnesses.

(7) For the purpose of any application in England for an adoption order, the court shall, subject to Adoption Rules, appoint some person to act as guardian ad litem of the infant upon the hearing of the application with the duty of safeguarding the interests of the infant before the court.

(8) Where the person so appointed is an officer of a local authority the court may authorise the authority to incur any necessary expenditure; but nothing in this section shall be deemed to authorise the court to appoint an officer of a local authority to act as guardian ad litem except with the consent of that authority.

NOTES

This section now has effect as if—

(a) in subsection (3) thereof the reference to Part I of the 1958 Act included references to sections 34 and 35 thereof (under which the right of a parent, adoption society or local authority to remove an infant from the care and possession of a person who has applied for an adoption order cannot be exercised without the leave of the court) ; and

(b) subsection (5) thereof included applications for the leave of the court under the said section 34 or the said section 35 among the applications for the hearing and determination of which otherwise than in open court provision may be made by Adoption Rules (Children and Young Persons Act, 1963, s. 54, p. 113, *ante*).

Application.—The application is to be made in the prescribed manner, and may only be made by a person domiciled in England or Scotland; see s. 1 (1), *ante*. Sub-s. (1) does not apply in relation to an application for an adoption order by a person not ordinarily resident in Great Britain, but such an application may be made, in England, to the High Court or the county court; see s. 12 (2), *post*.

A county court or juvenile court may make an adoption order in respect of a child who is the subject of a custody order in the Divorce Court without the prior discharge of the custody order; see *Crossley* v. *Crossley*, [1953] P. 97; [1953] 1 All E. R. 891.

" Previous application."—See Rule 5 of the Adoption (High Court) Rules, 1971, p. 1156, *post*; Rule 6 of the Adoption (County Court) Rules, 1959, p. 1129, *post*, and Rule 6 of the Adoption (Juvenile Court) Rules, 1959, p. 1109, *post*.

" Affidavit."—See Rule 17 of the Adoption (Juvenile Court) Rules, 1959, p. 1112, *post*; Rule 17 of the Adoption (County Court) Rules, 1959, p. 1131, *post*, and Rule 8 of the Adoption (High Court) Rules, 1971, p. 1157, *post*.

The use of affidavits in juvenile courts may avoid the necessity of calling a witness or witnesses to establish the identity of the infant who is the subject of the application with documents signifying consent to adoption, and with a birth certificate.

" Magistrates' court."—By Rule 1, p. 1109, *post*, applications are to be made to a juvenile court.

For definition of " juvenile court," see s. 45 of the Children and Young Persons Act, 1933, p. 51, *ante*.

S. 47 (2) of that Act, p. 53, *ante*, deals with the places at which juvenile courts are to be held and with the persons who may be admitted. Adoption proceedings in juvenile or county courts must be heard *in camera*, and representatives of the press must not be admitted. See Rule 16 of the Adoption (Juvenile Court) Rules, 1959, p. 1112, *post*; Rule 16 of the Adoption (County Court) Rules, 1959, p. 1131, *post*, Rule 3 of the Adoption (High Court) Rules, 1971, p. 1156, *post*, allows all proceedings under the Act to be disposed of in Chambers.

" Resides."—See the note " Reside " to s. 1, p. 1028, *ante*; also note " Residence " at p. 162, *ante*. The residence must, of course, be *bona fide*, and not a pretence for the purpose of selecting a particular tribunal.

The question sometimes arises where there is a change of residence after the forms of application have been filed and the date of hearing fixed so that when the application is heard the applicants and the infant no longer reside within the jurisdiction of the court. It is suggested that if jurisdiction existed when the court fixed the time for the hearing and appointed the guardian *ad litem* it is not unreasonable to hear the case and not to insist upon proceedings being undertaken *de novo* within the new jurisdiction.

" Juvenile court."—In the case of *Re J. S. (an Infant)*, [1959] 3 All E. R. 856; 124 J. P. 89, an appeal was allowed and a new trial ordered on the two grounds that it had not been " ensured " that the court was properly constituted (see note to

Rule 11 of the Juvenile Courts (Constitution) Rules, 1954, p. 472, *ante*), and that no note of evidence had been taken. Roxburgh, J., held that it was essential that a note of the evidence of the appellants before the juvenile court should be before the appellate court, and as no note had been taken by the justices' clerk, and as affidavit evidence by him as to what took place would not be acceptable, a new trial would be ordered.

"**Guardian ad litem.**"—For provisions as to appointment, etc., see Rules 6, 7, 15, 16 and Sched. II of the Adoption (High Court) Rules, 1971, pp. 1157 *et seq., post;* Rules 8, 9, 10, 11, 29 and Sched. II of the Adoption (County Court) Rules, 1959, p. 1129, *post,* and Rules 8, 9, 11 and Sched. II of the Adoption (Juvenile Court) Rules, 1959, p. 1110, *post.* As to the choice of a guardian *ad litem,* see observations of Roxburgh, J., in *Re A. B.,* [1948] 2 All E. R. 727. In many areas probation officers act as guardians *ad litem.* It is their duty to do this, if requested by or on behalf of a court (r. 31 of the Probation Rules, 1965, p. 527, *ante.)* The duties of a guardian *ad litem* are not confined to those set out in Sched. II to the Rules. His duty is "to safeguard the interests of the infant before the court". For practice in the High Court see the White Book.

On appeal to the High Court, the guardian *ad litem* appointed by a magistrates' court, or by a county court, is the guardian *ad litem* for the purposes of the appeal (*Re S. (an Infant),* [1959] 2 All E. R. 675).

Definitions.—For " England ", " infant " and " court ", see s. 57 (1), *post;* for " adoption order ", see s. 1 (1), *ante,* and s. 57 (1), *post,* in conjunction with s. 53 (4), *post;* and for " local authority ", see s. 28 (1), *post.*

Rules under this section.—See pp. 1109 *et seq., post.*

Where the Director of Social Services is appointed guardian *ad litem* he may carry out his duties and appear before the court personally or by any other officer or servant of the authority who assists the director in the exercise of his functions; Rule 7 (2) of the Adoption (High Court) Rules, 1971, p. 1157, *post,* and Rule 8 (3) of the Adoption (County Court) Rules, 1959, p. 1129, *post,* and of the Adoption (Juvenile Court) Rules, 1959, p. 1110, *post.*

Justices of the Peace Act, 1949, s. 15.—See 18 Halsbury's Statutes 3rd Edn., 82.

10. Appeals from magistrates' courts in England.—(1) Where, on an application made in England to a magistrates' court, the court makes or refuses to make an adoption order, an appeal shall lie to the High Court.

(2) So much of subsection (1) of section sixty-three of the Supreme Court of Judicature (Consolidation) Act, 1925, as requires an appeal from any court or person to the High Court to be heard and determined by a divisional court shall not apply to appeals under this section.

NOTES

Procedure.—See Order 55 of the Rules of the Supreme Court, Rule 3, p. 1261, *post.*

Appeals under this section are assigned to the Family Division (Administration of Justice Act, 1970, s. 1 and Sched. I.

Circumstances in which appellate court may review decision of justices.— In an appeal by a county council, whose children's officer was appointed guardian *ad litem,* from an order made by justices, it was held :

(i) that the principles regarding the welfare of infants acted on by the court in appeals relating to guardianship, custody, care and control of infants were equally applicable in determining whether the making of a particular adoption order would be for the welfare of an infant, and though the court would interfere where, *e.g.* the justices had erred in law or their findings of fact were not justified by the evidence, if they had not so erred, the court would only interfere with the exercise of their discretion in what appeared to be a very clear case;

(ii) although adoption societies and local authorities regarded severance from the natural parents as being of primary importance, there was no mandatory requirement of that nature in the Adoption Act, 1958;

(iii) the court should not take the view that it must always and necessarily be detrimental to an infant to be adopted by a man who had against him a conviction of indecent assault.

The appeal was dismissed. *Re G. (D.M.) (An Infant)*, [1962] 2 All E. R. 546; 126 J. P. 363; followed in *Re B. (M.F.) (An Infant)*, [1972] 1 All E. R. 898, C. A.

Documents to be supplied.—The confidential report of the guardian *ad litem* should be sent to the judge's clerk. The clerk to the justices should take a note of any questions and answers during the hearing before the justices and this note should be supplied to the court, *per* Roxburgh, J., in *Re J. S. (an Infant)*, [1959] 3 All E. R. 856; 124 J. P. 89.

Definitions.—For " England ", see s. 57 (1), *post*, and for " adoption order ", see s. 1 (1), *ante*, and s. 57 (1), *post*, in conjunction with s. 53 (4), *post*.

Supreme Court of Judicature (Consolidation) Act, 1925, s. 63 (1). See 25 Halsbury's Statutes, 3rd Edn., 708.

Interim order.—See note " Appeal against interim order " to s. 8, p. 1042, *ante*.

11. *(Applies to Scotland.)*

12. Modification of foregoing provisions in the case of applicants not ordinarily resident in Great Britain.—(1) An adoption order may, notwithstanding anything in this Act, be made on the application of a person who is not ordinarily resident in Great Britain; and in relation to such an application—

(a) subsection (5) of section one of this Act does not apply; and

(b) subsection (2) of section three of this Act applies with the substitution of the word " living " for the word " resident ".

(2) Subsection (1) of section nine and subsection (1) of section eleven of this Act do not apply in relation to an application for an adoption order by a person not ordinarily resident in Great Britain, but such an application may be made, in England to the High Court or the county court, and in Scotland to the Court of Session or the sheriff court.

(3) Where an application for an adoption order is made jointly by spouses who are not, or one of whom is not, ordinarily resident in Great Britain, the notice required by subsection (2) of section three of this Act (as modified by subsection (1) of this section) may be given by either of the applicants; and the provisions of subsection (1) of that section shall be deemed to be complied with if they are complied with in the case of one of the applicants and the applicants have been living together in Great Britain for at least one of the three months mentioned in that subsection.

(4) This section does not affect the construction of subsection (1) of the said section three in its application to any joint application to which subsection (3) of this section does not apply.

NOTES

Jurisdiction.—Application can be made only to the High Court or the county court—sub-s. (2).

" Notwithstanding anything."—See s. 1 (5), *ante*.

" Living."—This word, used as distinguished from residing, and in the whole context of the section, seems to indicate something of a purely temporary nature, the parties having no real residence in this country.

"**Great Britain.**"—*I.e.*, England, Scotland and Wales; see the Union with Scotland Act, 1706, 6 Halsbury's Statutes 3rd Edn., 501, and the Wales and Berwick Act, 1746, s. 3, 32 Halsbury's Statutes 3rd Edn., 412.

Domicil outside Great Britain.—On appeal to the Court of Appeal from a judgment of a county court making a full adoption order in favour of applicants not domiciled in Great Britain it was held that sub-s. (1) (p. 1046, *ante*) of this section was subject to the overriding provision in s. 1 (1) that the proposed adopting parent must be domiciled in England, and, therefore, where an applicant domiciled outside the jurisdiction makes an application under s. 53 (p. 1078, *post*), it is only a provisional order under s. 53 that the court is empowered to make, and a full adoption order, if made, is a nullity for want of jurisdiction. *Re R. (An Infant)*, [1962] 3 All E. R. 238; 126 J. P. 498.

The appeal was heard in camera, and the judgment was reported with leave of the court.

"**Jointly by spouses.**"—See s. 1 (2), (3), *ante*.

"**One of the three months.**"—In *Re M. (an Infant)*, [1965] Ch. 203; [1964] 2 All E. R. 1017; 128 J. P. 522, it was held, on an application for a provisional adoption order, that the requirements of sub-s. (3) of this section were not satisfied where the applicants had lived together in Great Britain for one month during the period of six months, but not during the period of three months, immediately preceding the order.

Definitions.—For "adoption order", see s. 1 (1), *ante*, and s. 57 (1), *post*, in conjunction with s. 53 (4), *post*; and for "England", see s. 57 (1), *post*.

Effects of adoption orders

13. Rights and duties of parents and capacity to marry.— (1) Upon an adoption order being made, all rights, duties, obligations and liabilities of the parents or guardians of the infant in relation to the future custody, maintenance and education of the infant, including all rights to appoint a guardian and (in England) to consent or give notice of dissent to marriage, shall be extinguished, and all such rights, duties, obligations and liabilities shall vest in and be exercisable by and enforceable against the adopter as if the infant were a child born to the adopter in lawful wedlock; and in respect of the matters aforesaid (and, in Scotland, in respect of the liability of a child to maintain his parents) the infant shall stand to the adopter exclusively in the position of a child born to the adopter in lawful wedlock.

(2) In any case where two spouses are the adopters, the spouses shall in respect of the matters aforesaid, and for the purpose of the jurisdiction of any court to make orders as to the custody and maintenance of and right of access to children, stand to each other and to the infant in the same relation as they would have stood if they had been the lawful father and mother of the infant and the infant shall stand to them in the same relation as to a lawful father and mother.

(3) For the purpose of the law relating to marriage, an adopter and the person whom he has been authorised to adopt under an adoption order shall be deemed to be within the prohibited degrees of consanguinity; and the provisions of this subsection shall continue to have effect notwithstanding that some person other than the adopter is authorised by a subsequent order to adopt the same infant.

(4) The references in subsection (3) of this section to an adoption order include references to an order authorising an adoption made under the Adoption of Children Act (Northern Ireland), 1950, or any enactment of the Parliament of Northern Ireland for the time being in force.

NOTES

" Parents."—See s. 1 (4), *ante,* and the note to that section.

" Consent or give notice of dissent to marriage."—For the right of parents to consent or give notice of dissent to marriage, see the Marriage Act, 1949, s. 3 and Second Schedule, pp. 1215, 1218, *post.* Where the adopter refuses his consent to the marriage of an adopted child, such child would have the right to apply to a court of summary jurisdiction under s. 3 of the Marriage Act, 1949, p. 1215, *post.*

" Two spouses."—As to adoption by two spouses, see s. 1 (2), (3), *ante;* and see *Crossley* v. *Crossley,* [1953] P. 97; [1953] 1 All E. R. 891, in which it was decided that any previous custody order made in respect of the child in favour of his former parent terminates on adoption.

" Law relating to marriage."—See, generally, the Marriage Act, 1949, 17 Halsbury's Statutes, 3rd Edn., 44.

" Prohibited degrees of consanguinity."—By s. 2 of the Marriage Act, 1835, all marriages celebrated after the passing of that Act between persons within the prohibited degrees of consanguinity or affinity were to be absolutely null and void. That Act was repealed by s. 79 (1) of, and Part I of the Fifth Schedule to, the Marriage Act, 1949; 17 Halsbury's Statutes 3rd Edn., 44 and s. 2 thereof re-enacted in s. 1 (1) of, and Part I of the First Schedule to, the Act of 1949. See, generally, 19 Halsbury's Laws, 3rd Edn., 782–785.

Family allowances, national insurance.—For the purposes of family allowances and national insurance an adopted child counts as the legitimate child of the adopter or adopters ; see the Family Allowances Act, 1965, s. 17 (4) ; 23 Halsbury's Statutes, 3rd Edn., 745, and the National Insurance Act, 1965, s. 114 (2) (a).

Fatal accidents.—For the purposes of the Fatal Accidents Acts, 1846 to 1908, a person is deemed to be a parent or child of a deceased person notwithstanding that he was only related to him in consequence of adoption, and, accordingly, in deducing any relationship which under the provisions of those Acts is included within the meaning of the expressions " parent " and " child " any adopted person is to be treated as being, or as having been, the legitimate offspring of his adopters; see the Law Reform (Miscellaneous Provisions) Act, 1934, s. 2 (1), (4), 23 Halsbury's Statutes, 3rd Edn., 788, in conjunction with s. 58 (2) and para. 10 of the Fifth Schedule, *post.*

Pensions.—An adopted child is a child within the meaning of the Superannuation Act, 1949, 24 Halsbury's Statutes, 3rd Edn., 843; see ss. 4 (3) (*b*), 63 (1), (4) of that Act; and *cf.* s. 58 (2) and para. 10 of the Fifth Schedule, *post.*

Criminal liability.—As to criminal liability of an adopter for causing or encouraging the prostitution of, intercourse with, or indecent assault on, an adopted girl under sixteen, see the Sexual Offences Act, 1956, s. 28, p. 396, *ante.*

Effect on affiliation order.—See s. 15, p. 1049, *post.*

Change of name.—Apparently an adoption order could always effect a change of surname. See a ruling of a Chancery judge noted at 107 J. P. N. 157. See also note to s. 21, p. 1056, as to change of Christian name.

In the case of *Re T.* (*otherwise H.*) (*An Infant*), [1963] Ch. 238 ; [1962] 3 All E. R. 970, it was held that if there were a right to change an infant's surname it rested primarily with the father as the natural guardian of the person of the infant and that an order granting the custody to the mother did not deprive the father of his rights. The court declared a deed-poll ineffective to change the infant's name and directed the mother to take such steps as were necessary to ensure that the infant was called by his proper name as before that deed.

Definitions.—For " adoption order ", see s. 1 (1), *ante,* and s. 57 (1), *post,* in conjunction with s. 53 (4), *post;* and for " guardian ", " infant " and " England ", see s. 57 (1), *post.*

14. Friendly societies, insurance, etc.—(1) For the purposes of the enactments for the time being in force relating to friendly societies, collecting societies or industrial insurance companies, an adopter shall be deemed to be the parent of the infant whom he is authorised to adopt under an adoption order.

(2) Where, before the making of an adoption order in respect of an infant, the natural parent of the infant has effected an insurance with any such society or company for the payment, on the death of the infant, of money for funeral expenses, the rights and liabilities under the policy shall by virtue of the adoption order be transferred to the adopter and the adopter shall, for the purposes of the said enactments, be treated as the person who took out the policy.

(3) In section eleven of the Married Women's Property Act, 1882, and section two of the Married Women's Policies of Assurance (Scotland) Act, 1880 (which make provision as to policies of assurance effected for the benefit of children) references to a person's children shall include, and be deemed always to have included, references to children adopted by that person under an adoption order.

NOTES

Enactments relating to friendly societies, collecting societies and industrial insurance companies.—For the relevant enactments, see 14 Halsbury's Statutes, 3rd Edn., 255 et seq.

"Parent."—See s. 1 (4), ante, and the note to that section.

Definitions.—For "infant", see s. 57 (1), post; and for "adoption order", see s. 1 (1), ante, and s. 57 (1), post, in conjunction with s. 53 (4), post.

Married Women's Property Act, 1882, s. 11.—See 17 Halsbury's Statutes, 3rd Edn., 116.

15. Affiliation orders, etc.—(1) Where an adoption order is made in respect of an infant who is illegitimate, then, unless the adopter is his mother and the mother is a single woman, any affiliation order or decree of affiliation and aliment in force with respect to the infant, and any agreement whereby the father of the infant has undertaken to make payments specifically for the benefit of the infant, shall cease to have effect, but without prejudice to the recovery of any arrears which are due under the order, decree or agreement at the date of the adoption order.

(2) After an adoption order has been made in respect of an infant who is illegitimate, no affiliation order or decree of affiliation and aliment shall be made with respect to the infant unless the adoption order was made on the application of the mother of the infant alone.

(3) Where an adoption order is made in respect of an infant committed to the care of a local authority by a care order (other than an interim order) in force under the Children and Young Persons Act, 1969, the care order shall cease to have effect.

(4) Where an adoption order is made in respect of an infant in respect of whom a resolution is in force under section two of the Children Act, 1948 or section sixteen of the Social Work (Scotland) Act, 1968, (which sections provide for the assumption by local authorities of parental rights in certain circumstances) the resolution shall cease to have effect.

(5) The references in this section to an adoption order include references to an order authorising an adoption made under the Adoption of Children Act (Northern Ireland), 1950, or any enactment of the Parliament of Northern Ireland for the time being in force.

NOTES

This section is printed as amended by the Social Work (Scotland) Act, 1968, and the Children and Young Persons Act, 1969, s. 72 (3), (4) and Scheds. V and VI.

Marriage.—The provision for the automatic termination of the affiliation order etc., on marriage (see s. 12 (2) of the repealed 1950 Act) is not re-enacted.

Notice to court which made affiliation order.—By Rule 23 of the Adoption (High Court) Rules, 1971, p. 1160, *post*, the guardian *ad litem*, by Rule 23 of the Adoption (County Court) Rules, 1959, p. 1132, *post*, the registrar, and by Rule 24 of the Adoption (Juvenile Court) Rules, 1959, p. 1113, *post*, the justices' clerk is required to serve notice of the making of an adoption order in respect of an infant who is illegitimate (unless the applicant is his mother and a single woman), on any other court which appears to him to have made an affiliation order which is still in force.

Definitions.—For " adoption order ", see s. 1 (1), *ante*, and s. 57 (1), *post*, in conjunction with s. 53 (4), *post*; for " infant " and " father ", see s. 57 (1), *post*; and for " local authority ", see s. 28 (1), *post*.

Children and Young Persons Act, 1969.—For provisions relating to the committal of infants to care of a local authority, see Part I, pp. 124 *et seq.*, *ante*.

Children Act, 1948, s. 2.—See p. 884, *ante*.

16. English intestacies, wills and settlements.—(1) Where, at any time after the making of an adoption order, the adopter or the adopted person or any other person dies intestate in respect of any real or personal property (other than property subject to an entailed interest under a disposition to which subsection (2) of this section does not apply), that property shall devolve in all respects as if the adopted person were the child of the adopter born in lawful wedlock and were not the child of any other person.

(2) In any disposition of real or personal property made, whether by instrument inter vivos or by will (including codicil) after the date of an adoption order—

    (a) any reference (whether express or implied) to the child or children of the adopter shall, unless the contrary intention appears, be construed as, or as including, a reference to the adopted person;

    (b) any reference (whether express or implied) to the child or children of the adopted person's natural parents or either of them shall, unless the contrary intention appears, be construed as not being, or as not including, a reference to the adopted person; and

    (c) any reference (whether express or implied) to a person related to the adopted person in any degree shall, unless the contrary intention appears, be construed as a reference to the person who would be related to him in that degree if he were the child of the adopter born in lawful wedlock and were not the child of any other person.

(3) Where under any disposition any real or personal property or any interest in such property is limited (whether subject to any preceding limitation or charge or not) in such a way that it would, apart from this section, devolve (as nearly as the law permits) along with a dignity or title of honour, then, whether or not the disposition contains an express reference to the dignity or title of honour, and whether or not the property or some interest in the property may in some event become severed therefrom, nothing in this section shall operate to sever the property or any

interest therein from the dignity, but the property or interest shall devolve in all respects as if this section had not been enacted.

(4) The references in this section to an adoption order include references to an order authorising an adoption made under the Adoption of Children Act (Northern Ireland), 1950, or any enactment of the Parliament of Northern Ireland for the time being in force.

NOTES

"**Adoption order.**"—For meaning, see s. 1 (1), *ante,* and s. 57 (1), *post*, and note that, by virtue of s. 53 (4), *post*, this section does not apply to a provisional adoption order.

"**Dies intestate.**"—" Intestate " includes a person who leaves a will but dies intestate as to some beneficial interest in his real or personal estate; see s. 55 (1) (vi) of the Administration of Estates Act, 1925, 13 Halsbury's Statutes, 3rd Edn., 38. Where a person has disposed of property by will, but the disposition fails, he dies intestate in respect of that property; see *Re Ford, Ford* v. *Ford*, [1902] 2 Ch. 605; *Re Cuffe, Fooks* v. *Cuffe*, [1908] 2 Ch. 500. See, further, *Re Skeats, Thain* v. *Gibbs*, [1936] 2 All E. R. 298; [1936] Ch. 683.

For priority of right to a grant of administration where an adopter or adopted person dies intestate, see the Non-Contentious Probate Rules, 1954, S.I. 1954 No. 796, r. 21.

"**Entailed interest.**"—See, generally, as to entailed interests, 27 Halsbury's Laws, 2nd Edn., 688 *et seq.*

Foreign adoption.—In the case of a foreign adoption it was held by Vaisey, J., in *Re Wilson, Grace* v. *Lucas*, [1954] 1 All E. R. 997, that the capacity of an adopted child to succeed to property was a matter to be determined, not by the law governing the adoption, but by the law governing the succession, which, in the case of personal property, was the law of the deceased's domicil; an adoption order made under a foreign jurisdiction could not be brought either expressly or by implication within the provisions or principles of the Adoption Act, 1950, s. 13 (1). See also *Re Marshall, Barclay's Bank, Ltd.* v. *Marshall*, [1957] Ch. 507; [1957] 3 All E. R. 172, C. A.

In *Re Valentine's Settlement, Valentine* v. *Valentine*, [1965] Ch. 831; [1965] 2 All E. R. 226 (Salmon L.J., dissenting), it was held that an English court would not recognize the adoption order of a court of a foreign country as conferring on an adopted infant the status of being a child of the adopting parents unless the adopting parents were domiciled (or, *per* Danckwerts, L.J., regarded by English law as domiciled) in the foreign country at the time of the adoption order. In that case the adopting parents were not domiciled in South Africa at the time the adoption orders were made, and accordingly neither adopted child could by English law take under the settlement of the adopting father. The Adoption Act, 1968, p. 1089, *post*, has not yet been brought into force, when it is, see s. 2, (2), p. 1089, *post*.

Inheritance (family provision).—An adopted child may be a dependant for the purposes of the Inheritance (Family Provision) Act, 1938; see the definitions of " son " and " daughter " in s. 5 (1) thereof, 13 Halsbury's Statutes, 3rd Edn., 118.

"**Disposition . . . made . . . after the date of the adoption order.**"—The term " disposition " means in the case of a will, the will itself, and the effective date is that of the making of the will, and not that of the death of the testator; see *Re Gilpin, Hutchinson* v. *Gilpin*, [1953] 2 All E. R. 1218; [1954] Ch. 1.

"**Reference . . . to the child or children of the adopter.**"—Even where sub-s. (2) is not applicable, the reference to a child may, nevertheless, have to be construed as referring to an adopted child; see *Re Fletcher, Barclays Bank, Ltd.* v. *Ewing*, [1949] 1 All E. R. 732; [1949] Ch. 473, where the testator knew that the adopter was incapable of bearing children; and see also *Re Gilpin, Hutchinson* v. *Gilpin, ubi supra*; *Best* v. *Best*, [1955] 2 All E. R. 839; [1956] P. 76. (variation of marriage settlement in favour of an adopted child when child of marriage born subsequent to adoption); *Re Wilby*, [1956] 1 All E. R. 27; [1956] P. 174 (person adopted abroad and dying intestate domiciled in England—adoptive mother not entitled to administration).

Death duties.—For the purposes of the rates of death duties, an adopted child is treated as the lawful child of the adopter; see the Adoption of Children Act, 1926, s. 5 (3), (4), as amended by the Finance Act, 1949, s. 52, Sch. XI, Part IV, p. 1023, *ante.*

Protection of statutory tenants.—An adopted child, even though not legally adopted, may, for the purposes of the Rent Restriction Acts, succeed to a statutory tenancy as a member of the tenant's family, within the meaning of s. 12 (1) (*g*) of the Increase of Rent and Mortgage Interest (Restrictions) Act, 1920, see *Brock* v. *Wollams,* [1949] 1 All E. R. 715; [1949] 2 K. B. 388, C. A. The wording of the Act of 1920 is "such member of the tenant's family". This Act is repealed and the Rent Act, 1968 makes similar provision as Sched. I, *ibid.*, provides "where . . . a person who was a member of the original tenant's family".

Marriage settlement.—In the case of *Purnell* v. *Purnell,* [1961] P. 141; [1961] 1 All E. R. 369, it was held that the court had jurisdiction to vary a marriage settlement by admitting an adopted child to benefit provided that anything which the natural children of the marriage were called on to give up was sufficiently compensated. In that case the settlement was made before the passing of the Adoption Act, 1950 (now repealed) and the infant had not been adopted at the time of the settlement, and for these reasons no rights were conferred on the infant by that Act, or by the Adoption Act, 1958.

Legitimation.—The revocation of an adoption order under s. 1 of the Adoption Act, 1960, p. 1085, *post,* or under s. 26 of the Adoption Act, 1958, p. 1059, *post,* shall not affect the operation of ss. 16 and 17 of the last mentioned Act in relation to an intestacy which occurred, or a disposition which was made, before the revocation. See s. 1 (2) of the Adoption Act, 1960, p. 1085, *post.*

" Contrary intention."—The contrary intention required to satisfy the words " unless the contrary intention appears " in sub-s. (2) (b) might appear from the surrounding circumstances which carried conviction to the mind of the court, but the effect of surrounding circumstances, if that was relied on to establish a contrary intention must be really cogent and convincing. (*Re Jones' Will Trusts, Jones* v. *Squire,* [1965] Ch. 1124; [1965] 2 All E. R. 828).

See also *Re Jebb (deceased), Ward-Smith* v. *Jebb and others,* p. 1023, *ante.*

17. Provisions supplementary to s. 16.—(1) For the purposes of the application of the Administration of Estates Act, 1925, to the devolution of any property in accordance with the provisions of the last foregoing section, and for the purposes of the construction of any such disposition as is mentioned in that section, an adopted person shall be deemed to be related to any other person being the child or adopted child of the adopter or (in the case of a joint adoption) of either of the adopters—

(a) where he or she was adopted by two spouses jointly, and that other person is the child or adopted child of both of them, as brother or sister of the whole blood;

(b) in any other case, as brother or sister of the half-blood.

(2) For the purposes of subsection (2) of the last foregoing section, a disposition made by will or codicil shall be treated as made on the date of the death of the testator.

(3) Notwithstanding anything in the last foregoing section, trustees or personal representatives may convey or distribute any real or personal property to or among the persons entitled thereto without having ascertained that no adoption order has been made by virtue of which any person is or may be entitled to any interest therein, and shall not be liable to any such person of whose claim they have not had notice at the time of the conveyance or distribution; but nothing in this subsection shall

prejudice the right of any such person to follow the property, or any property representing it, into the hands of any person, other than a purchaser, who may have received it.

(4) Where an adoption order is made in respect of a person who has been previously adopted, the previous adoption shall be disregarded for the purposes of the last foregoing section in relation to the devolution of any property on the death of a person dying intestate after the date of the subsequent adoption order, and in relation to any disposition of property made, or taking effect on the death of a person dying, after that date.

(5) The references in this section to an adoption order shall be construed in accordance with subsection (4) of the last foregoing section.

NOTES

"**Adopted by two spouses jointly.**"—See s. 1 (2), (3), *ante.*

Blood relationship.—Sub-s. (1) makes a natural distinction between the effect of adoption by two spouses, which creates an artificial blood relationship between the child and both the adopters, and adoption by one spouse which creates the relationship with that one and not with the other.

"**Convey or distribute . . . conveyance or distribution.**"—This covers the case where property is appropriated by personal representatives, and retained by them *qua* trustees or beneficiaries; *cf. Clegg* v *Rowland* (1866), L. R. 3 Eq. 368.

Trustees, etc.—Sub-s. (3) protects trustees and personal representatives from liability towards unknown adopted children, and thus relieves them from any obligation to make exhaustive enquiries on the subject. The rights of the adopted child are not taken away, and he may pursue any remedy available if he has not been given some share in property to which he considers he is entitled.

Second adoption.—Where there has been a second adoption, this cancels the former adoption so far as the provisions of s. 13 are concerned, and these apply only to the relationships created by the second adoption.

"**Adoption order.**"—For meaning, see s. 1 (1), *ante,* and s. 57 (1), *post;* and note that by virtue of s. 53 (4), *post,* this section does not apply to a provisional adoption order. Note also sub-s. (5) of this section.

Legitimation.—See note to s. 16, p. 1051, *ante.*

Administration of Estates Act, 1925 (c. 23).—13 Halsbury's Statutes, 3rd Edn., 38.

18. (*Applies to Scotland.*)

19. Citizenship.—(1) Where an adoption order is made in respect of an infant who is not a citizen of the United Kingdom and Colonies, then, if the adopter, or in the case of a joint adoption the male adopter, is a citizen of the United Kingdom and Colonies, the infant shall be a citizen of the United Kingdom and Colonies as from the date of the order.

(2) The references in this section to an adoption order include references to an order authorising an adoption under the Adoption of Children Act (Northern Ireland), 1950, or any enactment of the Parliament of Northern Ireland for the time being in force.

NOTES

"**Citizen of the United Kingdom and Colonies.**"—Citizenship of the United Kingdom and Colonies is dealt with in ss. 4 *et seq.* of the British Nationality Act, 1948, 28 Halsbury's Statutes, 2nd Edn., 142, in conjunction with ss. 3 (1) and 5 of the Ireland Act, 1949, 4 Halsbury's Statutes, 3rd Edn., 670. See also Adoption

Act, 1964, s. 1 (3), p. 1086, *post.* *Cf.* also the India (Consequential Provision) Act, 1949, 4 Halsbury's Statutes, 3rd Edn., 330, and the Pakistan (Consequential Provision) Act, 1956, 4 Halsbury's Statutes, 3rd Edn., 331. Whether adoption by a citizen of one of the Dominions confers Dominion citizenship depends, no doubt, on Dominion law.

British nationality.—Where a husband and wife applied to adopt a Frenchman aged twenty in order that he might acquire British nationality it was held that although the court was satisfied that an adoption order would be for the welfare of the infant it would, in the exercise of its discretion, decline to make an adoption order, because on the facts the applicants did not stand in *loco parentis* to the infant and the adoption sought was an "accommodation" adoption which was not within the intendment of the Adoption Act, 1958 (*Re A. (An Infant)*, [1963] 1 All E. R. 531; 127 J. P. 209).

Definitions.—For "adoption order", see s. 1 (1), *ante*, and s. 57 (1), *post*; and note sub-s. (2) of this section, and s. 53 (4), *post*, by virtue of which this section does not apply to a provisional adoption order. For "infant", see s. 57 (1), *post*.

Registration

20. Adopted Children Register (England).—(1) The Registrar General shall maintain at the General Register Office a register, to be called the Adopted Children Register, in which shall be made such entries as may be directed to be made therein by adoption orders, but no other entries.

(2) In England, a certified copy of an entry in the Adopted Children Register, if purporting to be sealed or stamped with the seal of the General Register Office, shall, without any further or other proof of that entry, be received as evidence of the adoption to which it relates and, where the entry contains a record of the date of the birth or the country or the district and sub-district of the birth of the adopted person, shall also be received as aforesaid as evidence of that date or country or district and sub-district in all respects as if the copy were a certified copy of an entry in the Registers of Births.

(3) The Registrar General shall cause an index of the Adopted Children Register to be made and kept in the General Register Office; and every person shall be entitled to search that index and to have a certified copy of any entry in the Adopted Children Register in all respects upon and subject to the same terms, conditions and regulations as to payment of fees and otherwise as are applicable under the Births and Deaths Registration Act, 1953, and the Registration Service Act, 1953, in respect of searches in other indexes kept in the General Register Office and in respect of the supply from that office of certified copies of entries in the certified copies of the Registers of Births and Deaths.

(4) The Registrar General shall, in addition to the Adopted Children Register and the index thereof, keep such other registers and books, and make such entries therein, as may be necessary to record and make traceable the connection between any entry in the Registers of Births which has been marked "Adopted" pursuant to the next following section or any enactment at the time in force, and any corresponding entry in the Adopted Children Register.

(5) The registers and books kept under subsection (4) of this section shall not be, nor shall any index thereof be, open to public inspection or search, and the Registrar General shall not furnish any person with any

information contained in or with any copy or extract from any such registers or books except under an order of any of the following courts, that is to say—

(a) the High Court;

(b) the Westminster County Court or such other county court as may be prescribed; and

(c) the court by which an adoption order was made in respect of the person to whom the information, copy or extract relates.

(6) In relation to an adoption order made by a magistrates' court, the reference in paragraph (c) of subsection (5) of this section to the court by which the order was made includes a reference to a court acting for the same petty sessions area.

NOTES

Registrar General; General Register Office.—See ss. 1 and 2, respectively, of the Registration Service Act, 1953, 27 Halsbury's Statutes, 3rd Edn., 1055.

" Such entries as may be directed."—See s. 21, *infra*, and for amendment of adoption orders and rectification of the Adopted Children Register, see s. 24, *post*.

" Certified copy."—See as to the position when an adoption order has been amended, s. 24 (6), *post*.

Search.—The fee for a general search is £2, and that for a certified copy of an entry in the Register is 25p on registration and 40p subsequently; see the Births and Deaths Registration Act, 1953, s. 30 (2), 27 Halsbury's Statutes, 3rd Edn., 1021, and S.I. 1968 No. 1242.

Although extracts from the Register are obtainable by members of the public, it will be impossible in ordinary circumstances for anyone to trace the origin and the original birth certificate of an adopted child. In exceptional circumstances, where for instance succession to property or title may be involved, the Registrar-General will be able to supply the necessary information to persons entitled to it. See also the provision in the Rules as to the supply of duplicates or copies of adoption orders by special direction of courts.

" Prescribed."—*I.e.*, by Adoption Rules; see s. 9, *ante*, and s. 57 (1), *post*. At the time of going to press no other county court has been prescribed for the purposes of sub-s. (5) (*b*).

Definitions.—For " adoption order ", see s. 1 (1), *ante*, and s. 57 (1), *post*, in conjunction with s. 53 (4), *post*; and for " England " and " court ", see s. 57 (1), *post*.

Births and Deaths Registration Act, 1953.—27 Halsbury's Statutes, 3rd Edn., 1021.

Registration Service Act, 1953.—27 Halsbury's Statutes, 3rd Edn., 1055.

21. Registration of English adoptions.—(1) Every adoption order made by a court in England shall contain a direction to the Registrar General to make in the Adopted Children Register an entry in the form set out in the First Schedule to this Act, and (subject to the next following subsection) shall specify the particulars to be entered under the headings in columns 2 to 6 of that Schedule.

(2) For the purposes of compliance with the requirements of the last foregoing subsection,—

(a) where the precise date of the infant's birth is not proved to the satisfaction of the court, the court shall determine the probable date of his birth and the date so determined shall be specified in the order as the date of his birth;

     (b) where the country of birth of the infant is not proved to the satisfaction of the court, then, if it appears probable that the infant was born within the United Kingdom, the Channel Islands or the Isle of Man, he shall be treated as having been born in England, and in any other case the particulars of the country of birth may be omitted from the order and from the entry in the Adopted Children Register;

and the names to be specified in the order as the name and surname of the infant shall be the name or names and surname stated in that behalf in the application for the adoption order, or, if no name or surname is so stated, the original name or names of the infant and the surname of the applicant.

     (3) The particulars to be entered in the Adopted Children Register under the heading in column 2 of the First Schedule to this Act shall include, in the case of an infant born in England, the registration district and sub-district in which the birth took place; and where the infant was born in England but the registration district and sub-district in which the birth took place is not proved to the satisfaction of the court, or where the infant is treated by virtue of paragraph (b) of subsection (2) of this section as born in England, he shall be treated for the purposes of this subsection as born in the district and sub-district in which the court sits.

     (4) Where upon any application to a court in England for an adoption order in respect of an infant (not being an infant who has previously been the subject of an adoption order made by a court in England under this Act or any enactment at the time in force) there is proved to the satisfaction of the court the identity of the infant with a child to whom an entry in the Registers of Births relates, any adoption order made in pursuance of the application shall contain a direction to the Registrar General to cause the entry in the Registers of Births to be marked with the word " Adopted ".

     (5) Where an adoption order is made by a court in England in respect of an infant who has previously been the subject of an adoption order made by such a court under this Act or any enactment at the time in force, the order shall contain a direction to the Registrar General to cause the previous entry in the Adopted Children Register to be marked with the word " Re-adopted ".

     (6) Where an adoption order is made by a court in England, the prescribed officer of the court shall cause the order to be communicated in the prescribed manner to the Registrar General, and upon receipt of the communication the Registrar General shall cause compliance to be made with the directions contained in the order.

NOTES

     "Adopted Children Register."—This is maintained by the Registrar General under s. 20 (1), *ante*. For provisions as to amendment of adoption orders and rectification of the register, see s. 24, *infra*, and for provision as to marking of entries in the case of provisional adoption orders, see s. 53 (6), *post*.

     Date of birth.—The court is bound, it seems, to state an actual date, however difficult it may be to guess within weeks or even months what that precise date is. The evident object of this is to spare children from the suspicion that they are illegitimate and perhaps foundlings, which naturally arises when a certificate gives " on or about " some date in place of a precise date.

     Change of name.—Sub-s. (2) seems to ratify a practice which has existed in many courts of allowing adopters to change both the christian name and the surname of the infant.   Strictly, however, it seems that where a child has been baptized its christian name cannot be changed on adoption, although additional christian names may be given; see *Re Parrott*, [1946] Ch. 183; [1946] 1 All E. R. 321.   See also *Practice Direction*—Infant—Change of surname—Enrolment of Deed Poll, [1969] 3 All E. R. 288.

"**United Kingdom.**"—See the note to s. 6, *ante*.

"**Registration district and sub-district.**"—See s. 5 (1) of the Registration Service Act, 1953, 27 Halsbury's Statutes, 3rd Edn., 1021.

"**Registers of Births.**"—See, in particular, ss. 1 (1) and 25 of the Births and Deaths Registration Act, 1953, 27 Halsbury's Statutes, 3rd Edn., 1021.   For provisions as to marking of entries of adopted children, see regs. 37 and 38 of the Registration of Births, Deaths and Marriages Regulations, 1968, S.I. 1968 No. 2049, p. 1148, *post*.   For provisions as to cancellation of the making of entries under sub-s. (4) of this section, see s. 24 (2), (3), (4), (5), *post*, and for marking in the case of provisional adoption orders, see s. 53 (6), *post*.

"**Prescribed officer; prescribed manner.**"—*I.e.*, prescribed by Adoption Rules; see s. 9, *ante*, and s. 57 (1), *post*.

Birth certificate in shortened form.—Under s. 33 of the Births and Deaths Registration Act, 1953, 27 Halsbury's Statutes, 3rd Edn., 1045, birth certificates may be obtained in shortened form, containing no particulars relating to parentage or adoption.   See the Birth Certificate (Shortened Form) Regulations, 1968 (S.I. 1968 No. 2050 and Regs. 81 and 82 of the Registration of Births, Deaths and Marriages, Regulations, 1968 (S.I. 1968 No. 2049).   Regulation 4 of the Regulations relates *inter alia* to the issue of such a shortened certificate in respect of an adopted person.

As to short certificate of baptism see the Baptismal Register Measure, 1961 ; p. 1299, *post*.

Interim order.—An interim order is deemed not to be an adoption order for the purposes of this Act, s. 8, *ibid.*, p. 1042, *ante*, and a copy should not be sent to the Registrar General.

Definitions.—For " adoption order ", see s. 1 (1), *ante*, and s. 57 (1), *post*, in conjunction with s. 53 (4), *post*; for " court ", " England " and " infant ", see s. 57 (1), *post*.

22, 23. (*Apply to Scotland.*)

24. Amendment of orders and rectification of Registers.—(1) The court by which an adoption order has been made may, on the application of the adopter or of the adopted person, amend the order by the correction of any error in the particulars contained therein, and may—

(a) if satisfied on the application of the adopter or of the adopted person that within one year beginning with the date of the order any new name has been given to the adopted person (whether in baptism or otherwise), or taken by him, either in lieu of or in addition to a name specified in the particulars required to be entered in the Adopted Children Register in pursuance of the order, amend the order by substituting or adding that name in those particulars, as the case may require;

(b) if satisfied on the application of any person concerned that a direction for the marking of an entry in the Registers of Births, the Register of Births or the Adopted Children Register included in the order in pursuance of subsection (4) or subsection (5) of section twenty-one or subsection (4) or subsection (5) of section twenty-three of this Act was wrongly so included, revoke that direction.

(2) Where an adoption order is amended or a direction revoked under subsection (1) of this section, the prescribed officer of the court or, in Scotland, the clerk of the court, shall cause the amendment to be communicated in the prescribed manner to the Registrar General or, as the case may be, the Registrar General for Scotland, who shall as the case may require,—

(a) cause the entry in the Adopted Children Register to be amended accordingly; or

(b) cause the marking of the entry in the Registers of Births, the Register of Births or the Adopted Children Register to be cancelled.

(3) Where an adoption order is quashed or an appeal against an adoption order allowed by any court, the court shall give directions to the Registrar General or the Registrar General for Scotland to cancel any entry in the Adopted Children Register, and any marking of an entry in that Register, the Registers of Births or the Register of Births, as the case may be, which was effected in pursuance of the order.

(4) Where the Registrar General is notified by the Registrar General for Scotland that an adoption order has been made by a court in Scotland in respect of an infant to whom an entry in the Registers of Births or the Adopted Children Register relates, the Registrar General shall cause the entry to be marked " Adopted (Scotland) ", or, as the case may be, " Re-adopted (Scotland) "; and where, after an entry has been so marked, the Registrar General is notified as aforesaid that the adoption order has been quashed, or that an appeal against the adoption order has been allowed, he shall cause the marking to be cancelled.

(5) Where the Registrar General for Scotland is notified by the Registrar General that an adoption order has been made by a court in England in respect of an infant to whom an entry in the Register of Births or the Adopted Children Register maintained by the Registrar General for Scotland relates, the Registrar General for Scotland shall cause the entry to be marked " Adopted (England) " or, as the case may be, " Re-adopted (England) "; and where, after an entry has been so marked, the Registrar General for Scotland is notified as aforesaid that the adoption order has been quashed, or that an appeal against the adoption order has been allowed, he shall cause the marking to be cancelled.

(6) Where an adoption order has been amended, any certified copy of the relevant entry in the Adopted Children Register which may be issued pursuant to subsection (3) of section twenty of this Act shall be a copy of the entry as amended, without the reproduction of any note or marking relating to the amendment or of any matter cancelled pursuant thereto; and a copy or extract of an entry in any register, being an entry the marking of which has been cancelled, shall be deemed to be an accurate copy if and only if both the marking and the cancellation are omitted therefrom.

(7) In relation to an adoption order made by a magistrates' court, the reference in subsection (1) of this section to the court by which the order has been made includes a reference to a court acting for the same petty sessions area.

NOTES

Venue, juvenile court.—Application is to be made to a juvenile court acting for the same petty sessions area as the juvenile court which made the adoption order. See Rule 27 of the Adoption (Juvenile Court) Rules, 1959, p. 1113, *post.*

Procedure.—The proper procedure would appear to be to treat the application as if it were a complaint for an order and to give interested parties the opportunity to make representations at the hearing. See Rule 27, p. 1113, *post.*

The notice sent to the Registrar General by the justices' clerk will presumably reproduce the adjudication entered in the court register.

Sub-s. (1): Correction of any error.—In *R.* v. *Chelsea Juvenile Court Justices (Re an Infant)*, [1955] I All E. R. 38 ; 119 J. P. 59, it was laid down that this section gave the court power in the widest terms to correct any error and was not a mere slip rule. In that case an adoption order had been made in respect of a child who was in the care of a local authority. The adopter subsequently had reason to doubt the accuracy of the particulars of age and identity and applied to the justices for correction of the errors. The justices considered they had no jurisdiction. An order of mandamus was issued directing them to hear the application.

" Adopted Children Register."—This is maintained by the Registrar General under s. 20 (1), *ante.* For the marking of entries therein, see s. 21, *ante,* and for the marking of entries in the case of provisional adoption orders, see s. 53 (6), *post.*

" Registers of births."—See the note to s. 21, *ante.* For the marking of entries therein, see s. 21 (4), (6), *ante,* and for the marking of entries in the case of provisional orders, see s. 53 (6), *post.*

Sub-s. (2): " Prescribed officer "; " prescribed manner."—The prescribed officer in proceedings in juvenile courts is the justices' clerk. See Rule 27 of the Adoption (Juvenile Court) Rules, 1959, p. 1113, *post.*

The form of application to be used is Form No. 12, *ibid.,* p. 1126, *post.*

" Registrar General."—See s. 1 of the Registration Service Act, 1953, 27 Halsbury's Statutes, 3rd Edn., 1055.

25. Registration and certificates of baptism.—Where a child in respect of whom an adoption order has been made is baptised, the entry to be made in the register under section three of the Parochial Registers Act, 1812, or, as the case may be, the certificate to be transmitted under section four of that Act, shall describe the child as the adopted son or daughter of the person or persons by whom he or she was adopted, instead of as the son or daughter of the natural parents.

NOTES

" Adoption order."—For meaning, see s. 1 (1), *ante,* and s. 57 (1), *post,* in conjunction with s. 53 (4), *post.*

Parochial Registers Act, 1812, ss. 3, 4.—10 Halsbury's Statutes 3rd Edn., 182.

Children baptised before adoption.—See directive issued by the Archbishops of Canterbury, York and Wales to diocesan bishops and registrars, p. 1175, *post.* Local registrars will be asked to inform parents about the facilities provided by the Baptismal Register Measure, 1961, when they attend to give information for the re-registration of the birth in pursuance of s. 14 of the Births and Deaths Registration Act, 1953 (Letter from General Register Office dated September 4, 1961).

Entries in Marriage Registers.—See directive above, p. 1175, *post.*

Legitimation following adoption

26. Legitimation: revocation of adoption orders and cancellations in Registers.—(1) Where any person adopted by his father or mother alone has subsequently become a legitimated person on the marriage of his father and mother, the court by which the adoption order was

made may, on the application of any of the parties concerned, revoke that order.

(2) Where an adoption order is revoked under this section, the prescribed officer of the court or, in Scotland, the clerk of the court, shall cause the revocation to be communicated in the prescribed manner to the Registrar General or, as the case may be, the Registrar General for Scotland, who shall cause to be cancelled—

(a) the entry in the Adopted Children Register relating to the adopted person; and

(b) the marking with the word " Adopted " (or, as the case may be, with that word and the word " (Scotland) " or " (England) ") of any entry relating to him in the Registers of Birth or the Register of Births;

and a copy or extract of an entry in any register, being an entry the marking of which is cancelled under this section, shall be deemed to be an accurate copy if and only if both the marking and the cancellation are omitted therefrom.

(3) In relation to an adoption order made by a magistrates' court, the reference in subsection (1) of this section to the court by which the order was made includes a reference to a court acting for the same petty sessions area.

NOTES

Intestacies, dispositions.—The revocation of an adoption order under this section shall not affect the operation of ss. 16 and 17 of the Adoption Act, 1958, in relation to an intestacy which occurred, or a disposition which was made, before the revocation. See s. 1 (2) of the Adoption Act 1960, p. 1085, *post*.

Section 1 of the Adoption Act, 1960, shall be construed as one with this section; and any reference in the Adoption Act, 1958, to s. 26 of that Act or to sub-s. (1) of that section shall be construed as including a reference to sub-s. (1) of s. 1 of the Adoption Act, 1960. See s. 1 (3) *ibid.*, p. 1085, *ante.*

Legitimacy Acts.—For the Legitimacy Acts, 1926 and 1959, see pp. 1299 *et seq.*, *post.*

Venue, juvenile court.—See note to s. 24, p. 1059, *ante.*

" Prescribed officer"; " prescribed manner."—See note to s. 24, p. 677, *ante.*

" Registrar General."—See s. 1 of the Registration Service Act, 1953, 27 Halsbury's Statutes, 3rd Edn., 1055.

Procedure.—See note to s. 24, p. 1059, *ante.*

" Adopted Children Register."—This is maintained by the Registrar General under s. 20 (1), *ante.* Entries are made under s. 21, *ante*, and provision for rectification of the Register is made by s. 24, *ante.*

" Registers of births."—See the note to s. 21, *ante*, and see as to marking of the word " Adopted ", ss. 21 (4), 24 (4), (5), *ante.*

Adoption Act, 1960.—S. 1 of the Adoption Act, 1960, p. 1085, *post*, is to be construed as one with this section.

Definitions.—For " father " and " court ", see s. 57 (1), *post*; and for " adoption order ", see s. 1 (1), *ante*, and s. 57 (1), *post*, in conjunction with s. 53 (4), *post.*

27. Legitimation: marking of entries on re-registration of births.—Without prejudice to the provisions of section twenty-six of this Act, where, after an entry in the Registers of Births or the Register of Births has been marked with the word " Adopted " (with or without the addition of the word " (Scotland) " or " (England) ") the birth is re-registered under section fourteen of the Births and Deaths Registration Act, 1953, or section two of the Registration of Births, Deaths, and Marriages (Scotland) (Amendment) Act, 1934 (which provide for the re-registration of the birth of legitimated persons), the entry made on the re-registration shall be marked in the like manner.

NOTES

" **Registers of births.**"—See the note to s. 21, *ante*, and see as to the marking of the word " Adopted ", ss. 21 (4), 24 (4), (5), *ante*.

Births and Deaths Registration Act, 1953, s. 14.—27 Halsbury's Statutes 3rd Edn., 1021.

Baptism.—As to the annotation of entries in the Register of Baptism see the Baptismal Registers Measure, 1961, pp. 1299 *et seq., post*.

PART II

LOCAL AUTHORITIES AND ADOPTION SOCIETIES

28. Local authorities.—(1) The local authorities for the purposes of this Act are, in England, the councils of counties and county boroughs and, in Scotland, the councils of counties and large burghs within the meaning of the Local Government (Scotland) Act, 1947; and for the purposes of this Act any small burgh within the meaning of that Act shall be included in the county in which it is situated.

(2) Every such local authority have power to make and participate in arrangements for the adoption of children.

NOTES

" **Counties.**"—The administrative counties in England and Wales are the adminis-trative counties named in Part I of the First Schedule to the Local Government Act, 1933, 19 Halsbury's Statutes, 3rd Edn., 393 ; s. 1 (2) (a) of the Act of 1933.

" **County boroughs.**"—These are the boroughs named in Part II of the First Schedule to the Local Government Act, 1933, 19 Halsbury's Statutes, 3rd Edn., 393 ; see s. 1 (2) (b) of that Act.   As to London the reference to a county borough is to be construed as a reference to the council of a London borough and the Common Council (London Government Act, 1963, s. 47 ; 20 Halsbury's Statutes, 3rd Edn. 504).

" **Make and participate in arrangements.**"—The Secretary of State may make regulations with respect to the exercise by local authorities of their functions of making or participating in arrangements for the adoption of children; see s. 32 (3), *post*.

Social Services committees.—For the discharge of functions of local autho-rities under Part II of this Act through Social Services committees or joint com-mittees, see s. 2 and Sched. I of the Local Authorities Social Services Act, 1970, p. 927, *ante*.

Definitions.—For " England ", see s. 57 (1), *post*; and for " make arrangements for the adoption of children ", see s. 57 (2), *post*.

29. Restriction on making arrangements for adoption.—(1) It shall not be lawful for any body of persons to make any arrangements for the adoption of an infant unless that body is a registered adoption society or a local authority.

(2) It shall not be lawful for a registered adoption society or local authority by whom arrangements are made for the adoption of an infant

to place him in the care and possession of a person who proposes to adopt him if an adoption order in respect of the infant could not lawfully be made in favour of that person.

(3) Every person who—

(a) takes any part in the management or control of a body of persons which exists wholly or in part for the purpose of making arrangements for the adoption of infants and which is not a registered adoption society or a local authority; or

(b) is guilty of a contravention of subsection (1) or subsection (2) of this section;

shall be liable on summary conviction to imprisonment for a term not exceeding six months or to a fine not exceeding one hundred pounds or to both.

(4) In any proceedings for an offence under paragraph (a) of subsection (3) of this section, proof of things done or of words written, spoken or published (whether or not in the presence of any party to the proceedings) by any person taking part in the management or control of a body of persons, or in making arrangements for the adoption of infants on behalf of the body, shall be admissible as evidence of the purpose for which that body exists.

(5) The court by which a person is convicted of a contravention of subsection (2) of this section may order the infant in respect of whom the offence was committed to be returned to his parent or guardian or to the registered adoption society or local authority.

NOTES

"**If an adoption order . . . could not lawfully be made.**"—No adoption order may be made in favour of a person who does not satisfy the conditions laid down in s. 2, *ante*, or (apart from provisional adoption orders under s. 53) who is not domiciled in England or Scotland; see s. 1 (1), *ante*.

"**Summary conviction.**"—Summary jurisdiction and procedure are now mainly governed by the Magistrates' Courts Act, 1952, 21 Halsbury's Statutes, 3rd Edn., 181, and the Magistrates' Courts Act, 1957, 21 Halsbury's Statutes, 3rd Edn., 316. For time limit on prosecutions, see s. 104 of the Act of 1952, and the Magistrates' Courts Rules, 1968. Proceedings may be taken by a local authority; see s. 54 (2), *post*.

"**Not exceeding six months.**"—As the maximum term of imprisonment which may be imposed exceeds three months, the defendant, if he appears personally, may claim trial by jury under s. 25 of the Magistrates' Courts Act, 1952, p. 276, *ante*.

Disobedience to order under sub-s. (5).—Apparently this should be dealt with under s. 54 of the Magistrates' Courts Act, 1952.

Officers, etc., of bodies corporate.—The liability of these in respect of offences by such a body is stated in s. 54 (1), p. 1079, *post*.

Definitions.—For "body of persons", "registered adoption society" and "infant", see s. 57 (1), *post*; for "local authority", see s. 28 (1), *ante*; for "adoption order", see s. 1 (1), *ante*, and s. 57 (1), *post*, in conjunction with s. 53 (4), *post*; and for "make any arrangements for the adoption of an infant", see s. 57 (2), *post*.

30. Registration of adoption societies.—(1) Subject to the following provisions of this Part of this Act, where an application is made in the prescribed manner by or on behalf of an adoption society to the local authority in whose area the administrative centre of the society is situated and there is furnished therewith the prescribed information relating to the activities of the society, the local authority shall, on payment by the society of such fee (not exceeding one pound) as may be prescribed, register the society under this Part of this Act.

(2) Any question where the administrative centre of an adoption society is situated shall be determined by the Secretary of State, whose determination shall be final.

(3) A local authority shall not register an adoption society under this Part of this Act unless the authority are satisfied, by such evidence as the authority may reasonably require, that the society are a charitable association.

(4) A local authority may refuse to register an adoption society under this Part of this Act, if it appears to the authority—

(a) that the activities of the society are not controlled by a committee of members of the society who are responsible to the members of the society;

(b) that any person proposed to be employed, or employed, by the society for the purpose of making any arrangements for the adoption of children on behalf of the society is not a fit and proper person to be so employed;

(c) that the number of competent persons proposed to be employed, or employed, by the society for the purpose aforesaid is, in the opinion of the authority, insufficient having regard to the extent of the activities of the society in connection with that purpose; or

(d) that any person taking part in the management or control of the society or any member of the society has been convicted of an offence under this Part of this Act, Part II of the Adoption Act, 1950, or the Adoption of Children (Regulation) Act, 1939, or of a breach of any regulations made under this Part of this Act, the said Part II, or the said Act of 1939.

(5) A local authority may at any time cancel the registration of an adoption society on any ground which would entitle the authority to refuse an application for the registration of the society, or on the ground that the society are no longer a charitable association, or on the ground that the administrative centre of the society is no longer situated in the area of the authority.

NOTES

"**Prescribed manner**"; "**prescribed information**"; "**prescribed fee.**"—*I.e.*, prescribed by regulations made by the Secretary of State; see ss. 32 (1), 57 (1), *post*. For the relevant provisions, see the Adoption Agencies Regulations, 1959, pp. 1100 *et seq.*, *post*.

"**Administrative centre.**"—If the registration is cancelled only because of a change of address the society can of course apply for registration in the district into which it has moved. Any question as to its administrative centre may be finally determined by the Secretary of State; sub-s. (2).

"**Secretary of State.**"—For the meaning of this expression, see the Interpretation Act, 1889, s. 12 (3), 32 Halsbury's Statutes, 3rd Edn., 439.

Refusal or cancellation of registration.—For procedure where a local authority propose to refuse an application for registration or to cancel a registration, see s. 31 (1)–(3), *infra*, and for appeals, see s. 31 (4)–(6), *post*.

Definitions.—For " adoption society " and " charitable association ", see s. 57 (1), *post*; and for " local authority ", see s. 28 (1), *ante*.

Adoption Act, 1950, Part II.—That Part is in effect replaced by Part II of this Act, and the Act of 1950 is repealed by s. 59 (2) and the Sixth Schedule, *post*.

Adoption of Children (Regulation) Act, 1939.—That Act was repealed by s. 46 (1) of, and the Fourth Schedule to, the Adoption Act, 1950.

31. Procedure and right of appeal.—(1) Where a local authority propose to refuse an application for registration made to them by or on behalf of an adoption society or to cancel the registration of an adoption society, the local authority shall give to the society not less than fourteen days' notice in writing of their intention to do so.

(2) Every such notice shall state the grounds on which the authority intend to refuse the application or to cancel the registration, as the case may be, and shall contain an intimation that, if within fourteen days after the receipt of the notice the society inform the authority in writing that they desire to do so, the authority will, before refusing the application or cancelling the registration, as the case may be, give to the society an opportunity of causing representations to be made to the authority by or on behalf of the society.

(3) If the local authority, after giving to the society an opportunity of causing such representations as aforesaid to be made, decide to refuse the application for registration or to cancel the registration, as the case may be, they shall give to the society notice in writing of their decision.

(4) Any adoption society aggrieved by the refusal of an application for registration, or by the cancellation of their registration, by a local authority may—

(a) in England, appeal to the Crown Court by a notice of appeal given within twenty-one days after notice in writing of the decision has been given to the society;

(b) *(applies to Scotland.)*

(5) [*Repealed by the Courts Act, 1971, s. 56 and Sched. XI, Part IV.*]

(6) Where the registration of an adoption society is cancelled by a local authority, the adoption society shall, for the purposes of this Part of this Act, be deemed to be registered under this Part of this Act during the period within which an appeal against the cancellation may be brought under this section and, if such an appeal is brought, until the determination or abandonment of the appeal.

NOTES

" Application for registration."—See s. 30 (1), *ante*.

" Representations."—Presumably the local authority is not bound to hear witnesses or to hold any kind of hearing. The representations may, no doubt, be written, but there would seem to be no reason why the local authority should not hear representatives of the society if it think fit.

" Refuse an application."—An application must be refused in accordance with s. 30 (3), *ante*, and may be refused in accordance with s. 30 (4), *ante*.

" Cancel the registration."—A registration may be cancelled in accordance with s. 30 (5), *ante*.

" Not less than fourteen days."—*I.e.*, not less than fourteen clear days must intervene between the day on which the notice is given and that on which the application is refused or the registration cancelled; see *Re Hector Whaling, Ltd.*, [1936] Ch. 208; [1935] All E. R. Rep. 302; and see also *McQueen* v. *Jackson*, [1903] 2 K. B. 163.

" **Notice.**"—This may be given by post; see s. 55, *post.*

" **Notice of appeal.**"—It is to be noted that the period during which notice may be given is twenty-one days which now corresponds with the provisions for appeals from magistrates' courts. The notice must be in writing and addressed to the appropriate officer of the Crown Court and to any other party to the appeal. (Crown Court Rules, 1971, r. 7 (2)).

" **Within twenty-one days.**"—The day on which notice of the decision is given is not to be reckoned; see *Goldsmiths' Co.* v. *West Metropolitan Rail. Co.*, [1904] 1 K. B. 1, C. A., and *Stewart* v. *Chapman*, [1951] 2 All E. R. 613.

Definitions.—For " local authority ", see s. 28 (1), *ante*; and for " adoption society " and " England ", see s. 57 (1), *post.*

32. Adoption societies regulations, etc.—(1) The Secretary of State may make regulations for any of the purposes set out in the Third Schedule to this Act and for prescribing anything which by this Part of this Act (including that Schedule) is authorised or required to be prescribed.

(2) Any person who contravenes or fails to comply with the provisions of regulations made under subsection (1) of this section shall be liable on summary conviction to a fine not exceeding twenty-five pounds and, in the case of a second or subsequent conviction, to a fine not exceeding fifty pounds.

(3) The Secretary of State may make regulations with respect to the exercise by local authorities of their functions of making or participating in arrangements for the adoption of children, and such regulations may make provision, in relation to local authorities who exercise those functions, for purposes corresponding with the purposes for which the Secretary of State has power under subsection (1) of this section to make regulations in relation to registered adoption societies.

NOTES

Third Schedule.—See p. 1084, *post.*

" **Secretary of State.**"—For the meaning of this expression, see the Interpretation Act, 1889 (c. 63), s. 12 (3), 32 Halsbury's Statutes, 3rd Edn., 439. The Advisory Council on Child Care does not advise the Secretary of State on matters connected with the discharge of his functions under sub-s. (3) of this section; see s. 43 (1) of the Children Act, 1948 (c. 43), 17 Halsbury's Statutes, 3rd Edn., 538, as amended by s. 58 (1) and the Fourth Schedule, *post.*

" **Any person.**"—For additional provisions as to offences by bodies corporate, see s. 54 (1), *post.*

" **Summary conviction.**"—See the note to s. 29, *ante.*

" **Second or subsequent conviction.**"—See note at p. 26, *ante.*

"**Local authorities . . . making or participating in arrangements.**"—*I.e.*, under s. 28 (2), *ante.*

Definitions.—For " prescribed " and " registered adoption society ", see s. 57 (1), *post*; for " making arrangements for the adoption of children ", see s. 57 (2), *post*; and for " local authority ", see s. 28 (1), *ante.*

Regulations.—The power to make regulations is exercisable by statutory instrument; see s. 56 (1), *post.*

See the Adoption Agencies Regulations, 1959, p. 1100, *post.* These relate both to adoption societies and to local authorities who make or participate in arrangements for the adoption of children.

As to Scotland see the Adoption Societies (Scotland) Regulations, 1959, S.I. 1959 No. 773 as amended by the Adoption Agencies (Scotland) Regulations, 1961, S.I. 1961 No. 1270.

33. Inspection of books, etc., of registered adoption societies.— (1) A local authority may at any time give notice in writing to any registered adoption society which has been registered by the authority under this Part of this Act, or to any officer of such a society, requiring that society or officer to produce to the authority such books, accounts and other documents relating to the performance by the society of the function of making arrangements for the adoption of infants as the authority may consider necessary for the exercise of the powers conferred on the authority by subsection (5) of section thirty of this Act.

(2) Any such notice may contain a requirement that any information to be furnished in accordance with the notice shall be verified by statutory declaration.

(3) Any person who fails to comply with the requirements of a notice under this section shall be liable on summary conviction to imprisonment for a term not exceeding three months or to a fine not exceeding fifty pounds or to both.

NOTES

"**Notice.**"—Notice may be given by post; see s. 55, *post.*

"**Registered under this Part of this Act.**"—*I.e.,* in pursuance of s. 30, *ante.*

"**Statutory declaration.**"—*I.e.,* a declaration made by virtue of the Statutory Declarations Act, 1835, 12 Halsbury's Statutes, 3rd Edn., 804; see the Interpretation Act, 1889, s. 21, 32 Halsbury's Statutes, 3rd Edn., 450.

"**Summary conviction.**"—See the note to s. 29, *ante.*

Definitions.—For " local authority ", see s. 28 (1), *ante;* and for " registered adoption society " and " infant ", see s. 57 (1), *post.*

"**Person.**"—This would include a registered adoption society. Such a body might be corporate or unincorporate; see definition of " body of persons " in s. 57, p. 1080, *post,* and see Interpretation Act, 1889, s. 19; 32 Halsbury's Statutes, 3rd Edn., 449.

Part III

Care and Possession of Infants Awaiting Adoption

34. Restriction on removal by parent or guardian after giving consent.—While an application for an adoption order in respect of an infant is pending in any court, a parent or guardian of the infant who has signified his consent to the making of an adoption order in pursuance of the application shall not be entitled, except with the leave of the court, to remove the infant from the care and possession of the applicant, and in considering whether to grant or refuse such leave the court shall have regard to the welfare of the infant.

NOTES

"**Parent.**"—See s. 1 (4), *ante,* and the note to that section.

Consent to the making of an adoption order signified.—See as to consents, s. 4, *ante.*

" **Leave of the court.**"—See r. 31A of the Adoption (Juvenile Courts) Rules, 1959, p. 1114, *post*, and Form 14 p. 1126, *post*; r. 27A of the Adoption (County Courts) Rules, 1959, p. 1133, *post*, and Rule 27 of the Adoption (High Court) Rules, 1971, p. 1161, *post*.

Definitions.—For "adoption order ", see s. 1 (1), *ante*, and s. 57 (1), *post*, in conjunction with s. 53 (4), *post*; and for " infant ", " court " and " guardian ", see s. 57 (1), *post*.

35. Return of infants placed by adoption societies and local authorities.—(1) Subject to subsection (2) of this section, at any time after an infant has been delivered into the care and possession of any person in pursuance of arrangements made by a registered adoption society or local authority for the adoption of the infant by that person, and before an adoption order has been made on the application of that person in respect of the infant—

    (a) that person may give notice in writing to the society or authority of his intention not to retain the care and possession of the infant; or

    (b) the society or authority may cause notice in writing to be given to that person of their intention not to allow the infant to remain in his care and possession.

(2) After an application has been made for an adoption order in the case of an infant, no notice shall be given in respect of that infant under paragraph (b) of subsection (1) of this section except with the leave of the court.

(3) Where a notice is given to an adoption society or local authority by any person, or by such a society or authority to any person, under subsection (1) of this section, or where an application for an adoption order made by any person in respect of an infant placed in his care and possession by such a society or authority is refused by the court or withdrawn, that person shall, within seven days after the date on which notice was given or the application refused or withdrawn, as the case may be, cause the infant to be returned to the society or authority, and the society or authority shall receive the infant.

(4) Where the period specified in an interim order made under section eight of this Act (whether as originally made or as varied under subsection (4) of that section) expires without an adoption order having been made in respect of the infant, subsection (3) of this section shall apply as if the application for an adoption order upon which the interim order was made had been refused at the expiration of that period.

(5) It shall be sufficient compliance with the requirements of subsection (3) of this section if the infant is delivered to, and is received by, a suitable person nominated for the purpose by the adoption society or local authority.

(6) Any person who contravenes the provisions of this section shall be liable on summary conviction to imprisonment for a term not exceeding six months or to a fine not exceeding one hundred pounds or to both; and the court by which the offender is convicted may order the infant in respect of whom the offence is committed to be returned to his parent or guardian or to the registered adoption society or local authority.

NOTES

"**Has been delivered.**"—A registered adoption society or local authority by whom arrangements are made for the adoption of an infant may not place him in the care and possession of a person who proposes to adopt him if an adoption order in respect of the infant could not lawfully be made in that person's favour; see s. 29 (2), *ante*.

For further provisions as to adopted children in the care of local authorities, see s. 36, *infra*.

"**Notice.**"—This may be given by post; see s. 55, *post*.

"**Within seven days.**"—*Cf.* the note " Within twenty-one days " to s. 31, *ante*.

In *Re C. S. C. (an Infant)*, [1960] 1 All E. R. 711; 124 J. P. 260, where Roxburgh, J., discharged an adoption order on appeal, he held that the court had no jurisdiction to order a stay.

"**Any person.**"—For additional provisions as to offences by bodies corporate, see s. 54 (1), *post*.

"**Summary conviction**"; "**not exceeding six months.**"—See the notes to s. 29, *ante*.

"**Court may order.**"—Disobedience to such an order could, it is submitted, be dealt with under s. 54 of the Magistrates' Courts Act, 1952, 21 Halsbury's Statutes, 3rd Edn., 230.

Definitions.—For " infant ", " registered adoption society " and " court ", see s. 57 (1), *post*; for " adoption order ", see s. 1 (1), *ante*, and s. 57 (1), *post*, in conjunction with s. 53 (4), *post*; for " local authority ", see s. 28 (1), *ante*; and for " arrangements made ", see s. 57 (2), *post*.

Leave of the court.—See note to s. 34, p. 1067, *ante*, for the appropriate Adoption Rules.

36. Further provisions as to adoption of children in care of local authorities.—(1) Where notice of intention to apply for an adoption order is given in pursuance of subsection (2) of section three of this Act in respect of an infant who is for the time being in the care of a local authority, not being an infant who was delivered into the care and possession of the person by whom the notice is given in pursuance of such arrangements as are mentioned in subsection (1) of section thirty-five of this Act, the said section thirty-five shall apply as if the infant had been so delivered, except that where the application is refused by the court or withdrawn the infant need not be returned to the local authority unless the local authority so require.

(2) Where notice of intention is given as aforesaid in respect of any infant who is for the time being in the care of a local authority then, until the application for an adoption order has been made and disposed of, any right of the local authority to require the infant to be returned to them otherwise than in pursuance of the said section thirty-five shall be suspended; and while the infant remains in the care and possession of the person by whom the notice is given—

> (a) no contribution shall be payable (whether under a contribution order or otherwise) in respect of the infant by any person liable under section eighty-six of the Children and Young Persons Act, 1933, or section seventy-eight of the Social Work (Scotland) Act, 1968, to make contributions in respect of him (but without prejudice to the recovery of any sum due at the time the notice is given); and

(b) subsections (2) and (3) of section eleven of the Family Allowances Act, 1945 (which provide that certain children in the care of a local authority shall not be treated as included in any family for the purposes of that Act) shall not apply in relation to the infant,

unless twelve weeks have elapsed since the giving of the notice without the application being made or the application has been refused by the court or withdrawn.

(3) Where notice of intention to apply for an adoption order is given as aforesaid in respect of any infant who is for the time being in the care of a local authority, and is given to a local authority other than the local authority in whose care the infant is, the authority to whom the notice is given shall inform that other authority of the receipt of the notice.

NOTES

This section is printed as amended by the Social Work (Scotland) Act, 1968, Sched. VIII.

Definitions.—For " infant " and " court ", see s. 57 (1), *post*; for " local authority ", see s. 28 (1), *ante*; and for " adoption order ", see s. 1 (1), *ante*, and s. 57 (1), *post*, in conjunction with s. 53 (4), *post*.

Children and Young Persons Act, 1933, s. 86.—See p. 67, *ante*.

Family Allowances Act, 1945, s. 11 (2), (3).—This Act is repealed by S. L. R. (Consequential Repeals) Act, 1965; 23 Halsbury's Statutes, 3rd Edn., 411. See now s. 11 of the Family Allowances Act, 1965; 23 Halsbury's Statutes, 3rd Edn., 745.

PART IV

SUPERVISION OF CHILDREN AWAITING ADOPTION OR PLACED WITH STRANGERS

NOTE

Juvenile courts.—S. 47 (2) of the Children and Young Persons Act, 1933, p. 53, *ante*, does not apply to proceedings under this Part of this Act. See s. 47 of the Adoption Act, 1958, p. 1075, *post*.

37. Meaning of protected child.—(1) Subject to the following provisions of this section, where—

(a) arrangements are made for placing a child below the upper limit of the compulsory school age in the care and possession of a person who is not a parent, guardian or relative of his, but who proposes to adopt him and another person, not being a parent or guardian of his, takes part in the arrangements; or

(b) notice of intention to apply for an adoption order in respect of a child is given under subsection (2) of section three of this Act,

then, while the child is in the care and possession of the person first mentioned in paragraph (a) of this subsection or, as the case may be, of the person giving the notice mentioned in paragraph (b) thereof, he is a protected child within the meaning of this Part of this Act.

(2) A child is not a protected child while the child is in the care of any person in any of the circumstances mentioned in subsections (2) or (4) of

section two of the Children Act, 1958, or paragraphs (b) to (e) of subsection (3) of that section.

(3) A child is not a protected child by reason of any such notice as is mentioned in paragraph (b) of subsection (1) of this section while he is in the care of any person in any such school, home or institution as is mentioned in subsection (3) of section two of the Children Act, 1958, nor while he is liable to be detained, subject to guardianship or resident as mentioned in subsection (4) of that section.

(4) A protected child ceases to be a protected child on the making of an adoption order in respect of him or on his attaining the age of eighteen, whichever first occurs.

(5) A child in the care and possession of two spouses one of whom is a parent, relative or guardian of his shall be deemed for the purposes of this Part of this Act to be in the care and possession of that one of them.

NOTES

This section is printed as amended by the Mental Health Act, 1959, the Mental Health (Scotland) Act, 1960, the Social Work (Scotland) Act, 1968, and the Children and Young Persons Act, 1969, ss. 52 (4), 72 (3), (4) and Scheds. V and VI.

" **Upper limit.**"—The upper limit of the compulsory school age is now fifteen years, but provision is made for its extension when practicable to sixteen years; see the Education Act, 1944, s. 35, p. 252, *ante*. See also as to registered pupils at special schools, s. 38 (1), *ibid.*, p. 255, *ante*; and see also s. 114 (6), *ibid.*, p. 270, *ante*, and s. 9 of the Education Act, 1962, p. 273, *ante*.

" **Parent.**"—See s. 1 (4), *ante*, and the note to that section.

" **Protected child.**"—Any inspector appointed under s. 103 of the Children and Young Persons Act, 1933, p. 79, *ante*, may enter any place where a protected child within the meaning of Part IV of this Act is being maintained and inspect the place and the child; see s. 54 (2) of the Children Act, 1948, p. 919, *ante*.

General effects of the amendments to sub-s. (2).—The general effects of the amendments in sub-ss. (4) and (5) of s. 52 of the Children and Young Persons Act, 1969, to the Adoption Act, 1958, and the Children Act, 1958, are that in future the Adoption Act provisions will apply to all children placed with a view to adoption, and only to such children, and in all other cases the Children Act, 1958, will apply. When a child is the subject of a supervision order under the Children and Young Persons Act, 1969, the "protected child" provisions are unnecessary and this is allowed for by the exception in sub-s. (4) of s. 2 of the Children Act, 1958.

Definitions.—For " compulsory school age ", " guardian " and " relative ", see s. 57 (1), *post*; for " adoption order ", see s. 1 (1), *ante*, and s. 57 (1), *post*, in conjunction with s. 53 (4), *post*; and for " takes part in the arrangements ", see s. 57 (2), *post*.

Children Act, 1958, Part I, s. 2.—See pp. 956, *ante*.

38. Duty of local authority to secure well-being of protected children.—It shall be the duty of every local authority to secure that protected children within their area are visited from time to time by officers of the authority, who shall satisfy themselves as to the well-being of the children and give such advice as to their care and maintenance as may appear to be needed.

NOTES

" **Local authority.**"—For meaning, see s. 28 (1), *ante*; and for discharge of functions of local authorities under Part IV of this Act through Social Service Committees, see s. 2 and Sched. I of the Local Authority Social Services Act, 1970, pp. 927 *et seq.*, *ante*.

" **Protected children.**"—See s. 37, *ante*, and the note "Protected child" thereto.

" **Visited.**"—Refusal to allow the visiting of a protected child by a duly authorised officer of a local authority is an offence under s. 44 (1) (*b*), *post*, penalties for which are prescribed by s. 44 (2), *post*.

39. Power to inspect premises.—Any officer of a local authority authorised to visit protected children may, after producing, if asked to do so, some duly authenticated document showing that he is so authorised, inspect any premises in the area of the authority in which such children are to be or are being kept.

NOTES

"**Local authority.**"—See the note to s. 38, *ante*.

" **Protected children.**"—See s. 37, *ante*, and the note " Protected child " thereto.

" **After producing, if asked to do so.**"—This does not mean that the right of entry can only be exercised if there is someone to whom the document can be produced; see *Grove* v. *Eastern Gas Board*, [1951] 2 All E. R. 1051; 116 J. P. 15, C. A.

" **Duly authenticated document.**"—See the Public Health Act, 1936, s. 284, 26 Halsbury's Statutes, 3rd Edn., 349. See also *London County Council* v. *Farren*, [1956] 2 All E. R. 401, C. A., and *Tennant* v. *London County Council* [1957], 121 J. P. 428, C. A.

" **Inspect any premises.**"—Refusal to allow the inspection of premises is an offence under s. 44 (1) (*b*), *post*, for which penalties are prescribed by s. 44 (2), *post*.

40. Notices and information to be given to local authorities.—(1) Subject to subsection (2) of this section, where arrangements are made for the placing of a child in the care and possession of any person and by reason of the arrangements the child would be a protected child while in the care and possession of that person, every person taking part in the arrangements shall give notice in writing of the arrangements to the local authority for the area in which the person in whose care and possession the child is to be placed is living.

(2) A notice under subsection (1) of this section need not be given by the person in whose care and possession the child is to be placed, nor by a parent or guardian of the child.

(3) A notice under subsection (1) of this section shall be given not less than two weeks before the child is placed as mentioned in that subsection, except that where the child is so placed in an emergency, the notice may be given not later than one week after the child is so placed.

(4) Where a person who has a protected child in his care and possession changes his permanent address he shall, not less than two weeks before the change, or, if the change is made in an emergency, not later than one week after the change, give written notice specifying the new address to the local authority in whose area his permanent address is before the change, and if the new address is in the area of another local authority, the authority to whom the notice is given shall inform that other local authority and give them such of the particulars mentioned in subsection (6) of this section as are known to them.

(5) If a protected child dies, the person in whose care and possession he was at his death shall within forty-eight hours of the death give to the local authority notice in writing of the death.

(6) A person who has or proposes to have a protected child in his care and possession shall at the request of the local authority give them the following particulars, so far as known to him, that is to say, the name, sex and date and place of birth of the child, and the name and address of every person who is a parent or guardian or acts as a guardian of the child or from whom the child has been or is to be received.

NOTES

"**Protected child.**"—See s. 37, *ante,* and the note thereto.

"**Notice.**"—The notices required by the section may be given by post; see s. 55, p. 1080, *post.* Failure to give a notice within the time specified or knowingly making or causing or procuring another person to make any false or misleading statements in a notice is an offence under s. 44 (1) (*a*), *post,* for which penalties are prescribed by s. 44 (2), *post.* Proceedings may be taken by a local authority; see s. 54 (2), p. 1080, *post.*

"**Local authority.**"—See the note to s. 38, *ante.*

"**Parent.**"—See s. 1 (4), *ante,* and the note to that section.

"**Not less than two weeks.**"—See the note "Not less than fourteen days", to s. 31, *ante.*

Definitions.—For " guardian ", see s. 57 (1), *post;* for " taking part in the arrangements ", see s. 57 (2), *post;* and for " in the care and possession ", see s. 37 (5), *ante.*

41. Power of local authority to prohibit placing of child.—Where
arrangements are made for the placing of a child in the care and possession of any person, and by reason of the arrangements the child would be a protected child while in the care and possession of that person, then, if neither a registered adoption society nor a local authority took part in the arrangements and it appears to the authority to whom notice is to be given under the last foregoing section that it would be detrimental to the child to be kept by that person in the premises in which he proposes to keep him, they may by notice in writing given to that person prohibit him from receiving the child in those premises.

NOTES

"**Protected child.**"—See s. 37, *ante,* and the note thereto.

"**Local authority.**"—See the note to s. 38, *ante.*

"**Notice in writing.**"—See as to local authority notices, s. 49, *post.*

Prohibition.—For right of appeal against a prohibition, see s. 42, *infra;* for removal to a place of safety of a child kept in contravention of a prohibition, see s. 43, *infra,* and for offences and penalties in connection with prohibitions, see s. 44, *post.*

Definitions.—For " registered adoption society ", see s. 57 (1), *post;* for " took part in the arrangements ", see s. 57 (2), *post;* and for " in the care and possession ", see s. 37 (5), *ante.*

42. Appeal to juvenile court against prohibition under section 41.
—(1) A person aggrieved by a prohibition imposed under the last foregoing section may, within fourteen days from the date on which he is notified of the prohibition, appeal to a juvenile court.

(2) The notice by which a prohibition is imposed under that section shall contain a statement informing the person on whom it is imposed of his right to appeal against the prohibition and of the time within which he may do so.

(3) (*Applies to Scotland.*)

NOTES

" **Person aggrieved.**"—See, in particular, on the meaning of this expression, *R*. v. *London Quarter Sessions, Ex parte Westminster Corporation*, [1951] 1 All E. R. 1032; 115 J. P. 350; *R.* v. *Surrey Quarter Sessions, Ex parte Lilley*, [1951] 2 All E. R. 659; and *R.* v. *Lancashire Quarter Sessions Appeal Committee, Ex parte Huyton-with-Roby Urban District Council*, [1954] 3 All. E. R. 225.

" **Within fourteen days.**"—*Cf.* the note " Within twenty-one days " to s. 31, *ante*.

Appeal.—The appeal is by way of complaint; see Magistrates' Courts Rules, 1968, rule 30.

" **Juvenile court.**"—See the note to s. 9, *ante*, and s. 47, *post*.

43. Removal of protected children from unsuitable surroundings.

—(1) If a juvenile court is satisfied, on the complaint of a local authority, that a protected child is being kept or is about to be received by any person who is unfit to have his care, or in contravention of any prohibition imposed by the local authority under section forty-one of this Act, or in any premises or any environment detrimental or likely to be detrimental to him, the court may make an order for his removal to a place of safety until he can be restored to a parent, relative or guardian of his, or until other arrangements can be made with respect to him; and on proof that there is imminent danger to the health or well-being of the child the power to make an order under this section may be exercised by a justice of the peace acting on the application of a person authorised to visit protected children.

(2) An order under this section may be executed by any person authorised to visit protected children or by any constable and may, be executed on a Sunday.

(3) A local authority may receive into their care under section one of the Children Act, 1948, or, as the case may be section fifteen of the Social Work (Scotland) Act, 1968, any child removed under this section, whether or not the circumstances of the child are such that they fall within paragraphs (a) to (c) of subsection (1) of the said section one or, as the case may be, the said section fifteen and notwithstanding that he may appear to the local authority to be over the age of seventeen.

(4) Where a child is removed under this section the local authority shall, if practicable, inform a parent or guardian of the child, or any person who acts as his guardian.

(5) (*Applies to Scotland.*)

NOTES

This section is printed as amended by the Statute Law Repeals Act, 1969, and the Social Work (Scotland) Act, 1968, ss. 95, 97, 98 and Sched. VIII.

" **Juvenile court.**"—See the note to s. 9, *ante*, and s. 47, *post*.

" **Local authority.**"—See the note to s. 38, *ante*.   Local authorities are required to make provision, in homes provided by them under Part II of the Children Act, 1948, for the reception and maintenance of children removed to a place of safety under this section; see s. 51 of the Children Act, 1948, p. 917, *ante*.

" **Protected child.**"—See s. 37, *ante*, and the note thereto.

" **Appeal.**"—An appeal from an order lies to quarter sessions under s. 48, *post*.

" **Parent.**"—See s. 1 (4), *ante*, and the note to that section.

" **Visit protected children.**"—See s. 38, *ante*.

"**Order for his removal.**"—Refusal to comply with an order for removal or obstruction of any person in the execution of such an order is an offence under s. 44 (1) (d), *post*, for which penalities are prescribed by s. 44 (2), *post*. The order must specify a period, not exceeding twenty-eight days, beyond which the child must not be detained in a place of safety without being brought before a juvenile court (Children and Young Persons Act, 1963, s. 23, p. 95, *ante*).

Place of safety.—For further provisions see s. 23 of the Children and Young Persons Act, 1963, p. 95, *ante*.

London Government Act, 1963.—Transfers, see note to s. 1 of the Children's Act, 1948, p. 881, *ante*.

Definitions.—For " place of safety ", " relative " and " guardian ", see s. 57 (1), *post*.

Children Act, 1948, s. 1.—See p. 880, *ante*.

44. Offences under Part IV.—(1) A person shall be guilty of an offence if—

    (a) being required, under any provision of this Part of this Act, to give any notice or information, he fails to give the notice within the time specified in that provision or fails to give the information within a reasonable time, or knowingly makes or causes or procures another person to make any false or misleading statement in the notice or information;

    (b) he refuses to allow the visiting of a protected child by a duly authorised officer of a local authority or the inspection, under the power conferred by section thirty-nine of this Act, of any premises;

    (c) he keeps any child in any premises in contravention of a prohibition imposed under this Part of this Act;

    (d) he refuses to comply with an order under this Part of this Act for the removal of any child or obstructs any person in the execution of such an order.

(2) A person guilty of an offence under this section shall be liable on summary conviction to imprisonment for a term not exceeding six months or a fine not exceeding one hundred pounds or both.

NOTES

"**Give any notice or information.**"—*I.e.*, under s. 40 (1), (4), (5), *ante*.

"**Knowingly.**"—Knowledge is an essential ingredient of the offence, and must be proved by the prosecution; see, generally, *Gaumont British Distributors, Ltd.* v. *Henry*, [1939] 2 All E. R. 808 ; 103 J. P. 256, and *R.* v. *Hallam*, [1957] 1 All E. R. 665. *Cf. Sherras* v. *De Rutzen* (1895), 59 J. P. 440.

"**Refuses to allow the visiting.**"—See s. 38, *ante*; also s. 45, *infra*.

"**Refuses to allow . . . the inspection.**"—See also s. 45, *infra*.

"**Protected child.**"—See s. 37, *ante*, and the note thereto.

"**Local authority.**"—See the note to s. 38, *ante*.

"**Prohibition imposed under this Act.**"—*I.e.*, under s. 41, *ante*.

"**Order for the removal of any child.**"—*I.e.*, under s. 43 (1), *ante*.

"**Obstructs.**"—Obstruction need not involve physical violence; see, in particular, *Borrow* v. *Howland* (1896), 74 L. T. 787, and *Hinchliffe* v. *Sheldon*, [1955] 3 All E. R. 406. In fact, there is authority for saying that anything which makes it more difficult for a person to carry out his duty amounts to obstruction ; see *Hinchliffe* v.

Sheldon, supra. Yet, standing by and doing nothing is not obstruction unless there is a legal duty to act; see *Swallow* v. *London County Council,* [1916] 1 K. B. 224; and contrast *Baker* v. *Ellison,* [1914] 2 K. B. 762.

" **Summary conviction**"; " **not exceeding six months.**"—See the notes to s. 29, p. 1061, *ante.*

45. Extension of power to issue warrants to search for and remove a child.—For the purposes of section forty of the Children and Young Persons Act, 1933, or section forty-seven of the Children and Young Persons (Scotland) Act, 1937 (which enable a warrant authorising the search for and removal of a child to be issued on suspicion of unnecessary suffering caused to, or certain offences committed against, the child), any refusal to allow the visiting of a protected child or the inspection of any premises by a person authorised to do so under this Part of this Act shall be treated as giving reasonable cause for such a suspicion.

NOTES

" **Refusal to allow visiting.**"—See ss. 38 and 44 (1) (*b*), *ante.*
" **Protected child.**"—See s. 37, *ante*, and the note thereto.
" **Inspection of any premises.**"—See ss. 39 and 44 (1) (*b*), *ante.*
Children and Young Persons Act, 1933, s. 40.—See p. 47, *ante.*

46. Avoidance of insurances on lives of protected children.—A person who maintains a protected child shall be deemed for the purposes of the Life Assurance Act, 1774, to have no interest in the life of the child.

NOTE

Life Assurance Act, 1774.—See 17 Halsbury's Statutes (3rd Edn.) 827.

47. Sittings of juvenile courts in proceedings under Part IV.— Subsection (2) of section forty-seven of the Children and Young Persons Act, 1933 (which restricts the time and place at which a sitting of a juvenile court may be held and the persons who may be present at such a sitting) shall not apply to any sitting of a juvenile court in any proceedings under this Part of this Act.

NOTES

" **Juvenile court.**"—See the note to s. 9, *ante.* Such sittings as come under this section are held in open court.
Children and Young Persons Act, 1933, s. 47 (2).—See p. 53, *ante.*

48. Appeal to the Crown Court.—An appeal shall lie to the Crown Court from any order made under this Part of this Act by a juvenile court or any other magistrates' court within the meaning of the Magistrates' Courts Act, 1952.

NOTES

" **Juvenile court.**"—See the notes to ss. 9 and 47, *ante.*
Procedure on appeal.—See Magistrates' Courts Act, 1952, ss. 83 *et seq.*, and the Magistrates' Courts Rules, 1968.
Magistrates' Courts Act, 1952.—For the meaning of " magistrates' court " in that Act, see s. 124 (1) thereof, 21 Halsbury's Statutes, 3rd Edn., 181.

49. Authentication of documents.—(1) Any notice by a local authority under this Part of this Act may be signed on behalf of the authority by the clerk of the authority or by any other officer of the authority authorised in writing to sign such a notice.

(2) Any notice purporting to bear the signature of the clerk of a local authority or any officer stated therein to be authorised by the authority to sign notices under this Part of this Act shall be deemed, until the contrary is proved, to have been duly given by the authority.

NOTE

Local authority.—See the note to s. 38, *ante.*

PART V

MISCELLANEOUS AND GENERAL

50. Prohibition of certain payments.—(1) Subject to the provisions of this section, it shall not be lawful to make or give to any person any payment or reward for or in consideration of—

(a) the adoption by that person of an infant;

(b) the grant by that person of any consent required in connection with the adoption of an infant;

(c) the transfer by that person of the care and possession of an infant with a view to the adoption of the infant; or

(d) the making by that person of any arrangements for the adoption of an infant.

(2) Any person who makes or gives, or agrees or offers to make or give, any payment or reward prohibited by this section, or who receives or agrees to receive or attempts to obtain any such payment or reward, shall be liable on summary conviction to imprisonment for a term not exceeding six months or to a fine not exceeding one hundred pounds or to both; and the court may order any infant in respect of whom the offence was committed to be removed to a place of safety until he can be restored to his parents or guardian or until other arrangements can be made for him.

(3) This section does not apply to any payment made to an adoption society or local authority by a parent or guardian of an infant or by a person who adopts or proposes to adopt an infant, being a payment in respect of expenses reasonably incurred by the society or authority in connection with the adoption of the infant, or to any payment or reward authorised by the court to which an application for an adoption order in respect of an infant is made.

NOTES

" **Payment or reward.**"—The court before making an adoption order must be satisfied that the applicant has not received or agreed to receive, and that no person has made or given or agreed to make or give to the applicant, any payment or other reward in consideration of the adoption except such as the court may sanction; see s. 7 (1) (c), *ante.*

When the court sees fit to sanction a payment or reward, the facts will be stated in the order itself; see Form 9 of the Adoption (Juvenile Court) Rules, 1959, p. 1124, *post.*

" **Adoption of an infant.**"—See, in particular, s. 1, *ante.*

" **Consent required.**"—*I.e.,* by s. 4, *ante.*

"**Summary conviction**"; "**not exceeding six months.**"—See the notes to s. 29, p. 1062, *ante*.

"**Parents.**"—See s. 1 (4), *ante*, and the note to that section.

Definitions.—For "infant", "court", "place of safety", "guardian" and "adoption society", see s. 57 (1), *post*; for "adoption order", see s. 1 (1), *ante*, and s. 57 (1), *post*, in conjunction with s. 53 (4), *post*; for "local authority", see s. 28 (1), *ante*; and for "making . . . arrangements", see s. 57 (2), *post*.

51. Restriction upon advertisements.—(1) It shall not be lawful for any advertisement to be published indicating—

  (a) that the parent or guardian of an infant desires to cause the infant to be adopted; or

  (b) that a person desires to adopt an infant; or

  (c) that any person (not being a registered adoption society or a local authority) is willing to make arrangements for the adoption of an infant.

(2) Any person who causes to be published or knowingly publishes an advertisement in contravention of the provisions of this section shall be liable on summary conviction to a fine not exceeding fifty pounds.

NOTES

"**Parent.**"—See s. 1 (4), *ante*, and the note to that section.

"**Any person.**"—For additional provisions as to offences by bodies corporate, see s. 54 (1), *post*.

Definitions.—For "guardian", "infant" and "registered adoption society", see s. 57 (1), *post*; for "make arrangements for the adoption of an infant", see s. 57 (2), *post*; and for "local authority", see s. 28 (1), *ante*.

52. Restriction on removal of infants for adoption outside British Islands.—(1) Except under the authority of an order under section fifty-three of this Act, it shall not be lawful for any person to take or send an infant who is a British subject out of Great Britain to any place outside the British Islands with a view to the adoption of the infant (whether in law or in fact) by any person not being a parent or guardian or relative of the infant; and any person who takes or sends an infant out of Great Britain to any place in contravention of this subsection, or makes or takes part in any arrangements for transferring the care and possession of an infant to any person for that purpose, shall be liable on summary conviction to imprisonment for a term not exceeding six months or to a fine not exceeding one hundred pounds or to both.

(2) In any proceedings under this section, a report by a British consular officer or a deposition made before a British consular officer and authenticated under the signature of that officer shall, upon proof that the officer or the deponent cannot be found in the United Kingdom, be admissible as evidence of the matters stated therein, and it shall not be necessary to prove the signature or official character of the person who appears to have signed any such report or deposition.

(3) In this section "the British Islands" means the United Kingdom, the Channel Islands and the Isle of Man.

(4) (*Applies to Scotland.*)

NOTES

" **Any person.**"—For additional provisions as to offences by bodies corporate, see s. 54 (1), *post.*

" **Makes . . . arrangements.**"—For the meaning of these words, see s. 57 (2), p. 1082, *post.*

Care and possession.—See the note to s. 3, p. 1030, *ante.*

"**British subject.**"—British nationality is now governed by the British Nationality Act, 1948, 1 Halsbury's Statutes, 3rd Edn., 861, as amended by, in particular, the British Nationality Act, 1958, 1 Halsbury's Statutes, 3rd Edn., 894, in conjunction with ss. 3 (1) and 5 of the Ireland Act, 1949, 4 Halsbury's Statutes, 3rd Edn., 670. See also, as to citizenship, s. 19, *ante.* By s. 57 (3), *post,* this Act applies to citizens of the Republic of Ireland as it applies to British subjects, and references in this Act to British subjects are to be construed accordingly.

" **Great Britain.**"—See the note to s. 12, *ante.*

" **Parent.**"—See s. 1 (4), *ante,* and the note to that section.

" **Summary conviction**"; "**not exceeding six months.**"—See the notes to s. 29, *ante.*

" **Consular officer.**"—For definition, see the Interpretation Act, 1889, s. 12 (20), 32 Halsbury's Statutes, 3rd Edn., 440.

" **Cannot be found.**"—A person who has died "cannot be found"; *cf. Re Dutton's Patents* (1923), 67 Sol. Jo. 403. The same appears to apply to any person whose whereabouts are unknown; see *Re Hulme's Trusts* (1887), 57 L. T. 13; and *cf. Rhymney Iron Co.* v. *Gelligaer District Council,* [1917] 1 K. B. 589. Note that it is sufficient that the person in question cannot be found in the United Kingdom.

" **United Kingdom.**"—See the note to s. 6, *ante.*

Emigration with consent of Secretary of State.—This section does not apply in the case of any infant emigrating under the authority of the Secretary of State given under s. 17 of the Children Act, 1948 which relate to the emigration of persons who are in the care of a local authority (Children and Young Persons Act, 1963, s. 55, p. 114, *ante*).

Definitions.—For " infant ", " guardian " and " relative ", see s. 57 (1), *post.* Note as to " the British Islands ", sub-s. (3) of this section.

53. Provisional adoption by persons domiciled outside Great Britain.—(1) If the court is satisfied, upon an application being made by a person who is not domiciled in England or Scotland, that the applicant intends to adopt an infant under the law of or within the country in which he is domiciled, and for that purpose desires to remove the infant from Great Britain either immediately or after an interval, the court may, subject to the provisions of this section, make an order (in this section referred to as a provisional adoption order) authorising the applicant to remove the infant for the purpose aforesaid, and giving to the applicant the custody of the infant pending his adoption as aforesaid.

(2) An application for a provisional adoption order may be made, in England to the High Court or the county court, and in Scotland to the Court of Session or the sheriff court.

(3) A provisional adoption order may be made in any case where, apart from the domicile of the applicant, an adoption order could be made in respect of the infant under Part I of this Act, but shall not be made in any other case.

(4) Subject to the provisions of this section, the provisions of this Act, other than this section and sections sixteen, seventeen and nineteen, shall apply in relation to a provisional adoption order as they apply in relation

to an adoption order, and references in those provisions to adoption, to an adoption order, to an application or applicant for such an order and to an adopter or a person adopted or authorised to be adopted under such an order shall be construed accordingly.

(5) In relation to a provisional adoption order section three of this Act shall have effect as if for the word " three ", both where it occurs in sub-section (1) and where it occurs in subsection (2), there were substituted the word " six ".

(6) Any entry in the Registers of Births, the Register of Births or the Adopted Children Register which is required to be marked in consequence of the making of a provisional adoption order shall, in lieu of being marked with the word " Adopted " or " Re-adopted " (with or without the addition of the word " (Scotland) " or " (England) ") be marked with the words " Provisionally adopted " or " Provisionally re-adopted ", as the case may require.

NOTES

" **Not domiciled in England or Scotland.**"—Under s. 1 (1), *ante*, the applicant for an adoption order must be domiciled in England or Scotland.

See note, " Domicile outside Great Britain," to s. 12, p. 1047.

For the law relating to domicile, see 7 Halsbury's Laws, 3rd Edn., 14 *et seq*.

" **Great Britain.**"—See the note to s. 12, *ante*.

" **Adoption.**"—The reference to adoption in sub-s. (1) includes adoption in law or in fact, and a provisional order can apparently be granted to applicants who cannot adopt the infant in the country of domicile. See the reference to adoption in law or in fact in s. 52 (1), *ante*.

Duration.—The section does not impose a time limit on the order, and it will remain in force until superseded, *e.g.*, by an adoption order made abroad, or quashed.

Devolution of property.—The provisions of the Act as to devolution of property do not apply to provisional adoption orders.

Citizenship.—Citizenship is not changed by a provisional adoption order.

Jurisdiction.—Application cannot be made to a juvenile court.

Religious faith.—In an appeal to the Court of Appeal against the refusal of a county court judge to make a provisional order, it was held that the judge exercised his discretion wrongly in holding that it was not in the interests of the infant, born to a girl of Protestant faith, to be adopted by the applicants for the reason that they were of the Jewish faith, and in failing adequately to consider the welfare of the infant. (*Re G. (An Infant)*, [1962] 2 Q. B. 141 ; [1962] 2 All E. R. 173 ; 126 J. P. 340, (C.A.)).

Registers of Births.—See the note to s. 21, *ante*, and as to marking of entries, see ss. 21 (4), 24 (4), (5), *ante*.

" **Register of Births.**"—This refers to a register kept in Scotland.

" **Adopted Children Register.**"—This is maintained under s. 20 (1), *ante*. As to marking of entries therein, see ss. 21 (5), 24 (4), (5), *ante*.

Sub-s. (5): " three ".—See note " One of the three months " to s. 12, p. 1047, *ante*.

Definitions.—For " court ", " England " and " infant ", see s. 57 (1), *post*; and for " adoption order ", see s. 1 (1), *ante*, and s. 57 (1), *post*, in conjunction with sub-s. (4) of this section.

54. Offences.—(1) Where any offence under Part II, Part III, Part IV or Part V of this Act committed by a body corporate is proved to have been committed with the consent or connivance of, or to be attributable to any neglect on the part of, any director, manager, member of the committee, secretary or other officer of the body, he, as well as the body, shall be deemed to be guilty of that offence and shall be liable to be proceeded against and punished accordingly.

(2) Proceedings for an offence under Part II, Part III, Part IV or Part V of this Act may, in England, be taken by a local authority.

NOTES

Onus of proof.—The director or other person must be proceeded against, and, of course, be given the same rights as any other defendant. The prosecution must prove that the offence was committed by the body corporate, and must also prove the consent, connivance or neglect of the other defendant.

Definitions.—For " England ", see s. 57 (1), *post*; and for " local authority ", see s. 28 (1), *ante*.

55. Service of notices, etc.—Any notice or information required to be given under this Act may be given by post.

NOTES

" By post."—As this section is permissive only, it is clear that where notice is given otherwise than by post and received by the person to whom it is given, this is good service; *cf. Re Sharpley and Manby's Application*, [1942] 1 All E. R. 66.

Postal service may be effected by ordinary registered post or recorded delivery; see *T. O. Supplies (London), Ltd.* v. *Jerry Creighton, Ltd.*, [1951] 2 All E. R. 992. By the Interpretation Act, 1889, s. 26, where a document is authorised or required to be served by post, whether the expression "serve" or the expression "give" or "send" or any other expression is used, then, unless the contrary intention appears, the service shall be deemed to be effected by properly addressing, prepaying, and posting a letter containing the document, and unless the contrary is proved to have been effected at the time at which the letter would be delivered in the ordinary course of post. See as to non-delivery, *R.* v. *London Quarter Sessions, Ex parte Rossi*, [1956] 1 All E. R. 670, C. A.; *Beer* v. *Davies*, [1958] 2 All E. R. 255; 122 J. P. 344, and *Layton* v. *Shires*, [1959] 3 All E. R. 587; 124 J. P. 46.

56. Rules and Regulations.—(1) Any power to make rules or regulations conferred by this Act on the Lord Chancellor or the Secretary of State or the Court of Session shall be exercisable by statutory instrument.

(2) The Statutory Instruments Act, 1946, shall apply to a statutory instrument containing an act of sederunt made for the purposes of this Act as if the act of sederunt had been made by a Minister of the Crown.

NOTES

Rules.—The Lord Chancellor has power to make rules under s. 9 (3), *ante*; and note the definition of " prescribed " in s. 57 (1), *post*.

Regulations.—The Secretary of State has power to make regulations under s. 32 (1), (3), *ante*; and note the definition of " prescribed " in s. 57 (1), *post*.

Statutory Instruments Act, 1946.—32 Halsbury's Statutes, 3rd Edn., 668. As to laying these instruments before Parliament, see the Laying of Documents before Parliament (Interpretation) Act, 1948.

57. Interpretation.—(1) In this Act, unless the context otherwise requires, the following expressions have the meanings hereby respectively assigned to them, that is to say—

" adoption order " has the meaning assigned to it by section one of this Act;

" Adoption Rules " has the meaning assigned to it by subsection (2) of section nine of this Act;

" adoption society " means a body of persons whose functions consist of or include the making of arrangements for the adoption of children;

" body of persons " means any body of persons, whether incorporated or unincorporated;

" charitable association " means a body of persons which exists only for the purpose of promoting a charitable, benevolent or philanthropic object, whether or not the object is charitable within the meaning of any rule of law, and which applies the whole of its profits (if any) or other income in promoting the objects for which it exists;

" compulsory school age ", in relation to England, has the same meaning as the Education Acts, 1944 to 1953 and, in relation to Scotland, means school age as defined in the Education (Scotland) Acts, 1939 to 1956;

" court " means a court having jurisdiction to make adoption orders;

" England " includes Wales;

" father", in relation to an illegitimate infant, means the natural father;

" guardian ", in relation to an infant, means a person appointed by deed or will in accordance with the provisions of the Guardianship of Minors Act, 1971, or by a court of competent jurisdiction to be the guardian of the infant;

"infant" means a person under eighteen years of age, but does not include a person who is or has been married;

"place of safety" means a community home provided by a local authority, a controlled community home, police station, or any hospital, surgery or other suitable place the occupier of which is willing temporarily to receive a child; and in Scotland has the same meaning as in the Social Work (Scotland) Act, 1968;

" prescribed ", in Part I of this Act, means prescribed by Adoption Rules or an act of sederunt under section eleven of this Act, and except in Part I of this Act, means prescribed by regulations made by the Secretary of State;

" registered adoption society " means an adoption society registered under Part II of this Act;

*   *   *   *   *

" relative ", in relation to an infant, means a grandparent, brother, sister, uncle or aunt, whether of the full blood or half blood or by affinity, and includes—

> (a) where an adoption order has been made in respect of the infant or any other person under any enactment (including any enactment of the Parliament of Northern Ireland) any person who would be a relative of the infant within the meaning of this definition if the adopted person were the child of the adopter born in lawful wedlock;
> (b) where the infant is illegitimate, the father of the infant and any person who would be a relative of the infant within the meaning of this definition if the infant were the legitimate child of his mother and father.

(2) For the purposes of this Act, a person shall be deemed to make arrangements for the adoption of an infant or to take part in arrangements for the placing of a child in the care or possession of another person, if (as the case may be)—

(a) he enters into or makes any agreement or arrangement for, or for facilitating, the adoption of the infant by any other person, whether the adoption is effected, or is intended to be effected, in pursuance of an adoption order or otherwise; or

(b) he enters into or makes any agreement or arrangement for, or facilitates, the placing of the child in the care or possession of that other person;

or if he initiates or takes part in any negotiations of which the purpose or effect is the conclusion of any agreement or the making of any arrangement therefor, or if he causes another to do so.

(3) This Act applies to citizens of the Republic of Ireland as it applies to British subjects, and references in this Act to British subjects shall be construed accordingly.

(4) Any reference in this Act to any other enactment shall be construed as a reference to that enactment as amended by any subsequent enactment.

NOTES

This section is printed as amended by the Guardianship of Minors Act, 1971, the Social Work (Scotland) Act, 1968, the Children and Young Persons Act, 1969 and the Family Law Reform Act, 1969.

"**Court.**"—For the courts which may make adoption orders, see s. 9 (1), *ante*.

"**Infant.**"—For construction of the expression "under eighteen years of age", see the note " Attained the age " to s. 2, *ante*.

"**Prescribed.**"—See for the express power to make Adoption Rules, s. 9, *ante*, and for the express power to make regulations, s. 32 (1), (3), *ante*.

"**Registered adoption society.**"—Where the registration of an adoption society is cancelled by a local authority, the adoption society is deemed, for the purposes of Part II of the Act, to be registered under that Part during the period within which an appeal against the cancellation may be brought under s. 31, *ante*, and if such an appeal is brought, until the determination or abandonment thereof; see s. 31 (6), *ante*. The Act has effect in relation to an adoption society registered under Part II of the Adoption Act, 1950 (c. 26), or the Adoption of Children (Regulation) Act, 1939 (c. 27), as if it were registered under Part II of this Act; see s. 59 and para. 8 of the Fifth Schedule, *post*.

"**British subjects.**"—See the note " British subject " to s. 52, *ante*.

"**Relative.**"—" By affinity " means by marriage, and sexual intercourse without marriage does not create affinity; see *Wing* v. *Taylor* (*falsely calling herself Wing*) (1861), 2 Sw. & Tr. 278. As to relation by half-blood, see 17 Halsbury's Laws, 2nd. Edn., 681, and cases there cited.

"**Compulsory school age.**"—See s. 114 (1) of the Education Act, 1944, p. 270, *ante*, in conjunction with ss. 35 and 38 (1) thereof, pp. 252, 255, *ante*, and the Education Act, 1962, s. 9, p. 273, *ante*.

Guardianship of Minors Act, 1971.—See Division 4, pp. 1193 *et seq.*, *post*.

Children Act, 1948, Part II.—See pp. 892 *et seq.*, *ante*. A local authority is required to plan for the provision and maintenance of community homes for the accommodation of children in care (s. 36 of the Children and Young Persons Act, 1969).

58. Amendment and adaptation of enactments.—[*Not reproduced.*]

59. Transitional provisions and repeals.—[*Not reproduced.*]

NOTE

Interpretation Act, 1889 (c. 63), s. 38.—See 24 Halsbury's Statutes, 2nd Edn. 229.

60. Short title, extent and commencement.—(1) This Act may be cited as the Adoption Act, 1958.

(2) This Act (except section nineteen, and so much of section fifty-eight as repeals section sixteen of the Adoption Act, 1950) does not extend to Northern Ireland.

(3) This Act comes into force on the first day of April, nineteen hundred and fifty-nine.

NOTE

Adoption Act, 1950, s. 16.—That section is reproduced in s. 19, *ante.*

SCHEDULES

Section 21   FIRST SCHEDULE

FORM OF ENTRY IN ADOPTED CHILDREN REGISTER IN ENGLAND

1	2	3	4	5	6	7	8
No. of entry	Date and country of birth of child	Name and surname of child	Sex of child	Name and surname, address and occupation of adopter or adopters	Date of adoption order and description of court by which made	Date of entry	Signature of officer deputed by Registrar General to attest the entry

SECOND SCHEDULE

[*Applies to Scotland*]

PURPOSES FOR WHICH ADOPTION SOCIETIES REGULATIONS MAY BE MADE

1. For regulating the conduct of negotiations entered into by or on behalf of registered adoption societies with persons who, having the care and possession of infants, are desirous of causing the infants to be adopted, and in particular for securing—

    (a) that, where the parent or guardian of an infant proposes to place the infant at the disposition of the society with a view to the infant being adopted, he shall be furnished with a memorandum in the prescribed form explaining, in ordinary language, the effect, in relation to his rights as a parent or guardian, of the making of an adoption order in respect of the infant, and calling attention to the provisions of this Act and of any rules made thereunder relating to the consent of a parent or guardian to the making of such an order, and to the provisions of this Act relating to the sending or taking of infants abroad; and

    (b) that, before so placing the infant at the disposition of the society, the parent or guardian shall sign a document in the prescribed form certifying that he has read and understood the said memorandum.

2. For requiring that the case of every infant proposed to be delivered by or on behalf of a registered adoption society into the care and possession of a person proposing to adopt him shall be considered by a committee (to be called a " case committee ") appointed by the society for the purpose and consisting of not less than three persons.

3. For prescribing, in the case of every such infant as aforesaid, the inquiries which must be made and the reports which must be obtained by the society in relation to the infant and the person proposing to adopt him for the purpose of ensuring, so far as may be, the suitability of the infant and the person proposing to adopt him respectively, and, in particular, for requiring that a report on the health of the infant signed by a fully registered medical practitioner must be obtained by the society.

4. For securing that no such infant shall be delivered into the care and possession of a person proposing to adopt him by or on behalf of the society until that person has been interviewed by the case committee or by some person on their behalf, until a representative of the committee has inspected any premises in Great Britain in which the person proposing to adopt the infant intends that the infant should reside permanently, and until the committee have considered the prescribed reports.

5. For requiring a registered adoption society to furnish to the registration authority by whom the society was registered the prescribed accounts and the prescribed information relating to the activities of the society.

6. For making provision for the care and supervision of infants who have been placed by their parents or guardians at the disposition of adoption societies.

7. For prohibiting or restricting the disclosure of records kept by registered adoption societies and making provision for the safe keeping of such records when they are no longer required.

NOTES

" **Adoption societies regulations.**"—These are now the Adoption Agencies Regulations, 1959, pp. 1100 *et seq., post.*

" **Parent.**"—See s. 1 (4), *ante*, and the note to that section.

" **Consent of a parent or guardian.**"—See s. 4, *ante*, and as to rules, see the note " Consent " to that section, and the notes " Prescribed manner " and " Such class as may be prescribed " to s. 6, *ante*.

" **Care and possession.**"—See note to s. 3, p. 1030, *ante*.

"Provisions . . . relating to the sending or taking of infants abroad."—See ss. 52 and 53, *ante*.

"Fully registered medical practitioner."—See the note to s. 7, *ante*.

"Great Britain."—See the note to s. 12, *ante*.

Definitions.—For "registered adoption society", "infant", "guardian", "prescribed" and "adoption society", see s. 57 (1), *ante*; and for "adoption order", see ss. 1 (1) and 57 (1), *ante*, in conjunction with s. 53 (4), *ante*.

FOURTH SCHEDULE   Section 58

CONSEQUENTIAL AMENDMENTS OF ENACTMENTS

[*Not reproduced ; the enactments are printed as amended.*]

FIFTH SCHEDULE   Section 59

TRANSITIONAL PROVISIONS

[*Not reproduced.*]

SIXTH SCHEDULE   Section 59

ENACTMENTS REPEALED

[*Not reproduced ; effect has been given to the repeals in the enactments as reproduced.*]

ADOPTION ACT, 1960

[8 & 9 Eliz. 2, c. 59]

An Act to amend the law with respect to the revocation of adoption orders in cases of legitimation, and to make further provision in connection with the revocation of such orders under section twenty-six of the Adoption Act, 1958.   [*29th July, 1960*]

1.—Further provision for revocation of adoption orders in cases of legitimation.—(1) Where any person legitimated by virtue of section one of the Legitimacy Act, 1959, had been adopted by his father and mother before the commencement of that Act, the court by which the adoption order was made may, on the application of any of the parties concerned, revoke that order.

(2) The revocation of an adoption order under this section, or under section twenty-six of the Adoption Act, 1958, shall not affect the operation of sections sixteen and seventeen of that Act in relation to an intestacy which occurred, or a disposition which was made, before the revocation.

(3) This section shall be construed as one with section twenty-six of the Adoption Act, 1958; and any reference in that Act to that section or to subsection (1) of that section shall be construed as including a reference to subsection (1) of this section.

2. Short title and extent.—(1) This Act may be cited as the Adoption Act, 1960.

(2) This Act does not extend to Northern Ireland.

NOTES

Legitimacy Act, 1959, s. 1.—See p. 1297, *post.*
Adoption Act, 1958, s. 26.—See p. 1059, *ante.*

ADOPTION ACT, 1964
[1964, c. 57]

An Act to provide for effect to be given to certain adoption orders made outside Great Britain ; to facilitate the proof of adoption orders in different parts of the United Kingdom ; and for connected purposes. [16th July, 1964]

1. Extension of enactments referring to adoption.—(1) Any provision (however expressed) in any enactment passed before the commencement of this Act under which a person adopted in pursuance of an adoption order is for any purpose treated as the child of the adopter, or any other relationship is deduced by reference to such an order, shall have effect, as respects anything done or any event occurring after the commencement of this Act,—

(a) if it extends only to adoptions in pursuance of orders made in the United Kingdom, as extending also to adoptions in pursuance of orders made, whether before or after the commencement of this Act, in the Isle of Man or in any of the Channel Islands ;

(b) if it extends only to adoptions in pursuance of orders made in England or in Great Britain, as extending also to adoptions in pursuance of orders made, whether before or after the commencement of this Act, elsewhere in the United Kingdom or in the Isle of Man or in any of the Channel Islands ;

and section 17 (3) of the Adoption Act, 1958 and section 24 (2) of the Succession (Scotland) Act, 1964 (which enable trustees and personal representatives to convey or distribute property among the persons entitled thereto without ascertaining that no adoption order has been made which affects any interest therein) shall extend to any such order as is mentioned in this subsection.

(2) An order authorising adoption made outside Great Britain after the commencement of this Act shall also have the same effect as an adoption order—

(a) for the purposes of section 14 (2) (transfer of rights under certain insurance policies) and 25 (entries in parochial registers of baptism) of the said Act of 1958, if the order is made in Northern Ireland ; and

(b) for the purposes of those sections and of section 15 (effect on affiliation orders &c.) of that Act, if the order is made in the Isle of Man or in any of the Channel Islands.

(3) An order authorising adoption made in the Isle of Man or in any of the Channel Islands shall have the same effect for the purposes of section 19 of the said Act of 1958 (citizenship) as an adoption order, if it is made after the commencement of this Act; and if such an order was made before the commencement of this Act in respect of a person who would have become a citizen of the United Kingdom and Colonies at the date of the order had this Act been then in force, he shall be a citizen of the United Kingdom and Colonies as from the commencement of this Act.

(4) Where a person adopted in pursuance of an order made, whether before or after the commencement of this Act, in Northern Ireland, the Isle of Man or in any of the Channel Islands has subsequently become a legitimated person, and the order is then revoked, the revocation shall not affect the operation of sections 16 to 17 of the said Act of 1958, or sections 23 and 24 of the said Act of 1964, as extended by subsection (1) of this section, in relation to an intestacy which occurred, or a disposition which was made, before the revocation.

(5) Any such provision as is mentioned in subsection (1) of this section which, by virtue of subsection (4) of section 53 of the said Act of 1958, applies in relation to orders under that section shall, as respects anything done after the commencement of this Act, apply also in relation to similar orders made, whether before or after the commencement of this Act, in Northern Ireland, the Isle of Man or any of the Channel Islands, and shall be construed accordingly; and any such order made after the commencement of this Act shall also have the same effect as an adoption order for the purposes of the provisions mentioned in subsection (2) of this section.

NOTE

This section provides that adoption orders made in Northern Ireland, the Isle of Man or the Channel Islands are to have effect as if made in Great Britain.

2. Evidence of adoptions etc.—(1) Any document which under section 20 (2) or section 22 (2) of the Adoption Act, 1958, or section 14 (9) of the Adoption of Children Act (Northern Ireland) 1950 or any corresponding enactment of the Parliament of Northern Ireland for the time being in force is receivable as evidence of any matter in any part of Great Britain or in Northern Ireland shall be so receivable also in the rest of Great Britain, or, as the case may be, in Great Britain.

(2) In section 1 (3) of the Fatal Accidents Act, 1959, the words from " and for the purpose " to the end are hereby repealed.

NOTE

This section fills a gap in the Adoption Act, 1958, by providing that extracts from the Adopted Children Register may be receivable as evidence in any part of Great Britain and Northern Ireland.

3. Registration of adoptions outside Great Britain.—(1) Where the Registrar General or the Registrar General for Scotland is notified by the authority maintaining a register of adoptions in Northern Ireland, the Isle of Man or any of the Channel Islands that an order has been made in that country authorising the adoption of an infant to whom an entry in the Registers of Births (or, as the case may be, the Register of Births) or the Adopted Children Register relates, he shall cause the entry to be marked with the word " Adopted " or " Re-adopted ", as the case may require, followed by the name, in brackets, of the country in which the order was made.

(2) Where, after an entry has been so marked, the Registrar General or the Registrar General for Scotland is notified as aforesaid that the order has been quashed, that an appeal against the order has been allowed or that the order has been revoked, he shall cause the marking to be cancelled ; and a copy or extract of an entry in any register, being an entry the marking of which is cancelled under this subsection, shall be deemed to be an accurate copy if and only if both the marking and the cancellation are omitted therefrom.

(3) The preceding provisions of this section shall apply in relation to orders corresponding to orders under section 53 of the said Act of 1958 as they apply in relation to orders authorising the adoption of an infant ; but any marking of an entry required by virtue of this subsection shall consist of the word " Provisionally " followed by the words mentioned in sub-section (1) of this section.

(4) Without prejudice to subsections (2) and (3) of this section, where, after an entry in the Registers of Births or the Register of Births has been marked in accordance with this section, the birth is re-registered under section 14 of the Births and Deaths Registration Act, 1953 or section 2 of the Registration of Births, Deaths and Marriages (Scotland) (Amendment) Act, 1934 (re-registration of birth of legitimated persons), the entry made on the re-registration shall be marked in the like manner.

NOTE

Registration Regulations.—See Regulation 37 of the Registration of Births, Deaths and Marriages Regulations, S.I. 1968 No. 2049, p. 1148, *post*.

4. Short title, citation, construction and extent.—(1) This Act may be cited as the Adoption Act, 1964.

(2) This Act, the Adoption Act, 1958 and the Adoption Act, 1960 may be cited together as the Adoptions Acts, 1958 to 1964.

(3) This Act shall be construed as one with the Adoption Act, 1958.

(4) This Act, except so far as it extends the operation of section 19 of the Adoption Act, 1958, does not extend to Northern Ireland.

ADOPTION ACT, 1968
[1968 c. 53]

ARRANGEMENT OF SECTIONS

Further provision for adoption in Great Britain

An Act to make provision for extending the powers of courts in the United Kingdom with respect to the adoption of children; for enabling effect to be given in the United Kingdom to adoptions effected in other countries and to determinations of authorities in other countries with respect to adoptions; and for purposes connected with the matters aforesaid.

[26th July, 1968]

Further provision for adoption in Great Britain

1. Further power to make adoption orders.—(1) Subject to the provisions of this Act, the court may, upon an application made in the prescribed manner by a qualified person or qualified spouses, make an order under this section (in this Act referred to as an adoption order) authorising the applicant or applicants to adopt a qualified infant.

(2) An adoption order may be made notwithstanding that the infant is already adopted under an adoption order or otherwise.

NOTES

Definitions.—"Qualified infant", "qualified person", "qualified spouses", "adoption order". Court means the High Court or the Court of Session. See s. 11, *post*.

"Qualified person".—The definition includes a person who resides in Great Britain and is a United Kingdom national who could apply for an adoption order under s. 1 of the Adoption Act, 1958 (if domiciled in England or Scotland), but includes also a person who could not so apply. The restriction imposed by s. 3(2) of the 1968 Act will apparently apply only to applications which could not be made under the 1958 Act.

"Adoption order".—See restriction imposed by s. 3(5), *post*.

2. Application of Adoption Act, 1958, etc., to adoption orders.
(1) Subject to the provisions of this section, the Adoption Act, 1958, shall have effect as if any reference in that Act to an adoption order within the meaning of that Act, other than a reference in the provisions mentioned in subsection (2) of this section, included a reference to an adoption order within the meaning of this Act.

(2) The aforesaid provisions of the Act of 1958 are sections 1(1) to (4), 9(1) and (5), 10(1), 11(1) and (3), 12(1) and (2), 13(4), 15(5), 16(4), 17(5), 19(2), 20(6), 24(7) and 26(2) and (3).

(3) The Act of 1958 as modified by subsection (1) of this section shall have effect in relation to an adoption order and a proposed adoption order subject to the following further modifications—

    (a) the following provisions shall be omitted, that is to say, section 9(2) to (4) and (6), section 11(2), in section 14(3) the words "and be deemed always to have included" and in section 57(1) the definitions of "adoption order", "Adoption Rules" and "infant";

    (b) any reference to Adoption Rules or the court within the meaning of that Act or to an act of sederunt under that Act shall respectively be construed as a reference to rules and the court within the meaning of this Act and to an act of sederunt under this Act;

    (c) in section 7(1)(a) the reference to the Act of 1958 shall include a reference to this Act and in section 8(3) the reference to section 3 of that Act shall include a reference to section 3(1) of this Act;

    (d) in section 12, for so much of subsection (1) as precedes paragraph (a) there shall be substituted the words "In relation to an application for an adoption order made by an applicant who is not or applicants who are not ordinarily resident in Great Britain".

(4) Sections 4 to 6 of the Act of 1958 (which relate to consents) shall not apply to an adoption order proposed to be made in respect of an infant who is not a United Kingdom national.

(5) In any enactment passed before the date on which this subsection comes into force, other than an enactment contained in the Adoption Acts, 1958 to 1964, any reference to an adoption order within the meaning of the Act of 1958 or to adoption or a person adopted under that Act or such an order shall respectively be construed as including a reference to, or to adoption or a person adopted under, an adoption order within the meaning of this Act.

NOTES

Definitions.—See s. 11, *post*.

Adoption Act, 1958.—See pp. 1026 *et seq. ante.*

3. Restrictions on making of adoption orders.—(1) An adoption order shall not be made on the application of a person who is not a United Kingdom national or of spouses who are not United Kingdom nationals if the adoption which would be effected by the order is prohibited by a provision of the internal law of the country of which the person is a national or the spouses are nationals, being a provision specified in an order of the Secretary of State as one notified to the Government of the United Kingdom in pursuance of the provisions of the Convention relating to prohibitions on an adoption contained in the national law of the adopter.

(2) An adoption order shall not be made in pursuance of an application made at time when the applicant or applicants and the infant are United Kingdom nationals and reside in Great Britain or a specified country.

(3) An adoption order shall not be made in respect of an infant who is not a United Kingdom national—

(a) except in accordance with the provisions, if any, relating to consents and consultations of the internal law relating to adoption of the country of which the infant is a national; and

(b) where the application for the order is made by one of two spouses, unless the other spouse consents to the application or the court dispenses with his or her consent on being satisfied as to any of the matters mentioned in section 5(4) of the Act of 1958.

(4) The reference to consents and consultations in paragraph (a) of subsection (3) of this section does not include a reference to consent by and consultation with the applicant for the order and members of the applicant's family (including his or her spouse), and for the purposes of that subsection may consents be proved in the prescribed manner and the court shall be treated as the authority by whom, under the law mentioned in that paragraph, consents may be dispensed with and the adoption in question may be authorised; and where the provisions there mentioned require the attendance before that authority of any person who does not reside in Great Britain, that requirement shall be treated as satisfied for the purposes of the said subsection (3) if—

(a) that person has been given a reasonable opportunity of communicating his opinion on the adoption in question to the proper officer or clerk of the court, or to an appropriate authority of the country in question, for transmission to the court; and

(b) where he has availed himself of that opportunity, his opinion has been transmitted to the court.

(5) An adoption order shall not be made unless the applicant for the order is a qualified person or the applicants for the order are qualified spouses not only at the time of the application but also immediately before the order is made.

(6) Except in the case of an adoption by qualified spouses, an adoption order shall not be made authorising more than one person to adopt a qualified infant.

NOTES

Definitions.—See s. 11, *post*. Adoption order in this subsection has the meaning assigned to it by s. 1, *ante*. The exclusion in sub-s. (2) does not prevent an application for an order under the Act of 1958; however if the applicants are not domiciled in England or Scotland, they are ineligible under both Acts.

Sub-s. (2).—See note "Qualified person" to s. 1, *ante*.

Recognition of adoptions and adoption proceedings taking place overseas

4. Extension of enactments to certain adoptions made overseas.— (1) Subject to sections 5 and 6 of this Act, any provision (however expressed) in any enactment passed before the date on which this section comes into force under which a person adopted in pursuance of an adoption order within the meaning of the Act of 1958 is for any purpose treated as the child of the adopter, or any other relationship is deduced by reference to such an order, shall have effect as respects anything done or any event occurring on or after that date as extending to an overseas adoption.

(2) Subject as aforesaid, the following provisions of the Act of 1958, that is to say, sections 14(2), 15(1) to (4), 17(3), 19(1) and 25 (which relate respectively to insurance for funeral expenses, affiliation orders, distribution of property, citizenship and registers of baptism) and section 23(5) of the Succession (Scotland) Act, 1964 (which defines "adoption order" for the purposes of Part IV of that Act), shall have effect as if any reference to an adoption order within the meaning of the Act of 1958 included a reference to an overseas adoption.

(3) In this Act "overseas adoption" means an adoption of such a description as the Secretary of State may by order specify, being a description of adoptions of infants appearing to him to be effected under the law of any country outside Great Britain; and an order under this subsection may contain provision as to the manner in which evidence of an overseas adoption may be given.

NOTE

Secretary of State's Order.—No order has been made at the time of going to press.

5. Recognition of determinations made overseas in adoption proceedings.—(1) Where an authority of a convention country or a specified country having power under the law of that country—

(a) to authorise or review the authorisation of a convention adoption or a specified order; or

(b) to give or review a decision revoking or annulling a convention adoption, a specified order or an adoption order,

makes a determination in the exercise of that power, then, subject to section 6 of this Act and any subsequent determination having effect under this subsection, the determination shall have effect in Great Britain for the purpose of effecting, confirming or terminating the adoption in question or confirming its termination, as the case may be.

(2) In this Act "convention adoption" means an overseas adoption of a description designated by an order under section 4(3) of this Act as that of an adoption regulated by the Convention.

NOTES

Definitions.—See s. 11, *post.*

Overseas adoption.—See s. 4(3), *ante.*

6. Annulment, etc., of certain adoptions and determinations made overseas.—(1) The court may, upon an application under this subsection, by order annul a convention adoption—

(a) on the ground that at the relevant time the adoption was prohibited by a notified provision, if under the internal law then in force in the country of which the adopter was then a national or the adopters were then nationals the adoption could have been impugned on that ground;

(b) on the ground that at the relevant time the adoption contravened provisions relating to consents of the internal law relating to adoption of the country of which the adopted person was then a national, if under that law the adoption could then have been impugned on that ground;

(c) on any other ground on which the adoption can be impugned under the law for the time being in force in the country in which the adoption was effected.

(2) Where a person adopted by his father or mother alone by virtue of a convention adoption has subsequently become a legitimated person on the marriage of his father and mother, the court may, upon an application under this subsection by the parties concerned, by order revoke the adoption.

(3) The court may, upon an application under this subsection—

(a) order that an overseas adoption or a determination shall cease to be valid in Great Britain on the ground that the adoption or determination is contrary to public policy or that the authority which purported to authorise the adoption or make the determination was not competent to entertain the case;

(b) decide the extent, if any, to which a determination has been effected by a subsequent determination.

(4) Any court in Great Britain may, in any proceedings in that court, decide that an overseas adoption or a determination shall, for the purposes of those proceedings, be treated as invalid in Great Britain on either of the grounds mentioned in subsection (3) of this section.

(5) Except as provided by this section, the validity of an overseas adoption or a determination shall not be impugned in proceedings in any court in Great Britain.

NOTE

Definitions.—See s. 11, *post*, and s. 7(4), *post*.

7. Provisions supplementary to section 6.—(1) Any application for an order under section 6(3)(b) or a decision under section (6)(3)(b) of this Act shall be made in the prescribed manner and within such period, if any, as may be prescribed.

(2) No application shall be made under subsection (1) or subsection (2) of section 6 of this Act in respect of an adoption unless immediately before the application is made the person adopted or the adopter resides in Great Britain or, as the case may be, both adopters reside there.

(3) In deciding in pursuance of section 6 of this Act whether such an authority as is mentioned in section 5(1) of this Act was competent to entertain a particular case, a court shall be bound by any finding of fact made by the authority and stated by the authority to be so made for the purpose of determining whether the authority was competent to entertain the case.

(4) In section 6 of this Act and this section—

"determination" means such a determination as is mentioned in section 5(1) of this Act;

"notified provision" means a provision specified in an order of the Secretary of State as one in respect of which a notification to or by the Government of the United Kingdom was in force at the relevant time in pursuance of the provisions of the Convention relating to prohibitions contained in the national law of the adopter; and "relevant time" means the time when the adoption in question purported to take effect under the law of the country in which it purports to have been effected.

NOTES

Prescribed manner.—This means prescribed by rules, see s. 11, *post.* No Rules had been made at the time of going to press.

Miscellaneous and general

8. Registration.—(1) The direction contained in an adoption order in pursuance of section 21 of the Act of 1958 (under which the Registrar General is required to register adoptions in the Adopted Children Register) shall include an instruction that the entry made in that register in consequence of the order shall be marked with the words "Convention order".

(2) If the Registrar General is satisfied that an entry in the Registers of Births relates to a person adopted under an overseas adoption and that he has sufficient particulars relating to that person to enable an entry in the form set out in Schedule 1 to the Act of 1958, as modified by this subsection, to be made in the Adopted Children Register in respect of that person, he shall—

(a) make such an entry in the Adopted Children Register; and

(b) if there is a previous entry in respect of that person in that register, mark the entry (or if there is more than one such entry the last of them) with the word "Re-adopted" followed by the name in brackets of the country in which the adoption was effected; and

(c) unless the entry in the Registers of Births is already marked with the word "Adopted" (whether or not followed by other words), mark the entry with that word followed by the name in brackets of the country aforesaid;

and for the purposes of this subsection the said Schedule 1 shall have effect as if column 6 were headed "Date and place of adoption".

(3) If the Registrar General is satisfied—

(a) that an adoption order or an overseas adoption has ceased to have effect, whether on annulment or otherwise; or

(b) that any entry or mark was erroneously made in pursuance of subsection (2) of this section in any register mentioned in that subsection,

he may cause such alterations to be made in any such register as he considers are required in consequence of the cesser or to correct the error; and where an entry in such a register is amended in pursuance of this subsection, any copy or extract of the entry shall be deemed to be accurate if and only if it shows the entry as amended but without indicating that it has been amended.

(4) Without prejudice to subsection (3) of this section, where an entry in the Registers of Births is marked in pursuance of subsection (2) of this section and the birth in question is subsequently re-registered under section 14 of the Births and Deaths Registration Act, 1953 (which provides for re-registration of the birth of a legitimated person) the entry made on re-registration shall be marked in the like manner.

(5) In the application of this section to Scotland—

(a) for any reference to the Registrar General or the Registers of Births there shall be substituted respectively a reference to the Registrar General of Births, Deaths and Marriages for Scotland and the register of births;

(b) for the references to section 21 of and Schedule 1 to the Act of 1958 there shall be substituted respectively references to section 23 of and Schedule 2 to that Act;

(c) in subsection (2), for the words "column 6 were headed" there shall be substituted the words "item 6 were entitled"; and

(d) in subsection (4), for the reference to section 14 of the Births and Deaths Registration Act, 1953, there shall be substituted a reference to section 20(1)(c) of the Registration of Births, Deaths and Marriages (Scotland) Act, 1965.

9. Nationality.—(1) If the Secretary of State by order declares that a description of persons specified in the order has, in pursuance of the Convention, been notified to the Government of the United Kingdom as the description of persons who are deemed to possess the nationality of a particular convention country, persons of that description shall, subject to the following provisions of this section, be treated for the purposes of this Act as nationals of that country.

(2) Subject to section 7(3) of this Act and subsection (3) of this section, where it appears to the court in any proceedings under this Act, or to any court by which a decision in pursuance of section 6(4) of this Act falls to be given, that a person is or was at a particular time a national of two or more countries, then—

(a) if it appears to the said court that he is or was then a United Kingdom national, he shall be treated for the purposes of those proceedings or that decision as if he were or had then been a United Kingdom national only;

(b) if, in a case not falling within paragraph (a) above, it appears to the said court that one only of those countries is or was then a convention country, he shall be treated for those purposes as if he were or had then been a national of that country only;

(c) if, in a case not falling within paragraph (a) above, it appears to the said court that two or more of those countries are or were then convention countries, he shall be treated for those purposes as if he were or had then been a national of such one only of those convention countries as the said court considers is the country with which he is or was then most closely connected;

(d) in any other case, he shall be treated for those purposes as if he were or had then been a national of such one only of those countries as the said court considers is the country with which he is or was then most closely connected.

(3) A court in which proceedings are brought in pursuance of section 6 of this Act shall be entitled to disregard the provisions of subsection (2) of this section in so far as it appears to that court appropriate to do so for the purposes of those proceedings; but nothing in this subsection shall be construed as prejudicing the provisions of section 7(3) of this Act.

(4) Where, after such inquiries as the court in question considers appropriate, it appears to the court in any proceedings under this Act, or to any court by which such a decision as aforesaid falls to be given, that a person has no nationality or no ascertainable nationality, he shall be treated for the purposes of those proceedings or that decision as a national of the country in which he resides or, where that country is one of two or more countries having the same law of nationality, as a national of those countries.

(5) Where an adoption order, a specified order or an overseas adoption ceases to have effect, either on annulment or otherwise, the cesser shall not affect the status as a citizen of the United Kingdom and Colonies of any person who, by virtue of section 19(1) of the Act of 1958, became such a citizen in consequence of the order of adoption.

NOTES

Definitions.—See s. 11, *post.*

Order.—No order had been made at the time of going to press.

10. Supplemental.—(1) In any case where the internal law of a country falls to be ascertained for the purposes of this Act by any court and there are in force in that country two or more systems of internal law, the relevant system shall be ascertained in accordance with any rule in force throughout that country indicating which of the systems is relevant in the case in question or, if there is no such rule, shall be the system appearing to that court to be most closely connected with the case.

(2) Except as otherwise expressly provided by this Act, nothing in this Act shall be construed as depriving an adoption effected outside Great Britain, or a determination made outside Great Britain with respect to such an adoption, of any recognition falling to be accorded to it under the law of England and Wales or Scotland apart from this Act.

(3) In section 1(4) of the Act of 1958 (which enables an adoption order to be made under that Act notwithstanding that a previous adoption order under it has been made in respect of the relevant infant) the references to an order previously made and to the previous and last previous order shall be construed as including references to an adoption order under this Act, a specified order and an overseas adoption; and in section 46(2) of the Matrimonial Causes Act, 1965 and section 99(2) of the Superannuation Act, 1965 (which provide for the interpretation of references to adoption in those Acts) the references to an enactment of the Parliament of Northern Ireland corresponding to the Act of 1958 shall be construed as including references to an enactment of that Parliament corresponding to this Act, and in the said section 99(2) the reference to an adoption order within the meaning of the Act of 1958 shall be construed as including a reference to an adoption order made under any enactment in force in any of the Channel Islands or the Isle of Man and corresponding to section 1 of this Act.

NOTES

For s. 1(4) of the Adoption Act, 1958, see p. 1026, *ante.*

Recognition apart from this Act.—*I.e.*, under laws relating to succession to property, custody of children etc.

11. Interpretation.—(1) In this Act the following expressions have the following meanings unless the context otherwise requires, that is to say—

"the Act of 1958" means the Adoption Act, 1958;

"adoption order" has the meaning assigned to it by section 1 of this Act;

"the Convention" means the Convention mentioned in the preamble to this Act;

"convention adoption" has the meaning assigned to it by section 5(2) of this Act;

"convention country" means any country (excluding Great Britain and a specified country) for the time being designated by an order of the Secretary of State as a country in which, in his opinion, the Convention is in force;

"the court" means the High Court or the Court of Session;

"internal law", in relation to any country, means the law applicable in a case where no question arises as to the law in force in any other country;

"overseas adoption" has the meaning assigned to it by section 4(3) of this Act;

"prescribed" means prescribed by rules or, in Scotland, by act of sederunt;

"qualified infant" means a person who—

(a) is under eighteen years of age on such date as the Secretary of State may by order specify and is not and has not been married; and

(b) is a United Kingdom national or a national of a convention country and resides in Great Britain, a specified country or a convention country;

"qualified person" means a person who either resides in Great Britain and is a United Kingdom national or a national of a convention country or resides in a convention country or a specified country and is a United Kingdom national;

"qualified spouses" means two persons married to each other in a case where—

(a) both reside in Great Britain and each is a United Kingdom national or a national of a convention country; or

(b) both are United Kingdom nationals and each resides in Great Britain, a specified country or a convention country;

"reside" means habitually reside and "resides" shall be construed accordingly;

"rules" means rules made under section 12(1) of this Act;

"specified country" means, for the purposes of any provision of this Act, any of the following countries, that is to say, Northern Ireland, any of the Channel Islands, the Isle of Man and a colony, being a country designated for the purposes of that provision by order of the Secretary of State or, if no country is so designated, any of those countries;

"specified order" means an adoption order made under any enactment in force in a specified country and corresponding to section 1 of this Act; and

"United Kingdom national" means, for the purposes of any provision of this Act, a citizen of the United Kingdom and Colonies satisfying such conditions, if any, as the Secretary of State may by order specify for the purposes of that provision.

(2) Any reference in this Act to any enactment is a reference to it as amended, and includes a reference to it as applied, by or under any other enactment including this Act.

NOTES

Definitions.—See also s. 7(4), *ante*.

Order.—No order has been made at the time of going to press.

12. Rules and orders, etc.—(1) Provision in regard to any matter to be prescribed under this Act, or under Part I of the Act of 1958 in its application to adoption orders and proposed adoption orders, and dealing generally with all matters of procedure and incidental matters arising out of this Act or the said Part I and for carrying this Act or the said Part I into effect shall be made, in England and Wales, by rules made by the Lord Chancellor and, in Scotland, by act of sederunt; and the rules or act of sederunt may include provision—

 (a) for applications for adoption orders to be heard and determined otherwise than in open court;

 (b) for excluding or restricting the jurisdiction of any court where an application for an adoption order within the meaning of this Act or the Act of 1958 has been refused by that or any other court.

(2) Any power to make orders or rules under this Act shall be exercisable by statutory instrument, and any statutory instrument made by virtue of this subsection (except an instrument containing only orders under the provisions of sections 3(1) and 9(1) and the provisions defining "notified provision" in section 7(4) and "convention country" and "specified country" in section 11(1) or under any of those provisions) shall be subject to annulment in pursuance of a resolution of either House of Parliament.

(3) An order made under any provision of this Act (except section 14(2)) may be revoked or varied by a subsequent order under that provision.

(4) Any order or rules made under this Act may make different provision for different circumstances and may contain such incidental and transitional provisions as the authority making the order or rules considers expedient.

(5) References to an order in subsections (2) to (4) of this section do not include references to an order of a court.

NOTE

No rules or orders had been made at the time of going to press.

13. Powers of Parliament of Northern Ireland.—Notwithstanding anything in the Government of Ireland Act, 1920, the Parliament of

Northern Ireland shall have power to make laws for purposes similar to the purposes of the foregoing provisions of this Act other than section 9(5) and the provisions extending section 19(1) of the Act of 1958.

14. Short title, commencement and extent.—(1) This Act may be cited as the Adoption Act, 1968.

(2) This Act shall come into force on such date as the Secretary of State may by order appoint, and different dates may be appointed under this subsection for different purposes of this Act.

(3) This Act, except the provisions extending section 19(1) of the Act of 1958 and except sections 9(5) and 13 and this section, does not extend to Northern Ireland.

NOTE

No order had been made bringing any part of the Act into force at the time of going to press.

SECTION 4.—STATUTORY RULES, ORDERS AND INSTRUMENTS, OFFICIAL CIRCULARS, ETC.

CONTENTS

THE ADOPTION AGENCIES REGULATIONS, 1959

[S.I. 1959 No. 639]

1.—(1) An application by or on behalf of an adoption society to a local authority to be registered under section thirty of the Adoption Act, 1958, shall be in the form set out in the First Schedule to these Regulations, or in a form to the like effect, and shall give the information therein required to be given.

(2) The fee to be paid by an adoption society under the said section thirty in respect of its registration shall be twenty shillings.

2. If a registered adoption society changes the address of the administrative centre of the society, the society shall notify the local authority which has registered the society of the change.

3.—(1) Every registered adoption society shall, within twelve months of the date of registration and thereafter at least once in every period of twelve months, furnish to the local authority which has registered the society—

(a) the accounts of the society for that period duly certified by an independent auditor;

(b) a return in the form set out in the Second Schedule to these Regulations or in a form to the like effect: and

(c) a copy of the society's latest annual report.

(2) For the purposes of this Regulation " independent auditor " means a person who is—

    (a) a chartered accountant or a member of an association or society of accountants incorporated before the date on which these Regulations come into operation; and

    (b) not a member, representative or officer of the society or of the society's case committee, or a relative of, or in partnership with, any such member, representative or officer.

4. Before an infant is placed at the disposition of a registered adoption society with a view to his being adopted, the society shall secure that the parent or guardian proposing so to place the infant is furnished with a memorandum in the form set out in the Third Schedule to these Regulations, and signs and returns to the society a certificate in the form set out in the said Third Schedule, or a form to the like effect, certifying that he had read and understood the said memorandum.

5. No infant shall be placed by or on behalf of a registered adoption society in the care and possession of a person proposing to adopt him until—

    (a) the society have, so far as is reasonably practicable, ascertained the particulars set out in the Fourth Schedule to these Regulations;

    (b) the society have obtained a report by a fully registered medical practitioner as to the health of the infant in the form set out in the Fifth Schedule to these Regulations, or in a form to the like effect;

    (c) the person proposing to adopt the infant has been interviewed by or on behalf of the society's case committee;

    (d) any premises in Great Britain in which that person intends that the infant shall reside permanently have been inspected by or on behalf of the society's case committee;

    (e) the society's case committee have inquired of the local authority in whose area these premises are situated whether the authority have reason to believe that it would be detrimental to the infant to be kept by that person in those premises; and

    (f) the society's case committee, after considering all the information obtained in pursuance of the foregoing paragraphs of this Regulation, have approved of the infant's being so placed.

6.—(1) Every registered adoption society shall make adequate arrangements for the supervision of every infant placed by or on behalf of the society in the care and possession of a person proposing to adopt him until that person gives notice under subsection (2) of section three of the Adoption Act, 1958, of his intention to apply for an adoption order in respect of the infant; and in particular shall arrange that every such infant is visited by a representative of the society within one month after being so placed and thereafter as often as the society's case committee deem necessary.

(2) The representative shall after each visit make a report to the case committee as to the welfare of the infant.

(3) Where an infant has been placed by or on behalf of a registered adoption society in the care and possession of a person proposing to adopt him and—

    (a) a serological test of the infant's blood for syphilis made after he had attained the age of six weeks has not been previously made, the society shall make arrangements for such a test of his blood to be carried out by, and a report thereon obtained from, a fully registered medical practitioner as soon as practicable after the said placing and the infant has attained the age of six weeks ; or

(b) the infant has not attained the age of two years and an examination of his urine for phenylpyruvic acid made after he had attained the age of six weeks has not been previously made, the society shall make arrangements for an examination of the infant's urine for the said acid to be carried out by, and a report thereon obtained from, a fully registered medical practitioner as soon as practicable after the said placing and the infant has attained the age of six weeks.

and the society shall furnish a copy of any report obtained under this paragraph to the person proposing to adopt the infant to which it relates.

7. Any information obtained by any member, officer or representative of a registered adoption society or of the society's case committee in the course of negotiations entered into by or on behalf of the society with a person proposing to place an infant at the disposition of the society with a view to his being adopted, or with a person proposing to adopt him, shall be treated as confidential and shall not be disclosed except so far as may be necessary for the purpose of proceedings under the Adoption Act, 1958, or for the proper execution of his duty or to a person who is authorised in writing by or on behalf of the Secretary of State to obtain the information for the purposes of research.

8. Every registered adoption society shall ensure that—

(a) none of their records or other documents relating to the negotiations mentioned in Regulation 7 of these Regulations are readily accessible to unauthorised persons;

(b) the said records and other documents are, unless the Secretary of State otherwise directs, preserved for at least twenty-five years.

9. Regulations 4 to 8 of these Regulations shall apply to a local authority making or participating in arrangements for the adoption of infants as they apply to a registered adoption society, except that any reference therein to the case committee of a registered adoption society shall be construed as a reference to the local authority.

NOTE
Production of records and giving of evidence, directions by court.—See Practice Direction dated February 8th, 1968, p. 1172, *post.*

10.—(1) References in these Regulations to a registered adoption society's case committee means the committee of the society appointed for the purpose of considering the case of an infant proposed to be placed by or on behalf of the society in the care and possession of a person proposing to adopt him.

(2) A case committee shall, so far as practicable, include one man and one woman and shall consist of not less than three persons each of whom shall be competent to judge whether the proposed placing is likely to be in the interests of the infant.

11. References in these Regulations to an adoption order or to a person proposing to adopt an infant shall be construed as including references to a provisional adoption order or a person proposing to apply for such an order.

12. The Interpretation Act, 1889, shall apply to the interpretation of these Regulations as it applies to the interpretation of an Act of Parliament.

13. The Adoption Societies Regulations, 1943, and the Adoption Societies Regulations, 1950, are hereby revoked.

14.—(1) These Regulations may be cited as the Adoption Agencies Regulations, 1959, and shall come into operation on the seventeenth day of April, 1959.

(2) These Regulations shall not extend to Scotland.

NOTE

These Regulations were made on April 6, 1959, under s. 32 of the Adoption Act, 1958 (p. 1065, *ante*), they are printed as amended by the Adoption Agencies Regulations, 1961, S.I. 1961 No. 900 and the Adoption Agencies Regulations, 1965, S.I. 1965 No. 2054. See Home Office Circular No. 278/1965, p. 1177, *post*.

As to a list of Adoption Societies whose registration had been reported to the Home Office, and a list of local authorities in England and Wales that act as Adoption Societies, see Home Office Circular dated August, 1970, p. 1185, *post*.

Regulation 1   FIRST SCHEDULE

APPLICATION FOR REGISTRATION OF ADOPTION SOCIETY

To the   Council.   I/We the undersigned hereby apply to have the adoption society called   registered under section thirty of the Adoption Act, 1958.

Particulars of the society:—

1. State date of establishment of society, and give particulars of any previous registration or application for registration...
....
....

2. State full postal address of the society's administrative centre ....
....
....

3. Give addresses of any other offices of the society ....
....
....

4. Give particulars of any activities of the society, other than those relating to the adoption of children; and state whether the society applies the whole of its profits (if any) or other income in promoting the objects for which it exists; and attach a copy of the instrument governing the society's activities and a statement of the society's accounts ....
....

5. Give the full name, address and occupation of each member of the committee controlling the activities of the society; and state how the committee is appointed and how it controls the activities of the society; and attach a copy of the rules governing the constitution of the society ....
....
....

6. Give the full name, address and occupation of each member of the society's case committee and his qualifications or experience for that purpose ....
....
....

7. Give the full name, address and occupation of every individual employed or proposed to be employed by the society, whether paid or unpaid, for the purpose of making any arrangements for the adoption of infants and his qualifications or experience for that purpose ....
....
....

8. If any person taking part in the management or control of the society or any member of the society has been convicted of an offence under Part II of the Adoption Act, 1958, Part II of the Adoption Act, 1950, or the Adoption of Children

(Regulation) Act, 1939, or of a breach of any regulations made under those enactments, give his name and particulars of his offence.......................................

....

....

I/We hereby declare that the above particulars are correct to the best of my/our knowledge and belief.

<blockquote>
Signature   ....

Address   ....

....

Position in the society   ....
</blockquote>

SECOND SCHEDULE   Regulation 3 (1)

ANNUAL RETURN

Return to the   *Council from the registered adoption*
society called   *for the year ended*

1. Give the full postal address of the society's administrative centre ....

....

....

2. State whether there has been any change in the objects for which the society exists and whether the society has applied the whole of its profits (if any) or other income in promoting the objects for which it exists.......................................

....

....

3. Give the full name, address and occupation, of each member of the committee controlling the activities of the society; and state whether there has been any change in the rules governing the constitution of the society ....

....

....

4. Give the full name, address and occupation, of each member of the society's case committee and his qualifications or experience for that purpose ....

....

....

5. Give the full name, address and occupation, of every individual employed by the society, whether paid or unpaid, for the purpose of making any arrangements for the adoption of infants and his qualifications or experience for that purpose ...

....

....

6. If any person taking part in the management or control of the society or any member of the society has been convicted of an offence under Part II of the Adoption Act, 1958, Part II of the Adoption Act, 1950, or the Adoption of Children (Regulation) Act, 1939, or of a breach of any regulations made under those enactments, give his name and particulars of his offence.......................................

....

....

7. Give the number of cases dealt with by the society under the following heads:—

(*a*) number of applications from persons wishing to adopt an infant ....

....

....

(b) number of infants offered to the society with a view to their being adopted, but not accepted by the society ....

....

....

(c) number of infants accepted by the society with a view to their being adopted ....

....

....

(d) number of infants placed by or on behalf of the society in the care and possession of persons proposing to adopt them ....

....

....

(e) number of infants so delivered in respect of whom adoption orders or provisional adoption orders had not been made ....

....

....

(f) number of adoption orders or provisional adoption orders made in respect of infants who were so placed during the period to which the return relates

....

....

(g) number of adoption orders or provisional adoption orders made in respect of infants who were so placed before the period to which the return relates

....

....

8. Give, under the following heads, the number of infants who, at the end of the period to which the return relates, had been placed at the disposition of the society with a view to their being adopted but had not been placed in the care and possession of persons proposing to adopt them:—

(a) number of infants in the care and possession of the society ....

....

....

(b) number of infants boarded out by the society ....

....

....

(c) number of other infants ....

....

....

9. Number of case committee meetings...

....

....

I/We hereby declare that the above particulars are correct to the best of my/our knowledge and belief.

Signature...

Address ....

....

Position in the society ....

THIRD SCHEDULE   Regulation 4

ADOPTION OF CHILDREN

Explanatory Memorandum

This memorandum is addressed to the parent (a term which does not include the natural father of an illegitimate child) or guardian of a child who is about to be legally adopted.

A person proposing to adopt your child has to apply to a court for an adoption order. Before making an order, the court will have inquiries made by a person called the guardian ad litem to see whether it would be in the interests of the child that he should be adopted by the proposed adopters. The court will also require to know whether you (and any other parent or guardian of the child) consent.   The court cannot make an adoption order without your consent unless it dispenses with your consent on the ground that you have abandoned, neglected or persistently ill-treated the child, or that you have failed without reasonable cause to discharge your obligations as a parent or guardian, or on the ground that you have unreasonably withheld your consent. The court may also dispense with consent on the ground that the parent or guardian cannot be found or is incapable of giving consent (for instance by reason of being insane).

You will be asked to sign a form of consent which can be shown to the court as evidence of your consent. This form will either give the names of the persons wishing to adopt the child or, if they wish to conceal their identity, will refer to them by a number. If you want to know what sort of people they are, you can ask the adoption society or local authority that is arranging the adoption.

Do not sign the form of consent unless you are quite sure that you are willing that your child should be adopted by these persons. If the court makes an adoption order, your rights as a parent or guardian will be transferred to the adopters and they will become in law the child's parents. You will then have no further right to see the child or to have the child returned to you. If the adopters live abroad, they will probably take the child abroad with them after obtaining an order.

If you do not know the names of the proposed adopters, but wish your child to be brought up in a particular religious faith, you may give your consent on condition that they propose to bring up your child in that faith.

If you sign the form of consent and then, before the adoption order is made, you wish to withdraw your consent, you should inform the court. But the proposed adopters are entitled to refuse to hand back your child to you unless you obtain the permission of the court.

You are not allowed to receive any money for giving your consent.

CERTIFICATE

To (name of adoption society or local authority)

I hereby certify that I have received from you a memorandum headed " Adoption of Children. Explanatory Memorandum ", from which I have detached this certificate of acknowledgment; and I further certify that I have read the memorandum and understand it.

Signature   ....

Address   ....

....

Date ....

FOURTH SCHEDULE   Regulation 5 (a)

PARTICULARS TO BE ASCERTAINED

PART I

Particulars relating to the infant

1. Name.

2. Date and place of birth.

3. If baptised, date and place of baptism and denomination.

4. If not baptised, religious persuasion of the infant's father and mother.

5. Name, address and age of the infant's father and mother. If either is dead, date of death.

6. If either the father or mother has any other children, the age and sex of each child.

7. Whether there is any history of tuberculosis, epilepsy, mental illness or other disease in either the father's or mother's family.

8. Why the infant is offered for adoption and whether he has previously been so offered.

9. Whether the mother consents to the infant's being adopted, and, if not, her reasons for not consenting.

10. If the infant is legitimate, whether the father consents to the infant's being adopted, and, if not, his reasons for not consenting. If the infant is illegitimate, whether the father (if known) has any objection to the infant's being adopted.

11. The names and addresses of the infant's guardians (if any), how and by whom they were appointed, and whether they consent to the infant's being adopted, and, if not, their reasons for not consenting.

12. Whether any other body or person has the rights and powers of a parent of the infant and whether that body or person has any objection to the infant's being adopted.

13. Whether the infant has any right to, or interest in, any property.

14. Whether an insurance policy for the payment on the death of the infant of money for funeral expenses has been effected.

PART II

Particulars relating to the proposed adopters

1. Names.

2. Address.

3. Dates of birth.

4. Religious persuasion.

5. Occupation.

6. Whether the proposed adopters are ordinarily resident in Great Britain, and, if not, the address at which they are ordinarily resident.

7. Whether the proposed adopters are domiciled in England, Wales or Scotland, and, if not, the country in which they are domiciled.

8. If the proposed adopters intend to apply for a provisional adoption order, whether they intend to adopt the infant in law or in fact in the country in which they are domiciled.

9. If there are two proposed adopters, the date and place of the proposed adopters' marriage, and whether either proposed adopter has previously been married and, if so, whether that marriage was dissolved or annulled.

10. If there is only one proposed adopter, whether that person is married, and, if so, why the spouse does not join in the application, and whether he consents to the infant's being adopted, and, if not, his reasons for not consenting.

11. Particulars of all members of the proposed adopters' household and their relationship (if any) to the proposed adopters.

12. The accommodation in the proposed adopters' home and the condition of the home.

13. The means of the proposed adopters.

14. The wishes of the proposed adopters as to the age and sex of the child they wish to adopt.

15. The names and addresses of two persons selected by the proposed adopters to whom reference can be made as to their character

16. Whether either of the proposed adopters has previously—

    (a) notified a local authority of his intention to adopt an infant;
    (b) applied to an adoption society or local authority with a view to adopting an infant;
    (c) had in his care and possession a foster child within the meaning of section 2 of the Children Act, 1958, who has been removed under section 7 of that Act;

(d) been prohibited from keeping a foster child under section 4 of that Act;
(e) had in his care and possession a protected child who has been removed under section 43 of the Adoption Act, 1958; or
(f) been prohibited from keeping a protected child.

FIFTH SCHEDULE   Regulation 5 (b)

MEDICAL REPORT AS TO HEALTH OF INFANT

Child's name .... Date of birth .... Sex ....

Weight.............................. Height................................

General condition ....
Skin ....
Eyes (including vision) ....
Ears (including hearing) ....
Nose and throat ....
Speech ....
Cardio-vascular system ....
Respiratory system..
Alimentary system...
Genito-urinary system (including examination of urine for albumen, and sugar
....
Skeletal and articular system (including examination for congenital dislocation
of hip) ....
Nervous system (including fits)..
Lymphatic system ....
Any other comments ....
Is the child physically normal having regard to his age? ....

B   Are there any items in the child's history or examination which suggest that he may be mentally abnormal having regard to his age? ....
....

C   Particulars of any illnesses from which the child has suffered ....
....

D   If known,
Weight at birth (if child is under one year of age) ....
Details of birth, including result of mother's serological tests for syphilis ...
....

Particulars, with dates, of vaccination or immunisation against—
Tuberculosis (state result of Mantoux test or whether child has been successfully vaccinated with B.C.G. vaccine)....................................
Smallpox ....
Diphtheria ....
Whooping cough ....
Poliomyelitis ....
Tetanus (active) ....
Any other disease ....

E   (i) (*To be completed only in the case of a child at least six weeks old at the time of the test*)
Result of suitable serological test of the child's blood for syphilis (please specify test) ....
(ii) (*To be completed only in the case of a child at least six weeks and under two years old at the time of the examination*)
Result of examination of the child's urine for phenylpyruvic acid...........•••
.............................•••••••

F   I examined the child on the .... day of ...., 19......

Signature.....................................Address ....

Qualifications ....
....

THE ADOPTION (JUVENILE COURT) RULES, 1959

[S.I. 1959 No. 504 (L.5)]

1.—(1) An application shall be in Form 1, and shall be made to a juvenile court acting for the petty sessions area in which the applicant or the infant resides at the date of the application by delivering it, or sending it by post, to the clerk to the justices for that area, together with all documents referred to in the application as attached thereto.

(2) The applicant shall supply to the justices' clerk a copy of his application at the same time as he makes his application.

2. If any person proposing to apply to a juvenile court for an adoption order desires that his identity be kept confidential, he may, before making his application, apply to the justices' clerk for a serial number to be assigned to him for the purposes of the proposed application, and the clerk shall assign a number to him accordingly.

3. Except where the applicant, or one of the applicants, is the father or mother of the infant or the infant has reached the upper limit of the compulsory school age, every applicant shall supply to the justices' clerk at the same time as he makes his application the certificate of a fully registered medical practitioner as to his health; and for the purposes of such certificate Form 2 may be used.

NOTE

Compulsory school age.—See s. 35 of the Education Act, 1944, p. 252, *ante*, and the definition in s. 57 of the Adoption Act, 1958, p. 1080, *ante*.

4.—(1) Any report on the health of the infant which is to be used for the purposes of an application shall be supplied by the applicant to the justices' clerk at the same time as he makes his application.

(2) The report may, if the applicant so desires, be in Form 3.

NOTE

See note 4 to Form 3. Even in cases where the applicant does not provide a report it is open to the court to require evidence as to the infant's health in order to determine that the adoption order would be for the welfare of the infant.

5.—(1) Any document signifying the consent of any person to the making of an adoption order for the purposes of section six of the Adoption Act, 1958, shall be in Form 4.

(2) If the said document is executed outside the United Kingdom, it shall be sufficiently attested for the purposes of subsection (3) of the said section six if it is attested by any of the following persons:—

    (a) any person for the time being authorised by law in the place where the document is executed to administer an oath for any judicial or other legal purpose;

    (b) a British consular officer;

    (c) a notary public; or

    (d) if the person executing the document is serving in any of the regular armed forces of the Crown, an officer holding a commission in any of those forces.

6. If it appears that the applicant has previously made an application in respect of the same infant to the High Court, a county court or a juvenile court, and that that court, after having heard the case, dismissed the application on its merits, the court shall not proceed with the application unless it is satisfied that there has been a substantial change in the circumstances since the previous application.

NOTE

A juvenile court is no longer absolutely precluded, as was formerly the case, from entertaining an application where the applicant has previously applied in respect of the same infant to the High Court or a county court.

7. If owing to special circumstances any application appears to the court to be more fit to be dealt with by the High Court, the court may, at any stage of the proceedings, refuse, on that ground expressly, to proceed with the application.

NOTE

The special circumstances should apparently have reference to the difficulty of the points of law involved and not to the social position or means of the parties. Reference may be made to the remark of Gorell Barnes, P., in *Dodd* v. *Dodd*, [1906] P. 189; 70 J. P. 163 in relation to a similar provision in another statute.

8.—(1) Subject to the provisions of Rules 6 and 7 of these Rules, the court shall, as soon as practicable after an application is made, appoint a guardian *ad litem* of the infant and shall furnish him with a copy of the application, together with the documents attached thereto.

(2) The person appointed guardian *ad litem* shall be—

 (a) if the local authority concerned consents, the children's officer of a local authority or an officer or servant of that authority who assists the children's officer in the exercise of his functions;

 (b) a probation officer; or

 (c) if in any particular case the court considers that it is not reasonably practicable, or that it would be undesirable, to appoint one of the aforesaid persons, some other person who appears to the court to be suitably qualified:

  Provided that no person shall be appointed guardian *ad litem* if—

   (i) he has the rights and powers of a parent of the infant, or has taken part in the arrangements for the adoption of the infant; or

   (ii) he is a member, officer or servant of a local authority, adoption society or other body of persons which has the rights and powers of a parent of the infant or which has taken part in the arrangements for the adoption of the infant.

(3) Where the children's officer of a local authority is appointed guardian *ad litem*, he may carry out his duties and appear before the court personally or by any other officer or servant of that authority who assists the children's officer in the exercise of his functions.

NOTES

Duties of probation officer as guardian *ad litem*.—See r. 31 of the Probation Rules, 1965, p. 528, *ante*.

High Court.—As to the duties of the guardian *ad litem* when application is made to dispense with the consent of parent or guardian, see Adoption (High Court) Rules, 1971, rule 9, p. 1157, *post*.

9.—(1) With a view to safeguarding the interests of the infant before the court the guardian *ad litem* shall, so far as it is reasonably practicable—

 (a) investigate all circumstances relevant to the proposed adoption, including the matters alleged in the application and those specified in the Second Schedule to these Rules; and

 (b) perform such other duties as are specified in the said Schedule or as the court may direct.

(2) On completing his investigations the guardian *ad litem* shall make a confidential report in writing to the court.

(3) With a view to obtaining the directions of the court on any particular matter, the guardian *ad litem* may, at any time, make such interim report to the court as appears to him to be necessary.

NOTE

In *Re J. S. (an Infant)*, [1959] 3 All E. R. 856; 124 J. P. 89, Roxburgh, J., held that the parties in an application for an adoption order had no right to see the confidential reports except in so far as the justices or (on appeal) the judge thought fit to disclose their contents at the hearing, and the justices were right in refusing to forward copies to the applicants. It was, however, the duty of the justices to forward them to the judge's clerk for the information of the appellate court.

10. At the time of appointing the guardian *ad litem*, the court shall fix a time for the hearing of the application.

11.—(1) After the time of the hearing of the application has been fixed, the court shall serve a notice in Form 5 on the applicant.

(2) If the guardian *ad litem* reports to the court that in his opinion the infant is able to understand the nature of an adoption order, the court shall inform the applicant that the personal attendance of the infant at the hearing of the application is required.

12.—(1) After the time of the hearing of the application has been fixed, the court shall serve a notice in Form 6 on the following persons:—

    (a) every person, not being an applicant, whose consent to the making of the adoption order is required under subsection (1) of section four of the Adoption Act, 1958;

    (b) any person having the rights and powers of a parent of the infant by virtue of section seventy-five of the Children and Young Persons Act, 1933, or sub-paragraph (1) of paragraph 12 of the Fourth Schedule to that Act or section three of the Children Act, 1948;

    (c) any person liable by virtue of any order or agreement to contribute to the maintenance of the infant;

    (d) the local authority to whom the applicant has given notice of his intention to apply for an adoption order under subsection (2) of section three of the Adoption Act, 1958;

    (e) any local authority or adoption society named in the application or in a form of consent as having taken part in the arrangements for the adoption of the infant;

    (f) any other person, not being the infant, who in the opinion of the court ought to be served with notice of the hearing of the application.

(2) Any person on whom a notice is required to be served under the foregoing provisions of this Rule shall be a respondent to the application.

NOTES

The guardian *ad litem* should inform the court, by an interim report in accordance with rule 9, *supra*, of any person who the court might consider ought to be served with notice. It should be noted that there is no power to dispense with the serving of the notice.

Persons to be served.—See note to Rule 10 of the Adoption (County Court) Rules, 1959, p. 1130, *post*. It should be noted that this was an appeal against a county court decision. See also the note " Cannot be found " at p. 1034, *ante*.

13. The court shall not make an adoption order or an interim order except after the personal attendance before the court of the applicant:

Provided that where the application is made by two spouses jointly, the court may dispense with the personal attendance of one of the applicants if the application is verified by a declaration made by that applicant and attested by a justice of the peace, a justices' clerk within the meaning of section twenty-one of the Justices of the Peace Act, 1949, or, if made outside the United Kingdom, by a person specified in paragraph (2) of Rule 5 of these Rules.

14. If the applicant has been informed that the personal attendance of the infant at the hearing is required, the court shall not make an adoption order or an interim order unless—

    (a) the infant has so attended or the court decides that there are special circumstances making his attendance unnecessary; and

    (b) the court is satisfied that the infant has been informed of the nature of the order.

15. If a serial number has been assigned to the applicant under Rule 2 of these Rules, the proceedings shall be conducted with a view to securing that he is not seen by, or made known to, any respondent who is not already aware of his identity, except with his consent.

16. Notwithstanding anything in section forty-seven of the Children and Young Persons Act, 1933, every application shall be heard and determined in camera.

17.—(1) Where proof of the identity of the infant is required for any purpose, any fact tending to establish his identity with an infant to whom a document relates may be proved by affidavit.

(2) Where any such fact is proved by affidavit, the attendance of a witness at the hearing to prove that fact shall not be compelled unless the fact is disputed or for some special reason his attendance is required by the court.

18.—(1) Where the determination of an application is postponed and an interim order is made, the court shall, on making the order or at any time thereafter but not less than one month before the expiration of the period during which the applicant has the custody of the infant in accordance with the interim order and whether or not the applicant makes an application for the purpose, fix a time for the further hearing of the application.

(2) On fixing a time for the further hearing of an application, the court shall—

    (a) serve on the applicant a notice in Form 7; and

    (b) serve on each respondent to the application a notice in Form 8.

NOTES

It may be necessary at the resumed hearing to make persons respondents who were not respondents at the original hearing.

It should be noted that there is no power to dispense with the serving of the notice.

19. An adoption order shall be drawn up in Form 9.

20.—(1) Within seven days after the making of an adoption order the justices' clerk shall send a copy of the order to the Registrar General.

(2) The copy sent to the Registrar General shall be drawn up on paper thirteen inches long by eight inches wide, and shall have a margin to be left blank, not less than one inch wide, on the left side of the face of the paper and a similar margin on the right side of the reverse of the paper.

21. Within seven days after the making of an adoption order the justices' clerk shall serve on the applicant an abridged copy of the adoption order in Form 10 signed by a member of the court.

NOTE

The applicant must be served with an abridged copy, and he is entitled by Rule 23, *post*, to a full copy of the order in addition.

22.—(1) An interim order shall be drawn up in Form 11.

(2) Within seven days after the making of an interim order the justices' clerk shall serve on the applicant a copy of the order.

NOTE

Copies of interim orders should not be sent to the Registrar General.

23.—(1) The justices' clerk shall not supply a copy of an adoption order or of an interim order or an abridged copy of an adoption order except—

    (a) in accordance with the provisions of Rules 20, 21 and 22 of these Rules; or

    (b) on the request of the Registrar General or the applicant or one of the applicants; or

    (c) on the application of any other person under an order of a juvenile court acting for the same petty sessions area as the juvenile court which made the adoption order or interim order.

    (d) on the request of another juvenile court, a county court or the High Court.

(2) This Rule applies to an adoption order or interim order made under the Adoption Act, 1950, or any enactment repealed by that Act as it applies in relation to an adoption order or interim order made under the Adoption Act, 1958.

(3) A juvenile court shall not request another juvenile court, a county court or the High Court to furnish a copy of an adoption order under paragraph (1) (d) of this Rule or under any other Adoption Rule corresponding to that paragraph except in the case of an infant born in England who had been adopted in England before 1st April 1959 and in respect of whom the registration district and sub-district in which he was born would not otherwise be proved to the satisfaction of the first mentioned court for the purposes of section 21 (3) of the Adoption Act, 1958.

24. Where an adoption order is made in respect of an infant who is illegitimate, then, unless the applicant is his mother and she is a single woman, the justices' clerk shall serve notice of the order on any other court which appears to him to have made an affiliation order or decree of affiliation and aliment which is still in force with respect to the infant.

25. On the determination of an application or on the making of an interim order, the justices' clerk shall serve notice to that effect on all parties who were not present when the court made its determination or order.

26. On the determination of an application or on the making of an interim order, the court may make such order as to costs as it thinks just, and in particular may order the applicant to pay—

    (a) the out-of-pocket expenses incurred by the guardian *ad litem*, and

    (b) the expenses incurred by any respondent in attending the hearing,

or such part of those expenses as the court thinks proper.

27.—(1) Any application made under section twenty-four of the Adoption Act, 1958, for the amendment of an adoption order or the revocation of a direction to the Registrar General or under section twenty-six of the said Act for the revocation of an adoption order shall be in Form 12, and shall be made to a juvenile court acting for the same petty sessions area as the juvenile court which made the adoption order concerned by delivering it or sending it by post to the clerk to the justices for that petty sessions area.

(2) Notice of the application shall be given by the court to such persons (if any) as the court specifies.

(3) Where an adoption order is amended or a direction revoked under subsection (1) of the said section twenty-four or an adoption order revoked under the said section twenty-six, the justices' clerk shall send to the Registrar General a notice specifying the date of the adoption order and the names of the adopter and of the adopted person as given in the Schedule to the adoption order and either stating the amendments to the adoption order made by the court or informing him of the revocation of the direction or adoption order, as the case may be:

Provided that where an order made under the Adoption of Children Act, 1926, is amended, the said notice shall specify in a form similar to the Schedule to Form 9 all the particulars to be entered in the Adopted Children Register.

28. Such part of the register kept in pursuance of rules made under the Magistrates' Courts Act, 1952, as relates to proceedings under Part I of the Adoption Act, 1958, shall be kept in a separate book and shall contain the particulars shown in Form 13; and the book shall not contain particulars of any other proceedings except proceedings under the Adoption Act, 1950, or any Act repealed by that Act.

29. The book kept in pursuance of Rule 28 of these Rules and all other documents relating to the proceedings mentioned in that Rule while they are in the custody of the court shall be kept in a place of special security.

30. Any information obtained by any person in the course of, or relating to, proceedings under Part I of the Adoption Act, 1958, shall be treated as confidential and shall be disclosed if, but only if,—

    (a) the disclosure is necessary for the proper exercise of his duties, or
    (b) the information is requested—

        (i) by a court or public authority (whether within Great Britain or not) having power to authorise an adoption for the purpose of the discharge of its duties in that behalf, or

        (ii) by a person who is authorised in writing by or on behalf of the Secretary of State to obtain the information for the purposes of research.

31. Any respondent, being a local authority or other body of persons, may appear and be heard at proceedings under Part I of the Adoption Act, 1958, by any officer or servant of that authority or body duly authorised in that behalf.

31A.—(1) A person wishing to apply to the court to grant leave for the removal of an infant from the care and possession of an applicant under section 34 or section 35 of the Adoption Act, 1958 (hereafter in this Rule referred to as "the said person") shall give notice in Form 14 to the court by delivering it, or sending it by post, to the clerk to the justices for the petty sessions area hearing the application for the adoption order.

(2) The court shall serve on the applicant and on each respondent to the application for the adoption order (other than the said person) a copy of the said notice.

(3) The court shall fix a time for hearing the application under this Rule and shall serve notice of the time on the said person and on the applicant and each respondent (other than the said person) to the application for the adoption order; and the applicant and each such respondent shall be a respondent to the application under this Rule.

(4) If a serial number has been assigned to the applicant under Rule 2 of these Rules, the proceedings under this Rule shall be conducted with a view to securing that, except with his consent, he is not seen by, or made known to, any other respondent to the application under this Rule, or to the said person, if he is not aware of his identity.

(5) (a) Rules 7, 16, 25 and 26 of these Rules shall apply to proceedings under this Rule as they apply to an application for an adoption order.

(b) Rule 28 of these Rules shall apply to proceedings under this Rule as it applies to proceedings under Part I of the Adoption Act 1958, except that the requirement as to the particulars to be shown may be modified so far as circumstances require ; and Rule 29 of these Rules shall apply accordingly.

(c) Rules 30 and 31 of these Rules shall apply to proceedings under this Rule as they apply to proceedings under Part I of the Adoption Act, 1958.

NOTE

" **Duly authorised.**"—In most cases the officer will no doubt produce a written authority signed on behalf of the local authority. He should if necessary be asked to give evidence on oath.

32. Unless otherwise directed, service of a document under these Rules—

(a) on a corporation or a body of persons may be effected by delivering it at, or sending it by post to, the registered or principal office of the corporation or body of persons;

(b) on any other person may be effected by delivering it to him or by sending it by post to him at his last known or usual place of abode.

NOTES

It is no longer the duty of the guardian *ad litem* to serve notices. This is now the duty of the court or the justices' clerk. See Rules 12, 25, *ante*.

The Rule does not provide for service by leaving the document with some other person for him at the respondent's address.

33. Save in so far as special provision is made by these Rules, proceedings on an application shall be regulated in the same manner as proceedings on complaint, and accordingly for the purposes of this Rule the application shall be deemed to be a complaint, the applicant to be a complainant, the respondents to be defendants and any notice served under these Rules to be a summons; but nothing in this Rule shall be construed as enabling a warrant of arrest to be issued for failure to appear in answer to any such notice.

NOTE

The parties may be legally represented; see the Magistrates' Courts Act, 1952, s. 99.

34. The court shall serve on the guardian ad litem a copy of every notice served on an applicant or respondent.

35. In these Rules a form referred to by number means the form so numbered in the First Schedule to these Rules or a form to the like effect, and any such form may be used with such variation as the circumstances may require.

36. These Rules shall apply only to proceedings under Parts I and III of the Adoption Act, 1958, before magistrates' courts.

37.—(1) In these Rules the following expressions have the meanings hereby assigned to them unless the context otherwise requires:—

" application " means an application for an adoption order and " applicant " shall be construed accordingly;

" determination of an application " includes a refusal to proceed with the application under Rule 7 of these Rules or a withdrawal of the application;

" infant " means the infant whom the applicant is applying to adopt;

" interim order " means an interim order made under section eight of the Adoption Act, 1958;

" regular armed forces of the Crown " means the Royal Navy, the regular forces as defined by section two hundred and twenty-five of the Army Act, 1955, the regular air force as defined by section two hundred and twenty-three of the Air Force Act, 1955, the Women's Royal Naval Service, Queen Alexandra's Royal Naval Nursing Service and Voluntary Aid Detachments serving with the Royal Navy.

(2) The Interpretation Act, 1889, shall apply to the interpretation of these Rules as it applies to the interpretation of an Act of Parliament.

38.—(1) The Adoption of Children (Summary Jurisdiction) Rules, 1949, and the Adoption of Children (Summary Jurisdiction) Rules, 1952, are hereby revoked.

(2) These Rules shall apply in relation to an application made before 1st April, 1959, the hearing of which or any other duty or business in connection with which has not been completed before the said date as they apply to applications made on or after that date, so however that no inquiry or certificate shall be required which would not have been required by the rules in force immediately before that date and any inquiry, application, appointment or order made, notice issued, consent given, declaration made or attested or other thing done in relation to such an application shall be deemed to have been made, attested, issued, given or done under these Rules.

39.—(1) These Rules may be cited as the Adoption (Juvenile Court) Rules, 1959.

(2) These Rules shall come into operation on the first day of April, 1959.

Dated this 19th day of March, 1959.

NOTE

These Rules were made under s. 15 of the Justices of the Peace Act, 1949, as extended by s. 122 of the Magistrates' Courts Act, 1952, and s. 9 of the Adoption Act, 1958, p. 662, *ante*. They are printed as amended by the Adoption (Juvenile Court) Rules, 1965, S.I. 1965 No. 2072. See Home Office Circulars 22, 277 and 278, pp. 1177, *et seq., post*.

FIRST SCHEDULE

FORMS

Form 1   Rule 1

Application for adoption order

This Form must be lodged in duplicate, but duplicates of the attached documents need not be lodged. Every paragraph must be completed or deleted, as the case may be.

To the   Juvenile Court

PART I

Particulars of applicant(s)

1. Name of [first] applicant in full ....
   Address ....
   Occupation...
   Date of birth ....
   Relationship (if any) to infant ....
   [Name of second applicant in full ....
   Address ....
   Occupation...
   Date of birth ....
   Relationship (if any) to infant ....

2. I am/We are resident in England or Wales and domiciled in England or Wales/Scotland.

3. I am a widow/widower/unmarried/I am married to.....................................
of../We are married to each other and our marriage certificate (or other evidence of marriage) is attached.

*4. The consent of my husband/wife to the making of an adoption order authorising me to adopt the infant is attached *or* I request the court to dispense with the consent of my husband/wife on the ground that he/she cannot be found/is incapable of giving his/her consent/we have separated and are living apart and the separation is likely to be permanent.

5. I/We attach a certificate as to my health/the health of each of us signed by a fully registered medical practitioner[1].

*Delete if a joint application or if applicant not married.

PART II

Particulars of infant

6. Name in full[2] ....

7. The infant is of the............sex and is not and has not been married.

8. The infant is the person to whom the attached birth or adoption certificate relates/the infant was born in..., on or about
....................................[3].

9 I/We attach a report as to the health of the infant made by a fully registered medical practitioner[4].

10. The infant is the child[5] of
Name of mother...
Address ....
and Name of father[6]...
Address ....

11. The guardian[7], if any, of the infant is
Name...
Address ....

12. I/We attach a document/documents signifying the consent of the infant's mother/father/guardian to the making of an adoption order authorising me/us to adopt the infant.

13. I/We request the court to dispense with the consent of the infant's mother/father/guardian on the ground that......................................[8].

14. The following body or person has the rights and powers of a parent of the infant[9];—
Name ....
Address ....

15. The following person is liable by virtue of an order of a court or an agreement to contribute to the maintenance of the infant—
Name ....
Address ....
Particulars of court order or agreement:
Name of court.....................................
Date of order ....
or Date of agreement............................

16. If an adoption order is made in pursuance of this application the infant is to be known by the following names:—
Surname ....
Other names ....

PART III

General

17. The infant was received into my/our care and possession on the   day of   , 19 , and has been continuously in my/our care and possession since that date.

18. I/We notified the   Council on the   day of   , 19   , of my/our intention to apply for an adoption order in respect of the infant[10].

19. I have not made/Neither of us has made a previous application for an adoption order in respect of the infant *or* (name of applicant)   made an application No............ to the   court on the   day of   , 19   , which was dealt with as follows   [11].

20. I/We have not received or given any reward or payment for, or in consideration of, the adoption of the infant or for giving consent to the making of the adoption order except as follows: [12]

21. As far as I/we know, no person or body has taken part in the arrangements for placing the infant in my/our care and possession except:

Name ....
Address ....

22. For the purposes of this application reference may be made to
of   [13].

23. I/We desire that my/our identity should be kept confidential.   The serial number of this application is   [14].

I/We being desirous of adopting the infant hereby apply for an adoption order in respect of the infant.

(Signature(s))......................................
Dated the   day of   , 19   .

Notes:

[1] A separate medical certificate is required in respect of each applicant except that no certificate need be supplied if the applicant, or one of the applicants, is the father or mother of the infant or the infant is, at the date of the application, above the upper limit of the compulsory school age.

[2] Enter the surname and other names as shown in the infant's birth certificate, or, if the infant has previously been adopted, his adoption certificate.   If the infant has no birth or adoption certificate, enter the surname and other names by which the infant was known before being placed for adoption.

[3] If the infant has a birth or adoption certificate, this should be attached.   If the infant does not have any such certificate, enter the date and place of birth so far as is known.

[4] As the court may require up-to-date information about the health of the infant, a medical report should be attached unless the applicant, or one of the applicants, is a parent or relative of the infant or the infant is at the date of the application above the upper limit of the compulsory school age.   If the infant is less than one year old at the date of the application, the report should have been made not more than one month before that date.   If the infant is one year old or more at that date, the report should have been made not more than six months before that date.   A form for this purpose is prescribed: Adoption (Juvenile Court) Rules, 1959, r. 4, Sch. 1, Form 3.

[5] If the infant has previously been adopted, give the names of his adoptive parents and not those of his natural parents.

[6] Enter the name of the father, if known.

[7] Guardian means a person appointed by deed or will in accordance with the provisions of the Guardianship of Infants Acts, 1886 and 1925, or by a court of competent jurisdiction to be the guardian.

[8] The consent of a parent or guardian may be dispensed with if the court is satisfied that that person has abandoned, neglected or persistently ill-treated the infant, or has persistently failed without reasonable cause to discharge the obligations of a parent or guardian, or cannot be found, or is incapable of giving his consent or is withholding his consent unreasonably.

[9] This entry should be deleted except where some person or body has the rights and powers of a parent of the infant by virtue of section 75 of, or paragraph

12 (1) of the Fourth Schedule to, the Children and Young Persons Act, 1933, or section 3 of the Children Act, 1948.

[10] Notice does not have to be given if the applicant or one of the applicants is a parent of the infant or if at the time of the hearing the infant will be above the upper limit of the compulsory school age.

[11] The court cannot proceed with an application if a previous application made by the same applicant in respect of the same infant has been heard and dismissed on its merits, unless there has been a substantial change in the circumstances since the previous application.

[12] Any such payment or reward is illegal except payment to an adoption society or local authority in respect of their expenses incurred in connection with the adoption.

[13] Where the applicant, or one of the applicants, is a parent of the infant or a relative as defined in the Adoption Act, 1958, s. 57 (1), no referee need be named.

[14] If the applicant wishes his identity to be kept confidential, he may obtain a serial number from the justices' clerk and this should be entered; otherwise this entry should be deleted.

Rule 3   Form 2

Medical certificate as to health of applicant

I examined...on.. and have formed the opinion that he is physically, mentally and emotionally suitable to adopt a child.

Signature......................................   Date.....................
Qualifications ....
Address ....

Rule 4   Form 3

Medical report as to health of infant

Note

This Form is for a medical report on a child who may be adopted. The report is for the benefit of the adopters and the court. In order that the adopters may benefit fully from the report, it is important that the certifying doctor should explain to the adopters the nature and extent of any disability or abnormality disclosed by the examination which might affect their decision whether or not to adopt the child.

Child's name .... Date of birth............................

Sex................. Weight...........................Height......................

A   General condition.
     Skin.
     Eyes (including vision).
     Ears (including hearing).
     Nose and throat.
     Speech.
     Cardio-vascular system.
     Respiratory system.
     Alimentary system.
     Genito-urinary system (including examination of urine for albumen and sugar.
     Skeletal and articular system (including examination for congenital dislocation
        of hip).
     Nervous system (including fits).
     Lymphatic system.
     Any other comments.
     Is the child physically normal having regard to his age?

B   Are there any items in the child's history or examination which suggest that
     he may be mentally abnormal having regard to his age?

C   Particulars of any illness from which the child has suffered.

D   If known.
     Weight at birth (if child is under one year of age).
     Details of birth, including result of mother's serological tests for syphilis.
     Particulars, with dates, of vaccination or immunisation against—
        Tuberculosis (state result of Mantoux test or whether child has been successfully vaccinated with B.C.G. vaccine).
        Smallpox.
        Diphtheria.
        Whooping cough.
        Poliomyelitis.
        Tetanus (active).
        Any other disease.

E   (i) (*To be completed only in the case of a child at least six weeks old at the time of the test*)
Result of suitable serological test of the child's blood for syphilis (please specify test) ....

(ii) (*To be completed only in the case of a child at least six weeks and under two years old at the time of examination*)
Result of examination of the child's urine for phenylpyruvic acid...........
....

F   I examined the child on the............day of..............................., 19..., and I have informed the adopters of the state of health of the child disclosed by the examination.

Signature ....   Address ....

Qualifications ....

Form 4   Rule 5

Consent to adoption order

1. I understand that an application for an adoption order has been or is to be made in respect of A.B. [to whom the birth/adoption certificate now produced and shown to me marked " A " relates] [1] (hereinafter called the infant) by C.D./C.D. and E.D. *or* by a person or persons identified in the petty sessions area of
under the serial number   (hereinafter called the applicant) [2].

2. I am * the mother [3]/father [4]/guardian [5] of the infant.

3. I understand that the effect of an adoption order will be to deprive me permanently of my rights as a parent or guardian and to transfer them to the applicant: in particular I understand that, if an order is made, I shall have no right to see or get in touch with the infant or to have the infant returned to me.

4. I further understand that the court cannot make an adoption order without the consent of each parent or guardian of the infant unless the court dispenses with a consent on the ground that the person concerned has abandoned, neglected or persistently ill-treated the infant, or cannot be found, or is incapable of giving consent, or is unreasonably withholding consent or has persistently failed without reasonable cause to discharge the obligations of a parent or guardian.

5. I further understand that, when the application for an adoption order is heard, this document may be used as evidence of my consent to the making of the order unless I inform the court that I no longer consent [6].

6. I hereby consent to the making of an adoption order authorising the adoption of the infant by the applicant [on condition that the religious persuasion in which the infant is proposed to be brought up is   ] [7].

7. As far as I know, no person or body has taken part in arranging for the infant to be placed in the care and possession of the applicant except—[8]

     Full name ....

     Address ....

         ....

                Signature.................................

                Address ....

                ....

* Delete all except the appropriate description.

Paragraphs 1, 2, 6 and 7 of this Form having been duly completed, this Form was signed by the above-mentioned person before me at
on the   day of   , 19 .

Signature ....
Full name ....
Description [9] ....

Warning. It is an offence to receive or give any reward or payment for, or in consideration of, the adoption of the infant or for giving consent to the making of an adoption order, other than a payment to a local authority or adoption society for their expenses incurred in connection with the adoption.

Notes:

[1] Insert the surname and other names of the infant as shown in the infant's birth certificate, or, if the infant has previously been adopted, his adoption certificate. If the infant has no birth or adoption certificate, enter the surname and other names by which the infant was known before being placed for adoption. The words in square brackets should be deleted except where the consenting party is the mother or father of the infant and the infant's birth or adoption certificate has not already been identified by the other parent.

[2] Insert either the name of the applicant or the serial number assigned to the applicant for the purpose of the application.

[3] The consent of the mother cannot be given before the infant is six weeks old.

[4] " Father " does not include the natural father of an illegitimate infant.

[5] " Guardian " means a person appointed by deed or will in accordance with the provisions of the Guardianship of Infants Acts, 1886 and 1925, or by a court of competent jurisdiction to be the guardian.

[6] Notice of the making of the application and of the court by which it is to be heard will be given. After the making of the application the consenting parent or guardian cannot remove the infant from the care and possession of the applicant except with the leave of the court.

[7] Delete the words in square brackets if the applicant is named or if the applicant is not named but the consenting party does not desire to impose a condition as to the religious upbringing of the infant.

[8] Enter the name of any local authority, adoption society or person who is known to have arranged, or to have taken part in the arrangements, for the infant to be placed in the care and possession of the applicant.

[9] In England or Wales the consent should be signed before a justice of the peace, or a justices' clerk or a duly authorised county court officer. In Scotland, it should be signed before a justice of the peace or a sheriff. In Northern Ireland it should be signed before a justice of the peace. Outside the United Kingdom, it should be signed before a person authorised to administer an oath for any judicial or legal purpose, a British consular officer, a notary public, or, if the person signing it is serving in the armed forces, a commissioned officer.

Rule 11   Form 5

Notice to applicant of time of hearing

In the [county of   . Petty Sessional Division of   ].
To A.B. of   .

I hereby give notice that your application for an adoption order to be made in respect of (name of infant) will be heard before the Juvenile Court sitting at
on the   day of   , 19 , at   o'clock in
the [county] aforesaid and that your attendance [and that of   (name of infant)] is required.

[Take note that an adoption order or interim order cannot be made until the infant has been informed of the nature of the order.*]

*Delete unless attendance of infant is required.

Dated the   day of   , 19 .

(Signature)
Justice of the Peace for the [county] first
above-mentioned or Clerk of the Court.

Form 6   Rule 12

Notice to respondent of application for adoption order

In the [county of   . Petty Sessional Divison of   ].
To A.B. of   .

I hereby give notice that—

  (1) an application has been made by (name and address of applicant) *or* under
      the serial number...............for an adoption order to be made in respect
      of (identify the infant);

  (2) C.D. of   has been appointed guardian *ad litem*;

†(3) the application will be heard before the Juvenile Court sitting at
      on   the   day of   , 19 , at   o'clock   in   the
      [county] aforesaid and you may then appear and be heard on the question
      whether an adoption order should be made.

OR

†(3) the application will be heard before the Juvenile Court sitting at   ,
      You may appear before the court and be heard on the question whether
      an adoption order should be made. If you wish to appear, write to the
      Clerk of the Court at   on or before the   day of
      , 19 , in order that a time may be fixed for your appearance.

[*(4) While the application is pending you are not entitled, if you have signified
      your consent to the making of an adoption order in pursuance of the
      application, to remove the infant from the care and possession of the
      applicant except with the leave of the court.]

**(5) The court has been requested to dispense with your consent on the ground
      that...

Dated the   day of   , 19 .

(Signature)
Justice of the Peace for the [county] first
above-mentioned or Clerk of the Court.

It would assist the court, if you would complete and return the attached reply
form.

Reply Form

         To the Clerk of the   Juvenile Court
         (Address) ....

               ....

I have received notice of the hearing of the application for an adoption order in
respect of   an infant.

I ‡do/do not wish to oppose the application. I ‡do/do not wish to appear and
be heard on the question whether an adoption order should be made.

Date ....   Signature ....
                          Address ....
                          ....

---

† The second alternative should be struck out except where the applicant desires that
his identity should not be disclosed *to the person to whom the notice is given*, in which case
the first alternative should be struck out.
  * Delete except where notice is addressed to a parent or guardian.
 ** Delete if inapplicable.
  ‡ Delete one or other alternative.

Rule 18 (2) (a)   Form 7
Notice to applicant of time of further hearing after interim order made
In the [county of   . Petty Sessional Division of   ].
To A.B. of   .

I hereby give notice that your application for an adoption order to be made in respect of   (name of infant) will be further heard before the Juvenile Court sitting at   on the   day of   , 19 , at   o'clock in the [county] aforesaid and that your attendance [and that of (name of infant)] is required.

‡[Take notice that an adoption order or interim order cannot be made unless the court is satisfied that the infant has been informed of the nature of the order.]

Dated the   day of   19

                              (Signature)
                              Justice of the Peace for the [county] first
                              above-mentioned or Clerk of the Court.

Rule 18 (2) (b)   Form 8
Notice to respondent of time of further hearing after interim order made
In the [county of   . Petty Sessional Division of   ].
To A.B. of   .

I hereby give notice that the application by   (state name and address of applicant) *or* under the serial number   for an adoption order to be made in respect of   (*identify the infant*) will be further heard before the Juvenile Court sitting at

*on the   day of   , 19 , at   o'clock in the [county] aforesaid; and you may then appear and be heard on the question whether an adoption order should be made.
OR

*and you may appear before the court and be heard on the question whether an adoption order should be made. If you wish to appear, write to the Clerk of the Court at   on or before the   day of   , 19 , in order that a time may be fixed for your appearance.

Dated the   day of   , 19 .
                              (Signature)
                              Justice of the Peace for the [county] first
                              above-mentioned or Clerk of the Court.

It would assist the court, if you would complete and return the attached reply form.

Reply Form

          To the Clerk of the   Juvenile Court
          (Address) ....
                    ....

I have received notice of the further hearing of the application for an adoption order in respect of   an infant.

I †do/do not wish to oppose the application. I †do/do not wish to appear and be heard on the question whether an adoption order should be made.

          Date ....   Signature ....
                                               Address ....
                                                       ....

‡ Delete unless attendance of infant at further hearing is required.
* The second alternative should be struck out except where the applicant desires that his identity should *not be disclosed to the person to whom the notice is given*, in which case the first alternative should be struck out.
† Delete one or other alternative.

Form 9   Rule 19

Adoption Order (Adoption (J.C.) Rules, 1959, r. 19)

In the [county of   .   Petty Sessional Division of   ].

Whereas an application has been made by   of   occupation (hereinafter called the applicant) for an adoption order in respect of *(enter names and surname as shown in birth certificate or Adopted Children Register or, if not so shown, by which infant was known before being placed for adoption)* an infant of the   sex the child/adopted child of (hereinafter called the infant);

And Whereas the name or names and surname by which the infant is to be known are

And Whereas the court is satisfied that the applicant is qualified in accordance with the provisions of the Adoption Act, 1958, to adopt the infant and that all conditions precedent to the making of an adoption order by the court have been fulfilled;

It is ordered that the applicant be authorised to adopt the infant;

[And as regards costs, it is ordered that   ;]

[And the precise date of the infant's birth not having been proved to the satisfaction of the court, it is determined that the probable date of the infant's birth was   ;

The country of birth of the infant not having been proved to the satisfaction of the court, the infant shall be treated as having been born in England [Wales]/the particulars of the country of birth shall be omitted from the Schedule to this Order;

The registration district and sub-district in which the infant was born not having been proved to the satisfaction of the court, the infant shall be treated as having been born in the   registration district and the   sub-district;]

And it is directed that the Registrar General shall make in the Adopted Children Register an entry recording the particulars set out in the Schedule to this Order;

And it having been proved to the satisfaction of the court that the infant is identical with [to whom the entry numbered   made on the   day of   19 , in the Registers of Birth for the registration district of   and sub-district of   in the county of relates] [to whom the entry numbered   made on the   day of   , 19 , in the Adopted Children Register relates] it is directed that the said entry in the Registers of Birth be marked with the word " Adopted "/the Adopted Children Register be marked with the word " Re-adopted ".

[The following payment or reward is sanctioned   .]

Dated the   day of   , 19 .

(Signature)

Justice of the Peace for the [county] first above-mentioned.

SCHEDULE

Date and country of birth	Registration district and sub-district	Name and surname of infant	Sex of infant	Name and surname, address and occupation of adopter or adopters	Date of adoption order and description of court by which made

NOTE

The sex of the child should be shown in the Appendix as "male" or "female" and not as "boy" or "girl". See Home Office Circular No. 167/1969.

Rule 21   Form 10
              Adoption Order (*Adoption* (*J.C.*) *Rules*, 1959, *r.* 21)

In the [county of   . Petty Sessional Division of   ].
Whereas an application has been made by   of   (hereinafter called the applicant) for an adoption order in respect of   (*enter
names and surname as shown in birth certificate or Adopted Children Register or, if
not so shown, by which infant was known before being placed for adoption*) (hereinafter
called the infant);
     It is ordered that the applicant be authorised to adopt the infant;
     And it is directed that the Registrar General shall make in the Adopted Children
Register an entry recording the particulars set out in the Schedule to this Order.
     Dated the   day of   , 19 .

                                        Justice of the Peace for the [county]
                                        first above-mentioned.

                              SCHEDULE

Date and country of birth	Registration district and sub-district	Name and surname of infant	Sex of infant	Name and surname, address and occupation of adopter or adopters	Date of adoption order and description of court by which made

Rule 22   Form 11

                              Interim order

     In the [county of   . Petty Sessional Division of   ].
Whereas an application has been made by   of   (hereinafter called the applicant) for an adoption order in respect of   (*enter
names and surname of infant as shown in birth certificate or Adopted Children Register
or, if not so shown, by which infant was known before being placed for adoption*), an
infant of the   sex (hereinafter called the infant);
     And Whereas the court is satisfied that the applicant is qualified in accordance
with the provisions of the Adoption Act, 1958, to adopt the infant and that all
conditions precedent to the making of an interim order by the court have been
fulfilled;
     It is ordered that the determination of the application be postponed and that
the applicant do have the custody of the infant until the   day of
          , 19 , by way of a probationary period;
     [On the following terms namely: *]
     [And as regards costs, it is ordered that   ;]
     [And that the application shall be further heard on   .
     Dated the   day of   , 19 .
                                        (Signature)
                                        Justice of the Peace for the [county]
                                        first above-mentioned.

     * Provision may be made for the maintenance, education and supervision of the welfare
of the infant and otherwise.
                              NOTE
See note to form 9.

Form 12   Rule 27

Application to amend or revoke adoption order

To the.............................Juvenile Court.

1. Identification of adoption order to be amended or revoked—
Name of adopters ....
Date of adoption order...
Name of infant adopted ....

2. Particulars of applicant—
Name ....
Address ....
....
State relationship to adopted person or, if no such relationship, state reason
for application ....

3. If application is made under s. 24 of the Adoption Act, 1958, state the amendments desired, and the facts relied on in support of the application.....................
....
....

4. If application is made under s. 26 of the Adoption Act, 1958, state the facts
relied on in support of the application.
....
....

I apply for the adoption order to be amended or revoked in accordance with this
application.

Dated the   day of   , 19 .

(Signature)   .

Form 13   Rule 28

Register of Adoptions

In the [county of   .   Petty Sessional Division of   ].

No.	Date of deci- sion	Name and address of applicant	Names of infant prior to adoption	Sex of infant	Age of infant	Names of infant after adoption	Minute of decision	Signature of justice adjudi- cating

Form 14   Rule 31A

Notice asking for leave of court to remove infant from prospective adopters

In the [county of   .   Petty Sessional Division of   ].
Whereas an application has been made by   (*name and address
of applicant*) *or* under the serial number for an adoption order to be made in respect
of   (*identify the infant*) :
I hereby give notice that—

*(a) I, the parent/guardian of the infant, seek the leave of the court to remove
the infant from the care and possession of the applicant :

*(b) The......................(*insert the name of local authority or adoption society*) seek the leave of the court to give notice of their intention

* Delete one or other alternative (see note).

not to allow the infant to remain in the care and possession of the applicant:

The grounds on which the leave of the court is sought are as follows:

Date...................... Signature.................................

Address ....

....

Note. A notice can be given only by a parent or guardian of the infant who has consented to the making of an adoption order or by a registered adoption society or local authority which has placed the infant with the prospective adopters or by a local authority if the infant is in the care of a local authority. In the first case delete alternative (b) and state your relationship to the infant: in the other two cases delete alternative (a) and state the name of the adoption society or local authority.

Rule 9   SECOND SCHEDULE

PARTICULAR DUTIES OF GUARDIAN AD LITEM

1. The guardian *ad litem* shall interview the applicant and shall ascertain—
   (a) particulars of all members of the applicant's household and their relationship (if any) to the applicant;
   (b) particulars of the accommodation in the applicant's home and the condition of the home;
   (c) the means of the applicant;
   (d) whether the applicant suffers or has suffered from any serious illness and whether there is any history of tuberculosis, epilepsy or mental illness in the applicant's family;
   (e) in the case of an application by one only of two spouses, why the other spouse does not join in the application;
   (f) whether any person specified in the application as a person to whom reference may be made is a responsible person and whether he recommends the applicant with or without reservations;
   (g) whether the applicant understand the nature of an adoption order and, in particular, that the order, if made, will render him responsible for the maintenance and upbringing of the infant.
   (h) why the applicant wishes to adopt the infant;
   (i) such other information, including an assessment of the applicant's personality and, where appropriate, that of the infant, as has a bearing on the mutual suitability of the applicant and the infant, and on the ability of the applicant to bring up the infant;
   (j) the applicant's religious persuasion, if any.

2. The guardian *ad litem* shall ascertain and inform the applicant—
   (a) whether the infant has been baptised and, if so, the date and place of baptism;
   (b) what treatment the infant has received with a view to immunising him against disease;
   (c) whether the infant has any right to, or interest in, any property;
   (d) whether an insurance policy for the payment on the death of the infant of money for funeral expenses has been effected.

3.—(1) The guardian *ad litem* shall, as soon as is reasonably practicable, ascertain whether the infant is able to understand the nature of an adoption order.
(2) If the guardian *ad litem* is of opinion that the infant is able to understand the nature of an adoption order, he shall forthwith inform the court of his opinion and ascertain whether the infant wishes to be adopted by the applicant.

4. The guardian *ad litem* shall interview either in person or by an agent appointed by him for that purpose—
   (a) every individual who is a respondent to the application; and
   (b) every individual who appears to him to have taken part in the arrangements for the adoption of the infant.

5.—(1) The guardian *ad litem* shall obtain from every respondent to the application, not being an individual, such information concerning the infant as they have in their possession and which they consider might assist the court in deciding whether or not the infant should be adopted by the applicant.

(2) Where such information is given in the form of a written report, the guardian *ad litem* shall append it to his own report to the court.

6. The guardian *ad litem* shall ascertain when the mother of the infant ceased to have the care and possession of the infant and to whom the care and possession was transferred.

7. The guardian *ad litem* shall ascertain that every consent to the making of an adoption order authorising the adoption of the infant by the applicant is freely given and with full understanding of the nature of an adoption order.

8. If either parent of the infant is dead, the guardian *ad litem* shall forthwith inform the court if he learns of any relation of the deceased parent who wishes to be heard by the court on the question whether an adoption order should be made.

9. Where the infant is illegitimate but no-one is liable as the putative father to contribute to his maintenance by virtue of any order or agreement, the guardian *ad litem* shall forthwith inform the court if he learns of any person claiming to be the father who wishes to be heard by the court on the question whether an adoption order should be made.

10. The guardian *ad litem* shall forthwith inform the court if he learns of any other person or body who wishes, or ought in his opinion, to be heard by the court on the question whether an adoption order should be made.

11. The guardian *ad litem* shall draw the attention of the court to any difference in age between the applicant and the infant which is less than the normal difference in age between parents and their children.

NOTE

In Home Office letter HO 52/59 D2 dated March 25, 1959, sent to clerks to justices, juvenile courts are recommended to provide applicants, through the guardian *ad litem* or otherwise with a simple statement about the effect of an adoption order. A note that might serve for this purpose was appended to the letter and is reproduced at p. 1173, *post.*

THE ADOPTION (COUNTY COURT) RULES, 1959

[S.I. 1959 No. 480 (L.4)]

Commencement of proceedings

1.—(1) An application to a county court for an adoption order shall be made by filing in the office of the appropriate court an originating application in Form 1.

(2) The proposed adopter shall be the applicant and the persons mentioned in Rule 10 shall be the respondents.

(3) Save as provided in Rule 8 no person shall be served with a copy of the application.

(4) The notice to be served on every respondent shall be in Form 2 and a copy shall be served on the guardian *ad litem.*

(5) A note of service or non-service shall be indorsed on a copy of Form 2.

2. If any person proposing to apply to a county court for an adoption order desires that his identity be kept confidential, he may, before filing an originating application, apply to the registrar for a serial number to be assigned to him for the purposes of the proposed application, and the registrar shall assign a number to him accordingly.

3. Except where the applicant or one of the applicants is the mother or father of the infant or the infant has reached the upper limit of the compulsory school age, every applicant for an adoption order shall file with his application a certificate of a fully registered medical practitioner as to his health; and, if the applicant so desires, Form 3 may be used for the purposes of such certificate.

4.—(1) Any report on the health of the infant which is to be used for the purposes of an application for an adoption order shall be filed with the application.

(2) The report may, if the applicant so desires, be in Form 4.

5.—(1) Any document signifying the consent of any person to the making of an adoption order for the purposes of section 6 of the Act shall be in Form 5 and, if executed before the commencement of the proceedings, shall be filed with the originating application.

(2) If the document is executed outside the United Kingdom, it shall be sufficiently attested for the purposes of subsection (3) of the said section 6 if it is attested by any of the following persons:—

(a) any person for the time being authorised by law in the place where the document is executed to administer an oath for any judicial or other legal purpose;

(b) a British consular officer;

(c) a notary public; or

(d) if the person executing the document is serving in any of the regular armed forces of the Crown, an officer holding a commission in any of those forces.

6. If it appears that the applicant has previously made an application for an adoption order in respect of the same infant to the High Court, a county court or a magistrates' court and that that court, after having heard the case, dismissed the application on its merits, the registrar shall bring the matter to the attention of the judge and shall not proceed with the application unless the judge is satisfied that there has been a substantial change in the circumstances since the previous application.

7. If owing to special circumstances any application appears to the judge to be more fit to be dealt with by the High Court, he may, at any stage of the proceedings, refuse, on that ground expressly, to proceed with the application.

NOTE

See note to Rule 7 of the Adoption (Juvenile Court) Rules, 1959, p. 1110, *ante*.

Appointment and functions of guardian ad litem

8.—(1) Subject to the provisions of Rules 6 and 7, the registrar shall, as soon as practicable after the making of an application for an adoption order, appoint a guardian *ad litem* of the infant and serve on him a copy of the originating application together with the documents attached thereto.

(2) The person to be appointed guardian *ad litem* shall be—

(a) if the local authority concerned consents, the children's officer of a local authority or an officer or servant of that authority who assists the children's officer in the exercise of his functions;

(b) a probation officer, or

(c) if in any particular case the registrar considers that it is not reasonably practicable or that it would be undesirable to appoint one of the aforesaid persons, some other person who appears to the registrar to be suitably qualified:

Provided that no person shall be appointed guardian *ad litem* if—

(i) he has the rights and powers of a parent of the infant or has taken part in the arrangements for the adoption of the infant; or

(ii) he is a member, officer or servant of a local authority, adoption society or other body of persons which has the rights and powers of a parent of the infant or which has taken part in the arrangements for the adoption of the infant.

(3) Where the children's officer of a local authority is appointed guardian *ad litem*, he may carry out his duties and appear before the court personally or by any other officer or servant of that authority who assists the children's officer in the exercise of his functions.

NOTE

Duties of probation officer as guardian *ad litem*.—See r. 31 of the Probation Rules, 1965, p. 528, *ante*.

9.—(1) With a view to safeguarding the interests of the infant before the court the guardian *ad litem* shall, so far as is reasonably practicable—

    (a) investigate all circumstances relevant to the proposed adoption, including the matters alleged in the originating application and those specified in the Second Schedule to these Rules; and

    (b) perform such other duties as are specified in the said Schedule or as the court may direct.

(2) On completing his investigations the guardian *ad litem* shall make a confidential report in writing to the court.

(3) With a view to obtaining the directions of the court on any particular matter, the guardian *ad litem* may at any time make such interim report to the court as appears to him to be necessary.

NOTE

" **Confidential report.**"—See note to Rule 9 of the Adoption (Juvenile Court) Rules, 1959, p. 1111, *ante*.

Duties of guardian *ad litem*.—As to the duties of the guardian *ad litem* under this Rule, see Adoption Application No. 41/61 (No. 2) noted at p. 1032, *ante*.

10. At the time of appointing the guardian *ad litem*, the registrar shall fix a time for the hearing of the application and shall serve a notice in Form 2 on the following persons:—

    (a) every person, not being an applicant, whose consent to the making of the order is required under section 4 (1) of the Act;

    (b) any person having the rights and powers of a parent of the infant by virtue of section 75 of the Children and Young Persons Act, 1933, or paragraph 12 (1) of the Fourth Schedule to that Act or section 3 of the Children Act, 1948;

    (c) any person liable by virtue of any order or agreement to contribute to the maintenance of the infant;

    (d) the local authority to whom the applicant has given notice of his intention to apply for an adoption order under section 3 (2) of the Act;

    (e) any local authority or adoption society named in the application or in a form of consent as having taken part in the arrangements for the adoption of the infant;

    (f) any other person, not being the infant, who in the opinion of the court ought to be served with notice of the hearing of the application;

and any person upon whom a notice is required to be served under this Rule shall be a respondent to the application.

NOTE

In re B. (an Infant), [1958] 1 Q. B. 12; [1957] 3 All E. R. 193, C. A., the Court of Appeal held that it had jurisdiction to hear an appeal by a mother who lived in Australia and had not been served with notice, as she could have been a party to the county court proceedings. The adoption order was set aside and the case sent back for rehearing.

11. Where the guardian *ad litem* reports to the court that in his opinion the infant is able to understand the nature of an adoption order, the registrar shall serve on the applicant a notice in Form 6.

Attendance of parties and hearing of application

12. The judge shall not make an adoption order or an interim order except after the personal attendance of the applicant before him:

Provided that where the application is made by two spouses jointly, the judge may dispense with the personal attendance of one of the applicants if the originating application is verified by an affidavit sworn by him in accordance with the provisions of section 84 of the County Courts Act, 1934 (or, if he is outside the United Kingdom, by a declaration made by him and attested by a person specified in Rule 5 (2) of these Rules).

13. Where the applicant has been served with a notice in Form 6, the judge shall not make an adoption order or an interim order unless—

(a) the infant has attended personally before him or it appears to the judge that there are special circumstances making the infant's attendance unnecessary; and

(b) the judge is satisfied that the infant has been informed of the nature of the order.

14. If a serial number has been assigned to the applicant under Rule 2 of these Rules, the proceedings shall be conducted with a view to securing that he is not seen by or made known to any respondent who is not already aware of his identity, except with his consent.

NOTE

Dispensing with consent.—See Practice Direction dated March 24, 1961, p. 1172, *post.*

15.—(1) Where the infant whom the applicant desires to adopt is identified in the originating application by reference to a birth certificate which is the same, or relates to the same entry in the Registers of Births, as a birth certificate exhibited to a form of consent, the infant whom the applicant desires to adopt shall be deemed, unless the contrary appears, to be identical with the infant to whom the form of consent refers.

(2) Where the infant has previously been adopted, the foregoing paragraph of this Rule shall have effect as if for the references to a birth certificate there were substituted references to a certified copy of an entry in the Adopted Children Register and as if for the reference to the Registers of Birth there were substituted a reference to that Register.

16. Every application for an adoption order shall be heard and determined in camera.

17.—(1) An applicant for a provisional adoption order shall provide evidence of the law of adoption in the country in which he is domiciled.

(2) An affidavit as to that law, sworn by a person who is conversant with it and who practises, or has practised, as a barrister or advocate in that country or is a duly accredited representative of the government of that country in the United Kingdom, shall, if filed with the originating application, be admissible without any such notice as is required by Order XX, Rule 5, of the County Court Rules having been given.

NOTE

Provisional orders are dealt with in s. 53 of the Adoption Act, 1958, p. 1078, *ante.*

18. Any respondent being a local authority or other body may appear and be heard by any officer or servant of the authority or body duly authorised in that behalf.

19.—(1) Where the determination of an application is postponed and an interim order is made, the registrar shall, not less than one month before the expiration of the period specified in the order, if no time has previously been fixed, fix a time for the further hearing of the application.

(2) When the time for the further hearing of an application is fixed, the registrar shall serve a notice in Form 7 on the applicant and shall serve a notice in Form 8 on every respondent and a copy thereof on the guardian *ad litem*.

Form and transmission of orders

20.—(1) An adoption order shall be drawn up in Form 9, and within 7 days after the making of the order the registrar shall send a copy to the Registrar General and deliver or send an abridged copy in Form 10 to the applicant.

(2) The copy sent to the Registrar General shall be drawn up on paper 13 inches long by 8 inches wide, and shall have a margin to be left blank, not less than one inch wide, on the left side of the face of the paper and a similar margin on the right side of the reverse.

21. An interim order shall be drawn up in Form 11, and within 7 days after the making of the order the registrar shall deliver or send a copy to the applicant.

22.—(1) The registrar shall not supply a copy of an adoption order or of an interim order or an abridged copy of an adoption order except—

    (a) in accordance with the provisions of the last two foregoing Rules;
    (b) at the request of the Registrar General or the applicant or one of the applicants;
    (c) on the application of any other person under an order of the judge, or
    (d) at the request of another county court, a juvenile court or the High Court.

(2) The foregoing paragraph applies to an adoption order or an interim order made under the Adoption Act, 1950, or any enactment repealed by that Act, as it applies to an adoption order or interim order made under the Adoption Act, 1958.

(3) A county court shall not request another county court, a juvenile court or the High Court to furnish a copy of an adoption order under paragraph (1) (d) of this Rule or under any other Adoption Rule corresponding to that paragraph except in the case of an infant born in England who had been adopted in England before 1st April 1959 and in respect of whom the registration district and sub-district in which he was born would not otherwise be proved to the satisfaction of the first mentioned court for the purposes of section 21 (3) of the Act.

23.—(1) Where an adoption order is made or refused or an interim order made, the registrar shall serve notice to that effect on all parties who were not present when the order was made or refused.

(2) Where an adoption order is made in respect of an infant who is illegitimate, then, unless the applicant is his mother and she is a single woman, the registrar shall serve notice of the order on any court which appears to him to have made an affiliation order or a decree of affiliation and aliment which is still in force with respect to the infant.

Costs

24. On the determination of an application for an adoption order or on the making of an interim order, the judge may make such order as to costs as he thinks just, and in particular may order the applicant to pay—

    (a) the out-of-pocket expenses incurred by the guardian *ad litem*,
    (b) the expenses incurred by any respondent in attending the hearing,

or such part of those expenses as the judge thinks proper.

Amendment and revocation of adoption orders

25.—(1) An application under section 24 of the Act for the amendment of an adoption order or the revocation of a direction to the Registrar General, or under section 26 of the Act for the revocation of an adoption order, may be made *ex parte* in the first instance, but the judge may require notice of the application to be served on such persons as he thinks fit.

(2) Where the application is granted, the registrar shall send to the Registrar General a notice specifying the date of the adoption order and the names of the adopter and of the adopted person as given in the Schedule to the adoption order and either stating the amendments to the adoption order made by the court or informing him of the revocation of the direction or adoption order as the case may be:

Provided that where an adoption order made under the Adoption of Children Act, 1926, is amended, the said notice shall specify in a form similar to the Schedule to Form 9 all the particulars to be entered in the Adopted Children Register.

Keeping of documents and information

26. All documents relating to proceedings under the Act, or any enactment repealed by the Act, shall, while they are in the custody of the court, be kept in a place of special security.

27. Any information obtained by any person in the course of, or relating to, proceedings under the Act shall be treated as confidential and shall be disclosed if, but only if,—

(a) the disclosure is necessary for the proper exercise of his duties, or

(b) the information is requested—

    (i) by a court or public authority (whether within Great Britain or not) having power to authorise an adoption, for the purpose of the discharge of its duties in that behalf, or

    (ii) by a person who is authorised in writing by or on behalf of the Secretary of State to obtain the information for the purposes of research.

Application for return of infant

27A.—(1) An application—

(a) under section 34 of the Act for leave to remove an infant from the care and possession of a person who has applied for an adoption order, or

(b) under subsection (2) of section 35 of the Act for leave to give notice under subsection (1) (b) of that section,

shall be made on notice to the registrar in accordance with Order 13, Rule 1, of the County Court Rules.

(2) The registrar shall serve a copy of the notice on the guardian *ad litem* of the infant and on every party to the application for the adoption order other than the person applying for such leave.

(3) Every application for such leave shall be heard and determined in camera.

(4) Where leave is refused—

(a) Rule 24 shall apply as if the application for leave were an application for an adoption order, and

(b) the registrar shall serve notice of the refusal on all parties who were not present when the application for leave was determined.

(5) Where leave is granted, the judge may treat the hearing of the application as the hearing of the application for an adoption order and refuse an adoption order accordingly.

Service of documents

28. Unless otherwise directed, any document under these Rules may be served—

    (a) on a corporation or a body of persons, by delivering it at, or sending it by post to, the registered or principal office of the corporation or body;

    (b) on any other person, by delivering it to him, or by sending it by post to him at his last known or usual place of abode.

NOTE

In the case of *Re L. (An Infant)*, (1963), *Times*, March 12, the father of a legitimate infant, a Spaniard resident in Spain, refused service of a notice sent to him by registered post, and the letter sent to him was returned marked " Return to sender ".

The Master of the Rolls said that it was clearly necessary to serve the father and that the court would nominate the British Consul to effect service in accordance with Order 11, rule 11 of the Rules of the Supreme Court.

Application of County Court Rules

29. Subject to these Rules, the County Court Rules shall apply to proceedings in a county court under the Act, so, however, that notwithstanding the provisions of Part II of Order V of those Rules, it shall not be necessary, unless the judge otherwise directs, to appoint a guardian *ad litem* for an infant respondent to an application for an adoption order.

Interpretation

30. In these Rules, unless the context otherwise requires—

    " the Act " means the Adoption Act, 1958;

    " adoption order " includes a provisional adoption order within the meaning of section 53 of the Act;

    " the appropriate court " in relation to an application for an adoption order means the county court for the district in which the applicant or the infant resides, and " judge " and " registrar " mean the judge and registrar of that court;

    " interim order " means an interim order made under section 8 of the Act; and

    " regular armed forces of the Crown " means the Royal Navy, the regular forces as defined by section 225 of the Army Act, 1955, the regular air force as defined by section 223 of the Air Force Act, 1955, the Women's Royal Naval Service, Queen Alexandra's Royal Naval Nursing Service and Voluntary Aid Detachments serving with the Royal Navy.

31. In these Rules a form referred to by number means the form so numbered in the First Schedule to these Rules or a form to the like effect, and any such form may be used with such variations as the circumstances may require.

32. The Interpretation Act, 1889, shall apply to the interpretation of these Rules as it applies to the interpretation of an Act of Parliament.

Revocation

33. The Adoption of Children (County Court) Rules, 1952, are hereby revoked.

34. Notwithstanding anything in these Rules, any application to a county court for an adoption order which is pending at the date of the commencement of these Rules may, so far as is consistent with the provisions of the Act, be proceeded with and determined in accordance with the Rules in force immediately before that date.

Citation and commencement

35. These Rules may be cited as the Adoption (County Court) Rules, 1959, and shall come into force on the first day of April, nineteen hundred and fifty-nine.

Dated the 19th day of March, 1959.

NOTES

These Rules are made under s. 9 of the Adoption Act, 1958, p. 1043, *ante*. They are printed as amended by the Adoption (County Court) (Amendment) Rules, 1965, S.I. 1965 No. 2070. See Home Office Circular No. 22/1966, p. 1182, *post*.

FIRST SCHEDULE
FORM No. 1
Rule 1 (1)

ORIGINATING APPLICATION FOR AN ADOPTION ORDER OR A PROVISIONAL ADOPTION ORDER

In the .... County Court
No. ....

IN THE MATTER OF the Adoption Act, 1958
and
IN THE MATTER OF .... [¹] an infant.

[This Form must be filed in duplicate, but duplicates of the attached documents need not be filed. Every paragraph must be completed or deleted, as the case may be.]

I, the undersigned .... /We the undersigned ...., being desirous of adopting [or obtaining a provisional adoption order in respect of] .... [¹], an infant, under the Adoption Act, 1958, hereby give the following particulars in support of my/our application.

PART I

Particulars of the applicant[s]

1. Name of [first] applicant in full ....
   Address [²] ....
   Occupation ....
   Date of birth ....
   Relationship (if any) to the infant ....

[2. Name of second applicant in full ....
   Address [²] ....
   Occupation ....
   Date of birth ....
   Relationship (if any) to the infant...]

3. I am/We are resident and domiciled in England or Wales/Scotland
[*or* I am/We are domiciled in England or Wales/Scotland but not ordinarily resident in Great Britain]
[*or* I am/We are not domiciled in England or Wales or Scotland].

4. I am unmarried/a widow/widower/I am married to .... of ....
/We are married to each other and are the persons to whom the attached marriage
certificate (or other evidence of marriage) relates.

[5. The consent of my husband/wife to the making of an adoption order/a
provisional adoption order in pursuance of my application is attached   [*or* I request
the judge to dispense with the consent of my husband/wife on the ground that
.... [³]].] [⁴]

[6. A certificate as to my/our health, signed by a fully registered medical practitioner, is attached.] [⁵]

PART II

Particulars of the infant

7. The infant is of the .... sex and is not and has not been married.
He/She was born on the .... day of ...., 19..., and is the
person to whom the attached birth/adoption certificate [⁶] relates [or was born on
or about the .... day of ...., 19..., in ....] [⁷]

[8. A report on the health of the infant [⁸], made by a fully registered medical
practitioner on the .... day of ...., 19..., [⁹] is attached.]

9. The infant is the child/adopted child [¹⁰] of .... [¹¹] whose last known
address was .... [*or* deceased] and .... [¹²] whose last known
address was .... [*or* deceased].

[10. The guardian[s] of the infant is/are .... of .... [and
.... of ....]] [¹³]

11. I/We attach a document/documents signifying the consent of the said
.... [¹⁴] to the making of an adoption order/a provisional adoption order
in pursuance of my/our application.

[12. I/We request the judge to dispense with the consent of .... on the
ground that .... [¹⁵].]

[13. The .... Council [*or* ....] of .... has/have the
rights and powers of a parent of the infant.] [¹⁶]

[14. .... of .... is liable by virtue of an order made by the
.... court at .... on the .... day of ....,
19..., [*or* by an agreement dated the .... day of ...., 19...,] to
contribute to the maintenance of the infant.] [¹⁷]

15. If an adoption order/a provisional adoption order is made in pursuance of
this application, the infant is to be known by the following names:—

Surname ....

Other names ....

PART III

General

16. The infant was received into my/our care and possession on the ....
day of ...., 19..., and has been continuously in my/our care and possession
since that date.

[17. I/We notified the .... Council on the .... day of
................., 19..., of my/our intention to apply for an adoption order/a provisional adoption order in respect of the infant.] [¹⁸]

18. I have not made/Neither of us has made a previous application for an adoption order/a provisional adoption order in respect of the infant [except an application No. ...... made to the .... court at .... which was heard
on the .... day of ...., 19..., and was dealt with as follows
.................] [¹⁹]

19. I/We have not received or given any reward or payment for, or in consideration of, the adoption of the infant or for giving consent to the making of the adoption
order/provisional adoption order [except as follows ....] [²⁰]

20. As far as I/we know, no person or body has taken part in the arrangements for placing the infant in my/our care and possession [except ....] [²¹]

[21. For the purposes of this application reference may be made to .... of ....] [²²]

[22. I/We desire that my/our identity should be kept confidential and the serial number of this application is ....] [²³]

[23. I/We intend to adopt the infant under the law of or within .... [²⁴] and for that purpose I/we desire to remove the infant from Great Britain.] [²⁵]

I/We accordingly apply for an adoption order/a provisional adoption order in respect of the infant.

Dated this .... day of ...., 19...

Signature(s).............................

....

Notes:

[¹] Enter the first name[s] and surname as shown in any certificate referred to in entry No. 7; otherwise enter the first name[s] and surname by which the infant was known before being placed for adoption.

[²] Insert the applicant's address and, where he is not ordinarily resident in Great Britain, the place abroad where he ordinarily resides.

[³] The consent of the applicant's spouse may be dispensed with if the court is satisfied that he or she cannot be found or is incapable of giving his or her consent or that the spouses have separated and are living apart and the separation is likely to be permanent.

[⁴] This entry should be deleted if the application is made jointly by husband and wife or the applicant is unmarried.

[⁵] A separate medical certificate is required in respect of each applicant. There is an official form (Form No. 3) which may be used for this purpose. No certificate, however, need be supplied if the applicant, or one of the applicants, is the father, or mother of the infant or the infant has reached the upper limit of the compulsory school age.

[⁶] If the infant has previously been adopted, a certified copy of the entry in the Adopted Children Register should be attached and not a certified copy of the original entry in the Registers of Births.

[⁷] Where a certificate is not attached, enter the place (including country) of birth, if known.

[⁸] As the court may require up-to-date information as to the health of the infant, a medical report should be attached unless the applicant, or one of the applicants, is a parent or relative of the infant or the infant has reached the upper limit of the compulsory school age. There is an official form (Form No. 4) which may be used for this purpose.

[⁹] If the infant is less than one year old on the date of the application, the report should have been made not more than one month before that date. If the infant is one year old or more on that date, the report should have been made not more than six months before that date.

[¹⁰] If the infant has previously been adopted, give the names of his adoptive parents and not those of his natural parents.

[¹¹] Enter mother's name.

[¹²] Enter name of father, if known.

[¹³] Guardian means a person appointed by deed or will in accordance with the provisions of the Guardianship of Infants Acts, 1886 and 1925, or by a court of competent jurisdiction, to be a guardian.

[¹⁴] Enter the names of the persons mentioned in entries No. 9 and 10 except, in the case of an illegitimate infant, his father.

[¹⁵] The consent of a parent or guardian may be dispensed with if the court is satisfied that the person whose consent is required has abandoned, neglected or persistently ill-treated the infant, or has persistently failed without reasonable cause to discharge the obligations of a parent or guardian, or cannot be found, or is incapable of giving his consent or is withholding his consent unreasonably.

[¹⁶] This entry should be deleted except where some person or body has the rights and powers of a parent of the infant by virtue of section 75 of the Children and Young Persons Act, 1933, or paragraph 12 (1) of the Fourth Schedule to that Act, or section 3 of the Children Act, 1948.

[¹⁷] This entry should be deleted except where some person or body is liable to maintain the infant under a court order or agreement.

[¹⁸] Notice does not have to be given if the applicant or one of the applicants is a parent of the infant or if at the time of the hearing the infant will have reached the upper limit of the compulsory school age.

[¹⁹] The court cannot proceed with the application if a previous application made by the same applicant in respect of the same infant has been heard and dismissed on its merits, unless there has been a substantial change in the circumstances since the previous application.

[²⁰] Any such payment or reward is illegal except payment to an adoption society or local authority in respect of their expenses incurred in connection with the adoption.

[²¹] Enter the name of any local authority, adoption society or individual who has taken part in the arrangements for placing the infant in the care and possession of the applicant with a view to his adoption.

[²²] Where the applicant, or one of the applicants, is a parent of the infant or a relative as defined by section 57 (1) of the Adoption Act, 1958, no referee need be named.

[²³] If the applicant wishes his identity to be kept confidential, the serial number obtained under Rule 2 of the Adoption (County Court) Rules, 1959, should be given; otherwise this entry should be deleted.

[²⁴] Where the application is for a provisional adoption order, insert the country in which the applicant is domiciled. The applicant must provide evidence of the law of adoption in that country. For this purpose an affidavit as to that law, sworn by a person who is conversant with it and who practises, or has practised, as a barrister or advocate in that country or is a duly accredited representative of the Government of that country in the United Kingdom, will be admissible if filed with the application.

[²⁵] This entry should be deleted except where the application is for a provisional adoption order.

FORM NO. 2

Rule 1 (4)

NOTICE OF AN APPLICATION FOR AN ADOPTION ORDER OR A PROVISIONAL
ADOPTION ORDER

[General Title—Form 1]   (Seal)

To .... of ....

Whereas an application for an adoption order/a provisional adoption order in respect of .... [¹], an infant of the .... sex born on the .... day of ...., 19..., has been made [by .... and ....] [²] *or* [under the serial number ....];

And whereas .... of .... has been appointed guardian *ad litem* of the said infant:
Take notice:

A. [³] [that the said application will be heard at the .... County Court at .... on the .... day of ...., 19..., at .... o'clock, and that you may then appear and be heard on the question whether an adoption order/a provisional adoption order should be made.]

B. [³] [That if you wish to appear and be heard on the question whether an adoption order/a provisional adoption order should be made, you should give notice to the court on or before the .... day of ...., 19..., in order that a time may be fixed for your appearance.]

[And further take notice that while the said application is pending, a parent or guardian of the infant who has already signified his consent to the making of the adoption order must not, except with the leave of the judge, remove the infant from the care and possession of the applicant[s].

[And further take notice that the court has been requested to dispense with your consent to the making of the adoption order/provisional adoption order on the ground that [5]][6].

It would assist the court if you would complete the attached form and return it to me.

Dated the .... day of ...., 19...

Registrar.

Notes :

[1] Enter the name[s] and surname of the infant as shown in the heading of Form No. 1.

[2] The name of the applicant must not be given where a serial number is specified in the originating application (entry No. 22) and the notice is addressed to an individual other than the spouse of the applicant. In that case complete the second entry in square brackets.

[3] Paragraph A should be completed and paragraph B struck out where the notice is addressed to a local authority, an adoption society, any other body of persons or the spouse of the applicant, or where the applicant does not desire his identity to be kept confidential (see the originating application, entry No. 22). Where a serial number is specified in that entry and the notice is addressed to an individual respondent other than the spouse of the applicant, paragraph A must be struck out and paragraph B completed.

[4] Delete words in square brackets except where the notice is addressed to a parent or guardian of the infant.

[5] Enter the grounds specified in Form 1 (entry No. 12).

[6] Delete the words in square brackets if inapplicable.

.... Perforation ....

To the Registrar of the .... County Court.

No. ....
I have received notice of the application for an adoption order/a provisional adoption order in respect of .... an infant.

I *do/do not wish to oppose the application.

I *do/do not wish to appear and be heard on the question whether an adoption order/a provisional adoption order should be made.

....
(Signature)

....
(Date)

....
(Address)

FORM No. 3

Rule 3

MEDICAL CERTIFICATE AS TO HEALTH OF APPLICANT

I examined .... on .... and have formed the opinion that he is physically, mentally and emotionally suitable to adopt a child.

Signature ....   *Date*.........................

Qualifications ....

Address..

FORM No. 4

Rule 4

MEDICAL REPORT ON HEALTH OF INFANT

Note :

This form is for a medical report on a child who may be adopted. The report is for the benefit of the adopters and the court. In order that the adopters may benefit fully from the report, it is important that the certifying doctor should

* Delete one or other alternative.

explain to the adopters the nature and extent of any disability or abnormality disclosed by the examination which might affect their decision whether or not to adopt the child.

Child's name .... Date of birth ....

Sex .... Weight .... Height ....

A   General condition
     Skin
     Eyes (including vision)
     Ears (including hearing)
     Nose a nd throat
     Speech
     Cardio-vascular system
     Respiratory system
     Alimentary system
     Genito-urinary system (including examination of urine for albumen and sugar)
     Skeletal and articular system (including examination for congenital dislocation
       of hip)
     Nervous system (including fits)
     Lymphatic system
     Any other comments
     Is the child physically normal having regard to his age?

B   Are there any items in the child's history or examination which suggest that
     he may be mentally abnormal having regard to his age?

C   Particulars of any illness from which the child has suffered.

D   If known,
     Weight at birth (if child is under one year of age)
     Details of birth, including result of mother's serological tests for syphilis.
     Particulars, with dates, of vaccination or immunisation against—
       Tuberculosis (state result of Mantoux test or whether child has been
         successfully vaccinated with B.C.G. vaccine)
       Smallpox
       Diphtheria
       Whooping cough
       Poliomyelitis
       Tetanus (active)
       Any other disease

E   (i) (*To be completed only in the case of a child at least six weeks old at the time of
     the test*)
     Result of suitable serological test of the child's blood for syphilis (please specify
     test)   ....
     (ii) (*To be completed only in the case of a child at least six weeks and under two
     years old at the time of the examination*)
     Result of examination of the child's urine for phenylpyruvic acid............
     ....

F   I examined the child on the .... day of ...., 19..., and I
     have informed the adopters of the state of health of the child disclosed by
     the examination.

Signature ....   *Date*............................

Qualifications ....

Address..

FORM NO. 5   Rule 5

CONSENT TO AN ADOPTION ORDER OR A PROVISIONAL ADOPTION ORDER

[General Title—Form 1]

Whereas an application is to be/has been made by ..../and ....
[*or* under the serial number] [²] for an adoption order/a provisional adoption order
in respect of .... [¹], an infant;

[And whereas the infant is the person to whom the birth certificate [³] now
produced and shown to me marked " A " relates] [⁴]:

I, the undersigned .... of ...., being [⁵] the mother [⁶]/father [⁷]/ guardian [⁸] of the infant, hereby state as follows:—

1. I understand that the effect of an adoption order will be to deprive me permanently of my rights as a parent/guardian and to transfer them to the applicant[s] [*or* I understand that the effect of a provisional adoption order will be to enable the applicant[s] to remove the infant from Great Britain for the purpose of adopting him/her abroad and to give the applicant[s] custody of the infant pending his/her adoption]; and in particular I understand that, if an order is made, I shall have no right to see or get in touch with the infant or to have him/her returned to me.

2. I further understand that the court cannot make an adoption order without the consent of each parent or guardian of the infant unless the court dispenses with a consent on the ground that the person concerned has abandoned, neglected or persistently ill-treated the infant, or cannot be found, or is incapable of giving consent, or is unreasonably withholding consent or has persistently failed without reasonable cause to discharge the obligations of a parent or guardian.

3. I further understand that, when the application for an adoption order is heard, this document may be used as evidence of my consent to the making of the order unless I inform the court that I no longer consent [⁹].

4. I hereby consent to the making of an adoption order/a provisional adoption order in pursuance of the application [on condition that the religious persuasion in which the infant is proposed to be brought up is ....] [¹⁰].

5. As far as I know, no other person or body has taken part in the arrangements for placing the infant in the care and possession of the applicant[s] [except .... of ....] [¹¹].

....
(Signature)

This form, duly completed, was signed by the said .... before me [¹²] at .... on the ....day of .... 19...

Signature ....
Address ....
Description...

Warning. It is an offence to receive or give any reward or payment for, or in consideration of, the adoption of the infant or for giving consent to the making of an adoption order, other than a payment to a local authority or adoption society for their expenses incurred in connection with the adoption.

Notes:

[¹] Insert the name[s] and surname as known to the consenting party.

[²] Insert either the name of the applicant or the serial number assigned to the applicant for the purpose of the application.

[³] If the infant has previously been adopted, a certified copy of the entry in the Adopted Children Register should be attached and not a certified copy of the original entry in the Registers of Births; and the description of the consenting party should include the words " by adoption " where appropriate.

[⁴] Delete the words in square brackets except where the consenting party is the mother or father of the infant and the birth certificate has not already been identified by the other parent.

[⁵] Delete all but one of the descriptions which follow.

[⁶] The mother's consent cannot be given before the infant is six weeks old.

[⁷] " Father " does not include the natural father of an illegitimate child.

[⁸] " Guardian " means a person appointed by deed or will in accordance with the provisions of the Guardianship of Infants Acts, 1886 and 1925, or by a court of competent jurisdiction, to be guardian of the infant.

[⁹] Notice will be given of the making of the application and of the court by which it is to be heard. After the making of the application the consenting parent or guardian cannot remove the infant from the care and possession of the applicant except with the leave of the court.

[¹⁰] Delete the words in square brackets if the applicant is named or if, although the applicant is not named, the consenting party does not desire to impose a condition as to religious upbringing.

[¹¹] Enter the name of any local authority, adoption society or person who is known to have arranged, or to have taken part in the arrangements, for the infant to be placed in the care and possession of the applicant.

[¹²] In England or Wales the document should be signed before a justice of the peace, a duly authorised county court officer or a justices' clerk and in Scotland before a justice of the peace or a sheriff. In Northern Ireland it should be signed before a justice of the peace. Outside the United Kingdom it should be signed before a person authorised to administer an oath for any judicial or legal purpose, a British consular officer, a notary public or, if the person signing it is serving in the armed forces, a commissioned officer.

FORM NO. 6   Rule 11

NOTICE TO APPLICANT THAT THE INFANT'S PRESENCE IS REQUIRED AT THE HEARING

[*General Title—Form No. 1*]   (Seal)

To .... of ....
Whereas an application has been made by you for an adoption order/a provisional adoption order in respect of the above-named infant;
And whereas the said application will be heard at the .... County Court at .... on the .... day of ...., 19..., at .... o'clock:
Take notice that no order can be made unless the infant is present at the hearing and the court is satisfied that he has been informed of the nature of the order.
Dated the .... day of ...., 19...

Registrar.

FORM NO. 7   Rule 19 (2)

NOTICE TO APPLICANT OF FURTHER HEARING OF AN APPLICATION FOR AN ADOPTION
ORDER OR A PROVISIONAL ADOPTION ORDER

[*General Title—Form No. 1*]   (Seal)

To .... of ....
Whereas an application has been made by you for an adoption order/a provisional adoption order in respect of the above-named infant;
And whereas the determination of the said application was postponed and an interim order was made by the judge on the .... day of ...., 19...:
Take notice that the said application will be further heard before the judge at .... on the .... day of ...., 19..., at .... o'clock;
[And take notice that no order can be made unless the infant is present at the further hearing and the judge is satisfied that he has been informed of the nature of the order.] [¹]
Dated .... day of ...., 19...

Registrar

Note:
[¹] Delete except where the applicant has previously been served with a notice in Form No. 6 or where the judge otherwise directs.

FORM NO. 8   Rule 19 (2)

NOTICE TO RESPONDENT OF FURTHER HEARING OF AN APPLICATION FOR AN ADOPTION
ORDER OR A PROVISIONAL ADOPTION ORDER

[*General Title—Form No. 1*]   (Seal)

To .... of ....

Whereas an application for an adoption order/a provisional adoption order in respect of .... [¹], an infant of the .... sex born on the .... day of ...., 19..., was made [by ,.................... and ....] [²] *or* [under the serial number ....];

And whereas .... of .... was appointed guardian ad litem of the said infant;

And whereas the determination of the said application was postponed and an interim order made by the judge on the .... day of .... 19..., Take notice:

A[³] [That the said application will be further heard before the judge at .... on the .... day of ...., 19..., at .... o'clock, and that you may then appear and be heard on the question whether an adoption order/a provisional adoption order should be made.]

B[³] [That if you wish to appear and be heard on the question whether an adoption order/a provisional adoption order should be made, you should give notice to the court on or before the .... day of ...., 19..., in order that a time may be fixed for your appearance.]

It would assist the court if you would complete the attached form and return it to me.

Dated the .... day of ...., 19...

Registrar.

Notes:

[¹] Enter the name[s] and surname of the infant as shown in the heading of Form No. 1.

[²] The name of the applicant[s] must not be given where a serial number is specified in the originating application (entry No. 22) and the notice is addressed to an individual other than the spouse of the applicant. In that case complete the second entry in square brackets.

[³] Paragraph A should be completed and paragraph B struck out where the notice is addressed to a local authority, an adoption society, any other body of persons or the spouse of the applicant, or where the applicant does not desire his identity to be kept confidential (see the originating application, entry No. 22). Where a serial number is specified in that entry and the notice is addressed to an individual respondent other than the spouse of the applicant, paragraph A must be struck out and paragraph B completed.

.... Perforation ....

To the Registrar of the .... County Court.

No. ....

I have received notice of the further hearing of the application for an adoption order/a provisional adoption order in respect of ...., an infant.

I *do/do not wish to oppose the application.

I *do/do not wish to appear and be heard on the question whether an adoption order/a provisional adoption order should be made.

....
(*Signature*)

....
(*Date*)   ....
                                        (*Address*)

FORM No. 9

Rule 20 (1)

ADOPTION ORDER OR PROVISIONAL ADOPTION ORDER (I)   (Seal)

[*General Title—Form No. 1*]

Whereas an application has been made by .... of ...., whose occupation is ...., [and ...., his wife] (hereinafter called the

* Delete one or other alternative.

applicant[s]) for an adoption order/a provisional adoption order in respect of
.... [¹], an infant of the .... sex, the child/adopted child of
.... [and ....];

And whereas the court is satisfied that the applicant is/applicants are qualified in accordance with the provisions of the Adoption Act, 1958, to be granted an adoption order/a provisional adoption order in respect of the infant and that all conditions precedent to the making of such an order have been fulfilled:

It is ordered that the applicant[s] be authorised to adopt the infant [or that the applicant[s] be authorised to remove the infant from Great Britain for the purpose of adopting him/her under the law of or within the country in which the applicant is/applicants are domiciled and that the applicant[s] do have the custody of the infant pending his/her adoption as aforesaid];

[And the following payment or reward is sanctioned ....;]

[And as regards costs it is ordered that ....;]

[And whereas the precise date of the infant's birth has not been proved to the satisfaction of the court but the court has determined the probate date of his/her birth to be the .... day of ...., 19...;]

[And whereas the country of birth of the infant has not been proved to the satisfaction of the court [but it appears probable that the infant was born within the United Kingdom, the Channel Islands or the Isle of Man];]

[And whereas the infant was born in England/Wales but the registration district and sub-district in which the birth took place have not been proved to the satisfaction of the court;]

[And whereas it has been proved to the satisfaction of the court that the infant is identical with .... to whom the entry numbered .... made on the .... day of ...., 19..., in the Registers of Births for the registration district of .... and sub-district of .... in the county of .... relates [or with .... to whom the entry numbered .... and dated the .... day of ...., 19..., in the Adopted Children Register relates];]

[And whereas the name or names and surname stated in the application as those by which the infant is to be known are ....:]

It is directed that the Registrar General shall make in the Adopted Children Register an entry recording the particulars set out in the Schedule to this order;

[And it is further directed that the aforesaid entry in the Registers of Births/Adopted Children Register be marked with the word " Adopted "/" Re-adopted "/" Provisionally adopted "/" Provisionally re-adopted "] [²].

Dated this .... day of .... 19...

Registrar.

SCHEDULE

Date [³] and country [⁴] of birth of child	Registration district and sub-district [⁵]	Name and surname of child [⁶]	Sex of child [⁷]	Name and surname, address [⁸] and occupation of adopter or adopters	Date of adoption order [⁹] and description of court by which made

Notes:

[¹] Enter the name[s] and surname of the infant as shown in the heading of Form No. 1.

[²] This paragraph should be deleted where the infant is not proved to be identical with a child to whom an entry in the Registers of Births or Adopted Children Register relates.

[³] Where the precise data of the infant's birth is not proved, enter the date determined by the court to be the probable date.

[⁴] Where the country of the infant's birth is not proved, the particulars of the country of birth may be omitted unless it appears probable that the infant was born within the United Kingdom, the Channel Islands or the Isle of Man. In that event enter England or Wales, as the case may be, as the country of birth.

[⁵] Where the infant was born in England or Wales but the registration district and sub-district in which the birth took place are not proved, or where the infant is treated in accordance with Note [⁴] as born in England or Wales, enter the district and sub-district in which the court sits.

[⁶] Enter the name or names and surname stated in Form No. 1 as those by which the infant is to be known or, if no name or surname is so stated, the original name or names of the infant and the surname of the applicant.

[⁷] Enter " boy " or " girl ", as the case may be.

[⁸] If the applicant is not ordinarily resident in Great Britain, enter the place abroad where he ordinarily resides.

[⁹] In the case of a provisional adoption order enter the words " Provisional adoption order " followed by the date of the order and the name of the court.

Rule 20 (1)   FORM NO. 10

ADOPTION ORDER OR PROVISIONAL ADOPTION ORDER (II)

[*General Title—Form No. 1*]

Whereas an application has been made by .... of ....
[and ...., his wife,] for an adoption order/a provisional adoption order in respect of .... [¹], an infant:

It is ordered that the applicant[s] be authorised to adopt the infant [*or* that the applicant[s] be authorised to remove the infant from Great Britain for the purpose of adopting him/her under the law of or within the country in which the applicant is/the applicants are domiciled and that the applicant[s] do have the custody of the infant pending his/her adoption as aforesaid];

And it is directed that the Registrar General shall make in the Adopted Children Register an entry recording the particulars set out in the Schedule to this order.

Dated this .... day of ...., 19...

Registrar.

SCHEDULE [²]

Date and country of birth of child	Registration district and sub-district	Name and surname of child	Sex of child	Name and surname, address and occupation of adopter or adopters	Date of adoption order and description of court by which made

Notes:

[1] Enter the name[s] and surname of the infant as shown in the heading of Form No. 1.

[2] Enter in the Schedule the particulars set out in the Schedule to Form No. 9.

FORM No. 11   Rule 21

INTERIM ORDER

[General Title—Form No. 1]

Whereas an application has been made by .... of ....
[and ...., his wife] (hereinafter called the applicant[s]) for an adoption order/a provisional adoption order in respect of .... [1], an infant;

And whereas the court is satisfied that the applicant is/the applicants are qualified in accordance with the provisions of the Adoption Act, 1958, to be granted an adoption order/a provisional adoption order in respect of the infant and that all conditions precedent to the making of such an order have been fulfilled:

It is ordered that the determination of the application be postponed and that the applicant[s] do have the custody of the infant until the .... day of ...., 19..., by way of a probationary period [*or* that the determination of the application be postponed to the .... day of ...., 19..., and that the applicant[s] do have the custody of the infant until that day by way of a probationary period] [upon the following terms, namely ....].

[And as regards costs it is ordered that ....].

[And it is ordered that the application be further heard before the judge at .... on the .... day of ...., 19..., at .... o'clock.]

Dated this .... day of ...., 19...

Registrar.

Note:

[1] Enter the name[s] and surname of the infant as shown in the heading to Form No. 1.

SECOND SCHEDULE   Rule 9

PARTICULAR DUTIES OF THE GUARDIAN AD LITEM

1. The guardian *ad litem* shall interview the applicant and shall ascertain—

    (a) particulars of all members of the applicant's household and their relationship (if any) to the applicant;

    (b) particulars of the accommodation in the applicant's home and the condition of the home;

    (c) the means of the applicant;

    (d) whether the applicant suffers or has suffered from any serious illness and whether there is any history of tuberculosis, epilepsy or mental illness in the applicant's family;

    (e) in the case of an application by one only of two spouses, why the other spouse does not join in the application;

    (f) whether any person specified in the application as a person to whom reference may be made is a responsible person and whether he recommends the applicant with or without reservations;

(g) whether the applicant understands the nature of an adoption order and, in particular, that the order, if made, will render him responsible for the maintenance and upbringing of the infant.

(h) why the applicant wishes to adopt the infant :

(i) such other information, including an assessment of the applicant's personality and, where appropriate, that of the infant, as has a bearing on the mutual suitability of the applicant and the infant and on the ability of the applicant to bring up the infant ;

(j) the applicant's religious persuasion, if any.

2. The guardian *ad litem* shall ascertain and inform the applicant—

(a) whether the infant has been baptised and, if so, the date and place of baptism;

(b) what treatment the infant has received with a view to immunising him against disease;

(c) whether the infant has any right to, or interest in, any property;

(d) whether an insurance policy for the payment on the death of the infant of money for funeral expenses has been effected.

3.—(1) The guardian *ad litem* shall, as soon as is reasonably practicable, ascertain whether the infant is able to understand the nature of an adoption order.

(2) If, in the guardian's opinion, the infant is able to understand the nature of an adoption order, the guardian shall forthwith inform the court and ascertain whether the infant wishes to be adopted by the applicant.

4. The guardian *ad litem* shall interview either in person or by an agent appointed by him for the purpose every individual who is a respondent or who appears to him to have taken part in the arrangements for the adoption of the infant.

5.—(1) The guardian *ad litem* shall obtain from every respondent, not being an individual, such information concerning the infant as they have in their possession and which they consider might assist the court in deciding whether or not the infant should be adopted by the applicant.

(2) Where such information is given in the form of a written report, the guardian *ad litem* shall append it to his own report to the court.

6. The guardian *ad litem* shall ascertain when the mother of the infant ceased to have the care and possession of the infant and to whom the care and possession was transferred.

7. The guardian *ad litem* shall ascertain that every consent to the making of an adoption order in pursuance of the application is freely given and with full understanding of the nature and effect of an adoption order.

8. Where either parent of the infant is dead, the guardian *ad litem* shall forthwith inform the court if he learns of any relation of the deceased parent who wishes to be heard by the court on the question whether an adoption order should be made.

9. Where the infant is illegitimate but no one is liable as the putative father to contribute to the maintenance of the infant by virtue of any order or agreement, the guardian *ad litem* shall forthwith inform the court if he learns of any person, claiming to be the father, who wishes to be heard by the court on the question whether an adoption order should be made.

10. The guardian *ad litem* shall forthwith inform the court if he learns of any other person or body who wishes or ought in his opinion to be heard by the court on the question whether an adoption order should be made.

11. Where the applicant is not ordinarily resident in Great Britain, the guardian *ad litem* shall endeavour to obtain a report on the applicant's home and living conditions from a suitable agency in the country in which he is ordinarily resident.

12. The guardian *ad litem* shall draw the attention of the court to the difference in age between the applicant and the infant if it is less than the normal difference in age between parents and their children.

THE REGISTRATION OF BIRTHS, DEATHS AND MARRIAGES REGULATIONS, 1968
[S.I. 1968 No. 2049]

NOTE

For interpretation of terms see Regulation 2.
The Registration of Marriages (Welsh Language) Regulations, 1971 (S.I. 1971 No. 129) makes provision for the use of forms in the Welsh language.

PART V

RE-REGISTRATION OF BIRTHS OF LEGITIMATED PERSONS

Attendance of parent

26. Where under Section 14 of the Act the Registrar General authorises the re-registration of the birth of a legitimated person, a parent of the legitimated person shall, if required by the Registrar General, attend personally within such time as the Registrar General may specify at the office of the registrar of births and deaths for the sub-district in which the birth occurred.

Relevant date for particulars

27. The provisions of regulation 17 shall apply to this Part of these regulations except that the surname to be recorded in respect of the mother of a child shall be her surname immediately after her marriage to the father.

Making of entry where parent attends

28.—(1) The registrar of the sub-district in which such a birth occurred shall read or show to the parent the particulars entered in the Registrar General's authority, and if it appears that there is any error or omission therein shall correct it in such manner as the Registrar General may direct.

(2) The registrar shall in the presence of the parent copy the particulars recorded in the spaces of the authority into the corresponding spaces of the entry so, however, that where any particular has been corrected in pursuance of paragraph (1) he shall enter only the particular as corrected, omitting any incorrect particular which has been struck out.

(3) The registrar shall enter in the register the qualification of the informant as "father" or "mother", as the case may be, and call upon the parent to verify the particulars as entered and to sign the entry.

(4) The registrar shall enter the date on which the entry is made and add the words "On the authority of the Registrar General".

(5) When the registrar has signed the entry in space 16 he shall add his official description.

Making of declaration where parent does not attend

29.—(1) A parent who is in England or Wales may with the consent of the Registrar General verify the particulars required to be registered on the re-registration of the birth of a legitimated person by making and signing before a registrar other than the registrar for the sub-district in which the birth occurred a declaration of the particulars, on a form provided for the purpose by the Registrar General; and any such declaration shall be attested by the registrar before whom it was made and sent by him to the registrar for the sub-district in which the birth occurred.

(2) A parent who is not in England or Wales may with the consent of the Registrar General verify the particulars required to be registered as aforesaid by making and signing before an authority specified in paragraph (3), (4) or

(5), as the case may be, and sending to the Registrar General, a declaration of the particulars on a form provided for the purpose by the Registrar General.

(3) In the case of a parent who is in Scotland, Northern Ireland, the Isle of Man, the Channel Islands or any other country of the Commonwealth or in the Irish Republic, the authorities before whom a declaration may be made are a notary public and any other person lawfully authorised to administer oaths in that country or place.

(4) In the case of a parent who is not in England or Wales or in any country or place mentioned in paragraph (3), the authorities before whom a declaration may be made are one of Her Majesty's consular officers, a notary public and any other person lawfully authorised to administer oaths in that country or place; but a declaration made before an authority other than one of Her Majesty's consular officers shall be authenticated by such an officer, if the Registrar General so requires.

(5) In the case of a parent who is a member of Her Majesty's Forces and who is not in the United Kingdom, the authorities before whom a declaration may be made shall include any officer who holds a rank not below that of Lieutenant-Commander, Major, or Squadron-Leader.

Making of entry in pursuance of declaration

30.—(1) On receiving the Registrar General's authority and consent to re-register a birth under regulation 29 and the declaration made for the purposes thereof, the registrar for the sub-district in which the birth occurred shall copy the particulars recorded in the spaces of the declaration into the corresponding spaces of the entry and shall enter the qualification of the informant as "father" or "mother", as the case may be; and he shall enter in space 14 the name of the declarant in the form in which it is signed in the declaration and shall add the words "by declaration dated......." and the date on which the declaration was made and signed.

(2) After entering such particulars the registrar shall complete the entry in the manner provided in regulation 28(4) and (5).

NOTE

This regulation is printed as amended by the Births, Deaths and Marriages (Amendment) Regulations, 1969, S.I. 1969 No. 1811.

Making of entry when particulars not verified by parent

31. Where so directed by the Registrar General the registrar for the sub-district in which the birth of a legitimated person occurred shall re-register the birth in such manner as the Registrar General in his authority may direct although the particulars to be registered are not verified by a parent; and in any such case the registrar shall enter in the space for the signature the words "On the authority of the Registrar General" without any further entry in that space.

Noting of previous entry

32. The superintendent registrar or the registrar having the custody of the register in which the birth was previously registered shall, when so directed by the Registrar General, note the previous entry of the birth with the words "Re-registered under section 14 of the Births and Deaths Registration Act, 1953 on............", inserting the date of re-registration, and shall make a certified copy of the previous entry, including a copy of the note, and send the copy to the Registrar General.

Certified copies of re-registered entries

33. Where application is made to a registrar or a superintendent registrar for a certified copy of the entry of the birth of a legitimated person whose birth has been re-registered in a register in his custody, he shall supply a certified copy of the entry of re-registration; and no certified copy of the previous entry shall be given except under the direction of the Registrar General.

Declaration in respect of a person born at sea

34. Where information is furnished to the Registrar General for the re-registration of the birth of a legitimated person who was born at sea and whose birth was included in a return sent to the Registrar General, a parent of the legitimated person may verify the particulars required to be registered on the re-registration of the birth of that person by making and signing a declaration of such particulars, on a form provided by the Registrar General for the purpose, before any registrar in England and Wales or such authority specified in regulation 29(3), (4) or (5) as may be applicable, and sending that declaration to the Registrar General.

Entry in respect of a person born at sea

35. A person deputed for the purpose by the Registrar General, on receiving his authority to re-register the birth of a legitimated person who was born at sea and whose birth was included in a return sent to the Registrar General, shall make the entry in a register to be kept at the General Register Office in form 4, in such manner as the Registrar General may direct.

Noting of previous entry

36. Where an entry is made under regulation 35, a person deputed as aforesaid shall note any previous record of the birth in the custody of the Registrar General with the words "Re-registered under section 14 of the Births and Deaths Registration Act, 1953, on.......", inserting the date of re-registration, and shall send a copy of the previous record, including a copy of the note, certified under the seal of the General Register Office, to the authority from whom that record was received by the Registrar General.

PART VI

BIRTH ENTRIES OF ADOPTED CHILDREN

Marking of birth entry of adopted child

37.—(1) A superintendent registrar or a registrar shall, when so directed by the Registrar General acting pursuant to the Adoption Acts, 1958 to 1968—

    (a) mark any entry specified in the direction with the word "Adopted" or, as the case may be, the words "Provisionally adopted", followed immediately, if the direction so specifies, by the name, in brackets, of the country in which the adoption order was made;

    (b) add his signature and official description; and

    (c) make and send to the Registrar General a certified copy of the entry showing the marking.

(2) A superintendent registrar or a registrar shall, when so directed by the Registrar General acting pursuant to the Adoption Acts, 1958 to 1968—

    (a) strike through any marking as to adoption in the margin of any entry specified in the direction and underneath write, as may be specified in the direction, the words "Adoption order quashed", "Adoption order revoked", "Appeal against adoption order allowed", or "Direction for the marking of this entry revoked";

(b) add his signature and official description; and

(c) make and send to the Registrar General a certified copy of the entry showing the cancelled marking and the note with respect to its cancellation.

Reproduction of marking in certified copy

38. Where a certified copy of an entry of birth relating to an adopted person is given under the provisions of sections 30, 31, or 32 of the Act (which relate to searches of registers and indexes) the certified copy shall include a copy of the marking made in pursuance of regulation 37(1).

NOTES

These regulations were made by the Registrar General on December 18, 1968, under powers conferred on him by various statutes and came into operation on April, 1, 1969.

Registration of adoptions outside Great Britain.—See s. 3 of the Adoption Act, 1964, p. 1029, *ante.*

THE REGISTRATION OF BIRTHS, DEATHS AND MARRIAGES (AMENDMENT) REGULATIONS, 1969

[S.I. 1969 No. 1811]

PART I

RE-REGISTRATION OF BIRTHS

Title and commencement

1.—(1) These regulations may be cited as the Registration of Births, Deaths and Marriages (Amendment) Regulations, 1969 and shall come into operation on 1st January, 1970.

(2) These regulations and the Registration of Births, Deaths and Marriages Regulations, 1968, shall be construed as one and may be cited together as the Registration of Births, Deaths and Marriages Regulations, 1968 and 1969.

Interpretation

2.—(1) The Interpretation Act, 1889, shall apply to the interpretation of these regulations as it applies to the interpretation of an Act of Parliament.

(2) In these regulations—

"the principal regulations" means the Registration of Births, Deaths and Marriages Regulations, 1968;

"the Act of 1969" means the Family Law Reform Act, 1969.

Officers before whom written statements may be made

3. The officer before whom a written statement for the purposes of section 27(4) of the Act of 1969 may be made shall be—

(a) in a case where not more than 3 months have elapsed since the date of the birth of the child, any registrar of births and deaths other than the registrar of births and deaths for the sub-district in which the birth occurred; or

(b) in any other case, any superintendent registrar.

Re-registration on joint information of parents

4. Where under section 27(2) (a) of the Act of 1969 the Registrar General authorises the re-registration of the birth of an illegitimate child at the joint request of the mother and the person acknowledging himself to be the father of the child—

(a) if the parents attend, pursuant to the authority of the Registrar General, before the registrar for the sub-district in which the birth occurred, within 3 months after the date of the birth, to give information for the re-registration of the birth, the registrar shall—

(i) ascertain from the parents the particulars to be registered concerning the birth and enter them in spaces 1 to 13 in the register in the presence of the parents in accordance with the authority of the Registrar General;

(ii) call upon the parents to verify the particulars entered and to sign the entry in space 14;

(iii) enter the date on which the entry was made and add the words "On the authority of the Registrar General";

(iv) sign the entry in space 16 and add his official description.

(b) if the parents attend, pursuant to the authority of the Registrar General, within 3 months after the date of the birth before any other registrar, or after 3 months have elapsed since the date of the birth, before any superintendent registrar, that officer shall—

(i) call upon the parents to make and sign a declaration in the form of Schedule 1;

(ii) attest the declaration and deliver it to the registrar of the sub-district in which the birth occurred.

(c) upon receiving the authority of the Registrar General to re-register a birth under paragraph (b) of this regulation and the declaration made in pursuance thereof, the registrar for the sub-district in which the birth occurred shall—

(i) copy the particulars recorded in the spaces of the declaration into the corresponding spaces of the entry and shall call upon the parents to sign the entry in space 14 of the register or, if they are not present, shall enter in space 14 the names of the parents in the form in which they are signed in the declaration and shall add the words "by declaration dated......" inserting the date on which the declaration was made and signed;

(ii) enter the date on which the entry was made and add the words "On the authority of the Registrar General";

(iii) if not more than 3 months have elapsed since the date of birth of the child, sign the entry in space 16 of the register and add his official description;

(iv) if more than 3 months have elapsed since the date of birth of the child, make the entry in the presence of the superintendent registrar of the district in which the birth occurred and the superintendent registrar and the registrar shall sign the entry and add their official descriptions.

Re-registration on mother's information and father's statutory declaration

5.—(1) Where under section 27(2)(b) of the Act of 1969 the Registrar General authorises the re-registration of the birth of an illegitimate child at the request of the mother of the child—

(a) a declaration in the form of Schedule 2 shall be made by the mother before one of the officers specified in regulation 3 or, if not more than 3 months have elapsed since the date of the birth of the child, before the registrar of the sub-district in which the birth occurred;

(b) the declaration shall be attested by the officer before whom it was made;

(c) where the declaration is attested by a superintendent registrar, or a registrar other than the registrar for the sub-district in which the birth occurred, the officer who attested it shall deliver it to that registrar together with the authority of the Registrar General and a statutory declaration made by the person who is to be shown in the register as the father, acknowledging himself to be the father of the child.

(2) Upon receiving the documents specified in the foregoing sub-paragraph the registrar for the sub-district in which the birth occurred shall—

(a) copy the particulars recorded in the spaces of the declaration made by the mother into the corresponding spaces in the register;

(b) call upon the mother to verify the particulars as entered and to sign the entry in space 14 or, is she is not present, shall enter her name in space 14 in the form in which it is signed in the declaration made by her and add the words "by declaration dated......" inserting the date on which her declaration was made and signed;

(c) add in space 14 the words "Statutory declaration made by...... on ......" inserting the full name of the person acknowledging himself to be the father and the date on which the statutory declaration was made and signed by him;

(d) enter the date on which the entry was made and add the words "On the authority of the Registrar General";

(e) if not more than 3 months have elapsed since the date of birth of the child, sign the entry in space 16 and add his official description;

(f) if more than 3 months have elapsed since the date of the birth, make the entry in the presence of the superintendent registrar of the district in which the birth occurred and the superintendent registrar and registrar shall sign the entry and add their official descriptions.

Noting of entries

6. The superintendent registrar or registrar having custody of the register in which the birth was previously registered shall, when so directed by the Registrar General, note the previous entry relating to the birth with the words "Re-registered under section 27 of the Family Law Reform Act, 1969, on......" inserting the date of the re-registration and make a certified copy of that entry, including a copy of the note, and send the copy to the Registrar General.

Welsh version

7.— [*Not reproduced.*]

PART II

AMENDMENT OF THE PRINCIPAL REGULATIONS

Signatures

8.—[*Substitutes a new paragraph for regulation 20(2) of the principal regulations —not included.*]

Declarations

9.—[*Not reproduced.*]

Signature in entry after declaration

10. In regulation 30(1) of the principal regulations there shall be inserted between the words "space 14" and "the words" the words "the name of the declarant in the form in which it is signed in the declaration and shall add".

NOTE

For Regulation 30 see p. 1149, *ante*.

SCHEDULE 1

DECLARATION FOR THE REGISTRATION OF A BIRTH

Regulation 4(b)(i)

Births and Deaths Registration Act, 1953, ss. 6 and 9
Family Law Reform Act, 1969, s. 27

CHILD	
1. Date and place of birth	
2. Name and surname	3. Sex
FATHER	
4. Name and surname	
5. Place of birth	
6. Occupation	
MOTHER	
7. Name and surname	
8. Place of birth	
9. (a) Maiden surname	(b) Surname at marriage if different from maiden surname
10. Usual address (if different from place of child's birth)	
INFORMANT	
11. Name and surname (if not the mother or father)	12. Qualification
13. Usual address (if different from that in 10 above)	

For use (a) where the informants give information out of the sub-district of the child's birth or (b) in any case where more than 3 months have elapsed since the date of birth of the child.

We. . . . ., being qualified under the Births and Deaths Registration Act, 1953 to give information for the registration of the birth of the above named child, DO SOLEMNLY DECLARE that the particulars above are those which are required to be registered concerning such birth, according to the best of our knowledge and belief, and request that the name of the father of the child be entered in the register of births as in space 4 above.

Signatures.................... .... Date................

Signed and declared by the above-named declarants in the presence

of...

Registrar of Births and Deaths/Superintendent Registrar

...............Sub-district ....District

SCHEDULE 2
DECLARATION FOR THE REGISTRATION OF A BIRTH

Regulations 5(1)(a), 8. *Family Law Reform Act*, 1969, *s.* 27

CHILD		
1. Date and place of birth		
2. Name and surname		3. Sex
FATHER		
4. Name and surname		
5. Place of birth		
6. Occupation		
MOTHER		
7. Name and surname		
8. Place of birth		
9. (a) Maiden surname	(b) Surname at marriage if different from maiden surname	
10. Usual address (if different from place of child's birth)		
INFORMANT		
11. Name and surname (if not the mother or father)	12. Qualification	
13. Usual address (if different from that in 10 above)		

For use where the child is illegitimate and the mother produces a statutory declaration of paternity made by the father.

I,........................DO SOLEMNLY DECLARE that I am the mother of the child the particulars of whose birth are specified above and that the person named in space 4 above is the father of the child; and I request that his name should be recorded as such in the register of births.

Signature.......................... Date.........................

Signed and declared by the above-named declarant in the presence of...........

Registrar of Births and Deaths/Superintendent Registrar

................................Sub-district ....District

SCHEDULES 3, 4 AND 5

These Schedules relate to forms in Welsh and are not reproduced.

NOTE

These Regulations were made by the Registrar General on December 17, 1969, under s. 20 of the Registration Service Act, 1953, ss. 9, 10 and 39 of the Births and Deaths Registration Act, 1953, and other powers, and came into operation on January 1, 1970.

THE ADOPTION (HIGH COURT) RULES, 1971
[S.I. 1971 No. 1520 (L.34)]

Citation, commencement and interpretation

1.—(1) These Rules may be cited as the Adoption (High Court) Rules, 1971 and shall come into operation on 1st October 1971.

(2) In these Rules, unless the context otherwise requires—

"the Act" means the Adoption Act, 1958;

"adoption order" includes a provisional adoption order within the meaning of section 53 of the Act;

"interim order" means an interim order made under section 8 of the Act;

"the minor" means in relation to any proceedings the person whom the applicant proposes to adopt;

"registrar" means a registrar of the Family Division of the High Court;

"regular armed forces of the Crown" means the Royal Navy, the regular forces as defined by section 225 of the Army Act, 1955, the regular air force as defined by section 223 of the Air Force Act, 1955 and any women's service administered by the Defence Council;

a rule referred to by number means the rule so numbered in these Rules and a form referred to by number means the form so numbered in Schedule 1 to these Rules or a form to the like effect.

(3) The Interpretation Act, 1889, shall apply to the interpretation of these Rules as it applies to the interpretation of an Act of Parliament.

NOTE

These rules are made under s. 9 of the Adoption Act, 1958, as amended by s. 54 of the Children and Young Persons Act, 1963.

Application of Supreme Court Rules and powers of registrar

2.—(1) Subject to the provisions of these Rules and of any enactment the Rules of the Supreme Court shall apply with the necessary modifications to proceedings in the High Court under the Act.

(2) For the purposes of paragraph (1) of this Rule any provision of these Rules authorising or requiring anything to be done shall be treated as if it were a provision of the Rules of the Supreme Court.

(3) Unless the contrary intention appears, any power which by these Rules is to be exercised by the Court may be exercised by the registrar.

Commencement and conduct of proceedings

3.—(1) An application to the High Court for an adoption order shall be made by originating summons in Form 1 issued out of the Principal Registry of the Family Division. The proposed adopter shall be the applicant and the minor shall be the respondent.

(2) All proceedings in the High Court under the Act may be disposed of in chambers.

Application for a serial number

4. If any person proposing to apply to the High Court for an adoption order desires that his identity shall be kept confidential he may, before taking out an originating summons, apply to the Senior Registrar of the Family Division, for a serial number to be assigned to him for the purposes of the proposed application and a number shall be assigned to him accordingly.

Effect of previous proceedings

5.—(1) Subject to the next following paragraph an application for an adoption order shall not be entertained by the High Court if a previous application by the same applicant in respect of the same minor has been made to the High Court, a county court or a juvenile court and that court, after hearing the application, has refused it on its merits.

(2) An application for an adoption order may be entertained by leave of the Court, notwithstanding the refusal of a previous application, if the judge is satisfied that since that refusal there has been a substantial change in the relevant circumstances.

(3) An application for leave under the last preceding paragraph shall be included in the originating summons and a statement of the facts on which the applicant relies in support of the application shall be exhibited to the affidavit referred to in Rule 8.

Appointment of guardian ad litem

6. Subject to the provisions of Rule 7, the Official Solicitor shall, if he consents, be the guardian *ad litem* of the minor for the purposes of the application and a copy of the summons shall be served on him.

7.—(1) If the Official Solicitor does not consent to act as guardian *ad litem*, or if the applicant desires that some other person should be appointed to act as guardian, the originating summons must ask for the appointment of a guardian *ad litem* and must be supported by an affidavit by the applicant stating the facts. The court may thereupon appoint as guardian *ad litem* any person who appears to be suitably qualified.

(2) Where the director of social services of a local authority is appointed as guardian *ad litem*, he may carry out his duties and appear before the court personally or by any other officer of that authority who assists him in the exercise of his functions.

NOTE
Duties of probation officer as guardian *ad litem*.—See r. 31 of the Probation Rules, 1965, p. 528, *ante.*

Evidence in support of application

8. Evidence in support of an application for an adoption order shall be given by means of an affidavit in Form 2.

9.—(1) Any document signifying the consent of a person to the making of an adoption order for the purposes of section 6 of the Act shall be in Form 3 and, if executed before the date of the applicant's affidavit referred to in Rule 8, shall be exhibited to that affidavit.

(2) If the document is executed outside the United Kingdom, it shall be sufficiently attested for the purposes of section 6 (3) of the Act if it is attested by any of the following persons:—

  (a) any person for the time being authorised by law in the place where the document is executed to administer an oath for any judicial or other legal purpose;
  (b) a British consular officer;
  (c) a notary public; or

(d) if the person executing the document is serving in any of the regular armed forces of the Crown, an officer holding a commission in any of those forces.

(3) Where a parent or guardian of the minor has not signified his consent to the making of an adoption order and the applicant intends to ask the court to dispense with such consent on any of the grounds specified in section 5 of the Act, there shall be exhibited to the affidavit referred to in Rule 8 a statement of the facts on which the applicant intends to rely.

10. Except where the applicant or one of the applicants is the mother or father of the minor or the minor has reached the upper limit of the compulsory school age, there shall be exhibited to the affidavit referred to in Rule 8 a certificate of a fully registered medical practitioner as to the applicant's health; and, if the applicant so desires, Form 4 may be used for the purposes of such certificate.

11.—(1) Any report on the health of the minor which is to be used for the purposes of an application for an adoption order shall be exhibited to the affidavit referred to in Rule 8.

(2) The report may, if the applicant so desires, be in Form 5.

12.—(1) The affidavit referred to in Rule 8 shall be filed within fourteen days after the issue of the originating summons, and the applicant shall serve a copy of the affidavit and of the documents exhibited to it on the guardian *ad litem*.

(2) Where the documents exhibited to the affidavit include a statement of the facts referred to in Rule 9 (3) the registrar shall, where practicable, inform the parent or guardian of the application to dispense with his consent and send him a copy of that statement:

Provided that, where a serial number has been assigned to the applicant under Rule 4, no information given or document supplied to a parent or guardian under this paragraph shall include any reference to the applicant otherwise than by that serial number.

13.—(1) An applicant for a provisional adoption order shall provide evidence of the law of adoption in the country in which he is domiciled.

(2) The Court may accept as evidence of that law an affidavit sworn by a person who is conversant with it and who practises, or has practised, as a barrister or advocate in that country or is a duly accredited representative of the Government of that country in the United Kingdom.

(3) Where the applicant intends to make use of any such affidavit, he shall file it with the affidavit referred to in Rule 8.

Notice of application

14. On the filing of the affidavit referred to in Rule 8, the registrar shall send a notice in Form 6 to any parent or guardian of the minor who has signified his consent to the making of an adoption order.

Duties of the guardian ad litem

15.—(1) With a view to safeguarding the interests of the minor before the court the guardian *ad litem*, shall, so far as is reasonably practicable—

(a) investigate all circumstances relevant to the proposed adoption, including the matters alleged in the applicant's affidavit and those specified in Schedule 2 to these Rules, and

(b) perform such other duties as are specified in the said Schedule or as the court may direct.

(2) On completing his investigations the guardian *ad litem* shall make a confidential report in writing to the court.

(3) With a view to obtaining the directions of the court on any particular matter the guardian *ad litem* may at any time make such interim report to the court as appears to him to be necessary.

NOTE

See R. S. C., O. 80, r. 2 (2). The function of the guardian *ad litem* is to represent the child "in the ordinary course of proceedings", he does not act in a custodial capacity. See note to rule 9, p. 1111 *ante*, as to confidential reports.

Hearing of the application

16. When the guardian *ad litem* has made his report to the court pursuant to Rule 15 (2) the registrar, after giving such directions (if any) as he thinks necessary, shall fix a date for the hearing of the application by a judge.

17. When the date for the hearing has been fixed the registrar shall serve a notice in Form 7 on the following persons, that is to say:—

  (a) every person, not being an applicant, whose consent to the making of the order is required under section 4 (1) of the Act;
  (b) any person or body having the rights and powers of a parent of the minor by virtue of section 24 of the Children and Young Persons Act, 1969 or section 3 of the Children Act, 1948;
  (c) unless otherwise directed, any person liable by virtue of any order or agreement to contribute to the maintenance of the minor;
  (d) the local authority to whom the applicant has given notice of his intention to apply for an adoption order under section 3 (2) of the Act;
  (e) any local authority or adoption society named in the application or in a form of consent as having taken part in the arrangements for the adoption of the minor;
  (f) any other person or body who in his opinion ought to be served with notice of the hearing of the application.

18. On the hearing of the application, any person on whom notice is required to be served under the last foregoing Rule may attend and be heard on the question whether an adoption order should be made. A local authority or other body may be represented by any officer or servant of the authority or body duly authorised in that behalf.

19. If a serial number has been assigned to the applicant under Rule 4, the proceedings shall be conducted with a view to securing, so far as possible, that he is not seen by or made known to any party who is not already aware of his identity except with his consent.

20. Where the determination of an application is postponed and an interim order is made without a date being fixed for the further hearing, the registrar shall, at least two months before the expiration of the period specified in the interim order, fix the date for the further hearing of the application and shall, unless otherwise directed, serve notice thereof in Form 8 on every person on whom notice is required to be served by Rule 17.

Form and transmission of orders

21.—(1) Within seven days after an adoption order has been drawn up the registrar shall send a copy to the Registrar General and to the applicant.

(2) Within seven days after an interim order has been drawn up the registrar shall send a copy to the applicant.

22.—(1) The registrar shall not supply a copy of an adoption order or of an interim order except—

    (a) in accordance with the provisions of Rule 21;

    (b) at the request of the Registrar General or the applicant or one of the applicants;

    (c) on the application of any other person under an order of a judge; or

    (d) at the request of a county court or juvenile court.

(2) Paragraph (1) of this Rule applies to an adoption order or an interim order made under the Adoption Act, 1950, or any enactment repealed by that Act, as it applies to an adoption order or interim order made under the Act.

(3) The High Court shall not request a county court or juvenile court to furnish a copy of an adoption order under any Adoption Rule corresponding to paragraph (1) (d) of this Rule except in the case of a minor born in England who had been adopted in England before 1st April 1959 and in respect of whom the registration district and sub-district in which he was born would not otherwise be proved to the satisfaction of the High Court for the purposes of section 21 (3) of the Act.

23.—(1) Where an adoption order is made or refused, or an interim order is made, the registrar shall serve notice to that effect on all parties on whom notice of the hearing was served under Rule 17.

(2) Where an adoption order is made in respect of a minor who is illegitimate, then, unless the applicant is his mother and the mother is a single woman, the registrar shall serve notice of the order on any court which appears to him to have made an affiliation order or a decree of affiliation and aliment which is still in force with respect to the minor.

Amendment and revocation of adoption orders

24.—(1) An application under section 24 (1) of the Act for the amendment of an adoption order or the revocation of a direction to the Registrar General, or under section 26 of the Act for the revocation of an adoption order, may be made *ex parte* in the first instance in the proceedings in which the adoption order was made, but the court may require notice of the application to be served on such persons as it thinks fit.

(2) Where the application is granted, the registrar shall send to the Registrar General a notice specifying the date of the adoption order and the names of the adopter and of the adopted person as given in the Schedule to the adoption order and either stating the amendments to the adoption order made by the court or informing him of the revocation of the direction or adoption order as the case may be:

Provided that where an adoption order made under the Adoption of Children Act, 1926, is amended, the said notice shall specify all the particulars to be entered in the Adopted Children Register.

Disclosure of information

25. Any information obtained by any person in the course of, or relating to, proceedings under the Act shall be treated as confidential and shall be disclosed if, but only if,—

    (a) the disclosure is necessary for the proper exercise of his duties, or

(b) the information is requested—

> (i) by a court or public authority (whether within Great Britain or not) having power to authorise an adoption, for the purpose of the discharge of its duties in that behalf, or
> (ii) by a person who is authorised in writing by or on behalf of the Secretary of State to obtain the information for the purposes of research.

Custody and inspection of documents

26.—(1) All documents relating to proceedings under the Act, or any enactment repealed by the Act, shall, while they are in the custody of the court, be kept in a place of special security.

(2) Save as required or authorised by any provision of these Rules or of any enactment, no document filed or lodged with the court in proceedings under the Act shall be open to inspection by any person, and no copy of any such document, or of any extract from any such document, shall be taken by or issued to any person.

Application for return of infant

27.—(1) An application—

> (a) under section 34 of the Act for leave to remove a minor from the care and possession of a person who has applied for an adoption order, or
> (b) under section 35 (2) of the Act for leave to give notice under section 35 (1) (b) of the Act,

shall be made to a judge by summons.

(2) The registrar shall, not less than seven clear days before the day appointed for the hearing of the summons, serve a copy of the summons on the guardian *ad litem* and on every party to the application for the adoption order.

(3) Where leave is refused, the registrar shall serve notice of the refusal on every party to the application for the adoption order.

(4) Where leave is granted, the judge may treat the hearing of the application as the hearing of the application for an adoption order and refuse an adoption order accordingly.

28. Unless otherwise directed, any document under these Rules may be served—

> (a) on a corporation or body of persons, by delivering it at, or sending it by post to, the registered or principal office of the corporation or body;
> (b) on any other person, by delivering it to him, or by sending it by post to him at his usual or last known address.

Use of forms

29. The forms in Schedule 1 to these Rules may be used in the cases to which they are applicable with such variations, if any, as the circumstances may require.

Revocation of Rules and transitional provisions

30. The Adoption (High Court) Rules, 1959, and the Adoption (High Court) (Amendment) Rules, 1965, are hereby revoked, so however that an application for an adoption order which is pending at the date of the commencement of these Rules may be proceeded with and determined in accordance with the Rules in force immediately before that date if and in so far as the more convenient disposal of the application so requires.

SCHEDULE 1

FORM No. 1

Rule 3

ORIGINATING SUMMONS FOR AN ADOPTION ORDER OR A PROVISIONAL ADOPTION
ORDER

In the High Court of Justice   19   , No.
    Family Division

IN THE MATTER OF................[¹] a minor

and

IN THE MATTER OF the Adoption Act, 1958

Let.................of..................attend at the Royal Courts of Justice,
Strand, London W.C.2, on a date to be fixed for the hearing of the application
of...............of..................for an order:—

[1. That a guardian *ad litem* be appointed for the purpose of safeguarding the
interests of the said...............][²]

[2. That the application be entertained notwithstanding that a previous application made by the same applicant in respect of the same minor has been refused by
the High Court [*or* as the case may be]][³].

3. That the applicant be authorised to adopt [or be granted a provisional adoption
order in respect of] the said...............

4. That the costs of this application be provided for.

Dated the...............day of..............., 19....

This summons was taken out by...............of.....................
solicitor for the above-named..................

Notes:
    [¹] Enter the name(s) and surname which the minor is to bear after the adoption.
    [²] Delete if the Official Solicitor has consented to act as guardian *ad litem*.
    [³] Delete if inapplicable.

FORM No. 2

Rule 8

AFFIDAVIT IN SUPPORT OF APPLICATION FOR AN ADOPTION ORDER OR A
PROVISIONAL ADOPTION ORDER[¹]

[*Heading as in Form* **1**]

[Every paragraph must be completed or, if it is not applicable, deleted]

I,................ of .... /We, ... of
.... being desirous of adopting [or obtaining a provisional adoption
order in respect of] ...., a minor, under the Adoption Act, 1958,
hereby make oath and say that the particulars set out in paragraphs 1 to ....
of this affidavit are true:—

PART I

Particulars of the applicant(s)

1. Name of [first] applicant in full ....
   Address[³] ....
   Occupation ....
   Date of birth ....
   Relationship (of any) to the minor ....

2. Name of second applicant in full ....
Address[3] ....
Occupation ....
Date of birth ....
Relationship (if any) to the minor ....

3. I am/We are resident and domiciled in England and Wales/Scotland

[*or* I am/We are domiciled in England and Wales/Scotland but not ordinarily resident in Great Britain]

[*or* I am/we are not domiciled in England and Wales or Scotland].

4. I am unmarried/a widow/widower/I am married to.......................
of................./We are married to each other and are the persons described as..................and..................in the marriage certificate (or other evidence of marriage) exhibited to this affidavit.

[5. The consent of my husband/wife to the making of an adoption order/a provisional adoption order in pursuance of my application is exhibited to this affidavit [*or* I request the judge to dispense with the consent of my husband/wife on the ground that.................................. [4].]][5]

[6. A certificate as to my/our health, signed by a fully registered medical practitioner, is exhibited to this affidavit.][6]

PART II

Particulars of the infant

7. The minor is of the............sex and is not and has not been married. He/She was born on the.............day of................, 19...., and is the person to whom the birth/adoption certificate[7] exhibited to this affidavit relates [*or* was born on or about the ....day of..............., 19...., in ....][8]

[8. A report on the health of the minor[9], made by a fully registered medical practitioner on the.............day of..............., 19...., [10] is exhibited to this affidavit.]

9. The minor is the child/adopted child[11] of.............[12] whose last known address was.........................[*or* deceased] and............ ....[13] whose last known address was............................ ....[*or* deceased].

[10. The guardian(s) of the minor is/are ....
of .... [and ....
of...........................]].[14]

11. A document/Documents signifying the consent of the said...............
.........[15] to the making of an adoption order/a provisional adoption order in pursuance of my/our application is/are exhibited to this affidavit.

[12. I/We request the judge to dispense with the consent of.................
on the grounds set out in the statement exhibited to this affidavit.][16]

[13. The...................Council [*or*...................................]
of .... has/have the rights and powers of a parent of the minor.]
[17]

[14. ....of..................is liable by virtue of an order made by the................court at..................on the.........day of..
..............., 19...., [*or* by an agreement dated the................day of ....19....,] to contribute to the maintenance of the minor.][18]

15. If an adoption order/a provisional adoption order is made in pursuance of this application the minor is to be known by the following names—

Surname.....................

Other names ....

PART III
General

16. The minor was received into my/our care and possession on the...........
day of..................., 19...., and has been continuously in my/our care and
possession since that date.

[17. I/We notified the .... Council on the...................
day of....................., 19...., of my/our intention to apply for an adoption
order/a provisional adoption order in respect of the minor.][19]

[18. I have not made/Neither of us has made a previous application for an adoption order/a provisional adoption order in respect of the minor.]

[19. A previous application No...........was made to the ....
court by .... in respect of the minor, which was heard on the
.............day of................., 19...., and was dealt with as follows
.... A statement of the changes in the relevant circumstances on which I/we rely in accordance with Rule 5 of the Adoption (High Court)
Rules, 1971 is exhibited to this affidavit.][20]

20. I/We have not received or given any reward or payment for, or in consideration of, the adoption of the minor or for giving consent to the making of the adoption
order/provisional adoption order [except as follows ....][21]

21. As far as I/we know, no person or body has taken part in the arrangements
for placing the minor in my/our care and possession [except ....][22]

[22. For the purposes of this application reference may be made to..............
of...................][23]

[23. I/We desire that my/our identity should be kept confidential and the serial
number of this application is.....................][24]

[24. I/We intend to adopt the minor under the law of or within ....[25]
and for that purpose I/we desire to remove the minor from Great Britain.][26]

Sworn etc.

This affidavit is filed on behalf of the applicant(s).

Notes:

[1] The marriage certificate and other documents referred to in this affidavit should be
separately exhibited.

[2] Enter the first name(s) and surname as shown in any certificate referred to in paragraph 7; otherwise enter the first name(s) and surname by which the minor was known
before being placed for adoption.

[3] Insert the applicant's present address and, where he is not ordinarily resident in Great
Britain, the place abroad where he ordinarily resides.

[4] The consent of the applicant's spouse may be dispensed with if the court is satisfied
that he or she cannot be found or is incapable of giving his or her consent or that the spouses
have separated and are living apart and the separation is likely to be permanent.

[5] This paragraph should be deleted if the application is made jointly by husband and
wife or the applicant is unmarried.

[6] A separate medical certificate is required in respect of each applicant. There is an
official form (Form No. 4) which may be used for this purpose. No certificate, however,
need be supplied if the applicant, or one of the applicants, is the father or mother of the
minor or the minor has reached the upper limit of the compulsory school age.

[7] If the minor has previously been adopted, a certified copy of the entry in the Adopted
Children Register should be supplied and not a certified copy of the original entry in the
Registers of Births.

[8] Where a certificate is not supplied, enter the place (including country) of birth, if
known.

[9] As the court may require up-to-date information as to the health of the minor, a
medical report should be supplied unless the applicant, or one of the applicants, is a parent
or relative of the minor or the minor has reached the upper limit of the compulsory school
age. There is an official form (Form No. 5) which may be used for this purpose.

[10] If the minor is less than one year old on the date of the application, the report should
have been made not more than one month before that date. If the minor is one year old
or more on that date, the report should have been made not more than six months before
that date.

[11] If the minor has previously been adopted, give names of his adoptive parents and not those of his natural parents.

[12] Enter mother's name.

[13] Enter name of father, if known.

[14] Guardian means a person appointed by deed or will in accordance with the provisions of the Guardianship of Minors Act, 1971 or by a court of competent jurisdiction, to be a guardian.

[15] Enter the names of the persons mentioned in paragraphs 9 and 10 except, in the case of an illegitimate minor, his father.

[16] The consent of a parent or guardian may be dispensed with if the court is satisfied that the person whose consent is required has abandoned, neglected or persistently ill-treated the minor, or has persistently failed without reasonable cause to discharge the obligations of a parent or guardian, or cannot be found, or is incapable of giving his consent or is withholding his consent unreasonably.

[17] This paragraph should be deleted except where some person or body has the rights and powers of a parent of the minor by virtue of section 24 of the Children and Young Persons Act, 1969 or section 3 of the Children Act, 1948.

[18] This paragraph should be deleted where some person or body is liable to maintain the minor under a court order or agreement.

[19] Notice does not have to be given if the applicant or one of the applicants is a parent of the minor or if at the time of the hearing the minor will have reached the upper limit of the compulsory school age.

[20] The court cannot entertain the application if a previous application made by the same applicant in respect of the same minor has been heard and dismissed on its merits, unless there has been a substantial change in the circumstances since the previous application.

[21] Any such payment or reward is illegal except payment to an adoption society or local authority in respect of their expenses incurred in connection with the adoption.

[22] Enter the name of any local authority, adoption society or individual who has taken part in the arrangements for placing the minor in the care and possession of the applicant with a view to his adoption.

[23] Where the applicant, or one of the applicants, is a parent of the minor, or a relative as defined by section 57 (1) of the Adoption Act, 1958, no referee need be named.

[24] If the applicant wishes his identity to be kept confidential, the serial number obtained under Rule 4 of the Adoption (High Court) Rules, 1971, should be given; otherwise this paragraph should be deleted.

[25] Where the application is for a provisional adoption order insert the country in which the applicant is domiciled. The applicant must provide evidence of the law of adoption in that country. For this purpose the judge may accept an affidavit as to that law, sworn by a person who is conversant with it and who practises, or has practised, as a barrister or advocate in that country or is a duly accredited representative of the Government of that country in the United Kingdom. Any such affidavit must be filed with this affidavit.

[26] This paragraph should be deleted except where the application is for a provisional adoption order.

FORM No. 3

Rule 9

CONSENT TO AN ADOPTION ORDER OR A PROVISIONAL ADOPTION ORDER

Whereas an application is to be/has been made by ....
/and ....[or under the serial number][1] for an adoption order/a provisional adoption order in respect of ....[2], a minor;
[And whereas the minor is not less than six weeks old;][3]
[And whereas the minor is the person to whom the birth certificate[4] now produced and shown to me marked "A" relates][5]:

I, the undersigned .... of................ being [6] the mother/father[7]/guardian[8] of the minor, hereby state as follows:—

1. I understand that the effect of an adoption order will be to deprive me permanently of my rights as a parent/guardian and to transfer them to the applicant(s), [or I understand that the effect of a provisional adoption order will be to enable the applicant(s) to remove the minor from Great Britain for the purpose of adopting him/her abroad and to give the applicant(s) custody of the minor pending his/her adoption]; and in particular I understand that, if an order is made, I shall have no right to see or get in touch with the minor or to have him/her returned to me.

2. I further understand that the court cannot make an adoption order without the consent of each parent or guardian of the infant unless the court dispenses with a

consent on the ground that the person concerned has abandoned, neglected or persistently ill-treated the minor, or cannot be found, or is incapable of giving consent, or is unreasonably withholding consent or has persistently failed without reasonable cause to discharge the obligations of a parent or guardian.

3. I further understand that, when the application for an adoption order is heard, this document may be used as evidence of my consent to the making of the order unless I inform the court that I no longer consent[9].

4. I hereby consent to the making of an adoption order/a provisional adoption in pursuance of the application [on condition that the religious persuasion in which the minor is proposed to be brought up is ....][10].

5. As far as I know, no other person or body has taken part in the arrangements for placing the minor in the care and possession of the applicant[s] [except........ ....][11].

$$\text{.................}$$
(Signature)

This form, duly completed, was signed by the said .... before me[12] at ....on the................day of................, 19.....

Signature............................
Address ....
Description ....

Warning. It is an offence to receive or give any reward or payment for, or in consideration of, the adoption of the minor or for giving consent to the making of an adoption order, other than a payment to a local authority or adoption society for their expenses incurred in connection with the adoption.

Notes:

[1] Insert either the name of the applicant or the serial number assigned to the applicant for the purpose of the application.

[2] Insert the name[s] and surname as known to the consenting party.

[3] Delete the words in square brackets except where the consenting party is the mother. The mother's consent cannot be given before the child is six weeks old.

[4] If the minor has previously been adopted, a certified copy of the entry in the Adopted Children Register should be attached, and not a certified copy of the original entry in the Registers of Births; and the description of the consenting party should include the words "by adoption" where appropriate.

[5] Delete the words in square brackets except where the consenting party is the mother or father of the minor and the birth certificate has not already been identified by the other parent.

[6] Delete all but one of the descriptions which follow.

[7] "Father" does not include the natural father of an illegitimate child.

[8] "Guardian" means a person appointed by deed or will in accordance with the provisions of the Guardianship of Minors Act, 1971, or by a court of competent jurisdiction, to be guardian of the minor.

[9] Notice will be given of the making of the application and of the court by which it is to be heard. After the making of the application the consenting parent or guardian cannot remove the minor from the care and possession of the applicant except with the leave of the court.

[10] Delete the words in square brackets if the applicant is named or if, although the applicant is not named, the consenting party does not desire to impose a condition as to religious upbringing.

[11] Enter the name of any local authority, adoption society or person who is known to have arranged, or to have taken part in the arrangements, for the minor to be placed in the care and possession of the applicant.

[12] In England and Wales the document should be signed before a justice of the peace, a duly authorised county court officer or a justices' clerk and in Scotland before a justice of the peace or sheriff. In Northern Ireland it should be signed before a justice of the peace. Outside the United Kingdom it should be signed before a person authorised to administer an oath for any judicial or legal purpose, a British consular officer, a notary public or, if the person signing it is serving in the armed forces, a commissioned officer.

FORM No. 4

Rule 10

MEDICAL CERTIFICATE AS TO HEALTH OF APPLICANT

I examined ....on................. and have formed the opinion that he is physically, mentally and emotionally suitable to adopt a child.

Signature .... *Date*...............

Qualifications ....

Address..

FORM No. 5

Rule 11

MEDICAL REPORT ON HEALTH OF MINOR

Note:

This form is for a medical report on a child who may be adopted. The report is for the benefit of the adopters and the court. In order that the adopters may benefit fully from the report, it is important that the certifying doctor should explain to the adopters the nature and extent of any disability or abnormality disclosed by the examination which might affect their decision whether or not to adopt the child.

Child's name..................................... Date of Birth ....

Sex..............Weight...............Height..............

A General condition.
  Skin.
  Eyes (including vision).
  Ears (including hearing).
  Nose and throat.
  Speech.
  Cardio-vascular system.
  Respiratory system.
  Alimentary system.
  Genito-urinary system (including examination of urine for albumen and sugar).
  Skeletal and articular system (including examination for congenital dislocation of hip).
  Nervous system (including fits).
  Lymphatic system.
  Any other comments.
  Is the child physically normal having regard to his age?

B Are there any items in the child's history or examination which suggest that he may be mentally abnormal having regard to his age?

C Particulars of any illnesses from which the child has suffered.

D If known,
  Weight at birth (if child is under one year of age).
  Details of birth, including result of mother's serological tests for syphilis.
  Particulars, with dates, of vaccination or immunisation against—
    Tuberculosis (state result of Mantoux test or whether child has been successfully vaccinated with B.C.G. vaccine).
    Smallpox.
    Diphtheria.
    Whooping cough.
    Poliomyelitis.
    Tetanus (active).
    Any other disease.

E (i) (To be completed in the case of a child at least six weeks old at the time of the test.)
    Result of suitable serological test of the child's blood for syphilis (please specify test)..

(ii) (To be completed in the case of a child over six days, excluding the day of his birth, and under two years old at the time of the test.)
Result of test of the child's blood for the purpose of estimating the level of phenylalanine therein ....

F   I examined the child on the .... day of ....
19...., and I have informed the adopters of the state of health of the child disclosed by the examination.

Signature...   *Date*................

Qualifications ....

Address...

FORM No. 6

Rule 14

NOTICE OF AN APPLICATION FOR AN ADOPTION ORDER OR A PROVISIONAL
ADOPTION ORDER

To............... of...[¹]
Whereas an application has been made [by ..../
...................and.....................][²] *or* [under the serial number
...................] for an adoption order/a provisional adoption order in
respect of..................[³], a minor;

Take notice that while the said application is pending you must not, except with the leave of the judge, remove the minor from the care and possession of the applicant. Application for such leave may be made at the Principal Registry of the Family Division, Somerset House, Strand, London, W.C.2.

Dated the..................day of................., 19....

....
Registrar

Notes:

[¹] Enter the name and address of any parent or guardian of the minor who has signified his consent to the making of an adoption order or a provisional adoption order.
[²] The name of the applicant must not be given where a serial number is specified in Form 2 (paragraph 23). In that case complete the second entry in square brackets.
[³] Enter the name(s) and surname as known to the person to whom the notice is given.

FORM No. 7

Rule 17

NOTICE OF HEARING OF AN APPLICATION FOR AN ADOPTION ORDER OR A
PROVISIONAL ADOPTION ORDER

To .... of ....
Whereas an application has been made [by ..../
.... and ....][¹] *or* [under the
serial number ....] for an adoption order/a provisional adoption
order in respect of.....................[²], a minor;

Take notice:

A. [³] [That the said application will be heard at the Royal Courts of Justice, Strand, London W.C.2., on the....................day of....................,
19...., at..........o'clock, and that you may then attend and be heard on the question whether an adoption order/a provisional adoption order should be made.]

B. [³] [That if you wish to attend and be heard on the question whether an adoption order/a provisional adoption order should be made, you should notify me on or before the.................day of................, 19...., in order that a time may be fixed for your attendance.]

[And further take notice that the court has been requested to dispense with your consent to the making of the adoption order/provisional adoption order on the grounds..][⁴] [⁵]

It would assist the court if you would complete the attached form and return it to me.

Dated the.................day of................, 19....

....
Registrar

Notes:

[¹] The name of the applicant must not be given where the notice is addressed to an individual and a serial number is specified in Form 2 (paragraph 23). In that case complete the second entry in square brackets.

[²] Enter the name(s) and surname as known to the person to whom the notice is given.

[³] Form A should be completed and Form B struck out where the notice is addressed to a local authority, an adoption society, any other body of persons or the spouse of the applicant, or where the applicant does not desire his identity to be kept confidential (see Form 2, paragraph 23). Where a serial number is specified in that paragraph and the notice is addressed to an individual, Form A must be struck out and Form B completed.

[⁴] Enter the grounds specified in Form 2 (paragraph 5) or refer to the statement exhibited to Form 2 (paragraph 12) as the case may be.

[⁵] Delete if inapplicable.

.... Perforation................

To:—The Senior Registrar, Principal Registry of the Family Division, Somerset House, Strand, London W.C.2.

I have received notice of the hearing of the application for an adoption order/a provisional adoption order in respect of................a minor.

I* do/do not wish to oppose the application.
I* do/do not wish to attend and be heard on the question whether an adoption order/a provisional adoption order should be made.

*delete one or other alternative

....
(Signature)

....
(Date)

....
(Address)

FORM No. 8

Rule 20

NOTICE OF FURTHER HEARING OF AN APPLICATION FOR AN ADOPTION ORDER OR A PROVISIONAL ADOPTION ORDER

To.................................of ....
Whereas an application has been made [by................................/
............................and.......................][¹] *or*
[under the serial number................] for an adoption order/a provisional adoption order in respect of........................., a minor[²];

And whereas the determination of the said application was postponed and an interim order was made by the judge on the....................day of........
.........., 19.....

Take notice:

A.[3] [That the said application will be further heard before the judge at the Royal Courts of Justice, Strand, London, W.C.2, on the...............day of ...., 19...., at...........o'clock and that you may then attend and be heard on the question whether an adoption order/a provisional adoption order should be made.]

B.[3] [That if you wish to attend and be heard on the question whether an adoption order/a provisional adoption order should be made, you should notify me on or before the..................day of.................., 19...., in order that a time may be fixed for your attendance.

It would assist the court if you would complete the attached form and return it to me.

Dated the...................day of.................., 19....

....
Registrar

Notes:

[1] The name of the applicant must not be given where the notice is addressed to an individual and a serial number is specified in Form 2 (paragraph 23). In that case complete the second entry in square brackets.

[2] Enter name(s) and surname as known to the person to whom the notice is given.

[3] Form A should be completed and Form B struck out where the notice is addressed to a local authority, an adoption society or any other body of persons or where the applicant does not desire his identity to be kept confidential (see Form 2, paragraph 23). Where a serial number is specified in that paragraph and the notice is addressed to an individual, Form A must be struck out and Form B completed.

.... Perforation....................

To:—The Senior Registrar, Principal Registry of the Family Division, Somerset House, Strand, London, W.C.2.

I have received notice of the further hearing of the application for an adoption order/a provisional adoption order in respect of.................., a minor.

I* do/do not wish to oppose the application.
I* do/do not wish to attend and be heard on the question whether an adoption order/a provisional adoption order should be made.

*delete one or other alternative

....
(Signature)

....
(Date)   *(Address)*

SCHEDULE 2

Rule 15

PARTICULAR DUTIES OF THE GUARDIAN AD LITEM

1. The guardian *ad litem* shall interview the applicant and shall ascertain—

   (a) particulars of all members of the applicant's household and their relationship (if any) to the applicant;
   (b) particulars of the accommodation in the applicant's home and the condition of the home;
   (c) the means of the applicant;
   (d) whether the applicant suffers or has suffered from any serious illness and whether there is any history of tuberculosis, epilepsy or mental illness in the applicant's family;

   (e) in the case of an application by one only of two spouses, why the other spouse does not join in the application;

   (f) whether any person specified in the application as a person to whom reference may be made is a responsible person and whether he recommends the applicant with or without reservations;

   (g) whether the applicant understands the nature of an adoption order and, in particular, that the order, if made, will render him responsible for the maintenance and upbringing of the minor;

   (h) why the applicant wishes to adopt the minor;

   (i) such other information, including an assessment of the applicant's personality and, where appropriate, that of the minor, as has a bearing on the mutual suitability of the applicant and the minor and on the ability of the applicant to bring up the minor;

   (j) the applicant's religious persuasion, if any.

  2. The guardian *ad litem* shall ascertain and inform the applicant—

   (a) whether the minor has been baptised and, if so, the date and place of baptism;

   (b) what treatment the minor has received with a view to immunising him against disease;

   (c) whether the minor has any right to, or interest in, any property;

   (d) whether an insurance policy for the payment on the death of the minor of money for funeral expenses has been effected.

  3. The guardian *ad litem* shall ascertain whether the minor is able to understand the nature of an adoption order and, if he is, whether he wishes to be adopted by the applicant.

  4. The guardian *ad litem* shall interview either in person or by an agent appointed by him for the purpose every individual to whom notice is required to be given under Rule 17 or who appears to the guardian *ad litem* to have taken part in the arrangements for the adoption of the minor.

  5.—(1) The guardian *ad litem* shall obtain from every person, not being an individual, to whom notice is required to be given under Rule 17 such information concerning the minor as they have in their possession and which they consider might assist the court in deciding whether or not the minor should be adopted by the applicant.

  (2) Where such information is given in the form of a written report, the guardian *ad litem* shall append it to his own report to the court.

  6. The guardian *ad litem* shall ascertain when the mother of the minor ceased to have the care and possession of the minor and to whom the care and possession was transferred.

  7. The guardian *ad litem* shall ascertain that every consent to the making of an adoption order in pursuance of the application is freely given and with full understanding of the nature and effect of an adoption order.

  8. Where either parent of the minor is dead, the guardian *ad litem* shall inform the court if he learns of any relation of the deceased parent who wishes to be heard by the court on the question whether an adoption order should be made.

  9. Where the minor is illegitimate but no one is liable as the putative father to contribute to the maintenance of the minor by virtue of any order or agreement, the guardian *ad litem* shall inform the court if he learns of any person, claiming to be the father, who wishes to be heard by the court on the question whether an adoption order should be made.

  10. The guardian *ad litem* shall inform the court if he learns of any other person or body who wishes or ought in his opinion to be heard by the court on the question whether an adoption order should be made.

  11. Where the applicant is not ordinarily resident in Great Britain, the guardian *ad litem* shall endeavour to obtain a report on the applicant's home and living conditions from a suitable agency in the country in which he is ordinarily resident.

  12. The guardian *ad litem* shall draw the attention of the court to the difference in age between the applicant and the minor if it is less than the normal difference in age between parents and their children.

PRACTICE DIRECTION

Chancery Division

Adoption—Consent of parent or guardian—Dispensing with consent—Evidence—Practice—Adoption Act, 1958, s. 5.

An applicant for an adoption order who wishes the court to dispense with the consent of a parent or guardian must set out in a statement or statements separately exhibited to the affidavit in support, the evidence on which he intends to rely. It shall be the duty of the guardian *ad litem* (unless otherwise directed) to take steps to inform the parent or guardian of the application to dispense with his or her consent and of the date of the hearing of the application before the master, and to send him or her a copy of the statement or statements of evidence lodged by the applicant in support of the application.

In the event of an applicant for an adoption order subsequently putting forward a further ground for dispensing with the consent of a parent or guardian, a copy of the statement or statements of evidence lodged by the applicant in support of the further ground shall also be sent to the parent or guardian by the guardian *ad litem*.

If a serial number has been assigned to the applicant in accordance with r. 3 of the Adoption (High Court) Rules, 1959, the memorandum identifying the statement as an exhibit to the applicant's affidavit must omit the applicant's name and the proposed adoptive name of the infant, and any reference to the applicant in the statement must be by the serial number and not by name. In such case the guardian *ad litem* must also warn the applicant or his solicitors that, if he attends the appointment before the master, it may not be possible to prevent the parent or guardian from discovering his identity.

This direction supersedes the direction issued by Russell, J., on March 24, 1961.

November 13, 1967.   [1967] 3 All E. R. 992.

NOTE

The major part of this direction has since been incorporated in the Adoption (High Court) Rules, 1971, p. 1156, *ante.*

PRACTICE DIRECTION

Chancery Division

Adoption—Practice—Directions—Production of records and giving of evidence by adoption society or local authority—Contested applications—Adoption Agencies Regulations, 1959, reg. 7, as amended by Adoption Agencies Regulations, 1965.

In contested proceedings under (a) Adoption Act, 1958, (b) Law Reform (Miscellaneous Provisions) Act, 1949, and (c) Guardianship of Infants Acts, 1886 and 1925, any adoption society or department of a local authority which has been concerned with the placing for adoption of the infant or with its care or supervision may be faced with a request by a party to the proceedings to produce its records or give evidence. So far as applications under the Adoption Act, 1958, are concerned, reg. 7 of the Adoption Agencies Regulations, 1959, provides that information obtained by any member, officer or representative of a registered adoption society or local authority shall be treated as confidential and shall not be disclosed except for the purpose of proceedings under the Adoption Act, 1958, or for the proper execution of his duty. Regulation 7 of the Adoption Agencies Regulations, 1959, does not extend to applications for wardship or guardianship of infants, but notwithstanding that, in such applications societies and local authorities may be in possession of information which they would normally consider should be treated as confidential.

In any such case a society or authority which is a party to proceedings may (in default of agreement between all the parties) apply in the proceedings to the court for directions as to what records and information should be made available to the court. Where it is not a party it may require the person seeking production to make application on its behalf. If the court is of opinion that disclosure of records or information to the parties would be harmful to the infant concerned, then directions may be given for such records or information to be made available to the court in the form of a confidential report.

The practice in adoption cases with regard to the provision of information to the Official Solicitor as guardian *ad litem* for the purpose of his report is unaffected.

February 8, 1968   [1968] 1 All E. R. 762.

Appendix to Home Office letter HO53/59   *Dated March 25*, 1959

EXPLANATORY MEMORANDUM TO BE GIVEN TO APPLICANTS FOR ADOPTION ORDERS

1. When the court considers your application for an adoption order, it will want to know whether the child is old enough to understand about adoption and, if so, whether you have told him about your application. If the court thinks the child is old enough to understand, you must tell him before the order can be granted.

2. If the child is still too young, it is best to decide to tell him as soon as he can begin to understand or as soon as he begins to ask questions, which is normally at the age of four or five. You can then gradually tell him more as he grows older. You may prefer not to tell him anything; but that would be unwise, because he would be likely to find out himself sooner or later and if you had not told him the discovery might be a great shock. If you find it difficult to tell him, the local children's officer or the adoption society, if a society arranged the adoption, may be able to help you, but he ought to be told by you.

3. When the court makes an adoption order, all the rights, duties, obligations and liabilities of the natural parents with regard to the child will be transferred to you.

4. After the adoption order is made, if you die (or anyone in your family dies) without leaving a will the child will be eligible to inherit just as he would if he had been a legitimate child born to you. If you or any of your relatives have already made wills and want to include the child as if he had been born into the family it would be well to seek legal advice.

5. When a married couple adopt a child jointly and the husband is a citizen of the United Kingdom and Colonies, the adoption order makes the child a citizen of the United Kingdom and Colonies (if he is not one already). When one person alone adopts a child and he or she is a citizen of the United Kingdom and Colonies, the granting of the adoption order has the same effect.

6. If the court makes an adoption order, you will be given, or sent within seven days, an abridged copy of the order. You are also entitled to receive, if you ask for it, a full copy of the order, which includes particulars of the child's original parentage (thus disclosing illegitimacy if he is illegitimate). The abridged copy omits these particulars but it is headed " Adoption order "

and you may prefer to use the abridged copy to show to anyone who needs to see the adoption order but whom you do not want to know all the particulars.

7. When an adoption order is made, the court directs the Registrar General to enter in the Adopted Children Register particulars of the adoption (quoting only the child's new name if his name has been changed). The Registrar General will send you, soon after he has received the copy of the order from the court a short certificate of the entry in the Register; this will be issued free of charge, but the fee for any additional short certificate will be [15p] and a full certified copy of the entry [40p]. These certificates are generally acceptable for most purposes where a birth certificate is required.

8. If the child is under five years of age and you have not received a welfare milk token and a vitamin token book for him, you should apply to the local office of the Ministry of Pensions and National Insurance producing, if you have one, the note handed to you by the adoption society or local authority about the previous token books.

9. If the court makes an adoption order and you wish the child to be registered with a doctor under the National Health Service, you should fill in the form below and take it to the doctor of your choice as soon as possible after the order is made. When the doctor accepts the child for inclusion in his list, arrangements will be made to send you a medical card in the child's new name (if there is a change of name) with a new National Health Service number which cannot be linked in any way with the child's previous identity. If you have the child's old medical card you should destroy it. It is important in the child's future interests that you should use the form whether or not the adoption involves any change of name or change of doctor.

Form E.C.58C

National Health Service

To be completed by parent

Child's surname ....

Child's forenames ....

Date of birth ....

Home address ....

....

Application to be placed on the list of Dr. ....

Signature of parent ....   Date ....

To be completed by doctor

I accept the child named above for inclusion in my list.

Signed ....   Date ....

Enter D here if supplying drugs

Enter distance here if claiming mileage

NOTE

Registration under the National Health Service of children awaiting adoption.—
See Home Office Circular No. 205/1965, p. 1182, *post*. The explanatory memorandum as printed has been amended in accordance with Home Office Circular No. 167/1969 dated August 15, 1969.

ADOPTED PERSONS

The Archbishops of Canterbury, York and Wales draw the attention of the clergy and laity in their Provinces to the following arrangements:

ENTRIES IN BAPTISMAL REGISTERS AND CERTIFICATES OF BAPTISM

For Children Baptized after Adoption

The entry in Baptismal Registers required by law is thus defined in the Adoption Act, 1958, s. 25 :

" Where a child in respect of whom an adoption order has been made is baptized, the entry to be made in the register under section three of the Parochial Registers Act, 1812, or, as the case may be, the certificate to be transmitted under section four of that Act, shall describe the child as the adopted son or daughter of the person or persons by whom he or she was adopted, instead of as the son or daughter of the natural parents."

For Children Baptized before Adoption

The baptism will have been recorded in the normal way in the Register of the parish church in which it was solemnized. In order to avoid the difficulties which might arise from the production of a certificate of this entry later in life, the following provision has been made :

(a) The person arranging the adoption will obtain from the minister of the parish where the child was baptized a full certificate of the entry in the baptismal register.

(b) The adopting parents (or someone acting on their behalf) will then cause this to be registered in a Diocesan Register of the Baptism of Persons Subsequently Adopted, and obtain in exchange for it a special Certificate of Baptism, signed by the Bishop or a person appointed by him, bearing the forename/s and surname by which the child is to be known as shown on the certified copy of the entry in the Adopted Children Register, and the date but not the place of baptism. The Diocesan Register will be that of the diocese of the parish in which the child was baptized. A small charge may be made. The full certificate from the Adopted Children Register must be sent with the application; it will be returned. The address for applications may be obtained from the Diocesan Handbook, from the agency that arranged the adoption, or from The Secretary, Church of England Committee for Liaison with the Social Services, Church House, Dean's Yard, London, SW1.

(c) The original full certificate will be kept with the Register.

(d) The special Certificate can be issued also for persons baptized and adopted before this provision was made. Application should be made as in paragraph (b) above.

ENTRIES IN MARRIAGE REGISTERS

The Clergy are recommended to follow the practice suggested by the Registrar General in his *Suggestions for the Guidance of the Clergy*, 1959, para. 26, 27 (p. 7), as follows :

" 26. Normally the particulars to be entered (*i.e.* in cols 7 and 8) are those of the natural father of the party, whether the party was of legitimate or illegitimate birth; but if the party was adopted by order of a Court in the United Kingdom, the particulars of the adoptive father may be entered, without qualification, if furnished by the party. If, however, the party is known by a surname different from that of his adoptive father and the name and surname of the adoptive father are entered in column 7 the words " Adoptive parent" in brackets may be entered after the surname if so desired by the party. Where a woman was authorized by the Court to be the sole adopter, the name of that woman may, at the request of the party, be inserted in column 7, followed by the words " Adoptive parent " in brackets after her surname.

27. Should the party show any reluctance to furnish particulars for insertion in these columns the clergyman need not press his inquiries, but he should draw a line through the column to show that the information was not supplied. He must not in any circumstances insert any words, such as " Not known ", " Illegitimate ", etc., in explanation of the omission of the particulars."

NOTES

This leaflet was revised in 1966 and the words " forename/s and surname by which the child is to be known as shown on the certified copy of the entry in the Adopted Children Register " were substituted for the words in previous leaflets "Child's Christian name(s), new surname ".

Catholics.—We are informed that each Catholic Diocese has arrangements for the registration of baptism and that the directions in the leaflet issued by the three Anglican Archbishops will serve to provide these facilities for Roman Catholic adopters. The Diocesan Official responsible for the Register is usually the Chancellor at the Diocesan Curial Offices. There are no directives about entries in Marriage Registers, although paragraph 27 (referred to in the leaflet) always applies already.

ADOPTION OF JEWISH CHILDREN

The following is an extract from a letter dated January 20, 1960, sent by Mr. Barnett Janner, now Sir Barnett Janner, M.P., President of the Board of Deputies of British Jews, to the Secretary of the Association of Municipal Corporations. Copies were later sent by the Secretary to town clerks, with additional copies for the attention of children's officers.

I hope it will be possible through you to bring to the notice of the municipal corporations and adoption societies the religious difficulties sometimes tragic in their consequence, which arise in cases of the adoption of children by Jewish couples. The difficulties arise because the Ecclesiastical Authorities will not sanction the marriage of persons in an orthodox Synagogue unless both parties are Jews according to Jewish law, and in the vast majority of cases of adopted children it is impossible to find proof many years later.

To avoid such difficulties and heartbreak, and in accordance with the principle that the welfare of the child is paramount, it is essential that Jewish adoptive parents should be advised before adopting a child to consult the Beth Din (Jewish Ecclesiastical Court), so as to make sure that the child to be adopted is Jewish. The Beth Din keeps a register of adopted children, so that when the question of marriage arises the existence of such registration will prevent any difficulties. The fact that a child has been brought up in a Jewish home does not by itself constitute Jewishness in the ecclesiastical meaning of the word.

Home Office Circular No. 89/1961.   *Dated May 17, 1961.*

THE ADOPTION AGENCIES REGULATIONS, 1961

1. I am directed by the Secretary of State to send you the enclosed copy of the Adoption Agencies Regulations, 1961, which came into operation on 1st June, 1961.

2. Under the Adoption Agencies Regulations, 1959, a child may not be placed by or on behalf of a registered adoption society or a local authority with a prospective adopter until a medical report in the form set out in the Fifth Schedule has been obtained. That report requires, among other things, the entry of the result of a test of the child's blood for syphilis made six weeks or later after birth ; and there has in consequence been doubt whether it was open

to a registered adoption society or a local authority to place a child with a prospective adopter before the child attained the age of six weeks. The amending Regulations remove that doubt.

3. The medical report in the principal Regulations also requires the entry of the result of an examination of the child's urine for phenylpyruvic acid. The Secretary of State is advised that this examination is unreliable if performed before the child is six weeks old and unnecessary after the child is two years old. The amending Regulations provide for amendment of the form of medical report so that the examination is required only if the child is less than two years old and, if required, must be made after the child has attained the age of six weeks.

4. The new paragraph (3) added to Regulation 6 of the principal Regulations makes provision for the case where the child is placed with a prospective adopter before the test for syphilis or examination for phenylpyruvic acid has been made, and requires that the test or examination shall be made as soon as practicable after the child has been placed and attains the age of six weeks. The registered adoption society or the local authority must give a copy of the report of the test or examination to the prospective adopter. The provisions of the new paragraph will apply not only to children placed on or after 1st June but also to any child previously placed if the adoption order has not been made.

5. Extra copies of this circular and the Regulations are enclosed for the Chief Financial Officer and the Children's Officer.

NOTE

This circular was sent to Clerks of County Councils and to Town Clerks.

Home Office Circular No. 278/1965　　　　　　*Dated December* 21, 1965.

THE ADOPTION (JUVENILE COURT) RULES, 1965 AND THE ADOPTION AGENCIES REGULATIONS, 1965

1. I am writing to draw your attention to the Adoption (Juvenile Court) Rules, 1965 and the Adoption Agencies Regulations, 1965, copies of which are enclosed.

2. These amend, respectively, the Adoption (Juvenile Court) Rules, 1959 and the Adoption Agencies Regulations, 1959. The Regulations and Rule 2 of the Rules come into operation on 1st January, 1966. The remaining Rules come into operation on 1st March, 1966.

3. The Regulations permit information obtained by an adoption agency about individual cases to be disclosed to a person who is authorised in writing by or on behalf of the Secretary of State to obtain it for the purposes of research. This provision is the outcome of discussions with associations representing bodies concerned with adoption about the need for research, and the terms on which information in confidential records kept by courts, local authorities and adoption societies should be available to research workers. The view was taken that a central authority should be responsible for examining the credentials of research workers, for ensuring that genuine and worthwhile research was intended by the person who wanted access to records and that uniform safeguards were imposed.

4. A research worker applying for an authority under this provision will be asked to comply with the following conditions:

(a) adequate notice should be given to the local authority officer concerned of the research worker's proposed visit;

(b) nothing calculated to identify any individual involved in a particular adoption should be published (the Home Office would require to see material to be published as a result of the research) ;

(c) the research worker should sign an undertaking under the Official Secrets Acts which would render him liable to prosecution if he made unauthorised disclosures ; and

(d) proposals to approach any of the parties involved in an adoption, details of which had been obtained during the research, should be discussed with the Home Office, and implemented only under such conditions as the Home Secretary might stipulate.

5. In many cases, a research worker contemplating research into adoption will be in touch with the Home Office from the outset. Where the research is local in character, the Department will consult the local authority concerned before considering whether to grant an authority. This cannot, of course, be done in the case of research on a national scale which is planned in close association with the Home Office. Local authorities will be informed, either individually or by circular of the grant of any authority which affects their courts. If a request is made to your authority for access to confidential adoption records for research purposes, the inquirer should be told to approach the Under Secretary of State at the above address.

6. Provision for the disclosure of information obtained by officers of courts is made in Rule 2 of the Adoption (Juvenile Courts) Rules, 1965, and in corresponding rules for the High Court and the county courts.

The Rules

7. Rule 1 does not concern local authorities. The other rules contain provisions which are of concern to officers of local authorities carrying out adoption work or acting as guardians *ad litem*.

8. Rules 3, 4, and 7 make provision for the procedure to be followed where leave of the court is sought under sections 34 and 35 of the Adoption Act, 1958 to remove a child from the care and possession of prospective adopters. Section 54 of the Children and Young Persons Act, 1963 extended to proceedings of this kind the power to make rules of procedure.

9. Rule 5 makes amendments to the Rules corresponding to the amendments made by the Adoption Agencies Regulations 1961 to the form of medical report required by the Adoption Agencies Regulations, 1959.

10. Rule 6 stems from comments made by Mr. Justice Roxburgh in the case *In re E. (an infant)* reported in *The Times* on 24th and 25th March, 1960. In that case the consent of both parents to their child's adoption had been dispensed with by the juvenile court hearing the applications. He said :

" It seems to me extraordinary that a person's consent can be dispensed with when he has not even been told that an application for that purpose is being made. I am not thinking of people who cannot be found ; I mean a person who can be and is served with a notice which does indicate that he can oppose the adoption order, but does not indicate that it is an application to have his consent dispensed with."

Courts have no doubt acted on the comments made in that case. The Rule now makes an appropriate addition to the relevant forms.

11. Rule 8 facilitates the United Kingdom subscribing to a Convention on the Adoption of Children now before the Council of Europe. The draft Convention, which aims at harmonising the adoption laws of member states, would call for no changes in the Adoption Act, 1958. Requirements of the Convention would, however, have some bearing on the duties of the guardian *ad litem* appointed by

a court, and the Rule makes formal additions to the schedule of their duties.   In practice, most guardians *ad litem* probably already comply with these requirements.

12. Corresponding provision to the Rules has been made in Rules applying to the High Court and county courts.   A copy of the county court rules is enclosed.

13. An extra copy of this circular is enclosed for the use of the Children's Officer.

NOTE

Issued to the councils of counties, county boroughs and London Boroughs in England and Wales.

Home Office Circular No. 277/1965.   *Dated December 21, 1965 (Extracts).*

THE ADOPTION (JUVENILE COURT) RULES, 1965

1. I am writing to draw your attention to the Adoption (Juvenile Court) Rules, 1965, a copy of which is enclosed, and to suggest certain minor changes of adoption procedure that can be made administratively.

2. . . .

3. Rule 1 remedies a difficulty that has sometimes been met in complying, in the case of children being re-adopted, with the requirement of section 21 (3) of the Adoption Act 1958 that the registration district and sub-district in which the child was born in England or Wales should be entered in the Adopted Children Register.   In such cases, the court normally has before it a copy of the entry in the Adopted Children Register relating to the previous adoption. If that adoption took place before 1st April 1959, the copy would normally give the court no indication of the registration district and sub-district in which the child was born, and, without further inquiry, the court would not be in a position to give appropriate directions to the Registrar General.   The Rule ensures that a juvenile court can supply, in such circumstances, on the request of another juvenile court, a county court or the High Court, a copy of an adoption order which would disclose the details required.

4. Rule 2 widens the circumstances in which information about an adoption is to be disclosed.   First, the amending Rule requires information to be given if a court or public authority (in any part of the world) having power to authorise an adoption requires it for the purpose of the discharge of its duties.   Second, the amending Rule requires information to be disclosed to a person who is authorised in writing by or on behalf of the Secretary of State to obtain it for the purposes of research.   This provision is the outcome of discussions with associations representing bodies concerned with adoption about the need for research, and the terms on which information in confidential records kept by courts, local authorities and adoption societies should be made available to research workers.   The view was taken that a central authority should be responsible for examining the credentials of research workers, for ensuring that genuine and worthwhile research was intended by the person who wanted access to records and that uniform safeguards were imposed.

5. . . .

6. In many cases, a research worker contemplating research into adoption will be in touch with the Home Office from the outset.   Where the research is local in character, the Department will consult the court concerned before considering whether to grant an authority.   This cannot, of course, be done in the case of research on a national scale which is planned in close association with

the Home Office. Clerks to justices will be informed, either individually or by circular, of the grant of any authority which affects their courts. If a request is made to you for access to confidential adoption records for research purposes, the inquirer should be told to approach the Under Secretary of State at the above address.

    7. ...

    8. ...

    9. ...

    10. ...

Other matters

11. The General Register Office find discrepancies from time to time in the details from adoption orders which the Registrar General is required to enter in the Adopted Children Register. In order to save the time of clerks to justices the General Register Office in correspondence and to ensure that the Adopted Children Register is kept on a uniform basis, it would be helpful if the practices suggested in the Appendix to this circular could be adopted by all juvenile courts.

NOTE

This circular was sent to clerks to justices.

APPENDIX

THE ADOPTION (JUVENILE COURT) RULES, 1959

Schedule 1

Form 9

    (a) When evidence is produced of the child's birth in a country other than the United Kingdom, the Isle of Man or the Channel Islands, the best course is to strike out in the body of the adoption order the alternatives relating to place of birth and to insert in column 1 of the Schedule the name of the country. Column 2 of the Schedule should be completed only where the birth occurred in England or Wales.

The Schedule to Forms 9 and 10

    (b) *Column 1.*—Country of birth. Section 21 (2) (b) of the Adoption Act, 1958 enables a court to treat a child whose country of birth is not proved to the satisfaction of the court, as having been born in England if it appears probable that he was born within the United Kingdom, the Channel Islands or the Isle of Man. For this purpose, England includes Wales (section 57 (1) of the Act). The body of Form 9 provides for the insertion of either England or Wales. When, in such a case, the registration district and sub-district in which the court sits is inserted in column 2 of the Schedule, the assumed country of birth should be stated in column 1 as Wales if the court sits in Wales, and England if it is English.

    (c) *Column 3.* Name and Surname of the child. Enter the name or names and surname by which the child is to be known and not his original name, unless no change is to be made.

    (d) *Column 4.* Sex of child. Enter " boy " or " girl " as the case may be rather than " male " or " female ".

    (e) *Columns 5 and 6.* Descriptions of the " occupation " of the adopters and the court making the order sometimes cause difficulties. Vague terms for occupations such as " Employee " or " Factory Worker " should be avoided if possible ; a simple description of the court is all that is needed.

The examples set out opposite illustrate these points.

DATE AND COUNTRY OF BIRTH	REGISTRATION DISTRICT AND SUB-DISTRICT	NAME AND SURNAME OF INFANT	SEX OF INFANT	NAME AND SURNAME ADDRESS AND OCCUPATION OF ADOPTER OR ADOPTERS	DATE OF ADOPTION ORDER AND DESCRIPTION OF COURT BY WHICH MADE
Twenty Sixth December 1965 England	District Bath Sub-District Bath North	John Joseph Smith	Boy	Alfred Smith of 6 Fig Tree Avenue Abingdon, Berkshire. Labourer in Wire Mill and [1] Joan Smith Shop Assistant	Twenty Second June 1964 [2] Abingdon Juvenile Court

[1] The words " Wife " " Housewife " or " of same address " are not needed.
[2] The full title of the court " Juvenile Court for the Petty Sessional Division of Abingdon " is not needed.

Sixth July 1963 Jersey Channel Islands		Deborah Jones	Girl	Charles Hector Jones 60 Beacon Hill, Grimsby, Major, Regular Army and Mary Jones	Second December 1963 [1] Grimsby Juvenile Court

[1] The full title of the court " Grimsby County Magistrates' Juvenile Court sitting at the Court House Brighowgate Grimsby " is not needed.

Twenty Seventh December 1940 Federal German Republic		Penelope Mitchell	Girl	Ronald Brian Joseph Mitchell of 12 Nord Strasse, Munich and 22 London Road, Stafford. Representative Electrical Engineers and Phyllis Mitchell	Fourth October 1965 Stafford Juvenile Court

Fourth January 1964 Isle of Man		John Brown	Boy	George Brown 3, The Ridgeway, Mosborough, Yorkshire. Truck Driver Flour Mill and Margaret Brown	Fourth March 1965 Eckington Juvenile Court

NOTE

The Registrar General has drawn the attention of the Home Office to the Registration of Births, Deaths and Marriage Regulations, 1968, which came into operation on April 1, 1969, and which consolidated with amendments the earlier Regulations. The new Regulations do not prescribe how the sex of a child shall be registered, and the Registrar General is now making the entry "male" or "female" in the birth records instead of "boy" or "girl" as formerly prescribed. It follows that the same change must be made in the Adopted Children Register otherwise short certificates issued from that register could be identified as related to adopted persons. In future, therefore, the sex of the child should be shown in the schedule to Forms 9 and 10 of the Rules as "male" or "female", as the case may be, and not as "boy" or "girl". The examples given on p. 2 of the appendix to the circular require correction in column 4. (Home Office Circular No. 167/1969 dated August 15, 1969.)

Home Office Circular No. 22/1966   *Dated February 3, 1966 (Extracts).*

THE ADOPTION (JUVENILE COURT) RULES, 1965, THE ADOPTION (COUNTY COURT) (AMENDMENT) RULES, 1965

I am directed by the Secretary of State to draw to your attention the Adoption (Juvenile Court) Rules, 1965 (S.I. 1965 No. 2072) and the Adoption (County Court) Rules, (S.I. 1965 No. 2070), which amend the Adoption (Juvenile Court) Rules, 1959 and the Adoption (County Court) Rules, 1959, respectively. Rule 2 of the Juvenile Court Rules and the corresponding Rule 3 of the County Court Rules came into operation on 1st January 1966. The remainder come into operation on 1st March 1966. The Rules which are of particular interest to a probation officer who is appointed guardian *ad litem* are as follows.

2. . . .

3. . . .

4. . . .

5. . . .

6. The additional items of information which the Rule requires the guardian *ad litem* to ascertain are:

    (a) why the applicant wishes to adopt the infant;
    (b) such other information, including an assessment of the applicant's personality and, where appropriate, that of the infant, as has a bearing on the mutual suitability of the applicant and the infant, and on the ability of the applicant to bring up the infant;
    (c) the applicant's religious persuasion, if any.

7. The guardian *ad litem* is also required by the Rule to draw the attention of the court to any difference in age between the applicant and the infant if it is less than the normal difference in age between parents and their children.

8. The Secretary of State suggests that a set of the Adoption Rules should be available for reference in each probation office where they are likely to be needed.

NOTE

This circular was sent to secretaries of Probation Committees (copies to all probation Officers for information).

Home Office Circular No. 205/1965.   *Dated September 9, 1965.*

REGISTRATION UNDER THE NATIONAL HEALTH SERVICE OF CHILDREN AWAITING ADOPTION

1. Paragraph 9 of the explanatory memorandum included as the Appendix to Home Office Circular No. 53/1959 of 25th March, 1959, about the Adoption

Rules described a procedure for the registration of a child who is to be adopted with a doctor under the National Health Service. The arrangement by which the appropriate form, which is part of the explanatory memorandum, is given by the courts to applicants for adoption orders does not provide for the situation of prospective adopters who may wish to have the child registered or re-registered with their doctor under the name by which the child is to be known as soon as he is received into their care and possession. The purpose of this letter is to invite the help of local authorities in remedying this position.

2. Most prospective adopters have an obligation under section 3 (2) of the Adoption Act, 1958, to notify the local authority of their intention to adopt. In the ordinary course, they give notice as soon as they receive the child and this may be some time before they apply for an adoption order. Once notice has been given the local authority has an obligation under section 38 to secure that the child is visited from time to time by officers of the authority who shall satisfy themselves as to his well-being and give such advice as to his care and maintenance as may appear to be needed. Your authority may be willing to agree that the officers carrying out these duties could conveniently draw the attention of prospective adopters to the arrangements for registration by handing them a copy of the enclosed form. Where the local authority have themselves arranged the placing of the child or have received notice of the placing of the child under section 40, they will no doubt arrange for the prospective adopters to be given the form at the earliest possible stage. The use of this specially numbered form, although it does not mention adoption, sets in train a procedure whereby the child's previous medical history is transferred to his record in his new name whilst avoiding unnecessary disclosure of his new name.

3. A supply of the forms is enclosed. More can be obtained from the local executive council of the National Health Service who will be willing to answer any questions about registration arrangements.

4. In a few instances, prospective adopters who have applied for an adoption order will not be granted one and under the new arrangements they may have already registered the child with a doctor in his intended new name. If the local authority knows that an adoption order has not been granted, it would assist the Ministry of Health if the authority would notify the National Health Service Central Register, Smedley Hydro, Southport, Lancashire, so that Health Service records can be corrected as necessary. Preferably the child's medical card should be sent but if it is not available, the information which should be given to the Central Register is the name by which the child was to have been known, his date of birth, and the National Health Service number (if the local authority know it).

5. Records kept by local authorities—for example, health visiting record cards—sometimes link the child's old and new identities. Local authorities will no doubt wish to ensure that any records they keep (apart from confidential adoption records) should not disclose an adopted child's previous identity: when an adoption is known to have taken place new records in the new name should be substituted for those in the old, which should be destroyed.

6. Extra copies of this circular and its enclosure are sent for the information of the Children's Officer and Medical Officer of Health. Copies have also been sent to the Clerk and Medical Officers of Health of authorities exercising delegated health and welfare functions.

NOTE

Issued to the councils of counties, county boroughs and London boroughs in England and Wales.

E.C. 58B

(For issue to a person who
intends to adopt a child)

NATIONAL HEALTH SERVICE

If you have in your care a child whom you intend to adopt, and wish to register or re-register the child with a doctor under the National Health Service, you should fill in the form below and take it to the doctor of your choice. When the doctor accepts the child as a patient, arrangements will be made for you to receive a medical card in the child's new name (if there is a change of name) and with a new National Health Service number which cannot be linked in any way with the child's previous records.

You will notice that there is no reference to adoption in the form itself; please detach it from these notes and use it on its own.

You may have registered the child already with your doctor, using a form provided by the doctor or the Executive Council. If so, you should re-register the child, using the form below if you want to ensure that the special arrangements are made for keeping the adoption confidential.

You may also have received from the Court to which you have applied for an adoption order a form like the one below. If so, and if you have used it, there is no need to fill in the form below. If the Court gives you a form after you have used this one, do not complete it.

If you have the old medical card, you should destroy it when you receive the new one.

E.C. 58B

NATIONAL HEALTH SERVICE

To be completed on behalf of the child

Names by which ⎫ Surname ....
the child is
to be known ⎬ Forenames ....

Date of Birth...

Home Address...

....

Application to be placed on the list of Dr...

Signature of Applicant on behalf of the child...

Date...................................

Doctor's Code No...................................

To be completed by doctor

I accept the child named above for inclusion in my list

Signed...   Date...........................

If claiming a Rural Practice Payment

If Supplying Drugs
Enter D here

Enter distance from main surgery
to patient's residence and inform
Executive Council if claiming for
other than ordinary distance

LIST OF ADOPTION SOCIETIES WHOSE REGISTRATION HAS BEEN REPORTED TO THE HOME OFFICE

Note: The names of the Societies are listed under the areas in which their administrative headquarters are situated, though their activities are not necessarily confined to those areas.

ENGLAND

REGISTRATION AREA	NAME AND ADDRESS OF SOCIETY
BEDFORDSHIRE	Northampton Diocesan Catholic Child Protection and Welfare Society St. Francis Home, 37 Brook Green, London, W.6
BERKSHIRE Reading	Oxford Diocesan Council for Social Work 48 Bath Road, Reading
CAMBRIDGESHIRE	Cambridge Association for Social Welfare 9 Petersfield, Cambridge
CHESHIRE Birkenhead	Diocesan Children's Rescue Society 111 Shrewsbury Road, Birkenhead
Chester	Chester Diocesan Moral Welfare Adoption Society 3 Abbey Green, Chester
DERBYSHIRE Derby	Derby Diocesan Council for Social Work Diocesan House, 3 College Place, Derby
DEVON Exeter	Exeter Diocesan Council for Family and Social Welfare St. Olave's Church House, Marcy Arches Street, Exeter
Plymouth	Plymouth R.C. Diocesan Children's Rescue Society Fr. David Rossiter, The Presbytery, Shortlands, Cullompton, Devon
DORSET	St. Gabriel's Adoption Society 18 Dorchester Road, Weymouth, *or* Health Centre, Westham Road, Weymouth
DURHAM	Durham Diocesan Adoption Society Hallgarth House, Hallgarth Street, Durham
South Shields	Jarrow Deanery Moral Welfare Association 29 King Street, South Shields
Sunderland	Sunderland Social Service Welfare Committee 33 Norfolk Street, Sunderland
ESSEX	Wel-Care 126 New London Road, Chelmsford (formerly Chelmsford Diocesan Moral Welfare Association)
GLOUCESTERSHIRE Bristol	Bristol and Somerset Family Welfare Adoption Society 70 Pembroke Road, Clifton, Bristol 8 Clifton Catholic Children's Society 58 Alma Road, Clifton, Bristol 8
Gloucester	Gloucester Diocesan Council for Social Work College Chambers, College Court, Gloucester

REGISTRATION AREA	NAME AND ADDRESS OF SOCIETY
HAMPSHIRE	The Diocese of Portsmouth R.C. Child Welfare Society 100 Wilton Avenue, Southampton
Portsmouth	Portsmouth Diocesan Council for Social Work 152 Highbury Grove, Cosham, Portsmouth
HERTFORDSHIRE	St. Albans Diocesan Council for Social Work Holywell Lodge, 41 Holywell Hill, St. Albans
LANCASHIRE	Lancaster, Morecambe and District Moral Welfare Association 7 Queen Street, Lancaster Ashton-under-Lyne Adoption Society 105 Wellington Road, Ashton-under-Lyne
Liverpool	Lancashire and Cheshire Child Adoption Council 72 Rodney Street, Liverpool 1 Liverpool Catholic Children's Protection Society 150 Brownlow Hill, Liverpool
Manchester	Manchester and District Child Adoption Society Gaddum House, 16/18 Queen Street, Manchester 2 Salford Catholic Protection and Rescue Society Inc. 390 Parrs Wood Road, Didsbury, Manchester 20
Oldham	Oldham Adoption Society 3 Bertha Street, Shaw, Oldham
Preston	Lancaster Diocesan Protection and Rescue Society 218 Tulketh Road, Preston
Salford	Manchester Diocesan Adoption Society 27 Blackfriars Road, Salford 3
LEICESTERSHIRE Leicester	Diocese of Leicester Council for Social Work 3A West Street, Leicester
LINCOLNSHIRE Lincoln	Lincoln Diocesan Board for Social Work Jews Court, Steep Hill, Lincoln
LONDON BOROUGHS Camden	Baptist Union Adoption Society 4 Southampton Row, W.C.1 Church Adoption Society 4A Bloomsbury Square, W.C.1
Croydon	Mission of Hope Birdhurst Lodge, South Park Hill Road, South Croydon Southwark Catholic Children's Society Russell Hill Road, Purley, Surrey
Haringey	Homeless Children's Aid and Adoption Society 54 Grove Avenue, Muswell Hill, N.10
Islington	National Children's Home and Orphanage Highbury Park, N.5
Kensington and Chelsea	Crusade of Rescue 73 St. Charles Square, Ladbroke Grove, W.10
Lambeth	Church of England Children's Society Old Town Hall, Kennington Road, S.E.11
Redbridge	Dr. Barnardo's Tanners Lane, Barkingside, Ilford

REGISTRATION AREA	NAME AND ADDRESS OF SOCIETY
Southwark	Independent Adoption Society 160 Peckham Rye, London, S.E.22
Westminster	National Adoption Society 47A Manchester Street, Nr. Baker Street, London, W.1 National Children Adoption Assoc. (Inc.) 71 Knightsbridge, S.W.1 International Social Service of Great Britain 70 Denison House, 296 Vauxhall Bridge Road, London, S.W.1 The Phyllis Holman Richards Adoption Society 11 Wilton Place, Knightsbridge, London, S.W.1
NORTHUMBERLAND Newcastle-upon-Tyne	Northern Counties Adoption Society Room 15, 5 Saville Place, Newcastle-upon-Tyne 1 Hexham and Newcastle Diocesan Rescue Society "St. John Bosco", Dene Brow, 9 Jesmond Park West, Newcastle-upon-Tyne 7
NOTTINGHAMSHIRE Nottingham	Catholic Children's Society 7 Colwick Road, West Bridgford, Nottingham Southwell Diocesan Board of Moral Welfare Warren House, 1 Plantagenet Street, Nottingham
SOMERSET Bath	Western National Adoption Society 1 John Street, Bath
STAFFORDSHIRE	Lichfield Diocesan Association for Family Care 23 Greengate Street, Stafford
SUSSEX EAST	Chichester Diocesan Association for Family Social Work Diocesan Church House, 9 Brunswick Square, Hove 2
SUSSEX WEST	Worthing and District Council of Social Service Methold House, 7/9 North Street, Worthing
WARWICKSHIRE Coventry	Father Hudson's Homes Adoption Society Coleshill, Birmingham St. Faith's Shelter Dudley Lodge, 143 Warwick Road, Coventry
WORCESTERSHIRE	Worcester Diocesan Association for Family and Social Service 12 Severn Terrace, Worcester
YORKSHIRE—NORTH RIDING Middlesbrough	Middlesbrough Diocesan Rescue Society 4 Oakfield Road, North Ormesby, Middlesbrough
YORKSHIRE—WEST RIDING Bradford	Bradford Diocesan Family Welfare Committee Church House, North Parade, Bradford 1
Doncaster	Doncaster and District Child Adoption Society 40 Nether Hall Road, Doncaster
Leeds	Leeds Diocesan Rescue Protection and Child Welfare Society Carmel House, Houghley Lane, Leeds 13
Sheffield	Sheffield and District Child Adoption Association (Incorporated) 57 Upper Hanover Street, Sheffield 3

REGISTRATION AREA	NAME AND ADDRESS OF SOCIETY
York	York Adoption Society
	29 Marygate, York

WALES

BRECONSHIRE	Swansea & Brecon Diocesan Moral Welfare Assn.
	57 Sketty Road, Uplands, Swansea
CAERNARVONSHIRE	
Bangor	Bangor Diocesan Adoption Society
	The Vicarage, Llandegai, Bangor
CARMARTHEN	St. David's Diocesan Moral Welfare Committee
	St. Peter's Church House, Nott Square, Carmarthen
DENBIGHSHIRE	Menevia Diocesan Rescue Society
	Bishop's House, Wrexham
GLAMORGAN	
Cardiff	Catholic Rescue Society
	The Presbytery of the Sacred Heart, Broad Street, Leckwith, Cardiff

LIST OF LOCAL AUTHORITIES IN ENGLAND AND WALES THAT ACT AS ADOPTION AGENCIES

Key: A. Indicated that local authority will place children only with prospective adopters resident in the council's area.

B. Indicates that local authority will accept for placing only children resident in the council's area.

Correspondence and enquiries about adoption should be addressed to the Children's Officer for the local authority concerned at the address given below.

LOCAL AUTHORITY			ADDRESS OF CHILDREN'S OFFICER
			ENGLAND—COUNTIES
Cambridgeshire and Isle of Ely			Children's Department, 19 Gloucester Street, Cambridge
Cornwall			County Hall, Station Road, Truro
Cumberland			Children's Department, 23 Portland Square, Carlisle
Devon			County Hall, Topsham Road, Exeter
Dorset			County Hall, Dorchester
Durham	A	B	County Hall, Durham
Essex		B	Liverpool Victoria House, London Road, Chelmsford
Hampshire		B	The Castle, Winchester
Hertfordshire	A		"Balsams", Queen's Road, Hertford
Isle of Wight			County Hall, Newport, Isle of Wight
Kent (with Canterbury)			Springfields, Maidstone
Lancashire	A	B	East Cliff County Offices, Preston
Lincs (Lindsey)			Children's Department, 37 Newland, Lincoln
Monmouthshire			Children's Department, Cambria House, Caerleon
Northamptonshire		B	Children's Department, 53 Billing Road, Northampton
Nottingham	A	B	County Hall, West Bridgford, Nottingham
Oxfordshire	A	B	Children's Department, The Moors, Kidlington, Oxford
Somerset			Children's Department, Bedford House, Park Street, Taunton

STATUTORY INSTRUMENTS, ETC.

LOCAL AUTHORITY			ADDRESS OF CHILDREN'S OFFICER
Suffolk East		B	Rope Walk, Ipswich
Suffolk West		B	3 Honey Hill, Bury St. Edmunds
Surrey	A	B	County Hall, Kingston-on-Thames
Sussex East	A		P.O. Box 5, County Hall, St. Anne's Crescent, Lewes
Warwickshire			Shire Hall, Warwick
Westmorland			County Hall, Kendal
Wiltshire			Children's Department, 5 Polebarn Gardens, Polebarn Road, Trowbridge

ENGLAND—COUNTY BOROUGHS

Barrow-in-Furness		B	52 Paradise Street, Barrow-in-Furness
Birmingham		B	Beaufort House, 91 Lionel Street, P.O. Box 93, Birmingham 3
Blackpool			Children's Department, Sefton Street, Blackpool
Bolton		B	Children's Department, Civic Centre, Bolton
Bootle		B	41 Merton Road, Bootle
Bristol		B	U.T.F. House, Kings Square, Bristol 2
Burnley		B	Children's Department, Town Hall, Burnley
Bury	A	B	Children's Department, 7 Manchester Road, Bury
Carlisle			Children's Department, Civic Centre, Carlisle
Chester			Children's Department, Old School House, Princess Street, Chester
Coventry			New Council Offices, Earl Street (South Side), Coventry
Derby		B	King's Chambers, Queen Street, Derby
Doncaster		B	York House, Cleveland Street, Doncaster
Gateshead		B	Children's Department, Family Advice Centre, 16 Regent Terrace, Gateshead 8
Gloucester			Children's Department, 27 Brunswick Road, Gloucester
Huddersfield	A	B	Children's Department, Ramsden House, 4th Floor, New Street, Huddersfield
Kingston-upon-Hull			Children's Department, 65 Mytongate, Kingston-upon-Hull
Leeds		B	Children's Department, 229 Woodhouse Lane, Leeds 2
Liverpool			Children's Department, Brougham Terrace, Liverpool 6
Manchester		B	Town Hall, Manchester 2
Newport			9 Gold Tops, Newport
Northampton		B	Children's Department, School Buildings, Campbell Square, Northampton
Nottingham	A	B	Children's Department, 126 Mansfield Road, Nottingham
Oxford		B	Children's Department, 77–79 George Street, Oxford
Plymouth			Children's Department, Municipal Offices, Lockyer Street, Plymouth
Portsmouth		B	Children's Department, 51 Kent Road, Southsea, Portsmouth
Preston		B	Children's Department, Guildhall Offices, Guildhall Street, Preston
Reading		B	Children's Department, 7 Cheapside, Reading
Rochdale		B	Children's Department, "Walmsley House", 131 Manchester Road, Rochdale
Rotherham			54 Hollowgate, Rotherham

LOCAL AUTHORITY		ADDRESS OF CHILDREN'S OFFICER
St. Helen's	B	Children's Department, 90 Hardshaw Street, St. Helen's
Sheffield	B	New Oxford House, Barkers Pool, Sheffield
Southampton		Marland House, Civic Centre, Southampton
Stockport		Children's Department, The Old Rectory, Churchgate, Stockport
Stoke-on-Trent	B	Children's Department, 11 Hartshill Road, Stoke-on-Trent
Walsall		Children's Department, Hatherton House, Lower Forster Street, Walsall
Warrington		Children's Department, Museum Street, Warrington
West Bromwich		Children's Department, P.O. Box 40, Town Hall, Lombard Street, West Bromwich
Wigan		Children's Department, Civic Buildings, Parsons Walk, Wigan
Wolverhampton		Children's Department, 49 Waterloo Road, Wolverhampton

LONDON BOROUGHS

Barking	B	Children's Department, 28–30 Ripple Road, Barking, Essex
Barnet	A	Children's Department, Town Hall, Friern Barnet, N.11
Bexley		Western House, Gravel Hill, Bexleyheath, Kent
Bromley		Children's Department, Park House, Bromley, Kent
Camden		Children's Department, 38/50 Bidborough Street, London, W.C.1
Ealing	B	Children's Department, 26 Castlebar Road, Ealing, London, W.5
Greenwich	B	Children's Department, Riverside House, Beresford Street, London, S.E.18
Hackney	B	Children's Department, 1 Hoxton Street, London, N.1
Hammersmith		Children's Department, Old Town Hall, Fulham Broadway, London, S.W.6
Havering		Children's Department, Langton's Billet Lane, Hornchurch, Essex
Hillingdon (In conjunction with Hounslow and Richmond-upon-Thames)		Children's Department, Old Bank House, High Street, Uxbridge, Middlesex
Hounslow (In conjunction with Hillingdon and Richmond-upon-Thames)		Children's Department, Great West Road, Brentford, Middlesex
Islington	B	Children's Department, 341/5 Holloway Road, London, N.7
Lambeth	B	Children's Department, Blue Star House, 234/44 Stockwell Road, London, S.W.9
Lewisham	B	Eros House, Rushey Green, Catford, London, S.E.6
Merton		Children's Department, 116 Kingston Road, London, S.W.19
Newham	B	Children's Department, 99 The Grove, London, E.15
Redbridge	B	Children's Department, 17/23 Clements Road, Ilford, Essex

LOCAL AUTHORITY		ADDRESS OF CHILDREN'S OFFICER
Richmond-upon-Thames (In conjunction with Hillingdon and Hounslow)		Children's Department, Town Hall, Richmond
Tower Hamlets (with City of London)	B	Children's Department, Archer House, 193/197 Bow Road, London, E.3
Wandsworth	B	Children's Department, Municipal Buildings, Wandsworth High Street, London, S.W.18
City of Westminster	B	Children's Department, Westminster City Hall, Victoria Street, London, S.W.1

WALES—COUNTIES

Breconshire	B	County Children's Department, Breconshire County Council, Captain's Walk, Brecon
Carmarthen	A B	Children's Department, 2 Church Street, Carmarthen
Denbighshire (with Flintshire)		Children's Department, Llanrhydd Street, Ruthin, Denbighshire
Flintshire (with Denbighshire)		Children's Department, Shire Hall, Mold, CH7 6NN
Glamorganshire		Glamorgan County Council Offices, Greyfriars Road, Cardiff
Pembrokeshire		County Offices, Haverfordwest

WALES—COUNTY BOROUGHS

Cardiff	City of Cardiff Municipal Offices, Greyfriars Road, Cardiff

GUARDIANSHIP AND MARRIAGE OF MINORS AND DOMESTIC PROCEEDINGS

CONTENTS

SECTION 1.—INTRODUCTORY NOTE

Since the passing of the Guardianship of Infants Act, 1925, jurisdiction under that Act and the Act of 1886, became exercisable by the High Court, County Courts, and Courts of Summary Jurisdiction. Magistrates, it is often said, must have statutory authority for every judicial act they perform. This is certainly true of guardianship proceedings, and whereas the High Court has inherent powers, apart from statute, in relation to the guardianship of minors, magistrates have no such inherent powers. Therefore, while they must follow any decision of the High Court upon the statutes, they must not assume that they can exercise a like power in any case, unless it is clear that the judge was acting under these statutes only, and not by virtue of his greater powers.

Proceedings usually arise out of a dispute between parents, between parent and guardian, or between guardians. Whatever be the ground of the proceedings, the first and paramount consideration must be the welfare of the minor. This, the established practice, was laid down in the 1925 statute itself, and re-enacted in the Guardianship of Minors Act, 1971, which repeals and consolidates the latter Acts.

The powers of Courts of Summary Jurisdiction, though less than those of the High Court and the County Court are considerable. It cannot be doubted that they are important. Where parents are at variance over their children, the welfare of the children is endangered, and in seeking to arrive at the best solution of the problem the court is taking a step which may to a considerable extent determine the future of the children. Time and attention devoted to the hearing of these cases are well spent.

Proceedings under these Acts are domestic proceedings under the Magistrates' Courts Act, 1952 (sections 56 to 58, 60 to 61, pp. 1220 *et seq.*, *post*, and see section 119 (3); 21 Halsbury's Statutes, 3rd Edn., 187), and therefore heard under conditions of restricted publicity. Magistrates may, however, exercise their discretion under the Rules and hear such cases *in camera*, if they are satisfied that this will be in the interests of the minor.

Consent to the marriage of a minor, formerly dealt with in the Act of 1925, is now dealt with in the Marriage Act, 1949; see p. 1215, *post*.

It is the duty of a probation officer if so requested by or on behalf of a court to make a report to the court with a view to assisting it in making an order or provision with respect to the custody, maintenance or education of a child under these Acts. See r. 31 (b) of the Probation Rules, 1965, p. 528, *ante*.

While the consolidation of these earlier Acts is timely, there are still a number of reforms which would be welcomed. There are anomalies between the provision of the Act of 1971 and the Matrimonial Proceedings (Magistrates' Courts) Act, 1960 especially in relation to the care, custody and supervision of children. There is no provision whereby a report under the Probation Rules (*ante*) may be received in evidence without the consent of the parties (*cf.* s. 4 (3) of the Act of 1960). Finally it should be noted that the powers of a guardian are the same as "under the Tenures

Abolition Act, 1660". Seemingly a redefinition of a guardian's powers was considered but rejected apparently on the ground that the law at present is well understood and to amend it might introduce difficulties not hitherto raised.

Appeals from magistrates' courts under the Act of 1971 are assigned to the Family Division of the High Court by the Administration of Justice Act, 1970. As regards matrimonial proceedings the Divorce Reform Act, 1969 and the Matrimonial Proceedings and Property Act, 1970 have made substantial changes in the law and practice of the High Court. These reforms and the creation of the Family Division of the High Court have yet to be matched by corresponding provisions in magistrates' courts. It is necessary, therefore, for a time, for magistrates to be concerned with the concept of the "matrimonial offence". The Law Commission is at present examining the anomalies in the situation and their report may be expected shortly.

SECTION 2.—GUARDIANSHIP OF MINORS

GUARDIANSHIP OF MINORS ACT, 1971

ARRANGEMENT OF SECTIONS

An Act to consolidate certain enactments relating to the guardianship and custody of minors.

[17th February, 1971]

General principles

1. Principle on which questions relating to custody, upbringing etc. of minors are to be decided.—Where in any proceedings before any court (whether or not a court as defined in section 15 of this Act)—

(a) the custody or upbringing of a minor; or

(b) the administration of any property belonging to or held on trust for a minor, or the application of the income thereof,

is in question, the court, in deciding that question, shall regard the welfare of the minor as the first and paramount consideration, and shall not take into consideration whether from any other point of view the claim of the father, or any right at common law possessed by the father, in respect of such custody, upbringing, administration or application is superior to that of the mother, or the claim of the mother is superior to that of the father.

NOTES

"Welfare of the infant."—See note to s. 44 of the Children and Young Persons Act, 1933, p. 50, *ante*. It is to be noticed that the welfare of the infant though the first and paramount consideration is only one amongst several other considerations. The parent, unless he has shown himself unfit to have custody, has generally a right to the custody of his own child; see *Re Thain, Thain* v. *Taylor*, [1926] Ch. 676, C. A.

In the case of *Re Collins (an Infant)*, [1950] Ch. 498; [1950] 1 All E. R. 1057, the Court held that this section was not confined to a case where both parents were living and the issue was between them, and that there was no warrant for the paramountcy of the (deceased) father's religion. See an article at 114 J. P. N. 307. See also *Chipperfield* v. *Chipperfield*, [1952] 1 All E. R. 1360; 116 J. P. 337. For a case in which it was held by Roxburgh, J., that an order of justices appointing a sister of the infant to be joint guardian with the father, a widower, in order that she could later apply for sole custody be quashed as not being for the benefit of the infant, see *Re H.* (1959), *Times*, November 6.

See also note "Mother" to s. 9, p. 1202, *post*.

Wishes of the child.—In the High Court an infant who is of sufficient age and intelligence is often questioned as to his wishes. Justices should of course follow the same practice.

For a case in which the Court of Appeal took into account the wishes of a girl aged eleven, see *D.* v. *D.* (1958), *Times*, March 21.

Religious persuasion.—See note at p. 168, *ante*.

"Custody."—As to whether a court of summary jurisdiction can order strangers to give up child to parent, see articles at 101 J. P. N. 417 and 107 J. P. N. 445.

"Father's right."—Father's common law right to control infant children re-affirmed by Cassels, J., in an enticement case (*Lough* v. *Ward*, [1945] 2 All E. R. 338).

In the case of *W.* v. *W. and C.*, [1968] 3 All E. R. 408, it was stated that it is a general principle, in questions of custody, that it is better for a boy of eight years of age, other things being equal, to be with his father rather than his mother, even if he has been with his mother up to that age; but see *Re C. (A.) (an infant)*, C. v. C., [1970] 1 All E. R. 309.

2. Equal right of mother to apply to court.—The mother of a minor shall have the like powers to apply to the court in respect of any matter affecting the minor as are possessed by the father.

NOTE

Father.—Both father and mother may apply for an order for custody of or access to the minor (s. 9, p. 1201, *post*).

Appointment, removal and powers of guardians

3. Rights of surviving parent as to guardianship.—(1) On the death of the father of a minor, the mother, if surviving, shall, subject to the provisions of this Act, be guardian of the minor either alone or jointly with any guardian appointed by the father; and—

(a) where no guardian has been appointed by the father; or
(b) in the event of the death or refusal to act of the guardian or guardians appointed by the father,

the court may, if it thinks fit, appoint a guardian to act jointly with the mother.

(2) On the death of the mother of a minor, the father, if surviving, shall, subject to the provisions of this Act, be guardian of the minor either alone or jointly with any guardian appointed by the mother; and—

(a) where no guardian has been appointed by the mother; or
(b) in the event of the death or refusal to act of the guardian or guardians appointed by the mother,

the court may, if it thinks fit, appoint a guardian to act jointly with the father.

NOTES

No guardian appointed by mother.—See *Re H., supra.*

Father.—See s. 14 (3), *post.*

Shall . . . be guardian.—By s. 18 (3) Matrimonial Proceedings and Property Act, 1970 a parent who is declared to be unfit to have the custody of a child of the family, shall not, on the death of the other parent, be entitled as of right to the custody or guardianship of that child.

4. Power of father and mother to appoint testamentary guardians.—(1) The father of a minor may by deed or will appoint any person to be guardian of the minor after his death.

(2) The mother of a minor may by deed or will appoint any person to be guardian of the minor after her death.

(3) Any guardian so appointed shall act jointly with the mother or father, as the case may be, of the minor so long as the mother or father remains alive unless the mother or father objects to his so acting.

(4) If the mother or father so objects, or if the guardian so appointed considers that the mother or father is unfit to have the custody of the minor, the guardian may apply to the court, and the court may either—

(a) refuse to make any order (in which case the mother or father shall remain sole guardian); or

(b) make an order that the guardian so appointed—

      (i) shall act jointly with the mother or father; or

      (ii) shall be the sole guardian of the minor.

(5) Where guardians are appointed by both parents, the guardians so appointed shall, after the death of the surviving parent, act jointly.

(6) If under section 3 of this Act a guardian has been appointed by the court to act jointly with a surviving parent, he shall continue to act as guardian after the death of the surviving parent; but, if the surviving parent has appointed a guardian, the guardian appointed by the court shall act jointly with the guardian appointed by the surviving parent.

NOTES

See s. 10, p. 1205, *post*, as to the powers of the court to make and vary orders under subsection (4) of this section.

"Maintenance."—Includes education; see s. 20 (2), p. 1212, *post*.

Guardianship on death of parent.—The word "father" in ss. 4 and 5 does not, apparently, include putative father; but see s. 14 (3) *post*. The word "mother" appears to include the mother of an illegitimate child. She may appoint a guardian; see *Re A., S.* v. *A.* (1940), 164 L. T. 230. By s. 10, p. 1205, *post*, where there is a sole guardian to the exclusion of the mother or father, the powers of the court may be exercised at any time and include a power to vary or discharge an order.

Appointment by deed or will.—The appointment of a guardian by will would be proved by production of probate. Where appointment is by deed, the deed would have to be produced and examined. It must be stamped (*Fengl* v. *Fengl*, [1914] P. 274; 84 L. J. P. 29).

Enforcement.—See note to s. 13, p. 1207, *post*.

Attachment of earnings.—See note to s. 13, p. 1207, *post*.

Illegitimate infant.—By s. 14 (3), p. 1207, *post*, it is provided that a person who is the natural father of an illegitimate infant and who is entitled to his custody by virtue of an order in force under s. 9, as applied by that section, shall be treated as if he were the lawful father of the infant; but any appointment of a guardian made by virtue of that subsection under s. 4 (1) of this Act shall be of no effect unless the appointer is entitled to the custody of the infant immediately before his death.

Father.—See s. 14 (3), *post*.

5. Power of court to appoint guardian for minor having no parent etc.—(1) Where a minor has no parent, no guardian of the person, and no other person having parental rights with respect to him, the court, on the application of any person, may, if it thinks fit, appoint the applicant to be the guardian of the minor.

(2) A court may entertain an application under this section to appoint a guardian of a minor notwithstanding that, by virtue of a resolution under section 2 of the Children Act, 1948, a local authority have parental rights with respect to him; but where on such an application the court appoints a guardian the resolution shall cease to have effect.

NOTES

"Having parental rights."—Examples are a local authority under a care order (s. 20 Children and Young Persons Act, 1969) and a local authority by virtue of a resolution under s. 2 Children Act, 1948.

Father.—See s. 14 (3), *post*.

6. Power of High Court to remove or replace guardian.—The High Court may, in its discretion, on being satisfied that it is for the welfare of the minor, remove from his office any testamentary guardian or any guardian appointed or acting by virtue of this Act, and may also, if it deems it to be for the welfare of the minor, appoint another guardian in place of the guardian so removed.

7. Disputes between joint guardians.—Where two or more persons act as joint guardians of a minor and they are unable to agree on any question affecting the welfare of the minor, any of them may apply to the court for its direction, and the court may make such order regarding the matters in difference as it may think proper.

NOTE

See s. 11, *post* as to the power of the court to make and vary orders under this section.

8. Continuation of certain powers of guardians. 1660 c. 24.—Every guardian under this Act shall have all such powers over the estate and person or over the estate (as the case may be) of a minor as any guardian appointed by will or otherwise has under the Tenures Abolition Act, 1660 or otherwise.

Orders for custody and maintenance

9. Orders for custody and maintenance on application of mother or father.—(1) The court may, on the application of the mother or father of a minor (who may apply without next friend), make such order regarding—

(a) the custody of the minor; and

(b) the right of access to the minor of his mother or father,

as the court thinks fit having regard to the welfare of the minor and to the conduct and wishes of the mother and father.

(2) Where the court makes an order under subsection (1) of this section giving the custody of the minor to the mother, the court may make a further order requiring the father to pay to the mother such weekly or other periodical sum towards the maintenance of the minor as the court thinks reasonable having regard to the means of the father.

(3) An order may be made under subsection (1) or (2) of this section notwithstanding that the parents of the minor are then residing together, but—

(a) no such order shall be enforceable, and no liability thereunder shall accrue, while they are residing together; and

(b) any such order shall cease to have effect if for a period of three months after it is made they continue to reside together.

(4) An order under subsection (1) or (2) of this section may be varied or discharged by a subsequent order made on the application of either parent or (in the case of an order under subsection (1)) after the death of either parent on the application of any guardian under this Act.

NOTES

"Maintenance."—Includes education; see s. 20, p. 1212, *post*.

In determining the amount, regard must be had to the means of the mother as well as to those of the father (*Re T. (an Infant)*, [1953] 2 All E. R. 830; 117 J. P. 517).

Maintenance to continue until 21.—See s. 12, *post*.

The Court.—This is defined in s. 15, p. 1207, *post*.

Application by mother.—The mother may apply without next friend. Before the passing of the Married Women's Property Act, 1882, a married woman had to sue by next friend, but after the passing of that Act it was possible for her to proceed without next friend, and apparently she may so apply under this Act, even if she herself is a minor.

Application by father.—It is arguable that a deed of separation between the parents, with conditions as to custody of a child, is not a bar to an application under these Acts; see a question and answer at 101 J. P. N. 417.

"Access."—It sometimes happens that the party not having custody desires an order, as to access but not custody. There seems no reason why such an order should not be made.

As to access by a mother who has committed adultery, see *Stark v. Stark and Hitchins*, [1910] P. 190; 79 L. J. P. 98; *B. v. B.*, [1924] P. 176; 93 L. J. P. 84, and *Re A. and B. (Infants)*, [1897] 1 Ch. 786; 66 L. J. Ch. 592. It appears that even where a parent has committed adultery there may be circumstances in which it is still for the welfare of the infant that such parent should have access to, or even custody of the infant. See also an article at 99 J. P. N. 528. For a review of the cases in which access may be denied see *C. v. C.* (1971), *Times*, May 28; and *M. (P.) v. M. (C.)* (1971), 115 Sol. Jo. 444 (C. A.).

Venue.—In courts of summary jurisdiction, the venue was formerly where the respondent to the application resides; *R. v. Sandbach Justices, Ex parte Smith*, [1951] 1 K. B. 62; [1950] 2 All E. R. 781; 114 J. P. 514, but see now s. 15 (1), p. 1207, *post*.

"Minor."—A minor is a person under eighteen years of age. A person becomes eighteen years of age at the commencement of the relevant anniversary of his birth (Family Law Reform Act, 1969, s. 9 (1)). The infant himself may make application, see Rules of the Supreme Court, and it would seem he may apply in the lower courts.

Illegitimate children.—By s. 14 (1), p. 1207, *post*, orders relating to custody and access, but not to maintenance, may be made under the section in respect of illegitimate children. Maintenance is a matter for proceedings under the Affiliation Proceedings Act, 1957.

"Mother."—In the case of an illegitimate child, the mother is not considered to have the same rights as the mother of a legitimate child; see *Barnardo v. McHugh*, [1891] A. C. 388; 55 J. P. 628; and other cases; but she is liable to maintain it and has a better right to its custody, in ordinary circumstances, than any one else (see, however, *Re A. (an Infant)*, [1955] 2 All E. R. 202). Further, she can appoint a guardian; see Schedule to the Guardianship of Infants Act, 1925, repealed and replaced by Sched. II to the Marriage Act, 1949, p. 1218, *post*.

In *Re B. (An Infant)*, [1962] 1 All E. R. 872 it was held that there is no settled rule of law that, where the custody of an infant is in question, a child of tender years should remain in the custody of the mother.

See also *Re L. (An Infant)*, [1962] 3 All E. R. 1 in which Lord Denning, M.R., said : " while a judge is right to give great weight to the welfare of the children, and indeed to make it, as the statute says, the first and paramount consideration, he must nevertheless remember that while it is the paramount consideration it is not the sole consideration.

In *H. v. H. and C.*, [1969] 1 All E. R. 262 the father was awarded custody and care and control since in all the circumstances it would have been very upsetting to remove a child suddenly from a house to which he was used. *Per* Salmon, L.J.,: "From the point of view of common sense and ordinary humanity, all things being equal the best place for any small child is with its mother." *Per curiam*: in cases of this nature the judge should in addition to receiving evidence of an affidavit see the parties concerned as the question of custody and the presenting of evidence is very often a decisive matter.

In *Re F. (an infant)*, [1969] 2 Ch. 238; [1969] 2 All E. R. 766, Megarry, J., referred to the case of *Re L. (an infant)*, *supra*, and said that the court should consider and weigh all the circumstances that are of any relevance, giving the welfare of the infant especial weight. Nevertheless, this process cannot be analysed or carried out according to any formula, and must depend on the exercise of a judicial discretion after all relevant factors have been considered.

" **Father.**"—The putative father of an illegitimate child may apply for an order as to custody or access; see s. 14 (1), p. 1207, *post*.

In *Re H. (Infants)* (1965), 109 Sol Jo. 575, the Court of Appeal dismissed an appeal by the mother of two illegitimate infants from the decision of Pennycuick, J., in chambers affirming the order of the St. Albans' justices giving custody of the children to their putative father. The Master of the Rolls said that he was not sure that the mother of an illegitimate child had a legal claim superior in law to that of the putative or natural father, when one considered the statutes and particularly the Legitimacy Act, 1959. Winn, L.J., concurring, said that he accepted the submission that by force of s. 3 (1) of the Legitimacy Act, 1959, (now re-enacted in s. 14 (1), *post*), in any proceedings under s. 5 of the Guardianship of Infants Act, 1886 (now this section), by force of s. 1 of the Act of 1925 (now s. 1 of this Act), the meaning of the word "father" was to be taken to comprise not only a lawful father but a putative father, so far as the latter meaning might have relevance.

Contents of orders.—In courts of summary jurisdiction the Magistrates' Courts Act and Rules, 1968 apply. See also the Guardianship of Infants (Summary Jurisdiction) Rules, 1925, p. 1258, *post*. It is suggested that where the proceedings relate to several infants there should be a separate order in respect of each.

Custody to third party.—In *J. v. C.*, [1970] A. C. 668; [1969] 1 All E. R. 788, the infant born of Spanish parents was placed with foster parents who later returned to Spain, taking the infant with them. He returned to the foster parents in 1961, and on the application of the foster parents was taken into care in October 1961. The natural parents then applied for the return of the child, and the local authority took proceedings to make the infant a ward of court. An order was made in July 1965 by Ungoed-Thomas, J., that the foster parents should have care and control of the infant. In May 1968 the natural parents applied for care and control. The case again appeared before Ungoed-Thomas, J., who made no order, thus in effect continuing in force the order of 1965. The Court of Appeal upheld the order of 1965 and the natural parents appealed to the House of Lords, where it was held: the judge having applied the right principles in the exercise of his discretion, the appeal would be dismissed, because—

(i) whatever may have been the position in law before the passing of the Guardianship of Infants Act, 1925, by s. 1 of that Act the first and paramount consideration in custody matters was the welfare of the infant; and the latter part of that section did not call for, or imply, any construction on the natural meaning of the first part so as to limit its application to disputes between parents;

(ii) since there were substantial differences between an adoption order and an order giving care and control of an infant, it could not validly be argued that the judge's order was in effect an adoption order which, by reason of lack of parental consent, he would not have had jurisdiction to make;

(iii) although the existence of an order of a foreign court would not in itself prevent an English court from making an order with regard to the welfare of the infant, since no order had been made by a Spanish court no consideration of comity would prevent the court from exercising its jurisdiction.

On whom order to be served.—A copy of the order should be served on each respondent to the application and on any person in whose custody the infant is for the time being. See s. 13, p. 1206, *post*.

Effect of marriage of minor.—By s. 2 of the Marriage Act, 1949, p. 1215, *post,* a marriage solemnized between persons either of whom is under the age of sixteen shall be void. The marriage of a minor daughter puts an end to the guardianship of the parents at common law; see *Mendes* v. *Mendes* (1747), 3 Atk. 619; 1 Ves. Sen. 89.

Whether this is so in the case of a minor son is open to doubt. It may be noted, however, that under s. 3 of the Marriage Act, 1949, which deals with consent to the marriage of a minor, a minor who is a widower or widow is excluded from the operation of the Section. In any case marriage would, however, be a ground upon which application for discharge of an order under the Act could be entertained.

Reference may be made to articles at 104 J. P. N. 35 and 108 J. P. N. 14.

" **Costs.**"—In courts of summary jurisdiction justices have a general power to order payment of costs, under s. 55 of the Magistrates' Courts Act, 1952, and enforcement will be under that Act.

Against whom proceedings may be taken.—The Acts deal with matters in issue between persons having a right to lawful custody of an infant, and it is doubtful whether proceedings can be taken under these Acts against a stranger who not being a parent or guardian retains possession of an infant. The remedy would be in the High Court, to which application might be made for *habeas corpus*.

See a question and answer (No. 4) at 101 J. P. N. 417.

Variation of orders.—This section does not require that there should be fresh evidence to justify variation. Generally, it is unlikely that a court would vary its order except upon new circumstances being proved, or upon evidence coming to light which was not available when the order was made. As to *res judicata*, see *R.* v. *Middlesex Justices, Ex parte Bond*, [1933] 1 K. B. 72; 96 J. P. 487 and *Re F. (W.) (an Infant)*, [1969] 2 Ch. 269; [1969] 3 All E. R. 595; 133 J. P. 723. However, the welfare of the infant being the first and paramount consideration, it might be proper for magistrates to vary an order even where the additional evidence could have been given at the original hearing.

In *Skinner* v. *Carter*, [1948] Ch. 387; [1948] 1 All E. R. 917; 112 J. P. 329, the Court of Appeal held that it was not competent for justices to challenge an adoption order which they were informed was made in favour of "spouses" who were bigamously married, and reversed the decision of Vaisey, J. ([1948] 1 All E. R. 42), discharging an order made by justices under the Guardianship of Infants Acts, 1886 and 1925, for the maintenance of an adopted infant by the "guardian" who was the male adopter.

As to the evidence necessary to support an application to vary, see *Re Wakeman, Wakeman* v. *Wakeman*, [1947] Ch. 607; [1947] 2 All E. R. 74; 111 J. P. 373 in which Jenkins, J., said "I think too that the absence from s. 3 (4) of the Act (now s. 9 (4) of this Act) of any express reference to fresh evidence suggests that the court was intended to have greater latitude in dealing with applications under that subsection than it has under analogous statutory provisions which expressly require the production of fresh evidence."

So far as maintenance is concerned there is also the general power conferred by s. 53 of the Magistrates' Courts Act, 1952; 21 Halsbury's Statutes, 3rd Edn., 187, to revoke, revive or vary an order made by a court of summary jurisdiction for the periodical payment of money.

Venue for variation.—In *Re D. (an Infant)*, [1953] 2 All E. R. 1318, C. A.; 118 J. P. 25, justices for E. had made an order dealing with custody, access and maintenance. Later the husband applied to the W. justices, in whose area he then resided, for the variation of the order, asking for certain provisions as to care and control. The Court of Appeal held that the W. justices had jurisdiction to vary the order, under s. 1 (1) of the Guardianship and Maintenance of Infants Act, 1951 (now s. 15 (1) of the Act). As to venue when one party lives in Scotland see s. 15, *post*.

What court may vary.—Where the High Court has dealt, or is dealing with, a question of custody a court of summary jurisdiction should usually refrain from acting, but see the case of *Vigon* v. *Vigon and Kuttner*, [1929] P. 157; 93 J. P. 112. See, however, *Re C. and C. (Infants)* (1952), *Times*, 10th December, in which it was held that there was no impropriety in proceedings before justices being continued where the High Court had granted an interim injunction restraining the father of infants from taking them out of the jurisdiction.

Children Act, 1948.—Where an order of any court is in force giving the custody of a child to any person, the foregoing provisions of this Part of this Act (*i.e.*, ss. 1 to 5 of the Children Act, 1948, pp. 880 *et seq.*, *ante*) shall have effect in relation to the child as if for references to the parents or guardian of the child or to a parent or guardian of his there were substituted references to that person (*ibid.*, s. 6 (2) p. 890, *ante*).

Legal Aid.—Legal aid will be available to any person to whom a certificate has been issued under the Legal Aid (General) Regulations, 1971: S.I. 1971 No. 62.

Ward of court.—A guardian when in complete agreement with other guardians is not a suitable respondent to a summons to make an infant a ward of court. (*Practice Note*, [1962] 1 All E. R. 156).

Taking infant out of the jurisdiction.—When an infant is the subject of a custody order (or a care and control order) made by the High Court which provides that the infant may not go or be taken out of the jurisdiction without the leave of the court, or is the subject of an injunction restraining persons from taking the infant out of the jurisdiction, the assistance of the Home Office is available to prevent the unauthorised removal of the infant, see *Practice Note*, [1963] 3 All E. R. 66, dated July 15, 1963.

Infant out of the jurisdiction.—The English courts may make an order notwithstanding the child is outside the jurisdiction, *Philips* v. *Philips* (1944), 60 T. L. R. 395, C. A., *Delph* v. *Delph* (1955), *Times*, April 26. (The Hague Convention on Recognition of Divorces and Legal Separation, adopted October, 1968, does not apply to orders for the custody of children).

Custody. Division of custody rights.—In the case of *Re W.* (*J.C.*) (*An Infant*), [1963] Ch. 556; [1963] 2 All E. R. 706, the mother of an infant appealed against a magistrates' order that the custody of the infant should be given to the father but that the child's care and control should be given to the mother. Mr. Justice Pennycuick held that the magistrates had no power to make such an order.

The father appealed to the Court of Appeal against that decision, and it was held that the magistrate had power to make the order. The appeal was allowed and the decision of the magistrate restored ([1964] Ch. 202; [1963] 3 All E. R. 459; 127 J. P. 529 (C.A.)) but as to split orders under the Matrimonial Proceedings (Magistrates' Courts) Act, 1960 see *Wild* v. *Wild*, [1969] P. 33; [1968] 3 All E. R. 608; 132 J. P. 572.

10. Orders for custody and maintenance where person is guardian to exclusion of surviving parent.—(1) Where the court makes an order under section 4 (4) of this Act that a person shall be the sole guardian of a minor to the exclusion of his mother or father, the court may—

    (a) make such order regarding—

        (i) the custody of the minor; and
        (ii) the right of access to the minor of his mother or father,

    as the court thinks fit having regard to the welfare of the minor; and

    (b) make a further order requiring the mother or father to pay to the guardian such weekly or other periodical sum towards the maintenance of the minor as the court thinks reasonable having regard to the means of the mother or father.

(2) The powers conferred by subsection (1) of this section may be exercised at any time and include power to vary or discharge any order previously made under those powers.

NOTES

Father.—See s. 14 (3), *post*.

Maintenance to continue until 21.—See s. 12, *post*.

11. Orders for custody and maintenance where joint guardians disagree.—The powers of the court under section 7 of this Act shall, where one of the joint guardians is the mother or father of the minor, include power—

    (a) to make such order regarding—

        (i) the custody of the minor; and

        (ii) the right of access to the minor of his mother or father,

    as the court thinks fit having regard to the welfare of the minor;

    (b) to make an order requiring the mother or father to pay such weekly or other periodical sum towards the maintenance of the minor as the court thinks reasonable having regard to the means of the mother or father;

    (c) to vary or discharge any order previously made under that section.

NOTE

Maintenance.—See s. 12, *post*.

12. Orders for maintenance of persons between 18 and 21.—(1) An order under section 9, 10 or 11 of this Act for the payment of sums towards the maintenance of a minor may require such sums to continue to be paid in respect of any period after the date on which he ceases to be a minor but not extending beyond the date on which he attains the age of twenty-one; and any order which is made as aforesaid may provide that any sum which is payable thereunder for the benefit of a person who has ceased to be a minor shall be paid to that person himself.

(2) Subject to subsection (3) of this section and to section 14 (4) of this Act, where a person who has ceased to be a minor but has not attained the age of twenty-one has, while a minor, been the subject of an order under this Act or under any enactment repealed by this Act, the court may, on the application of either parent of that person or of that person himself, make an order requiring either parent to pay—

    (a) to the other parent;

    (b) to anyone else for the benefit of that person; or

    (c) to that person himself,

in respect of any period not extending beyond the date when he attains the said age, such weekly or other periodical sum towards his maintenance as the court thinks reasonable having regard to the means of the person on whom the requirement is imposed.

(3) No order shall be made under subsection (2) of this section, and no liability under such an order shall accrue, at a time when the parents of the person in question are residing together, and if they so reside for a period of three months after such an order has been made it shall cease to have effect.

(4) An order under subsection (2) of this section may be varied or discharged by a subsequent order made on the application of any person by whom payments were required to be made under the previous order.

13. Enforcement of orders for custody and maintenance.—(1) Where an order made by a magistrates' court under this Act contains a provision committing to the applicant the legal custody of any minor, a copy of the order may be served on any person in whose actual custody the minor may for the time being be, and thereupon the provision may, without prejudice to any other remedy open to the applicant, be enforced under section 54 (3) of the Magistrates' Courts Act, 1952, as if it were an order of the court requiring that person to give up the minor to the applicant.

(2) Any person for the time being under an obligation to make payments in pursuance of any order for the payment of money under this Act shall give notice of any change of address to such person (if any) as may be specified in the order, and any person failing without reasonable excuse to give such a notice shall be liable on summary conviction to a fine not exceeding £10.

(3) An order of a magistrates' court for the payment of money under this Act may be enforced in like manner as an affiliation order, and the enactments relating to affiliation orders shall apply accordingly with the necessary modifications.

NOTE

Enforced ... as an affiliation order.—See Magistrates' Courts Act, ss. 74–76, 1952, and Magistrates' Courts Rules, 1968. See also Attachment of Earnings Act, 1971, s. 1 and Sched. I. Orders for payment of maintenance under ss. 9 (2), 10 (1), 11, or 12 (2) are all maintenance orders to which that Act applies.

Illegitimate children

14. Application of Act to illegitimate children.—(1) Subject to the provisions of this section, subsection (1) of section 9 of this Act shall apply in relation to a minor who is illegitimate as it applies in relation to a minor who is legitimate, and references in that subsection, and in any other provision of this Act so far as it relates to proceedings under that subsection, to the father or mother or parent of a minor shall be construed accordingly.

(2) No order shall be made by virtue of subsection (1) of this section under subsection (2) of the said section 9.

(3) For the purposes of sections 3, 4, 5 and 10 of this Act, a person being the natural father of an illegitimate child and being entitled to his custody by virtue of an order in force under section 9 of this Act, as applied by this section, shall be treated as if he were the lawful father of the minor; but any appointment of a guardian made by virtue of this subsection under section 4 (1) of this Act shall be of no effect unless the appointor is entitled to the custody of the minor as aforesaid immediately before his death.

(4) No order shall be made under section 12 (2) of this Act requiring any person to pay any sum towards the maintenance of an illegitimate child of that person.

Jurisdiction and procedure

15. Courts having jurisdiction under this Act.—(1) Subject to the provisions of this section, "the court" for the purposes of this Act means—

(a) the High Court;

(b) the county court of the district in which the respondent (or any of the respondents) or the applicant or the minor to whom the application relates resides; or
(c) a magistrates' court having jurisdiction in the place in which any of the said persons resides.

(2) A magistrates' court shall not be competent to entertain—

(a) any application (other than an application for the variation or discharge of an existing order under this Act) relating to a minor who has attained the age of sixteen unless the minor is physically or mentally incapable of self-support; or
(b) any application involving the administration or application of any property belonging to or held in trust for a minor, or the income thereof.

(3) A county court or magistrates' court shall not have jurisdiction under this Act in any case where the respondent or any of the respondents resides in Scotland or Northern Ireland—

(a) except in so far as such jurisdiction may be exercisable by virtue of the following provisions of this section; or
(b) unless a summons or other originating process can be served and is served on the respondent or, as the case may be, on the respondents in England or Wales.

(4) An order under this Act giving the custody of a minor to the mother, whether with or without an order requiring the father to make payments to the mother towards the minor's maintenance, may be made, if the father resides in Scotland or Northern Ireland and the mother and the minor in England or Wales, by a magistrates' court having jurisdiction in the place in which the mother resides.

(5) It is hereby declared that a magistrates' court has jursidiction—

(a) in proceedings under this Act by a person residing in Scotland or Northern Ireland against a person residing in England or Wales for an order relating to the custody of a minor (including, in the case of proceedings by the mother, an order requiring the father to make payments to the mother towards the minor's maintenance);
(b) in proceedings by or against a person residing in Scotland or Northern Ireland for the revocation, revival or variation of any such order.

(6) Where proceedings for an order under subsection (1) of section 9 of this Act relating to the custody of a minor are brought in a magistrates' court by a woman residing in Scotland or Northern Ireland, the court shall have jursidiction to make any order in respect of the minor under that subsection on the application of the respondent in the proceedings.

NOTES

Powers of magistrates' court.—Such courts have no inherent powers in relation to guardianship, such as are possessed by the High Court but must rely on statutory authority. In particular it is to be noted that a court cannot make an order in respect of an infant of sixteen years of age and upwards, unless the infant is mentally or physically incapable of self-support, nor can the court deal with questions of property administration.

This section allows, however, that the court may vary an order even though the infant is over sixteen years of age.

A married woman who applies for an order under the Matrimonial Proceedings (Magistrates' Courts) Act, 1960 may also apply for an order under this Act in respect of the custody and maintenance of the children of the marriage, as she is entitled to have the benefit of both statutes. *Re Kinseth, Kinseth* v. *Kinseth,* [1947] 1 All E. R. 201.

It is permissible to discharge an order for custody and maintenance under the Matrimonial Proceedings (Magistrates' Courts) Act, 1960 (see p. 1224, *post*), and to make a fresh order under the Guardianship of Infants Acts (now this Act) (*Flood* v. *Flood,* [1948] 2 All E. R. 712; 112 J. P. 416).

The making of orders under both statutes is less likely to be applied for now that the limits of maintenance have been repealed and in view of the provisions of s. 4 of the Act of 1960.

Venue.—If the mother and the infant reside in England or Wales the English court in whose jurisdiction the mother resides has jurisdiction even when the father resides in Scotland or Northern Ireland. Either parent residing in Scotland or Northern Ireland may apply to a court in England for an order, or the revocation, revival or variation of an order, the English court has jurisdiction in the latter case to hear a summons against a respondent residing in Scotland. Where there is an application for an order under s. 9 (1) by a woman residing in Scotland the court has power to make any order under that subsection on the application of the respondent.

A summons under s. 2 of the Maintenance Orders Act, 1950, must be served personally; *ibid.,* s. 15.

See notes " Variation of orders " and " Venue for variation " at p. 1204, *ante.*

Enforcement of order.—A provision as to custody may be enforced by *habeas corpus.* Where an order has been made by a court of summary jurisdiction, a copy may be served on any person having actual custody of the infant, and if such person fails to obey the order he can be dealt with under s. 54 of the Magistrates' Courts Act, 1952. It is suggested that the clause in the order should be worded.— "that the mother do grant the father access to the said . . .". The advantage of this is that it is a definite order which can be enforced under s. 54.

A maintenance order made by a court of summary jurisdiction under this Act is enforceable in the same manner as an affiliation order. There is no appeal against the enforcement by justices of maintenance arrears: *Re Stern (An Infant), Stern* v. *Stern,* [1950] Ch. 550; [1950] 2 All E. R. 160; 114 J. P. 361.

Second application in respect of same infant.—Where a court has determined and dismissed an application on its merits, the matter is not *res judicata.* See *Re F. (W.) (an infant),* [1969] 2 Ch. 269; [1969] 3 All E. R. 595; 133 J. P. 723 in which it was held that although the first decision before the justices did not make the matter *res judicata* and therefore they had jurisdiction to hear the second summons, nevertheless since no further evidence was there adduced, it was not proper for them to have heard the second application and they ought to have stopped the second hearing as soon as they realised that no further evidence was to be adduced.

Duration of order.—It is sometimes argued from the decision in *Re Witten (An Infant)* (1887), 57 L. T. 336; 3 T. L. R. 811, that the court has a discretion as to the period the order is to remain in force. It will in any event cease when minority ceases. Note the limitation upon the jurisdiction of courts of summary jurisdiction in sub-s. (2).

Custody order already in existence.—Where an order as to custody is in force in respect of the infant, under the Summary Jurisdiction (Separation and Maintenance) Acts, it would not seem proper for a court of summary jurisdiction to make an order as to custody, but possibly it might make an order as to access.

Children Act, 1948.—See note at p. 1204, *ante,* as to the effect of the Children Act, 1948, where a court order is in force giving the custody of a child to any person.

Procedure.—Proceedings under this Act, other than those for enforcement or variation of orders for the payment of money, are domestic proceedings to which ss. 56 to 61 of the Magistrates' Courts Act, 1952, pp. 1220 *et seq.*, *post*, apply. They may be heard *in camera*, in the interests of the infant, see the Rules.

"Amount of order."—Small maintenance payments within the meaning of s. 65 of the Income and Corporation Taxes Act, 1970, must be made without deduction of income tax (sub-s. (2), *ibid.*).

It is pointed out in H.O. Circular No. 180/46, dated July 31, 1946, that it is not inconsistent with the principle of the Family Allowances Act, 1945, that a woman shall receive a family allowance in addition to any sum (including the maximum sum) to be paid under an order.

16. Appeals and procedure.—(1) Where any application has been made under this Act to a county court, the High Court shall, at the instance of any party to the application, order the application to be removed to the High Court and there proceeded with on such terms as to costs as it thinks proper.

(2) An appeal shall lie to the High Court from any order made by a county court under this Act.

(3) Subject to subsection (4) of this section, where on an application to a magistrates' court under this Act the court makes or refuses to make an order, an appeal shall lie to the High Court.

(4) Where an application is made to a magistrates' court under this Act, and the court considers that the matter is one which would more conveniently be dealt with by the High Court, the magistrates' court may refuse to make an order, and in that case no appeal shall lie to the High Court.

NOTES

Appeal and transfer to High Court.—The appeal conferred by sub-ss. (2) and (3) is to the Family Division of the High Court.

It is submitted that where some point of unusual importance or difficulty arises, it may be proper to refuse to make any order, leaving the applicant to apply to the High Court.

The parties have no right to have a case transferred to the High Court from a court of summary jurisdiction (*Beaumont* v. *Beaumont*, [1938] Ch. 551 ; [1938] 2 All E. R. 226). It is doubtful whether a case could be stated upon a point of law, though *Peagram* v. *Peagram*, [1926] 2 K. B. 165 ; 90 J. P. 136, is sometimes quoted in support of the view that a case can be stated.

In *Re L*——, [1951] 1 All E. R. 912 ; 115 J. P. 271, it was decided that justices might refer to the High Court an application to vary an existing order.

A further appeal lies to the Court of Appeal, and apparently leave to appeal is not necessary (*Re W. (an Infant)*, [1953] 2 All E. R. 1337, C. A.).

The appellant's solicitor should apply for a statement of the reasons for the decision complained of, and lodge it with the judge's clerk when obtaining an appointment for the purpose of obtaining the judge's direction as to the hearing of the appeal, in accordance with *Practice Direction*, [1955] 1 All E. R. 784.

Expediting appeals.—In *Clark* v. *Clark* (1971), 115 Sol. Jo. 76, practitioners were reminded that in appeals relating to children it was always open to apply to the Clerk of the rules for the hearing to be expedited.

Where on an appeal from a decision of magistrates' court which is by way of rehearing, the court is empowered to draw inferences of fact, the discretion is still that of the magistrates. If, however, circumstances have so changed that the substratum of the magistrates' decision no longer exists, then unless the case is such that it ought to be remitted for rehearing, the appellate court exercises an unfettered discretion *de novo* on the facts as they exist at the time of the appeal. But if that substratum still exists, the appellate court must put into the scales the facts as found by magistrates, together with any relevant new facts, and then seek to exercise a discretion in the same way as it appears that the magistrates would have done had the full facts been before them, *per* Megarry, J., in *Re B. (T. A.) (an infant)*, [1971] Ch. 270; [1970] 3 All E. R. 705; 135 J. P. 7.

But see also *Re O. (infants)*, [1971] Ch. 748; [1971] 2 All E. R. 744, C. A. This was an appeal from a decision ordering a rehearing in a case where justices had awarded custody, without the benefit of a welfare report, to the father. Davies, L.J. took the view that "the law now is that if an appellate court is satisfied that the decision of the court below is wrong, it is its duty to say so and act accordingly ... I am quite unable to subscribe to the view that a decision must be treated as sacrosanct because it was made in the exercise of discretion; so to do might well perpetuate injustice ... "

Stay of order.—As to stay pending appeal, see *Re S. (an Infant)*, [1958] 1 All E. R. 783; 122 J. P. 245, to the effect that when an order involves transfer of custody a stay should be granted pending appeal, or the court should generally postpone its operation for a few days. In *B. (B.) v. B. (M.)*, [1969] P. 103; [1969] 1 All E. R. 891, it was decided that justices had power to grant a stay of execution in cases under the Matrimonial Proceedings (Magistrates' Courts) Act, 1960, and should grant a stay unless there were reasons of urgency for affecting a change of custody. The importance of granting a stay in appropriate cases is illustrated by the case of *Re Desmerault* (1971), *Times*, February 11. Later in an address to magistrates (1971), *Times*, June 12, the Lord Chancellor said magistrates should hesitate to disturb the *status quo* and pointed to the advisability of the court taking the initiative and granting a stay of execution.

Cases already before the High Court.—

A circular issued by the senior Registrar of the Divorce Registry, reproduced by permission of the President at 115 J. P. N. 676 is as follows:—

" At a meeting of Judges convened by the President to consider this matter, the following conclusion was reached:

" It is considered that while it is right and proper when the issue of custody is actually pending in a divorce suit that the justices should adjourn the guardianship summons on the lines laid down in *Higgs* v. *Higgs* ([1941] 1 All E. R. 214; 105 J. P. 119) and *Knott* v. *Knott* ([1935] P. 158; 99 J. P. 329), there is no ground restricting the concurrent jurisdiction of the magistrates' courts in a guardianship case when the issue of custody has not been raised in the divorce suit merely because it is open to a spouse to take appropriate steps to enable him or her to raise the question of custody in the divorce suit. It is felt that the provision in s. 7 (3) of the Guardianship of Infants Act, 1925 (now 16 (3) of this Act) affords a sufficient safeguard to any spouse who desires, however belatedly, to have issue of custody decided in the High Court."

17. Saving for powers of High Court and other courts.—(1) Nothing in this Act shall restrict or affect the jurisdiction of the High Court to appoint or remove guardians or otherwise in respect of minors.

(2) Nothing in section 15 (4), (5) or (6) of this Act shall be construed as derogating from any jurisdiction exercisable, apart from those provisions, by any court in England or Wales; and it is hereby declared that any jurisdiction conferred by those provisions is exercisable notwithstanding that any party to the proceedings is not domiciled in England and Wales.

Supplementary

18. Consequential amendments, repeals and savings.—(1) The enactments specified in Schedule 1 to this Act shall have effect subject to the amendments there specified, being amendments consequential on this Act.

(2) The enactments specified in Schedule 2 to this Act are hereby repealed to the extent specified in the third column of that Schedule.

(3) Any application, order or other thing made, done or having effect under or for the purposes of an enactment repealed by this Act and pending or in force immediately before the commencement of this Act shall be deemed to have been made or done under or for the purposes of the corresponding enactment in this Act; and any proceeding or other thing begun under any enactment so repealed may be continued under this Act as if begun thereunder.

(4) So much of any document as refers expressly or by implication to any enactment repealed by this Act shall, if and so far as the nature of the subject-matter of the document permits, be construed as referring to this Act or the corresponding enactment therein, as the case may require.

(5) Nothing in this section shall be taken as prejudicing the general application of section 38 of the Interpretation Act, 1889 with regard to the effect of repeals.

19. [*This section is now spent*].

20. Short title, interpretation, extent and commencement.—(1) This Act may be cited as the Guardianship of Minors Act, 1971.

(2) In this Act "maintenance" includes education.

(3) References in this Act to any enactment are references thereto as amended, and include references thereto as applied, by any other enactment.

(4) This Act—

   (a) so far as it amends the Maintenance Orders Act, 1950, extends to Scotland and Northern Ireland;
   (b) so far as it amends the Army Act, 1955 and the Air Force Act, 1955, extends to Northern Ireland,

but, save as aforesaid, extends to England and Wales only.

(5) This Act shall come into force at the expiration of the period of one month beginning with the day on which it is passed.

Section 18 (1)   SCHEDULE 1

CONSEQUENTIAL AMENDMENTS

[In so far as these amendments affect the Acts printed in this book they have been incorporated in the texts of the provisions affected.]

SCHEDULE 2   Section 18 (2)
REPEALS

[In so far as these repeals affect the Acts printed in this book they have been incorporated in the texts of the provisions affected.]

CUSTODY OF CHILDREN ACT, 1891

[54 & 55 Vict. c. 3]

An Act to amend the Law relating to the Custody of Children.

[26th March 1891.]

ARRANGEMENT OF SECTIONS

1. Power of court as to production of child.—Where the parent of a child applies to the High Court or the Court of Session for a writ or order for the production of the child, and the Court is of opinion that the parent has abandoned or deserted the child, or that he has otherwise so conducted himself that the Court should refuse to enforce his right to the custody of the child, the Court may in its discretion decline to issue the writ or make the order.

2. Power to court to order repayment of costs of bringing up child.—If at the time of the application for a writ or order for the production of the child, the child is being brought up by another person, or is boarded out by the guardians of a poor law union, or by a parochial board in Scotland, the Court may, in its discretion, if it orders the child to be given up to the parent, further order that the parent shall pay to such person, or to the guardians of such poor law union, or to such parochial board, the whole of the costs properly incurred in bringing up the child, or such portion thereof as shall seem to the Court to be just and reasonable, having regard to all the circumstances of the case.

3. Court in making order to have regard to conduct of parent.— Where a parent has—

(a) abandoned or deserted his child ; or
(b) allowed his child to be brought up by another person at that person's expense, or by the guardians of a poor law union, for such a length of time and under such circumstances as to satisfy the Court that the parent was unmindful of his parental duties ;

the Court shall not make an order for the delivery of the child to the parent, unless the parent has satisfied the Court that, having regard to the welfare of the child, he is a fit person to have the custody of the child.

4. Power to court as to child's religious education.—Upon any application by the parent for the production or custody of a child, if the Court is of opinion that the parent ought not to have the custody of the child, and that the child is being brought up in a different religion to that in which the parent has a legal right to require that the child should be brought up, the Court shall have power to make such order as it may think fit to secure that the child be brought up in the religion in which the parent has a legal right to require that the child should be brought up. Nothing in this Act contained shall interfere with or affect the power of the Court to consult the wishes of the child in considering what order ought to be made, or diminish the right which any child now possess to the exercise of its own free choice.

5. Definitions of " parent " and " person."—For the purposes of this Act the expression " parent " of a child includes any person at law liable to maintain such child or entitled to his custody, and " person " includes any school or institution.

6. Short title.—This Act may be cited as the Custody of Children Act, 1891.

NOTES

By s. 1, p. 1213, *ante,* the court is to regard the welfare of the child as the first and paramount consideration.

The reference to the guardians of a poor law union should no doubt be treated, now that the poor law has been abolished, as a reference to the Supplementary benefits commission or to a local authority, as the case may be.

SECTION 3.—MARRIAGE OF MINORS

INTRODUCTORY NOTE

By the Age of Marriage Act, 1929 (now s. 2 of the Marriage Act, 1949), it was enacted that no marriage could lawfully take place between parties either of whom was under sixteen years of age. Above that age, a minor needs the consent of his parents or guardians, but if such consent cannot be obtained or is refused, application may be made to the court, and if the court gives consent such consent is of the same effect as if it had been given by the parent.

The question of consent to the marriage of a minor was formerly dealt with in the Guardianship of Infants Act, 1925, s. 9. That section was repealed by the Marriage Act, 1949, and replaced by s. 3 of that Act.

MARRIAGE ACT, 1949
[12, 13 & 14 Geo. 6, c. 76]

*   *   *   *

2. Marriages of persons under sixteen.—A marriage solemnized between persons either of whom is under the age of sixteen shall be void.

NOTE

Void marriage.—The invalidity of a marriage where the girl is under sixteen does not make the man guilty of an offence against s. 6 or s. 14 of the Sexual Offences Act, 1956 (sexual intercourse or indecent assault), if he reasonably believes she is his lawful wife; *ibid.*, ss. 6, 14.

3. Marriages of persons under twenty-one.—(1) Where the marriage of an infant, not being a widower or widow, is intended to be solemnized on the authority of a certificate issued by a superintendent registrar under Part III of this Act, whether by licence or without licence, the consent of the person or persons specified in the Second Schedule to this Act shall be required:

Provided that—

(a) if the superintendent registrar is satisfied that the consent of any person whose consent is so required cannot be obtained by reason of absence or inaccessibility or by reason of his being under any disability, the necessity for the consent of that person shall be dispensed with, if there is any other person whose consent is also required; and if the consent of no other person is required, the Registrar General may dispense with the necessity of obtaining any consent, or the court may, on application being made, consent to the marriage, and the consent of the court so given shall have the same effect as if it had been given by the person whose consent cannot be so obtained;

(b) if any person whose consent is required refuses his consent, the court may, on application being made, consent to the marriage, and the consent of the court so given shall have the same effect as if it had been given by the person whose consent is refused.

(2) The last foregoing subsection shall apply to marriages intended to be solemnized on the authority of a common licence, with the substitution of references to the ecclesiastical authority by whom the licence was granted for references to the superintendent registrar, and with the substitution of a reference to the Master of the Faculties for the reference to the Registrar General.

(3) Where the marriage of an infant, not being a widower or widow, is intended to be solemnized after the publication of banns of matrimony then, if any person whose consent to the marriage would have been required under this section in the case of a marriage intended to be solemnized otherwise than after the publication of the banns, openly and publicly declares or causes to be declared, in the church or chapel in which the banns are published, at the time of the publication, his dissent from the intended marriage, the publication of banns shall be void.

(4) A clergyman shall not be liable to ecclesiastical censure for solemnizing the marriage of an infant after the publication of banns without the consent of the parents or guardians of the infant unless he had notice of the dissent of any person who is entitled to give notice of dissent under the last foregoing subsection.

(5) For the purposes of this section, " the court " means the High Court, the county court of the district in which any applicant or respondent resides, or a court of summary jurisdiction having jurisdiction in the place in which any applicant or respondent resides and rules of court may be made for enabling applications under this section—

(a) if made to the High Court, to be heard in chambers;
(b) if made to the county court, to be heard and determined by the registrar subject to appeal to the judge;
(c) if made to a court of summary jurisdiction, to be heard and determined otherwise than in open court,

and shall provide that, where an application is made in consequence of a refusal to give consent, notice of the application shall be served on the person who has refused consent.

(6) Nothing in this section shall dispense with the necessity of obtaining the consent of the High Court to the marriage of a ward of court.

NOTES

This section is a re-enactment, with modifications, of s. 9 of the Guardianship of Infants Act, 1925. Section 36 (1) of the Interpretation Act, 1889; 32 Halsbury's Statutes, 3rd Edn., 456, applies. The section is printed as amended by the Family Law Reform Act, 1969, s. 2 (2).

"**Infant.**"—See s. 1 (2) Family Law Reform Act, 1969, and s. 78 (1) of the Marriage Act, 1949, as amended.

Consents required.—Adoptive parents will be treated as parents, whose consent is required; see Adoption Act, 1958, s. 13 (1), p. 1047, *ante.*
Where a local authority has passed a resolution in accordance with s. 2 of the

Children Act, 1948, assuming parental rights and powers in respect of a child in its care, the consent of that local authority should be obtained. This applies only while the resolution remains in force, which cannot be after the infant has attained the age of 18. As to an infant subject to a care order, see the Children and Young Persons Act, 1969, p. 124, *ante*. Notice would no doubt be served on the parent as well as the local authority.

The same consents are required when the marriage is intended to be solemnised under the Marriage (Registrar General's Licence) Act, 1970 (s. 3, *ibid*.).

Consent where parent, etc., is absent or inaccessible or under disability.— The procedure in such a case necessarily differs from that where consent is refused. If there is no respondent upon whom a notice is required to be served, the application must be heard *ex parte*, and if there are no respondents to such application, the question formerly arose whether the county court or the magistrates' court had jurisdiction to entertain it. The section now defines "the court" as the High Court, the county court of the district in which any applicant or respondent resides, or a court of summary jurisdiction having jurisdiction in the place in which any applicant or respondent resides and the effect of the amendment is that either the county court or the magistrates' court may deal with such an application.

Absence or inaccessibility it is submitted must not be too widely interpreted. A person may be accessible, although he is in a place in which a notice cannot be served effectively upon him. It may be quite possible to communicate with him. Absence is no doubt meant to include the case of a person whose whereabouts is unknown or uncertain.

The point is that it must be impossible to obtain consent. A prisoner of war or a person in enemy occupied territory is almost certainly inaccessible. Disability may be from lunacy or some similar cause.

The first part of proviso (a) deals with cases in which the superintendent registrar and not the court is concerned. If consent of A and B is required, and A is inaccessible, the registrar may act on the consent of B, but if B is also inaccessible the question arises, must he dispense with both consents, or does the case come within the second part of the proviso, under which either the Registrar-General or the court can exercise a discretion, the Registrar-General dispensing with consent or the court granting it.

It is sometimes argued that the word " person " should be interpreted as " person or persons," and that where two consents are required, and both persons are inaccessible, the case falls within the second part of proviso (a), and not the first part. See articles at 109 J. P. N. 315, and 110 J. P. N. 402.

Where the marriage is intended to be solemnised under the Marriage (Registrar General's Licence) Act, 1970 the superintendent registrar shall not be required to and the Registrar General may, dispense with the consent of that person, whether or not there is any other person whose consent is also required (s. 6, *ibid*.).

Where consent refused.—In courts of summary jurisdiction, notices are to be served as if they were summonses. Consequently a notice cannot be served in any part of the British Isles where a summons issued in England could not be served. In such cases application may be made to the High Court. See a question and answer at 104 J. P. N. 491.

The hearing in a court of summary jurisdiction is a domestic proceeding governed by the Magistrates' Courts Act, 1952, ss. 56 to 61, pp. 1220 *et seq., post*. The court may go still further and under the Rules hear the case *in camera*. As the hearing is as if the application were a complaint for an order, evidence should be taken on oath and cross-examination permitted. Procedure on the hearing of a complaint is laid down in the Magistrates' Courts Act, 1952, s. 45; 32 Halsbury's Statutes, 2nd Edn., 458. A full note of the proceedings is desirable. The consent, if given, should be in writing and signed as an order. In this respect the provisions of s. 2 (3) Family Law Reform Act, 1969, p. 1306, *post*, should be noted.

The High Court.—*I.e.* the Family Division, (Administration of Justice Act, 1970, s. 1 and Sched. I).

County court.—Applications to the court should be made by originating application under Order VI, Rule 4 of the County Courts Rules, 1936; S. R. & O. 1936 No. 626/L. 17, as amended. For further details, see the County Court Practice.

Rule 10 of the Supreme Court, 1965, Order No. 55, p. 1265, *post*, provide for the removal of applications to the High Court and for appeals to that court.

Retracting consent.—As a parent can retract a consent to marriage (*Hodgkinson v. Wilkie* (1795), 1 Hag. Con. 262), it would seem that a court can also do so upon a fresh application and fresh evidence.

Costs.—It is doubtful whether on an application for consent to marriage a court of summary jurisdiction has power to award costs. See a question and answer at 103 J. P. N. 743.

Marriage by banns.—As to marriages intended to be solemnized after the publication of banns, where a person entitled to give notice of dissent has given such notice, it appears that the consent of the court would not avail and that, therefore, justices should not entertain an application. The point is discussed at 114 J. P. N. 121.

Appeal.—It was held in a case under the Guardianship of Infants Act, 1925, that there is no appeal where the justices refuse consent to marry: *Re Queskey*, [1946] Ch. 250; [1946] 1 All E. R. 717; 110 J. P. 272.

Rules of procedure.—The existing Rules, made under the Guardianship of Infants Acts are continued in force by virtue of s. 79 (2) of this Act; 17 Halsbury's Statutes, 3rd Edn., 44.

Enquiries.—It is the duty of a probation officer, if requested by the court, to make enquiries with respect to an application under this section. See r. 31 (e) of the Probation Rules, 1965, p. 527, *post.*

SECOND SCHEDULE   Section 3

CONSENTS REQUIRED TO THE MARRIAGE OF AN INFANT BY COMMON LICENCE OR SUPERINTENDENT REGISTRAR'S CERTIFICATE

1. Where the Infant is Legitimate

Circumstances	*Person or Persons whose consent is required*
1. Where both parents are living:	
(a) if parents are living together;	Both parents.
(b) if parents are divorced or separated by order of any court or by agreement;	The parent to whom the custody of the infant is committed by order of the court or by the agreement, or, if the custody of the infant is so committed to one parent during part of the year and to the other parent during the rest of the year, both parents.
(c) if one parent has been deserted by the other;	The parent who has been deserted.
(d) if both parents have been deprived of custody of infant by order of any court.	The person to whose custody the infant is committed by order of the court.
2. Where one parent is dead:	
(a) if there is no other guardian;	The surviving parent.
(b) if a guardian has been appointed by the deceased parent.	The surviving parent and the guardian if acting jointly, or the surviving parent or the guardian if the parent or guardian is the sole guardian of the infant.
3. Where both parents are dead.	The guardians or guardian appointed by the deceased parents or by the court under section 3 or 5 of The Guardianship of Minors Act, 1971.

II. WHERE THE INFANT IS ILLEGITIMATE

Circumstances	*Person whose consent is required*
If the mother of the infant is alive.	The mother, or if she has by order of any court been deprived of the custody of the infant, the person to whom the custody of the infant has been committed by order of the court.
If the mother of the infant is dead.	The guardian appointed by the mother.

MAGISTRATES' COURTS ACT, 1952

[15 & 16 Geo. 6 & 1 Eliz. 2, c. 55]

*　　　*　　　*　　　*　　　*

Domestic proceedings

56. Domestic proceedings and constitution of courts.—(1) In this
Act the expression " domestic proceedings " means proceedings—

(a) under the Guardianship of Minors Act, 1971;

(b) under the Summary Jurisdiction (Separation and Maintenance)
Acts, 1895 to 1949;

(c) under section three or section four of the Maintenance Orders
(Facilities for Enforcement) Act, 1920;

(d) under subsection (3) of section four of the Family Allowances
Act, 1945, or under that subsection as applied by subsection (2)
of section nineteen of the National Insurance Act, 1946;

(e) under section three of the Marriage Act, 1949,

other than proceedings for the enforcement of an order made under any
of the enactments mentioned in paragraphs (a) and (b) of this subsection,
or for the variation of any provision for the payment of money contained
in an order made under any of those enactments, or in an order made or
confirmed under the enactments mentioned in paragraph (c) of this
subsection.

(2) A magistrates' court when hearing domestic proceedings shall be
composed of not more than three justices of the peace, including, so far
as practicable, both a man and a woman.

NOTES

This section is printed as amended by the Guardianship of Minors Act, 1971.

Affiliation proceedings.—By s. 5 of the Legitimacy Act, 1959, domestic proceedings include applications for an affiliation order under the Affiliation Proceedings
Act, 1957, s. 44 of the National Assistance Act, 1948, or s. 26 of the Children Act,
1948, other than proceedings for enforcement, etc.

Justices of the Peace for the City of London.—These do not exercise jurisdiction in domestic proceedings, which are dealt with by the Metropolitan stipendiary
magistrates and justices for the Inner London area, see s. 119 (3) of this Act.

Revocation, revival and variation of orders.—See s. 8 (3) of the Matrimonial
Proceedings (Magistrates' Courts) Act, 1960, p. 1233, *post.*

57. Sittings of magistrates' courts for domestic proceedings.—
(1) The business of magistrates' courts shall, so far as is consistent with
the due dispatch of business, be arranged in such manner as may be
requisite for separating the hearing and determination of domestic proceedings from other business.

(2) No person shall be present during the hearing and determination by a magistrates' court of any domestic proceedings, except—

    (a) officers of the court;

    (b) parties to the case before the court, their solicitors and counsel, witnesses and other persons directly concerned in the case, and other persons whom either party desires to be present;

    (c) solicitors and counsel in attendance for other cases;

    (d) representatives of newspapers or news agencies;

    (e) any other person whom the court may permit to be present, so, however, that permission shall not be withheld from a person who appears to the court to have adequate grounds for attendance.

(3) When hearing domestic proceedings, a magistrates' court may, if it thinks it necessary in the interest of the administration of justice or of public decency, direct that any persons, not being officers of the court or parties to the case, the parties' solicitors or counsel, or other persons directly concerned in the case, be excluded during the taking of any indecent evidence.

(4) Where the same parties are parties to domestic proceedings and to proceedings for the enforcement of an order made under the Summary Jurisdiction (Separation and Maintenance) Acts, 1895 to 1949, or the Guardianship of Minors Act, 1971, or made or confirmed under the Maintenance Orders (Facilities for Enforcement) Act, 1920, or for the variation of any provision for the payment of money contained in an order made or confirmed under any of those Acts, and the proceedings are heard together by a magistrates' court, the provisions of the last two preceding subsections shall, unless the court otherwise determines, have effect as if the whole of those proceedings were domestic proceedings.

(5) The powers conferred on a magistrates' court by this section shall be in addition and without prejudice to any other powers of the court to hear proceedings *in camera*.

(6) Nothing in this section shall affect the exercise by a magistrates' court of the power to direct that witnesses shall be excluded until they are called for examination.

NOTE

" **In camera.**"—See the Guardianship of Infants (Summary Jurisdiction) Rules, 1925, p. 1258, *post*.

Where an appeal is brought against a decision of a court which had power to sit in private, the court hearing the appeal shall have power to sit in private during the proceedings on the appeal (Domestic and Appellate Proceedings (Restrictions of Publicity) Act, 1968, s. 1).

58. Newspaper reports of domestic proceedings.—(1) It shall not be lawful for the proprietor, editor or publisher of a newspaper or periodical to print or publish, or cause or procure to be printed or published, in it any particulars of domestic proceedings in a magistrates' court other than the following, that is to say,—

    (a) the names, addresses and occupations of the parties and witnesses;

  (b) the grounds of the application, and a concise statement of the
      charges, defences and counter-charges in support of which
      evidence has been given;
  (c) submissions on any point of law arising in the course of the pro-
      ceedings and the decision of the court on the submissions;
  (d) the decision of the court, and any observations made by the
      court in giving it.

(2) Any person acting in contravention of this section shall be liable
on summary conviction to imprisonment for a term not exceeding four
months or a fine not exceeding one hundred pounds or both.

(3) No prosecution for an offence under this section shall be begun
without the consent of the Attorney General.

(4) Nothing in this section shall prohibit the printing or publishing of
any matter in a newspaper or periodical of a technical character *bona fide*
intended for circulation among members of the legal or medical professions.

NOTE

Trial by jury.—In proceedings for an offence against this section, the defendant, if
he appears, has a right to claim trial by jury, in accordance with s. 25, p. 276, *ante*.

*   *   *   *

60. Report by probation officer on means of parties.—(1) Where
in any domestic proceedings in which an order may be made for the
periodical payment of money by any person, or in any proceedings for
the enforcement or variation of any such order, or in any proceedings in
any matter of bastardy, a magistrates' court has requested a probation
officer to investigate the means of the parties to the proceedings, the
court may direct the probation officer to report the result of his investigation to the court in accordance with the provisions of this section:
    Provided that in the case of any such domestic proceedings no direction
to report to the court shall be given to a probation officer under this
subsection until the court has determined all issues arising in the proceedings other than the amount to be directed to be paid by such an
order.

(2) Where the court directs a probation officer under this section to
report to the court the result of any such investigation as aforesaid, the
court may require him—

  (a) to furnish to the court a statement in writing about his investiga-
      tion, which shall be read aloud in the presence of such parties
      to the proceedings as may be present at the hearing; or
  (b) to make an oral statement to the court about his investigation.

(3) Immediately after the statement of the probation officer has been
read aloud or made, as the case may be, under the last preceding subsection, the court shall ask each party to the proceedings whether he or
she objects to anything contained in the statement; and where objection
is made the court shall require the probation officer to give evidence on
oath about his investigation.

(4) Any statement made by a probation officer in a statement furnished
or made by him under subsection (2) of this section, or any evidence

which he is required to give under subsection (3) of this section, may be received by the court as evidence, notwithstanding anything to the contrary in any enactment or rule of law relating to the admissibility of evidence.

NOTES

This section is printed as amended by the Legitimacy Act, 1959, s. 5 (2).

It is important to observe carefully the restriction imposed by the proviso to sub-s. (1), see *Higgs* v. *Higgs*, [1941] 1 All E. R. 214; 105 J. P. 119.

Matrimonial Proceedings (Magistrates' Courts) Act, 1960.—For the application of that Act to sub-s. (1) of this section see s. 4 (8) of the above mentioned statute, p. 1233, *post*.

" **Determined all issues.**"——The exercise by the court of its special powers under s. 4 (1) of the Matrimonial Proceedings (Magistrates' Courts) Act, 1960, p. 1231, *post* are excepted.   See s. 4 (8), *ibid*.

61. Examination of witnesses by court.—Where in any domestic proceedings, or in any proceedings for the enforcement or variation of an order made in domestic proceedings, or in proceedings in any matter of bastardy, it appears to a magistrates' court that any party to the proceedings who is not legally represented is unable effectively to examine or cross-examine a witness, the court shall ascertain from that party what are the matters about which the witness may be able to depose or on which the witness ought to be cross-examined, as the case may be, and shall put, or cause to be put, to the witness such questions in the interests of that party as may appear to the court to be proper.

MATRIMONIAL PROCEEDINGS (MAGISTRATES' COURTS) ACT, 1960
[8 & 9 Eliz. 2, c. 48]
ARRANGEMENT OF SECTIONS

An Act to amend and consolidate certain enactments relating to matrimonial proceedings in magistrates' courts and to make in the case of other proceedings the same amendments as to the maximum weekly rate of the maintenance payments which may be ordered by a magistrates' court as are made in the case of matrimonial proceedings.   [29th July, 1960.]

1. Jurisdiction of magistrates' court in matrimonial proceedings.—(1) A married woman or a married man may apply by way of complaint to a magistrates' court for an order under this Act against the other party to the marriage on any of the following causes of complaint arising during the subsistence of the marriage, that is to say, that the defendant—

(a) has deserted the complainant; or

(b) has been guilty of persistent cruelty to—

    (i) the complainant; or

    (ii) an infant child of the complainant; or

    (iii) an infant child of the defendant who, at the time of the cruelty, was a child of the family; or

(c) has been found guilty—

    (i) on indictment, of any offence which involved an assault upon the complainant; or

    (ii) by a magistrates' court, of an offence against the complainant under section twenty, forty-two, forty-three or forty-seven of the Offences against the Person Act, 1861, being, in the case of the said section forty-two, an offence for which the defendant has been sentenced to imprisonment or any other form of detention for a term of not less than one month; or

    (iii) of, or of an attempt to commit, an offence under any of sections one to twenty-nine of the Sexual Offences Act, 1956, or under section one of the Indecency with Children Act, 1960, against an infant child of the complainant, or against an infant child of the defendant who, at the time of the commission of or attempt to commit the offence, was a child of the family; or

(d) has committed adultery; or

(e) while knowingly suffering from a venereal disease has insisted on, or has without the complainant being aware of the presence of that disease permitted, sexual intercourse between the complainant and the defendant; or

(f) is for the time being an habitual drunkard or a drug addict; or

(g) being the husband, has compelled the wife to submit herself to prostitution or has been guilty of such conduct as was likely to result and has resulted in the wife's submitting herself to prostitution; or

(h) being the husband, has wilfully neglected to provide reasonable maintenance for the wife or for any child of the family who is, or would but for that neglect have been, a dependant; or

(i) being the wife, has wilfully neglected to provide, or to make a proper contribution towards, reasonable maintenance for the husband or for any child of the family who is, or would but for that neglect have been, a dependant, in a case where, by reason of the impairment of the husband's earning capacity through age, illness, or disability of mind or body, and having regard to any resources of the husband and the wife respectively which are, or should properly be made, available for the purpose, it is reasonable in all the circumstances to expect the wife so to provide or contribute.

(2) A magistrates' court shall have jurisdiction to hear a complaint under this section—

(a) if at the date of the making of the complaint either the complainant or the defendant ordinarily resides within the petty sessions area for which that court acts; or

(b) except in the case of a complaint by virtue of paragraph (c) of the foregoing subsection, if the cause of complaint arose wholly or partly within the said petty sessions area; or

(c) in the case of a complaint by virtue of the said paragraph (c), if the offence or attempt to which the complaint relates occurred within the said petty sessions area.

(3) The jurisdiction conferred by the last foregoing subsection—

(a) shall, subject to section 11 of the Administration of Justice Act, 1964, and any determination of the committee of magistrates' thereunder, be exercisable notwithstanding that the defendant resides in Scotland or Northern Ireland if the complainant resides in England and the parties last ordinarily resided together as man and wife in England; and

(b) is hereby declared to be exercisable where the complainant resides in Scotland or Northern Ireland if the defendant resides in England:

Provided that nothing in this subsection shall be construed as enabling a court to include in an order under this Act against a person residing in Scotland or Northern Ireland a provision such as is mentioned in paragraph (a) of subsection (1) of section two of this Act.

NOTES

This section is printed as amended by the Administration of Justice Act, 1964; 21 Halsbury's Statutes, 3rd Edn., 345.

" **Other form of detention.**"—*E.g.*, detention in a detention centre under s. 4 of the Criminal Justice Act, 1961, p. 402, *ante*, or borstal training under s. 20 of the Criminal Justice Act 1948, p. 305, *ante*, or s. 28 of the Magistrates' Courts Act, 1952, p. 307, *ante*.

" **Magistrates' court shall have jurisdiction.**"—The general provision as to jurisdiction made by s. 44 of the Magistrates' Courts Act, 1952, does not apply.

In *Kaye* v. *Kaye*, [1965] P. 100; [1964] 1 All E. R. 620; 128 J. P. 193, it was held that a magistrates' court had jurisdiction to entertain maintenance proceedings notwithstanding that proceedings for wilful neglect to maintain were current in the High Court, but, save in exceptional cases, the justices should, as a matter of discretion adjourn the proceedings before them for the High Court proceedings to be decided. In this case the wife's application remained on the file of the High Court at the time when she applied to magistrates for an order. The magistrates' order was set aside and the case remitted to a fresh panel for a rehearing at which, if the wife did not discontinue the High Court proceedings it would be open to the husband to contend that the justices should not hear the case.

" Resides."—See first part of note " Residence " at p. 162, *ante*.

England.—This includes Wales; see the Wales and Berwick Act, 1746 (32 Halsbury's Statutes, 3rd Edn., 412).

Definitions.—For " child," " child of the family," " dependant," " drug addict," " habitual drunkard " and " petty sessions area," see s. 16 (1), p. 238, *post*.

Indecency with Children Act, 1960, s. 1.—See p. 398, *ante*.

Notice to parent of child (other than a party) of court's power to make provision with regard to children.—See Rule 4 of the Magistrates' Courts (Matrimonial Proceedings) Rules, 1960, p. 1269, *post*.

For form of notice see Form 4 in the Schedule to the Rules, p. 1273, *post*.

Legal aid.—Legal aid will be available to any person to whom a certificate has been issued under the Legal Aid (General) Regulations, 1971, S.I. 1960 No. 62, as amended, and the Legal Aid and Advice Act, 1949 (Commencement No. 10) Order, 1961, S.I. 1961 No. 554.

Wilful neglect to provide reasonable maintenance.—As to the court's power on finding neglect to provide reasonable maintenance for a child to make an order for provision for the wife see *Northrop* v. *Northrop*, [1968] P. 88; [1967] 2 All E. R. 961, C. A.

Adultery.—As to the standard of proof where a child's legitimacy is in issue see *F.* v. *F.*, [1968] 1 All E. R. 242, at p. 247; *Preston-Jones* v. *Preston-Jones*, [1951] A. C. 391, at pp. 400, 401; [1951] 1 All E. R. 124, at p. 127.

2. Order by magistrates' court in matrimonial proceedings.—

(1) Subject to the proviso to subsection (3) of section one of this Act and to the provisions of this section and of section four of this Act, on hearing a complaint under the said section one by either of the parties to a marriage the court may make an order (in this Act referred to as a " matrimonial order ") containing any one or more of the following provisions, namely—

(a) a provision that the complainant be no longer bound to cohabit with the defendant (which provision while in force shall have effect in all respects as a decree of judicial separation);

(b) a provision that the husband shall pay to the wife such weekly sum as the court considers reasonable in all the circumstances of the case;

(c) where, by reason of the impairment of the husband's earning capacity through age, illness, or disability of mind or body, it appears to the court reasonable in all the circumstances so to order, a provision that the wife shall pay to the husband such weekly sum as the court considers reasonable in all the circumstances of the case;

(d) a provision for the legal custody of any child of the family who is under the age of sixteen years;

(e) if it appears to the court that there are exceptional circumstances making it impracticable or undesirable for any such child as aforesaid to be entrusted to either of the parties or to any other individual, a provision committing the care of the child to a specified local authority, being the council of the county or county borough in which the child was, in the opinion of the court, resident immediately before being so committed;

(f) if, in the case of any child committed by the order to the legal custody of any person, it appears to the court that there are exceptional circumstances making it desirable that the child should be under the supervision of an independent person, a provision that the child be under the supervision—

    (i) of a probation officer appointed for or assigned to the petty sessions area in which in the opinion of the court the child is or will be resident; or

    (ii) of a specified local authority, being the council of a county or county borough;

(g) a provision for access to any child of the family by either of the parties or by any other person who is a parent of that child, in a case where the child is committed by the order to the legal custody of a person other than that party or parent;

(h) a provision for the making by the defendant or by the complainant or by each of them, for the maintenance of any child of the family, of weekly payments, being—

    (i) if and for so long as the child is under the age of sixteen years, payments to any person to whom the legal custody of the child is for the time being committed by the order, or by any other order made by a court in England and for the time being in force, or, during any period when the child is in the care of a local authority under the order, to that local authority;

    (ii) if it appears to the court that the child is, or will be, or if such payments were made would be, a dependant though over the age of sixteen years, and that it is expedient that such payments should be made in respect of that child while such a dependant, payments to such person (who may be the child or, during any such period as aforesaid, the local authority) as may be specified in the order, for such period during which the child is over that age but under the age of twenty-one years as may be so specified.

(2) Where, on a complaint under section one of this Act, the court makes a matrimonial order on the ground that the defendant is for the time being an habitual drunkard or a drug addict, and the order contains such a provision as is mentioned in paragraph (a) of the foregoing subsection, then, if in all the circumstances, and after giving each party to the proceedings an opportunity of making representations, the court thinks it proper so to do, the court may include in that order—

(a) if the complainant is the husband, a provision such as is mentioned in paragraph (b) of the foregoing subsection; or

(b) if the complainant is the wife, a provision such as is mentioned in paragraph (c) of that subsection;

but save as aforesaid the said paragraph (b) or (c) shall not authorise the court to require any payment such as is therein mentioned to be made by the complainant.

(3) The court hearing a complaint under section one of this Act shall not make a matrimonial order containing a provision such as is mentioned in paragraph (a), (b) or (c) of subsection (1) of this section—

(a) on the ground that the defendant has committed an act of adultery, unless the court is satisfied that the complainant has not condoned or connived at, or by wilful neglect or misconduct conduced to, that act of adultery; or

(b) where the complainant is proved to have committed an act of adultery during the subsistence of the marriage, unless the court is satisfied that the defendant has condoned or connived at, or by wilful neglect or misconduct conduced to, that act of adultery.

(4) The court shall not make an order containing—

(a) such a provision as is mentioned in paragraph (d) or (e) of sub-section (1) of this section in respect of any child with respect to whose custody an order made by a court in England is for the time being in force;

(b) such a provision as is mentioned in paragraph (e), (f) or (g) of the said subsection (1) in respect of any child who is already for the purposes of Part II of the Children Act, 1948, in the care of a local authority;

(c) such a provision as is mentioned in the said paragraph (f) or (g) in respect of any child in respect of whom the order contains such a provision as is mentioned in the said paragraph (e).

(5) In considering whether any, and if so what, provision should be included in a matrimonial order by virtue of paragraph (h) of subsection (1) of this section for payments by one of the parties in respect of a child who is not a child of that party, the court shall have regard to the extent, if any, to which that party had, on or after the acceptance of the child as one of the family, assumed responsibility for the child's maintenance, and to the liability of any person other than a party to the marriage to maintain the child.

NOTES

This section is printed as amended by the Maintenance Orders Act, 1968.

Scotland, Northern Ireland.—Sub-s. (1) (a) is excluded by the proviso to s. 1 (3), *ante,* in the case of defendants residing in Scotland or Northern Ireland.

" Age of sixteen."—See note " Attained the age," at p. 53, *ante.*

" Resident."—See first part of note at p. 162, *ante.*

England.—This includes Wales; see note, p. 1047, *ante.*

Definitions.—For " child," " child of the family," " dependant," " drug addict," " habitual drunkard," " matrimonial order " and " petty sessions area," see s. 16 (1), p. 1238, *post.* As to " matrimonial order," note also sub-s. (1) of this section.

Children Act, 1948, Part II.—See pp. 892 *et seq., ante.*

Notice to local authority with regard to child.—See Rule 1 of the Magistrates' Courts (Matrimonial Proceedings) Rules, 1960, p. 1268, *post.*

For form of notice see Form No. 1 in the Schedule to the Rules, p. 1272, *post.* A local authorities functions in relation to supervision of a child are assigned to the Social Services Committee (Local Authority Social Services Act, 1970).

Substitution of new supervisor for child.—See Rule 2, *ibid.,* p. 1268, *post.*

For form of notice of appointment of new supervisor, see Form No. 2 in the Schedule to the Rules, p. 1272, *post.*

Maintenance by post.—See Home Office Circular dated October 6, 1971, No. 214/1971.

Liability of putative father to maintain.—In *Roberts* v. *Roberts*, [1962] P. 212; [1962] 2 All E. R. 967, 126 J. P. 438 it was held that the word " extent " in sub-s. (5) of this section was not used with temporal significance, and that as the husband had assumed full responsibility for the child's maintenance, albeit only for four months, the relevant extent of his responsibility was accordingly full. It was also held that the putative father was " under liability " (in the sense of being " answerable for ") the maintenance of the child within this subsection, although no affiliation order had been made, since the fact of the child having been a member of his household within twelve months after its birth was *prima facie* evidence that he had paid money for its maintenance for the purposes of s. 2 (1) (b) of the Affiliation Proceedings Act, 1957.

Per curiam in such a case the justices should adjourn their final adjudication in order to allow the wife to take affiliation proceedings.

Child of the family.—In *Bowlas* v. *Bowlas*, [1965] P. 450; [1965] 3 All E. R. 40; 129 J. P. 523, it was held: (i) although the mere fact that a man married a woman with children, and set up home with her, might be sufficient evidence that he accepted the children as members of the new family constituted by the marriage, yet in the present case careful investigation was required before drawing from the fact of marriage with knowledge of the children and of their position the inference that the husband accepted them as members of the new family and had accepted responsibility for their maintenance: (ii) the justices had not considered "the extent, if any" to which the husband had assumed responsibility for the children's maintenance, having regard particularly to the liability of the wife's former husband to maintain the children; accordingly the case would be remitted to a fresh panel of justices for re-hearing.

In *Dixon* v. *Dixon*, [1967] 3 All E. R. 659; 132 J. P. 123 it was held that there could not be acceptance of a child into a family without some mutual arrangement between the spouses and that the mutual arrangement must be an arrangement that the child should be treated by both spouses as the child of both.

In *S. (P. D.)* v. *S. (E.)* (1971), *Times*, July 19, the Court of Appeal laid down five principles:

   (a) if there was to be acceptance by a non-parent, the actual parent must offer the child for acceptance,

   (b) the question must be answered at the date of marriage,

   (c) an intention expressed before marriage might be withdrawn *before marriage* if there was a subsequent change of mind,

   (d) acceptance on the occasion of marriage was final and could not be withdrawn,

   (e) the test whether he had assumed responsibility was objective, not subjective, therefore, the fathers' liability to contribute to a child's maintenance need not be by judgment order, but extended to any enforceable liability.

It is possible that the Law Commission which is considering the discrepancies between this Act and the definition of "child of the family" in the Matrimonial Proceedings and Property Act, 1970, will recommend changes.

Access.—Where a custody order had been made by magistrates giving custody of the infant to the wife, with reasonable access by the husband, and the access in fact offered by the wife was unsatisfactory it was held that the husband's application by originating summons under the Law Reform (Miscellaneous Provision) Act, 1949, to make the infant a ward of court and for directions as to care and control of the infant was misconceived, and that his proper course was to apply to the magistrates for more specific orders relating to access (*Re K. (K. J. S.) (an infant)*, [1966] 3 All E. R. 154).

Assessment of amount.—In assessing the quantum of maintenance the magistrates should not merely decide on the global sum necessary for the support of a mother and child and then divide it haphazardly between them; they should decide separately what sum is reasonable in all the circumstances for the support of each child and of the mother and should order accordingly (*Northrop* v. *Northrop*, [1966] 3 All E. R. 797, at p. 800).

Adulterous mother.—In *Mounter* v. *Mounter* (1971), *Guardian*, June 15, the Court of Appeal held that it is better for a 2 year old boy to be with his mother, though she is living with another man, than to be cared for by his father in the evening and by a baby sitter in the day time, although said to be happy. *Cf. G.* v. *G.* (1971), *Times*, April 27, where access was granted to a father but prohibiting his mistress to be present when the children stayed overnight between 8 p.m. and 10 a.m. Cases of this nature depend to a very large extent on their particular facts.

3. Supplementary provisions with respect to order for care or supervision of child.—(1) Before including in a matrimonial order a provision committing a child to the care of a local authority, the court shall inform the authority of their proposal so to do and hear any representations from the authority, including any representations as to the inclusion in the order by virtue of paragraph (h) of subsection (1) of section two of this Act of provision for payments to the authority.

(2) Upon the inclusion in a matrimonial order of a provision committing a child as aforesaid—

(a) Part II of the Children Act, 1948 (which relates to the treatment of children in the care of a local authority) except section seventeen thereof (which relates to arrangements for the emigration of such children); and

(b) for the purposes only of contributions by the child himself at a time when he has attained the age of sixteen and is engaged in remunerative full-time work, Part III of that Act (which relates to contributions towards the maintenance of children in the care of a local authority),

shall apply as if the child had been received by the local authority into their care under section one of that Act.

(3) While such a provision as aforesaid remains in force with respect to any child, the child shall continue in the care of the local authority notwithstanding any claim by a parent or other person.

(4) Any such provision as aforesaid shall cease to have effect as respects any child when the child attains the age of eighteen years.

(5) Each parent or guardian of any child for the time being in the care of a local authority under a matrimonial order shall give notice to the authority of any change of address of that parent or guardian, and any person who without reasonable excuse fails to comply with this subsection shall be liable on summary conviction to a fine not exceeding ten pounds.

(6) Where a matrimonial order provides for a child to be under the supervision of a probation officer, that officer shall be selected in like manner as if the order were a probation order.

[*Repealed by the Local Authority Social Services Act, 1970. See now s. 2, and Sched. I, ibid.*]

(8) For the purposes of any matrimonial order providing for a child to be under the supervision of a probation officer or of a local authority, without prejudice to section eight of this Act, provision may be made by rules for substituting from time to time a probation officer appointed for or assigned to a different petty sessions area, or, as the case may be, a different local authority, if in the opinion of the court the child is or will be resident

in that petty sessions area or, as the case may be, in the area of that authority.

(9) Any provision of a matrimonial order that a child be under the supervision of a probation officer or local authority shall cease to have effect as respects any child when the child attains the age of sixteen years.

NOTES

This section is printed as amended by the Criminal Justice Act, 1967, Sched. III, and the Local Authorities Social Services Act, 1970.

" **Resident.**"—See first part of note at p. 162, *ante.*

Definitions.—For " child," " matrimonial order," " petty sessions area " and "rules," see s. 16 (1), p. 1238, *post.*

Children Act, 1948.—See pp. 880 *et seq., ante.*

Rules.—See the Magistrates' Courts (Matrimonial Proceedings) Rules 1960, Rule 2, p. 1268, *post.*

4. Special powers and duties with respect to children.—(1) Where the court has begun to hear a complaint—

   (a) under section one of this Act; or
   (b) for the variation of a matrimonial order—

      (i) by the revocation, addition or alteration of provision for the legal custody of a child; or
      (ii) by the revocation of a provision committing a child to the care of a local authority or a provision that a child be under the supervision of a probation officer or local authority; or

   (c) for the revocation of a matrimonial order consisting of or including any such provision as aforesaid.

then, whether or not the court makes the order for which the complaint is made, but subject to subsections (4) and (5) of section two of this Act and subsection (6) of this section, the court may make a matrimonial order containing, or, as the case may be, vary the matrimonial order so that it contains, any provision such as is mentioned in paragraphs (d) to (h) of subsection (1) of the said section two which, after giving each party to the proceedings an opportunity of making representations, the court thinks proper in all the circumstances; and the court shall not dismiss or make its final order on any complaint in a case where the powers conferred on the court by this subsection are or may be exercisable until it has decided whether or not, and if so how, those powers should be exercised.

(2) Where, on hearing such a complaint as aforesaid or a complaint for the variation of a matrimonial order by the revocation, addition or alteration of provision for access to a child, the court, after it has made any decision which falls to be made on the complaint with respect to any provision such as is mentioned in paragraphs (a) to (c) of subsection (1) of section two of this Act, is of the opinion that it has not sufficient information to make the decision required by the foregoing subsection or, as the case may be, to make a decision as to access to the child, the court may call for a report, either oral or in writing, by a probation officer, or by such an officer of a local authority as is mentioned in subsection (7) of section three of this Act, with respect to such matters as the court may

specify, being matters appearing to the court to be relevant to that decision.

(3) Any statement which is or purports to be a report in pursuance of the last foregoing subsection shall be made, or if in writing be read aloud, before the court at a hearing of the complaint, and immediately after it has been so made or read aloud the court shall ask whether any party to the proceedings who is present or represented by counsel or solicitor at the hearing objects to anything contained therein; and where objection is made—

(a) the court shall require the officer by whom the statement was or purported to be made to give evidence on oath with respect to the matters referred to therein; and

(b) any party to the proceedings may give or call evidence with respect to any matter referred to in the statement or in any evidence given by the officer.

(4) Subject to the next following subsection, the court may take account of any statement made or read aloud under the last foregoing subsection and of any evidence given under paragraph (a) of that subsection, so far as that statement or evidence relates to the matters specified by the court under subsection (2) of this section, notwithstanding any enactment or rule of law relating to the admissibility of evidence.

(5) A report in pursuance of subsection (2) of this section shall not include anything said by either of the parties to a marriage in the course of an interview which took place with, or in the presence of, a probation officer with a view to the reconciliation of those parties, unless both parties have consented to its inclusion; and if anything so said is included without the consent of both those parties as part of any statement made or read aloud under subsection (3) of this section, then, unless both those parties agree otherwise, that part of the statement shall, for the purposes of the giving of evidence under the said subsection (3) and for the purposes of subsection (4) of this section, be deemed not to be contained in the statement.

(6) On the hearing of a complaint under section one of this Act in the case of which there is a child of the family who is not a child of both the parties, other than a child with respect to whose custody an order made by a court in England is for the time being in force—

(a) subsections (1) and (3) of this section shall have effect as if any person who, though not a party to the proceedings, is a parent of that child and who is present or represented by counsel or solicitor at the hearing were a party to the proceedings; and

(b) if any such person is not so present or represented, the court shall not make a matrimonial order on the complaint unless it is proved to the satisfaction of the court, on oath or in such other manner as may be prescribed by rules, that such steps have been taken as may be so prescribed with a view to giving notice to that person of the making of the complaint and of the time and place appointed for the hearing:

Provided that nothing in paragraph (b) of this subsection shall require notice to be given to any person as the father of an illegitimate child unless that person has been adjudged by a court to be the father of that child.

(7) Where for the purposes of this section the court adjourns the hearing of any complaint, then, subject to subsection (2) of section forty-six of the Magistrates' Courts Act, 1952 (which requires adequate notice of the time and place of the resumption of the hearing to be given to the parties), the court may resume the hearing at the time and place appointed notwithstanding the absence of both or all of the parties.

(8) In any proceedings in which the powers conferred on the court by subsection (1) of this section are or may be exercisable, the question whether or not, and if so how, those powers should be exercised shall be excepted from the issues arising in the proceedings which, under the proviso to subsection (1) of section sixty of the Magistrates' Courts Act, 1952, must be determined by the court before the court may direct a probation officer to make to the court under that section a report on the means of the parties.

NOTES

Variation, revocation of a matrimonial order.—As to the revocation and variation of matrimonial orders, see ss. 8, 10, *infra*.

England.—This includes Wales; see note, p. 1226, *ante*.

Definitions.—For " child," " matrimonial order " and " rules," see s. 16 (1), p. 829, *post*.

Rules.—See the Magistrates' Courts (Matrimonial Proceedings) Rules, 1960, pp. 1268, *et seq.*, *post*.

Notice to parent of child (other than a party) of court's power to make provision with regard to children.—See Rule 3 of the Magistrates' Courts (Matrimonial Proceedings) Rules, 1960, p. 1268, *post*.
For form of notice see Form No. 3 in the Schedule to the Rules, p. 1272, *post*.

Non-cohabitation clause.—A non-cohabitation clause is inappropriate in a justices' order based on the ground of wilful neglect to provide reasonable maintenance, if there is no other circumstance which makes a separation order necessary for the protection of the wife or children. See *Vaughan* v. *Vaughan*, [1963] 2 All E. R. 742, 746; 127 J. P. 404.

Enquiries : sub-s. (2).—It is the duty of a probation officer if requested by the court to make a report with respect to the matters specified in this sub-s. See r. 31 (c) of the Probation Rules, 1965, p. 527, *ante*.

*   *   *   *

8. Revocation, revival and variation of orders.—(1) Subject to section four of this Act, section fifty-three of the Magistrates' Courts Act, 1952 (which provides for the revocation, revival or variation, by order on complaint, of an order of a magistrates' court for the periodical payment of money) and the proviso to subsection (1) of section fifty-five of that Act (which relates to costs on the hearing of such a complaint) shall apply for the purpose of the revocation, revival or variation of any matrimonial or interim order as if that order were an order for the periodical payment of money, whether or not it is in fact such an order; and a complaint for the said purpose may be heard whatever the time at which it is made; and for the avoidance of doubt it is hereby declared that for the purposes of this Act the expression " variation " in relation to any order includes the addition to that order of any provision authorised by this Act to be included in such an order:
Provided that, without prejudice to the powers and duties of the court

under section four of this Act, nothing in this section shall authorise the making of a complaint—

(a) for the variation of an order by the addition of a provision committing a child to the care of a local authority or providing for a child to be under the supervision of a probation officer or local authority; or

(b) for the revival of any such provision as aforesaid which has ceased to be in force; or

(c) for the variation of a provision committing a child to the care of a local authority.

(2) Where on a complaint for the revocation of a matrimonial order it is proved that the parties to the marriage in question have resumed cohabitation or that the party on whose complaint the order was made has during the subsistence of the marriage committed an act of adultery, the court shall revoke that order:

Provided that—

(a) the court shall not be bound by reason of such a resumption of cohabitation to revoke any provision of the order such as is mentioned in the proviso to subsection (1) of section seven of this Act;

(b) the court shall not revoke the order by reason of such an act of adultery as aforesaid—

(i) except at the request of the person who was the defendant to the proceedings n which the order was made; or

(ii) if the court is of the opinion that the person aforesaid has condoned or connived at, or by wilful neglect or misconduct conduced to, that act of adultery,

and shall not be bound by reason of that act of adultery to revoke any provision of the order included therein by virtue of paragraphs (d) to (h) of subsection (1) of section two of this Act.

(3) The court before which there fall to be heard any proceedings for the variation of a provision for the payment of money contained in a matrimonial or interim order may, if it thinks fit, order that those proceedings and any other proceedings being heard therewith shall be treated for the purposes of the Magistrates' Courts Act, 1952, as domestic proceedings; and that Act shall thereupon have effect accordingly notwithstanding anything in subsection (1) of section fifty-six thereof; and no appeal shall lie from, or from the refusal of, an order under this subsection.

NOTES

"**May be heard whatever the time at which it is made.**"—This provision prevents the usual six months' limitation laid down by s. 104 of the Magistrates' Courts Act, 1952, from applying.

"**Domestic proceedings.**"—For special provisions relating to domestic proceedings, see Section 4, pp. 1231 *et seq., ante.*

Definitions.—For " child," " interim order " and " matrimonial order," see s. 16 (1), p. 1238, *post.*

Notice to person outside United Kingdom of complaint for revocation, etc., of order.—See Rule 5 of the Magistrates' Courts (Matrimonial Proceedings) Rules, 1960, p. 1269, *post*.

For form of notice see Form No. 5 in the Schedule to the Rules, p. 1273, *post*.

Defendants to complaint for revocation, revival or variation of order.—See Rule 7 of the Magistrates' Courts (Matrimonial Proceedings) Rules, 1960, p. 1270, *post*.

*   *   *   *

10. Parties to complaint for variation, etc.—(1) A complaint by virtue of section eight of this Act for the revocation, revival or variation of a matrimonial or interim order may be made in the following cases by the following persons in addition to the parties to the marriage in question, that is to say—

(a) where a child of the family is not a child of both the parties to the marriage, a complaint relating to any provision with respect to the child such as is mentioned in paragraph (d) or (g) of subsection (1) of section two of this Act may be made by any person who, though not one of the parties to the marriage, is a parent of the child;

(b) a complaint relating to payments under the order such as are mentioned in paragraph (h) of the said subsection (1) may be made by any person to whom such payments fall, or upon the making of the order for which the complaint is made would fall, to be made;

(c) where under the order a child is for the time being committed to the legal custody of some person other than one of the parents or to the care of a local authority, a complaint relating to any provision with respect to the child such as is mentioned in the said paragraph (d) or (g) may be made by any person to whose legal custody the child is committed by the order or who seeks the legal custody of the child by the complaint;

(d) where under the order a child is for the time being under the supervision of a probation officer or local authority, the probation officer or local authority may make a complaint relating to any provision with respect to the child such as is mentioned in the said paragraphs (d), (g) and (h) ;

(e) a complaint for the revocation of a provision of the order committing a child to the care of a local authority may be made by that local authority or by any person to whose legal custody the child is for the time being committed by the order or who by the same complaint also seeks the legal custody of the child;

(f) a complaint for the variation or revocation of a provision of the order that a child be under the supervision of a probation officer or local authority may be made by that probation officer or local authority, or by any person to whose legal custody the child is for the time being committed by the order or who by the same complaint also seeks the legal custody of the child.

(2) Provision may be made by rules as to what persons shall be made defendants to any such complaint as aforesaid; and where in the case of any such complaint there are two or more defendants, the powers of the

court under subsection (1) of section fifty-five of the Magistrates' Courts Act, 1952, shall be deemed to include power, whatever adjudication the court makes on the complaint, to order any of the parties to pay the whole or part of the costs of all or any of the other parties.

NOTES

Definitions.—For " child," " child of the family," " interim order," " matrimonial order " and " rules," see s. 16 (1), p. 1238, *post*.

Rules.—See the Magistrates' Courts (Matrimonial Proceedings) Rules, 1960, pp. 1268, *et seq.*, *post*.

*   *   *   *

13. Enforcement, etc.—(1) The payment of any sum of money directed to be paid by an order made by virtue of this Act may be enforced in the same manner as the payment of money is enforced under an affiliation order.

(2) Without prejudice to section fifty-two of the Magistrates' Courts Act, 1952 (which relates to the power of the court to direct payments to be made through the clerk of a magistrates' court), the court making an order by virtue of this Act for payment of a periodical sum by one person to another may direct that it shall be paid to some third party on that other person's behalf instead of directly to that other person; and, for the purposes of any order made by virtue of this Act, the said section fifty-two shall have effect as if, in subsection (2) thereof, for the words " the applicant for the order " in the first place where those words occur there were substituted the words " the person to whom the payments under the order fall to be made ".

(3) Where an order made by virtue of this Act contains a provision committing a child to the legal custody of any person, or to the care of a local authority, a copy of the order may be served on any other person in whose actual custody the child for the time being is; and thereupon that provision may, without prejudice to any other remedy which may be available, be enforced under subsection (3) of section fifty-four of the Magistrates' Courts Act, 1952, as if it were an order of the court requiring that other person to give up the child to the person to whom the legal custody of the child is committed or, as the case may be, to the local authority.

(4) Any person for the time being under an obligation to make payments under any order made in proceedings brought by virtue of this Act shall give notice to such persons, if any, as may be specified in the order of any change of address; and any person who without reasonable excuse fails to comply with this subsection shall be liable on summary conviction to a fine not exceeding five pounds.

(5) A person shall not be entitled to enforce through the High Court or any county court the payment of any arrears due under an order made by virtue of this Act without the leave of that court if those arrears became due more than twelve months before proceedings to enforce the payment of them are begun.

(6) The court hearing an application for the grant of leave under subsection (5) of this section may refuse leave, or may grant leave subject to such restrictions and conditions (including conditions as to the allowing of time for payment or the making of payment by instalments) as that court

thinks proper, or may remit the payment of such arrears or any part thereof.

(7) An application for the grant of leave under the said subsection (5) shall be made in such manner as may be prescribed by rules of court.

NOTES

This section is printed as amended by the Criminal Justice Act, 1967, Sched. III, and s. 32 of the Matrimonial Proceedings and Property Act, 1970.

Enforcement as under affiliation order.—See notes to s. 87 of the Children and Young Persons Act, 1933, p. 69, *ante*.

13A. Orders for repayment in certain cases of sum paid after cessation of order by reason of remarriage.—(1) Where—

(a) an order to which this section applies or a provision thereof has ceased to have effect by reason of the remarriage of the person entitled to payments under the order, and

(b) the person liable to make payments under the order made payments in accordance with it in respect of a period after the date of such remarriage in the mistaken belief that the order or provision was still subsisting,

no proceedings in respect of a cause of action arising out of the circumstances mentioned in paragraphs (a) and (b) above shall be maintainable by the person so liable or his or her personal representatives against the person so entitled or her or his personal representatives, but on an application made under this section the court may exercise the powers conferred on it by the following subsection.

This section applies to an order in relation to which subsection (4) of section 7 of this Act, as amended by the Matrimonial Proceedings and Property Act, 1970, applies.

(2) The court may order the respondent to an application made under this section to pay to the applicant a sum equal to the amount of the payments made in respect of the period mentioned in subsection (1) (b) of this section or, if it appears to the court that it would be unjust to make that order, it may either order the respondent to pay to the applicant such lesser sum as it thinks fit or dismiss the application.

(3) An application under this section may be made by the person liable to make payments under an order to which this section applies or his or her personal representatives and may be made against the person entitled to payments under the order or her or his personal representatives.

(4) An application under this section may be made in proceedings in the High Court or a county court for leave to enforce, or the enforcement of, the payment of arrears under an order to which this section applies, but except as aforesaid such an application shall be made to a county court, and accordingly references in this section to the court are references to the High Court or a county court, as the circumstances require.

(5) An order under this section for the payment of any sum may provide for the payment of that sum by instalments of such amount as may be specified in the order.

(6) The jurisdiction conferred on a county court by this section shall be exercisable by a county court notwithstanding that by reason of the

amount claimed in an application under this section the jurisdiction would not but for this subsection be exercisable by a county court.

(7) Section 13 (1) and (2) of this Act shall not apply to an order under this section.

(8) The clerk of a magistrates' court to whom any payments under an order to which this section applies are required to be made, and the collecting officer under an attachment of earnings order made to secure payments under the first mentioned order, shall not be liable—

(a) in the case of that clerk, for any act done by him in pursuance of the first mentioned order after the date on which that order or a provision thereof ceased to have effect by reason of the remarriage of the person entitled to payments under it, and

(b) in the case of the collecting officer, for any act done by him after that date in accordance with any enactment or rule of court specifying how payments made to him in compliance with the attachment of earnings order are to be dealt with,

if, but only if, the act was one which he would have been under a duty to do had the first mentioned order or a provision thereof not ceased to have effect as aforesaid and the act was done before notice in writing of the fact that the person so entitled had remarried was given to him by or on behalf of that person, the person liable to make payments under the first mentioned order or the personal representatives of either of those persons.

(9) In this section "collecting officer", in relation to an attachment of earnings order, means the officer of the High Court, the registrar of a county court or the clerk of a magistrates' court to whom a person makes payments in compliance with the order.

NOTE

This section is added by the Matrimonial Proceedings and Property Act, 1970, s. 31.

*   *   *   *

15. Increase of maintenance payments which may be ordered under other Acts.—[*Repealed by the Maintenance Orders Act*, 1968, s. 3, *p.* 1242, *post.*]

16. Interpretation.—(1) In this Act, save where the context otherwise requires, the following expressions have the following meanings respectively, that is to say—

" child ", in relation to one or both of the parties to a marriage, includes an illegitimate or adopted child of that party or, as the case may be, of both parties, but does not include a child adopted by some other person or persons, and " parent ", in relation to any child, shall be construed accordingly; and " adopted " means adopted in pursuance of an adoption order made under the Adoption Act, 1958, or any enactment repealed by that Act or by the Adoption Act, 1950, or under any corresponding enactment of the Parliament of Northern Ireland;

" child of the family ", in relation to the parties to a marriage, means—

(a) any child of both parties; and

(b) any other child of either party who has been accepted as one of the family by the other party;

NOTE

"**Child of the family.**"—See note, p. 1229, *ante*.

" dependant " means a person—

(a) who is under the age of sixteen years; or

(b) who, having attained the age of sixteen but not of twenty-one years, is either receiving full-time instruction at an educational establishment or undergoing training for a trade, profession or vocation in such circumstances that he is required to devote the whole of his time to that training for a period of not less than two years; or

(c) whose earning capacity is impaired through illness or disability of mind or body and who has not attained the age of twenty-one years;

" drug addict " means a person (not being a mentally disordered person within the meaning of the Mental Health Act, 1959) who, by reason of the habitual taking or using, otherwise than upon medical advice, of any drug to which any of the provisions of the Dangerous Drugs Act, 1951, for the time being applies—

(a) is at times dangerous to himself or to others, or incapable of managing himself or his affairs; or

(b) so conducts himself that it would not be reasonable to expect a spouse of ordinary sensibilities to continue to cohabit with him;

"habitual drunkard " means a person (not being a mentally disordered person within the meaning of the Mental Health Act, 1959) who, by reason of habitual intemperate drinking of intoxicating liquor—

(a) is at times dangerous to himself or to others, or incapable of managing himself or his affairs; or

(b) so conducts himself that it would not be reasonable to expect a spouse of ordinary sensibilities to continue to cohabit with him;

" interim order " means an order under section six of this Act and includes any order made by virtue of section eight of this Act varying or reviving an order under the said section six;

" matrimonial order " means an order under section two of this Act and includes any order made by virtue of section eight of this Act varying or reviving an order under the said section two;

" petty sessions area " has the same meaning as in the Magistrates' Courts Act, 1952;

" rules " means rules made under section fifteen of the Justices of the Peace Act, 1949.

(2) Save where the context otherwise requires, any reference in this Act to any enactment shall be construed as a reference to that enactment as amended by or under any subsequent enactment, including this Act.

NOTES

"**Age of sixteen.**"—See note, "Attained the age" at p. 53, *ante.*

Adoption Act, 1958.—See p. 1026, *ante.*

Adoption Act, 1950.—That Act is repealed and replaced by the Adoption Act, 1958.

Mental Health Act, 1959.—See pp. 442 *et seq., ante.*

17. Expenses.—There shall be defrayed out of moneys provided by Parliament any increase attributable to this Act in the sums payable out of moneys so provided under any other enactment.

*   *   *   *

19. Short title, extent and commencement.—(1) This Act may be cited as the Matrimonial Proceedings (Magistrates' Courts) Act, 1960.

(2) This Act, except for subsection (1) of section fourteen and the repeal of sections one and five of the Maintenance Orders Act, 1950, shall not extend to Scotland or to Northern Ireland.

(3) This Act shall come into force on such day as the Secretary of State may by order made by statutory instrument appoint.

SCHEDULE

ENACTMENTS REPEALED

[*The Schedule repeals* inter alia *certain words in s.* 126 *of the Magistrates' Courts Act,* 1952. *This section is printed, as amended, at p.* 386, ante.]

MATRIMONAL CAUSES ACT, 1965
[1965, c. 72]

36. Power to commit children to care of local authority.—(1) Where the court has jurisdiction by virtue of this Part of this Act, to make an order for the custody of a child and it appears to the court that there are exceptional circumstances making it impracticable or undesirable for the child to be entrusted to either of the parties to the marriage or to any other individual, the court may if it thinks fit make an order committing the care of the child to the council of a county, county borough or London borough or the Common Council of the City of London (hereafter in this section referred to as "the local authority"); and thereupon Part II of the Children Act, 1948 (which relates to the treatment of children in the care of a local authority) shall, subject to the provisions of this section, apply as if the child had been received by the local authority into their care under section 1 of that Act.

(2) The authority specified in an order under this section shall be the local authority for the area in which the child was, in the opinion of the court, resident before the order was made to commit the child to the care of a local authority, and the court shall before making an order under this

section hear any representations from the local authority, including any representations as to the making of an order for payments for the maintenance and education of the child.

(3) While an order made by virtue of this section is in force with respect to a child, the child shall continue in the care of the local authority notwithstanding any claim by a parent or other person.

(4) An order made by virtue of this section shall cease to have effect as respects any child when he becomes eighteen, and the court shall not make an order committing a child to the care of a local authority under this section after he has become seventeen.

(5) In the application of Part II of the Children Act, 1948 by virtue of this section—

(a) the exercise by the local authority of their powers under sections 12 to 16 of that Act (which among other things relate to the accommodation and welfare of a child in the care of a local authority) shall be subject to any directions given by the court ; and

(b) section 17 of that Act (which relates to arrangements for the emigration of such a child) shall not apply.

(6) It shall be the duty of any parent or guardian of a child committed to the care of a local authority under this section to secure that the local authority are informed of his address for the time being, and a person who knowingly fails to comply with this subsection shall be liable on summary conviction to a fine not exceeding ten pounds.

(7) The court shall have power from time to time by an order under this section to vary or discharge any provision made in pursuance of this section.

NOTE

This section is printed as amended by the Criminal Justice Act, 1967, Sched. III.

Part II of the Children Act, 1948.—See pp. 892 *et seq., ante.*

Wards of court.—Section 7 Family Law Reform Act, 1969, p. 1309, *post*, provides for the committal of wards of court to the care of a local authority. See Part II of the Children Act, 1948, p. 892, *ante.*

37. Power to provide for supervision of children.—(1) Where the court has jurisdiction by virtue of this Part of this Act to make an order for the custody of a child and it appears to the court that there are exceptional circumstances making it desirable that the child should be under the supervision of an independent person, the court may, as respects any period during which the child is, in exercise of that jurisdiction, committed to the custody of any person, order that the child be under the supervision of an officer appointed under this section as a welfare officer or under the supervision of a local authority.

(2) Where the court makes an order under this section for supervision by a welfare officer, the officer responsible for carrying out the order shall be such probation officer as may be selected under arrangements made by the Secretary of State; and where the order is for supervision by a local authority, that authority shall be the council of a county, county borough

or London borough selected by the court and specified in the order or, if the Common Council of the City of London is so selected and specified, that Council.

(3) *Repealed by the Local Authority Social Services Act, 1970. See now s. 2 and Sched. I, ibid.*]

(4) The court shall not have power to make an order under this section as respects a child who in pursuance of an order under the last foregoing section is in the care of a local authority.

(5) Where a child is under the supervision of any person in pursuance of this section the jurisdiction possessed by a court to vary any order made with respect to the child's custody, maintenance or education under this Part of this Act shall, subject to any rules of court, be exercisable at the instance of that court itself.

(6) The court shall have power from time to time by an order under this section to vary or discharge any provision made in pursuance of this section.

NOTES

This section is printed as amended by the Local Authority Social Services Act, 1971.

" **Children Act, 1948, s. 39.**"—See p. 927, *ante.*

" **Supervision.**"—As to supervision by a probation officer see r. 32 of the Probation Rules, 1965, p. 527, *ante.* Section 6 of the Matrimonial Proceedings (Children) Act, 1958, is repealed by the Matrimonial Causes Act, 1965 and replaced by s. 37 of that Act.

Wards of court.—See s. 7 (4) Family Law Reform Act, 1969, which applies the provisions of sub-s. (2) and (3) of this section to wards of court under the supervision of a welfare officer or local authority.

As to transfer of supervision see Home Office Circular No. 131/1968, p. 694, *ante.*

*   *   *   *

MAINTENANCE ORDERS ACT, 1968
[1968 c. 36]

An Act to amend the enactments relating to matrimonial guardianship and affiliation proceedings so far as they limit the weekly rate of the maintenance payments which may be ordered by magistrates' courts.

[July 3, 1968]

1. Increase of maximum payments for children.—The enactments described in the Schedule to this Act shall have effect subject to the amendments specified in the second column of that Schedule, being amendments removing the limits of fifty shillings and seven pounds ten shillings imposed by those enactments upon the weekly rate of the payments for the maintenance of a child, and for the maintenance of a party to a marriage, which may be required by order of a magistrates' court thereunder.

2. Supplementary.—Any order made by a magistrates' court before the date of the commencement of this Act may be varied so as to include, from the date of the variation, provision for the payment of such increased sums as would have been lawful if the order had been made after the first mentioned date.

3. Short title, extent, commencement and repeal.—(1) This Act may be cited as the Maintenance Orders Act, 1968.

(2) This Act does not extend to Scotland or Northern Ireland.

(3) This Act shall come into force at the expiration of the period of one month beginning with the day on which it is passed.

(4) Section 15 of the Matrimonial Proceedings (Magistrates' Courts) Act, 1960 is hereby repealed.

SCHEDULE

ENACTMENTS AMENDED

The Guardianship of Infants Act, 1925. (15 & 16 Geo. 5. c. 45.)	In section 7, in subsection (1), paragraph (c) of the proviso shall be omitted.
The Affiliation Proceedings Act, 1957. (5 & 6 Eliz. 2. c. 55.)	In section 4, in paragraph (a) of subsection (2), the words "not exceeding fifty shillings a week" shall be omitted.
The Matrimonial Proceedings (Magistrates' Courts) Act, 1960. (8 & 9 Eliz. 2. c. 48.)	In section 2, in paragraphs (b) and (c) of subsection (1), the words "not exceeding seven pounds ten shillings" shall be omitted; and in paragraph (h) of that subsection for the words from "payments by way of a weekly sum" to "fifty shillings" there shall be substituted the words "weekly payments".

NOTE

Guardianship of infants.—See now Guardianship of Minors Act, 1971. The Act is printed as amended by the Administration of Justice Act, 1970, and the Matrimonial Proceedings and Property Act, 1970.

MATRIMONIAL PROCEEDINGS AND PROPERTY ACT, 1970

[1970 c. 45]

The Matrimonial Proceedings and Property Act, 1970, came into force on January 1, 1971. Those provisions which relate particularly to the subjects included in this work are reproduced. Sections 3, 17, 18 and 19 replace ss. 33–35 of the Matrimonial Causes Act, 1965, and together with ss. 36 and 37 of the 1965 Act are the main provisions affecting the protection and custody of children. It is the duty of the probation officer, if so requested by or on behalf of a court to make a report to the court with respect to the custody, maintenance or education of a child under Part III of the 1965 Act (see now ss. 17–19, below).

3. Financial provision for child of the family in cases of divorce, etc.—(1) Subject to the provisions of section 8 of this Act, in proceedings for divorce, nullity of marriage or judicial separation, the court may make any one or more of the orders mentioned in subsection (2) below—

    (a) before or on granting the decree of divorce, of nullity of marriage or of judicial separation, as the case may be, or at any time thereafter;

    (b) where any such proceedings are dismissed after the beginning of the trial, either forthwith or within a reasonable period after the dismissal.

(2) The orders referred to in subsection (1) above are—

    (a) an order that a party to the marriage shall make to such person as may be specified in the order for the benefit of a child of the family, or to such a child, such periodical payments and for such terms as may be so specified;

    (b) an order that a party to the marriage shall secure to such person as may be so specified for the benefit of such a child, or to such a child, to the satisfaction of the court, such periodical payments and for such term as may be so specified;

    (c) an order that a party to the marriage shall pay to such person as may be so specified for the benefit of such a child, or to such a child, such lump sum as may be so specified.

(3) Without prejudice to the generality of subsection (2) (c) above, an order under this section for the payment of a lump sum to any person for the benefit of a child of the family, or to such a child, may be made for the purpose of enabling any liabilities or expenses reasonably incurred by or for the benefit of that child before the making of an application for an order under this section to be met.

(4) An order under this section for the payment of a lump sum may provide for the payment of that sum by instalments of such amount as may be specified in the order and may require the payment of the instalments to be secured to the satisfaction of the court.

(5) While the court has power to make an order in any proceedings by virtue of subsection (1) (a) above, it may exercise that power from time to time; and where the court makes an order by virtue of subsection (1) (b) above in relation to a child it may from time to time make a further order under this section in relation to him.

5. Matters to which court is to have regard in deciding what orders to make under ss. 2, 3 and 4.—(1) It shall be the duty of the court in deciding whether to exercise its powers under section 2 or 4 of this Act in relation to a party to the marriage and, if so, in what manner, to have regard to all the circumstances of the case including the following matters, that is to say—

(a) the income, earning capacity, property and other financial resources which each of the parties to the marriage has or is likely to have in the foreseeable future;

(b) the financial needs, obligations and responsibilities which each of the parties to the marriage has or is likely to have in the foreseeable future;

(c) the standard of living enjoyed by the family before the breakdown of the marriage;

(d) the age of each party to the marriage and the duration of the marriage;

(e) any physical or mental disability of either of the parties to the marriage;

(f) the contributions made by each of the parties to the welfare of the family, including any contribution made by looking after the home or caring for the family;

(g) in the case of proceedings for divorce or nullity of marriage, the value to either of the parties to the marriage of any benefit (for example, a pension) which, by reason of the dissolution or annulment of the marriage, that party will lose the chance of acquiring;

and so to exercise those powers as to place the parties, so far as it is practicable and, having regard to their conduct, just to do so, in the financial position in which they would have been if the marriage had not broken down and each had properly discharged his or her financial obligations and responsibilities towards the other.

(2) Without prejudice to subsection (3) below, it shall be the duty of the court in deciding whether to exercise its powers under section 3 or 4 of this Act in relation to a child of the family and, if so, in what manner, to have regard to all the circumstances of the case including the following matters, that is to say—

(a) the financial needs of the child;

(b) the income, earning capacity (if any), property and other financial resources of the child;

(c) any physical or mental disability of the child;

(d) the standard of living enjoyed by the family before the breakdown of the marriage;

(c) the manner in which he was being and in which the parties to the marriage expected him to be educated or trained;

and so to exercise those powers as to place the child, so far as it is practicable and, having regard to the considerations mentioned in relation to the parties to the marriage in paragraphs (a) and (b) of subsection (1) above, just to do so, in the financial position in which the child would have been if the marriage had not broken down and each of those parties had properly discharged his or her financial obligations and responsibilities towards him.

(3) It shall be the duty of the court in deciding whether to exercise its powers under the said section 3 or 4 against a party to a marriage in favour of a child of the family who is not the child of that party and, if so, in what manner, to have regard (among the circumstances of the case)—

    (a) to whether that party had assumed any responsibility for the child's maintenance and, if so, to the extent to which, and the basis upon which, that party assumed such responsibility and to the length of time for which that party discharged such responsibility;

    (b) to whether in assuming and discharging such responsibility that party did so knowing that the child was not his or her own;

    (c) to the liability of any other person to maintain the child.

Additional powers of court to make orders requiring party to marriage to make payments to other party, etc.

6. Neglect by party to marriage to maintain other party or child of the family.—(1) Either party to a marriage may apply to the court for an order under this section on the ground that the other party to the marriage (in this section referred to as the respondent)—

    (a) being the husband, has wilfully neglected—

        (i) to provide reasonable maintenance for the applicant, or

        (ii) to provide, or to make a proper contribution towards, reasonable maintenance for any child of the family to whom this section applies;

    (b) being the wife, has wilfully neglected to provide, or to make a proper contribution towards, reasonable maintenance—

        (i) for the applicant in a case where, by reason of the impairment of the applicant's earning capacity through age, illness or disability of mind or body, and having regard to any resources of the applicant and the respondent respectively which are, or should properly be made, available for the purpose, it is reasonable in all the circumstances to expect the respondent so to provide or contribute, or

        (ii) for any child of the family to whom this section applies.

(2) The court shall not entertain an application under this section unless it would have jurisdiction to entertain proceedings by the applicant for judicial separation.

(3) This section applies to any child of the family for whose maintenance it is reasonable in all the circumstances to expect the respondent to provide or towards whose maintenance it is reasonable in all the circumstances to expect the respondent to make a proper contribution.

(4) Where the child of the family to whom the application under this section relates is not the child of the respondent, then, in deciding—

    (a) whether the respondent has been guilty of wilful neglect to provide, or to make a proper contribution towards, reasonable maintenance for the child, and

    (b) what order, if any, to make under this section in favour or for the benefit of the child,

the court shall have regard to the matters mentioned in section 5 (3) of this Act.

(5) Where on an application under this section it appears to the court that the applicant or any child of the family to whom the application relates is in immediate need of financial assistance, but it is not yet possible to determine what order, if any, should be made on the application, the court may order the respondent to make to the applicant until the determination of the application such periodical payments as the court thinks reasonable.

(6) Where on an application under this section the applicant satisfies the court of any ground mentioned in subsection (1) above, then, subject to the provisions of section 8 of this Act, the court may make such one or more of the following orders as it thinks just, that is to say—

    (a) an order that the respondent shall make to the applicant such periodical payments and for such term as may be specified in the order;

    (b) an order that the respondent shall secure to the applicant, to the satisfaction of the court, such periodical payments and for such term as may be so specified;

    (c) an order that the respondent shall pay to the applicant such lump sum as may be so specified;

    (d) an order that the respondent shall make to such person as may be specified in the order for the benefit of the child to whom the application relates, or to that child, such periodical payments and for such term as may be so specified;

    (e) an order that the respondent shall secure to such person as may be so specified for the benefit of that child, or to that child, to the satisfaction of the court, such periodical payments and for such term as may be so specified;

    (f) an order that the respondent shall pay to such person as may be so specified for the benefit of that child, or to that child, such lump sum as may be so specified.

(7) Without prejudice to the generality of subsection (6) (c) and (f) above, an order under this section that the respondent shall pay a lump sum—

    (a) may be made for the purpose of enabling any liabilities or expenses reasonably incurred in maintaining the applicant or any child of the family to whom the application relates before the making of the application to be met;

(b) may provide for the payment of that sum by instalments of such amount as may be specified in the order and may require the payment of the instalments to be secured to the satisfaction of the court.

Further provisions relating to orders under sections 2, 3, 4 and 6

7. Duration of certain orders made in favour of party to marriage and effect of remarriage.—(1) The term to be specified in any order made by virtue of section 2 (1) (a) or (b) of this Act or section 6 (6) (a) or (b) thereof shall be such term, being a term beginning not earlier than the date of the making of an application for the order in question and lasting not longer than the maximum term, as the court thinks fit.

(2) In subsection (1) above "the maximum term" means—

(a) in the case of an order made by virtue of the said section 2 (1) (a) in proceedings for divorce or nullity of marriage, the joint lives of the parties to the marriage or a term ending with the date of the remarriage of the party in whose favour the order is made, whichever is the shorter;

(b) in the case of an order made by virtue of the said section 2 (1) (b) in any such proceedings, the life of that party or a term ending with the date of the remarriage of that party, whichever is the shorter;

(c) in the case of an order made by virtue of the said section 2 (1) (a) in proceedings for judicial separation or made by virtue of the said section 6 (6) (a) the joint lives of the parties to the marriage;

(d) in the case of an order made by virtue of the said section 2 (1) (b) in proceedings for judicial separation or made by virtue of the said section 6 (6) (b), the life of the party in whose favour the order is made.

(3) Where an order is made by virtue of the said section 2 (1) (a) or (b) in proceedings for judicial separation or by virtue of the said section 6 (6) (a) or (b) and the marriage of the parties affected by the order is subsequently dissolved or annulled but the order continues in force, the order shall, notwithstanding anything in it, cease to have effect on the remarriage of the party in whose favour it was made, except in relation to any arrears due under it on the date of such remarriage.

(4) If after the grant of a decree dissolving or annulling a marriage either party to that marriage remarries, that party shall not be entitled to apply for an order under section 2 or 4 of this Act against the person to whom he or she was married immediately before the grant of that decree unless the remarriage is with that person and that marriage is also dissolved or annulled or a decree of judicial separation is made on a petition presented by either party to that marriage.

8. Provisions as to powers of court to make orders in favour of children and duration of such orders.—(1) Subject to subsection (3) below—

(a) no order under section 3, 4 (a) or 6 of this Act shall be made in favour of a child who has attained the age of eighteen; and

    (b) the term for which by virtue of an order under the said section 3
        or 6 any payments are to be made or secured to or for the benefit
        of a child may begin with the date of the making of an applica-
        tion for the order in question or any later date but shall not
        extend beyond the date when the child will attain the age of
        eighteen.

    (2) The term for which by virtue of an order under the said section 3
or 6 any payments are to be made or secured to or for the benefit of a
child shall not in the first instance extend beyond the date of the birthday
of the child next following his attaining the upper limit of the compulsory
school age unless the court which makes the order thinks it right in the
circumstances of the case to specify a later date therein.

    For the purposes of this subsection the upper limit of the compulsory
school age means the age that is for the time being that limit by virtue
of section 35 of the Education Act, 1944 together with any Order in
Council made under that section.

    (3) The court may make such an order as is mentioned in subsection
(1) (a) above in favour of a child who has attained the age of eighteen,
and may include in an order made under the said section 3 or 6 in relation
to a child who has not attained that age a provision extending beyond the
date when the child will attain that age the term for which by virtue of
the order any payments are to be made or secured to or for the benefit
of that child, if it appears to the court that—

    (a) that child is, or will be, or if such an order or provision were
        made would be, receiving instruction at an educational estab-
        lishment or undergoing training for a trade, profession or
        vocation, whether or not he is also, or will also be, in gainful
        employment; or
    (b) there are special circumstances which justify the making of the
        order or provision.

    (4) Any order made by virtue of section 3 (2) (a) of this Act or section
6 (6) (d) thereof shall, notwithstanding anything in the order, cease to
have effect on the death of the person liable to make payments under the
order, except in relation to any arrears due under the order on the date
of such death.

    13. Validity of maintenance agreements.—(1) If a maintenance
agreement includes a provision purporting to restrict any right to apply
to a court for an order containing financial arrangements, then—

    (a) that provision shall be void; but
    (b) any other financial arrangements contained in the agreement
        shall not thereby be rendered void or unenforceable and shall,
        unless they are void or unenforceable for any other reason (and
        subject to sections 14 and 15 of this Act), be binding on the
        parties to the agreement.

    (2) In this and the next following section—

    "maintenance agreement" means any agreement in writing made,
        whether before or after the commencement of this Act, between
        the parties to a marriage, being—

(a) an agreement containing financial arrangements, whether made during the continuance or after the dissolution or annulment of the marriage; or

(b) a separation agreement which contains no financial arrangement in a case where no other agreement in writing between the same parties contains such arrangements;

"financial arrangements" means provisions governing the rights and liabilities towards one another when living separately of the parties to a marriage (including a marriage which has been dissolved or annulled) in respect of the making or securing of payments or the disposition or use of any property, including such rights and liabilities with respect to the maintenance or education of any child, whether or not a child of the family.

14. Alteration of agreements by court during lives of parties.— (1) Where a maintenance agreement is for the time being subsisting and each of the parties to the agreement is for the time being either domiciled or resident in England and Wales, then, subject to subsection (3) below, either party may apply to the court or to a magistrates' court for an order under this section.

(2) If the court to which the application is made is satisfied either—

(a) that by reason of a change in the circumstances in the light of which any financial arrangements contained in the agreement were made or, as the case may be, financial arrangements were omitted from it (including a change foreseen by the parties when making the agreement), the agreement should be altered so as to make different, or, as the case may be, so as to contain, financial arrangements, or

(b) that the agreement does not contain proper financial arrangements with respect to any child of the family,

then, subject to subsections (3), (4) and (5) below, that court may by order make such alterations in the agreement—

(i) by varying or revoking any financial arrangements contained in it, or

(ii) by inserting in it financial arrangements for the benefit of one of the parties to the agreement or of a child of the family,

as may appear to that court to be just having regard to all the circumstances, including, if relevant, the matters mentioned in section 5 (3) of this Act; and the agreement shall have effect thereafter as if any alteration made by the order had been made by agreement between the parties and for valuable consideration.

(3) A magistrates' court shall not entertain an application under subsection (1) above unless both the parties to the agreement are resident in England and Wales and at least one of the parties is resident in the petty sessions area (within the meaning of the Magistrates' Courts Act, 1952)

for which the court acts, and shall not have power to make any order on such an application except—

(a) in a case where the agreement includes no provision for periodical payments by either of the parties, an order inserting provision for the making by one of the parties of periodical payments for the maintenance of the other party or for the maintenance of any child of the family;

(b) in a case where the agreement includes provision for the making by one of the parties of periodical payments, an order increasing or reducing the rate of, or terminating, any of those payments.

(4) Where a court decides to alter, by order under this section, an agreement by inserting provision for the making or securing by one of the parties to the agreement of periodical payments for the maintenance of the other party or by increasing the rate of the periodical payments which the agreement provides shall be made by one of the parties for the maintenance of the other, the term for which the payments or, as the case may be, so much of the payments as is attributable to the increase are or is to be made under the agreement as altered by the order shall be such term as the court may specify, but that term shall not exceed—

(a) where the payments will not be secured, the joint lives of the parties to the agreement or a term ending with the remarriage of the party to whom the payments are to be made, whichever is the shorter;

(b) where the payments will be secured, the life of that party or a term ending with the remarriage of that party, whichever is the shorter.

(5) Where a court decides to alter, by order under this section, an agreement by inserting provision for the making or securing by one of the parties to the agreement of periodical payments for the maintenance of a child of the family or by increasing the rate of the periodical payments which the agreement provides shall be made or secured by one of the parties for the maintenance of such a child, then, in deciding the term for which under the agreement as altered by the order the payments or, as the case may be, so much of the payments as is attributable to the increase are or is to be made or secured for the benefit of the child, the court shall apply the provisions of section 8 (1), (2) and (3) of this Act as if the order to which this subsection relates were an order under section 3 of this Act.

(6) For the avoidance of doubt it is hereby declared that nothing in this or the last foregoing section affects any power of a court before which any proceedings between the parties to a maintenance agreement are brought under any other enactment (including a provision of this Act) to make an order containing financial arrangements or any right of either party to apply for such an order in such proceedings.

NOTES

"**To a magistrates' court.**"—Application is by way of complaint and summons. Magistrates' Courts Rules, 1968, r. 87.

"Child of the family."—Section 27 provides that child of the family means " . . . a child who has been *treated* by both of those parties . . . " This is a different definition to that contained in s. 13 of the Matrimonial Proceedings (Magistrates' Courts) Act, 1960, see p. 1236, *ante*.

In *W. (R. J.)* v. *W. (S. J.)*, [1971] 3 All E. R. 303, it was held that, where a husband is not the father of his wife's child that child is a child of the family if it has been treated as such by both husband and wife and in this connection lack of knowledge on the part of one or both parties of the facts relating to paternity is immaterial (*R.* v. *R.*, [1968] P. 414; [1968] 2 All E. R. 608, distinguished. Statement in Rayden on Divorce 11th Edition, p. 867 approved).

Protection, custody, etc., of children

17. Restrictions on decrees for dissolution, annulment or separation affecting children.—(1) The court shall not make absolute a decree of divorce or of nullity of marriage, or make a decree of judicial separation, unless the court, by order, has declared that it is satisfied—

> (a) that for the purposes of this section there are no children of the family to whom this section applies; or

> (b) that the only children who are or may be children of the family to whom this section applies are the children named in the order and that—

>> (i) arrangements for the welfare of every child so named have been made and are satisfactory or are the best that can be devised in the circumstances; or

>> (ii) it is impracticable for the party or parties appearing before the court to make any such arrangements; or

> (c) that there are circumstances making it desirable that the decree should be made absolute or should be made, as the case may be, without delay notwithstanding that there are or may be children of the family to whom this section applies and that the court is unable to make a declaration in accordance with paragraph (b) above.

(2) The court shall not make an order declaring that it is satisfied as mentioned in subsection (1) (c) above unless it has obtained a satisfactory undertaking from either or both of the parties to bring the question of the arrangements for the children named in the order before the court within a specified time.

(3) If the court makes absolute a decree *nisi* of divorce or of nullity of marriage, or makes a decree of judicial separation, without having made an order under subsection (1) above the decree shall be void but, if such an order was made, no person shall be entitled to challenge the validity of the decree on the ground that the conditions prescribed by subsections (1) and (2) above were not fulfilled.

(4) If the court refuses to make an order under subsection (1) above in any proceedings for divorce, nullity of marriage or judicial separation, it shall, on an application by either party to the proceedings, make an order declaring that it is not satisfied as mentioned in that subsection.

(5) This section applies to the following children of the family, that is to say—

    (a) any minor child of the family who at the date of the order under subsection (1) above is—

        (i) under the age of sixteen, or

        (ii) receiving instruction at an educational establishment or undergoing training for a trade, profession or vocation, whether or not he is also in gainful employment; and

    (b) any other child of the family to whom the court by an order under that subsection directs that this section shall apply;

and the court may give such a direction if it is of opinion that there are special circumstances which make it desirable in the interest of the child that this section should apply to it.

(6) In this section "welfare", in relation to a child, includes the custody and education of the child and financial provision for him.

NOTES

"**Child of the family.**"—See s. 27, p. 1255, *post*, and note to s. 14, p. 1251, *ante*.

"**The decree shall be void.**"—Where there is a dispute as to whether a child is a child of the family the question must be decided by the judge and the court may of its own motion appoint the Official Solicitor as guardian *ad litem*; Divorce Rule CVIII (1).

18. Orders for custody and education of children affected by matrimonial suits.—(1) The court may make such order as it thinks fit for the custody and education of any child of the family who is under the age of eighteen—

    (a) in any proceedings for divorce, nullity of marriage or judicial separation, before, by or after the final decree;

    (b) where such proceedings are dismissed after the beginning of the trial, either forthwith or within a reasonable period after the dismissal;

and in any case in which the court has power by virtue of this subsection to make an order in respect of a child it may instead, if it thinks fit, direct that proper proceedings be taken for making the child a ward of court.

(2) Where an order in respect of a child is made under this section, the order shall not affect the rights over or with respect to the child of any person, other than a party to the marriage in question, unless the child is the child of one or both of the parties to that marriage and that person was a party to the proceedings on the application for an order under this section.

(3) Where the court makes or makes absolute a decree of divorce or makes a decree of judicial separation, it may include in the decree a declaration that either party to the marriage in question is unfit to have the custody of the children of the family.

(4) Where a decree of divorce or of judicial separation contains such a declaration as is mentioned in subsection (3) above, then, if the party to

whom the declaration relates is a parent of any child of the family, that party shall not, on the death of the other parent, be entitled as of right to the custody or the guardianship of that child.

(5) While the court has power to make an order in any proceedings by virtue of paragraph (a) of subsection (1) above, it may exercise that power from time to time; and where the court makes an order by virtue of paragraph (b) of that subsection with respect to a child it may from time to time until that child attains the age of eighteen make a further order with respect to his custody and education.

(6) The court shall have power to discharge or vary an order made under this section or to suspend any provision thereof temporarily and to revive the operation of any provision so suspended.

NOTES

Unfit to have the custody.—By s. 3 of the Guardianship of Minors Act, 1971, on the death of one parent, the other would normally have guardianship of the child.

Welfare report.—See the remarks of Davies, L.J., in *W.* v. *W.* (1971), 115 Sol. Jo. 367. In *H.* v. *H. and C.*, [1969] 1 All E. R. 262, C. A., it was emphasised that questions of custody, care and control cannot be determined without oral evidence of the parties and their witnesses. In the former case the county court judge had decided on affidavit evidence, and although there were separate welfare officers reports on the two parties, neither officer had seen the other party or compared the respective accommodation.

19. Orders for custody of children in cases of neglect to maintain.—(1) Where the court makes an order under section 6 of this Act, the court shall also have power from time to time to make such orders as it thinks fit with respect to the custody of any child of the family who is for the time being under the age of eighteen; but the power conferred by this section and any order made in exercise of that power shall have effect only as respects any period when an order is in force under that section and the child is under that age.

(2) Section 18 (2) and (6) of this Act shall apply in relation to an order made under this section as they apply in relation to an order made under that section.

NOTES

Section 6 of this Act.—*I.e.*, neglect by party to marriage to maintain other party or child of the family.

Education until 21.—See s. 8 (3).

27. Interpretation.—(1) In this Part of this Act—

"adopted" means adopted in pursuance of—

        (a) an adoption order made under the Adoption Act, 1958, any previous enactment relating to the adoption of children, the Adoption Act, 1968 or any corresponding enactment of the Parliament of Northern Ireland; or

        (b) an adoption order made in the Isle of Man or any of the Channel Islands; or

(c) subject to sections 5 and 6 of the Adoption Act, 1968, an overseas adoption within the meaning of section 4 of that Act;

"child", in relation to one or both of the parties to a marriage, includes an illegitimate or adopted child of that party or, as the case may be, of both parties;

"child of the family", in relation to the parties to a marriage, means—

(a) a child of both of those parties; and

(b) any other child, not being a child who has been boarded-out with those parties by a local authority or voluntary organisation, who has been treated by both of those parties as a child of their family;

"the court" (except where the context otherwise requires) means the High Court or, where a county court has jurisdiction by virtue of the Matrimonial Causes Act, 1967, a county court;

"custody", in relation to a child, includes access to the child;

"education" includes training.

(2) For the avoidance of doubt it is hereby declared that references in this Part of this Act to remarriage include references to a marriage which is by law void or voidable.

(3) Any reference in this Part of this Act to any enactment is a reference to that enactment as amended by or under any subsequent enactment, including this Act.

INCOME AND CORPORATION TAXES ACT, 1970
[1970 c. 10]

*   *   *   *   *

Special types of payment

65. Small maintenance payments.—(1) In this section "small maintenance payments" means payments under an order made by a court in the United Kingdom—

(a) by one of the parties to a marriage (including a marriage which has been dissolved or annulled) to or for the benefit of the other party to that marriage for that other party's maintenance, or

(b) to any person for the benefit of, or for the maintenance or education of, a person under 21 years of age, not being such a payment as is mentioned in paragraph (a) above,

being (subject to subsection (5) below) payments which—

(i) are for the time being required by the order (whether as originally made or as varied) to be made—

(A) weekly at a rate not exceeding £7 10s. 0d. per week, or
(B) monthly at a rate not exceeding £32 10s. 0d. per month, and

(ii) would, apart from this section, fall within section 52 or 53 above (deduction of income tax from annual payments),

and "small maintenance order" means an order providing for the making of small maintenance payments.

(2) Notwithstanding anything in the said section 52 or 53, small maintenance payments shall be made without deduction of income tax.

(3) Any sums paid in or towards the discharge of a small maintenance payment shall be chargeable under Case III of Schedule D, but the tax shall (notwithstanding anything in sections 119 to 121 of this Act) be computed in all cases on the payments falling due in the year of assessment, so far as paid in that or in any other year.

(4) A person making a claim in that behalf shall be entitled, in computing his total income for any year of assessment for any of the purposes of the Income Tax Acts, to deduct sums paid by him in or towards the discharge of any small maintenance payments which fall due in that year; and, for the purposes of section 25 of this Act (personal reliefs not to be given in respect of charges on income), any amount which can be deducted under this subsection in computing the total income of a person shall be

treated as if it were income the tax on which that person is entitled to charge against another person.

(5) The Treasury may from time to time, by order made by statutory instrument subject to annulment in pursuance of a resolution of the House of Commons, increase the amount of £7 10s. 0d. and the amount of £32 10s. 0d. in subsection (1) (i) above, either as respects payments within paragraph (a) of that subsection, or as respects payments within paragraph (b) thereof, or as respects both.

(6) An order under subsection (5) above which increases, or further increases, the said amount of £7 10s. 0d. for a class of payments shall increase, or further increase, the amount of £32 10s. 0d. for that class of payments so that it is 52 twelfths of the weekly amount or, if that does not give a convenient round sum, such other amount as appears to the Treasury to be the nearest convenient round sum; and an order under that subsection may contain provision whereby it—

    (a) does not in general affect payments falling due in the year of assessment in which it comes into force under small maintenance orders made before its coming into force, but

    (b) in the case of a small maintenance order which was made before that time but is varied or revived after that time, does apply in relation to payments falling due under that order at any time after the variation or revival.

(7) Where a court—

    (a) make or revive a small maintenance order, or

    (b) vary or revive an order so that it becomes, or ceases to be, a small maintenance order, or

    (c) change the persons who are entitled to small maintenance payments,

the court shall furnish to the Board, in such form as the Board may prescribe, particulars of the order or variation, as the case may be, the names of the persons affected by the order, and, so far as known to the court, the addresses of those persons.

In this subsection—

    "the persons affected", in relation to a small maintenance order, means the person liable to make the payments under the order and any person for the time being entitled to the payments, and

    reference to the variation of an order include references to the making of an order changing the persons entitled to the payments thereunder.

SECTION 6.—STATUTORY INSTRUMENTS, ORDERS, RULES AND PRACTICE DIRECTIONS

CONTENTS

THE GUARDIANSHIP OF INFANTS (SUMMARY JURISDICTION) RULES, 1925

[S. R. & O. 1925, No. 960/L.24]

1. These Rules may be cited as the Guardianship of Infants (Summary Jurisdiction) Rules, 1925.

2. These Rules shall come into operation on the 1st October, 1925.

3.—(1) The power of a court of summary jurisdiction to do any act or thing authorised to be done by such court under the Guardianship of Infants Acts, 1886 and 1925, except as regards the consent authorised to be given under section 9 of the Guardianship of Infants Act, 1925, shall be exercised by an order upon complaint in accordance with the Summary Jurisdiction Acts.

Provided that, if the court considers it expedient in the interests of the infant, it may decide to hear the proceedings *in camera*.

[(2) Annulled by S. R. & O. 1944, No. 1206/L. 43.]

4.—(1) Application for the consent of a court of summary jurisdiction to the marriage of an infant, under section 9 of the Guardianship of Infants Act, 1925, may be made personally, either verbally or in writing, to a justice of the peace, or to a court of summary jurisdiction, and thereupon such justice or court may issue a notice of such application, and of the time and place appointed for the hearing of the application, directed to the person who has refused consent.

(2) Such notice shall be served on the person to whom it is directed in the same manner as if it were a summons issued under the Summary Jurisdiction Acts.

(3) The court of summary jurisdiction shall hear such application in the same manner as if it were hearing a complaint for an order under the Summary Jurisdiction Acts.

(4) The court shall have power to hear such application *in camera* if it considers it expedient in the interests of the infant that the application should not be heard and determined in open court.

1258

NOTES

Procedure.—Proceedings have not been assigned to juvenile courts. They are " domestic proceedings," by virtue of s. 56 of the Magistrates' Courts Act, 1952, p. 1220, *ante.*

Summary Jurisdiction Acts.—The relevant sections of these Acts are repealed by the Magistrates' Courts Act, 1952. See now Part II of that Act, 21 Halsbury's Statutes, 3rd Edn., 181, and the Magistrates' Courts Rules, 1968.

Consent to marriage is now dealt with by s. 3 of the Marriage Act, 1949, p. 1215, *ante,* which replaced s. 9 of the Guardianship of Infants Act, 1925. These Rules which were made under the repealed s. 7 (2) of the Guardianship of Infants Act, 1925, remain in force by virtue of s. 79 (2) of the Marriage Act, 1949; 17 Halsbury's Statutes, 3rd Edn., 97.

THE COUNTY COURT RULES, 1936

[S. R. & O. 1936, No. 626/L.17]

ORDER XLVI. Rules 1, 2, 9 and 14

The Guardianship of Infants Acts, 1886 and 1925

1.—(1) All proceedings under the Guardianship of Infants Acts, 1886 and 1925, shall be heard and determined in chambers unless the court otherwise directs.

2. Where application is made under paragraph (2A) of section 4 of the said Act of 1925, for the appointment of the applicant to be guardian of an infant who has been received into the care of a local authority under section 1 of the Children Act, 1948, the court shall, not less than 14 days before the day fixed for the hearing, serve a copy of the application and a notice in Form 26 upon the local authority and the authority shall be entitled to appear on the hearing of the application.

Marriage Act, 1949

9.—(1) Every application under section 3 of the Marriage Act, 1949, for the consent of the court to the marriage of an infant shall be heard and determined in chambers unless the court otherwise directs.

(2) The application may be heard and determined by the registrar.

(3) A copy of the application and a notice in Form 26 shall, not less than 7 clear days before the day fixed for the hearing, be served on every person whose consent is required to the marriage and who has refused his consent.

(4) Notwithstanding the provisions of Rule 2 of Order 3 it shall not be necessary for the application to be made by the applicant's next friend unless the court so directs.

Maintenance Orders Act, 1950

14.—(1) In this Rule—

" this Act " means the Maintenance Orders Act, 1950;

"maintenance order" means an order for the payment of weekly or other periodical sums made by a county court under section 3 (2) or 5 (4) of the Guardianship of Infants Act, 1925.

(2) The prescribed officer of the county court for the purposes of sections 17, 22, 23 and 24 of this Act shall be the registrar.

(3) An application under Part II of this Act for the registration of a maintenance order in the sheriff court in Scotland or the court of summary jurisdiction in Northern Ireland, within the jurisdiction of which the defendant appears to be, shall be made to the registrar of the county court in which the maintenance order was made, by lodging in the office of that court an affidavit by the applicant (together with a copy thereof) stating:—

(a) the date of the maintenance order, the name of the person liable to make payments thereunder, and the amount of the weekly or other periodical payments ordered therein;

(b) the address in the United Kingdom of the person liable to make payments under the maintenance order;

(c) the reason why it is convenient that the maintenance order should be enforceable in Scotland or in Northern Ireland, as the case may be;

(d) the amount of any arrears due to the applicant under the maintenance order; and

(e) that the maintenance order is not already registered under this Act.

(4) If it appears to the registrar that the person liable to make payments under the maintenance order resides in Scotland or Northern Ireland and that it is convenient that the maintenance order should be enforceable there, he shall send a certified copy of the maintenance order and the applicant's affidavit to the sheriff-clerk of the sheriff court in Scotland or, as the case may be, to the clerk of the court of summary jurisdiction in Northern Ireland, having jurisdiction in the place in which the person liable to make payments under the maintenance order appears to be.

(5) On being notified of the registration of the maintenance order in the court to which the certified copy has been sent, the registrar shall make a note thereof in the books of the court relating to the maintenance order.

(6) Where a maintenance order registered in a court in Scotland or Northern Ireland is varied or discharged by the court which made it, the registrar shall send a certified copy of the order varying or discharging the maintenance order to the sheriff-clerk, or as the case may be, the clerk of the court in which the maintenance order is registered.

(7) Upon receipt of a notice of variation of the maintenance order or of cancellation of the registration of the maintenance order by the court in which it is registered, the registrar shall make a note thereof in the books of the court relating to the maintenance order.

(8) An application to the county court under section 22 (5) of this Act to adduce evidence in connection with a maintenance order registered in Scotland or Northern Ireland shall be made on notice in accordance with the provisions of Order XIII.

FORM 26

Notice to Respondent of day on which matter will be heard.
Order 6, Rule 6 (1) (c) (ii)

[Actions.]

		In the	County Court.
			No. of
			Plaint
BETWEEN		A.B.	*Plaintiff,*
		and	
		C.D.	*Defendant.*

[Matters.]

In the   County Court.

No.

IN THE MATTER OF [*here state the title of any Act, other than the County Courts Act, 1934, by which the Court is given power to entertain the proceedings.*]

AND IN THE MATTER OF [*here refer to the trust, settlement or other particular matter in respect of which the proceedings are brought.*]

BETWEEN   *A.B.*   *Applicant,*
                                                         [or *Petitioner*],
                                                         [or *Appellant*],
                                            and
                                           C.D.   *Respondent.*

[*or as the case may be.*]

Take notice that this matter will be heard at a Court to be holden at on the   day of   19 , at the hour of   in the noon, and that if you do not attend at the time and place above-mentioned, such Order will be made as the Judge thinks just.

A sealed copy of the originating application is hereto annexed.

NOTES

These Rules are printed as amended by the County Court (Amendment) Rules, 1951 and 1960.

For details of procedure and forms, reference should be made to the County Court Practice and the Encyclopaedia of Court Forms and Precedents in Civil Proceedings, title Infants, Vol. IX, pp. 473 *et seq.*

Consent to marriage.—See note, p. 1259, *ante.*

RULES OF THE SUPREME COURT, 1965
ORDER 55

APPEALS TO HIGH COURT FROM COURT, TRIBUNAL OR PERSON: GENERAL

Application

1.—(1) Subject to paragraphs (2), (3) and (4), this Order shall apply to every appeal which by or under any enactment lies to the High Court from any court, tribunal or person.

(2) This Order shall not apply to an appeal by case stated.

(4) The following rules of this Order shall, in relation to an appeal to which this Order applies, have effect subject to any provision made in relation to that appeal by any other provision of these rules or by or under any enactment.

Court to hear appeal

2. An appeal to which this Order applies shall be heard and determined by a Divisional Court of the Queen's Bench Division except where by some other provision of these rules or by or under any enactment it is required to be heard and determined by a Divisional Court of another Division or by a single judge.

NOTE

Appellate jurisdiction under s. 11 of the Guardianship of Minors Act, 1971, the Matrimonial Proceedings (Magistrates' Courts) Act, 1960, and s. 10 of the Adoption Act, are amongst the matters assigned to the Family Division by s. 1 and Sched. I of the Administration of Justice Act, 1970.

Bringing of appeal

3.—(1) An appeal to which this Order applies shall be by way of rehearing and must be brought by originating motion.

(2) Every notice of the motion by which such an appeal is brought must state the grounds of the appeal and, if the appeal is against a judgment, order or other

decision of a court, must state whether the appeal is against the whole or a part of that decision and, if against a part only, must specify the part.

(3) The bringing of such an appeal shall not operate as a stay of proceedings on the judgment, determination or other decision against which the appeal is brought unless the Court by which the appeal is to be heard or the court, tribunal or person by which or by whom the decision was given so orders.

NOTE

As to applications for leave to adduce further evidence see *Practice Direction*, [1967] 2 All E.R. 1232.

Service of notice of motion and entry of appeal

4.—(1) The persons to be served with notice of the motion by which an appeal to which this Order applies is brought are the following:—

(a) if the appeal is against a judgment, order or other decision of a court, the registrar or clerk of the court and any party to the proceedings in which the decision was given who is directly affected by the appeal;

(b) if the appeal is against an order, determination, award or other decision of a tribunal, Minister of the Crown, government department or other person, the chairman of the tribunal, Minister, government department or person, as the case may be, and every party to the proceedings (other than the appellant) in which the decision appealed against was given.

(2) The notice must be served, and the appeal entered, within 28 days after the date of the judgment, order, determination or other decision against which the appeal is brought.

(3) In the case of an appeal against a judgment, order or decision of a court, the period specified in paragraph (2) shall be calculated from the date of the judgment or order or the date on which the decision was given.

(4) In the case of an appeal against an order, determination, award or other decision of a tribunal, Minister, government department or other person, the period specified in paragraph (2) shall be calculated from the date on which notice of the decision was given to the appellant by the person who made the decision or by a person authorised in that behalf to do so.

Date of hearing of appeal

5. Unless the Court having jurisdiction to determine the appeal otherwise directs, an appeal to which this Order applies shall not be heard sooner than 21 days after service of notice of the motion by which the appeal is brought.

Amendment of grounds of appeal, etc.

6.—(1) The notice of the motion by which an appeal to which this Order applies is brought may be amended by the appellant, without leave, by supplementary notice served not less than 7 days before the day appointed for the hearing of the appeal, on each of the persons on whom the notice to be amended was served.

(2) Within 2 days after service of a supplementary notice under paragraph (1) the appellant must lodge two copies of the notice in the office in which the appeal is entered.

(3) Except with the leave of the Court hearing any such appeal, no grounds other than those stated in the notice of the motion by which the appeal is brought or any supplementary notice under paragraph (1) may be relied upon by the appellant at the hearing; but that Court may amend the grounds so

stated or make any other order, on such terms as it thinks just, to ensure the determination on the merits of the real question in controversy between the parties.

(4) The foregoing provisions of this rule are without prejudice to the powers of the Court under Order 20.

Powers of court hearing appeal

7.—(1) In addition to the power conferred by rule 6(3), the Court hearing an appeal to which this Order applies shall have the powers conferred by the following provisions of this rule.

(2) The Court shall have power to receive further evidence on questions of fact, and the evidence may be given in such manner as the Court may direct either by oral examination in court, by affidavit, by deposition taken before an examiner or in some other manner.

(3) The Court shall have power to draw any inferences of fact which might have been drawn in the proceedings out of which the appeal arose.

(4) It shall be the duty of the appellant to apply to the judge or other person presiding at the proceedings in which the decision appealed against was given for a signed copy of any note made by him of the proceedings and to furnish that copy for the use of the Court; and in default of production of such a note, or, if such note is incomplete, in addition to such note, the Court may hear and determine the appeal on any other evidence or statement of what occurred in those proceedings as appears to the Court to be sufficient.

Except where the Court otherwise directs, an affidavit or note by a person present at the proceedings shall not be used in evidence under this paragraph unless it was previously submitted to the person presiding at the proceedings for his comments.

(5) The Court may give any judgment or decision or make any order which ought to have been given or made by the court, tribunal or person and make such further or other order as the case may require or may remit the matter with the opinion of the Court for rehearing and determination by it or him.

(6) The Court may, in special circumstances, order that such security shall be given for the costs of the appeal as may be just.

(7) The Court shall not be bound to allow the appeal on the ground merely of misdirection, or of the improper admission or rejection of evidence, unless in the opinion of the Court substantial wrong or miscarriage has been thereby occasioned.

ORDER 90

MISCELLANEOUS PROCEEDINGS IN THE FAMILY DIVISION

I. GENERAL

Interpretation

1. In this Order, "principal registry" means the principal registry of the Family Division, and "registrar" means a registrar of that Division.

Assignment and commencement of proceedings

2. All proceedings to which this Order relates shall be assigned to the Family Division and, except as provided by rules 3 and 5, shall be begun in the principal registry.

II. PROCEEDINGS CONCERNING MINORS

Application to make minor a ward of court

3.—(1) An application to make a minor a ward of court must be made by originating summons issued out of the principal registry or out of a district registry as defined by the matrimonial causes rules.

(2) Where there is no person other than the minor who is a suitable defendant, an application may be made *ex parte* to a registrar for leave to issue either an *ex parte* originating summons or an originating summons with the minor as defendant thereto; and, except where such leave is granted, the minor shall not be made a defendant to an originating summons under this rule in the first instance.

(3) Particulars of any summons under this rule issued in a district registry shall be sent by the district registrar to the principal registry for recording in the register of wards.

When minor ceases to be a ward of court

4.—(1) A minor who, by virtue of section 9 (2) of the Law Reform (Miscellaneous Provisions) Act, 1949, becomes a ward of court on the issue of a summons under rule 3 shall cease to be a ward of court—

   (a) if an application for an appointment for the hearing of the summons is not made within the period of 21 days after the issue of the summons, at the expiration of that period;
   (b) if an application for such an appointment is made within that period, on the determination of the application made by the summons unless the Court hearing it orders that the minor be made a ward of court.

(2) Nothing in paragraph (1) shall be taken as affecting the power of the Court under section 9 (3) of the said Act to order that any minor who is for the time being a ward of court shall cease to be a ward of court.

(3) If no application for an appointment for the hearing of a summons under rule 3 is made within the period of 21 days after the issue of the summons, a notice stating whether the applicant intends to proceed with the application made by the summons must be left at the registry in which the matter is proceeding immediately after the expiration of that period.

Applications under Guardianship of Minors Act, 1971

5. Where there is pending any proceeding by reason of which a minor is a ward of court, any application under the Guardianship of Minors Act, 1971 (hereafter in this Part of this Order referred to as "the Act of 1971") with respect to that minor may be made by summons in that proceeding, but except in that case any such application must be made by originating summons issued out of the principal registry or out of a district registry as defined by the matrimonial causes rules.

Defendants to guardianship summons

6.—(1) Where the minor with respect to whom an application under the Act of 1971 is made is not the plaintiff, he shall not, unless the Court otherwise directs, be made a defendant to the summons or, if the application is made by ordinary summons, be served with the summons, but, subject to paragraph (2) any other person appearing to be interested in, or affected by, the application shall be made a defendant or be served with the summons, as the case may be, including, where the application is made under section 5 of the Act of 1971 with respect to a minor who has been received into the care of a local authority under section 1 of the Children Act, 1948, that authority.

(2) The Court may dispense with service of the summons (whether originating or ordinary) on any person and may order it to be served on any person not originally served.

Guardianship proceedings may be in chambers

7. Applications under the Act of 1971 may be disposed of in chambers.

Applications for consent to marriage

8.—(1) Subject to paragraph (2), the provisions of this Order relating to applications under the Act of 1971 shall apply with the necessary modifications to applications under section 3 of the Marriage Act, 1949 for obtaining the Court's consent to the marriage of a minor.

(2) Where an application under the said section 3 is made in consequence of a refusal to give consent to a marriage every person who has refused consent shall be made a defendant to the summons and rule 6 (1) shall not apply.

Appeals and applications affecting minors

9.—(1) Every appeal to the High Court—

    (a) under section 16 (2) or (3) of the Act of 1971 from a county court or magistrates' court, or

    (b) under section 10 of the Adoption Act, 1958 from a magistrates' court,

shall be heard and determined by a Divisional Court of the Family Division.

(2) Order 55, rule 4 (2), shall apply to any appeal under this rule, and subject thereto, rule 16 of this Order (except paragraph (2) thereof) shall apply with the necessary modifications to any such appeal as it applies to appeals under the Matrimonial Proceedings (Magistrates' Courts) Act, 1960.

(3) After entry of an appeal from a county court or magistrates' court under the Act of 1971 the Divisional Court may, on an application made *ex parte* or otherwise, make any order with respect to the custody or maintenance of the minor in question pending the appeal or otherwise as it thinks proper.

Removal of guardianship proceedings from a county court

10.—(1) An application for an order under section 16 (1) of the Act of 1971 for the removal of an application from a county court into the High Court shall be made by an originating summons issued out of the principal registry and, unless the Court otherwise directs, the summons need not be served on any person.

(2) The application may be heard by a registrar, but, if an order is made for the removal to the High Court of an application to the county court, that application shall be heard by a single judge of the Family Division.

(3) Where an order is made under the said section 16 (1), the plaintiff must send a copy of the order to the registrar of the county court from which the proceedings are ordered to be removed.

(4) On receipt by the proper officer of the documents referred to in Order 16, rule 19, of the County Court Rules, 1936, that officer must forthwith file the said documents and give notice to all parties that the application removed is proceeding in the High Court.

(5) The application so removed shall proceed in the High Court as if it had been made by originating summons issued out of the principal registry.

Drawing up and service of orders

11. The provisions of the matrimonial causes rules relating to the drawing up and service of orders shall apply to proceedings under this Part of this Order as if they were proceedings under those rules.

Jurisdiction of registrars

12.—(1) In proceedings to which this Part of this Order applies a registrar may transact all such business and exercise all such authority and jurisdiction as may be transacted and exercised by a judge in chambers.

(2) Paragraph (1) is without prejudice to the power of the judges to reserve to themselves the transaction of any such business or the exercise of any such authority or jurisdiction.

III. OTHER PROCEEDINGS

Application for declaration affecting matrimonial status

13.—(1) Where, apart from costs, the only relief sought in any proceedings is a declaration with respect to the matrimonial status of any person, the proceedings shall be begun by petition.

(2) The petition shall state—

(a) the names of the parties and the residential address of each of them at the date of presentation of the petition;

(b) the place and date of any ceremony of marriage to which the application relates;

(c) whether there have been any previous proceedings between the parties with reference to the marriage or the ceremony of marriage to which the application relates or with respect to the matrimonial status of either of them and, if so, the nature of those proceedings;

(d) all other material facts alleged by the petitioner to justify the making of the declaration and the grounds on which he alleges that the Court has jurisdiction to make it;

and shall conclude with a prayer setting out the declaration sought and any claim for costs.

(3) Nothing in the foregoing provisions shall be construed—

(a) as conferring any jurisdiction to make a declaration in circumstances in which the Court could not otherwise make it, or

(b) as affecting the power of the Court to refuse to make a declaration notwithstanding that it has jurisdiction to make it.

(4) This rule does not apply to proceedings to which rule 14 applies.

Application under section 39 of Matrimonial Causes Act, 1965

14.—(1) A petition under section 39 of the Matrimonial Causes Act, 1965 shall, in addition to stating the grounds on which the petitioner relies, set out the date and place of birth of the petitioner and the maiden name of his mother, and, if the petitioner is known by a name other than that which appears in the certificate of his birth, that fact shall be stated in the petition and in any decree made thereon.

(2) The petition shall be supported by an affidavit by the petitioner verifying the petition and giving particulars of every person whose interest may be affected by the proceedings and his relationship to the petitioner:

Provided that if the petitioner is under 16, the affidavit shall, unless otherwise directed, be made by his next friend.

(3) An affidavit for the purposes of paragraph (2) may contain statements of information or belief with the sources and grounds thereof.

(4) On filing the petition, the petitioner shall issue and serve on the Attorney-General a summons for directions as to the persons, other than the Attorney-General, who are to be made respondents to the petition.

(5) It shall not be necessary to serve the petition on the Attorney-General otherwise than by delivering a copy of it to him in accordance with subsection (6) of the said section 39.

(6) The Attorney-General may file an answer to the petition within 21 days after directions have been given under paragraph (4) and no directions for trial shall be given until that period has expired.

(7) A respondent who files an answer shall at the same time lodge in the divorce registry as many copies of the answer as there are other parties to the proceedings and a registrar shall send one of the copies to each of those parties.

Further proceedings on petition under rule 13 or 14

15.—(1) Unless a judge otherwise directs, all proceedings on any petition to which rule 13 or 14 relates shall take place in London.

(2) Subject to rules 2, 13 and 14 and paragraph (1) of this rule, the matrimonial causes rules shall apply with the necessary modifications to the petition as if it were a petition in a matrimonial cause.

Appeals under the Matrimonial Proceedings (Magistrates' Courts) Act, 1960

16.—Every appeal to the High Court under the Matrimonial Proceedings (Magistrates' Courts) Act, 1960 shall be entered by lodging two copies of the notice of motion in the principal registry.

(2) Order 55, rule 4 (2), shall apply to the appeal as if for the period of 28 days therein specified there were substituted a period of 6 weeks.

(3) Notwithstanding anything in Order 10, rule 5, notice of the motion need not be served personally.

(4) On entering the appeal or as soon as practicable thereafter, the appellant shall, unless otherwise directed, lodge in the principal registry—

    (a) two certified copies of the summons and of the order appealed against,
    (b) two copies of the clerk's notes of the evidence,
    (c) two copies of the justices' reasons for their decision,
    (d) a certificate that notice of the motion has been duly served on the clerk and on every party affected by the appeal, and
    (e) where the notice of the motion includes an application to extend the time for bringing the appeal, a certificate (and a copy thereof) by the appellant's solicitor, or the appellant if he is acting in person, setting out the reasons for the delay and the relevant dates.

(5) If the clerk's notes of the evidence are not produced, the Court may hear and determine the appeal on any other evidence or statement of what occurred in the proceedings before the magistrates' court as appears to the Court to be sufficient.

(6) The Court shall not be bound to allow the appeal on the ground merely of misdirection or improper reception or rejection of evidence unless, in the opinion of the Court, substantial wrong or miscarriage of justice has been thereby occasioned.

(7) A registrar may dismiss an appeal to which this rule applies for want of prosecution or, with the consent of the parties, may dismiss the appeal or give leave for it to be withdrawn, and may deal with any question of costs arising out of the dismissal or withdrawal.

NOTE

For notes on the above Rules, see the *Annual Practice*, and for forms, see the *Encyclopædia of Court Forms and Precedents in Civil Proceedings*, title "Infants," Vol. IX, pp. 473 *et seq.* (Butterworths).

THE MAGISTRATES' COURTS (MATRIMONIAL PROCEEDINGS) RULES, 1960

[S.I. 1960 No. 2229]

Notice to local authority with regard to child

1. At least ten days before including in a matrimonial order a provision committing a child to the care of a local authority the court shall cause notice in the form numbered 1 in the Schedule to these Rules to be delivered or sent by post to that authority.

Substitution of new supervisor for child

2.—(1) Where a matrimonial order provides for a child to be under the supervision of a probation officer appointed for or assigned to a petty sessions area or under the supervision of a local authority, and the court is of the opinion, upon representations made to it orally or in writing by or on behalf of a probation officer appointed for or assigned to that area or, as the case may be, by or on behalf of that local authority, that the child is or will be resident in a petty sessions area other than that for which the probation officer has been appointed or to which he is assigned or, as the case may be, in the area of another local authority, the court may vary the order by substituting a probation officer appointed for or assigned to the other petty sessions area, or, as the case may be, by substituting the other local authority.

(2) Where the court varies a matrimonial order in accordance with this Rule, the court shall cause a notice in the form numbered 2 in the Schedule to these Rules to be given or sent by post—

    (a) to the person to whom the legal custody of the child is committed by the matrimonial order ; and

    (b) in duplicate, to the clerk to the justices for the petty sessions area, or, as the case may be, the local authority, substituted by the order under this Rule,

and shall cause the probation officer or local authority by or on whose behalf the representations were made to be informed that the order has been so varied.

Notice to parties of court's power to make provision with regard to children

3. In a case where the special powers of the court under section four of the Act to make provision with regard to any child of the family of the parties are or may be exercisable, the clerk of the court shall—

    (a) upon the making of a complaint under section one or section eight of the Act, cause a notice in the form numbered 3 in the Schedule to these Rules to be given to the complainant ;

    (b) upon the issue of a summons after the making of such a complaint as aforesaid, cause a similar notice to be served on the defendant with the summons.

Notice to parent of child (other than a party) of court's power to make provision with regard to children

4.—(1) In the case of a complaint under section one of the Act where—

(a) there is a child of the family of the parties who is not a child of both parties ; and

(b) the court is required, under subsection (6) of section four of the Act, to take steps with a view to giving notice of the complaint, and of the time and place appointed for the hearing, to any person who, though not one of the parties, is a parent of that child,

the court may make a matrimonial order on the complaint in accordance with paragraph (b) of the said subsection (6) if there has been read aloud before the court at the hearing of the complaint a statement signed by the clerk of the court that the steps required by the following paragraphs of this Rule have been taken with a view to giving notice to the parent as aforesaid.

(2) Subject to the next following paragraph, the steps required by this Rule are the following :—

(a) before the summons is issued on the complaint the complainant shall be required to say whether or not there is a child of the family who is not a child of both the parties and in respect of whom a notice is required to be given to his parent under subsection (6) of section four of the Act, and, if there is, to give the name and address of that parent so far as this information is known to, or can in the opinion of the clerk conveniently be obtained by, the complainant ;

(b) at least ten days before the hearing at which the court proposes to make a matrimonial order on the complaint the clerk shall cause a notice in the form numbered 4 in the Schedule to these Rules to be sent by post addressed to any such parent as is referred to in sub-paragraph (a) of this paragraph whose name and address are known to the clerk, whether from information given by the complainant in accordance with that sub-paragraph or otherwise.

(3) Where, after notice has been sent to a parent in accordance with sub-paragraph (b) of the last foregoing paragraph, the hearing at which the court proposes to make a matrimonial order in accordance with this Rule is adjourned, the court may make the order at the adjourned hearing if it is satisfied that reasonable steps have been taken to give the parent adequate notice of the time and place thereof.

Notice to person outside United Kingdom of complaint for revocation, etc., of order

5.—(1) Where a complaint is made by virtue of section eight of the Act for the revocation, revival or variation of a matrimonial or interim order and the defendant does not appear at the time and place appointed for the hearing of the complaint but the court is satisfied that there is reason to believe that he has been outside the United Kingdom during the whole of the period beginning one month before the making of the complaint and ending with the date of the hearing, then, subject to paragraph (2) of this Rule, the court may, if it thinks it reasonable in all the circumstances to do so, proceed to hear and determine the complaint in accordance with subsection (2) of section nine of the Act if it is proved to the satisfaction of the court that the complainant has taken any of the following steps to give notice to the defendant of the making of the complaint and of the time and place aforesaid, that is to say :—

(a) has caused a notice in the form numbered 5 in the Schedule to these Rules to be delivered to the defendant ; or

(b) has caused a notice in the form aforesaid to be sent by post addressed to the defendant at his last known or usual place of abode or at his place of business or at such other address at which there is ground for believing that it will reach him ; or

(c) has caused a notice summarising the effect of that in the form aforesaid to be inserted in one or more newspapers on one or more occasions.

(2) Where it is proposed to take any such steps as are mentioned in sub-paragraph (b) or (c) of the preceding paragraph, the complainant shall apply for directions to a justice of the peace acting for the same petty sessions area as that of the court by which the complaint is to be heard, and the taking of such steps shall be effective for the purposes of this Rule only if they were taken in accordance with the directions given by the said justice.

(3) Paragraph (1) of Rule 55 of the Magistrates' Courts Rules, 1952, shall apply for the purpose of proving the delivery of a written notice in pursuance of sub-paragraph (a) of paragraph (1) of this Rule as it applies for the purpose of proving the service of a summons.

In relation to a solemn declaration made outside the United Kingdom, paragraph (1) of the said Rule 55, as applied by this paragraph, shall have effect as if for the reference to the authorities mentioned in the said paragraph (1) there were substituted a reference to a consular officer of Her Majesty's Government in the United Kingdom, or any person for the time being authorised by law, in the place where the declarant is, to administer an oath for any judicial or other legal purpose.

(4) Paragraph (2) of the said Rule 55 shall apply for the purpose of proving the sending of a written notice in pursuance of sub-paragraph (b) of paragraph (1) of this Rule, or the insertion of a notice in a newspaper in pursuance of sub-paragraph (c) thereof, as it applies for the purpose of proving the service of any process, provided, as respects the insertion of a notice in a newspaper, that a copy of the newspaper containing the notice is annexed to the certificate

Certificate by clerk when maintenance payments are forwarded abroad.

6.—A complainant for the revocation or variation of a matrimonial order under which payments fall to be made by the complainant to the defendant through the clerk of a magistrates' court may supply to that clerk for such a certificate as is mentioned in subsection (4) of section nine of the Act, and, if the facts warrant it, the clerk shall supply such a certificate to the complainant in the form numbered 6 in the Schedule to these Rules.

Defendants to complaint for revocation, revival or variation of order

7.—(1) Where a complaint is made by virtue of section eight of the Act for the revocation, revival or variation of a matrimonial or interim order, the persons to be made defendants to the complaint in accordance with subsection (2) of section ten of the Act shall be the following persons (not being the complainant), that is to say, the parties to the marriage in question and the persons specified in the following paragraphs of this Rule.

(2) Where the complaint relates to a provision of the order for the legal custody of a child, the following persons shall be made defendants to the complaint :—

(a) any person who, though not a party to the marriage in question, is a parent of the child ;

(b) any person to whose legal custody the child is for the time being committed by the order ;

    (c) where under the order the child is for the time being committed to the care, or under the supervision, of a local authority, that local authority;

    (d) where under the order the child is for the time being under the supervision of a probation officer, that probation officer.

The father of an illegitimate child shall not be treated as a parent of that child for the purposes of sub-paragraph (a) of this paragraph unless he has been adjudged by a court to be the father of that child.

(3) Where the complaint is for the revocation of a provision committing a child to the care of a local authority, the persons specified in sub-paragraphs (a), (b) and (c) of the foregoing paragraph shall be made defendants to the complaint.

(4) Where the complaint is for the revocation or variation of a provision that a child be under the supervision of a probation officer or a local authority, the following persons shall be made defendants to the complaint :—

    (a) the persons specified in sub-paragraphs (a) and (b) of paragraph (2) of this Rule;

    (b) the probation officer or local authority under whose supervision the child is for the time being under the order;

    (c) if the complaint is for the variation of the provision, the probation officer or local authority whom it is sought by the complaint to substitute for the officer or authority specified in the last foregoing sub-paragraph.

(5) Where the complaint relates to a provision for access to a child, the following persons shall be made defendants to the complaint :—

    (a) the persons specified in sub-paragraphs (a) and (b) of paragraph (2) of this Rule;

    (b) where under the order the child is for the time being committed to the care, or under the supervision, of a local authority, that local authority;

    (c) where under the order the child is for the time being under the supervision of a probation officer, that probation officer.

(6) Where the complaint relates to a provision for payments for the maintenance of a child, any person to whom such payments fall to be made shall be made a defendant to the complaint.

Interpretation

8.—(1) In these Rules " the Act " means the Matrimonial Proceedings (Magistrates' Courts) Act, 1960.

(2) Section sixteen of the Act shall apply to the interpretation of these Rules as it applies to the interpretation of the Act.

(3) The Interpretation Act, 1889, shall apply to the interpretation of these Rules as it applies to the interpretation of an Act of Parliament.

(4) Any reference in these Rules to a form in the Schedule to these Rules shall include a reference to a form to the like effect with such variations as the circumstances may require.

Citation and commencement

9. These Rules may be cited as the Magistrates' Courts (Matrimonial Proceedings) Rules, 1960, and shall come into operation on the first day of January, 1961. Dated the first day of December, 1960.

NOTE

These rules were made by the Lord Chancellor under the Justices of the Peace Act, 1949, s. 15 as extended by the Magistrates' Courts Act, 1952, s. 122.

SCHEDULE
Forms

1

Notice to local authority of proposal to commit a child to their care
(M.P. (M.C.) Act, 1960, ss. 2 (1) (e), 3 (1).)

In the [county of   .   Petty Sessional Division of   ].
Before the Magistrates' Court sitting at
To the   [County] [Borough] Council.

Proceedings are pending under the Matrimonial Proceedings (Magistrates' Courts) Act, 1960, before this Court between A.B., of   , and B.B., of   .

Notice is hereby given that the Court proposes to commit the following children of the family of the parties ot the care of the council, namely :—

C.B., D.B., and E.F.

If the council wishes to make any representations in this matter, including representations about payments to the council for the maintenance of the said children, the Court will hear such representations on   day the day of   , 19   , at the hour of   o'clock in the   noon.

Dated the   day of   , 19   .

J.C.,
Clerk of the Magistrates' Court.

2

Notice of appointment of new supervisor for child
(M.P. (M.C.) Act, 1960, ss. 2 (1) (f), 3 (8).)

In the [county of   .   Petty Sessional Division of   ].
Before the Magistrates' Court sitting at   .

To A.B., to whom the legal custody of C.B. has been committed by a matrimonial order.

To the clerk to the justices for the   petty sessions area.
[*or* To the   [County] [Borough] Council].

By a provision dated the   day of   , 19   , of the matrimonial order mentioned above, C.B., then of   , was placed under the supervision of a probation officer for the   petty sessions area [*or* of the   [County] [Borough] Council].

You are hereby given notice that the Court, being of the opinion that the child is now [*or* will be] resident in the   petty sessions area [*or* the area of the   [County] [Borough] Council] at   , has varied the provision so that the child shall be under the supervision of a probation officer for that petty sessions area [*or* of that council].

Dated the   day of   , 19   .

J.C.,
Clerk of the Magistrates' Court.

3

Notice to parties of Court's power to make provision with regard to children
(M.C. (M.P.) Rules, 1960, r. 3.)

Parties to complaints under the Matrimonial Proceedings (Magistrates' Courts) Act, 1960, are informed that at the hearing of such a complaint the Court has power to make provision for any of the following purposes as regards any child of both parties or any child of one party who has been accepted by the other as one of the family: (a) custody (which may be awarded to either party or to a third person); (b) access to the child by either or both of the parties (or anybody else who is a parent of the child); (c) the payment of maintenance for the child by either or both of the parties.

In certain exceptional circumstances the Court may commit the child to the care of the county or county borough council or place him under the supervision of a probation officer or of the council.

The Court may exercise these powers whether the complaint asks for any provision about the child or not and whether any other order is made on the complaint or the complaint is dismissed.

At the hearing of the complaint the Court will hear anything the parties may wish to say on these matters.

The Court cannot make its final decision on the complaint until it has decided whether or not, and if so how, to exercise these powers.

4

Notice to parent of child (other than a party) of Court's power to make provision with regard to children (M.P. (M.C.) Act, 1960, s. 4 (1), (6).)

In the [county of . Petty Sessional Division of].
To D.E.

You are hereby given notice that proceedings are pending under the Matrimonial Proceedings (Magistrates' Courts) Act, 1960, between A.B. and B.B. and it has been stated that their family includes a child C.B. whose parents are [A.B.] and yourself but who has been accepted as one of the family by (B.B.].

If this information is correct, the Court has power to make provision at the hearing for any of the following purposes as regards C.B.: (a) custody (which may be awarded to either party or to a third person, including yourself; (b) access to the child by either or both of the parties or yourself; (c) the payment of maintenance for the child by either or both of the parties.

In certain exceptional circumstances the Court may commit the child to the care of the county or county borough council or place him under the supervision of a probation officer or of the council.

The hearing will take place on day the day of ,
19 , at the hour of in the noon before the Magistrates' Court sitting at .

At the hearing the Court will hear anything which you may, as a parent of the child, wish to say on these matters. For this purpose you may appear in person or be represented by a barrister or solicitor. Whether you exercise this right or not, you cannot be ordered to pay any of the parties' costs.

Dated the day of , 19 .

J.C.,
Clerk of the Magistrates' Court.

5

Notice to person outside United Kingdom of complaint for revocation, etc.
(M.P. (M.C.) Act, 1960, s. 9 (2), (3).)

In the [county of . Petty Sessional Division of
To A.B.

A complaint has been made by me the undersigned this day [or on the day of , 19 ,] to the Magistrates' Court sitting at under section 8 of the Matrimonial Proceedings (Magistrates' Court) Act, 1960, that the matrimonial [or interim] order made by that Court on the day of , 19 , should be [revoked] [or revived] [or varied by].

The complaint will be heard by that Court on day the day of , 19 , at the hour of in the noon.

You may appear in person or be represented by a barrister or solicitor at the hearing. If you do neither, the Court may, if it thinks it reasonable, deal with the case in your absence.

[*To be completed in a case where the complaint is for the revocation or variation of a provision for the making of payments by the complainant to the defendant and is based on the defendant's prolonged absence abroad as mentioned in s. 9 (3) of the M.P. (M.C.) Act, 1960.* At the hearing I intend to satisfy the Court that there is reason to believe that during the period of six months immediately preceding the making of the complaint you were continuously outside the United Kingdom or were not in the United Kingdom on more than thirty days. If the Court is satisfied of this, it may, after having regard to any communication to the Court in writing from you, revoke the order for payments by me to you or reduce the amount of the payments. If you wish to make any written communication, you should do so by letter addressed to the clerk of the   Magistrates' Court at (*address*) so that it will reach him before the hearing.]

(Signed) B.B.

Dated the   day of   , 19 .

6

Certificate by clerk when maintenance payments are forwarded abroad
(*M.P. (M.C.) Act, 1960, s. 9 (4)*.)

I, J.C., the clerk to the Magistrates' Court sitting at   , through whom payments fall to be made by A.B. to B.B. under a matrimonial order made by the Magistrates' Court sitting at   , on the   day of   , 19 , hereby certify that (a) during the period from the day of   , 19 , to the   day of   , 19 , every payment made under the order has been forwarded by me to an address outside the United Kingdom, namely   ; and (b) during the period from the   day of   , 19 , to the day of   , 19 , the said B.B. has not, to my knowledge, been in the United Kingdom at any time [*or* on more than thirty days, namely from the day of   , 19 , to the   day of   , 19].

Dated the   day of   , 19 .

J.C.

NOTE

These Rules were made by the Lord Chancellor on December 1, 1960, under s. 15 of the Justices of the Peace Act, 1949, as extended by s. 122 of the Magistrates' Courts Act, 1952; they came into force on January 1, 1961.

Home Office Circular No. 10/1970.   *Dated February 2, 1970.*

INCOME TAX AND SMALL MAINTENANCE PAYMENTS

I am directed by the Secretary of State to refer to section 205 of the Income Tax Act, 1952, as amended by section 17 of the Finance Act, 1968.

2. It has been brought to the Secretary of State's attention that there may be doubt whether the limits for "small maintenance payments" of £7 10s. a week or £32 10s. a month, as defined in section 205(1)(i) of the Income Tax Act, 1952, apply to the total payments made to a wife under a maintenance order, where payments are ordered for the wife and for a child or children of whom she has custody, or individually to each payment in favour of each beneficiary under an order.

3. The Secretary of State has no authority to give a binding interpretation of the law on this subject, but, after consultation with the Board of Inland Revenue, he is of the opinion that the question whether payments required under a maintenance order to be made for the benefit of any person are "small

maintenance payments", within the meaning of sections 205–207 of the Income Tax Act, 1952, falls to be decided by reference to the amount of the payments ordered to be made for that person's benefit, and without regard to the amount of any payments required by the same order to be made for the benefit of other persons. Accordingly, a maintenance order which provides for the payment for any person's benefit of maintenance payments within the limits specified in section 205(1)(i) of the Act is to be treated as a small maintenance order for the purposes of sections 205–207 so far as it relates to those payments; but it is not to be treated as a small maintenance order in relation to payments in excess of those limits which are ordered to be made for the benefit of another person. Thus, where, for example, a maintenance order is made for a sum to be paid to a wife for her own benefit and for further sums to be paid to her for the benefit of two children of whom she has custody, the limits specified in section 205(1)(i) of the Act should be applied separately to the payments for the wife and for each child.

NOTE

Although this circular refers to the Act of 1952 now repealed, the wording is similar to that in s. 65, Income and Corporation Taxes Act, 1970.

This circular was sent to Clerks to the Justices.

Home Office Circular No. 140/1971.   *Dated June* 25, 1971.

DISCLOSURE OF ADDRESSES FROM OFFICIAL RECORDS TO FACILITATE PROCEEDINGS FOR MAINTENANCE

1. I am directed by the Secretary of State to refer to Home Office Circulars No. 123/65 and No. 39/67 (as amended by No. 96/68), which described the arrangements for the disclosure of addresses from the records of a number of government departments for the purpose of maintenance proceedings. These arrangements (which have recently been referred to in Parliament and elsewhere) have been modified in certain respects since the earlier circulars were issued and, as modified, are described in this circular. Circulars No. 123/65, No. 39/67 and No. 96/68 are hereby revoked.

2. Although the Secretary of State recognises that the records available may not assist in tracing defendants, he nevertheless hopes that clerks will make the fullest use of these sources of information where it is possible that they could be of assistance. He would be grateful therefore if clerks will seek an address from the records whenever they think this would serve a useful purpose or a complainant asks them to do so, provided that they are satisfied that sufficient particulars are available to make possible the identification of the defendant. He would like to take this opportunity of thanking clerks for their co-operation.

Application for addresses—general

3. Arrangements for access to be given to departmental records apply to any proceedings, either initial or for enforcement, which include a claim for the payment of maintenance, brought under the Maintenance Orders (Facilities for Enforcement) Act, 1920, the Maintenance Orders Act, 1950, the Magistrates' Courts Act, 1952, the Affiliation Proceedings Act, 1957, the Maintenance Orders Act, 1958, the Matrimonial Proceedings (Magistrates' Courts) Act, 1960, the Matrimonial Proceedings and Property Act, 1970, the Guardianship of Minors Act, 1971, and, as from 2 August 1971, the Attachment of Earnings Act, 1971. The records available are those of the Department of Health and Social Security, the Ministry of Defence, and the Passport Office.

4. For proceedings in magistrates' courts the address is given to clerks to justices only on the understanding that it will be used solely for the purpose of

proceedings and will not be made known to the complainant or to anyone else except in the normal course of proceedings. Departments are not normally prepared to disclose the address to the complainant or to her solicitor, unless she is in receipt of supplementary benefit, when the address will, if necessary, be given to her solicitor by the Department of Health and Social Security, to enable proceedings to be taken.

5. If particulars of the person whose address is sought can be reliably identified in their records, the departments are prepared to furnish the address to the clerk to the justices upon receipt of a letter from him requesting that it be furnished and certifying:—

    (i) that the order is in existence and that its enforcement is frustrated because the defendant cannot be traced; or

    (ii) that a complaint for an order has been made, and that a summons would be issued if the address of the defendant could be ascertained, or that a summons has been issued but cannot be served because the defendant cannot be traced.

Department of Health and Social Security records—general

6. The principal records available are those held by the Records Branch of the Department of Health and Social Security at Newcastle and the National Health Service Central Register at Southport. The records at Newcastle are the most likely source of an up-to-date address. Changes of address may become known from new addresses shown on National Insurance contribution cards surrendered annually on expiry or because an insured person has made a claim for benefit. It should be noted, however, that changes of addresses are not always shown on surrendered contribution cards. Records of persons registered for general medical services in the National Health Services are kept at the National Health Service Central Register and by liaison with N.H.S. Executive Councils the Central Register can provide the address at the time the person concerned last registered for such medical services. A person may move but keep the same doctor and hence these records may vary considerably in their reliability as a source of a recent address. It is accordingly suggested that applications should be addressed in the first instance to Records Branch at Newcastle; if the application does not produce a useful address, resort should then be had to the National Health Service Central Register. If, however, the complainant is receiving supplementary benefit it will be advisable to refer in the first place to the Manager of the local Social Security (Supplementary Benefits) Office in order to avoid possible duplication of enquiries.

Social Security records

7. Applications to the Department of Health and Social Security should be addressed to the Liaison Officer, Records Branch, Department of Health and Social Security, Newcastle on Tyne. The possibility of identifying the record of a particular defendant will depend largely on what identifying particulars are furnished to the Department and an address will not be supplied unless the Department is satisfied from the particulars furnished that the record of the defendant has been reliably identified. The complainant should therefore be asked to give as much information as possible before application is made and the particulars given to the Department should, if possible, include the following:—

    (i) the defendant's surname and full Christian names or forenames;

    (ii) the exact date of his birth or, if not known, his approximate age;

    (iii) his National Insurance number (if known);

 (iv) the exact date of the marriage and spouse's Christian names or forenames;

 (v) the defendant's last known address with the date when he was living
there;

 (vi) any other known addresses with dates;

 (vii) if the defendant is a war pensioner, his war pension number and service
particulars (if known).

8. The Department will be prepared to search if given full particulars of the
defendant's name and date of birth, but clearly the chances of accurate identification are increased by the provision of more identifying information.

9. The Secretary of State suggests that to facilitate subsequent tracing of
records, clerks should consider the possibility of asking defendants to provide
their National Insurance number at the time a maintenance order is made
(though there is of course no statutory power for a court to require this information to be supplied at that time).

National Health Service records

10. Applications for disclosure of an address from the Health Service records
should be made to the National Health Service Central Register, Smedley's
Hydro, Southport, Lancashire. All requests should, if possible, be accompanied
by the following information:—

 (i) the defendant's surname and full Christian names or forenames;

 (ii) the exact date of his birth or, if not known, his approximate age;

 (iii) his national health service number (if known);

 (iv) his home address as it was in 1939;

 (v) any subsequent known addresses with dates.

Records of the Passport Office and Ministry of Defence—general

11. Applications for the disclosure of addresses should be made to the Passport
Office or to the Ministry of Defence if either the principal records (*i.e.* those of
the Department of Health and Social Security described above) have failed to
reveal an address or there are strong grounds for believing that the defendant
may have made a recent application for a passport or that he is or has recently
been a serving member of the Army, Navy or Air Force.

Passport Office records

12. Applications to the Passport Office should be addressed to the Chief
Passport Officer, Passport Office, Clive House, Petty France, London, S.W.1
and, if possible, the following information should be provided:—

 (i) the defendant's surname and full Christian names or forenames;

 (ii) the exact date of his birth or, if not known, his approximate age;

 (iii) his place of birth;

 (iv) his occupation;

 (v) whether he is known to have travelled abroad, and, if so, the destination and dates;

 (vi) his last known address with the date he was living there;

 (vii) any other known address with dates.

Ministry of Defence records

13. Application to the Ministry of Defence should be addressed as follows:—

(i) Soldiers (all ranks)	Ministry of Defence, C2 Army Department, Old War Office Building, Whitehall, LONDON, S.W.1
(ii) Naval officers and ratings	Ministry of Defence, Naval Law Division, Old Admiralty Building, Whitehall, LONDON, S.W.1

    (iii) Air Force officers   Ministry of Defence, AR 8b (R.A.F.),
        (serving or retired)   Adastral House, Theobald's Road, LONDON,
                                    W.C.1
    (iv) Airmen or ex-airmen   The Air Officer Commanding, R.A.F. Record
                                    and Pay Office, Eastern Avenue, Barn-
                                    wood, GLOUCESTER

14. As much of the following information as possible should be provided:—

    (i) the defendant's surname and full Christian names or forenames;
    (ii) his exact date of birth or, if now known, his approximate age;
    (iii) his date of entry into the Service, his rank, official number, and, if he is no longer serving, his date of discharge. It would be helpful if the regiment or corps of a soldier could also be given;
    (iv) any other relevant information such as the last known address.

NOTE

This circular was sent to Clerks to the Justices.

Home Office Circular No. 214/1971.   *Dated October* 6, 1971.

PAYMENT OF MAINTENANCE BY POST

1. I am directed by the Secretary of State to say that representations have been made to him that maintenance should ordinarily be paid out from the collecting office through the post, except where the recipient asks for payment in cash. After considering views expressed by the Justices' Clerks Society and the London Magistrates' Clerks' Association he considers it desirable that this should become the general practice. Accordingly, the Magistrates' Courts Rules Committee will be invited in due course to approve an amendment of Rule 32 (2) of the Magistrates' Courts Rules, 1968 (which gives the clerk to the justices discretion at the request of the person entitled to receive the payments under a maintenance order (the payee) to pay maintenance by post). This amendment will have the effect of requiring the clerk to pay maintenance by post unless the payee indicates that she prefers to collect it personally from the court. We propose to include words designed to protect the justices' clerk against unreasonable requests or conduct; but the intention is that the choice as to method of payment should rest with the payee.

2. The Secretary of State is aware that, although many courts are already making payments by post, many others are not, and that these will need time to make any administrative changes in staffing and accounting procedures that are necessary. He therefore has in mind that the proposed amendments of the Rule might come into force in the summer of 1972. In the meantime he would be grateful if clerks to justices will use the intervening period to implement the new proposals in advance of formal imposition by Rule.

3. The Secretary of State wishes to draw attention to certain matters of administration, practice, and procedure relating to payment of maintenance by cheque through the post, which are set out in the following paragraphs.

Arrangements for encashing cheques

4. It has been the experience of clerks who have adopted payment by cheque that most payees, even if without bank accounts, have experienced little difficulty in practice in encashing cheques. In some areas this has been done by the court making arrangements for women to encash their cheques at the local branches of a particular bank and the bank has accepted responsibility for verifying the endorsement on the cheque from a specimen signature which is provided by the court making the order. Clerks may wish to consider similar arrangements and to give general advice to payees on this matter.

Anonymity of cheques

5. It is desirable for cheques not to carry on their face any indication of the reason for which the payment is being made (*e.g.* the words "Maintenance Account" or "Court Collecting Officer"). The use of cheques without any such identifying matter is to be preferred.

Dispatch of payments

6. Payments received should be dispatched to reach the payee as soon as conveniently possible. Delay in sending payments can cause hardship to the payee. The practice of accumulating payments in the collecting office is to be deprecated.

Receipts

7. The Home Office Auditors have advised that from an audit point of view the practice of sending out a separate receipt with the cheque to be returned by the payee before further payment is made is undesirable. If payment is made by crossed cheque, provided that the bank is instructed to return paid cheques and these are filed in the collecting office as proof of payment, the auditors would require no other receipt, since the passage of the cheque un-endorsed through a bank account shows that the payee is still alive and a signature endorsing the cheque to a tradesman, for example, may be compared with a signature on the court papers. It is suggested that clerks who wish to be certain that the payee is still alive may do so by other means than by requiring a receipt for each payment made, for example by requiring the payee in person to certify periodically that she is the person entitled to the payments.

Cost of payment

8. The Secretary of State takes the view that the cost of payment by post by cheque may reasonably be borne by the court. If the payee requests that payment be made in cash through the post by registered envelope, it would be proper to require her to bear the expense of such method of payment; but, in view of the expense and trouble to her of payment by registered post, payment by this method is obviously unattractive.

Telephone queries on availability of maintenance

9. The Secretary of State is informed that some courts refuse to answer telephone inquiries about the availability of maintenance. It appears from his consultations that the general opinion, which the Secretary of State shares, is against this practice and he hopes that Magistrates' Courts Committees and clerks to justices will, in consultation, be able to make such arrangements as are necessary to ensure that personal inquiries are answered.

Advice on other matters

10. If personal collection of maintenance ceases to be the general practice, the opportunity for women to seek advice over the collecting office counter will be diminished. The Secretary of State hopes that clerks to justices will take steps to ensure that there are adequate facilities at their offices for answering questions about all matters relating to maintenance orders.

11. The Secretary of State appreciates that payment of maintenance by cheque as the normal practice may involve courts in additional expenditure, but he is informed that some courts who are using this method of payment

have found compensating advantages and economies in the relief and redeployment of the collecting office staff. He is, in any case, of the opinion that the primary consideration is for the courts to provide the service which is most convenient to the payee, and he hopes that Magistrates' Courts Committees, in considering how to effect the changes necessitated by the proposed amendment of Rule 32, will keep this objective in mind.

NOTE

This circular was sent to the Clerk to the Justices and the Clerk to the Magistrates' Courts Committee.

DIVISION 5

LEGITIMACY

LEGITIMACY

CONTENTS

INTRODUCTORY NOTE

Before the coming into operation of the Legitimacy Act, 1926, English law did not recognise the legitimation of a child, born illegitimate, by the subsequent marriage of his parents to one another. It was generally true to say once a bastard always a bastard, with all the disadvantages that this state involved. Towards the turn of the century, however, public opinion became less inclined to acquiesce in this visiting of the sins or indiscretions of the parents upon the children, and the harshness and injustice of the law in this respect were to a large extent remedied by the passing of the Act of 1926, under which legitimation by subsequent marriage was subject to the condition that at the time of the birth of the child neither parent was married to a third party; later this condition was repealed by the Legitimacy Act, 1959, which made other alterations in the law.

As to the presumption of legitimacy of a child born during wedlock, see the case of *F.* v. *F., Times*, June 18, 1959. The Family Law Reform Act, 1969, s. 26, provides that such a presumption may in any civil proceedings be rebutted by evidence which shows that it is more probable than not that that person is illegitimate or legitimate as the case may be. The Act further amends s. 10 of the Births, Deaths Registration Act, 1953, so that a birth may be registered with an entry of the father's name without his being present and signing, if the mother so requests and on production of a declaration by the mother as to the father of the child and a declaration from the father acknowledging that fact.

Where a declaration of legitimacy is desired, application may be made to the High Court or to a county court, but in various proceedings the fact of legitimation by subsequent marriage may be proved and acted upon without there being in existence any such declaration. The question whether a child is legitimate or illegitimate may have to be decided in connection with, for example, proceedings for adoption or for obtaining orders under the Guardianship of Minors Act, 1971 or the Matrimonial Proceedings (Magistrates' Courts) Act, 1960. The investigation of such questions has become easier and more satisfactory now that the rule in *Russell* v. *Russell*, [1924] A. C. 687, has been abolished by legislation, and the two persons who know most about it, and who may be perfectly truthful witnesses, are competent to give evidence as to access or non-access.

By virtue of s. 39 of the Matrimonial Causes Act, 1965, p. 1302, *post*, any British subject may, if domiciled in England or Northern Ireland apply by petition to the High Court or county court for a decree declaring his legitimacy, or that the marriage of his parents or grandparents or himself was a valid marriage.

The whole subject of legitimacy and legitimation is dealt with fully in Halsbury's Laws of England (3rd Edn.) Volume 3, Part II.

Provision is made in Part III of the Family Law Reform Act for the use of blood tests in determining paternity. Although this would seem to give magistrates' courts the power to order blood tests in proceedings under the Affiliation Orders Act, 1957, regard should be had to the remarks of Lord Hodson in S. v. S., [1970] 3 All E. R. 107, H. L., "Parliament, cannot have intended to confer an unfettered discretion to order blood tests on magistrates' and county courts. In that case it was said that since the Family Law Reform Act, 1969, had placed both legitimate and illegitimate children on a par in property social prejudice had vanished, it was best that the truth should out." Principles and authorities which applied to custody cases did not necessarily apply to paternity cases where there might be a conflict between the child's interest and the general requirements of justice, that no available evidence should be suppressed. No person, it was said, should go from the court with a sense of grievance and injustice; if he did, he was unlikely to treat a child found legitimate on partial evidence with proper parental affection.

As to property rights of illegitimate children, see now Part II of the Act of 1969, p. 1310, *post*.

LEGITIMACY ACT, 1926
[16 & 17 Geo. 5, c. 60]

ARRANGEMENT OF SECTIONS

An Act to amend the law relating to children born out of wedlock.

[15th December, 1926.]

1. Legitimation by subsequent marriage of parents.—(1) Subject to the provisions of this section, where the parents of an illegitimate person marry or have married one another, whether before or after the commencement of this Act, the marriage shall, if the father of the illegitimate person was or is at the date of the marriage domiciled in England or Wales, render that person, if living, legitimate from the commencement of this Act, or from the date of the marriage, whichever last happens.

(2) [*Repealed by the Legitimacy Act, 1959.*]

(3) The legitimation of a person under this Act does not enable him or his spouse, children, or remoter issue to take any interest in real or personal property save as is hereinafter in this Act expressly provided.

(4) The provisions contained in the Schedule to this Act shall have effect with respect to the re-registration of the births of legitimated persons.

NOTES

Repeal.—Sub-s. (2) was repealed by the Legitimacy Act, 1959; see s. 1 (2) of that Act, p. 1297, *post.*

Custody order, legitimated child.—Whether a court could make an order as to the custody of a legitimated child under the Summary Jurisdiction (Separation and Maintenance) Acts, 1895–1949, or under the Guardianship of Infants Acts, 1866 and 1925, without a formal declaration of legitimacy was formerly open to doubt; but in *M.* v. *M.,* [1946] P. 31, *sub nom. Millard* v. *Millard and Addis,* [1945] 2 All E. R. 525, it was held that a legitimated child could be the subject of a custody order by the Divorce Court, though there had been no declaration of legitimacy. In *Colquitt* v. *Colquitt,* [1948] P. 19; [1947] 2 All E. R. 50; 111 J. P. 442, it was held by a Divisional Court that it was within the jurisdiction of justices to make an order for custody under the Summary Jurisdiction (Separation and Maintenance) Acts,

1895–1949 in respect of "a child legitimated by the provisions of this section although no petition had been presented on behalf of the child under s. 2, and no declaration had been made under s. 188 of the Supreme Court of Judicature (Consolidation) Act, 1925". See also *B.* v. *A.-G.* (*N. E. B. intervening*), [1965] P. 278; [1965] 1 All E. R. 62.

Domicile.—See note at p. 1026, *ante*, and see *Scappaticci* v. *A.-G.*, [1955] 1 All E. R. 193.

As to the effect of legitimation upon the nationality of a child in certain cases, see s. 23 of the British Nationality Act, 1948.

Evidence of legitimation.—In *MacDarmaid* v. *A.-G.*, [1950] P. 218; [1950] 1 All E. R. 497, the petitioner was born in 1894, father and mother married in 1925, father previously married in 1886, first wife last seen in 1891. It was held that the onus was on the petitioner to show that the first wife was not alive in 1894.

Foreign marriage.—See *Starkowski* (by his next friend) v. *A.-G.*, [1953] 2 All E. R. 1272, H. L.

Void marriage.—See the Legitimacy Act, 1959, s. 2 (1), p. 1297, *post*.

Date from which legitimation effective.—In *Kruhlak* v. *Kruhlak* (*No. 2*), [1958] 2 All E. R. 294; 122 J. P. 360, it was held that a decree of divorce is effective from the beginning of the day on which it is pronounced. Therefore a child born to the woman some hours before a decree was pronounced was born to her when she was unmarried, and it was legitimated by her subsequent marriage to the father.

Adoption.—As to the revocation of adoption orders when a person adopted by his father and/or mother becomes a legitimated person on the marriage of his father and mother, see s. 26 of the Adoption Act, 1958, p. 1059, *ante*, and s. 1 of the Adoption Act, 1960, p. 1085, *ante*.

2. [*Repealed by the Matrimonial Causes Act*, 1950.]

3. Rights of legitimated persons, etc., to take interests in property.—(1) Subject to the provisions of this Act, a legitimated person and his spouse, children or more remote issue shall be entitled to take any interest—

  (a) in the estate of an intestate dying after the date of legitimation ;
  (b) under any disposition coming into operation after the date of legitimation ;
  (c) by descent under an entailed interest created after the date of legitimation ;

in like manner as if the legitimated person had been born legitimate.

(2) Where the right to any property, real or personal, depends on the relative seniority of the children of any person, and those children include one or more legitimated persons, the legitimated person or persons shall rank as if he or they had been born on the day when he or they became legitimated by virtue of this Act, and if more than one such legitimated person became legitimated at the same time, they shall rank as between themselves in order of seniority.

(3) Where property real or personal or any interest therein is limited in such a way that, if this Act had not been passed, it would (subject or not to any preceding limitations or charges) have devolved (as nearly as the law permits) along with a dignity or title of honour, then nothing in this Act shall operate to sever the property or any interest therein from such dignity, but the same shall go and devolve (without prejudice to the preceding limitations or charges aforesaid) in like manner as if this Act had not been passed. This subsection applies, whether or not there is

any express reference to the dignity or title of honour and notwithstanding that in some events the property, or some interest therein, may become severed therefrom.

(4) This section applies only if and so far as a contrary intention is not expressed in the disposition, and shall have effect subject to the terms of the disposition and to the provisions therein contained.

NOTES

Disposition . . . after the date of legitimation.—See Family Law Reform Act, 1969, s. 15 (4), for the exclusion of this paragraph in respect of dispositions made after January 1, 1970.

"Relative seniority."—For the exclusion of this subsection see s. 15 (4) of the Family Law Reform Act, 1969.

Probate Rules.—As to the order of priority for grant of administration in case of intestacy, see the Non-Contentious Probate Rules, 1954, S.I. 1954 No. 796 (L.6), rule 21 (1) (ii).

Letters of administration.—As to the rights of a legitimated person, his spouse, children or remoter issue to take an interest, see Chapter VI of *Tristram and Coote's Probate Practice*, 23rd Edition, p. 204.

4. Succession on intestacy of legitimated persons and their issue.

—Where a legitimated person or a child or remoter issue of a legitimated person dies intestate in respect of all or any of his real or personal property, the same persons shall be entitled to take the same interests therein as they would have been entitled to take if the legitimated person had been born legitimate.

5. Application to illegitimate person dying before marriage of parents.

—Where an illegitimate person dies after the commencement of this Act and before the marriage of his parents leaving any spouse, children or remoter issue living at the date of such marriage, then, if that person would, if living at the time of the marriage of his parents, have become a legitimated person, the provisions of this Act with respect to the taking of interests in property by, or in succession to, the spouse, children and remoter issue of a legitimated person (including those relating to the rate of death duties) shall apply as if such person as aforesaid had been a legitimated person and the date of the marriage of his parents had been the date of legitimation.

6. Personal rights and obligations of legitimated persons.

—(1) A legitimated person shall have the same rights, and shall be under the same obligations in respect of the maintenance and support of himself or of any other person as if he had been born legitimate, and, subject to the provisions of this Act, the provisions of any Act relating to claims for damages, compensation, allowance, benefit, or otherwise by or in respect of a legitimate child shall apply in like manner in the case of a legitimated person.

(2) Where the marriage leading to the legitimation of a child took place before the fourth day of January, nineteen hundred and twenty-six, and the father of the child died before that date, the child shall, for the purpose of determining rights to pension or additional allowance under the Widows', Orphans' and Old Age Contributory Pensions Act, 1925, be deemed to have been a child of the marriage living at that date :

Provided that nothing in this subsection shall confer any right to claim any payment in respect of any period prior to the date of legitimation.

7. Death duties.—Where a legitimated person or any relative of a legitimated person takes any interest in real or personal property, any duty which becomes leviable after the date of legitimation shall be payable at the same rate as if the legitimated person had been born legitimate.

NOTE

This section is printed as amended by the Finance Act, 1949.

8. Provisions as to persons legitimated by extraneous law.— (1) Where the parents of an illegitimate person marry or have married one another, whether before or after the commencement of this Act, and the father of the illegitimate person was or is, at the time of the marriage, domiciled in a country, other than England or Wales, by the law of which the illegitimate person became legitimated by virtue of such subsequent marriage, that person, if living, shall in England and Wales be recognised as having been so legitimated from the commencement of this Act or from the date of the marriage, whichever last happens, notwithstanding that his father was not at the time of the birth of such person domiciled in a country in which legitimation by subsequent marriage was permitted by law.

(2) All the provisions of this Act relating to legitimated persons and to the taking of interests in property by or in succession to a legitimated person and the spouse, children and remoter issue of a legitimated person (including those relating to the rate of death duties) shall apply in the case of a person recognised as having been legitimated under this section, or who would, had he survived the marriage of his parents, have been so recognised ; and, accordingly, this Act shall have effect as if references therein to a legitimated person included a person so recognised as having been legitimated.

(3) [*Applies to Scotland.*]

NOTES

Domicile.—See note at p. 1026, *ante*, and see *Scappaticci* v. *A.-G.*, [1955] 1 All E. R. 193.

In the case of *In re Hurll, Angelini* v. *Dick*, [1952] 2 All E. R. 322, it was held that s. 8 (1) of this Act was limited in its application to a person whose father was not at the time of the birth of such person domiciled in a country in which legitimation by subsequent marriage was permitted by law.

9. Right of illegitimate child and mother of illegitimate child to succeed on intestacy of the other.—[*Repealed by the Family Law Reform Act*, 1969. *See now s.* 14, *ibid.*]

10. Savings.—(1) Nothing in this Act shall affect the succession to any dignity or title of honour or render any person capable of succeeding to or transmitting a right to succeed to any such dignity or title.

(2) Nothing in this Act shall affect the operation or construction of any disposition coming into operation before the commencement of this Act, or affect any rights under the intestacy of a person dying before the commencement of this Act.

11. Interpretation.—For the purposes of this Act, unless the context otherwise requires :—

> The expression " legitimated person " means a person legitimated by this Act ;
>
> The expression " date of legitimation " means the date of the marriage leading to the legitimation, or where the marriage occurred before the commencement of this Act, the commencement of this Act ;
>
> The expression " disposition " means an assurance of any interest in property by any instrument whether inter vivos or by will ;
>
> The expression " intestate " has the same meaning as in the Administration of Estates Act, 1925, and " will " includes " codicil " ;
>
> The expression " entailed interest " has the same meaning as in the Law of Property Act, 1925.

12. Short title and commencement.—(1) This Act may be cited as the Legitimacy Act, 1926.

(2) [*Repealed by the S. L. R. Act, 1950.*]

(3) The provisions of this Act shall, save as therein otherwise expressly provided, extend only to England and Wales.

NOTE

Scotland.—See the Legitimation (Scotland) Act, 1968.

SCHEDULE

REGISTRATION OF BIRTHS OF LEGITIMATED PERSONS

1. [*Repealed.*]

2. It shall be the duty of the parents of a legitimated person, or, in cases where re-registration can be effected on information furnished by one parent and one of the parents is dead, of the surviving parent, within the time hereinafter specified, to furnish to the Registrar-General information with a view to obtaining the re-registration of the birth of that person ; that is to say :—

> (a) If the marriage took place before the commencement of this Act, within six months of such commencement ;
>
> (b) If the marriage takes place after the commencement of this Act, within three months after the date of the marriage.

3. [*Repealed.*]

4. The failure of the parents or either of them to furnish information as required by this schedule in respect of any legitimated person shall not affect the legitimation of that person.

5. [*Repealed.*]

6. Any parent who fails to give information as required by this Schedule shall be liable on summary conviction to a fine not exceeding forty shillings and any sum paid to the Secretary of State in pursuance of section twenty-seven of the Justices of the Peace Act, 1949, in respect of a fine recovered under this paragraph shall be deemed to be Exchequer moneys within the meaning of that section and shall be paid by the Secretary of State into the Exchequer.

NOTES

Regulations.—See the Registration of Births, Deaths and Marriages Regulations, 1968, p. 1148, *ante.*

This Schedule is printed as amended by the Births and Deaths Registration Act, 1953; 27 Halsbury's Statutes, 3rd Edn., 1021. Paras. 1, 3 and 5 were replaced by s. 14 of that Act.

By the Legitimation (Re-registration of Birth) Act, 1957, this Schedule is extended to apply to all persons legitimated by the subsequent marriage of their parents whether or not the legitimation was effected under the Legitimacy Act, 1926; *infra.*

Parochial registers.—As to the annotation of parochial registers of baptisms in cases of persons legitimated after baptism, see the Baptismal Registers Measure, 1961, p. 1299, *post.*

LEGITIMATION (RE-REGISTRATION OF BIRTH) ACT, 1957

[5 & 6 Eliz. 2, c. 39]

An Act to extend the operation of section fourteen and paragraph (d) of section thirty-six of the Births and Deaths Registration Act, 1953, and of the Schedule to the Legitimacy Act, 1926; and for purposes connected with that matter. [17th July, 1957]

1. Re-registration of births of legitimated persons.—(1) Section fourteen of the Births and Deaths Registration Act, 1953, and the Schedule to the Legitimacy Act, 1926 (which relate to the re-registration of births of persons legitimated by the subsequent marriage of their parents) shall apply and be deemed always to have applied in relation to all persons recognised by the law of England and Wales as having been legitimated by the subsequent marriage of their parents, whether or not their legitimation, or the recognition thereof, was effected by the last mentioned Act:

Provided that where—

(a) the marriage by which a person is legitimated took place before the passing of this Act; and

(b) the said Schedule would not apply or have applied in relation to him but for this Act,

the time limited by paragraph 2 of the said Schedule for the furnishing to the Registrar General of information with a view to obtaining the re-registration of the birth of that person shall not expire until three months from the passing of this Act.

(2) In the said section fourteen, and in paragraph (d) of section thirty-six of the Births and Deaths Registration Act, 1953, the words " within the meaning of the Legitimacy Act, 1926 " are hereby repealed wherever they occur.

2. Short title.—This act may be cited as the Legitimation (Re-registration of Birth) Act, 1957.

NOTE

For the schedule to the Legitimacy Act, 1926, see p. 864, *ante.*

Regulations.—See the Registration of Births, Deaths and Marriages Regulations, 1968, Part V, p. 1148, *ante.*

LEGITIMACY ACT, 1959
[7 & 8 Eliz. 2, c. 73]

An Act to amend the Legitimacy Act, 1926, to legitimate the children of certain void marriages, and otherwise to amend the law relating to children born out of wedlock. [29th July, 1959]

1. Amendment of Legitimacy Act, 1926.—(1) Subsection (2) of section one of the Legitimacy Act, 1926 (which excludes the operation of that Act in the case of an illegitimate person whose father or mother was married to a third person at the time of the birth) is hereby repealed.

(2) In relation to an illegitimate person to whom it applies by virtue of this section, the Legitimacy Act, 1926, shall have effect as if for references to the commencement of that Act there were substituted references to the commencement of this Act.

NOTES
Commencement of Act.—The Act came into force on October 29, 1959.

Adoption orders, revocation.—As to the revocation of adoption orders made in respect of persons legitimated by this section see s. 1 of the Adoption Act, 1960, p. 1085, *ante.*

2. Legitimacy of children of certain void marriages.—(1) Subject to the provisions of this section, the child of a void marriage, whether born before or after the commencement of this Act, shall be treated as the legitimate child of his parents if at the time of the act of intercourse resulting in the birth (or at the time of the celebration of the marriage if later) both or either of the parties reasonably believed that the marriage was valid.

(2) This section applies, and applies only, where the father of the child was domiciled in England at the time of the birth or, if he died before the birth, was so domiciled immediately before his death.

(3) This section, so far as it affects the succession to a dignity or title of honour, or the devolution of property settled therewith, applies only to children born after the commencement of this Act.

(4) This section does not affect any rights under the intestacy of a person who died before the commencement of this Act, and does not (except so far as may be necessary to avoid the severance from a dignity or title of honour of property settled therewith) affect the operation or construction of any disposition coming into operation before the commencement of this Act.

(5) In this section the following expressions have the meanings hereby assigned to them, that is to say—

> " void marriage " means a marriage, not being voidable only, in respect of which the High Court has or had jurisdiction to grant a decree of nullity, or would have or would have had such jurisdiction if the parties were domiciled in England;
>
> " disposition " has the same meaning as in the Legitimacy Act, 1926;

and any reference in this section to property settled with a dignity or title of honour is a reference to any real or personal property, or any interest in such property, which is limited by any disposition (whether subject to a preceding limitation or charge or not) in such a way as to devolve with the dignity or title as nearly as the law permits, whether or not the disposition contains an express reference to the dignity or title and whether or not the property or some interest in the property may in some event become severed from it.

(6) [*Repealed by the Matrimonial Causes Act, 1965*].

NOTES

Domicile.—This has been defined as the place in which a man has had his fixed and permanent home, and to which whenever he is absent he has the intention of returning.   Domicile may be by birth or by choice.

Commencement of Act.—See note to s. 1, *ante*.

" Disposition."—For definition, see s. 11 of the Legitimacy Act, 1926, p. 1295, *ante*.

Declaration.—Where a child alleges that he is entitled to be treated as the legitimate child of his parents under this section on the ground that he was born after his parents had been through a ceremony of marriage which either or both of whom reasonably believed to be a valid marriage, he should present his petition under the Matrimonial Causes Act, 1950, s. 17 (1) and not 17 (2) on the ground that what is required is a declaration of legitimacy and not a declaration of legitimation (there having been no ceremony of marriage between his parents subsequent to his birth (*Sheward* v. *A.-G.*, [1964] 2 All E. R. 324).   Section 17 (1), (2) are repealed and replaced by s. 39 (1), (2) of the Matrimonial Causes Act, 1965.

" Reasonably believed."—The test whether a party " reasonably believed " that the marriage was valid is an objective test, and reasonable grounds for the belief must be shown.   *Hawkins* v. *A.-G.*, [1966] 1 All E. R. 392.

Dictum of Lord Parker, C.J., in *R.* v. *King*, [1963] 3 All E. R. 565, applied.

3. Custody and guardianship of illegitimate infants.—[*Repealed by the Guardianship of Minors Act, 1971.   See now s. 14, ibid.*]

4. Applications, &c., under s. 1 of Affiliation Proceedings Act, 1957.—An application under section one of the Affiliation Proceedings Act, 1957, may be made by a woman who was a single woman at the date of the birth of the child whether or not she is a single woman at the time of the application and the reference to a single woman in section two of that Act (which relates to the time within which such application may be made) shall be construed accordingly.

NOTES

" Single woman."—Formerly, a woman making application for an affiliation order had to prove her status as a single woman at the date of her application, but this is not now necessary provided that she proves that she was a single woman at the date of the birth of the child.   There are various decisions on the meaning of the expression " single woman " which are to be found noted in *Chislett's Affiliation Proceedings* and *Stone's Justices' Manual*.

Legal Aid.—Legal aid will be available to any person to whom a certificate has been issued under the Legal Aid (General) Regulations, 1971, S.I. 1971 No. 62 and the Legal Aid and Advice Act (Commencement No. 10) Order, 1961, S.I. 1961 No. 554.

5. Procedure on applications for affiliation orders.—(1) The proceedings which are domestic proceedings within the meaning of the Magistrates' Courts Act, 1952, shall include proceedings on an application

for an affiliation order made under the Affiliation Proceedings Act, 1957, section forty-four of the National Assistance Act, 1948, or section twenty-six of the Children Act, 1948 (other than proceedings for the enforcement, revocation, revival or variation of an affiliation order), and section fifty-six of the said Act of 1952 (which defines " domestic proceedings ") shall have effect accordingly.

(2) In subsection (1) of section sixty of the Magistrates' Courts Act, 1952, the words " or of proceedings for an affiliation order " are hereby repealed.

NOTE
" **Domestic proceedings.**"—For the relevant sections of the Magistrates' Courts Act, 1952, see pp. 1220 *et seq.*, *ante.*

6. Extent, short title, commencement, and saving.—(1) This Act shall not apply to Scotland or Northern Ireland.

(2) This Act may be cited as the Legitimacy Act, 1959.

(3) This Act shall come into force on the expiration of three months beginning with the day on which it is passed.

(4) It is hereby declared that nothing in this Act affects the Succession to the Throne.

NOTE
Commencement.—This Act was passed on July 29, 1959.

BAPTISMAL REGISTERS MEASURE, 1961
[9 & 10 Eliz. 2 No. 2]

A Measure passed by the National Assembly of the Church of England to provide for the annotation of parochial registers of baptisms in cases of persons legitimated after baptism, and for the issue of short certificates of baptism in certain cases, and for purposes connected with the matters aforesaid. [*3rd August,* 1961]

1. Annotation of entries.—(1) A custodian of registers of baptisms maintained under section three of the Parochial Registers Act, 1812, shall, without any fee, make the prescribed annotation in any such register in his custody against any entry shewing the baptism of a person who has been legitimated since he was baptised, if the following conditions are satisfied :—

  (a) there is produced to the custodian by an interested person a certified copy of an entry in a register, which is maintained under the Births and Deaths Registration Act, 1953, or which is in the custody of the Registrar General, being an entry in which the birth of the baptised person is re-registered as that of a legitimated person ; and

  (b) the interested person identifies to the custodian, in the registers of baptism in his custody, the entry shewing baptism which is alleged to require annotation ; and

(c) the custodian is satisfied that the said certified copy relates to the birth of the person whose baptism is recorded in the entry so identified to him :

Provided that nothing in this section shall require any custodian to allow any search to be made in any register of baptisms without payment of such fees as may be lawfully demanded by him.

(2) In this section " prescribed annotation " means the form of words set forth in Part I of the Schedule to this Measure or a form of words substantially to the like effect.

(3) Any certificate of the baptism of any person (other than a short certificate of baptism given under the succeeding section) given in respect of an entry in a register of baptisms which has been annotated in accordance with the provisions of this section shall set out the annotation which appears on the register in full.

2. Short certificates of baptism.—(1) A custodian of registers of baptisms shall, in any case in which before the passing of this Measure he would have given a certificate of the baptism of any person compiled from the registers in his custody, give, at the request of the person paying the fee for the certificate, a short certificate of baptism in the form set out in Part II of the Schedule to this Measure, or in a form substantially to the like effect, and shall complete the certificate with the particulars set forth in the said Part of the Schedule.

(2) A short certificate of baptism given under this section shall be valid for all purposes for which a certificate of the baptism of any person compiled from a register of baptisms would have been valid before the passing of this Measure and, without derogation from the generality of the foregoing, all such short certificates which purport to be signed by the custodian of the register of baptisms from which the certificate is compiled shall be received as evidence of the baptism to which the certificate relates, without any further or other proof of such entry.

(3) The fee payable to the custodian giving a short certificate of baptism under this section shall be such sum as may be fixed by such persons or authorities as may from time to time have power to fix fees for searches of registers of baptisms, and until such fee is fixed a sum of one shilling and sixpence.

3. Interpretation.—In this Measure :—

the expression " custodian " means the rector, vicar, curate or officiating minister of any parish or chapelry who by virtue of section five of the Parochial Registers Act, 1812, has custody of registers of baptisms and the chief officer of any diocesan record office and any diocesan registrar who, by virtue of the Parochial Registers and Records Measure, 1929, has the custody of such registers ;

the expression " interested person " means the legitimated person in question, or either of his parents, or any other person who satisfies the custodian that he has a reasonable personal or other interest in the matter.

4. Short title.—This Measure may be cited as the Baptismal Registers Measure, 1961.

NOTE

Catholics.—We are informed that the Bishops have decided on a uniform practice for entries in Baptismal Registers of children born out of wedlock and subsequently made civilly legitimate, as follows :

" Before making the entry in the register the priest of the place of baptism must:
(a) have been shown the civil re-registration of birth [on the authority of the Registrar General] ;
(b) have possession of the Catholic marriage certificate of the parents, and
(c) be satisfied that the parents were free to marry at the time of the child's birth (Canon 1116)."

The priest may then re-register the child's baptism using the name of the father and making cross-references with the previous entry.   Where these three conditions are not fulfilled but civil legitimation has taken place, a marginal note may be added to the original baptismal entry to the effect that " this child was subsequently civilly legitimated and is now known as . . . (father's name) ".   If in such a case a baptismal certificate is called for, a short form may be used : " I hereby certify that according to the records of . . . (parish title) . . . (name) was baptised on . . . (date)".

SCHEDULE

PART I   Section 1

Certificate showing re-registration of birth,
          produced to me this   day of   19 ,
showing father's name as A.   B.
                                      (signed)

Officiating Minister   ⎫
Officer in charge of   ⎪
      diocesan record office ⎬ or as the case may be.
Diocesan Registrar   ⎭

PART II   Section 2

CERTIFICATE OF BAPTISM

   I hereby certify from the records of the parish of (1)
that (2)
was baptised according to the rites and ceremonies of the Church of England
on the   day of   in the year of Our Lord 19 .
                        (signed)
                        Rector, vicar, curate, minister of
                   or
                        Chief Officer of the diocesan record office of the Diocese of
                   or
                        Registrar of the Diocese of
The particulars to be inserted in the numbered spaces of the form are :

(1) The name of the parish or other place of which the register of baptisms in question is or was the register.   If the place is not a parish the word parish is to be struck out and other appropriate words are to be substituted therefor.

(2) The Christian names of the baptised person as recorded in the entry followed by the surname of his father as recorded in the entry or if more than one such surname is so recorded or if his mother appears from the entry to have borne a different surname at the date of his

baptism, such one of those surnames of his father or mother as the applicant may request. If an annotation has been made against the entry in the register, by virtue of section one of this Measure the surname is to be that recorded in the annotation. If there is no such annotation and no entry appears in the column for the fathers' name in the register the surname to be inserted is the surname of the baptised persons' mother appearing from the entry to have been used by her at the date of baptism or, if more than one such surname is so recorded, such one of them as the applicant may request.

MATRIMONIAL CAUSES ACT, 1965
[1965 c. 72]

*   *   *   *

11. Legitimacy of children of annulled marriages.—Where a decree of nullity is granted in respect of a voidable marriage, any child who would have been the legitimate child of the parties to the marriage if at the date of the decree it had been dissolved instead of being annulled shall be deemed to be their legitimate child.

*   *   *   *

PART IV

MISCELLANEOUS AND GENERAL

Miscellaneous

39. Declarations of legitimacy, etc.—(1) Any person who is a British subject, or whose right to be deemed a British subject depends wholly or in part on his legitimacy or on the validity of any marriage, may, if he is domiciled in England or Northern Ireland or claims any real or personal estate situate in England, apply by petition to the court for a decree declaring that he is the legitimate child of his parents, or that the marriage of his father and mother or of his grandfather and grandmother was a valid marriage or that his own marriage was a valid marriage.

(2) Any person claiming that he or his parent or any remoter ancestor became or has become a legitimated person may apply by petition to the court, or may apply to a county court in the manner prescribed by county court rules, for a decree declaring that he or his parent or remoter ancestor, as the case may be, became or has become a legitimated person.

In this subsection " legitimated person " means a person legitimated by the Legitimacy Act, 1926, and includes a person recognised under section 8 of that Act as legitimated.

(3) Where an application under the last foregoing subsection is made to a county court, the county court, if it considers that the case is one which owing to the value of the property involved or otherwise ought to

be dealt with by the High Court, may, and if so ordered by the High Court shall, transfer the matter to the High Court ; and on such a transfer the proceeding shall be continued in the High Court as if it had been originally commenced by petition to the court.

(4) Any person who is domiciled in England or Northern Ireland or claims any real or personal estate situate in England may apply to the court for a decree declaring his right to be deemed a British subject.

(5) Applications to the court (but not to a county court) under the foregoing provisions of this section may be included in the same petition, and on any application under the foregoing provisions of this section (including an application to a county court) the court or the county court shall make such decree as it thinks just, and the decree shall be binding on Her Majesty and all other persons whatsoever, so however that the decree shall not prejudice any person—

(a) if it is subsequently proved to have been obtained by fraud or collusion : or

(b) unless that person has been given notice of the application in the manner prescribed by rules of court or made a party to the proceedings or claims through a person so given notice or made a party.

(6) A copy of every application under this section and of any affidavit accompanying it shall be delivered to the Attorney-General at least one month before the application is made, and the Attorney-General shall be a respondent on the hearing of the application and on any subsequent proceedings relating thereto.

(7) Where any application is made under this section, such persons as the court or county court thinks fit shall, subject to rules of court, be given notice of the application in the manner prescribed by rules of court, and any such persons may be permitted to become parties to the proceedings and to oppose the application.

(8) No proceedings under this section shall affect any final judgment or decree already pronounced or made by any court of competent jurisdiction.

(9) The court (including a county court) by which any proceedings under this section are heard may direct that the whole or any part of the proceedings shall be heard in camera, and on application for a direction under this subsection shall be heard in camera unless the court otherwise directs.

NOTES

This section is printed as amended by the Domestic and Appellate Proceedings (Restriction of Publicity) Act, 1968, s. 2 (1), (2).

S. 8 of the Legitimacy Act, 1926.—See p. 1294, *ante.*

In camera.—Prior to the 1968 Act, *supra,* the determination of legitimacy by legal proceedings was in public. See *B. (otherwise P.)* v. *A.-G.,* [1967] P. 119; [1965] 3 All E. R. 253.

The court.—Proceedings in the High Court are assigned to the Family Division. Administration of Justice Act, 1970, s. 1 and Sched. I.

❋   ❋   ❋   ❋

FAMILY LAW REFORM ACT, 1969
[1969 c. 46]

ARRANGEMENT OF SECTIONS

Part I

Reduction of Age of Majority and Related Provisions

Part II

Property Rights of Illegitimate Children

Part III

Provisions for use of Blood Tests in Determining Paternity

An Act to amend the law relating to the age of majority, to persons who have not attained that age and to the time when a particular age is attained; to amend the law relating to the property rights of illegitimate children and of other persons whose relationship is traced through an illegitimate link; to make provision for the use of blood tests for the purpose of determining the paternity of any person in civil proceedings; to make provision with respect to the evidence required to rebut a presumption of legitimacy and illegitimacy; to make further provision, in connection with the registration of the birth of an illegitimate child, for entering the name of the father; and for connected purposes.   [25th July, 1969.]

PART I

REDUCTION OF AGE OF MAJORITY AND
RELATED PROVISIONS

1. Reduction of age of majority from 21 to 18.—(1) As from the date on which this section comes into force a person shall attain full age on attaining the age of eighteen instead of on attaining the age of twenty-one; and a person shall attain full age on that date if he has then already attained the age of eighteen but not the age of twenty-one.

(2) The foregoing subsection applies for the purposes of any rule of law, and, in the absence of a definition or of any indication of a contrary intention, for the construction of "full age", "infant", "minor", "minority" and similar expressions in—

(a) any statutory provision, whether passed or made before, on or after the date on which this section comes into force; and

(b) any deed, will or other instrument of whatever nature (not being a statutory provision) made on or after that date.

(3) In the statutory provisions specified in Schedule 1 to this Act for any reference to the age of twenty-one years there shall be substituted a reference to the age of eighteen years; but the amendment by this subsection of the provisions specified in Part II of that Schedule shall be without prejudice to any power of amending or revoking those provisions.

(4) This section does not affect the construction of any such expression as is referred to in subsection (2) of this section in any of the statutory provisions described in Schedule 2 to this Act, and the transitional provisions and savings contained in Schedule 3 to this Act shall have effect in relation to this section.

(5) The Lord Chancellor may by order made by statutory instrument amend any provision in any local enactment passed on or before the date on which this section comes into force (not being a provision described in paragraph 2 of Schedule 2 to this Act) by substituting a reference to the age of eighteen years for any reference therein to the age of twenty-one years; and any statutory instrument containing an order under this subsection shall be subject to annulment in pursuance of a resolution of either House of Parliament.

(6) In this section "statutory provision" means any enactment (including, except where the context otherwise requires, this Act) and any order, rule, regulation, byelaw or other instrument made in the exercise of a power conferred by any enactment.

(7) Notwithstanding any rule of law, a will or codicil executed before the date on which this section comes into force shall not be treated for the purposes of this section as made on or after that date by reason only that the will or codicil is confirmed by a codicil executed on or after that date.

2. Provisions relating to marriage.—(1) In the following enactments, that is to say—

- (a) section 7 (c) of the Foreign Marriage Act, 1892 (persons under 21 intending to be married by a marriage officer to swear that necessary consents have been obtained);
- (b) paragraph 2 (c) of Part I of the Schedule to the Marriage with Foreigners Act, 1906 (persons under 21 seeking certificate to swear that necessary consents have been obtained);
- (c) section 78 (1) of the Marriage Act, 1949 (definition of "infant" as person under the age of 21),

for the words "twenty-one years" there shall be substituted the words "eighteen years".

(2) In subsection (5) of section 3 of the said Act of 1949 (which defines the courts having jurisdiction to consent to the marriage of an infant)—

- (a) for the words "the county court of the district in which any respondent resides" there shall be substituted the words "the county court of the district in which any applicant or respondent resides"; and
- (b) after the words "or a court of summary jurisdiction" there shall be inserted the words "having jurisdiction in the place in which any applicant or respondent resides".

(3) Where for the purpose of obtaining a certificate or licence for marriage under Part III of the said Act of 1949 a person declares that the consent of any person or persons whose consent to the marriage is required under the said section 3 has been obtained, the superintendent registrar may refuse to issue the certificate or licence for marriage unless satisfied by the production of written evidence that the consent of that person or of those persons has in fact been obtained.

(4) In this section any expression which is also used in the said Act of 1949 has the same meaning as in that Act.

3. Provisions relating to wills and intestacy.—(1) In the following enactments, that is to say—

    (a) section 7 of the Wills Act, 1837 (invalidity of wills made by persons under 21);

    (b) sections 1 and 3 (1) of the Wills (Soldiers and Sailors) Act, 1918 (soldier etc. eligible to make will and dispose of real property although under 21),

in their application to wills made after the coming into force of this section, for the words "twenty-one years" there shall be substituted the words "eighteen years".

(2) In section 47 (1) (i) of the Administration of Estates Act, 1925 (statutory trusts on intestacy), in its application to the estate of an intestate dying after the coming into force of this section, for the words "twenty-one years" in both places where they occur there shall be substituted the words "eighteen years".

(3) Any will which—

    (a) has been made, whether before or after the coming into force of this section, by a person under the age of eighteen; and

    (b) is valid by virtue of the provisions of section 11 of the said Act of 1837 and the said Act of 1918,

may be revoked by that person notwithstanding that he is still under that age whether or not the circumstances are then such that he would be entitled to make a valid will under those provisions.

(4) In this section "will" has the same meaning as in the said Act of 1837 and "intestate" has the same meaning as in the said Act of 1925.

4. Maintenance for children under Guardianship of Infants Acts to continue to age of 21.—[*Repealed by the Guardianship of Minors Act, 1971. See now s.* 12, *ibid.*]

5. Modification of other enactments relating to maintenance of children so as to preserve benefits up to age of 21.—(1) For the purposes of the Inheritance (Family Provision) Act, 1938, the dependants of a deceased person shall continue to include any son who has not attained the age of twenty-one; and accordingly—

    (a) in subsection (1) (c)* of that Act for the words "infant son" there shall be substituted the words "a son who has not attained the age of twenty-one years";

    (b) in subsection (2) (c)* of that Act for the words "in the case of an infant son, his attaining the age of twenty-one years" there shall be substituted the words "in the case of a son who has not attained the age of twenty-one years, his attaining that age".

(2) Where a child in respect of whom an affiliation order has been made under the Affiliation Proceedings Act, 1957 has attained the age of eighteen and his mother is dead, of unsound mind or in prison—

    (a) any application for an order under subsection (2) or (3) of section 7 of that Act directing that payments shall be made under the affiliation order for any period after he has attained that age may be made by the child himself; and

---

* *sic.* Clearly this refers to s. 1 of the Inheritance (Family Provision) Act, 1938.

(b) the child himself shall be the person entitled to any payments directed by an order under that section to be so made for any such period as aforesaid.

(3) [*Repealed by the Matrimonial Proceedings and Property Act,* 1970.]

6. Maintenance for wards of court.—(1) In this section "the court" means any of the following courts in the exercise of its jurisdiction relating to the wardship of children, that is to say, the High Court, and "ward of court" means a ward of the court in question.

(2) Subject to the provisions of this section, the court may make an order—

(a) requiring either parent of a ward of court to pay to the other parent; or

(b) requiring either parent or both parents of a ward of court to pay to any other person having the care and control of the ward,

such weekly or other periodical sums towards the maintenance and education of the ward as the court thinks reasonable having regard to the means of the person or persons on whom the requirement is imposed.

(3) An order under subsection (2) of this section may require such sums as are mentioned in that subsection to continue to be paid in respect of any period after the date on which the person for whose benefit the payments are to be made ceases to be a minor but not beyond the date on which he attains the age of twenty-one, and any order made as aforesaid may provide that any sum which is payable thereunder for the benefit of that person after he has ceased to be a minor shall be paid to that person himself.

(4) Subject to the provisions of this section, where a person who has ceased to be a minor but has not attained the age of twenty-one has at any time been the subject of an order making him a ward of court, the court may, on the application of either parent of that person or of that person himself, make an order requiring either parent to pay to the other parent, to anyone else for the benefit of that person or to that person himself, in respect of any period not extending beyond the date when he attains the said age, such weekly or other periodical sums towards his maintenance or education as the court thinks reasonable having regard to the means of the person on whom the requirement in question is imposed.

(5) No order shall be made under this section, and no liability under such an order shall accrue, at a time when the parents of the ward or former ward, as the case may be, are residing together, and if they so reside for a period of three months after such an order has been made it shall cease to have effect; but the foregoing provisions of this subsection shall not apply to any order made by virtue of subsection (2) (b) of this section.

(6) No order shall be made under this section requiring any person to pay any sum towards the maintenance or education of an illegitimate child of that person.

(7) Any order under this section, or under any corresponding enactment of the Parliament of Northern Ireland, shall be included among the orders

to which section 16 of the Maintenance Orders Act, 1950 applies; and any order under this section shall be included among the orders mentioned in section 2 (1) (d) of the Reserve and Auxiliary Forces (Protection of Civil Interests) Act, 1951.

(8) The court shall have power from time to time by an order under this section to vary or discharge any previous order thereunder.

NOTE

This section is printed as amended by the Administration of Justice Act, 1970, s. 54 and Sched. XI, and the Courts Act, 1971.

7. Committal of wards of court to care of local authority and supervision of wards of court.—(1) In this section "the court" means any of the following courts in the exercise of its jurisdiction relating to the wardship of children, that is to say, the High Court, and "ward of court" means a ward of the court in question.

(2) Where it appears to the court that there are exceptional circumstances making it impracticable or undesirable for a ward of court to be, or to continue to be, under the care of either of his parents or of any other individual the court may, if it thinks fit, make an order committing the care of the ward to a local authority; and thereupon Part II of the Children Act, 1948 (which relates to the treatment of children in the care of a local authority) shall, subject to the next following subsection, apply as if the child had been received by the local authority into their care under section 1 of that Act.

(3) In subsection (2) of this section "local authority" means one of the local authorities referred to in subsection (1) of section 36 of the Matrimonial Causes Act, 1965 (under which a child may be committed to the care of a local authority by a court having jurisdiction to make an order for its custody); and subsections (2) to (6) of that section (ancillary provisions) shall have effect as if any reference therein to that section included a reference to subsection (2) of this section.

(4) Where it appears to the court that there are exceptional circumstances making it desirable that a ward of court (not being a ward who in pursuance of an order under subsection (2) of this section is in the care of a local authority) should be under the supervision of an independent person, the court may, as respects such period as the court thinks fit, order that the ward be under the supervision of a welfare officer or of a local authority; and subsection (2) of section 37 of the said Act of 1965 (ancillary provisions where a child is placed under supervision by a court having jurisdiction to make an order for its custody) shall have effect as if any reference therein to that section included a reference to this subsection.

(5) The court shall have power from time to time by an order under this section to vary or discharge any previous order thereunder.

NOTE

This section is printed as amended by the Local Authority Social Services Act, 1970, and the Courts Act, 1971.

Home Office Circular No. 215/1969/H1 dated October 31, 1969, points out that the Act contains no provision for the supply of reports to the court by welfare officers in cases where the possibility of an order under this section is under consideration but if the court requests such a report it should of course be provided.

It also points out that the relevant effect of the reference to s. 37 (2) of the Act of 1965, when read with Rule 32 of the Probation Rules, 1965 is that the welfare officer will be a probation officer appointed for, or assigned to, the petty sessions area in which the ward for the time being resides.

8. Consent by persons over 16 to surgical, medical and dental treatment.—(1) The consent of a minor who has attained the age of sixteen years to any surgical, medical or dental treatment which, in the absence of consent, would constitute a trespass to his person, shall be as effective as it would be if he were of full age; and where a minor has by virtue of this section given an effective consent to any treatment it shall not be necessary to obtain any consent for it from his parent or guardian.

(2) In this section "surgical, medical or dental treatment" includes any procedure undertaken for the purposes of diagnosis, and this section applies to any procedure (including, in particular, the administration of an anaesthetic) which is ancillary to any treatment as it applies to that treatment.

(3) Nothing in this section shall be construed as making ineffective any consent which would have been effective if this section had not been enacted.

9. Time at which a person attains a particular age.—(1) The time at which a person attains a particular age expressed in years shall be the commencement of the relevant anniversary of the date of his birth.

(2) This section applies only where the relevant anniversary falls on a date after that on which this section comes into force, and, in relation to any enactment, deed, will or other instrument, has effect subject to any provision therein.

12. Persons under full age may be described as minors instead of infants.—A person who is not of full age may be described as a minor instead of as an infant, and accordingly in this Act "minor" means such a person as aforesaid.

PART II

PROPERTY RIGHTS OF ILLEGITIMATE CHILDREN

14. Right of illegitimate child to succeed on intestacy of parents, and of parents to succeed on intestacy of illegitimate child.—(1) Where either parent of an illegitimate child dies intestate as respects all or any of his or her real or personal property, the illegitimate child or, if he is dead, his issue, shall be entitled to take any interest therein to which he or such issue would have been entitled if he had been born legitimate.

(2) Where an illegitimate child dies intestate in respect of all or any of his real or personal property, each of his parents, if surviving, shall be entitled to take any interest therein to which that parent would have been entitled if the child had been born legitimate.

(3) In accordance with the foregoing provisions of this section, Part IV of the Administration of Estates Act, 1925 (which deals with the distribution of the estate of an intestate) shall have effect as if—

(a) any reference to the issue of the intestate included a reference to any illegitimate child of his and to the issue of any such child;

(b) any reference to the child or children of the intestate included a reference to any illegitimate child or children of his; and

(c) in relation to an intestate who is an illegitimate child, any reference to the parent, parents, father or mother of the intestate were a reference to his natural parent, parents, father or mother.

(4) For the purposes of subsection (2) of this section and of the provisions amended by subsection (3) (c) thereof, an illegitimate child shall be presumed not to have been survived by his father unless the contrary is shown.

(5) This section does not apply to or affect the right of any person to take any entailed interest in real or personal property.

(6) The reference in section 50 (1) of the said Act of 1925 (which relates to the construction of documents) to Part IV of that Act, or to the foregoing provisions of that Part, shall in relation to an instrument inter vivos made, or a will or codicil coming into operation, after the coming into force of this section (but not in relation to instruments inter vivos made or wills or codicils coming into operation earlier) be construed as including references to this section.

(7) Section 9 of the Legitimacy Act, 1926 (under which an illegitimate child and his issue are entitled to succeed on the intestacy of his mother if she leaves no legitimate issue, and the mother of an illegitimate child is entitled to succeed on his intestacy as if she were the only surviving parent) is hereby repealed.

(8) In this section "illegitimate child" does not include an illegitimate child who is—

(a) a legitimated person within the meaning of the said Act of 1926 or a person recognised by virtue of that Act or at common law as having been legitimated; or

(b) an adopted person under an adoption order made in any part of the United Kingdom, the Isle of Man or the Channel Islands or under an overseas adoption as defined in section 4 (3) of the Adoption Act, 1968.

(9) This section does not affect any rights under the intestacy of a person dying before the coming into force of this section.

15. Presumption that in dispositions of property references to children and other relatives include references to, and to persons related through, illegitimate children.—(1) In any disposition made after the coming into force of this section—

(a) any reference (whether express or implied) to the child or children of any person shall, unless the contrary intention appears, be construed as, or as including, a reference to any illegitimate child of that person; and

(b) any reference (whether express or implied) to a person or persons related in some other manner to any person shall, unless the contrary intention appears, be construed as, or as including, a reference to anyone who would be so related if he, or some other person through whom the relationship is deduced, had been born legitimate.

(2) The foregoing subsection applies only where the reference in question is to a person who is to benefit or to be capable of benefiting under the disposition or, for the purpose of designating such a person, to someone else to or through whom that person is related; but that subsection does not affect the construction of the word "heir" or "heirs" or of any expression which is used to create an entailed interest in real or personal property.

(3) In relation to any disposition made after the coming into force of this section, section 33 of the Trustee Act, 1925 (which specifies the trusts implied by a direction that income is to be held on protective trusts for the benefit of any person) shall have effect as if—

(a) the reference to the children or more remote issue of the principal beneficiary included a reference to any illegitimate child of the principal beneficiary and to anyone who would rank as such issue if he, or some other person through whom he is descended from the principal beneficiary, had been born legitimate; and
(b) the reference to the issue of the principal beneficiary included a reference to anyone who would rank as such issue if he, or some other person through whom he is descended from the principal beneficiary, had been born legitimate.

(4) In this section references to an illegitimate child include references to an illegitimate child who is or becomes a legitimated person within the meaning of the Legitimacy Act, 1926 or a person recognised by virtue of that Act or at common law as having been legitimated; and in section 3 of that Act—

(a) subsection (1) (b) (which relates to the effect of dispositions where a person has been legitimated) shall not apply to a disposition made after the coming into force of this section except as respects any interest in relation to which the disposition refers only to persons who are, or whose relationship is deduced through, legitimate persons; and
(b) subsection (2) (which provides that, where the right to any property depends on the relative seniority of the children of any person, legitimated persons shall rank as if born on the date of legitimation) shall not apply in relation to any right conferred by a disposition made after the coming into force of this section unless the terms of the disposition are such that the children whose relative seniority is in question cannot include any illegitimate children who are not either legitimated persons within the meaning of that Act or persons recognised by virtue of that Act as having been legitimated.

(5) Where under any disposition any real or personal property or any interest in such property is limited (whether subject to any preceding

limitation or charge or not) in such a way that it would, apart from this section, devolve (as nearly as the law permits) along with a dignity or title of honour, then, whether or not the disposition contains an express reference to the dignity or title of honour, and whether or not the property or some interest in the property may in some event become severed therefrom, nothing in this section shall operate to sever the property or any interest therein from the dignity or title, but the property or interest shall devolve in all respects as if this section had not been enacted.

(6) This section is without prejudice to sections 16 and 17 of the Adoption Act, 1958 (which relate to the construction of dispositions in cases of adoption).

(7) There is hereby abolished, as respects dispositions made after the coming into force of this section, any rule of law that a disposition in favour of illegitimate children not in being when the disposition takes effect is void as contrary to public policy.

(8) In this section "disposition" means a disposition, including an oral disposition, of real or personal property whether inter vivos or by will or codicil; and, notwithstanding any rule of law, a disposition made by will or codicil executed before the date on which this section comes into force shall not be treated for the purposes of this section as made on or after that date by reason only that the will or codicil is confirmed by a codicil executed on or after that date.

16. Meaning of "child" and "issue" in s. 33 of Wills Act, 1837.—(1) In relation to a testator who dies after the coming into force of this section, section 33 of the Wills Act, 1837 (gift to children or other issue of testator not to lapse if they predecease him but themselves leave issue) shall have effect as if—

(a) the reference to a child or other issue of the testator (that is, the intended beneficiary) included a reference to any illegitimate child of the testator and to anyone who would rank as such issue if he, or some other person through whom he is descended from the testator, had been born legitimate; and

(b) the reference to the issue of the intended beneficiary included a reference to anyone who would rank as such issue if he, or some other person through whom he is descended from the intended beneficiary, had been born legitimate.

(2) In this section "illegitimate child" includes an illegitimate child who is a legitimated person within the meaning of the Legitimacy Act, 1926 or a person recognised by virtue of that Act or at common law as having been legitimated.

18. Illegitimate children to count as dependants under Inheritance (Family Provision) Act, 1938.—(1) For the purposes of the Inheritance (Family Provision) Act, 1938, a person's illegitimate son or daughter shall be treated as his dependant in any case in which a legitimate son or daughter of that person would be so treated, and accordingly in the definition of the expressions "son" and "daughter" in section 5 (1) of that Act, as amended by the Family Provision Act, 1966, after the words "respectively include" there shall be inserted the words "an illegitimate son or daughter of the deceased".

(2) In section 26 (6) of the Matrimonial Causes Act, 1965 (which provides, among other things, for the word "dependant" to have the same meaning as in the said Act of 1938 as amended by the said Act of 1966), after the words "as amended by the Family Provision Act, 1966" there shall be inserted the words "and the Family Law Reform Act, 1969".

(3) This section does not affect the operation of the said Acts of 1938 and 1965 in relation to a person dying before the coming into force of this section.

PART III

PROVISIONS FOR USE OF BLOOD TESTS IN DETERMINING PATERNITY

20. Power of court to require use of blood tests.—(1) In any civil proceedings in which the paternity of any person falls to be determined by the court hearing the proceedings, the court may, on an application by any party to the proceedings, give a direction for the use of blood tests to ascertain whether such tests show that a party to the proceedings is or is not thereby excluded from being the father of that person and for the taking, within a period to be specified in the direction, of blood samples from that person, the mother of that person and any party alleged to be the father of that person or from any, or any two, of those persons.

A court may at any time revoke or vary a direction previously given by it under this section.

(2) The person responsible for carrying out blood tests taken for the purpose of giving effect to a direction under this section shall make to the court by which the direction was given a report in which he shall state—

- (a) the results of the tests;
- (b) whether the party to whom the report relates is or is not excluded by the results from being the father of the person whose paternity is to be determined; and
- (c) if that party is not so excluded, the value, if any, of the results in determining whether that party is that person's father;

and the report shall be received by the court as evidence in the proceedings of the matters stated therein.

(3) A report under subsection (2) of this section shall be in the form prescribed by regulations made under section 22 of this Act.

(4) Where a report has been made to a court under subsection (2) of this section, any party may, with the leave of the court, or shall, if the court so directs, obtain from the person who made the report a written statement explaining or amplifying any statement made in the report, and that statement shall be deemed for the purposes of this section (except subsection (3) thereof) to form part of the report made to the court.

(5) Where a direction is given under this section in any proceedings, a party to the proceedings, unless the court otherwise directs, shall not be entitled to call as a witness the person responsible for carrying out the

tests taken for the purpose of giving effect to the direction, or any person by whom any thing necessary for the purpose of enabling those tests to be carried out was done, unless within fourteen days after receiving a copy of the report he serves notice on the other parties to the proceedings, or on such of them as the court may direct, of his intention to call that person; and where any such person is called as a witness the party who called him shall be entitled to cross-examine him.

(6) Where a direction is given under this section the party on whose application the direction is given shall pay the cost of taking and testing blood samples for the purpose of giving effect to the direction (including any expenses reasonably incurred by any person in taking any steps required of him for the purpose), and of making a report to the court under this section, but the amount paid shall be treated as costs incurred by him in the proceedings.

21. Consents, etc., required for taking of blood samples.—(1) Subject to the provisions of subsections (3) and (4) of this section, a blood sample which is required to be taken from any person for the purpose of giving effect to a direction under section 20 of this Act shall not be taken from that person except with his consent.

(2) The consent of a minor who has attained the age of sixteen years to the taking from himself of a blood sample shall be as effective as it would be if he were of full age; and where a minor has by virtue of this subsection given an effective consent to the taking of a blood sample it shall not be necessary to obtain any consent for it from any other person.

(3) A blood sample may be taken from a person under the age of sixteen years, not being such a person as is referred to in subsection (4) of this section, if the person who has the care and control of him consents.

(4) A blood sample may be taken from a person who is suffering from mental disorder within the meaning of the Mental Health Act, 1959 and is incapable of understanding the nature and purpose of blood tests if the person who has the care and control of him consents and the medical practitioner in whose care he is has certified that the taking of a blood sample from him will not be prejudicial to his proper care and treatment.

(5) The foregoing provisions of this section are without prejudice to the provisions of section 23 of this Act.

22. Power to provide for manner of giving effect to direction for use of blood tests.—(1) The Secretary of State may by regulations make provision as to the manner of giving effect to directions under section 20 of this Act and, in particular, any such regulations may—

(a) provide that blood samples shall not be taken except by such medical practitioners as may be appointed by the Secretary of State;
(b) regulate the taking, identification and transport of blood samples;
(c) require the production at the time when a blood sample is to be taken of such evidence of the identity of the person from whom it is to be taken as may be prescribed by the regulations;
(d) require any person from whom a blood sample is to be taken, or, in such cases as may be prescribed by the regulations, such

other person as may be so prescribed, to state in writing whether he or the person from whom the sample is to be taken, as the case may be, has during such period as may be specified in the regulations suffered from any such illness as may be so specified or received a transfusion of blood;

(e) provide that blood tests shall not be carried out except by such persons, and at such places, as may be appointed by the Secretary of State;

(f) prescribe the blood tests to be carried out and the manner in which they are to be carried out;

(g) regulate the charges that may be made for the taking and testing of blood samples and for the making of a report to a court under section 20 of this Act;

(h) make provision for securing that so far as practicable the blood samples to be tested for the purpose of giving effect to a direction under section 20 of this Act are tested by the same person;

(i) prescribe the form of the report to be made to a court under section 20 of this Act.

(2) The power to make regulations under this section shall be exercisable by statutory instrument which shall be subject to annulment in pursuance of a resolution of either House of Parliament.

23. Failure to comply with direction for taking blood tests.—(1) Where a court gives a direction under section 20 of this Act and any person fails to take any step required of him for the purpose of giving effect to the direction, the court may draw such inferences, if any, from that fact as appear proper in the circumstances.

(2) Where in any proceedings in which the paternity of any person falls to be determined by the court hearing the proceedings there is a presumption of law that that person is legitimate, then if—

(a) a direction is given under section 20 of this Act in those proceedings, and

(b) any party who is claiming any relief in the proceedings and who for the purpose of obtaining that relief is entitled to rely on the presumption fails to take any step required of him for the purpose of giving effect to the direction,

the court may adjourn the hearing for such period as it thinks fit to enable that party to take that step, and if at the end of that period he has failed without reasonable cause to take it the court may, without prejudice to subsection (1) of this section, dismiss his claim for relief notwithstanding the absence of evidence to rebut the presumption.

(3) Where any person named in a direction under section 20 of this Act fails to consent to the taking of a blood sample from himself or from any person named in the direction of whom he has the care and control, he shall be deemed for the purposes of this section to have failed to take a step required of him for the purpose of giving effect to the direction.

24. Penalty for personating another, etc., for purpose of providing blood sample.—If for the purpose of providing a blood sample for a test required to give effect to a direction under section 20 of this Act any person personates another, or proffers a child knowing that it is not the child named in the direction, he shall be liable—

    (a) on conviction on indictment, to imprisonment for a term not exceeding two years, or

    (b) on summary conviction, to a fine not exceeding £400.

25. Interpretation of Part III.—In this Part of this Act the following expressions have the meanings hereby respectively assigned to them, that is to say—

    "blood samples" means blood taken for the purpose of blood tests;

    "blood tests" means blood tests carried out under this Part of this Act and includes any test made with the object of ascertaining the inheritable characteristics of blood;

    "excluded" means excluded subject to the occurrence of mutation.

PART IV
MISCELLANEOUS AND GENERAL

26. Rebuttal of presumption as to legitimacy and illegitimacy.— Any presumption of law as to the legitimacy or illegitimacy of any person may in any civil proceedings be rebutted by evidence which shows that it is more probable than not that that person is illegitimate or legitimate, as the case may be, and it shall not be necessary to prove that fact beyond reasonable doubt in order to rebut the presumption.

NOTE

In *T. (H.)* v. *T. (E.)*, [1971] 1 All E. R. 590, the dictum of Lord Reid in *S.* v. *S.*, [1970] 3 All E. R. at p. 109 was applied, and it was held that the presumption of legitimacy only had effect where either no evidence was led to the contrary or the evidence was so evenly balanced that the court was unable to reach a decision on it, for even weak evidence must prevail over the presumption if there was no evidence to counter-balance it.

27. Entry of father's name on registration of birth of illegitimate child.—(1) In section 10 of the Births and Deaths Registration Act, 1953 (which provides that the registrar shall not enter the name of any person as the father of an illegitimate child except at the joint request of the mother and the person acknowledging himself to be the father and requires that person to sign the register together with the mother) for the words from "except" onwards there shall be substituted the words "except—

    (a) at the joint request of the mother and the person acknowledging himself to be the father of the child (in which case that person shall sign the register together with the mother); or

    (b) at the request of the mother on production of—

        (i) a declaration in the prescribed form made by the mother stating that the said person is the father of the child; and

        (ii) a statutory declaration made by that person acknowledging himself to be the father of the child."

(2) If on the registration under Part I of the said Act of 1953 of the birth of an illegitimate child no person has been entered in the register as

the father, the registrar may re-register the birth so as to show a person as the father—

    (a) at the joint request of the mother and of that person (in which case the mother and that person shall both sign the register in the presence of the registrar); or

    (b) at the request of the mother on production of—

        (i) a declaration in the prescribed form made by the mother stating that the person in question is the father of the child; and

        (ii) a statutory declaration made by that person acknowledging himself to be the father of the child;

but no birth shall be re-registered as aforesaid except with the authority of the Registrar General and any such re-registration shall be effected in such manner as may be prescribed.

(3) A request under paragraph (a) or (b) of section 10 of the said Act of 1953 as amended by subsection (1) of this section may be included in a declaration under section 9 of that Act (registration of birth pursuant to a declaration made in another district) and, if a request under the said paragraph (b) is included in such a declaration, the documents mentioned in that paragraph shall be produced to the officer in whose presence the declaration is made and sent by him, together with the declaration, to the registrar.

(4) A request under paragraph (a) or (b) of subsection (2) of this section may, instead of being made to the registrar, be made by making and signing in the presence of and delivering to such officer as may be prescribed a written statement in the prescribed form and, in the case of a request under the said paragraph (b), producing to that officer the documents mentioned in that paragraph, and the officer shall send the statement together with the documents, if any, to the registrar; and thereupon that subsection shall have effect as if the request had been made to the registrar and, if the birth is re-registered pursuant to the request, the person or persons who signed the statement shall be treated as having signed the register as required by that subsection.

(5) This section shall be construed as one with the said Act of 1953; and in section 14 (1) (a) of that Act (re-registration of birth of legitimated person) the reference to section 10 of that Act shall include a reference to subsection (2) of this section.

NOTES

Officers before whom written statements may be made. See the Registration of Births, Deaths and Marriages (Amendment) Regulations, 1969, Reg. 3, p. 1151, *ante.*

Re-registration on joint information of parents.—See the Registration of Births, Deaths and Marriages (Amendment) Regulations, 1969, Reg. 4, p. 1151, *ante.*

Re-registration on mother's information and father's statutory declaration.—See the Registration of Births, Deaths and Marriages (Amendment) Regulations, 1969, Reg. 5, p. 1152, *ante.*

28. Short title, interpretation, commencement and extent.—(1) This Act may be cited as the Family Law Reform Act, 1969.

(2) Except where the context otherwise requires, any reference in this Act to any enactment shall be construed as a reference to that enactment as amended, extended or applied by or under any other enactment, including this Act.

(3) This Act shall come into force on such date as the Lord Chancellor may appoint by order made by statutory instrument, and different dates may be appointed for the coming into force of different provisions.

(4) In this Act—

(a) section 1 and Schedule 1, so far as they amend the British National-ity Act, 1948, have the same extent as that Act and are hereby declared for the purposes of section 3 (3) of the West Indies Act, 1967 to extend to all the associated states;

(b) section 2, so far as it amends any provision of the Foreign Mar-riage Act, 1892 or the Marriage with Foreigners Act, 1906, has the same extent as that provision;

(c) section 6 (7), so far as they affect Part II of the Maintenance Orders Act, 1950, extend to Scotland and Northern Ireland;

(d) section 10, so far as it relates to the Civil List Act, 1952, extends to Scotland and Northern Ireland;

(e) section 11, so far as it relates to the Employers and Workmen Act, 1875, extends to Scotland;

(f) section 13 extends to Northern Ireland;

(g) section 19 extends to Scotland;

but, save as aforesaid, this Act shall extend to England and Wales only.

NOTE

This section is printed as amended by the Guardianship of Minors Act, 1971, s. 18 (2) and Sched. 2.

The Family Law Reform Act, 1969 (Commencement No. 1) Order, 1969, S.I. 1969 No. 1140, p. B286, *post*, brought into force from January 1, 1970, Parts I, II and IV and the Schedules. Part III was brought into force by the Family Law Reform Act, 1969 (Commencement No. 2) Order 1971, S.I. 1971 No. 1857, as from March 1, 1972. See also the Blood Tests (Evidence of Paternity) Regulations 1971, (S.I. 1971 No. 1861), and the Magistrates' Courts (Blood Tests) Rules 1971, (S.I. 1971 No. 1991) both of which are also operative from March 1, 1972. It has not been possible to include these instruments in this volume.

SCHEDULE 3

TRANSITIONAL PROVISIONS AND SAVINGS

*   *   *   *

Wardship and custody orders

3.—(1) Any order in force immediately before the commencement date—

(a) making a person a ward of court; or

(b) under the Guardianship of Infants Acts, 1886 and 1925, or under the Matrimonial Causes Act, 1965 or any enactment repealed by that Act, for the custody of, or access to, any person, which is expressed to continue in force until the person who is the subject of the order attains the age of twenty-one, or any age between eighteen and twenty-one, shall have effect as if the reference to his attaining that age were a reference to his attaining the age of eighteen or, in relation to a person who by virtue of the principal section attains full age on the commencement date, to that date.

(2) This paragraph is without prejudice to so much of any order as makes provision for the maintenance or education of a person after he has attained the age of eighteen.

INDEX

D.

DAMAGES—
magistrates' court, in, 387
parent may be ordered to pay, 59
provision as to in probation order, 290

DANGER—
burning, exposure to risk of, 24
dangerous performance, meaning of, 41
                    prohibition of, 33–34
juvenile exposed to moral, 10 *et seq.*

DEATH—
approved school, in, notice of, 465
children's home, in, notice of, 981
detention centre, in, information to family, 492
duties, payment of, by legitimated person, 1293, 1294
              effect of adoption, 1023, [1052]
foster child, of, notice of, 959
        parent, of, 985
inmate of reception centre, of, 486
protected child, of, 1071
remand home, in, notice of, 470
sentence of, not pronounced on person under eighteen, 57–58
            pardon from, term of imprisonment, after, 419

DECEASED CHILD. *See also* DEATH.
burial, 898
cremation, local authority's power to arrange, 898
expenses of persons attending funeral, 901
funeral expenses, recovery from parent, 898

DEFECTIVE. *See* MENTAL DISORDER.

DEPOSITION—
juvenile, of, admissibility in evidence, 49
           power to take out of court, 49

DETENTION. *See also* IMPRISONMENT.
absentees of, 179
age for, 402, 403
borstal in, removal from prison, after, 416
        training for, 305
community home, in, [58], 177
definition, 418
extension of enactments to young offenders, 435
fine, in default of payment of, 59, 145, 314–315, 405, 493
grave crimes, for, 177
juvenile, of, before criminal proceedings, 42
          for grave crimes, 57
limitation upon, order for, 402
medical treatment during, 379
one day, for, 385
order, care order substituted for, [58]
place of safety, time limitation, [965], [1074]
release from, 175
remand home, in, 64, [391]
           time limitation, [965], [1074]
removal from, for judicial purposes, 413
Scotland, removal from, after, 417
        sentence of, in, 418
Secretary of State, by order of, 62
temporary, pending transfer to borstal institution, 391
term of, consecutive, 405, 418
time limitation, [405], 406
transfer to another part of U.K., after release from, 412
            to serve, 411

DETENTION CENTRE—
advisory council on penal system, report of, 840
accommodation in, 483
after-care of inmates, 492
appellants, provisions relating to, 496
baby, mother's right to have with her, 484
Board of Visitors, investigations by, 487–488
                            provisions relating to, 497–499
boys between 14 and 17, for, 846
classification and grading, 483
clothing of inmates, 495
                  inventory of, 484
                  return of, on release, 485
commitment to, time limit, 405
complaints by inmates, 489
death of inmate, 485
              information to family, 492
default in payment of money, detention for, 493
                          time limit, 405
diet, examination by Board of Visitors, 499
    general provisions as to, 495
    recommendations as to, 494
    restricted, 487
discipline in, 486
disregarding period while unlawfully at large, 392
drink and tobacco, prohibition of, 489
education of inmates, 490
employment of inmates, 490
family relationships, maintenance of, 492
girls, for, [403]
gratuities to staff prohibited, 497
hospital, equipment of, at, 493
hygiene in, 495
letters, writing and receiving, 492
                    additional, 499
      written by appellant, 496
library, provision of, 492
medical attention, inmate requiring, 496
             examination of inmates, 484
             Officer, duties of, 493, 494
money sent to detainee, retention of, 409
offences against rules of, 409
          by inmates, 487
physical welfare of inmates, 493
prison sentence instead, order for, 406
provision of, 390
recall to, 421
release from, special days, 409
             supervision after, 406, 421
religion, change of, approval by Board of Visitors, 499
religious observances in, 491
remission of punishment, 488
          sentence, 486
removal from, 484
        for judicial purposes, 413
restraints, authorised by Board of Visitors, 499
        use of, 488
rules for management of, 391
search of inmates, 484
        members of staff, 497
        persons entering or leaving, 490
staff, obligations of, 496
suicidal inmates, 494
transfer to, from prison, 416, 417
unauthorised articles, removal of, 487
           what are, 489
unlawfully at large from, in another part of U.K., 414–415
visitors, restrictions on, 490
visits to inmates, 492, 493
           additional, 499

EMPLOYMENT—*continued.*
    detention centre, of inmates of, 490
    entertainments, in.   *See* ENTERTAINMENTS.
    factories and mines, in, 41
    juveniles, of, prosecution for offences arising from, 32–33
    licensed betting office, in, 422
    local education authority, notice to be given to, 263
    persons under eighteen, of, byelaws regulating, 30–31
    restriction on, of child under 18, 31, [32], [105], 508
    school children, of, restrictions on, 266–277
    street trading, in, of person under sixteen, 31, 41

ENTERTAINMENTS.   *See also* PERFORMANCES.
    abroad, licence for, 109
        offences in connection with, 38
        restrictions on person under eighteen, 35 *et seq.*
    amateur, child taking part in, [105]
    child taking part in, licence for, 105, 109
            false statement in, 108
        restrictions on, 103
        rules relating to, contravention of, 108
    dangerous, licence for training, 108
    rehearsals, licence not required for, [106]
    safety of children at, 25

ENTRY—
    power of, where offence suspected, 40

ESCAPE—
    approved school from, 786
    arrest without warrant in case of, 392
    assisting, liability for, 408
    boarded out child, of, 888
    period of sentence, disregarding time while at large, 392
    place of safety, from, 234
    remand home, from, 470

EVIDENCE—
    adoption, of consent to, 1038, 1039
    age, of.   *See* AGE.
    appeal tribunal, before, 976
    approval of approved school, of, 80
    authentication of documents, 81, 269
    by–laws, of, 39
    care proceedings, in, 577
    certificate of exemption as, 262
        medical practitioner, 98
    child, of, corroboration of, [18], 45, [399]
        five years of age, [45]
        in committal proceedings, [98]
        sexual offences case, 675, 676
    consular report as, 39, 1077
    cruelty to person under sixteen, of, 10 *et seq.*
    deposition admissible as, 49, 550–551, 553
    illegitimacy, of, 1029
    indecent, 675
        exclusion of persons from court during, 1221
    juvenile, of, power to clear court during, 44, 677
            prohibit publication, 46, 675
    mental deficiency, of, 454
    order of, 553–554
        court, of, 80–81
    previous conviction of, proof of, 533
    probation order, of failure to comply with, 284
    sexual offences case, age of child, 677
            committal proceedings, 676
            expulsion of public, 678
            protection of child, 678. *See also* SEXUAL OFFENCES.

EVIDENCE—*continued.*
    spouse of accused person, by, 27, 399
            under Sexual Offences Act, [397]
    wages, of, 78
    writing, in, necessity for, 550
    written statements, in committal proceedings, 432–434
            criminal proceedings, 558–559

EXPOSURE—
    child, of, meaning of, [17]
    person under sixteen, of, 10
    risk of burning, to, 24, 87

F.

FAMILY ALLOWANCES—
    adoption, application for, effect of, 1069
            effect of, [1048]
    cessation of, when child received into care, [884]
    child in care of local authority, [886]

FAMILY LAW REFORM ACT, 1969...1305 *et seq.*
    arrangement of sections, 1304–1305

FATHER. *See* PARENT.

FEEBLE MINDED. *See* MENTAL DISORDER.

FINE—
    assisting person to escape, for, 408
    child, in respect of, limitation on, 277
    county college, for offence relating to, 263
    cruelty for, 101
    default in payment of, 404, [405]
    definition of, 387
    detainees, outstanding, against, 697–702
    detention in default of payment of, 314–315, 318, 404
            in detention centre, 493
        lieu of, 59
    enforcement of payment of, 320–321
    gaming offences, for, 425
    harbouring or concealing juvenile offender, for, 112
    increase of, certain offences, for, 101, 103
    intoxicating liquor, in relation to, 427, 428
    limitation on amount of, [60], [277]
    maximum, for breach of probation order, [285]
        on summary conviction, [34], [35]
    nominal, 372
    notice of, when required, [556]
    parent may be ordered to pay, 60
    payment of, after imprisonment, effect of, 315
        order to attend at attendance centre, 374
    probation order, for breach of, 283
    restriction on amount of, [60]
    supervision order in addition to, 316

FINGER-PRINTS—
    taking of, 147, 382, 435

FIREARM—
    acquisition and possession of, by minors, 437
    ammunition, definition of, 439
    certificate as to, 436
    definition, 439
    members of rifle club, 437
    offences in relation to, 437–439
    prohibition against possession of, [59]
    shooting gallery, at, 438

FIREARMS ACT, 1968...436 *et seq.*

G.

GUARDIANSHIP OF MINORS—*continued.*
introductory note, 1195–1196
maintenance, order for, 1128
   enforcement of, 560, 1136
    powers of court of summary jurisdiction to award, 1126
marriage of infant, effect on, [1203]
order, enforcement of, 1136
procedure, county court, 1259
  in chambers, 1259
  High Court, 1261
  summary jurisdiction, 1258
registration of maintenance order, 1259
welfare of child paramount consideration, [1032], [1033]

GUARDIANSHIP OF INFANTS RULES—
County Court Rules, 1259
Summary Jurisdiction Rules, 1925...1258

GUARDIANSHIP OF MINORS ACT, 1971...1198 *et seq.*
arrangement of sections, 1197

GUILT—
finding of, replaces conviction for juveniles, 62
plea of, 52

H.

HARMFUL PUBLICATIONS—
forfeiture of, power to order, 394
importation of, prohibition of, 395
meaning of, 394
proceedings in respect of, institution of, 393–395
search warrant in respect of, 394

HEALTH SERVICES AND PUBLIC HEALTH ACT, 1968...951 *et seq.*

HEALTH VISITOR—
duties of, 877

HOME OFFICE SCHOOLS. *See* APPROVED SCHOOL.

HOME PROVIDED BY LOCAL AUTHORITY. *See also* LOCAL AUTHORITY
accommodating children in care of the authority, 896
accommodation of children in, 893
appointment of persons having charge, 896
direction that premises shall not be used as, 896
duty to provide, 892
premises unsuitable, 896
  used for, regulations as to, 894
regulations as to conduct of, 894, 979 *et seq.*
  not conducted in accordance with, 896
religious instruction, 896, 980
safety, provision for child removed to place of, 917
Secretary of State may order closure, 896
temporary reception accommodation in, 895
    time limit for child in, 896

HOMICIDE—
child charged with, 166

HOMOSEXUAL ACT—
prohibition on trial by jury, 276

HOSPITAL—
allowance in respect of child in, 1006
compulsory admission to, 445–447
definition, 951
discharge from, restrictions on, 450
Nurseries and Child-Minders Regulation Act, exemption under, 948

HOSPITAL—*continued*.
    order, appeal against, 453–454
        care proceedings, form for, 599
            Crown Court, by, 432
          effect of, 448–449
          juvenile court, by, 448
          mentally disordered persons, as to, 542
          parental rights after, 444
          restriction on discharge, 451, 456
    prisoners, removal to, 454, 455
    resident of hostel or home going to, [280]

HOSTEL—
    hospital, resident going to, [280]
    local authority, not provided by, maintenance of children in, 893
    probation. *See* PROBATION.
    terms upon which child maintained in, 893
    who may be accommodated in, 899

HUSBAND—
    evidence of, admissibility of, 27

I.

IDIOT. *See* MENTAL DISORDER.

ILLEGITIMATE CHILD—
    adoption of, effect on affiliation order, 1049
    approved school, at, affiliation order in respect of, 70
    birth, re-registration of, 1152
    care order, subject of, [70]
    custody of, [12], [1202], [1291]
        wishes of parents as to, [882]
    dependants, as, 1313, 1314
    evidence of illegitimacy, [1029], 1317
    guardianship of, [1200], 1207
    legitimation of. *See* LEGITIMATION.
    local authority, in care of, maintenance of, 903–905
    parent of, meaning of, [28], 397
    property rights of, 1310–1313
    putative father, rights of, [1032]
    registration of birth of, entry of father's name, 1317, 1318
    relative of, meaning of, 1023

ILL-TREATMENT—
    meaning of, [15–16]
    medical treatment, lack of, amounting to, [16]
    person under sixteen, of, 10 *et seq.*, 47

IMPRISONMENT—
    approved school, transfer to, from, 62
    borstal, in lieu of, 401, [402]
        transfer between, and, 308–309, [385]
    consecutive term, as single, 419
    definition, 418
    fine, in lieu of, 314–315, 318–319, 493
    first offender, of, [373], [385]
    juveniles, of, restrictions on, 372, [380], 385
    limitations upon, 400
    magistrates' court, by, restrictions on, [380], 385
    means inquiry before, 315
    medical treatment, prisoner requiring, 389
    one day's, 372
    pardon, after, from death sentence, 419
    photographing and measuring prisoners, 388
    place of safety, whether prison included, [83]
    prison, rules for management of, 391–392
    prisoner removal for judicial or other purposes, 389
    recall to, 401

LOCAL AUTHORITIES AND LOCAL EDUCATION AUTHORITIES (ALLOCATION OF FUNCTIONS) REGULATIONS, 1951...977–979

LOCAL AUTHORITY—
  abandoned child, duty to provide for, 880 *et seq.*
  accounts of, 916, 931–932
  acquisition of land by, 920
  adoption, arrangements for, by, 1061. *See also* ADOPTION ; ADOPTION ORDER.
    research regarding, 110
  altered county, transfer of functions from, 1002
  approved school, contributions to, by, 73
    duty to provide, 66
  arrears order, person liable under, information from, 100
  boarding-out children. *See* BOARDED OUT CHILDREN ; BOARDING-OUT.
  child beyond control, duty concerning, 92
    in care of, accommodation of, 893
      affiliation order in respect of, 903–906
      after-care of, 912
        placement, 729
      boarding out of, 893, 894
      burial or cremation of, 898, 901
      code cards by, 738–740
      contributions to maintenance of, 110, 902
      court orders in respect of, 890–892
      divorce court, by order of, 1240
      duty of parents to maintain contact, 891
        to act, 167, 168, 892
      emigration of, 898, [1078]
      expenses of education, 978–979
      family allowance in respect of, 1069
      general duties towards, 892
      guarantee of apprenticeship deeds of, 111
      liability for maintenance, 887
      matrimonial order in respect of, 1227
      not foster child, 957
      orders for committal to, of, 161, 162
      persuading to run away, 888
      powers concerning, [884]
      provision of homes for, 895–896
      religion of, [885], 887
        where boarded out, 894
    child in care of, transfer to successor authority, 1002
      visits by parents of, 901
      voluntary home, placed in, 897
      ward of court, committal of, to, 1309
  children, care of, for purposes of, defined, 914
  children's homes provided by, administration of, 979 *et seq*
  common council, functions as, [1026]
  community home, detention by, in, [58]
    provision of accommodation in, 899
  complaint against, for access to child, 1271
  council of altered county, expenses, 1002
      responsibility, 1013
    dissolved county, transfer of functions, 1000, 1001
    London borough, functions as, [880], [956], [1026]
  definition of, [91], 518
    in relation to foster children, 969
      probation, 293
  dissolved council, expenses of, 1013
    county, in, 1010
      meaning of, 1004
  education, for, definition of, 248, 270
  financial assistance by, to child formerly in care, 115
  foster child, duty as to, 198, 956
      failure to comply with requirements as to, 967
      power as to, 960
      removal on complaint of, 964
  grant by Exchequer to, 79
    for education, 110
    to voluntary organisation by, 916

LOCAL HEALTH AUTHORITY—
child-minders, duty to keep register of, 936
inspection of nurseries by, 946 *et seq.*
meaning, 876
medical practitioner approved by, 447, 454
mentally disordered child, guardianship of, 457
       in care of, 443
mothers and young children, duties to, 876
notification by registered child-minder on acquisition of new home, 944
nurseries, duty to keep registers of, 939
orders in respect of nurseries and child-minders, 946
prosecution of offences under Nurseries and Child-Minders Regulation Act, 947
requirements as to registered nurseries and child-minders, 942
          breach, 944
          variation, 943

LONDON—
application of provisions as to local authorities to, 75
borough of, function as local authority, [1026]
by-laws street trading, as to, 670, 671
City of, local authority, as, 76
county borough, reference to, [1061]
employment of children, by-laws as to, [30], 468–472
juvenile courts in, 54
non-application of Juvenile Courts (Constitution) Rules to, 474
police authority in, definition of, 82

LONDON AUTHORITIES (CHILDREN) ORDER, 1965...998
explanatory notes, 1012 *et seq.*

LONDON GOVERNMENT RE-ORGANISATION—
children's service, changes in, 1010
dissolved county borough council, responsibilities of, 1012
effects on children in care, 1009
     children's officers, 1009
     supervision orders, 1009
London County Council, changes in, 1009–1010
         successor authorities, choice of, 999
             notification to, of transfer of cases,
        transfer of children in care of, 999, 1009, 1010   [1012, 1013
        functions, 999
successor authority, appointment of, 1009
        supervision of children, 1009
transitional arrangements relating to children, 1009–1010

LUNACY. *See* MENTAL DISORDER.

M.

MAGISTRATES' COURT—
appeal to, 556
adjournment of inquiry by, 378
appeal from, in relation to foster child, 966
application of money found on defaulter, 314
arrears order, making of, 99
committal for sentence by, 554–555
committee of, 121, 122
fine in respect of child, limitation on, 277, 318
forms to be used in, 540–550
guardianship proceedings, jurisdiction in, 1208
imprisonment by, restrictions on, 385
jurisdiction over children, 94, 298
means inquiry by, 315
recognizance, forfeiture of, 317

MAGISTRATES' COURTS ACT, 1952...275 *et seq.*, 378 *et seq.*, 1220 *et seq.*

MAGISTRATES' COURTS (CHILDREN AND YOUNG PERSONS) RULES, 1970...571 *et seq.*
forms, schedule of, 581–614

MAGISTRATES' COURTS (FORMS) RULES, 1968...540 *et seq.*

MAGISTRATES' COURTS (MATRIMONIAL PROCEEDINGS) RULES, 1960...1268 *et seq.*
    forms under, 1272

MAINTENANCE—
    age 21, up to, modification of enactments, 1307
    agreements, alteration of, powers of courts as to, 1250, 1251
            definition of, 1249
            validity of, 1249
    amount of, assessment of, 1229
    approved school children home on leave, for, 798
    guardian by, to exclusion of parent, 1205
    local authority, contributions by, 73
    maximum payment, increase of, 1242
    order for, 1227
            enforcement of, 1206–1207, 1236
                    by attachment of earnings, [70], [906]
           of person between 18 and 21, 1206
           registration of, 1259, 1260
        of, application of parent, 1201
    payment abroad, certificate of, 1274
            of, by post, 1278
    person under supervision in non-approved hostel, 686
                    private house, for, 683
    Probation Committee, contribution towards, 685
    probationer, for, at Brentwood Recuperative Centre, [686]
                  Crowley House, 685
                  Elizabeth Fry Home, 685
    recovery of, after cessation by re-marriage, 1237–1238
    small, payments, definition, 1256
            income tax payable, 1256, 1275
    ward of court, of, 1308

MAINTENANCE ORDERS ACT, 1968...1242 *et seq.*

MANSLAUGHTER, 11–12, [19], 58

MARRIAGE—
    adoption, effect of, 1047
    age for, 1306
    consent to, by court, 1059
    declaration of, validity of, 1302
    infant, of, consents required, 1215, 1258
            guardianship, [1203]
    person under sixteen, of, 1215
    settlement, variation of, [1052]
    void, act done by virtue of, not offence, [1215]
        legitimacy of child of, 1297

MARRIAGE ACT, 1949...1215–1219

MATRIMONIAL CAUSES—
    child born on day of divorce, [1292]
        of annulled marriage, status of, 1302
            family, arrangements as to, 1252–1254
                financial provision for, 1244–1246
        placed in care of local authority, [892], 1240
        supervision of, 1241
    financial provision for child of family, 1244–1246
    local authority, notice to, 1268
    orders in relation to, duration of, 1248, 1249
    probation officer, notice to, 1268

MATRIMONIAL CAUSES ACT, 1965...1240 *et seq.*, 1302 *et seq.*

MATRIMONIAL ORDER—
    application for, 1224

PRISON. *See also* IMPRISONMENT.
    committal of person under 17 on remand, to, [307]
    definition of, 420
    offence against rules of, 409
    removal from, to borstal, 416

PRISON ACT, 1952...308 *et seq.*, 388 *et seq.*

PROBATION. *See also* SUPERVISION ORDER.
    after-care, 683
    commission of further offence during, 286-287
    committee, flat rate contributions by, 685
            fund for probationers, maintenance of, 685
            maintenance contributions, by, 682, 685
            payment for person under supervision in private house, 682, 683
    consent of offender to, 279
    contributions to maintenance during, 530–532
    costs, order for payment of, 290
    effect of conviction, 291
    employment during, 529
    expenses of probationer, payment of, 532
    grants to probationer, payment of, 531
    home or hostel, admission to, restrictions on, 478
            definition of, 292
            future pattern of, 687 *et seq.*
            maintenance charge to residents, 692
            management of, 292
            medical care in, 480
            notice of resident going to hospital, [281]
            residence in, 279
            rules for management of, 477–482
    institution, inspection of, 293
            residence in, 279
    juvenile offender becoming seventeen during, 54
    local authority, definition of, 293
            while juvenile in care of, 890
    mental treatment, requirement as to, 281
                  breach of, 284
    order, abolition of, under 17, [278]
        amendment of, 283, 295, 530
        appeal, made on, 295
        breach of requirement of, 283, 284, [285], [288] 290, 373, [375]
        compensation or damages, provision as to, 290
        contents of, 279
        conviction, not to be, 291
        definition of, 481
        discharge of, 283, 295
        fresh, power to make, [285]
        magistrates' court, by, 298
        miscellaneous provisions, 302
        provision of copies of, 279–280
        quashing of, [404]
        review of, 283
        Scotland, by court in, 298
            offender residing in, 289
        substitution of conditional discharge for, 301
        when made, [890]
    payment of damages or compensation in addition to, 279, 280
    period permissible, 279
    powers of court to order, 278 *et seq.*
    residence, offender in England, 297
            Scotland, 289
        requirement as to, 279, 282
            expenses of, 532
    rules, 477 *et seq.*, 526 *et seq.*
    security for good behaviour during, 290
    sentence for original offence, effect of, 284
        meaning of, 294, [295]

R.

YOUNG PERSON—*continued.*
    education of, prevention of by vagrancy, 23–24
    employment of, abroad, 35 *et seq.*
                licence and regulation, 108, 471–472
                licensed betting office, in, 422
                restrictions on, 29 *et seq.*, 266–267
                street trading, for, 31, 41
    evidence of, power to clear court during, 44
    financial assistance to, by local authority, 115
    fine, order to parent to pay, 59–60
    hearing of information against, 94, [95]
    homicide, guilty of, 146
    identification of, in reports of proceedings, 46
    imprisonment of, restrictions on, 372
                by magistrates' court, 380, 427
    intoxicating liquor in relation to, 427 *et seq.*   *See also* INTOXICATING LIQUOR.
    mental deficiency.   *See* MENTAL DISORDER.
    metal, old, purchasing from, 23
    moral danger, exposed to, 10 *et seq.*
    protection of, from publicity in court proceedings, 148–149, 675–676
    publications harmful to, 393 *et seq.*   *See also* HARMFUL PUBLICATIONS.
    removal from undesirable surroundings of, 50
    street trading by, 31
    summary trial of, 144
    tobacco, sale of, to, 21–22
    treatment of, 145–146
    vagrant, wandering with, 23–24
    warrant to search for or remove, 47.   *See also* WARRANT.
    welfare of, duty of court to consider, 50

YOUTH TREATMENT CENTRES—
    facilities of, 855 *et seq.*

MADE AND PRINTED IN GREAT BRITAIN BY WILLIAM CLOWES & SONS, LIMITED, LONDON, BECCLES AND COLCHESTER